D1363855

UNDER THE EDITORSHIP OF

Meyer F. Nimkoff

THE FLORIDA STATE UNIVERSITY

SOVIET SOCIETY

A Book of Readings

Edited by

Alex Inkeles HARVARD UNIVERSITY

Kent Geiger TUFTS UNIVERSITY

HOUGHTON MIFFLIN COMPANY, BOSTON
THE RIVERSIDE PRESS, CAMBRIDGE, MASSACHUSETTS

HOUGHTON MIFFLIN COMPANY · BOSTON

HOUGHTON MIFFLIN COMPANY, BOSTON
THE RIVERSIDE PRESS, CAMBRIDGE, MASSACHUSETTS

Printed in the U.S.A.

Preface

A large part of the most impressive results of scholarship in the field of Soviet studies is scattered in journals not readily accessible except to the student working at a major library. This book makes a substantial selection of such outstanding work easily available. At the same time it seeks to meet another need, that for a single source in which the student or general reader can find a thorough and reliable picture of Soviet society as a whole.

In lecturing to various groups in universities and in the community we have repeatedly been asked to suggest a single work in which could be found a comprehensive description of the main institutional features of the Soviet system, a realistic account of the patterns of daily life of the people, and sound interpretations and evaluations of that information. Perhaps because the field of Soviet studies is so young, most scholars working in it have chosen to give first priority to writing the more specialized and technical monographs necessary to give any branch of learning a firm foundation. We do have some excellent studies of a more general nature, but these are in most cases written from the perspective of a single discipline such as political science or economics and necessarily leave out of account many important institutions and features of the system. There is, therefore, substantial need for a systematic general survey of Soviet society as a whole, of social organization and patterns of interaction over the entire range of institutions and settings which make up the Soviet system. We have attempted to approximate that goal in this book of readings.

The orientation which guided us in making our selection was distinctly socio-

v

logical. Our objective was to convey an impression of the Soviet Union as a complete society, a social system, and not merely a modern political state, or a planned economy, or a totalitarian dictatorship. Within this framework the first principle guiding our choices was comprehensiveness. Our outline was developed so that every important feature of the Soviet system and social life within it would at some point receive at least brief comment. Since we were not assembling an encyclopedia we could, of course, achieve that objective only within strict limits. Often the treatment of one sub-field has to stand for a much larger realm. We had room, for example, for an article on the development and control of literature, but were obliged to forgo separate pieces on sculpture and painting as well. This omission seems warranted because the regime's policies and actions with regard to sculpture and painting have been broadly comparable with those adopted in regard to literature. Since the control of music has not produced the same deleterious effects, however, we include a separate report on its fate under Soviet control.

Our second objective was to stress development, the unfolding of Soviet policy and the emergence of Soviet institutions out of the interplay of forces represented by Soviet ideology, practical necessity, and the qualities of the people and institutions inherited from the pre-Revolutionary society. We therefore favored articles of broad sweep, general surveys with an explicitly interpretative or analytic orientation. In the process we hope that our readers will be made aware of Soviet history, of its fascinating although often stark and even terrifying past. We mean thereby not only to do justice to historical fact. In our opinion it is not possible to understand the contemporary situation without reference to the past from which it developed. The Soviet past was, however, much more grim than are present conditions. An exclusively historical account, therefore, runs the risk of giving a misleading picture of Soviet life as it is today. We have sought to strike a balance between these elements, giving the system its due in those realms in which it has accomplished notable advances.

At the same time that we sought to do justice to the past, we have not allowed it to overshadow the reality of the contemporary system. Virtually all of the fundamental changes in Soviet society made in the post-Stalin era are fully discussed. Well over half of the items included were published after the death of Stalin and deal extensively with changes and developments since that time. But it is unwise to pursue such changes too closely. To do so would produce a collection of quickly outdated news bulletins rather than a series of articles of lasting significance. We have felt it important to emphasize the enduring features characterizing the system and the general principles guiding its development. This provides the only sound basis for interpreting the flow of current events as the system adjusts and develops to meet new conditions. Inevitably some of the facts described at the time the particular articles were written no longer apply today. To guide our readers the year of publication is displayed beneath the title of each article. We have, in addition, often called attention in our introductory notes to important changes subsequent to the appearance of certain articles. And where major changes in administration, organization, or policy have occurred we have supplemented the article describing the earlier situation with one summarizing recent developments.

Basic facts and figures and details of organization and administration have not been neglected. They have, however, been kept to the minimum necessary for general orientation and as a background for the more analytical papers to which we have assigned the central place. For more detailed technical descriptions, such as those dealing with the organization of government organs or the mechanisms used for setting prices, the materials we present would have to be supplemented with an appropriate text or monograph. The importance we attach to analytic materials also accounts for the fact that we did not include documentary sources, such as the Communist Manifesto, the Soviet Constitution, or the Resolutions of Communist Party Congresses. In any event such materials are easily accessible in the several published collections of documents cited in the bibliographies we have supplied. The two speeches by Khrushchev we include are exceptions to this rule, but even they are more or less analytic and not merely documentary. In any event, their unique significance for understanding the current scene will serve to justify their inclusion.

To convey a vivid sense of the concrete and an awareness of the patterns of life as they are experienced by Soviet citizens in all walks of life was our third chief object. We have given particular attention to materials which highlight the interaction between individuals and between individuals and the system. Each section is, wherever appropriate, concluded with a concrete description, or a sociological "role analysis," of the activities of the most significant actors in the particular social realm — factory manager, lawyer, worker or peasant, parent and student. The brief excerpts from the Soviet press, mainly letters to the editor and didactic short stories, serve the same purpose of exposing the less formal, the more intimate and natural side of daily life in the Soviet Union.

Since we felt it crucial to provide a comprehensive survey of Soviet social institutions we could not use the absolute merit of each article as our sole criterion of selection. We made our choices in part on the basis of what the selection contributed to the book as a whole. As a result we were obliged to omit many articles which we and others in the field regard as "classic" pieces which broke important new ground or exerted particular influence on the direction of research on Soviet affairs. For the same reason we did not attempt to secure representation for all the important contributors to Soviet studies, although a high proportion of the most outstanding are in fact represented. At times, however, a well-known scholar appears in our collection writing on a topic other than that with which the bulk of his research has dealt. Many have been given much less space than their importance in the field would ideally require.

Although we drew overwhelmingly on scholarly journals — some thirty are represented — in a few instances where the material was peculiarly suited to our purposes we have taken extracts from books and articles appearing in more popular magazines. Out of respect for the complexity of the subject and the efforts of the distinguished scholars and authors, we have, with a few minor exceptions, presented only complete and unabridged articles as they were originally published. In those cases in which Russian words appear in the text, the system of transliteration used in the original has ordinarily been retained. Most Russian words have been defined when they first appear in transliteration, but to avoid any possible confusion we have included a glossary of Russian terms at the back of the book. Finally, to help guide the reader, we have inserted in several articles appropriate subheadings which did not appear in the original.

The logic underlying the over-all arrangement of the material will be self-evident. The precise location of any particular article must, however, always contain an element of the arbitrary. Most of the articles are broad-ranging pieces which touch on a variety of problems and contain a number of themes. This is in the nature of the social system as well as in the nature of scholarly writing. No one article or section exhausts what the book has to say about any given topic. Although each piece is self-contained, it should be read in the context of the chapter and the chapter-section in which it appears. Some topics not explicitly mentioned in the Table of Contents are nevertheless extensively dealt with in several articles. Foreign policy, for example, is not a subject heading, but it is dealt with at length in articles on "The System in Perspective," those under the heading "A Forward Look," and at several other points. To aid those who wish to correlate or compare the different comments made by several authors on the same subject, we have provided an index. In addition, there are carefully selected suggestions for further reading for those wishing to learn more about particular institutions or issues. We hope that altogether the collection of articles will give the reader a concrete as well as accurate and fairly complete understanding of the history, structure, and functioning of Soviet society.

We have received assistance from many persons and several institutions in bringing these selections together. First, of course, to the authors and publishers of the original writings we are most grateful for their generosity in allowing us to reproduce their work. We are grateful to Lawrence J. Silverman for collecting an initial bibliography of the journal-length literature on the Soviet Union published in English up to 1954 and for his evaluations of a good portion of the items. To the Russian Research Center of Harvard University we are indebted for considerable material assistance in the way of typing services during the time this book of readings was carried as a Center project. We owe a special debt of thanks to Dr. Marshall D. Shulman, Associate Director, who gave vigorous encouragement to the idea of such a book. We also want to thank those of our colleagues who made suggestions while the book was in preparation and who offered criticisms of our format and selections. For this we are especially indebted to Betty B. Burch, Robert A. Feldmesser, Mark G. Field, Barrington Moore, Jr., and Talcott Parsons. For efficient and responsible typing we are obliged to Mrs. Mabel F. Adams of the Tufts University Sociology Department, to Annette French, Mary Towle, Mrs. Jeanne M. Maloney, and especially to Miss Rose DeBenedetto of the Russian Research Center. Mrs. Helen W. Parsons, Administrative Assistant of the Russian Research Center, was helpful in many ways, as was Mrs. Nancy Boyden of her staff. Finally, we are indebted for assistance in proofreading and the preparation of the index to Miss Joan L. Carnes of Jackson College, Tufts University, and for preparation of the glossary to Mr. Sanford R. Lieberman of Harvard University.

April 1961   **Alex Inkeles**
                                                        Kent Geiger

Contents

Chapter II · Ideology and Power

Chapter V · **Everyday Living**   493

Chapter VI · **A Forward Look**   632

SOVIET SOCIETY

Backgrounds

History may well define the Russian Revolution of 1917 and its aftermath as the most important event of the twentieth century. Yet like most very complex events its essence seems especially difficult to grasp. Churchill's description of the Soviet Union as "a riddle, wrapped in a mystery, inside an enigma" made it clear that even the most perceptive men in the highest places, equipped with the best resources, felt frustrated in their effort to discover what went on behind Russia's "iron curtain." Since Churchill's remark we have had the benefit of an enormous amount of energetic and penetrating research into all aspects of Soviet life. Furthermore, as a result of Khrushchev's "secret" speech on Stalin and the subsequent publication of minutes of the plenary sessions of the Central Committee of the Communist Party, we can claim to have come far toward understanding what were previously the most impenetrable of the mysteries — the character of Stalin, the nature of his motivation, and the pattern of interpersonal relations in the inner reaches of the Kremlin.

Yet we continue to feel that no one really has the key to Soviet behavior. Perhaps there is no master key. Does not something of the same difficulty beset us when we confront any major historical event: Can we grasp *the* essence of the French Revolution? Is there any one way to "sum up" the impact of the rise of America on the modern world? The emergence of grand theories is probably inevitable when men are confronted by phenomena as challenging as is the Soviet system. Indeed, such theories may be necessary to provide a framework for analysis. But if we remain on the level of grand theory, much of the concrete reality of any society will escape us. We need sharp distinctions between expedient changes in administration and basic changes in the larger social system,

3

between events and processes, between external and internal policy, between what actually was done and our assumptions about the motivation underlying such action. Although the sweeping general theories about Soviet internal and foreign policy have dominated the scene, most research on the Soviet Union is concerned with facts which are perhaps more mundane but happily are also more amenable to social science analysis. Speculation about the inner life of the Kremlin may be the dazzling segment of Soviet studies which catches the public eye, but as with the iceberg the larger and more substantial part of the structure lies below the surface. One can of course be confused by too many guideposts as well as by too few. To comprehend the development of Soviet agriculture, to assess the role of terror in Soviet life, to understand the changes in Soviet family life, we must see them in the context of Soviet history and approach them in their socio-political setting — a setting which includes a whole complex of forces which have been operative in shaping Soviet society.

It is always a great temptation to those interested in the more glamorous facts of political life — especially when they are so colorful and so often bizarre, as in the Soviet case — to skip entirely over the mundane facts of geography, natural resources, and population composition in order to come directly to grips with the raw facts of power. We do not feel that the materials of nature can so readily be by-passed. We hardly agree with the geopolitical school, which holds that Soviet behavior is largely predetermined by the facts of Russia's resources and geographical position. Nevertheless, we feel it important to recognize that the natural and human materials are not merely the base on which Soviet society rests. They have in important ways supported, limited, and even channeled and shaped its development. The facts are, furthermore, neither so simple nor so obvious as many imagine them to be.

The Soviet regime began not only with territory and people taken over from Tsarist Russia, but also with the greater part of the social structure of its predecessor. One of the most common misconceptions about the Soviet Union is found in the image of its progress through time. Many have the impression that somehow, around 1917, after a cataclysmic birth trauma which shook the whole world, the Soviet system emerged whole, in all its complexity, and has "been with us" ever since. Equally common is the assumption that the Soviet Union as we know it today is the end product of the gradual unfolding of a master plan smoothly carried out over the years by Lenin and Stalin. Neither assumption bears much relation to the reality of Soviet development, which has been complex and uneven, characterized by periods of relative stability alternating with times of the most rapid change, by sudden stops and startling leaps, and by all manner of twists and turns. To follow Soviet events at all intelligently it is essential to be familiar with the broad outlines of Soviet development. Many of the papers appearing in later chapters in this collection will again review the history of Soviet affairs from the perspective of some particular problem, but as a general guide we present in this chapter a series of papers especially selected to reveal in broad outline the stages of Soviet development.

The forces which were at work through those stages have been many and complex and the products diverse. Both the forces and the results are dealt with at length in the individual contributions to this book. But it is useful, and perhaps essential, to have some general view, some broad perspective, as a framework for evaluating the individual elements in the total picture. We have therefore given a great deal of space in this introductory chapter to papers which provide an overview of the system. Taken together, the papers of this chapter remind us that no single simple view can encompass the complexity of the Soviet system. It is no mystery — and it does yield meaning when subjected to careful social science analysis. Yet it also represents a unique historical outcome of the interplay of geography, history, cultural tradition, revolutionary ideology, power politics, and economic necessity. One can find in it plan and confusion, order and chaos, intelligence and stupidity, the rational and the irrational — in short, all the elements of the human scene. The particular combination is unique, but the elements are universal in human society.

NATURAL AND HUMAN RESOURCES

1

Industrial and Agricultural Resources*

Chauncy D. Harris

(1955)

A large land mass full of rich natural resources is in itself no guarantee of economic development. Indeed, the Japanese case is often cited to support the argument that natural riches are not necessary to industrial development. While resources may be neither a sufficient nor even necessary cause of economic progress, it cer-

* Reprinted from "USSR Resources: Heavy Industry" and "USSR Resources: Agriculture," *Focus,* Vol. 5 (February 1955), pp. 1–6 and Vol. 5 (May 1955), pp. 1–6, by permission of the author and the American Geographical Society. The maps appearing in the original article have been omitted.

tainly helps to have them in ample supply. Professor Harris reveals the great extent of Soviet resources, and also exposes some sobering limitations they present, especially as regards agriculture. The significance of such natural limits is, of course, greatly influenced by the regime's willingness to invest in any sector of the economy, and Professor Harris keeps us sensitive not only to the influence of resources on politics, but of politics on resources. Some of the articles in Chapter III go into more detail about how the Soviet leaders have used their resources.

To realize just how vast the Soviet Union is, let us remember that it is three times the size of the United States, is larger than the whole of North America, and covers one-sixth of the continental surface of the globe. The northernmost tip lies close to the North Pole; the southernmost border touches far-off Iran and Afghanistan. The greatest east–west distance is more than 6,000 miles. When it is noon on the Polish frontier, it is 11 P.M. on the shores of Bering Strait; by way of comparison, when it is noon in San Francisco, it is only 3 P.M. in New York City. On the basis of its size alone, one might venture to guess that the Union's total resources are immense.

Twenty-five years ago the Soviet Union was mainly an agricultural country. Its power and mineral resources had barely been touched.

The basic aim of the Soviet regime, as expressed by Stalin in 1925, was to transform this agrarian state into an industrial giant — as quickly as possible. First, the government socialized all means of production, and then initiated (in 1928) a succession of Five-Year Plans, all of which have stressed the development of industry, particularly heavy industry.

Undeniably the Soviet Union has made spectacular gains in this respect. Production of both coal and steel — the two most important elements in heavy industry — has multiplied nearly ten times during this period; the Union has risen from a minor position to second rank in the world today. If the same percentage rates of increase were to continue for the next quarter of a century, the Soviet Union would produce more coal and steel than all the rest of the world! This is unlikely, of course.

In 1928, Soviet coal output was only 34 million metric tons, less than one-tenth that of Germany and the United Kingdom together; by 1953 it had risen to 320 million metric tons, nearly equal to the combined total for these two highly industrialized countries, and not far below the output of the United States (440 million metric tons).

In 1928, the Soviet Union produced 4 million metric tons of steel, less than one-fifth as much as the United Kingdom and Germany together; in 1953 it succeeded in producing 38 million metric tons, about 15 per cent more than the combined efforts of these two countries. It still has a long way to go, however, before reaching the United States level, which stood at 101 million metric tons in 1953.

What special conditions have made possible this stupendous growth in Soviet heavy industry?

First of all, it should be noted that such an explosive expansion is not unique. The United States underwent a similar period of rapid development some time ago; the increase in amount of production that the Soviet Union has achieved in 25 years took but a little longer in the United States.

Secondly, Soviet heavy industry has been able to borrow technology from the West and thus has largely bypassed a period of slow experimentation.

Thirdly, the Government has had the power to determine economic policies. By severely limiting expenditures for food, clothing, and shelter, it was able to concentrate investment and labor on heavy industry, and thereby achieved a world record in rate of expansion: the rate of growth of the total economy is another matter and is not here considered. By heavy taxation the government accumulated vast funds for industrial investment, and two-thirds of this investment was devoted to heavy industry.

Agriculture, milked by the government, stagnated. The standard of living suffered; according to a recent American study, real wages in the Soviet Union declined precipitately during the early Five-Year Plans and only now are once again approaching the level of 1928. The amount of housing in cities is reported to have decreased from 64 square feet of floor space per person in 1928 to 46 square feet in 1953. The *average* urban family of five has a one-room apartment 12 by 19 feet. Consumer and light industries were utterly neglected.

The long-range possibilities for continued Soviet expansion of heavy industry depend on many factors, such as the size, skill, and motivation of the labor force, technology, capital in the form of installed facilities for production and transportation, financial resources, management, market, and general economic development. We shall here concern ourselves, however, only with the basic natural resources of energy and metals. One provides the power and the other the tool through which the power is applied. But first we need to make clear certain principles.

Mineral Resources

Known mineral resources do not set ultimate limits. Many reserve figures are little more than working inventories. As known deposits are exhausted, more intensive effort may locate new ones. Furthermore, the technology of mineral exploration and exploitation is improving all the time. Secondly, shortage of a single raw material is rarely critical. Other materials can generally be substituted. Thirdly, the Soviet Union has demonstrated a remarkable ability to limit consumer consumption when it so wishes.

The total energy resources (fuel and water power) of the Soviet Union are estimated to constitute 23 per cent of the total world resources (as compared with 29 per cent for the

United States). According to these estimates, the United States and the Soviet Union together have more than half the energy resources of the entire world.

The areal distribution of Soviet energy resources, however, is in general unfavorable. Most of the people live in the European part of the Union, but 90 per cent of both the coal and the water-power resources lie in the Asiatic part. This maldistribution may be one reason why the government has encouraged, and even forced, an eastward migration of population and industry.

A very large proportion (94 per cent) of Soviet fuel reserves are in the form of coal; peat represents only 4 per cent, and all other fuels (petroleum, natural gas, and oil shale) merely 2 per cent. Coal provides about 70 per cent of the energy currently produced, petroleum and fuel wood most of the rest. We shall here consider only coal, petroleum, and water power.

Soviet coal reserves, estimated at the astronomical figure of 1,650,000 million tons, are sufficient to meet the foreseeable needs of the country for many centuries to come. Of the major producing fields — the Donets, the Kuznetsk, the Moscow Basin, the Urals, and Karaganda — the Donets Basin has by far the best location in respect to markets of all the deposits of high-grade coal. Probably because of this, it has been the largest producer since the rise of modern coal mining, even though it possesses only 5 per cent of the reserves. Before World War II it was producing considerably more coal than all the other fields together. Its proportion has now dropped to about one-third of the total, but its actual output has climbed to 100 million metric tons (about the same as the bituminous-coal production of Pennsylvania).

The Kuznetsk Basin, the second most important field, has the largest reserves of good-quality coal in the Union, and, among the Siberian fields, it has the best location, best quality, and largest proved reserves. The locational handicap of Soviet coals is well illustrated by the fact that Kuznetsk coal is shipped to Central Asia and to the Urals, both about 1,500 miles away. In so long a journey 40 per cent of the coal is consumed in its own transportation.

The Moscow Basin and some of the Ural basins produce lignite rather than bituminous coal, but production increased sharply during and after the war because of their proximity to major markets. The Karaganda field, opened in the 1930's in the sparsely settled steppes, provides good-quality coking coal (though high in ash) and is closer to the Magnitogorsk steel industry than the faraway Kuznetsk.

One of the major problems of Soviet metallurgy is a shortage of good-quality coking coal. Much of the coking coal used is high in sulphur and in ash; recovery of coke per ton of coking coal is slightly more than 50 per cent, as compared with 76 per cent in the United States. Another problem is the fact that much of the Donets coal lies in thin seams, few of them being more than a yard thick; extraction costs are therefore high, and are likely to keep on rising.

Estimates of the Soviet share of total world reserves of petroleum range from 5 per cent according to *World Oil* to 59 per cent according to Soviet sources. Suffice it to say that geological conditions from the Caspian Sea northward to the Urals are favorable for large deposits of petroleum; undoubtedly, new oil fields will be discovered and exploited.

At the moment, however, the relative importance of petroleum in the Soviet Union is declining; coal is becoming the principal industrial fuel. Fifty years ago the amount of fuel obtained from petroleum equaled that from coal; by 1950 it had fallen to less than one-quarter as much, indicating a trend in direct opposition to that of the United States, where petroleum and natural gas are being increasingly used in place of coal.

Furthermore, nothing comparable to the dramatic discovery and exploitation of the oil fields in America and along the Persian Gulf has taken place in the Soviet Union in the last few decades, and consequently it has not been able to maintain its former rank among world producers. In 1901 the Soviet Union was producing half of the world's petroleum; by 1946 its share had dropped to 6 per cent. In 1953, when it produced 52 million metric tons (330 million barrels), its share had risen to only 8 per cent, in spite of the emergence of the *Second* Baku.

Although never in enemy hands during World War II, the old Baku, for long the world's leading oil field, declined during the war owing to a shortage of labor and materials, especially steel needed for new drilling. It has never fully recovered because several of the early-developed pools have been exhausted. Such fields as Grozny and Maikop have also declined, for similar reasons, and are now only moderately productive, as are the fields of Nebit-Day and Emba on the Caspian Sea, and Okha on Sakhalin.

As a result of the discovery of good oil horizons at greater depths, the Second Baku (really an umbrella name for three widely spaced districts) has been growing rapidly; in fact, it is now the largest Soviet producer. The three oil districts are located near the cities of Ufa and Molotov on the western flank of the Ural Mountains, and Kuibyshev, on the Volga River.

Several of the longest and largest rivers in the world cross the Soviet Union, yet its waterpower resources are less developed than those of any major power: only about 3 per cent of the potential is utilized. The Fourth Five-Year Plan called for the production of 12 billion kw-h in 1950 from hydroelectric plants. Great projects now under way at Kuibyshev and Stalingrad on the Volga, and elsewhere, are expected nearly to triple hydroelectric-power production, but even then it will lag far behind that of the United States (96 billion kw-h in 1950), or of Western Europe, or of Canada. The failure to push the development of hydroelectric power in the Soviet Union is a direct result of the highly unfavorable areal distribution of water-power resources (which are mainly in eastern Siberia thousands of miles from the large population centers), and the great seasonal variations in flow in the rivers (many are subject to tremendous floods after spring thaws; many are frozen for months at a stretch) coupled with the heavy costs required for hydroelectric-power installations.

Turning now from energy to metals, let us consider the Sovet Union's position with respect to iron, copper, aluminum, lead, and zinc — the principal metalliferous ores of industrial significance. Very few countries have large reserves of all these ores, and most countries import a fraction of their needs for one or more of them. The Soviet Union, however, is driving for self-sufficiency in all strategic materials.

The measured reserves of iron ore that could be utilized under existing technological and economic conditions are sufficient to last for about a century at current rates of consumption. About two-thirds of these reserves are found in three major deposits: Krivoy Rog, Kerch, and Magnitogorsk. The most pressing problem with respect to iron ore in the Soviet Union, as it is in the Mesabi Range of the United States, is the approaching exhaustion of high-grade ore and the consequent necessity of turning to lower-quality ores that require concentration before use. The little-used Kerch ores, the largest measured reserve, average only 35 per cent iron content; they are powdery and must be sintered as well as concentrated. Both Krivoy Rog and Magnitogorsk, by far the largest producers of high-quality iron ore, are reported to be approaching depletion of the best ores.

The Soviet Union has moderate reserves of copper ore, thought to be enough to last several decades at present rates of production. Like American copper deposits, the two principal deposits, at Dzhezkazgan and Kounradski, have a low copper content and are remote from markets. Probably because of technological difficulties the Soviet Union has regularly had to import large quantities of copper to supplement domestic supplies.

Soviet resources of bauxite (the ore for aluminum) are believed to be modest in spite of recent development of sizable deposits at Krasnaya Shapochka and Kamensk in the Urals. Their utilization requires vast amounts of electric power, which fact may be one reason for the construction of large hydroelectric-power stations on the Volga and its tributaries. An important portion of Soviet needs is supplied by the extensive high-grade bauxite deposits of Hungary, now drawn into the Soviet orbit.

The largest reserves of lead and zinc are in the Altay Mountains, but total known resources are modest, and at present rates of production they may soon be exhausted. Lead and zinc needs have long been met partly by imports, most of which probably now come from Poland.

The enormous size of the Soviet Union creates special problems for heavy industry. Many parts of the country are far from cheap sea transport and therefore even bulky commodities must be transported over vast distances by relatively expensive overland hauls.

One measure of the energy needed to overcome the space friction involved in operating the Soviet economy is the consumption of fuel in transportation. It is estimated that Soviet railroads require about 30 per cent of all coal produced. Smaller countries of Western Europe, such as the United Kingdom and Germany, use only a third as high a proportion of their coal in railroad transport.

One way in which the government is attempting to solve the distance problem and to economize on transportation is by encouraging as much regional self-sufficiency as possible. Thus the government has called for the development of local sources of raw materials near existing markets, of food production in industrial districts, and of manufacturing in agricultural areas. The growing of wheat in the central industrial district and the development of cotton textile factories in Central Asia are cases in point.

The total physical resources of energy and metalliferous ores in the Soviet Union appear to be sufficient for several decades of further expansion in heavy industry. But the cost of utilizing these resources is another matter! The real costs of producing coal and iron ore, for example, appear to be rising as the high-quality, easily mined, and accessible deposits become depleted and less favorable ones must be used. It is well to remember, however, that in no other country in the world has so high a proportion of the total national income been poured into the development of heavy industry, and, to judge by past experience, one may predict that the government will be willing to pay the high price necessary for its continued growth.

In contrast to rapidly expanding Soviet industry, Soviet agriculture has been relatively stagnant. The lack of progress in agriculture rests on two sets of factors: the harsh physical environment and the unfavorable human conditions under which farming has been carried on.

Soils and Weather

The most significant physical features limiting agriculture in the Soviet Union are directly or indirectly climatic. It is helpful to remember that the Soviet Union and North America are about equal in area (8½ million square miles) and in population (200 millions) and that in each an agricultural heartland abuts vast wastelands climatically unsuited to cultivation. In North America this heartland extends from the Atlantic Seaboard westward to about the hundredth meridian and reaches from the Gulf of Mexico northward to the southern fringe of Canada. A corresponding agricultural heartland in the Soviet Union, called the Fertile Triangle, stretches from corners at Leningrad on the Baltic Sea and Odessa on the Black Sea to somewhat east of the Ural Mountains.

These heartlands are bordered on the north by immense expanses too cool for regular farming and on the east or west sides by immense arid or semi-arid plains too dry for non-irrigated crops. But in the Soviet Union the heartland is somewhat smaller than in North America, and a smaller total area is in crops: 386 million acres as compared with 440 million (1952). Furthermore, the average crop yields in the Soviet Union fall short of those in North America. Consequently, the agricultural production of the U.S.S.R., though large in total quantity compared with that of any other individual country, remains far below that of North America.

Two critical features underlie the climatic handicaps of the Soviet Union: high latitudinal position and great longitudinal extent. The Soviet Union occupies a more northerly position than North America. The fiftieth parallel lies poleward of any part of the continental United States; yet it marks approximately the southern boundary of the eastern half of the Soviet Union. The southern boundary of the western part of the Union lies at about the fortieth parallel, that is in about the latitude of Denver. Only tiny segments of the mainland of North America are north of the seventieth parallel; yet about half of the Soviet Arctic coast lies north of this latitude. As a result of its northerly location, the taiga (northern coniferous forests) and the bleak treeless Arctic tundra are more extensive in the U.S.S.R. than in Alaska, Canada, and Greenland; altogether such areas cover five and a half million square miles, or nearly two-thirds of the entire Soviet Union, compared with less than half of North America.

The northern frontier of agriculture is limited not by a single climatic factor, but rather by a refractory combination of climatically related features: a cool, short, irregular growing season; infertile podzol soils; poor drainage; and permafrost (permanently frozen subsoil).

The bitterly cold winters do not necessarily preclude farming but the summertime growing season is short and the weather often raw. Crop failures are frequent. The problems created by the shortness of the growing season and the moist cool weather of harvest time near the northern edge of cultivation have been solved to some extent by ancient grain-ripening kilns and by modern drying machinery on collective farms. By way of partial compensation for the short summer, however, the high latitude produces unusually long days. At the Arctic Circle the longest period of continuous daylight is, of course, 24 hours on June 21. But even at 60° north (the latitude of Leningrad, or Seward, Alaska) the period of continuous daylight is nearly 19 hours at the summer solstice.

The podzol soils of these northern areas are deficient in soluble plant foods, low in colloids, poor in structure, and highly acidic. Heavy manuring and liming are necessary to sustain agriculture; but the cost of such operations is scarcely justified in areas of low yields.

Poor drainage and bogs characterize large areas. The West Siberian lowland is the largest flat space on the face of the globe. Poor drainage there results not only from low stream gradients but also from the northward course of the rivers. Since the mouths of the rivers are frozen for longer periods than the headwaters, the downrushing spring melt waters flood widely over the level plains and linger well into the summer. In other areas, for example, near Moscow and Leningrad, poor drainage results from glacial derangement of the terrain; moraines deposited by the glaciers block many stream valleys and thus form lakes, bogs, and marshes.

Permafrost covers nearly half of the Soviet Union. In permafrost areas only a thin surface layer thaws in summer. The impervious frozen subsoil prevents drainage, and poses difficult problems for both farming and building operations.

Extreme continentality results from the great longitudinal extent of the Soviet Union from 20° E. to 170° W. In the Western Hemisphere a comparable distance would be from

western Alaska eastward to the coast of Norway. Because of this great east–west elongation, much of the Soviet Union is thousands of miles from any body of water that might exert an ameliorating influence on the climate (the Arctic Sea is, of course, covered by ice during most of the year).

The continentality, together with the northerly location, occasions extremes of temperature, a short growing season, and a dearth of moisture. In the eastern parts of the country the average January temperature falls to more than 40° F. below zero (−58° at Verkhoyansk). The coldness of the interior hinders the overwintering of crops or fruit trees; spring grains rather than winter grains therefore become the staple crop. Continental conditions also give rise to the relative absence of spring and fall. Winter and summer are virtually the only two seasons. Farm operations, such as planting, must be telescoped into the shortest possible period. The average frost-free season decreases eastward from 160 days at Leningrad to 130 at Moscow and only 95 at Irkutsk (near Lake Baykal). A high variability in the length of the frost-free season from year to year goes hand in hand with the dangerous risk of unseasonable late frosts in spring or early frosts in fall.

The amount of precipitation also decreases sharply eastward from the Baltic coast. Long before the winds from the west penetrate deeply into the continental interior, they have lost much of their moisture. Siberia, lacking a nearby source of moisture such as the Gulf of Mexico provides for interior North America, is prevailingly dry. Were it not so cold, it would be mostly a desert.

Agricultural Output

Any expansion of the agricultural frontier toward the dry southeast is risky because of the low total rainfall, the high variability from year to year, and the occasional occurrence of desiccating winds called *sukhovey*. In the continental interior, in Soviet Central Asia, about a million square miles are covered by deserts and semi-arid steppes where rainfall is utterly inadequate for crops. Even in the less arid Middle and Lower Volga region, only an occasional year has enough moisture for crops; complete crop failures are frequent. The dreaded *sukhovey* may destroy within a single day a promising crop resulting from a year of adequate rainfall; plants simply wilt, as the roots cannot supply sufficient moisture to balance the high transpiration rates caused by the blasts of hot air with very low relative humidities.

This combination of coolness and dryness deprives the Soviet Union of agricultural regions similar to the richest American ones — the Corn Belt and the Cotton Belt, both of which are favored by warm moist climates. No major Soviet region combines a long, warm growing season with adequate precipitation. Most of the warm southernmost part of the Union is plagued by an acute shortage of moisture.

The Fertile Triangle, the agricultural heartland, has a cool continental semi-arid climate similar to that of the spring wheat region of the Prairie Provinces of Canada and the Dakotas of the United States. These areas are characterized by relatively low crop yields per acre, high variability of yields from year to year, a severely restricted range of crops, and little possibility of increasing yields through more intensive farming. Odessa, on the warm southern margin of the Triangle, is as far north as Duluth, Minnesota. Actually, its summer temperatures are somewhat higher than those of Duluth, being more nearly those of Omaha, Nebraska. But its annual precipitation is about ten inches less than either Duluth or Omaha. Because of the short growing season and the relatively meager and irregular rainfall, farming in the Fertile Triangle, as in the American spring wheat region, is heavily dominated by grains, mainly wheat, rye, and oats. The richest soils of the Soviet Union, the fertile chernozems (blackearths), stretch in a broad sweeping band along the semi-arid southeastern edge of the Triangle, but their productivity is hampered by the scanty and uncertain rainfall.

Partly as a result of a short growing season and meager rainfall and partly as a result of poor farming methods, Soviet yields per acre are low. Estimates indicate an average wheat yield per acre of about 12 bushels (compared with 17 in the United States) and of corn of 17 bushels (compared with 40 in the United States).

A map of the sown areas depicts clearly the vastness of the noncultivated spaces in the Soviet Union. The perennial question is whether the frontiers of present cultivation cannot be pushed farther into these gigantic unfarmed expanses. The amount of cultivated land in the Union has been increasing at a moderate rate for many decades. Some tracts not now cultivated certainly could be put under the plow. A tremendous, feverish, and dangerous campaign is currently under way to cultivate 70 million acres of new semi-arid land in Western Siberia, Kazakhstan, the Urals, the Volga region, and the North Caucasus during the three years 1954–1956. Although the absolute physical limits of agriculture have not been reached, the economic limits on both the cool and the dry margins doubtless have been attained or overreached in many areas. Much land now tilled is as poor as the abandoned farmland of the Appalachian Mountains or the Dust Bowl in the United States.

While the physical conditions in the Soviet Union are relatively intractable, they alone by no means explain the sickly state of Soviet agriculture. Human factors are also important, particularly in the low yields per acre on existing farmland.

The human factors depressing agricultural production emanate especially from government policy. The government has favored heavy industry at the expense of agriculture. In order to secure funds and food to support a tempestuous upsurge in heavy industry, the government has implemented a series of oppressive tax and control devices in agriculture.

The first sweeping change effected by the government and bitterly opposed by the farmers was the collectivization of agriculture throughout the entire country by the combining of all farm units into giant collective and state farms. Except for small garden plots, individual peasant holdings were eliminated. Though it did not increase agricultural production, the change did provide a mechanism by which the state could collect a larger proportion of the farm output and thereby feed the urban workers engaged in the industrialization of the country. Agricultural machinery was concentrated in machine and tractor stations owned and operated by the state. Thus the government, through its control of harvesting machinery, was able to take actual physical possession of a large fraction of the total crop. At the time of collectivization farm income dropped precipitately; real farm income may not yet have recovered sufficiently to equal the pre-collectivization levels of a quarter century ago.

Hopes for increased production have been blighted by the extremely low prices paid to farmers. Much of the agricultural output has been acquired by the government at very low prices fixed by the state, only to be sold later at relatively high prices to consumers. The mark-up has been, in effect, a burdensome tax, by which the government has rapidly amassed huge sums to be invested in heavy industry. According to an official Soviet report in 1953, farm receipts on livestock farms for the entire Soviet Union average only five rubles per workday unit, equivalent in actual purchasing power to about 35 cents. A laborer on the average Soviet livestock farm must work three full days in order to make enough to purchase one dozen eggs at Moscow retail prices. That low prices have had a depressing effect on agricultural production is evidenced by the growth of the few branches of agriculture that have been granted high prices. Industrial crops, such as cotton, have been so favored.

Agricultural production generally has fallen far short of announced plans. Thus in spite of ambitious goals for rapidly increasing the number of livestock, sharp decreases have actually occurred. In the period 1928 to 1953, the number of cattle fell from 66.8 to 56.6 million (cows from 33.2 to 24.3 million) and the number of sheep and goats from 114.6 to 109.9 million (on January 1 for comparable areas). The number of hogs rose slightly from 27.7 to 28.5 million. Average milk production per cow is less than half as high as in the United States.

Recent agricultural trends in the Soviet Union contrast sharply with those in the United States. Total Soviet farm output has been sluggish for the last 25 years, while farm output in the United States has risen steeply, increasing by about 40 per cent in the last 15 years. Per capita output of edible animal products in the Soviet Union, such as meat and milk, has actually declined by about 30 per cent in a quarter century. Industrialized countries usually have better diets than agrarian ones, but in spite of industrialization the Soviet Union still has a poorer diet than the under-developed nonindustrial countries of southern and eastern Europe.

Recent policy changes in the Soviet Union hold out some hope for the consumer and the farmer. If the plans for improving the lot of the farmers and for increasing production, announced in 1953, 1954, and 1955, are really carried out, agricultural production may show more gains in the future than in the recent past. But serious environmental problems will persist.

2

Trends in Soviet Population History*

Frank Lorimer

(1944)

The richest of natural resources and the most exceptional organization become productive only in so far as there are people in significant numbers, with appropriate skills, located in the right places. The availability of great reserves of under-employed manpower was an essential precondition for Soviet economic development. But in the process of development the initial population was transformed. It also paid a very heavy price for the speed and intensity of change. Dr. Lorimer reviews the interaction between population and social change from 1917 down to World War II.

The rise and progress of the Union of Soviet Socialist Republics has been conditioned by unique geographical, demographic and cultural circumstances.[1] The Marxian thesis that socialism could not be established in one country, though based on acute observations, proved fallacious under these conditions. Most obvious is the factor of space, the territory of the Soviet Union being the largest in the world under one political administration. Associated

* Reprinted from "Recent Population Trends in the Soviet Union," *American Sociological Review*, Vol. 9 (1944), pp. 219–222, by permission of the author and the American Sociological Association.
[1] Based on data and analysis in *The Population of the Soviet Union: History and Prospects*, published by the League of Nations, Geneva, 1946, by the same author. See also *The Future Population of Europe and the Soviet Union*, by Notestein, Taeuber, Kirk, Coale and Kiser, Geneva: League of Nations, 1944.

with the factor of space are wealth and diversity of natural resources. The particular stage of economic and cultural development in the Russian Empire at the time of the Revolution was no less important. Four-fifths of the people were peasants; the middle class was small and scattered; the urban proletariat, though relatively small, was sufficiently numerous to become politically dominant under skillful leadership. At the time of the first Soviet Census in 1926, when the occupational structure of the population was not radically different from that in the late pre-revolutionary period, there were 4 million workers and employees in manufacturing, mining, construction and transportation, and a somewhat larger number of employed persons in various other fields, including agriculture and crafts, trade and public services. The combination of great resources and incipient industrial progress set the stage for a phenomenal expansion of industry under centralized economic control. By January, 1939, there were over 14 million workers and employees in manufacturing, mining, construction and transportation, and about 15 million employed persons in other fields. The progress of education and the arts advanced with equal rapidity among people half of whom (persons ten years of age and over) had been completely illiterate in 1926. Thus the shocks and strains of violent changes were absorbed in the constructive force of a rising industrial nation and a new dynamic culture.

A low ratio of population to resources in the Russian plain has been one of the major assets of the Soviet Union, as of the United States and Canada. In the interpretation of economic achievements, this factor is naturally minimized, both by Russians and by Americans, in favor of emphasis on personal and social characteristics; but its importance is very real. As it happens, the U.S.S.R. and North America (from Panama to the Arctic) are practically identical in area and in number of inhabitants. The historical conditions responsible for the low density of population in America are potent. The factors which inhibited the growth of population in the Russian plain until a few centuries ago are less commonly understood. An ancient accumulation of agrarian population in the territory now occupied by the Soviet Union would have required the effective occupation of the black soil prairies; but these remained a no-man's-land from prehistoric times to the middle of the seventeenth century — locked between the antagonistic cultures of the village people in the northern forests and the nomads of the Asiatic steppes. Meanwhile, the civilizations of Central Asia and the Transcaucasus remained isolated and circumscribed. After this deadlock was broken by the forest dwellers, stimulated in the arts of peace and destruction by contact with Western Europe, the Russian population spread out and increased rapidly in number. But the interval between this time and the present was too brief to permit the formation of a dense population. Russia, like North America, has the added advantage of extensive territory which is incapable of supporting a large agricultural population, but which supplies important resources for modern industry.

Population Growth

Excluding non-Russian nationalities to the south and east, the Russian population rose from about 18 million persons in 1725 to over 90 million persons in 1900 — while its land base was being extended southward into Central Russia, the Ukraine, the middle and lower Volga valleys, the Crimea and the North Caucasus, and very slowly at first and then more rapidly, into Siberia, the margins of the Asiatic Steppes, and the Far East. Diverse nationalities in the Caucasus, the Volga-Ural region, Siberia, the Asiatic steppes, and Central Asia were encompassed by the Russian Empire, but remained largely unassimilated. The integration of these diverse nationalities in the life of the Soviet Union evidences the wisdom of the Soviet leaders and the constructive force of the Revolution.

Natural increase in European Russia in the late Imperial period proceeded at a high, constant rate (about 17 per thousand per year). The increase of population in the U.S.S.R. reached a peak (around 20 per thousand) in the early Soviet period, dropped sharply during the late twenties and early thirties, then rose again in 1937–1938 to the height of the earlier peak. It apparently remained near that point to the time of the German invasion. The population of the U.S.S.R. increased from 147 million at the First All-Union Census, December 1926, to 170 million persons at the second (published) census, January 1939 — representing an average annual increase of 12.3 per thousand.

Conditions associated with the first World War and the Revolution, above all the epidemics and famine which followed in their wake, wiped out the normal increase of a ten-year period — causing an estimated deficit of 28 million persons in the Soviet population as of 1926. Nevertheless, the natural increase of the Russian people was so high that the population in the U.S.S.R. area was 38.6 per cent higher in 1926 than in 1897 (at the time of the only complete Imperial census).

It is difficult to chart exactly the movement of births and deaths in the Soviet Union during the inter-census period, because official vital statistics for these years have never been published. Apparently the birth rate fell from about 45 per thousand in 1927 to about 30 per thousand in 1935, then rose to 33.8 in 1936, 39.6 in 1937, and 38.3 in 1938. The sharp decline reflects rapid cultural change, urbanization, and extensive resort to the abortion clinics. The abrupt rise reflects the curtailment of and final suppression of the abortion clinics (except service on therapeutic or eugenic grounds), the strengthening of marriage bonds, and an extended program of benefits to mothers and children. The drop in the birth rate, described here as indicated by indirect evidence, may appear unreasonably precipitous — but the associated conditions were unique. The evidence at our disposal indicates that the general death rate in the U.S.S.R., 1926–27, was about 26 per thousand (after correction for estimated under-registration, and adjustment for areas not covered in the statistics at that time). It was distinctly lower, but still high in 1938, i.e., 17.8 per thousand — indicating infant mortality well over 100 deaths under 1 year per thousand live births. Even on these assumptions as regards births and deaths, there remains a deficit of about 4 million persons in population growth during the inter-census period. This must be attributed to excess deaths in connection with the program for the settlement of the nomads in the Asiatic steppe region, the collectivization drive, and hazards associated with the initial tempo of industrial construction — or the hypothesis that mortality near the beginning and end of this period was above the rates indicated by the best available evidence.

One cannot safely assume that the future course of fertility and mortality in the Soviet Union will conform to the pre-war European experience, especially as regards fertility. It is, however, unlikely that fertility will fall *more* rapidly or mortality *less* rapidly than in past European experience. Projections of future population growth for the U.S.S.R. based on the assumption that changes in specific vital rates will parallel declines of fertility and mortality in European experience would, therefore, seem to provide *minimum* estimates. Even on this assumption, the expected future growth of the Soviet population stands in sharp contrast to that of Western Europe. Leaving war losses and boundary changes out of account, the expected movement of population within the January 1939 borders of the U.S.S.R., is a rise from 173.8 million in January 1940 to 251 million persons in 1970. The expected change in the combined population of northwestern and central Europe (including the British Isles, France, Germany, Austria, Hungary, Czechoslovakia, the low countries, and the Scandinavian — but not Poland, Lithuania, Latvia or Estonia) during the same period and on the same assumptions, is a decrease from 230 million in 1940 to 222 million persons in 1970.

The effect of the war on the Soviet population cannot be measured at this time. If we arbitrarily assume that the population of the U.S.S.R. within the January 1939 borders will be 20 million less than otherwise expected in 1945, and distribute this hypothetical loss by age and sex on certain arbitrary but reasonable assumptions, we can carry the projection forward along the lines already described. The expected U.S.S.R. population in 1970 on this basis is 222 million persons. On the hypothesis that the territory of the Soviet Union will be bounded in the West by the Curzon Line and will include Estonia, Latvia, Lithuania, Bessarabia and Northern Bukovina, the expected 1970 population, adjusted for war losses in proportion to the arbitrary hypothesis defined above, will be somewhere in the vicinity of 244 million persons. The population projected to 1970 for all other European areas, combined, *without* adjustment for war losses, is 392 million persons (222 million in the various Northwestern and Central European countries, as defined above; 86 million in the Iberian Peninsula and Italy; 84 million in other parts of Poland and the Balkan countries).

Composition of Population

The age and sex structure of the Soviet population reflects the irregularities of population movements in this area during the last thirty years. However, the trend toward rapid increase, the very high fertility and the rather high mortality generally characteristic of its previous demographic history predominate over these irregularities. Forty-five per cent of the whole Soviet population was under 20 years of age in 1940. The corresponding proportion will presumably be less in future years, but it is unlikely to drop to the figure already characteristic of Northwestern and Central Europe (32 per cent), whereas the corresponding proportion for the latter region may fall to a much lower figure before 1970. Conversely, the proportion of aged persons is now very low in the U.S.S.R.; even with an appreciable rise, it will remain relatively low for several decades. The proportion of young adults 20–44 years will remain constant — except for effect of war on the number of young male adults. The number of males, relative to females, in this critical age group was, however, abnormally low in the U.S.S.R. in 1940 — the estimated ratio being 90 males per 100 females between 20 and 45 years of age. With the hypothetical adjustment for war losses, described above, this ratio (which would otherwise rise) falls to 82 in 1945 — rising gradually thereafter until a normal balance (around 100) is restored some 25 years hence. On the other hand, the U.S.S.R. had an extraordinarily large numbers of youths in 1940, born during the early peak in births, 1923–1928 (especially 1924–1927). This great cohort of youth has already contributed significantly to the triumph of Soviet arms, and will constitute a key source of strength in post-war reconstruction. The number of young men passing the threshold of their eighteenth year will fall off in the late 1940's and early 1950's. Then a new, larger cohort of youth will enter the scene. After making all due allowances for errors inherent in such estimates, it is certain that the Soviet Union will be characterized in the immediate future by a rapidly growing and predominantly young population.

The eastward trend of the Soviet population both during the inter-war period and at forced tempo during the war has been widely publicized. Numerically, the movement from rural areas to cities has been far greater and no less significant. These two major redistribution trends are closely related. They represent the shift from a loosely coordinated, predominantly agrarian structure to a diverse, well-balanced and integrated economy, tapping the potential resources of a vast domain. This transition was in its initial stages when it was temporarily interrupted by the war. Soviet energies during the next decade must be directed in large part to the reconstruction of industries and homes wrecked by war. It does not follow that all of this reconstruction must take place on the old sites, though much of it will. Reconstruction can also be affected in part through new construction in areas that were previously underdeveloped. One can be sure that these undertakings will be planned with primary reference to future opportunities. The movements of people will follow the directives of economic planning. Soviet industry is still in the formative stage. The next quarter-century will witness extremely interesting developments in this respect, with related cultural and political changes.

3

A Comparison of the Current Population in the U.S.S.R. and U.S.A.*

John F. Kantner

(1959)

Dr. Kantner brings our survey of the population question up to date, bringing to bear the results of the latest census. He does so from the perspective of comparisons of the Soviet and American populations, which reveal that they are now markedly more alike in size and

* Reprinted from "Basic Demographic Comparisons Between the U.S.S.R. and the United States," *Comparisons of the United States and Soviet Economies*, Part I (1959), pp. 54–68, paper submitted to the Subcommittee on Economic Statistics of the Joint Economic Committee, Eighty-sixth Congress, First Session, Washington, D.C., by permission of the author.

"quality" than was the case before World War II.

Preliminary results from the recent population census of the U.S.S.R., together with certain related information, afford the best opportunity in 20 years for comparing the population of the U.S.S.R. and the United States. The two countries have followed quite divergent courses during these years, with the result that in some respects they are less alike than before the war. In other respects, notably in total population, these two countries have become more alike. The following review of current information on the population of the U.S.S.R. points up some of these similarities and contrasts. Until more complete data are available, however — data such as those which are to be ready around the end of 1959[1] — analysis is necessarily limited and conclusions correspondingly tentative.

I. Total Size and Growth

A. The Size of the Total Population

Before the war the population of the U.S.S.R. within its present boundaries was

---

[1] The release of preliminary data is to be followed by more detailed tabulations of the same items plus data on such matters as age and sex, nationality, native language, marital status, educational attainment, social group, and means of subsistence, occupation, and type of economic activity.

larger by 46 per cent than the population of the United States. Today, however, the Soviet population exceeds that of the United States by only 18 per cent, even though throughout most of the postwar period official statistics show a more rapid rate of natural increase for the U.S.S.R. than for the United States.

The explanation of the very low rate of growth of the U.S.S.R. population is of course the heavy losses and deficit of births inflicted on the Soviet Union by the war.

B. Evaluation of Total Population

The total population reported by the Soviet census is lower than many observers had expected. The senior engineer and executive officer of the Central Statistical Administration's machine accounting division, D. K. Zhak, in discussing plans for tabulating census results, anticipated a population in the neighborhood of 215 million.[2] The announced total also is more than a million short of the population that would have been reached if the officially estimated population of 200.2 million in 1956[3] had grown according to the officially reported

---

[2] D. K. Zhak, *Mekhanizirovannaya razrabotka materialov perepisey naseleniya S.S.S.R.* ["Mechanical Processing of the Material from the U.S.S.R. Census of Population"], Moscow, 1958, p. 116.

[3] Tsentral'noye Statisticheskoye Upravleniye pri Sovete Ministrov S.S.S.R., *Narodnoye khozyaystvo S.S.S.R.* ["National Economy of the U.S.S.R."], Moscow, 1956, p. 17.

TABLE 1   *Total Population of the U.S.S.R. and United States and Per Cent Increase, 1939–1959**

COUNTRY	POPULATION		PER CENT INCREASE, 1939–1959
	1939	1959	
U.S.S.R.	190.7[a]	208.8[a]	9.5
United States..........	131.0[b]	177.2[c]	35.3
U.S.S.R. .... United States..........	1.46	1.18	

* In this and subsequent tables, data for Alaska and Hawaii are not included.

[a] *Izvestiya*, May 10, 1959. The 1959 population as reported to the nearest thousand is 208,826,000.

[b] U.S. Department of Commerce, Bureau of the Census, *Statistical Abstract of the United States, 1958*, p. 5, No. 2.

[c] Interpolation between estimated population in 1957, *ibid.*; average of projected values for 1969, *ibid.*, p. 6, No. 3.

rates of natural increase. And since the 1956 figure, especially its urban component, has been characterized as possibly too low[4] there seemed to be good reason to expect a figure larger than 210 million.

Aside from these prior expectations, there are no unchallengable grounds for rejecting the census results. An examination of the preparations for the census and the plans for its conduct reveals no obvious shortcomings but rather shows a thoroughgoing concern for completeness of coverage.[5] The most likely major exclusion, the military, are stated to be included in the figures that have been released.

If past experience can be relied on, we should not expect major revisions of the preliminary census total.

C. Growth of the Soviet Population

The United States is not expected to attain a population as large as the present Soviet population before 1970.[6] The future growth of both countries will be largely a matter of natural increase,[7] that is, an excess of births over deaths. Unlike the United States during its

---

[4] M. Ya. Sonin, "Ob aktual'nykh voprosakh vosproizvodstva trudovykh resursov S.S.S.R." ["On Actual Problems of the Reproduction of Labor Resources in the U.S.S.R."], in *Voprosy sotsialisticheskovo vosproizvodstva* ["Problems of Socialist Reproduction"], Moscow, 1958, p. 258. In this source, Sonin refers to total population only. In another source he stated his belief that the urban population was too low.

[5] On the first canvass of the population 207,752,000 persons were enumerated; this was followed by a second visit which added another 285,000 persons to the total. Finally, a checking out of schedules which had been filled out for persons who were temporarily absent at the time of the enumerator's visit yielded an additional 789,000.

[6] The average of the four series of Bureau of the Census projections of the total population for 1970 is 211,006,000. Series III projection for 1970 is 208,199,000 and assumes a moderate decline in the level of fertility. (U.S. Department of Commerce, Bureau of the Census, *Statistical Abstract of the United States, 1958*, pp. 6–7.) The population projected for the U.S.S.R. in 1970 falls in the range between 237 and 259 million. See U.S. Department of Commerce, Bureau of the Census, *Estimates and Projections of the Population of the U.S.S.R.: 1950 to 1976*, by Arthur A. Campbell and James W. Brackett, Series P–95, No. 52, Washington, 1959.

[7] Since the war, net annual immigration to the

period of basic industrial development, the U.S.S.R. has not been able to rely upon immigration to supply its manpower needs but has had to raise its own. In its 40-year history the U.S.S.R. has acquired approximately 20 million persons through annexation — all since 1939 — and a number of these have entered into the streams of eastward migration within the country. Coincidentally, this figure is close to the number of immigrants who entered the United States during the 40 years prior to the passage of the restrictive immigration legislation of 1924.

1. *Natural Increase.* — In 1957 the rate of natural increase in the Soviet Union was 17.5 per thousand, compared to 15.7 per thousand in the United States. These may be compared to natural increase rates of 13.4 and 8.6, respectively, for 1940 (see Table 2). Thus, while growth rates for both countries have risen, the U.S. rate has shown a greater increase. In 1940, for example, the rate of natural increase in the United States amounted to only 64 per cent of the rate in the Soviet Union, while in 1957 it was 90 per cent (see Table 3).

Interestingly, rises in the growth rate for the respective countries stem basically from different origins. In the U.S.S.R. both birth and death rates have declined, but the decline in the death rate has been much greater than the decline in the birth rate. In the United States, on the other hand, while the death rate declined somewhat, a modest rise (30 per cent) in the birth rate was the major contribution to the higher growth rates. Neither the U.S.S.R. nor the U.S. rates of natural increase are high when contrasted to many of the world's underdeveloped countries, but they are more than double the rates for the countries of Western Europe, largely because of the difference in birth rates.

Taking reported rates at face value and leaving out war years, the U.S.S.R. natural increase rate shows no decided trend either downward or upward during the Soviet period.

United States has fluctuated between 150,000 to 350,000 per year. The U.S.S.R. has not reported any statistics on immigration. It has put forth considerable effort in recent years to persuade emigrés to return from abroad, but it seems unlikely that this would be a major source of growth in the future.

TABLE 2   Vital Rates of the U.S.S.R. and the United States: Selected Years, 1913–57

YEAR	U.S.S.R.				UNITED STATES			
	Rate per 1,000 population			Infant mortality rate[1]	Rate per 1,000 population			Infant mortality rate[1]
	Birth	Death	Natural increase		Birth	Death	Natural increase	
1913	47.0	30.2	16.8	273	[2]29.5	[2]13.2	[2]16.3	[2]99.9
1940	31.7	18.3	13.4	184	19.4	10.8	8.6	47.0
1950	26.5	9.6	16.9	81	24.1	9.6	14.5	29.2
1951	26.8	9.6	17.2	84	24.9	9.7	15.2	28.4
1952	26.4	9.3	17.1	75	25.1	9.6	15.5	28.4
1953	24.9	9.0	15.9	68	25.0	9.6	15.4	27.8
1954	26.5	8.9	17.6	68	25.3	9.2	16.1	26.6
1955	25.6	8.2	17.4	60	25.0	9.3	15.7	26.4
1956	25.0	7.5	17.5	47	25.2	9.4	15.8	26.0
1957	25.3	7.8	17.5	45	25.3	9.6	15.7	26.3

[1] Deaths of infants under 1 year of age per 1,000 births.
[2] Rates for 1915. Death rate for 1913 is 13.8.
Source: U.S.S.R.: *Vestnik Statistiki*, No. 10, 1958, p. 93, United States: Various editions of *Statistical Abstract of the United States.*

The present level is slightly above the rate in 1913 but the tendency between 1913 and 1940 was in the other direction. The only way to guess at the prospective course of natural increase, therefore, is to examine its two components: the death rate and the birth rate.

2. *The Death Rate.* — The death rate of 7.5 per thousand which was reported along with the census results is not the lowest in the world as claimed, but is nevertheless an impressively low rate. It represents real gains in Soviet science, medicine, and sanitation, and also reflects a favorable age and sex structure of the population.

If the United States death rates[8] for individual age-sex groups are assumed for the population of the U.S.S.R.,[9] a death rate of 6.4 per thousand results. Comprising this with the U.S.S.R. crude rate of 7.5 strongly sug-

[8] Rates for 1955 were used. See United Nations *Demographic Yearbook, 1957.*
[9] The population used for this exercise was an estimated distribution for 1958 prepared by the Foreign Manpower Research Office, Bureau of the Census. The structure of this estimated population is consistent with all known facts about the Soviet population but there is, of course, no guarantee that it is a completely accurate reproduction.

gests lower mortality for specific age and sex groups in the United States than in the Soviet Union.

Additional evidence that mortality in the U.S.S.R. has not reached the level of the United States comes from a comparison of infant mortality rates, one of the most sensitive indicators of the general level of health in a population. The Soviet infant mortality rate as reported for 1957 (45 per thousand live births)[10] exceeds that of the United States (26) by 73 per cent. It is about the level of the prewar U.S. rate and very close to the present rates for Italy and Japan. Nevertheless, a rate of 45 per thousand for the U.S.S.R. represents a striking decline from its prewar level of 184 per thousand, which is higher than the rates currently reported for any of the underdeveloped countries of the world. It is clear that the U.S.S.R. has partaken fully of the worldwide revolution in medicine and public health. This is clear also from the life expectancy figures which have been released. The expectation of life at birth reported for

[10] *Vestnik statistiki* ["Statistical Herald"], No. 10, 1958, p. 93.

TABLE 3 Comparison of Vital Rates for the U.S.S.R. and the United States: 1940 and 1957

COUNTRY	1940			1957		
	Birth	Death	Natural Increase	Birth	Death	Natural Increase
1940 rate = 100:						
U.S.S.R.	100	100	100	80	43	131
United States	100	100	100	130	89	183
U.S.S.R. rate = 100:						
U.S.S.R.	100	100	100	100	100	100
United States	61	59	64	100	123	90

Source: Table 2.

the U.S.S.R. in 1955–56[11] was 63 years for males and 69 years for females. In the United States, male life expectation attained a comparable level in 1941, but the average length of life for females did not reach 69 years until after the war. Since the end of the war 3 years have been added to the average length of life of U.S. males; the average length of life of U.S. females has been stretched by 5 years. The expectation of life at birth for the United States in 1956 was 67 years for males and 73 years for females. Thus, although the U.S.S.R. has not yet achieved the low levels of mortality of the United States, the picture from the official figures is of impressive gains.

Another relevant aspect of the mortality situation in the U.S.S.R. is the amount of variation in the death rate between different parts of the country. In 1955 the crude death rate[12] varied from a low of 6.6 in the Republic of Georgia to 11.9 for Estonia.[13] Crude death rates in the United States in the same year ex-

hibit an almost identical range of variation: 6.6 for Utah to 11.7 for New Hampshire. Age appears to be a factor in explaining these variations in both cases, although for the Soviet Union our only measure of age composition is the ratio of voters — persons 18 years of age and over — to total population. Thus, the relatively high death rate for Estonia would seem to be associated with the fact that almost 8 out of 10 persons in that republic are 18 years of age or older. In the Republic of Georgia, where the lowest death rate is found, approximately 6 out of 10 are 18 years and over. The difference between the extreme death rates in the United States is also associated with difference in age. In New Hampshire 67 per cent of the population is 18 years and over while in Utah the figure is 58 per cent.[14]

A more important point, however, is the fact that if we eliminate from consideration the two areas of the Soviet Union with the highest death rates and the oldest populations — Estonia and Latvia[15] — the death rates for all

[11] *Dostizheniya sovetskoy vlasti za sorok let v tsifrakh* ["Accomplishment of the Soviet Regime Over 40 Years, in Figures"], Moscow, 1957, p. 345. Very little is known about the data from which these life expectancy values were computed. The construction of new Soviet life tables is planned for 1961 using data from the recent population census.

[12] A crude rate is based upon the total number of events of some type occurring to a stated population during a given period of time. Refined rates measure events among more restricted populations in order to exclude the influence of certain variables.

[13] Rates for Uzbekistan and Turkmenistan are not available.

[14] U.S. Department of Commerce, Bureau of the Census, "Estimate of the Civilian Population by Broad Age Groups for States and Selected Outlying Areas: July 1, 1957," *Current Population Reports*, Series P–25, No. 194. The difference in age composition between these two States is more clearly brought out by comparing the population 65 years and over: New Hampshire, 11.1 per cent; Utah, 6.3 per cent.

[15] Latvia's death rate in 1955 was 10.5. Seventy-two per cent of the population of Latvia was 18 years of age and over. In both the ratio of deaths to total population and the ratio of voters to total population, Latvia ranks second to Estonia.

the remaining areas are below the lowest ever reached by the United States. With the differences between the two countries in infant mortality and average length of life favoring the United States, the indicators again point to a young population as a principal ingredient in the low Soviet death rates. Inaccuracies in the statistics themselves cannot be dismissed as a reason for the low death rates reported by the U.S.S.R. We have no definite information, however, that would lead us to believe that deaths are less accurately reported than the population figures to which they are related.

With no high death rate areas susceptible to easy victories, the future course of the Soviet death rate would seem to be an upstream struggle against an aging population, for the declines in age-specific mortality which are to be expected cannot be counted on to fully counteract a trend toward a higher crude death rate. This trend will be reinforced by a balancing out of the number of men and women in the population. Death rates are higher among men than women, and thus the present deficit of U.S.S.R. males acts to hold down the general death rate.[16] As the gap between the number of men and women closes, the crude rate will tend to rise.

3. *The Birth Rate.* — The announced Soviet birth rate (25 births per thousand population) is very close to that which has been recorded for the United States in recent years. Both the Soviet and United States birth rates have been fairly stable since 1950. The difference is that the U.S.S.R. birth rate has never regained its prewar level whereas the current U.S. rate is as high as any that has been recorded since before World War I. Very different demographic dynamics, therefore, underlie the surface similarity of the United States and U.S.S.R. crude birth rates.

In the United States, for example, there is relatively little geographic variation in the crude rates outside of several States in the South and Southwest where the birth rate exceeds 30 per thousand.[17] These States, however, currently account for only 5 per cent of the births. In the U.S.S.R., on the other hand, much greater geographic variation in the birth rate is encountered. Areas with birth rates greater than 30 in 1955 accounted for nearly one-quarter of all births. Younger populations, balanced sex ratios, and higher age-specific fertility rates are no doubt all involved in these high birth rates. Most of the high birth rate areas in the U.S.S.R. are found in the republics of central Asia and Transcaucasia. Continued social and economic change in these areas can be expected to have a downward effect on the birth rate.

As in the United States, so it is in the Soviet Union that the birth rates in rural areas are higher than in urban areas. In this connection, therefore, it is important to note that about 60 per cent of Soviet families are rural families.[18] It is nearly the reverse in the United States, where in 1957 over 60 per cent of the families were urban.[19] As Soviet farmers continue to move to the city and as the countryside becomes urbanized, a tendency toward lower birth rates is expectable.

Marriage in the U.S.S.R. has to contend with a difficult housing situation — more of a barrier perhaps in urban than in rural places. Perhaps equally important in its effect on the proportion married is the imbalance between the sexes. As it affects the birth rate, however, this is of diminishing importance since the sexes in the most fertile years (under 32) are now stated to be equal. The marriage rate of 12 per thousand is relatively high (the U.S. rate in 1957 was 8.9) and undoubtedly reflects this balance of the sexes in the marriageable ages. The marriage rate and the birth rate do not always move together and it is risky, therefore, to put any emphasis on the probable future decline in the Soviet marriage rate.[20]

To forecast the results of the various factors impinging on the birth rate is hazardous.[21]

---

[16] For more on the age and sex composition of the Soviet population, see Section III below.
[17] *Statistical Abstract, 1958*, p. 58.

[18] *Planovoye khozyaystvo* ["Planned Economy"], No. 6, 1955, p. 55.
[19] *Statistical Abstract, 1958*, p. 47. The percentage reported is 63.3. This is an understatement of the urban proportion since it refers only to places which were urban in 1950.
[20] The nature of the Soviet marriage rate is not perfectly clear since the handling of common-law marriages is unknown. There is besides, perhaps, some tendency toward inflation in the rate, since marriage certificates are useful in obtaining housing allocations in certain areas.
[21] For a discussion of the factors which might be expected to influence future Soviet fertility, see Chapter 3 [not included in the present selection — Eds.].

There is much high fertility potential to be reduced in central Asia and among rural families. However, the great unknowns are the relative number of married persons now and in the future, and the extent to which arbitrary family limitation will be practiced in the future.[22]

If we can assume that the Soviet birth rate already reflects the impact of an increased marriage rate and an increase in the proportion of the population married, the net effect from all other influences would be toward a lower crude birth rate in the future.

D. Summary of Growth Prospects

Only the most tentative and cautious conclusions about the future rate of natural increase can be drawn from a consideration of the present birth and death rates reported for the U.S.S.R. There is some reason, however, to expect an increase in the over-all death rate due to the aging of the population and an expectable increase in the proportion of males in the population. Such an increase would most likely be moderated by a further decline in age-specific mortality, but if the present reported levels of infant mortality and life expectation are correct, such gains would have a minor effect on the total number of deaths. There is not enough information for a convincing analysis of Soviet fertility. However, the large proportion of rural families and the high birth rates of the underdeveloped areas within the Soviet Union are threats to a sustained, high level of the national birth rate.

With a slight rise in the death rate and some decline in fertility, the natural increase rate of the Soviet Union could easily fall below that of the United States at the present time. More importantly, however, the implication of a diminished rate of natural increase for the U.S.S.R., and even of a closer correspondence in the over-all size of the Soviet Union and the United States, depends upon the ecological and

---

22 Abortions have been legalized in the Soviet Union since 1955. No stipulations other than proper medical and sanitary safeguards are made. Abortions have been reported to exceed 30 per cent of the live births in recent years. Concern over the high rate of abortions appears to have stimulated serious Soviet interest in contraception. See report of Abraham Stone in *Science,* Vol. 127, May 16, 1958.

social organization of each population aggregate.

II. *Redistribution of the Population*

Changes in the geographic distribution of the Soviet population between 1939 and 1959 reflect two major trends — movements from west to east and from rural territory to urban areas. Both movements continue trends established in the previous intercensal period, 1926–39. Like comparable movements in the United States, they indicate a nation undergoing rapid industrialization and making adjustments to utilize its resources more fully.

A. *Total Population*

The census results show some striking increases in the population of Eastern regions of the U.S.S.R. A gain of 70 per cent was reported for the total population of the Far East, 32 per cent for eastern Siberia, 33 per cent for the Urals, 53 per cent for Kazakhstan, and 42 per cent for Kirgiziya — as compared with an increase of 9.5 per cent in the total. Despite these high rates of increase, however, the absolute shift of population from west to east has been quite moderate. Seventy per cent of the Soviet population now lives west of the Urals. Before the war, the population in this part of the country, which constitutes only 21 per cent of the total area, was 76 per cent of the total (Table 4).

The only three regions which showed a decrease in population between the censuses were the central European part of the R.S.F.S.R. (around Moscow), Belorussia, and Lithuania. Of these three, the central European region was the big loser, with a net loss of 3.2 million.

A rough comparison of this west-east shift in the U.S.S.R. to population shifts in the United States between 1940 and 1957 indicates that the movement of the Soviet population to the east has been greater than the westward movement in the United States (Table 5). In 1940, 69 per cent of the population lived east of the Mississippi in 29 per cent of the total area. By 1957 the proportion of the population east of the Mississippi had dropped slightly to 67 per cent.

These figures do not reveal the dramatic increase which occurred in the Pacific region (comprising California, Oregon, and Washington), which increased by 8.7 million be-

TABLE **4**   *Percentage Distribution of the Area and Population of the U.S.S.R., by Western and Eastern Regions, 1939 and 1959*

REGION	AREA	POPULATION					
		Total		Urban		Rural	
		1939	1959	1939	1959	1939	1959
Total.........	100.0	100.0	100.0	100.0	100.0	100.0	100.0
West of the Urals .	21.0	75.5	69.8	76.1	68.6	75.2	70.9
Urals and east	78.9	24.5	30.2	23.9	31.4	24.8	29.1

Source: Area — Informatsionno-Statisticheskiy Otdel Prezidiuma Verkhovnovo Soveta SSSR, *SSSR Administrativno-territorial'noye deleniye soyuznykh respublik na 1 yanvarya 1958 goda* ["U.S.S.R. Administrative-Territorial Divisions of the Union Republics on January 1, 1958"], Moscow, 1958, pp. 13–483.
1939 Population — *Izvestiya*, May 10, 1959; Tsentral'noye Statisticheskoye Upravleniye, *Sovetskaya torgovlya* ["Soviet Trade"], Moscow, 1957, pp. 312–332.
1959 Population — *Izvestiya*, May 10, 1959.

tween 1940 and 1957, or by more than 89 per cent. This was a much larger increase than was registered by any of the Soviet economic regions; the largest gain there was 70 per cent for the Far East. Other regions of the United States which showed marked gains were the Mountain region, 54 per cent; South Atlantic, 38 per cent; and East North Central, 32 per cent.

Two conclusions thus emerge: (1) Certain areas within the U.S.S.R. — especially those east of the Urals — have exhibited remarkable rates of growth since the prewar period in spite of only a moderate increase of the total population. These rates of increase have been equaled by several areas in the United States during roughly the same period. (2) The rapid growth of the Soviet east has produced a very moderate eastward shift in the population. In the United States, using the traditional east-west dividing line of the Mississippi, differential regional growth has not appreciably affected the prewar east-west population balance.

The eastward shift of some 16 million persons between 1939 and 1959 occurred as the result of both migration and natural increase, their relative importance being difficult to evaluate. Millions of people were moved to the Urals and other eastern areas during the war, and many never returned to their homes. Thousands of servicemen demobilized since

World War II have also settled in the east. The greatest source of migration, however, has been the planned — often forced — resettlement of both families and single persons from the cities and villages of the European west to the new lands of the east. Soviet sources carry daily reports of families — often thousands of families — who have undertaken a pioneering venture beyond the Urals. A certain number of these migrants return to their former homes, but it seems clear that large numbers have become permanent residents in the east.

Other factors producing the population shift have been the relatively smaller civilian war losses of the regions east of the Urals, and a higher rate of natural increase which characterized these areas before and since the war.

It is probable that the eastward shift of the Soviet population will continue for some time. The current 7-year plan contains provisions for an accelerated development of the east, and a planned flow of both industrial and agricultural labor to take part in the new programs is to be expected. This, together with higher rates of natural increase, should produce a steady, gradual shift of Soviet population to the east.

B. Urban Population

The urban population of the U.S.S.R. increased from 60.4 to 99.8 million between

TABLE **5** *Percentage Distribution of the Area and Population of the United States, East and West of the Mississippi River: 1940, 1950, and 1957*

REGION	AREA	POPULATION							
		Total			Urban		Rural		
		1940	1950	1957	1940	1950	1940	1950	
Total.........	100.0	100.0	100.0	100.0	100.0	100.0	100.0	100.0	
East of the Mississippi	29.1	69.2	68.1	67.0	74.0	70.4	63.1	64.6	
West of the Mississippi	70.9	30.8	31.9	33.0	26.0	29.6	36.9	35.4	

Source: Area — U.S. Bureau of the Census, *Statistical Abstract of the United States: 1958* (79th edition), Washington, D.C., p. 160. Population — *Ibid.*, pp. 10, 13, and 23. 1957 data are provisional figures for July 1.

1939 and 1959, a gain of more than 65 per cent. Compared with the increase of 9.5 per cent in the total population, this is an impressive change. It bespeaks a torrential flow of population from rural to urban areas as a concomitant of rapid industrialization.

Nevertheless, the process of urbanization in the U.S.S.R. has slowed down markedly in comparison with that of the previous intercensal period, 1926–39. Both the annual increment to the urban population and the annual rate of increase are below comparable figures for the earlier period. Between 1939 and 1959 the average annual increment to the urban population was 2.0 million, or half a million less than the annual average increment of 2.5 million between 1926 and 1939. The annual rate of increase, 1939–59, was 3.3 per cent, while the rate for the period 1926–39 was 9.4 per cent. In the most recent period the absolute annual average increase of the Soviet urban population seems to have attained its prewar level but the rate of increase is still around half the average prewar rate despite the fact that the annual increase in the index of industrial output is higher now than before the war.

The Soviet urban population at present is slightly greater than the U.S. urban population at the time of the 1950 census, but probably only about three-fourths of the present urban population of the United States.[23] Stated in terms of the numbers of persons leading a non-agricultural way of life, the differences between this country and the U.S.S.R. are even more extreme. Approximately 85 per cent of rural families in the U.S.S.R. are farm families whereas in the United States the figure is 35 per cent.[24] Thus, while the urban population of the United States probably exceeds the urban population of the Soviet Union by about one-fourth, the estimated nonagricultural population of the United States is one-third greater than that of the U.S.S.R.

The shift of the Soviet urban population to the east has been comparable to that of the total population, as is shown by the data in Table 4. Although there have been some tremendous increases in the number of urban residents in eastern regions, 68.6 per cent of the Soviet urban population still lives west of the Urals.

In all of the eastern regions of the R.S.F.S.R. the urban population increased more than 100 per cent — including a gain of nearly 150 per cent in the Far East. The republics of central Asia showed similar gains — Kirgizia and Tadzhikstan both had increases of more than 150 per cent — while the urban population of Kazakhstan grew by 141 per cent.

23 According to recent estimates by Resources for the Future, Inc., the U.S. urban population in 1960 will be 126,600,000, or 70.5 per cent of the total U.S. population.

24 Based on data in U.S. Bureau of the Census, *Statistical Abstract of the United States, 1957* (78th edition), Washington, D.C., 1957, p. 15; and Tsentral'noye Statisticheskoye Upravleniye pri Sovete Ministrov S.S.S.R., *Narodnoye khozyaystvo S.S.S.R. v 1956 godu* ["National Economy of the U.S.S.R. in 1956"], Moscow, 1957, pp. 19, 105, and 203.

Increases in the western areas were smaller, percentagewise, but greater in numbers of persons. All of the western regions registered urban population increases of more than 30 per cent, with a 36.6 per cent growth in the populous center, around Moscow, and much larger increases in the smaller Baltic and Transcaucasian republics.

The growth of urban population in the U.S.S.R. has been the result of three processes: migration, administrative action, and natural increase. Although the exact share of the increase attributable to each source is not known, it is certain that migration from rural areas has played the greatest role. Since the 1920's there has been a steady flow in this direction, and the rural reservoir is still large.

Administrative action, or a change from rural to urban status by decree, has been another important factor, particularly in the last few years. Between 1939 and 1959 there was a net increase of 1,857 urban places in the U.S.S.R. — 503 new cities and 1,354 new urban-type settlements. Of these, 128 cities and 499 settlements were added in the 3 years between January 1956 and January 1959.[25]

The Soviet Union has a greater number of cities with a population above 50,000 than the United States, 299 in 1959 compared with 232 in the United States in 1950.[26] Of these, the U.S.S.R. had 25 in the size group of 500,000 and above, and the United States had 18. There has been little change in this comparison since before World War II, when the U.S.S.R. had 221 cities with a population of 50,000 or more, and the United States had 199.

C. Rural Population

The other side of the picture of population change in the Soviet Union is the decrease of the rural population. During the intercensal period the number of rural inhabitants dropped by nearly 21 million, or by 16 per cent of the total in 1939. As a proportion of the total population, it declined from 68 per cent in 1939 to 52 per cent in 1959.

Rural inhabitants in the United States, on the other hand, increased by 7.9 per cent be-

tween 1940 and 1950, or from 57.2 to 61.8 million — using the 1940 concept of urban. (If the 1950 definition of urban were used for both 1940 and 1950 the increase in rural population would be somewhat less.) This is consistent with the longtime trend for rural population in the United States which has shown an increase in every decade since the earliest years despite losses in some of the Central States. Unlike the U.S.S.R., where for at least 30 years rural areas have lost population to urban areas, the U.S. rural population, through natural increase and immigration, has managed to supply people to the cities and still increase in size.

The continuing Soviet efforts to develop agriculture in the east, and especially the "virgin lands" campaign which began in 1954, have involved the movement of hundreds of thousands of persons to the east. In 1956 it was announced that more than 350,000 persons had settled in the "virgin lands,"[27] and since that time the movement of both single persons and families has continued. Nevertheless, the shift of rural population eastward has not been great.

It was only in Kazakhstan and in three central Asiatic republics (Uzbek, Tadzhik, and Kirgiz) that the rural population increased. In all eastern regions of the R.S.F.S.R. the rural population decreased. The conclusion which these data suggest is that a large share of the Soviet eastward migration has gone to urban areas, and that within the eastern regions themselves there has been an extensive rural-urban movement.

In the west, all regions but one lost rural population between 1939 and 1959. The Moldavian Republic showed an increase of 5.5 per cent, but the losses in other areas ranged up to a high of 31 per cent in the center, around Moscow.

The slight geographic shift eastward of the U.S. rural population between 1940 and 1950 — from 63 to 65 per cent east of the Mississippi — was of a fundamentally different nature than the eastward shift of the rural population of the U.S.S.R. American farmers west of the Mississippi did not open up new agricultural areas in the east but became part of the rural-urban movement within their own

---

[25] *Narodnoye khozyaystvo* . . ., p. 33, and *Izvestiya*, May 10, 1959.
[26] *Izvestiya*, May 10, 1959, and *Statistical Abstract, 1957*, p. 19.

---

[27] *New York Times*, April 8, 1956.

areas and to other parts of the country. The number of farms and acres of harvested cropland have generally declined in the eastern part of the United States.

III. *Population Composition*

A. *The Sex Ratio*

One of the most significant disclosures of the Soviet census is the low proportion of males in the total population. Females outnumber males by 20 million, a greater imbalance than is shown in any earlier Soviet census.

TABLE 6   *Males per 100 Females, U.S.S.R. and United States, Selected Years*

YEAR	MALES PER 100 FEMALES	
	U.S.S.R.	United States
1926	93.4	103.1
1939	91.9	100.8
1959	81.9	[1]98.0

[1] Includes Armed Forces overseas.

The low sex ratio of 1926 reflects the losses and birth deficits of World War I and the Revolution. To this was added the effects of the calamitous period of collectivization of the 1930's, which depressed the ratio even further in 1939. The present nadir of the sex ratio — the lowest reported for any country in the world except East Germany — is a simple measure of the demographic cost of World War II. Low birth rates during World War II and the longer average length of life of women have been secondary contributors to the low Soviet sex ratio.

B. *Age Composition*

No direct 1959 census information on the age structure of the Soviet population has so far been released. The number of persons 18 years of age and over enumerated in the census has not yet been announced. An approximation to the size of this group is given by the number of voters[28] registered for the March 1959 elections.

---

[28] Legal voting age in the U.S.S.R. is 18.

The ratio of voters (approximately 137 million) to total population when compared with ratios of the same type for earlier years reveals an upward tendency, denoting a decline in the relative size of the preadult population as well, perhaps, as an aging of the adult population due to the increase in the average length of life[29] (Table 7).

TABLE 7   *The Ratio of Registered Voters to Total Population in the U.S.S.R.: Selected Years*

YEAR	VOTERS PER 100 OF THE POPULATION
1939	55
1950	62
1951	62
1955	63
1958	65
1959	65

The only other available indication of the current age composition of the Soviet population is the statement that there are an equal number of males and females under 32 years of age.[30] This is possibly a statement that should not be taken too literally, for in addition to a probable rounding error, it is likely that the number of women reporting themselves as under 32 is somewhat inflated due to the almost universal tendency among women toward polite understatement of age. In general, however, the statement makes sense, since it is the population under 32 that escaped the heaviest mortality of the last war.

The population 18 to 31 years of age in 1959 was born during the years from 1928 to 1941. These are years for which we have some information about births, and if our guesses about the deaths suffered by this group are not too bad, we would expect approximately 53 million persons in the age group 18–31 in 1959. Those 32 and above would therefore equal 84 million (137 million voters minus 53 million 18–31 years of age).

---

[29] Nondemographic factors such as the political amnesties of 1953–56 have helped to increase this ratio but do not appear capable of explaining it.

[30] *Izvestiya*, May 10, 1959.

TABLE 8 *Estimated Current Sex Ratios by Age for the U.S.S.R. and the United States*

	MALES PER 100 FEMALES			MALES PER 100 FEMALES	
AGE	U.S.S.R. 1959	United States, 1960	AGE	U.S.S.R. 1959	United States, 1960
All ages	82	98	45 to 49 years	53	95
			50 to 54 years	62	96
Up to 4 years	105	104	55 to 59 years	64	94
5 to 9 years	104	104	60 to 64 years	60	91
10 to 14 years	104	104	65 to 69 years	58	88
15 to 19 years	104	103	70 years and over	51	79
20 to 24 years	104	102	Under 15 years	104	104
25 to 29 years	91	99	15 to 59 years	77	98
30 to 34 years	80	97	60 years and over	56	85
35 to 39 years	60	96	32 years and over	60	93
40 to 44 years	50	96			

Putting these pieces together with the reported total number of males and females, we arrive at the surprising — and of course very tentative — conclusion that in the ages 32 and above there were more than 5 women for every 3 men (see Table 8).[31] The implied sex ratio of 60 is more than 10 points below that for East Germany, indicating, if true, that the decimation of Soviet troops exceeded that of any other belligerent. The common observation of women doing men's work in the U.S. S.R. needs no further confirmation than the figures here cited.

By adding some more tentative figures to those already considered, we get, in Table 9, a broad profile of the Soviet population in 1959, contrasted with current estimates for the United States.

The preschool population of the U.S.S.R. is approximately 20 per cent greater than that of the United States, according to our rough calculations. This is about as might be expected from a comparison of the estimated number of births in the two countries in recent years. In 1956, estimated births in the U.S.S.R. exceeded the number of U.S. births by 19.6 per cent.

The number of children now receiving their elementary and secondary training (ages 7–17), among whom are the coming generation of scientists and technicians, is not greatly different between the two countries. The reason, of course, is that this group includes those born between 1942 and 1946 when the birth rate was relatively high in the United States and extremely low in the Soviet Union.

Comparison within the young adult age groups (18 to 31) must be made very cautiously since there are reasons to believe that the Soviet figure may be exaggerated.[32] There seems little question, however, that the draft-age population in the Soviet Union exceeds that of the United States by a greater margin than is suggested by the differences in the total population. This does not necessarily mean that the pool of manpower available for military services is that much larger in the U.S. S.R. The relative scarcity of older men re-

[31] The detailed distribution by age in Table 7 . . . has been obtained by adjusting earlier estimates to conform to the new census information. For a full description of the procedures by which the detailed estimates are made, see Campbell and Brackett, *op. cit.*

[32] If the sex ratio for ages 32 and over is raised, the population 32 and over will be increased and the number 18–31 would have to fall in order to be compatible with the total number of voters. This would imply that our estimate of the survivors of births, 1928–41, was too high. This is a readily admitted possibility since the mortality of the war period is still very unclear.

TABLE **9**   *Estimated Age Distribution of the Population of the U.S.S.R. and the United States: 1959 (Absolute Figures in Millions)*

AGE	U.S.S.R.		UNITED STATES[1]	
	Number	Per Cent	Number	Per Cent
All ages	208.8	100.0	180.1	100.0
0 to 6 years	[2]33.0	15.8	27.6	15.3
7 to 17 years.....................	[3]38.8	18.6	36.7	20.4
18 to 31 years	[4]53.0	25.4	32.7	18.2
32 years and over.................	[5]84.0	40.2	83.1	46.1

[1] Estimates for 1960. See *Statistical Abstract, 1958*, pp. 6–7.

[2] Survivors of estimated births 1953–58. See U.S. Bureau of the Census, *Estimates and Projections of the Population of the U.S.S.R.: 1950 to 1976*, Series P–95, No. 52.

[3] Residual. Children enrolled in grades 1–10, the vast bulk of whom are in the age group 7 to 17, are estimated to have numbered approximately 30 million in 1959. The implied school participation rate $\frac{30.0}{38.8} = 0.77$ is reasonable.

[4] Estimated survivors of births, 1928–41. See U.S. Bureau of the Census, *op. cit.*

[5] Registered voters in 1959 all-union elections minus estimated population, 18–31.

quires industry and agriculture to draw upon these men. The greater need for industrial and agricultural manpower in the Soviet Union, due to a lower level of labor productivity, also necessarily increases labor demand.

Comparison of numbers in the final age group is nearly meaningless because of the vast differences in sex composition. To a considerable extent, this already maimed group in the Soviet Union is the one on which the present generation of school children must depend. And they must depend for the most part upon those under 50 — the group most seriously affected by the war and among whom the proportion of married families with both parents present will undoubtedly be low. For these age groups in the United States in 1957 married persons comprised over 80 per cent — a qualitatively and quantitatively different dependency situation.

We might expand this discussion of the "working age" population by drawing upon more detailed estimates of the age and sex composition of the Soviet population prepared by the U.S. Bureau of the Census. These estimates suggest that the Soviet population of "working age," taken here to be 15 to 59 years,

numbered almost 131 million in 1959, 57 million men and 74 million women (see Table 10). The U.S. population in this group numbered about 99 million divided about equally between men and women.

By 1966, the projections point to a working-age population of about 138 million for the U.S.S.R. and 109 million for the United States. While the male population in this age range in the Soviet Union is expected to show a greater increase than the female portion (9 per cent for males compared to only 2.2 per cent for females), it is not expected to grow as much as that for the United States (10.7 per cent for males, 10.5 per cent for females).

To the extent that these estimates of the Soviet age distribution have any validity — and in certain respects, as we have noted, they are not unreasonable — they tend to confirm the over-all census total. That is, they can be accommodated by it. This is not to say that there may not be an error of several million in the reported totals. It does, however, reinforce our earlier conclusion that there is no compelling reason to reject the results which have so far been released. More than that we cannot say until more data become available.

TABLE **10** Comparison of the "Working Age" Population (15 to 59 Years) for the U.S.S.R. and the United States: 1958/1959 and 1965/1966 (in Thousands)

GROUP	SOVIET UNION			UNITED STATES		
	Population		Per Cent change	Population		Per Cent change
	Jan. 1, 1959	Jan. 1, 1966		July 1, 1958	July 1, 1965	
Both sexes......	130,887	137,628	5.2	98,596	109,054	10.6
Male	56,785	61,911	9.0	48,744	53,966	10.7
Female	74,102	75,717	2.2	49,850	55,088	10.5

Source: United States, 1958: Appendix Tables E and F and *Statistical Abstract of the United States: 1959*, p. 24.

STAGES OF SOVIET DEVELOPMENT

4

Historical Background of the Russian Revolution*

E. H. Carr

(1953)

E. H. Carr, probably the most eminent of historians of the Soviet period, reminds us that the Bolshevik Revolution did not come "like a thunderclap out of a clear sky," but reflected forces going back at least to the emancipation of the serfs and before that to the Decembrist officers' revolt of 1825. It is hotly debated whether or not Tsarist Russia possessed an adequate social base for a democratic evolution which might have taken place had it not been for the violence on which Bolshevism insisted and which it engendered. The weight of opinion is with Mr. Carr in arguing that under Tsarist autocracy appropriate institu-

* Reprinted from "The Background of Revolution," *Current History*, Vol. 25 (1953), pp. 65–69, by permission of the author and the publisher.

tions on which to rest democratic development had not had time to evolve — leaving that "void of chaos and anarchy" into which the Bolsheviks leapt.

The Bolshevik revolution of October 1917 did not come like a thunderclap out of a clear sky. It had been preceded eight months earlier by the February revolution which overthrew the Czar and set up a liberal republican government. The February revolution was not only the product of two-and-a-half years of frustration and disorganization in the First World War; it was also an echo of the short-lived revolution of 1905 which had followed defeat in the Russo-Japanese War, and which now seemed in retrospect like a dress rehearsal for the major event of 12 years later.

The 1905 revolution had behind it a long trail of incipient or abortive revolutionary movements, beginning with the so-called "December" conspiracy of 1825 — an officers' mutiny aiming at a palace revolution. The distant, faintly heard rumble of revolution had been the background of Russian history and, still more, of Russian literature and thought, all through the nineteenth century.

If, however, one seeks a convenient and arbitrary starting point for the story of 1917, the best landmark to take is the emancipation of the serfs by Czar Alexander II in 1861. The emancipation was an attempt to break up the feudal structure of Russian society, and to introduce into the primitive peasant economy the beginnings of industrial development on modern Western lines. In Marxist terminology, it was the first stage of the Russian bourgeois revolution — the same process set on foot in Western Europe by the French Revolution and its economic concomitant, the Industrial Revolution.

It was, like one previous important attempt to transform and modernize the basis of Russian life under Peter the Great, a revolution from above. The impulse came from within the ruling class, from a group of courtiers who had the ear of the Czar. Its motive was to remedy the chronic inefficiency and backwardness revealed by the Crimean War, and, by bringing the Russian administrative, military, and economic machine up to date, to enable Russia once more to hold her own among the European powers.

But it was also a revolution from above designed, as Alexander II confessed, to forestall a revolution from below. In this respect it enjoyed a real, though equivocal, success. Short though it fell of meeting the needs and demands of the peasants, it went far enough to put an end to the long series of peasant revolts which had marked the course of Russian history.

But in so doing, it made certain that the Russian Revolution, when it came, would be infinitely more profound and more far-reaching. The emancipation and its consequences, direct and indirect, determined the course and character of the revolution of 1917.

By breaking the legal fetters which riveted the peasant to the land, the emancipation created the raw material of an industrial proletariat, and made possible the development of a "free" labor market. In other words, it played the same role in Russian history as the enclosures played in the early stages of the industrialization of Great Britain. The process developed slowly, and gathered momentum only in the 1890's, when the international conjunction of forces gave birth to a Franco-Russian alliance, and stimulated an abundant flow of French capital investment to Russia for the purpose of building up Russia's industrial and military strength.

Peculiar Development

Under these impulses Russian industry, and especially heavy industry, developed in the 20 years before 1914 at an astonishingly rapid rate. But the same impulses gave a peculiar twist to the industrialization of the Russian economy. First of all, large-scale Russian industry almost from the moment of its birth was geared to the production of "war potential," including railway construction, rather than to the needs of a consumer market. It was "planned" in the sense that it depended primarily on government orders, not on spontaneous market demand; it was financed by loans accorded for political reasons rather than for the traditional "capitalist" motive of earning commercial profits. In these respects it anticipated much that was to happen in Russia under the Five Year Plans 30 years later.

Secondly, the tardy arrival of industrialization in Russia meant that it skipped over many of the earlier stages through which the much slower growth of industrialization had passed in Western Europe — the gradual transformation from the single-handed craftsman to the small workshop, and from the first primitive factory to the giant agglomeration employing hundreds and thousands of workers.

When modern Russian industry was born at the end of the nineteenth century, it immediately assumed the characteristic modern shape of the large-scale factory. Already before 1914, one quarter of all Russian industrial workers worked in factories employing more than one thousand persons each. In Germany the corresponding proportion was only 8 per cent; in Great Britain it was lower still. Russian industry, the youngest in Europe and in other respects the most backward, was the most advanced in respect of the concentration of production in large-scale units.

This hot-house development of Russian industry produced a social structure sharply differentiated from that of the older industrial communities of Western Europe, and falsified the prognostications of those Marxists who assumed that Russia would imitate, at a long interval of time, but without substantial modifications, the experience of the West and travel the Western democratic and capitalist road.

History, as commonly happens, failed to repeat itself. The rapidity and belatedness of Russian industrial development shaped the human factor on both sides of industry on distinctive lines of its own. In the West, something of the spirit of the earlier entrepreneur, attentive to the changing conditions of the market and in close personal contact with his workers, survived even in the manager of modern industry. In Russia, the industrial manager was from the first the administrator, the organizer, the bureaucrat. In the West, the industrial worker contrived to retain, even in the age of mass production, something of the personal skills and independent spirit of the artisan. In Russia, the vast majority of the new generation of industrial workers were still peasants in factory clothes.

A "gray mass" of peasants had been transformed overnight into a gray mass of factory workers. But to drive the peasant into the factories and force on him the rigors of factory routine required — before, as after, the revolution of 1917 — a harsh and relentless discipline which shaped relations between industrial management and industrial worker on lines of a sharply defined class hostility. Weak and backward as it was, the Russian proletariat provided far more fertile soil than the advanced proletariats of the West for the proletarian revolution.

The factories had, however, touched only the fringes of the Russian peasantry. When the revolution took place, more than 80 per cent of the population still lived on the land. The emancipation had freed the peasant from a legal status which had become an intolerable anachronism. But it had not solved the agrarian problem.

The peasant commune as a collective organ of cultivation was less, rather than more, efficient when the rights of the landowner had been abrogated; and the annuities now payable by the peasant proved not less onerous in practice than the obligation formerly owed by him to the landowner. What the emancipation did was to give the exceptionally capable, industrious, or fortunate peasant the opportunity to rise out of the ruck and prosper at the expense of his less provident fellows, to acquire livestock and implements, to hire a worker or two, and set up as a petty landowner on his own — in a word, to become a *kulak*.

To encourage the *kulak* was the purpose of the Stolypin reform of 1908 in the system of land tenure, described by its author as a "wager on the strong." But, once again, too little was done and the time was too short. The prosperity of a few was enhanced at the expense of the increasing misery of many. The emancipation seemed to have staved off the revolution by lifting the burdens of serfdom from the shoulders of the peasant. But, in liberating him, it had destroyed the traditional structure of society and created no other. The peasant, cast adrift, could not make a revolution for himself. But he could, as the sequel showed, easily be harnessed to a revolution made by others.

Belated Reform

The political history of the Russian autocracy in the half century before 1914 reveals the same insecure and transitional character. Just as the emancipation of the serfs was a belated attempt to modernize the Russian economy on Western lines, so the political reforms which accompanied it were an attempt to bring an obsolete system of government up to date by borrowing and adapting Western liberal and democratic institutions. The courts were reformed, rudimentary social services were established, and an enlightened — though scarcely democratic — machinery of local self-government was grafted on to the rigid age-old trunk of autocratic power.

But, just as the Russian economy developed in a forcing house at a temperature maintained by pressures from without, so the political reforms grew not from the strength of their own indigenous roots, but under alien impulses from the West. They were accepted, reluctantly and with suspicion, by the rulers of Russia. Rarely has there been so striking a confirmation of Tocqueville's dictum that the foundations of revolution are laid when a ruling class loses confidence in its own right to rule.

It would be foolish to argue that Russia was inherently incapable of developing an industrial capitalist economy, or liberal democratic institutions, or of producing a commercially and democratically minded middle class and a thrifty and responsible "labor aristocracy" (to borrow Engels' convenient phrase). All these things had happened in the West. But, for history to repeat itself in Russia, it would have been necessary to isolate Russia from the external pressures of the West, so that events there could follow their own natural course of development.

What was not possible was to telescope into

a period of fifty years the evolution of Russia from a primitive feudal society into a modern industrial democracy. Yet this is what was required if Russia was to catch up the time-lag and confront the Western Powers as their peer. Hence, in the ding-dong battle waged throughout this period of Russian history between the traditionalists and the reformers (or revolutionaries), between those who thought that things were moving too fast for stability and those who thought they were not moving fast enough to catch up with the modern world, both sides were right.

Things were not moving nearly fast enough to put Russia on terms of material equality with the Western Powers. But the traditional supports of autocracy were being hacked away far too rapidly and ruthlessly for the halting efforts of those who were trying to raise pillars of society and government to replace them.

The story of the fifty years before 1914 explains why, when the revolution came, the whole edifice collapsed with a startling suddenness, leaving behind it a void of chaos and anarchy with hardly any constructive forces in sight. In 1905 defeat in the Japanese war almost gave the autocracy its *coup de grace*. The proletariat of Petrograd revolted and tasted a brief moment of power in the first Petrograd Soviet. The liberals reiterated their demand for constitutional reform, and obtained promises which were not kept. The army hesitated, and stood firm.

A naval mutiny did not spread. Smoldering peasant discontents broke out, but too sporadically and too late to affect the issue. It was a trial of strength. But, once more, the concessions made, the reforms undertaken or promised, while they did not go far enough to allay the revolutionary ferment, went more than far enough to complete the discrediting of autocratic government. After 1905 the autocracy was a self-confessed failure.

When the storm broke in Petrograd in February 1917, friend and foe alike were overwhelmed by the suddenness and completeness. The old order collapsed, not because new claimants for power were pushing it aside, but through its own inherent rottenness. No intermediate period of compromise with the decaying monarchy, such as occurred at the beginning of the French Revolution, was possible. Abdication was from the first the all

but universal demand; attempts to secure continuity by substituting the brother or young son of the fallen Czar failed through lack of any broad basis of support.

Out of this void two potential governments emerged; the Provisional Government of the liberal intelligentsia, pledged to some form of constitutional government and using the watchwords of democracy, and the Petrograd Soviet, a revival of 1905, claiming to speak in the mystic name of "the revolution."

Dual Power

But neither of these forces was united or determined enough to govern a nation at war in the throes of an inextricable economic and military crisis. From February to October, 1917, in conditions of ever increasing chaos, Russia lived under the so-called "dual power" — an uneasy compromise of mutual and grudging toleration between the Provisional Government and the regime of the Soviets (for these had sprung up, spontaneously and anarchically, all over Russia).

The Bolsheviks were at the outset a tiny majority in the Soviets. These were everywhere dominated by the peasant party of the Social Revolutionaries; in Petrograd and Moscow the Bolsheviks were, at first, outnumbered even by the Mensheviks. It was not till September that the Bolsheviks obtained a majority in the Petrograd and Moscow Soviets; almost everywhere else they remained in a minority till after the revolution.

Nor at the start were the Bolsheviks themselves united. Like everyone else, they had underestimated the breakneck spread of events in Russia, and assumed that the revolution there, having overthrown the Czar, would pass through its constitutional and capitalist phase. Only Trotsky, who had seen the revolution of 1905 at closer quarters than any of the other leaders, clearly realized that the basis for the intermediate stage, corresponding to the liberal democracy of the Western world, was lacking in Russia.

By the time Lenin returned from exile to Petrograd in April 1917 he had come round independently to the same view, and forced it on his at first wavering colleagues. The record of events between the February and October revolutions of 1917 reveals that the Bolsheviks seized power, not because this was part of their original intention, and not because they had at first any large measure of support for such a policy. They seized power because the intermediate democratic regime which they, in common with all the other revolutionaries, had expected to see established, proved impotent.

This was the situation that Trotsky had foreseen, and which Lenin diagnosed from Switzerland in the first days after the February revolution. It is, of course, true that the Bolsheviks played their part in discrediting the Provisional Government and the parties in the Soviet which later joined the government coalition. But their power and their following were at first extremely small; and they could have made little headway against a government of even moderate strength and determination.

Like the February revolution, the October revolution was almost bloodless. In Petrograd there was no resistance worth the name. The Bolsheviks won because, once the Czar was overthrown, they were the only group who consistently showed confidence in their ability to seize and maintain power. Every middle road seemed to be blocked.

The dilemma which had opened the road to power for the Bolsheviks continued to beset the new regime when power had fallen into its hands. The feverish attempt to catch up the time-lag which separated the Russian economy from that of the West had proved fatal to the Russian autocracy. It had frustrated the ambitions of Russian liberals. The attempt had now to be made once more in the new conditions. No Marxist had hitherto believed that it was possible to make the transition, politically or economically, to socialism except in a community which had already passed through the stages of developed democracy and capitalism.

If Lenin and the early Bolsheviks now believed this possible, if they believed that backward Russia could catch up and surpass the rest of Europe, it was because they also believed that the proletarian revolution was imminent in Europe, and that the advanced worker could come to the aid of his more backward Russian colleagues.

When the hope of European revolution faded, the Bolshevik regime was faced once more with the old unsolved dilemma. How could the gap between autocracy and socialism be bridged in a country which had never

had time to learn the lessons of bourgeois democracy? How could an advanced socialist order be built in a predominantly peasant country which had never possessed the resources in capital equipment and trained workers proper to a fully fledged capitalist economy? What would be the fate of the attempt of a socialist economy in Russia to catch up and overtake the economic development of the Western world — an attempt which had already proved incompatible with the survival of Russian autocracy and with the hopes of Russian democracy? The answer to these questions was to provide the central theme of the history of the Soviet period.

5

From Lenin Through Stalin*

Waldemar Gurian

(1952)

Prof. Gurian's compact but thorough review of the stages of Soviet development carries us from 1917, through World War II, to the year just prior to Stalin's death. Although he highlights the shifts and turns in Soviet policy, Prof. Gurian differs with many analysts who see elements of discontinuity in this sequence. He sees it as unified by an underlying theme: the drive by Lenin and Stalin to establish, preserve, and expand the power of the totalitarian state.

1917–1921: War Communism and NEP

A brief survey of the various phases of the Soviet regime will give a general picture of its development. In the first months of propaganda decrees and the destruction of traditional groups and institutions, Lenin began to change from a negative policy of destroying the old regime and its heritage to a policy of building up the instruments of power for the

* Reprinted from "The Development of the Soviet Regime," *Bolshevism: An Introduction to Soviet Communism* (1952), pp. 42–54, University of Notre Dame Press, by permission of the publisher.

new regime. His acceptance of the peace treaty of Brest-Litovsk† and his emphasis upon order and discipline prove that Lenin realized the necessity of taking existing conditions into account. There was some hesitation before socialization of industrial enterprises occurred;[1] for Lenin and the party had believed that it would be sufficient for the workers to control and direct the bourgeois capitalists. But this control proved unworkable and the regime was forced to seize the enterprises.

However, even Lenin, despite his basic realism, sometimes inclined toward utopian projects, such as that aiming at a quick transformation of society with the help of a universal labor service and the abolition of money payment.[2] At the same time, he realized the necessity for educating the masses as well as the representatives of the new regime. The role of non-Bolshevik specialists was stressed, as was the necessity for learning from the technical experiences of the past.

The first period, which combined utopian experiments and decrees with attempts at a realistic approach, prepared the organization of a strong political power and the imposition of discipline on the masses; soon it developed into the period of civil war and so-called War Communism (1918–1920). During this second period Communist policy was dominated by the need to crush the various White armies.[3] These armies received support, first from some German military circles, who in 1918 opposed the policy of the German Foreign Office and aided efforts to destroy General Krasnov's Red regime. After the disappearance of Imperial Germany, the Allies aided the White Russian armies. Despite the collapse of the original hopes that the confiscatory policies of this period would achieve the quick construction

of a socialist-communist society, these policies did make it possible for the Communists to conduct and win the civil war. For, though production had decreased to a minimum, confiscation proved a sufficient means of obtaining supplies for the Red army.

The defeat in the war against Poland (1920), the well-known uprising in Kronstadt (the naval port of Petrograd), and the lesser known peasants' revolts in Central Russia, caused Lenin to call for a retreat after the Red victory in the civil war. The White armies had suffered annihilating defeats; they had been unable to coordinate their operations because they were weakened by conflicts between democratic and moderate-socialistic politicians on the one side, and the conservative military leadership on the other; they did not receive, despite many promises, enough support from abroad; and they often incensed the masses of the people — workers in industrial areas and peasants, particularly in Siberia — by seeming to favor the return to an outdated pre-revolutionary social order.

On the other hand, Lenin realized that the exhausted and tired masses needed a return to normal conditions after their sacrifices and sufferings during the civil war. He realized, too, that a quick transformation of World War I into a world revolution would not take place. The collapse of Imperial Germany and of the Hapsburg Dual Monarchy did not result in the rise of Communist regimes; the Soviet regimes in Bavaria and Hungary were of brief duration. The Soviets were unable to reconquer the Baltic States and to impose a Communist government upon Poland, though they did succeed in establishing a Ukrainian Soviet Republic and, later, in conquering the Menshevik Republic of Georgia.

Lenin's foreign policy, like his domestic policy, had a dual character from the beginning. The Third International, founded in Moscow in 1919, aimed to prepare and organize revolution outside Russia by unifying the various pro-Communist groups and directing the development of the various Communist parties.[4] The Comintern imposed 21 points upon parties wishing to join; it kept authority in its own hands and excluded socialist leaders it re-

---

† [In March 1918 the Soviet Government signed a separate peace treaty with the Central Powers. It ended Russian participation in World War I, but imposed enormous losses of territory, population, and natural and capital resources upon the new Bolshevik regime. — *Eds.*]
[1] M. Dobb, *Soviet Economic Development since 1917* (London, 1948).
[2] Lenin, *Sotchinenia* ["Works"], Vol. XXII (3rd. ed., Moscow, 1929), pp. 168 f.
[3] W. H. Chamberlin, *The Russian Revolution, 1917–1921* (New York, 1937); G. Stewart, *The White Armies* (New York, 1933).

---

[4] F. Borkenau, *World Communism* (New York, 1939).

garded as untrustworthy. But at the same
time treaties were concluded by the Soviet
regime with capitalist governments, and the
independence of the Baltic States was recognized, for the Soviet government realized that
its attempt to impose communist government
upon these states, after the German collapse of
1918, had failed. Poland received territorial
concessions by the treaty of Riga, after the
Soviet armies were routed at Warsaw. The
treaty of Rapallo established friendly relations
with Germany and permitted the utilization
of German military experience by the Red
Army. The treaty was concluded in 1922 with
the Weimar Republic,[5] though this regime had
originated from a defeat imposed upon German pro-Communists. The realistic policy of
Rapallo did not end revolutionary expectations
and policies; the Soviet leaders tried — though
without success — to establish Communist
domination in Germany, while the Weimar
Republic was weakened by the Ruhr conflict of
1923. This realistic foreign policy, however,
was based not only upon calculations of Russian national interest, but also took into consideration the limits of Soviet strength as well
as the decline of revolutionary enthusiasm and
fluidity in the world after 1920. However,
despite their realism, Soviet leaders did not
give up hope for a world revolution in the long
run.

They simply shifted their emphasis from
the aim of rapid world revolution starting in
Western countries to the aim of increasing and
enhancing the power of the existing Soviet
regime. During the Brest-Litovsk crisis, Lenin
stressed the importance of the fact that the
Soviet regime was in being — the healthy first-
born child of the world revolution. Work for
the world revolution became more and more
identified with a foreign policy that guaranteed
the security of the Soviet Union and strengthened its power. This foreign policy with its
maneuvers and shifts was the product of the
delay in the coming of the world revolution.
While waiting for this revolution the Soviet
regime had to be strengthened; it had to learn
from the experiences and technical achievements of other powers and nations. As Lenin

---

[5] E. H. Carr, *German–Soviet Relations Between
the Two World Wars, 1919–1939* (Baltimore,
1951).

has put it: "We must utilize Capitalism in
order to build Socialism." Soviet leaders recognized the usefulness of economic relations with
capitalist states just as they accepted as a fact
the power of Imperial Germany in the Brest-
Litovsk period. The Soviet leaders recognized
the temporary necessity for the co-existence
of the Soviet and the capitalist world; they expected that as the Soviet world would progress
and grow stronger, the capitalist world would
decay and grow weaker. The weak links in the
capitalistic chain should be discovered. Lenin's
analysis of Imperialism overcame the traditional Marxian belief that the revolution must
result from a prior development of Capitalism
to maturity in the industrialized countries with
a strong proletariat. According to Lenin, the
revolution could be brought about in colonial,
exploited regions which were trying at the
same time to accomplish a bourgeois-nationalist
liberation. The doctrinaire utopianism of
Bolshevism did not exclude shifting power
politics; on the contrary, it imposed them.
The Bolshevik regime had to maneuver in order to survive until proper conditions —
namely, its own strength and the weakness of
the other powers — would permit a new advance.

1921–1927: Stalin's Rise to Power

The whole period of 1921–1927 can be
characterized as a period in which the Soviet
regime tried to gain strength for such a new
advance. This period opened with Lenin's
introduction of the New Economic Policy
(NEP), designed to make concessions to the
tired and exhausted masses. A limited free
market and private trade were admitted in the
interest of the peasants. Lenin even offered
"concessions" to foreign capitalists in order to
make investments in Soviet Russia attractive
to them — a policy which did not have the
success expected. Principles of calculation and
the stringencies of legalistic rules were emphasized and introduced, replacing the former
policies of confiscation without regulations,
which had aided in winning the civil war. But
the "commanding positions" remained in the
hands of the party. The nationalized economy
controlled the sector into which private initiative was admitted. Banks, big enterprises, and
foreign trade remained under the control of
the Soviet state. No other parties were per-

mitted alongside the Bolshevik party. A committee which was organized in the hunger-catastrophe of 1922 was dissolved when its non-Bolshevik members tried to gain independent influence. The Che-Ka was rechristened G-P-U; but even under formal legal supervision, it retained its basically unlimited powers. The consolidation of the regime advanced.

The loose confederation of Soviet Republics — of which the Russian and Ukrainian were the most important ones — was held together by the solidarity and unity of the Communists; it was replaced in 1924 by the Soviet Union. The U.S.S.R. was nominally a federation, but in reality, despite the explicit statement of its constitution about the right of secession, it continued to concentrate power in Moscow. True, this tendency towards centralization was camouflaged by a policy which opposed the remnants of Tsarist Great Russian chauvinism. In the Ukrainian Soviet Republic a policy of Ukrainization was favored. Former Ukrainian nationalist leaders, like the historian Hrushevsky, were permitted to participate in public life. But also in the period of apparent concessions to non-Russian nationalism the authority of the leadership in the party was strengthened. The tenth party congress, on Lenin's initiative, forbade factional groupings inside the party.[6] Lenin had tired of opposition groups, like the so-called worker opposition, which protested against increasing bureaucratization of the party and of public life. But Lenin could afford some controversial discussions inside the party. His authority had become so undisputed that he could successfully utilize at the same time men like Stalin and Trotsky even though they were estranged by their bitter quarrels during the civil war.

During Lenin's illness (he was incapacitated in 1922 and died in 1924), an internal struggle about who was to succeed him developed within the party leadership. Upon Zinoviev's suggestion Stalin had been made secretary general of the party in 1922. He used this office to bring the party machine, step by step, under his control. Together with Kamenev and Zinoviev, two typical Bolshevik intellectuals,

he prevented Trotsky from becoming Lenin's heir and helped reduce his influence in the party. Then Stalin turned against his allies of the first hour and in their turn deprived them of power. Now they joined with Trotsky, opposing Stalin in a bloc. But it was too late. Stalin could use the party machine against the opposition; the party voted always in Stalin's favor and did not listen to the arguments of the opposition. Of course, all competitors in the fight for power cited Lenin as the highest infallible authority. Zinoviev had coined the expression "Leninism" and had tried to discredit Trotsky by utilizing Lenin's old polemics against him. It is remarkable that Stalin moved very cautiously during this time and disallowed "bloodletting in the Party."[7] He refused to sacrifice the rightist Bukharin to Zinoviev, who demanded his head. In 1927 the opposition was expelled from the party; its leaders submitted more or less eagerly to the official line; and Trotsky was exiled (1929) from the Soviet Union.

1927–1936: Totalitarian Planning and the Stalin Constitution

The Bolsheviks under Stalin organized and consolidated their complete control of the Soviet Union according to a definite totalitarian pattern. The Five Year plans for the organization of production and the acceleration of industrialization were put into operation. After 1929, Stalin, against the opposition of rightists Tomsky, Bukharin, and Rykov, carried out the collectivization of agriculture from above, using every form of compulsion.[8] For millions of people, this policy resulted in death through hunger, or in deportation to labor camps.[9] For Stalin was determined to destroy the independence of the peasants who had threatened the process of industrialization by their refusal to supply cities with foodstuffs. The peasants were forced into *kolkhozes* controlled by party officials and had to fulfill production

---

[6] Lenin, *Sotchinenia,* Vol. XXVI (3rd. ed., Moscow, 1930), p. 588. *Selected Works,* Vol. IV, n. 131 ff. 1.

[7] Stalin, *Ob opposizii* (Moscow, 1928), p. 226.
[8] That has been recognized by Stalin himself in his warning against dizziness from success. *Sotchinenia,* Vol. XII (Moscow, 1949), p. 191. f.
[9] N. Jasny states: "At gun point, with sacrifices of millions of lives and by sending other millions in concentration camps, almost 100 million peasants and their families were herded into the Kholkhos," *Soviet Studies,* Vol. III, No. 2 (Oxford, October 1951), 161.

quotas imposed from above. They were forced to adopt agricultural machinery in order to form a market for the products of the industrial plants; the government organized and controlled the centers (stations) for the machines.

The millions deported as forced labor brought a change in the activities of the GPU.[10] Its concentration camps had served to isolate active or potential enemies of the regime; now these camps became enterprises for economic and colonizing purposes. The Baltic–White Sea canal had served as a preparatory experiment for the exploitation of forced labor; now deportees, political and criminal prisoners, could be used on a much larger scale in the almost unpopulated regions of Northern Europe as well as of Asiatic Russia. In other words, terror was now combined with economic planning. The chance to become members of the camp's administrative as well as directing group, and the carefully planned proportion between the amount of work performed and the amount of food given were destined to increase the productivity of forced labor. The official propaganda, of course, presented the camps and the regions of exile as places where antisocial persons could be rehabilitated and transformed into socially useful persons and valuable members of the socialist community.

During this period when the U.S.S.R. became definitely organized as a totalitarian state, foreign policy was, until 1933, dominated by the fear that the Western powers might again intervene against the Soviet regime as they did after World War I. The U.S.S.R. denounced the League of Nations, to which it did not belong, as a hypocritical pseudo-moral institution organized in order to prepare and justify such an intervention. The Soviet Union cooperated with Germany for economic reasons as well as to prevent united action by a united capitalist front. The treaty of Rapallo developed into the treaty of Berlin in 1926. The Comintern through its lack of success lost its prestige and

independence, and became more and more clearly an instrument of Soviet foreign policy. This was confirmed by Trotsky's attempts to use it as a weapon against Stalin's policy — they failed completely. More and more emphasis was put on relations with China, and the U.S.S.R. made a great impression on the Chinese when it abandoned the unequal treaties and privileges Russia had received from them. The Soviets also supported the Chinese movement for national liberation, though their hopes to cooperate with the Kuomintang failed after the death of Sun Yat Sen (the founder of the Chinese Republic), because Chiang Kai-shek broke with Moscow. But a Communist party was permanently established in China. It accepted the basic tenets of Leninism, although it tried to utilize specific features of the agrarian crisis in China in order to seize power.[11] Having regained the Russian Asiatic territories, lost in the first years after the establishment of the Soviet regime, the Soviet Union adopted a very cautious policy toward Japan, giving up its privileges in Manchuria — the Soviet leaders were anxious to avoid an open external conflict.

A new period of Soviet foreign policy started in 1934 when Hitler's Nazi regime became definitely established in Germany. Fearing a Nazi crusade, the Soviet Union turned to the West. A military alliance with France was concluded; membership in the League of Nations was asked for and received; diplomatic recognition by the United States at the end of 1933 was highly appreciated. These policies gave rise to the belief that the Soviet Union was on the way to democratization. This belief was also encouraged by the preparation and acceptance of the Stalin Constitution (1936). This document not only omitted revolutionary statements but granted equal rights to all Soviet citizens, whereas previously certain groups — for example Tsarist officials and priests — were deprived of such rights or franchise. The new appreciation of Russia's past (demonstrated by the condemnation of the late historian, Pokrovsky, who stressed the role of commercial capitalism in Russian history and denounced the sins of the Tsarist re-

---

[10] Cf. D. Dallin and B. Nikolaevsky, *Forced Labor in the Soviet Union* (New Haven, 1947). Of the many books of former inmates of Soviet camps most revealing is the introductory survey of M. Rozanov's *Zavoevately bielych piaten* (Posev, Limburg, 1951), V-XXXVI.

---

[11] B. I. Schwartz, *Chinese Communism and the Rise of Mao* (Cambridge, 1951).

gime),[12] also strengthened the erroneous opinion of many that the Soviet Union had abandoned, under Stalin's leadership, its world revolutionary designs. It was believed that Stalin was exclusively interested in a powerful Russian state. Had not Stalin emphasized, from the beginning of his fight with Trotsky, the necessity of building up socialism in one country, whereas his adversary upheld the necessity of "permanent revolution," believing that uprisings abroad were required for the existence of the Soviet regime?

1936–1939: The Great Purge and the Turn to Hitler's Germany

Those who believed the Soviet Union was on its way to democracy regarded the collectivization of agriculture as the last application of mass terror. But the hope that the Soviet Union was on the road to democracy was soon shaken. In 1936, even before the Stalin Constitution was put into force, bloody purges were inaugurated, directed against old Bolsheviks, distinguished party members, officials, and generals.[13] Potential as well as actual enemies of Stalin's regime became the

victims. Close friends of Lenin, like Kamenev and Zinoviev, made startling public confessions and were sentenced to death. The execution of other leading Bolsheviks, like Karakhan and Enukidse, was made known by brief notices; leading military men, such as Marshall Tukhatchevsky and General Yakir, were executed after secret trials; others, like Marshalls Jegorov and Bluecher, simply disappeared. Jagoda, who for many years had been the head of the political police and had prepared the first great trial of the purge, admitted abjectly and publicly the most heinous crimes; the peak of this period was named "Ezhovschina" after Jagoda's successor, Ezhov, who ruthlessly performed countless liquidations and arrests until he, too, finally vanished from public life.

The great purge from 1936 to 1938 definitely established Stalin's absolute control over the Party. Those Communists who had known and opposed him as one of Lenin's lieutenants disappeared. Intellectuals like the former emigres, inclined to discussion and skepticism, were now replaced by "apparatchiki" (men of the apparatus) who carried out orders without any hesitation. Party doctrine for them consisted in formulas applied in accordance with the interpretation and meaning determined by the highest authorities.

The great purge stabilized definitively a totalitarian rule by an omnipotent Soviet leadership. Perpetuating itself by controlling everything with the help of a subservient

---

12 With some exaggeration K. Mehnert claims that, with the condemnation of Pokrovsky — after his death (1932) — and the publication of Stalin's and Molotov's decree on teaching history of May 16, 1934, a new period in Bolshevik ideology started. (Cf. his interesting study *Weltrevolution durch Weltgeschichte*, Schriftenreihe der Deutschen Europa Akademie, Heft 9, Kitzingen, 1951). About the persecution of the Pokrovsky School, cf. A. Ouralov, *Staline au Pouvoir* (Paris, 1951) pp. 114–135. Cf. also S. Yakobson, "Postwar Historical Research in the Soviet Union" in Philip E. Mosely, ed., "The Soviet Union Since World War II" (*The Annals of the Academy of Political and Social Science*, Philadelphia, 1949); G. Kagan "La crise de la science historique russe," *Revue Historique*, 1940; G. von Rauch, "Die sowjetische Geschichtsforschung heute," *Die Welt als Geschichte*, XI (1951), Heft 4.
13 F. L. Schuman, *Soviet Politics at Home and Abroad* (New York, 1946) gives (on pp. 261 ff.) a long though incomplete list of the prominent victims of the purge. "The number of little people who were purged cannot be estimated" (p. 262). On the one hand, F. L. Schuman believes that "the portrait of conspiracy spread on the Soviet court record" is "closer to reality than any alternative explanation" (264); on the other hand, he states: "The Soviet authorities preferred to see

a thousand innocents liquidated rather than see a traitor escape." (268) Lists of those who had to be arrested were drawn up according to "objective criteria": membership in non-Communist parties — even before the rise of the Soviet regime, e.g., the security organs received orders to arrest certain percentages of the population. Another feature was the ultimate purge in their turn of the purgers of the first stages. Almost all Caucasian colleagues of Beria, who headed the NKVD in the Caucasus until he became Ezhov's successor, disappeared. Cf. the many books describing the great purge: particularly revealing are A. Ouralov, *op. cit.*, and A. Weissberg, *The Accused* (New York, 1951). Weissberg was a foreign Communist who lived in the U.S.S.R. as a leading expert in physics. — Three members of Stalin's Politburo disappeared during the purge [G. K. Schueller, *The Politburo* (Stanford, 1951).]

bureaucracy, it pretended (and still pretends) to fulfill and interpret authoritatively an absolutely true doctrine. But, as we have seen, this development was not a break with Lenin's principles; Stalin's extension of terroristic methods to the party was only an application of these principles. Stalin had instruments for establishing his regime which Lenin, fighting for a conquest of power, obviously did not yet have. Stalin had an additional motive for using these instruments, for despite all the adulation bestowed upon him after 1929, he did not have the unquestioned authority in the party enjoyed by Lenin. Stalin realized after the assassination of his lieutenant Kirov that the opposition against him in the party had only been driven underground, and that continued terror would be required to make his position secure.

Soviet foreign policy was, on the whole, rather on the defensive from the end of the civil war until Hitler's rise to power in 1933. The danger of an attack by Nazi Germany was countered by a shift in Soviet foreign policy. The friendly relations established with Western powers and the membership in the League of Nations (1934) were attempts to win support for the Soviet Union against Nazi Germany.[14] The cooperation of communists with moderate socialists in so-called popular fronts was undertaken for the same purpose, although the latter had been formerly denounced as the worst traitors and as "social fascists."

1939–1945: Soviet Policies During World War II

But the turn to the West was discouraged by the Munich conference of 1938, to which the U.S.S.R. was not invited. The West, led by Chamberlain, the prime minister of appeasement, made concessions to Hitler. Therefore, in the spring of 1939 Litvinov, the foreign commissar, who was the symbol of anti-Nazi Western orientation, was dismissed. From August 1939, by means of the non aggression pact negotiated by Litvinov's successor, Molotov, and Hitler's foreign minister, Ribbentrop, the Soviet Union tried to exploit Hitler's aggression for its own security and benefit, opening the gate for German aggression against Poland, which caused World War II.[15] This

pact promised Soviet neutrality in the case of German aggression, and accordingly assured the Nazis of no involvment in a dangerous two-front war. In a secret annex the pact provided that, if Germany expanded to the East, the Soviet Union would be compensated by the partition of Poland; the whole of Eastern Europe was divided into spheres of interest.

What had been obvious for years in Soviet internal policies was now confirmed by the Union's foreign policy. What really mattered was the preservation and the expansion of the power of the totalitarian state; the existence and constant strengthening of this state were seen by the Soviet leaders as the best instrument and the safest guarantee for the coming victory of socialism and communism everywhere in the world. The communist attempts to conquer power by internal revolutions had failed outside the U.S.S.R., regardless of the activities of the Third International. In the U.S.S.R., on the contrary, power had not only been achieved but stabilized and expanded. Therefore, the Soviet party and the Soviet Union became exemplary in all respects; everything serving its existence and strength was good. The Leninist political religion had created and justified the totalitarian state (the dictatorship of the proletariat represented by the party), and this totalitarian state had developed from a means to an end in the present era.

The victory of socialism and the communist party had been accomplished in the U.S.S.R. and was accompanied by a surge of Soviet nationalism — its victories and grand purpose entitled the U.S.S.R. to universal leadership and to unlimited self-glorification.[16]

In 1941 Hitler's attack forced the Soviet Union to fight on the side of the Allies. The

---

[14] Cf. M. Beloff, *The Foreign Policy of Soviet Russia, 1929–1941*, Vol. I (New York, 1949).

[15] M. Beloff, *op. cit.*, Vol. II (New York, 1950); E. H. Carr, *German Soviet Relations Between the Two World Wars, 1919–1939* (Baltimore, 1951). Source books are *Nazi–Soviet Relations: 1931–1941* (Department of State, Washington, 1948), and Alfred Seidl (ed.), *Beziehungen zwischen Deutschland und der Sowjetunion* (Tubingen, 1949). Cf. also A. Rossi, *The Russo-German Alliance* (Boston, 1951).

[16] In the conflict with Marshal Tito the Cominform (declaration of June 28, 1948) stated that the criticism made by the Central Committee of the Soviet Party must be accepted by the Yugoslav Party. *The Soviet–Yugoslav Dispute* (London, 1948), p. 65.

war was conducted as a great patriotic war; and the dissolution of the Third International in 1943 seemed to confirm the end of Soviet interest in world revolution. But as soon as the military defeat of the Nazis appeared certain, Soviet power politics came again into the open. These tactics were warranted not so much by the claim that they served the coming communist classless society as by the assertion that they were the necessary means of protecting the Soviet Union against hostile actions and menacing interventions by the Western powers, particularly the United States, the leading imperialist power. Soviet expansionism was favored by the general situation at the end of World War II. Soviet control of Central Europe and the Balkans as well as the extraordinary prestige of Soviet military power were advantageous for the domination of the Soviet Union on the one hand; on the other hand they increased fear of threatening world revolution. Their basic doctrinal approach made the Soviet leaders regard the world as necessarily split into two camps. They believe that one of these camps, the capitalist-imperialist one, of course, must collapse in the end, though only after a long and protracted struggle.

Since 1945: The Cold War

Soviet expansionism led to the cold war with the United States and the West. The capitalist Allies of World War II inherited the role of Hitler as the main enemy of the socialist world. The revolutionary situations created by the war had to be exploited. The Soviet Union expanded and organized its power by establishing its system of satellites, by encouraging the victory of the communist party in China, by harrassing the imperialistic world with attacks and local wars such as that in Korea, and by intensifying and exploiting all conflicts such as those precipitated by the rise of Asiatic and Mid-Eastern nationalisms against colonial powers.

The circle is closed — the world revolution is now a function of Soviet expansionist foreign policy and the successes of Soviet foreign policy serve the world revolution. In Europe the Soviet-controlled satellite states increase the power of the U.S.S.R.; and in Asia the Soviet-supported Chinese communist party wins the civil war. A few defeats are suffered, of course: Marshal Tito of Yugoslavia breaks

away from Soviet control; the policies of expansionism and non-cooperation result in reactions. The Truman doctrine is directed against further Soviet expansion and is implemented economically by the Marshall Plan and militarily by the Atlantic Pact. The attempt of the North Korean satellite to take over South Korea permits the United Nations (under the leadership of the United States) to prove that new attempts at expansion will be met with armed resistance. Despite endless declarations that it is for peace and disarmament whereas the United States and the Atlantic powers are for aggression and armament, the Soviet Union continues to lose influence over world public opinion as well as over the international labor movement. But the Stalinist policy emphasizes the power of the Soviet Union, and its military might continues to inspire fear in spite of all military and political countermeasures involved in the so-called policy of containment.[17]

The Soviet Union expects in the long run to win the cold war without risking a shooting war on a global scale. Soviet exploitation of conflicts among other powers and the burdens of the armament race will assure and intensify world-wide social and political crises. Internal conflicts in the capitalist camp will compensate for Soviet technical and economic inferiority.

6

The U.S.S.R. Under Khrushchev*

Isaac Deutscher

(1959)

Our capsule history of the Soviet Union is carried forward through the post-Stalin years by Isaac Deutscher, noted biographer of both

17 For the policy of containment cf. G. F. Kennan, "The Sources of Soviet Conduct," first printed in *Foreign Affairs,* July 1947 . . . [Reprinted in the present volume, Article 10, pp. 90–99. — Eds.]
* Reprinted, with the permission of the author and the publisher, from *Russia in Transition,* rev. ed., by Isaac Deutscher, published by Grove Press, Inc., Chapter 5, pp. 80–88. Copyright © by Hamish Hamilton Ltd., 1957; Copyright © by Grove Press, Inc., 1960.

Trotsky and Stalin. Although Mr. Deutscher has usually been identified with the more optimistic interpretation of the possibilities for a democratization of Soviet totalitarianism, he appears here in a more cautious mood, stressing the paradox between Khrushchev's reforms, which take the system further from the Stalinist model, and his personal triumph and power, which take the system back toward Stalinism.

[In 1959] the Twenty-First Congress of the Soviet Communist Party assembled in Moscow almost three years after Khrushchev's "secret speech" at the Twentieth Congress. For the Soviet Union and the other Communist-ruled countries these were eventful years, crowded with reforms, counter-reforms, inner party struggles, turmoil, and confusion. Khrushchev's "secret" speech was, of course, the formative event of the period: it reverberated through all subsequent developments. Whatever the formal agenda of the Twenty-First Congress — officially it was convened only to endorse the new Seven Year Plan — the essential question before it was whether or not Communism was to follow the signposts set up three years earlier. How much of the Stalinist orthodoxy was still valid and how much was discarded?

Inevitably, these questions had produced controversy and splits. It is now officially admitted that, despite the pretence of unanimity maintained at the Twentieth Congress, the party leaders were then deeply divided over all major issues, as in truth they had been even earlier. It was only while the Twentieth Congress was in session that the Central Committee authorized Khrushchev to make his revelations about Stalin; and only a small majority of the Committee voted for this momentous decision. Nearly half the members, led by Molotov and Kaganovich, fought desperately, and till the last moment, to save the idol and the dogmas of Stalinism. What was at stake was the system of government and party leadership, and not merely Stalin's good or bad name. None of the major administrative, economic, and social changes that have since been introduced in the Soviet Union could have been even contemplated as long as the party was shackled by Stalinist orthodoxy. Khrushchev's "secret" speech was the prelude to the long series of reforms that filled the interval between the two Congresses.

Three-Stage Development

The story of the interval, however, is full of contradictions and paradoxes. It falls into, at least, three major chapters: the first was brought to a close by the Polish and Hungarian upheavals in October and November 1956. The second ended with the expulsion from the Central Committee of Molotov, Malenkov, and Kaganovich in June 1957. The third and last chapter, leading up to the Twenty-First Congress, could be divided into several subchapters; its story is of the greatest complexity and confusion.

In the first period the movement for de-Stalinization developed almost openly and assumed great explosive force. It met deep and widely felt needs; it evoked a powerful popular response; and it aroused boundless hopes. The range of the movement, however, was relatively limited, at least as far as the Soviet Union was concerned. It was primarily political in character. Its emphasis was on inner party reform, collective leadership, and freedom of inner party criticism — in a word, on the replacement of the Stalinist "bureaucratic centralism" by the Leninist "democratic centralism." These were also the months of the "thaw" in literature and in the arts, and of an intense ferment of ideas in academic circles. From month to month de-Stalinization made startling conquests in vital but narrowly circumscribed fields. The intelligentsia led the movement, while the bureaucracy was divided against itself; but the mass of the working class, not to speak of the peasantry, remained largely inarticulate. Therein lay the weakness of the movement. Yet its momentum was strong enough to force Molotov, Kaganovich, and their adherents into a deep retreat. They could only watch events in alarm and warn the Central Committee that it was losing control over the situation.

The Hungarian rising gave the Stalinist diehards the opportunity to rally and to go over to the offensive. They denounced Khrushchev as the unwitting inspirer of the rising and the prompter of revisionism, who had jeopardized Communist rule in Eastern Europe and exposed the Soviet Union itself to dangerous shocks. The perils they spoke of were real enough; and so all the leaders, de-Stalinizers as well as Stalinists, were seized with panic. In the course of eight months Molotov and Kaganovich pressed home the attack and succeeded in regaining much of the ground they had lost. Khrushchev was compelled to call a halt to the debunking of the Stalin era, to declare war on revisionism, and to try and discipline the restive intelligentsia. But it was impossible to undo the effects of the Twentieth Congress and to make people forget his disclosures about Stalinist misrule. Too much discontent and disillusionment were pent up in all social classes. The workers began to react against the privileges of the bureaucracy, against social inequality, and against the old, severe industrial discipline. The peasants refused to increase agricultural production, which was disastrously low and threatened to impede industrial progress.

The party leadership had reason to fear that the disgruntled intelligentsia (whose ranks had been politically strengthened by the release from concentration camps and the rehabilitation of old heretics and "enemies of the people") might appeal to the workers and peasants and set in motion a genuine popular opposition. Something had to be done to dispel the popular discontent — at least a new wage policy and a new approach to collective farming were needed.

Thus, even if only to be able to call an effective halt to political and ideological de-Stalinization, Khrushchev had to carry de-Stalinization into the fields of economic and social policy. Moreover, the Hungarian and Polish upheavals had put a severe strain on the Soviet economy. It had become necessary to prop up economically the tottering or shaky Communist governments of Eastern Europe and to step up the output of consumer goods in the Soviet Union as well as in the other Communist countries. But it was well nigh impossible to achieve this and at the same time to maintain a rapid rate of development in heavy industry, and to force the pace in the nuclear arms race, under the old over-centralized and rigidly bureaucratic system of economic administration.

Khrushchev set out to break up that system and to replace it by the Regional Economic Councils, to enhance the status of the Trade Unions, and to accord new rights to factory councils and factory committees. By means of local initiative and responsibility he hoped to increase the efficiency of the entire industrial machinery. Acting on the same principle, he released the collective farms from bureaucratic tutelage, transferred to them the property of the Machine Tractor Stations, abolished compulsory food deliveries, and offered the farmers all sorts of material incentives.

Resistance to Khrushchev

The Stalinist die-hards put up a stubborn resistance to this series of reforms. They relied on the backing of Moscow's powerful industrial bureaucracy and on the caution and fear that had seized large sections of the party machine since the Hungarian rising. In June 1957 Molotov and Kaganovich were on the point of bringing their counter-offensive to a successful conclusion. Strengthened by the adherence of Malenkov and Shepilov, de-Stalinizers of the previous period, and by Bulganin's hesitations, they obtained a majority within the Presidium of the Central Committee and carried a motion deposing Khrushchev from the post of the party's First Secretary. This was to have put an end to the "Period of Troubles" and risky experiments.

At this point, though, Khrushchev appealed from the Presidium to the Central Committee. If the records of that session of the Committee were to be published, the effect, at least in the Soviet Union, might be almost as shocking as was that of Khrushchev's "secret" speech. The debates were stormy. The antagonists charged one another with working for the ruin of the Soviet Union and Communism; and for the occasion each side dragged skeletons from the family cupboards. At one point, for instance, while Khrushchev dwelt on his adversaries' responsibility for the Great Purges of the 1930's — the topic invariably recurring in all secret debates since Stalin's death — he pointed at Molotov and Kaganovich and exclaimed: "Your hands are stained with the blood of our party leaders and of innumerable innocent Bolsheviks!" "So are yours!" Molotov and Kaganovich shouted back at him. "Yes, so are mine," Khrushchev replied, "I admit this. But during the purges I was merely carrying out your orders. I was not then a member of the Politbureau and I bear no responsibility for its decisions. You were."

Thus, Khrushchev went on playing on the revulsion against Stalinism; and this was indeed strong enough to assure his success. The Central Committee expelled Molotov, Kaganovich, and Malenkov from its midst (but not from the party) and it confirmed Khrushchev in office. Essentially, the vote reflected the majority's conviction that it was impossible for the party to go on ruling the country as before and that the reforms advocated by Khrushchev were sound and overdue. The new and modern economy and structure of society could no longer be reconciled with the old administrative and political superstructure.

It was no accident that in June 1957 Marshal Zhukov threw his weight behind Khrushchev. Perhaps more strongly than any other group, the officers corps had resented the Stalinist purges; and it was convinced of the urgency of economic and administrative reform. Zhukov himself undoubtedly entertained high ambitions — in the months which followed the June session he spoke the language of a Soviet de Gaulle. In the following November it was his turn to be expelled from the Central Committee, and at the Twenty-First Congress Marshall Malinovsky, his successor as Defense Minister, declared that Zhukov had "tried to set himself up as a new Bonaparte."

Consequences of Victory

Yet, how paradoxical is the outcome of all these disputes and showdowns! On the one hand, Khrushchev's triumph over his adversaries has enabled him to go ahead with his reforms, every one of which takes the Soviet Union further and further away from the Stalinist system of government. On the other, his triumph appears to have driven the party, politically, a long way back towards Stalinism. By eliminating his adversaries, Khrushchev appears to have destroyed the post-Stalinist "collective leadership" and to have become the party's sole master. This "dialectically contradictory" and ambiguous outcome of all the recent struggles was strikingly demonstrated in the December sessions of the Central Committee and of the Supreme Soviet, which were convened in preparation for the Twenty-First Congress. An immense amount of new legislation was placed before these two bodies. Nearly all of it had been designed to demonstrate that the break with Stalinism was continuing, was deepening, and was spreading to ever new spheres of Soviet life. The new Seven Year Plan did not aim only at approaching the level of American

industry. Its special feature was the new emphasis on the need for the "harmonious" development of producer and consumer industries; and this necessitated some slowing down in the rate of the over-all development. The Plan made important concessions to consumer interests. It also marked a further departure from Stalin's anti-egalitarian policy: it provided for a steady narrowing of the gap between high and low incomes; and for a shortening of working hours in industry and the gradual introduction, within the coming decade, of a working week of 30–35 hours.

In apparent contrast to this egalitarian trend was Khrushchev's school reform, also passed in December, which partly curtailed universal secondary education. The truth was that the Soviet educational system had, in its unparalleled growth, run ahead of the social system as a whole and had outrun the nation's resources. Every year millions of young people, their secondary education completed, knocked at the doors of the universities and were turned away. The universities, where expansion could not possibly keep pace with expansion in secondary education, were unable to accommodate so many candidates; and the rush of the young to the universities threatened to starve industry of manpower. Khrushchev was now chasing the mass of Soviet youth from the university gate to the factory bench; and he was anxious to stop the rush to the universities at an earlier stage — at the secondary school. But he met with widespread, and more than usually articulate, opposition; and he had to compromise. He increased budgetary grants for education by as much as 50 per cent, declared that the retrenchment in secondary education was only temporary or denied that there would be any retrenchment; and he had to dwell on the egalitarian character of the polytechnical school, where theoretical education was to be combined with productive labor.

The principle of de-Stalinization, however, was most strikingly evident in the project of the new Criminal Code, which its sponsor introduced to the Supreme Soviet as an act of legislation designed to "liquidate the shameful heritage of the past." The Code had been under debate for many years; and the project was the resultant of conflicting viewpoints. It did not go so far as the most liberal of Soviet jurists had expected, but it did go a very long way towards transforming a police state into a state "ruled by law." It deprived the political police of the powers to sentence, imprison, and deport citizens. Henceforth no one was to be sentenced otherwise than by a normal court in open trial. Penalties were reduced. Guilt by association, the "category" of the "enemy of the people," the co-responsibility of the defendant's relatives, the penalty of the deprivation of citizenship, and many similar features of the old Code were abolished. No defendant could be charged with "terrorism" unless there was *prima facie* evidence of an actual attempt at political assassination.

Under such a Code it would have been impossible for Stalin ever to produce his *univers concentrationnaire*, to stage any of his great purges and the Moscow trials, and even to deport Trotsky to Alma Ata and Constantinople. As if to stress the meaning of the new Code, General Serov, the grim old policeman, was replaced as chief of State Security by the ex-Comsomol leader Shelepin.

Yet — and here was the greatest paradox — the ghosts of the Great Purges seemed to be crowding back into the Central Committee's conference hall in December 1958, when Bulganin made his "confession of guilt," denouncing Molotov, Malenkov, and Kaganovich, and extolling Khrushchev's merits; and when the Central Committee rejected this "confession" as "hypocritical and inadequate," and Rudenko, Vyshinsky's successor as State Prosecutor, spoke about the "*crimes* of the anti-party group." The spectacle was evidently staged in order to bring pressure to bear on Molotov and his associates and to make them appear before the Twenty-First Congress in sackcloth and ashes, with confessions similar to those that Stalin's adversaries were once forced to make. For a moment it looked as if the party were back if not in 1936, the year of the Zinoviev trial, then at least in 1930–34, the years when the stage was being set for the Great Purges.

But the clock was not and could not be turned back by a quarter of a century. At the Central Committee Rudenko may have spoken in Vyshinsky's voice, demanding the heads of the Leader's enemies; but Khrushchev himself would not or dared not make that demand. A few weeks later, in January 1959, while the Twenty-First Congress was in session, the issue was at the center of an intense struggle behind the scenes; and the noises off

stage could be heard in full Congress, even in speeches made from the rostrum. Spiridonov, the leader of the Leningrad organization, insisted that Malenkov, Molotov, and Kaganovich, should appear before the Congress, "lay down arms," and recant. Mikoyan, however, ridiculed those anxious to see a repetition of such Stalinist practices and urged the Congress to consider the controversy with the "anti-party group" as closed. In effect, Molotov and his friends refused to humiliate themselves and did not "lay down arms" and the Congress did not give Khrushchev a free hand for a showdown in the Stalinist style. The majority evidently responded to Mikoyan's appeal and preferred to wind up this inner party feud with a little vituperation against the Opposition but without any of the old "bloodthirsty" threats. This was the year 1959, after all. It was only three years since Khrushchev had denounced the Stalinist witch-hunts, "confessions," and terror; and the denunciation was still ringing in the ears of the Twenty-First Congress.

THE SYSTEM IN PERSPECTIVE

7

Ten Theories in Search of Soviet Reality*

Daniel Bell

(1958)

To provide some sense of the range of efforts to "fit" the Soviet Union to some theory, and to counsel appropriate caution with regard to such efforts, we present Daniel Bell's sprightly

* Reprinted from "Ten Theories in Search of Reality: The Prediction of Soviet Behavior in the Social Sciences," *World Politics*, Vol. 10 (April 1958), pp. 327–365, by permission of the author and the Center of International Studies at Princeton University.

survey of the theories of leading Sovietologists and Kremlinologists. Any single theory is likely to be so global, it must neglect so much and simplify so much else, as to become not the total explanation it set out to be but inevitably merely another one-sided view claiming to be the complete picture. To use Mr. Bell's metaphor "from such heights the terrain of politics, its ridges and gullies, become flattened, and the weary foot-traveler finds few guides to concrete problems."

I

Surely, more has been written about the Russian Revolution and the ensuing forty years of Soviet rule than about any comparable episode in human history.† The bibliography of items on the French Revolution occupies, it is said, one wall of the Bibliothèque Nationale. A complete bibliography on the Soviet Union — which is yet to be compiled and may never be because of the geometric rate at which it multiplies — would probably make that earlier cenotaph to scholarship shrink the way in which the earlier tombs diminished before the great complex at Karnak.

And yet how little of this awesome output has stood the test of so short a span of time! If hell, as Thomas Hobbes once said, is truth seen too late, the road to hell must now be paved twice over with the thousands of books claiming to discover the "truth" about Russia — while the tortures of the damned are reserved for those, diplomats especially, who committed the fates of millions in the confident belief that they could predict correctly the way in which the Soviet rulers would respond.[1]

In the last ten years there has been, presumably, a new sophistication, and an extraordinary amount of research and writing on Soviet society, particularly in the United States. Some of this research has come from Russian defectors; most of it has been done in special institutes set up by government or

foundation research grants in an effort to obtain reliable knowledge about Soviet behavior. We have seen, too, the entry of new disciplines — anthropology, sociology, and psychiatry — into the study of political phenomena. In some instances these newer approaches have claimed to provide a total understanding of Soviet behavior; in others, to supplement existing explanations. So thick and heavy is this research that an outside observer, seeking to push his way through the marshes, often finds himself mired (as that wonderful Russian onomatopoetic evocation has it) in *splosh*. And one is bogged down further by the fact that much of this newer research is couched in a special jargon which owes allegiance to other modes of discourse than the common tongue. (As R. P. Blackmur has said of the "New Criticism," the terminology rigidifies in the course of time and the "normal pathology of a skill becomes a method, and the method a methodology.")

In this article, the writer has attempted a description and, in representative cases, a detailed assessment of these methodologies. This is not a "national estimate" of Russian capabilities and weaknesses, social, military, or economic, such as is made by the National Security Council. Nor is it a "survey" of empirical research. The writer has sought to distinguish ten approaches in social theory, each of which, despite some shading or overlap, represents a coherent judgment of Soviet behavior. It is hoped that by "reading" each against the other, some sense of the crucial differences, analytical or methodological, may emerge. Beyond that, such a reading may aid in the formulation of the two judgments which are essential in any stock-taking — namely: (1) Which theories or approaches have "stood up" in explaining events, and which have not? (2) If one were a policy-maker, which research would one underwrite in the future, and why?

II. *Enter Pirandello*

Hegel once said that what was reasonable was real. Each of the theories to be discussed seems reasonable, yet not wholly real. Something may be wrong with Hegel, the theories, or both. The reader will have to be the judge.

A. *Characterological Theories*

(1) *Anthropological.* Beginning with the

† This article is a revision of a paper presented at a conference on "Changes in Soviet Society," held at Oxford, June 24–29, 1957, under the joint auspices of St. Antony's College, Oxford, and the Congress for Cultural Freedom.

[1] *Pace* President Roosevelt, who wrote on the flyleaf of his personal copy of Joseph E. Davies' *Mission to Moscow:* "This book will last." Richard H. Ullman, "The Davies Mission and United States-Soviet Relations, 1937–1941," *World Politics,* IX, No. 2 (January 1957), p. 220.

work of Ruth Benedict, and taken up by Linton and Kardiner, Margaret Mead, and Clyde Kluckhohn, contemporary anthropologists have developed the concept of "culture and personality." The argument is that members of a given culture share certain common, sufficiently distinct ways of handling emotional drives and regulating social conduct which form a unique life style that differs, often markedly, from the life style of other cultural groups. The "norms" of the group specify how an individual must manage the key tensions generated in social living (i.e., attitudes to authority, frustration of impulses, aggression, etc.) and how the social controls against violations of those norms (i.e., mechanisms of guilt and shame, disposal of repressed hate, etc.) operate.

Margaret Mead,[2] Geoffrey Gorer and John Rickman,[3] and Henry V. Dicks[4] have sought to apply these "culture and personality" concepts to Russian behavior. Gorer, particularly, has gained a certain notoriety for what skeptics have dubbed "diaperology." Together with the late John Rickman, a respected British psychiatrist who had lived in Russia during World War I, Gorer argued that the maternal practice of tightly swaddling the Russian infant produces a privation-gratification cycle. This predisposes the "Great Russian" national character to pendulum swings of submissiveness and violent eruption, of apathy and diffuse persecutory anxiety, of "oral" greed and abstinence.[5] This accounts, too, for the willingness of the Russian adult to submit to brutal authority.

---

[2] Margaret Mead, *Soviet Attitudes to Authority*, New York, 1951.
[3] Geoffrey Gorer and John Rickman, *The People of Great Russia*, London, 1949.
[4] Henry V. Dicks, "Observations on Contemporary Russian Behavior," in *Human Relations*, v, No. 2 (1952), pp. 111–75.
[5] A dichotomy, like an atom once split, can seemingly be multiplied indefinitely. Thus Dinko Tomasic, in his study of *The Impact of Russian Culture on Soviet Communism* (Glencoe, Ill., 1953), finds that Russian national character is a bisect of two contrasting influences, that of the "power-seeking and self-oriented nomadic horsemen of the Eurasian steppes" and of the "anarchic and group-oriented [Slavic] tillers of the land." One can also point to antinomies, such as Gordon Wasson's discovery that Russians are mycophiles and Anglo-Saxons are mycophobes.

Dicks's work is more specific. A British psychiatrist at the Tavistock Institute (he set up the War Office Selections Boards), Dicks's generalizations are based, principally, on long interviews with Russian defectors. The outstanding trait of Russian personality, says Dicks, is its ambivalence. On one side is the omnivorousness, the tendency to rush at things and to "swallow them whole," the need for quick and full gratification, the spells of manic omnipotence, the anarchic demand for abolition of all bounds and limitations. On the other, the melancholy closeness and suspicion, the anxious and sullen submissiveness, the "moral masochism and grudging idealization of a strong and arbitrary authority which is thought of as the only safeguard against the excesses of Russian nature." Authority, thus, if it is to be *authority*, must be hard, deprivational, arbitrary, and capricious; if the *vlast* were weak, nobody would obey it.

Against the traditional untidiness, lack of system, and formlessness of the Russian masses is the contrasting behavior of the elite. It has to be puritanical, in full control of all sentimentality and self-indulgence, and strong enough to renounce the gratifications which "traditional" Russian character seeks. At important points there are congruities. The people expect and the elite satisfies the image of authority as severe, arbitrary, and fickle. The system, further, permits the most authoritarian fraction of the population "to act out their introjected bad-object relations" — i.e., to step into the shoes of a hated, yet, deep down, secretly identified-with father figure (Tsar, landlord, etc.). "By this hypothesis," says Dicks, "I would explain the rise in Soviet Russia of a rigid, gold-braided, intensely status-conscious and anxious bureaucracy, which is winning in the struggle against the very tendency originally successfully attacked by the new system and its founders during the Revolution."[6]

But this very transformation of goals, on a conscious or an unconscious level, provides the "salient" divergence between the Soviet system and the traditional Russian culture-pattern. For the elite, faced with the need of quickly producing a new type of technological and managerial personality, "is using the impetus of its own imperfectly assimilated and

---

[6] Dicks, *op. cit.*, p. 171.

conflict-laden goal-drives to force and mould the people into a new cultural norm." Since the greater the pressure, the more intensive the inner conflicts, the elite "projects its own compulsive and sadistic authoritarian dominance needs on to foreign outgroups." Thus it creates a psychological situation of "encirclement" and attributes all failures to the work of the external enemy. "It is difficult to estimate," says Dicks, "how much of this paranoid behavior is the result of conscious design and how much is the effect of an inner compulsion due to cultural-psychological forces into which the top leaders have little insight. In this respect, I can only refer to the amazing discovery of the psychiatric pictures presented by a comparable power clique whom we were able to study: Hitler's entourage. We had assumed a cynical and cold-blooded exploitation of this paranoid dynamic by people like Goebbels and Himmler — and we found they were its victims."[7]

The acceleration of industrialization, says Dicks, will increase the tensions between the elite and the people. The coercions are "resented and stored up against the regime," the deprivations in the name of some ultimate and impersonal good are interpreted as "withdrawal of love and nurturance." But such unconscious rage also leads to a sense of guilt for having defied authority, and this becomes projected onto the elite (i.e., it creates a feeling, at all levels, that the elite is angry at the masses and wants to punish them), leading to an increase in the atmosphere of "persecutory anxiety and diffuse fear (*strakh*)." The guilt thus also reduces a tendency to strike out at, or oppose, the regime.

(2) *Psychoanalytic.* An attempt to analyze not Russian but Bolshevik character structure, particularly as exemplified in the Politburo, has been made by Nathan Leites in his RAND study, underwritten by the U.S. Air Force.[8] But Leites' work goes beyond the mere codification of behavior in operational terms. In guarded, almost esoteric fashion, Leites undertakes a psychoanalytic explanation which is fairly breathtaking in its attempt. Bolshevik elite behavior is seen in contrast to that of the nineteenth-century intelligentsia. The latter were moody, nervous, soul-searching,

brooding, introspective. "The Bolshevik" is rigid, suspicious, unyielding, ever-aggressive. This character is stamped in the primal image of Lenin, and is derived, psychoanalytically speaking, as a "reaction-formation" to fears of death and latent homosexual impulses. (Since Leites' massive work — 639 pages — is the most ambitious attempt yet to read an "operational code" of Bolshevik behavior, particularly in international strategy, a more detailed exposition of the theory is undertaken in Section III below.)

B. Sociological Theories

(3) *The Social System.* This socio-psychological theory, developed at Harvard in the Russian Research Center, and expressed most concisely in the recent book by Raymond Bauer, Alex Inkeles, and Clyde Kluckhohn,[9] seeks to identify the functionally relevant "operating characteristics" of the Soviet system — e.g., the overcommitment of resources to particular objectives; "storming"; the refusal to allow independent concentration of power — and the effect of these behavior patterns on the various social groups. In this fashion, the authors seek to locate the points of strain in the Soviet system. (Because it is the summary volume of the largest single research project on Soviet behavior, it is discussed in greater detail in Section IV below.)

(4) *Ideal Types.* This approach, exemplified largely in the writings of Barrington Moore, Jr., at Harvard[10] (though it has influenced the thinking of W. W. Rostow at M.I.T. and Henry Dicks at Tavistock), sets up a number of models for the organization of power in a society, and seeks to establish how far any society, and the Russian in particular, can go in its commitment to one or another of these forms.

According to Moore, power and position in a society are held in one of a combination of three ways: (a) *traditional:* power and position are transmitted through the family or kinship system, from father to son; (b) *rational-technical:* power and position are at-

---

[7] *Ibid.*

[8] Nathan Leites, *A Study of Bolshevism,* Glencoe, Ill., 1954.

[9] Raymond A. Bauer, Alex Inkeles, and Clyde Kluckhohn, *How the Soviet System Works,* Cambridge, Mass., 1956.

[10] Barrington Moore, Jr., *Terror and Progress — USSR,* Cambridge, Mass., 1954, and *Soviet Politics: The Dilemma of Power,* Cambridge, Mass., 1950.

tained by an individual on the basis of skill and technical ability, regardless of the status of one's parent; (c) *political:* power and position are awarded on the basis of loyalty to a political leader, party, or clique.

The use of any one criterion limits the range of workable alternatives for the solution of other problems. Rationality emphasizes that technical competence should be the criterion for employment. But the nature of power struggles demands that jobs should go to the faithful, to the commissar rather than the manager, while purges, the most drastic expression of politics, remind individuals that obedience is the first law of the Soviet system. Meanwhile, traditionalism is still the "natural" mode of the peasantry, and, *sub rosa,* within large sections of Soviet industry, for family and informal ties have become a necessary means of protection against arbitrary orders.

The political criterion of power in Russia (e.g., the commissars in the army, the control functions of the party in relation to industry) has been employed too ruthlessly, says Moore, at the expense, even, of sacrificing large classes of technicians and experienced army officers (the *Yezhovschina*). The power of the dictator to intervene arbitrarily at any point in the administrative hierarchy creates a level of insecurity which an ongoing system may find difficult to maintain. The choice now, Moore feels, lies between "creeping rationality" or traditionalism, or some combination of both.

Since the Soviet Union is intent on industrialization, the rationalizing elements are likely to become more deeply embedded in the society: this would mean that technical criteria would replace political decisions, jobs would be allocated according to skill, career expectations would have a higher degree of stability, family privileges could be passed on to the children. In turn, the power and prestige of the industrial manager, the engineer, and the technician would rise, and the share in power and prestige held by the "control" apparatus — the party and the secret police — would decline.

An alternative evolution in a traditionalist direction, which Moore finds politically "somewhat more plausible," would mean that the party and military elements would retain control, but arbitrary intervention would diminish as personal cliques and machines within the bureaucracy become the focal point of loyal-

ties. Such a development would also imply a rise in local autonomy and a resistance to innovation and change.

Plausible as these alternatives seem, if there is any sense to Khrushchev's vast "decentralization" scheme, it would seem to mean the reassertion of a political criterion, rather than economic rationality, in the handling of economic affairs. Genuine economic decentralization, as Richard Lowenthal points out,[11] would leave the party as a parasitic appendix to the economy. Despite the absorption of managers into the party, the division of function between managers and party whips has been a source of conflict; and this was utilized by Malenkov, speaking for the managerial group. What Khrushchev, whose strength has been in the party secretariats, has now done is to create a union of function, whereby the party secretaries, at the Republic and regional levels, will be responsible for the economic performance of the plan. As Lowenthal concludes: "It is the 'irrational' Khrushchev with his party bosses, and not the 'rational' Malenkov with his managers and economic administration, who has won the latest round; and the reason is to be found precisely in the logic of self-preservation of the party regime. . . ."[12] If Moore is correct, such logic may yet lead to economic crises; but that remains to be seen.

C. Political Theories

(5) *Marxist.* Expressed most directly by Isaac Deutscher, this approach sketches a theory of Soviet development based on the proposition that the level of productive power always acts as a constraint on the possibilities of action. It argues that the Stalinist dictatorship was a historically "necessary" stage, therefore, in overcoming the resistance of the masses to industrialization, but that once this social stage has been achieved, the dictatorial apparatus will "come into social conflict" with the requirements of the new, higher stage of economic development.[13]

As developed by Deutscher — agreement can be found in the writings of E. H. Carr —

---

[11] "The Permanent Revolution Is on Again," *Commentary,* XXIV, No. 2 (August 1957), pp. 105–12.
[12] *Ibid.,* p. 109.
[13] Isaac Deutscher, *Russia: What Next?,* London, 1953.

the year 1920 represented the crossroads of the revolution:[14] the working class was exhausted, demoralized, shrunken to half its size, anxious for relaxation; in a free election, the Bolsheviks would have been ousted; only the iron will of the Bolshevik leadership saved the revolution, at the expense of putting down democracy in the party (i.e., suppressing the Workers' Opposition faction, the "levelers or Utopian dreamers"). The result was an anomaly, a workers' revolution without working-class support. The rationale for this paradox was "historical necessity" — i.e., that nationalized property represented a higher stage of social development and therefore had to be defended, even against the workers.

The theory, *sans* Stalinist apologetics, had its origin in Trotsky's *The New Course* (1923) and later *The Revolution Betrayed* (1937). There Trotsky argued that in the growth of bureaucracy Russia faced a crisis: either the release of productive forces from the heavy hand of bureaucracy, or a "Thermidor," a return to some capitalist form, state or otherwise. Deutscher, at this point, feels otherwise. The backwardness of the peasant masses and their reluctance to make the sacrifice for industrialization, he says, required the harsh measures and iron discipline of Stalinism. But with the progress that was achieved in the 1930's, says Deutscher, the Stalinist terrorism and "primitive magic" had outlived their "usefulness" and were coming into conflict with the "new needs of Soviet society." Industrialization, he believes, "tends to awaken the democratic aspirations of the masses," while the "phenomenal growth of Soviet wealth . . . tends to soften class privileges, and the orthodoxy, the iron curtain and the elaborate mythology of Stalinism tend to become socially useless. . . . Stalinism is untenable in this expanding society at its present level of productive forces."[15]

This theme, with a greater emphasis on the working class as a "political power of a magnitude hitherto unknown in Russian history," has been expanded by Deutscher in a recent publication.[16] The post-Stalin reforms, he

notes, are reforms from "above," intended largely to provide some security for the bureacracy. But the working class, particularly the skilled elements in engineering (which employs about one-third of Russia's industrial manpower), is now displaying long-suppressed egalitarian aspirations. This is evident in the revision of the old "progressive" piece-rate system, the narrowing of wage differentials, the introduction of a new pension scheme, and the abolition of all tuition fees in education.

This egalitarian drive — which is reinforced by the formal ideology that the workers are the ruling power in the country — says Deutscher, must come into conflict with the bureaucracy, which will seek to maintain its privileges and to preserve the status quo. And such an impending conflict must create a problem for a regime. With the power of the secret police diminished, there is only the army as the guardian of the order. But the army, rather than keeping order for the benefit of the party, sooner or later will do so on its own account. "In other words," concludes Deutscher, "the strains and stresses caused by a stormy revival of mass movements lacking leadership and clear political purpose, may lead to the establishment of a dictatorship of the Bonapartist type. All the more so as the military could hardly view with indifference a situation in which they must see a threat to Russia's positions of power and to all the strategic gains she won in the last war."[17]

It is highly debatable whether industrialization leads to a striving for *freedom* (even though it may lead to a demand by workers for a greater distributive share of wealth), or whether the expansion of wealth tends to diminish class privileges. *Relative* scarcities in the Soviet Union are bound to exist for a long period, however "phenomenal" the growth of Russian productivity. And the congealing of class privileges may become the real brake on any relaxation of the dictatorship, although key social groups at the top may win a measure of security. Certainly, in the downfall of Zhukov, the military has, for the time being at least, once again come under the control of the party. Deutscher clearly underestimated the role of the party, and in *Russia: What Next?* (published in 1953) failed even once to mention Khrushchev — so remote was he from

[14] Isaac Deutscher, *The Prophet Armed: Trotsky, 1879–1921,* New York, 1954.
[15] *Russia: What Next?,* pp. 123, 125.
[16] Isaac Deutscher, "Russia in Transition," *Universities and Left Review,* 1, No. 1 (Spring 1957), pp. 4–12.

[17] *Ibid.,* p. 12.

the inner-elite struggles. What is relevant, however, for this presentation is that in Deutscher's scheme of analysis there is a clearly determinable sense (whether substantively right or wrong) of a mainspring of change; and thus it focuses attention on the question which all social theory must confront — the sources of change in social systems.

(6) *Neo-Marxist.* Leading out of Trotsky's discussion of the nature of Soviet society, a group of theorists argued that Russia, despite nationalized property, was no longer a workers' state, but a new social form — namely, "bureaucratic collectivism."[18] The distinction has been important for the political orientations of the Marxist parties and sects. The orthodox Trotskyites, for example, claimed that Russia, although a "degenerated" workers' state, was, because of nationalized property, "historically progressive" and therefore worth defending in the event of a conflict with capitalist powers. The dissident Trotskyites, claiming that a new exploitative class society had been established, took a "neither-nor," "third camp" position. Analytically — i.e., in terms of its predictive utility — the scheme is of less value. The neo-Marxists, in their analysis of the future

[18] The first book to insist that Russia was a new class state — calling it "bureaucratic collectivism" — was that of Bruno R., *La Bureaucraticisation du Monde,* Paris, 1939. The theme was debated in the Menshevik press in the early 1940's, with the late Theodor Dan arguing in *Novy Put* that Russia was still a workers' state, and Rudolf Hilferding and Solomon Schwarz arguing the contrary in the *Vestnik.* (Dan, following the invasion of Russia, gave qualified support to the Russian regime.) Hilferding's argument, a classic statement of the neo-Marxist position, was printed in the *Modern Review,* 1, No. 4 (June 1947), pp. 266–71, under the title, "State Capitalism or Totalitarian State Economy," while Schwarz's data appeared later in his article, "Heads of Russian Factories," in *Social Research,* IX, No. 3 (September 1942), pp. 315–33, and in his collaborative effort with Gregory Bienstock and Aaron Yugow, *Management in Russian Industry and Agriculture,* New York, 1944. The debate was carried over into the Trotskyite press in the 1940's, principally in the *New International* and the *Fourth International* in New York. Trotsky's last argument is contained in the collection entitled *In Defense of Marxism* (*Against the Petty-bourgeois Opposition*), New York, 1942. The revisionist position can be found in James Burnham's *The Managerial Revolution,* New York, 1941, and Max Schachtman's introduction to the revised edition of Trotsky's *The New Course,* New York, 1943.

course of events in the Soviet Union, would tend to use the same terms as the Marxist analysts.

(7) *Totalitarian.* Expressed most forcefully in the categories of political philosophy by Hannah Arendt,[19] this theory argues that a radically new social form, different from tyranny, dictatorship, or authoritarianism, was created in Germany and exists now in Russia. The essentially new fact of totalitarianism is that all intermediate or secondary institutions between the leader and the "masses" have been eliminated, and that the ruler, unrestrained by legal or political checks, rules by terror. The theory, as applied to the Soviet Union by Bertram D. Wolfe, holds that no essential change in the nature of the regime is possible and that totalitarianism, through an inner "ideo-logic" of its own, can never relinquish its combative posture vis-à-vis democratic societies.

This argument was developed by Wolfe in his paper prepared for the Oxford Conference and published in the August 1957 issue of *Commentary.* Since his paper was subject to detailed challenge by Raymond Aron at the conference, it was not discussed in my paper as originally prepared. But in terms of my frame of reference, one point can be noted: as a "working tool" to explain specific political situations, the theory of totalitarianism, which Mr. Wolfe draws from Karl Wittfogel's *Oriental Despotism* (New Haven, Conn., 1957), is too sweeping. From such heights the terrain of politics, its ridges and gullies, become flattened and the weary foot-traveler finds few guides to concrete problems. Even on a simpler, intuitive basis, one can question the basic assumption of the theory — namely, that society becomes completely atomized and rule is anomic and direct. In a *crisis* situation, a state can fragment all social life and through terror, perhaps, mold a people to its will. But can a society live in permanent crisis? Can it hold such a rigid posture, without either exploding into war or relaxing? The basis of all social life requires not only a minimum of personal security, but the reasonable expectation by parents that their children will be educated, develop careers, and so forth. To

[19] Hannah Arendt, *The Origins of Totalitarianism,* New York, 1951 (published in England as *The Burden of Our Times*).

that extent, a tendency toward "normalization" is at work in any crisis state.

(8) *Kremlinological.* These speculations, identified principally with the writings of the late Franz Borkenau and of Boris Nicolaevsky, focus primarily on the power struggle within the core elite and seek to identify the shifting coalitions ("who is doing-in-whom") within the Kremlin as a basis for predicting political events. While open to easy satire, it is the supercilious who mock it at their peril, as the *New York Post* once learned when it scoffed at the speculations arising from the fact that all the Bolshevik leaders *but* Beria had appeared en masse at the Bolshoi Ballet. "Perhaps Beria doesn't like ballet," said the *Post* archly. Perhaps he didn't, but we never had the opportunity to find out, for two days later came the announcement that Beria had been arrested as a traitor.

In one form or another, Kremlinology is practiced today by every foreign office and by most journalists. Its emphasis is largely on personality and power groups, and less on the social systems and the way such systems can or cannot constrain these leaders. (See Section V for an enlargement of this discussion.)

D. Historical Theories

(9) *Slavic Institutions.* Represented in an earlier generation by Nicholas Berdyaev, Sir Bernard Pares, and Sir John Maynard, and today to some degree by Edward Crankshaw, Ernest Simmons, and Werner Philipp (of the Free University of Berlin), this school states that much of contemporary Russian behavior can be accounted for by traditional Slavic character and institutions. "Too often we forget," said Professor Ernest Barker, in introducing Maynard's *The Russian Peasant: And Other Studies* (London, 1942), "that Russia, with all her changes, still largely remains the same." The theme is elaborated in Sir John's book: "All Russian regimes have been sudden and arbitrary. . . . Old Russia was always rough, with its Siberian exiles. . . . Planning . . . a characteristic feature of the new regime, is not as new at first glimpse as it looks to be. . . . Even the 'Party' — that misnomer of the vocation of leadership — is not really new: but rather a new application of an ancient institution: the priesthood . . ." etc., etc.

One finds a similar argument in the November 1951 lecture by Professor Werner Philipp on the "Historical Presuppositions of Political Thought in Russia," inaugurating the Osteuropa Institute of Berlin.[20] As a reviewer summarizes Professor Philipp's argument: "Conditions and traditions have produced a definite political mentality in Russia which goes back for several centuries. . . . The Russian distrust of the West, the cult and consciousness of the precedence of the community over the individual, the recognition of the unlimited power of governmental authority over society, and the discrepancy between political reality and the professed ideal aim, all these phenomena of Soviet thought and life have their roots in conditions which developed in Russia between the beginning of the thirteenth and the end of the sixteenth century."[21] The theme of an "eternal Russia" is propounded, too, by Crankshaw in his *Cracks in the Kremlin Wall* (New York, 1951).

To argue that the roots of Soviet life go down deep in the Russian past is not, of course, to justify those practices (although the argument lends itself sometime to apologetics, and in the 1930's and 1940's apologists like Bernard Pares or Maurice Hindus did justify Russian behavior in such terms). But like the characterological theories ("parallel travelers," one might call them), the Slavophile theory argues in effect that since Soviet institutions were shaped by historical social forms, and since they are deeply rooted in the traditions of the people, they will change only slowly.

(10) *Geo-political.* This school, which had some vogue during World War II (e.g., Nicholas Spykman at Yale, and William T. R. Fox's *The Super-Powers,* New York, 1944) and still has some supporters, holds that Russian foreign policy is dictated primarily by long-range strategic interests deriving from its position as a great land-mass power, and that its contemporary political aspirations (e.g., in the Middle East) reflect the historic drives of Great Russian policy. The school generally tends to minimize ideology (viz., Walter Be-

---

[20] Horst Jablonowski and Werner Philipp, eds., *Forschungen zur ost-europäischen Geschichte,* Vol. I, Berlin, 1954.
[21] Hans Kohn in the *Russian Review,* XIV, No. 4 (October 1955), p. 373.

dell Smith's introduction to the Marquis de Custine *Diaries,* New York, 1951), and to see Russian policy primarily as a function of strategic power position. To some extent, the policy views of George Kennan (see his Princeton University lectures, *Realities of American Foreign Policy,* Princeton, N.J., 1954) and those of Henry Kissinger are shaped by these considerations.

III. Kto-Kovo — *The Id and Ego of Bolshevism*

During the truce negotiations in Korea, a slim book, *The Operational Code of the Politburo,* by Nathan Leites, was used by the American negotiators as a tactical manual. Leites' research, embodied in the larger *Study of Bolshevism,* was sponsored by the U.S. Air Force's Project RAND. The fact that RAND has given strong support to the pioneering method of Leites (which is now being applied to the study of French politics) makes a more detailed examination of his work worthwhile.

Leites begins by attempting to define "Bolshevik character" as a type distinct in social history. The attempt to define historic character is not unique. (We have the image, somewhat overworked these days, of the "inner-directed Protestant.") What makes Leites' work unique are the novel categories he chooses and, above all, his method. There is no observation of behavior. Like Max Weber, who drew his "Protestant ethic" from the writings of Luther, Calvin, Baxter, and others, Leites scans the writings of Lenin and Stalin to infer similar norms which guide the Bolshevik Party. He reads the Bolshevik character as a "reaction" to the Oblomovs, who slept away their lives; to the Rudins, the high-flown talkers but never-doers; to the indecisive, soul-sick, moody students. The Bolshevik, as Boris Pilnyak put it, is "against the old peasant roots of our old Russian history, against its aimlessness, its non-teleological character . . . against the philosophy of Tolstoy's Karataev." The moral training of the Russian intelligentsia stressed both the prohibition against egotism and the prohibition against "dirtying oneself." Chekhov once said, "If all Socialists are going to exploit the cholera for their own ends, I shall despise them." But, for the Bolshevik, refusal to use bad means is merely an expression of sentimentality and stupidity; in Bolshevik doctrine, the worst egotist is precisely he who refuses to soil his hands. The party strives for humanity, and "purity" lies not in a personal refusal to act immorally but in dedication to the party. In such dedication the individual finds his defense against both egotism and personal impurity.

In contrast to the Russian intelligentsia, who spoke of ultimate things and sacred values, the Bolsheviks maintain silence about the sacred. Against the vice of outpouring emotion, the Bolsheviks uphold the virtue of reserve. Against the older Russian tendency to depressed passivity, introspection, nervous impressionability, and excited babbling, against the protracted searching for metaphysical truths and the posing of unanswerable questions — against all these, there is the determinism of history, the certainty of purpose, the commitment to action, the ability to avoid taking personal offense, the "masculinity" of action. Against the fear of a life with nothing to strive for, a life filled with uncontrollable, impulsive gratifications which arouse anxiety and guilt and thus lead to the famous Russian flirtation with death — Gorky tells how in his youth boys would lie immobile on a railroad track while trains passed over them — against this there are the constant goals of work and the party. Death is merely the point at which one has outlived one's *usefulness.* Of the suicide of Marx's son-in-law, Paul Lafargue, Lenin wrote: ". . . if one cannot work for the party any longer, one must be able to look truth in the face and die like the Lafargues."

Out of such elements of ethics and moral temper emerges, in Leites' view, the "operational code in politics." For Bolshevism, all politics is summed up in the formula, *kto-kovo* — literally, "who-whom," but in its most radical sense, "who kills whom." Political relations are between dominators and dominated, between users and used. There can be no neutrals. If politics is *kto-kovo,* then all political strategies are guided by this fundamental rule: one pushes to the limit, one refuses to be provoked, one acts when one is ready, etc.

Stated in these gross terms, the precepts become political commonplaces, akin to the generalized precepts of military strategists or the maxims of Machiavelli. What gives Leites' analysis its special point and quality are the nuances of detail: the Bolshevik use of procedural points for trading; the expectations that personal insults will be taken politically and not personally (Vishinsky contemptuously calls Romulo "an empty barrel" in the UN General Assembly and then sends roses to a reception at Romulo's home); the role of provocations, and the like.

This same rigidity and calculatedness of behavior the Bolsheviks ascribe to their adversaries. The "big bourgeoisie" are seen as the Bolsheviks see themselves — i.e., as *serious*, calculating men who, wielding power, obey the "laws" of power. Political acts are not accidental; any act of the opposing ruling class can only be a hostile move in the constant war whose final outcome must be the annihilation of one side or the other. For the petty bourgeoisie, on the other hand, particularly the liberals, the Bolsheviks have only deep contempt; they are sentimental, given to illusions, deceived by the content of ideologies, moralistic — in short, fundamentally *unserious*.

Is "Bolshevik" character the same as it was fifty years ago? In important respects, yes; Leites believes that there are certain invariant patterns. Before 1917, Bolshevism as a small party faced a hostile state; now, in its view, it faces a hostile world — its basic posture remains the same. Prerevolutionary behavior toward rival political organizations once displayed itself in small cafés and drafty meeting halls; now its scene is the great assembly halls of world politics: the same behavior repeats itself. The preoccupation with procedural issues — arising from the belief that a small point will "inevitably" grow into a big one and must not be conceded — which was manifested by Lenin in regard to the constitution of the editorial board of *Iskra* in 1900 (when he was "coexisting" with rival Social Democrats) was duplicated in intra-party disputes in 1921 and, again, at international negotiations at Yalta, San Francisco, and the Conference of Foreign Ministers in 1945.

The political consequence of this analysis is inescapable: if politics is *kto-kovo*, then "coexistence" as a sustained *modus vivendi* is impossible. Leites sums it up flatly: ". . . a 'settlement' in Western terms, with outside groups — an agreement sharply and indefinitely reducing the threat of mutual annihilation — is inconceivable, [although] agreements with them, codifying the momentary relationship of forces, must always be considered and

often concluded."[22] But the party "maintains a full awareness of the basic conflict," and at the strategic moment presses forward again. Promises, as Lenin said, are like pie crusts, "made to be broken."

But let us now look more closely at Leites' use of psychoanalytic insight, for the novelty of his book lies there. To say, as Leites does, that the sources of Bolshevik character lie in a reaction to the extreme temper of the Russian intelligentsia in the nineteenth century is still to write history without the help of Freud; Lenin and his co-workers were perfectly *conscious* of their attempts to reverse traditional patterns of Russian character, to overcome Karataev and Oblomov. But when Leites speaks of the Bolshevik character as a "reaction-formation" to *unconscious*, overwhelmingly powerful wishes, he is approaching politics in a way that was impossible before psychoanalysis.

Two principal drives, according to Leites, explain Russian intellectual character: preoccupation with death, and latent passive homosexual impulses. (Tolstoy, for example, could not endure the idea of death or sex.) The Russian intellectual displayed a fascination with death that is terrifying to the Bolshevik. Against that fascination, the Bolshevik defense is to minimize death by work and, more important, to express a kind of personal omnipotence through the dissolution of the self into the all-embracing, undying party. Thus, Leites writes, "The earlier Russian feeling that life is empty because of death has been replaced by the Bolshevik feeling that death is empty and small and unable to interfere with life."[23]

The code of work becomes all-important. It is a basic defense against threatening feelings. Krupskaya, Lenin's wife, tells of the time in exile when Lenin was absorbed for hours in playing chess. "On his return to Russia Vladimir Ilyich abandoned chess-playing. 'Chess gets hold of you too much, and hinders work . . . ,'" he said. "From his early youth," she continues, "Vladimir Ilyich was capable of giving up whatever activity hindered his main work." In exile, many political refugees went often to the cinema, while others, scorning this mode of enjoyment, preferred to take

---

[22] *A Study of Bolshevism*, p. 527.
[23] *Ibid.*, p. 137.

physical exercise in walking. The group divided, said Krupskaya, into cinemists and anti-cinemists, who were jokingly called "anti-Semites." "Volodya," wrote Krupskaya to Lenin's mother, "is a decided anti-cinemist and a fierce walker."[24]

The theme of latent homosexuality, lying deep in the arcanum of psychoanalysis, is seen as a pervasive yet repressed element of Russian intellectual desire. In Dostoevsky, the utmost demonstration of emotion by the usually overwrought and emotionally charged characters is to embrace and clasp one another. To Bolshevism, the fantasy of men embracing each other is repulsive and frightening. When Lenin described those once close to him who had now made common cause with his enemies, he would say that they "kissed" and "embraced" one another. ("The Scheidemannites kiss and embrace Kautsky." — "The followers of Bernstein are impudently blowing kisses to [Plekhanov].")

To Leites, a further significant clue lies in the number of Lenin's intimate friendships which ended in violent ruptures. These included Struve, a close collaborator in the 1890's; Potresev, an early *Iskra* associate; Plekhanov, Lenin's "ambivalently loved master" who "capitulated" to the Mensheviks; Aleksinsky, perhaps Lenin's most intimate associate in the years after 1905, who later denounced him as a German agent; and Malinovsky, the Bolshevik whip in the Duma, of whom Lenin said, "He will not be another Aleksinsky," and who turned out to be a police agent.

"One might speculate — " says Leites, "the data discussed here allow no more than that — whether the Bolshevik insistence on, in effect, killing enemies and being killed by them is not in part an effort to ward off fear-laden and guilty wishes to embrace men and be embraced by them. This hypothesis is consistent with the existence of certain pervasive Bolshevik trends described in this study: the fear of being passive, the fear of being controlled and used, the fear of wanting to submit to an attack. Once one denies one's wish to kiss by affirming one's wish to kill, this is apt to reinforce one's belief in the enemy's wish to kill by virtue of the mechanism of projection, probably heavily used by the Bolsheviks."[25]

[24] *Ibid.*, pp. 135, 261.
[25] *Ibid.*, pp. 403–4.

On the basis of what documentation can one make such sweeping inferences? Even if we fully accept the psychoanalytic theories, how does one validate these judgments without putting the Bolshevik leaders on the couch, so to speak? Leites' method is to examine the imagery, fantasy, and characteristic literary metaphors employed by Bolshevik leaders, and the fictional models in Russian literature with which the Bolsheviks identify, or those they assail. Russian literature and the Russians' attitude toward it seem to make this possible. In few cultures have fictional characters become so sharply defined national types: Dostoevsky's gallery — the Karamazov's, Raskolnikov, Myshkin, Verkhovensky; Turgeniev's Rudin, Gogol's Chichikov, Goncharov's Oblomov, Chekov's multifarious characters. These are all models which are accepted or rejected by Russians as psychological masks.

Taking off from these literary sources, Leites draws on Freudian theory to highlight the latent meanings of specific imagery. For example, fear of impotence, fear of being beaten (in Stalin's famous speech to the managers of Soviet industry in 1931, the image of beating or being beaten occurs eleven times in a single paragraph), fear of contamination, of embraces, of annihilation, jokes about "cleaning out" the party, fear of being used as a "tail," etc. As chief evidence for his theories Leites relies on the marshaling of images, in a vast profusion. The result is a strange and fascinating medley of quotations — roughly three thousand cited for various points.

This method of analysis immediately provokes a charge of "reductionism" — namely, that all ideas are seen as being *au fond* something more primitive. Thus, Lenin's fierce attack on solipsism is seen as expressing panic about annihilation, while his attack on the "spontaneity of the masses" is seen as a defense against desires for impulsive, orgiastic gratification. In what sense, one may ask, is the primitive impulse behind an idea more "real" than the idea itself? This is a difficulty one often encounters in connection with psychoanalytic thinking. It is obvious that the psychological impulse *behind* an idea is no test of its truth; the test of truth comes *after* the idea has originated. Yet we have learned not to scoff at these hidden mainsprings, *for we are dealing less with the ideas than with the way in which they are held and used.* What Leites is arguing is that any view held with stubbornness, exaggeration, and intensity — as all Communist views are held — and which violently rejects all rational tests, raises the presumption that it may constitute a defense against strong unconscious wishes or fears which stand in contradiction to the idea. To follow a pronouncedly masculine profession like soldiering does not label a man as a "latent homosexual," but if we find him compulsively, violently, and beyond reason insisting on his military posture, "common sense" permits us to suspect that he may be afraid of being less a man than he would like to appear.

Granting even the validity of the psychoanalytic method in the study of personality, we must still ask whether it can legitimately be extended into the analysis of politics.

Erich Fromm has argued, in *Escape from Freedom* (New York, 1941), that the sadomasochistic character, typical of the German middle class, found an outlet in the Nazi Party. T. W. Adorno and his associate authors of *The Authoritarian Personality* (New York, 1950) have pointed to the rigid, compulsive individuals who seek authoritarian values. Harold Lasswell, in the early *Psychopathology and Politics* (Chicago, 1930), sought to show how the political arena acts as a displacement of personal needs. (For example, adolescents, feeling guilty about sex strivings, find sublimation in the generalized "love" appeal of political movements that emphasize brotherhood.) In these studies, characteristic of modern social science, the social structure is taken as fundamental and the personality components are seen as the responses.

Leites' view, however, goes beyond this. He says, in effect, that *character determines politics.* Since the mainspring of Bolshevism is action, the movement, by impressing its character on others, transforms all politics and, in the end, the social structure itself as well. (Compare the purposeful Bolshevik-type organization with interest-group parties, or tepid ideological parties, to see the difference.) Bolshevism, in this sense, can be considered as one of the few successful movements of pure will in history; its only competitors in this respect are certain religious orders. Because, in modern life, ideas (abstract, philosophical conceptions of truth) have become transformed

into ideologies (active strivings to implement a creed as truth), Leites' type of analysis is possible, reflecting as it does a social reality. For ideologies are, in effect, attempts to unite ideas, behavior, and character; they demand a hardening of commitment. The Communist (or the Fascist, or the kibbutznik, or the 100 per cent American) is not only supposed to believe certain things; he is supposed to act, to *be* something, and, in acting, to fix his character. If one is "serious," one "lives" one's ideology. Thus ideology may be said to presuppose character.[26]

What determined Bolshevik character? Leites stops short of an answer to this question, possibly because the purpose of his book lies elsewhere — he is interested in describing the pattern of Bolshevik action in order to develop a practical way of counteracting communism. Whether or not his picture of this operational code is a true one is, he argues, independent of the origins of Bolshevik impulses. Formally he is correct, for the code's validity depends upon its internal consistency, upon its confirmation by other analysts using the same data, and finally upon its usefulness in making predictions. Yet, intellectually the sources of that code are important, for only by tracing them can we have a complete model of social analysis.

The conventional answer regarding Bolshevik character is that the conspiratorial nature of the conditions of underground work in the days before the revolution — the environment — shaped the peculiar structure of the Bolshevik elite and its unique code and discipline. But there were other parties, Marxist and Social Revolutionary, which operated in the same environment. And the ideological debates between Lenin and Martov in 1903 on the nature of the party membership antedated the development of "party work": Martov argued that a Social Democrat was one who sympathized generally with the party's program, while Lenin argued that only a professional revolutionary, only a conspirator, could be a party member. Thus the pattern was prefigured in the thinking of Lenin.

Leites, it seems to me, would be forced to

---

[26] This may explain the intensity of the feelings of ex-Communists toward the party. Though they are free of the ideology, the rigid personality pattern remains.

argue that the Bolshevik pattern was a product of will. Further, if he is to be consistent with the psychoanalytic approach, he would have to argue that *it was the character of Lenin, the "primal father," which shaped the party* (his followers did call themselves Leninists) *rather than the party organization and the environment which shaped Lenin* and the other Bolsheviks. And it was the will of Lenin alone which altered the party's politics, as in the crucial decisions in April and July 1917. The Bolshevik Party, more than any other party in history, has demonstrated the nature of will. It was, and is, one of the most highly self-conscious movements in history. Its patristic writings are not only canonical; they are also "training documents" in the tempering of a "hard core" party membership. Individuals may join from a variety of motives, but all must be stamped in the mold or driven out. The splits and expulsions (becoming blood purges after power is achieved) which characterize Communist parties may thus be seen not as mere ideological or even power fights but as a *process of personality selection.*

With the Leites study we come full circle in the theories of history and politics. It was the fashion a hundred years ago to ascribe historical change to "great men" and the force of their personalities. Subsequently we interpreted history in terms of abstract "social forces" — population pressure, search for markets, etc. — which somehow, but never fully understandably, translated themselves through individual actors into tangible events. The glaring inadequacies of these deterministic theories have led to the reintroduction of psychological and, through Freudian influence, of characterological explanations. Even ex-Marxists have not been immune. Is not the current fashionable theory of the "primacy of politics" over economic forces simply a smuggled-in psychological theory of "power"? Most attempts to explain the situation in Russia today find expression in the "power" formula. But actually the formula of "power" explains little. It tells nothing about different tactics, different social groups, the different purposes for which power will be used. If a psychological theory of politics is to be employed, then the Leites view — with its emphasis on character as blending a power drive with ideology — is, in spite of all its limitations and uncertainties, far more subtle and imaginative than

the contraband psychology of the political scientist.

However, two questions remain to be asked of the method: How are continuities of character established, and how, and with what difficulties, does an elite group impress its character upon a country?

In the Leites model, as we have seen, there is the implication that the initial change in the character of the intelligentsia — the emergence of Bolshevism — was a reaction-formation, and that the character of the "primal father" determined its political course. If that was true of Lenin, how does it apply to Stalin and to his heirs? In his study of *Hamlet*, Ernest Jones remarks that there are two kinds of sons: those who reject their fathers, and those who take over and internalize the essential characteristics of the father, often caricaturing his features in the process.[27] From this point of view, Stalin was the son who took over the lineaments of the father. The touches, however, were grosser. Where in Lenin's time it was the party that had the monopoly on foresight, under Stalin it became a group within the party, and eventually the Leader alone, in whom all wisdom resided. Devices once reserved for the enemy — particularly deception and terror — were exercised on the masses which the party claimed to represent, and later against rivals within the party itself. Lenin had opposed personal touchiness and insisted on the irrelevance of personal prestige; Stalinism reacted intensely to minor slights, but only after giving them a political interpretation. Lenin opposed bragging; the Stalinist regime went in for the greatest self-glorification in history. Lenin opposed the creation of "scandals" in the party; Stalin liquidated the party cadres under the most fantastic charges.

These changes in Bolshevik behavior *do not necessarily reflect changes in the unconscious wishes and fears* which Leites posits as the ultimate sources of the Bolshevik character. Psychological *defense* patterns may change — indeed, they often *must* change as older defenses become inadequate. But when such changes take place on a broad political scale, they become extremely important, and we are bound to ask why the changes in defense

27 *Hamlet* . . . with a Psycho-analytic Study by Ernest Jones, M.D., London, 1947, p. 22. The argument is elaborated in Jones' *Hamlet and Oedipus*, New York, 1951, pp. 83–90.

mechanisms have occurred, why *these* particular changes, and what further changes are likely to occur. Here Leites offers little assistance. His theory deals with the dynamics of Bolshevism in the process of its formation, but once Bolshevism has come to birth, the model, as he presents it, is static. Take, for example, the initial turning on Stalin by Khrushchev and company. One could say that this, in turn, represents a reaction to the overbearing, almost paranoid Stalin; or there may be more "rational" explanations: the need to win mass support, etc. Further, how are we to explain the seeming "openness" and marked vulgarity of Khrushchev's character? We have no guide in the model itself to the possibility or the nature of the change.

The static quality of the model comes in part from its methodology. The basic outlines of Bolshevik character are drawn not from the empirical world of action, but from the abstract canons of Bolshevik doctrine. In itself this is not too great a fault, since the doctrine itself is evident. The greater fault of the theory — and, paradoxically, its strength — lies in the fact that, starting from static doctrine, it posits a static force called "character" and then gathers all human action into that one hedgehog force.[28] But how often in social action does character or will actually impose itself on events? People live largely in social systems, and they are "chained" to one another in complex ways. All of us, no doubt, would like to impose our "character" on the world, but in practice we find ourselves forced to modify our demands to conform with *possibilities*. Leites may thus be claimed to have given his concept of "character" a false autonomy, and in applying this concept to politics — which is *par excellence* a phenomenon of change within possibilities — to have falsified the nature of the subject.

IV. *How the Harvard System Works*

Turning now to the sociological approach: the study by three Harvard social scientists — Raymond A. Bauer, Alex Inkeles, and Clyde

---

[28] As George Ivask has said, if all men may be divided into foxes and hedgehogs, they may also be divided, following the satire of Saltykov-Schedrin, into boys with pants and boys without pants. If Lenin wore pants, is Khrushchev without them?

Kluckhohn — is the best that contemporary sociology offers, and on this score alone merits attention. Their book, *How the Soviet System Works*, is a revised presentation of a report, *Strategic Psychological Strengths and Vulnerabilities of the Soviet Social System*, that was prepared for the U.S. Air Force, the agency which commissioned and paid for the five years' research that went into the study. In one respect, the study illustrates the hazards of such sponsored research, since the authors found themselves under pressure to produce a "popular" book which the Air Force sponsors could show to their own controllers. The result is not a happy combination: "theses" are condensed and presented with only partial documentation; the book is written in an attempted vernacular style which just does not come off. The project, based on systematic interviewing of defectors, drew data from 329 extended life-history interviews, including detailed personality tests; 435 supplementary interviews; almost 10,000 questionnaires on special topics; 2,700 general questionnaires, and 100 interviews and psychological tests, administered for control purposes, to a matched group of Americans. In all, 33,000 pages of data were accumulated. These, together with the list of over fifty specialized unpublished studies and thirty-five published articles on which the authors drew in preparing the book, indicate how rich their source materials were.

Economic and political matters were not considered to be within the scope of the project. The key concept was that of the "social system," and this is the heart of the Harvard contribution. A social system is simply the characteristic ways in which societies, or subgroups, organize their activities to achieve specific goals. Since the resultant institutions or behavior patterns are linked, in meaningful fashion, presumably variations in one area are accompanied by regular — and determinate — variations in others. (Thus a change in the rate of capital accumulation, one of the fundamental determinants of an economic system, must precipitate changes in the rate of consumption, etc.) In the social system, reorganization of the structure of authority in the factory would presumably entail corresponding changes in the organization of the school system, the family, etc. For example, when Stalin introduced one-man rule and tight labor discipline in the factories in 1931, one could imagine a manager, confronted with a disrespectful student from a "progressive" school, asking, "What kind of a hooligan is this?" and insisting that school methods be changed so that students would learn obedience. The educational commissars, however, confronted with "wild" children from broken homes, would be forced to demand that the family be strengthened and divorce be made more difficult. And so, in linked fashion, we find the reintroduction of older, traditional forms of authority.[29] Yet such social change may become self-defeating, for as repression in the factory becomes pervasive, individuals need to find protection and do so in close family ties. And thus, after a while, the regime begins to complain about undue familialism. This example oversimplifies a social process, but it is not unjust.

The Harvard group has concentrated, however, not on locating change in the conventional institutions of society — family, political system, education, industry — but on the typical adaptive patterns of behavior which regulate the life of the ruled. These "central patterns" are: the need to conform to an explicit ideology; the refusal to allow independent sources of power; the centralization of all planning and control; the overcommitment of resources to particular objectives; the use of terror and forced labor; "storming" as a method of reaching objectives; the tolerance of evasions which fulfill the plan — e.g., *blat* (the network of informal deals) — etc. On the basis of these "operating characteristics," the Harvard group seeks to identify the general strengths and weaknesses of the *system*. Weaknesses: there are no orderly processes of succession in office; economic growth in heavy industry is disproportionate to that in consumer industries; there are constant purges and insecurities. Strengths: the atomization of resistance; the Russians' ignorance of the realities of the outside world; the deep loyalties to the system on the part of the managerial groups.

One trouble with this approach is that one

---

29 The example has been adapted from Alex Inkeles, "Understanding a Foreign Society: A Sociologist's View," *World Politics*, iii, No. 2 (January 1951), pp. 269–80.

does not know, actually, which of these "operating characteristics" are central and which are not, for the Harvard group seems to lack an organizing principle which determines the selections. Is "forced labor," for example, an "inherent" aspect of the system, or a fortuitous element which got out of hand and may be discarded? And, if the latter, how is the judgment made? — on the basis of the fact that the terror has become self-defeating or that it is uneconomic, or because of moral disapprobation from the outside, or what? Moreover, if one seeks to forecast the "likely responses . . . of various segments of the Soviet leadership" in order to gauge the degree of loyalty and disaffection among the major social groups, the "central patterns" may be of less importance than an accurate definition of the different interests of such segments and of their power vis-à-vis other interest groups. The question is, what do we look for in a mode of analysis?

A mode of analysis is a function of the particular categories one uses to group together related characteristics. In political theory, one can classify regimes, as Aristotle did, as monarchies, oligarchies, or democracies; or, as Max Weber did, as traditional, rational, and charismatic. One's purpose dictates one's perspectives. The danger is that one tends to think of categories as realities rather than as theoretical constructs. This error has been appallingly true of Marxist thought, which in rudimentary fashion first employed the concept of a social system. Since in a simple Marxist model of capitalism, classes are formed in relation to the means of production, to the simple-minded Communist there could be no exploitation in Russia since the "people" owned the factories and there were, therefore, no exploiting classes. Hence, too, the fierce doctrinal debates as to whether Russia was a "workers' state," a "degenerated workers' state," or what.

But, given all these pitfalls, the gain in trying to define the *essential* nature of a system is that one can locate the causal factors (in modern jargon, the independent variables), the changes in which affect all other parts of the system. (To Marx, for example, the essential nature of capitalism is the compulsion to accumulate and reinvest. Crises are deemed inevitable because of ensuing gaps between consumption and production, because of overproduction, and because of the falling rate of profit, which is a function, presumably, of high capital and low labor inputs.)

The Harvard group, however, shrinks from seeking to specify the motor forces in the social system as they have conceived it. "It is difficult, if not impossible," they say, "to assign a rank order of importance to those operating characteristics since they constitute an interlocking system in which each has implication for the other."[30] Apart from the fact that one may question the "tightness" of such interlocks" (what, for example, is the link between "storming" and "forced labor" as characteristics of the system?) or even the congruence of the different "operating characteristics," *is it so difficult to single out the factor of prime importance?* Is it not quite clear, really, that the Soviet system is characterized, essentially, by the centralized control of political power, that it is a *command* system, with few institutional checks, and that all other aspects of the system — the refusal to allow independent power, the overcommitment of resources, etc. — derive from that fact?

But, once that is admitted, a large element of indeterminacy has to be admitted as well. For, in such a command system, the decisions of a few men — and, in the case of Stalin, of one — become decisive in changing the nature of the system. If Bukharin, rather than Stalin, had won, would not Russia be a different society? Or if Malenkov, rather than Khrushchev, had kept power, would not the profile of Russia be somewhat different today? The development of Soviet society depends thus on the nature of Soviet political developments.

If this be true, then, in seeking to understand the Soviet Union we are back to Kremlinology, the endlessly fascinating and often exasperatingly occult game of charting the petty protocol at the dinner table or seeing who is called on to speak at the Supreme Soviet, and in what sequence, in order to guess who is "on first."

The essential fact is that the Harvard system, lacking a sense of motor, cannot locate the sources of change in the system. While it is important to know the "limits" of social action (e.g., how far one can push recalcitrant peasants before offering new incentives; or

which groups have the greatest potential for independent action), in *politics* one has to know who composes a ruling group, how the group arrives at a decision, how the claims of subordinate groups are adjudicated, and so on. For in a society like Russia, where institutional and behavior patterns are not autonomous, a "social system" has no meaning unless it can be defined within the context of politics.

V. *Who Eats Before Whom*

The basic assumption of Kremlinology is that every move at the Russian *verkhuska* is shot through with the struggle for protocol, prestige, and power. Thus the manifest need to decentralize the Russian economy because of the increasing inability of a single center to direct the operation of 300,000 enterprises becomes a problem as well of whose power is increased and whose power is reduced by such a shift. Thus, not in the final analysis, but in the immediate one, all rational-technical criteria bow to the political. And thus, in analyzing any move of Russian policy, we are forced to thread our way through the Byzantine intrigues which are spun in such power fights.

The real problem arises, first, in the definition of the contending power groups and, second, in the way we identify the alignments of individuals, particularly subordinates. One approach has been to define power groups in "functional" terms — e.g., party, army, secret police, state bureaucracy, etc. — and to locate spokesmen for those groups from the positions they hold. Thus the late Franz Borkenau, a leading practitioner of Kremlinology, wrote in the *New Leader* of May 6, 1957: "Since Stalin's death, an undisguised struggle has raged between Khrushchev as representative of the Party dictatorship and one-time Premier Georgi Malenkov as spokesman of the managers' demand for independence. Over the last four years, the managers have been making more and more effective demands for greater decentralization in the economy. Hence, Khrushchev and his ally Lazar Kaganovich have devised this scheme as a circuitous plan for undermining the managerial class." In a later article (June 3), Kaganovich was seen as standing on the sidelines, rather than at Khrushchev's side.

There are several difficulties with this sweeping type of statement. A word like "man-

---

[10] Bauer, Inkeles, and Kluckhohn, *op. cit.*, p. 20.

agers" contains a basic ambiguity. Are the managers the men who head the factories in the field, the heads of economic ministries in Moscow, or the planners in the Gosplan? If the "managers" include all three categories, is there an identity of interests among them? (Surely one would expect considerable friction between a factory seeking greater control over its own activities and a ministry in Moscow.) And, if not, which of the three are the real "managers"? A second difficulty arises from mechanically countering bloc with bloc. While it is true that there are often interest conflicts between functional groups, the very nature of a political power struggle carried on by small cliques and coteries requires the power figure to have his allies within *all* groups. Thus the fight may not be simply "managers" vs. "party," or "army" vs. "party," but may cut across these groupings. Is the army, for example, a unitary interest group (united on what interests?) or does Zhukov line up with X and Koniev with Y and Vasilievsky with Z? From what we know of armies elsewhere, certainly such internal conflicts and differing outside alliances take place — e.g., in the U.S. Army, the Marshall-Eisenhower group vs. MacArthur. The problem, then, is to locate those issues on which the army would stand united and those on which its top officers would divide. And, in so doing, one faces the problem of determining what it is that ties cliques and coteries together: school affiliation, loyalties to one who has made promotion possible, differences in generation, common wartime or service experiences, etc., etc.

Nor can one say that ideology determines alignments, for on key policy issues — consumer goods vs. heavy industry, tough or soft line toward the West, tough or soft line toward the satellites — there may be no unitary ideology which dictates a consistent attitude toward such issues. Malenkov may have wanted relaxation at home so as to be more tough with the West. Moreover, a top figure will often switch ideological sides opportunistically in a bid for support. Certainly Stalin's history is instructive in this regard. (The question is often put: does Khrushchev represent the "Stalinist" faction or does Malenkov? The difficulty with these formulations is that what we are observing is the break-up of a faction and, in such a highly personal situation, few

of the formal sociological criteria for charting allegiances seem to hold.)

Even greater difficulties are faced in the task of locating the links of support down the line. Every foreign office and propaganda organization maintains extensive biographical dossiers on members of the Soviet elite in an effort to keep track of the shifting personnel as a means of measuring the relative strength of the contenders at the top. And often, as the example cited below shows, the method is highly tenuous.[31] How far one can go with

31 The *Radio Liberation Daily Information Bulletin* of May 14, 1957, carried the following news item, headed "Andropov — Head of the Satellite Countries Department of the CC":

"*Pravda* for May 12, 1957 twice mentions the former ambassador of the USSR in Hungary, Yu. V. Andropov, as 'head of a department of the Central Committee of the CPSU.' According to the *Pravda*, Andropov was present at Khrushchev's reception for the government delegation from the Mongolian People's Republic and also at a lunch given by Bulganin in honor of the same delegation.

"Although the Tass reports do not state precisely which department Andropov controls, it may be assumed that it is the fairly secret satellite countries department (even its official name is not known).

"In the past, B. N. Ponomarev, who was invariably called 'a member of the Central Committee of the CPSU' usually took part in such receptions and banquets in honor of party and government delegations from the satellite countries. The position occupied by Ponomarev has never been mentioned anywhere. In this connection it is interesting to note that at the lunch given by Bulganin and Khrushchev in honor of the Albanian party and government delegation on April 12th this year (*Pravda*, 13th April 1957) the order of those who attended was as follows:

". . . Serov — Ponomarev — Palgunov — Nikitin. . . .

"At the lunch which was recently given by Bulganin for the Mongolian delegation, the order of protocol was as follows:

". . . Serov — Andropov — Nikitin — Palgunov. . . .* [FOOTNOTE: * The protocol order at the reception given by Khrushchev was as follows: Gromyko — Pisarev (ambassador in Mongolia) — Andropov; however, it should be remembered that according to protocol, at a reception for a foreign delegation, the Soviet ambassador of the country concerned is always given the place of honor, whether or not he actually merits it 'on the protocol ladder'.]

"Despite all these facts, it would be premature to conclude that Ponomarev has been replaced by

this detailed, yet mechanical, scoring is open to question. One observer, in reviewing Boris Meissner's *Das Ende des Stalin-Mythos,* complains: ". . . he believes that he can say of any party functionary, from the top on down through lower ranks, whether he is a Khrushchev or a Malenkov man, a supporter of this or that tactical nuance of party policy. Very often these assertions are based on extraneous biographical information. Whoever served under Malenkov at some time in the past must, in Meissner's opinion, be considered a Malenkov adherent in all present-day situations. Whoever worked with Khrushchev twenty years ago in the Ukraine still must be his confidant today."[32]

And sometimes the same event — in this instance, the appointment of one F. R. Kozlov to the key post of candidate member of the party Presidium — is interpreted in diametrically opposite fashion. Harrison Salisbury, in the *New York Times* of February 16, 1957, reported that Kozlov was a member of a group to which Mr. Pervukhin belonged, and was "probably an adherent of Mr. Malenkov." Kozlov, said Salisbury, was one of the authors of the key propaganda documents of the "doctors' plot" of 1953; and one can surmise, therefore, in line with the logic of Kremlinology,

that Malenkov was one of the directors of the plot. But Richard Lowenthal commented a day later in the *London Observer:* "Mr. Khrushchev's inner-party position has been reinforced not only by Mr. Shepilov's return to the party Secretariat, but by the promotion of Frol Romanovich Kozlov, the first secretary of the Leningrad region, to candidate membership of the party Presidium. . . . Having returned to obscurity during the early Malenkov era, he was at the end of 1953 promoted by Khrushchev's personal intervention to take the place of Malenkov's protégé, Andrianov, as head of the Leningrad party organization." And, by equal logic, since Kozlov had signaled the campaign of vigilance at the start of the "doctor's plot," Khrushchev was thus tied to the execution of the plot.

This is not to say that the method is wrong, but that someone's information is inadequate. (For the record, Mr. Lowenthal was right about Kozlov, and Salisbury wrong.) How excruciatingly difficult the problems of Kremlinology can be is seen from a report in the *New York Times* of August 10, 1957, which stated that the U.S. State Department simply did not know who was running the Soviet foreign office and writing its *démarches.* Said the report:

> The State Department has been trying for some time without success to solve a new Kremlin riddle.
>
> The question: Who is the man who really operates Soviet foreign policy? who is the Soviet opposite number to Secretary of State Dulles? . . .
>
> It is argued that Mr. Khrushchev and Marshal Bulganin have been away from Moscow so much, unaccompanied by foreign policy experts, that they cannot possibly have had time to "mind the store" during recent months.
>
> Yet the State Department feels that the quality of Soviet diplomacy has improved noticeably during this period and now shows an unusual degree of sophistication in its understanding of the West. . . .
>
> The Secretary has asked the United States intelligence agencies to examine the evidence, but so far the investigators have drawn a complete blank. . . .
>
> The effect in Washington is to make it extremely difficult for the State Department to appraise either the Soviet Union's present in-

---

Andropov, because Ponomarev is also to some extent connected with the international communist movement. (For example he was a member of the delegation of the CPSU to the Fourteenth Congress of the French Communist Party in July 1956.) A more probable explanation is that an 'international division of labor' has been carried out in the Central Committee; Ponomarev will henceforth maintain contact only with those Communist parties outside the orbit, while Andropov deals with the satellites.

"*Bearing in mind the fact that Andropov was released ('in connection with a transfer to other work' — Pravda 7 March 1957) in the course of a reshuffle of senior officials of the Ministry of Foreign Affairs which was begun by Shepilov immediately before his withdrawal from the post of Minister of Foreign Affairs, there can be no doubt to whom Andropov owes his promotion* (on the 'protocol ladder' he is now several stages above his former chief — V. V. Kuznetsov, first deputy Minister of Foreign Affairs — see *Pravda,* 12 May, 1957)."

[32] Immanuel Birnbaum, "Destalinization: Motives and Consequences," *Problems of Communism,* vi, No. 1 (January-February 1957), p. 41.

tentions or the probable future of its foreign policy.

Consider, too, the dilemma of the Kremlinologist in having to make spot interpretations of a major change in the status of leading personnel when the announcement of the change itself offers no clue as to its meaning. Thus, the day after a terse announcement appeared that Marshal Zhukov had been relieved of his post, Harry Schwartz, the *New York Times* specialist, began his story in this fashion: "Two principal possibilities have emerged from Marshal Georgi K. Zhukov's removal yesterday as Soviet Defense Minister: a substantial decline in his real power or a step toward his promotion in the Soviet hierarchy" (October 27, 1957).

One can sympathize with these occupational hazards. Henry Adams, in his *Autobiography,* remarks that when he was in London during the American Civil War, serving as secretary to his father, the United States Minister, he was making reports on the splits in British Cabinet opinion — reports which became the basis of American policy (e.g., the Mason-Sliddel affair), and which, he felt, were based on firsthand information. Twenty years later, when the Cabinet papers were opened, he found to his dismay that his reports had been completely wrong. Shortly after the revolt in Budapest, Hugh Gaitskell raised the question in the House of Commons whether the Russians had been emboldened to intervene because of the news of Eden's action at Suez. The question, even if Gaitskell intended it only to press a political advantage, was not an unfair one. It would be important to know if this were so. Is there an answer? We have no access to sources.

But one *can* raise a question regarding method, at least as to the way in which Kremlinology has been applied. Put most simply, Kremlinology often becomes the obverse side of the Bolshevik mentality — that is, it becomes over-deterministic. The characteristic fact about Bolshevik mentality is its refusal to admit of accident and contingency. Everything has a reason, a preordained motive. Hence the sinister refrain in Bolshevik rhetoric: "It is no accident, comrade, no mere *accident,* that . . ." or, "Why at this time, why at *this particular moment,* does the enemy

choose . . . ?" And so all such questions lead, with insidious intent, to the ultimate question: *kto-kovo,* who is using whom? One is reminded of the episode some years back when two Ukrainian delegates to the UN wandered into a small New York delicatessen during a hold-up and, failing to understand the command of the robbers, one of them was shot in the thigh. Vishinsky, either to embarrass the United States, or because he was truly suspicious, rejected the explanation of the New York police department that, since it was a hold-up, the shooting could not have been political. "How could it have been a hold-up?" he asked. "It was a *small* delicatessen." In wealthy, capitalist America, who would bother to hold up a *small* store?

One sometimes finds a similar logic among the Kremlinologists. Every move — both of personnel in the power conflicts within, and of policy in the international arena without — is seen as a carefully plotted, conspiratorially conceived, predetermined plan whose every consequence is anticipated; every move has a secret meaning which detailed charting of protocol and word counting can uncover.[33]

---

[33] Imagine what the Kremlinologist and/or the psychoanalyst could do with the statement of Indian Ambassador K. P. S. Menon, the last foreigner to see Stalin alive, that at the interview Stalin occupied himself throughout the entire session with making doodles — of wolves.

Perhaps the most extraordinary attempt to trace Soviet elite maneuverings by means of "Kremlinological" methods is the RAND study of Myron Rush, *The Rise of Khrushchev,* Washington, D.C., 1958. In 1955, Rush observed that Khrushchev's title as first secretary of the party (*pervi sekretar*), which normally appeared in the Russian press in lower case, suddenly was given in *Pravda,* of May 25, 1955, as *Pervi Sekretar.* (The next day, the capital S was diminished, but the capital P retained, and the title appeared thereafter as *Pervi sekretar.*) From a clue as slim as this, and from others which at first glance might seem to be equally tendentious (e.g., Khrushchev's emulation of Stalin's use of the word *otriskoi,* or "belching forth," to characterize Malenkov as a right deviationist), Rush argued, in a paper prepared for RAND at that time, that Khrushchev was beginning to make his bid for power, and that he would use Stalin's ladder, the party secretariat apparatus, in his ascent. For some detailed questioning of Mr. Rush's reasoning, see my review of his book in *Problems of Communism,* VII, No. 2 (March–April 1958).

But from what we know of every chancellery in the world, few campaigns in political (or even military) affairs are ever calculated with such precision. And the analyst who fails to consider contingency runs the same risk as the Bolshevik in overdetermining the political game.

And with one more step we come full circle. Whatever the importance of power at the top, no group of power figures, however absolute their rule, can wield infinite power. The problem with the Kremlinological approach is the same as with that of Leites. Every attempt to impose one's will has to take into account the finite limits of natural resources and the recalcitrance of human institutions[34] — but how?

---

[34] Insufficient attention has been paid, for example, to the techniques of evasion practiced by Soviet scientists in carrying out their work in accordance with the common fund of scientific knowledge. Alexander Weisberg-Cybulski, who was editor of the physics journal in the Soviet Union, and later a director of an institute in Kharkov, before being jailed in the 1937–1938 purges, tells the highly amusing story of how, in the journal articles, research advances in Russia were attributed, out of political necessity, to the wisdom derived from dialectical materialism and of the problems that confronted the editors when the German Academy of Science asked for the secret of the new method. (See *Science and Freedom*, proceedings of the Hamburg Conference, London, 1955.)

More recently, Ivan D. London has noticed wholesale evasions of *partinost* in science: "For example, it is not difficult to show, on the basis of items abstracted from speeches, prefaces, introductory paragraphs, etc., that in the Soviet Union the whole development of physiology of the sense organs was prescribed by the Communist Party in order to provide a 'concrete basis for Lenin's theory of reflection' and to meet the 'demands of practice': industrial, medical, and military, the latter two in particular. Yet a detailed scrutiny of the technical literature, the published minutes of various meetings, conferences, etc., over the years reveals little to suggest that the serious programs of research in the field of sensory physiology in the Soviet Union have been really influenced, in any respect, by either practical considerations or Party dicta. Of course, superficially there may seem to be a planned compliance with practical programmatic aims — after all, 'Soviet language' fulfills, besides communicative, also prophylactic functions — but any sensory physiologist who is alert to his subject will recognize the dust-in-the-eyes purpose of certain parts of research pro-

VI. *The One Road and the Many — Exit Pirandello*

Now that we have investigated many roads, are there some which can lead us to reality better than others? (Says a passage in the Talmud: "If you don't know where you are going, any road will take you there.") Perhaps a few distinctions — and questions — are in order.

A. *The Different Moments*

There should be a clear distinction between the types of change which take place: between changes in Soviet society (the social system) and in Soviet politics, although in crucial moments one is dependent on the other. The difference is one of distinguishing between a process and an event; or, to revive an old distinction of the crusty sociologist William Graham Sumner, between *crescive* and *enacted* change.

Crescive changes are those which surge, swell, go on willy-nilly, and develop with some measure of autonomy. They variously derive from organic growth of tradition, or from changes in values (e.g., the decision of people to have fewer children or more), or from technical imperatives, once a key decision has been taken (e.g., the need for training more engineers, once a country industrializes).

Enacted changes are the conscious decisions or intents of legislators or rulers (e.g., the declaration of war, the collectivization of agriculture, the location of new industry, etc.) Those who enact change have to take into account the mores of the people and the resources at their disposal, but these serve only as limiting, not determining, factors.

Sociological analysis is most sure when it deals with crescive changes. These can be identified, their drift charted, and, like iceberg floes, their course and even their break-up specified more readily than others. But sociological analysis often fails in predicting political decisions. There are in history what Hegel called the "unique moments," and, in calling the turn, not pure reason but practical judgment (that unstable compound of informa-

grams. . . ." ("Toward a Realistic Appraisal of Soviet Science," *Bulletin of the Atomic Scientists*, XIII, No. 5, May 1957, p. 170.)

tion, intuition, and empathy) has to take hold. Bolshevism has been par excellence a movement minutely conscious of the past and supremely aware of the tactical and strategic nuances of events. It has been this constant awareness of "unique moments" (the "revolutionary situation," as Lenin first conceived it) and its ability to adapt its timing to the changing situation that have given Bolshevism its unique political advantage in the past.

B. The Problem of Prediction

The nature of the changes which one describes conditions the kinds of prediction one can make. One can define, and predict, the limits of broad crescive changes (e.g., if one knows the resource pattern of the Soviet Union — amount of arable land, minerals, manpower — one can make a guess about the slowdown in the rate of economic growth), but in predicting the short-run policy turns one comes up against the variabilities of accident, folly, and simple human cantankerousness. The situation is reminiscent of two radicals in the 1920's debating the future course of Soviet politics. "The objective situation," said one, "requires that Trotsky do so and so and so and so." "Look," replied the other, "you know what Trotsky has to do, and I know what Trotsky has to do, but does Trotsky know?"

One of the key problems in the analysis of power is the mode of succession. In the Soviet system, as opposed to a constitutional regime, there seems to be no formal definition of legitimacy, and no system of investiture of power. In seeking to duplicate Stalin's rise, Khrushchev used the party secretariat as a power lever. But in doing so he was taking a big gamble. In the war years and after, Stalin had emphasized his governmental and military titles rather than his party position. At the time of his death in 1953, Stalin was only one of nine party secretaries, but was, uniquely, the Chairman of the Council of Ministers of the USSR. Malenkov relinquished his post as party secretary, when forced to make a choice, and sought to legitimize his authority through the post of Premier and the Council of Ministers. It is the measure of Khrushchev's shrewdness that he assumed correctly that, despite the rise of the technical and military classes, the mechanics of political power had not changed essentially since the 1930's. Yet

can we assume that these "laws of mechanics" will hold in the naming of Khrushchev's successor? How do we define the balance of forces and predict the direction in which they will tip?

And yet, given all these problems and pitfalls, it would be a forward step in the social sciences if a group of Soviet experts were, at regular intervals, to make predictions at different levels of probable Soviet developments and state the reasons for their inference. (Bauer, Inkeles, and Kluckhohn, for example, stated that the collegial system of power in Russia *could* stabilize itself; Rush said that it would not, and predicted Khrushchev's bid for power.[35]) By systematic review of the predictions, the successes and failures, one could probably obtain a more viable operational model of Soviet behavior.

C. The Role of the Irrational

In social theory, the weight of analysis has always been thrown on the side of the rational explanation. The presumption (cf. Moore, Rostow, Deutscher, Aron, etc.) is that a society ultimately makes its choices on the basis of the rational alternatives which confront it. But how much meaning can one make of the role of pique (e.g., Tito's anger, as reported in the Dedijer biography,[36] at the fact that "we were treated like Komsomols," or Khrushchev's resentment at being forced by Stalin to dance the *Gopak*) in explaining the precipitateness or intensity of political acts? And, taking into account the researches of Leites, what weight can be given to the role of emotional components, conscious or unconscious, as a clue to political stance? Is it simply that rationality dictates the political course, and emotions the choler, or what?

D. Myth and Monolith

One difficulty with analysis in social science is that it deals with categories, not people. In recent analyses of the Communist movement, particularly in the United States, the movement has been seen as a monolith, with each adherent a disciplined soldier or a "true believer" ready always to follow orders of "the party."

[35] Bauer, Inkeles, and Kluckhohn, *op. cit.*, p. 239; Rush, *op. cit.*, p. 21.
[36] Vladimir Dedijer, *Tito*, New York, 1953, p. 327.

To some extent, the West itself has been seduced by the very image of "the Bolshevik" with which the Communist rulers have sought to mold the "new" Soviet man. For, like any human group, the Communists have not been immune to personal rivalries and, more important, they have not been immune to the inherent factionalism which besets all radical movements. In fact, one might argue that factionalism, if only the need at times to chop off a "left" wing or a "right" wing, has been necessary in order for the party to maintain a myth of inviolate correctness. Certainly, however, the strains and factions of earlier years (the defections of Levi, Ruth Fischer, Brandler, Thalheimer, Souvarine, Rappaport, Rosmer, Bordiga, Silone, Cannon, Lovestone, Wolfe) have had their counterparts — although the struggles were more hidden and suppressed — in the defections and expulsions and murders of Marty, Tillon, Lecoeur, Hervé, Cucchi, Magnani, Reale, Tito, Petkov, Gomulka, Rajk, Nagy, and thousands of others. In fact, not monolithism but factionalism has been a basic law of the Communist movement. And we have failed to see this and exploit it. For from general political experience — whether it be in the trade union movement or political parties — we know that ruling groups rarely collapse, but fall through the defection of key power figures who control substantial followings. This was the experience of the CIO with the "Communist problem" in the United States, and the meaning of Tito, Nagy, and (perhaps) Gomulka in the international Communist movement.

But more than a tactical inability to exploit the fissures and cracks is involved. In the character approach, and in Kremlinology, too, there has often been a "false concreteness." One saw all Communists as "the enemy," as "the Bolshevik," and any unrest, particularly in the satellites, purely as power conflicts between rival leaders. But there was more than this. There was also the simple recalcitrance and the simple decency of the human being which lay underneath. Who becomes the *apparatchik*, seduced by sadism and power, and who does not; who the bureaucrat and who the lurking idealist; who the Rakosi and who the Gyulya Hay — this question is not, as we saw in Poland and Hungary in 1956, a closed book.

We can now see, in retrospect, the real meaning of the first Nagy regime in 1954–1955, how the momentum gathered when people were able to communicate with each other, exchange experiences, and realize that some hope of change was possible.[37] But why did almost all the specialists in Soviet affairs fail to catch the significance of those clues in 1954–1955? Was it because they were so mesmerized by the thought of "power" alone as the singular clue to the meaning of social conflict as to forget its impact on people?

Having said this, we must also recognize that political events do not return in the same trajectory. Having failed to catch the "unique moment," we are apt to forget that the moment may not return. The lesson of the last few years, from East Berlin to Budapest, is that a "thaw" breaks up glaciers and log jams, creates rifts and fissures, and sends massive floes down the sea of history. But have not the Russians — who are more sensitive than most to the lessons of history — seen this as well and, learning from these events, may they not have decided that, if they can help it, there will be no more thaws?

E. The Word and the Deed

Every society, every social organization, lives for certain goals which, in considerable measure, are dictated by its ideology. We know — to use an example from modern trade union experience — that many individuals act quite pragmatically when their doctrinaire ideological goals conflict with the ongoing reality, and they compromise accordingly. Yet, when called upon to take a stand on issues far removed from their immediate experience, the only vocabulary, the only rhetoric, the only categories of analysis or even simple formulae

---

[37] We realize, too, the profound wisdom of de Tocqueville: ". . . it is not always when things are going from bad to worse that revolutions break out. On the contrary, it oftener happens that when a people which has just put up with an oppressive rule over a long period of time without protest suddenly finds the government relaxing its pressure, it takes up arms against it. . . . Patiently endured so long as it seemed beyond redress, a grievance comes to appear intolerable once the possibility of removing it crosses men's minds. For the mere fact that certain abuses have been remedied draws attention to the others and they now appear more galling. . . ." Alexis de Tocqueville, *The Old Regime and the French Revolution,* Anchor ed., New York, 1955, pp. 176–77.

available to them are the old ideological banners. They use them and become trapped; for ideology is a hardening of commitment, a freezing of opinion.

Since the Bolshevik ideology is the only formal canon of Soviet intentions that we have, an answer to this question is of prime importance: To what extent are the Soviet leaders committed to the formal Bolshevik ideology (e.g., the incompatibility of compromise, the attribution to capitalism of inherent imperialist aims, etc.), and to what extent are they prepared to modify it on the basis of experience and reality?

The answers are contradictory: (1) If one accepts the "characterological evidence" (e.g., Dicks, Leites), compromise is precluded. The rigid psychological postures and even paranoid suspicions of the Soviet rulers make it difficult for them to appraise realistically the changes in the Western world. (2) An extreme Kremlinologist might say that the Soviet rulers are cynical and regard the ideology simply as a necessary myth for the masses. (3) A geopolitical theorist, taking a completely rationalist view, would argue that strategic interests rather than ideology determine the behavior of Soviet rulers. (4) The weight of some evidence (see pp. 29–35 of the Bauer, Inkeles, and Kluckhohn book) is that ideology, even though cynically used by the Soviet rulers, is a real factor in the way they think and in the formulation of their goals.

But all this was before Khrushchev. While in the fields of literature and the arts the party has moved to reassert *partinost* (ideological control), in other fields practical considerations rather than ideology seem to determine policy. Soviet economists, for example, in conformity with the Marxist theory of value, could not admit of the productivity of capital, or utilize the interest rate to measure the rational allocation of capital. But even under socialism capital scarcities exist, and if cost economies were to be achieved, some disguised techniques had to be created in order to carry out the functions of the interest rate. After the war, these evasions of dogma were attacked by the ideologists. "In the hot debate which followed," writes Robert Campbell, "the conflict between the very real problem of the planners and the demand of purity in doctrine was made quite clear. The Soviet leaders faced an impasse; one of the central assumptions of Marxist economic theory had been proved wrong by their own experience, and they were faced with a painful choice between ideology and rational expediency. . . . So long as Stalin was alive, no official line emerged to break the deadlock. About a year after his death, however, the Gordian knot was cut, and cut in such a way as to constitute a surrender of orthodoxy to reality."[38]

In the field of agriculture, Khrushchev has taken the dramatic, drastic step of abolishing the machine and tractor stations, which, in the Stalinist scheme, represented a giant step forward in the elimination of the peasantry, and is turning their equipment over to the *kolkhozes*. And we can surmise that, in the fields of nuclear physics and other strategic specializations, the pressure to squeeze all theories into the ritualistic formulae of dialectical materialism has diminished.

And yet, at some point — but where? — some essential aspects of the regnant ideology — but which? — must be maintained, for without a central belief system with some continuity, disintegrative opinions begin to spread (e.g., Poland). Nothing demonstrates better the incalculable effects of such opinion — and of the role of single events in politics — than the corrosive effects of the Khrushchev speech denigrating Stalin. Once the charade is exposed, how can the large masses of people — particularly the youth — retain any belief, when the leadership itself has destroyed the moral and psychological basis of believing? Paradoxically, this may lead the rulers to an even more intensive effort to assert the validity of the central features of the ideology. A movement is never more fanatical than "when prophecy fails," or when hypocrisy is exposed, for in an effort to still the panicking doubts of the believers, it redoubles its efforts to assert the fundamentals of the faith.[39] And however cynical a ruling group may become about the "myths" that are necessary for the masses, in such situations they may find themselves psychologically trapped by the verbal formulae

[38] Robert W. Campbell, "Some Recent Changes in Soviet Economic Policy," *World Politics,* IX, No. 1 (October 1956), p. 8.

[39] In this connection, see the interesting study, *When Prophecy Fails,* by Leon Festinger, Henry W. Riecken, and Stanley Schacter, Minneapolis, Minn., 1956.

they employ, and act as if the ideology were real.

F. Foreign and Domestic

In the past, a determining factor in the behavior of foreign Communist parties, and in the policy of the Soviet government, has been the internal power struggles in the Soviet party. But one can argue now that the primary motives of internal Soviet development (e.g., the continued emphasis on heavy industry) are in reflex to the tense world situation. In any assessment, how do the Soviet rulers weigh these considerations?

Both the characterological and the geo-political approach state, in effect, that whatever the internal developments in the Soviet Union, Soviet policy will be combative and expansionist, and that internal and external calculations affect only the timing of aggressive moves. But this leads, with deliberate intent, to the question which is the purpose of this visit: To what extent is the Soviet system a qualitatively new phenomenon, subject to its own laws and indestructible from within; to what extent can the Soviet Union evolve gradually from within into a more stable, normal society?

The approaches broadly labeled characterological, Kremlinological, and totalitarian would argue the former, while the sociological (including M. Aron's variant in the paper presented to the Oxford Conference) and the neo-Marxist, plus some of the historical school, would argue the latter proposition.

Derivative questions immediately arise: Was Stalin an aberration, or does communism, by its very nature (e.g., vanguard party, dictatorship of the proletariat, Bolshevik ideology), take one through a period of the Stalinist type even without a Stalin? Can Communist regimes in Europe, and especially in Asia, "leap directly" to a mellowed phase without going through the type of upheaval which Russia experienced? Are the repressive phases merely a function of forced industrialization? At this stage the author, like Pirandello pursuing the illusion of reality, is tempted, almost, to repeat the ten theories which first set him off in search of reality. But, except for a coda, the play is done:

There is one large variable which these theories, in the nature of things, cannot adequately take into account — the behavior of the free world, which is the most important

"reality factor" limiting the freedom of action of the Communist leaders. Here the role of social science becomes characteristically ambiguous. For the theories we have been discussing are designed to shape the behavior of the free world in its opposition to communism, but in so doing they set up the risk of a self-confirming hypothesis whereby we, because of our judgment of how the Communists may be expected to act, adopt policies forcing them to confirm or negate that judgment. (Just as the Russians force us into similarly prefigured molds.) This is always a danger, but we can minimize it if we remember that no matter how far our social science sophistication has come, it cannot take the place of that practical flexibility which is demanded by two necessary humilities: an awareness of the limitations of our knowledge, and of the openness of history.

8

Marxist Ideology and Soviet Reality*

Barrington Moore, Jr.

(1945)

Any sharp separation between the stages of Soviet development and the content of the ongoing process of social change must necessarily be arbitrary and somewhat artificial. The following three contributions, providing an overview of the system, therefore all review a good deal of history in the process of addressing themselves to one of the more fundamental general questions we may ask about the Soviet experience. Dr. Moore assesses the role played by ideology in Soviet development. This has been a perennial question among students of Soviet society, and one of the most popular among journalists and casual observers of the Soviet scene. Many deny that Marxism or ideology has played any significant role at all. Others read Soviet history as if it were little more than the unfolding of the detailed blue-

* Reprinted from "Some Readjustments in Communist Theory," *Journal of the History of Ideas*, Vol. 6 (1945), pp. 468–82, by permission of the author and the publisher.

print fully laid down by Marx. Dr. Moore shows us some of the subtleties of the complex interplay between ideology and political reality. This is a theme we will return to in Chapter II. For now we limit ourselves to the observation that Dr. Moore's analysis would hardly lead us to believe that the Marxist blueprint, standing alone, is an adequate guide to a description of Soviet social reality.

Introduction

Social scientists and popular writers on political and social affairs have frequently discussed the role of ideas in bringing about a change in human behavior and the institutions of a given society. A review of the literature shows that social scientists have come to two nearly opposite conclusions concerning the influence of ideas, ideals, and ethical systems on behavior and social institutions.

One group has concluded that ideas are relatively insignificant, and that wholesale changes in the structure and functioning of a society do not come about through the influence of ideas, but are solely the product of changes in environmental conditions, the level of technology, the characteristics of neighboring societies, and similar concrete factors.[1] The other school, while not necessarily denying the importance of these factors, asserts that changes in the behavior, institutions, and structure of a society are to a very large extent the result of philosophies and ideas that have gained currency in it.[2]

---

[1] See William Graham Sumner, *Folkways* (Boston, 1906), 87, 99; and for a contrary view by the same author, *Essays of William Graham Sumner*, edited by A. G. Keller and M. R. Davie (New Haven, 1934), 169; A. G. Keller, *Societal Evolution* (Revised edition, New York, 1931), *passim*, and esp. 52; Vilfredo Pareto, *The Mind and Society* (Trans. by Andrew Bongiorno and Arthur Livingston, New York, 1935), Vol. III, 1112, 1300 ff., Vol. IV, 1542; William Fielding Ogburn, *Social Change* (New York, 1931), 364; George Lundberg, *Foundations of Sociology* (New York, 1939), 222.

[2] See Robert M. MacIver, *Society* (New York, 1931), 521, 523, and his *Social Causation* (Boston, 1942), 281, 301; Lester Frank Ward, *The Psychic Factors of Civilization* (Second edition, Boston, 1906), *passim* and esp. Chap. VIII and p. 282; Robert Briffault, *Rational Evolution* (New York, 1930), *passim*, and esp. 271, 279; Karl Mannheim, *Ideologie und Utopie* (Bonn, 1929), *passim*,

The data afforded by the success of one wing of the Marxist movement in carrying out a revolution in Russia and stabilizing its power for a little over a generation provide a convenient case study by which it is possible to check current generalizations and suggest certain modifications in them. While it is not possible by means of a single case study to prove one of two alternative hypotheses, which would require testing against a large number of cases, one may arrive at fruitful corrections of present theories in this fashion. In addition, the case of Marxist theory and practice, affecting the daily life of the inhabitants of more than one-sixth of the surface of the earth, has independent significance for students of contemporary society.

Within the space of this paper only a few of the key concepts of Marxism, as interpreted by Lenin and his followers, can be examined in this fashion, setting out their form before the Revolution, and then noting both behavior and the form of Marxist-Leninist-Stalinist doctrine after the Revolution.

Marxist-Leninist Theory Prior to 1917

Marxist-Leninist theory in the period prior to the Russian Revolution may be summarized under the following points: (1) the transfer of the means of production to the State; (2) the elimination of the old ruling class that owned and directed the means of production; (3) the simplicity and lack of skill-requirements believed characteristic of the managerial and directive functions to be taken over by the proletariat; (4) the abolition of special rewards for performance of managerial and technical services; (5) the necessity and inevitability of a world-wide proletarian revolution, culminating in the Communist Society and the withering away of the State; (6) the danger and delay to this revolution and to the real interests of the working class that would be caused by certain democratic movements and institutions, which could, however, be made into stepping stones for the coming revolution; (7) the necessity for the working class to put its class interests ahead of national interests; (8) in the case of Russia, the granting of a right of seces-

---

Mensch und Gesellschaft im Zeitalter des Umbaus (Leiden, 1935), 12, 167–169, *Diagnosis of Our Time* (London, 1943), 87, 90. The last author falls somewhere between the two groups.

sion to its constituent nations, the elimination of ethnic privileges and disabilities, and the granting of a limited cultural autonomy.[3] Of these points numbers three, four, and five, which contain the essence of Marxian equalitarianism, require some elaboration to be clear to contemporary readers.

Lenin was convinced that the problems of industrial management were so simple that any literate file clerk could carry out managerial functions.[4] Here is what he says in one passage:

> Capitalist culture has *created* large scale production, factories, railways, the postal service, telephones, etc., and *on this basis* the great majority of functions of the old "state power" have become so simplified and can be reduced to such simple operations of registration, filing and checking that they can be easily performed by every literate person, and it will be possible to perform them for "workmen's wages," which circumstances can (and must) strip those functions of every shadow of privilege, of every appearance of "official grandeur."[5]

Lenin was very specific on the point of abolishing the sharp wage differentials of capitalist society. Again he remarked:

> Our immediate aim is to organize the *whole* of national economy on the lines of the postal

system, so that the technicians, managers, bookkeepers, as well as *all* the officials shall receive salaries no higher than "workmen's wages," all under the control and leadership of the armed proletariat.[6]

While Lenin recognized the necessity for industrial discipline, "subordination," "control," and "managers," he was of the opinion that managerial functions could be rotated, performed by each individual in turn so that they would no longer be the functions of a special stratum of the population.[7]

It is not so widely known that neither Marx nor Lenin believed in the feasibility or desirability of complete equality of consumption. Lenin quotes Marx to the effect that in the early stages of the Communist Society the distribution of goods would be according to the amount of work performed by the individual, which would, they claimed, lead to inequalities, as no two human individuals performed the same amount of work.[8]

As is well known, Marx and Lenin believed that the necessary preliminary to the Communist Society was a violent revolution by the proletariat. Almost a century ago, in the Communist Manifesto of 1848, Marx spoke of the revolution as if it were just around the corner, anticipating that it would occur in a country with a developed industrial proletariat such as Germany, or possibly in France.[9] Both writers believed that the proletariat should make use of democratic movements in order to overthrow the "reactionary feudal" regimes, and then in turn "crush, smash to atoms, wipe off the face of the earth" the "bourgeois democratic" movements in order to take power themselves.[10]

At the same time Lenin drew a clear distinction between the immediately attainable Socialist society, and the eventual goal of Communism. Lenin believed that certain economic inequalities, and from his point of view, inequalities, would remain during the "transition

[3] These points are made in the following works: (1) V. I. Lenin, *The State and Revolution* (Moscow, Leningrad, 1935), 55. This book was written in 1917. (2) *Ibid.*, 31. (3) *Ibid.*, 47. (4) *Ibid.*, 52, 53, 90. (5) See the concluding paragraphs of the *Communist Manifesto*, available in *Capital, The Communist Manifesto and Other Writings*, by Karl Marx, with an introduction by Max Eastman (New York, 1932), 355; and in the same volume, *Address of the Central Authority to the Communist League, April, 1850*, 357, 363; *The Civil War in France*, 401, 404–405. Also Lenin, *op. cit.*, 24, 27, 29, 32, 35, 41, 58. (6) *Communist Manifesto*, in Marx, *op. cit.*, 354–355, *Address of the Central Authority*, 359, 362, 366, Lenin, *op. cit.*, 96–97. (7) Lenin, "On the Right of Nations to Self-Determination," written February, 1914, in *Selected Works* (London, 1936), IV, 260, 262, 265, 290, 293. J. Stalin, "Marxism and the National Question," written in 1913, in *Marxism and the National and Colonial Question* (Moscow, 1940), 15, 30, 37, 46, 49. (8) Stalin, *op. cit.*, 50–51.

[4] V. I. Lenin, *The State and Revolution*, 97, 98.

[5] *Ibid.*, p. 47. Italics in original.

[6] *Ibid.*, 53.

[7] *Ibid.*, 52.

[8] *Ibid.*, 90.

[9] See the concluding paragraphs of *The Communist Manifesto*, in Marx, *op. cit.*, 355, and *Address of the Central Authority to the Communist League*, 357, 363.

[10] Marx, *op. cit.*, 354–355, 359; Lenin, *The State and Revolution*, 24, 27, 29, 32, 35, 41, 58, 96–97.

from capitalism to Communism" and in the "first phase of Communist Society." In defining the eventual aim as "From each according to his ability, to each according to his needs," he remarked:

> By what stages, by what practical measures humanity will proceed to this higher aim — we do not and cannot know.[11]

Similarly in the political field, Marxist-Leninist theory prior to 1917 stressed the concept of the eventual "withering away of the State." The withering away of the State, according to Lenin, demands as its economic prerequisite the freeing of productive powers by the expropriation of private property in the means of production, and the abolition of the distinction between mental and physical labor.[12] According to this theory economic conditions will eventually be such that the need for government will disappear. What will remain will be the purely administrative functions of accounting and control, previously exercised by capitalist managerial personnel. At this point the State will disappear.[13] Until it is reached, says Lenin, there is no genuine freedom:

> While the State exists there is no freedom. When freedom exists there will be no State.[14]

Though the preceding points cover the outstanding features of Marxist-Leninist theory as a political and economic program, it is impossible to consider here others that are perhaps equally important and which underwent very significant modifications after the Revolution, such as views on the agricultural and peasant question, and on religion.

Marxist-Leninist-Stalinist Theory and Practice: 1917–1944

With the success of the Revolution of 1917 Lenin and his followers won the opportunity to put their theories into practice. While it is out of the question to review all the changes in both theory and practice that have taken place since 1917, certain shifts stand out.

The distinguishing feature of contemporary Soviet economic institutions is that the means

of production have become the property of the State, very much in the fashion advocated by pre-Revolutionary theory. The industrial means of production, mines, factories, and railways are State property. Agriculture is operated on a collective basis, though members of collective farms retain small plots and some livestock for their individual use.

This situation did not come about overnight, nor is it necessarily one that will endure. After the disastrous economic collapse that accompanied the first few years of Communist rule, due to the ravages of the Civil War as well as to the upheaval attendant upon the Communists' efforts to put their theories into practice, in 1921 Lenin called a retreat in the New Economic Policy, permitting a partial revival of private trade, and other semi-capitalist measures. But it is clear that Lenin himself did not consider this move in any other light than a temporary retreat, and search for a new route toward the goal of Socialism, and eventually Communism.[15] After Lenin's death, and beginning in 1928, a program of industrialization was put into effect, for which Stalin is given much of the credit. This program, the well-known series of Five Year Plans, did much toward converting Russia into a modern industrial power, in which, however, the main means of production belong to the State.

If we may consider the first point of Marxist-Leninist economic theory, the transfer of the means of production to the State, to have been carried out in practice, there remain important modifications in the other points concerning the simplicity of managerial functions and the consequent removal of salary differentials as a technique for attracting managerial ability, as well as a means of eliminating class distinctions. The modifications were made first in practice, and later justified by a readjustment in theory.

Significantly, the first readjustment in salary differentials took place in the Communist Party, with the abolition in 1929 of a maximum on the income or wages to be received by

---

[11] Lenin, *op. cit.*, 96.
[12] *Ibid.*, 92.
[13] *Ibid.*, 98–99.
[14] *Ibid.*, 92.

[15] See his "Notes of a Publicist," written in 1922, and "Five Years of the Russian Revolution and the Prospects of the World Revolution," Report delivered at the Fourth Congress of the Communist International, November 13, 1922, in *Selected Works* (London, 1938), Vol. X.

a Party member.[16] Two years later Stalin asserted that the cause of a heavy turnover of labor in the factories, amounting to 30 to 40 per cent a year, was the "leftist" practice of wage equalization, and ordered the drawing up of wage scales to distinguish between skilled and unskilled labor, and heavy and light work.[17]

Likewise in 1931 Stalin admitted the widespread inefficiency of proletarian management, pointing out that the working class must create its own technically trained group.[18] Although the number of individuals with technical training had greatly increased, the problem of obtaining adequate managerial skill was evidently not solved even by 1939. At the Eighteenth Party Congress Molotov in scathing language referred to the "economic illiteracy" of managers who considered it beneath their dignity to examine a balance sheet, or to learn what their products cost the State.[19] In an effort to increase productive efficiency, the power of the factory director has been steadily increased, and that of the Party organization within the factory and of the trade union representatives steadily reduced, until now the director's powers on paper at least equal or surpass those of an American factory manager.[20]

---

16 The abolition took place in a roundabout way. A decree of the Party Central Committee and Central Control Commission announced that the income of Party members was not to exceed the Party maximum (not defined in the decree) except in the following cases: (1) Communists working immediately on production and construction, workers, craftsmen, specialists, and organizers working in . . . factory management, and (2) literary and artistic workers and inventors. See decree, "On the Regulation of Working Activity and Income of Communists," text in *Izvestia TSK VKP* (B), official organ of the Party Central Committee, No. 13, May 15, 1929, p. 28. In actual practice these cases included nearly all of those in which it was possible for a Party member to earn more than the Party maximum.
17 Stalin, "New Conditions–New Tasks in Economic Construction," speech delivered at a Conference of Business Executives, June 23, 1931 in *Problems of Leninism* (Moscow, 1941), 371–372.
18 *Ibid.*, 378.
19 Reported in *Moscow News*, March 22, 1939, p. 15.
20 Solomon M. Schwarz, "Heads of Russian Factories," *Social Research*, Vol. 9, No. 3, September 1942, pp. 315–333.

The ideological accompaniment to these measures for locating, rewarding, and strengthening managerial talent has been for the Party to stress those passages in Marx and Lenin that stated opposition to contemporary varieties of equalitarian Socialism. Secondly, the Party reminds the masses that Lenin and Marx did not believe that the first stages of the Socialist State would bring about equality of consumption. Finally, the Soviet authorities point out that even the eventual aim of "To each according to his needs" is by no means a strictly equalitarian doctrine. At the same time Lenin's equally frequent and strongly-worded remarks about the simplicity of managerial functions, as merely accounting and control that any literate person could perform for "workmen's wages," are carefully avoided in present-day speeches and writings by Russian leaders.

In 1934 in his report to the Seventeenth Party Congress Stalin sharply reminded his followers that "Marxism means not the equalization of individual requirements and individual life, but the abolition of classes. . . ."[21] Likewise he extended these views to agricultural problems, saying:

> There can be no doubt that the confusion in the minds of certain Party members concerning Marxian Socialism, and their infatuation with the equalitarian tendencies of agricultural communes are as like as two peas to the petty bourgeois views of our Leftist blockheads, who at one time idealized the agricultural commune to such an extent that they even tried to set up communes in factories where skilled and unskilled workers, each working at his trade, had to pool their wages in a common fund, which was then shared out equally. You know what harm these infantile equalitarian exercises of our "Left" blockheads caused our industry.[22]

So far there has been no real development of a symbolism and mythology praising the virtues and accomplishments of the efficient technical specialist and industrial manager as such, corresponding to that surrounding the Edison type of inventor and captain of industry in American culture. It is no exaggeration to say that Soviet policy toward these groups

---

21 Stalin, *Problems of Leninism*, 521.
22 *Ibid.*, 522.

has alternated between flattering them and shooting them. Part of the dilemma was caused by the fact that in the early days of the regime many of these individuals were survivors from the Tsarist regime whose loyalty was questionable. From the beginning the official attitude has been at best almost entirely the negative one that good Bolsheviks are not suspicious of efficient experts and administrators. The symbolism of efficiency and energy associated with the captain of industry in the United States has been reserved for the Communist Party member. To do things "in a Bolshevik manner" is to do them capably and energetically. After the forced draft educational program that endeavored to turn out a sufficient number of qualified managerial and technical personnel, a strong effort was made to improve the orthodox indoctrination of these persons, especially through the discussion and study of the latest official history of the Communist Party, published in 1938, which strongly criticized Trotsky and other opponents of Stalin. It was thought to be impossible for a man to be a good administrator unless he had a proper grounding in Marxist-Leninist theory.[23] In 1939 at the Eighteenth Congress Stalin asserted that the new intelligentsia created by the Bolsheviks should be trusted by them, a remark that is difficult to take at its face value, since previous similar statements had been followed by purges of these individuals, including not only the old but also the new Soviet intelligentsia.[24] However, there are some slight indications that during the war the prestige of the managerial group has been rising: for example *Pravda* in announcing awards for production corresponding to the American "E for Excellence" always gives the name of the factory director.

On the question of social classes the official Party pronouncement is that they have practically disappeared. Socialism has arrived, Stalin and other Party leaders assert. The resolutions of the Eighteenth Congress of 1939 proclaimed:

The Socialist society of the U.S.S.R. consists now of two friendly classes — the workers and the peasants — between which the borders are being wiped out and gradually disappearing, as they are between these classes and the intelligentsia.[25]

Similarly the differences between intellectual and physical work are officially stated to be disappearing.[26] Thus the stress on what one might term the non-equalitarian aspects of Marxism-Leninism has by no means gone so far as to omit the dictum about the disappearance of social classes.

How closely the claim concerning the disappearance of social classes corresponds to the facts is largely a matter of definition. Nearly all writers on the Soviet Union agree that one may distinguish several social groups in the U.S.S.R., varying from the high government, Party, or Army official, down through the petty clerical worker, to the skilled and finally unskilled manual laborer. Though not nearly as immense as in capitalist countries, the differences in income between these social groups have increased since the beginning of the Five Year Plans until some persons now receive over ten times as much cash income, in addition to other perquisites, such as the use of an automobile, a good apartment, etc., as do ordinary workers. More significant from the point of view of distinction between social classes is that these groups differ from each other in dress, codes of etiquette and behavior, and that there are even indications of an incipient class endogamy. As one instance among many, one may cite a recent one-act play, based upon the relationship between a promising young architect and the daughter of an educated man. The architect is proud of the fact that his father was an illiterate muzhik, but uncertain whether or not he can marry the girl. In her company, he is ill at ease, especially when she

[23] S. Kaftanov, "On the Soviet Intelligentsia," *Bolshevik*, No. 2, January, 1939, p. 58. (In Russian.)
[24] Stalin, *Problems of Leninism,* 644, 654, 663; for earlier similar statements by Stalin see 382 ff. and his speech at the 15th Party Congress in 1927 in the *Stenographic Report* (Moscow, Lenin-

grad, 1928), 65, the latter in Russian.
[25] The *CPSU (b)* in *Resolutions and Decisions of Congresses, Conferences, and Plenums of the Central Committee* (Politizdat, 1941), II, 725. (In Russian.)
[26] *Partinoe Stroitel'stvo (Party Construction),* the name since 1929 of the official journal of the Party Central Committee, formerly *Izvestia TSK VKP (b),* "Introduction," No. 18, September, 1940, p. 6.

criticizes his clothes.[27] Yet there are no reliable data with which this writer is familiar to show that these culturally distinct social groups have yet started to become hereditary. There is some indication that the grouping is too new to show signs of such a development. For instance the membership of the Communist Party, which is heavily weighted with high government officials, Army leaders, and industrial managers, was in 1960 composed of 70 per cent persons who had been in the Party for ten years or less, and only 30 per cent who had been in for a longer period. If there is a distinct upper stratum, it is a group whose activity dates since the time when power became centralized in Stalin's hands.[28]

Stalin's program of "socialism in one country" and the development of Russia as an industrial power by no means involved the discard of revolutionary ideology and symbolism.

Standard world revolutionary slogans continued to be part of official statements of the Communist Party of the Soviet Union until 1941. In 1938, among the slogans of the twenty-first anniversary of the October Revolution were "Down with capitalism" and "Long live the proletarian revolution in the entire world."[29] Again in 1939, shortly after the Party Congress, a prominent article in the official publication of the Party's Central Committee boasted of the accomplishments of Socialism in the U.S.S.R., stating that the workers' standard of living was constantly falling in the capitalist countries. The article continued by claiming that, "the international proletariat of the entire world rallies still more closely and strongly around the Communist International," and raised the cry for a "complete victory of the world-wide proletarian Socialist revolution."[30] In 1941 the Party's May Day slogans referred to the Commuist International, the international bonds of the working class, international proletarian solidarity, and so forth, but made no reference to world revolution.[31] This was the last May Day prior to the German attack of June 22, 1941.

Since then the idea of a future revolution has been dropped from official propaganda. Even on the twenty-fifth anniversary of the October Revolution the slogans of the Party's Central Committee made no reference to a hypothetical future revolution.[32] The 1943 issues of *Pravda*, official Party daily, likewise fail to mention a coming revolution. Even the Communist International itself was disbanded in May of 1943.

A detailed analysis of Communist attitudes toward democracy and democratic movements since the October Revolution would lead us too far afield. The problem has been one of Soviet relationships with sovereign states, instead of the pre-Revolutionary one of the relationship between a revolutionary group and its competitors for the allegiance of the so-called working class. The official attitude toward the United States, Great Britain, and France, and by extension toward democracy, has varied in accord with the exigencies of Soviet foreign policy, a relationship that may be observed in the ideology and foreign policy of other states. While the Soviet Union now identifies itself with what are usually termed democratic powers, the United States and Great Britain, in the war of "freedom-loving peoples" against "Hitlerite aggression,"[33] as late as 1940 an official man-

---

[27] P. Yal'tsev, "Success," in *Short Plays* (Moscow, Leningrad, 1937). (In Russian.) Another interesting fictional study is the short story by Pavel Nilin, "Matvei Kuz'mich," in *Golden Hands* (Moscow, 1939), based on the theme of the relation between a self-made man and his father. (Also in Russian.)

[28] For statistics on the Communist Party see G. Malenkov, "Report of the Credentials Commission," XVIII Congress, *Moscow News*, March 27, 1939, p. 2. For some of the more important materials and interpretations on the growth of social classes, in addition to Schwartz, *op. cit.*, see Sidney and Beatrice Webb, *Soviet Communism, A New Civilization?* (New York, 1936), II, 795–796, for orthodox pro-Soviet interpretation; L. Yvon, *URSS telle qu'elle est* (Paris, 1938), with much first-hand cultural data, though anti-Soviet, *passim;* Leon Trotsky, *The Revolution Betrayed* (trans. by Max Eastman, New York, 1937), esp. 102, 125, 133–134, 155–156; L. E. Hubbard, *Soviet Labour and Industry* (London, 1942), 185 ff., 222, good on purely economic factors.

[29] *Partiinoe Stroitel'stvo*, No. 21, November 1, 1938, p. 3.

[30] "Raise the banner of international proletarian solidarity," *Partiinoe Stroitel'stvo*, No. 9, May, 1939, p. 14.

[31] *Bolshevik*, No. 7–8, April, 1941, p. 1.

[32] *Bolshevik*, No. 19–20, October, 1942, pp. 5 ff.

[33] Stalin, "Order of the Day," May 1, 1942, in a collection of his wartime speeches, *The War of National Liberation* (New York, 1942), 52.

ual on the rights and obligations of the Soviet citizen stated: "The second imperialist war has shown the complete bankruptcy of bourgeois democracy."[34]

Communist doctrine and practice concerning democracy as an internal policy for the Soviet Union after the Revolution represents the interplay of two aspects of Marxist-Leninist-Stalinist theory with the actual facts of political and economic tensions in the U.S.S.R. We have already noted that one aspect of Marxist-Leninist theory prior to the Revolution was that democracy would be more free and representative in the Socialist than in the bourgeois states. A second aspect of this doctrine is its negative evaluation of free speech, the free interplay of ideas, civil liberties, and the like. Marx, Lenin, and Stalin follow a single tradition of vitriolic and savage attacks on theoretical and political opponents, even though Lenin occasionally admitted past errors. Stalin was one of the early users, if not the coiner, of the term, "rotten liberalism," which he applied to an editor's action in 1931 in permitting a discussion of certain of Lenin's and Trotsky's policies before the 1917 Revolution.[35]

Yet Stalin could claim that the new Constitution of 1936 represented the "victory in the U.S.S.R. of full and thoroughly consistent democracy."[36] The claim is based partly on a definition and interpretation of democracy that is quite different from that current in the United States and Great Britain, if indeed one could find a universally acceptable definition in these two countries. The Soviet definition likewise stresses personal freedom, but does so in terms of guarantees of employment, economic security, and the elimination of the "exploitation of man by man."[37] Stalin explains the apparent unanimity of political opinion in

the U.S.S.R. and the absence of competing political parties, the usual feature of other democratic states, as due to the fact that parties in such countries represent hostile social classes, which have been eliminated in the US.S.R.[38]

It is obvious from the purges, which struck most heavily just after the promulgation of the new constitution, that this last explanation does not accord completely with the facts, and that hostility, even if not based on tensions between social classes, still existed. On other aspects of the general practice of Soviet democracy one finds that while the masses are not free to participate in the formulation of national policy, they are encouraged to criticize its actual execution. Similarly, although nation-wide Soviet elections are so nearly unanimous as to arouse justified suspicions that they do not represent the actual state of opinion, there is evidence that on local matters, even within the tightly disciplined Communist Party, there is a fairly frequent overturn of minor officials through open elections.[39]

Communist political doctrines and practices concerning nationalism have also changed somewhat since the Revolution, although the change is not as marked as many popular articles and newspaper commentators assert. In general, Communist theory and practice from 1917 to 1941 condemned ethnic prejudice, recognized and encouraged regional autonomy, at the same time that it kept this autonomy sharply within the limits of the patterns set by the general Soviet economic structure and the political interests of Great Russia, or the U.S.S.R., as a whole. In 1921 Stalin, reversing earlier precepts, stated that the demand of the border regions to secede from Russia must be rejected.[40] On the same occasion he advocated the development of local national schools, national theaters, national ed-

[34] Y. Oumansky, *Basic Rights and Obligations of Citizens of the U.S.S.R.* (Moscow, 1940), 5. (In Russian.)

[35] Stalin, "Some Questions Concerning the History of Bolshevism, Letter to the Editors of *Proletarskaya Revolyutsia*," *Problems of Leninism*, 388–400.

[36] Stalin, "On the Draft Constitution of the U.S.S.R.," Report delivered at the Extraordinary Eighth Congress of Soviets of the U.S.S.R., November 26, 1936, *op. cit.*, 589.

[37] *Ibid.*, 572–573; Oumansky, *op. cit.*, 1 and *passim*.

[38] Stalin, *op. cit.*, 579.

[39] W. H. Chamberlin, *The Russian Enigma* (New York, 1943), 151–153; N. de Basily, *La Russie sous les Soviets* (Paris, 1938), 158; for an instance of local elections see, "Some Results of the Elections of Party Organs — From Materials of the Division of Leading Party Organs of the Central Committee of the CPSU (b)," *Bolshevik*, No. 10, May 15, 1937, p. 6.

[40] Stalin, "The Policy of the Soviet Government on the National Question in Russia," in *Marxism and the National and Colonial Question*, 69.

ucational institutions, and the raising of the cultural level of the masses of the border regions, much of which was later carried out in practice.[41] Six years later he warned that this regional cultural autonomy must not be allowed to assume the character of a fight against "Moscow" or "against Russian culture and its supreme achievement — Leninism."[42] During the purges that preceded the Party Congress of 1939 many of the leaders of Union Republics and smaller political units inhabited by national minorities were reported to have been shot.

Since the war there has been a marked increase in the use of purely Russian patriotic symbolism, coinciding with the almost complete disappearance of Marxian revolutionary appeals. The adoption of a new anthem for the U.S.S.R. is but one of the more striking features of this development.[43] Along with Lenin, older Russian heroes and figures, Pushkin, Tolstoy, Suvorov, Dimitry Donskoi, are used by Stalin in his patriotic appeals to the nation.[44]

At the same time that there has been an increase in Russian nationalist symbolism, and a revival of Pan-Slavism, shown by the formation of the All-Slav Committee in Moscow, there has been a careful avoidance of any ideological appeals that smacked of the Tsarist policy of forced Russification of Slavic and non-Slavic peoples. Stalin has condemned German racial theories, and claimed that the "strength of the Red Army lies in the fact that . . . it has been brought up in the spirit of the equality of all races and peoples."[45] The fight of the Red

Army has been presented as an effort to prevent the Germans from enslaving "Russians, Ukrainians, Byelorussians, Lithuanians, Letts, Estonians, Uzbeks, Tatars, Moldavians, Georgians, Armenians, Azerbaidjanians, and the other free peoples of the Soviet Union."[46] Thus the emphasis of the new nationalism, the new Pan-Slavism, is on the common struggle against Nazi Germany, and is free of invidious and ethnocentric references to other nationalities.

A comparison between Marxist-Leninist theory prior to the Revolution with the same theory today shows the following items to have been dropped or modified: (1) the belief in a coming world-wide proletarian revolution; (2) the belief in the simplicity of managerial functions and the lack of any necessity of increased economic rewards to attract managerial skill; (3) the belief in democracy as a stepping-stone to Socialism, which has been replaced by a policy towards other governments and social movements more clearly based on the territorial interests of the U.S.S.R. During the same period three other important items have remained without substantial modification: (1) the belief in the necessity for the transfer of the means of production to the society as a whole; (2) the belief in the end of a system of social classes; (3) the belief in the desirability of cultural autonomy for national minorities, provided the autonomy does not interfere with major Great Russian economic or political aims.

It is also clear that the retention, modification, or abandonment of several items of belief can be traced to specific concrete circumstances and behavior, such as the disappearance of world revolutionary ideology due to the German attack and the U.S.S.R.'s need for outside assistance, or the abandonment of certain equalitarian economic ideas due to the necessity for developing industrial discipline and efficiency. Furthermore it is significant that one idea, the transfer of the means of production to the society as a whole, was carried out in actual practice despite the necessity for a temporary retreat, during the NEP, and despite a high cost in human suffering.

Meanwhile we must remember that changes in both Communist doctrine and practice have by no means come to an end, and that it is

---

[41] *Ibid.*, 72; Sidney and Beatrice Webb, *op. cit.*, I, 139–159.

[42] Stalin, "Extract from a Letter to Comrade Kaganovich and Other Members of the Central Committee of the Communist Party of the Ukraine," *op. cit.*, 202.

[43] The former "Internationale" has been adopted as the official Communist Party song.

[44] An interesting sidelight is provided by the way in which the war has rehabilitated the reputation of a man such as Plekhanov, an early Russian Marxist, who strongly opposed Lenin's defeatist policy in the last Russo-German conflict. Anathematized until 1941, he was mentioned by Stalin along with Lenin, Gorky, Tschaikowsky, as one of the heroes of the "great Russian nation." See *The War of National Liberation*, 29.

[45] Stalin, "Order of the Day," on the occasion of the twenty-fourth anniversary of the founding of the Red Army, February 23, 1942, *op. cit.*, 44.

[46] Stalin, Speech of July 3, 1941, *op. cit.*, 13. Similar themes, though of course limited to Slavs, may be found in *Slavyane*, Russian language publication of the All-Slav Committee.

impossible to look upon the contemporary situation as a final product that will undergo no further development.

Some Tentative Theoretical Conclusions

From the point of view of general theory concerning the relationship between ideas and institutional behavior, the most obvious point evident from a brief survey of Marxist-Leninist-Stalinist theory is that the theory was put into practice insofar as the transfer of the means of production to the society as a whole is concerned. This fact would make it appear at first glance that the role of ideas is or can be determinative in producing social change.

However, several qualifications must be noted. In the first place, Marxist-Leninist theory almost certainly would not have arisen without the prior conditions of the industrial revolution. In the second place, a more general view of the economic and cultural history of the Western world since the middle of the last century would show that there has been a universal trend toward giving the national government powers of control over economic processes. The trend has gone further in some countries, namely the totalitarian ones, than in the democratic ones, but is evident in all of them. Thus Marxist-Leninist theory was in line with the types of adjustment that were being tried in this culture area during the past few generations.

This observation suggests the modification of any theory of the relationship between ideas and institutional behavior in order to take into account the nature of the specific idea considered. Social scientists have perhaps been in error in considering the problem from too general a point of view. The question is not whether ideas influence behavior, so much as whether a specific idea can influence behavior. Other well-documented cases, such as the vicissitudes of various Utopian societies or even the effort of the Catholic Church to enforce sacerdotal celibacy, show that certain ideas could not be put into practice, except in a limited fashion, and that adjustments and modifications, along the lines of legal fictions are necessary.[47]

Another readily observable point in the history of Marxist-Leninist theory and practice

[47] Henry C. Lea, *History of Sacerdotal Celibacy in the Christian Church* (London, 1932), Chap. XXXII.

is that readjustments in behavior and practice on several occasions precede readjustments in theory and doctrine. Thus it is quite clear that concrete behavior influences philosophical theory, and that circumstances can produce changes in ideas.

With these modifications in mind, the relationship between ideas and behavior can perhaps be stated along the following lines. As it is impossible to prove any relationship from an analysis of a single case, which is valuable only as a check on current theories and as a means of suggesting modifications in them, the relationship can be put only in the terms of a hypothesis, subject unquestionably to considerable further checking and modification.

The relationship between ideas and institutional structures and behavior is probably a reciprocal one. Ideas are social inventions, probably subject to the same limitations pointed out by Ogburn and others as applying chiefly to technical inventions, namely the cultural base must be present before a new invention can be made. In the case of any specific mechanical invention, such as the steam engine, a cultural base consisting of a whole series of prior inventions, such as the control of fire, the wheel, control of metals, etc., is required. This explains why inventions occur nearly simultaneously in different parts of the same culture area. The same principle evidently applies to ideas. Not only is a whole series of technological inventions necessary before an idea such as Marxism is possible, but also a series of ideas has to win currency in advance of an intellectual invention. It is well known that Marx did not make up his theories out of whole cloth, but that he modified the ideas of previous writers and added new points of his own.

A feature of this reciprocal relation between ideas and institutional structures or behavior is the observable fact of a considerable mortality among ideas. This mortality is paralleled in the field of technological inventions, for which a given society may have no use at the time they are invented, as in the case of Leonardo da Vinci, or which may be superseded by inventions that are better adapted to the purposes set by the society. The bow and arrow, the electric automobile and the sailing vessel, are familiar examples of this process in the technological field. Sometimes the techniques disappear entirely, as in the case of certain "lost arts." In the case of ideas we have seen how certain features of Marxism-Leninism, such as equality of wages, have tended to disappear from current doctrine because they were not adapted to a specific situation.

At the same time it is evident that after an idea has been invented, it influences the behavior of those who adopt it, since new behavior and new adjustments to concrete circumstances are made by these individuals within the framework of the idea. Thus Stalin and his followers carried out the industrialization of Russia on a collectivist basis instead of on a capitalist one, which had already begun to make some headway before the Revolution. A degree of flexibility is given in carrying out these adjustments by the power of behavior to modify ideology, and through devices such as legal fictions. But it seems likely that this flexibility has definite limits. The limitations are not necessarily due to any psychological factors, but may be due to the fact that each change in doctrine and each readjustment in practice leaves a residue of unsatisfied and unreconciled individuals.[48]

If this interpretation of the connection between ideas and institutional behavior is valid, or indeed if there is any regularly observable connection between symbol output and behavior, the behaviorists who wish to disregard ideas altogether are depriving themselves of a potentially useful tool of prediction and analysis.

To be successful, predictions of the future behavior of a given social group would probably have to take into account the following factors: a knowledge of the group's ideology, which would have to be combined with information concerning the group's social composition and consequent interests or combination of interests; knowledge of its past behavior; and, most difficult of all, knowledge of the general cultural and social situation in which the group will have to function. In the present state of the social sciences it is extremely difficult to make more than crude estimates of these factors. In particular, the weighting and the significance of each of the different factors is difficult to ascertain in the absence of strict

experimental controls. One cannot put the Roman Empire in a test tube, add a little Christianity, and watch whether it declines and falls. Furthermore, history is an inadequate laboratory notebook. But there appears to be at least a considerable probability that ideas determine reactions to events, and are in turn modified by them. That such hypotheses are of more than academic interest, and that on their verification or disproof depends intelligent human adjustment to the world around us, needs no repetition here.

9

Social Change and Cultural Stagnation

Isaiah Berlin*

(1957)

An alternative lens for putting Soviet society in focus is offered by Isaiah Berlin. Again it is an idea which demands our attention, an idea rooted in Russian culture — the all-embracing view of communal life which leaves little room for notions such as the inviolability of persons and provides ideal soil for the eventual rise of a totalitarian society. However extensive the Soviet creation of new political and economic forms, Professor Berlin argues, the system has produced "a long blank page in the history of Russian culture." In the course of his subtle, complex, and far-ranging characterization, Professor Berlin also stresses the distinctive qualities of Soviet society as a unique political invention of Stalin.

I

One of the most arresting characteristics of modern Russian culture is its acute self-consciousness. There has surely never been a society more deeply and exclusively preoccupied with itself, its own nature and destiny. From the eighteen-thirties until our own day the

---

[48] As some acute observers have pointed out, this fact played a role in the purges that followed the adoption of the Constitution.

* Reprinted, with a few revisions by Mr. Berlin, from "The Silence in Russian Culture," *Foreign Affairs*, Vol. 36 (1957), pp. 1–24, by permission of the author and the publisher. (Copyright, 1957, by the Council on Foreign Relations.)

subject of almost all critical and imaginative writing in Russia is Russia. The great novelists, and a good many minor novelists too, as well as the vast majority of the characters in Russian novels, are continuously concerned not merely with their purposes as human beings or members of families or classes or professions, but with their condition or mission or future as Russians, members of a unique society with unique problems. This national self-absorption is to be found among novelists and playwrights of otherwise very different outlooks. An obsessed religious teacher like Dostoevsky, a didactic moralist like Tolstoy, an artist regarded in the West as being dedicated to timeless and universal psychological and aesthetic patterns like Turgenev, a "pure" unpolitical writer, careful not to preach, like Chekhov, are all, and throughout their lives, crucially concerned with the "Russian problem." Russian publicists, historians, political theorists, writers on social topics, literary critics, philosophers, theologians, poets, first and last, all without exception and at enormous length, discuss such issues as what it is to be a Russian; the virtues, vices, and destiny of the Russian individual and society; but above all the historical role of Russia among the nations; or, in particular, whether its social structure — say, the relation of intellectuals to the masses, or of industry to agriculture — is *sui generis*, or whether, on the contrary, it is similar to that of other countries, or perhaps, an anomalous, or stunted, or an abortive example of some superior Western model.

From the eighties onwards a vast, now unreadably tedious, mass of books, articles, pamphlets began to flood upon the Russian intelligentsia, mostly concerned to prove either that Russia is destined to obey unique laws of its own — so that the experience of other countries has little or nothing to teach it — or, on the contrary, that its failures are entirely due to an unhappy dissimilarity to the life of other nations, a blindness to this or that universal law which governs all societies, and which Russians ignore at their peril. The writers of Western countries, as often as not, produce their works of art or learning or even day-to-day comment (even in America where there exists similar self-consciousness, though not on so vast a scale) without necessarily tormenting themselves with the question whether their

subject matter has been treated in its right historical or moral or metaphysical context. In Russia, at any rate since the second half of the nineteenth century, the reverse obtained. There no serious writer could think of taking a step wtihout concerning himself with the question whether his work was appropriately related to the great ultimate problems, the purposes of men on earth. The duty of all those who claimed to have the insight to understand, and the moral courage to face, their personal or social or national condition was always the same: in the first place to relate the relevant problems to the path which the given society (i.e., Russian, and only after that, human) was inexorably pursuing (if one was a determinist), or should be pursuing (if one thought one had freedom of choice), at the particular historical (or moral or metaphysical) stage of its development.

No doubt the Romantic doctrines, particularly in Germany, with their emphasis on the unique historical missions of different groups of men — Germans, or industrialists, or poets — which dominated European literature and journalism in the eighteen-thirties and forties, are partly responsible for this pervasive Russian attitude. But it went further in Russia than elsewhere. This was partly due to the fact that the effective advance of Russia to the center of the European scene (after the Napoleonic wars) coincided with the impact of the Romantic Movement; it derived partly from a sense of their own cultural inferiority, which made many educated Russians painfully anxious to find a worthy part of their own to play — worthy, above all, of their growing material power in a world that was apt to look down upon them, and cause them to look down upon themselves, as a dark mass of benighted barbarians ruled by brutal despots and good only for crushing other freer, more civilized peoples. Again there may be, as some writers maintain, a strong craving for teleological and indeed eschatological systems in all societies influenced by Byzantium or by the Orthodox Church — a craving that the Russian priesthood, lacking as it conspicuously did the intellectual resources and tradition of the Western churches, could not satisfy, at any rate in the case of the better educated and critically inclined young men.

Whatever the truth about its origins, the

state of mind of virtually all Russian intellectuals in the nineteenth and early twentieth centuries (there were some exceptions) was dominated by the belief that all problems are interconnected, and that there is some single system in terms of which they are all in principle soluble; moreover, that the discovery of this system is the beginning and end of morality, social life, education; and that to abandon the search for it in order to concentrate upon isolated or personal ends, say, the pursuit of knowledge, or artistic creation, or happiness, or individual freedom for their own sakes, is wilful, subjective, irrational, egoistic, an immoral evasion of human responsibility. This attitude is characteristic not merely of the left-wing Russian intelligentsia, but of the outlook of civilized Russians of all shades of political opinion, spread widely both in religious and in secular, in literary and in scientific circles. Almost any philosophical system that affected to give a comprehensive answer to the great questions found a marvellously, indeed excessively, enthusiastic welcome among these eager, overresponsive, idealistic, impeccably consistent, sometimes only too rigorously logical thinkers.

And the systems were not slow in arriving. First came German historicism, particularly in its Hegelian form, which conceived of history as the essential, indeed the only genuine science. True, Hegel looked on the Slavs with contempt as "unhistorical," and declared that (like the "extinct" Chinese civilization) they had no part to play in the march of the human spirit. This part of Hegel was quietly ignored, and adequate room made in the universal schema for the Slavs in general, and (on the authority of Hegel's formidable rival, Schelling) for the Russians in particular. After the infatuation with Schiller, Fichte, Hegel, and other German Idealists came a similar faith in French social prophets — Saint-Simon, Fourier, and their many disciples and interpreters, who offered cut-and-dried "scientific" plans of reform or revolution for which some among their Russian disciples, with their will to believe in literal inspiration, were ready to lay down their lives. This was followed by many another *Lebensphilosophie* — inspired by Rousseau, by Comtian Positivism, Darwinism, neo-mediaevalism, Anarchism, which in Russia went far beyond their Western prototypes.

Unlike the West, where such systems often languished and declined amid cynical indifference, in the Russian Empire they became fighting faiths, thriving on the opposition to them of contrary ideologies — mystical monarchism, Slavophil nostalgia, clericalism, and the like; and under absolutism, where ideas and daydreams are liable to become substitutes for action, ballooned out into fantastic shapes, dominating the lives of their devotees to a degree scarcely known elsewhere. To turn history or logic or one of the natural sciences — biology or sociology — into a theodicy; to seek, and affect to find, within them solutions to agonizing moral or religious doubts and perplexities; to transform them into secular theologies — all that is nothing new in human history. But the Russians indulged in this process on a heroic and desperate scale, and in the course of it brought forth what today is called the attitude of total commitment, at least of its modern form.

Over a century ago Russian critics denounced European civilization for its lack of understanding. It seemed to them characteristic of the morally desiccated, limited thinkers of the West to maintain that human activities were not all necessarily interconnected with each other — that what a man did as a writer was one thing and what he did as a citizen was another; that a man might be a good chemist and yet maltreat his family or cheat at cards; that a man might compose profound music and yet hold stupid or immoral political views that were no business of the critics or of the public. This notion of life, according to Russians of almost all shades of opinion, was artificial and shallow and flew to pieces before the deeper insight of the all-embracing view, according to which the life of individuals and the life of their institutions was one and indivisible. Every faculty and element in the individual were in a state of constant interplay; a man could not be one thing as a painter and another as a citizen, honest as a mathematician and false as a husband; it was impossible to draw frontiers between any aspects of human activity, above all between public and private life. Any attempt to insulate this or that area from the invasion of outside forces was held to be founded upon the radical fallacy of thinking that the true function and purpose of a human being does not penetrate every one of his acts and relationships — or worse still, that men had, as men, no specific function or purpose at all. It followed that whatever most fully embodies this ultimate total human purpose — the State, according to the Hegelians; an elite of scientists, artists, and managers, according to the followers of Saint-Simon or Comte; the Church, according to those who leaned towards ecclesiastical authority; an elected body of persons embodying the popular or national will, according to democrats or nationalists; the class designated by "history" to free itself and all mankind, according to Socialists and Communists — this central body had a right to invade everything. The very notion of the inviolability of persons, or of areas of life, as an ultimate principle was nothing but an effort to limit, to narrow, to conceal, to shut out the light, to preserve privilege, to divide and insulate human beings from one another, to build walls between a man and his neighbor, or, worse still, a man and the truth (for the truth is always social) — and therefore the central source of error, weakness, and vice.

The doctrine that there is one truth and one only, which the whole of one's life should be made to serve, one method, and one only, of arriving at it — this ancient and familiar doctrine can take many shapes. But even in its most idealistic and unworldly forms, it is, in essence, totalitarian. Even those critical versions of it which permit doubts about the nature of the central truth, or about the best method of its discovery, or the title of its preachers, allow none about the right and the duty, once it is established, to make everyone and everything obey it; they allow no intrinsic virtue to variety of opinion or conduct as such; indeed, the opposite. For there can be no more than one truth, one right way of life. Only vice and error are many. Consequently, when Marxism finally came to Russia in the seventies and eighties it found an almost ideal soil for its seeds.

II

Marxism contained all the elements which the young *révoltés* in Russia were looking for. It claimed to be able to demonstrate the proper goals of human existence in terms of a pattern of history of which there was "scientific" proof. The moral and political values which it preached could, so it claimed, be determined "objectively," that is to say, not in terms of the subjective and relative and unpredictable attitudes of different individuals or classes or cultures, but in terms of principles which, being "founded" on the "objective behavior of things," were absolute and alone led to the salvation and liberation of all men to the degree to which they were rational. It preached the indissoluble oneness of men and institutions. It claimed, just as the eighteenth century French philosophers had in effect claimed, that all real, that is to say soluble, problems were fundamentally technological; that the ends of man — what human beings could be, and, if they knew their true interests, would necessarily want to be — were given by the new scientific picture of the universe. The only problem was how to realize these ends. This was not a moral or political problem but a technical task: that of finding and using the right means for the "demonstrably" valid, universal goal; a problem of engineering.

Stalin's famous and most revealing phrase about intellectuals as "engineers of human souls" was faithfully derived from Marxist premises. The duty of intellectuals was to elucidate the correct social goals on the basis of a "scientific" analysis of society and history; and then, by means of education, or "conditioning," so to attune the minds of their fellow citizens that they grasped demonstrated truths and responded accordingly, like the harmonious constituents of a properly regulated and efficiently functioning mechanism. The simile which Lenin used in one of his most famous statements of political doctrine — *State and Revolution* — according to which the new free society, liberated from the coercion of one class by another, would resemble a factory or workshop in which the workers did their jobs almost out of mechanical habit, was a piece of imagery drawn from this technocratic view of human life. The watchwords were efficiency, tidiness, security, freedom for the good to do what they wanted; this last being necessarily one and the same goal for all those who were rational and knew the truth, not freedom to do anything whatever, but only what is right — the only thing which any rational being can wish to do — that which alone will make for true, everlasting universal happiness. This is an old Jacobin doctrine, and indeed much older —

in its essentials as old as Plato. But no one, perhaps, had believed it quite so naively or fanatically in any previous age.

During the decade that followed the October Revolution these principles — the moral and metaphysical foundations of totalitarianism — were genuinely accepted, at any rate by some among the Communist leaders. Whatever the personal shortcomings of Trotsky or Zinoviev or Bukharin or Molotov or the heads of the secret police, and perhaps even of Stalin at this stage, there is no reason for doubting the sincerity or depth of their convictions or principles. A great many disagreements arose, of course, but they were concerned not with ends but with means; when they went sufficiently far they were stigmatized as deviations. Thus Trotsky thought that there was a danger of a too-well-entrenched bureaucracy which would function as a brake — like all vested interests — upon the progress of the Revolution which needed agents who were more imaginative, more bloody, bold and resolute — men not tempted to stop halfway on the path of the world revolution. The so-called Workers' Opposition objected to the concentration of authority in the hands of the Central Committee of the Communist Party, and wanted more equality, and more democratic control exercised by workers' organizations. The Right-Wing Deviationists thought that over-rapid collectivization of agriculture would produce a degree of economic dislocation, pauperization, and ruin likely to be more damaging to the Soviet economy than the adoption of a slower pace in the harsh process of liquidating peasant property and its defenders together with other so-called survivals of the capitalist regime; and advocated a less urgent tempo and milder measures. There were disagreements as to how far the army might be used in the regimentation of industry. There were memorable disagreements about foreign policy and the policy toward Communists abroad.

The acutest of all disagreements occurred, perhaps, on the cultural front: there were those who thought that any "slap in the face" (as it used to be called) to the bourgeois culture of the West, in whatever form — aggressive futurism and modernism in the arts, for example, or any violent revolt against tradition — was *eo ipso* an expression of Bolshevism, in so far as it was a blow at the Western establishment,

lowered its morale, and undermined its moral and aesthetic foundations. A good deal of experiment, sometimes bold and interesting, at other times merely eccentric and worthless, occurred at this time in the Soviet Union in the guise of cultural warfare against the encircling capitalist world. This was the "Cultural Bolshevism," particularly popular in Germany, against which Communist policy later so sternly set its face. For one thing the audacities of the cultural Bolsheviks were, as might be expected, the personal acts of individual artists and therefore found little favor in the eyes of those members of the Party for whom Communism meant belief in the task of creating a specifically proletarian culture by means of collective action, and for whom the aberrations of the *avant garde* poets, painters, and producers were merely so much individualist eccentricity — an *outré* and decadent perversion of the very bourgeois civilization which the Revolution was out to destroy. Lenin, be it noted, disliked all forms of modernism intensely: his attitude to radical artistic experiment was bourgeois in the extreme. But he made no attempt to enforce his aesthetic views, and, under the benevolent patronage of the Commissar of Education, Lunacharsky, a poor critic and playwright but a sincere opponent of open barbarism, the controversies continued unabated. There were splits within factions: the champions of "proletarian" culture could not agree on whether it was to be produced by individual men of gifts who distilled within themselves the aspirations of the proletarian masses, actual and potential, acting, as it were, as their mouthpieces or rather megaphones; or whether, as the extremer ideologists proclaimed, individuals as such had no part at all to play in the new order, for the art of the new collectivist society must itself be collective. These latter in effect believed that works of art must be written collectively by groups, and criticism — reviews, directives — by squads of critics, bearing collective responsibility for their work, each member being an anonymous component of a social whole. Again, some maintained that the business of proletarian art was to present the new reality in an intenser form, to heighten it if necessary by the inventions of the socialism-impregnated imagination; others thought that the business of artists was strictly utilitarian: to help with the making of Communist society by documentary reportage of the new life — the building of factories, collective farms, power stations, the destruction of the old installations, the production of the essentials of the socialist economy — tractors, combines, uniform food, identical clothing, mass-produced houses, books, above all good, happy, uncomplicated, standard human beings.

One could go on to multiply examples; the point I wish to make is that these "programmatic" controversies were, in the first place, genuine; that is to say, the contending parties, on the whole, believed what they were saying, and the disagreements between them could justly be described as real differences in the interpretation of an accepted Marxist doctrine. Moreover they were, to some degree, carried on in public; and, most important of all, they were differences not about ends but about means. The ends had become universally accepted since the opponents and doubters had been eliminated or silenced. The intransigence of the Comintern in dealing with foreign Communist and still more Socialist parties, and merciless heresy hunts, probably derived, for the most part, from the honest belief that these parties might compromise on the central truth — on the dogma of what constituted the desired society — or else that they had chosen, or might choose, paths that could lead away, however imperceptibly at first, from these sacred and undisputed goals.

It was its own conception of itself that divided Bolshevism so sharply from its parent, Western Marxism — a conception which made it not merely a set of political or social or economic beliefs or policies, but a way of life, all-penetrating and compulsory, controlled absolutely by the Party or the Central Committee of the Party in a way for which little authority can be found even in the most extreme pronouncements of Marx and Engels. This was the "Tsarism in reverse," which Herzen in the early fifties had gloomily and accurately predicted that Communism in Russia would become, and which it owes primarily to the personality of Lenin himself. No doubt the conditions of Russian life, which molded both him and it, in part created the need for religious certainty and messianic doctrine which Marxism provided. But the authoritarian element is among Lenin's specific contributions — the conception of the Party as a sect ruled ruth-

lessly by its elders and demanding from its members the total sacrifice upon its altar of all that they most cherished (material goods, moral principles, personal relationships), the more defiant and horrifying to tender-minded morality the better. It was this streak of stony fanaticism enlivened by a sardonic humor and vindictive trampling upon the liberal past that unnerved some of Lenin's socialist colleagues and attracted such disciples as Stalin and Zinoviev.

It was part and parcel of this vision of the millennium, disguised as a rational doctrine, to ignore the fact that as a scientific theory, claiming to be able to explain and predict social and economic change, Marxism had, by the beginning of the twentieth century, been refuted by events in ways which have been described too often and too fully to be worth recapitulation. In the West, efforts to save the theory from intellectual bankruptcy, some orthodox, some heretical, were from time to time made by conscientious socialists and others. In Russia this was, by and large, not required. In Russia, especially after the October Revolution, Marxism had become a metaphysics, professedly resting on an analysis of history but stubbornly ignoring all awkward facts, designed by force or persuasion to secure conformity to a set of dogmatic propositions with its own esoteric, half-intelligible terminology, its own "dialectical" techniques of argument, its own clear and rigid *a priori* notions of what men and society must, at whatever cost, be made to be.

One of the most striking differences between the Soviet Union and the West was (and is) that in Russia those who were defeated in these internal Soviet controversies were liable from the very beginning of the regime — even before the official beginning of the terror — to be at best silenced, at worst punished or executed. Yet even these Draconian measures did not make the controversies less real. Indeed they had the opposite effect — the fact that the fruit of victory was power, and of defeat elimination, added an element of violent excitement to the duels in which the antagonists had so much to lose or win. I do not mean to assert that all or even the majority of those engaged in these febrile and perilous controversies were persons of integrity or moved by disinterested motives; a great deal of ruthless or desperate fighting for position or survival, with little regard for the professed principles of Marxism, was evident enough in Russia in the twenties. But at least some sort of wage was paid by vice to virtue; the protagonists in these struggles still felt traditionally obliged to advance some kind of theoretical justification for their conduct, and since some of them seemed to believe deeply in what they said, the issues were at times matters of genuine principle. This was most obviously the case on the "cultural front," which has at all times yielded the most reliable symptoms of what was going on in other spheres of Soviet life. Moreover, among the controversialists, men of remarkable gifts and temperament were to be found, and their attitudes, whether honest or opportunist, were those of exceptional human beings. Lunacharsky, Vorovsky, Averbakh were not, by any possible standard, critics of the first water, but they possessed a genuine revolutionary eloquence; Bukharin, Trotsky, Radek were as thinkers negligible, but one of them was a man of genius, and the others were at the very least gifted agitators. And among the creative writers and artists there still were some figures of the first rank who had not emigrated, or had returned. This alone made the twenties memorable, not only in Russian history but in Russian culture.

To all this Stalin put an abrupt end, and a new phase began.

III

The ideological policy of Stalin's regime is a fascinating topic, deserving separate study to itself, which no one has yet attempted seriously, and toward which I should like only to make one or two suggestions.

Once it had become clear to Stalin and his henchmen that an early world revolution was not to be expected, and that the doubtless inevitable fulfillment of Marxist prophecies in the capitalist world might take place at a time and in ways very different from those which the earlier, more optimistic founding fathers had prophesied, he concentrated upon three interconnected purposes. Firstly, the perpetuation of the Bolshevik regime, and in particular of those of its leaders who were prepared to accept his own authority. Secondly, the maintenance and increase of Soviet power, political, economic, and military, in a hostile world, by every possible means short of those entailing a radical change in the Soviet system itself. And thirdly, the elimination of all factors, whether at home or abroad, likely to jeopardize either of these two central purposes, whether or not such elimination was consistent with Marxism, Socialism, or any other ideological attitude.

Stalin has at times been compared to Napoleon. It is, on the whole, a fanciful and misleading comparison. Stalin did not suppress or pervert the Bolshevik Revolution as Napoleon "liquidated" the Jacobins. There never was a Thermidor (still less a Brumaire) in the Russian Revolution: neither in the mid-twenties (where Trotsky naturally placed it), nor after the assassination of Kirov, nor after the death of Stalin. But there is something also in this analogy that is illuminating. To ask whether Stalin was a faithful Marxist or even a faithful Leninist is like asking whether Napoleon believed in the ideals or ideas of the French Revolution. Napoleon was sufficiently a child of the Revolution to be instinctively opposed to everything connected with the pre-revolutionary regime, and to wish to come to terms with some of its survivals solely for limited periods and for reasons of expediency. Just as Napoleon took it for granted that the relics of feudalism in Europe were doomed beyond recall, that the dynastic principle was not worth respecting, that nationalism was a force that must be used, that centralization and uniformity were policies favorable to his rule and the like, so it may be assumed that Stalin was Marxist and Leninist enough to believe that capitalism was inescapably doomed to be destroyed by its own "internal contradictions," although it might here and there engage in a desperate struggle for survival, whether it realized this or not and however useless such a struggle might be. Similarly Stalin probably accepted the tactical corollary that wherever such "contradictions" reached the acute stage, those who wished to survive and inherit the earth must seek to exacerbate these critical situations and not to palliate them; whereas in situations where these contradictions had not yet reached a critical point the path of prudence on the part of the members of the new society, i.e., the Communists, was not to promote premature risings but to bore from within and concentrate on Popular Fronts and Trojan

Horses of various kinds. It is clear that he genuinely believed that the future of human society was inevitably collectivist and not individualist; that the power of religion and the churches was collapsing; that control of economic power was more important (i.e., capable of effecting greater changes or stopping them) than, say, nationalist sentiment or political power; and in all these respects he was, of course, a true, if exceedingly crude follower of Marx. But if it be asked whether he was a Marxist in the sense in which Lenin undoubtedly was one — i.e., of believing that as the result of the dreadful birth pangs a new world would be born in which men would in some sense be freer or more reasonable than before, capable of developing their faculties on a vastly more productive scale, living in a world without wars, starvation and oppression — it seems doubtful whether he troubled himself with such questions any more than the Emperor Napoleon reflected about the ultimate validity of any of the ideals of the French Revolution. And, to his intellectual credit be it said, Stalin paid little enough regard — even by way of lip service — to the many utopian elements in Lenin's outlook.

It is, perhaps, a second point of similarity with Napoleon that Stalin firmly grasped a truth which perhaps Napoleon was the first among secular rulers fully to realize and act upon, namely that discussion of ideas — disputes about issues apparently remote from politics, such as metaphysics or logic or aesthetics — was, by promoting the critical spirit, in principle more dangerous to despotic regimes engaged in a struggle for power than belief in any form of authoritarianism. Napoleon's open hostility to the *Idéologues* — the empiricists and positivists of his day — is well known. He openly preferred the implacable legitimist and ultramontane Bonald, who abused him and would have no truck with him, to the politically mild and conformist liberal, Destutt de Tracy. Similarly Stalin, when he felt himself securely in power, decided to put an end to all ideological controversy as such in the Soviet Union. He did this by proclaiming one school to be victorious over all others (it does not historically matter which). The new directive was that the business of the intelligentsia — writers, artists, academics, and so forth — was not to interpret, argue about,

analyze, still less develop or apply in new spheres, the principles of Marxism, but to simplify them, adopt an agreed interpretation of their meaning, and then repeat and ingeminate and hammer home in every available medium and on all possible occasions the self-same set of approved truths. The new Stalinist values were similar to those proclaimed by Mussolini: loyalty, energy, obedience, discipline. Too much time had been wasted in controversy, time which could have been spent in promoting enforced industrialization or educating the new Soviet man. The very notion that there was an area of permissible disagreement about the interpretation of even unquestioned dogma created the possibility of insubordination; this, beginning indeed in spheres remote from the centers of power — say, musical criticism or linguistics — might spread to more politically sensitive areas and so weaken the drive for economic and military power for which no sacrifice was too great or too immoral. The celebrated Marxist formula — the unity of theory and practice — was simplified to mean a set of quotations to justify officially enunciated policies. The methods taken to suppress the least symptom of independence on the part of even the most faithful Stalinist intellectuals (let alone so-called deviationists or unreconstructed relics of older dispensations) — and, let it be added, the success of these methods — are a phenomenon without parallel in the recorded history of human oppression.

The result has been a long blank page in the history of Russian culture. Between 1932 and, say, 1945, or indeed 1955, it would not be too much to say that — outside natural science — scarcely any idea or piece of critical writing of high intrinsic value was published in Russia, and hardly any work of art — scarcely anything genuinely interesting or important in itself and not merely as a symptom of the regime or of the methods practiced by it, that is to say, as a piece of historical evidence.

This policy was, perhaps, chiefly due to Stalin's personal character. He was a half-literate member of an oppressed minority, filled with resentment against superior persons and intellectuals of all kinds, but particularly against those articulate and argumentative socialists whose dialectical skill in the realm of theory must have humiliated him often both before the Revolution and after it, and of whom Trotsky was only the most arrogant and brilliant representative. Stalin's attitude toward ideas, intellectuals, and intellectual freedom was a mixture of fear, cynical contempt, and sadistic humor that took the form (a touch of Caligula) of discovering to what grotesque and degrading postures he could reduce both the Soviet and foreign members of his cowering congregation. After his death this policy has on occasion been defended by his heirs on the ground that when an old world is being destroyed and a new world brought into being, the makers and breakers cannot be expected to have any time for the arts and letters, or even ideas, which must, at any rate for the moment, suffer what befalls them without protest.

It is interesting to ask how such absolute subservience, and for so long a period, could have been secured on the part of an intelligentsia which had after all not merely contributed the very term to the languages of Europe, but had itself played so prominent and decisive a role in bringing about the victory of the Revolution. Here was a body of persons the blood of whose martyrs had been the seed of the entire revolutionary movement, a body to which Lenin, far more than Marx, had assigned a leading role in the task of subverting the old order and of keeping the new one going; and yet, when it was crushed, not a mouse stirred: a few indignant voices abroad, but inside the Soviet Union silence and total submission. Mere intimidation, torture, and murder should not have proved sufficient in a country which, we are always told, was not unused to just such methods and had nevertheless preserved a revolutionary underground alive for the better part of a century. It is here that one must acknowledge that Stalin achieved this by his own original contributions to the art of government — inventions that deserve the attention of every student of the history and practice of government.

IV

The first invention has been called "the artificial dialectic."[1] It is well known that according to the systems of Hegel and of Marx

events do not proceed in direct causal sequence but by means of a conflict of forces — of thesis and antithesis — ending in a collision between them, and a Pyrrhic victory, in the course of which they eliminate each other, and history takes "a leap" to a new level, where the process, called dialectical, begins once again. Whatever may be the validity of this theory in any other sphere, it has a very specific applicability to revolutionary situations.

As every student of the subject must know, the principal practical problem before those who have successfully brought off a large-scale revolution is how to prevent the resultant situation from collapsing into one of two opposed extremes. The first — let us call it Scylla — is reached when the zealots of the revolution, observing that the new world which the revolution was meant to create has somehow not yet come to pass, seek for explanations, culprits, scapegoats, blame it on criminal weakness or treachery on the part of this or that group of their agents or allies, declare the revolution in mortal peril and start a witch hunt which presently develops into a terror, in the course of which various groups of revolutionaries tend to eliminate each other successively, and social existence is in danger of losing the minimum degree of cohesion without which no society can continue to be. This process tends to be checked by some form of counter-revolution, which is brought on by a desperate effort on the part of the majority, whose security is threatened, to preserve itself and achieve stability, an instinctive social recoil from some imminent-looking collapse. This is what occurred during the great French Revolution, to some extent during the Commune of 1871, in some parts of Eastern Europe in 1918, and might have occurred in 1848 had the extreme left-wing parties begun to win. The mounting spiral of terror was, in fact, what Trotsky was suspected of wishing to promote.

The opposite extreme — Charybdis — is subsidence into a weary indifference. When the original impetus of the revolution begins after a time to ebb, and people seek a respite from the terrible tension of the unnatural life to which they have been exposed, they seek relief, comfort, normal forms of life; and the revolution slides by degrees into the ease, *Schlamperei*, moral squalor, financial chicanery, and general corruption of the kind which

---

[1] See "Stalin and the Art of Government," by O. Utis, *Foreign Affairs*, January 1952, in which Stalin's method of retaining power is discussed.

marked, for example, the French Directoire; or else subsides into some conventional dictatorship or oligarchy, as has happened so often in Latin America and elsewhere. The problem for the makers of the revolution, therefore, is how to keep the revolution going without falling foul of either the Scylla of utopian fanaticism or the Charybdis of cynical opportunism.

Stalin should be credited with having discovered and applied a method which did, in fact, solve this particular problem in a certain sense. Theoretically, history or nature (as interpreted by Hegel or Marx) should, by pursuing its own dialectical process, so develop that these opposites collide at the crucial stage, forcing reality to ascend a creative spiral instead of collapsing into one-sided forms of bankruptcy. But since history and nature at times evidently tend to nod, man must from time to time come to the aid of these impersonal agencies. The government, as soon as it sees signs of the fatal hankering after the fleshpots of the older life, must tighten the reins, intensify its propaganda, exhort, frighten, terrorize, if need be make examples of as many conspicuous backsliders as may be required to stop the rout. Malingerers, comfort-lovers, doubters, heretics, other "negative elements" are eliminated. This is the "thesis." The rest of the population, duly chastened, dominated by terror rather than hope or desire for gain or faith, throw themselves into the required labors, and the economy bounds forward for a while. But then the elite of the revolutionary zealots, the fanatical terrorists, the simon-pure heart of the Party, who must be genuinely convinced of the sacred duty of cutting off the rotten branches of the body politic, inevitably go too far. If they did not, if they could stop in time, they would not have been the kind of people to perform the task of inquisition with the desperate zeal and ruthlessness required; hypocrites, half-believers, moderates, opportunists, men of cautious judgment or human feeling are of no use for this purpose, for they will, as Bakunin had warned long ago, compromise halfway. Then the moment arrives when the population, too terrorized to advance, or too starved, becomes listless, downs tools, and efficiency and productivity begin to drop off; this is the moment for clemency. The zealots are accused of having gone too far, they are accused of oppressing the people, and — always a popular move — they are in their turn publicly disciplined, that is, in Stalin's heyday, purged and executed. Some small increase of freedom is allowed in remote fields — say, that of literary criticism or poetry or archaeology, nothing so near the center of things as economics or politics. This is the "antithesis." The people breathe again, there is optimism, gratitude, talk of the wisdom of their rulers now that their eyes have been opened to the "excesses" of their unfaithful servants, hope of further liberties, a thaw; production leaps up, the government is praised for returning to some earlier, more tolerant ideal, and a relatively happier period ensues.

This once more leads to the inevitable relaxation of tension, slackening of discipline, lowering of productive effort. Once more there is (the new thesis) a call for a return to ideological purity, for the reestablishment of fundamental principles and loyalties, for the elimination of the parasitical saboteurs, self-seekers, drones, foreign agents, enemies of the people who have in some way managed to creep into the fold. There is a new purge, a new spurt of ideological fanaticism, a new crusade, and the heads of the counter-revolutionary hydra (the new antithesis) have to be cut off once again.

In this way the population is, as it were, kept perpetually on the run, its development proceeds by a zigzag path, and individual self-preservation depends on a gift for perceiving at which precise moment the central authority is about to order a retreat or an advance, and a knack for swiftly adjusting oneself to the new direction. Here timing is all. A miscalculation, due to inertia or political insensitiveness, or, worse still, political or moral conviction, causing one to linger too long on a road that has been condemned, must almost always, particularly if persisted in, mean disgrace or death.

It cannot be denied that by this deliberate policy of carefully timed purges and counter-purges of various intensities, of contraction and expansion, Stalin did manage to preserve in being a system that cannot be actively approved or felt to be natural by most of those concerned, and indeed to keep it going for a longer period than that for which any other revolution has, thus far, managed to survive. Although the method, to be successful, requires the master hand of its inventor, it appears to have survived him. Despite the grave shocks to the system caused by the struggle for power among Stalin's successors, the emergence into the open of conflicts and factions, the risings of oppressed peoples in the West totally unforeseen in Moscow, the "artificial dialectic" appears to be functioning still. The succession, in strict sequence, during the last five years, of "liberal" and repressive moves by the Soviet rulers, both at home and abroad, although no longer conducted with the virtuosity (or the deep personal sadism) of Stalin, has too much regularity of pattern to be unintended. The hypothesis advanced by the author to explain only Stalin's own methods of government seems to fit his successors.

The method is an original political invention, and Stalin deserves full credit for it. One of its deliberate by-products has been the total demoralization of what is still in the U.S.S.R. called the intelligentsia — persons interested in art or in ideas. In the worst moments of Tsarist oppression there did, after all, exist some areas of free expression; moreover, one could always be silent. This was altered by Stalin. No areas were excluded from the Party's directives; and to refuse to say what had been ordered was insubordination and led to punishment. "Inner emigration" requires the possibility of the use of one's mind and means of expression at least in neutral ways. But if one's chances of sheer survival have been made dependent on continuous active support of principles or policies which may seem absurd or morally abhorrent; and if, moreover, the whole of one's mental capacity is taxed by the perpetual need to chart one's course in fatally dangerous waters, to manoeuvre from position to position, while one's moral fiber is tested by the need to bow one's head low not to one but to many capricious, unpredictably changing divinities, so that the least inattention, slackness, or error costs one dear — then there is less and less possibility of thinking one's own thoughts, or of escaping into an inner citadel in which one can remain secretly heterodox and independent and know what one believes. Stalin went further. He forbade more than a minimum degree of official intercommunication between one academic faculty and another, between laboratory and institute, and successfully prevented the growth of any center of

intellectual authority, however humble and obedient, however fraudulent and obscurantist. No priesthood of dialectical materialism had been allowed to arise, because no discussion of theoretical issues was permitted; the business of the Academy of Sciences or the Institute of Red Professors or the Marx-Engels Institute was to quote Marx in supporting Stalin's acts: the doctrine, he or some other member of the Politbureau (certainly not a professor), would supply for himself.

Where there is an official church or college of augurs, with its own privileges and mysteries, there is a relatively fenced-off area, with walls within which both orthodoxy and heresy can flourish. Stalin set himself to repress ideas as such — at a very high cost, be it added, not merely in terms of the basic education of Soviet citizens (not to speak of disinterested intellectual activity, "pure" research and so on), but even in the useful and applied sciences which were gravely handicapped by the lack of freedom of discussion and suffered an abnormally high admixture of adventurers, charlatans, and professional informers. All this was effective in stifling every form of intellectual life to a far greater degree than was realized by even the most hostile and pessimistic observers in the West, or, for that matter, by Communist Parties outside the Soviet orbit. To have created such a system is a very striking achievement on Stalin's part, whose importance should not be underrated. For it has also nearly crushed the life out of what once was one of the most gifted and productive societies in the world. At any rate for the time being.

V

There is yet a second consequence of this system which is worthy of remark, namely that most of the standard vices so monotonously attributed by orthodox Marxists to capitalism are to be found in their purest form only in the Soviet Union itself. Most readers of [*Foreign Affairs*] will be familiar with such stock Marxist categories as capitalist exploitation, the iron law of wages,[2] the transformation of human beings into mere commodities, their alienation from their human essence, the skimming off of

---

[2] The phrase is Lassalle's, but the general conception is certainly part of Marx's doctrine.

surplus value by those who control the means of production, the dependence of the ideological superstructure on the economic base, and other Communist phrases. But where do these concepts best apply?

Economic exploitation is a phenomenon that has been familiar enough in the West; but there is no society in which one body of men is more firmly, systematically, and openly "exploited" by another than the workers of the Soviet Union by their overseers. True, the benefits of this process do not go to private employers or capitalists. The exploiter is the state itself, or rather those who effectively control its apparatus of coercion and authority. These controllers — whether they act as Party officials or state bureaucrats or both — act far more like the capitalists of Marxist mythology than living capitalists in the West today. The Soviet rulers really do see to it that the workers are supplied with that precise minimum of food, shelter, clothing, entertainment, education, and so forth that they are thought to require in order to produce the maximum quantity of the goods and services at which the state planners are aiming. The rest is skimmed off as surplus value far more conveniently and neatly than it can ever have been detached in the unplanned West. Wages are regulated in the most "iron" way possible — by the needs of production. Economic exploitation here is conducted under laboratory conditions not conceivable in Western Europe or America.[3] It is again in the Soviet Union that official professions of "ideology" — principles, slogans, ideals — correspond least to actual practice. It is there, too, that some intellectuals can most truly be described as lackeys (some sluggish and reluctant, others filled with a kind of cynical delight and pride in their own virtuosity) of the ruling group. It is there, far more obviously than in the West, that ideas, literature, works of art act as "rationalizations" or smoke screens for ruthless deeds, or means of escape from the contemplation of crimes or follies, or as opium for the masses. It is there that the

state religion — for that is what the dead and fossilized "dialectical materialism" of the official Soviet philosophers has, in effect, more or less avowedly become — is nothing but a consciously used weapon in the war against the enemy, within and without; and lays no claim to "objective" truth.

The materialist theory of history teaches us that the primary factors that determine the lives of individuals and societies are economic, namely the relationships of human beings in the productive system; while such cultural phenomena as their religious, ethical, political ideas, their judicial and political institutions, their literature, arts, scientific beliefs and so forth belong to various tiers of the "superstructure," that is, are determined by — are a function of — the "base." This celebrated and justly influential doctrine, embodying as it does a great deal that is new, important, illuminating, and by now very widely accepted, has, nevertheless, never been easy to fit in detail to any given society or period of history in the past. Every attempt to apply it narrowly[4] always encountered too many exceptions: if these were to be explained away, they usually had to be stretched till the theory became too vague or encrusted with too many qualifications to retain any utility. But it holds only too faithfully of Soviet society. There it is absolutely clear to everyone what is part of the base and what is part of the superstructure. Writers, artists, cultural workers can have no illusions about which level of the pyramid they constitute. Economic, military and other "material" needs really do wholly determine — because they are deliberately made to determine — ideological phenomena, and not vice versa. It is not nature nor history that has produced this situation, but a piece of highly artificial engineering, by which Stalin and his officials have transformed the Russian Empire.

It is an extraordinary irony of history that categories and concepts invented to describe Western capitalism should turn out to fit most

---

[3] Mr. Milovan Djilas corroborates this forcibly in his book *The New Class* (New York, Praeger, 1957). Whether the system is to be called state capitalism (the state being anything but a democracy) or a "degenerate worker's state" or a naked autocracy is a question of the most appropriate label. The facts themselves are not in doubt.

[4] Say, to demonstrate that the writings of Thomas Love Peacock could not possibly have arisen save in the economic conditions of early nineteenth century England; and that these conditions in their turn made such writings as those of, let us say, Mr. Aldous Huxley (or others like him) inevitable when the process entered a later phase of the dialectic.

closely its mortal enemy. But this is scarcely an accident, a *lusus historiae*. Every student of the Russian Revolution knows that the issue that divided the Bolsheviks most deeply from the orthodox Marxists — the Mensheviks — was the practicability of an immediate transition to socialism. The Mensheviks maintained that according to any interpretation of Marx, genuine socialism could be established only in a society which had reached a high degree of industrialization — where the organized proletariat formed the majority of the population, and was, through the working of the "inexorable" and mounting "contradictions" of economic development, in a position to "expropriate the expropriators" and initiate socialism. No one could maintain that this stage had yet been reached in the Russian Empire. But the Bolsheviks, mainly under Trotsky's inspiration, claimed that instead of semi-passively waiting for capitalism (a bourgeois republic) to do the job, leaving the workers insufficiently protected from the free play of "history," "nature," etc. — this process could be controlled by a proletarian dictatorship; Russia could be made to go through the stages demanded by the "dialectic of history" under hothouse conditions regulated by the Communist Party. This was to be the famous "transitional" period of the dictatorship of the proletariat — the artificial or controlled equivalent of "natural" capitalist development in the West: two roads leading equally to full-blown Communism, but the Russian corridor less painful because not left to the vagaries of "nature," but planned by men in control of their own fate owing to their possession of the "scientific" weapon of Marxist theory and able, therefore, to "shorten the birth pangs" by a well executed revolution. If, like Lenin, one begins with fanatical faith in the correctness of the Marxist analysis of history, the fact that it does not fit too well even the capitalist West, which it was designed to describe, will make little difference. If the pattern does not correspond to the facts, the facts must be made to tally with the pattern. Russia in 1917 was not an advanced capitalist society. Its proletariat was relatively feeble. But the dialectic of history cannot be cheated. Unless Marxism rested on a gigantic fallacy there could be no salvation without the equivalent of the capitalist phase. Hence the corresponding phenomena had to

be synthetically produced — made to emerge by artificial means.

This can sometimes be done with success, as in Japan, for example. But the Japanese followed the light of reason and experience. They modernized themselves by the methods that seemed to work best, without being chained to a dogmatic theory. They achieved their purpose not without brutalities, but rapidly and with spectacular success. An economic program adapted to specifically Russian conditions was not open to Lenin and his followers. They were compelled by their fidelity to the Marxist classics to subordinate their practical judgment to the demands of theory: the social and economic development of Russia had to proceed by fixed steps whose order was laid down by the Marxist manuals. This created appalling — and avoidable — handicaps that were overcome at a terrible human cost. Russia *had* to go through phases which, according to Marx, Western capitalism passed during and after its industrial revolution. Russian reality had to be altered to resemble a model constructed, not too competently, to account for the progress of a society very unlike itself. The society was vivisected, as it were, to fit a theory which began its life as no more than the explanation of the evolution of another society. Something which was designed to be at once a description and a warning became normative: a theory intended to account for the development and behavior of Western Europe in the nineteenth century had been turned into a blueprint for Eastern Europe in the twentieth.

Actions founded upon errors of social observation do not necessarily end badly. There is, for all to see, that part of American constitutional development which was inspired by Montesquieu's mistaken interpretation of British political theory and practice. Lenin's error proved more costly. Russia was precipitated into unheard-of horrors of industrialization largely because Marx had — with much justice — drawn a dark picture of Western capitalism and was understood to hold that no society could escape something analogous.[5]

_____

[5] I do not, of course, wish to imply the untenable propositions that (a) the industrialization of Russia would not have occurred without the determination to impose Marxist doctrines, or that (b) it

The imposition of the Bolshevik system upon an economically retarded country is a unique monument to the power of a few men's wills and their sovereign contempt for history and empirical evidence; and a blood-curdling interpretation of the Unity of Theory and Practice.

VI

Faced with crises and the possibility of collapse, Lenin executed a partial retreat. And his successors, under the pressure of events, substituted various practical makeshifts and realistic devices and policies in place of the extravagant utopian design which dominates Lenin's thinking. Nevertheless the violent break with reality that is at the heart of the Bolshevik Revolution can evidently not be eliminated without causing the regime to collapse; at any rate no serious attempt to do so has ever been made. For this reason Soviet society is not, in the normal sense, a civil society at all.

The purpose of normal human societies is in the first place to survive; and, after that, to satisfy what Mill called "the deepest interests of mankind," that is to say, to satisfy at any rate a minimum number of men's normal desires after their basic needs are satisfied — say, for self-expression, happiness, freedom, justice. Any government which realizes these values to a reasonable degree is held to fulfill its function. These are not the principal ends of Soviet society, or of its government. Conditioned by its revolutionary origins, it is organized to achieve objectives, to respond to challenges, win victories. Like a school, a team of players, still more like an army on the

march, it is a specialized institution designed for specific purposes that must be made explicit to its members by the leaders. Soviet life is constructed to strive for goals. It makes little difference what the particular goals may be — military or civil, the defeat of the enemy within or without, or the attainment of industrial objectives — announced goals there must be, if Soviet society is to continue to be. The leaders understand this well, and whether or not they are to be regarded as prisoners of their own system, they know that they must continue to exhort their subjects to greater and greater endeavors if they are to avoid the disintegration of the regime. They are in the position of army commanders in a war, who realize that unless their troops see a minimum amount of active service, the discipline, the *esprit de corps*, the continued existence of the armies as fighting units cannot be guaranteed.

The leaders of the Soviet Union, for all we know, may well by now be hankering after peaceful existence, may be looking for ways of safely abandoning the exiguous splendors and unending cruelties and miseries of the regime in order to subside into "normal" life. If they harbor any such desires, they know that in the short run, at least, this is not practicable. For Soviet society is organized not for happiness, comfort, individual liberty, justice, personal relationships, but for combat. Whether they wish it or not, the drivers and controllers of this immense train cannot now halt it or leap from it in mid-course without risk of destruction. If they are to survive and above all remain in power, they must go on. Whether they can replace parts of it while it is moving, and so transform it (themselves) into something more humane and less destructive and dangerous to themselves and mankind, remains to be seen. The symptoms are not all discouraging. At any rate that must be the hope of those of us who do not think war inevitable.

In the meanwhile those forced marches toward socialization have discredited the tradition of social idealism and liquidated the intelligentsia connected with it, perhaps more decisively than unaided persecution could have done. Nothing destroys a minority movement more effectively than the official adoption, and inevitable betrayal and perversion, of its ends by the state itself. There are cases where nothing succeeds less well than success.

---

was, or is, regrettable. Nor is the rapid pace of the expansion of the industrial base something to be lamented *per se*. My thesis is that the methods adopted by the masters of the Soviet Union were inhumanly — and gratuitously — cruel and wasteful of lives and resources, and that this sprang from doctrinaire blindness more than out of objective conditions, the personal character of the early Bolshevik leaders, or ignorance, whether inevitable or not. And, moreover, that this outlook and this way of doing things did great, lasting, and avoidable harm to the education and moral and intellectual condition of its survivors, which underdeveloped countries, faced with analogous problems today, and anxious both to increase their national and military power and to raise their living standards, need not inflict.

10

The Sources of Soviet Conduct*

George F. Kennan

(1947)

In this paper by George F. Kennan, we turn again to the role of guiding ideas, this time to the more esoteric elements of Marxist ideology. But Mr. Kennan also stresses the influence of circumstances — of the opportunities of the historic moment. Many of his assumptions about the weakness of the Soviet system and the limits on its further development have not been borne out by subsequent events. Yet his statement remains a challenging interpretation of Soviet conduct, and the great influence it has exerted on American and general Western policy and orientation toward the Soviet Union during the long period of the "containment" policy makes it a document every student of Soviet affairs should know.

The political personality of Soviet power as we know it today is the product of ideology and circumstances: ideology inherited by the present Soviet leaders from the movement in which they had their political origin, and circumstances of the power which they now have exercised for nearly three decades in Russia. There can be few tasks of psychological analysis more difficult than to try to trace the interaction of these two forces and the relative role of each in the determination of official Soviet conduct. Yet the attempt must be made if that conduct is to be understood and effectively countered.

It is difficult to summarize the set of ideological concepts with which the Soviet leaders came into power. Marxian ideology, in its Russian-Communist projection, has always been in process of subtle evolution. The ma-

* Reprinted from "Sources of Soviet Conduct," Foreign Affairs, Vol. 25 (1947), pp. 566–582, by permission of the author and the publisher. (Copyright, 1947, by the Council on Foreign Affairs.) At the time of original publication, the author was indicated only as "X". The author was later identified as Mr. Kennan.

terials on which it bases itself are extensive and complex. But the outstanding features of Communist thought as it existed in 1916 may perhaps be summarized as follows: (a) that the central factor in the life of man, the factor which determines the character of public life and the "physiognomy of society," is the system by which material goods are produced and exchanged; (b) that the capitalist system of production is a nefarious one which inevitably leads to the exploitation of the working class by the capital-owning class and is incapable of developing adequately the economic resources of society or of distributing fairly the material goods produced by human labor; (c) that capitalism contains the seeds of its own destruction and must, in view of the inability of the capital-owning class to adjust itself to economic change, result eventually and inescapably in a revolutionary transfer of power to the working class; and (d) that imperialism, the final phase of capitalism, leads directly to war and revolution.

The rest may be outlined in Lenin's own words: "Unevenness of economic and political development is the inflexible law of capitalism. It follows from this that the victory of Socialism may come originally in a few capitalist countries or even in a single capitalist country. The victorious proletariat of that country, having expropriated the capitalists and having organized Socialist production at home, would rise against the remaining capitalist world, drawing to itself in the process the oppressed classes of other countries."[1] It must be noted that there was no assumption that capitalism would perish without proletarian revolution. A final push was needed from a revolutionary proletariat movement in order to tip over the tottering structure. But it was regarded as inevitable that sooner or later that push be given.

For 50 years prior to the outbreak of the Revolution, this pattern of thought had exercised great fascination for the members of the Russian revolutionary movement. Frustrated, discontented, hopeless of finding self-expression — or too impatient to seek it — in the confining limits of the Tsarist political system, yet lacking wide popular support for their

[1] "Concerning the Slogans of the United States of Europe," August 1915. Official Soviet edition of Lenin's works.

choice of bloody revolution as a means of social betterment, these revolutionists found in
Marxist theory a highly convenient rationalization for their own instinctive desires. It afforded pseudo-scientific justification for their
impatience, for their categoric denial of all
value in the Tsarist system, for their yearning
for power and revenge and for their inclination
to cut corners in the pursuit of it. It is therefore no wonder that they had come to believe
implicitly in the truth and soundness of the
Marxian-Leninist teachings, so congenial to
their own impulses and emotions. Their sincerity need not be impugned. This is a phenomenon as old as human nature itself. It has
never been more aptly described than by
Edward Gibbon, who wrote in *The Decline
and Fall of the Roman Empire:* "From enthusiasm to imposture the step is perilous and
slippery; the demon of Socrates affords a
memorable instance how a wise man may deceive himself, how a good man may deceive
others, how the conscience may slumber in a
mixed and middle state between self-illusion
and voluntary fraud." And it was with this
set of conceptions that the members of the
Bolshevik Party entered into power.

Now it must be noted that through all the
years of preparation for revolution, the attention of these men, as indeed of Marx himself,
had been centered less on the future form which
Socialism[2] would take than on the necessary
overthrow of rival power which, in their view,
had to precede the introduction of Socialism.
Their views, therefore, on the positive program
to be put into effect, once power was attained,
were for the most part nebulous, visionary, and
impractical. Beyond the nationalization of industry and the expropriation of large private
capital holdings there was no agreed program.
The treatment of the peasantry, which according to the Marxist formulation was not of the
proletariat, had always been a vague spot in
the pattern of Communist thought; and it remained an object of controversy and vacilla-
tion for the first ten years of Communist
power.

The circumstances of the immediate post-
revolution period — the existence in Russia
of civil war and foreign intervention, together

[2] Here and elsewhere in this paper "Socialism"
refers to Marxist or Leninist Communism, not to
liberal Socialism of the Second International variety.

with the obvious fact that the Communists
represented only a tiny minority of the Russian people — made the establishment of dictatorial power a necessity. The experiment
with "war Communism" and the abrupt attempt to eliminate private production and
trade had unfortunate economic consequences
and caused further bitterness against the new
revolutionary regime. While the temporary
relaxation of the effort to communize Russia,
represented by the New Economic Policy, al-
leviated some of this economic distress and
thereby served its purpose, it also made it evident that the "capitalistic sector of society" was
still prepared to profit at once from any relaxation of governmental pressure, and would,
if permitted to continue to exist, always constitute a powerful opposing element to the
Soviet regime and a serious rival for influence
in the country. Somewhat the same situation
prevailed with respect to the individual peasant who, in his own small way, was also a
private producer.

Lenin, had he lived, might have proved a
great enough man to reconcile these conflicting
forces to the ultimate benefit of Russian society, though this is questionable. But be that
as it may, Stalin, and those whom he led in
the struggle for succession to Lenin's position
of leadership, were not the men to tolerate
rival political forces in the sphere of power
which they coveted. Their sense of insecurity
was too great. Their particular brand of fanaticism, unmodified by any of the Anglo-
Saxon traditions of compromise, was too fierce
and too jealous to envisage any permanent
sharing of power. From the Russian-Asiatic
world out of which they had emerged they
carried with them a skepticism as to the possibilities of permanent and peaceful coexistence of rival forces. Easily persuaded of their
own doctrinaire "rightness," they insisted on
the submission or destruction of all competing
power. Outside of the Communist Party, Russian society was to have no rigidity. There
were to be no forms of collective human activity or association which would not be dominated by the Party. No other force in Russian
society was to be permitted to achieve vitality
or integrity. Only the Party was to have structure. All else was to be an amorphous mass.

And within the Party the same principle
was to apply. The mass of Party members
might go through the motions of election, de-

liberation, decision, and action; but in these motions they were to be animated not by their own individual wills but by the awesome breath of the Party leadership and the over-brooding presence of "the word."

Let it be stressed again that subjectively these men probably did not seek absolutism for its own sake. They doubtless believed — and found it easy to believe — that they alone knew what was good for society and that they would accomplish that good once their power was secure and unchallengeable. But in seeking that security of their own rule they were prepared to recognize no restrictions, either of God or man, on the character of their methods. And until such time as that security might be achieved, they placed far down on their scale of operational priorities the comforts and happiness of the peoples entrusted to their care.

Now the outstanding circumstance concerning the Soviet regime is that down to the present day this process of political consolidation has never been completed and the men in the Kremlin have continued to be predominantly absorbed with the struggle to secure and make absolute the power which they seized in November 1917. They have endeavored to secure it primarily against forces at home, within Soviet society itself. But they have also endeavored to secure it against the outside world. For ideology, as we have seen, taught them that the outside world was hostile and that it was their duty eventually to overthrow the political forces beyond their borders. The powerful hands of Russian history and tradition reached up to sustain them in this feeling. Finally, their own aggressive intransigence with respect to the outside world began to find its own reaction; and they were soon forced, to use another Gibbonesque phrase, "to chastise the contumacy" which they themselves had provoked. It is an undeniable privilege of every man to prove himself right in the thesis that the world is his enemy; for if he reiterates it frequently enough and makes it the background of his conduct he is bound eventually to be right.

Now it lies in the nature of the mental world of the Soviet leaders, as well as in the character of their ideology, that no opposition to them can be officially recognized as having any merit or justification whatsoever. Such opposition can flow, in theory, only from the hostile and incorrigible forces of dying capitalism. As long as remnants of capitalism were officially recognized as existing in Russia, it was possible to place on them, as an internal element, part of the blame for the maintenance of a dictatorial form of society. But as these remnants were liquidated, little by little, this justification fell away; and when it was indicated officially that they had been finally destroyed, it disappeared altogether. And this fact created one of the most basic of the compulsions which came to act upon the Soviet regime: since capitalism no longer existed in Russia and since it could not be admitted that there could be serious or widespread opposition to the Kremlin springing spontaneously from the liberated masses under its authority, it became necessary to justify the retention of the dictatorship by stressing the menace of capitalism abroad.

This began at an early date. In 1924 Stalin specifically defended the retention of the "organs of suppression," meaning, among others, the army and the secret police, on the ground that "as long as there is a capitalist encirclement there will be danger of intervention with all the consequences that flow from that danger." In accordance with that theory, and from that time on, all internal opposition forces in Russia have consistently been portrayed as the agents of foreign forces of reaction antagonistic to Soviet power.

By the same token, tremendous emphasis has been placed on the original Communist thesis of a basic antagonism between the capitalist and Socialist worlds. It is clear, from many indications, that this emphasis is not founded in reality. The real facts concerning it have been confused by the existence abroad of genuine resentment provoked by Soviet philosophy and tactics and occasionally by the existence of great centers of military power, notably the Nazi regime in Germany and the Japanese Government of the late 1930's, which did indeed have aggressive designs against the Soviet Union. But there is ample evidence that the stress laid in Moscow on the menace confronting Soviet society from the world outside its borders is founded not in the realities of foreign antagonism but in the necessity of explaining away the maintenance of dictatorial authority at home.

Now the maintenance of this pattern of Soviet power, namely, the pursuit of unlimited authority domestically, accompanied by the cultivation of the semi-myth of implacable foreign hostility, has gone far to shape the actual machinery of Soviet power as we know it today. Internal organs of administration which did not serve this purpose withered on the vine. Organs which did serve this purpose became vastly swollen. The security of Soviet power came to rest on the iron discipline of the Party, on the severity and ubiquity of the secret police, and on the uncompromising economic monopolism of the state. The "organs of suppression," in which the Soviet leaders had sought security from rival forces, became in large measure the masters of those whom they were designed to serve. Today the major part of the structure of Soviet power is committed to the perfection of the dictatorship and to the maintenance of the concept of Russia as in a state of siege, with the enemy lowering beyond the walls. And the millions of human beings who form that part of the structure of power must defend at all costs this concept of Russia's position, for without it they are themselves superfluous.

As things stand today, the rulers can no longer dream of parting with these organs of suppression. The quest for absolute power, pursued now for nearly three decades with a ruthlessness unparalleled (in scope, at least) in modern times, has again produced internally, as it did externally, its own reaction. The excesses of the police apparatus have fanned the potential opposition to the regime into something far greater and more dangerous than it could have been before those excesses began.

But least of all can the rulers dispense with the fiction by which the maintenance of dictatorial power has been defended. For this fiction has been canonized in Soviet philosophy by the excesses already committed in its name; and it is now anchored in the Soviet structure of thought by bonds far greater than those of mere ideology.

II

So much for the historical background. What does it spell in terms of the political personality of Soviet power as we know it today?

Of the original ideology, nothing has been officially junked. Belief is maintained in the basic badness of capitalism, in the inevitability of its destruction, in the obligation of the proletariat to assist in that destruction and to take power into its own hands. But stress has come to be laid primarily on those concepts which relate most specifically to the Soviet regime itself: to its position as the sole truly Socialist regime in a dark and misguided world, and to the relationships of power within it.

The first of these concepts is that of the innate antagonism between capitalism and Socialism. We have seen how deeply that concept has become imbedded in foundations of Soviet power. It has profound implications for Russia's conduct as a member of international society. It means that there can never be on Moscow's side any sincere assumption of a community of aims between the Soviet Union and powers which are regarded as capitalist. It must invariably be assumed in Moscow that the aims of the capitalist world are antagonistic to the Soviet regime, and therefore to the interests of the peoples it controls. If the Soviet Government occasionally sets its signature to documents which would indicate the contrary, this is to be regarded as a tactical manoeuvre permissible in dealing with the enemy (who is without honor) and should be taken in the spirit of *caveat emptor*. Basically, the antagonism remains. It is postulated. And from it flow many of the phenomena which we find disturbing in the Kremlin's conduct of foreign policy: the secretiveness, the lack of frankness, the duplicity, the wary suspiciousness, and the basic unfriendliness of purpose. These phenomena are there to stay, for the foreseeable future. There can be variations of degree and of emphasis. When there is something the Russians want from us, one or the other of these features of their policy may be thrust temporarily into the background; and when that happens there will always be Americans who will leap forward with gleeful announcements that "the Russians have changed" and some who will even try to take credit for having brought about such "changes." But we should not be misled by tactical manoeuvres. These characteristics of Soviet policy, like the postulate from which they flow, are basic to the internal nature of Soviet power, and will be with us, whether in the foreground or the background, until the internal nature of Soviet power is changed.

This means that we are going to continue for a long time to find the Russians difficult to deal with. It does not mean that they should be considered as embarked upon a do-or-die program to overthrow our society by a given date. The theory of the inevitability of the eventual fall of capitalism has the fortunate connotation that there is no hurry about it. The forces of progress can take their time in preparing the final *coup de grâce*. Meanwhile, what is vital is that the "Socialist fatherland" — that oasis of power which has been already won for Socialism in the person of the Soviet Union — should be cherished and defended by all good Communists at home and abroad, its fortunes promoted, its enemies badgered and confounded. The promotion of premature, "adventuristic" revolutionary projects abroad which might embarrass Soviet power in any way would be an inexcusable, even a counter-revolutionary act. The cause of Socialism is the support and promotion of Soviet power, as defined in Moscow.

This brings us to the second of the concepts important to contemporary Soviet outlook. That is the infallibility of the Kremlin. The Soviet concept of power, which permits no focal points of organization outside the Party itself, requires that the Party leadership remain in theory the sole repository of truth. For if truth were to be found elsewhere, there would be justification for its expression in organized activity. But it is precisely that which the Kremlin cannot and will not permit.

The leadership of the Communist Party is therefore always right, and has been always right ever since in 1929 Stalin formalized his personal power by announcing that decisions of the Politburo were being taken unanimously.

On the principle of infallibility there rests the iron discipline of the Communist Party. In fact, the two concepts are mutually self-supporting. Perfect discipline requires recognition of infallibility. Infallibility requires the observance of discipline. And the two together go far to determine the behaviorism of the entire Soviet apparatus of power. But their effect cannot be understood unless a third factor be taken into account: namely, the fact that the leadership is at liberty to put forward for tactical purposes any particular thesis which it finds useful to the cause at any particular moment and to require the faithful and unquestioning acceptance of that thesis by the members of the movement as a whole.

This means that truth is not a constant but is actually created, for all intents and purposes, by the Soviet leaders themselves. It may vary from week to week, from month to month. It is nothing absolute and immutable — nothing which flows from objective reality. It is only the most recent manifestation of the wisdom of those in whom the ultimate wisdom is supposed to reside, because they represent the logic of history. The accumulative effect of these factors is to give to the whole subordinate apparatus of Soviet power an unshakeable stubbornness and steadfastness in its orientation. This orientation can be changed at will by the Kremlin but by no other power. Once a given party line has been laid down on a given issue of current policy, the whole Soviet governmental machine, including the mechanism of diplomacy, moves inexorably along the prescribed path, like a persistent toy automobile wound up and headed in a given direction, stopping only when it meets with some unanswerable force. The individuals who are the components of this machine are unamenable to argument or reason which comes to them from outside sources. Their whole training has taught them to mistrust and discount the glib persuasiveness of the outside world. Like the white dog before the phonograph, they hear only the "master's voice." And if they are to be called off from the purposes last dictated to them, it is the master who must call them off. Thus the foreign representative cannot hope that his words will make any impression on them. The most that he can hope is that they will be transmitted to those at the top, who are capable of changing the party line. But even those are not likely to be swayed by any normal logic in the words of the bourgeois representative. Since there can be no appeal to common purposes, there can be no appeal to common mental approaches. For this reason, facts speak louder than words to the ears of the Kremlin; and words carry the greatest weight when they have the ring of reflecting, or being backed up by, facts of unchallengeable validity.

But we have seen that the Kremlin is under no ideological compulsion to accomplish its purposes in a hurry. Like the Church, it is dealing in ideological concepts which are of long-term validity, and it can afford to be patient. It has no right to risk the existing achievements of the revolution for the sake of vain baubles of the future. The very teachings of Lenin himself require great caution and flexibility in the pursuit of Communist purposes. Again, these precepts are fortified by the lessons of Russian history: of centuries of obscure battles between nomadic forces over the stretches of a vast unfortified plain. Here caution, circumspection, flexibility and deception are the valuable qualities; and their value finds natural appreciation in the Russian or the oriental mind. Thus the Kremlin has no compunction about retreating in the face of superior force. And being under the compulsion of no timetable, it does not get panicky under the necessity for such retreat. Its political action is a fluid stream which moves constantly, wherever it is permitted to move, toward a given goal. Its main concern is to make sure that it has filled every nook and cranny available to it in the basin of world power. But if it finds unassailable barriers in its path, it accepts these philosophically and accommodates itself to them. The main thing is that there should always be pressure, unceasing constant pressure, toward the desired goal. There is no trace of any feeling in Soviet psychology that that goal must be reached at any given time.

These considerations make Soviet diplomacy at once easier and more difficult to deal with than the diplomacy of individual aggressive leaders like Napoleon and Hitler. On the one hand, it is more sensitive to contrary force, more ready to yield on individual sectors of the diplomatic front when that force is felt to be too strong, and thus more rational in the logic and rhetoric of power. On the other hand, it cannot be easily defeated or discouraged by a single victory on the part of its opponents. And the patient persistence by which it is animated means that it can be effectively countered not by sporadic acts which represent the momentary whims of democratic opinion but only by intelligent long-range policies on the part of Russia's adversaries — policies no less steady in their purpose, and no less variegated and resourceful in their application, than those of the Soviet Union itself.

In these circumstances it is clear that the main element of any United States policy toward the Soviet Union must be that of a long-term, patient but firm and vigilant containment of Russian expansive tendencies. It is important to note, however, that such a policy has nothing to do with outward histrionics: with threats or blustering or superfluous gestures of outward "toughness." While the Kremlin is basically flexible in its reaction to political realities, it is by no means unamenable to considerations of prestige. Like almost any other government, it can be placed by tactless and threatening gestures in a position where it cannot afford to yield even though this might be dictated by its sense of realism. The Russian leaders are keen judges of human psychology, and as such they are highly conscious that loss of temper and of self-control is never a source of strength in political affairs. They are quick to exploit such evidences of weakness. For these reasons, it is a *sine qua non* of successful dealing with Russia that the foreign government in question should remain at all times cool and collected and that its demands on Russian policy should be put forward in such a manner as to leave the way open for a compliance not too detrimental to Russian prestige.

III

In the light of the above, it will be clearly seen that the Soviet pressure against the free institutions of the Western world is something that can be contained by the adroit and vigilant application of counter-force at a series of constantly shifting geographical and political points, corresponding to the shifts and manoeuvres of Soviet policy, but which cannot be charmed or talked out of existence. The Russians look forward to a duel of infinite duration, and they see that already they have scored great successes. It must be borne in mind that there was a time when the Communist Party represented far more of a minority in the sphere of Russian national life than Soviet power today represents in the world community.

But if ideology convinces the rulers of Russia that truth is on their side and that they can therefore afford to wait, those of us on whom that ideology has no claim are free to examine objectively the validity of that premise. The Soviet thesis not only implies complete lack of control by the West over its own economic destiny, it likewise assumes Russian unity, discipline, and patience over an infinite period. Let us bring this apocalyptic vision down to earth, and suppose that the Western world finds the strength and resourcefulness to contain Soviet power over a period of ten to fifteen years. What does that spell for Russia itself?

The Soviet leaders, taking advantage of the contributions of modern technique to the arts of despotism, have solved the question of obedience within the confines of their power. Few challenge their authority; and even those who do are unable to make that challenge valid as against the organs of suppression of the state.

The Kremlin has also proved able to accomplish its purpose of building up in Russia, regardless of the interests of the inhabitants, an industrial foundation of heavy metallurgy, which is, to be sure, not yet complete but which is nevertheless continuing to grow and is approaching those of the other major industrial countries. All of this, however, both the maintenance of internal political security and the building of heavy industry, has been carried out at a terrible cost in human life and in human hopes and energies. It has necessitated the use of forced labor on a scale unprecedented in modern times under conditions of peace. It has involved the neglect or abuse of other phases of Soviet economic life, particularly agriculture, consumers' goods production, housing, and transportation.

To all that, the war has added its tremendous toll of destruction, death, and human exhaustion. In consequence of this, we have in Russia today a population which is physically and spiritually tired. The mass of the people are disillusioned, skeptical, and no longer as accessible as they once were to the magical attraction which Soviet power still radiates to its followers abroad. The avidity with which people seized upon the slight respite accorded to the Church for tactical reasons during the war was eloquent testimony to the fact that their capacity for faith and devotion found little expression in the purposes of the regime.

In these circumstances, there are limits to the physical and nervous strength of people themselves. These limits are absolute ones, and are binding even for the cruelest dictatorship, because beyond them people cannot be driven. The forced labor camps and the other agencies of constraint provide temporary means of compelling people to work longer hours than their own volition or mere economic pressure would dictate; but if people survive them at all they become old before their time and must be considered as human casualties to the demands of dictatorship. In either case their best powers are no longer available to society and can no longer be enlisted in the service of the state.

Here only the younger generation can help. The younger generation, despite all vicissitudes and sufferings, is numerous and vigorous; and the Russians are a talented people. But it still remains to be seen what will be the effects on mature performance of the abnormal emotional strains of childhood which Soviet dictatorship created and which were enormously increased by the war. Such things as normal security and placidity of home environment have practically ceased to exist in the Soviet Union outside of the most remote farms and villages. And observers are not yet sure whether that is not going to leave its mark on the over-all capacity of the generation now coming into maturity.

In addition to this we have the fact that Soviet economic development, while it can list certain formidable achievements, has been precariously spotty and uneven. Russian Communists who speak of the "uneven development of capitalism" should blush at the contemplation of their own national economy. Here certain branches of economic life, such as the metallurgical and machine industries, have been pushed out of all proportion to other sectors of economy. Here is a nation striving to become in a short period one of the great industrial nations of the world while it still has no highway network worthy of the name and only a relatively primitive network of railways. Much has been done to increase efficiency of labor and to teach primitive peasants something about the operation of machines. But maintenance is still a crying deficiency of all Soviet economy. Construction is hasty and poor in quality. Depreciation must be enormous. And in vast sectors of economic life it has not yet been possible to instill into labor anything like that general culture of production and technical self-respect which characterizes the skilled worker of the West.

It is difficult to see how these deficiencies can be corrected at an early date by a tired and dispirited population working largely under the shadow of fear and compulsion. And as long as they are not overcome, Russia will remain economically a vulnerable, and in a certain sense an impotent, nation, capable of exporting its enthusiasms and of radiating the strange charm of its primitive political vitality but unable to back up those articles of export by the real evidences of material power and prosperity.

Meanwhile, a great uncertainty hangs over the political life of the Soviet Union. That is the uncertainty involved in the transfer of power from one individual or group of individuals to others.

This is, of course, outstandingly the problem of the personal position of Stalin. We must remember that his succession to Lenin's pinnacle of pre-eminence in the Communist movement was the only such transfer of individual authority which the Soviet Union has experienced. That transfer took 12 years to consolidate. It cost the lives of millions of people and shook the state to its foundations. The attendant tremors were felt all through the international revolutionary movement, to the disadvantage of the Kremlin itself.

It is always possible that another transfer of pre-eminent power may take place quietly and inconspicuously, with no repercussions anywhere. But again, it is possible that the questions involved may unleash, to use some of Lenin's words, one of those "incredibly swift transitions" from "delicate deceit" to "wild violence" which characterize Russian history, and may shake Soviet power to its foundations.

But this is not only a question of Stalin himself. There has been, since 1938, a dangerous congealment of political life in the higher circles of Soviet power. The All-Union Congress of Soviets, in theory the supreme body of the Party, is supposed to meet not less often than once in three years. It will soon be eight full years since its last meeting. During this period membership in the Party has numerically doubled. Party mortality during the war was enormous; and today well over half of the Party members are persons who have entered since the last Party congress was held. Meanwhile, the same small group of men has carried on at the top through an amazing series of national vicissitudes. Surely there is some reason why the experiences of the war brought

basic political changes to every one of the great governments of the West. Surely the causes of that phenomenon are basic enough to be present somewhere in the obscurity of Soviet political life, as well. And yet no recognition has been given to these causes in Russia.

It must be surmised from this that even within so highly disciplined an organization as the Communist Party there must be a growing divregence in age, outlook, and interest between the great mass of Party members, only so recently recruited into the movement, and the little self-perpetuating clique of men at the top, whom most of these Party members have never met, with whom they have never conversed, and with whom they can have no political intimacy.

Who can say whether, in these circumstances, the eventual rejuvenation of the higher spheres of authority (which can only be a matter of time) can take place smoothly and peacefully, or whether rivals in the quest for higher power will not eventually reach down into these politically immature and inexperienced masses in order to find support for their respective claims? If this were ever to happen, strange consequences could flow for the Communist Party: for the membership at large has been exercised only in the practices of iron discipline and obedience and not in the arts of compromise and accommodation. And if disunity were ever to seize and paralyze the Party, the chaos and weakness of Russian society would be revealed in forms beyond description. For we have seen that Soviet power is only a crust concealing an amorphous mass of human beings among whom no independent organizational structure is tolerated. In Russia there is not even such a thing as local government. The present generation of Russians have never known spontaneity of collective action. If, consequently, anything were ever to occur to disrupt the unity and efficacy of the Party as a political instrument, Soviet Russia might be changed overnight from one of the strongest to one of the weakest and most pitiable of national societies.

Thus the future of Soviet power may not be by any means as secure as Russian capacity for self-delusion would make it appear to the men in the Kremlin. That they can keep power themselves, they have demonstrated. That they can quietly and easily turn it over to others remains to be proved. Meanwhile, the hardships of their rule and the vicissitudes of international life have taken a heavy toll of the strength and hopes of the great people on whom their power rests. It is curious to note that the ideological power of Soviet authority is strongest today in areas beyond the frontiers of Russia, beyond the reach of its police power. This phenomenon brings to mind a comparison used by Thomas Mann in his great novel *Buddenbrooks*. Observing that human institutions often show the greatest outward brilliance at a moment when inner decay is in reality farthest advanced, he compared the Buddenbrook family, in the days of its greatest glamour, to one of those stars whose light shines most brightly on this world when in reality it has long since ceased to exist. And who can say with assurance that the strong light still cast by the Kremlin on the dissatisfied peoples of the Western world is not the powerful afterglow of a constellation which is in actuality on the wane? This cannot be proved. And it cannot be disproved. But the possibility remains (and in the opinion of this writer it is a strong one) that Soviet power, like the capitalist world of its conception, bears within it the seeds of its own decay, and that the sprouting of these seeds is well advanced.

IV

It is clear that the United States cannot expect in the foreseeable future to enjoy political intimacy with the Soviet regime. It must continue to regard the Soviet Union as a rival, not a partner, in the political arena. It must continue to expect that Soviet policies will reflect no abstract love of peace and stability, no real faith in the possibility of a permanent happy coexistence of the Socialist and capitalist worlds, but rather a cautious, persistent pressure toward the disruption and weakening of all rival influence and rival power.

Balanced against this are the facts that Russia, as opposed to the Western world in general, is still by far the weaker party, that Soviet policy is highly flexible, and that Soviet society may well contain deficiencies which will eventually weaken its own total potential. This would of itself warrant the United States entering with reasonable confidence upon a policy of firm containment, designed to confront the Russians with unalterable counter-force at every point where they show signs of encroaching upon the interests of a peaceful and stable world.

But in actuality the possibilities for American policy are by no means limited to holding the line and hoping for the best. It is entirely possible for the United States to influence by its actions the internal developments, both within Russia and throughout the international Communist movement, by which Russian policy is largely determined. This is not only a question of the modest measure of informational activity which this government can conduct in the Soviet Union and elsewhere, although that, too, is important. It is rather a question of the degree to which the United States can create among the peoples of the world generally the impression of a country which knows what it wants, which is coping successfully with the problems of its internal life and with the responsibilities of a World Power, and which has a spiritual vitality capable of holding its own among the major ideological currents of the time. To the extent that such an impression can be created and maintained, the aims of Russian Communism must appear sterile and quixotic, the hopes and enthusiasm of Moscow's supporters must wane, and added strain must be imposed on the Kremlin's foreign policies. For the palsied decrepitude of the capitalist world is the keystone of Communist philosophy. Even the failure of the United States to experience the early economic depression which the ravens of the Red Square have been predicting with such complacent confidence since hostilities ceased would have deep and important repercussions throughout the Communist world.

By the same token, exhibitions of indecision, disunity, and internal disintegration within this country have an exhilarating effect on the whole Communist movement. At each evidence of these tendencies, a thrill of hope and excitement goes through the Communist world; a new jauntiness can be noted in the Moscow tread; new groups of foreign supporters climb on to what they can only view as the band wagon of international politics; and Russian pressure increases all along the line in international affairs.

It would be an exaggeration to say that American behavior unassisted and alone could exercise a power of life and death over the

Communist movement and bring about the early fall of Soviet power in Russia. But the United States has it in its power to increase enormously the strains under which Soviet policy must operate, to force upon the Kremlin a far greater degree of moderation and circumspection than it has had to observe in recent years, and in this way to promote tendencies which must eventually find their outlet in either the break-up or the gradual mellowing of Soviet power. For no mystical, Messianic movement — and particularly not that of the Kremlin — can face frustration indefinitely without eventually adjusting itself in one way or another to the logic of that state of affairs.

Thus the decision will really fall in large measure in this country itself. The issue of Soviet-American relations is in essence a test of the over-all worth of the United States as a nation among nations. To avoid destruction the United States need only measure up to its own best traditions and prove itself worthy of preservation as a great nation.

Surely, there was never a fairer test of national quality than this. In the light of these circumstances, the thoughtful observer of Russian–American relations will find no cause for complaint in the Kremlin's challenge to American society. He will rather experience a certain gratitude to a Providence which, by providing the American people with this implacable challenge, has made their entire security as a nation dependent on their pulling themselves together and accepting the responsibilities of moral and political leadership that history plainly intended them to bear.

SUGGESTIONS FOR FURTHER READING

Natural and Human Resources

BALZAK, S. S., V. F. VASYUTIN, and YA. G. FEIGIN, *Economic Geography of the U.S.S.R.* New York: The Macmillan Company, 1949.

> Translation of an authoritative prewar Soviet text, also interesting for the Marxist context in which the subject is discussed.

CRESSEY, GEORGE B., *How Strong Is Russia? A Geographical Appraisal.* Syracuse, N.Y.: Syracuse University Press, 1954.

LORIMER, FRANK, *The Population of the Soviet Union: History and Prospects.* Geneva: League of Nations, 1946.

> Detailed and comprehensive, with methods of gathering and treating data fully described.

Population Trends in Eastern Europe, the U.S.S.R., and Mainland China. Proceedings of the Thirty-sixth Annual Conference of the Milbank Memorial Fund, New York, November 4–5, 1959.

> Contains two articles, "Recent Demographic Trends in the U.S.S.R." by John F. Kantner, and "Problems of Manpower and Industrialization in the U.S.S.R." by Warren W. Eason.

SHIMKIN, DEMITRI B., *Minerals: A Key to Soviet Power.* Cambridge, Mass.: Harvard University Press, 1953.

Stages of Soviet Development

BERDYAEV, NICHOLAS, *The Origin of Russian Communism*. London: Geoffrey Bles, Ltd., 1948.

The philosophical and characterological background to Soviet ideology.

BLACK, CYRIL E. (ed.), *The Transformation of Russian Society: Aspects of Social Change Since 1861*. Cambridge, Mass.: Harvard University Press, 1960.

Papers written for a conference held in Harriman, New York, April 25–27, 1958.

CARR, E. H., *A History of Soviet Russia*. New York: The Macmillan Company, 1950–58.

Six volumes of this detailed topical treatment have appeared, dealing with the years from 1917–1926.

MAYNARD, JOHN, *Russia in Flux*. New York: The Macmillan Company, 1948.

A sympathetic account by a British scholar who was well acquainted with Tsarist Russia.

RAUCH, GEORGE VON, *A History of Soviet Russia*, rev. ed. New York: Frederick A. Praeger, Inc., 1958.

A straightforward historical summary.

SCHUMAN, FREDERICK L., *Russia Since 1917: Four Decades of Soviet Politics*. New York: Alfred A. Knopf, 1957.

A history and an interpretation of the Soviet experience.

SIMMONS, ERNEST J. (ed.), *Continuity and Change in Russian and Soviet Thought*. Cambridge, Mass.: Harvard University Press, 1955.

Essays on literature, economics and other topics.

TIMASHEFF, NICHOLAS S., *The Great Retreat: The Growth and Decline of Communism in Russia*. New York: E. P. Dutton and Co., 1946.

A sociological interpretation of the drastic shift in Soviet policy in the 1930's.

The System in Perspective

BAUER, RAYMOND A., and ALEX INKELES, *The Soviet Citizen: Daily Life in a Totalitarian Society*. Cambridge, Mass.: Harvard University Press, 1959.

Social psychological data based largely on the materials gathered from Soviet refugees by the Harvard Project on the Soviet Social System.

BAUER, RAYMOND A., ALEX INKELES, and CLYDE KLUCKHOHN, *How the Soviet System Works*. Cambridge, Mass.: Harvard University Press, 1956.

Emphasis is on the "operating characteristics" of the system and their effects.

DALLIN, ALEXANDER (ed.), *Soviet Conduct in World Affairs*. New York: Columbia University Press, 1960.

An authoritative selection of readings.

FITZSIMMONS, THOMAS, *et al., U.S.S.R.: Its People, Its Society, Its Culture.* New Haven: Human Relations Area Files Press, 1960.

A comprehensive survey which gives a lot of attention to informal patterns.

HENDEL, SAMUEL (ed.), *The Soviet Crucible.* New York: D. Van Nostrand Co., Inc., 1959.

Readings on the many sides of Soviet government.

KULSKI, W. W., *The Soviet Regime: Communism in Practice,* rev. ed. Syracuse, N.Y.: Syracuse University Press, 1959.

A topical and thematic analysis, with Soviet publications serving as the main source materials.

McCLOSKY, HERBERT, and JOHN E. TURNER, *The Soviet Dictatorship.* New York: McGraw-Hill Book Company, Inc., 1960.

An analytical as well as historical account of Soviet politics.

ROSTOW, W. W., *et al., The Dynamics of Soviet Society.* New York: W. W. Norton & Company, Inc., 1952.

A general survey, giving special attention to sources of cohesion, tension, and instability.

WEBB, BEATRICE and SIDNEY, *Soviet Communism: A New Civilization?,* 2 vols. New York: Charles Scribner's Sons, 1938.

Still a classic in scope of coverage and in presentation of Soviet-approved viewpoints.

II

Ideology and Power

Regardless of the specific substantive area under study, students of Soviet society seem to reflect one or the other of two rather opposed tendencies. We may label these schools — meaning to be as non-pejorative as possible — the "realists" and the "institutionalists." The realists insist that information coming out of the Soviet Union is intended mainly as propaganda to becloud and befog the observer. They hold that the institutionalists are dealing only with the facade, the cover hiding the reality of the system underneath, a system which has its distinctive, indeed unique, character.

On ideology, realists make a distinction between the public, open, "exoteric" slogans and directives, and the actually operating, but hidden and covert or "esoteric" ideology which truly guides the system. They recognize that the Soviet Union has "laws" and claims to acknowledge the rule of law, but they question whether it is at all meaningful to speak of law under Soviet conditions where absolute political rulers can, whenever they deem it necessary, put aside the law and have done so repeatedly. They question how reasonable it is to discuss the policy of the Soviet *state*, when in fact there is no sovereign power in the Soviet Union except for the Communist Party. Realists would object to discussing the mobilization of public opinion in the U.S.S.R. — arguing that public opinion assumes individuals with access to information, free to make up their own minds, and possessed of the means of relating to each other or banding together to express their common views. In this sense, the realists hold, there *is* no such thing as public opinion in the Soviet Union. Realists also tend to be pessimists about the future of Soviet society — that is, to believe there is little prospect for an enduring liberalization, let alone democratization, of Soviet totalitarianism.

The institutionalists, on the other hand, tend to take the formal institutional structure of Soviet society much more seriously, even though they do not necessarily accept it at face value. They stress that no country can long run without some degree of order, regularity, and calculability, and that this makes many institutions — like the law, courts, government agencies, the family, the community, the university — indispensable even to a totalitarian regime. They argue, further, that over time these institutions come to have a certain degree of autonomy, even of inviolability, as the effective performance of the system comes more and more to depend on their functioning. The dictatorship may at first only pay lip service to them, but in time it becomes dependent on them, then limited and constrained, and finally becomes a prisoner or even a servant of the established regular institutions. When this argument is carried to its ultimate conclusion, it suggests that the dictatorship and totalitarianism must eventually become "eroded," and be replaced by a stable, orderly, responsible, and perhaps even democratic order.

The editors of this volume agree with the institutionalists in at least one respect. We believe that Soviet society and its history cannot be understood without reference to Marxist ideology and its adoption and revision by Lenin. This is not to say that we assume any "straight-line" relation — a one-to-one correspondence between Marxist-Leninist ideology and Soviet institutions. On the contrary, we interpret most of those institutions as the product of a complex interaction between traditional Russian ways, the pressure of circumstances, the power aspirations of Soviet leaders, and the "world view" carried in their heads and perhaps in their hearts. But ideas have been part of this complex process, and in the Soviet case more prominent than in most of the previous outstanding cases of modern national development.

Whatever the role of ideas and ideology in Soviet development, we must recognize that it was outstandingly a revolution "from above." Such a revolution, largely imposed by a tightly knit core of deeply committed leaders, could not be carried out without some special means, some unique instrument of rule. The Communist Party, in its distinctive role as a kind of civilian army in politics, represents probably the single most important institution in Soviet development. Its principles of organization, its methods of recruiting and training members, its relations with other institutions and the people are crucial features of Soviet social structure. No one can presume to understand Communist society unless he has grasped the nature and role of the Party in the Soviet system.

At the same time, the organization and direction provided by the Communist Party could not in itself suffice for the task of transforming traditional rural Russian society into the modern intensely industrialized Soviet system. The Party might be the "driving belt," but it had to be attached to some machinery, and over time the Soviet Union has developed the full array of governmental institutions to execute the unique features of the Party's policy as well as to perform the routine functions that fall to government in any modern society.

These, too, are a part of Soviet reality, and a complete picture of the Soviet scene must assign them a prominent place.

The fact that the revolution was one "from above" posed a distinct problem for the Soviet leadership. They could not count on mass or popular support, let alone enthusiasm, for the majority of the programs they introduced and indeed imposed on the Soviet people. The Party sought to meet this deficiency by two seemingly contradictory measures — a massive program of persuasion to win support for its program and practice, and a massive campaign of terror to coerce the people into doing what the Party wanted them to do. The program of mass persuasion goes on unabated; the terror is now much muted. To understand the Soviet past, consideration of this more violent aspect of the Soviet political system is indispensable; to understand the future it must certainly be given at least serious attention. There are some students of Soviet affairs who believe a return to a more Stalinesque type of repression is highly likely, even "necessary" to the rulers. Many others argue that the system can function quite well without terror, relying on a system of censorship and relatively mild controls. The outcome will be important not only to Soviet citizens but to all the world. We return to this problem and give it more extensive consideration in our last chapter. In the present chapter we take the necessary earlier step of becoming familiar with the role of ideology and the structure of power in the Soviet Union.

THE ROLE OF IDEAS

11

The Appeal of Communist Ideology*

Donald G. MacRae

(1951)

We have already seen that, whether or not ideology played an important role in shaping the course of Soviet affairs, the topic certainly

* Reprinted from "The Bolshevik Ideology: The Intellectual and Emotional Factors in Communist Affiliation," *The Cambridge Journal*, Vol. 5 (1951), pp. 164–177, by permission of the author and Bowes and Bowes Limited.

occupies a central place in the debates among specialists on Soviet affairs. Our first contributor to this chapter on Ideology and Power returns to the issue again. Mr. MacRae seeks to explain the appeal of Marxist ideology. He is not, however, concerned with the "truth" or the "scientific" adequacy of the theory so much as with its essential emotional attraction. Neglect of the fact that Marxist ideology is for many people mainly a "world view," a general orientation and perspective, has muddled many discussions of the relation of the Communist blueprint and Soviet reality. Many analysts, having proved to their own satisfaction that the Soviet system does not accord with the formal requirements of Marxist-Leninist ideology, have on this basis rather too hastily concluded that ideology plays no role in Soviet affairs.

In what follows I attempt to treat Marxism in its Bolshevik form not as a system or method, but as an ideology, not as a corpus of knowledge, but as a constellation of concepts in the minds of men. In doing this I hope to fill the gap that has been left by such recent and excellent studies as those of Carew Hunt, Plamenatz, and Arnold,[1] and to answer some of the questions not dealt with by, for example, Towster or Inkeles.[2] My problem is that of the appeal of Bolshevism as a politico-social creed; and the question I want to consider is, why men moved by honest and generous sentiments associate themselves with the thought-world and institutions of international Communism.[3] In short, my proposal is to treat Bolshevism sociologically, as an ideological fact, and not merely as a possibly "true" account of the worlds of nature and of man. There are plenty of studies of the validity of various portions of Marxism, but there is no great value in them for us. The objective "truth" of Islam or Calvinism is not of much help in deciding why men are Mahometans or Presbyterians, and only at the end of this paper is the veristic element in Bolshevik theory considered, and then merely in its relevance to the social operation of the ideology. Just as the historian of Islam would discount, not as intrinsically unimportant but as beside the point, the divine inspiration claimed for the new creed which, in many ways a Christian heresy, and developed on the oppressed and semi-barbarous marches of Mediterranean civilization, was to conquer in just over a century one-sixth of the land surface of the globe, so the sociologist must treat Bolshevism today. Certainly Bolshevism claims the status and the prestige of science and calls on its predictive success as witness of its veridicity, but many writers have observed how a prophecy may ensure its own fulfilment,[4] and it is my purpose here to consider the character of the appeal of Bolshevism altogether apart from its status as sociology, economics, or philosophy.

The Claim of Bolshevism to Scientific Status

The claim to scientific status has been mentioned, so we may begin with its ideological significance. Science and the mental habits of the scientist have acquired the most enormous of prestiges by their empirical success in explaining, controlling, and adapting the world of nature. The ascription of being scientific is the ascription simultaneously of truth and of power. This has been realized in many fields from Christian Science to the "race science" of the Nazis or the advertisement of patent medicines. As a result, the claim of Bolshevism to be a science and/or to be the truly scientific method, has great emotive force. That Marxism professes a materialist philosophy reinforces this position, for the most spectacular of the sciences, and (before 1896) the most theoretically complete and self-sufficient, was undoubtedly physics, with which philosophical materialism at most times has been profoundly associated.

But Marxism is a science of a special sort: its foundations are not empirical or inductive,[5] but Hegelian; and the development of Marx's own thought would provide a sceptical but sympathetic biographer wtih a valuable subject. Marxists claim the natural sciences as their allies, accepting "mechanical" explanations save at crucial points. Here, where the laboratory scientist finds explanation incomplete or difficult and problems unsolved, the "dialectic" is appealed to and used to dissolve all mysteries.

The dialectic is well-fitted to this function, as most occasions can be forced into the triadic frame of thesis–antithesis–synthesis,

---

[1] R.N. Carew Hunt, *The Theory and Practice of Communism*, London, 1950. J. Plamenatz, "Deviations from Marxism," *Political Quarterly*, Vol. XXI, 1950; "The Communist Ideology," *Political Quarterly*, Vol. XXI, 1951. G. J. Arnold, "Stalinism," *Political Quarterly*, Vol. XXII, 1950.

[2] J. Towster, *Political Power in the USSR*, New York, 1948. A. Inkeles, *Public Opinion in Soviet Russia: A Study in Mass Persuasion*, Cambridge (USA), 1950.

[3] A rather different question which is closely related to the one I discuss, and which partly overlaps with it, concerns why people actually join Communist parties and why the membership of such parties fluctuates so widely in non-Communist countries. I do not think a general answer is possible here. All sorts of questions of fear, possible advantage, indignation, or despair are at work, and these are matters that should be studied in terms of the specific histories of the various Communist parties. Such histories hardly exist in a serious form, though something has been done for Germany and more for France — e.g., in the work of Zévaès, Rossi, Monnerot, and Walter.

[4] E.g., Edward Gibbon, *Decline and Fall*, Vol. I, Ch. 1, where Gibbon discusses the legend of Terminus.

[5] Cf. Karl Marx's doctoral dissertation, *Differenz der democritischen epicurischen Naturphilosophie,* Jena, 1841.

and as its categories of transition, opposition, contradiction, and interpenetration are ill-defined and wide enough to make merely verbal explanation easily accessible to anyone who has acquired the appropriate vocabulary. The dialectic, therefore, not merely associates Marxism and science, it makes Marxism appear as a kind of super-science.

The scientific prestige extends further. Marxism claims to be a science of society and, consequently, of man. This sociology no doubt has virtues, which have often been pointed out, but here I am concerned only with its ideological significance. It is important to realize that *to most Marxists no knowledge of alternative, objective thought about society is available.* This is true of manual workers in the West who can well appreciate the world of physical science in their daily life and work, but it has an additional importance in technologically backward areas. Here the slow spread of industry, the social dislocation which this spread nevertheless entails, and the desire for technological and scientific power, all enormously enhance the appeal of Bolshevism to local skilled workers and discontented intellectuals. Where technological inferiority and hope deferred in industrial progress cause despair, there the social technique and promise of Bolshevism provide a social substitute involving only human organization, and Marx is seen as the provider of an accessible short cut by his science of society and the social revolution to a world of technological and industrial achievement.

To correct one technology by another — a social one — is part of the appeal of Marxism to the proletariat: in colonial countries this promise is reinforced by the claim that an industrial order is possible (without the pains of birth and growth) by the use of a social technique backed by the repute of science in areas where science is still half-magic.[6]

In all this of course is a truth: science by giving understanding and knowledge *does* increase human power, and this is already to some degree true of academic social science. The veridical elements in Marxist social theory

buttress the whole ideological structure, and the triumph of Bolshevism is guaranteed to the believer by the same forces which keep the stars

> . . . rank on rank
> The army of unalterable law.

Marxism as Messianic Religion

What this name of science guarantees is very simple and very old, and many Marxists have denounced those who remark and comment on the identity which can be observed between their creed and a Messianic and Apocalyptic religion. Bukharin, for instance, wrote: "one of the most widespread forms of ideological class struggle against Marxism is its treatment as an eschatological doctrine, with all its accompaniments of chiliasm, of soteriology, of myth. . . . All these analogies are playing with words."[7]

Now, in so far as these analogies are intended as criticisms of the objective validity of Marxist reasoning, Bukharin's criticism is to the point, but any account of Marxism as a social doctrine, animating a social movement, and which is concerned with Marxism as a myth in Sorel's sense — the affirmation of a readiness to *act* — must see in these analogies a profound relevance. The Bolshevik testament is a Christian heresy whose God is personified history, pronouncing judgment on the unjust in the thunder of revolution and the smoke of battle, and delivering them not in some far future but here, now. History, as in St. Augustine or Calvin, is the story of divine judgment moving under the hands of men to its one conclusion. And what is more, Marxists have recognized this: the language of the Bible breaks through the *Communist Manifesto* where the "expropriators are expropriated," or in the sudden anger of the Preface to the *Critique of Political Economy*, and Engels in his *Peasant War in Germany* recognizes his kin with Munzer as English Marxists have more recently recognized (or thought they recognized) theirs with Winstanley and the Diggers of the English revolution. The emotive appeal is that of a religion of salvation and damnation supported by a crabbed, a Tal-

---

[6] The word "magic" is used strictly — i.e., in the sense of Frazer's *Golden Bough,* where magic is a false technology, an erroneous attempt to command the forces of nature and society.

[7] N. I. Bukharin (and others), *Marxism and Modern Thought,* p. 3.

mudic, theology. And this can be said without prejudice, to the value of Marx's contributions to history, the social sciences, and to politics. What has led Bolshevism in our time to dominate some eight hundred million human beings is the subtle alliance of what can be recognized as a modicum of scientific truth with a salvationist religion.

If we examine the parallel in more detail we will find it close and illuminating. Marxism is a religion of the dispossessed and discontented, and it promises them relief *because* of their condition. The very forces of the capitalist historical process that result in poverty and in misery at the same time prepare the judgment of the revolution, and this judgment is a true correction of time in which the mighty are cast down, and the lowly exalted. The consummation of time is guaranteed by history, but history is not justified by faith alone, but by words. Emotively at least Bolshevism is deterministic: like all deterministic creeds its rigor arouses in the believers the most resolute and patient action and thus their acts confirm the faith, and the faith the acts.

The goal of time is the reign of the saints, the dictatorship of the proletariat, a time of justice without mercy. Beyond the state, "withered away," lies the realm of mercy, of "truly human history," of love and comradeship, in fact, of anarchy as understood by Godwin, Bakunin, and Kropotkin.[8] The goal of anarchy, of the innocence of human relations unconstrained by law, is the goal of the return to Eden and to the restoration of the Natural Man of the *philosophes*. It is an aboriginal dream of humanity.

But not merely does Bolshevism promise the wrath to come and paradise beyond, it gives the most powerful of motives, fear and hope, to those who would join. The victory of the revolution is inevitable: therefore let those who can purge their class-guilt join with the proletariat and escape the judgment. Moreover, as Lenin argued,[9] since the revolution needs, if not bourgeois leaders, at least leaders drawn from the bourgeoisie, they may hope for power in doing so. Bolshevism provides the exhilarating knowledge of under-

standing, of being "in on" the secrets of social destiny. It also provides a threat.

The minatory aspect of the prophecy is clear: the dross-heap of history waits for those who hesitate or choose wrongly. And all choice, but that of Communism, *is* wrong: the historical process, the dialectic, the prestige of science warrant the victory of the Marxist proletariat. The actual character of the reign of the saints, of the Dictatorship of the Proletariat, where the Communist Party has come to power, has profoundly and of set purpose[10] confirmed the threat. It may not for long in a Communist country be of advantage to have been on the winning side, but it is certain perdition to have sided with the losers. The very knowledge of probable danger within the fold, coupled with the conviction of certain danger without, produces a vertiginous delight in the more sophisticated Marxist.

But the primary attraction of Marxism cannot be to the sophisticated, though there can be no doubt that Marxism exercises a peculiar fascination over those who are susceptible to the worst intellectual heresy of our age: the romanticism of violence. (This is especially true because the individual who might well be afraid of his own inclinations in this direction can excuse himself to himself by the generosity of his goal and the "scientifically" established fact that history and society are intrinsically brutal and predetermined.) The main appeal is not here, however; it is the simple one of the Messiah and the Apocalypse.

In the writings of Marx and Engels the eschatological center is hidden and qualified by an enormous commentary on politics which are now out-of-date, economics that is now irrelevant, philosophy that was always largely verbal trickery, science now outmoded, and a historical sociology of economic and other institutions still of high value. Lenin and the early Bolsheviks drew a distinction, which has since been maintained between Propaganda, between the dissemination of total understanding of a situation among the few, and the Agitation of a limited number of principles of action among the many. In these terms the

---

[8] Cf. in particular K. Marx, *Les prétendues scissions de l'Internationale*, 1872.

[9] Lenin, *Collected Works*, (2nd ed.), Vol. LV, pp. 383–91.

[10] Cf. Trotsky, *The Defence of Terrorism*. (This book, originally published in 1921, re-appeared with a new introduction — London, 1935 — after Trotsky had become a victim of the methods he justified. He retracts nothing.)

history of Bolshevik thought and the history of Bolshevik expression (which has largely conditioned that thought) has been that of the replacement of Propaganda by Agitation. This is not merely visible in the transition from the language of the young Marx — antithetical, epigrammatic, brilliant and brutal — to the leaden repetitions of Marshal Stalin or Mr. Molotov. It can be seen in the transition to Agitation within the U.S.S.R. since 1917, and in the growth of that extraordinary and now international jargon based on the recapitulation and recombination of some sixty or seventy phrases with which we are all familiar,[11] and which has so thoroughly debased a number of the most common and necessary words of political discourse.

This simplification into dogma of the apocalypse has an enormous appeal, especially in backward territories. There the mere fact that it is a simplification, a pre-digestion of a "science" which gives hope, is immensely attractive.[12] Marxism does not merely give access in tabloid form to Western culture; it gives, at the same time, a feeling of superiority to it. The psychological oppression of the West is reversed by Bolshevism, and a felt inferiority can triumph in observing the inevitable judgment whereby the last shall be first, the first last. The Bolshevik makes great use of local history and local pride in his propaganda. He reveals the "inwardness" of what "really happened, and turns to the surface a new pride in a new knowledge of the achievements of the oppressed. He gives in fact, the "ancient lowly" a history and therefore a pedigree and a dignity. Objectively much of this is admirable and useful, but it reinforces the millenarian faith which is central to the mass propaganda and success of Communism.

Bolsheviks have always been ready, in Lenin's phrase, to denounce "Marxist bookworms and braggarts," and this attitude to the professional intellectual can be seen with absolute clarity in Vyshinsky's cross-examination of Bukharin.[13] No doubt, whatever the merits of the case, the success of Lysenko has been helped by the picture of the "new Soviet man," rising, from outside the institutions of orthodox science, to denounce these institutions. Bolshevism can take advantage of popular ambivalence to the work of mind and turn from scholasticism to simplicity and back again in its argument with ease. The popular reverence for learning and the popular confidence in the untutored wisdom of the masses are equal and supporting notes in the chord of Marxism.

In countries where there is a tradition of an inspired book — Bible, Koran, Confucian classics, etc. — Marxism with its texts of varying difficulty can play much the same social role, but with the added interest that at least as long as Marshal Stalin lives the texts are not complete. The possession of such texts has many advantages. The first is the use of them, various in origin and date and subject, to provide a mosaic of accepted doctrine which may in fact embody a good argument or conceal a bad or absent one. No Communist can be omniscient: but, sufficiently learned in Bolshevik literature, he can appear very near it, and the consistency of his vocabulary will suggest a consistency and coherence of thought reassuring both to him who commands it and to him who reads or listens. Combined with the fact that the Communist Party nearly always has a "line" on every subject, this dialectical readiness is very impressive, especially in societies not highly verbally sophisticated.

Secondly, in an organization in which the purge is an accepted institution and in which a change in policy can often be equated with a treachery *ex ante*, the ascription of this crime to textual misinterpretation or distortion is very

---

[11] The fountainhead is in Marshal Stalin's own writings and the *History of the CPSU (b)* (Moscow, 1939). The most developed contemporary instance is the Bucharest organ of the Cominform, *For a Lasting Peace and a People's Democracy.*
[12] In such areas the idea of progress does not come, as so often in the West, as dead and false, but as new and exciting and true. "Progressive" is still an attribute of virtue for the Eastern intellectual and the Western manual worker, and Marxism is "progressive." With this is linked, but it is another subject, the Marxist praise for Youth and faith in the young — similar points could also be made about the emancipation of women.

---

[13] V. *Report of Court Proceedings in the Case of the Anti-Soviet "Bloc of Rightists and Trotskyites,"* Moscow, March 2nd–13th, 1938, p. 421 *et seq.* (Peoples Commissariat of Justice of the U.S.S.R.). A recent and milder case concerns the reactions of the Hungarian Communist Party to the critic and philosopher Lukacs; in English, v. Jozesf Revai, *Lukacs and Socialist Realism,* London, 1950.

convenient.[14] It can be argued, though never as nakedly as this, that if Marxism is the one true scientific method, then any failure in the world of practice must be because of an incorrect application of theory; but, as the theory is claimed to be very simple, such error can only be the consequence of malignancy. The firing squad is no inappropriate institution to close such a syllogism. In fact by arguing that Marxism is very simple when it is, in fact, very complex and uncertain, people can be easily convinced of inadequacy or guilt.

Thirdly, there is in Marxism a ladder of knowledge, a *scala scientiae*, which is closely but not uniformly correlated with party position. The study of Marxism is repeatedly stressed as desirable in Communist circles, and eminence in the party (by catching the notice of its officials) turns often on dialectical ability in defence of some new change in the line or of some overtly difficult or unpopular policy. The whole institutional structure of the party, which is not under discussion here, facilitates this process in the recruitment of the Communist elite. The mechanisms of denunciation and demotion turn largely on learned criticism, and the *furor theologicus* since Marx (with some slight help from Engels) wrote *Die heilige Familie* has been a feature of Communist polemic. Marxism, as has already been said, gives a confidence in "being in on" things, and "with" them. There are degrees in this, and the double ladder of knowledge and office within Communist parties makes the ascent of these degrees desirable — especially as they give not merely understanding but power and personal security.[15]

The Role of the Intellectual

This is not all. The intellectual in the present century has increasingly found himself

> . . . a stranger and afraid
> In a world I never made.

14 Cf. the series of verbatim reports of state trials from that of the Industrial Party to 1938 in the U.S.S.R. and the more recent east-European trials of Petkov, Rajk, Kostov and Vogeler, all of which are available in English translation.
15 An interesting and rather touching example of this, showing also the part of practical work in the economic field, will be found in F. Dubkovetsky, *Advancing to Communism: Notes of a Pioneer of Collective Farming in the Ukraine,* Moscow, 1950.

The Communist Parties, East and West, have offered two kinds of human and one of cosmic comradeship. To be an intellectual in the West is (for Britain at least, in 1951 it would be better to say, was) to be *déclassé* either upward or downward. In one case he was ashamed and resentful of his original class, in the other for his original class. Membership of a Communist Party provides the microcosm of a classless society and comradeship in it. Secondly it provides a sense of unity with the oppressed, and for those who are *déclassé* downward it provides an expiation and, in day to day political work, a genuine personal atonement, for feelings of class guilt. Thirdly it provides a comradeship, a pantheist and Whitmanesque camaraderie, with the universe. It is a poor joke perhaps which equates "anomie" with the opposite of bonhomie, but for the Western intellectual there is a sense in which this was exactly the truth about the substitution which adherence to Communism offered. It made man at one with society not as constituted but as it must be, and at one with the universe in which he lived. This is no small gift. In the East the intellectual far more than in the West is always *déclassé*, and this is particularly true of Asia and Africa. Bolshevism plays the same part there as it did throughout the West in the 1930's but to a smaller degree today. But it does more: as suggested earlier, it promises hope and dignity, and these not merely for a class but for a people as a whole. At the same time it gives a concrete vision of personal power to which the gateway is an understanding of the Marxist theory. In the East the sacred books clearly guarantee a deliverance, on earth and now, to men and areas where this faith had hitherto been chimeric and attenuated beyond hope.

Conspiracy is part of the tradition of Communist organization. To be a member of a conspiracy is in some sense to have a private revelation, a knowledge denied all others outside the group. It involves sacrifice, a payment of those vicarious psychological debts that cling inevitably to man as a social animal. Not all — in England probably not many — Communists are engaged in conspiracy, but there is a habit of mind which goes with the very possibility of conspiracy, of "going underground" (even where illegality is not involved), which alters the structure of knowledge in the head of the Communist. And it encourages the emergence of a "double" morality, whereby the party member can display entirely different "in-group" and "out-group" behavior.

Inside the party group we saw the double ladder of promotion by words and by works. The words are inevitably often casuistry and this applies both in mass-work, where all is not revealed to the audience, and in work in the branch or cell, where the major premises of action and of discourse are essentially tacit even if known. Again the mind is compartmentalized, and when we add to this the linguistic debasement of the Bolshevik thought world, the psychological impact of membership is such that the Communist becomes capable of a range of intellectual behavior hitherto impossible to him. He accepts contradictions and denies facts in a way disconcerting to the non-Bolshevik, and frequently he does this in good faith. Even where words have constant denotations between Communist and non-Communist, they may bear entirely different connotations. Moreover, in a sense unusual outside the party organization, they may change connotation with context at high speed and with baffling consequences. And it is here, where we deal with Orwell's "Double-think," that predictions of Communist behavior go most astray.[16] It is not only in vocabulary but in usage that anyone who has to deal with Communists should be trained. "Double-think" is also double-edged, and the Communists frequently are its dupes — though no doubt they gain more than they lose from the practice.

The Bolshevik's contempt for personal freedom sharply separates him from the traditions of the English, American, and French revolutions. Many thinkers — Burke, Brownson, Tocqueville, Acton, and Burckhardt, for ex-

---

[16] George Orwell in *1984* was very shrewd on this point, but he made "Double-think" unnecessarily formal, overt, and planned. Such a system would in fact be socially unworkable. In general, Orwell is an inadequate guide to Communism. Disraeli said that a public school is a microcosm of society, and Orwell seems often merely to translate his experience of Eton (with some reference to the wartime B.B.C. and the post-1945 world) into the future as the image in little of his coming society. This may sound far-fetched, but a comparison of *1984* and Mr. Cyril Connolly's *Enemies of Promise* will perhaps justify it. It is clear that Orwell was unaware of the parallel.

ample — have postulated a profound incompatibility between liberty and equality. To those who accept this view, Bolshevism is but another example of the passion for equality making vain the hope of liberty. But, whatever the truth of this view is, the Bolshevik sacrifice of liberty is made possible and acceptable by intellectual mechanisms which reinforce each other. Both of these are buttressed by the fact that, in a world in which responsibility seems to grow as power lessens, freedom is a burden; and Bolshevism is a system which excludes much of the weight of personal choice. I say "excludes," but to the Communist a better word might be "postpones." After the revolution, after the dictatorship of the proletariat, comes freedom, but a freedom that does not burden, for human nature will have been re-made to innocence, and human life remoulded to simplicity. Until then humanity must be re-educated by history and by the chief agent of history, the Communist Party. In the name of education how many crimes have been committed! This argument, however, is a sop to the Communist who is genuinely concerned with the problem of freedom. He can also accept it because, after all, Marxism shows there is such an inevitable, if grim, period which cannot be avoided. (No Communists take seriously Lord Keynes's phrase that in the long run we are all dead, and in this is part of their strength.) Casuistry, too, suggests that there "is more than one kind of freedom," and that the freedoms of the person and expression are comparatively unimportant to most of mankind as compared with the blessings of a just economy.

This is the second mechanism whereby freedom can be, not rejected, but removed from among the practical problems of the present. For most of mankind throughout the world's history the economic problem has been primary and economic techniques have been such that non-economic aspiration has not been open to any but the few. I do not believe that mind is a reflex of economic circumstance, but it was an accurate insight of Marx to see that it is often so. By offering economic advantage and economic equality simultaneously, Communism brings a hope that is both material and psychological — the belief that after the revolution bellies will be fuller and the contumely of wealth no longer present to mock honest poverty.[17] Among industrial workers throughout the old world this is a significant hope, but in the peasantries of Asia and Africa it is more, and it is welcomed with the zeal of religious conversion. The liberties of person and expression are among the highest of human values, but in countries used to despotism tempered by anarchy and corruption, they must seem flat and irrelevant when so much remains to be done for equality and an equal advance to a modest plenty.

Again we encounter that ideological strength in Bolshevism whereby contraries can be held together in the mind. There are three ways in which the compartmentalized psychology of the Communist can do this: by use of an ambiguous vocabulary, by use of the dialectic, and by a careful juggling with the priorities of the Bolshevik future. In countries remote from the West the whole process can be carried on the more freely, for it is not easy to believe good of one's conquerors, while Western administrators have seldom mirrored the more profound social content of their societies, and to believe in the evil and the approaching doom of the West is to believe more readily in the future of one's own land. In all this the greatest political invention, however imperfectly realized, of Europe is forgotten and liberty is the victim of motives which, however mistaken, are at least strong and understandable.

Prophets, Leaders, and Devils

The prestige of a science, the promise of a revelation, the hope of equality, are all seen against a succession of prophets and leaders. The exciting drama of Bolshevik ideology comes right in history through the intermediary of a royal line of prophet beings succeeding in success not by birth nor by appointment as did the Antonines, but by a divine election where history replaces God. Marx certainly took himself with preternatural seriousness as a thinker and a leader (though less so as a man), and Engels when Marx was safely dead became much more pontifical than before. Lenin was in dead earnest in all he did and

Trotsky was undeniably vain, but it was only after 1924 that deification and personal adulation became part of the institutional structure of Bolshevik leadership.

This transition was important. The dangers of split and internal feud within the ranks of a revolutionary organization become much more serious in their possible consequences once power has been attained, and at the same time the difficulties of concrete policy decisions, and the possibility of disagreement about these, greatly increases. Marxism by its combination of ambiguity and theology offers a field for protracted internal argument which can lead to real differences on policy. Also Marxism is complex and it is not always easily practicable to deduce the appropriate act from the doctrine in any given situation. As a result an infallible leader solves many problems. He maintains unity of thought and action and saves the ordinary party member many of the difficulties and dangers of thought. In those areas where there is a tradition of divine leadership his presence is a reassurance and a guarantee.[18]

But it is not enough to have a leader of this sort; he must be placed in a succession — a succession which, coming last in time, he will crown. This is the role of Marshal Stalin. Errors, however, will still be made, policies changed, and the "monolith" of the party (to use a favorite phrase) will be revealed as spurious unless a scapegoat can be found. In addition the danger of all despots is the palace revolution; men who have made one revolution may make another. The institution of the purge and the incarnate personal enemy therefore occupies a place in the ideology.

Bolshevism has many devils, and men in the misery of this condition enjoy an enemy. Orwell, I think, was wrong in believing that a Trotsky-devil is necessary to a Bolshevik society which still has external enemies, but Trotsky was undoubtedly necessary if the thir-

---

[17] The perpetration of economic inequality inside the U.S.S.R. can be explained as a transient necessity and contrasted with the allegedly (and quite plausibly) greater inequities of other societies.

[18] When the edge of the sword of poverty was biting into the bone,
Lenin Pasha arose
And, facing the Sultan and all the rich, he said,
"I am a friend of the poor and a brother to all the poor.
Come, we shall fight to the death!"
(From an Armenian poem quoted by W. Kolarz, *Stalin and Eternal Russia*, London, 1944).

ties were to be weathered by Bolshevism. He is still useful, but the foreign capitalist is more permanent and useful, especially with his retinue of "Social-Fascist fakers," and internal class-enemies and Kulaks. In denouncing these as at once dangerous and futile, Bolshevik invective is found in its most typical forms.

With regard to these incarnate devils, the purge serves a double purpose — it guarantees the vigilance and care of the leadership, and it frightens those who are even momentarily dissident. Confession, leaving no doubt, no possibility of public expostulation, makes assurance doubly sure save where a Radek, double-tongued, or an obdurate Kostov, is in the dock.

The ideology of course finds its succession of father-figures and leaders, and its list of traitorous "fiends,"[19] from Vogt and Bakunin to Tito, inconvenient in the conversion of the sophisticated. On the other hand the intellectually sophisticated persons who join without belief in this aspect of things are rendered malleable by a consciousness of guilt, and of failure in "Communist understanding." Those who are repelled would not make good party members anyway.

This structure of concepts with its ambiguities and its logic, its gods and devils, its promises and threats, could never survive, far less expand, had it no foundation in the social realities of the age and in the aspirations of men. In fact the injustice against which Communism appeals is often real even where most unavoidable, and the sense that ancient wrongs are remediable comes with the strength of intoxication to all who are or who feel oppressed. In its day to day work, because it does not need to fear office with a trouble-

some opposition, the Communist organizations of non-Communist countries can be alert and fearless in finding grievances and pertinacious in demanding remedies even where none can exist. On issues where there is no over-riding Russian fiat, local parties can make use of Marxism as a guide to social reality, to the weak places and the sore spots of society. In these they will effect much, for Marxism, imperfect as science, is diagnostically useful and the grip it gives on the vital processes of society is genuine enough. Communist parties can always attain some measure of sociological realism by virtue of the more important aspects of Marxist thought so long as Russia does not interfere. In addition they can be patient in the promise of victory and the knowledge that with victory they have the right, the duty, and the means to destroy all rivals. Recruited predominantly from the workers and peasants, Communists know where the shoe in fact pinches, though often the ideology forbids the full exploitation or even comprehension of this knowledge. The normal consequence, however, is the strengthening of the hold on the political situation if the leaders are not too casuistical or intellectualized to understand the led.

But even with the limited but real strength which the genuinely scientific part of Marxist sociology gives, with the ancient grievances of many and the dazzle of the ideology, Marxism could be expected to have only a limited attractiveness (especially for the unsophisticated) if it made no appeal to charity, to good-will, and to a disinterested desire to emancipate mankind. Religious fanaticism often, it is true, dispenses with these motives and yet makes converts; but its path is not made easier on this account. And it is at this point that Marxism is particularly interesting. In the literature of Marxism hatred plays a far larger part than love, and disinterestedness is dismissed as a "bourgeois" illusion. The language of "bourgeois" ideals appears, but its use is admittedly disingenuous: justice is part of "double-think" and comradeship is a concept as much of exclusion as of alliance. Indeed, universal charity is expressly postponed to another world, to the millenium, and the less said about it in the present circumstances of the world the better: it is an enervating preoccupation. The immediate appeal is to a desire to be on the win-

---

[19] "Trotsky-Bukharin fiends. . . . Whiteguard pigmies, whose strength was no more than that of a gnat. . . . These Whiteguard insects forgot that the real masters of the Soviet country were the Soviet people, and that the rykovs, bukharins, zinovievs and kamenevs [sic] were only temporary employees of the state, which could at any moment sweep them out from its offices as so much useless rubbish. These contemptible lackeys of the fascists. . . . Trotsky-Bukharin fiends. . . . Bukharin Trotsky gang. . . ." *History of the CPSU* (*b*), Moscow, 1939, pp. 347–8. Cf. G. F. Alexandrov and others, *Joseph Stalin, A Short Biography,* Moscow, 1947, p. 136.

ning side in a battle with the intolerable world. And the unlikely vision is offered of a world of peace and loving kindness springing (dialectically, we must suppose) from the practice of hatred and brutality.

And yet, there is no doubt that the Marxist ideology can appeal to men moved by a large and genuine compassion. How this can be is difficult to determine. It is improbable that there is here nothing but illusion, that the charitable man can find inspiration in Marxism only when he is also preternaturally gullible. And since the charity is often as innocent and genial and straightforward as it can be, it is not enough to recognize in Marxism only the perverted love which conceals itself in cruelty. What seems more likely is that at this important point Marxism is drawing upon emotions, foreign to it, which have a real and important place in our civilization and also in the larger socialist tradition. In short, to many the appeal of Marxism springs from the reflection of a less restricted emotional world which the ideology throws back because of the ambiguous brightness of its surface. And often it is the discovery that this is no part of the ideology, but the image of a world outside, which moves a man to disgust and to desert what he once found so appealing.

12

The "Withering Away of the State" in Theory and Practice*

Robert V. Daniels

(1953)

To say that Soviet leaders are influenced by the Marxist-Leninist world view is not to say that they treat it with hallowed reverence. As Professor Daniels makes very plain in his detailed review of Soviet theory on the role of the state, classical Communist theory, appropriately transmuted, is regularly used merely as

* Reprinted from "The State and Revolution: A Case Study in the Genesis and Transformation of Communist Ideology," *American Slavic and East European Review*, Vol. 12 (1953), pp. 22–43, by permission of the author and the publisher.

a rationalization of the harsh realities of the Soviet regime.

By common agreement among virtually all political complexions, Lenin's *State and Revolution* is accepted as the core of his doctrine of revolution and the proletarian dictatorship.[1] A striking indication of the importance and contemporary relevance attributed to the work has been its use as evidence in the trials of the leaders of the American Communist party for conspiring to overthrow the government. And to the present Soviet commentator no less than to his bitterest adversary, *State and Revolution* sets up the premises from which the Soviet reality of today is considered to be the logical conclusion.

Yet this reasoning cannot be sustained on the basis of logic alone. *State and Revolution* is a work conforming neither to Lenin's previous thought nor to his subsequent practice. It stands as a monument to its author's intellectual deviation during the year of revolution, 1917. Nevertheless, the ideas of *State and Revolution*, permeated with an idealistic, almost utopian spirit, were made to serve as the reference point for rationalizing the subsequent evolution of the Soviet State in an entirely different direction.

In *State and Revolution* Lenin developed in detail for the first time a political program to be followed by the proletarian dictatorship after the expected revolutionary victory. The plan was not complicated in its outlines. It comprised three main provisions for the ordering of the new body politic: (1) the destruction of the repressive machinery of the bourgeois state; (2) the establishment of a real democracy of the working class, with political representatives strictly subordinate to the will of the masses; (3) transference of the tasks of administration directly into the hands of the masses. Lenin summarized the new regime thus:

> The workers, having conquered political power, will break up the old bureaucratic apparatus, they will shatter it to its very foundations, until not one stone is left upon another; and

[1] The preparation of this article was supported by the Russian Research Center of Harvard University, at which the author was formerly a Research Fellow.

they will replace it with a new one consisting of these same workers and employees, *against* whose transformation into bureaucrats measures will at once be undertaken, as pointed out in detail by Marx and Engels: (1) not only electiveness, but also instant recall; (2) payment no higher than that of ordinary workers; (3) immediate transition to a state of things when *all* fulfill the functions of control and superintendence, so that *all* become "bureaucrats" for a time, and *no one*, therefore, can become a "bureaucrat."[2]

Such would be the constitution of the regime which would liquidate the remnants of the bourgeois order, superintend the socialist reorganization of the economy, and pave the way for the transition to the stateless society of communism.

Lenin Shifts Position

State and Revolution, the most developed product of Lenin's thought in 1917, stands in sharp contrast to the main substance of "Leninism" expressed previously and subsequently. This is suggested by the fact that in *State and Revolution* the "party" in the abstract, as an element in the theory of the revolutionary process, is mentioned exactly *once,* and then only obliquely.[3] The central position which the party otherwise usually held in Lenin's thought hardly needs to be stressed. A glance at Lenin's earlier writings readily reveals his accustomed emphasis on the role of the party in the revolutionary movement, and indicates moreover the contrast in organizational spirit with *State and Revolution.* In his famous pamphlet *Čto delat'?* (What Is to Be Done?) Lenin declared, ". . . the spontaneous struggle of the proletariat will not become a genuine 'class struggle' until it is led by a strong organization of revolutionaries," i.e., the party.[4] The party was characteristically for Lenin the

key element in the process of revolution. Within it, ". . . as regards the ideological and practical direction of the movement and the revolutionary struggle of the proletariat, the greatest possible centralization is necessary. . . . To lead the movement we must have the smallest possible number of the most single-minded groups, of professional revolutionaries tested by experience."[5] Far removed is this from the faith in the masses of 1917.

Lenin's characteristic post-revolutionary attitude was typified in the theses which he presented on behalf of the Central Committee of the Communist Party to the Ninth Party Congress in March, 1920 — "iron discipline," "obedience of labor," "centralization of economic administration," were terms in which he described the only course he saw open to the proletarian dictatorship in Russia. He declared frankly that ". . . the elective principle must be replaced by the principle of *selection.*"[6] A year later, at the Tenth Congress, Lenin summed up his current political philosophy in a single phrase, as he denounced the criticisms of the Workers' Opposition: ". . . the dictatorship of the proletariat is impossible except through the Communist Party."[7]

These remarks are only cited as illustrations of the prevailing patterns of Lenin's political thought at various times. They should show sufficiently the extent to which *State and Revolution* is an aberration. The change in Lenin in 1917 was not, however, confined to theory; in his day-to-day political activity, his ideas of tactics, and in his relations with his fellow-revolutionaries in the Bolshevik party, Lenin displayed a shift in 1917 closely corresponding to the temporary modification of his overall political outlook.

Understanding this extensive political change in Lenin is difficult within the limits of the usual conception of the history of the Bolshevik party. Ordinarily the party's pattern of development is seen as a straight line of unfolding Leninist strategy, flanked in either di-

---

[2] *State and Revolution* (New York, 1932), pp. 91–92.

[3] *Ibid.,* pp. 28–29. Lenin is arguing for the leadership of Marxists as against opportunists, and asserts, "By educating a workers' party, Marxism educates the vanguard of the proletariat. . . ." The latter term as well, though a familiar element of Communist jargon, is rarely used by Lenin here; he speaks simply of "the proletariat."

[4] Lenin, *Collected Works* (New York, 1929), II, Book II, 208.

[5] "Pis'mo k tovarišču o nasikh organizacionnykh zadacakh," *Socinenija* (4th ed., Moscow, 1946–1950), VI, 221.

[6] *Protokoly s'ezdov i konferencij vsesojuznoj kommunističeskoj partii(b) Devjatyj s'ezd RKB(b)* (Moscow, 1934), p. 532.

[7] *Protokoly . . . : Desjatyj s'ezd RKP(b),* (Moscow, 1933), p. 128.

rection by deviations which split off. These in the early period dissipate themselves or rejoin the main stream, while in the later period they come to final grief in physical liquidation. This scheme is superficial and inadequate; actually, it corresponds closely to the official Communist picture of the history of the party. More accurately the party should be understood as comprising two fairly distinct lines of thought and policy, extending almost from the inception of the party to the political destruction of the Left Opposition in 1927.[8] The dominant stream of Bolshevism was the Leninist — the familiar doctrine and organization which the party's founder represented up until 1917 and from 1918 on, and of which Stalin inherited the headship. The other ideological and political tendency was represented by various left-wing groups. From this designation it should not be assumed that the Leninist wing was particularly "rightist"; the latter was rather distinguished by its organizational "hardness." Essentially the Leninist and leftist streams of thought originated in separate though partially coincident splits from the prevailing Social-Democratic orthodoxy in two different dimensions — organizational hardness, and programmatic leftism. For a time many followers of these two tendencies believed themselves to be in the same camp, until disagreements arose after the revolution of 1905. However, a large number of future Left Oppositionists, from Trotsky on down, remained outside the Bolshevik ranks as late as 1917.

Between the two wings of the party there were clear-cut and consistent differences of outlook. The leftists stressed the egalitarian and anarchistic social goals of the revolution and pressed for their rapid realization; the Leninists stressed the means of struggle and the organization of power which they considered necessary for the attainment of the goals. The leftists were revolutionary idealists, the Leninists revolutionary pragmatists. In their backgrounds, the leftists tended to be middle class intellectuals; the Leninists, proletarian or peasant and non-intellectual; the

Leninists were less likely to have had experience as émigrés in the West. Understandably, then, the leftists tended toward a theoretical and international outlook, the Leninists toward a practical and national view.

Although the leftist tendency did not enjoy such strength or continuity as did the Leninist, it was nevertheless expressed fairly consistently over the years by a succession of opposition groups — the Otzovists, Ultimatists, and Vperëdists during the period 1907–1912, the "Left Bolsheviks" during the war years, the Left Communists in 1918, the Democratic Centralists and the Workers' Opposition during the period of War Communism, the Trotskyists in 1921 and again from 1923 to 1927. In 1917, the leftist group for a time stepped out of its oppositionist role, and became the dominant force in the party. This was due not only to the revolutionary situation and the influx of the non-Bolshevik leftists, but also to the fact that Lenin himself shifted from the Leninist wing to the leftist wing of the party! This is why Lenin's April Theses were such a shock to the cautious Leninism of the majority of the people from the underground Bolshevik organization. Proceeding and gaining momentum, the leftist upsurge carried the party through 1917 and, overriding objections on the part of some of Lenin's formerly closest disciples consummated the victory of October. *State and Revolution*, placed in its proper context as the most complete formulation of the leftist program, begins to make some sense.

Sources of the New Program

What were the sources of the egalitarian and anarchistic program set forth by Lenin in *State and Revolution*, and in particular why did he stress so much the question of "smashing" the bourgeois state? Up until 1916 Lenin, in company with most of his Social-Democratic contemporaries, had given little or no attention to the problems treated in *State and Revolution*, or to the works of Marx and Engels in which they were originally discussed. Quite suddenly, in late 1916 and early 1917, he developed an avid interest in these matters, and commenced the study and writing which eventually took published form in *State and Revolution*. This sudden focus of attention on the theory of the revolutionary state immediately preceded Lenin's shift over to the left-

---

[8] This interpretation has been developed at length by the present author in a doctoral dissertation, "The Left Opposition in the Russian Communist Party, to 1924," Harvard University, 1950.

ist stream of Bolshevik thought, and was apparently instrumental in precipitating his change of outlook.

The principal credit for inspiring the new trend in Lenin's political thought belongs to Nikolaj Bukharin, later an eminent Communist theoretician, leader of the Right Opposition against Stalin, and finally shot in 1938. Up to 1918 Bukharin was the chief leader of the left-wing Bolsheviks. In 1916 he wrote a number of extremely interesting articles on the relation of the state to the Socialist revolution. The influence which these had on Lenin was indicated in the collection of Lenin's notes and miscellaneous writings, *Leninskij Sbornik* (Lenin Collection), published in 1924, in an editorial note appended to the materials relating to this period:

> Under the pseudonym of "Nota Bene" N. I. Bukharin placed in No. 6 of the journal "The Youth International" [Jugendinternationale] an article on the question of the state, in which he subjected to criticism the "commonly held" but in fact Kautskian interpretation of the teaching of Marx on the state. It was precisely this article which induced Vladimir Il'ich to occupy himself more closely with the corresponding question. From the article prepared by Vladimir Il'ich . . . arose his work *State and Revolution*.[9]

In the body of his letter to Alexandra Kollontay of February 17, 1917, to which the above note referred, Lenin wrote:

> I am preparing . . . an article on the question of the relation of Marxism to the state. I have already come to conclusions more sharply against Kautsky than against Bukharin. . . .[10]

The article by Bukharin to which Lenin referred was "Der imperialistische Raubstaat," which appeared in *Jugendinternationale* on December 1, 1916. It was one of a series of articles in which Bukharin developed the idea that a fundamental task of the proletarian revolution was the literal destruction of the existing bourgeois state. The rationale of this program Bukharin set forth most profoundly in another article, where he revealed what in retrospect can be seen as amazing prophetic insight. This was "Teorija imperialističeskogo gosudarstva" (The Theory of the Imperialist State), an essay so apt as an analysis of a major social trend of the twentieth century that its virtual oblivion imperatively should be remedied.[11]

Bukharin in this article advanced the thesis that in the era of imperialism a new form of political and social organization was evolving out of bourgeois society. "Militaristic state capitalism," he termed this incipient new order, under which

> the state power . . . sucks in almost all areas of production; it not only embraces the general conditions of the exploitative process; the state becomes more and more a direct exploiter, which organizes and directs production, as a collective capitalist.[12]

The ultimate result of this tendency would be ". . . a new Leviathan, in comparison with which the fantasy of Thomas Hobbes seems like child's play."[13] Socialism, in Bukharin's mind, had nothing in common with the totalitarian, bureaucratic state whose possible evolution he foresaw.

> Socialism is the regulation of production directed by *society*, not by the state . . . it is the abolition of class contradictions, not their intensification.[14]

---

[9] *Leninskij Sbornik* (Moscow, Lenin Institute, 1924), II, 284, note 7. This volume was published under the editorial direction of Leo Kamenev, who at that time was included together with Bukharin among the political "ins" of the Communist Party.

[10] *Ibid.*, pp. 282–83.

[11] Bukharin originally wrote this article in the middle of 1916 with the intention of publishing it in the semi-periodical *Sbornik Sotsial-Demokrata* edited by Lenin, but the article was rejected. It ultimately appeared in 1925 in *Revoljucija prava* (Moscow, Communist Academy), Sbornik I. In a note attached to the article at the time of publication (p. 5, note 1), Bukharin advanced as the explanation for the original rejection the surmise that the editorial board "did not consider it possible to publish the article because it felt that there were developed here incorrect views about the state." In contrast to this, Lenin said in his letter to Kollontay of February, 1917 (*Leninskij Sbornik*, II, 283), that it was simply the lack of funds which prevented the publication of the next number of the *Sbornik*, in which Bukharin's article was already scheduled to be included. This may indicate that Lenin was moving towards Bukharin's left-wing position faster than the latter thought.

[12] *Revoljucija prava*, I, 21.

[13] *Ibid.*, p. 30.

[14] *Ibid.*, p. 26.

The proletarian revolution is not simply the midwife of the new socialist society which is bound to come forth at some moment from the shell of capitalistic society; there are two alternative successors to capitalism — "militaristic state capitalism," under which the whole force of social organization bears down on the proletariat to exploit it, where "the worker is transformed into a slave" — *or* socialism.

> Theoretically, there can be two possibilities here: either the workers' organizations, like all the organizations of the bourgeoisie, will merge into the state-wide organization and be transformed into a simple appendage of the state apparatus, or they will outgrow the framework of the state and burst it from within, as they organize their own state power (the dictatorship [of the proletariat]).[15]

The proletarian revolution was assigned the crucial task of forcing the development of society out of the course toward state capitalism, and into the course toward socialism. (Bukharin, to his personal misfortune, was of course unaware of the possibility that a successful proletarian revolution might fail to divert the course of history and, under certain conditions, actually accelerate the evolution of the Leviathan which he so feared.)

The tactical conclusion which Bukharin derived from his theory of contemporary social evolution was ultra-radical, ". . . a general attack on the ruling bandits. In the developing revolutionary struggle the proletariat destroys the state organization of the bourgeoisie. . . ."[16] This dictum was echoed by Lenin in *State and Revolution:* "A revolution must not consist in a new class ruling, governing with the help of the old state machinery, but in this class *smashing* this machinery and ruling, governing by means of *new* machinery."[17]

With this attitude toward the old political order Bukharin and Lenin were following in the footsteps of certain left-wing European Marxists, notably the Dutch Social-Democrat Anton Pannekoek, an astronomer by profession, but by avocation a revolutionary theorist. Pannekoek posed the thesis that

> The state power is not a simple neutral object

in the class struggle; it is a weapon and a fortress of the bourgeoisie, the strongest support, without which the bourgeoisie could never retain its place.[18]

This view was the basis for his contention that

> The struggle of the proletariat is not simply a struggle against the bourgeoisie *over* the state power as an object, but a struggle *against* the state power. . . . The content of this revolution is the destruction and dissolution of the state's means of force by the proletariat's means of force.[19]

The State Machinery and the Class Struggle

Underlying the emphasis which Pannekoek, Bukharin, and (following them) Lenin placed on revolution as an act of smashing the state, was an aspect of Marxian political theory which was subject to a great deal of misunderstanding. This was the question of the relation of the state machinery to the class struggle; specifically, was the existence of the political power exclusively a product of the class struggle? As popularly understood the doctrine of Marxism is simple; the state is nothing more than the organ of the ruling class to suppress the masses and maintain the conditions of exploitation.[20] Bukharin, for example, even in "The Theory of the Imperialist State," defined the state thus:

> From the point of view of Marxism, the state is nothing other than the greatest general organization of the ruling classes, the basic function of which consists of the preservation and extension of the exploitation of the oppressed classes.[21]

---

[15] *Ibid.,* p. 30.

[16] *Ibid.,* pp. 31–32.

[17] *State and Revolution,* p. 96.

[18] "Imperializm i zadači proletariata," published in Russian translation in Lenin's journal *Kommunist* No. 1–2 (Geneva, 1915), p. 74. Strangely enough, the ideas which it developed seem not to have come to Lenin's own attention until Bukharin took them up later.

[19] "Massenaktion und Revolution," *Die Neue Zeit,* July 12, 19, and 26, 1912. This article had much direct influence on Lenin at the end of 1916, as the materials in *Leninskij Sbornik,* Vol. XIV, indicate.

[20] R. N. Carew-Hunt, *The Theory and Practice of Communism: An Introduction* (New York, 1951), pp. 64–65.

[21] *Revoljucija prava,* I, 7.

Lenin, in *State and Revolution*, is on this point quite clear: no class conflict, no state.[22]

Reference to the original sources of the theory, however, reveals a different implication. Engels, in *The Origin of the Family, Private Property, and the State*, explained the development of political institutions thus:

> The state, then, is by no means a power forced on society from the outside. . . . It is simply a product of society at a certain stage of evolution. It is the confession that this society has become hopelessly divided against itself, has entangled itself in irreconcilable contradictions which it is powerless to banish. In order that these contradictions, these classes with conflicting economic interests, may not annihilate themselves and society in a useless struggle, a power becomes necessary that stands apparently above society and has the function of keeping down the conflicts and maintaining "order." And this power, the outgrowth of society, but assuming supremacy over it and becoming more and more divorced from it, is the state.[23]

Engels made here a point that most of his successors never really grasped: that the class struggle explains the *origin* of the state, but not necessarily its *continued existence*. Once established, the state organization tends to become its own *raison d'être*, and can exist more and more independently of the conditions which originally produced it. To be sure, the state continues to play a role in the class struggle:

> The state is the result of the desire to keep down class conflicts, but having arisen amid these conflicts, it is as a rule the state of the most powerful economic class that by force of its economic supremacy becomes also the ruling political class and thus acquires new means of subduing and exploiting the oppressed masses.[24]

This and other tasks which the state is called upon to perform simply increase the power, scope, and independence of the state organization:

> This public power of coercion . . . increases in the same ratio in which the class antagonisms

become more pronounced, and in which neighboring states become larger and more populous. A conspicuous example is modern Europe, where the class struggles and wars of conquest have nursed the public power to such a size that it threatens to swallow the whole society. . . .[25]

Here Engels took account of a particularly important aspect of the modern state — as a unit in an anarchistic international society, with the consequent pressures of defense and/or aggrandizement — an aspect ignored almost totally in most Marxist thought on the state, but an aspect which nevertheless played a key role in Soviet political rationalizations after the revolution.

Marx himself employed the idea that the state can become an independent source of evil in society, apart from any given ruling class. This was the tendency which he observed in France, whose government until 1848 had been

> . . . a mere tool in the hands of the dominant class. Not until the second Bonaparte rose to power, does the State seem to have become completely independent. As against bourgeois society, the State machine has fortified itself so thoroughly that the chief of the Society of December the Tenth [Louis Bonaparte's brownshirts] can function as its director. . . .[26]

Later on, Marx analyzed the Bonaparte dictatorship of the Second Empire as an instance of the particular independence which the state power was able to acquire at a time when the contending social classes, in this case bourgeoisie and proletariat, were nearly evenly balanced in strength.

> . . . it was the only form of government possible at a time when the bourgeoisie had already lost, and the working class had not yet acquired, the faculty of ruling the nation.[27]

The interesting point here lies in Marx's reference to "ruling the nation," which by the implication of this context represents some kind of a social function which has to be carried on entirely apart from the class struggle. This suggests that the class struggle theory of the state was all along supposed to be understood in a limited sense, as referring only to that aspect of social organization which con-

---

[22] *State and Revolution*, pp. 10–11.
[23] *The Origin of the Family, Private Property, and the State* (Chicago, 1902), p. 206.
[24] *Ibid.*, p. 208.

[25] *Ibid.*, p. 207.
[26] *The Eighteenth Brumaire of Louis Bonaparte* (New York, 1926), pp. 130–31.
[27] *The Civil War in France* (Chicago, n.d.), p. 42.

cerned the means by which one class repressed another. Close analysis of *State and Revolution* reveals that Lenin, by way of the restricted definitions which he employs, made precisely this tacit assumption.

Proceeding from the recognition that the state power could become dangerously independent, Marx drew upon the experience of the Paris Commune for a prescription of the course of action which should be taken to ensure a successful proletarian revolution. In *The Civil War in France* he outlined the measures which would have to be taken in order to end permanently the threat to the proletariat posed by the old state institutions, and to

> . . . restore to the social body all the forces hitherto absorbed by the state parasite feeding upon, and clogging the free movement of, society.[28]

Complete democratic control over all political functions was to be assured by election of all officials, the right of immediate recall of elected officials, limitation of the salaries of all government officials to the level of workmen's wages, local and municipal autonomy as far as practicable, and above all the replacement of all police and military formations by the national guard, i.e., the collectivity of the population, the "armed people."[29]

Marx commented on the program of the Commune itself:

> The few but important functions which still would remain for a central government . . . were to be discharged by Communal, and therefore strictly responsible agents. . . . While the merely repressive organs of the old governmental power were to be amputated, its legitimate functions were to be wrested from an authority usurping pre-eminence over society itself, and restored to the responsible agents of society. Instead of deciding once in three or six years which member of the ruling class was to represent the people in Parliament, universal suffrage was to serve the people, constituted in Communes, as individual suffrage serves every other employer in the search for the workmen and managers in his business. . . . nothing could be more foreign to the spirit of the Commune than to supersede universal suffrage by hierarchic investiture.

> . . . the Commune . . . was a thoroughly expansive political form, while all previous forms of government had been emphatically repressive. Its true secret was this. It was essentially a working-class government, the product of the struggle of the producing against the appropriating class, the political form at last discovered under which to work out the economic emancipation of Labor.[30]

Engels, in his 1891 introduction to *The Civil War in France*, went even further in his political conclusions:

> The Commune was compelled to recognize from the outset that the working class, once come to power, could not carry on business with the old state machine; that, in order not to lose again its own position of power which it had but just conquered, this working class must, on the one hand, set aside all the old repressive machinery previously used against itself, and on the other, *safeguard itself against its own deputies and officials* by declaring them all, without any exception, subject to recall at any moment. . . . What had been the characteristic attribute of the former state? Society had created its own organs to look after its common interests, originally through simple division of labor. But these organs at whose head was the state power, had in the course of time, in pursuance of their own special interests, transformed themselves from the servants of society into the masters of society. . . .[31]

In this manner Engels derived from his conception of the independent existence of the state an imperative directive for action to protect the socialist society. The state is not ultimately a derivative of the class struggle, but was (in Engels' Rousseauan phraseology) "created" by "society" "to look after its common interests." The class aspect is an auxiliary feature, acquired in the course of history. Hence there is no reason to conclude that with the termination of the class struggle by a proletarian revolution, the state will necessarily wither away; it simply ceases to be an organ of *class* repression, because there are no more classes to be repressed by each other. Not only does the state still exist; it continues to be a threat to the successful establishment of a socialist so-

---

[28] *Ibid.*, p. 47.
[29] *Ibid.*, p. 42.

[30] *Ibid.*, pp. 45–48.
[31] *The Civil War in France* (New York, 1940), p. 20.

ciety because of the possibility of "transforming itself into the master of society." Therefore it is imperative for the proletariat to take the measures which Marx outlines, in order that the institutions which must exist to carry out necessary social functions will not be able to dominate the population which they are supposed to serve.

> Against this transformation of the state and the organs of the state from servants of society into masters of society — a process which had been inevitable in all previous states — the Commune made use of two infallible remedies. In the first place, it filled all posts — administrative, judicial, and educational — by election on the basis of universal suffrage of all concerned, with the right of these electors to recall their delegate at any time. And in the second place, all officials, high or low, were paid only the wages received by other workers.[32]

This action by the Commune Engels hailed as the "shattering of the former state power and its replacement by a new and really democratic state."[33]

Lenin had no sooner acquainted himself with the program of smashing the bourgeois state than he incorporated it wholeheartedly into his scheme of the revolutionary process. The idea of smashing the state proved quickly to be irresistible to Lenin as a set of political tactics. However, he failed to grasp the basic rationale of the smashing dictum — protection of society against the dangerous independence of the state machinery — and as a result he allowed the entire program of mass control over the exercise of political power to be vitiated after his party came to power. Lenin did not go beyond the narrow class-determined conception of the state. This simple view, justifying all the rigorous measures taken in the name of the dictatorship of the proletariat, and assuring the ultimate prospect of the withering away of the state and political coercion, was the generally accepted premise of the political doctrine of the Communist Party. (The subtleties of Marx and Engels about the broader aspects of political institutions have remained in a convenient oblivion as far as Communist theoreticians have been concerned.)

In *State and Revolution* Lenin followed Engels on the withering of the narrowly conceived state:

> . . . once the majority of the people *itself* suppresses its oppressors, a "special force" for suppression is *no longer necessary.* In this sense the state *begins to wither away.* Instead of a privileged minority . . . the majority can itself directly fulfill all these functions; and the more the discharge of the functions of state power devolves upon the people generally, the less need is there for the existence of this power.[34]

It was, however, only to the state in the narrow sense, as an instrument for class repression, that Lenin applied the dicta of smashing and democratic controls (measures originally designed for application to the state in the broad sense to keep it from becoming the "master of society"). His shift after the October Revolution to his characteristically greater emphasis on pragmatic and power considerations was foreshadowed even in *State and Revolution* as he revealed his readiness to yield, outside the realm of the narrowly "political," to pressures for the maintenance of a strong institutional authority and for the retention of the old bureaucractic and managerial personnel. The anarchistic ideal, he reasoned, was rendered utopian in economic affairs by the actual development of the conditions of production under industrialism:

> Take a factory, a railway, a vessel on the high seas . . . is it not clear that not one of these complex technical units, based on the use of machines and the ordered cooperation of many people, could function without a certain amount of subordination and, consequently, without some authority or power?[35]

Lenin was frank in recognizing the preferred position which this requirement conferred on trained technical and managerial personnel inherited from the old regime:

> We need good organizers in banking, and in the work of combining enterprises (in these matters the capitalists have more experience, and work is done more easily with experienced people); we need more and more engineers, agronomists, technicians, scientific experts of every kind. . . . Probably, we shall only gradu-

---

[32] *Ibid.,* p. 21.
[33] *Ibid.*

[34] *State and Revolution,* p. 37.
[35] *Ibid.,* p. 52.

ally bring in equality for all work, leaving a temporary higher rate of pay for such specialists during the transition period, but we shall put them under an all embracing workers' control. . . . As for the organizational form of the work, we do not invent it, we take it ready-made from capitalism. . . .[36]

The prospects for a flourishing institutional structure outside the context of the withering political state were indicated by Lenin in his speech to the First Congress of Economic Councils in May, 1918:

> There is no doubt that the further the conquests of the October Revolution advance . . . the greater and higher will become the role of the economic councils, which alone among all state institutions will preserve for themselves a lasting place that will become all the more permanent the nearer we come to the establishment of a socialist system, the less we need a purely administrative apparatus, an apparatus engaged only in government, strictly speaking. This apparatus is doomed, after the resistance of the exploiters has definitely been smashed, after the toilers have learned to organize socialist production — this apparatus of administration in the proper, narrow, restricted sense of the word, this apparatus of the old state is doomed to die; but an apparatus of the type of our Supreme Economic Council is destined to grow, develop, and become strong, fulfilling all principal active functions of an organized society.[37]

This was yet another effort to reconcile the narrow, strictly class conception of the state with the patent necessity of over-all social organization and authority to direct the growingly complex affairs of modern society. The "state" might wither away, to be sure, but the scope of "state" and "withering" were being progressively constricted.

Beyond the October Revolution

Very rapidly after the October Revolution the dominant orientation of the party and its leadership shifted from program and ideals to the problems of organizing and defending political power; the party again rose to the forefront in the Bolshevik system of thought. Most party members ceased to take the program of *State and Revolution* seriously, at least not in their day-to-day activity. This neglect became general under the pressure of the civil war. The soviets, supposedly embodying the control measures of the 1917 program, fell into abeyance, as the locus of real political power shifted to the party and especially to the higher organs of the party. Military and economic stress, the practical and military orientation of the party, the necessity of recourse to bureaucratic methods to make the government, economy, and army function, and the limitations in the program itself as understood, all combined to defeat the democratic spirit of the revolutionary ideology and to facilitate the formation of a new bureaucratic, hierarchical political order.

A rearguard action, hopeless under these conditions, was fought by the leftist opposition groups in the party — the Workers' Opposition and the Democratic Centralists — to defend the spirit of *State and Revolution* against the bureaucratic expediencies which the majority of the party was freely condoning. All thought of formally limiting political authority from below was dismissed by most Communists. Strong state power, under the firm control of the party as the vanguard of the proletariat, was held to be the indispensable instrument of the dictatorship of the proletariat in carrying through the socialist revolution and suppressing the resistance of the dispossessed classes.

The theory of the state as the instrument of the dictatorship of the proletariat in the period of transition, consolidation, and building of socialism served effectively to put out of mind the real problems of the relation of the state to society and the dangers of the state becoming independent of mass control and the "master of society." It was in this theoretical context, or lack of context, that the Soviet State, independent of any popular control or class domination, did in fact become the "master of society," realizing more accurately that one could ever expect the fears expressed by Marx and Bukharin.

This institutional evolution has been mirrored in ideology. Changes in the field of political theory provide a striking illustration

---

36 "Will the Bolsheviks Retain State Power?" *Collected Works* (New York, 1932), XXI, Book II, 33.

37 *Sočinenija* (3rd ed., Moscow, 1935), XXIII, 36.

of the post-revolutionary transformation in Soviet thinking. From the view of the state as a necessary evil destined to wither away after the revolutionary social transformation was accomplished, party doctrine has shifted around 180 degrees, to extol the state as the highest form of social organization and a great creative force.

Like most of the theoretical content of party ideology, the doctrine of the state remained substantially unchanged from the Revolution to 1929. The extensive evolution in political practice and institutions which took place up to that time, the decline of the soviets and the rise of the party, were subsumed under the category of the dictatorship of the proletariat, which was still officially expected to lead into the withering away of the state when the resistance of remnants of the exploiting classes had been finally overcome. The one potentially significant development was Stalin's theory of socialism in one country, which, in asserting the possibility of socialism being achieved under conditions of capitalist encirclement, contained in embryo a justification for the retention of the state under socialism to meet the needs of defense.

Some foretaste of the state of mind which was later to prevail was provided by developments on the theory of the political role of the party, which accompanied the consolidation of power in the hands of Stalin and the party secretariat. The dynamic scheme whereby the revolution was to be made in the ultimate interest of the whole population, by the workers, under the leadership of the vanguard of the proletariat, the party, was transformed into a static pattern for the organization of the revolutionary regime in a sharply stratified and hierarchical form.

. . . the party is not only indispensable to the proletariat for the establishment of the dictatorship. It becomes even more necessary after the seizure of power in order to maintain the dictatorship of the proletariat, to consolidate and enlarge it with a view to inaugurating a completely socialized order. . . . The proletarian masses must be imbued with the spirit of discipline and organization; . . . the proletarian masses must be inoculated against the harmful influence of the petty bourgeoisie,

must be prevented from acquiring petty-bourgeois habits and customs.[38]

Thus did Stalin demonstrate his distrust of the masses, who could not be relied on to behave in a socialist fashion without external compulsion. Stalin was in practice coming to consider the party, and conscious top-level political leadership, as the prime mover of history (a not unnatural attitude toward the role which he himself was coming to play). It was the party, rather than spontaneous economic evolution, which must be looked to primarily for the preparation of "the conditions for the inauguration of socialist production."[39]

State and Revolution *under Stalin*

In 1930 Stalin first explicitly modified the doctrine of the withering-away of the state.

We are in favor of the state dying out, and at the same time we stand for the strengthening of the dictatorship of the proletariat, which represents the most powerful and mighty authority of all forms of state which have existed up to the present day. The highest possible development of the power of the state, with the object of preparing the conditions of the dying out of the state: that is the Marxist formula. Is it "contradictory"? Yes, it is "contradictory." But this contradiction is a living thing, and completely reflects Marxist dialectics.[40]

Four years later, Stalin strengthened this view by incorporating the experience of the violent imposition of central power which characterized the period of the first Five Year Plan and collectivization:

It goes without saying that a classless society cannot come of itself, spontaneously, as it were. It has to be achieved and built by the efforts of all the working people, by strengthening the organs of the dictatorship of the proletariat, by intensifying the class struggle, by abolishing classes, by eliminating the remnants of the

---

[38] Stalin, "Foundation of Leninism" (1924), in *Leninism* (New York, 1928), pp. 169–70.
[39] *Ibid*.
[40] Political Report to the Sixteenth Party Congress (1930), *Leninism* (New York, 1933), II, 402.

capitalist classes, and in battles with enemies both internal and external.[41]

Worries about the state power becoming dangerously independent were dispersed by the narrow class conception of the state which Marxists by this time accepted almost universally. The Soviet State was the state of the working class, and hence by definition could do naught but serve the interests of the proletariat. The stronger the state and the party, the better would the interests of the proletariat be served. From this it followed that the idealistically-minded oppositionists in the party who from time to time ventured to protest the growing centralization of power were "objectively" undermining the revolutionary cause and rendering themselves liable to appropriate measures of discipline. As to the ultimate disposition of the state with its manifest bureaucratic tendencies, the final achievement of communism would automatically cause the withering of the state and all its problems. Evidently there were growing misgivings in the party over this, for Stalin found it necessary to discredit the concern felt by some Bukharinists, apparently over the failure of the state to begin to show signs of withering away. Referring to "a little confusion and . . . unhealthy sentiments among a section of party members," he asserted:

. . . they began to reason in this way: If it is classless society, then we can relax the class struggle, we can relax the dictatorship of the proletariat, and get rid of the state altogether, since it is fated to die out soon in any case. They dropped into a state of moon-calf ecstasy, in the expectation that soon there will be no classes, and therefore no class struggle, and therefore no cares and worries, and therefore we can lay down our arms and retire — to sleep and to wait for the advent of classless society. (General laughter.) It goes without saying that if this confusion of mind and these non-Bolshevik sentiments obtained a hold over the majority of our Party, the Party would find itself demobilized and disarmed.[42]

In accord with actual political developments, the role of political power and organization was moving to the forefront of Communist theory.

It was on the basis of the above pronouncements of Stalin that party spokesmen were able to argue the continued need to strengthen the state when, with the introduction of the Constitution of 1936, socialism was declared to have been achieved. ". . . all the exploiting classes have now been eliminated," Stalin declared; there remained three cooperating groups, workers, peasants, and the "Soviet intelligentsia."[43]

Nevertheless, the struggle against the remnants of the exploiting classes had to be intensified:

The specific gravity of the hostile elements in our Soviet structure is unusually low, almost equal to zero, but even so these elements can resort to the sharpest forms of struggle with us.[44]

"Vigilance against the enemies of the Soviet State" provided the theoretical heading under which was subsumed in all its ramifications the Great Purge.

For a definitive new theory of the state, the party had to wait until Stalin got around to making a statement. This he did at the Eighteenth Party Congress in 1939.[45] He was faced with the problem of developing a more convincing rationalization for the obviously permanent Leviathan state whose construction had just been completed, a political order which blatantly contravened the withering prognosis of Marxian theory.

At the Congress, Stalin casually and sketchily indicated the outlines of his new theory of the Soviet state. Once he had spoken, his words were seized upon in the now familiar pattern, and broadcast, amplified, elaborated upon, interpreted and canonized into the body of infallible revolutionary truth: "Comrade

---

[41] "Report to the Seventeenth Party Congress" (1934), *Problems of Leninism* (English ed., Moscow, 1940), pp. 517–18.
[42] *Ibid.*, p. 518.

[43] Stalin, "On the Draft Constitution of the USSR," *Problems of Leninism* (Moscow, 1940), pp. 564–67.
[44] M. Mitin, "O likvidacii klassov v SSSR i socialističeskom, vsenarodnom gosudarstve," *Pod znamenem Marksizma*, No. 5 (1936), p. 8.
[45] *Problems of Leninism* (Moscow, 1940), pp. 656–63.

Stalin raised the Marxist-Leninist doctrine of the state to a new, higher level," was the theme running through all these commentaries.[46]

Comrade Stalin certainly did raise the Marxist-Leninist doctrine of the state to a new, higher level. He raised it from the level of a superstructural dependence on economic forces and class contradictions, a temporarily necessary evil from the standpoint of revolution, to the level of a prime mover of history and a positive social good. We now have, at every turn in Soviet writings, "The Soviet state, a state of a new type, the most democratic in the world, the chief instrument for the overcoming of class differences and for the preparation of the material and spiritual prerequisites for the transition to communism."

By one of the typically labored feats of common sense which pass for genius in the Soviet Union, Stalin brought the Marxian theory of the state down to Soviet earth by recalling some of the most prosaic aspects of the state which had been abstracted out of the realm of the political by the restricted class conception of the state.

Without the pretentiousness which the significance of his remarks might have justified, Stalin began his cursory re-examination of the political theory of the Soviet state by considering the obvious question, why has the state not begun to wither away? The very posing of such a question, he asserted, indicated an erroneous approach to the whole problem, by people who followed theory too literally without regard to the complexities of practice. Vyshinsky had in an article published shortly before been much harsher with the questioners; treachery, he termed it, to suppose that

> . . . the process of the withering of the state will be realized not through the maximum strengthening of the state power of the proletariat, but through the weakening of this power.[47]

Stalin had particularly in mind the implications of the international context in which socialism was being built in the Soviet Union; the necessity of the state for national defense

was obvious. Whether consciously or not, he was taking advantage of one of the serious weaknesses of the ordinary narrow Marxist view of the state; he pointed to very real considerations — such as defense — which were not taken into account in the narrow class theory of the state, but which could hardly be denied. These considerations he used to justify political developments which would seem inexplicable if not intolerable from the old point of view. In this way Stalin undertook to correct the doctrine of the withering of the state as formulated by Engels. He contended that Engels had reasoned in abstraction from the international context, with his assumption of the simultaneous victory of socialism in most or all states. However, Stalin was either partially ignorant of Engels' views, or chose to distort them. Engels had specifically referred to international pressures in accounting for the growth of the supra-class aspects of the state as the master of society. The socialist revolution would necessarily have to be international, in order to eliminate the needs of defense which so encouraged the tendency toward bureaucracy. This point, however, had been entirely overlooked in all the discussions on socialism in one country.

Having established the orthodoxy of the socialist revolution in national isolation, Stalin was able to justify all the features of the traditional state which were associated with national security — he referred particularly to the army, intelligence service, and penal institutions. In fact, the whole of Stalin's new political theory can be described as the shift from the narrow class theory of the state back to the broad conception of the state as an institution of social service, compulsion, and action, standing above classes (though of course influenced by the class structure of society). Stalin was simply recognizing the emergence of the supra-class state which Marx, Engels, and Bukharin warned against. But in his evaluation of this state he differed diametrically with them.

An almost conventional and common-sense attitude was suggested in Stalin's description of the development of the Soviet state and its functions, a development which he broke down into two phases: phase one, to the elimination of the exploiting classes; phase two, afterwards. The state in phase one had three func-

[46] See, for example, the collection *Učenie Lenina-Stalina o gosudarstve* (Voronež, 1940).
[47] "Lenin i Stalin o gosudarstve i prave," *Bol'ševik*, No. 1 (1939), p. 34.

tions: (1) the familiar work of the dictatorship of the proletariat, suppressing the exploiting classes; (2) national defense — following logically from the doctrine of socialism in one country; (3) a new idea — the beginnings of "the economic-organizing and cultural-educational work of the organs in our state, which had as its goal the development of the sprouts of a new, socialist economy and the reeducation of people in the spirit of socialism." (Here we can see the complete divergence from Marxism, in conceiving of economic and cultural development as the results of political organization and action.) This positive role of the state was completely foreign to the narrow class view of the state. The functions described here had earlier been thought of as the nonpolitical administrative operations which would devolve upon society as the state withered away; this was, for example, the course envisaged by Lenin in his speech on the economic councils in May, 1918.

In phase two,

> The function of military suppression within the country fell off, died away, for the exploiters were annihilated, there are no more exploiters left to suppress. In place of the function of suppression the state has taken on the function of defense of socialist property from thieves and embezzlers of the people's goods.

Even if euphemistically, Stalin was forced to recognize in his theoretical system the extreme tensions in Soviet society and the need for the regime to rely on police repression. The second function, defense, continues under phase two, while the third, the development of the economy and educational work by the state, becomes fully extended.

Finally, Stalin asked himself the crucial question:

> Will we also retain the state even in the period of communism?
>
> Yes, it will be retained, if the capitalist encirclement is not liquidated. . . .
>
> No, it will not be retained but will die away, if the capitalist encirclement is liquidated, if it is replaced by a socialist encirclement.
>
> Thus do matters stand on the question of the socialist state.

And thus have matters stood ever since, with innumerable commentaries on Stalin's brief statement, but with no positive contributions

to the theory save Stalin's own contained in his article "On Marxism in Linguistics" in June, 1950. Earlier constructions of Marxist political theory have been recast in the spiirt of Stalin's broad conception of the state as independent of class society and charged with a variety of positive roles. Typical of this effort to reinterpret Communist doctrine is a recent article by one V. V. Nikolaev,[48] which amounted to an exercise in tying together in a chain of historical logic both the present Soviet regime and the Bolshevik program of 1917. As is characteristic in the application of Communist ideology to the rationalization of the Soviet regime, the connection was established with the use of broad ideological categories — "socialism," "democracy," "classless," "mass participation" — terms which were always loose and whose practical content was subjected to drastic change. This accomplished the formal identification of present practice and the ideal of *State and Revolution*. Effectively suppressed were the vast substantive differences between them which had resulted from two decades of the most rapid social change.

The new Stalinist conception of the state was an adaptation of theory to reality, a correction of the narrow Marxist approach which had been overwhelmed by events. In the Soviet Union there was a state, independent of classes and the class struggle, growing more powerful as "class" (though not "strata") differences were supposed to be disappearing; moreover, this state was not the mere product or reflection of deeper economic and social conditions — it had become a prime mover of history. Accordingly, Stalin could revise the basic Marxist conception of the social process and revolution, as he did in discussing the problem of base and superstructure (referring especially to the political organs of society) in relation to language:

> The superstructure is generated by the base, but this by no means signifies that it merely reflects the base, that it is passive, neutral and indifferent to the fate of its base, to the fate of classes, to the character of the system. On the contrary, having put in an appearance, it then becomes a most active force which has contributed vigorously to the formation and con-

---

[48] "V. I. Lenin o sovetskom gosudarstve," *Voprosy filosofii*, No. 2 (1950).

solidation of its base, takes all steps to assist
the new order to drive the old base and the
former classes into the dust and liquidate
them.[49]

Marx has been turned on his head. Bukharin
has been shot. The Leviathan has come into
its own.

THE COMMUNIST PARTY

13

Development and Functioning of the Party*

Barrington Moore, Jr.

(1944)

*The bald fact of the Communist Party's dom-
inance in Soviet affairs largely precludes any
major difference of opinion concerning its role.
In the selections we present on the Party,
therefore, we rather by-pass this issue, concentrating on explorations of the organization
of the Party, the functions it actually performs,
the composition of its membership, and the
elements of continuity and change in its development. Professor Moore provides the main
outline, bringing his survey down to the end
of World War II. While quite well aware
of the raw facts of power in Party affairs, he
gives more recognition than do many others to
the ability of the lower Party organs to manage
their own affairs.*

What happens to a revolutionary group
when it has been in power for over a genera-

49 "On Marxism in Linguistics," Pravda, June 20,
1950; translated in the Current Digest of the
Soviet Press, July 17, 1950.
* Reprinted from "The Communist Party of the
Soviet Union: 1928-44," American Sociological
Review, Vol. 9 (1944), pp. 267-278, by permis-
sion of the author and the American Sociological
Association.

tion and forced to face the problems of governing a large modern nation? Has the Communist Party of the Soviet Union, traditionally
associated with the underdog, developed into
some variety of ruling class? Or is it merely
a non-hereditary elite? If so, what are the
more important characteristics of this elite?
How do they exercise their control over the
life of the people? How are policy and leadership determined within this group? Are the
leaders and their policy democratically controlled by the Party membership, as many
apologists for the Soviets have claimed, or is
the Party merely the passive tool of a cruel
and ruthless dictatorship, as many disillusioned
leftists and liberals have asserted? The present
paper[1] is an effort to present a partial answer
to these and certain other similar questions,
which are significant both from the point of
view of sociological theory and practical politics, two fields which are enriched by mutual
contact.

Basic to an understanding of the Communist
Party of the Soviet Union is the fact that since
1928 the U.S.S.R. has been engaged in an industrial and agricultural revolution directed by
the Party. Prior to the Five Year Plans, the
Soviet Union inherited from Tsarist Russia a
country that was chiefly agricultural. During
the twelve year period, 1928–1940, Soviet
industrial output increased 7.5 times.[2] Simi-

1 The primary sources are: (1) Stenographic reports of the Party Congresses of 1927, 1930, 1934,
and 1939. The complete stenographic report of the
1939 Congress is not available in Washington.
Therefore it is necessary to rely on newspaper texts
of these speeches. They may be found in the
March 1939 issues of Pravda, the official Party
daily. A few of the more important speeches are
available in English in Moscow News. (2) The
official journal of the Party's Central Committee,
Partiinoe Stroitel'stvo (Party Construction), before 1929 known as Izvestia TSK VKP (b)
(News of the Central Committee of the Communist Party of the Soviet Union). Bolshevik,
also an official journal with more emphasis on
Party theory than on Party practice, is useful.
Pravda has been consulted for more recent material. (3) Stalin, J., Problems of Leninism (Moscow, 1941) a translation of his most important
speeches. (In citing sources in Russian the author
has translated the titles of all articles and decrees,
giving the official position of the writer where it
was known.)
2 A. Yugow, Russia's Economic Front for War and
Peace (New York, 1942) p. 15.

larly, the system of agriculture was changed from one of private ownership of land, which had persisted beyond the period of the Bolshevik Revolution, to a collective system in 1939 covering 99.3 per cent of all lands under cultivation.[3]

Social Composition of the Party

One of the most striking facts about the Party's composition is that during the period of industrialization and agricultural collectivization there has been a very heavy overturn in the membership. Compared with the Party of 1928, it is practically a new group. In 1939 only 8.3 per cent of the membership was made up of persons who had entered the Party prior to the heroic period, that is before 1920.[4] But 70 per cent entered the Party after 1929 and the end of open disputes over policy, which closed with Stalin's victory over Trotsky. These figures show clearly that the Party is not a hereditary group.

As might be anticipated, the members are predominantly young. The distribution of the ages of the delegates, who were probably somewhat older and more experienced than the membership as a whole, at the Eighteenth Conference in 1941[5] was as follows:

Of a total of 457 delegates
under 35 there were 163 delegates or 35.6%
from 36–40 there were 195 delegates or 42.8%
from 41–50 there were 90 delegates or 19.8%
over 50 there were 8 delegates or 1.8%[6]

At first glance the occupational composition presents a paradox. The Communist Party of the Soviet Union has never at any time been composed primarily of industrial workers. The paradox is explained by the fact that before the Revolution the Party was engaged chiefly in preparing for a revolution rather than in attempting to win economic concessions for the workers within the framework of capitalist society, while after the Revolution it has functioned largely as a controlling body. However, the Party anxiously endeavored to maintain a proportion of proletarian workers in its ranks and for some time kept statistics on it, published at the various Congresses. The following figures are available for what they are worth concerning the proportion of workers in the Party. By "working class kernel" is meant, presumably, men with working class backgrounds but not necessarily engaged at the time in manual labor.

1926 working class kernel 58.4%
    workers from production 35.7%
1927 working class kernel 57.8%
    workers from production 40.8%
1930 working class kernel 68.2%
    workers from production 48.6%
1934 working class kernel 60.0%
    workers from production 9.3%
1939 figures not published[7]

At the last Congress in 1939 a new constitution of the Party was adopted, which abandoned the old entrance requirements that had favored industrial workers, on the grounds that social origins no longer mattered since the politico-moral unity of the people had been achieved and class differences eliminated in the U.S.S.R.[8]

What is more probable is that the Party leaders had been fighting a losing battle to keep up the proportion of workers from production, and did not wish to give statistical evidences of failure. This interpretation is strengthened by a decree that mentions recruiting difficulties even in big industrial establishments[9] and by two other decrees of the

---

[3] *Ibid.*, p. 46.

[4] G. Malenkov, "Report of the Credentials Commission," XVIII Congress, *Moscow News*, March 27, 1939, p. 2.

[5] Party Congresses and Conferences are similar in function, and are in the form of conventions of elected delegates. In the early period the two types of conventions alternated with each other. Both types of gatherings have become increasingly rare.

[6] N. Shatalin, "Report of Mandate Commission," at XVIII Conference, *Bolshevik*, No. 3–4, February, 1941, p. 57.

[7] L. M. Kaganovich, Speech at XVI Congress, *Stenographic Report* (Moscow, Leningrad, 1931), p. 83; the 1934 figures refer only to the delegates at the Congress, and would probably be somewhat weighted against workers from production. See Ezhov, Speech, XVII Congress, *Stenographic Report* (Moscow, 1934), p. 303.

[8] See "The Constitution of the CPSU (b); Second Lecture, Membership in the Party," *Partiinoe Stroitel'stvo*, No. 7, April 1940, p. 27.

[9] Decree of the Central Committee of March 4, 1938, "On the Work of the Party Organizations in Taking New Members into the CPSU(b)," *Partiinoe Stroitel'stvo*, No. 6, March 15, 1938, p. 61.

same year that discriminated against technical specialists by putting them into the category of workers for whom there were the stiffest entrance requirements, along with lavatory and locker room attendants.[10]

If by 1939 the Party had given up the pretense of being a Party of manual laborers, it had not yet become a Party composed exclusively of persons holding managerial positions in industry and agriculture. In January of 1937 managerial personnel numbered 1,751,000 in the U.S.S.R. as a whole,[11] while two years later the Party had only 1,588,852 members and 888,814 candidates. Despite statements by some writers on Soviet affairs to the effect that all persons in control positions are Party members[12] it is impossible for these two figures, nearly equal in size, to refer to the same body of people. Descriptions of the day-to-day operations of the Party, which will be frequently cited in other sections of this paper, make it clear that there exists a sizable portion of the membership that is made up not only of managerial personnel but of manual workers in both industry and agriculture, as well as persons with minor supervisory functions, such as foremen, shop superintendents, and the like.

No figures are known to the writer which show the proportion of Party members holding managerial positions. However, it is safe to estimate that they constitute not less than 50 and not more than 70 per cent of the Party. Of these perhaps a half are former manual laborers. This estimate is based on the observation that since 1928 managerial positions have been given chiefly to Party members.

Soviet figures in 1936 show that the industrial managerial group was composed almost entirely of Party members, which had come to be the case soon after the beginning of the Five Year Plans.

In 1923 29% of factory directors were
CPSU(b) members

In 1924 48% of factory directors were
CPSU(b) members

In 1929 93% of factory directors were
CPSU(b) members

In 1931 100% of factory directors were
CPSU(b) members

In 1936 97.5% of factory directors were
CPSU(b) members.[13]

The preference for giving managerial positions to Party members was criticized at the Eighteenth Conference in 1941.[14] Similarly, a decree of the Party Central Committee of March 4, 1938 criticized the regional (*oblast*)[15] committee for failure to promote non-Party individuals to managerial positions. The decree stated that the local Party organizations "correctly" promoted non-Party workers only to second rank and technical duties, but that there prevailed also in many places the incorrect system of limiting all managerial positions in the *oblast* and *rayon* to Party members[16] and re-

---

[10] "On the Order of Acceptance into the Party of Lenin and Stalin," Consultation column, *Partiinoe Stroitel'stvo*, No. 23, December 1, 1938, pp. 60–62, and references to decree of February 16, 1938.
[11] Molotov, Speech at XVIII Congress, *Moscow News*, March 22, 1939, p. 17. Space considerations prevent reproduction of the occupational breakdown of this total.
[12] See, for instance, M. Gordon, *Workers Before and After Lenin* (New York, 1941), p. 96; W. H. Chamberlin, *The Russian Enigma* (New York, 1943), p. 143.

[13] Figures 1923–1929 based on a sample of 1300 directors or less, 1931 figures refer to factories with over 500 workers, though the figure of 100 per cent was said to be nearly the case for U.S.S.R. as a whole; 75 per cent of these men were said to have working class origin. (Kaganovich, Speech at XVI Congress, *Stenographic Report*, p. 79; A. Loshkin, "Factory Management," *Bolshaya Sovetskaya Entsiklopediya* (Moscow, 1932), Vol. 25, p. 751. Figures for 1936 from *SSSR Strana Sotsializma* (Moscow, 1936), p. 94. (*The USSR, Country of Socialism*).
[14] Resolutions of the XVIII Conference, "The Organizational Tasks of Party Organizations in the Field of Industry and Transportation," *Bolshevik*, No. 3–4, February 1941, p. 64.
[15] The Party is divided into administrative subdivisions corresponding to those of the U.S.S.R. as a whole. For a good description of the U.S.S.R. subdivisions see Sidney and Beatrice Webb, *Soviet Communism: A New Civilization?* (New York, 1936), Vol. I, Chap. 2, where the terms are explained. In 1939 the Party had 11 Central Committees, 1 for each Union Republic, 6 territorial (*kray*) committees, 30 area (*okrug*) committees, 212 city city committees, 336 city district (*rayon*) committees, 3479 rural district (*rayon*) committees, and 113,060 primary Party organizations. See Stalin, *Problems of Leninism*, p. 650. In addition there is the All Union Central Committee, usually referred to simply as the Central Committee.
[16] Decree of the Central Committee of the CPSU (b) of March 4, 1938, "On the Promotion of Non-Party Persons to Managerial, Soviet, and Economic Work," *Partiinoe Stroitel'stvo*, No. 6, March 15, 1938, p. 62.

peats earlier criticisms of this practice made by Stalin.

Possibly because the membership of the Party was becoming too heavily weighted on the side of managerial personnel, a situation which was contrary to Leninist precepts, the leaders have permitted a large influx of new members since 1939. In 1941 the membership had risen from the 1939 figure of 2,477,666 (including candidates) to 3,876,885 (including candidates).[17] An Associated Press dispatch of January 17, 1944, by Henry C. Cassidy reported that the total membership was now more than 4,600,000. A high proportion of the new members are soldiers of the Red Army. Although the Party has continually criticized the method of mass recruiting, it has continually engaged in it. Mass entry into the Party on the field of battle is now a common phenomenon. Seven hundred members at a time is reported as a typical instance of present recruiting methods.[18] It is safe to interpret this as a method of increasing the soldier's stake in the Soviet Union, as well as increasing the Party's control over the Army, which has been shaky at several crucial periods.[19]

Role of the Party in Economic Life

One of the main problems faced by the Russians in their drive to construct a new form of society was the establishment of industrial discipline, along with the training and discovery of adequate managerial leadership.[20] In 1931, three years after the beginning of the First Five Year Plan, Stalin stressed the need for a new industrial and technical intelligentsia. Earlier in the year he attributed failures in production to the fact that Bolsheviks had not mastered managerial technique, and carried on their management "by merely

signing papers."[21] Evidently a completely satisfactory solution has not yet been found, as complaints about inefficient management may still be found in the Russian press. Molotov's outburst at the Eighteenth Congress reveals clearly the type of problems with which the top Soviet leaders were dealing:

> An end must be put to this [mismanagement — BM], intensifying the struggle against mismanagement and losses of every kind along the whole front. It is necessary in practice to insure attention to economics, to the cost of the products turned out. It is necessary to know well what the work of each enterprise, of each organization costs the state. Meanwhile, even such executives are to be found among us as consider it beneath their dignity to examine the balance sheet, to study the accounts, to devote attention to cost accounting. It is necessary resolutely to put an end to this unconcern and economic illiteracy, as to an anti-state and anti-Bolshevik practice.[22]

Soon after the beginning of the Five Year Plan the Soviet authorities began in earnest to strengthen the position of the factory manager and to make him personally responsible for progress of production under his direction.

Prior to the Five Year Plans, collegium management, i.e., management by a large board of proletarian directors, was the prevailing practice in the administration of an industry as a whole, distinguished from the administration of a particular factory. Within the factory itself there existed the "triangle" composed of the director, the trade union representative, and the representative of the Communist Party cell.

The transfer of authority to the factory director was not a simple process to be marked by any single decree, and was accompanied by the process of trial and error, plus denial of error, that is often characteristic of social change. As early as 1920 the Party praised the general principle of individual, personal responsibility[23] and as late as 1927 Stalin praised

[17] Shatalin, op. cit., p. 56.

[18] P. Iudin, "Political Work at the Front," *Pravda*, April 9, 1943.

[19] For a detailed study of the growth of the Red Army and its relations with the Party, see D. F. White, *The Growth of the Red Army* (Princeton, 1944).

[20] For a study of the development and problems of the factory manager, see G. Bienstock, S. M. Schwarz, and A. Yugow, *Management in Russian Industry and Agriculture* (London and New York, 1944). This excellent work appeared after the present study was in type.

[21] J. Stalin, Speech delivered at a conference of business representatives, June 23, 1931, "New Conditions — New Tasks in Economic Construction," *Problems of Leninism* (Moscow, 1941), pp. 378–379; and, "The Tasks of Business Executives," speech delivered at the First All-Union Conference of Managers of Socialist Industry, February 4, 1931, *ibid.*, pp. 359–367.

[22] *Moscow News*, March 22, 1939, p. 15.

[23] Resolutions, IX Congress, *Stenographic Report* (Moscow, Leningrad, 1920), pp. 376–377, 387.

the principle of collegium management,[24] only to criticize it again in 1931.[25] The landmark marking the disappearance of the collegiums is probably the Seventeenth Congress of the Party in 1934.[26] The "triangle" was abandoned somewhat earlier. Its official demise took place in the decree of the Central Committee of September 7, 1929, intended to set up a system of one-man management (*edinonachalya*) within the factory.[27]

From later discussions in the press and Party decrees it is clear that the principle of one-man management (*edinonachalya*) has never been fully established. In 1934 among the theses on organizational problems presented to the Seventeenth Congress was the "extreme weakness of one-man management."[28] Again in 1941 the resolutions of the Eighteenth Conference refer to the necessity for strengthening the principle and putting it into actual practice.[29]

The present pattern of relationship between the Party and industrial management is the following, so far as can be determined from documentary sources. At the top of the administrative structure is the *Gosplan*, which, under instructions of the All-Union Central Committee of the Communist Party, issues the basic directions governing the plan and the economic life of the nation.[30] This central administrative apparatus for the nation-wide management of industry and agriculture has been changed frequently.[31] Below this central administrative apparatus are three bodies with somewhat more stable roles. They are (1) the regional (Republic, *oblast* or smaller) Party organizations; (2) the factory directors, and

(3) the primary Party organizations, formerly cells, within the factory. While other bodies and relationships exist, especially in transportation, the above three are the most important ones and will be analyzed below in some detail.

The regional Party organizations are responsible for all economic matters within their areas. "The Party committee of the *rayon*, city, and *oblast* Party organization carries full responsibility for the economic life of the *rayon*, city, or *oblast*."[32] Similarly the All-Union Central Committee in reprimanding one of the *oblast* committees for failure to pay sufficient attention to production in its area stated:

> Party committees bear direct responsibility before the Party for the condition of the work of production; they cannot remain unconcerned about whether an establishment works well or badly, whether the government plan is being fulfilled or is collapsing. This is the obvious and elemental truth.[33]

This role of general supervision is not a new one. Indeed the general pattern of Party–industry relations at the regional and local level appears to have been stabilized in the early 1930's and to have undergone relatively minor modifications since then. For instance, in 1931 a decree signed by Molotov and Stalin required the regional Party organizations to attend to various changes in accounting methods for industry in their particular areas. The bureaus of the local Party committees were expected to obtain from the heads of the branches of the banks in their area a report on how the changes had been carried out.[34] A contemporary example of the function of an *oblast* committee is that of Rostov, which in 1940 arranged for the subcontracting of items for farm machinery to aid a factory that was not fulfilling the plan. The *oblast* committee did this by calling to-

[24] Speech at XV Congress, *Stenographic Report* (Moscow, Leningrad, 1928), p. 69.
[25] *Problems of Leninism*, p. 387.
[26] Resolutions, *Stenographic Report*, p. 673.
[27] Decree of the Central Committee of the CPSU (b), "On Measures for the Regulation of the Management of Production and the Establishment of One-Man Management," in *Izvestia TSK VKP* (b), October 10, 1929, p. 23; A. Lokshin, "One-Man Management," *Bolshaya Sovetskaya Entsiklopediya* (Moscow, 1932), Vol. 24, p. 254, and "Factory Management," *Ibid.*, Vol. 25, p. 75.
[28] *Partiinoe Stroitel'stvo*, No. 1, January 1934, p. 3.
[29] *Bolshevik*, No. 3–4, February 1941, p. 61.
[30] Yugow, *op. cit.*, p. 231.
[31] For a succinct summary of these changes see M. T. Florinsky, *Toward an Understanding of the U.S.S.R.* (New York, 1939), pp. 174–180.

[32] N. Patolichev, Secretary of the Yaroslavsky *Oblast* Committee of the CPSU(b), "In the Center of Attention — Basic Problems of Production," *Partiinoe Stroitel'stvo*, No. 23–24, December 1940, p. 22.
[33] "The Orlovsky *Oblast* Committee of the CPSU (b) Takes Bad Care of Industry," in column "Questions of Economic Management," *Partiinoe Stroitel'stvo*, No. 17, September 1940, p. 41.
[34] "On New Measures for the Introduction of Business Accounting," decree of September 21, 1931, in *Partiinoe Stroitel'stvo*, No. 21, November 1931, pp. 79–80.

gether the factory directors, and the secretaries of the primary Party organizations within the factories, for their area.[35] During the siege of Leningrad the Party city committee in addition to its regular economic functions devoted considerable energy to teaching war techniques to the civil population.[36]

A key point at which the regional Party organization enters the pattern of relationships that govern industry is through its control over the selection of factory directors. Before the Five Year Plans it appears that the regional Party organizations, the primary Party organizations inside the factory, the national economic administrative organs, and the trade union organizations all had some part in the selection of the director, although the national economic administrative organs, which later became the People's Commissariats for various industries, were theoretically responsible.[37] In a commentary on the decree one writer makes the point that the national economic administrative organs have the right to select and discharge the factory directors, and that the workers' organizations do not have this right.[38] In 1930 the selection of all administrative economic leadership including the factory directors was brought under a special division of the Party's Central Committee set up for the purpose, and called the assignment division.[39] According to Kaganovich the selection of leadership had been done previously in a haphazard way by another subdivision of the

Central Committee, which had insufficient staff to devote proper attention to it.[40] Under the new arrangement the Communist Parties of the constituent national republics, and the various regional Party committees were to set up assignment divisions similar to those in the Party's Central Committee, which divisions were to do most of the real work of selection. This arrangement has remained basically the same up until the present, though there have been various modifications of form and of title. Thus in 1939 at the Eighteenth Congress Stalin recommended that there should be a Cadres Administration (as the Russians use it, cadres means leaders) of the Central Committee of the CPSU(b) and a corresponding cadres department in each of the republican, territorial, and regional Party organizations, a recommendation that was also presented in a speech by Zhdanov and enacted into the resolutions of the Congress.[41]

In practice it appears that the regional and the local Party committees work largely on their own in selecting managerial personnel. For example in 1939 the Moscow *oblast* committee of the Party cleaned out the management of the cotton industry, installing new young comrades as directors in twenty-six textile factories.[42] In another case a factory director was accused of nepotism, upon which the *rayon* committee of the Party took up the question "with the proper organizations," as a

---

35 A. Rozhkov, head of industrial division of Rostov *Oblast* Committee CPSU(b), "The Industrial Divisions of an *Oblast* Committee," *Partiinoe Stroitel'stvo*, No. 21, November 1940, pp. 53–57.
36 A. Pavlov, in charge of war section of Leningrad City Committee CPSU(b), writing in *Pravda*, February 20, 1943, p. 3.
37 See the discussion on this point in the decree of September 7, 1929, by the Central Committee "On Measures for the Regularization of the Management of Production and the Establishment of One-Man Management," in *Izvestia TSK VKP*(b), October 10, 1929, p. 25.
38 V. Ryabokon, "One-Man Management, the 'Triangle' and the Masses," *Partiinoe Stroitel'stvo*, No. 1, November 1929, p. 15.
39 *Raspredelitel'ny otdel.* See speech by Kaganovich before the Orgburo of the Central Committee, "On the Apparatus of the Central Committee of the CPSU(b)," *Partiinoe Stroitel'stvo*, No. 2, February 1930, pp. 9 ff. and accompanying decree on p. 71. For the various industrial sectors into which this division was further broken up see, *ibid.*, No. 3–4, February 1930, p. 86.

40 Kaganovich, *loc. cit.*
41 Stalin, *Problems of Leninism*, p. 653; "Changes in the Constitution of the CPSU(b), Resolution of the XVIII Congress of the CPSU(b) on the Speech of Comrade A. Zhdanov," in *VKP(b) v Rezoliutsiyakh i Resheniyakh ego S'ezdov, Konferentsii i Plenumov TSK* (Moscow, 1941), pp. 749–750. (*The CPSU(b) in Resolutions and Decisions of Its Congresses, Conferences and Plenums of the Central Committee*). It is obvious that on paper the role of the Party *Cadres* Administration and of the Peoples Commissariats in selecting managerial personnel overlap. The dilemma is more apparent than real, since the Party supplies or appoints nearly all important leaders in the Soviet Union. In 1939 Stalin mentioned (*op. cit.*, p. 652) the appointment by the Party of 500,000 persons to various posts, including non-Party ones. In the specific instances noted by this writer, managerial personnel has been appointed or removed by the Party through its regional organizations.
42 B. Chernousov, secretary of the Moscow *Oblast* Committee of the CPSU(b), "Promote Young Cadres Boldly and On Time!" *Partiinoe Stroitel'stvo*, No. 11, June 1939, pp. 42–43.

result of which a new director was installed.[43] Meanwhile the managers themselves are admonished that the decisions of the Congress do not free them from the necessity of being on the lookout for new leaders, and that they must not constantly call upon the Party cadres division for them.[44] This and other sources show that the Party cadres divisions also help to pick persons much lower in authority than the factory director, such as chiefs of shops, heads of shifts — positions that appear to correspond roughly to foremen in the United States.[45]

At first glance the role of the Russian factory director seems to have become quite similar to that of his counterpart in the United States, the factory manager. The Party has continued to strengthen the position of the factory director in the last few years. Its official statement on the factory director is:

> To him the Party and the government have entrusted the management of industry, and he is personally and fully responsible for his actions.[46]

The strengthening of the director's position has developed in part by decrees limiting the authority of the Party primary organization within the factory.[47] The primary Party organization, for example, does not have the right to reverse the orders of the factory administration; it does not have the right to give orders in its own name on matters affecting production; it does not have the right to demand that the director have his orders agree with those of the Party organization; it does not have the right to hire, fire, or transfer

workers, all of which functions are specifically reserved to the management.[48] A ukase of the Presidium of the Supreme Soviet, on June 26, 1940, among other provisions, forbade employees to leave an establishment without permission of the director, making the penalty a two- to four-month prison term.[49] But it is also clear that if the Party found it necessary to forbid these practices, they must have existed and been fairly widespread, an indication that the director's authority was limited in practice.

Early in 1940 the Party found it necessary to publish an article on the relation between directors, Party members in the factory, and ordinary rank and file workers, which criticized sharply the general lack of respect toward managerial personnel. The incidents it reports may be only locally significant, but they illuminate the cultural patterns governing these relationships. In one case the chief engineer told the head of the workshop, a Communist, to change some bench equipment. The latter refused. Then the engineer went down to the shop to give the order personally to the workmen, and over the head of the Communist in charge of the workshop. The latter in turn countermanded the engineer's order. In another case the director walking through the factory noticed a lot of dirt in one section. He asked the cleaning woman why it was so dirty. "Call that dirt," she replied. "If you call that dirt, you don't know what dirt really is! And if you don't like it, here, take the broom and clean it up yourself!"[50]

While it pays to be skeptical about items of self-criticism in the Soviet press, since the stream of self-condemnation is obviously turned off and on at will by those in authority, these incidents and the decrees cited make it quite plain that the pattern of worker–management relations is unlike that in the United States.

Of course the situation varies considerably from place to place, and in relation to the personality of the director. John Scott, a keen observer who worked for several years in the

---

[43] "Report of the Division of Cadres to the Plenum of the *Rayon* Committee," *Partiinoe Stroitel'stvo*, No. 21, November 1940, p. 60.
[44] "Introduction," *Partiinoe Stroitel'stvo*, No. 13, July 1939, p. 8.
[45] N. Shipulin, head of the sector of the *Cadres* Administration of the Central Com. CPSU(b), "On the Work of the Cadres Divisions" *Partiinoe Stroitel'stvo*, No. 21, November 1939, p. 29.
[46] "One-Man Management, and the Right of Control," *Partiinoe Stroitel'stvo*, No. 18, September 1940, p. 36.
[47] As is evident from the preceding paragraph, the regional Party organizations, as contrasted with the primary ones, have strong powers. It is likely that the former have increased in strength while the latter have decreased.

---

[48] *Ibid.*, p. 35.
[49] Text in *Partiinoe Stroitel'stvo*, No. 11–12, June 1940, p. 8.
[50] Y. Kapustin, Secretary of the Leningrad City Committee of the CPSU(b), "Strengthen One-Man Management in Every Possible Way," *Partiinoe Stroitel'stvo*, No. 16, August 1940, pp. 27–29.

great steel plant of Magnitogorsk, relates that the plant director was the "supreme commander" and "virtual dictator," who "controlled supplies, all plant administration, city construction and maintenance, public services, school construction, health service, and transport."[51] Here the relationship between the Party organization in the plant and the managerial personnel was a harmonious one:

> Administrative and technical questions were discussed at regular closed Party meetings, and inasmuch as most of the administrators were Party members, important decisions could be and were made.[52]

As we have seen that a high proportion of the managerial personnel in the U.S.S.R. belongs to the Party, it is probable that the situation described by Scott is widespread. Similarly *Pravda* describes in favorable terms the pattern of relationships in the more successful sections of the mining industry during the war, where the director of the mine and the Party organization consult with leading technical and engineering workers and Stakhanovites to discover weaknesses and make the right decisions for removing them.[53]

The role of the primary Party organizations within the factory was defined in the resolutions of the Party's Eighteenth Congress concerning changes in the Constitution of the CPSU(b). While the primary organizations are not supposed to concern themselves with management or interfere with management's functions in any way, they are expected to exercise a certain limited control over the conditions in any industrial or agricultural establishment in which they exist.[54] This situation represents a very modified continuation of some features of the old institution of the "triangle," whereby the Party cell shared authority with the trade union and the factory director.

The right of control is defined as the right of the primary Party organizations to acquaint themselves with the factory's accounts, etc., the right to hear the speeches and reports of the managers, the right to put questions to the management on factors hindering production, and the right to make recommendations concerning their correction. From the press accounts it appears that the last two points are the ones most stressed in actual practice.[55]

While the primary Party organizations are expressly warned to keep hands off the administration, it is clear that in practice they often perform functions that in a capitalist economy are associated with management or are the subject of bargaining between the management and the trade unions. The primary organizations concern themselves with questions of wage payment, promotions within a factory, the allocation of the labor supply, the use of equipment, and the obtaining of raw materials. Usually, the Party organization acts to avert a situation that is threatening to slow up production. In one case, which took place during the war, a factory director attempted to blame his failure to produce up to the plan on war conditions, pointing to the mountain of telegrams on his desk as proof of his efforts to obtain raw materials. The Party factory organization, with the help of the Party city committee, investigated and found that the supply division was buried in unnecessary paper work, as a result of which, forms showing that the materials had already been received lay around for weeks.[56]

---

[51] J. Scott, *Behind the Urals* (Cambridge, Mass., 1942), pp. 80–81.

[52] *Ibid.*, p. 152. Scott's information refers to the years 1933–1936 in these instances.

[53] Article by E. Kolishev, Secretary of Nizhne-Tagilsky City Committee, CPSU(b), in the issue for January 6, 1943, p. 3.

[54] "Changes in the Constitution of the CPSU(b), Resolution of the XVIII Congress of the CPSU(b) on the Speech of Comrade A. Zhdanov, Adopted Unanimously March 20, 1939," in *VKP(b) v Rezolyutsiyakh*, p. 751.

[55] See "One-Man Management and the Right of Control," *Partiinoe Stroitel'stvo*, No. 18, September 1940, p. 34.

[56] K. Khmelevsky, Secretary of the Molotov City Committee of the CPSU(b), "The City Committee of the CPSU(b) and Lagging Factories," *Pravda*, May 31, 1943, p. 3; for other illustrations see also O. Kozlov, Secretary of the Moscow *Rayon* Committee of the CPSU(b), "Party Organizations and Questions of Independence of Production," *Partiinoe Stroitel'stvo*, No. 23–24, December 1940, pp. 26–30; S. Masterov, head of the organizations and instructional section of the Leningrad City Committee of the CPSU(b), "Control of Primary Party Organizations in Practice," *ibid.*, No. 11, June 1939, p. 53; Y. Kapustin, then Secretary of the Party Committee of Kirov factory of the city of Leningrad, "On the Control of Primary Party Organizations in Establishments," *ibid.*, No. 5, March 1939, pp. 37–38.

Finally, the Party organizations have a series of functions that can best be described as inspirational. Communist workers are supposed to set an example to the other workers through superior energy and enthusiasm, and to indoctrinate the latter by explaining to them the aims, practices, and advantages of the socialist state. An official manual, issued for the assistance of Party workers during the war, explains the special task of the Party organization in the shop as being one of mobilizing the workers for the fulfillment of production plans, the development of socialist competition, and the carrying on of political work among the workers.[57] It appears that this psychological aspect of Party work has increased during the war, and that the Party devotes a great deal of time and energy to explaining to the factory workers and the population at large the nature of the enemy, the characteristics of fascism, and the implications of being subject to the Germans. The Party enlists non-Party sympathizers to assist in this work, and has issued detailed instructions on the most effective way of dealing with different types of audiences, so as to bring home to the individual just what a German victory would mean to him personally, and what he can do by his own efforts to contribute to a German defeat. Patriotic appeals, atrocity stories, and the like have largely taken the place here of the original Marxian revolutionary symbols.[58]

In agriculture the pattern of relationships is similar to that prevailing in industry. Soviet agriculture is organized into a series of collective farms around nuclei of machine tractor stations. The directors of the machine tractor stations, which are regarded as important political foci, are usually appointed by the regional Party organizations.[59]

A significant difference is the fact that the Party has a much smaller number of persons engaged in agricultural work than in industrial labor. In 1930, 50 per cent of the collective farms still lacked Party organizations.[60] Evidently with the growth of the collective farm movement the proportion dropped precipitously. By 1939 out of 243,000 collective farms only 12,000 had primary Party organizations, with a total membership, including candidates, of 153,000 persons, or an over-all average of one organization to every twenty farms. The situation is more startling in certain areas; for instance in the White Russian republic in a total of 9,665 collective farms there were only 44 primary organizations with a total membership of 614 persons.[61]

To some extent the difference is made up by using members of the Communist youth organizations, the Komsomols. They are required, according to the Party constitution, to carry out Party directives where there are no primary Party organizations. Among their functions, and those of the Party in the collective farms, are discussion and preparation of plans for sowing, for the repair of equipment, the development of separate branches of the economy (presumably crop diversification), the conditions of labor discipline, and the ubiquitous political and cultural work.[62]

Determination of Policy and Leadership Within the Party

In the course of adjustment to major economic and social problems posed by the drive towards industrialization and collectivization, the Party was bound to experience dissension due to the presentation of alternate solutions to these problems, as well as to the differences and conflicts between the various leaders of the Party. If one can predict anything with

---

[57] V Pomoshch' Partiinomu Rabotniku — Voprosi partiino-organizatsionnoi raboti — vypusk pervyi (Ogiz, Gospolitizdat, 1943), p. 1. (For the Assistance of a Party Worker — Questions of Party Organizational Work).

[58] See for instance Pamyatka Agitatora — o tom kak provodit besedy (Moskovsky Bolshevik, 1943) passim. (Handbook of an Agitator, How to Conduct a Discussion.)

[59] In January of 1936, according to SSSR Strana Sotsializma, p. 95, 98.2 per cent of these directors were themselves Party members. See also M. Benediktov, "The Tasks of Socialist Agricultural

Economy in 1943," Bolshevik, No. 5, March 1943, p. 14; M. Burmistenko, Secretary of the Central Committee of the Communist Party of the Ukraine, "On the Selection and Promotion of Cadres," Partiinoe Stroitel'stvo, No. 15, August 1939, p. 16; A. Pronin, "On the Directors of MTS," ibid., No. 17, September 1940, p. 52.

[60] Kaganovich, Speech at XVII Congress, Stenographic Report, pp. 556–557.

[61] Andreev, Speech at XVIII Congress, Pravda, March 14, 1939, p. 3.

[62] Pravda, January 20, 1943, p. 1.

certainty, it is that similar dissensions will arise as the Party faces new problems, and that the methods used to solve them in the past will continue to be used in the future and to undergo various modifications as they are put to use.

In theory the machinery for resolving internal dissensions into disciplined action is the system of democratic centralism. By democratic centralism, with which is usually coupled the slogan internal democracy, the Communists have meant: first, the right of every Party member to take whatever position he chose on problems facing the Party, and to try to persuade other members to follow his views, up to the point where policy was decided and the Party line laid down, usually at the Congress, after which the Party member was under the strictest discipline to carry out the Party line irrespective of his own personal views; secondly, the right of every Party member to elect the Party officers, and to be elected an officer of the Party.[63]

Democratic centralism, as officially defined, has not been the actual mechanism by which policy and leadership have been determined since 1928, and it is doubtful to what extent it represented actual behavior in the period 1917–1928. While differences over policy were frequent in the early Congresses, the Fifteenth Congress in 1927 was the last one in which any significant difference of opinion appeared. It was also the one at which the opposition was formally excluded from the Party.[64] The Congresses themselves, which were annual affairs after the Revolution, have been held with decreasing frequency. The Fourteenth was held in 1925, the Fifteenth in 1927, the Sixteenth in 1930, the Seventeenth in 1934, and the Eighteenth in 1939. Even the formally expressed right of free discussion within the Party before a decision had been reached, specifically guaranteed in the 1926 Party constitution, was in 1934 restricted to instances to be decided upon in advance by the Central Committee or the regional (*oblast* or republic) Party organiza-

tions.[65] The 1934 modification of the constitutional guarantee was meaningless. No discussion of major policy has taken place since 1928. From that date onward there has been no open criticism of Stalin or any of his major policies in the Party publications, and one may say with reasonable certainty, in the Soviet press as a whole. Therefore it is obvious that one must look elsewhere than in the open presentation of alternate solutions and policies and concomitant compromises for an explanation of the workings of the Party mechanism.

One key to an understanding of the mechanisms surrounding the determination of policy would be an exact knowledge of how economic and political conditions in the country were brought to the attention of the highest Party leaders, and the types of discussion that took place in the circles immediately surrounding Stalin before a decision was reached. In purely economic matters there exists a wide variety of official publications, of a general and regional nature, and of varying degrees of scientific reliability, which are of course available to policy makers, in addition to unpublished sources which undoubtedly put a little less varnish on the truth. Furthermore each Party organization is supposed to check on the work of the organizations lower in the hierarchy, which check is in itself a source of information on both economic and political conditions. Finally there are the reports of the secret police, now incorporated in the Commissariat of Internal Affairs. By the very nature of secret police work, this type of information is largely limited to scattered collections of rumors and unguarded statements torn from their context. However, in the absence of a free press, these collections may serve some purpose in banishing illusions that all is well, and even reveal to the discerning administrator the need for a serious change in policy.

As for the types of discussion and the persons that participate in the actual formation of policy, in the absence of memoirs one can only guess that major turns of policy, such as the Soviet German Non-Aggression Pact of August 23, 1939, are decided in consultation

---

[63] See the Party Statutes of 1926, 1934, 1939 in *VKP(b) v Rezoliutsiyakh.*

[64] See the *Stenographic Report;* also the resolution excluding the opposition reprinted in *VKP(b) v Rezolyutsiyakh,* p. 259.

[65] *VKP(b) v Rezolyutsiyakh,* pp. 88, 595, 758. The restriction was repeated in the 1939 Statutes.

with a very small number of persons. It is said that even Voroshilov, then chief of the Red Army, did not know of this decision until after it had been reached.

In other cases consultation occurs with a wider body of individuals from whom information is derived. In 1939 Kaganovich stated that the Central Committee made a whole series of decisions on the Constitution, elections in the state collective farms, and the improvement of Party work, after calling in people from the outside who were engaged in facing these problems, and discussing the matter with them.[66] While it may be necessary to take these claims with several grains of salt, as well as Stalin's frequent statements about the necessity for maintaining close contact with the masses,[67] they probably reflect practice as well as ideals.

It is much easier to see the mechanisms at work that produce a change of leadership than to perceive those which bring about a readjustment of policy, although of course the two are related. The feature that has caught the eye of the general public is the series of purges, executions, and demonstration trials that have in various forms been characteristic of the period of the Five Year Plans. From 1922–1929 there were no purges; from then on purges or executions were frequent until after the Eighteenth Congress. Their known effect has been on the top leadership of the Party. Thus, as Souvarine points out, of the directing staff of the Party during Lenin's lifetime, only Stalin is left alive today.[68] Although the purges and executions reached down to the rank and file of the Party, it is not known what proportion was shot, and what proportion was merely temporarily excluded. In the winter of 1938 60 to 70 per cent of the exclusions were annulled in Kursk, Kiev, Archangel and other places.[69] Contrasted with the purges and

executions, which are an outstanding way of changing and readjusting the leadership, is the device of cooption, which makes for continuity of leadership. By cooption is meant selection from above: if the members of a Party executive committee decide that a particular individual would be a desirable person to have on the committee they coopt him to membership. The extent to which this device is or was in use cannot be ascertained with any accuracy, though it has been the subject of frequent criticism by the leading organs of the Party. Cooption has been frequently criticized by leading Party organs as a practice which threatened to replace democratic centralism. Some of the sharpest criticism occurred just before the general elections to the Supreme Soviet in 1937.[70] In the Resolutions of the Eighteenth Congress the Party boasted of having suppressed the practice of cooption, a claim which, by the mere necessity of its proclamation, is almost certainly false.[71]

Despite the purges and the practice of cooption, and contrary to the impression of writers such as Souvarine, and to a lesser extent Eugene Lyons, who assert that the Soviet system is an unmitigated autocracy, there are abundant indications of the power of the lower sectors of the Party to manage their own affairs and to change their own officers by elective procedures. This autonomy has sharp and definite limits: a provincial Party committee that makes a poor decision or neglects some economic problem within its area, or that passes a resolution contrary to the general policy or line of the Party is told publicly and sharply by the Central Committee in Moscow to review the matter again and report back its new action or decision by a specific date. Nearly every issue of the Central Committee's publication, *Partiinoe Stroitel'stvo*, contains a reprimand along these lines. Similarly the provincial and regional organizations, by reviewing the minutes of the meetings of the local and primary Party organizations, correcting incorrect decisions, and by a system of travelling instructors, keep a

[66] Speech at XVIII Congress, *Pravda*, March 17, 1939, p. 6.

[67] *Problems of Leninism, passim.*

[68] B. Souvarine, *Stalin* (New York, 1939), pp. 634–637. These pages are largely lists of names of prominent Soviet leaders who "perished or disappeared without publicity" in 1938 alone.

[69] E. Schvarts, "The Suppression of Mass Cleansings of the Party," *Partiinoe Stroitel'stvo*, No. 5, March 1939, p. 34.

[70] Plenum of the Central Com. of February–March 1937, text in *VKP(b) v Rezolyutsiyakh*, pp. 653–655.

[71] *Ibid.*, p. 748.

sharp eye on the Party organizations within their area.[72] At times these limitations lead to a lack of initiative among the primary Party organizations, which are then criticized by the ones above them for perpetually waiting for a ukase before taking any action on a situation demanding immediate action.[73] But in many other cases there are strong indications of activity, usually along the lines of action or discussion to implement major policy decisions that have already been adopted by the Central Committee. As a typical example, the June 23, 1943, plenum of the Moscow *oblast* committee discussed (1) the preparation for sowing and harvesting, (2) the degree of fulfillment of the government plan for livestock breeding in the collective farms of two *rayons* in the *oblast*, and (3) the work of the city and *rayon* committee in taking in members during the first five months of 1943.[74] Regular gatherings of the membership of the local organizations also occur. At these gatherings the local Party official gives a report of his work, after which a debate follows in which a number of persons participate from the floor. Then a decision is voted as to whether the work is satisfactory. In some cases if the work is unsatisfactory, the officer or committee is not reelected.[75]

Summary and Conclusion

From the material presented here, it is clear

that the Party cannot be considered a hereditary class, or even an incipient one as yet, since most of its membership dates only from 1929. At the same time it is to a large extent an elite, that is, a group of persons holding control positions or offices in the Soviet social structure. In addition to holding many of these positions itself, the Party controls the selection of economic officers, down to the lowest rung, approximating that of foreman in American society.

Within this elite the determination of policy and leadership theoretically takes place through the mechanism of democratic centralism, from which there are in practice marked deviations, through the practice of cooption, the increasing infrequency of the Congresses, and the purges. Outside of a small circle close to Stalin, there is no discussion of major policy. At the level of the city Party organizations, and in smaller subdivisions, there is widespread discussion of how policy has been carried out, and free elections based on these discussions, which may result in the failure of the lower officials, whose work is unsatisfactory, to win reelection.

14

Social Characteristics of the Party Membership*

T. H. Rigby

(1957)

Mr. Rigby carries our Communist Party history down through the post-Stalin years, telling the story from the special perspective suggested by an analysis of the composition of its membership. We see that the membership has changed in response to changes in the conception of the Party's role and to transforma-

---

[72] Section "On Party Themes," *Partiinoe Stroitel'-stvo*, No. 23–24, December 1940, pp. 71–72; "Protocol of Party Gatherings and Sessions," *ibid.*, No. 21, November 1940, p. 66; L. Shuster, instructor of the Rostokinsky *Rayon* Committee of the CPSU(b), city of Moscow, "Remarks of an Instructor," *ibid.*, pp. 43–48; also decree of Central Com. "On Certain Measures in Connection with the Results of the Elections of Leading Party Organs," August 22, 1938, *ibid.*, No. 19–20, October 1938, p. 78.

[73] See as example L. Volkov, "A Superficial Approach to the Matter," from the *Pravda* correspondent for Ivanovskaya *oblast*, *Pravda*, April 10, 1943.

[74] *Pravda*, June 25, 1943, p. 2.

[75] Good reports of such meetings may be found in *Pravda*, April 2, 1943, on a meeting in Samarkand; and P. Nazarov, Secretary of the Sokol'nichesky *Rayon* Committee, CPSU(b), Moscow, "Accountability — Basis of Democratic Centralism," *Partiinoe Stroitel'stvo*, No. 9, May 1, 1938, pp. 48–49.

* Reprinted from "Social Orientation of Recruitment and Distribution of Membership in the Communist Party of the Soviet Union," *American Slavic and East European Review*, Vol. 16 (1957), pp. 275–290, by permission of the author and the publisher.

tions in the structure of Soviet society. How much the Party, in its turn, has been transformed by its changing composition is less evident, but may in the long run prove even more significant.

Four different conceptions of the role of the Communist Party of the Soviet Union can be discerned as having had an influence upon its recruitment policy at different periods. One or the other of these conceptions has dominated in each phase of the Party's growth, with the exception of the Civil War years and the period of World War II. In those two turbulent times a relatively open door policy prevailed, and devoted war service seems to have been the main criterion of suitability for membership.

The four different conceptions in order of adoption may be summarized as being: (1) the concept of the Party as the general staff of the socialist revolution, (2) the concept of the Party as a party of the proletariat, (3) the concept of the Party as the leading and directing force of Soviet society, and (4) the concept of the Party as an association of the "best people" of Soviet society.

The general staff concept was rested upon the expressed conviction that workers, if left to themselves to determine policy, could develop only "trade union consciousness." This concept was held primarily in the pre-revolutionary period. It implied that while every effort should be made to recruit reliable proletarian members, a warm welcome must also be accorded professional revolutionaries drawn from the "bourgeois intelligentsia" and capable of leading the workers on the basis of "socialist consciousness." The proletarian party concept followed to dominate the period of the years after the civil war, achieving its most thoroughgoing implementation in the late 1920's. In essence it held that the Party must be composed overwhelmingly of actual rank-and-file wage workers. Recruitment from other social and occupational groups was to be restricted severely. This concept declined in influence in practice after the late 1920's although it remained dogma until 1939.

The third and fourth concepts have come to have greatest current interest, and it is for this reason that the evidence set forth in this paper has been selected to relate to them. In contradistinction to the proletarian party concept the third concept of the Party as the lead-

ing and directing force of Soviet society has made for the incorporation within the Party of all occupational groups exercising authority in any field of productive, administrative, intellectual, or "public" activity. The adoption of this approach was preceded by a phase of mass expulsions, which reduced Party membership from three and a half millions in 1933 to under two millions in January 1938. In November 1936 recruiting was resumed, after a three-year halt, to the tune of a Central Committee decision stressing that henceforth enrolments must be on a strictly selective basis, with no more wholesale recruitment of workers of particular factories.[1] This decision and a further one circulated on July 14, 1938, calling for a stepping-up of enrolments and greater concentration on the "best people"[2] mark the turn toward mass recruitment of the new technical-bureaucratic "intelligentsia." This approach was dominant up to the outbreak of the war, receiving ideological justification at the Eighteenth Party Congress in March, 1939.[3]

In 1946 it was mentioned that in the prewar period corresponding in length to the war (i.e., from mid-1936 till June, 1941) 24 per cent of those enrolled were "workers."[4] Assuming the proportion of "peasants" to have been no higher than this (most indications are that it was lower), over half the new recruits to the Party in the period under consideration must have come under the official classification of "intelligentsia." When allowance is made for many of the "workers" and "peasants" being actually employed in white-collar posts,[5]

---

[1] See "Voprosy chlenstva v VKP(b)," *Partijnaja zhizn'*, No. 20 (1947), p. 80.
[2] See XVII S'ezd VKP(b), *Stenograficheskij otchet*, p. 577, where the 1938 decision is quoted by a Georgian Party official as authority for a roughly tenfold increase in the rate of recruitment of *kolkhoz* chairmen, doctors, agronomists and other "intelligentsia" groups.
[3] See Stalin's and Zhdanov's speeches to the Eighteenth Congress, especially *Problems of Leninism*, 11th edit., pp. 663–5, and the *Land of Socialism Today and Tomorrow*, pp. 181–3.
[4] Shamberg, "Some Questions of Intra-Party Work," *Partijnoe stroitel'stvo*, No. 4 (1946), p. 28.
[5] As figures quoted at the Eighteenth Congress make clear, in many places a half or more of the "peasant" and "worker" recruits may have been so employed. See XVIII S'ezd VKP(b), pp. 578, 586.

the preponderance of managerial, administrative, technical and professional personnel among those enrolled in the Party from 1937 to 1941 is obvious.

The Changing Social Character of the Party

The social character of the Party being created in this period was almost the direct antithesis of that officially aimed at in the decade following Lenin's death. In place of the conception of a thoroughly proletarian movement, with rank-and-file workers and poor peasants forming the vast majority, there was elevated the concept of an elite Party made up of those invested with authority by virtue of their commanding position, their experience, or their productive skill and energy.[6]

This new approach was somewhat obscured during the war, when the policy of enrolling in the Party servicemen who had distinguished themselves in battle brought a considerable influx of recruits from the humbler ranks of Soviet society. The proportion of workers among the new Party members rose from 24.4 per cent to 32.1 per cent.[7] To judge from the great expansion of Party strength on the collective farms during the postwar demobilization period, a similar rise must have taken place in the proportion of peasants recruited. At the same time, the enormous wartime losses of administrative and managerial cadres must have brought into action a factor which has operated throughout the history of

[6] For a detailed treatment of the social orientation of Party recruitment during these earlier periods, see Fainsod, *How Russia Is Ruled,* pp. 209-32.
[7] See Shamberg, *loc. cit.*

the CPSU to keep the proportion of production workers in the Party down: the promotion of "activist" workers and peasants to leading posts once they had attained Party status. Nevertheless, there can be little doubt that the mass wartime recruitment had the net result of giving the Party firmer roots in the lower reaches of Soviet society. For example, in 1949 there were five times as many Communists in the Moscow region working directly in production as in 1940.[8]

Broadening the Social Composition of the Membership

In the recruitment policy of the early postwar period there seems to have been a return to emphasis upon the Party's "leading and directing" role, with its concomitant concentration of recruitment among the intelligentsia. However, after 1948 there are clear indications of a steadily broadening approach. The breakdown of new members in Belorussia given in Table 1, provides the most striking evidence of this fact.

In 1951 the Party authorities in the town of Staliniri were rebuked because 70 per cent of recruits in the two previous years had been white-collar workers, and this percentage was said to be too high.[10] The aim seems to have been to bring up the number of skilled tradesmen in the factories and farms closer to parity

[8] *Moskovskij bol'shevik,* February 2, 1949.
[9] See figures given by Belorussian First Secretary Patolichev in his report to the Twentieth Congress of the Belorussian Communist Party, *Sovetskaja Belorussija,* September 22, 1952.
[10] See *Zarja Vostoka,* February 2, 1951.

TABLE 1 *Class Status of New Party Members in Belorussia, 1948–1952*[9]

YEAR	WORKERS AND COLLECTIVE FARMERS Per Cent	OFFICE WORKERS AND INTELLIGENTSIA Per Cent
1948	18.8	81.2
1949	40.4	59.6
1950	42.4	57.6
1951	43.9	56.1
January–June, 1952	49.8	50.2

in the Party with the number of administrative and professional personnel. Even in Moscow workers formed 34 per cent of those recruited in 1949–1951, while engineers and technicians constituted 33 per cent and administrators and professional people 27.5 per cent.[11] In 1952, 57 per cent of the Kirgiz CP were "workers" or "peasants."[12]

These figures bear witness to a major shift away from the concepts underlying recruitment in the years following the great purges. This brings us to the fourth concept of the Party as an association of the "best people" of Soviet society.

The term "best people" was also used in the preceding period, but nearly always in contexts linking it to high-status occupational groups. In the postwar years it developed wider connotations. As now employed it seems to imply that each occupational group has its own "best people," its natural leaders, who should become the representatives of the Party among their comrades, rallying them by word and example to support of the Party's policies.

After the Nineteenth Congress in October 1952, the level of new enrolments was cut back sharply, and there appears to have been a return to a narrower recruitment basis. Between October 1952 and January 1954, 57.4 per cent of the new candidates for membership in Belorussia were white-collar workers,[13] compared with 50.2 per cent in the first half of 1952.[14]

In many areas recruitment was entirely restricted to white-collar workers.[15] In Georgia, during 1953 only 19 of the 83 recruits in industrial Kutaisi and 40 of the 184 in Batumi were workers.[16] The keynote speeches in the 1954 Party congresses in these two republics and in the Ukraine[17] condemned this state of affairs, as did Khrushchev in his speech to the

Central Committee on February 23, 1954. Khrushchev, who was concerned in this speech mainly with the effects of the restrictive recruitment policy on the Party's strength in the *kolkhozes*, stated that in 585 rural districts not a single *kolkhoznik* had been recruited during 1953, and that only 16,620 of those who joined the Party in that year were *kolkhozniks*. "Many *raikoms* are paying no attention whatever to the question of recruitments," he said. "It is well known that in recent years the Party has been conducting a policy of restricting recruitment, but this does not mean that the recruitment of the foremost *kolkhozniks* must be stopped altogether. . . . This shortcoming must be eliminated."[18]

These statements mark the latest turning point in the Party's policy, initiating a return to the more liberal approach of the pre-Nineteenth Congress era. The rate of new enrolments rose sharply. In the Ukraine, Belorussia, Azerbaidzhan, Georgia, Armenia, Uzbekistan, Tadzhikistan and Kirgizia — the eight Union republics for which accurate figures are available — the average increase in Party membership between September 1952 and February 1954 was 1.2 per cent while between February 1954 and January 1956 it was 6.6 per cent.[19] Incomplete figures from other republics and regions of the R.S.F.S.R. indicate the same pattern, so that there is every reason to believe that these figures are broadly representative of the country as a whole. Allowing for the difference in length of the periods under comparison, there appears to have been something like a fourfold increase in the rate of recruitment after February 1954.

Along with this, the net is once more being cast more widely. In Belorussia, where again the most precise information is available, 61

[11] See *Moskovskaja pravda*, March 31, 1951.
[12] *Sovetskaja Kirgizija*, September 21, 1952. The trend was less marked in some areas than others. For example, white-collar workers and intelligentsia still represented 59 per cent of the Party organizations in Georgia in 1952. *Zarja Vostoka*, September 18, 1952.
[13] See *Sovetskaja Belorussija*, February 13, 1954.
[14] See Table I.
[15] *Sovetskaja Belorussija*, February 17, 1954.
[16] *Zarja Vostoka*, February 18, 1954.
[17] See *Pravda Ukrainy*, March 24, 1954.

[18] *Pravda*, March 21, 1954.
[19] Based on a comparative analysis of figures given in the republican press. Increases in the individual republics for the periods before and after February 1954 were as follows: Ukraine; before 3.1 per cent, after 7.4 per cent; Belorussia: before 1.25 per cent, after 12 per cent; Georgia: before 1.8 per cent, after 4.9 per cent; Azerbaidzhan: before 1.6 per cent, after 5.5 per cent; Armenia: before 2.2 per cent, after 5.3 per cent; Uzbekistan: before −.4 per cent, after 5.9 per cent; Kirgizia: before, −.5 per cent, after 4.6 per cent; Tadzhikistan: before, .8 per cent, after 7.3 per cent.

per cent of the candidates for Party membership in 1954 and 1955 were workers or collective farmers — 18 per cent more than in the post-Nineteenth Congress period.[20] In Rostov Province the recruitment of collective farmers was accelerated threefold in 1955.[21] Figures recently revealed from the Ukraine, Azerbaidzhan, Latvia, Tadzhikistan, and Armenia indicate the same trend.[22] Nevertheless, as was implied in many of the keynote speeches of the 1956 Union republic congresses, it is no easy matter to secure a substantial expansion of Party membership in the humbler ranks of Soviet society. Unless a big recruiting effort is made, working-class and peasant candidates are not numerous. Thus three of the ward committees of the CPSU in Baku were blamed for lack of zeal in recruiting workers, who represented only 41 out of 403 candidates in the Gorodskoj Borough, 54 of 169 in Dzerzhinskij Borough and 56 out of 515 in Voroshilovgrad Borough. In three rural districts of Azerbaidzhan, collective farmers made up only 17 out of 65, 14 out of 43 and 5 out of 35 candidates during 1954–55.[23] Only 11.4 per cent of post-Nineteenth Congress recruits in Stalingrad province were *kolkhozniks,* and in industrial Novosibirsk region only 32 per cent were workers.[24] In the Ukraine the Party second secretary Podgorny stated in January 1956 that in the mining region of Stalino only 3 per cent of Party members were coal-cutters and other mining tradesmen, while only 94 of the 2,000 mine tradesmen and mechanics in the city of Stalino were Communists.[25] Such facts are significant, but we should not allow them to conceal the real achievements of the policy of wider recruitment outside the intelligentsia since 1954.

This policy was reaffirmed in the Resolution of the Twentieth Congress on Khrushchev's

report,[26] and subsequently stressed in the Party press.[27]

The Postwar Increase in Rural Membership

Of all changes in the distribution of CPSU membership since World War II, none has been greater in scale and importance than the increase of Party strength in the countryside.

In the pre-Revolutionary period, the number of peasants who joined the Bolsheviks was insignificant, and they constituted only 7.5 per cent of the Party in 1917. The Civil War brought thousands of peasants into the Bolshevik ranks, so that by 1921 they represented fully a quarter of the membership. The proletariat-oriented recruitment of the 1920's did not favor such a rapid growth of peasant representation, and by 1930 the proportion of Party members who were of peasant origin had dropped off to 20 per cent.[28] This represented only half a million individuals, and taking into account the very large proportion who had already migrated to the towns or been promoted to administrative jobs, the Party's weakness among the farming sections of the population at the time of the collectivization will be appreciated. While the Party's numbers increased fourfold between 1922 and 1929, the number of Communists in the villages only doubled.[29]

The years 1930–1932 saw vigorous efforts to build up the rural cells, partly through local recruiting and partly through sending working-class Communists to the villages, and for the first time the growth of the Party membership in the villages outpaced that of the Party as a whole. Nevertheless, the distribution of Communists in the collectives remained dangerously thin. At the end of 1933, only 649

---

[20] See *Sovetskaja Belorussija,* January 27, 1956.
[21] See *Partijnaja zhizn,* No. 17, 1955, p. 7.
[22] See *Pravda Ukrainy,* January 20, 1956; *Bakinskij rabochij,* January 27, 1956; *Sovetskaja Latvija,* January 18, 1956; *Kommunist Tadzhikistana,* January 20, 1956; *Kommunist* (Erevan), January 20, 1956.
[23] *Bakinskij rabochij,* January 27, 1956.
[24] C. C. Secretary Suslov, as reported in *Pravda,* February 17, 1956.
[25] *Pravda Ukrainy,* January 23, 1956.

[26] The Resolution called for greater attention to recruitment. Empasis was to remain upon the quality rather than the number of recruits, but this was to involve enrolling "the foremost people, principally from among workers and collective farmers." See *Pravda,* February 25, 1956.
[27] For example, the leading article in *Pravda,* April 6, 1956, stated that "it is essential to obtain a decisive increase in the relative weight of workers and collective farmers among those enrolled in the Party."
[28] The above figures are taken from B.S.E. (1st ed.), XI, pp. 533–4.
[29] See *ibid.,* p. 535.

out of the 11,400 *kolkhozes* in the Leningrad Province had party cells,[30] while in the Western Province there was one district in which 85 per cent of the collective farms had not a single Communist, another district with 82 per cent, and a third with 90 per cent of their farms completely devoid of Communists.[31]

The large-scale recruitment which began at the end of 1936 was centered, as we have seen, mainly upon the intelligentsia, and although this term peripherally included the *kolkhoz* aristocracy, it brought no radical increase in the Party's strength on the farms prior to World War II. For example among the 7,201 recruits from November 1936 to March 1939 in the *rural* districts of Leningrad Province, only 1,177 were collective farmers.[32] At the time of the Eighteenth Congress, Party cells existed on only 12,000 *kolkhozes* — about 8 per cent of the total. There were 153,000 Communists on the collective farms, that is, every five farms had, on the average, three Party members among them.[33]

The great postwar expansion of Party strength in the countryside has been achieved in four phases:

(1) 1945–1946. Demobilization brought back to the villages thousands of young Communists who had joined the Party while serving in the armed forces.

(2) 1947–1949. Party forces in the countryside were redistributed and rural cells reorganized so as to transfer the greatest possible number of Communists to collective farm cells.

(3) 1950–1952. The reorganization of the collective farms, which drastically reduced their number, together with substantial peasant recruitment, greatly increased the average strength of the collective farm cells.

(4) September, 1953. This period brought the transfer of thousands of Communists from town to country and from early 1954, the resumption of large-scale recruitment.

By early 1947, the demobilization of wartime recruits had already brought a considerable reinforcement of Party strength in the countryside. However, this tended to be concentrated in the local administrative centers rather than on the farms. In one district of the Kaluga Province for example, there were over a thousand Communists, but only 10 per cent of these were actually engaged in agricultural production. Only four *kolkhozes* in the district had Party cells (a minimum of three members or candidates was required for the formation of a cell) and on 59 collective farms there were no Communists at all.[34] In a rural district of the Molotov Province, only 3 out of the 90 collective farms had Party organizations.[35] In Bryansk Province there were cells on only 353 out of the 2,928 collective farms.[36] A large number of Communists distributed in ones or twos among the farms had perforce to belong to "territorial primary Party organizations," that is, to cells covering a given geographical area rather than a particular production unit. In Orel Province three quarters of the rural Communists in 1947 were enrolled in territorial organizations.[37] In 85 per cent of the collective farms of the Kalinin Province the Communists belonged to territorial Party organizations centered about the village administration. At the same time over half of the Communists in these organizations were *kolkhoz* members.[38] This situation had serious disadvantages in the eyes of the Party leadership, which wanted the Communists on the collective farms to provide a rallying center in the productive and political campaigns and to serve as a counter-check on the farm administration and its chairman.

Small as it was, however, this proportion of collective farms with their own Party cells represented a significant advance. In the same Kalinin Province, for example, although only 10 per cent of the collective farms had Party cells, this was already three and a half times the wartime number.[39] In Kharkhov Province, the Ukraine, there were 498 collective farm Party organizations in 1941 with 4,382 members; in 1947 there were 1,117 with 7,605 members.[40] The Ukraine was an area of comparatively weak Party membership, and in other areas the growth of collective farm cells in the period immediately after the war was

30 *Partijnoe stroitel'stvo*, No. 1 (1934), p. 54.
31 Ibid., No. 2 (1934), p. 33.
32 See *Pravda*, March 21, 1939.
33 Andreev, in *Land of Socialism Today and Tomorrow*, p. 244.

34 See *Partijnaja zhizn'*, No. 9 (1947), p. 43.
35 See *Partijnaja zhizn'*, No. 11 (1947), p. 22.
36 See *Partijnaja zhizn'*, No. 9 (1947), p. 3.
37 *Partijnaja zhizn'*, No. 5 (1947), p. 27.
38 *Partijnaja zhizn'*, No. 7, (1947), p. 14.
39 Ibid.
40 *Partijnaja zhizn'*, No. 11 (1947), p. 34.

much more rapid. In the Orel Province, for example, between April 1, 1946, and March 1, 1947, they grew from 255 to 458, and their membership from 1,583 to 3,091.[41]

The years 1947–1949 saw an enormous proliferation of Party organizations on the collective farms, and a shifting of the center of gravity among rural Communists from the territorial to the farm organizations. The policy seems to have been to distribute Communists in each rural district in such a way as to secure the necessary minimum number of Communists to form a separate cell on the maximum number of collective farms. As early as February 1948, there was one district of Stalingrad Province which had Party organizations in all but one of its collective farms.[42] A month later Chkalov Province had organized Party organizations in 1,554 out of its 2,087 *kolkhozes*.[43] In the country as a whole, the number of rural Party organizations grew by 31,703 during 1947, and 25,579 of these were on collective farms. By early 1948, over 50 per cent of rural Party cells were on collective farms. A third of the *kolkhozes* of the Soviet Union then had their own Party organizations. There were many territories, provinces, and republics where the number was over half, and some in which it exceeded 85 per cent.[44]

The year 1949 saw the end of the second phase of the postwar campaign for expanding Party membership in the rural areas. Figures made public at Party congresses and conferences that year indicate the extent of the headway already made. In the Moscow Province *kolkhoz* Party cells increased from 153 before the war to 1,048 in 1949.[45] In the Ukraine, the increase was from 3,156 in 1940 to 13,280 in 1949.[46] In Georgia the number rose over the same period from 1,339 to 3,200.[47]

The number of *kolkhoz* cells was, however, expanding at a far greater rate than the num-

ber of *kolkhoz* Communists. Thus, while the number of collective farm organizations in the Ukraine had quadrupled since before the war, their total membership had scarcely more than doubled.[48] In Tadzhikistan the number of Party organizations in industrial enterprises increased by 150 per cent between 1940 and the end of 1948, while those in collective farms grew by 352 per cent. Yet the increase in total membership was practically the same in each — 297 per cent in industry and 319 per cent in the collective farms.[49] These facts indicate the relative weakness of many of the new collective farm cells, and confirm that the great increase in their number between 1947 and 1949 was due less to recruitment of new Party members than to a judicious disposal of those Communists already available in the rural areas.

The third phase brought the amalgamation of the smaller collective farms, which reduced their number from 254,000 in January 1950 to 97,000 in October 1952.[50] This made it possible to raise considerably the average strength of *kolkhoz* cells, a fact which is reflected in the proliferation of Party groups in the labor brigades and livestock farms of the *kolkhozes*,[51] and the steadily rising number of collective farm organizations with the necessary fifteen members to elect a bureau as well as a secretary.[52]

The years 1951 and 1952 also witnessed a big expansion of Party membership in the rural areas of the recently acquired Western borderlands. Between April 1951 and September 1952, the number of Moldavian Communists working in the countryside increased by 4,211 while those working in industry increased only by 1,049.[53] In Belorussia, 14,008 out of the 17,887 new members taken on from 1949 to 1952 were enrolled by the Party cells of collective farms or MTS.[54]

---

41 *Partijnaja zhizn'*, No. 5 (1947), p. 27.
42 *Partijnaja zhizn'*, No. 5 (1948), p. 20.
43 *Partijnaja zhizn'*, No. 7 (1948), p. 7.
44 *Partijnaja zhizn'*, No. 5 (1948), p. 21.
45 See G. M. Popov's report in *Moskovskij bol'shevik*, February 2, 1949.
46 See Khrushchev's report to the Sixteenth Congress of the Ukrainian Communist Party, *Pravda*, January 26, 1949.
47 See Charkviani's report to the Fourteenth Congress of the Georgian Communist Party, *Zarja Vostoka*, January 28, 1949.

48 Khrushchev, *loc. cit.*
49 See B. Gafurov's report to the Seventh Congress of the Tadzhik Communist Party, *Kommunist Tadzhikistana*, December 22, 1948.
50 See Malenkov's report at the Nineteenth Congress of the CPSU, *Pravda*, October 6, 1952.
51 See CPSU statutes, sec. 55, "On Party Groups."
52 *Pravda*, August 22, 1952, Nijazov, in *Pravda Vostoka*, September 20, 1952.
53 See L. I. Brezhnev, Report to the Fourth Congress of the Moldavian Communist Party, *Sovetskaja Moldavija*, September 20, 1952.
54 *Sovetskaja Belorussija*, September 22, 1952.

In the period following the September 1953 session of the Central Committee, tens of thousands of Communists were transferred to the villages from industrial and administrative jobs in the towns. In the Smolensk Province, over 2,000 Party members were switched from the towns to the rural districts,[55] while in Belorussia the number was 13,000.[56] While many of these received posts in the district Party and government offices, a large proportion went to work directly in the MTS, *kolkhozes,* and state farms.[57] No less than 30,000 senior Party members were posted as *kolkhoz* chairmen alone.[58] In the light of these and similar figures revealed during the Twentieth Congress and the local conferences and congresses preceding it, it would seem that at least 100,000 Communists must have been transferred to work in agriculture during 1954–1955. Meanwhile, as we have seen, the farms figured prominently in the Party recruitment campaign initiated in 1954. Of the 235 new Party cells formed in Latvia in 1954–1955, no less than 231 were in *kolkhozes.*[59] These two factors have produced a further substantial reinforcement of Communist forces in rural production units. In Belorussia, for example, in 1954–1955 the number of Party members directly employed in the *kolkhozes,* state farms, and MTS rose from 23,874 to 35,038 — i.e., by 47 per cent.[60] The steps taken in the postwar period to strengthen Communist forces in the villages have resulted in a metamorphosis of the Party's position in the *kolkhozes.* While only one *kolkhoz* in twelve had a primary Party organization in 1939, by September 1953, Party cells existed in 76,000 out of the 94,000 collective farms,[61] and by the beginning of 1956 only 7,356 were without a primary Party organization.[62] Realization of the goal of a Party

cell in every *kolkhoz* is now in sight.[63] While the total Party membership roughly trebled between 1939 and 1954, the number of Communists in the *kolkhozes* increased about sixfold.[64]

Occupational Area and Level of Party Members

No official analyses of the occupational distribution of the CPSU membership are available. However, partial breakdowns for certain areas and fields of activity have been given from time to time, and much can be learned from a comparison of these.

Industry. Bulganin stated in July 1955 that over 2,000,000 Party members were employed in industrial enterprises.[65] If Communists employed in mining, construction, lumbering, and transport were added, the number would probably be somewhat higher than 2,500,000. It is likely that about half of these are actual production workers. Of the 90,000 Communists in the coal industry, for example, 38,000 are employed underground.[66] In Georgia there were 8,309 "workers of the leading trades" enrolled in the Party between 1940 and 1948, compared with 5,156 managerial and technical employees.[67] In 1945 there were 1,675 Communists employed in the machine-tool industry in Baku, of whom 765 (45 per cent) were managerial and technical employees and 910 (55 per cent) were production workers.[68] Of

---

55 See *Pravda,* February 22, 1956.

56 *Sovetskaja Belorussija,* January 26, 1956.

57 Including 16,000 who were sent to stock-raising jobs on the farms. See *Partijnaja zhizn',* No. 9 (1955), 17.

58 See Kaganovich's speech in *Pravda,* January 21, 1956.

59 See *Sovetskaja Latvija,* January 18, 1956.

60 *Sovetskaja Belorussija,* January 26, 1956.

61 See Khrushchev, *O merakh dal'neishego razvitija sel'skogo khozaistva SSSR* (Gospolitzdat, 1953), pp. 4, 72.

62 See Aristov's speech in *Pravda,* February 17, 1956.

63 In Belorussia, an area of comparatively thin Party membership, the proportion of *kolkhozes* with Party cells rose from 56 per cent to 91.5 per cent between January 1954, and January 1956. See *Sovetskaja Belorussija,* January 26, 1956. The Baltic republics are the chief remaining area of weakness. Party cells have not yet been formed on 712 of the *kolkhozes* in Lithuania (*Sovetskaja Litva,* January 26, 1956). There are still collective farms in Estonia without a single Communist (*Pravda,* February 19, 1956).

64 For 1954 figures, see Khrushchev: *O dal'neishem uvelichenii proizvodstva zerna v strane i ob osvoenii celinnykh i zalezhnykh zemel'* (Gospolizdat, 1954), p. 58.

65 See *Pravda,* July 17, 1955.

66 Khrushchev's Report to the Twentieth Congress of the CPSU, *Pravda,* February 2, 1956.

67 See *Zarja Vostoka,* January 28, 1949. A significant proportion of the workers doubtless attained managerial or technical status at some time after joining the Party.

68 See *Partijnoe stroitel'stvo,* No. 3–4 (1945), p. 19.

industrial employees enrolled in the Moscow Party organization between 1949 and 1951, 48 per cent were managerial and technical and 52 per cent were production workers.[69] In Chkalov Province in 1955 there were 11,000 Communists employed in industrial enterprises, of whom a little over 4,000 were engaged in "the decisive sectors of production." Of over 1,000 Communists employed in the construction industry, 470 were working directly in production.[70] A deficiency of all these figures is that they give no indication of the proportion of Communist "workers in production" who hold foreman status.

Agriculture. In 1954, according to Khrushchev, of the 3,000,000 Communists located in the rural districts, 31 per cent were employed in *kolkhozes*, 8 per cent in MTS and 4.3 per cent in state farms.[71] Allowing for the subsequent stepping up of enrolments and the transfer of Communists to agriculture, there must now be about 1,000,000 Communists in the collective farms, a quarter million in the MTS, and approaching 150,000 in the state farms. How many of these work at the different levels of the farming hierarchy? In 1948 there was published the following official breakdown of collective farm Communists:[72]

Kolkhoz chairmen	13.8%
Brigade leaders	10.1%
Heads of livestock farms	4.7%
Tractor drivers	5.4%
Other farm workers (including team leaders)	47.9%
Miscellaneous (presumably comprising agronomists, bookkeepers, livestock specialists, storemen and other office personnel)	18.1%

Farm chairmen must now represent a much smaller proportion of *kolkhoz* Communists, and brigade leaders probably a larger one. The great expansion of rural cells must have brought some rise in the proportion of "team leaders" (*zvenevye*) and rank-and-file farm workers. Between them these probably make up over

half the *kolkhoz* Communists but, as in the case of industry, there is no way of isolating the rank-and-file employees from those of junior foreman status.

Administration. This category comprises officials employed in the central, republican, and local offices of the government, Party, trade unions, and *Komsomol*. Here again Khrushchev's February 1954 speech provides a useful starting figure. He said that 30 per cent of the 3,000,000 Communists in the rural districts of the U.S.S.R. (i.e., about 900,000 Party members) were employed in various public offices.[73] These would make up by far the largest contingent of Communists in the administrative category. No over-all figures for the higher levels of the administrative hierarchies are available. In 1951, 35 per cent of the Moscow City Party organization, or 131,000 Communists, were employed in government offices.[74] Moscow contains both the Union government and the government of the R.S.F.S.R., and the number of Communists working in government offices in the other republic capitals would not be at all comparable. In Tbilisi somewhat over a quarter of the delegates to the 1951 conference of the city Party organization were government or trade union officials. Trade union officials were probably 20–25 per cent of this number, and assuming the remainder to have been mostly delegates from the Party cells of government offices, this would suggest a total strength for the latter of about 10,000 Communists. Georgia is a relatively small republic, but it has a high rate of Party membership, so this figure is probably not very far from the average for Communists employed in government offices in the capitals of the national republics. If so, this group would total about 150,000. Allowing for government officials working at the city and regional levels, and for Party, *Komsomol*, and trade union officials working at levels above the district, the total number of

---

[69] See *Moskovskaja pravda*, March 31, 1951.
[70] *Partijnaja zhizn'*, No. 17 (1955), p. 25.
[71] Khrushchev, *O dal'neishem uvelichenii proizvodstva zerna . . .*, p. 58.
[72] See *Partijnaja zhizn'*, No. 5 (1948), p. 21.

[73] Khrushchev, *O dal'neishem uvelichenii proizvodstva zerna . . .*, p. 58. The Russian phrase used indicated that this covered not only government offices, but Party and other para-governmental bodies as well. However, it is not clear whether it also included the chairmen of village Soviets. Most of the 50,000 village Soviet chairmen appear now to be Party members.
[74] *Moskovskaja pravda*, March 31, 1951.

Communists in the administration category would apparently amount to about 1,500,000.

Armed Forces and Police. The armed forces have always represented one of the most important centers for "political education" and recruitment to the Party, not only during the Civil War and World War II, but also in time of peace. This is exemplified by the fact that while Communists represented 27 per cent of those taken into the army in 1930, they made up 57 per cent of this class when it was demobilized in 1932.[75] In 1938 no less than 101,310 persons serving in the army were enrolled as candidates for Party membership.[76] In 1934 over a quarter of all Red Army men were Party members.[77] In the Navy the proportion in 1939 was 17 per cent.[78] No such figures have been discovered for the postwar period, but it was stated that of the 640,000 members of the armed forces released in 1955, 145,000 (or 22 per cent) were Communists.[79] This would suggest a total of close on a million Communists in the armed forces as a whole.[80] It is difficult to estimate the number of Party members in the police (including the militia, security police, border troops, and internal security troops). Party representation is undoubtedly very high, but figures are not available on the total strength of these organizations. However, there are some leads on the number of Communists in the armed forces and police taken together. These elect delegates to republic Party conferences separate from the territorial Party organizations, though with the same rate of representation. Army and police delegates made up 12 per cent of the delegates to the 1949 Ukrainian congress, and 14 per cent of those to the 1952 congress in this republic.[81] They constituted 11.4 per

cent of the delegates to the Fourteenth Georgian Party Congress in 1949.[82] If these proportions are broadly representative for the country as a whole, they imply a total of somewhat under 1,000,000. This is a somewhat lower figure than that suggested by the earlier calculation, but in any case a figure in the vicinity of a million would appear a reasonable estimate of the number of Communists in the armed forces and police category.

"Culture." The term is used to cover persons working in educational, medical, and scientific research establishments, as well as the arts and entertainment. Seventeen per cent of the Leningrad regional Party organization were drawn from this category in 1952.[83] The percentage in most areas is undoubtedly well below this. In the Ukraine in 1952 it was 9 per cent.[84] It is probable that somewhat under three quarters of a million Party members come into this category. Teachers and doctors are probably the best represented occupational groups here. In 1947, there were 80,000 teachers and 40,000 doctors in the Party,[85] and these numbers must have risen since then.

These calculations are summed up in Table 2 below.[86]

Summary

In conclusion it may be said that postwar trends in the social composition of the Soviet Communist Party have diverged significantly from those pursued between 1936 and 1941. The concentration of Party membership in the "leading" sections of society has ceased to be the dominant feature of recruiting and allocation policy. While the predominance of the administrative-managerial bureaucracy has been maintained, the main stress has been

[75] N. Kirjaev, *Partija bol'shevikov v bor'be za ukreplenie sovetskoi armii v gody mirnogo socialisticheskogo stroitel'stva* (Moscow, 1951), p. 32.
[76] *Ibid.*, p. 34.
[77] *Ibid.*
[78] *Pravda*, March 22, 1939.
[79] *Pravda*, February 17, 1956.
[80] A. Avtorkhanov points out however (*Vestnik Instituta po izucheniiu SSSR*, No. 2 [19], 1956, p. 7) that Twentieth Congress delegates from the armed forces, as pictured in the press, numbered 116, and that if all military delegates appeared in the photograph, this would imply a figure of about 580,000 for Communists in the armed services.
[81] See *Pravda Ukrainy*, February 5, 1949, and September 26, 1952.

[82] *Zarja Vostoka*, January 29, 1949.
[83] *Leningradskaja pravda*, September 28, 1952.
[84] *Pravda Ukrainy*, September 25, 1952.
[85] See *Partijnaja zhizn'*, No. 20 (1947), p. 83.
[86] Some indirect confirmation of these results is derived from comparison with various local analyses published since 1952 (see *Pravda Ukrainy*, September 25, 1952; *Leningradskaja pravda*, September 28, 1952; *Krasnoe znamja*, February 13, 1954; *Sovetskaja Kirgizija*, September 21, 1952; *Sovetskaja Belorussija*, February 15, 1956); and by the fact that the estimates add up to a figure very close to the 7,215,505 given by Khrushchev at the Twentieth Congress as the size of the Party membership — see *Pravda*, February 15, 1956.

TABLE **2** *Estimated Occupational Distribution of C.P.S.U. Membership*

OCCUPATION	APPROXIMATE NUMBER	APPROXIMATE PERCENTAGE OF TOTAL MEMBERSHIP
Industry, mining, transport, etc..........................	2,600,000	36
(Junior foremen and rank-and-file workers).............	(1,300,000)	(18)
Agriculture (collective & state farms & MTS)................	1,400,000	19
(Junior foremen and rank-and-file workers).............	(750,000)	(10)
Political and administrative hierarchies...................	1,500,000	21

upon achieving adequate Party representation in other social and occupational groups. The farming population, as the most serious area of Party weakness, has come in for special attention. There is now no major section of Soviet society lacking a substantial hard core of Party members.

It is perhaps not too fanciful to perceive a parallel between these trends and the postwar modification (though not reversal) of the tendencies toward sharper class and status differentiation and reduced social mobility which were apparent in the latter 1930's. The impression created is that of a fairly stable and self-assured privileged class which, like the late Victorian bourgeoisie in England, seeks to extend its influence and certain benefits to the masses, with the object of achieving a new consensus confirming its privileges.

Immediately after the war, and for a period following the Nineteenth Congress, the recruitment figures suggest an approach to the Party's membership which runs counter to the main line of the postwar period. These spells of more restrictive recruitment may represent responses to temporary problems, e.g., in 1945–1947 to the need to assimilate and indoctrinate the masses of raw wartime recruits, and in 1952–1953 to the political uncertainty associated with the "doctor's plot" and the death of Stalin. The possibility cannot be excluded, however, that the rate and social orientation of the Party's growth is a subject on which differences of opinion exist within the Party leadership and that the postwar fluctuations in recruitment policy reflect shifts in the influence of particular leading individuals or groups.

15

The Komsomol: Youth Under Dictatorship*

Merle Fainsod

(1951)

We know from Mr. Rigby's discussion of the composition of the Communist Party that it has not always been the party of youth. The Komsomol, or Young Communist League, is the Party's answer to this challenge. Professor Fainsod analyzes one of the most important social distinctions in the contemporary U.S.S.R., that between the generations. He reveals not only the elaborate apparatus for mobilizing and

* Reprinted from "The Komsomols: A Study of Youth Under Dictatorship," *Ameican Political Science Review*, Vol. 45 (1951), pp. 18–40, by permission of the author and the American Political Science Association. Quotations from *Young Communists in the USSR*, translated by Virginia Rhine (Washington, 1950) are reprinted here with the permission of Public Affairs Press; quotations from *Youth in Soviet Russia*, by Klaus Mehnert (London & New York, 1933) are reprinted here with the permission of George Allen & Unwin Ltd. and Harcourt, Brace and Company.

indoctrinating the youth, but also the doubts which tend to erode their faith and belief.

One of the most striking characteristics of modern totalitarianism is the conscious attention which it devotes to the organization and indoctrination of youth.† The Soviet dictatorship is unique in having set the pattern of such activity; it has carried it on at a level of intensity and over a span of time unmatched by its now defunct Fascist and Nazi rivals. A third of a century has passed since the Bolsheviks rode to power in 1917; the membership of the Communist Party is today overwhelmingly composed of a generation which not only came of age since the Revolution but which also largely served its apprenticeship in the Young Pioneers and Komsomols. And waiting at the threshold of power is a new generation of approximately 10,000,000 Komsomols and 13,000,000 Pioneers, from whose ranks the Communist elite of the future is to be recruited.

What has been the history of this effort to assimilate and discipline the new generations? What manner of training are they receiving? What values does the present leadership seek to implant in them? What motives operate to induce affiliation with the Komsomols? How is the Komsomol organized? What are the activities of its membership? How are the oncoming waves of Soviet youth relating themselves to the society which has produced them? To what extent are they deeply loyal to the present regime? Is there evidence of disaffection among them, and if so, does this disaffection present any important threat to the stability of the regime itself?

To put these questions is not to suggest that anything resembling conclusive answers can be deduced from the available data. Interpretations of the moods and attitudes of Soviet youth run a spectacular gamut. The official view of the Party leadership is that the younger generation is fanatically and passionately devoted to Communism. The counter-claim of some ex-Soviet citizens in emigration is that the whole body of Soviet youth is ready to rise up in revolt against the regime at the first opportunity. What the available evidence does seem to demonstrate is that neither of these polar positions can stand serious scrutiny. Even a cursory reading of the literature of self-criticism in the Soviet press yields sufficient denunciations of political passivity in Komsomol circles to cast grave doubt on the official picture of Soviet youth as an embodiment of zealous orthodoxy. On the other hand, interviews with Soviet defectors and non-returners, many of whom themselves passed through the Komsomol school, testify to the continued presence, though in diminished degree, of a hard core of fanaticism in the Komsomol which makes it impossible to treat the younger generation as entirely lost to the Communist cause.

The observations which are reported here are based both on a consultation of official Soviet publications and on a series of interviews with some fifty Soviet defectors and non-returners who were at one time members of the Young Pioneers and Komsomol organizations.[1] There are serious problems of appraisal involved in reliance on either of these sources; taken together, however, they serve as a mutual corrective, and there are enough instances where the testimony is corroborative to induce some confidence in the results.

I. *The Growth and Development of the Komsomol*

To understand the problem of the generations in Soviet terms, one must view it in terms of the historical perspective in which it has evolved. Every generation bears the ineluctable stamp of the strategic historical experiences to which it has been exposed. The history of Soviet youth, and indeed of Soviet society, has

† The author wishes to acknowledge the very generous aid provided by the Russian Research Center, Harvard University, and the Human Resources Research Institute of the Air University in making this study possible. He also wishes to express a strong debt of gratitude to Mr. Paul W. Friedrich, who was associated with him in interviewing Soviet defectors in Germany and Austria and whose reports on interviews with former members of the Komsomol have contributed invaluable insights into their motivations for affiliation and the sources of disaffection among them.

[1] The interviews took place in Western Germany and Austria during the Summer and Fall of 1949. The great majority of those interviewed had left the Soviet Union during World War II; a small minority consisted of recent defectors from the Red Army and the Soviet Military Government in Germany. For a general treatment of the attitudes of Soviet non-returners and defectors, see Merle Fainsod, "Controls and Tensions in the Soviet System," *American Political Science Review,* Vol. 44, pp. 266–282 (June 1950).

been a unique tale of turmoil in a turbulent age. The Revolution, the Civil War and War Communism, the N.E.P., the Five Year Plans, Collectivization, the Great Purge of 1936–38, World War II, and the years of strain which followed have all left their marks on succeeding generations of youth. Over most of the period, life has been lived in an atmosphere attuned to crisis, of dangers real and fancied, of super-human demands on youth, of endless emergencies and constant strife and tension. The casualties have been high. The Revolution has consumed its children as well as its makers. Like most revolutionary movements which attempt a sharp break with the past, the Communist leadership has placed its primary reliance on youth to generate the momentum of innovation. It was Lenin who wrote long before the Revolution, "We mean to leave the collection of weary thirty-year old ancients, revolutionaries 'come to their senses,' and Social Democratic renegades to people like the Constitutional Democrats. We always mean to remain the Party for the youth of that class to which the future belongs."[2]

Prior to the Revolution, the Bolsheviks maintained no separate organization for the younger generation. The reason was an obvious one. The cadres of the Party were themselves largely recruited from among student and factory youth. Through these cadres the Party sought to penetrate and exercise influence on the circles of student and worker youth which sprang up sporadically in the period of the 1905 Revolution and the years thereafter.[3] Indeed, a resolution calling for such action among students, introduced by Lenin at the Second Congress of the Russian Social-Democratic Labor Party in 1903 (when the Bolsheviks and the Mensheviks were still organizationally united), represents the first recorded Party action in this area.[4] But until 1917, aspirations reached far beyond achievement, and

the Bolsheviks remained a small sectarian group with little in the way of mass influence, either among the youth or their elders.

Even after the outbreak of the March Revolution, the Bolsheviks were slow to assume the initiative in organizing an affiliated youth movement. In Petrograd, the storm center of revolutionary activity, the leadership in youth organization was taken by an idealistic young student, P. Shevtsov, who attempted to turn the energies of youth in a cultural and non-political direction. Under his auspices, a number of young workers in the Petrograd factories were banded together in a league called *Work and Light*, which repudiated the class struggle and called upon youth "to join no party, but to work together ourselves according to the precepts of brotherly feeling. Above all we must aspire to enter life intellectually and morally mature, with steadfast views on honor and duty. Let us therefore take the torch of learning into our hands, but in our hearts there shall be room only for endeavor towards the goodness and beauty of life."[5] The program of the league called for a great expansion of schools, the foundation of a university for working class youth, the establishment of clubs and theatres, youth hostels and excursions into the woods to share the joys of nature.

The vagueness of this program, removed as it was from the immediate realities of political and economic struggle, provided the Bolsheviks with their opportunity to make a vigorous counter-appeal to working class youth. They sent their representatives into *Work and Light,* but only with the objective of attacking its program, winning support for their own views, discrediting Shevtsov, and eventually taking over the direction of the young workers themselves. Under the leadership of the twenty-one-year-old Bolshevik V. Alexeiev, a *Socialist Association of Young Workers* was organized with a program based on the class struggle and calling for immediate measures to improve the working conditions of juvenile labor. Faced with a vigorous challenge from this group, Shevtsov's grip over his own league became increasingly feeble, and in August 1917, *Work and Light* was disbanded by a vote of its own members. Meanwhile, the *Socialist Association of Young Workers* had expanded into a city-wide organization of working-class youth with

---

[2] Quoted in Klaus Mehnert, *Youth in Soviet Russia* (London and New York, 1933), p. 49.
[3] *Bol'shaya Sovetskaya Entsiklopediya* [The Great Soviet Encyclopedia] (Moscow, 1930), Vol. 11, pp. 635–638.
[4] For a copy of this resolution see VKP(b), *O Komsomole i Molodyozhi* [On the Komsomol and Youth] (Moscow, 1938), p. 76. This volume is a valuable collection of the most important Party resolutions on the Komsomol for the period up to 1938.

---

[5] Mehnert, *op. cit.,* p. 53.

a program copied largely from the Bolshevik model. By December 1917, it had attained a membership of approximately 15,000.[6] In Moscow and other large industrial centers, organizations of young workers developed more slowly though the same process of Bolshevik penetration and capture of leadership repeated itself. By identifying themselves with the specific economic grievances of the young workers and calling for such popular reforms as the outlaw of child labor, the six-hour working day for young workers, the establishment of minimum wages, the provision of social insurance benefits, compulsory education free of charge until the age of sixteen, and the right to vote at the age of eighteen, the Bolsheviks succeeded in mobilizing considerable support among the more politically active working class youths in the large cities and, indeed, relied heavily on such support in their successful bid for power in November 1917.

The organization of a Communist youth affiliate on an all-Russian basis was delayed until almost a year after the November Revolution. The 176 delegates who foregathered for the First Congress of the Komsomol, or Communist Association of Youth, in Moscow from October 29 to November 4, 1918, represented an initial membership of only 22,100.[7] They were, as was to be expected, overwhelmingly Communist in their political sympathies, but also present was a scattering of non-Party youth as well as a few delegates from other left-wing groups still collaborating with the Communists. The major struggle at the Congress took place over the designation of the organization as Communist. There was fear expressed that this appellation would frighten youth away from affiliation, but these fears were swept aside by the majority. The Congress, although declaring itself an "independent" organization, expressed complete solidarity with the Party, and adopted the Communist tag by an overwhelming majority. At the Second Congress, meeting in October 1919, with 96,-000 members represented, the bond with the Party was drawn more tightly. Although the Komsomol was still declared to be an "autonomous" organization, the Congress not only expressed its adherence to the program and tactics of the Party, but recognized its Central Committee as immediately subordinate to the Central Committee of the Party.

During the Civil War period, all of the energies of the Komsomol were concentrated on the struggle against the Whites. The Komsomols were rushed to the front in successive mobilizations, where they functioned as agitators, commissars, and shock troops, to provide leadership and inspiration for less dependable conscripts. But through the end of 1919 they remained a relatively small band, and it was not until the prospects of victory brightened during 1920 that they began to take on the character of a mass organization. By the time of the Third Congress of the Komsomols in October 1920, membership had climbed to approximately 480,000.

The rapid growth in membership brought new problems to the fore. The Komsomol was not then as tightly controlled as it was later to become. It began to spawn deviations.[8] Even before the Second Congress, a group led by Dunayevski had been pressing for the organization of special sections of the trade unions reserved for young workers. This was denounced by the Party as an effort to pit the interests of young workers against their elders and as a syndicalist deviation detracting from the authority of the Komsomol organization itself. Dunayevski and others continued to urge wider mass participation in decision-making, but their claims were decisively rejected, and disciplinary measures were taken against the deviators. Restiveness under the central controls which were already beginning to consolidate themselves within the Komsomol found their expression in renewed demands for more organizational democracy and local autonomy. This position was strongly espoused by the so-called Ukrainian opposition, which also insisted on the exclusion of intellectuals from the Association. These oppositionist tendencies, which had their analogue in the Workers' Opposition within the Party itself, were sharply attacked and repudiated at the Third Komsomol Congress.

The Third Congress marked the beginning of the turn from war to peace. In addition to

[6] Bol'shaya Sovetskaya Entsiklopediya, Vol. 11, p. 638.
[7] Ibid., p. 640.

[8] Ibid., pp. 645–649; also VKP(b), O Komsomole i Molodyozhi, pp. 80–82.

adopting a new program and constitution for the Association, the Congress listened to Lenin sounding a new call: "The task before the elder generation of revolutionaries was comparatively simple. For them it was a matter of doing away with the bourgeoisie, of inspiring hatred for it among the masses, of awakening class-consciousness in the workers. The task before your generation is infinitely more complicated: the erection of the Communist society"[9] Lenin's injunction to the Congress to "learn, learn, learn," to master the knowledge that the despised capitalist society had accumulated, to practice discipline, and to seek proficiency in the prosaic tasks of school and workshop came as something of a shock. The shock was accentuated by the adoption of the New Economic Policy in the Spring of 1921.

After the romantic heroics of Civil War battlefields and War Communism, adjustment to the N.E.P. did not come easily. To many, N.E.P. appeared as a retreat from Socialism, a surrender after victory. Opposition to N.E.P. was lively and violent in Komsomol circles. A few of the more fanatic committed suicide in protest. Still others found it impossible to make the transition from military to civilian life and sank into a quagmire of despair as unhappy victims of the Revolution which they had helped create. Grumbling among young workers mounted as working conditions failed to register the improvement for which they had hoped and unemployment increased. Enthusiasm gave way to disenchantment, and the Komsomol organization itself underwent a crisis. By October 1922, the time of meeting of the Fifth Congress, membership had plummeted to 247,000, and Party leaders became seriously alarmed.[10]

From 1922 on, strenuous efforts were made to recapture and consolidate the loyalty of Soviet youth. One of the resolutions passed by the Fifth Congress provided for the organization of the Pioneer association to attract the pre-Komsomol generation and to condition and prepare it for Komsomol membership. Measures were taken to improve working conditions for young factory workers and to pro-

vide some degree of protection for them against unemployment by imposing a minimum quota of juveniles on every industrial undertaking.[11] The system of factory schools (FZU) was extended, thus making available a modicum of education to young workers in the factories. Efforts were also made to compensate for the weakness of the organization in the countryside by mobilizing Komsomol activists and sending them to the villages to recruit members and build up local organizations. Greater stress was placed on political indoctrination within the Red Army, where peasant youths called up for military service were more amenable to Komsomol blandishments than when exposed to cross-influences at home.

As a result of these measures, the tide was reversed. By January 1, 1924, the membership of the Komsomol again passed the 400,000 mark.[12] By January 1, 1925, after the so-called "Lenin Levy," when the Party appealed to the youth to commemorate Lenin's death by closing ranks, membership rose to a million. The second million was reached in 1927, on the eve of the Five Year Plan.[13]

While the later phase of the N.E.P. registered substantial gains in membership for the Komsomol, the period was not without its problems. The level of political literacy was low, particularly in rural areas. Among the more politically alert, the grey dullness of the N.E.P. was not calculated to stir enthusiasm. The strong response which the Trotsky opposition, and later the block of Zinoviev, Kamenev, and Trotsky, received from the more educated and politically conscious stratum of the Komsomol organization becomes explicable against this background. Trotsky's call for world revolution evoked stirring memories of the first days of the Revolution and drew on a militant tradition of activism which the N.E.P. was by way of thwarting. The purge of the Left opposition within the Party left its scar on the Komsomol, though, as events turned out, the wound responded to treatment.

The initiation of the Five Year Plan in 1928 aroused an outburst of zeal and fervor among the Komsomols for which only the period of Revolution and Civil War furnished a parallel.[14]

---

9 Mehnert, *op. cit.,* pp. 60–61.
10 *Bol'shaya Sovetskaya Entsiklopediya,* Vol. 11, p. 649.

11 *Ibid.,* pp. 649–650.
12 *Ibid.,* p. 649.
13 *Ibid.,* pp. 653–654.
14 See Mehnert, *op. cit.*

Here was an enterprise which in its immensity, its call for sacrifice, and its promise for the future was peculiarly suited to appeal to the idealism of youth. Komsomols were mobilized in the thousands to construct such industrial giants as the Stalingrad tractor factory, the Dnepropetrovsk electric station, and the new factories in the Urals and Siberia. They were drafted to work in the Don Basin when coal production lagged. They built a new industrial center on the Amur River in the Far East, named Komsomolsk in their honor. They were sent by the thousands to participate in collectivization, to liquidate the Kulaks, to help establish Kolkhozes, and to staff the new MTS (Motor-Tractor Stations). They set the pace as shock brigadiers, as Stakhanovite workers, and as leaders in socialist competition. They took upon themselves the task of stamping out illiteracy, and they crowded the newly established technical institutes to prepare themselves to become the engineers and industrial managers of the morrow.

The outpouring of energy was impressive, yet the almost superhuman demands which the Plan imposed on youth also exacted their toll. The initial delirium of dedication to a new industrial project in the wilderness was succeeded by the more prosaic routine of daily irritations compounded of poor food, crowded housing, and the constant spur to make bricks out of straw. The more tender-hearted among the Komsomols were broken by the harsh realities of dekulakization and famine in the villages. As the Soviet novelist Gladkov put it, "These years are very difficult for our young people. They burn out quickly, overwork themselves, and suffer from nervous troubles; at the age of eighteen or nineteen many are either stunted or dried up and old in spirit. No fewer than one-third of the patients in the sanitarium are Komsomolites, and they are all like aged, used-up people, who have gone through a great deal already."[15]

It was the hard and the tough who survived. The sensitive and the weak dropped out as casualties by the wayside. Their places were taken by representatives of the oncoming generation recruited from the Pioneers. The size of the Komsomol organization continued to expand. By the time of the Ninth Congress of

the Komsomols in 1931, membership reached the 3,000,000 mark. At the Tenth Congress in April 1936 the membership approximated 4,000,000.[16]

The mid-thirties marked an important turn in the membership policies and program of the Komsomol. Until that period, the Komsomol had been regarded as a relatively exclusive class organization with membership primarily recruited from proletarian elements in the cities and the poorer peasantry in the villages. Admission was regulated on the basis of social origin, and the Rules of the Komsomol described it as "a mass organization, proletarian in its essence, uniting in its ranks the broad strata of the foremost, class conscious and politically literate youth."[17] At the 1936 Congress the Rules were modified to liberalize the conditions of admission. The Komsomol was to be "a mass non-party organization, affiliated with the VKP(b) [the Party], which unites in its ranks the broad stratum of the progressive, politically literate toiling youth of the town and village" with entrance determined not on the basis of social origin but in terms of the broader criterion of loyalty to the Soviet regime.[18]

This deliberate decision to widen the base of the Komsomol was accompanied by a marked shift of program. With the initiation of the Five Year Plan, the whole weight of Komsomol activity had been turned in the direction of emergency economic activity — the construction of new industrial plants, the organization of Kolkhozes, and the whipping up of enthusiasm for the manifold enterprises embraced in the Plan. In the process the Communist education of the youth was being neglected. "Some of our regional committees," reported A. V. Kosarev, the Komsomol secretary, "had become, so to say, some sort of small, sickly economic Narkomats [ministries]. . . . We have to remember that our basic task is the organization and Communist

---

[15] *Ibid.*, p. 91.

[16] Julian Towster, *Political Power in the USSR* (New York, 1948), p. 140. Also "Twenty Years of the Komsomol," *Partiinoe Stroitel'stvo*, No. 16, pp. 52–59 (August 1938).
[17] A. A. Andreyev, "The Communistic Education of the Youth and the Tasks of the Komsomol," *Partiinoe Stroitel'stvo*, No. 9, p. 10 (May 1936).
[18] *Ibid.*

education of the youth and children."[19] Under the banner of Stalin's new watchword, "Cadres decide everything," the main task of the Komsomol was now declared to be Communist indoctrination of the youth. The Komsomols were not to participate in economic questions as actively as they had done before; their major attention was to be turned to the educational task. Programs were also to be developed to appeal more widely to youth. The Komsomol leadership was called upon to emphasize "cultural" as well as political work, to organize athletic competitions, ski excursions, musicales, dramatics, dances, and evening literary discussions in order to minister to the many-sided interests of youth and to attract its support. Under the impetus of these measures, membership grew sharply. By October 1939, it had climbed to 9,000,000.[20]

The late thirties brought trials and tribulations as well as successes. The Great Purge of 1936–38 had its maximum impact on the Party, but it also struck the Komsomols hard. The central apparatus of the Komsomol was decimated; A. V. Kosarev, the first secretary, was removed, and many of the top functionaries of the organization disappeared with him.[21] At the height of the Yezhovschina, a veritable reign of terror was unleashed among Komsomols as well as Party members. Denunciations were rife in all the local organizations. Expulsions took place in the hundreds and thousands as the N.K.V.D. relentlessly pursued the so-called "Trotskyite-Bukharinist-German-Japanese-Fascist spies, diversionists, murderers, double-dealers, hostile elements, and enemies of the people" who were alleged to have infiltrated the Komsomol organization.[22] By the Spring of 1938, the Party leadership was prepared to admit that many mistakes had been committed in the course of the wholesale expulsions, and efforts were made to repair some of the damage by punishing "slanderers responsible . . . for unjust accusations" and restoring such of the victims as still remained alive to their former status in the organization.[23] But the heritage of bitterness left by the purge persisted, and its continuing effects were visible in the pattern of motivations of Soviet defectors during and after World War II.

Not all of the effects of the purge, however, were negative. The havoc wrought by the purge among the older generation was much greater than among the youth. In the process, many responsible posts in both the Party and governmental hierarchy were vacated, and the Komsomol activists who survived the purge were presented with magnificent opportunities for rapid promotion and access to positions of influence and large responsibilities. These young Komsomols who were catapulted to power over the graves of their elders were welded to the regime and incorporated in its leadership group.

Other developments in the pre-war years served to generate discontent among some members of the Komsomol rank-and-file. On October 2, 1940, the government instituted a system of tuition fees for the last three years of secondary education and higher schools.[24] At the same time it also established a state labor reserve scheme by which up to a million youths per year between the ages of fourteen and seventeen were to be drafted for training as industrial workers.[25] The introduction of tuition fees meant that those students who could not qualify for scholarships or were unable to draw on family resources to support them had to abandon their hopes of higher education. The advantages conferred on the financially better-situated left a reservoir of

---

[19] A. V. Kosarev, "On the Reorganization of Komsomol Work," *Partiinoe Stroitel'stvo*, No. 14, p. 8 (June 1935).

[20] Towster, *op. cit.*, p. 140.

[21] See the attack in the editorial "Raise the Bolshevistic Vigilance of the Komsomol," *Partiinoe Stroitel'stvo*, No. 18, p. 8 (September 1937).

[22] See, e.g., O. Smirnov, "Reshaping the Work of the Komsomol," *Partiinoe Stroitel'stvo*, No. 12, pp. 23–27 (June 1937). See also P. Vershkov, "A Leninist-Stalinist Education for Soviet Youth," *ibid.*, No. 7, pp. 28–33 (April 1938) where some typical expulsion figures are cited. In the Komsomol organization of Georgia, 1577 persons were excluded in the third quarter of 1937. Of these,

1182 were denounced as "hostile elements." In the Omsk region during the same period, 1101 Komsomolites were excluded, of whom 731 were denounced as "hostile elements and double dealers."

[23] See Vershkov, *loc. cit.*, p. 28.

[24] *Sobranie Postanolenii i Razporyazhenii Pravitel'stva SSSR*, 1940, No. 27, Sec. 637; 1940, No. 29, Sec. 698.

[25] *Vedomosti Verkhovnogo Soveta SSSR*, 1940, No. 37.

bitterness among those who were forced to withdraw from the higher schools as a result of the decree. At the same time the restrictions on access to educational opportunity and freedom of occupational choice, involved in the labor draft, also induced frustration and discontent. While it is difficult to appraise the significance of the dissatisfaction produced by these measures, the testimony of young Soviet defectors and non-returners is virtually unanimous in stressing the growth of a mood of disillusionment and disenchantment in that segment of Soviet youth which was most adversely affected.

The success of the Soviet army in surviving the Nazi onslaught and pressing on to victory may suggest that the mood was a passing one, or that in any case it did not go deep enough or was not widespread enough to affect the will to fight. Yet the problem of the loyalty of Soviet youth to the regime cannot be disposed of with a mere reference to the pragmatic fact of Soviet victory. The mass surrenders of the early days of the War point to a serious problem of morale, as well as to difficulties of matériel and generalship. All of the evidence available through interviews indicates that the mass atrocities committed by the Nazis in the course of their Russian campaign and the contempt with which they treated the Slav *Untermenschen* had much to do with stiffening resistance. Hatred of the Nazis unleashed a genuine and widespread national upsurge of feeling, which the Party leadership was shrewd enough both to stimulate and exploit. Communist slogans were muted, and the wellsprings of national sentiment were tapped to the full. The bars of admission to Party and Komsomol were lowered for members of the armed forces; the millions who enrolled during the War responded primarily to patriotic appeals. By October 1945, the claimed membership of the Komsomol was 15,000,000, approximately half of the population in the eligible age group.[26]

Since the end of the War, there has been a sharp drop in Komsomol membership. The last precise data, released on the occasion of the Eleventh Congress of the Komsomol in March 1949 showed a membership roll of 9,283,289, a figure roughly equivalent to the

1939 membership.[27] No official explanations of this decline have been vouchsafed. The difficulty which has been encountered in compensating for the high attrition rate among war-enrolled Komsomols through new admissions, suggests a falling-off in the appeal of the Komsomol which may have considerable political significance. While the available evidence is too spotty to justify large-scale conclusions, it may be surmised on the basis of occasional hints thrown out in the Soviet press that some sectors of Soviet youth manifest a disturbing passivity toward Komsomol membership. Recent reports indicate considerable Party concern over the large number of automatic exclusions from the Komsomols as a result of non-payment of dues, failure to attend meetings, and unwillingness to discharge the social and political obligations that go with membership.[28] Since the Eleventh Congress (1949), the Komsomol leadership has been pursuing an intensified program of Communist indoctrination of the young and has centered a major portion of its activity on the schools. The slow growth in membership which has been reported since the Eleventh Congress may indicate that the organization is beginning to win back some of the ground which it has lost since the end of the war.[29]

The history of the Komsomols is a record of the persistent and strenuous efforts of the Party leadership to anchor itself as firmly as possible in the support of the oncoming Soviet generations. Despite these efforts, the experience of life under the Soviet regime has eroded

---

[26] Towster, *op. cit.*, p. 140.

[27] See "Report of Mandate Commission, Eleventh Congress of the Komsomol," *Molodoi Bol'shevik*, No. 8, p. 67 (April 1949).

[28] See, e.g., the following articles: V. Ershov, "Do Not Exclude Without Foundation but Educate" (On the Mistakes of the Kemerovsk Regional Committee), *Molodoi Bol'shevik*, No. 21, pp. 39–43 (November 1949); Resolutions of the Second Plenum of the Komsomol Central Committee on the Work of the Komsomol Organizations in the Sverdlovsk Region and the Stalingrad Tractor Factory, *ibid.*, No. 1, pp. 33–34 (January 1950); "On the Style of Work of the Molotovsk Regional Committee," *ibid.*, No. 9, pp. 30–37 (May 1950).

[29] *Molodoi Bol'shevik*, in No. 23 (December 1949), at p. 47, cites the Komsomol membership then as 9,676,000. This represents a gain of nearly 400,000 since the Eleventh Congress. Most recent accounts assume a membership of around 10,000,000.

loyalties, among the youth as well as their elders, and has made widespread use of repressive and disciplinary measures necessary. But it would be a mistake to assume, because terror and secret police are integral features of the Soviet regime, that the role of indoctrination as it expresses itself through the Komsomol or other channels can be dismissed as without significance. Each new generation as it grows to maturity offers the Party leadership a fresh opportunity to imprint its stamp upon it. The capacity of the totalitarian regime to mold the minds of the young while they are still plastic and malleable is a formidable weapon, the power of which should never be underrated.

II. *Training the Komsomols*

The process starts in the kindergarten, where children's play, singing, and story-telling are used, as a recent Soviet textbook put it, "to instill love of the Soviet fatherland, its people, its leaders, and the Soviet Army. . . ."[30] The child is first enrolled in the "Little Octobrists," where his education in civic responsibilities begins. At the age of nine, he becomes eligible for membership in the "Young Pioneers," where his political education begins to assume more significant proportions.[31] Membership in the Young Pioneers, which now runs between thirteen and fourteen million, is virtually universal in the eligible age group, nine to fifteen. Indeed, the drive to affiliate is so great in the early impressionable years that the threat of exclusion is frequently a sufficient sanction to discipline the most unruly. Entrance into the Pioneers is the occasion for an impressive initiation ceremony replete with symbolism and emblems calculated to appeal to the very young. The celebration is attended by all the Pioneers of the school, their leaders, teachers, the school director, and honored guests. As described in a recent account,[32] the assembly hall is decorated with portraits of Lenin and Stalin. The Pioneers march into the hall in quasi-military formation. One of

the honored guests, an Old Bolshevik, presents each initiate, arrayed in his new uniform, with his red kerchief, his Pioneer badge, and his membership card. As the presentation is made, the symbolism of kerchief and badge is explained. The three corners of the triangularly-folded kerchief stand for Party, Komsomol, and Pioneer, pillars of the Soviet state. The badge is decorated with a red flag on which are the hammer and sickle and a campfire of five logs burning with three flames. The five logs represent the continents of the earth; the three flames symbolize the Third International with its promise of the future world revolution. The new recruits are greeted with the slogan, "To battle for Lenin and Stalin — be ready!", and they reply in the slogan emblazoned on the Pioneer badge, "Always ready!", while rendering the Pioneer salute. The ceremony is concluded with speech-making, recitations, and songs designed to impress the initiates with their new estate.

Once enrolled in the Pioneers, the new member becomes part of a "link" of eight to twelve youngsters who elect their own leader. The "links" are united in a "brigade" with approximately forty members in the same or adjoining classes. Each brigade chooses its "council" of five to represent it and functions under a Komsomol leader who is designated to supervise and direct brigade activities. These activities vary with the age level of the Pioneers. In the younger classes, political inspiration at meetings largely takes the form of tales of the childhood of Lenin or Stalin or stories of heroism on the part of young Pioneers in the war against the Nazis. With older children, political instruction becomes more pointed. The biographies of Lenin and Stalin are studied more carefully with emphasis on their revolutionary activities. The heroic exploits of the Soviet army are celebrated; there are lectures on the Constitution, and national and international events are reviewed from the Party standpoint.

Political instruction in the narrow sense, however, is only one part of the Pioneer program. There are also a variety of organized activities such as excursions for nature study, to museums, and points of historical interest, athletic competitions, literary, dramatic, and musical evenings, and opportunities to pursue hobbies at school or at the so-called Houses of

[30] E. N. Medynskii, *Narodnoe Obrazovanie i SSSR* (Moscow, 1947), p. 32.
[31] For recent descriptions of Pioneer activities, see *Kommunisticheskoe Vospitanie v Sovetskoi Shkole* [Communist Education in the Soviet School] (Moscow, 1950), pp. 313–336.
[32] *Ibid.*, pp. 322 ff.

Pioneers, which are set aside as centers of Pioneer extra-curricular programs. There is the requirement to engage in socially useful work, which may embrace such diverse activities as helping to edit a wall newspaper for Pioneers, gathering scrap, working in the school garden or on a neighboring Kolkhoz, or even helping combat "religious prejudices" in the home. The tendency of these extra-curricular activities to compete with and even interfere with school programs has led to periodic protests by Soviet school authorities against overburdening the child with outside activities. The present tendency is to integrate Pioneer activities as closely as possible with the school, to emphasize classroom obligations as the first responsibility of the Pioneer, and to arrange the Pioneer program so that it supports, rather than comes into conflict with, the school curriculum.

The Pioneers are designed to take care of children between the ages of nine and fifteen. At the age of fourteen, however, the child becomes eligible for membership in the Komsomols, provided, of course, that he can satisfy the conditions for admission.[33] These conditions include recommendation by one member of the Communist Party or two Komsomols who have themselves been members of the organization for at least a year. Recommendation by the council of a Pioneer brigade counts as the equivalent of one recommendation by a Komsomol member. The candidate for admission must be approved both by the local Komsomol organization which he seeks to enter and by the district or town committee which exercises jurisdiction over that local organization.

Enrollment in the Komsomols is thus a much more selective process than membership in the Pioneers. Where the Pioneers operate as a virtually universal organization for all children in the eligible age group, not more than half of the students in the upper three classes of the ten-year school ordinarily join the Komsomols, and only about a quarter of those in the eligible age group (fourteen to twenty-six) are presently Komsomol members.

The Komsomol is the reservoir from which Party members will be recruited; and in the eyes of the Party leadership at least, this is the period of tutelage when qualifications can be sifted and political ardor tested. The Rules of the organization require each member to study Marxism-Leninism, to engage in constant efforts to raise his political literacy, to explain the political line of the Party to the broad masses of youth, to fulfill the decisions of the Party and Komsomol organizations, to participate actively in the political life of the country, to provide an example of socialist attitudes toward work and study, to protect socialist property, to struggle decisively against all breaches of socialist legality and order, to demonstrate political vigilance by guarding war and state secrets, to master the cultural, scientific and technical knowledge which will enable him to perfect his qualifications, to study military affairs, to be always ready to give all his strength and if necessary his life for the defense of his Socialist Fatherland, to seek to stamp out drunkenness, hooliganism, the remains of backward religious prejudices, and uncomradely attitudes toward women, to participate actively in the work of his Komsomol organization, to attend all meetings, and to fulfill all decisions swiftly and accurately.[34]

This is, of course, the proclamation of a Party ideal rather than a realistic description of the state of mind of a rank-and-file Komsomol initiate. There are Komsomol activists who seek to approximate the ideal-type, and who demonstrate all the hallmarks of ideological devotion and dedication. But, if the testimony of ex-Komsomol defectors is to be credited, this group constitutes a small minority, perhaps no greater than 10 to 20 per cent of the membership. The motives which inspire the others to affiliate tend to be both more earthy and more complex. For many careerism apparently plays a major role. The knowledge that Komsomol and Party membership opens the way to power and preferment in the Soviet system operates as a strong inducement for the ambitious to affiliate, even when ideological fervor burns low. Sometimes the attraction of membership is predominantly social; the young women among the Soviet non-returners tended especially to stress the

[33] See the revised rules adopted at the Eleventh Congress of the Komsomol, April 6, 1949. They are reprinted in full in *Molodoi Bol'shevik*, No. 9, pp. 19–24 (May 1949).

[34] *Ibid.*, pp. 19–20.

appeal of Komsomol-sponsored discussion clubs, excursions, dances, and musicales as contributing greatly to the attractions of membership. A number of ex-Komsomolites emphasized the pride which they felt in being singled out as of leadership calibre. Many who could not be counted among the more zealous activists reported that they had been so molded and formed by previous indoctrination that they simply accepted Komsomol membership as a natural expression of the role which they were expected to play in life. This attitude of uncritical acknowledgment of the existing structure of authority appears to be widespread and pervasive, at least until it is challenged by unhappy experiences in Soviet society, exposure to the West, or other sources of disenchantment.

III. *Organization of the Komsomols*

The organization of the Komsomols is closely modeled on the hierarchical pattern of its big brother, the Party.[35] At the bottom of the pyramid are the primary organizations in factories, collective farms, state farms, educational and other state institutions. Each primary organization must have at least three members and is established with the consent of the district or town committee which exercises supervision over it. Where the primary organization consists of more than a hundred members, it may be broken down into subgroups in shops of a factory, different faculties of a university, etc. Where the group has less than ten members, a secretary is selected to provide leadership. In larger groups a committee or bureau as well as a secretary serves as the directing nucleus. Both perform their Komsomol duties in addition to their regular employment. Full-time Komsomol secretaries are ordinarily assigned by the central apparatus only to important enterprises or institutions where there is a substantial membership and a program of work requiring the exclusive attention of a Komsomol functionary. In most cases the primary Komsomol organizations operate under the control of the district or town Komsomol committees and their secretaries; but in the armed forces and in institutions where special political sections have been established, the line of responsibility is directly to the head of the political section, or his assistant in charge of Komsomol activity. In units of the armed forces, the Komsomol organizations function under the immediate direction of the Assistant Commander for Political Affairs and in close collaboration with the Party organization in the unit. The chain of command in such cases runs through the armed forces hierarchy, rather than to the apparatus of district and regional Komsomol committees.

At the district or town level, supervisory power is concentrated in a committee which in turn elects a bureau and a number of secretaries. But, if the testimony of ex-Komsomols is to be credited, "election" is a euphemism so far as the secretaries are concerned. They report that the secretaries are full-time Komsomol functionaries who are assigned by higher echelons in the organization and are automatically confirmed in their responsibilities by the committees. The Rules of the Komsomol require that district or town secretaries be members or candidates for membership in the Party with two years of experience in Komsomol work. The key figure in the organization is the first secretary. The importance of the role is attested by the fact that, in 1949, 99 per cent of all first secretaries in towns and 95.2 per cent of all first secretaries in districts were Party members.[36] The first secretary exercises a general supervisory responsibility over all Komsomol work; more specific responsibilities such as the direction of Pioneers, activities in schools, factories, or collective farms, work with young women, physical culture and sports, military training, and organization and agitation are assigned to the other secretaries depending on their character and availability.

The next higher levels in the Komsomol hierarchy are the regional and republic organizations. Here the basic pattern of organization is essentially the same as below. There is the regional or central committee of the republic, a smaller bureau within it, and a full complement of secretaries with assigned responsibilities for different aspects of Komsomol activity. At this level secretaries are required to be Party members with at least three years of experience in the Komsomol. Operat-

---

[35] *Ibid.,* pp. 20–24.

[36] See the report of the Central Committee delivered to the Eleventh Congress by First Secretary N. A. Mikhailov, *ibid.,* No. 8, p. 36 (April 1949).

ing under them are substantial staffs of full-time Komsomol functionaries with specific responsibilities running the gamut of the organization's activities.

The central administrative organization of the Komsomol consisted in 1949 of a Central Committee of 103 members and 47 candidates, a control commission of 31 members, a bureau of 11 members, five secretaries, and a large secretariat, all of whom operate under the general direction of the First Secretary, N. A. Mikhailov.[37] Theoretically, the highest organ in the Komsomol is the All-Union Congress, which, according to the Rules, is required to meet at least once every three years. Until the Tenth Congress in 1936, meetings were held with reasonable regularity. There then ensued a thirteen-year break before the Eleventh Congress was finally assembled in 1949. The report of the Mandate Commission of the Eleventh Congress is revealing.[38] Of the 1362 delegates who participated, 548 were leading full-time Komsomol functionaries and only 126 were classified as workers and 126 as collective farmers; 953 delegates were either Party members or candidates; 669 were twenty-six years old or older, ordinarily the age when Komsomol membership expires; 195 of these were over thirty. While forty-four nationalities were supposed to be represented in the Congress, 850 delegates, or over 60 per cent, were Great Russians. The impression which is unmistakably conveyed is of an assembly dominated by a Party and Komsomol apparatus made up substantially of Party members masquerading as over-aged Komsomols and with a marked Great Russian coloration. As in the case of the Party, the Congress has become a rally of functionaries called together to ratify and applaud the decisions of the leadership.

According to the Rules, the Central Committee exercises policy direction between Congresses while the Control Commission watches over budget, personnel, and the execution of decisions. While both these bodies meet with reasonable frequency and in fact play a much more important role than the Congress, they

in turn operate under the direction of the First Secretary, N. A. Mikhailov, whose position as a member both of the Central Committee of the Party and of the Orgbureau gives him a status only below that of the Politbureau circle. It can be assumed that the top Party leadership has entrusted Mikhailov with the supervision of Komsomol affairs and that it is through him Party directives on Komsomol matters are transmitted and executed.

IV. *Activities of the Komsomols*

While the responsibilities of the Komsomol organization embrace a wide range of diversified activities, the emphasis, in contrast with the Pioneers, is much more heavily on the political. These activities include:

1. Political instruction of Komsomol members.
2. Political instruction and leadership supplied by the Komsomols to the Pioneers, to non-affiliated youth, and to other groups.
3. Military and para-military training and physical culture and sports.
4. Leadership and assistance in carrying out governmental and Party programs.
5. Social and cultural activity.

The political indoctrination of all Komsomol members is a central concern of the Party. As has already been observed, it begins seriously with the Pioneers and increases in scope and intensity as children grow older. No aspect of the school curriculum is without some political coloration, though in the upper grades instruction in history and the Soviet Constitution is used as the primary vehicle for instilling Party consciousness and loyalty. Ordinarily instructors in these areas are Party members or candidates. In the advanced institutes and universities, there will also be extensive programs of instruction in Ist-Mat (Historical Materialism) or Dia-Mat (Dialectical Materialism) as well as in allied political subjects. Such instruction is invariably entrusted to Party members. In addition, the Komsomol organization carries on an extensive program of political education under its own auspices. According to Mikhailov's report at the Eleventh Congress, in 1949 there were 237,-125 political circles and schools in which more than four million Komsomols were engaged in

[37] The membership of these bodies is listed in *ibid.*, No. 9, pp. 25–26 (May 1949).
[38] *Ibid.*, No. 8, pp. 66–72 (April 1949).

studying aspects of Marxism-Leninism.[39] In addition, he asserted that there were many engaged in self-study programs devoted to the official history of the Party, the works of Lenin and Stalin, and other political topics. This activity was directed by a corps of more than 200,000 propagandists, of whom more than 45 per cent were Party members. In the same report he indicated that *Komsomolskaya Pravda*, the central Komsomol journal, had a circulation of 700,000 and that *Pionerskaya Pravda*, the central Pioneer journal, was issued in editions of 1,000,000 copies. In addition, he cited the existence of thirty-seven Komsomol and seventeen Pioneer newspapers as well as eight Komsomol and fifteen children's magazines with a total circulation of around four million.[40]

The members of the Komsomols are not only indoctrinated; they are also required to indoctrinate. The Komsomols have a special responsibility for the Young Pioneers. Each Pioneer brigade has its assigned Komsomol leader, who not only supervises play and social activity, but is supposed to instill Communist consciousness in his charges. Komsomol activists are also assigned to Pioneer summer camps to undertake similar responsibilities; they are called upon to take the leadership in school assemblies in delivering reports and fiery speeches on current political themes; they serve as agitators to explain Party policy to the "backward" masses; they take an active speech-making role in pre-election campaigns, loan drives, and collections for a variety of revolutionary causes.

Komsomols are also expected to provide leadership in the area of physical culture, sports, and military training. The first obligation of the Komsomol, according to a recent Soviet text, is to prepare himself for service in the Soviet Army. "The Komsomol member must be a leading physical culturist."[41] Preparatory to their own military service, they are required to take an active role in the paramilitary "voluntary" societies which serve the various branches of the armed forces, Dosarm (army), Dosav (air) and Dosflot (navy).[42] In this capacity they engage in shooting practice, air raid drills, first aid, long marches, parachute and glider training, and political meetings at which the necessity for military preparedness is constantly reiterated.

The Komsomolite is also expected to serve as a model and example for the youth of the country by assisting his Party and government in every way. He is supposed to volunteer for the most strenuous and disagreeable tasks, to help with the harvest, to enlist for the new construction job, to work in the mines, or to go wherever his organization sends him. Whether he be in the factory or the school, he is expected to be an outstanding worker, a paragon of discipline, a stimulus to his associates, and a constant help to his superiors in carrying out their responsibilities. He is adjured to be constantly on guard against "enemies of the people"; ex-Komsomolites testify that the more zealous members of the organization are frequently enrolled by the Secret Police as "seksots," or informers, to report on their comrades and associates both inside and outside the Komsomol.

Finally, there is the area of social-cultural activity where the Komsomolite is expected to cultivate many-sided interests in order to make himself a "whole" man. This is the area which the less fervid members find most attractive, because of its relative removal from the political realm. The literary, dramatic, dancing, and singing groups which the Komsomol sponsors provide some relief from the incessant and concentrated political bombardment to which youth is exposed, but even these forms of social-cultural activity are far from being apolitical. Komsomolites participating in a series of evenings devoted to Pushkin discuss papers on such themes as "Pushkin and the Decembrists," "Pushkin on Capitalism," "Pushkin-Patriot," "Pushkin and the Present," and "Pushkin's Criticism of Amer-

---

[39] *Ibid.*, p. 27.
[40] *Ibid.*, p. 29.
[41] *Young Communists in the USSR*, translated by Virginia Rhine (Washington, 1950), p. 19.

[42] For descriptions of Komsomol relationships to Dosarm and Dosflot, see Major-General V. Golovkin, "Komsomol and Dosarm," *Molodoi Bol'shevik*, No. 22, pp. 31–35 (November 1949), and Rear Admiral I. Golubev-Monatkin, "Komsomol and Dosflot," *ibid.*, No. 14, pp. 35–39 (July 1950).

ica."[43] The dramatic groups read and produce plays from the contemporary Soviet repertoire which are heavily saturated with doctrinal content. Even the dancing and singing are partly organized around political themes. In the Soviet state there is no real escape from the long arm of ideological control.

V. Problems of Loyalty and Disaffection

What manner of man does the Komsomol seek to create and what values does the top Party leadership seek to implant in the minds of youth? A recent Soviet monograph entitled *Young Communists in the U.S.S.R.*, which describes the demands made on Komsomols, furnishes a vivid and even frightening insight into Party goals and purposes. "The most important task of the Komsomol organization," says the monograph, "is to maintain in all the youth Soviet patriotism, Soviet national pride, the aspiration to make our Socialist state ever stronger."[44] . . . "Whatever the Komsomol may do, with whatever works or studies he may occupy himself, he must always be prepared to enter the ranks of the Soviet Army at the first call of the Party and the Soviet government. . . ."[45] In civil, as well as military life, he must provide a shining example of self-sacrifice and discipline. The Komsomol is told that he lives in the greatest and most progressive country in the world, and that what gives his country its strength is the leadership of the Communist Party guided by the teachings of Marx, Engels, Lenin, and Stalin. "To study Marxism-Leninism is the duty and obligation of every Komsomol member."[46] Every Komsomol is obligated to carry out the policies of the Bolshevik Party steadily and consistently. "All his life must be subordinated to the great aim — the struggle for Communism."[47] . . . "It is completely correct to say that personal existence is politics."[48] . . . "The hero of our time, of our country, is the person who contributes to the welfare of the Soviet Socialist Motherland by his labor and exploits, and who is unselfishly devoted to the work of the Party of Lenin and Stalin, the work of Communism. He is a man who does not fear any enemies or difficulties; he is the builder of the new society."[49]

This image of the ideal Komsomolite with its stress on the virtues of disciplined obedience to Party dictates represents the ultimate value which the Party leadership seeks to inculcate. But the energies of youth, even under dictatorship, elude such tight constraints. In the words of the anonymous author of *Young Communists in the U.S.S.R.*, ". . . the survivals of the old way of life have still not been finally overcome. . . . The baneful influence of bourgeois ideology sometimes penetrates into the midst of our youth."[50]

It is no easy matter to come to any reliable judgments on the state of mind of Soviet young people, or more particularly, to appraise the extent of disaffection among them. In the absence of free access to the Soviet Union itself, judgments must necessarily be reached on the basis of self-criticism appearing in the Soviet press and on interviews with ex-Komsomolites and others in the Soviet emigration who have had extensive contacts with Soviet youth. The data derived from these sources do not lend themselves to sweeping conclusions or exact statistical formulations; at best when cautiously utilized, they point to the existence of certain stresses and weaknesses in the ability of the regime to command the loyalty of youth.

It is possible on the basis of interviews with defectors to identify situations which corrode faith and even categories of youth whose loyalty to the regime can be considered dubious. Children of parents who have been persecuted by the Soviet regime constitute such a group, though not all of them can be automatically classified as disloyal. They include such diverse elements as the descendants of the "former people" of Czarist times, the offspring of the Kulaks who were dispossessed in the course of collectivization, and the relatives of victims of the purges and of inmates of the

[43] See D. G. Popov, "The Work of Komsomol Organizations in the School," in *Kommunisticheskoe Vospitanie v Sovetskoi Shkole* (Moscow, 1950), p. 289.
[44] *Young Communists in the USSR*, p. 7.
[45] *Ibid.*, p. 16.
[46] *Ibid.*, p. 51.
[47] *Ibid.*, p. 77.
[48] *Ibid.*, p. 79.

[49] *Ibid.*, p. 82.
[50] *Ibid.*, p. 76.

forced labor camps. Many of these groups experienced persecution as children, which they never altogether forgot or forgave. Because they are regarded as suspect by the MGB, their career expectancies are limited, and such children tend to become covert opponents of the regime as they grow up. Even those who manage somehow to transcend the handicaps of their social background, to enter the Komsomol, and embark on promising careers in Soviet society, live with the constant fear that their pasts will rise up to plague them. Public affirmations of loyalty conceal inner torments and tensions.

The peasant youth in the villages and collective farms appears to be another category in which Communist indoctrination is at a relatively low level. Komsomol enrollment in rural areas has always been significantly lower than in the urban industrial centers; and despite constant efforts to improve the ratio, the villages remain a weak link in the chain.[51] It is in the countryside that cross-loyalties exert their most significant influence. The persistence among the older generation of antipathy to collectivization, memories of past suffering and present hardships, and strongly-ingrained religious attitudes leave an impress on the younger generation which Communist propaganda in the schools cannot wholly counteract or eradicate. Indeed, the relative weakness of the Communist apparatus in the villages contributes to the strength of family influences. As the youth are drained away from the villages for military service or industrial work, they are, of course, removed from family pressures and are subjected to more intensive Communist indoctrination. In the process, new converts are won for Komsomol and Party, but how genuinely and profoundly fun

damental attitudes shift is by no means clear.

Other youth elements whose loyalty can be regarded as, at least, dubious are those who were repatriated from Germany and Austria at the end of the War, or who saw service in the West as soldiers of the Red Army in the advance through Eastern and Central Europe, or who had duty later with the occupation forces or administration. The exposure to the West, with its opportunity to see how ordinary workers and farmers live abroad and to compare their relatively advanced standards with the low standards still prevailing in the Soviet Union, offered such a blatant contradiction to official Party propaganda about the West as inevitably to plant doubts and generate discontent. One of the problems of the Soviet regime in the post-war years has been to isolate and neutralize these centers of infection. The repatriates who have since escaped from the Soviet Union report that they were treated by the Soviet secret police with the utmost suspicion, that many of their compatriots were arrested and presumably shipped to forced labor camps, and that relatively few were permitted to resettle in their former homes. The demobilized soldiers and officers who related their discoveries in the West to friends and neighbors at the end of the War are also reported to have encountered serious difficulties. The sharp drop in Komsomol enrollment after 1945 may be interpreted, in part at least, as an index of attrition of loyalties among returning veterans. Similar problems, according to defector reports, have arisen in connection with the morale of occupation forces, although these reports also indicate that the regime in recent years has made the most strenuous efforts to screen troops assigned to occupation duty for political reliability, to subject them to the most intensive indoctrination, and to limit their contacts with local populations to an indispensable minimum. Even these efforts have not been altogether effective in stopping defection, nor can they prevent the gathering of impressions whose cumulative effect may be ideologically corrosive.

Disaffection may also be a product of individual, as well as group experiences. The youth who finds himself consigned to the State Labor Reserves when his own ambition is to go on to a higher education, the student

[51] A very recent illustration is furnished by a report on the amalgamation of collective farms in the Zagorskii district of the Moscow region appearing in *Molodoi Bol'shevik*, No. 17, pp. 56–60 (September 1950). Prior to the amalgamation in June 1950, Komsomol organizations existed in only 43 collective farms out of a total of 141. After the amalgamation, these Komsomol units were organized in 25 out of 32 collective farms. However, of the 141 new work brigades, only 30 contained Komsomol groups. It needs to be remembered that the Moscow region counts as one of the most advanced.

who is forced to give up his studies because he cannot afford to pay the necessary tuition fees, the university or institute graduate who is dissatisfied with the assignment which he receives on completion of his course of study, the young worker who cannot adjust to the tight labor discipline of the Soviet system with its severe penalties for absence and tardiness, the independent-minded young intellectual who is forced to suppress his views lest it cost him his career, the victims of denunciations and purges, the politically "backward" young people who find the constantly reiterated propaganda a bore and long for "bourgeois" comforts and gayety — these are only samples of Soviet life-situations which breed frustration and disillusionment, even when they are hidden under a surface show of compliance and affirmation.

Some corroboration of the existence of such attitudes among Soviet youth is available in official Soviet sources. The monograph *Young Communists in the U.S.S.R.* is loud in its denunciations of "bourgeois survivals among some of the youth."[52] . . . "It is necessary to unmask, to ridicule commonplace bourgeois tastes . . . unworthy of Soviet youth, by some youths and girls of rotten bourgeois 'culture'."[53] . . . "Such backward people are willing to declare: 'One's personal life is nobody's business; how I live concerns only myself and no one else'. . . . Such a point of view is profoundly incorrect and pernicious."[54] . . . "The remnants of the past find their expression also in various superstitions and prejudices which permeate youth."[55] These religious inclinations are referred to as a "delusion which poisons the hearts of young people . . ." and which must be combatted by "thoughtful and patient anti-religious propaganda."[56] The Komsomol is called upon to fight "against servility before the bourgeois West, and rotten apoliticalness."[57] Mikhailov, in his keynote speech to the Eleventh Congress of the Komsomol, was particularly critical of what he called the formalism of political work in the universities, and he sharply

attacked the apolitical and cosmopolitan influences of "several" Leningrad universities.[58] He picked out for special censure the tendency of some university graduates to try to evade assignments to areas far from the large cities and to wangle office rather than production assignments. At the December 1949 Plenum of the Central Committee, which followed the Eleventh Congress, considerable concern was expressed over the failure of several leading Komsomol organizations to recruit new members and the tendency of some of the existing membership to lose interest and drop out. The lag in rural recruitment was singled out as particularly unsatisfactory.[59]

Both official reports and the information supplied by ex-Soviet citizens indicate diversity in the attitude of different sectors of Soviet youth toward the regime. But they by no means agree on the quantitative distribution of these attitudes. In the official view, Soviet youth is overwhelmingly devoted and loyal, and it is only a small minority who are backward, indifferent, or hostile. The impression derived from interviews with ex-Komsomolites among the Soviet defectors is quite different. They agree that there is a firm nucleus of Komsomol activists who are genuine ideological converts. This group rarely loses faith and indeed may even become more fanatical as it grows older. It is from this element that the Party and the secret police recruit their most devoted cadres. Around this nucleus, in the view of defector informants, there is a much larger circle of youth who join the Komsomol and even go on into the Party, inspired by motivations which may be described as largely careerist in character. Overtly, they are pro-regime; they take an active part in political life, and go through the motions of conformity in order to make their way in Soviet society. But they lack the fanaticism of the first group. Their inner "real" political affiliation may embrace such widely different attitudes as passive acceptance of the regime, apathy, cynicism, or even

52 *Op. cit.*, p. 77.
53 *Ibid.*
54 *Ibid.*
55 *Ibid.*, p. 79.
56 *Ibid.*, p. 80.
57 *Ibid.*, p. 11.

58 *Molodoi Bol'shevik*, No. 8, p. 25 (April 1949).
59 See Resolutions of the Second Plenum of the Komsomol Central Committee on the Work of the Komosomol Organizations in the Sverdlovsk Region and the Stalingrad Tractor Factory, *Molodoi Bol'shevik*, No. 1, pp. 33–44 (January 1950).

bitterly suppressed resentment of the life-situations in which they find themselves. Such apt terms as "the outer cover" (*vneshnaya obolochka*) and "the reddish scale" (*krasno-vataya okalina*) have been coined to describe these careerists, with the implication that you don't have to scratch very deep to find the real animal. Yet so far as surface behavior goes, they give every evidence of being not only loyal, but active Soviet citizens.

Around this group there stretches the great outer circle of Soviet young people who never affiliate with the Komsomol and, who, in purely numerical terms, constitute the mass of Soviet youth. This circle includes such diverse elements as the bulk of young collective farmers, the majority of young workers in industry, and a substantial number of young intellectuals who evade membership even when the opportunity to affiliate is presented, sometimes at considerable risks to their future careers. It is not easy to generalize on the political attitudes of the non-Komsomolites, but, if defector evidence is to be trusted, they harbor the powers of inertia and apathy in Soviet society; they include much latent hostility to the regime; and they represent that sector in Soviet society where political indoctrination meets its most passive response.

The testimony of defectors, both young and old, is virtually unanimous in emphasizing a decline in the ideological élan of youth, as compared with the idealism of Civil War days or the great outpouring of energy and dedication which accompanied the first phase of the Five Year Plans. As Soviet society has crystallized into a militarized, authoritarian, and hierarchical pattern, the apocalyptic vision of the free, classless Communist utopia becomes an increasingly tarnished dream, with little power to stir the imagination or devotion of any except the very immature. There are still great goals to be attained, but they are essentially practical goals, the construction of new heavy industry, the building up of military strength, and the expansion of Soviet power. The problem of the regime is to harness the energies of youth to achieve these goals. In attempting to solve this problem, ideology is only one of many weapons, and not necessarily the most important.

Perhaps the most potent is the power of the regime to control the career expectancies of youth, to reward achievement which fits in with the goals of the leadership, and to punish deviant conduct with the most severe penalties. The system of incentives offers the highest prizes to those who manage to incorporate themselves into the leadership stratum of Party, secret police, army, and administration; it provides attractive emoluments for the intellectuals who are willing to sing the tunes of the regime; and it gives special bonuses to the managers, the engineers, and the shock brigadiers who distinguish themselves in production. It buttresses financial awards with a system of honorifics designed to be particularly attractive to the less sophisticated.

The obverse side of the medal is the use of fear and terror as political weapons. For the workers who lag in production there is the discipline of a wage system that consigns the laggard to the lowest minimum of subsistence. For all who deviate from the straight and narrow path of conformity to the leadership's demands, there is the omnipresent danger of arrest by the secret police and confinement in a forced labor camp. Whip and carrot combine to extirpate the slightest overt demonstration of opposition to the regime.

At the same time the regime is shrewd enough to understand that this system of rewards and punishments must be given ideological justification if it is to possess the minds as well as enlist the energies of youth. The appeal of the ultimate utopian goal is not wholly abandoned, even if it be less stressed and less effective. But blame for the postponement of its realization is placed on the continued existence of the cunning capitalist enemy without; the Soviet Union must be an armed fortress and live in a state of siege if it is to survive and triumph over the capitalist encirclement. At the same time Communist victories in Europe and Asia are used to support the promise that the ultimate world triumph will not be too long delayed, that the voice of the future is the voice of Communism, and that present sacrifices prepare the way for the Promised Land of plenty which will come afterwards.

Meanwhile, youth is told, it must work, obey, and learn to fight. The main enemy this time is the United States instead of the Nazis.

Every propaganda organ builds an image of the aggressive American imperialist as a barbaric replica of the Nazi out to dominate the world. The objective of this campaign is to channel all the genuine hatred which the Nazis provoked and all the frustration and aggression which accumulate within Soviet society against this new external enemy symbol of America. Soviet youth are warned that they must be prepared to make the sternest sacrifices to defend their homes and families, and preserve their Soviet fatherland, as a symbol of liberation and hope for the oppressed masses in capitalist-dominated countries.

This in its basic outlines is the indoctrination to which Soviet youth is being currently exposed. It is reiterated in every mass medium, in oral agitation, and in every nook and cranny of the Soviet educational and propaganda system. Its power to persuade those who caught a glimpse of the West may be questioned. There is abundant proof, both in the reports of defectors and in the series of post-war ideological purges and campaigns which have been directed against cosmopolitanism and adulation of the West, that it meets with some resistance in intellectual and, perhaps, other circles. But for the oncoming generation of youth, now almost totally sealed off from the West, insulated against outside contacts, and subject to exclusive manipulation by the Party leadership, the strength of the current appeal to the youth who have come of age since World War II should not be underestimated. In the years since the Revolution, the attrition of loyalties in the middle-aged and the old has been counter-balanced by the capacity of the regime, through the Komsomol and the Young Pioneers, to indoctrinate a part of each new generation of youth with its own values. Whether or not this indoctrination survives the trials and tribulations of later life, it has played and may continue to play a role of crucial significance in replenishing the life energies of the regime.

The apparent strength of totalitarianism is its capacity to mobilize the loyalties of impressionable youth. The weakness of the totalitarian regime only become fully evident after its downfall. The great paradox of totalitarianism is its inability to fulfill its own totalitarian aspirations. The monolithic façade conceals

tensions and grievances from which no Soviet generation is free. The fate of the Western world may well depend on the development of successful measures to undermine the indoctrination to which Soviet youth is exposed and to exploit the cleavages with which Soviet society is permeated.

16

A Voice from the Rank and File*

A Party Member in Pravda

(1958)

This brief letter of complaint from a Party member describing the formal and undemocratic conduct of local Party officials provides a minor but graphic illustration of those features of the system which contribute to dampening political fervor. Letters of this kind are called "letters of self-criticism" (samokritika) and are an important valve for releasing some of the tension which builds up in the system. The writer is ordinarily quite safe from reprisal if he is careful to attack only relatively minor officials and avoids calling in question any of the basic practices or institutions of Soviet Communism.

It is well known that during the last few years the Communist Party and its Central Committee have done a great job of restoring Leninist norms of inner-Party life and the principles of Party leadership. In particular, meetings of Communists and of Party aktivs are now much better run. This makes certain features of the work of our Stalin

---

* Reprinted from "Aktiv Meetings Should Not Be Conducted This Way," G. Shuvalev (letter from a Communist), *Pravda* (August 21, 1958), p. 2, translated in *Current Digest of the Soviet Press* Vol. 10, No. 34, pp. 20–21, published at Columbia University by the Joint Committee on Slavic Studies appointed by the American Council of Learned Societies and the Social Science Research Council. Used by permission of the publisher.

Borough Party Committee in the city of Nikolayev all the more intolerable.

It is known that Party *aktivs* are convened to discuss major Party and government decisions. The Party Statutes say that *aktivs* are to meet "not merely for show and not to approve these decisions formally and ceremonially but to subject them to genuine discussion." This provision of the statutes is violated in our borough.

One gets the impression that *aktiv* meetings are held in our borough not in order to mobilize Communists for the carrying out of Party decisions but merely as a matter of form — i.e., so that it can be reported to the city Party committee that meetings have been held. One sometimes leaves these meetings with a sense of vexation.

The success of any meeting depends to a large extent on preparation. The personnel of our borough Party committee cannot be reproached for neglecting preparation. On the contrary, the whole staff generally works on preparing for meetings. Instructors and officials write reports and compile lists of participants in the meetings; lists of speakers are drawn up in advance; draft resolutions are prepared. Naturally, the borough Party committee officials do not show up in the Party organizations on days when these details are being worked out. But what actually happens at the *aktiv* meetings?

The principal speaker reads his report in a monotonous voice, never lifting his eyes from the script. After this the other previously prepared speeches are read. When the list of speakers has been exhausted, the chairman (usually a secretary of the borough Party committee) announces, "It is moved that the discussion be closed." The participants are weary from listening to the speeches (ordinarily there are no intermissions) and they agree. Recognition is seldom granted anyone who is not on the list of speakers; if someone asks the chairman why he was not recognized, he is told that it was the will of the meeting.

Let me relate the melancholy tale of my last speech, at a Party *aktiv* meeting that was held in July of this year.

When preparations for the meeting were in progress, I reached an agreement with the borough Party committee instructor who was drawing up the list of speakers that I would be recognized. We also agreed on the content of my speech. Two days before the meeting, Comrade Lazarenko, director of the Party enlightenment office, came to see me, and the following exchange took place:

"Comrade Shuvalov, I understand that you are going to speak at the Party *aktiv* meeting," she said.

"Yes, I intend to speak."

"Do you have a copy of your speech that I may look over?"

"I have a copy, but why must I show it to you?"

"Comrade Budanov, secretary of the borough Party committee, has asked me to look at it."

The day before the meeting, Comrade Lazarenko asked me to drop in at the borough Party committee with my speech. I was received by Comrade Gavrilova, an instructor. She also asked to look over my speech. I refused.

As we were talking, a messenger from one of the city's factories brought in the typewritten text of the speech of another participant in the meeting. This gave Comrade Gavrilova a pretext for reproaching me:

"You see, Comrade Shuvalov, everyone is submitting his text to us."

And one more characteristic detail: as Comrade Gavrilova went over the Communist's speech, she deleted whole paragraphs without consulting him.

I was feeling bitter when I left Comrade Gavrilova, but this was not the end of my anguish. The day of the Party *aktiv* meeting, Comrade Davydova, secretary of the borough Party committee, called me in, and once more I refused to submit the text of my speech.

As a result of this incorrect preparation, the meeting turned out to be a formality. The principal speaker, the first secretary of the borough Party committee, read his report. The other speakers also read their speeches. The many people who attended the meeting listened to these readings without any particular interest.

I would like to call attention to another thing. It is known that presidiums are chosen to guide these meetings. But does a borough meeting need a presidium of 20 or 30 people?

It seems to me that a businesslike meeting should elect a small, businesslike presidium.

Moreover, the presidiums sometimes include, along with Communists in good standing, some people who do not belong there. For instance, Comrade Ignatchenko, former director of the Road Machinery Plant, has often been elected to our presidium. He was recently removed from his post for abuse of his position and as a crude person who has lost contact with the masses. The borough and city Party committees are well aware of Ignatchenko's "sins." And yet officials of the borough Party committee have continued to recommend this incompetent comrade to membership on meeting presidiums.

I tried to speak on this question at a borough Party conference, but even though I had been promised the floor, I was not recognized. I tried to speak at a plenary session of the borough Party committee, but I was not recognized there either. I hope *Pravda* will help me in this matter.

THE STATE

17

The Constitution, Governmental Organization, and Political Practice*

Alec Nove

(1949)

Although we acknowledge that the Soviet government is absolutely dominated by the Communist Party and serves merely as the administrative instrument for attaining the Party's objectives, we must nevertheless recognize that it is in its own right an enormous

---

* Reprinted from "Some Aspects of Soviet Constitutional Theory," *Modern Law Review*, Vol. 12 (1949), pp. 12–36, by permission of the author and Stevens and Sons, Limited.

institutional complex regulating in minutest detail the lives of over two hundred million people. Dr. Nove quite properly begins his survey of Soviet government by a restatement of the Soviet conception of its role, and through his detailed exploration of the government's structure reveals how well it in fact performs the functions which it was designed to fulfill.

1. The Purposes of the Soviet State Machine

It is a common failing of both friends and enemies of the U.S.S.R. to apply to Soviet institutions criteria of judgment which are quite irrelevant, both to the avowed purpose of these institutions and to their actual functioning. The aim of this paper is to examine the structure of, and the theories behind, the Soviet system of government, as these are viewed by *Soviet* constitutional theorists.[1]

It is impossible to appreciate Soviet ideas on the State, Law, or Justice, without some knowledge of the Marxist-Leninist terminology which all Soviet lawyers employ. This is no place for a general discussion of Marxist theory,

---

[1] Detailed expositions of Soviet constitutional theory and practice may be found in the following (Russian) works:

Vyshinski (ed.), *Soviet State Law* (*Sovetskoye gosudarstvennoye pravo*), Academy of Sciences (legal section), Moscow, 1938 (despite the date of publication, still an invaluable guide to official theory).

A. I. Denisov, *Soviet State Law* (Russian title as above), Ministry of Justice, Moscow, 1947.

Yevtikhiev and Vlasov, *Administrative Law* (*Administrativnoye pravo*), Ministry of Justice, Moscow, 1946.

(The above are textbooks for law students).

The Foundations of the Soviet State and Law (*Osnovy sovetskovo gosudarstva i pravo*), a symposium edited by Professors I. D. Levin and A. V. Karass on behalf of the Law Institute of the Academy of Sciences of the U.S.S.R., Moscow, 1947 (issued by the Ministry of Justice as a textbook for students *not* specializing in law, and largely a condensed version of other books).

Articles in the periodical *Soviet State and Law* (*Sovetskoye Gosudarstvo i Pravo*), published by the Legal section of the Academy of Sciences.

Various pamphlets and booklets on the Soviet State (mainly transcripts of lectures) issued in Moscow in 1946 and 1947.

Stenographic reports of the sessions of the Supreme Soviet.

Communist Party report and resolutions, works of Lenin and Stalin, Press articles, and so on.

so it will suffice to state simply that the following concepts are accepted as *axiomatic* by Soviet theorists in this field: —

(a) "The State always has been, and is, a coercive apparatus, with the help of which the ruling classes impose obedience on their 'subjects.' "[2] So long as capitalism survives, "the exploiting classes need political rule in order to maintain exploitation, i.e., the selfish interests of an insignificant minority against the vast majority of the people,"[3] and, indeed, "the more democratic (the capitalist State is), the cruder, the more cynical is this capitalist rule."[4] While the limited rights of the people under capitalist democracy make it worth defending against fascism, "this, however, in no way weakens the description of *any* bourgeois State . . . as an apparatus for the suppression and oppression of the toiling masses."[5]

(b) The Soviet State, too, is an instrument of suppression, of "dictatorship," wielded by the working class in alliance with the peasantry, i.e., by and in the interests of the mass of the people, towards the building of Communism. Although this State does, and must, restrict the freedom of those who oppose it, it is, by definition, "a million times more democratic than the most democratic bourgeois republic."[6] There is no contradiction, in Soviet eyes, between the Dictatorship of the Proletariat and democracy, because the dictatorship is wielded by and for the vast majority, in their own interest, through the Communist Party, which always represents their interests.

(c) As the State is an organ of class suppression, it follows that it must eventually "wither away" after classes are abolished.

(d) Laws are "forms by which the ruling class in the given society sets norms of behavior for all other classes, according to what profits and suits that ruling class."[7]

(e) Abstract justice, in any ethical sense, cannot be invoked as a basis of Law. Justice is itself purely relative; under capitalism there can only be "capitalist justice," and Soviet justice, as well as Soviet law, must express the

needs of a Socialist transformation of society.[8]

Both Marx and Lenin concentrated, in their theoretical formulations, on emphasizing the evil character of the bourgeois class State and class law, and this, allied to the theory of the withering away of the State, led to the rise in the twenties of a Soviet school of law which regarded the State and law almost apologetically, as a transient phenomenon. They interpreted the increasing preoccupation of the Soviet State with economic regulation as the beginning of the withering-away process. Professor Reissner went so far as to question whether there is any need to "dress up the proletarian dictatorship in some mysterious legal formulae."[9] Another leading Soviet lawyer of the period, Pashukanis, emphasized in his teachings that legal forms were a survival of the pre-Socialist, class epoch, about to wither away with the State. Much of Lenin's *State and Revolution* can be, and was, cited to support this view.

These theories were decisively rejected by 1936, and their advocates removed from any influence on affairs. Pashukanis, indeed, was liquidated as a "spy and wrecker," and his theories are now officially deemed to have been the means by which he deliberately sought to weaken the Soviet State for treasonable ends — a typically Soviet approach to the subject of political error.[10] In their place, new theoreticians produced the ideas which found their institutional expression in the "Stalin Constitution."

In the early years of the Soviet regime, Lenin and his colleagues were not unmindful of the need for "revolutionary socialist legality," in the sense that Soviet officials had to act in accordance with Soviet rules. However, in a period in which the small trader and the individual peasant farmer had to be painfully liquidated, the situation required administrative flexibility of a kind which did not take kindly to legal restraints. By 1935, however, these processes were complete. The State really did fully control the economic life of the U.S.S.R., and Stalin declared that the

[2] Vyshinski, p. 13.
[3] Lenin, *State and Revolution* (English ed., p. 21).
[4] Lenin, quoted by Vyshinski, p. 13.
[5] Vyshinski, p. 14. Emphasis his.
[6] Lenin, *Proletarian Revolution* (English 1935 ed., p. 30).
[7] Vyshinski, p. 21.

[8] A useful historical survey of Soviet law and justice is contained in Schlesinger, *Soviet Legal Theory* (Kegan Paul, 1945).
[9] Reissner, *Law*, Moscow, 1925.
[10] This view of Pashukanis and his school is fully developed in Vyshinski, pp. 58–61.

Socialist society had been built. No "exploiting classes" remained.

Clearly, the new and widespread tasks of the Soviet State, especially in the field of economic planning, required effective organization, effective obedience to the State authorities. Furthermore, a new degree of *social* stability (reflected by increased income differentiation, inheritance laws, life insurance policies, the greater stress on family life, and so on) had to find its reflection in the legal structure of the Union. "Stalin teaches us to strengthen Socialist legality, underlining all the importance to our further progress of the stability of Soviet laws. This idea of stability finds its reflection in the great Stalin constitution. . . ."[11]

This concept of the Soviet State is clearly quite at variance with the idea that it is about to wither away. Stalin himself was responsible for a reformulation of the official theory. "The withering away of the State will come not through the weakening of the power of the State, but through its uttermost strengthening, which is necessary for the purpose of completing the destruction of the remnants of the dying classes and to organize defence against the capitalist environment."[12] Only when people are willing to work without compulsion, drawing from the common pool in accordance with their needs, only when the capitalist States no longer threaten the security of the Union, will it be possible to think of the withering away of the State. These vast changes in the human character and the international situation cannot occur for a great many years, and meanwhile the U.S.S.R. "must proceed not by lessening the class struggle but by strengthening it."[13]

At the 18th congress of the Communist Party in 1939, Stalin formulated the tasks of the Soviet State as follows: "defence of the country against external aggression, protection of socialist property, economic-organizational and cultural development work," contrasting these functions with the task of liquidating hostile classes which played so large a role in Soviet affairs before 1936.[14] On this interpre-

tation, the coercive measures taken within the U.S.S.R. in the period following the promulgation of the Stalin Constitution were part of the "defence of the country against external aggression"; this accords with the official representation of all political opponents of the regime as agents of various foreign powers.

This is what Vyshinski's textbook has to say about the nature of the Constitution: "The dictatorship of the proletariat solves the problem of the proletarian revolution also with the help of law and in accordance with measures strictly defined by law, through administrative and judicial organs. The dictatorship of the proletariat is a power unlimited by any law. But the dictatorship of the proletariat, creating its own laws, uses laws, demands the observances of law and punishes breach of law. It does not entail anarchy or disorder; on the contrary, it entails strict order and firm government, acting on strict basic rules, set out in the fundamental law of the proletarian State, the Constitution. The problem of strengthening the power of the proletarian dictatorship faces the Soviet State in all its acuteness and strength. . . . The greatest expression of proletarian democracy, and at the same time the organic synthesis of the principles of proletarian dictatorship, is the Stalin Constitution."[15] Denisov echoes him, quoting Stalin's dictum: "The present Constitution leaves in being the dictatorship of the working class."[16]

While the Soviet State axiomatically represents "the highest form of democracy that is possible,"[17] all bourgeois States, whatever the party in power, inevitably act according to the juridical principles of the "dictatorship of the bourgeoisie."[18] (The English lawyer would be amused to see in Vyshinski's volume how easily English constitutional theories can be exploded. For instance, a quotation from Engels about the class prejudice of English country J.P.'s in 1875 is held to prove the utter hypocrisy of the whole contention that there is an independent judiciary in Great Britain!)

Soviet theorists make much of the democratic forms of the Stalin Constitution. This form, as we shall see, does not correspond in its content to Western democratic ideas. How-

11 Vyshinski, p. 54.
12 Stalin, *Leninism* (*Voprosy Leninisma*, Xth Russian ed., p. 509).
13 Stalin, *op. cit.*
14 Summary quoted from *Soviet Administrative Law*, p. 1; full version in stenographic account of XVIIIth congress of C.P. p. 717.

15 Vyshinski, pp. 50–51.
16 Stalin, *Voprosy Leninisma*, 11th Russian ed., p. 519.
17 Vyshinski, p. 51.
18 Levin and Karass, p. 89.

ever, it does not in the least follow that the Constitution is therefore a mere sham. It has a significant part to play in Soviet life, and so have the institutions it has called into being.

The reader who is unfamiliar with the Soviet Constitution may find some value in the following very condensed summary: a part (Articles 1–10) of the Constitution contains a series of sociological propositions which do not directly enter a lawyer's purview (e.g., "the U.S.S.R. is a Socialist State of workers and peasants," or "from each according to his ability, to each according to his work"). There is a section on basic rights and freedoms, to which allusion will be made later. Finally, there is a detailed account of the system of governmental organization. This is based on an elected assembly, the Supreme Soviet, which is divided into two houses, the Soviet of the Union (elected in proportion to the population by electoral districts throughout the Union) and the Soviet of Nationalities, in which the sixteen [now fifteen] Republics comprising the Union are represented equally, regardless of population, by twenty-five members each.[19] The two Houses meet normally for two sittings a year, each lasting less than one week. In between sessions, power is exercised by a joint standing committee of the two Houses, the Praesidium, subject to the ratification of important decisions by the Supreme Soviet. The Council of Ministers (formerly People's Commissars) is elected by the Supreme Soviet and is responsible to it and to the Praesidium. The general supervision over the administration of law (and the legality of administration) falls to the Attorney-General of the Union ("Generalni Prokuror"), who is appointed by the Supreme Soviet. The U.S.S.R. itself is, in law, a voluntary union of national republics, each with a constitution of its own. Finally, the interpretation of the constitution and of the laws is the responsibility of the Praesidium.

While there cannot be attempted in these few pages a detailed description of the Soviet system of government, it is of considerable interest to examine some individual features of the system outlined above, and to examine critically how Soviet theory and Soviet practice

deal with the traditional problems which face the constitutional lawyer: constitutional amendments, sovereignty, federalism, separation of powers, legislation and its enforcement, and so on.

2. *Constitutional Amendment*

A relative inflexibility of the Constitution is formally recognized by the requirement, in Article 146, of a two-thirds majority vote of both Houses for any amendment or new article.

This provision has not been of real importance for two reasons: the first is the fact, to be referred to later, that all voting in both Houses is always unanimous. The second lies in the fact that the Praesidium has, by decree, several times amended the Constitution, and the amendment *took effect* before its subsequent ratification. Thus numerous new Ministries were set up by Decree (*ukaz*) of the Praesidium (e.g., the Ministry of Rubber Industry on June 5, 1941, Ministry of Machine Tool Construction on October 14, 1945). As the setting up of Ministries affects the powers of the Republics of the Union, all Ministries are listed in Articles 77 and 78 of the Constitution; yet it was not until March 1946, that the requisite amendments were put before the Supreme Soviet, and were carried unanimously and without discussion.[20] Meanwhile the relevant Ministries had been functioning in their new form on the authority of the Praesidium. Another example among many may be cited: on the submission of the Supreme Soviet's Committee on New Legislation, the Praesidium promulgated on October 10, 1945, an *ukaz* changing the minimum age at which a deputy could be elected to the Supreme Soviet from eighteen to twenty-three, thus amending Article 135 of the Constitution. The wisdom of the measure is not in question, but it is interesting to note that the elections of 1946 were carried out with this *ukaz* in effective operation, and it was the newly-elected Supreme Soviet which ratified the change, *ex post factum*, unanimously and without discussion.[21] It is not unfair to conclude that formal constitutional rigidities have little chance of interfering with administrative ex-

---

[19] There is also special representation for 'autonomous republics' and for minor national subdivisions; these are themselves federal units of individual republics.

[20] See *Stenographic Account of the First Session of the Supreme Soviet*, Moscow, 1946.
[21] *Op. cit.*, Vol. 12.

pediency. Formally, only the Supreme Soviet can make laws; the Praesidium can only issue *ukazes*, which must be based on powers conferred by the Constitution or on existing legislation. It is clear from the above that in actual fact its *ukazes* can not only have the force of law but can also effectively amend the Constitution; formally, however, it is not till a vote of the Supreme Soviet is taken that the *ukaz* becomes a law (*zakon*).

Even the Council of Ministers has been known to ignore the Constitution. For instance, Article 121 of the 1936 Constitution guaranteed free secondary and higher education. In 1940 a ministerial order introduced fees. Article 121 was amended by the Supreme Soviet — in 1947.

3. Sovereignty and the Union Republics

The official teaching on Sovereignty is closely linked with the federal nature of the Soviet State, and it is convenient to treat both together. (For reasons of space the important subject of the "autonomous republics," i.e., federal subdivisions of the Union republics into which the U.S.S.R. is divided, is being left on one side.)

Sovereignty is defined as follows in Vyshinski's textbook: "the supremacy of State power, which makes it unlimited and independent within its own borders and independent in its relationship with other States."[22] Granted this definition, it must be said that Soviet theory advances a series of propositions which no lawyer outside its own borders would regard as mutually compatible. Thus: "In the U.S.S.R. Sovereignty belongs to the multinational Soviet people, who exercise it through its socialist State and through the supreme organs of State power,"[23] and again: "the supreme organs of State power in the U.S.S.R. . . . incarnating the will of the whole multinational Soviet people, fully and indivisibly exercise its sovereignty."[24] But at the same time "every Union republic is a sovereign State,"[25] "the Stalin Constitution confirmed . . . the sovereignty of the Union Republics,"[26] "the

Sovereignty of the U.S.S.R. does not contradict the sovereignty of the Union Republics."[27]

What reasons are given for this apparently untenable proposition? First, that the U.S.S.R. was formed on the basis of voluntary union, in which the union republics voluntarily surrendered certain powers to the central U.S.S.R. government. Secondly, that each republic has the formal right of secession from the Union (Article 17). Thirdly, that the boundaries of each republic cannot be altered save with its consent. Fourthly, that each union republic possesses all residuary powers, i.e., those not specifically granted to the center in Article 14 of the Constitution. Fifthly, that the republics participate in central decisions by sending their representatives to the Supreme Soviet, and in particular to the Soviet of Nationalities within it, and these decisions are (by definition!) in the general interest of all. Sixthly, each republic has the right to enter into relations with foreign States and to maintain its own military formations. Finally, that without the protection of the Union, the republics would not be able to defend their own sovereignty. "Bourgeois" teaching on the subject is false because: sovereignty never belongs to the people in reality, but only to the ruling class; and any but the largest States are not independent except in an unreal, formal sense.

The views of Vyshinski and his fellow-lawyers, summarized above, are not in accord with Soviet reality. Vyshinski is fond of judging "bourgeois" institutions by their real nature-in-action, as distinct from their formal-juridical nature, and it is only right to return the compliment by subjecting the "sovereignty" of the Union republics, two of which have separate representation within the UN, to a brief factual scrutiny: —

It is necessary to begin with a reference to two concepts: "democratic centralism" and "dual subordination," an understanding of which is essential in this context.

The term *democratic centralism* was originally coined to describe the form of organization which Lenin prescribed for the Bolshevik party: iron discipline and full obedience to the elected leadership. This system was also applied to the Soviet State: "Democratic centralism assumes, in the structure and in the ac-

---

22 Vyshinski, p. 262.
23 *Ibid.*
24 *Ibid.*, p. 292.
25 *Ibid.*, p. 263.
26 Levin and Karass, p. 130.

27 N.P. Farberov, *op. cit.*, p. 12.

tivity of the State machine, unity in essentials and variety in detail. . . . The necessity of unity is founded on common basic interests of all nationalities and administrative units of the Soviet State and of the State as a whole."[28] Or, put another way, the system implies "the strictest obedience to the directives of the Party and the government," while ensuring "fullest consideration of local conditions and peculiarities."[29]

The above principles find their organizational expression in the so-called system of *dual subordination*. At each level below that of the central government, one often finds State organs nominally responsible to two masters: one on its own level, and one above it. For example, the Council of Ministers of the Ukrainian republic is responsible *both* to the Council of Ministers of the U.S.S.R. *and* to the Supreme Soviet of the Ukraine; the Ukrainian Minister of Textile Industry is at one and the same time the Ukrainian subordinate of the Minister of Textile Industry of the U.S.S.R. *and* a member of the Ukrainian "cabinet"; the Kiev city health department is also the Kiev branch of the Ukrainian Ministry of Health, and so forth. Within this system, the orders of the center have all the legal force of a valid instruction from a hierarchical superior. From top to bottom, "the Soviet on a higher (hierarchical) level controls the inferior one, and the instructions of the higher Soviet are obligatory on the lower one; the former checks on the legality of the latter's actions, and is responsible for these actions."[30] The same degree of subordination applies to any administrative unit of the Union republics *vis-à-vis* its equivalent in Moscow. The fact that a republican minister, for instance, is responsible to the Cabinet of which he is a part, as well as to his superior on the U.S.S.R. level, must be viewed in the light of the fact that the Ukrainian cabinet collectively is fully subordinated to the U.S.S.R. cabinet.

It is with the above points in mind that one can appreciate the significance of the "residuary" nature of the powers of the republics, i.e., their right to do anything not specifically as-

signed to the center by virtue of Article 14 of the Constitution. It must be added that Article 14 defines the competence of the Union so vaguely that anything could be included within its orbit, and that in case of dispute the Praesidium is the sole arbiter of the Union's competence (there has, needless to say, been no dispute to date).

A brief mention of points relevant to the powers of the union republics will now be given below: —

(a) We have already seen how far the Councils of Ministers which each republic possesses are under the authority of the center. With a few exceptions of purely local significance, the individual ministries on republican level are branches of ministries in Moscow (these ministries are known as "union-republican"), operating under the principle of dual subordination. In these cases, the ministry at Union level "exercises its authority through identically-named ministries at union-republican level."[31] The degree of autonomy actually delegated by the center must vary considerably, but, for example, an economic ministry on republican level receives instructions from Moscow on "the organization of work, piecework norms, wages, financial organization and so on, the construction of new undertakings, the organization of raw material supplies, preparation of cadres, and so forth," and the ministry's budget and production plans require central approval.[32] It should be added that large industrial units of all-Union significance are controlled directly from Moscow.

(b) Even this limited degree of local autonomy applies to a small section of the Soviet State's activity, particularly in the economic field. Of the fifty economic ministries which existed in Moscow at the end of 1947, only fifteen were union-republican. The remaining thirty-five are known as "union ministries," i.e., ministries which conduct their affairs within the republics through subordinates who are responsible *only* to the center.

(c) Since 1944, some of the republics possess their own ministries of Foreign Affairs. Under the amended Constitution, "Foreign Affairs" is on the list of union-republican ministries, and the normal principle of hierarchical

---

[28] Denisov, p. 260.
[29] *Administrative Law*, p 17.
[30] Denisov, p. 261.

[31] *Administrative Law*, p. 27.
[32] *Ibid.*, p. 294.

subordination to the center, which is a normal feature of a union-republican ministry, must apply to this field. The textbook lays down that the center remains responsible for "the general rules concerning the relations of the individual union republics with foreign countries" and "for representing the Union as a whole in international relations."[33] It is difficult indeed to think of any subject which, say, the Ukraine could discuss with a foreign country without in some way affecting the Union as a whole — and therefore necessarily requiring the guidance of Moscow. "It is natural that the decisive rights in this field belong to the Union."[34]

(d) There is a Ministry of the Interior in each of the republics, but these are fully subordinate to the Minister in Moscow, having no responsibility whatever to the republican council of ministers. "In this respect the Ministry of the Interior is in the same position as a Union ministry."[35] The individual republics therefore have no control over the secret police formations, labor camps, convoy troops, frontier guards, and even fire brigades functioning on their territories.

(e) The "sovereign" republics are forbidden to alter their own administrative-territorial divisions, which are listed in Articles 22–29 of the *Union* Constitution.

(f) The budgets of the republics require approval by the center. (In 1946 all the sixteen republics' budgets combined totalled 63,000 million rubles, while the Union's budget was 320,000 million rubles.)

(g) The union-republics have, since 1944, the right to maintain their own armed forces. This is, on paper, an impressive manifestation of sovereignty. However, this is how the right is interpreted by a Soviet commentator: "The unity of the Army is now being still further strengthened, as the military formations of the union-republics will be component parts of the Army of the U.S.S.R. The Army of the Soviet Union must continue to be unquestionably one, unquestionably centralized. The whole Red Army will have a single set of regulations, a

single mobilization plan, a single command. The basic rules of organization of the armed forces will be laid down by the Union organs."[36]

(h) The supervision over the legality of administration within each republic's territory is carried out by the "Prokuror's" department. However, the officials of this department are appointed by, and are responsible to, the "Prokuror-General" of the U.S.S.R., and they are *not* in any way responsible to the republican authorities. The Prokuror is barred from challenging any acts of the *Central* Government.

(i) "The Council of Ministers of the Union republics are forbidden to undertake any reorganization of their administrative apparatus, to create new organizations or offices, or to alter the nomenclature or salaries of their officials, without the permission of the Central Establishments Commission" (in Moscow).[37]

(j) Most important of all, the Communist Party is highly centralized on an all-Union basis, and in a one-party State it is the degree of autonomy granted to local party functionaries which really determines the extent of local rights. The party statutes lay down that "on all questions, party groups are obliged strictly and undeviatingly to obey the decisions of the leading organs of the Party" (Paragraph 71) and this applies to the party leadership of a Union republic *vis-à-vis* the center.

There remains the formal right of secession from the Union. When the new Constitution was being discussed in 1936, Stalin said: "The U.S.S.R. is a voluntary Union of republics with equal rights. To omit from the Constitution the articles relating to freedom to secede from the U.S.S.R. would be a breach of the voluntary character of the Union."[38] It is certainly a tenable proposition to say that the republics have *equal* rights (whatever views one may hold as to the extent of these rights), but the right to secede is purely fictional, and must remain so for as long as public advocacy of

---

[33] *Ibid.*, p. 171.

[34] Levin and Karass, p. 137.

[35] *Administrative Law*, p. 192. Presumably this applies equally to the Ministry of State Security, formerly part of the Ministry of the Interior.

[36] N.P. Farberov, *The Sovereignty of the Union Republics*, transcript of lecture, published by *Pravda*, Moscow, 1946.

[37] *Administrative Law*, p. 40. (Even a rural district council in England has greater powers in this field!).

[38] *Report on the Draft Constitution of the U.S.S.R.*, Moscow, 1936.

secession remains a *de facto* criminal offence. No one with the slightest knowledge of U.S.S.R. politics would deny that if any Ukrainian (for instance) stood up in a meeting in Kiev to advocate independence for the Ukraine, he would court instant arrest. Indeed, Stalin himself has written the following revealing paragraph: "There are occasions when the right of self-determination contradicts another and higher right, the right of the working class to strengthen its power. In these cases — it should be frankly stated — the right of self-determination cannot and must not obstruct the rights of the dictatorship of the working class. The former must give way before the latter."[39]

Soviet federalism rests on the need to adjust the policies decided at the center to the varied national cultural and linguistic requirements of a vast country. "The toiling masses of each nation within the U.S.S.R. are free in deciding the national form of their participation in the common work of building Socialism."[40] Considerable local initiative in carrying out centrally-divised policies is encouraged, but strictly within the framework of these policies.

Soviet delegates at international conferences defend the principle of national sovereignty. It should be clear from the above that in Soviet parlance the Ukraine or Azerbaidjan are sovereign States. So long as Western lawyers judge Soviet lawyers' pronouncements at their *Western* linguistic value, they will be unable to follow their case.

4. The Communist Party and the Constitution

The position of the Communist Party in the Soviet State is the subject of much misunderstanding. The Webbs defined it as follows: "The party members who are office-bearers, and who are all pledged to complete obedience to the dictates of the Party authorities, have assumed as their main vocation the supreme direction of policy and the most important part of its execution, in every branch of public administration of the U.S.S.R. . . . The Communist party central committee, and especially the inner Politbureau which it appoints, not

only prescribes the line to be pursued by all party cells throughout the U.S.S.R., but also coordinates and directs the policy and executive action of the Council of People's Commissars and of all party members who constitute the most important part of the staffs in these commissariats. It is in this way, in fact, that is exercised the dictatorship of the proletariat."[41]

The Webbs wrote before the Stalin Constitution came into force. There is no doubt, however, that the above passage in no way underrates the role of the Party. Denisov's textbook, after comparing the Party with the heroes of Greek mythology, states the following: "Party leadership is the basis of the fruitful activity of each State and social organization, and of all these organizations taken together. They all take instructions from the Party, which has its members in the State and social organizations of the masses, forming the directing nucleus and ensuring that the given State or social organization carries out the decisions of the Party. That is why the opportunist 'theory' that non-party organizations should be independent of the Party organization, has been shown up by Lenin and Stalin as incorrect and harmful. . . . In general, the whole Soviet system and constitution rests on the directing role of the Party. . . . The Party controls the selection, distribution and training of the personnel of the whole Soviet State apparatus, and checks on the work of the organs of State and government. Not a single important decision is taken by the State organs of our country without previous instructions and advice from the Party."[42] The Communist Party is specifically mentioned in Article 126 of the Constitution, in which the following clear statement of its functions occurs: "The most active and conscious citizens from the ranks of the working class and other toilers join together in the All-Union Communist Party (Bolsheviks), which is the advance guard of the toilers in their struggle for the strengthening and development of the Socialist order and *constitutes the directing nucleus of all toilers' organizations, both social and governmental.*" Particular attention must be drawn to the last sentence (emphasis mine), because

---

[39] Stalin, *Marxism and the National-Colonial Question*, quoted by Denisov, p. 232.
[40] Vyshinski, p. 218.

[41] *Soviet Communism*, p. 354.
[42] Denisov, p. 191–2.

in it is to be found the key to all Soviet constitutional practice and the explanation of much of the theory. The leading role of the Party permeates all Soviet life. "The unity of the administration is ensured by the political leadership of the Party, whose directives and slogans *have the force of a practical decision which must be immediately carried out;* the executive organs carry out their functions in full accordance with the directives given by the Party."[43] A large proportion of the more important executive orders are published as coming jointly from the Council of Ministers and the Central Committee of the Party.

The Soviet theorists are, of course, right when they point out that their Constitution at least honestly emphasizes the supremacy of the Party, while Western constitutions usually ignore the existence of parties, although these are by no means without significance to the real working of any "bourgeois" constitution. But the existence of a highly-disciplined party with a long-term political monopoly creates a quite special situation, and, as we have seen, there is a profound sense in which a pronouncement of the Central Committee of the Party has practically the force of law, despite the oft-repeated desire of the Party leaders to carry out the task of government exclusively through the Soviet State machinery

The Party itself, like the Soviet State itself, is run on the basis of "democratic centralism," i.e., unquestioning obedience to orders from superior authority, which, however, is itself elected. There are some who hold that such a system gives to the Party chiefs powers over the process of election itself, and certainly the higher organs of the Party seem to be endowed with powers which one cannot see effectively challenged from below. It should be stated in this connection that while the Party statutes lay down that a Congress should be held every three years, no Congress has been held since 1939.

5. *The Constitutional Guarantees*

The freedoms guaranteed by the Constitution must be interpreted, and are interpreted by Soviet jurists, in the light of the nature and purpose of the Soviet State. Personal freedom, in the sense of freedom from want, is "guaranteed" by the provisions relating to old age

pensions, sick pay, freedom from unemployment, etc.[44] When it comes to such matters as freedom of the press, of meetings, demonstrations, or of speech, Article 126 of the Constitution makes these freedoms conditional upon their being used "in accordance with the interests of the toilers and with the aim of strengthening the Socialist order." Explaining these provisions, the textbook lays down: "In our State there is not, and of course cannot be, any freedom of speech, of the press, etc., for the enemies of Socialism." As for demonstrations, "in the U.S.S.R. the fullest initiative is granted to social and toilers' organizations, and in the first place to the directing nucleus of all these social and governmental organizations, the Communist Party."[45]

The Soviet jurist does not consider that these limitations in any way contradict his concept of democracy; he considers that the capitalist basis of the Western States makes nonsense of their formal constitutional guarantees, and that only in the U.S.S.R. (and the countries of the "new democracy" in Eastern Europe) is there to be found the material basis of real freedom, directed in the interests of the mass of the people.

However, it is difficult to see how Vyshinski would justify the immense precautions taken to make sure that unorthodox views do not find their way into print. The following quotation tells its own story: "Permits for obtaining and using duplicators and accessories thereto are granted by the local police department to the *head of the secret department* within the undertaking, office or organization acquiring the duplicator,[46] or, where there is no secret department to the head of the undertaking, office or organization. . . ." Once the permit is received, "the duplicator must be registered in the local office of 'Glavlit,' "[47] and "the sale of duplicators is permitted only with prior permission of the police department,

---

[43] *Administrative Law,* p. 6.

[44] But we have seen how one "guarantee," dealing with free higher education, was disregarded in 1940.

[45] Vyshinski, p. 555.

[46] Emphasis mine. No *individual* is entitled to acquire a duplicator. The "secret department" is the network of secret police agents which functions within most Soviet institutions. It is rare to find a reference to it in print.

[47] "Glavlit" is the body responsible for censorship of all published material, which must be submitted to it *before and after* its appearance.

while accessories may only be obtained on production of the duplicator's registration certificate, bearing a wax seal of the police department."[48]

6. The Separation of Powers

Soviet theorists strongly attack the theory of separation. "The basic content of the principle of the separation of powers in a bourgeois state consists of ensuring the independence of the executive, as the firmest prop of the power of the bourgeoisie, as against the elected representatives of the people, who at a time of wider franchise are less reliable from the point of view of bourgeois interests."[49] In Vyshinski's textbook, both Ramsay Muir's and Lord Hewart's criticisms of the growth of delegated legislation are quoted with approval.

Soviet theory insists on "the supremacy of the elected representative assembly in the Soviet State."[50] The Supreme Soviet, or its standing committee (the Praesidium), has supreme powers. "All other activities of the State are subordinate in character. Forms of subordinate powers are: the executive . . . the judiciary."[51] In accordance with these principles, the Ministers are appointed by, and are responsible to, the Supreme Soviet, while the Praesidium interprets the Constitution and the laws; the judges of the High Court and the Prokuror-General of the U.S.S.R. are also appointed by the Supreme Soviet.

The declared opposition of Soviet theorists to the principle of separating the powers arises, too, from the theoretical consideration that there is no need to protect different sections of the community against the State, or one part of the State against another. Such an idea would run counter to the present-day Soviet notion that Soviet society contains no internal contradictions. Indeed, the Soviet State is held literally to *embody the General will* in Rousseau's sense;[52] it must therefore be illimitable.

7. The Supreme Soviet and Its Praesidium

The Supreme Soviet requires a long article of its own. All that will be attempted here is a brief discussion of three aspects of its existence: its unanimity, the theory behind its second chamber, and its Praesidium.

It has already been stated that it is, in law, the sole body entitled to legislate for the whole Union.[53] This was not true of its predecessor under the 1924 constitution, the Congress of Soviets. This body, indirectly elected, met every two years, and was more like a mass meeting than a legislature (about 3,000 delegates attended). It elected a Central Executive Committee (*Vtsik*) of some 600 members, which met at more frequent intervals and exercised all the Congress's powers. When *Vtsik* was not in session, all its powers (including that of legislation) were exercised by its praesidium. Finally, the Council of People's Commissars was also empowered to pass valid laws.[54]

Although the Supreme Soviet is now of manageable size and not just a mass meeting, the Western observer cannot but be struck by its unanimity on *all* issues, including the election of its own officers and committees. This unanimity does not mean that there is no criticism. Reports of sessions are full of speeches calling for more and better construction projects in a given area, or demanding greater efficiency in various branches of the administration. These criticisms, however, are never taken to the point of registering a hostile vote (unless, of course, that vote is itself unanimous). Criticism concentrates on details of execution, but not on the policy itself.

Soviet theorists maintain that the Supreme Soviet is "a working institution, which does not spend time and energy on political quarrels and arguments . . . in its activity is expressed moral-political unity, a bolshevik businesslike approach."[55]

In fact, the practice of unanimity arises naturally from the one-party system. The large

[48] *Administrative Law,* p. 231. This is *not* a wartime security measure, as it already existed in 1935.
[49] Levin and Karass, p. 94.
[50] Levin, *The State System of a Socialist Democracy* (transcript of lecture), Moscow. 1946.
[51] Levin and Karass, p. 34.
[52] This analogy is developed at some length in an unsigned leading article in *Soviet State and Law,* 1946, No. 2.

[53] Art. 32; but the Praesidium and the Ministers have invaded this field (see above).
[54] The Webbs, *Soviet Communism,* or Batsell's *Soviet Rule in Russia* (Macmillan, N.Y., 1929), contains full descriptions of the pre-1936 system, seen from very different angles.
[55] *Soviet State and Law,* 1946, No. 2, p. 28.

majority of deputies are party members, and the others may be fairly described as fellow-travellers. In consequence, any disagreements are ironed out behind closed doors in meetings of the party group, and no doubt nominations to committees, etc., are similarly arranged, for only one name is generally put forward for any one vacancy.

Needless to say, Party control over the legislature is by no means peculiar to the Soviet Union! What *is* unique is the pursuit of the fetish of unanimity, even where (in the election of a minor committee, for example) it has no clear purpose. It might well have been argued that only under a socialist State could deputies cast their vote quite freely, unencumbered by vested interest or narrow party considerations. This is not, however, the line taken in the U.S.S.R., where the "sure compass" of dialectical materialism is held to provide one, "correct," answer to any problem, and where the Party controls all important appointments.

The "Second Chamber" of the Supreme Soviet, the Soviet of Nationalities, is composed of twenty-five representatives directly elected by the people of each of the Union republics, plus eleven from each autonomous republic, and lesser numbers from smaller national groupings. This represents in the highest organ of Soviet power the multinational principle of the Soviet state, and is intended to safeguard the specifically national interests of the various national groupings. Originating in a committee within the People's Commissariat of Nationalities, the Soviet of Nationalities was set up under the 1924 Constitution as a special section of the Central Executive Committee (*Vtsik*). The Soviet of Nationalities under the Stalin Constitution is fully the equal in all formal respects with the Soviet of the Union. At joint sessions the Speakers of the two Houses take the chair at alternate meetings. Deputies are elected to both Houses for four years, at the same general election. In case of disagreement between the two Houses, a joint committee (on which they are equally represented) is provided for in the Constitution; if after all efforts by this committee the Houses still disagree, the Praesidium dissolves them and there is a new election. For no reason other than the above can the Supreme Soviet be dissolved before the end of its term. In

practice, this provision is without significance, as both Houses have always been unanimously of the same opinion on any issue.

The *Praesidium* is, perhaps, the most original contribution of the U.S.S.R. to the practice of government.[56] It is composed of a chairman, sixteen vice-chairmen (one for every union republic), fifteen other members and a secretary, all elected at a joint session of the two Houses of the Supreme Soviet (Article 48). Its powers are: —

(a) *Legislative*. Although it has the formal right only to issue Decrees (*ukazi*), we have seen that in effect the Praesidium may legislate effectively by *ukaz* on any issue, and may expect its acts to be subsequently ratified by the Supreme Soviet. (In any case, being itself the interpreter of the Constitution, it is hardly likely to find itself guilty of illegal acts.)

(b) *Executive*. The Praesidium's functions under this head cover a field which, in most other countries, belongs either to the Cabinet or to the Head of the State. Thus it calls meetings of the Supreme Soviet, appoints and accepts resignations of Ministers (between sessions of the Supreme Soviet), declares war, appoints ambassadors, receives letters of credence from foreign envoys, exercises the prerogative of mercy, awards decorations, appoints and dismisses C.-in-C.s of the armed forces. Vyshinski stresses that the Chairman of the Praesidium has no powers, except those arising simply from his being the chairman; he takes the chair, he signs laws and ukazes, but he can issue no instructions save in the name of the Praesidium. "The Praesidium of the Supreme Soviet is the 'President-in-Commission' (*kollegialny president*) of the U.S.S.R."[57]

(c) *Judicial*. The Praesidium interprets the Constitution and the laws and has the power of declaring any act of the Union Ministry, or republican ministries, or any other administrative act, void if it deems them not to be in accordance with law.

The Praesidium is "accountable to the Supreme Soviet for all its activities."[58] The Praesidium has no right of veto over legislation, and cannot dissolve the Supreme Soviet

56 The "new democracies" in the Balkans have adopted some features of this institution.
57 *Vyshinski*, p. 311. The words are Stalin's.
58 *Ibid.*, p. 310.

save if the two Houses fail to agree. In practice, with the Supreme Soviet meeting at infrequent intervals, the Praesidium naturally has very wide powers, which it exercises without any instance of challenge or even question from its "master," the Supreme Soviet.

A member of the Praesidium who becomes a minister resigns from the Praesidium, but ministers can be deputies to the Supreme Soviet, though this is not always the case.[59]

8. *The Executive*

The *Council of Ministers* is responsible to, and is appointed by, the Supreme Soviet and its Praesidium, and its instructions must be based on either laws or ukazes issued by these bodies (Articles 66–67).[60] These instructions (*postanovlenia* — laying down norms, and *rasporyazhenia* — deciding a specific case) have the force of a statutory rule. There has been no case of a rule being challenged, but presumably such a challenge would have to go up for decision to the Praesidium. In practice the Council of Ministers must work closely with the Praesidium, as is inevitable in view of the wide powers of the latter.

Space forbids detailed inquiry into the powers of Ministers. Attention ought, however, to be drawn to the very large size of the Council of Ministers (nearly seventy strong). So large a body cannot attempt serious discussions on policy. Its real nature becomes apparent when the list of ministries is studied (Ministry for the Cinema, Ministry for Manufacture of Transport Equipment, Ministry for the Oilfields of the Eastern regions, Ministry of Cellulose and Paper Manufacture, to cite some examples). The bulk of rank-and-file ministers deal with economic sectors, within which they are in effect the senior managers. Their task is to issue orders to the industries they control in accordance with policy, and it is to a much smaller body that one must look

to discover who makes policy. It is surely no accident that under the Chairman (Stalin) there are eleven vice-chairmen of the Council of Ministers, who are all members or alternates of the powerful Political Bureau of the Communist Party. They must surely double the roles of Party and State leadership, and act as an inner Cabinet. Whereas in 1937 there were two vice-chairmen and eighteen ministers, there are now eleven vice-chairmen and sixty ministers, so it is reasonable to suppose that these vice-chairmen control groups of ministries. Some of them, like Molotov and Mikoyan, hold ministerial posts, while others (e.g., Malenkov, Andreyev) are without portfolio.

The Council of Ministers has attached to it a number of special Boards and Committees with wide powers (for instance those dealing with afforestation, radio transmission, religious affairs, as well as the Academy of Sciences and the Tass news agency. All are under the general authority of the Council of Ministers, and their chiefs have the right of "consultative voice" without a seat in the Cabinet.

In the composition of individual ministries one peculiarity is worth bringing out: in every ministry there is, under the Minister, a council (*kollegia*), to whom all important questions must be referred; this council is appointed not by the Minister but by the Council of Ministers. Its members consist of the Minister's deputies and of some high civil servants, and, if they disagree with the Minister, they have the right to appeal to the Council of Ministers. Indeed, before 1934 the *kollegii* issued instructions on their own responsibility; this caused confusion, and they were abolished, only to be revived in 1938 without the power of independent executive action. Only the Minister can issue a valid instruction for the Ministry as a whole.

One ministry is peculiar to the Soviet Union and deserves a brief special mention. This is the Ministry of State Control, born of a marriage between the Workers' and Peasants' Inspection and the Party's Central Control Committee. This Ministry has the double task of preventing abuses in the administrative machine, and of ensuring that orders given by the higher authorities are in fact carried out. Its officials have powers of access to all relevant documents, and "it is compulsory for all

---

[59] In 1938 Stalin himself was a member of the Praesidium, but he ceased to be a member when he became officially the Head of the Government. He remains a deputy, however. Ministers, whether they are or are not deputies, have the right to speak in either House.

[60] In practice the Council of Ministers, usually bracketed with the Central Committee of the Party, has issued Orders making new laws, and even (as we have seen) amending the Constitution.

ministries, commissions, departments and other organs" to provide "explanations, reports and all other information."[61] The Ministry has its men working throughout the administrative machine, at all levels (it even has its inspectors in military stores and army divisions). The Ministry's officials are empowered to take disciplinary action against offenders, or, in serious cases, to hand the case over to the Prokuror for criminal prosecution before the courts. The Ministry of State Control plays an important role in that system of inspection and cross-checking, which is a feature of Soviet administration (other "checkers" include the secret police, the Ministry of Finance, the Planning authorities and the Establishments commission).

9. Electoral Procedure

The procedure for *elections* to the Supreme Soviet is, on paper, fully consonant with the democratic principle. The legality of election procedure is watched over by a system of electoral commissions, who represent social societies and workers' organizations (the names of members are confirmed by the local Soviet in the area in which they function). A widely representative Central Electoral Commission, whose members are confirmed by the Supreme Soviet or its Praesidium, supervises the elections on a nationwide scale, and hears appeals against any decision by the local commissions. It renders a report on the conduct of the elections to the Mandates commissions of the two Houses of the Supreme Soviet.

Candidates may be nominated by "social organizations or societies of toilers — i.e., communist party organizations and other societies registered in accordance with the law."[62] Religious organizations are excluded.[63]

Now it has already been remarked that the Constitution itself lays down that the Communist party is "the directing nucleus of all social organizations and societies of toilers." It follows, then, that the candidate is effectively selected by the Communist Party (whether that candidate is himself a party member or not). In the two elections that

have been held to the Supreme Soviet since the promulgation of the Stalin Constitution (1938 and 1946), there has not been a single case of contested election. A Soviet lawyer would view that matter thus: "The moral and political unity of the whole Soviet people results in the fact that, in practice, only one candidate is nominated in each constituency, and he receives unanimous support from all social organizations and meetings of the working masses of the given area. . . . Soviet elections are a brilliant demonstration of Socialist Democracy in action."[64] Indeed, at the last election 99.7 per cent of the electors voted, and less than 1 per cent failed to vote for the official candidates. As a charmingly naive article put it, "not a single deputy in a bourgeois parliament . . . can ever have received or can ever receive such a majority. . . ."[65] At any rate, we must admit that the organization which gets people to the poll must be very efficient.

The Constitution provides for the recall of individual deputies by the electors if the latter are dissatisfied with them, but the mechanism for doing so has never been brought into being, and the right is purely theoretical to date.

10. A Note on the Judiciary and the Political Police

The Soviet judicial system requires an article of its own, and only the briefest reference will be made to its position in the constitutional structure of the Union. At the top of the hierarchy of people's and regional courts stands the Supreme Court (strictly the High Court) of the U.S.S.R. It is divided into five "collegia": civil, military, criminal, rail transport, and water transport. There is a President, sixty-eight judges and twenty-eight "assessors." The collegia are responsible for hearing appeals from the lower courts, which may be initiated by an aggrieved party or by the prosecutor (Prokuror); in addition, there are cases of national importance, for which the relevant collegium of the High Court acts as a tribunal of first instance. On these occasions, two assessors sit with the judge (as is the practice in the lower courts). The Mili-

---

[61] *Administrative Law,* p. 128.
[62] Art. 56 of the *Regulations on Elections to the Supreme Soviet of the U.S.S.R.*
[63] Vyshinski, p. 637.

[64] Levin and Karass, p. 215.
[65] *Soviet State and Law,* 1946, No. 2.

tary collegium heard the cases of Zinoviev and Bukharin during the purges, because it covers "cases of treason, espionage, sabotage, etc., by whomsoever committed,"[66] as well as appeals from courts martial. The Transport collegia hear appeals from the special transport courts, whose main task is to enforce labor discipline, and who appear to have powers similar to courts martial. The two transport and the military collegia are staffed by judges who have risen in the hierarchy of these special courts. From the decisions of the collegia there is no appeal (save to the Praesidium, which exercises the prerogative of mercy).

However, cases may be reviewed by the Plenum of the Supreme Court, which is a meeting of all the judges, attended also by the Prokuror-General and the Minister of Justice, held at least every two months. The Plenum reviews those judgments of the Collegia which are brought to its notice by the President of the Court or the Prokuror-General, and issues directives to the lower courts. These directives lay down the principles which the lower courts must follow in applying the laws, and frequently embody valuable safeguards for the public.[67]

The Supreme Court's powers to interpret laws arise primarily from its own case-work. In carrying out this function, however, it is subordinate to the Praesidium of the Supreme Soviet, which has the overriding right to interpret the Constitution and the laws.

The Supreme Court judges are appointed for five years by the Supreme Soviet, and Article 112 of the Constitution lays it down that they are "independent and subject only to the law."

As in most other Continental countries, the preparation of a case against the accused (including interrogation of witnesses, etc.) is undertaken by a judicial investigator (sledo-vatel) who operates under the guidance of the Prokuror. For political cases, however, the organs of the Ministry of State Security (i.e., the political police) act as judicial investigators, with the usual powers of interrogation and detention which such officials possess.

The Minister of Justice exercises a general supervision over the functioning of the courts. He may not intervene in the hearing of a case (save to overcome delays and red tape), but he "watches over the correctness of the application of the laws to civil and criminal cases."[68] If the Minister feels that a new instruction to the courts is called for, he puts a proposal to that effect before a meeting of the Plenum of the Supreme Court.

Space compels total omission of fascinating problems connected with procedure and application of the laws. But no review of Soviet constitutional practice can omit some reference to the Ministry of Home Affairs and the Ministry of State Security, usually known by their initials — M.V.D. (N.K.V.D.) and M.G.B. These two ministries were at one time one, and the exact boundary between their functions is a well-guarded secret. They jointly exercise the powers of the former O.G.P.U., and many more besides. There is nothing in the Constitution about the wide powers of arbitrary imprisonment practised by these ministries and their local organs. However, a series of laws and orders regulate their functions, and many pages of the textbook on Administrative Law are devoted to listing them. We have already seen that the M.V.D. and M.G.B. organs act as preliminary investigators of any political case. If they should come to the conclusion that a citizen is "socially dangerous," the "Special Council" (Os-oboe Soveshchanie) may exile him or confine him to a concentration camp for up to five years — and "control over the release of the detainee is exercised by the local organs of the M.V.D. in the area of exile or detention."[69] The Special Council at Union level consists of the Minister of the Interior, his highest subordinates and the Prokuror-General; the latter may appeal to the Council of Ministers against an unjust detention order. But if the security organs have built up a case against the accused (for instance, under the many sub-paragraphs of Article 58 of the Criminal Code, which define counter-revolutionary activities), he is tried and sentenced by the regular courts of the land. The choice seems to rest with the

66 Vyshinski, p. 471.
67 Schlesinger, op. cit., contains much information on the general work of the Soviet Courts.

68 Denisov, p. 314.
69 Administrative Law, pp. 191 and 245.

secret police, who undertake the preliminary examination.

The M.V.D. also exercises the functions of the Registrar-General, controls fire brigades, the uniformed police, a large and well-equipped Security Army, frontier guards, road-building, prisons, and concentration-labor camps. With the M.G.B., it is a power in the land; during the great purge of 1936–38 it was able to cause the total disappearance of deputies, Ministers, and even members of the Polit-bureau.

11. The "Prokuror"

The institution of *Prokuror* in the Soviet State has no clear parallel in Western countries. He is at one time the Public Prosecutor and the guardian over legality in the field of both administration and justice in the area in which he functions. The hierarchy of local Prokurors are appointed by, and are entirely subordinated to, the Prokuror-General of the U.S.S.R.; they are totally independent of the local or union-republican authority. The Prokuror-General is appointed by the Supreme Soviet for seven years, and we have seen that he plays his part in the plenums of the Supreme Court in determining the general "policy" of the Soviet Courts. He also personally prosecutes in important cases before the Supreme Court; thus Vyshinski, who was then the Prokuror of the U.S.S.R., prosecuted Zinoviev, Bukharin, etc., before the military collegium of the Supreme Court.

The Prokuror in the localities exercises the following functions:

(a) While "he does not settle administrative problems himself," the Prokuror "must see that the settlement of such problems by local State authorities corresponds to the provisions of the law." In case of any illegal instruction being issued by anyone, or of any illegal act or omission, the Prokuror's office must challenge the illegality, i.e., bring the matter to the notice of the next highest organ of State power. If the decision of this organ is also inconsistent with the law, it can be challenged in its turn. In this way "the problem can go up to the highest organs of the State, which then give a binding decision."[70] In acting thus, the Prokuror is expected both to use his personal initiative and to follow up complaints from citizens.

(b) In his capacity as Public Prosecutor, the Prokuror represents the State in all judicial proceedings. If in his view any decision of the court is wrong, he can challenge it and take the case to the next highest court, right up to the Supreme Court.[71]

(c) The sanction of the Prokuror or of a court is required for any arrest.

(d) The judicial investigators operate under his authority.

There is a close tie-up in practice between the Prokuror system and the Party and State security organs. "In order that it should be a strong and flexible weapon in the hands of the working-class dictatorship in its struggle for Communism, the Prokuror must work under the closest supervision of, and in the closest contact with, the party organizations which offer the most effective guarantees against local or personal influences."[72] In his task, he must cooperate "with the organs of the N.K.V.D. and with the courts in a decisive struggle against all remnants of the Trotsky-Bukharinite bandits, the hirelings of fascist intelligence services, spies, wreckers, thieves, hooligans" and so on.[73]

First and foremost, the Prokuror is "the guardian of Socialist legality, the executor of the policy of the Communist Party and Soviet power, a fighter in the cause of Socialism."[74] His position is deliberately intended to be outside the system of elective organs of State power in the various republics and the local government areas. He must watch over the local administration and the local machinery of justice, and keep them to the laws, ukazes, and directives of the supreme authorities of the Union. It is doubtful, in view of the above quotations, whether he is likely to protect the

---

[70] Vyshinski, p. 473.

[71] His right applies also to civil cases, and in criminal cases he has the right of appeal against a prisoner's acquittal. He may also undertake a civil case on behalf of a citizen if this is in the public interest. Recently, the right to appeal against a sentence "once it is legally in force" has been reserved to senior members of the hierarchy of Prokurors.

[72] Vyshinski (quoting Lenin), p. 473.

[73] *Ibid.*, p. 481. The political jargon is definitely "1938"; in 1948 there would be a reference to the Hirelings of Imperialist Warmongers.

[74] *Ibid.*, p. 484.

citizen in cases where "political unreliability" is involved, but a conscientious Prokuror can do much to defend citizens against abuse of power by local authorities or officials.

12. *The Citizen and the Administration*

The reader who has some knowledge of Continental law will be looking for a Russian equivalent of the special administrative courts, a Russian *"Conseil d'État"* for hearing citizens' cases against the State. There is, however, no hierarchy of this type of administrative courts in the U.S.S.R. State prosecution of citizens or officials for any serious offence not committed on the transport system is heard by the ordinary courts. The following means exist for an aggrieved Soviet citizen to obtain satisfaction against the State:

(a) The right of complaint. This is "the most important means of ensuring legality in Soviet administration." 'The right of complaint in the Soviet State has this essential characteristic, that . . . it is the means of defending the legal rights of citizens. . . ."[75] An elaborate procedure exists by which the complaint must be investigated within a given period of time, and the complainant is shielded from repressive acts save in cases of malicious and libellous complaints. The complaint may be addressed to the head of the office committing the alleged illegal act, or to the Prokuror, or to a State Control office (as well, of course, as through Party channels). If no satisfaction is obtained, the complainant may make representations to the next highest administrative level. The Party is enjoined to assist in this system of complaints, as its proper functioning helps to keep the administration on its toes.

(b) The right of appeal to the courts. This is limited in scope principally to "the prevention of breaches of Socialist legality in the levying of administrative fines and non-payment of taxes."[76] A variety of State and other institutions have the right of imposing fines (e.g., city officials of Moscow may fine citizens for non-compliance with by-laws). The accused has no right of appeal on the substance of the case; he may, however, refuse to pay the fine, and then the case is heard by the courts — who confine themselves to deciding whether the authority in question was *intra vires* in levying the fine and do not consider the rights and wrongs of the decision of the administrative organ. Where the fine is levied by an institution (e.g., by an office or factory for spoiled work), no appeal to the courts is possible, and the money owing is simply deducted from pay.

(c) The Prokuror, as already stated, watches over the legality of administrative acts. Citizens' complaints may be taken up, and the Prokuror's office may challenge the illegal act all the way up the administrative hierarchy, up to the Government and Ministries of the U.S.S.R., whose acts are not challengeable by the Prokuror-General.

(d) A hierarchy of State Arbitration Tribunals hear disputes between the various economic organizations of the State. Where an organization can persuade the Prokuror that it has been unfairly treated, the latter can appeal to the Chief Arbitrator, who is attached to the Council of Ministers. The decision of State arbitration tribunals is binding on both parties. Disputes within the same sphere of ministerial responsibility (e.g., between two trusts of the Ministry of Heavy Industry) are heard by the ministerial arbitration tribunal, whose decision is final. Arbitration is not relevant to cases "where one of the parties is below the other in the same hierarchy, as the orders of the superior organization are binding for its inferiors."[77] With all industry owned by the State, the significance of these Arbitration Tribunals is clearly much greater than they would have in this country.

It will be seen that outside of the small sector reserved to the courts, the citizen's rights against the State are confined to appeals to higher administrative instances, who are expected to reverse the decision complained of.[78] With the Party in control at each level, it may be said that this system, while affording

---

[75] *Administrative Law,* p. 137.
[76] *Administrative Law,* p. 117.

[77] *Ibid.,* p. 134.
[78] This applies to the *administration* at all levels, but not to economic undertakings; the latter are endowed with a legal personality, and may be participants in a civil action. Thus a citizen whose suit was ruined at a State-run dry-cleaning establishment may sue that establishment for damages before the ordinary courts.

protection against illegal acts by individuals, is helpless in the face of any Party-backed decisions, provided the Party organ is high enough in the hierarchy to wield the necessary influence.

13. Some Conclusions

The Soviet theory of State and Law follows logically enough from the premises on which it rests. If "the Party embodies the desires and yearnings [sic] of the people,"[79] then the constitutional forms which give the most efficient expression to the Party's policy represent a perfect form of democracy. If "there can be no conflict in Soviet society between law and morality because both represent the ideology and outlook of the whole monolithic Soviet society,"[80] then Soviet law axiomatically represents the General Will of the people. If the interests of the State, in the Soviet classless society, must always be identical with the interests of the individual, then the omnipotence of the State (and of the Party) is in itself a "guarantee of the maintenance of the interests of the individual."[81]

Of course, the above seems to the Western constitutional lawyer to be altogether too rosy a picture. The Party may become corrupted, as others have been before it, by the unchallenged exercise of absolute power. Its leaders may come to identify the furtherance of their own power or privileges, or considerations of administrative expediency, with the interests of the people. Many instances might be quoted of legislation which seems to have little connection with the desires of the masses of the people (for example, the imposition of a fine of up to a quarter of a worker's monthly wage for being more than twenty minutes late to work). Absolute power, in the nature of things, is liable to be abused, and Soviet constitutional theory and practice seem to be well fitted for such abuse.[82]

---

[79] Levin and Karass, p. 32.
[80] Op. cit., p. 36.
[81] Denisov, p. 119.
[82] It has come to notice that one of the books quoted in this article, Administrative Law, by Yevtikhiev and Vlasov, has been the subject of official criticism, and is to be rewritten by its authors. It is felt, nonetheless, that the quotations made are not without value.

18

Soviet Political Life After Stalin*

Cyril E. Black

(1958)

While acknowledging the massive structure of the Soviet governmental apparatus, and the importance of the functions it performs, we must be careful not to take the constitutional framework of Soviet government literally, particularly as it applies to matters like voting. Professor Black's intimate portrait of the political process is intended to help keep before us the unreal quality of Soviet democracy by describing the reality of the election procedures in the U.S.S.R.

A visitor to Russia today who has the opportunity to meet a representative cross-section of Soviet officials cannot fail to be impressed by a spirit of local initiative and self-confidence which is in significant contrast to the political style of the Stalin era. To some extent this impression may reflect Khrushchev's own animated personality. He can shift rapidly from a rather weary thoughtfulness to lively humor as he tries to gauge with his shrewd eyes the effect of his remarks, and he leaps from one subject to another with assurance and imagination. It is not without cause that in proposing Khrushchev's candidacy for premier on March 27 Voroshilov noted among many other qualifications that "his talks with political leaders of various countries and with representatives of the world press have considerably enlarged the circle of friends of our homeland and greatly increased the Soviet Union's prestige on the international scene."

The visitor need not, however, base his

---

* Reprinted from "Soviet Political Life Today," *Foreign Affairs*, Vol. 36 (1958), pp. 569–581, by permission of the author and the publisher. (Copyright, 1958, by the Council on Foreign Relations.)

judgment primarily on the personality of the boss of the Communist Party. There is much other evidence of the new spirit in which Russia's affairs have been conducted since the death of Stalin. The control of economic production, which in a sense is the Party's first order of business, has undergone a fundamental reorganization. In the field of industry, 141 all-union, union-republic, and republic ministries have been dissolved and their functions divided between 105 regional economic councils and the central planning bodies. In agriculture, during the past winter, the collective farms have been encouraged to purchase the agricultural machinery which in the past they have rented from the Machine-Tractor Stations. The latter are being converted into Repair and Techincal Stations, which will retain their service functions while relinquishing much of the centralized control which they have hitherto exerted over agricultural production.

The basic economic changes have been accompanied by a relaxation of overt police terror and apparently a significant depopulation of the slave labor camps. There has also been a marked increase in the frankness of public statements, and still more in unpublished speeches, as witness Khrushchev's attacks on Stalin at the Twentieth Party Congress. A flood of foreign tourists has been admitted since 1955, and there is good evidence of a willingness to engage in extensive exchanges with the United States and other Western countries of students, artists, and delegations representing a wide variety of professions.

The significance of these changes inevitably raises the question as to how far the assumptions about the Soviet political system that have been so firmly fixed in the thinking of the Western world in the past generation are still valid. Does the Party still have a firm hold on political power? Does political activity, as reflected, for instance, in the procedures of the Supreme Soviet, show any evolution from the practice of Stalin's time? How has the nature of Party controls changed under Khrushchev? What, indeed, are the capacities of the Soviet political system for evolution, given the pressures of rapid industrialization and the traditions of Russian society?

II

One impression left by even a cursory visit to the Soviet Union is that the Communist Party shows no signs of relinquishing its monopoly of power. The recent elections for the Supreme Soviet provided an impressive demonstration of the Party's control. The Supreme Soviet is a bicameral legislative body, with a Council of the Union of 738 deputies elected from districts representing every 300,000 of the population and a Council of Nationalities of 640 members representing on a proportional basis the various national administrative subdivisions of the U.S.S.R. In the elections on March 16, no less than 99.97 per cent of the 133,836,325 eligible voters went to the polls. Of these, only 580,641 exercised their right to vote against the regime by crossing out the names of the candidates for the Council of the Union; the number was 363,736 in the case of candidates for the Council of Nationalities. In the case of the Council of the Union, this negative vote was more than double the 247,897 negative votes cast in 1954. The 1958 figure nevertheless represents only 0.43 per cent of the total number of votes, and cannot be interpreted as a significant challenge to the regime. These electoral results are achieved by the assertion of effective Party controls — not advertised, but in the last analysis frankly acknowledged by Party officials — at each stage of the electoral process.

Under the direction of the Presidium of the Supreme Soviet, the elections are administered by a Central Electoral Commission. This body supervises electoral commissions for each of the major administrative divisions of the country, as well as for the electoral districts of each of the two Councils of the Supreme Soviet and for the voting precincts. The latter are the same for the two Councils, although the electoral districts do not coincide. These electoral commissions, which comprised a total of some 1,200,000 members in 1958, are made up of representatives of what are officially known as "public organizations," a term which includes all professional organizations of workers and employees, and organizations or societies representing cooperatives, the youth, and cultural, technical, and scholarly interests, as well as collective farms and the military. Of the recognized organizations in the Soviet Union, only the churches do not play a role in electoral activity. Each of these organizations, again with the exception of the churches, has its Party unit which is the directing element in all politcal matters. Indeed, the Party normally prefers to act through these public organizations rather than in its own name, although it is also represented on the electoral commissions.

This indirect exercise of Party authority through public organizations is the key to the process by which candidates are selected. Not less than 30 days before the date of the election, the electoral commissions organize a meeting in each of the electoral districts of the two Councils of the Supreme Soviet to nominate candidates. Before these formal nominating sessions, names of candidates have been put forward at meetings of one or more of the public organizations in the district. Thus a factory, a collective farm, a military unit or a branch of the Academy of Sciences — to name only a few of the possibilities — will on the initiative of its Party units suggest trustworthy candidates. How these various proposals are narrowed down to a single candidate for each electoral district is not clear from the public record, but a talk with a local Party secretary helps to clarify the situation. The Party, he will tell you, wants respected public figures as deputies to the Supreme Soviet — persons who are popular among their professional colleagues and at the same time trustworthy from the point of view of Party and State. The Party sees to it that from one to three such candidates are agreed upon at the formal nominating session, and it also sees that all but one of them decline to run for office when invited by the electoral commission. Indeed, when more than one candidate is nominated, one or two are generally national figures nominated for many districts. When these announce in which district they will run, the appropriate adjustments are made and the list of candidates is published.

The outcome of this process of selection is that one candidate, and only one, is nominated for each electoral district. This has been the case in all elections, national and local, since the existing electoral system was established under the Constitution in 1936. The official

rationale of this system is that Soviet society, unlike that of the "capitalist" states, is not divided by conflicting interests resulting from the exploitation of man by man. Since there is only one interest, there is need for only one candidate.

In so far as there is a political campaign in the Soviet Union, it is conducted during the last month before the election. The list of candidates has now been published, and every day the press carries election stories, biographical sketches of the candidates, reviews of the regime's accomplishments since the last election in 1954 and accounts of the meetings at which the candidates are presented to the voters. The number of times a candidate is able to appear in public will depend on how busy he is at his regular occupation, but he will at least put in an appearance at one formal meeting organized by the electoral commission in his district.

At a typical meeting of this sort in a provincial town, half a dozen speakers — including perhaps a scholar, a worker, an army officer, a housewife, a collective farmer, and even one or two school children — will extol the merits of the candidate. The candidate himself, who is seated on the stage with members of the electoral commission, then reviews the accomplishments of the government and promises to work for higher production and better living conditions. The audience has been brought together by the distribution of free tickets to the public organizations, and it claps politely at the end of each speech. There is no spontaneity or enthusiasm, however, and indeed there is an audible murmur of whispering and gossiping during the speeches. Even the candidate himself may chat and joke with his neighbors while his achievements are being praised a few feet away. The whole ceremony does not take more than an hour, and is followed by a concert or a variety show which seems to attract more spontaneous interest than the political part of the program. Climaxing these provincial meetings are those in Moscow, where the First Secretary of the Party and his principal colleagues give their pre-election addresses.

After all of this careful preliminary work, the election day itself holds little suspense. Elections are held on a Sunday with the polls open from 6:00 A.M. till midnight, and by noon most of the voters have cast their ballots. The cynics say that this gives the Party twelve hours to round up the rest of the voters. However this may be, it is a risky business to refrain from voting. Except for those who have avoided getting their names on the registration list (and this may be a sizable number in the larger cities where many are said to flaunt the strict limitations on residence), there is no more public way to defy the Party than to refrain from voting. Each voter presents his domestic passport at the registration desk, and his name is checked on the list of voters. He is then given two ballots, one for each Council of the Supreme Soviet, with the names of the single candidate already printed on them. All he has to do is to drop the ballots in the ballot box and he has fulfilled his obligation. For those who are travelling, there are ballot boxes on the trains and boats. Seven electoral districts for each Council are provided for members of the armed services stationed abroad, and even outposts in the Antarctic have their ballot boxes. Officials with portable ballot boxes visit the hospitalized and bedridden, and no stone is left unturned to get all of the voters to the polls. Considering the size of the country and the number of voters, 99.97 per cent is not a bad record.

A negative vote is somewhat less hazardous than failing to vote. Booths are available — some with easy chairs and potted flowers — but only a small fraction of the voters make use of them. Some may use a booth only to write a slogan praising the Party or to sign their names, a superfluous gesture. But the 580,641 and 363,736 adverse votes in the case of the Council of the Union and the Council of Nationalities respectively were cast by actually crossing out the names of the candidates. No substitution of names is valid. To cross out a name nevertheless constitutes defiance of the Party and requires courage. No formal record is kept of those who use the booths, but it would be easy for an election official to notice who entered one. It is difficult to tell whether scratching the name of a candidate is a sign of protest against the regime itself or simply represents a dislike of the individual candidate. The Party interprets it in this latter sense, and in the occasional instances in local elections where candidates are defeated by failing to receive 50 per cent of the votes the local authorities are blamed for failing to select popular and respected candidates.

III

The 1,378 candidates thus elected to the Supreme Soviet form an impressive cross-section of the Soviet elite. Official statements stress the popular origin of the deputies. It is claimed that 44.6 per cent are workers and collective farmers directly engaged in production and that more than 60 per cent are workers and peasants by social status. Another 26.4 per cent are women. The Western student, however, can see the other side of the coin. About one-half of the deputies are high Party and state officials, including ministers of the union and of the constituent republics, generals, police officials, bankers, and so on. Perhaps another quarter are managerial and professional personnel below the directing level, including many of the nominal workers and farmers who are in fact trade-union and collective-farm officials. At the same time, some 25 per cent of the deputies are genuine workers and farmers, selected by the Party to represent their stratum (as there are no "classes") because of their local prominence.

As a legislative body, the Supreme Soviet does not bear much resemblance to the American Congress. The members keep their regular full-time jobs, which in most cases are not seriously interrupted by their work as deputies. The Supreme Soviet normally holds two sessions a year of about ten days each, but a certain amount of this time is devoted to ceremony and organization and it has been estimated that the deputies have averaged no more than seven working days a year since the first session met in 1938. Since the death of Stalin this average has increased to about ten days a year. All bills are adopted unanimously and with little debate. Indeed, so far as the general public is concerned the Supreme Soviet appears to be little more than a bureau for legitimizing the directives of the Party.

Behind the scenes, however, there is more activity than meets the eye. There are nine Standing Committees — for each of the two Councils dealing with legislative proposals, the budget, foreign affairs, and credentials, and, in addition, one dealing with economic affairs for the Council of Nationalities alone. These review in advance most of the legislation presented to the Supreme Soviet at its various sessions. Their size varies, but in the newly elected Supreme Soviet some 259 deputies participate in the work of these Standing Committees, which may last for several weeks before sessions of the Supreme Soviet. Moreover, each bill examined by a Standing Committee is first drafted by an *ad hoc* subcommittee which includes deputies who are not necessarily members of the Standing Committee but who have specialized knowledge of the matter at hand. In addition, at the subcommittee level a wide range of governmental specialists may be called into consultation in the drafting of legislation. Only the final recommendations of the Standing Committees are published in the proceedings of the Supreme Soviet, and their procedures as well as those of the *ad hoc* subcommittees are not known from direct observation or official records. From the available accounts, however, it appears that at this level divergent views are expressed and divisions of opinions are recorded. It is possible that three or four hundred deputies may spend as much as several weeks in Moscow apart from the public sessions of the Supreme Soviet.

To the extent that such discussion takes place, the supreme Soviet should perhaps be regarded not as a rubber stamp but as having the function of formulating as legislation the directives of the Party. Much of the burden of this work is performed by the secretariat of the Presidium of the Supreme Soviet and by the smaller secretariats of the nine Standing Committees. But the deputies themselves also play a role in so far as the business before the Supreme Soviet comes within their special competence. At the same time, the existence of this preparatory work does not alter the fact that the Supreme Soviet drafts legislation rather than formulating policy. While legislative initiative is vested in a variety of institutions, these institutions, like the Supreme Soviet itself, are instruments of the Party. Indeed, since the appointment of Khrushchev as Chairman of the Council of Ministers on March 27, the unity of Party and state has been if possible closer than ever.

The question is sometimes raised as to why the Party bothers with elections and a parliament. It bothers with them because they are essential instruments of Party control. The

electoral process gives the average voter a sense of participation in the political process, and indeed it may in some subtle psychological fashion commit him to sharing responsibility for the Party's directives. The laws, in substance made by the Party, become public instruments through institutions in which all mature citizens participate. At the same time, the members of the Supreme Soviet are an important transmission belt for Party policy. When these respected citizens go back to their places of work after a session of the Supreme Soviet, they carry with them the prestige of the capital city. Nor are the Supreme Soviet deputies the only persons involved. In 1957, no less than 1,549,777 deputies were elected to local soviets. In addition, there are the 1,200,000 members of electoral commissions. While there is some overlapping, probably more than 2,000,000 citizens were thus associated with Party and government through the electoral process. Since many of these were not Party members, the local and national elections play an important role in promoting the acceptance of Party directives as national policy. Finally, the elections also provide an intensive period of propaganda for the national policies of the Party. While propaganda is a year-round process, in the month preceding the quadrennial election to the Supreme Soviet, hundreds of leading national figures in many walks of life join in a chorus of praise for the government's achievements and promises of better things to come.

IV

The political power which is not held by the voters and is not exercised by the Supreme Soviet is found, of course, in the Party, which is still firmly in the saddle. At the same time, while events since Stalin's death have shown no weakening of the Party's control over the political system, they have given evidence of significant changes in the spirit in which Party affairs are conducted — changes which have been reflected in the Party's method of control.

In the Stalin era the political leaders operated on the assumption that not only the population at large but even the bulk of the Party officials were hostile and untrustworthy. As Khrushchev recalled in his unpublished speech, 70 per cent of the members of the Party Central Committee in the late 1930's were arrested and shot. Stalin placed the entire administration of the country, including all major industrial enterprises, under a highly centralized bureaucracy in Moscow, which in turn was closely supervised by a ruthless police.

Under this system control from the center was assured, but it was bought at a very high price of inefficiency and over-bureaucratization. Since Stalin's death, control has devolved significantly from the central bureaucracy to the local organs of Party and administration. In the United States this shift has frequently been referred to as a "decentralization," but this term is not used in Russia. The Russians call it a "reorganization," and indeed it might better be referred to as a "recentralization."

This new and in many respects more dynamic centralization is achieved through the Party apparatus around the country, which like a central nervous system initiates all stimuli in the body politic. The police, through which Stalin used to terrorize local Party officials, no longer serve as the primary means of control. Khrushchev has built up his own cadres of local Party secretaries whom he is apparently able to trust. In talking with them, the casual visitor gains the impression that they understand and support the policies he has initiated. One senses that a degree of relaxation among higher Party officials around the country has replaced the paralyzing fear in which they must have lived in Stalin's day. One can imagine that they treat Khrushchev with deference when they visit him, but are able to argue with him on matters of policy without the apprehension that the police will knock on their door before the next day dawns.

Economic reorganization has strengthened the hands of the local Party organizations, and through them of the central organization of the Party as well. Similarly in agriculture, the new confidence in the collective farms reflects a great increase in the authority of the Party representatives in the collectives at the expense of the Machine-Tractor Stations, which were essentially an instrument of the central state bureaucracy.

It will take time to see how all of Khrushchev's innovations work out, but the main outlines of his political strategy seem to be clear enough. The surviving top leaders who worked for Stalin in the home office — notably Molotov, Kaganovich, Malenkov, and Bulganin — doubtless shared Stalin's distrust of the larger Party organization around the country. One can well imagine their remonstrating with Khrushchev that the confidence in local Party and administrative controls implied by his innovations was bound to undermine the authority of the central Party organization. Long isolated from local officials by many layers of state and Party bureaucracy, these leaders apparently felt that the demonstrated inefficiency of Stalin's way of doing things was a necessary price for the monolithic controls underlying the security of the political system. Khrushchev, whose career has been spent in the main away from the home office, was in much closer rapport with the new generation of officials.

Like Stalin before him, Khrushchev has bypassed competing Party leaders by building up his power through appointing local Party secretaries and members of the Central Committee and its staff. Yet the differences between the two are much greater than the similarities. Not only is Khrushchev 20 years older than was Stalin at a similar stage in his career, but the style of his regime is strikingly different. The significant relaxation of tensions within the Party and between the Party and influential non-Party segments of the population would seem to preclude under Khrushchev's regime sweeping purges such as those in the 1930's. It also appears likely that the sudden demise of Khrushchev woulld present less of a crisis to the Party than did the death of Stalin in 1953.

V

If the impression is correct that the Party is now more relaxed and self-confident than in Stalin's day, and that its control of the levers of political power is as firm as ever, what is the outlook for the further evolution of Soviet politics?

The greatest handicap to Western thinking is the tendency to measure Russia by Western standards. The number of telephones, radios, and cars per capita is compared with that in Europe and in the United States. It is assumed that Western democratic forms are inevitable in all modern countries, and that the longer they are delayed the stronger the opposition to the government must become. There is a whole school of thought devoted to seeking out tensions in the Soviet system, and squads of government officials try to exploit these tensions through propaganda. Tensions indeed there are in Russia, perhaps more than in most societies, and if comparable tensions existed in the West they might well cause an explosion. The struggle for power among Party leaders, especially when succession to the top leadership is in question, similarly gives rise to situations which in Western eyes must inevitably lead to widespread disorder. Yet the Soviet political system survived the death of Stalin without too much strife, and a successor to Khrushchev will doubtless be found when it becomes necessary to do so.

In thinking about Russia, perhaps only two assumptions can safely be made. One is that the traditions of Soviet politics are significantly different from those of the West, and the other is that we do not yet know enough about non-Western political systems to make any very accurate predictions about the evolution of Soviet politics. All we can do is to try to understand the ways in which Russia differs from Western societies, and to estimate the range of possibilities lying ahead.

Modern societies are produced by the interaction of historically formed traditions with the more or less universal imperatives of industrialization. Considering the significant differences between Russian traditions and those of the West, it would be prudent to expect that a modern Russia will not resemble very closely what we know as modern Western society. In many respects (to limit the comparison to the United States) Russian traditions have been the very opposite of ours. We have long been one of the wealthiest countries in the world, while Russia has been desperately poor by European standards. We have enjoyed almost complete national security between the defeat of the British at New Orleans in 1815 and the revelation of Soviet technical achievements by the sputniks in 1957. Russia, on the other hand, has been the battlefield of many nations from earliest times down to 1945. We started out with the freest institutions of Europe, while the Russians in wrestling with their problems drew on the experience of the Byzantine and Mongol empires and of the enlightened despots.

Human nature may be the same the world around, but political institutions are molded by the life experience of organized societies.

History has taught the Russians that poverty can be overcome only by subordinating the individual to the group, and that unless they have a strong government they will be over-run by foreign enemies. Only the state can bridge the gap between Russian poverty and individual and national security. The history of Russian politics is the history of state power, transformed through the centuries by a variety of influences and in fact accepted by most segments of public opinion. Indeed, the recognition and acceptance by the Bolsheviks of the role of state power was a significant factor in their victory in 1917.

Industrialization, or more broadly modernization, has had much the same impact on Russia as on other societies. Rapid industrialization began in the 1880's under the impetus of state policy, and its inexorable pressure has been felt ever since. The proportion of workers and of city dwellers in the population has grown. The organization of political and economic activity has become more centralized, with great emphasis on capital formation. Social mobility has increased and there has been an extensive mixing of ethnic groups. Literacy and popular education have grown by leaps and bounds. This has led to a secularization of thought and a general acceptance of change. Traditional values and family ties have been undermined, and national symbols have been developed to cope with the resulting psychological insecurities.

These pressures affected the later Tsarist empire as well as the more recent Soviet period, as they have influenced all societies under the impact of modernization. Indeed, it is fascinating to speculate whether Russia would be very much different today if the Communists had not come to power. The differences would probably be far less than are generally acknowledged, although it would be difficult to convince any Russian of this today. It should at least be recognized, however, that the impact of Communism has been more on the methods of modernization than on the quantitative results. Communism as we know it today can perhaps best be defined as the Soviet method of modernization, and it may never be possible to unravel the intricate interrelations within this ideology of Marxism, Leninism, the Russian revolutionary tradition, and, indeed, the ambitions, goals, and methods of Russian society in general. Each has played its role in forming the values and precedents which motivate Communist leadership, and each has in turn been altered by daily interaction with the practical problems of transforming Russia into a modern society.

Foreign affairs is the one phase of Soviet policy which still seems to be strongly if not predominantly influenced by the Marxism of the old-fashioned variety known to the West. It is perhaps natural that the further a problem is removed from practical Soviet knowledge, the more a solution is sought in ideology. One gains the impression in talking with Khrushchev and with younger members of the Soviet elite, even those who have visited the United States, that they have very little conception of our values and methods of work. What they see is an irrational, disorganized, confused society, with no clear table of organization and no ideology set forth in logical theses and interpreted in an official journal. They are at least as aware of the tensions in our society as we are of theirs, and they too have squads of government officials seeking to exploit these tensions through propaganda. They see a rising Soviet curve of production which must inevitably cross a declining American curve at some future time. They doubtless believe literally that Marx's predictions about the decline of what they call "capitalism" are as scientifically dependable as are the laws of natural science. They envisage a future world organized more or less the way the Soviet Union is organized today, with political and economic institutions adapted as necessary to unpredictable exigencies.

It follows that Soviet leaders do not expect to reach anything more than short-range agreement with "capitalist" governments, which are by nature transitory. As they see it, the decline of capitalism will be more rapid in an era of apparent peace than in one marked by Soviet threats. Khrushchev's disarming manner supports a policy designed to weaken NATO by removing the situation that called it into being. Encouragement of the idea of disarmament will tend to undermine the defense industries, which the Communists regard as the principal bulwark of "capitalist" prosperity. "Peaceful coexistence" is the name they give to their policy at this stage, although it might better be called "watchful waiting."

The only safe assumption one can make about Russia is that the Communist way of doing things is likely to survive for the foreseeable future. The ruthlessness of a future government is not likely to exceed that of Stalin's regime, and the degree of liberalization which may eventually result from Russia's achieving a new position of security will in all probability not be so great as to affect our policy. Perhaps the one way in which we can seriously influence Soviet politics is by seeing to it that Soviet leadership gets a better idea of what our world is like. While all peoples tend to judge the world by their own standards, and we no less than most, the Russians have a particularly narrow and doctrinaire view of foreign affairs. It may be that no fruitful negotiations will be possible until each side accepts the other as a going concern with indefinite chances of survival.

THE LAW

19

The Socio-political Setting of Soviet Law*

Nicholas S. Timasheff

(1952)

Government in the Soviet Union is today presumed to rest on law. But there are some analysts who hold that in the face of the absolute power of the Communist Party and its readiness to use the instruments of force and terror there is in fact no "law" in Russia. To keep us mindful of the influence of the socio-political setting on the nature and role of law we present Professor Timasheff's enumeration

---

* Abridged from "Soviet Law," *Virginia Law Review*, Vol. 38 (1952), pp. 871–884. Used by permission of the author and the publisher.

of some of the characteristic limits on Soviet law which have persisted through time.

Foreign legal systems belong to the number of the most difficult objects for observation, accurate description, and correct interpretation. The difficulty arises from the juxtaposition, in legal systems, of two elements. The form of the legal system is almost invariable. It always consists of normative propositions ascribing rights and duties to persons, physical and corporate, separating protected interests from those unprotected and imposing sanctions on the violators of its elements. The constancy of the legal form often lures the observer into the mistake of unwarranted identification of elements of a foreign legal system with elements of his own.

On the other hand, the legal system is the mirror of culture. Its content reflects the value system of the corresponding society, especially the value it ascribes to the person, to property, to the collectivity, political and nonpolitical, and to the nonmaterial goals of human endeavor. But culture is highly variable. A culture is always the culture of this particular society at this particular time, differing from the culture of another society or from the culture of the same society at another time. Hence, a foreign observer is often induced into the mistake of not recognizing similarities where they actually exist.

For many reasons, these difficulties appear with exceptional strength when Soviet law is being studied. Soviet law has been promulgated by men who, in principle, denied the value of the legal form, but had to recant and to restore it, adapting it to their goals. Soviet law reflects a culture based principally on a complete re-evaluation of values, and also on a partial restoration of the values of the past. Soviet law emerged on a scene which is part of the European, or Western one, but a peripheral part presenting many departures from that which one finds in its center. Furthermore, observation of Soviet law is now obstructed: the Iron Curtain separating the U.S.S.R. and its satellites from the rest of the world does not make any exception for the legal phase of their culture. During the past few years, export of the official collection of Soviet laws and almost all of the legal periodicals appearing in the Soviet Union has not been allowed.

The purpose of this article is to promote the understanding of Soviet law as it actually is. Soviet law is now 35 years old, and for the past 10 years has been remarkably static. Under these conditions, it is scientifically permissible to formulate a few principles identifying its nature and meaningfully locating it in the universe of past and present legal systems.

(1) Soviet law is the law of a society which has chosen, as its ideal, the socialist model of economic organization. Like every social ideal, the socialist one is centered around an assertion as to the best way of making men happy. For the socialists, the basic premise of happiness is the collectivization of the means of production. In its original form, collectivization was required to be complete; in our day, many socialists are satisfied with the collectivization of key industries and services.

Socialism is sometimes given another definition. Then, it is identified with planned economy.[1] Planning is, however, only a natural and not a necessary trait of a socialist society. Under the so-called "War Communism" (1917–1921), Russia's economy was socialist in that almost the totality of the means of production was collectivized; but there was no planning. On the other hand, there is much planning in societies which have not chosen socialism as the blueprint of their economic structure; e.g., the *plan Monnet* in France.

That Soviet law is socialist law is beyond doubt, since it creates an almost complete monopoly of the means of production in favor of the collectivity (in its political aspect). At two times, once around 1920 and again in the early thirties, the ideal seemed to have been achieved almost completely. From 1921–1929 there was a significant retreat called the New Economic Policy (NEP) which created a "two sectors economy" and a complex legal structure which was partly socialist and partly not. Since 1934–35 another retreat, on a much smaller scale, has exempted from state monopoly small plots of land individually tilled by the peasants, some cattle which they are allowed to breed individually, and small industrial tools which artisans (predominantly in the framework of co-operatives) are allowed to own. Officially, the collective farms are producers' co-operatives; in actuality, they are state enterprises presenting some peculiarities as to

---

[1] Berman, *Justice in Russia* 52 (1952).

the organization of management and the reward of the labor force.

(2) Soviet law is the law of a totalitarian society. The term "totalitarian" (and its opposite, liberal) refers to the extent of the auxiliary functions of the state, i.e., functions which go beyond its two necessary functions, which are protection against outside enemies and maintenance of "law and order." A society is totalitarian if the number of its auxiliary functions is so high that almost all human activities are regulated by the state. A society is liberal if the number of its auxiliary functions is so small that the state's activities are almost confined to their logical minimum. Since the regulation of activities by the state is effected by the law, the law of a totalitarian society displays a tendency to be inflated, with one exception: civil law co-ordinating the decentralized activities of the citizens is, by necessity, shrinking.

This is obviously the present condition of Soviet law. An enormous amount of legal regulations corresponds to that which, in a liberal society (e.g., in the United States) is achieved by the inner order of business corporations or even decided from case to case by those in command of them. Equally large is the scope of official regulation of cultural activities in such fields as literature, music, painting, movies, radio, etc. These regulations go so far that they create a state monopoly of these activities, with authors, composers, painters, and so on working as state functionaries.[2] On the other hand, the real content of Soviet civil law has shrunk far below the content of the Civil Code of 1922 which was enacted during the NEP.[3] Whole chapters of this Code and many sections of other chapters are now only "law in books," no longer "law in life."

(3) Soviet law is the law of a despotic society. A society is despotic if, in the relationship between the state and its citizens, the state ascribes to itself all the rights and imposes on its citizens a heavy burden of duties. A society is free if the opposite is the case. In a despotic state, criminal justice remains justice only as long as no political interest is involved; if it is, justice degenerates in oppression. On

the other hand, in a free society, cases may be decided against the state even when they involve its vital interests (e.g., the case of Judith Coplon). In a despotic state, administration is conducted mainly according to technical rules depending upon the political objectives of the rulers; on the contrary, in a free society, administration is carried out within rigid margins imposed by the law.

The despotic character of Soviet law is undeniable. Soviet jurisprudence treats justice as a branch of administration. Among the sources of law, "the policy of the communist party" is often mentioned. Judges are often rebuked and sometimes even demoted or dismissed for ignoring the objectives of such policies. Soviet criminal law and procedure bear manifest traits of despotism. The law of August 7, 1932, imposes the death penalty for the theft of goods in transit or the property of collective farms. A law of January 4, 1947, imposes prison terms of from 7 to 25 years for the theft of state property, and prison terms of from one to five years for not reporting such a theft. A law of June 8, 1934, punishes the family of a fugitive to a foreign country. A law of June 9, 1947, gives limitless extension to the crime of delivering state secrets. Most characteristic, however, is the law of December 4, 1934, concerning the trial of persons accused of terroristic actions: the investigation must be closed in 10 days, no counsel for defense is allowed, no appeal is possible, and a death sentence must be carried out immediately.

A complete denial of individual rights also permeates Soviet labor law. One has only to mention the law of December 20, 1938, concerning labor passports into which every dismissal of a worker must be entered and without which no one can be hired; the law of July 10, 1940, imposing 5 to 8 years in prison for factory managers and chief engineers for the manufacturing of goods of poor quality; the law of October 2, 1940, concerning the labor conscription of adolescents; and the law of the same day on the compulsory transfer of engineers, technicians, office employees, and skilled workers to any enterprise and any district.

(4) Soviet law is the law of a dictatorial society. A society is dictatorial if the political status of those in power is based upon a seizure of power and their ability to maintain it against attempts to dislodge its possessors (in contra-

[2] Inkeles, *Public Opinion in Soviet Russia* (1950).
[3] Bratus, "Some Problems Concerning the Draft Civil Code of the U.S.S.R.," 10 *Sovietskoye Gosudarstvo i Pravo* 11 (U.S.S.R., 1948).

distinction to the explicit consent of the governed in a democratic society or to the implicit tradition of obedience in old fashioned monarchies). Commonly, a dictatorial government must apply terroristic methods to exact obedience and prevent upheaval. Terrorism from above is expressed in vague definitions of political crimes, atrocious punishment of their perpetrators, poorly articulated rules of criminal procedure, the existence of multi-branched and omnipotent police, and the lack of guarantees for citizens suspected of disloyalty.

The dictatorial character of Soviet society and, *ergo*, Soviet law is beyond doubt. Even officially, the Soviet state embodies the stage of "the dictatorship of the proletariat" which is transitional between the bourgeois state enforcing "the law of the exploiters" and the beatitude of the stateless society of the Marxian dreams. The power position of the men in the Kremlin is founded only on the fact of the seizure of power by Lenin and his private army, the present-day state apparatus being nothing more than the extension in time and in scope of the latter.[4] This is well expressed in the electoral law and especially in the practice of elections characterized by these traits: (a) nominations for offices are made only by the ruling party or organizations designated and dominated by it; (b) only one slate of candidates is offered to the voters; (c) no "write-ins" are allowed; (d) voting is not so much a right as a duty of the citizens. Second, it is well expressed in the automatization of the masses through legislation and administrative practices which confine the rights of association and assembly to organizations led by the ruling party and meetings convoked by it. Together with the monopoly of the means of mass communication[5] and the terroristic character of Soviet criminal law,[6] these devices form an insuperable barrier against the rise of a social movement which could overthrow the existing government either by vote or by violence.

(5) Soviet law is the law of a society in cultural decay. This decay exists beyond doubt in the realms of science, philosophy, literature, music, and the arts. As a part of such a cul-

ture, Soviet law could not escape decay. More often than not, the legislative enactments of the Soviets are technically helpless. Soviet courts are manned by persons who could not compare, both as to legal training and the ability to think along legal lines, with the courts of pre-Revolutionary Russia. Trials before today's courts, especially criminal trials, reflect not only the despotic and dictatorial character of Soviet society, but strike the observer by their primitive character. Evidence is almost entirely confined to the confession of the defendant, as had been the case before the judicial reform of 1864, while after that reform a defendant who pleaded guilty could not be interrogated by the court or the prosecutor. Collections of the decisions of the supreme court appear seldom and in the form of thin booklets which do not display refined legal thought, while the decisions of the Senate of pre-revolutionary Russia were on a par with the decisions of the *cour de cassation* or the *Reichsgericht*. Legal publications are poor and servile; their main purpose is that of repeating and expanding that which just had been said in the Kremlin. The authority of Marx, Engels, Lenin, and Stalin has replaced that of the great jurists of the past, Roman, Western, or Russian. In addition to the "big four," only those are quoted who, at the time of the writing, are considered to be the best interpreters of the ideas of those in power. Before the revolution, the works of the great Russian jurists were animated by liberal views and often challenged the policies of the government.

(6) Soviet law is the law of a society which, after having broken with the national and historical tradition, undergoes a peculiar process of a partial restoration of that tradition.[7] In the realm of law, this process was conspicuous in the early years of the NEP, when all of a sudden codes of civil and criminal procedure, and others, were produced which were based mainly on hasty rewriting of pre-revolutionary laws adapted to the new situation. Around 1930, these codes were almost forgotten. But since the middle thirties, "legality" became one of the official slogans, and the codes were at least partly revived. In consequence, Soviet law, commonly in a deteriorated form, revives

---

[4] Timasheff, "Political Power in the Soviet Union," 14 *Review of Politics* 15 (1952).

[5] See § 2 *supra*.

[6] See § 3 *supra*.

[7] Timasheff, *The Great Retreat* (1946).

the legal tradition of pre-Revolutionary Russia so far as it is compatible with the new traits of Russian society reviewed above. Since the legal tradition of pre-Revolutionary Russia was part of the Western or European, on the surface Soviet law displays quite a few similarities to that of continental Europe. . . .

20

History and Spirit of Soviet Law*

Harold J. Berman

(1948)

Professor Berman reviews for us the several stages in Soviet thinking about the law. This survey suggests that despite the limits on law already described by Prof. Timasheff, the law does have a history of growing importance in Soviet theory and practice. Professor Berman also advances his own thesis on the "parental" quality in Soviet law, which the "realist" school has sharply criticized.

Revolution is the violent establishment of new law. Not only new rules of law but also new legal institutions, new categories and principles of law, new conceptions of justice are forged in the fire of revolutionary terror and civil war. To the victims and the onlookers, and often to the revolutionaries themselves, this law-creative process is not immediately apparent. On the one hand, all legality seems to be swallowed up in the whirlwind of destruction; on the other hand, a new heaven and new earth is proclaimed, in which all will live in brotherhood and harmony, without need of law. But when the smoke of violence settles, and the dust of utopia is wiped from the eyes, there remains — new law.

This is the only justification of revolution, and those who respect the legal system under which they live must also pay their respects to the revolution which created it. For in the West, at least, every great nation owes its law to a revolution. Even the United States, which created no new legal system but adopted instead the Common Law of England, was compelled to fight a Revolutionary War in order to secure to the American colonists "the rights of free Englishmen." The close dependence of the Code Napoleon on the French Revolution of 1789 is generally recognized. More controversial is the connection between the English Common Law and the English Revolution of 1640: the Puritans asserted that they were only "restoring" the medieval and Anglo-Saxon law which had been abrogated during 150 years of Tudor "depotism." Yet none would deny that this "restoration" was a step into the future, that it inaugurated a new era in the development of the English legal system. Likewise the so-called Reception of Roman Law in sixteenth century Europe was, in fact, a recreation rather than a mere reception of ancient law and was a direct result of the German Reformation of 1517. If we push further into the past, we find that the cornerstone of all the legal systems of Europe was the renovated Roman and Canon Law of the eleventh and twelfth centuries, which was a product of the Papal Revolution of 1075 and the consequent establishment of the Roman Catholic Church as a separate legal entity, distinct from secular law, with the Pope as its legal head and the Papal Curia as a court of last resort throughout Western Christendom.[1]

The Russian Revolution of 1917 seems to fall into the pattern of the great European revolutions. As with its predecessors, its original fury was unleashed against all legality, and its original vision was directed toward a society which would be free of the very idea of law. Like them, it has in the course of time settled down, and in settling down has invoked "stability of laws."[2] In fact, orthodox principles have been restored, since the mid-1930's, in

* Reprinted from "The Spirit of Soviet Law," *Washington Law Review*, Vol. 23 (1948), pp. 152–166, by permission of the author and the publisher.

---

[1] For the story of the European revolutions, see Rosenstock-Huessy, *Out of Revolution: The Autobiography of Western Man* (1938).

[2] Stalin, in a speech in 1936 to the Extraordinary Eighth Congress of Soviets, said: "We need stability of laws now more than ever." This became the chief slogan of the subsequent reforms.

one field of Soviet law after another.[3] Nevertheless, Soviet jurists claim that their law is "law of a new type, essentially different from all types of law known to history, particularly bourgeois law."[4] Despite many similarities between present-day Soviet law and, for example, American law — despite its striking resemblance especially to pre-revolutionary Russian law — Vyshinsky and other leaders of the Soviet legal profession assert emphatically that their law is "socialist in form and in content."

How can Soviet law be at the same time so similar and so different? The Soviet explanation is based on the intricacies of Marxist-Leninist-Stalinist theory. A simpler answer may be this: that both in form and in content there is a similarity in letter, a difference in spirit. Accepting this answer as a hypothesis, I propose to examine the spirit of Soviet law — first in the "revolutionary" period of 1917 to 1936, then in the "post-revolutionary" period from 1936 to the present — and to single out certain basic attitudes which underlie Soviet law today and give it a distinctive character.

I

On November 22, 1917, within a month after they had seized power, the Bolsheviks abolished the Tsarist courts and instructed judges of the new Soviet courts to apply Tsarist laws only insofar as those laws were not superseded by revolutionary law and were not in conflict with "revolutionary legal conscience." A year later, on November 30, 1918, a second statute on courts forbade every reference whatsoever to Tsarist laws.

The new government produced a host of revolutionary decrees in rapid succession. Most of these were directed to the abolition of pre-revolutionary legal institutions — inheritance, private property in land and the means of production, private trade, ecclesiastical control of family relations, and so forth. Others were designed to give positive recognition to proletarian power: thus a decree of November 16, 1917, provided that "the workers [in each enterprise] shall control the methods of production, the purchase and sale of the products and raw materials, their storage, and the finances of the business"; and the 1918 Constitution of the Russian Republic declared the State to be a "proletarian State," in which only the proletariat could vote for the Soviets. Still other of these early decrees, however, went beyond proletarian dictatorship and were thought of as measures ushering in Socialism itself, that is, a classless society. These included the nationalization of banks, of industry, of foreign trade, of houses; general compulsory labor; the establishment of state and cooperative trade; the distribution of all commodities by ration cards; moneyless transactions between state enterprises; the payment of wages partially in kind; the appropriation of farm surpluses in the villages; and the establishment of State farms.

This was what was later described as "the heroic period" of the Russian Revolution. War raged against counter-revolution from within and intervention from without. A system of revolutionary tribunals enforced what was officially termed the "Red Terror." At the same time, the imminent advent of world-wide Socialism — in the Marxian sense of a classless society — was preached and believed. "We are approaching the complete abolition of money," wrote Zinoviev in 1920. "The Communist Manifesto written by Marx and Engels is still to us today the gospel of the present revolution," stated Bukharin. Lenin himself wrote in 1918 that "our Revolution has succeeded in coming to immediate grips with the complete and practical realization of Socialism," and he spoke of Socialism in the villages as something already achieved. According to Trotsky,[5] "the Soviet government hoped and strove to develop these [early] methods of regimentation into a system of planned economy in distribution as well as production. In other words, from 'War Communism' it hoped gradually, but without destroying the system, to arrive at genuine Communism." Trotsky explains this by "the fact that all calculations at that time were based on the hope of an early victory of the revolution in the West."

The spirit of Soviet law in these first years,

---

[3] See articles by the present author on Soviet family law, criminal law, contract law, and property law, appearing in 56 *Yale Law Journal* 26 (1946), 56 *Yale Law Journal* 803 (1947), 35 *California Law Review* 101 (1947), 96 *University of Pennsylvania Law Review* 324 (1948).

[4] Cf. Kareva, "The Role of Soviet Law in the Education of Communist Consciousness," *Bolshevik*, No. 4 (1947). In Russian. P. 47.

[5] Trotsky, *The Revolution Betrayed*, 22.

from 1917 to 1921, was thus a spirit of nihilism on the one hand, and of apocalypticism on the other — of ruthless destruction of everything pre-revolutionary, and of glorious transition to a new order of equality and freedom *without* law. It was the spirit of Cheka, predecessor to OGPU and NKVD — and the spirit of anarchism in its literal significance. In spite of Lenin's warnings against "the sickness of leftism," the new Soviet law was afflicted with that congenital revolutionary disease.

With the introduction of the New Economic Policy in 1921, the radical legislation of the earlier period was repudiated as the product of a war emergency. "'War Communism' was necessitated by the war and by the ruin of the country," Lenin stated in a speech of April 9, 1921. "It was not and could not be a policy answering the economic needs of the proletariat. It was but a temporary measure." Again: "We went too far on the path of nationalization of commerce and industry, and in the suppression of local trade. Was it a blunder? Yes, without question."

The N.E.P. (New Economic Policy) was a retreat from a bankrupt War Communism; it was not, however, a retreat from the revolutionary principle of preparing Russia for Socialism, nor was Socialism conceived differently after the introduction of the N.E.P.; Lenin called it a "strategic" retreat. Money reappeared; state distribution was replaced by private trade; the peasants were given large measures of freedom on their individual farms and well-to-do peasants ("kulaks") emerged; private businessmen ("nepmen") were allowed to take over factories under a state licensing system; one-man management was restored as against workers' control. At the same time, there was strict supervision by the Workers and Peasants' State. Kulaks and nepmen were restricted, disfranchised, heavily taxed. A large "Socialist sector" of industry — the "commanding heights" of banking, insurance, large-scale transport, production of raw materials, foreign trade — remained in the hands of the State. By 1923, in fact, the strategic retreat was terminated (although the N.E.P. was not officially abandoned until 1928): wholesale trade was again taken out of private hands, very low prices were fixed by the State for its purchase of grain from the peasants, and the gradual return to socialism was inaugurated.

The encouragement of private initiative under the N.E.P., the restoration of the market, the desire to attract foreign capital made necessary the construction of a legal system. In addition it was realized that law could be very useful to the proletarian State, and with the temporary postponement of full Socialism there were no theoretical obstacles to either State or law. Therefore, in 1922 and 1923, numerous codes were hastily drawn up and enacted, including a Civil Code, Land Code, Criminal Code, Code of Civil Procedure, Code of Criminal Procedure, and a new Labor Code to replace that of 1918. Inheritance was restored, though with drastic limitations. A 1923 decree on State industrial enterprises established corporate independence for trusts. Meanwhile, a Judiciary Act of 1922 abolished the system of revolutionary tribunals and created a hierarchy of courts on the European model. The 1918 Family Code was replaced in 1926, and a new Criminal Code was issued in the same year.

The codes were in large measure copied from European examples, especially the German. There were, however, certain revolutionary provisions, especially in the Family Code and the Criminal Code. Also, "revolutionary legal conscience" remained the underlying principle for the decision of doubtful cases. Non-proletarians were consciously discriminated against both in private and public law. Underlying the whole system was the basic assumption that law is essentially an instrument of State policy, and that the State, in turn, is merely the "executive committee of the ruling class" — in this case, the proletariat.

N.E.P. law and N.E.P. legal theory were thus dominated by the spirit of temporary and impatient compromise with "bourgeois" principles of private rights and due process. Law was considered to be by its very nature oppressive. It was tolerated only because the advance to Socialism had been slowed down. In Lenin's words, "While there is a State, there is no freedom; when there is freedom, there will be no State."

In 1928 the N.E.P. compromise was abandoned; total planning was inaugurated as a means of rapid industrialization, militarization, and feverish collectivization. Gradualness was replaced by a gigantic leap. The immediate transformation of the Soviet Union into a classless Socialist society — independently of world revolution — was envisioned. Particularly, the Second Five-Year Plan of 1933–1937 had for its specific purpose the achievement of Socialism. As Premier Molotov put it to the Communist Party Conference which approved the draft of the Plan: "The leading idea of the Second Five-Year Plan is that all classes and their causes are to disappear by 1937 in the U.S.S.R." The Party Conference declared: "The chief political task of the Second Five-Year Plan is to do away with the capitalist elements and with classes in general; to destroy fully the causes giving rise to class distinctions and exploitation; to abolish the survivals of capitalism in the economy and the consciousness of the people; to transform the whole working population of the country into conscious and active builders of a classless society." This explicitly included the aim of "destroying the difference between the worker and the peasant" — that is, establishing a basic equality, a political and economic identity, between urban and rural workers."

Now for the first time positive content was given to the Marxist idea of the "withering away" of the State (and of law) under Socialism. Law as an instrument of the class-dominated State would be replaced by Plan as the manifestation of the will of a classless society. Through the Plan, all the characteristics of the original Marxist vision would be made manifest. Planning would eliminate exploitation, money, private property, the family as a legal entity, crime in the legal sense, the State itself. The Plan would give unity and harmony to all relationships. The Plan itself would not be an instrument of compulsion but simply an expression of rational foresight on the part of the planners, with the whole people participating and assenting.

The "withering away" of law under Socialism was actively anticipated during the First and Second Five-Year Plans. The N.E.P. codes became largely obsolete and were not replaced. In the cases and the statutes, and particularly in the vast structure of administration, what compromises had been made under the N.E.P. with the formality of law, with its basis in rights and duties, with its essential stability — were more and more surrendered in the name of economic expediency, rapidly shifting social policy, and administra-

tive flexibility. Underlying Soviet law in this period was the spirit of economic planning, the spirit of war Communism revived.

II

In 1936 it was officially announced by Stalin that Socialism had been achieved. The Proletarian dictatorship, properly speaking, was over; such classes as existed — the workers, the peasants, the intelligentsia — were "friendly" classes, not "hostile" economic classes in the Marxist sense. But instead of the "withering away" of money, property, the family, criminal sanctions, the State, law, there was a wholesale restoration of these "bourgeois" institutions on a new "socialist" basis. Stalin called for a Socialist State — to Marx and Lenin a contradiction in terms — supported by "stability of laws."

The full extent of this restoration has not generally been appreciated. It has been obscured by the purges which accompanied it, even though these can only be properly understood as the liquidation of those groups which had stood for the pre-restoration principles. It has been obscured by the war and the prewar preparations, which some have interpreted as giving a temporary emergency character to Soviet internal developments. It has been obscured by the Soviet fiction of continuity, which represents Russian history since 1917 as a single unbroken advance "according to Marx."

In whatever direction one turns, one finds a new spirit dominating Soviet institutions since the mid-1930's and the proclamation of the achievement of Socialism. In its cultural aspect, Soviet society has returned to Russian history, national traditions, patriotism; to strong bonds — legal and economic as well as spiritual — of family life; to a recognition of religion as having a legitimate role in the values of the people. Economically, the emphasis has been on competition and personal initiative both among workers, who since 1935 have been paid on a piece-rate (Stakhanovite) basis, and among managers, who since 1936 have been accorded a large measure of freedom of contract and may distribute extra profits as bonuses; efforts after 1928 to reestablish workers' control in new forms have been suppressed, and one-man management reemphasized in theory and practice; financial stability has been encouraged as a check on the overexuberance of production drives; within the planning system itself there has been increasing decentralization; business operations have been more and more freed from rigid control; earlier attempts to treat workers and peasants as a single economic unit have been abandoned, and instead a balance has been struck between their different interests. Politically, the 1936 Constitution removed the onerous franchise restrictions from non-proletarians; lines — admittedly wavy — have been drawn between legislative, administrative, and judicial functions; certain important administrative powers — for example, that of taxation — have been made reviewable in the courts; legality, due process of law, has been stressed in theory and has made important strides forward in practice.

There has been a return to the N.E.P. codes, which, though never formally rescinded, were fast losing their importance under the First and Second Five-Year Plans. A significant example of this is the requirement, first acknowledged in the late 1930's, that *Gosarbitrazh*, the special system of courts which hears cases involving State business enterprises, must decide disputes not merely in terms of the plans issued for those enterprises but also in terms of the Civil Code. This means that economic expediency, whether from the point of view of the public or that of the individual enterprise, is no longer sufficient to justify a breach of contract. *Pacta sunt servanda*, formerly challenged as a bourgeois fiction, is now proclaimed as a governing principle of Soviet Socialist contract law.[6]

Likewise in criminal law, the "bourgeois" rule of "no crime, no punishment, without a [previous] law" has been reasserted as a Socialist principle, and the famous doctrine of analogy severely limited.

Personal ownership — a category created by the 1936 Constitution as distinct from State and socialized ownership — has been increasingly extended and protected. Inheritance has been freed from crushing taxation and freedom of testation introduced. A judicial process of

divorce has been established for the first time since the Revolution.

A new Judiciary Act was promulgated in 1938 to lay the foundation for more orthodox trial procedure. Vyshinski, leader of the movement for the new Socialist law, has emphasized the need for "judicial culture" (that is, proper court procedure) and "judicial authority." "Judicial activity requires the deepest trust in the court," he stated in 1938.[7] "The judge must fight for that trust."

The spirit of Soviet law since 1936 — as revealed both before and after the war, in both the statutes and the court cases — is one of struggle for legality, for orthodoxy. It is a continuing struggle rather than an accomplished fact — for many reasons. One is Russia's historic backwardness in legal consciousness; Russian law has never played the same role as that of Western law, it has never been so highly developed or so highly valued. Another reason is that although the Revolution has "settled down" it has not stopped, and whenever it feels itself seriously threatened it tends to disregard the new legality. A third reason is that although *Law* has been raised to equal rank beside *Plan* — Law expressing the stability of the Soviet social order, Plan its dynamic quality — the equilibrium between the two is itself a shifting one. But despite these limitations, Soviet Socialist law is no myth. The condemnation of earlier theories which saw even in Soviet law a temporary instrument of class rule and suppression — and the ruthless purging of their authors — was no teapot tempest. In Soviet law since 1936 "the sickness of leftism" has once and for all been cast out.

III

Granting that law now plays a positive role in the Soviet social order, granting that traditional standards of law and justice have been grafted onto the Socialist planned economy, there remains the principal question: wherein is this Soviet law different; wherein does it justify the description "socialist in form and content"?

For better or worse — perhaps for better *and* worse — Soviet law, with all its ortho-

---

[6] Agarkov, "Debtor's Discharge from Liability When Performance Is Impossible [Under the Soviet Law]," 29 *Journal of Comparative Legislation* 9 (1947).

[7] Vyshinsky, *The Soviet Court and Socialist Administration of Justice* 53 (1938). In Russian.

doxy, has introduced new conceptions, new attitudes, and new spirit. This is not immediately apparent from reading the codes or studying Soviet legal theory. The codes are still the old ones of the N.E.P., amended but not fundamentally rewritten, despite the provision of the 1936 Constitution that new all-union codes are to replace the old republican ones. The theory is still rudimentary, consisting chiefly in a repudiation of the earlier theories and the repeated assertion that Soviet law "expresses the will of the whole Soviet people." In fact it has been suggested[8] that the reason for the unusual delay in drafting new codes is the confused state of legal theory, which has been "unable to find its bearings in the struggle between the exigencies of day-to-day life and the Marxian interpretation of Sovietism." Where, then, is the new spirit to be found? It may be found in part on the fringes of the written law and of the theory; in part in certain unique legal institutions — of which I shall describe two, the divorce procedure and the settlement of so-called pre-contract disputes; but chiefly in judicial practice, i.e., the cases themselves. Of what does the new spirit consist? It consists of a new attitude toward persons, toward the community, and toward the relationship of law to both.

(1) *The Cases.* The Judiciary Act of 1938, Article 3, states that "By all their activities the courts educate the citizens of the U.S.S.R. in the spirit of devotion to the Motherland and to the cause of Socialism, in the spirit of strict and undeviating observance of Soviet laws, of care for Socialist property, of labor discipline, of honesty toward State and public duty, of respect for the rules of Socialist common-life." This educational role of the courts involves a different conception of the person with respect to whom judgments are rendered, and of the community for which he is being educated. The Soviet litigant or accused is treated not merely as one possessing rights and duties, not merely as an independent individual who knows what he wants and must stand or fall by his own claim or defense; he is treated also as a dependent member of the collective group, a child or youth whom the law must not only protect but also guide and train. The Soviet judge speaks to

the litigant or accused in an unusual manner; he may upbraid or counsel him as a father, may explain to him what is right and what is wrong as if he were a child. If the defendant is a member of the Communist Party, the judge may forcefully recall to him that he bears a greater responsibility than others, that his light must shine among men as a beacon of the future Communist "good society." Although the parties may be represented by lawyers, and although the "adversary" character of the trial has received more stress in recent years, nevertheless the judicial contest is waged against the background of a more intimate relationship among all the participants, a relationship more akin to that of a family than to that of an impersonal "civil" society.

(2) *Divorce Procedure and the Settlement of Pre-Contract Disputes.* That the Soviet judge is like a father or teacher to those who come before him with their grievances is illustrated in the divorce procedure instituted in 1944. A Soviet citizen may file a petition for divorce with the People's Court, which summons the respondent and by conversation with respondent and petitioner seeks, first, to ascertain the motives for the divorce and, second, to reconcile the parties. If no reconciliation is effected, the petitioner may file a second petition for divorce with a higher court, which may grant the divorce.

In discussing the measures which the People's Court should take to reconcile the parties, Soviet commentators have stated:[9] "It is impossible to expect any ready-made recipes. Here experience, tact, and the authority of the court are necessary. Far from always do the spouses come into court with a firm decision to separate. Often the suit is the result of a recent quarrel, the product of impetuousness and not a thought-out decision. Some the court may reconcile by means of a quiet explanation of the incorrectness of their behavior; it may convince others of the necessity of explaining to each other in court and forgiving each other; and others it may give time for reconsideration. . . .

If the People's Judge is unsuccessful in ef-

[8] H. A. Freund, *Russia from A to Z*, 347 (1945).

[9] Tadevosian and Zagorye, "Practice of the Application of the Decree of the Presidium of the Supreme Soviet of the U.S.S.R. of July 8, 1944, in Cases of Dissolution of Marriage," 8 *Socialist Legality*, 1, 5 (1945). In Russian.

fecting a reconciliation, the case goes for trial in the higher court, where witnesses may be heard and arguments made. Official Soviet legislation gives no grounds for divorce; however, unofficial instructions which were sent to the judges at the time the new divorce law was enacted state that such factors as marital infidelity, desertion, cruelty, and the like, should be taken into consideration. The basic principle governing the court is that "divorce should be granted only in those cases where it is actually impossible to re-establish the broken family, where the breach between the spouses is so deep that it is impossible to reconcile them and to prolong their married life."[10] Thus where the spouses were married eight years and had three children, it was held that incompatibility was not a sufficient ground, though under other circumstances it might be. Likewise, where a man and wife, sixty-five and sixty-one years old respectively, had quarreled over how to bring up their grandchildren, a decree of divorce granted on that ground was overruled by the Supreme Court.

It is apparent that concepts of contract and tort play a very minor role in Soviet divorce law. Anglo-American doctrines of connivance, condonation, collusion, and recrimination would be entirely incomprehensible to the Soviet jurist, while the common American practice of granting uncontested divorces automatically would be equally alien. Soviet divorce law is designed to encourage actively and consciously the stability of marriage. These differences reflect a different conception of the nature of the family, and ultimately of the nature of the person, before the law. Soviet husbands and wives are, in effect, wards of the court, requiring encouragement and guidance in the path of socialist family life. The Soviet citizen is a child, a pupil; the law is his parent, his teacher.

The same spirit is manifest in regard to corporate persons. Here too there are important literal similarities, both in form and in content, between Soviet law and the law of non-socialist countries. Soviet State business enterprises have been recognized as independent legal entities, operating on a profit-and-loss basis, entering into contractual relations with each other. There is a surprising amount of inter-corporate litigation in Soviet courts, and the rules of contract, agency, bills and notes, sales, and so forth, upon which the decisions rest, would not shock an American lawyer. It is true that Soviet freedom of contract is limited by economic plans issued by superior economic organs, and that the court in interpreting a contract will look at the plan; however, this is not an absolute limitation, and insofar as the nature of business law is concerned, there is a similarity between the effect of planning on Soviet contract law and the effect of public policy and public control on American contract law. However, the spirit in which the Soviet rules are applied is a new one. Here again the law plays the role of father and educator.

An example of this is the judicial settlement of so-called pre-contract disputes. These are disputes which arise after the obligation to enter into a contract has been imposed by plans of distribution, where the parties thus obligated are unable to agree on the terms of the contract to be made. Either party may bring suit to have the disagreement resolved, or the dispute may be brought to court on the initiative of the Council of Ministers (which has promulgated the plan of distribution) or on the initiative of the court itself (a special court, *Gosarbitrazh*, whose judges are both jurists and economic experts). The court hears the parties and renders a decision — based on the plans, the general law, the so-called "basic conditions of supply" issued by superior economic organs, and the circumstances of the particular transaction — which in effect creates a contract between them.

Soviet jurists have found difficulty in interpreting the juridical nature of the planned obligation to contract. They have analogized it to the *pactum de contrahendo* of Roman law.[11] Perhaps the closest analogy in American law is the obligation to bargain collectively under the National Labor Relations Act. However, the Soviet court requires not merely that the parties attempt in good faith to reach an agreement, but also that the agreement reached conform to the interests of the economy as a whole. Conditions whereby one or both parties

---

10 H. A. Freund, *op. cit.,* 8 *supra* note (1945).

11 Cf. No. 2 Shkundin, "The Influence of Plan on Obligation," *Soviet State and Law,* 34, 37–8 (1947). In Russian.

attempt to escape subsequent liability for non-performance — as, for example, the right to be released from the contract if the supplier fails to receive certain materials from a third party, or the right unilaterally to decrease the quantity of goods to be delivered if the supplier receives orders from other enterprises — have been annulled in pre-contract cases, on grounds of what we would call "public policy."[12]

Soviet divorce procedure and pre-contract cases are examples of new legal institutions produced by the Russian Revolution. Here Soviet law differs in letter from that of other countries — both in form and in content. However, they are also illustrations of a different spirit which runs throughout Soviet law, underlying even those rules and institutions (of which there are many) that are identical in letter with our own. Soviet business enterprises in their commercial relations, like Soviet husbands and wives in their family relations, "go to school" to the law.

(3) *The Written Law.* The codes and statutes present a picture of Soviet law which in general is surprisingly similar to our own law, with differences chiefly in degree and emphasis. There is, course, a far greater degree of State ownership. Criminal law is emphasized much more strongly, especially as a means of deterring and punishing infringements of State economic policy. Administrative law predominates, the law of inheritance or of personal property is not very highly developed. Nevertheless, there is sufficient resemblance to give an American lawyer the feeling that he is in familiar territory.

On the fringes of the written law, however, may be detected evidences that this is "law of a new type." An example is the law concerning counter-revolutionary crimes. For the most part this resembles the usual law of treason; however, also prohibited is "counter-revolutionary propaganda and agitation," and, moreover, a necessary element is "counter-revolutionary intent," which may mean something more — or less — than the intent to overthrow the government by force. Reported cases of counter-revolutionary crimes are rare. In 1944,

however, a Soviet citizen charged with that offense was acquitted, the court stating "the witnesses incorrectly interpreted the true meaning of his opinion, relating to one of the most offensive episodes of the charge, concerning an evaluation of the Constitution of the U.S.S.R. . . . [I]t is clear that these opinions were not . . . evoked by any orientation against Soviet authority, which is an indispensable condition for finding them counter-revolutionary. . . ."[13]

How far the term "counter-revolutionary" has become synonymous with "anti-State" is difficult to determine. Insofar as a different type of society is implied, a society bound not simply by politics but by an idea to which politics is subservient, a society in revolution, there is involved a kind of law differing in spirit from our own.

(4) *Theory.* Prior to the upheaval of the mid-1930's, it was believed that by the creation of a new economic order there would inevitably be produced a new type of man. The emphasis was on economics and on techniques; law played an inferior role. Since 1936 the emphasis has been, in Stalin's words, on cadres — as opposed to technique. The advance from Socialism to Communism will be achieved, it is now thought, not by any fundamental change in the political or economic order, but by what is called "the perfection of man." Law is important, therefore, not merely in giving stability to the political and economic processes, but also in remaking Soviet man, strengthening him morally for the tasks of building the good Communist society.

On the fringes of Marxist theory, quite far removed from the original doctrine that law is a superstructure reflecting economic class interests, an insight into the attitudes underlying Soviet law may be gained. Soviet society is thought of as a moral or "moral-political" unity; its members are but youths and children, requiring training and education; Soviet law educates them to a Communist social-consciousness, "ingrafting upon them," in the words of a recent Soviet writer,[14] "high, noble feelings." However repressive the Soviet legal system may appear to the "reasonable man" of

---

[12] Cf. Berman, "Commercial Contracts in Soviet Law," 35 *California Law Review* 191, n. 42 and 225–27 (1947).

[13] Case reported in Hazard, *Materials on Soviet Law*, 3–4 (1948). Mimeographed.
[14] Kareva, *op. cit.*

American tradition, the importance of the underlying conception of *Law as a teacher* should not be minimized.

21

Soviet Property Law: A Case Study Approach*

John N. Hazard

(1953)

It helps considerably in understanding Soviet law to move down from the more general level of discussion to consider it in action through an examination of concrete cases, as Professor Hazard does in his review of Soviet property law. Here we can clearly see the interaction between ideological orientations and the power interests of the state on the one hand, and on the other the pressure toward calculability, certainty, order, and personal security in one's possessions.

Soviet jurists have always looked upon law as an instrument of social change.[1] It has been considered an instrument with which the Soviet leaders might mould a new social structure. Lenin expressed the idea simply in these words: "Law is politics."[2]

The subject of Soviet law and its relationship to social change is nowhere illustrated so well as in the measures taken over the past thirty years in the sphere of property law. The law of property is appropriate for examination for two reasons. Soviet jurists consider it the subject of primary importance in moulding a new social structure, and the subject has not been recently developed in detail in English language publications.

* Reprinted from "Soviet Property Law and Social Change," *British Journal of Sociology*, Vol. 4 (1953), pp. 1–13, by permission of the author and Routledge and Kegan Paul Limited.
[1] Some of the material in this paper appears in *Law and Social Change in the USSR*, published in 1953 by Stevens & Sons.
[2] V. I. Lenin, 14, *Sochineniya*, 2nd or 3rd edition, Moscow, 1923–7, p. 212.

Marxist Doctrine and Early Policies

The starting point for any consideration of Soviet property law must be Marxist doctrine, for it is in that doctrine that Soviet leaders say they find the inspiration for their policies. It is common knowledge that the Communist Manifesto focused attention upon property relationships as reflecting historical conditions and influencing future change. The Manifesto declared that "In a sense, the theory of the Communists may be summed up in a single sentence: Abolition of private property." Elsewhere in Marxist literature it is made clear that the words "private property" are given a special meaning. They do not refer to all private ownership of property but to private ownership of productive goods. Such ownership is declared by Marxists to be the key not only to economic power but to political power as well. Since their assumption of power in 1917, the Soviet leaders have repeated on all occasions that of all of the lessons they have learned from their Marxist heritage, the lesson on property ownership is the most important. They have concluded that never again can means of production be privately owned, at least in any quantity. They have concluded that the essential requirement for moulding a new social structure is state ownership of productive resources.

The reflection of this doctrinal principle in the early Soviet laws is too well known to require repetition in detail. The very first instruction to the judges following the revolution advised them to base their decisions upon the laws of the deposed government only to the extent that they had not been abolished by the revolution.[3] They were to search their revolutionary conscience and consciousness in plotting the new law. By March 1918, a second decree[4] forbade the use of any of the Tsarist laws, and required the judges to apply only the new laws of the revolutionary regime. If gaps existed, these were to be filled by the judge himself, using as a guide his revolutionary consciousness.

Some specific decrees struck down those

[3] Decree of 27 November 1917, *Sobr. Uzak.*, RSFSR, 1917–1918, No. 4, Art. 50, sec. 5.
[4] *Sobr. Uzak.*, RSFSR, 1917–18, No. 26, Art. 347, sec. 35.

Tsarist laws which were concerned with the ownership of productive goods.[5] Almost immediately after the revolution decrees transferred to the state ownership of the land, multiple dwellings, the merchant marine, banks, insurance companies, and basic industries. Stocks and bonds were annulled and the Tsarist law of inheritance was abolished.

It became clear that property as a source of income and power was no longer to be protected by law, except in small quantities such as small bank accounts, family dwellings, and the workshops of the artisans.

The attitude of the Soviet leaders toward the legal protection of ownership of productive goods was illustrated a few years after the revolution. The destruction of the civil war, following upon the disruption of the First World War, had reduced the economy of Soviet Russia to the point of danger to the new regime. The Soviet leaders found it necessary to plan an economic retreat from their basic principles. They called it a strategic retreat to indicate that it was to be but temporary. There were many heavy hearts, for some of the leaders thought that there might never be a return to the program of the revolution.

The Commissar of Justice found it necessary to explain the retreat to his fellow workers in his Ministry. In 1922 he said, somewhat regretfully, that a new civil code was to be promulgated, and he laid the blame at the door of France and England. He explained the problem in these words:[6]

> During the past year Soviet Russia has linked herself more and more with a number of countries by treaties. . . . As is well known, Lloyd George, when the question of the Genoa Conference was discussed, declared that Soviet Russia must be represented, but that it must establish a recognized system of legal norms which would permit other countries to have permanent relations with it.

Law in recognizable form meant, apparently,

protection of property ownership in productive goods, and it was being reintroduced only because it was necessary to entice French and English capital.

When Lenin announced the necessity of the strategic retreat to the New Economic Policy, he emphasized another factor, namely the necessity of restoring the domestic economy. The Civil Code became effective 1 January 1923, to introduce the protection of property. Within it were to be found the law relating to inheritance, to the protection of property from damage, to the doing of business, to the making of contracts of purchase and sale. Although much shorter than the civil codes of Western European countries, the new Soviet Russian civil code is in familiar form, for it was drafted with an eye on the French Civil Code.

The Soviet leadership was obviously fearful of the new law they were creating. Was it likely that the new civil code would become a Trojan horse, to be utilized by the hated bourgeois elements of society to regain power? Would it be possible for the bourgeoisie to misuse the rights granted by the new code to the disadvantage of the state and its new leaders?

In an effort to reduce the likelihood of such misuse of the code, the legal draftsmen introduced an article which has since become well known, the famous Article I. It read as follows:

> The law protects private rights, except as they are exercised in contradiction to their social and economic purpose.

By incorporating this principle, which had long been espoused by some of the legal philosophers of the West, the Soviet leaders hoped to make it possible for the politically minded judges to depart from the code when such departure seemed necessary to avoid harm to the regime.

Fear lest the new civil code be misused to the disadvantage of the regime was also reflected in the work of the courts. The Supreme Court of the Russian Republic found it necessary to caution judges in the application of those articles of the code which concerned the law of obligations. Since these were patterned after the articles of the French civil code, the

---

[5] For English translation, see Hazard and Weisberg, *Cases and Readings on Soviet Law*, New York, 1950, pp. 246–7.
[6] D. I. Kurskii, *Izbrannye Stati i Rechi*, Moscow, 1948, p. 69.

Supreme Court instructed the inferior courts, as follows:

> The Article to a certain extent is of exceptional character and is subject to restrictive and not amplifying application and interpretation.[7]

Again it was indicated that the new code was to be applied strictly, and was not to be used as the basis for developing through judicial decisions a broad concept of recovery for damage to property.

A bow was also made in the direction of the poor and against the wealthy, for one of the articles in the section having to do with the law of obligations said:

> Art. 411. In fixing compensation for the damage caused, the court shall in all cases take into consideration the financial position of both the injured party and the party who caused the damage.

This favoring of the poor against the wealthy went so far that in another section it was provided that if a wealthy person caused injury to a poor person, damages should be paid even if the person causing the injury were not at fault.[8]

This, then, was the law of the period of strategic retreat: a law which provided protection of property owners, but a law which permitted the conclusion that the leaders still were suspicious of its provisions and were even hostile to some of them.

With the introduction of the first Five Year Plan in 1928, the period of the strategic retreat approached its end. The tax rate on private enterprise was increased, and finally it was legislated out of existence in all but the most limited form. With this development in the process of social change, a renewed drive was evident to do away with property protection. It took the form of a belittling of the importance of the Civil Code. Although the Code was not repealed, it was indicated by the authors of Soviet textbooks that it would not long be of importance. Attention was turned to administrative law, called "economic law."[9]

Textbooks were rewritten with the new title of "economic law," and only at the end in the final chapters was there an exposition of the principles of civil law as found in the code. It was included rather apologetically, as being required because the principles were still the law of the land. Law school courses in civil law were renamed "economic law," and the law relating to contracts and inheritance and damages was included only in the final lectures. Students were advised that their practice would include such problems for a while, and they must know the law, but it was a dying field of law. All of this was done in expectation that the law would "wither away" in accordance with the prophecy of Engels.

The legal reasoning of the men who anticipated the early withering away of civil law has recently been set forth in a volume of translations published by the Association of American Law Schools in 1951.[10] It is unnecessary to develop the ideas at this point.

Work Incentive and Personal Property

During this period of the development of the Five Year Plans a new element entered the picture. It was the increased necessity to raise production. One of the promises of Communism was a level of production so high that every citizen could obtain from the state the goods that he needed. Yet, production was low, and vigorous steps were required to raise the productivity of the worker. The leadership decided upon the further development of the property incentive. Such a decision was not easy to make, because there had been many who had demanded egalitarianism in wage rates in the new society. The high officials were, under the rules of the early days of the revolution, to receive no more salary than the bench workmen. Equalization of wages was popular. Yet now it was to be cast aside under the requirement for greater production. Reliance upon any sense of social duty to obtain from workmen increased efforts had proved to be impossible. This sense of social duty had not developed as the early leaders had expected.

The period of sharply differentiated wages

---

[7] Civil Code, RSFSR, annotation to Art. 403.

[8] Art. 406.

[9] See Pashukanis and Gintsberg, *Khozyaistvennoe Pravo*, 2 vols., Moscow, 1934–5.

[10] See Lenin *et al.*, *Soviet Legal Philosophy*, Cambridge, Mass., 1951.

was introduced with the early 1930's. The old principle of egalitarianism was pushed aside, and the Soviet Encyclopedia stated "Socialism and egalitarianism have nothing in common."

What did this change in attitude mean for the development of the law? The leadership was awarding decorations to Alexei Stakhanov for increasing production and paying him very high wages. His ability to purchase the good things of life was emphasized in stories of his home and his family. He was but the prototype of the new hero, the workmen whose productivity was reflected in a high income. Yet incomes were valueless unless the recipients could purchase commodities. These commodities had to be subject to the protection of the law. Of what use was a commodity if the law did not permit its owner to recover it from a wrongful taker, or did not permit the owner to recover damages from a person who caused injury to it? Even further, of what use was a large income if a man could not be confident that he might transmit some part of it, at least, to his children?

The civil code was still in existence, giving all of this protection. It had not been repealed during the period when it was expected soon to wither away, but many parts of it had passed to a place of secondary importance. Now it was brought forth again with respect. The books which had been entitled "Economic Law" reappeared with new titles, even before there was time to make a change in substance. Many specialists have in their libraries the textbook of Rubinshtein which was reissued with the new title "Civil Law" to replace the old title "Economic Law." In time the books were rewritten, and the chapters on civil law which had been appearing at the end of the volume were expanded and made the subject of whole books.

Was there no fear that the civil code would not be used by bourgeois elements to undermine the regime? Conditions in society had changed since the early 1920's when the code had been enacted. The private enterprise of the period of the New Economic Policy had almost disappeared. Statistics show that only 2½ per cent of the adults in the U.S.S.R. were denied the right to vote in 1934 as a result of the restrictions of the constitution. Since these restrictions concerned primarily those who employed labor for profit, it was evident that by 1934 the persons with property in the bourgeois sense were relatively few. The class of wealthy persons of the old type had entirely disappeared.

Under the new policy of favoring the superior workman with higher wages, the new class of wealthy were not the class enemies of the past against whom there had been discriminatory policies in earlier years. The new wealthy were the favored workers, on whose production the leadership relied for success. Wealth was now a sign of one's contribution to society, and not a sign of one's potential danger. It is small wonder that the attitude toward the law protecting property and the property owner was to change.

The change in attitude toward the property owner is well illustrated by a paragraph taken from a textbook on civil law, published after the war in 1947. By that time the new attitude had gone so far that the authors found it possible to say:

> The opportunity to apply Article 406 (i.e., the article providing for liability of the wealthy even without fault) of the Civil Code under present circumstances is limited to very unusual cases. . . .[11]

The school of jurists who espoused the withering away of the state and of law had been ousted in 1937. It was explained by Stalin that they had not appreciated that the withering process could not occur by degrees, as they had supposed. It could occur only after the state and its law had been strengthened to prepare the way for the ultimate withering. Stalin's principal theoretical spokesman, P. Yudin, explained that the error had been made because of insufficient grounding in dialectical materialism, which teaches that great social changes occur not by direct transition from one phase to another but as the result of contradictions.

This is not the place to discuss the philosophical questions involved in the new theoretical explanation for the stability of law. Suffice it to say that law was placed in a new

---

[11] *Grazhdanskoe Pravo,* Moscow, 1947.

position, and civil law was given a respect which it had not enjoyed for some years.

Evidence of the fact that the fear of misuse of the civil code by hostile elements had waned is to be found in an article published after the war. Professor Agarkov informed his readers that even Article I of the civil code required rethinking. He said:

> About 1930, Article I ceased to interest both the practice of the courts and the literature on civil law. Not a single directive concerning Article I had been issued by the Supreme Court of the U.S.S.R. . . . The textbooks are characteristic . . . giving no analysis of Article I. . . .[12]

When it is remembered that this Article I had permitted the judge to disregard rights guaranteed by the civil code if he thought that the right was being exercised to the detriment of the regime, one can grasp the extent of the change in thinking. Now, apparently, the leadership was content to rest on the provisions of the code without fear that they would be misused by the new class of property owners.

Legal Protection of Property Rights

The inheritance tax was abolished, leaving in effect only a relatively small filing fee. This occurred in 1943, and soon after the inheritance laws were liberalized. Through a series of judicial decisions the Supreme Court indicated to the lower courts and to the public at large the attention it wished paid to property rights. When one considers that the judicial decisions of the courts in the U.S.S.R. are not required to be published, but appear only when the Supreme Court believes them to have importance as a directive to lower courts, these decisions acquire added meaning. A few of them will indicate the attitude of those who guide the destinies of the U.S.S.R.

The judicial decisions concerned the article of the civil code permitting an owner to recover his property even from a bona fide purchaser, provided that the property had been lost or stolen. The question before the court was whether this limited language could be extended to protect an owner in situations in which the property had not been lost or stolen within the technical meaning of these terms. Here are the facts of the first case:[13]

A Russian peasant women had transferred her cow to the Soviet army for evacuation to the rear as the Germans advanced. As the result of what seems almost a miracle the cow was not eaten by the army but was exchanged for meat from another peasant woman, who remained behind and was eventually engulfed by the German advance. By a second miracle the cow survived the German occupation, and when the Soviet army returned, it was still in the possession of the peasant woman.

The original owner returned with the troops of her country and saw the cow. She asked for its return, but its custodian refused to return it, saying that she had purchased it from the Soviet army in retreat. A court action was brought. The plaintiff failed to recover the cow in the court of first instance because the court thought that owners were protected against a bona fide purchaser only if the property had been lost or stolen. In the opinion of the court the cow had neither been lost or stolen.

The Supreme Court reversed the decision of the court of first instance, saying that the principles of the code should have been extended in this case. To be sure, the cow had not been lost or stolen, but the owner had been deprived of possession because of *force majeure*, represented by the military situation.

The second case concerned a cow which had been taken from its Russian owner by the German army. Later in the war it had been captured by the Soviet army. The Soviet army did not wish to eat it, nor did the troops wish to care for it, and so they delivered it to the nearest collective farm, saying that it was a trophy of war. The court of first instance decided that the cow belonged to the collective farm when action was brought by the original owner. The Supreme Court reversed the decision, saying that the rules of the civil code protected the owner even in such circumstances, and the cow was returned.

---

[12] N. M. Agarkov, *Izvestiya Akademii Nauk, SSSR, Otdelenie Ekonomiki i Prava*, 1946, No. 6, p. 424.

[13] See P. E. Orlovskii, *Praktika Verkhovnogo Suda SSSR po Grazhdanskim Delam v Usloviakh Otechestvennoi Voiny*, Moscow, 1944, pp. 17–18, and *Sudebnaya Praktika Verkhovnogo Suda*, SSSR, 1948, Vypusk I, p. 29.

In the third case action was brought by a former owner of a cow against the President of a collective farm, who had the cow in his possession. He defended the action by arguing that the owner had been deprived of her ownership because her son had collaborated with the Germans. The court of first instance rejected the suit, but the Supreme Court ordered a new trial, saying that the record of the trial in the court of first instance did not support the allegation that the owner's son had collaborated. On the contrary, it showed that he had been acquitted of the charge, and the cow should be returned to the owner.

In another action the provisions of the code concerning a contract of sale were tested. As in some other countries, the code provides that if a contract is made under circumstances in which advantage is taken of the "extreme want" of one of the parties, it may be set aside. Judicial decisions declared in the early years that both parties must know that such advantage is being taken and that the condition is not to be interpreted as permitting the setting aside of a contract which is not profitable. Something more than unprofitableness is required. In the present case,[14] the contract concerned the sale of a small private dwelling during the German occupation of the city of Kharkov. It seems that two persons had offered the owner of the house, who was an elderly man dying of starvation, some food and a small amount of money for the house. The offer had been accepted, and the house changed hands. Later the elderly man died. When the Soviet army returned to Kharkov, it brought with it the daughter of the elderly man who had died. She found the house in the possession of the people who claimed to have purchased it. They would not relinquish possession and she brought an action to recover the house as the rightful heir of the former owner.

The court considered the circumstances of the sale and reached the conclusion that it should be set aside. It believed that the purchasers had taken advantage of the elderly man's starvation, and that this was a situation of "extreme want" within the meaning of the civil code.

The cases of this character are numerous, but the few that have been given may indicate the current policies of the Soviet courts. Property of the kind indicated is being protected.

Limitations Upon Property Rights

In spite of the interest in protecting consumers' goods which are privately owned, there is no return to private ownership of large-scale productive property. Rumors circulating during the war that heroes of the Soviet army would be given plots of land on their return to the motherland proved not to be true. There have been no changes in the concept of state ownership of land. There has been no distribution of great industries to trusted henchmen. Industry has remained solely in the hands of the state in contradiction of another wartime rumor that the state managers would become the new owners after the war. Great economic wealth derived from the operation of landed estates or industry is impossible of achievement. Even the small opportunities offered the private individual to derive income from small-scale production have been reduced. In 1943, the provision permitting an artisan to employ one assistant was removed from the licensing act of the Ministry of Finance.[15] No one may now be licensed to produce and sell commodities if he employs labor.

Even the licences granted to artisans who work alone are limited to activity in which a profit cannot be obtained by any increase in value of the raw materials constituting the principal part of the item which is being produced. Thus, the processor of grain will not be licensed unless he receives his raw materials from his customer. He may not purchase grain on the open legal market and use it to make bread for sale. No processor of hemp, wool, or flax may obtain raw materials from the market. He may only obtain them from his customer.

Some activities are forbidden entirely, such as the manufacture of poisons, explosives, inflammable materials, and even cosmetics for what must be the obvious reasons. A sidelight is thrown on the Soviet definition of poisons by an additional provision which makes it impossible to obtain a licence to operate a print shop, or any duplicating machine. Clearly such

---

[14] *Sudebnaya Praktika Verkhovnogo Suda,* SSSR, 1948, Vypusk IV, p. 9.

[15] Instruction of 26 March 1936, as amended, printed as annotation to Art. 54, Civil Code RSFSR, August, 1948, edition, p. 170.

an operation might be used to evade the censorship rules. But these latter prohibitions do not concern the wealth-producing properties of private enterprise. They are most probably banned because of the immediate physical danger they represent to the citizen.

The activities of the independent middleman are also banned. A case will illustrate the attitude of the authorities.[16] Two citizens made a contract with a handicraft cooperative association to travel through the countryside to sell blackboards on which the names of exemplary farmers might be posted. Under the terms of the agreement the men were to receive a commission on all blackboards sold. They proceeded on their mission and were very successful. For two months during the summer of 1939 sales were made on which the commission would have been 18,077 rubles. To assure payment of their commissions, they withheld part of it when remitting the proceeds of the sales to their principals. Later they demanded the balance, and when it was refused, they brought suit.

Although the salesmen obtained judgment in the court of first instance, the Supreme Court reversed on the ground that the contract was illegal. The licensing act provided for no travelling salemen's contracts. The salesmen were ordered to pay over to the state the amount they had withheld on the ground that it was an unjust enrichment, and the cooperative association was denied thereby any benefit at the salesmen's expense under the illegal contract.

The case is unusually interesting because it seems to attack only the method of operation. The men could have been employees of the cooperative association on a salary. This salary could have been varied on the basis of the number of blackboards sold. The illegality was not in this but in the effort to make themselves independent contractors. They might have acquired thereby a source of income subject to less control than if they had been only wage earners.

The policy of the leadership against merchandising activities is also clearly indicated in the law. Under the criminal code it is a crime to buy goods for the purpose of resale at a profit.[17] Such an article, if adopted in England, would make it criminal to conduct the business of Regent Street. The protection accorded to property ownership of consumers' goods is not, therefore, to be extended to the person who wishes to conduct the business of the merchant.

Fear lest the danger of the merchant escape detection because of the difficulty of catching the individual engaged in buying and reselling at a profit gave rise to a remarkable order of the Supreme Court of the U.S.S.R. during the past war.[18] It was declared that a court might impute intent to comit the crime of speculation, i.e., buying with the intent to resell at a profit, from the fact that a citizen was found in possession of goods in quantities exceeding those required for his use and the use of his family.

Some judicial decisions will indicate how this ruling of the Supreme Court has been applied. A man was found in possession of 1090 pairs of women's stockings. This was thought to be an indication of his intention to resell them at a profit, and he was convicted of the crime of speculation and sentenced. The Supreme Court upheld the conviction, noting also that at the time the accused had been apprehended he was engaged in no socially useful work. Apparently, the Supreme Court believed that his lack of work was added reason to assume that he was a professional merchant and a criminal.[19]

Likewise, a man was convicted when apprehended in a marketplace with a large stock of goods and 12,000 rubles. He argued at the trial that he had purchased the goods to make gifts, and that he had had no intention of reselling them when apprehended. The trial court found that the prisoner had been released shortly before from prison for another offence. He had taken the train to a distant city and had purchased on the open market 400 jars of tobacco, 15 bottles of liquor, 14 pocket mirrors, and a large quantity of cigarette papers. In the opinion of the court this operation was that of a merchant and not a bearer of gifts. The Supreme Court affirmed the conviction.[20]

---

[16] *Sovetskaya Yustitsiya*, 1940, No. 16, p. 44.
[17] Criminal Code, RSFSR, Art. 107.

[18] Order of 10 February 1940, printed as annotation to Criminal Code, RSFSR, 1943 edition, p. 176.
[19] *Sotsialisticheskaya Zakonnost*, 1940, No. 9, p. 72.
[20] *Sudebnaya Praktika Verkhovnogo Suda*, SSSR, 1942, Vypusk I, p. 12.

The result is not always adverse to the defendant, as is indicated by two other decisions. A woman was tried because she had in her possession when apprehended 18 buckets, 10 saucepans, a basin, and 5 cups. She argued in her defence that these items had been purchased on her trip to the city with money given her by neighbors. She was only performing a courtesy to her neighbors and not committing a crime. She was convicted by the trial court, but the Supreme Court set aside the conviction on the ground that the evidence supported her claim.[21]

In another case a man was able to obtain his release when he proved that the items he had sold had been in use by his family, and they were sold only because they were no longer required. This fact was accepted as proving that he had no intent to become a merchant when he acquired the goods.[22]

Reliance has been placed not solely upon the criminal law to prevent the rise of commerce. One of the stated purposes of the ruble conversion law of 1947 was the penalizing of speculators.[23] The rate of exchange for old rubles was set at differing levels, depending upon whether the citizen kept his money in the bank or outside of it. It was the presumption of the law that a person who had gained his wealth by illegal means as a merchant feared to put it into a bank. Thus the rate of exchange was made to discriminate against the person who acquired property solely for the purpose of resale.

Some limitations on the use of property are suggested by a case having to do with a privately owned dwelling. An owner who had difficulty in evicting a tenant from her summer home in the country brought suit against the tenant. It was proved at the trial that the plaintiff owned an apartment in Moscow, which she used in the winter. The court of first instance held against the owner in the action for ejectment on the ground that the owner did not require the use of the space in the country, since she had space in the city. The Supreme Court of the U.S.S.R. reversed the decision on the ground that the country space was only for summer use and could not be considered as a second apartment.[24] The implication seems plain that if an owner of two permanent living places seeks to oust a tenant of one, he will not succeed, because the use of living space must be related to one's personal needs.

The case is included among those relating to property ownership only to fill out the picture. It is not peculiar to the Soviet system, because other systems of law have reached the same solution when housing space has been much in demand because of a severe shortage. Certainly the shortage of housing space is reason enough for the Soviet courts to take the position they do. It is hard to tell whether their position is also doctrinal and based upon their antagonism to the use of property for the purpose of gaining income.

Confiscation of property is occasionally a penalty for counter-revolutionary activity as determined by a court.[25] It is no longer a penalty for the violation of less fundamental rules, except in the cases well known to other systems, such as smuggling, the shipment of goods in violation of postal or freight regulations, and the possession of firearms and explosives. The policy of protecting property has extended to the development of a policy toward confiscation which is generally similar to that in effect in systems of law which have nothing to do with the Soviet approach. Similar rules to those in operation in the West are also in effect as regards the requisitioning of property for the use of the state. Compensation must be paid in an amount to be determined by an administrative tribunal. To be sure, this method of determination of value is not as popular in the common law world as is the determination by a court, but the difference could not be noted generally outside the common law world. No published reports permit the outsider to determine whether the determinations of value by the administrative board are fair.

For the property owner who acquires his wealth in the permitted activities, the law provides means even of accumulating wealth by

21 *Ibid.*, 1945, Vypusk VII (XXII), p. 10.
22 *Ibid.*, 1942, Vypusk I, p. 14.
23 *Sob. Post.*, SSSR, 1948, No. 1, Art. 1.

24 *Sotsialisticheskaya Zakonnost*, 1939, No. 8–9, p. 103.
25 Civil Code, RSFSR, Art. 70, and law of 28 March 1927, *Sobr. Zak.*, RSFSR, 1927, No. 38, Art. 248, Part III.

investment. Thus, the Savings Banks accept deposits on which the rate of interest is currently 5 per cent.[26] State Bonds are sold with the possibility of obtaining a return of many times the face amount as the result of a lottery drawing.

An Evaluation of Soviet Property Law

Considering the various provisions of the law, it is now evident that in the "bundle of rights" which constitute ownership, there are now present nearly all the rights known to the Western world. The owner of consumers' goods may recover damages if his property is injured. He may recover it from a wrongful possessor, and even from a bona fide purchaser in most instances. He may sell it when it is no longer required for the purpose for which it was acquired. He may bequeath it to his heirs. He may invest it in income-producing bank accounts and in lottery bonds of the state. He may even have a sale set aside if it is determined that unfair advantage was taken of his poverty. All of these rights are now more than likely to be protected by the civil code because Article I, permitting a court to ignore them if they are misused in the opinion of the court, is no longer being applied.

The principal limitation upon ownership is in the right to resell property which has been acquired solely for the purpose of resale. Another limitation is allied to this one, in that the artisan who obtains a licence to process goods may not, in most cases, purchase raw materials for the purpose of processing them for sale on the market. He must obtain them only from his customer.

In spite of this liberalization of the law relating to property, there remain the severe restrictions enacted at the time of the revolution on the ownership of producer's goods. No private individual may buy land or shares of stock in an industrial enterprise or invest in securities of some limited company or found a bank or insurance company. These activities are deemed to be not solely economic in character but to be related to political power. The law has not changed, even with the stress of

the war, to protect such rights.

To the legal historian and the comparative lawyer, the steps Soviet leaders have taken in the realm of property law are not entirely unfamiliar. On many occasions in the past, property law has been manipulated to achieve political effects desired by a regime. In many countries of the old world, and even in the new, a new regime has punished its enemies and rewarded its friends by appropriate changes in the law of property. The development of interest in the sphere of Soviet property law has been the careful distinction that has been drawn between types of property. Friends have been rewarded in a manner which seems hardly to have been imagined by Soviet leaders at the time of their revolution, but the rewards have not been indiscriminate.

Soviet leaders seem to have adhered carefully to their basic tenet of faith that property ownership is the key to political power. While the faithful producer has been rewarded in a manner which sometimes appears munificent, he has never been permitted to have that type of property which in the eyes of Soviet theorists would permit him to challenge the power of the regime. Not even the highest dignitaries of the regime have obtained such property rights, a fact which led Leon Trotsky in his *Revolution Betrayed* to argue that although a vast bureaucracy had been developed it could not be permanent. His reason was simple in that this bureaucracy had not acquired the ownership of the industries which they administered.

We of the West have come to the conclusion that many relationships other than those surrounding property ownership now have importance in creating positions of power. Undoubtedly, Soviet leaders now appreciate that fact, as evidenced by their care to control the trade unions, the cooperatives and other pressure groups, but the status of the law suggests that they still reserve the top place in the hierarchy of power for the traditional element. It is the element of private ownership of productive goods. The faithful will be rewarded by many things, wealth, position, medals, and privileges, but they will not be accorded an opportunity to become a new generation of landlords and industrialists.

---

[26] See Alec Cairncross, "The Moscow Economic Conference", *Soviet Studies,* 4 (1952), p. 113, at p. 126.

22

The Soviet Lawyer: An Occupational Profile*

Frederick Wyle

(1953)

As we have seen, the rule of law in the U.S.S.R. is far from absolute, being avowedly subordinate to decisions of the Communist Party. The diminished importance of the law in a totalitarian system is also made apparent in the fact that strikingly few among the top coterie of Communists have been lawyers or trained in the law. Mr. Wyle's article, based on interviews with former Soviet lawyers, helps further to make concrete the minor role of law by describing the functions and work atmosphere of the rank-and-file Soviet lawyer. In a personal communication, Mr. Wyle cautions us to bear in mind that his respondents were all talking about their experiences in the 1930's and that allowance should be made for any changes in the last twenty years.

Introductory Note. One method I have found useful in appraising the place of the Soviet lawyer in his society is to relate him to the two dominant phenomena of Soviet life. These are, first, the preservation and extension of control by the Communist Party and its leaders over as many aspects of life in the Soviet Union as possible, and second, the drive for industrial and agricultural production. There are, of course, other factors which go to determine the social role of an occupational group, even in the Soviet Union: the extent to which it renders a valuable service to other groups in the society, or the extent to which it symbolizes a value which is cherished by other groups of the society. In the Soviet

---

* Revised by Mr. Wyle from "The Soviet Lawyer: A Memorandum with Appended Case Notes" (June 1953), unpublished memorandum of the Project on the Soviet Social System (AF No. 33 (038)-12909), Russian Research Center, Harvard University. Used by permission of the author.

Union, the symbolic value of "law" and "lawyers," as representatives of a system of values revolving around "the law" as we know it, is relatively weak. The strongest indices to the role of the lawyer in Soviet society are furnished, therefore, as it seems to me, by reference to the prime activities of Soviet life: political control by the Party, and agricultural and industrial production.

The Soviet lawyer takes part in governmental control, and in agricultural and industrial production to only a minor extent, as will be shown below. From the point of view of the regime, he is a rather remote auxiliary, a tool for certain limited purposes with a limited usefulness. He is therefore not valued highly by the regime, the dispenser of social rewards. Neither does he stand high in the esteem of the population, by comparison with other professional groups of a roughly similar standing in the West. On the whole, one may say that the Soviet lawyer is a being without influence or substantial power, as power is regarded in the Soviet Union.

Comparative Ranking of Lawyer

In terms of popular esteem, governmental favor, and self-evaluation, the average Soviet lawyer ranks somewhere among skilled white-collar workers. He might be compared in social rank with a bookkeeper, some degrees below a chief bookkeeper of a substantial enterprise, or with a middle engineer; he ranks definitely below a doctor, a responsible engineer, or a university professor.

The Soviet lawyer is only rarely a member of the Communist Party, this in itself being a significant description of his relative lack of status in Soviet society. Aside from top-level government lawyers, he occupies almost no positions of trust and responsibility, and is hardly ever a member of prominent organizations such as soviets.

Whether some of the conclusions of this paper explain his rank or not, the fact seems to be that the lawyer ranks considerably lower in social status in the Soviet Union than he does in any other modern nation.

Types of Lawyers

In order to examine the lawyer's role in greater detail, it is well at this point to distinguish between two types of lawyers in the Soviet Union:

(1) The *jurisconsult* — A salaried employee of an enterprise, roughly corresponding to a company counsel, or a legal adviser to the director.

(2) The *advocate* — A member of a "collegium" of lawyers, engaged in law practice for private individual clients, on a fee basis, and within the framework of supervision and control of his collegium.

The Jurisconsult

(1) *Formal Functions.* The formal functions of a jurisconsult in, say, a productive enterprise, are those of rendering legal advice to the director — i.e., interpreting and correlating the regulations and law formally defining the rights and duties of the enterprise and the director; under certain circumstances, representing the enterprise in arbitration proceedings regarding disputes with other enterprises; assisting in contractual relations with other enterprises; and performing a number of more or less bureaucratic functions, such as setting pay schedules and rates in accordance with government regulations, supervising the observance of labor discipline, and bringing charges against offenders of labor discipline in the name of the enterprise, etc.

The jurisconsult is an employee of the enterprise. He received (during the thirties) from 300 to 500 rubles monthly in small enterprises, and from 600 to 800 rubles in the large enterprises. If he works for a large enterprise, he devotes his full time to it; most of those working for smaller enterprises have two or three, and often more, positions, despite a legal restriction on the number of jobs they may hold as "full-time" positions.

(2) *Limitations of Functions.* The jurisconsult attached to an economic enterprise is perhaps more aptly described by the title "regulations technician" than by that of legal adviser. As for the interpretation of economic regulations and orders, it seems to me that the director of the enterprise is glad enough to have someone to relieve him of a burden and a nuisance, but that it does not seem to anyone to be a matter of prime importance. The primary aim of the director is production, and the successful director often achieves his standing by resorting to extra-legal and illegal

devices which are more or less tolerated by the regime so long as the result is increased production without too great a disruption of other sectors of the economy.

In the manipulation of these extra-legal and illegal devices, such as swap, deal, hoarding, etc., the director does not seem to attach much importance to the jurisconsult. He does not seem to consult, at least to any appreciable extent, the jurisconsult as to whether he can "get away with it." The decisions as to whether to stay within the legal channels or not seem to be made by the power group of the factory without the participation of the jurisconsult, and by reference to other considerations than those of legality.

The power group includes the director, the chief bookkeeper, who juggles the books to present a favorable picture of the enterprise's financial health, the chief engineer or production man, and the local Party representative. The power group clearly does not include the jurisconsult. The *tolkach,* the "expediter," seems rather to be the man upon whom a great deal of the success of the enterprise in its extra-legal dealings depends. It is quite striking, for example, that the respondents in the managerial specialty interviews hardly ever mention the jurisconsult, while they describe in considerable detail the cooperation of the various other members of the power group to accomplish their extra-legal dealings. One has the impression that the enterprise's jurisconsult is more or less irrelevant to the important decisions, including "legal" decisions, made by the enterprise's power group.

In the negotiations of contracts, the jurisconsult likewise plays a very limited role. For the important sectors of the economy, model contracts are worked out in considerable detail, and in all sectors of the economy the contractual relations between enterprises are generally prescribed. There remains the working out of details, place of shipment, time of delivery, etc., all of which give rise to legal rights between enterprises, but which do not seem to be main considerations of the director. Relative to other factors making for the success of the industrial or commercial enterprise, the jurisconsult's function in the negotiation of the contracts seems negligible. Whether a "good deal" is achieved by an enterprise in the process of negotiation seems to be determined more by the over-all "rank" of the enterprise than by the skill of the negotiators, including the jurisconsult.

The jurisconsult performs duties most analogous to those of his Western colleagues in representing his enterprise in arbitration proceedings and in the courts. However, there are some reports that the directors rather than their jurisconsults handle the arbitration of important disputes. Respondents indicated that the arbitration boards (*Gosarbitrazh*) sometimes preferred to deal with the directors and scorned the jurisconsults as technical pettifoggers who had little relation to the "real" issues.

It would be assumed in the West that participation in arbitration and court cases should bring some measure of acknowledgment and social esteem to the jurisconsult. My present impression, however, is that while a jurisconsult who is successful in winning cases is mildly appreciated, the whole area of asserting rights under contracts is considered somewhat extraneous to the main business at hand, production.

As for the jurisconsult's bureaucratic functions, they are a cause for considerable strain and tension in the relations of the jurisconsult with the workers of the enterprise generally. It is his function to supervise, at least in part, the observance of the intensely unpopular labor discipline laws. He is thus the person who formally charges workers in court with violating the laws against lateness, absenteeism, and the like.

The jurisconsult also must make the hard decisions regarding issues of workers' rights such as overtime, pay rates, schedules, and so on, all of which are generally regarded by the workers in the Soviet Union much as they are regarded elsewhere. The jurisconsults themselves often have intense moral conflicts arising from their duty to "take to court" workers who have violated the rigid labor laws, and with whom the jurisconsults may be in complete or partial sympathy. In some cases, respondents report, the jurisconsults are able to hush up and cover up the violations. This is a dangerous business, however, since it exposes the jurisconsults themselves to charges of sabotaging labor discipline.

In terms of our original criteria of analyzing the role of the Soviet lawyer, it is this function of enforcing labor discipline which is the only duty of the jurisconsult involving the exercise of significant power. Furthermore, his discretion in such matters is severely limited by the general supervision exercised by the Party, to some extent by the procuracy, and by the director.

(3) *Role of Jurisconsult from Point of View of People — Social Standing.* On the whole, I have the impression that the workers of an enterprise regard the jurisconsult with a mixture of mild respect and mild animosity. He is not directly connected with production and is therefore often regarded as a white-collar "parasite." On the other hand, his education and knowledge are respected. His power is recognized as being very limited, and even if his intentions are thought to be good, little hope is placed in his ability to further the welfare of the workers. He of course represents the administration in those cases where the interests of the administration are adverse to those of the workers. In workers' suits for compensation, back pay, disability compensation, etc., he represents the evils of bureaucracy, and seems to be the focus for the animosity engendered by decisions on "dry," "legalistic" grounds. Even the press at times makes of him a scapegoat for "formalism," "bureaucratism" and fuddy-duddy obstructionism to production or good management—worker relations.

One redeeming factor is the occasional aid the jurisconsult gives to individuals within the enterprise regarding their legal troubles on the outside. This aid, of course, is not part of the official duties of the jurisconsult, and he gives it only rarely, generally at the instance of the director. One respondent said that he spent several hours each week at this sort of work — drawing up letters of complaint, or filing documents of various kinds, etc. Another respondent said that he rendered this sort of assistance to individuals only once every several months. This work is in the nature of a favor to individuals, rather than a normal function of the jurisconsult.

On balance, the opprobrium attaching to the jurisconsult as the administration's man seems to outweigh the esteem he may have gained with some workers through private favors. At best, he seems to be regarded as a "poor fish" who has to do his work regardless of how he feels about the things he does, "like everyone else." At worst, he is regarded as a "parasite" who is just one more bureaucrat feeding off the toil of the workers.

(4) *Role of Jurisconsult from Point of View of Regime.* The regime does not seem to value the jurisconsult particularly. In the enforcement of labor discipline, he seems to be considered a minor tool, chief reliance and responsibility being on the director and on the Party unit in the enterprise. He does help the director in achieving the sort of stability and regularity which in some areas is vital to any complex system, but since the area of free choice is so narrowly prescribed, the jurisconsult isn't a person whose judgment is particularly important in achieving orderliness, or success in production. One indication of the place of the jurisconsult in the eyes of the regime is a criticism in the press in 1940. The critic blasts the director for excessive liberality in distributing bonuses for achieving certain production norms: the director had gone so far as to distribute a bonus to his jurisconsult.

Perhaps the strongest indication of the role of the jurisconsult in the social structure as the regime views it, is the fact that very many of the jurisconsults in the late thirties seemed to have been formerly arrested persons, members of the pre-Revolutionary bourgeoisie, persons who were dismissed from some position in the arts, sciences, or administration because they were considered not politically trustworthy enough, and other products of "hostile class elements." It does not seem that a regime as hyper-sensitive to considerations of political loyalty as the Soviet would allow people of such questionable background to occupy a position which it felt to be of any influence or importance. No qualifying personal characteristics seemed to be required of the jurisconsults, so long as they satisfied the director to whom they were responsible that they knew their jobs. A low percentage, estimated variously as between 5 per cent and 20 per cent, of the jurisconsults were members of the Party. These considerations, and the relatively low salary, point to the conclusion that the jurisconsult is not particularly valued by the regime.

(5) *General Remarks on Jurisconsult.* The most striking thing in the respondents' testimony was the emphasis all of them laid on the political safety of the jurisconsult's job. With respect to the possibility of political repression, the jurisconsult is extraordinarily safe — safer, all the respondents agreed, than the director, the engineer, the chief bookkeeper, even than an agronomist, who may be blamed for crop failure in a bad year.

As long as the advice given by the jurisconsult was based on the appropriate regulations, the respondents stressed, nothing would happen to them. This would seem to coincide with their relatively small importance in the actual process of production and control. In any event, the job of jurisconsult seems to have been, in the difficult thirties, a little island of relative safety in the tempest-tossed sea of political surveillance.

Of course, jurisconsults of large enterprises and of important state agencies were somewhat more subject to political trends, but by and large, "a jurisconsult's job was not a dangerous one."

(6) *Summary on Jurisconsult — Advantages and Disadvantages.* Positive aspects are, first of all, political safety, and to a lesser extent, the considerable independence allowed to the jurisconsult in the pursuit of his daily duties; the association, however limited, with a "profession"; the rather important opportunity to travel to the large cities in pursuit of affairs of the enterprise, and the coincident opportunity to purchase scarce commodities; the fact of white-collar work and the intellectual nature of the work, at least in part.

Negative aspects seem to be a sense of professional frustration for those who were lawyers, or knew of the legal profession, in pre-Revolutionary days; a sense of futility and uselessness; the general low social standing as compared with people of lesser education and ability but greater involvement in the production or control processes; lack of esteem by the population and, particularly, by workers in the enterprise.

The respondents were unanimous in placing the doctor, the engineer, the university professor, and intellectuals and artists ahead of themselves in the social order.

The Advocate

(1) *Formal Functions.* The formal functions of the Soviet advocate are comparable to some extent, but only to some extent, with

those of a lawyer engaged in the general practice of law in this country. He is a member of the "collegia" of lawyers of his community, and the collegia, consisting of a dozen or several dozen lawyers generally, are supposed to take the cases which private clients bring to them. These matters might be apartment difficulties, divorce cases, compensation and salary cases, defenses in criminal actions, etc. However, even the most general comparison to a Western lawyer must be tempered by an examination of the context, which we will undertake below.

Another function of the Soviet lawyer, as he is endlessly reminded by the regime, is to educate the public whenever he has an opportunity to do so in the "spirit of the Marxist law." Often the occasion of a trial is regarded by the regime primarily as an opportunity for the advocate to deliver political speeches explaining concrete cases of individual deviant behavior in terms of current Soviet ideology. The exercise of the advocate's forensic talents in the narrow interests of his client is expected, if not to take second place, then certainly not to take precedence over the advocate's educational function.

The advocate's remuneration is based on a percentage of the rates which his collegium charges the client for his services. Although in form the collegium selects the lawyer for a client, generally the client will request the services of a particular advocate whose reputation is high. If the advocate is free, he will generally be assigned to the case. Thus, something like individual law practice results. However, the collegium is controlled by its secretary, who is a Party member, and whose duty it is to represent the interests of the Party and the regime in supervising the collegium. Final authority in assigning lawyers to particular cases is in the secretary.

There is great disparity in the income of different advocates. Income ranges from several hundred to several thousand rubles monthly, depending on the ability of the particular advocate. Advocates also have the function of defending persons accused of certain categories of (non-political) crimes. This duty is likewise assigned and controlled by the secretary of the collegium.

There is another function of the advocate, which, however, is limited to a very small group of the advocates, presumably the Party members. This is the defense of persons accused of political crimes and being tried either by the courts of the secret police or by closed sessions of the regular court either under prosecution by the secret police or under certain drastic articles of the penal law.

(2) *Limitations of Functions.* The chief limitation of the function of the Soviet advocate is inherent in the political structure of his society. The Soviet Constitution grants a number of civil rights to Soviet citizens, on condition that these rights are not exercised in contradiction of the social purposes for which they are granted. What constitutes a contradiction of the social purposes of these civil rights is decided by non-legal agencies of the regime in the first instance, and by the court system secondarily. The advocate has no influence on these decisions, nor can he predict with any degree of certainty what they will be. Furthermore, the agencies of internal security have overreaching power to take complete charge of any case of individual behavior which they consider to have political or counter-revolutionary significance, and in this event, all laws are suspended.

The functions of the advocate may be said to vary infinitely with the nature of the case in which his aid is sought — i.e., according to the place in the spectrum of political significance which the case occupies. In the case, for example, of two women bickering over the right to use a communal kitchen of an apartment which their families share, or in a minor suit of a worker for compensation for injury at his place of work, the advocate may be said to function almost on a par with his Western colleague. He will display forensic talent, wit, oratory, in short, he becomes an adversary of his client's opponent.

On the other hand, where the case is close to what the government views as sabotage of production, or a criminal charge which may have implications of anti-government sentiment or actions, the advocate becomes a modest, almost apologetic pleader for clemency.

In a case of political significance, there is usually a confession before the trial starts. Confessions are never questioned, so that the issue of guilt is settled long before the trial, and the only issue at the trial is the size of the penalty. Here the advocate will restrict himself to agreeing with the prosecution as to the heinousness of the crime, but urge extenuating circumstances such as youth, past service to the regime, or good intentions, in order to mitigate the sentence.

The range of cases from apolitical disputes to political offenses is infinite, and the freedom of the advocate to defend his client varies as infinitely. The exercise of judgment as to what degree of freedom is permissible in a particular trial is a fine art, perhaps one of the finest developed in the Soviet Union. The difficulty of this art is emphasized by the fact that in a society so governed by ideology and, to a large extent, fear, as the Soviet Union, any case can be politicized by a skillful prosecutor, if not by reference to the act committed, then by reference to the personalities involved in the situation. The very first question which the Soviet advocate asked of his client in the thirties, indeed, seems to have been not what he had done, but what his social background was. The social background of the client — and sometimes of the advocate — and the climate of political opinion, i.e., the atmosphere created by the regime at the moment, are more important in the decision of cases than such things as the degree of proof, the ability of the advocate, and even the judge's opinion as to what the facts of the situation may have been, it would seem. However, the same atmosphere of political pressure may be turned to one's advantage by a skillful and glib advocate. Indeed, one of the prime requirements for a successful advocate seems to be a good knowledge of Marxism-Leninism-Stalinism.

Another limitation on the function of the advocate as a representative of his client's interests is the participation of non-legal agencies in the decision of certain disputes. While it seems to be the exception rather than the rule, all the respondents report cases of the Party intervening by contacting the judge, who is subject to Party discipline, and dictating the decision of a particular case. This intervention is frowned upon by the regime in cases where only personal considerations are involved. However, since the Party is relied upon to keep the court system in line with general policy, it seems an inevitable concomitant of the Soviet judicial system. "Drives," "campaigns," and "attacks" to root out one or another form of individual behavior

regarded as contrary to the interests of the regime govern the atmosphere in which both court and advocate function. Stories abound of advocates who unwisely let their zeal for the interests of their client lead them into a hasty word, an inadvertent remark, and who repented of their lack of judgment in a concentration camp soon thereafter.

Aside from such political considerations, there are technical limitations on the advocate. The lack of firm precedents, the lack of adequate reporting of cases (even to the extent that precedent is admitted) and the generally low level of education of those associated with the judiciary, further limit what the West would regard as the proper function of a lawyer in the interests of his client.

(3) *Role of Advocate from Point of View of People — Social Standing.* In certain areas — the apolitical disputes over apartment houses, etc. — people seem to value the services of the advocate. However, the over-all impression is that people do not think highly of the official functions of the advocate in securing benefits for them.

In cases involving desperate issues of life and death, or long-term imprisonment, it is recognized that the advocate can do little but plead for clemency or mitigation of the sentence. In lesser cases of salary disputes, etc., people seem to resent the fees charged by the collegium in order to make available the services of an advocate. The fee for a rather simple case might be a week's wages, and many would-be private litigants simply cannot afford the fees of the collegium. The respondents estimated as from 60 per cent to 90 per cent the workers who appear in court to sue their enterprises without a lawyer. There appears to be no Soviet substitute for the American system of contingent fees, enabling a person without funds to obtain the services of a lawyer to be recompensed out of the recovery, if any. Many of the jurisconsults said that they were often ashamed of winning a case for the enterprise solely because of the ignorance of the worker on the other side and state that they felt sure that, if the worker had had an advocate, he would have won.

The chief popular appreciation of the advocate seems to be in an area which might be called "political power counseling." In cases of great seriousness, involving extreme penalties and the intervention of non-legal agencies, the advocate can do little in court. However, he often has a sensitive and broad understanding of the realities of political power in the society. He knows to whom to write, whom to attempt to bribe, what line of approach to take with regard to other agencies, and he may act as the conduit for bribes in some cases. He knows the appropriate formulas for the political atmosphere of the moment and what kind of attitude on the part of the citizen is permitted or desired by the regime. This understanding can be of considerable value to the advocate's client.

The advocate's intellectual finesse, his political understanding and "know-how," his sometimes considerable income, his role in the regime's use of the courts for propaganda, and his real, if limited, aid to the population at large — all seem to make for a somewhat higher place in the social order for the advocate than for the jurisconsult. An enlightened guess might place him, so far as the general population is concerned, higher than the jurisconsult, but still lower than the doctor or engineer, and probably the university professor.

(4) *Role of Advocate from Point of View of Regime.* The main functions of the advocate in which the regime is interested are two. First, he is expected to contribute to the education of the populace by his conduct at trials, expounding the principles of Marxism-Leninism and applying them to the particular facts of a particular case, thus showing the "real" social significance of cases of individual deviant behavior. Second, he aids in the preservation of stability in the non-political areas of Soviet life by his participation in the process of solving disputes in an ordered and legal way.

The more politically significant a particular case in court is, the greater the advocate's duty of public education and explanation. Soviet trials are heavily attended, and the function of educating the public to approved norms of behavior, by showing both the fault of a particular act and impressing the populace with the unpleasant consequences of similar acts, is one which all who are connected with the court system and trials are expected to fulfill. Party and secret police observers frequently attend the trials, as do representatives of the court administration, to see that this function

is properly carried out. It would seem also that the advocate has a strong professional interest in making long speeches of the kind desired by the regime, because only thus can he justify the propriety of showing clemency to his particular client, in terms of a "proper" consideration of ideology. The regime recognizes the usefulness of the advocate in the process of propaganda, and encourages his role in this respect.

As for the securing of nonpolitical rights of individuals, the advocate fulfills a role much like that of his counterpart in any modern nation. In cases such as apartment difficulties, or compensation claims, it is in the interest of the regime to have these disputes resolved by law and lawyers, and thus to avoid spending bureaucratic energies on affairs in which the regime has no particular interest. The regime's principal interest in such disputes as apartment allocation and divorce matters is to keep instability in these fields from affecting politically important areas such as industrial or agricultural production, or its own political control. However, the advocate does not seem to be viewed as entitled to particular respect or great rewards for this function. Of the two functions, propaganda and stabilization, the regime seems to regard propaganda as the more important.

In line with the greater importance of the advocate, as compared with the jurisconsult, there are some restrictions imposed upon entry into the collegium which are not applicable to the jurisconsult. There are some very minor educational qualifications, which can be substituted for by "practical" experience; the more important qualifications are political reliability and the proper background. Several jurisconsult respondents expressed a desire to have been advocates rather than jurisconsults, explaining that they were not considered reliable enough. The degree of their political safety is not rated as high by the advocates as by the jurisconsults, and Party membership seems to have been somewhat greater; the top estimate even for advocates, however, was still only 30 per cent. The majority of respondents estimated the percentage of party membership by advocates as much lower.

(5) *General Remarks on the Advocate.* A great deal depended on the personality of the advocate, the respondents say. A good

man, one with intellectual flexibility, a keen sense of the direction of the political wind, and above all, a good bluffer, could do a great deal and "get away with it." The advocate is engaged in the public manipulation of the symbols of ideological dogma. These can be powerful weapons in skillful hands. On the other hand, the advocate by the same token may offend others who wield power in a more secret and more effective way.

It would seem that the advocates retain a good deal of professional pride, at least those who have had some legal training. Many advocates are former judges or procurators who were fired for personal inefficiency or drunkenness, or some other non-political offense, and became advocates to make a living. However, since there seems to be a fairly effective selection of the best advocates by the clients, the professional pride of the few good ones has a chance to grow, and standards for the profession have a chance to develop. Also, there is some pride in being able to manipulate power factors in the society successfully. One respondent was most contemptuous in relating how another advocate (less skilled than the respondent, one may infer) was called to a secret session of an NKVD tribunal to defend a person accused of Trotskyism. The defense counsel defined Trotskyism to the judges in the course of his defense, but apparently incorrectly. He so frightened the judges by exposing them to his heretical theories that they promptly sent him off to Siberia. The respondent who told the story was highly contemptuous of his unlucky colleague's lack of skill. "And he called himself an advocate!"

(6) Summary on the Advocate — Advantages and Disadvantages. The chief positive aspects seemed to be professional pride, the rather heady spirit of one who flirts with danger but usually wins, the intellectual challenge of the job, the independent work method and situation, and in many cases, also, the relatively high earnings. The chief negative aspects seemed to be the sense of professional frustration and intellectual dishonesty, which may be said to increase with the degree of ability. The advocate sees extra-legal forces as the more important basis of decision in matters which he would like to see decided on legal grounds. Political danger is relatively higher than with the jurisconsult, but, it seems,

not yet as high as with the director or chief engineer. Another negative aspect is the relatively great demands made upon the advocate by the regime for the purposes of propaganda.

The Court System

The most striking thing reported by the respondents regarding the court system is the low level of education of the judges. This is borne out by official Soviet statistics. (In 1947 over 60 per cent of the judges were without any legal training.) Generally, the judge has the least legal education of the persons participating in a trial or law suit in a professional capacity; the state procurator often is the only person in the court room who has a Soviet legal education; the jurisconsult often has a good pre-Revolutionary legal education, or at least a good general education which enables him to educate himself fairly rapidly in the law; the advocates vary considerably, being generaly superior to the judge, however.

Another striking bit of testimony, again confirmed by Soviet published sources, is the tremendous overload of cases on the court. This leads to the disposition of many economic cases in a most summary manner — twenty, thirty, and more cases being disposed of in a day, many without the participation of any legal counsel.

The role of the assessors, the two lay judges elected popularly (but probably selected by the Party or other agencies of the regime), is generally agreed to be without any substantial significance. In rare cases, the assessors will disagree with the judge as to the punishment, and sometimes they will persuade him to reduce the sentence or even overrule him. Their ignorance of the law, the prestige of the judge who represents the state, and the pressure of too many cases, however, keep them from playing any significant role for the present.

The procurators and the judges are Party members, and the procurator seems to be the person who conveys the Party line as to particular "campaigns," etc., to the judge. If necessary, the judge uses this information to convince a hesitant assessor; however, this seems to be rarely necessary. Conferences of procurators and judges are held, and verbal instructions and exhortations create the political atmosphere.

The court system as such seems a fairly inferior agency of the government, reliance for political control and state security being in other agencies. The Ministry of Internal Security has its own tribunals, and will refer cases without political significance to the courts with recommendations as to which article of the criminal code is applicable, or try certain cases in closed sessions of the regular courts. The outcome of such security cases, one may speculate, is fairly well decided by the Ministry of Internal Security.

Interference of the Party with ordinary cases was discussed above. It seems the exception rather than the rule, unless a Party member is involved. In such a case, the Party may discipline its own members, or may turn him over to the court with recommendations, or may communicate with the judge and instruct his decision.

The Conditioning Influence of the Political System

The use of the word "lawyer" with reference to the Soviet scene, so much as we have done so, requires some comment. To an American, the word "lawyer" has certain functional connotations which it would be well not to attach readily to the Soviet lawyer. The problem of dissociating these functional connotations from the word "lawyer" is a difficult and delicate one, and does not seem to have been satisfactorily solved in the relevant American writings.

The functions of an American lawyer may be grouped roughly into two categories, constituting, of course, only the most general classification: (1) the prediction of the incidence of state force; (2) the structuring of social relations.*

In order to predict the incidence of state force on a given fact situation with some accuracy, the lawyer must depend on the political system. The political system must provide reasonable certainty and stability in the formulation and execution of the laws; assurance that the framework of established government will be observed; and some degree of assurance that established standards of legal procedure will be observed. The system must fur-

---

* The classification is that of Professor Lon Fuller of the Harvard Law School.

ther provide an independent and impartial judiciary, clear and explicit laws, some method for filling in the lacunae among the laws (whether called "precedent" or not), and some procedures for review and appeal to correct mistakes and prejudice.

It may be justly pointed out that the limitations inherent in any scheme for government by law, and in human judgment, will prevent a perfect system of law from being realized in any society. Certainly American laws can be in many significant respects much improved. Nevertheless, knowing that we cannot rely completely on the American lawyer's predictions, substantially we do rely on them. We trust, by and large, to the political system to provide the framework within which reasonably accurate predictions can be made.

In the Soviet context, this is not true. In certain types of cases which we have called non-political — apartment difficulties, divorce suits, compensation claims — the Soviet lawyer may predict somewhat more reliably than in cases involving political considerations. But even in these non-political areas, the existence of unlimited power in non-legal agencies and organizations conditions all predictions. Denunciation on false grounds; the secret power, or connections with power, of seemingly innocuous individuals; and the capacity by those who wield power to give "political" significance to a case and thus apply a different set of criteria and procedures to them — all these factors of Soviet life are part also of the Soviet lawyer's life and influence the manner in which he functions.

In order for the lawyer to fulfill the second in our classification of functions, the structuring of social relations, the political and social system must likewise provide a scope of freedom for such relations wide enough to allow for a meaningful choice among alternatives. The Soviet system provides no such scope.

There is discussion as to whether the American political system too has not begun to narrow the scope of individual choice mischievously. In any case, in the Soviet Union the choice is so narrow, the governmental prescription of social relations so detailed and exclusive, that the Soviet lawyer can be substantially excluded from the category of social architects. For it to be otherwise, the Soviet lawyer must await a fundamental change in his social system.

MASS PERSUASION AND ITS EFFECTS

23

Mobilizing Public Opinion*

Alex Inkeles

(1961)

The state and the law have never been regarded by the Communist leadership as sufficient to the task of ruling and of moving Soviet society forward toward the goals set by the Party. To mobilize the people a massive apparatus of propaganda and agitation has been deemed necessary, not only to create support — or at least the external semblance of it — but to prevent the free flow of ideas and the development of allegiances which might resist or at least detract from the monolithic consecration to the Party's goals which Communism demands. Our next offering describes in detail the Soviet apparatus for mobilizing opinion, and suggests some lines for evaluating its effectiveness.

The Communist Party of the Soviet Union has developed an elaborate and complex apparatus designed to shape the thinking of the Soviet people.[1] Highly centralized, carefully controlled, and vigorously utilized, this ap-

---

* Reprinted from "Mobilizing Public Opinion in Soviet Russia," to appear in the first issue (early 1961) of the *Annuaire* of the Centre de Recherches sur l'U.R.S.S. et les Pays de L'Est, Faculté de Droit et des Sciences Politiques et Économiques de Strasbourg, by permission of the publisher.
[1] Since this paper is meant to serve as a general survey, I have drawn heavily on materials published elsewhere by me, and particularly on *Public Opinion in Soviet Russia*, Cambridge: Harvard University Press, 1950, "The Russians Don't Hear," *The Atlantic Monthly*, January 1951, and "Recent Developments in Soviet Mass Communications," *Gazette: International Journal of the Science of the Press* (Leiden), 4: 285–97, 1958.

paratus is guided by a distinctive theory and is motivated by a single purpose — to mobilize popular support behind the domestic and foreign programs of the Soviet rulers. Full exposure of the role of force in Soviet society has been a desirable antidote to the unrealistic pictures of Soviet life so frequently drawn during the thirties and the years of World War II. But in so far as this emphasis leads us to neglect the role of persuasion in Soviet society, our net gain may be a small one. For we cannot have an adequate assessment of Soviet strengths and weaknesses unless we take full account of Soviet efforts at mass persuasion.

It is widely and mistakenly assumed in the West that Soviet leaders are "uninterested" in public opinion. In fact, Leninist theory and Soviet practice reveal a most intense interest in the state of popular thinking. The crucial difference between East and West in this regard lies not in the presence or absence of interest, but in the nature of that interest.

Leninist-Stalinist theory conceives of the Communist Party as an informed, conscious elite, armed by Marxist theory with knowledge of the laws of social development. Its position in relation to the masses of the population is summed up in the recurrent Leninist-Stalinist description of the Party as the general staff of the proletarian army. But, the characterization continues, just as the general staff is impotent unless it is certain of the obedience of the rank-and-file soldier, so the Communist Party cannot proceed unless it is sure of the requisite amount of support or at least "benevolent neutrality" on the part of the popular masses. From these considerations stemmed Lenin's description of the Soviet regime as resting on a balance of coercion and persuasion.

Thus, the Leninist-Stalinist interest in public opinion does not derive from any desire to gauge public opinion in order to follow it. Indeed, Stalin has indicated that the Communist organization cannot constitute a true revolutionary party "if it limits its activities to *a mere registration* of the sufferings and thoughts of the proletarian masses." The Bolshevik leader seeks to gauge the feelings of the masses solely to determine whether or not they will support a program of action by the class-conscious "vanguard" organized in the Communist Party. And in so far as they will not, it becomes the task of the Communist

Party to take necessary measures of propaganda and agitation to bring the masses to the requisite state of support of the Party's efforts. The instrument of coercion is of course always available in reserve or sufficiently in evidence to hasten the process of persuasion.

To effect its goals of mass persuasion in the Soviet Union the Communist Party has established a special Department of Propaganda and Agitation. Within the framework of policy decisions set down by the former *Politburo*, and now by the Presidium of the Party's Central Committee, the Department unifies and gives central direction to the multifarious activities designed to influence public opinion carried on by the Party, the government, and agencies like the trade unions. At every level of the Soviet territorial-administrative structure down to the factory or collective farm, each Party unit has an equivalent section to direct the local work of propaganda and agitation in conformity with central directives. These units must bring the decisions of the Party and government to the people, explain them, seek to win popular support for them, and effect the mobilization of the population to secure their fulfillment. Not only are they the chief channel of communication from the Party to the people, but they are also one of the main means by which intelligence on the state of popular thinking is conveyed to the Party leaders.

To fulfill its responsibilities the Department of Propaganda and Agitation is divided into a series of sectors, each with a distinct sphere of operations — "cultural enlightenment," the press and publishing, the radio, the film, art, science, education, and so on. There is no realm of intellectual endeavor, no form of organized activity that might conceivably influence public opinion, which the Party exempts from scrutiny and control by its Administration of Propaganda and Agitation. Its activities range all the way from handling difficult and sensitive questions of the interpretation of Marxist texts to explaining to the ordinary workers why their work regulations have been changed; and from selecting the nationwide slogans for the annual Revolutionary holidays, to the detailed criticism of some obscure handwritten "wall-newspaper" in an outlying factory or farm. Its function, of the broadest scope, is exercised at a national level, yet its impact through the equivalent local units is felt at the lowest reaches of the society and in the smallest matters.

Although the Communist Party's Department of Propaganda and Agitation is the crucial agency in the control of Soviet mass communications, it does not actually operate the bulk of the major media. This is in accord with the general Soviet practice of placing day-to-day administrative and operating responsibility in the hands of government agencies, in order to leave the Party's units free to concentrate on policy-determination and on the control and supervision of the operating agencies. Consequently, the prime responsibility for the regular operation of the media of mass communication is concentrated in a series of government agencies directly under the Council of Ministers of the U.S.S.R. These include agencies or special committees concerned with art, the radio, the cinema, and printing establishments, which along with several other similar organizations controlling libraries and museums, circuses, theaters and musical institutions, were all grouped under a new Ministry of Culture established in March 1953.

Bolshevik Agitations

The media of mass communication in the Soviet Union are not only adjusted, as they are everywhere, to the facts of population and geography, but are adapted as well to the social structure of the U.S.S.R. and to the special purposes of the Party. This is most strikingly illustrated in the regime's reliance on a unique system of oral agitation. The Party maintains a huge corps of Bolshevik agitators who regularly number two million, but whose ranks may swell to more than three million at the time of special campaigns such as those surrounding Soviet elections. The agitators are the part-time, unpaid, "volunteer" voice of the regime in the ranks of the masses of the population. Selected primarily from among Party members, it is their task to bring the message of the Party to the people through direct face-to-face contact. Before or after the change of shift or in the rest-period in the plants and on the farms, and even in the workers' dormitories or at their apartments, the agitator is expected to gather together small groups of his fellow workers or residents to conduct his agitation. Whether he reads aloud some article from the daily press, describes some important recent decision of the Party or government, leads a critical discussion of the work performance of his group, or exhorts them to greater effort, he speaks in each case as the voice of the Party.

The Party's utilization of several million agitators naturally serves as a major supplement to the traditional media of communication, which are by no means fully adequate to the task of reaching a population of more than 200 million scattered over some 8.5 million square miles of territory, and speaking well over one hundred different languages and dialects. But the significance of the Bolshevik agitator is much greater than his role as a supplement to the radio and press. Group agitation is an unusual means of mass communication whose significance should be better understood in the West. Like all agitation and propaganda, that of the Communist Party is designed to affect attitudes, and through attitudes to affect action. Contemporary American research indicates that a group setting, and particularly group discussion, is generally a more effective instrument for changing attitudes than are the radio and the newspaper. To a large extent the work of the Bolshevik agitator, since it includes regular contact in a group setting and provides an opportunity for limited group discussion, creates a situation which should be conducive to effective attitude-formation. Thus, through its utilization of the Bolshevik agitator the Communist Party has capitalized on what is probably one of the most effective of all instruments for mass communication.

In addition, the work of the agitator provides a personal link between the Party and the people, unlike the impersonal radio or newspaper. He serves as a convenient target against which his audience may, in limited degree, direct hostility and discontent which otherwise mght be directed, even though covertly, against the leaders of the regime itself. The agitator also serves as a constant source of information on the attitudes and state of mind of the population. He is expected to keep a careful account of the questions asked and the problems in which the workers show special interest. These are collected and collated at the local level, and are supposed to be passed

up the Party hierarchy to the highest echelons. Thus the corps of agitators serves the Party as a kind of substitute for a system of scientific public opinion testing, since such testing is obviously not possible under Soviet political conditions.

The Soviet Press

Although far from being as novel a system of mass communication as is the network of agitators, the Soviet press is a distinctive phenomenon among the major press networks of the world. It is in no sense a business venture; neither is it conceived of as an instrument for expressing the opinions of individual publishers, nor as a means of mirroring public opinion. In the Soviet Union the press is viewed as a major social force which must be adapted and harnessed to facilitate attainment of the goals of the Communist Party. Lenin spoke of the press as "a collective propagandist, agitator and organizer," and Stalin characterized it as a "driving belt" between the Party and the masses. Khrushchev has in turn declared: ". . . the press is our chief ideological weapon . . . called upon to rout the enemies of the working class." This conception has had an impact on every aspect of newspaper work in the Soviet Union.

Bolshevik theory rejects the notion of freedom of the press as it is understood in the West. Objectivity as a goal of journalistic effort is similarly rejected. The resultant conception of what is news is remarkably different from that held by Western journalists. The private affairs of prominent persons in political and artistic life, and many other elements which are important as news in the United States play no role in the Soviet newspaper. The main ingredients of Soviet news are those events which have come to characterize the effort of the Communist Party to cement its control of Soviet society and to press the people on against all obstacles towards rapid industrialization of the country. Thus, the Soviet newspaper is constantly full of reports on such matters as the progress of the sowing or harvesting campaigns, or the "difficulties" experienced in building new industrial plants. If a lathe operator in some obscure plant in the Urals succeeds in increasing his production by 40 per cent, that fact may become front page news as the Soviet newspapers everywhere take up the story in an effort to secure adoption of the new methods of work speed-up. Or, to take an example from the field of ideology, it is almost beyond conception that *The New York Times* would devote almost half of its column space for a period of a week to a national conference of biologists which had met to formulate a basic "policy line" for the scientific work of American biologists, and to affirm the essentially "American" character of the environmental as against the hereditary approach to genetics. Yet it was the precise equivalent that *Pravda* did during one week of 1948, and such events are regular occurrences in the Soviet press.

By 1958 there were almost 10,000 newspapers in the Soviet Union with a total circulation approaching 58 million for the average "collective" single issue, although a very large proportion are printed only once or at best two or three times per week. Of the total, some 5,000 are printed in languages other than Russian, as part of the effort to provide each nationality group its native-language press and thus assure its exposure to the message of the Party. In addition, the Soviet press is carefully divided along territorial-administrative lines. Thus, in addition to the Communist Party's *Pravda* published in Moscow, each of the Soviet republics and most of the major urban centers have their own *Pravda*, patterned after the parent *Pravda* in Moscow. The newspapers are also carefully divided along functional lines into special networks, each ranging from nationwide central to local papers, and each designed to reach a special audience on the basis of occupation, age, sex, etc. There are about 150 newspapers for the youth, for example, headed by *Komsomolskaya Pravda*, with a circulation of almost two and a half million.

The printed newspapers are supplemented by a network of hundreds of thousands of mimeographed and "wall newspapers," put out in a single handwritten or typed copy on the bulletin boards of factories, farms, and housing developments. They report on the production activities of their plant or farm, give suggestions for the improvement of particular work processes, criticize those workers or shops which are lagging behind, praise those whose work is outstanding, and carry local notices of various kinds. It is characteristic of Soviet policy that these "wall-newspapers" are not haphazard or uncontrolled phenomena, but are rather considered as integral parts of the total press apparatus, with regular part-time editors and "correspondents," all closely supervised by the local Party organizations. Like the Bolshevik agitator, the wall-newspaper has the advantage of flexibility and adaptability to local conditions and needs. It represents another striking example of the Party's intense effort to utilize all resources, however meager, to extend the coverage of the regular means of communication and to increase their effectiveness.

The regular press no less than the wall newspaper is expected to give special emphasis to its letters-to-the-editor columns, which constitute a major part of the Soviet institution of *samokritika* or "self-criticism." Through these letters the Soviet citizen is provided a kind of open season on bureaucrats. So long as they are careful to select targets not too high in the power-hierarchy, and avoid any appearance of criticizing the regime or basic Party policy, Soviet citizens may through these letters vent rather strongly worded complaints against the work of the government bureaucracy in such matters as supplying consumers' goods, and repairing and maintaining housing and public facilities. In this way the Party leaders utilize the media of mass communication as a carefully controlled means whereby the population may drain off some of the aggression generated by the frustration of Soviet life, without permitting these complaints to call the system as such into question.

Control and Censorship

The elaborateness of the structure of the Soviet press is more than matched by the system of control and censorship. The editor of every Soviet newspaper and journal, including the wall-newspaper, is carefully selected by the Communist Party, and the editors of the more important newspapers are members of the executive committee of the corresponding levels of the Party organization. Each newspaper's work is directly controlled by the Party unit at the same level and is supervised by the Party organization at the next higher level. Each of the larger newspapers is expected to supervise the work of the newspapers of lesser importance in the same specialized segment of the press network. Thus, the central labor paper *Trud* is assigned particular responsibility for supervising and criticizing the trade union newspapers at all lower levels. Finally, there is the supervision of the relevant press sections of the Department of Agitation and Propaganda, and of *Glavlit*, the government censorship agency. The Party thus seeks to ensure that the instructions it issues will be effectively carried out at all levels of the press, and that the newspapers will serve as instruments of the Party in mobilizing population.

In its turn, the radio in the Soviet Union is not regarded as being primarily either a source of amusement or a means of recreation for the population. Like the press, it is conceived of as being first and foremost a channel of communication between the Party and the people, another one of those driving belts by which the Party seeks to mobilize the population behind its control. Despite its recognition of the importance of radio as a means of mass communication, the Soviet regime has been far from successful in covering the nation with an adequate radio network. The entire country had only about 130 broadcasting stations in 1956 and in 1958 there was only one radio for every nine persons in the population. This compares favorably with the poorer European countries such as Italy, but it is far below the ratio of sets to population in France (1:5) and the United Kingdom (1:4).

But what it lacks in size the Soviet radio system largely compensates for in its unique structure. About 75 per cent of the equipment capable of receiving radio programs in the Soviet Union does not consist of radio sets at all, but is rather made up of wired speakers. Each speaker is connected with a local "exchange" — of which there were by 1958 almost 36,000 — much in the manner of a telephone system. The main function of these "exchanges" is to re-transmit over their wires regular broadcasts sent out by the main radio stations such as Radio Moscow. The striking fact about these exchanges and their wired speakers is that the radio owner cannot choose the station to which he will listen, but must listen to the program, generally the *one* program, which is transmitted over the wires of his exchange. Thus, the system of wired speakers gives the regime a powerful instrument for the control of what the Soviet radio audience

may hear. This effectively cuts off the vast majority of the Soviet radio audience from contact with all non-Soviet stations, including the Voice of America. Yet the regime is able to stay in constant contact with the population even under conditions of aerial bombardment, since programs sent over wires cannot be used as a guide by hostile airplanes. During World War II in besieged Leningrad, for example, the city government maintained constant radio contact with the population even during German air raids. The sets were left on at all times, and when no program was being broadcast a metronome kept the wire alive. When approaching danger created the need for making a special announcement, the speed of the metronome's beat was increased to call the attention of the people to their radio speakers.

At the same time the radio exchanges are able to send their own programs over the wires to their subscribers. Thus, in addition to the greater control which they make possible, the exchanges give the Soviet radio a high degree of flexibility in adjusting the content of its broadcasts to the precise composition of the local radio audience served by any exchange. In so far as the Party seeks to mobilize the mind and will of the population behind its programs, it must of course adjust its appeals to the composition of the various audiences and to the particular functions which diverse groups play in Soviet society. This type of adaptation is made possible by the structure of the Soviet radio network, and the fact that the director of each radio exchange can know the precise social composition of the audience which subscribes to his exchange. Frequently these audiences are highly homogeneous, being predominantly made up of the peasants of a particular area, or the workers of a given factory or industrial district. As a result, the director of the exchange is able carefully to select the programs carried over his exchange's wires to suit them to the composition of that audience, and to the tasks set for it by the Party and government.

After a slow start, television has begun to be widely presented as a supplement to the Soviet radio. In 1958 there were two million sets served by 25 stations, and it was planned that by 1960 there would be 75 stations and 8 million receivers. There is some reason to believe the extensive capital outlay required for television does not have strong support because the regime has not yet learned to use it effectively for propaganda purposes. So long as it is seen mainly as a potential source of amusement by the regime, it will reecive much less priority than the well-proved press and radio propaganda network.

The Soviet film industry, like so many other aspects of mass communication in the U.S.S.R., is characterized by intense efforts to make maximum use of extremely scarce resources. In 1939 the country boasted only about 3,000 film theaters as against almost 20,000 for the United States. But by placing projectors in clubs, schools, libraries, and other public places, and by utilizing almost 15,000 portable projectors to show films in the villages, the number of installations was brought to a total of over 30,000. As a result of such measures the 45,000 projectors in operation during 1950 were expected to reach an audience of 1,100 millions. The number of film projectors of all types rose to 63,000 by 1957, although of these 26,000 were portable and mainly of the 16 millimeter type for use in schools and for rural village screening. Screen fare is provided by more than thirty studios which produced a high of 90 feature films in 1957, still about one-third the number produced in the United States, Japan, and India. In early years the modest output of films had to be supplemented by repeatedly re-showing old Soviet films, all others being ideologically unacceptable. In the late 1950's safe films could be imported from the Soviet satellites, and the internal "thaw" also made it possible to show a few films from other countries.

The Soviet film is as closely controlled by the Party as are the radio and the newspaper. The film in the U.S.S.R. is yet another weapon in the propaganda arsenal of the regime. Thus, the Minister of Culture told film workers in 1958 that they must produce films which show "the reorganization of the management of industry . . . and the struggle of farm workers to outstrip the United States in per capita production of meat, milk, and butter." As one Soviet film writer dolefully complained, Soviet studios put out "very little in the way of comedy, and no satire at all."

The position of the manager of a radio station or a director of Soviet films is not unlike that of the newspaper editor. The film director, for example, is subject to the orders of the Minister of Culture, who himself is instructed by the Central Committee of the Party. The director is also held personally responsible for carrying out the instructions of the Party, and is supervised in this respect by the film section of the Department of Propaganda and Agitation. In addition, his work, along with every stage of the film-making process, is supervised by a special "Art Council," made up largely of personnel carefully selected by the Party to insure the ideological "correctness" of Soviet films.

The impact of such directives on Soviet film directors can well be imagined. Difficulties with ideological correctness of their work, as the Soviets phrase it, create such strains on the film producers as to seriously hamper their productivity. It is not surprising, for example, that film comedies have not been produced with any great success in the Soviet Union, for the Party has ordered that even the amusing material in any film "must organize the thoughts and feelings of the audience in the required proletarian direction." As a result of shifts in the Party line many films are abandoned in the midst of production, and others are completed but are never shown. A striking example was presented in the postwar period when the film *A Great Life*, after having gone through all the stages of film control and censorship was finally shown on the screen. It was then made the subject of a special Party decision, found to be "extremely weak artistically and ideologically perverted," and ordered withdrawn.

Literature and the Theater

Literature and the theater in the Soviet Union have also been largely subverted from their status as arts and converted into instruments of mass communication designed to effect the mobilization of the population in support of the rule of the Communist Party. Although their difference "in form" is acknowledged, the novel and the play are both assigned propaganda responsibilities only slightly different from those of the newspaper and radio. In the U.S.S.R. literature must serve the interests of "the people, the Party, and the state." It must enter into the ideological war with the defined enemies of the Soviet state, discharging an obligation, as Politburo member Zhdanov phrased it for the writers of Leningrad, "to return blow for blow against all this vile slander and these attacks upon our Soviet culture, [and] also boldly to attack bourgeois culture which is in a state of degeneration and decay."

Since the novel, story, and play are clearly not well suited to the communication of news or information, their function has been primarily expository and didactic. Thus, in its decision of August 26, 1946, "On the Repertory of the Dramatic Theater and on Measures for Its Improvement," the Central Committee of the Communist Party declared that it "places before the dramaturgists and workers of the theater the task of creating . . . works on the life of Soviet society and on Soviet man . . . representing in their plays and performances the life of Soviet society in its unceasing forward progress. . . ." And in its decision on literature in the same month the Party charged the Soviet writer with responsibility "to aid the government in the correct upbringing of the youth, answering its queries, raising up a new generation, optimistic, undaunted by difficulties, and ready to overcome all obstacles." Literature, continued the decision, must focus on and develop the picture of a single basic hero "the foremost man of socialist society, the Party and non-Party Bolshevik." In this hero are to be concentrated all the prime virtues of the new Soviet man, for this is a hero "suffused with feelings of socialist duty, love of motherland, of unlimited readiness to give all his strength to the affairs of Communism, a capable man, with unlimited possibilities for development, constantly perfecting himself morally, and energetically building socialist society."

Given the tasks of literature and the drama in the Soviet scheme, one need not encounter any great difficulty in anticipating the image of the writer which Soviet leaders hold. Characterized by Stalin as "engineers of the soul," they were placed by the wartime Party boss of ideological and artistic matters, Andrei Zhdanov, "on the forward fighting line . . . of the ideological front." These "ideological workers" are gathered together in the Union of Soviet Writers of the U.S.S.R., which, as one might expect, was not a spontaneous creation of Soviet writers. Rather, it was called into being by a resolution of the Central Committee of the Communist Party in 1934, as the chief organizational form through which the Party transmits its influence and exercises its

control over Soviet literature. Before the War the Union had about 3,000 members, 1,300 of them being members of nationalities other than Great Russian. These "nationality" representatives are also organized in Writers' Unions in each of the federal republics of the U.S.S.R. and in several of the national areas of lesser importance.

The Writers' Union constitutes the chief means utilized by the Communist Party to effect its direction of the activities of Soviet novelists and playwrights. The President of the Union has generally been a prominent Soviet writer, but at the same time a reliable and trusted Party member. To insure the "correctness" of the decisions of the Union, however, the Secretary has usually been a trusted Party official assigned to watch over the Party's interests even though he himself was not a writer or had only the most tenuous connection with professional literary activity. In addition to these measures, the Party exercises a continuing supervision over the work of writers through the columns of criticism in the major newspapers such as *Pravda* and *Isvestia*, and particularly through the newspaper *Literary Gazette*, which is assigned responsibility for the day-to-day policing of the Soviet literary realm. Finally, as will have been noted from the important decisions quoted above, the highest authorities of the Party intervene directly on occasion to check "mistaken and harmful tendencies" and to reorient Soviet writers in accordance with the current Party line. In extreme cases a writer may, of course, easily be silenced, either for a short period or permanently.

To carry the approved literary message to the people the Soviet regime maintains a vast structure of theaters and publishing houses. There are well over 900 professional theaters in the U.S.S.R., and a large proportion of these have permanent repertory companies. Of the total number of theaters somewhat under half present plays in languages other than Russian. Furthermore, so that no audience will be neglected, there are more than 150 professional children's theaters, about half of which present live actors and the other half puppets. Organizationally this theater network shows something of the specialization and centralization of authority which characterizes the Soviet press. There is, for example, a special Central Theater of the Red Army in Moscow, which regularly presents plays with military themes. This central theater sets a model for and supervises military theater companies at lower military unit and territorial levels. Furthermore, to reach the peasantry and others in areas without direct access to a regular theater, there are special traveling companies which tour the countryside. These are frequently summer companies formed from the lesser stars of the regular theaters. This entire theater network is managed by the Theater Administration of the Committee on Arts within the Ministry of Culture. The Administration appoints the director of all theaters except for the most important, the director of the largest central theaters being appointed directly by the Committee on Art with the approval of the higher Party organs.

The bulk of the important publishing activities in the Soviet Union are centered in a complex organization known as the Union of State Publishing Houses (*Ogiz*), which has generally incorporated *Goslitizdat*, the publishing house specializing in *belles-lettres*. This publishing house, of course, works according to plan as does the membership of the Union of Writers, and it may be severely castigated if it turns out fewer new titles of novels and plays than its plan requires. The publishing house operates directly under the supervision of the Department of Propaganda and Agitation of the Communist Party's Central Committee. Its activities are also closely supervised by the government censorship agency *Glavlit*, although ironically the censor located by *Glavlit* in each publishing house must be paid by the publishing house in which he works. Books which win the favor of the Party may be produced in fabulous numbers. For example, Ostrovsky's 1937 novel, *How Steel Was Tempered*, reached 4,600,000 copies by 1944. Similarly, the play *Front* by Korneichuk, which appeared at the most critical point of the war, was serialized in *Pravda*, reproduced in an enormous number of copies, and *simultaneously* played in several hundred different theaters across the Soviet Union. Thus the Party seeks to insure that literary work which meets its approval and serves its needs is given really mass circulation.

In addition to its utilization of the Bolshevik agitator, the newspaper, radio, film, novel, and play, the Communist Party in the Soviet Union has harnessed even the plastic and pictorial arts. The whole presents an imposing picture of universal adaptation of the media of mass communication to the Party's ends. And the Party has equally adapted to its purposes the content of Soviet mass communication. It is not, as many mistakenly believe, entirely taken up with heavy treatises on Marxist theory. The Party does not hesitate, indeed it is all too quick, to draw on such time-tested formulas as nationalism and patriotism.

Effectiveness of Soviet Propaganda

It is true, of course, that there are serious chinks in the Soviet propaganda armor. The agitators, for example, are caught between the direct pressures and hostilities of the population from below, and the constant pressure of the Party from above, demanding that they exhort and goad on the population to still greater efforts and sacrifice. As a result thousands each year abandon their work as agitators. Editors must constantly be reprimanded for ideological "deviations" in their newspapers, films cannot be shown, books must be withdrawn. And the regime is in many respects a prisoner of its own system. For in so far as it wishes to judge the state of popular thinking it must rely either on the secret police or on the reports of the agitators and the newspaper editors. It is to the advantage of the police to exaggerate the extent of discontent, for this keeps them in business. As for the editors and agitators, they are responsible for public opinion in their areas. To report the true facts is often to expose themselves to criticism and stronger forms of reprimand for falling down on the job. The result is that they frequently withhold the truth, or present false, glowing pictures of their success.

Despite such deficiencies, however, there remains the hard fact of the regime's absolute monopoly of mass communication, and its consequent ability to control what the Soviet citizen sees and hears about events in the outside world. The strength of this monopoly is nowhere better illustrated than in the efforts of the United States government to reach the Soviet people through the Voice of America. Those efforts began with a tremendous handicap. At least 75 per cent of the potential audience for the VOA in Russia could not hear the broadcasts for the simple reason that their wired speakers could not pick up *any* aerial broadcasts. Then even that part of the audience which could hear the broadcasts was largely cut off by Soviet jamming.

The most problematic aspect of Soviet mass communications has always been its effectiveness. Even under the best of conditions it is difficult to assess the effects of mass communication. In the face of the almost complete inaccessibility of the Soviet audience, the topic seemed to defy analysis. Since the war, however, we have recorded the testimony of many thousands of escapees from the Soviet terror who became refugees during and after World War II. Then after 1955 it was possible for scholars and others to travel more or less freely in certain Soviet cities. Although neither of these sources is an adequate substitute for systematic opinion sampling under conditions of free communication, they do enable us to venture much further in assessing the effects of Soviet mass communications.

Our latest studies have given rather definitive results for an assessment of the patterns of exposure to Soviet mass communications. Soviet sources have always been noticeably silent about the audiences for the mass media, hinting that all segments of the population alike are avid consumers of the regime's communications. Numerous studies of other industrial countries, however, consistently reveal that there are marked differences in the "communications behavior" of individuals differing in education and occupation. Our data lead us to conclude that this is true for Soviet society as for other industrial countries. Among those working in the intelligentsia, over 80 per cent read newspapers frequently, and more than 60 per cent "frequently" listened to the radio. By contrast, among skilled workers the comparable figures were only 43 and 36 per cent, respectively, and among peasants from the collective farms only 16 per cent were regular newspaper readers and only 7 per cent listened to the radio frequently. Obviously the regime was being very effective in reaching the well educated and responsible people, but was doing much less well among the middle ranks and apparently was hardly hitting the peasants at all with its main battery. Those who were escaping this first line of attack were not necessarily being caught on the second wave. On the contrary, we found that those who were often exposed to one type of official communication were also often exposed to other types, and vice versa. For example, those in

the intelligentsia were reached by the more "personalized" communications, such as meetings and agitation sessions, as much as three times more often than were the peasants and ordinary workers. A similar contrast prevailed with regard to the movies, which were attended "often" by 53 per cent of the intelligentsia as against 17 per cent of unskilled workers and 7 per cent of the peasants.

In so far as there is any connection between exposure to Soviet mass communication and acceptance of its message, we should expect a much higher proportion of convinced Soviet Communists among those with better education holding more responsible positions. Such indeed was the finding in our studies of former Soviet citizens. This is not to deny the dramatic evidence of student discontent which from time to time has reached us from the Soviet Union. This more "political" and vocal segment of the population may generate the most vivid evidence of unrest while yet being the group which has been most shaped and molded to the main patterns of Soviet thought. Indeed, on the basis of our studies with former Soviet citizens, my own travels in the Soviet Union, and the full accounts of my colleagues who were also there in 1955–56, I am led to eschew any one-sided estimate of the effectiveness of Soviet mass communications. The dominant impression I took away was of the imposing effectiveness of a completely controlled system of mass communications operating under virtually complete monopoly conditions. Yet at the same time I was filled with awe at the extraordinary persistence of the human drive for trustworthy information, and amazement at the capacity of individuals to work their way to a personal assessment of the truth even when they were surrounded on every side by an endless barrage of highly organized official propaganda.

With a few notable exceptions the media of mass communication appear to have been extraordinarily effective in shaping the pattern of thought about public issues among Soviet citizens. This ranges all the way from matters of general ideology to matters of fact. It reveals itself in the strength of belief in such ideas as the welfare state or the notion that a society needs strong guiding hands such as that provided by the Communist Party; in the conviction that Soviet accomplishments in various economic fields are superior to those of other countries; and in estimates of the treatment of the Negro in the United States, or in the assessment of the British Labour Party's desire for peace. It seems clear that where the reporting of the regime's mass communication monopoly does not run too patently counter to the direct experience of Soviet citizens or does not challenge their basic values, it has a powerful grip on the Soviet mind and shapes it pretty much to the official image. Very often the official line does, of course, run counter to the direct experiences of Soviet citizens. This was especially true during the years of greatest hardship before the war and immediately afterward. It continues true today when the Soviet citizens can see in many areas, such as housing, how the large promises of the regime fall far short of the needs of the population. Although now more tempered in its attack, the Soviet press continues in many of its comments on religion, the family, friendship, ethnic loyalty, and work, to urge a pattern not congenial to the traditional culture, and consequently one which finds little response in important segments of the Soviet audience.

The most serious weakness of the Soviet press and radio continues to lie in its being unfree, a mere agent of government policy rather than a medium for conveying news and expressing opinion. This forces it of necessity to be tendentious, repetitive, arid, and often palpably insincere and untrue. In the brief "thaw" before the regime cracked down again, we secured "from within" a few glimpses of this condition, as in the following comment by a writer in the *Literary Gazette*: "Sometimes the noisy rumble of the prepared texts of speeches at the Young Communist League meetings has drowned out the worried voices of young consciences. At times a deadening formalism made the carrying out of important propaganda assignments meaningless. It was important to place 'jackdaws' (check-marks) in a column of assignments. 'Done.' How many good crops were picked clean by such jackdaws."

My contacts with Soviet citizens in the U.S.S.R. left me, as it did most of my colleagues, with a strong impression of their extraordinary hunger for honest and straightforward information about the world outside — especially about Western Europe and the United States. It is a strange anomaly that

while continuing to jam the Voice of America and making the free circulation of foreign non-Communist magazines almost impossible, the Soviet government nevertheless decided to permit more than half a million Soviet citizens to go abroad in 1956, a not insignificant proportion to visit Western Europe. However carefully these tourists may have been selected on grounds of political reliability, their observations cannot fail to affect their opinions, and the opinions of others they will talk to. There is, of course, nothing which could effectively prevent the regime from withdrawing the privilege of foreign travel and from restricting travel inside the Soviet Union by visitors from non-Communist countries. Unless the terror returns to dam up these new currents of information and ideas, however, they will act to constrain the freedom of the official monopoly from arbitrarily dispensing arrant nonsense instead of information and will press it toward greater frankness and honesty. This will hardly give the Soviet citizen a free press, but it may prove a step on the road toward that still distant attainment of freedom of thought and communication in Soviet society.

24

Political Alienation Among Former Soviet Citizens*

Raymond A. Bauer

(1955)

The regime's massive effort at manufacturing a favorable opinion in support of its forced march into industrialization was by no means uniformly successful. The brutal facts of Soviet policy, the desperate pace of its program, and the harsh conditions it imposed on people contributed to turning many against the regime and greatly weakened the allegiance of others. Professor Bauer explores the sources of alienation from the Soviet regime, basing his analysis

* Reprinted from "Some Trends in Sources of Alienation from the Soviet System," *Public Opinion Quarterly*, Vol. 19 (1955), pp. 279–291, by permission of the author and the publisher.

on the testimony of former Soviet citizens. Many of the conditions he describes are, of course, historically limited. The Stalinist terror has largely been lifted, the Soviet standard of living has been steadily rising, and the whole tone of Soviet life greatly mellowed under the new dispensation. Yet it is evident from the letter by a Soviet student — which we present next — that the preservation of faith in the regime is an uncertain affair in the face of the stark realities of Soviet policy.

This article contains certain quantitative data which support a number of propositions about changes in sources of alienation from the Soviet system. These data derive from the interviews and questionnaires which were gathered from Soviet refugees in 1950–1951 by the Harvard Project on the Soviet Social System.[1] The propositions in themselves are not new. They were originally arrived at on the basis of a qualitative analysis of the life history interviews in our data, and have already been presented in that form in other documents.[2] Probably no one of these propositions is in itself novel among "Russian experts," but it is doubtful that they would be received with a high degree of consensus. Since the later statistical analyses yielded substantial quantitative confirmation of the earlier qualitative impressions, it seems worthwhile to report their verification. The value of these propositions lies not so much in giving a picture of what *has* happened in the Soviet Union, but rather as a characterization of the way in which

a population adjusts to a revolutionary social and political order and as a basis for predicting future developments in the Soviet Union and in other countries behind the Iron Curtain.

It goes without saying that there are exceedingly complicated methodological problems in the use of these data. A full discussion of the assumptions and precautions employed will soon be available in print.[3] For the purposes of this paper, however, it is perhaps sufficient to argue that since we are concerned with the process of alienation, the use of an alienated sample is justified without further explanation. Nor does the representativeness or unrepresentativeness of the sample on other dimensions than allegiance to the Soviet regime generally pose a problem, since no attempt is made to estimate population parameters in the U.S.S.R. We are concerned with trends and relationships where the relative magnitude and direction of differences count, but absolute magnitudes are less important. Furthermore, the data which are presented here must not be considered as in all instances *demonstrating* the points to be made. The statistics cited are backed in most instances by a considerable number of additional statistics, and by a good deal of qualitative evidence.

In the main, the tabular material is based on some 2700 questionnaires administered in Europe and in the United States. In two instances the data are based on smaller samples: one on 327 life history interviews, the other on a questionnaire sub-sample of approximately 700 cases. Even where the smaller samples are employed the differences with which we are dealing are sufficiently large and the trends so consistent within the data that employment of tests of statistical significance would be pedantry.

One limitation on these findings should be noted. The *younger* generation of which we speak is composed essentially of people who grew up after the Revolution but left the Soviet Union by 1943. For practical purposes the statistical findings end with that period. However, extended qualitative interviews with some eighty postwar refugees, the shared judgment of other groups of investigators who have dealt

[1] The work of this project was done under Air Force Contract No. 33(038)–12909.

[2] It is difficult to assign adequate credit to all the persons who contributed to this analysis. Many of the conclusions, in fact in many instances the very same quantitative analyses were arrived at independently by analysts working on separate problems. The two pieces of work which most parallel this present article, and to which I am also to a large degree indebted are:

David B. Gleicher, *The Meaning of Hostility*, mimeo, Cambridge, 1955 and — Alice Rossi, *Generational Differences in the Soviet Union*, submitted as a Ph.D. dissertation, Columbia University, 1955.

The earlier reports of our qualitative impressions were made in: Raymond A. Bauer, *The Psychologist and the Study of Soviet Political Allegience*, mimeo, Cambridge, 1953 and *The Social Psychology of Loyalty to and Disaffection from the Soviet Regime*, mimeo, Cambridge, 1954.

[3] Alex Inkeles and Raymond A. Bauer, *The Soviet Citizen: Daily Life in a Totalitarian Society*, Cambridge: Harvard University Press, 1960.

with various groups of postwar defectors, and an assessment of developments in the Soviet Union since the war based on official Soviet statements all indicate that the trends which the analysis uncovers would be accentuated in the youngest generation.

The main points to be made are:

1. Difficult conditions of day-to-day living probably produce hostility toward the Soviet order, but this type of hostility is seldom sufficient to produce alienation of sufficient intensity to cause a person to flee the system.

2. An accumulation of ideological opposition to the regime coupled with unsatisfactory life conditions probably is an effective force in alienation of the older, pre-Revolutionary generation; but for succeeding generations alienation depends more on some specific, personal conflict with the system which involves either rejection by the system or loss of faith in its power and influence.

3. Alienation from the Soviet system does not by any means involve rejection of all of its institutional features. As a matter of fact, as time passes, succeeding generations come to take its institutional features more or less for granted and blame the failures and faults of the system on the men who run it.

The Effect of Standard of Living

Everyone who follows the newspapers is aware of Mr. Malenkov's recent difficulties and in particular the controversy over whether or not more attention should be paid to consumer's goods in the Soviet Union and the satellite countries. One would probably need no more evidence than this to conclude that

the standard of living of the Soviet people is something less than they would desire. The qualitative interviews are saturated with complaints about food, clothing, housing, and conditions of work, and the quantitative data indicate that the low standard of living of the Soviet populace produces hostility toward the Soviet order.

Expression of hostility on various indices of hostility[4] was strongly correlated — independently and for all subgroups of the sample — with all the individual conditions of life on which our respondents reported: social class membership, pay, occupation, degree of satisfaction with the job, whether they thought the pay was commensurate with the job, etc.[5] Such relationships existed between reported conditions of day-to-day existence, criteria of hostility to the Soviet System such as atttudes toward the leadership, willingness to drop an A bomb on Moscow, etc., and an "index of distortion." Table 1 illustrates one of these relationships, between hostility and social class membership, and shows that the greatest hostility is expressed by those groups with the poorest standard of living.

The criterion of hostility employed in this table, the so-called index of distortion, was originally developed by Lee Wiggins of Colum-

---

[4] Obviously the entire sample must be regarded as in some sense hostile to the Soviet system. More properly our indices are indices of *relative* hostility. We are comparing the most hostile with the least hostile.

[5] These relationships are reported in detail in David B. Gleicher's *The Meaning of Hostility*, Cambridge mimeo, 1955.

TABLE 1 *The Relationship of Hostility to the Soviet Union to Social Class*

Social Group	Per Cent Expressing Moderate or Great Hostility*	Number
Intelligentsia.........	28%	(555)
Employees	30	(595)
Skilled workers	45	(228)
Ordinary workers	58	(381)
Peasants............	58	(290)

* Expression of hostility is related to the standard of living of the social class of which one is a member.

TABLE **2** *Relationship of Hostility Toward the Soviet Union to Arrest Experience and to Job Satisfaction*

PROPORTION OF PERSONS EXPRESSING MODERATE OR GREAT HOSTILITY			
Arrest History	Hostile	Job Satisfaction**	Hostile
Self arrested	52%	Low	55%
Family member arrested	47	So-so	46
No arrests	27	High	32

* In this and the following two tables, since hostility and job satisfaction are related to social group membership, social group is held constant by averaging the percentage figures obtained for each social group. This has the effect of giving equal weight to each group. The trends shown in these tables are of course revealed within each social group.
** It would seem that job-satisfaction, as a summary index of standard of living, is as highly correlated with hostility as is history of arrest to self or family.

bia University as an instrument of data control. Respondents were presented with a series of factual statements about the Soviet Union, such as that tractor production had increased, or literacy had improved. The intent of this was to put them on their mettle to see whether they would "tell the truth" even if it seemed to reflect favorably on the Soviet system. Extensive experience with this index indicated that it was an excellent measure of hostility to the Soviet system.

One may object that all of these items may be part of a generalized attitude toward the Soviet system, that persons hostile to the Soviet system will recall or report their life in the Soviet Union gloomily. If these people give a generally jaundiced picture of their life in the Soviet Union, they might also distort their reports of certain other items. They ought, for example, to be more likely to say they were always opposed to the Soviet system. But when they were asked this question there was no indication that hostility toward the Soviet system, as expressed on this "index of distortion," was in any way related to a disposition to report preferentially that one had always opposed the Soviet order. All-in-all, the weight of this statistical evidence supports the impression gained from the qualitative interviews, namely that the generally unsatisfactory conditions of life in the Soviet Union generate some measure of hostility toward the system.

Our contention, however, is that hostility generated from this source is seldom sufficient to produce alienation in great intensity. To support this contention we must turn our attention to other criteria of disaffection and to other sources of disaffection.

Standard of living is only one of the day-to-day circumstances of life which may produce hostility. There is also the impact of the political police. It is instructive to compare the relative impact of these two "determiners of hostility" on several criteria of alienation. As a measure of the individual's reaction to his standard of living we may use an index of job satisfaction, an index which is compounded of both subjective and objective aspects of his job situation. For the impact of the secret police, we have the respondent's report of whether he or a member of the family was ever arrested. The results are reported in Table 2. Obviously we are dealing here with very crude instruments, and the most that we can say from these data is that the two sources of hostility, dissatisfaction with one's job and having an arrest in the family, make about the same order of contribution to feelings of hostility to the system. About the same increment of "hostility" is found if we compare persons who say their standard of living was "better" or "worse" than that of the majority.

Table 3 represents still another attempt to assess the relative impact of arrest and standard of living on hostility to the Soviet system. The criterion of hostility employed here was the individual's assertion that he had wanted to leave or had attempted to leave the Soviet Union prior to his actual departure which was in fact involuntary in a majority of instances. The table was organized so that we might assess the effect of these two "determinants" of hostility independently of each other. When each "determinant" of hostility is held constant, the other effects a change of exactly 18 per cent in the proportion of persons reporting they *wanted* to leave the Soviet Union.[6] For example, among persons of the same degree of job satisfaction, those persons who reported an arrest to themselves or a member of their family were 18 per cent likely to be "hostile" on this criterion of hostility. Similarly, among persons of identical arrest status, those "dissatisfied" with their jobs were 18 per cent more likely to be hostile. There is a fairly marked relationship of about the same order of magnitude between one of our criteria of hostility to the system and these two "sources" of hostility, day-to-day conditions of life, and arrest by the Soviet secret police.

---

[6] The initial decision to use a two-way break and the choice of conventions in collapsing a number of other categories produced by accident these "perfect" results. Obviously it is improbable that such complete symmetry would be obtained if other conventions were employed.

Saying that one wanted to leave the Soviet Union is one thing, but actually leaving it voluntarily is another. More than half our sample reported that they had left involuntarily, having either been captured as soldiers, or forcibly evacuated from German occupied territory. Table 4 repeats Table 3 except that the reported *actual* departure is used as a criterion of alienation, in place of the reported *desire* to leave. There is an appreciable overlap of these two criteria, but as these data show they are far from identical. Whether or not a person was satisfied with his job, an arrest to himself or a member of his family increased sharply the probability of his reporting that he had left the Soviet Union voluntarily, whereas degree of job satisfaction has virtually no relationship to this more stringent criterion of alienation. I say "virtually" no relationship despite the fact that Table 4 contains a spuriously perfect result by accident of the way in which categories were combined. The question of "degree" of alienation is of course a difficult one with which to deal. The assumption that voluntary departure involves "more" alienation than wanting to leave or expressing

TABLE 3 *Relationship of Job Satisfaction and Arrest History to Desire to Leave the Soviet Union**

PER CENT CLAIMING TO HAVE WANTED AND/OR TRIED TO LEAVE				
	Dissatisfied with Job		Satisfied with Job	
	Per Cent	Numbers	Per Cent	Numbers
Arrest to self and/or family	78	511	60	434
No arrests	60	105	42	113

* This table was controlled by social class so as to give equal weight to each class.

TABLE 4 *Relationship of Job Satisfaction and Arrest History to Actual Mode of Departure Reported**

PER CENT CLAIMING VOLUNTARY DEPARTURE				
	Dissatisfied with Job		Satisfied with Job	
	Per Cent	Numbers	Per Cent	Numbers
Arrest to self or family	44	655	44	533
No arrest experience	27	120	27	146

* Controlled for class.

anti-Soviet attitudes has a good deal of *a priori* validity. That this assumption should result in these particular findings of course reenforces the faith in the initial assumption.

It should not be surprising that contact with the secret police in the form of an arrest to one's self or a member of one's family produces a higher degree of hostility and alienation than does a low standard of living. What is more interesting, however, is that both of these sources of alienation result in about the same order of "verbal hostility." But, assuming that in *most* instances reports of whether a person left voluntarily or involuntarily are "true," it is only arrest that has any appreciable effect on active alienation in the form of leaving voluntarily. We would not of course argue that active alienation takes place *only* among persons rejected by the system. We have, for example, not touched as yet on the question of ideological sources of opposition to the system. This will be taken up shortly. However, we have the distinct impression that, in the younger generation in particular, situational factors are becoming increasingly important as *the* effective source of alienation, that the younger generation becomes alienated not because of ideological opposition or dissatisfaction with his personal life conditions, but because something happens which gives him the status of a second-class citizen unable to pursue a normal career in Soviet society, or able to do so only under conditions of extreme anxiety in which he fears that his past will be held against him.

Generational Trends in Sources of Alienation

Whether in fact alienation on the basis of such situational factors as we mentioned above is in fact the *modal* pattern in the younger generation cannot be established with our data. However, there is strong quantitative evidence that the *trend* is very definitely in this direction.

The first piece of evidence has to do with the relative impact of arrest on alienation in the older and younger generation. Table 5 summarizes the relationship of arrest experience to voluntary departure within two age groups, those who were 21 or younger at the time of the Revolution, and those who were over 21 years old. We see that among the older generation about 50 per cent claim to have left voluntarily regardless of whether they had experienced an arrest to themselves or a member of their family or not. There is a slight relationship, but it is very modest. But among the younger generation the proportion claiming to have left voluntarily is about doubled for those persons who reported some direct contact with arrest — 49 per cent asserting they left voluntarily in contrast to 26 per cent among those who reported no direct contact with arrest. This suggests the older people may have been saturated with grievances to the point where an arrest in the family made some, but relatively little, difference in their degree of alienation from the regime. But in the younger generation it took the dramatic impact of such an event, threatening them with the permanent status of a second class citizen, to make them decide to depart voluntarily.

Let us remember this proposition for a moment, and turn to another of our qualitative impressions, that the loyalty of the younger generation is increasingly dependent on their image of the strength of the system. We concluded on the basis of our qualitative interviews that the younger people were proportionately prouder of the strength of the system, and, further, seeing no viable alternative to accommodate to it they repressed or suppressed their doubts about it rather than run the risk of open conflict with it. Loss of faith in strength of the system, we concluded, had two effects. It destroyed their pride and confidence in the system, and, it permitted them to let their suppressed doubts come to the surface.

We asked a group of people who had lived under the German occupation whether or not they thought during the first few years of the war the Germans would win. As Table 6 shows, young people who thought the Germans were going to win were more than twice as likely to have left voluntarily in comparison to those who did not expect German victory; whereas, people over forty-five appear to have been uninfluenced by this factor. Again, holding for only a minimum interpretation, we have additional evidence that situational factors affect voluntary departure in the younger generation much more strongly than in the older generation. Further more we shall see shortly that younger people cited exposure to the West frequently as a reason for turning against the system — an experience which our quali-

TABLE 5   *Voluntary Departure According to Arrest History and Age*

Arrest History	21 Years or Younger at Time of Revolution		Over 21 Years at Time of Revolution	
	Per Cent	Number	Per Cent	Number
Respondent arrested	49%	(140)	58%	(262)
Arrest in family only	38%	(731)	54%	(380)
Neither respondent nor family arrest	26%	(215)	45%	(51)

tative interviews showed to have produced disillusionment and lack of faith in the system.

All the foregoing evidence strengthens our contention that active alienation is based progressively less on ideological factors in the younger generation. But we have additional, more direct, evidence for this.

Our respondents were asked whether they had always been opposed to the Soviet regime or had once been in favor of it. If we hold social group membership constant (i.e., give equal weight to each group) we see in Table 7 that the younger people are considerably more likely to say they had at one time favored the regime. Among persons over fifty in 1950–51 (about 17 years old at the time of the revolution) 82 per cent claim always to have been opposed to the Soviet system. This is true of only 55 per cent of those persons born after 1920 (30 or younger in 1950–51). We cannot, of course, consider these to be good estimates of the proportion of people who actually favored or opposed the regime at one time, since the pressures of the interview situation must have biased the distribution of answers away from admitting even past support for the regime. These are minimal estimates of regime sup-

port. But these answers do reflect a marked trend over time, and the proportion of avowed one-time adherents continues to rise step by step among the younger groups. If we consider the strength of this trend, the direction of both response and sample bias in our data, and the evidence of our qualitative interviews, particularly with postwar escapes, we would seem to be well warranted in assuming that the majority of young Soviet citizens begin life with an initial acceptance of the system.

In Table 8 we have summarized the reasons people offered for being opposed to the regime, or for turning from it if they had once favored it. Several things strike us at a casual glance.

1. Persons who claim always to have been opposed to the regime are more likely to cite ideological reasons for their opposition. The rate at which ideological reasons were cited in general in answer to this question seems somewhat to inflate the role of ideological sources of alienation as judged by references to ideology in our oral interviews. This is to a great extent a function of the fact that the term "ideological" was very broadly defined and included such things as "absence of personal

TABLE 6   *Percentage Voluntary Departure According to Age and Opinion of German Chances for Victory*

German Chances for Victory	21 Years or Younger at Time of Revolution		Over 21 Years at Time of Revolution	
	Per Cent	Number	Per Cent	Number
Thought at beginning Germans would win..	46%	(309)	52%	(197)
Did not think Germans would win	19%	(119)	51%	(65)

TABLE **7** *Relationship of Age to Claiming Always to Have Been Opposed to the Soviet System*

Age in 1950	Per Cent Claiming Always to Have Been Opposed	Total
Under 30	55	499
31–40	61	643
41–50	72	534
50 & over ...	82	485

freedom" which are "ideological" only under the broadest possible definition of the term. However, this in no way affects our proposition that such reasons are cited most often by people who claim always to have been opposed to the regime.

2. Younger people are less likely to cite ideological reasons regardless of whether they claim always to have been opposed or not. Since they are also much less likely to claim always to have been opposed to the regime,

there are two reenforcing trends that indicate that ideological factors are less relevant for the defection of the young.

3. Distinctive reasons offered by the youngest group are reaction to police terror, and exposure to the West. The latter factor, as we know from our qualitative interviews, spelled disillusionment for many young Soviet citizens. They found they had been deceived by the regime, which pictured capitalist countries as impoverished.

TABLE **8** *Reasons for Turning Against the Soviet System or for Having Been Always Opposed to It, by Age*

AGE IN 1950	REASONS								TOTALS
	Terror	Agricultural and Other Econ. Policies	Standard of Living	Ideo.	Leaders	False Promises	Exp. to West	Other	
Persons Who Were Once in Favor:									
Under 30.....	36%	14%	7%	14%	3%	12%	26%	11%	225
31–40	37	25	13	26	4	10	18	12	248
41–50	29	37	11	30	7	12	6	12	148
50 & Over....	15	58	39	35	9	3	3	27	74
Persons Who Claimed Always to Have Been Opposed:									
Under 30.....	47%	20%	16%	48%	5%	5%	17%	14%	274
31–40	25	14	9	45	10	7	8	12	395
41–50	27	12	7	59	11	9	5	9	386
50 & Over....	28	14	5	64	12	7	3	6	411

Certain of these trends are inhibited in the youngest age group. In Table 7, the rate of decrease in the proportion of persons claiming always to have been opposed to the Soviet regime is somewhat decreased. In Table 8, I would call your attention to the group under 30 years of age in 1950 who claimed always to have been opposed; 47 per cent of them claim that the police terror was a source of opposition. Among those claiming always to have been opposed to the regime, this youngest group cites the police terror much more often than any other age group. The reason, I think is clear. These are the youngsters who were 17 years or younger during the period of the "Great Purges" in the late thirties, and the atmosphere of political terror hit them with particular strength before their political opinions were well formed. Even the oldest of them was probably only 15 years old when the purges started. Therefore, they are more likely to cite terror as a reason for being *always* opposed. Probably for the same reasons they continue to cite ideological reasons, such as lack of liberty, at a relatively high rate. They actually show a slight reversal of trend, with 48 per cent of this youngest group offering ideological reasons for being opposed, as compared to 45 per cent of the next older group. We are clearly dealing with the impact of historical events rather than with life cycle differences. To some extent this is an assurance that we are dealing with historical changes rather than with life-cycle phenomena. Of equal importance, if our inferences are correct, it would appear that the impact of specific historical events has repressed rather than augmented the trends we have been describing in our data. If there were available a comparable sample of persons who grew up *after* the "Great Purges" we would expect that the proportion who were once in favor of the system would be higher than any of the age groups in our present sample, and the proportion of persons citing ideological reasons would be lower.

All-in-all the trend over time appears to be quite strong that the younger a Soviet refugee is the less likely he is to cite an ideological reason for turning against the regime. The import of this finding is further bolstered by data not reported in this table. We found that among people who had once been in favor of the regime (again holding social class constant) the younger were about twice as likely to cite some direct personal experience as the reason for turning against the system (something that happened to themselves) as were the older people.

The Focus of Alienation

From *what* are people alienated? Is it the leadership? The "system" in some abstract way? Do they reject the social and economic forms of Soviet society?

We have been tempted at times to say that alienation is not from "the system" but from the regime, from the men who run the system. The complication in this statement, however, is that "the system" is thought of by Soviet refugees in a very diffuse way as encompassing the leadership, the police terror, a variety of other totalitarian features, and a few such economic forms as the collective farm system. The most accurate statement that could be made I suppose is that in their thinking "the system" is that to which they are opposed, and that which they favor is regarded as outside "the system." One thing the data establish beyond a doubt is that alienation from the Soviet order does not constitute an undifferentiated rejection of all the institutional forms that we ordinarily associate with that society. Even the most alienated of Soviet refugees seemed to approve of the welfare state in principle. Almost everybody was opposed to the collective farm system, and the police terror. But, on the other hand, almost everybody favored state ownership of the basic economy and social welfare practices, such as socialized medicine. This held true regardless of how "alienated" a person was as judged by a wide variety of criteria of alienation.

There were some inter-group differences in the types of social and economic institutions one favored. Members of the intelligentsia, for example, were twice as likely to favor return of light industry to private ownership as were the peasants and ordinary workers. Differences such as these, however, seemed to be entirely a function of social class and not of extent of alienation from the Soviet order.

In Table 9 we see an interesting illustration of the extent to which hostility to "the system" does not necessarily mean rejection of specific institutional features. At one point in the questionnaires respondents were asked what features of the Soviet system they would keep if the present regime were overthrown. A considerable proportion were so opposed to "the Soviet system" in general that they said they would keep nothing. This proportion ranged from a quarter of the intelligentsia to a half of the peasantry, a finding that confirms what we reported earlier, that the lower classes expressed more "verbal" hostility to the system. But at other points in the questionnaire the very same people who said they would "keep nothing" of the system indicated that they favored in principle such institutions as state ownership of transport and communications, of heavy industry, and favored government guaranteed work. We see in Table 9 that a minimum of 80 per cent of persons who said they would keep "nothing" of the system favored such institutional aspects of it, and that these proportions were virtually identical with those of persons who had specified something to keep. Again the same sort of result was obtained on a variety of indices of alienation. We saw above, for example, that exposure to arrest had a marked effect on the rate of voluntary departure from the Soviet Union — our most stringent criterion of hostility. Yet it had virtually no effect on attitudes toward such social and political institutions as we have been talking about.

With all of the appropriate reservations it is nevertheless true that the Soviet citizen tends to blame the failures of the system on the men who operate it rather than on its social, economic, and to some extent even po-

litical institutions — again making exception of the collective farm system and the secret police. Furthermore, this trend is increasing in time. Alice Rossi, in her study of generational differences among our respondents, found that the younger people were more inclined to favor the institutional structure of Soviet society — state ownership, control, and planning, and welfare institutions — and simultaneously more inclined to favor violent treatment to the Soviet leaders in the event of the overthrow of the regime.[7] This would suggest that the younger people are increasingly disposed to blame the failures of the system on the leaders and less on the institutions. There is an interesting confirmation of this in data assembled by Mrs. Rossi and presented in Table 10. This table shows the proportions of respondents who said that the Soviet Union would have been better if there had been a different leadership. Despite the small number of cases — these data come from our oral interviews rather than from the written questionnaires — there is a strong tendency for the younger people of both upper and lower social groups to be more likely to feel that the responsibility for things lies with the leadership rather than with the institutions. Final reenforcement for this notion can be found in Table 8 where we find a steep decline in the citation of government agricultural and economic policies as a reason for turning against the regime.

Alienation varies in its intensity, its origins,

---

[7] Alice Rossi, op. cit.

TABLE 9 — *Comparison of People Who Said They Would "Keep Nothing" in the Soviet System with Other Respondents on Their Acceptance of Specific Institutional Features in Other Contexts*

Favors:	Said Would "Keep Nothing"		Specified Some Things to Keep	
	Per Cent	Number	Per Cent	Number
1. State ownership of transport and communications	84	540	90	1144
2. State ownership of heavy industry	82	541	87	1144
3. Government guarantee of work	85	539	85	1132

TABLE **10**   *Proportions Saying Soviet Union Would Have Been Better if There Had Been Different Leadership*

Age in 1950	Intelligentsia—White-Collar		Workers—Peasants	
	Per Cent	Number	Per Cent	Number
Under 35........	49	(43)	55	(44)
36–45	35	(46)	44	(25)
Over 45........	32	(54)	27	(26)

and its focus. Furthermore, in a population exposed to a new social and political order there will be profound changes in each of these dimensions of alienation between successive generations. I have argued that the younger generations of Soviet citizens have come progressively to accept the Soviet system initially, and turn from it, if they do, because they have been rejected by it and/or have lost faith in its strength rather than for ideological reasons, or because they are dissatisfied with general conditions of life. Although the data presented here cannot be considered rigid proof of these propositions, they do support the qualitative impressions derived from the analysis of life history interviews with refugees. The propositions rest on the convergent impact of several sorts of data. The accumulated weight of several sources of evidence pointing strongly in the same direction permits confidence in these conclusions.

25

Ferment Among the Youth*

An Anonymous Soviet Student

(1957)

We have already referred to this letter as evidence that the sources of alienation in Soviet

* Excerpts from a letter written by a Soviet student in January 1957, first pubished in *Forum*, an Austrian monthly (February 1957) and translated in *The Nation* (April 6, 1957), p. 297. Reprinted with permission of both publishers.

society are not all in the Stalinist past. The agitation reflected in this letter is no longer visible on the surface in the U.S.S.R. today, but the readiness to question, which it reveals, must be assumed to be still there.

Moscow

November 30, 1956, is a memorable day for us Russian students; some say, a historic day. After Professor B. E. Syroechkovich's required lecture on Marxism-Leninism (in Moscow State University) there followed the usual discussion, during which a student . . . posed a question of decisive importance, perhaps the question which will determine the destiny of our form of Marxism: How was it possible for a general strike to occur in a Socialistic state — to speak plainly, in the Hungarian People's Democracy — since a general strike against a workers' and peasants' government was impossible?

Professor Syroechkovich was only able to give as an answer what we could read in our daily newspapers. For a discussion at the university level this was too little. He began to speak about the terror of Horthy-fascistic officers and diversionist Western imperialists, but his words were drowned in the protests of the students, who proved to him with a flood of Lenin quotations that he had not attempted to answer the actual question. . . . The discussion became noisy and confused and the professor preferred to withdraw. . . .

On the following day the notice boards of the Komsomol organization of the University carried hand-written sheets demanding an honest report and a frank discussion of the situation in Hungary. By lecture time, the notices had been removed, but their contents spread that morning from mouth to mouth.

At midday fresh notices were posted announcing a meeting of the Komsomol, at which the "shameful" events of the previous day were to be discussed. The meeting took place in the Ostrovsky Clubroom and was opened by Linkov, the secretary of the Komsomol Organization. His first remark necessarily acted as a provocation to most of those present: he declared that it was the Komsomol's duty to avoid in the future "such excesses as had degraded the academic halls" the day before. The result was only that a new "excess" immediately developed. In a quickly improvised vote, "The Hungarian Question in the Light of Marxism-Leninism" was declared the only item on the agenda and thus the control of the discussion was wrested from the officers. The very first speaker spoke of an "over-bureaucratized system" which had estranged itself from the masses and was therefore trying to maintain itself with the methods of the recently unmasked Beria.

This referred to Hungary, but the comparison with the Soviet Union was obvious and was even . . . spoken of openly: if the conclusions reached by the Twentieth Party Congress are not followed up, must we not expect a similar development here and will not our workers rise one day under the banner of Lenin against those who have developed into their bourgeois, bureaucratic exploiters? When Linkov objected to these "anti-party sentiments," and tried to get the floor from the speaker, he encountered such vehement opposition among the students that he left the hall together with his associates. But the discussion continued and even involved several activists of the Komsomol. . . .

On December 3 the administration actually expelled 140 students because of "khuligans-tvo" (rowdyism) and at the same time announced that the lectures on Marxism-Leninism would be suspended until after the New Year's holidays.

It was the first time in the history of the Moscow University that the administration found itself forced to suspend lectures because the teaching staff was not equal to dealing with questions which might arise in the discussions. The student body recognized in this a victory which they had bullied out of the Komsomol. Contrary to the expectations of the Komsomol secretaries, who counted on an

ebbing of excitement, the discussions in the clubs and student quarters continued. . . .

The significance which the Komsomol attributed to the discussions at the university had the interesting result that similar discussions broke out in other places too. In the middle of December, the Komsomol activists of the Moscow army district were forced to convene in order to deal with similar developments in the garrison. We in Moscow also heard of occurrences at the Leningrad universities. . . . Lively discussions are also in progress at the universities in Kiev, Kharkov, Sverdlovsk, Novosibirsk, and even in central Asia, in Tashkent.

Almost the whole of the Soviet youth has been seized by the wave of discussions. This is undoubtedly one of the most interesting political movements to have emerged since Stalin's death. Significantly enough, however, it was not started by the men in power, not "from above," but spontaneously and from within the Socialistic camp itself. Probably the solution to this movement will also have to be found within the Socialistic camp, a solution which those above can advance but can hardly hinder. . . .

26

Rumor Takes Over*

From a Story in Pravda

(1957)

It sometimes seems that the effort to control opinion and prevent the circulation of rumor only serves to generate it even more rapidly. Most rumors tend to undermine the effectiveness of the controlled mass media, and therefore are not reported in the official press except in the most guarded way. But the less

* Reprinted from "The Rumor Mill: 'Auntie Says,'" (feuilleton), Sem. Narinyani, *Pravda* (Dec. 26, 1957), p. 3, translated in *Current Digest of the Soviet Press*, Vol. 9, No. 52, p. 18, published at Columbia University by the Joint Committee on Slavic Studies appointed by the American Council of Learned Societies and the Social Science Research Council. Used by permission of the publisher.

serious variety is sometimes used, as in this story, as part of the campaign against all rumor.

Three girls from the watch factory came running in to the newspaper's office after work. They were excited. They were alarmed.

"Tell us, is it true?"

"What are you talking about?"

"About the new money made out of nylon. They say that after New Year's the old money will be called in, and one nylon ruble will be issued in exchange for four and a half paper rubles."

"That's a strange rate of exchange, isn't it?"

"It's because nylon is more expensive than paper."

"It's stronger, too," one of the girls interjected.

"Nonsense. There's no need to change our ruble. It's already strong and stable."

"It may be strong, but it's unhygienic," the first girl said.

"And nylon is washable; fewer people will get the flu after the exchange, they say."

"To be hygienic you should wash your hands, not your money."

"But just the same, tell me — is there or isn't there going to be an exchange after New Year's?

"Who gave you the idea there would be?"

"It's what they're saying."

"Who, for instance?"

"Tamara Polikarpovna, for instance. She sells soda water at the factory lunch counter."

"And you believed her?"

"They believed her — I didn't," the third girl broke in, speaking for the first time. "So I brought them down here."

"Then there isn't going to be any nylon money?" asked the first girl.

"No."

"Nylon or any other kind? No exchange at all?"

"None at all."

"I can't understand it," the girl said, shrugging her shoulders. "What reason would Tamara Polikarpovna have to spread false rumors?"

"Oh, a good reason! When flighty, weak-willed people hear such rumors, they begin to lose their heads. They hurry to the stores and buy up all kinds of things they don't need. And later Tamara Polikarpovna buys the stuff

from them for next to nothing and resells it at a pretty profit."

"There, what did I tell you?" the third girl said, turning triumphantly to her companions.

The girls glanced at one another, laughed at their gullibility and hurried off. There is no need to worry about these young ladies — they won't be taken in by rumors the next time.

Oh, Tamara Polikarpovna, Tamara Polikarpovna! This isn't the first feuilleton we've written about you this year, or the first year we've written about you, for that matter. Yet you go right on the same old way, a true agent of the OTS marketplace news service (*Odna tyotka skazala* — "Auntie says"), as people called the rumor mill during the war.

It turns out that the OTS news service uses male gossips as well as female ones. A letter reached us from Taganrog concerning one Makar Makarovich Krivorotov. Makar Makarovich lives in a fine apartment, among whose appurtenances is a bathtub. Makar Makarovich rarely takes a bath in the tub, however, preferring to use it for storage. It is always filled with something or other; once it contained a five-year supply of matches, then it was calico, after the calico it was oil cake. Later Makar Makarovich filled his tub with kerosene, then with sunflower-seed oil, then with bolts of cloth. At one time Makar Makarovich even collected horse collars, though he never owned a horse in his life. At present Makar Makarovich's much put-upon bathtub is filled with sugar.

"What's the idea?"

"The price is going up — haven't you heard?" Makar Makarovich even knows how much it's going up — seven rubles 25 kopeks a kilogram for lump sugar, five rubles 40 kopeks a kilo for granulated.

"Who told you so?"

In reply, Makar Makarovich merely runs a comb through his hair meaningfully, though he has hardly enough hair left to make it worth the effort.

"I have nothing to say, and there's no need to say anything. I know it, and that's enough," is what the gesture signifies.

This tribute of gossips is indestructible. They not only know and believe but make up and spread lies of all descriptions. Everything around them is moving, progressing, but they are just as they were ten, twenty, or forty years ago. Life is in ferment around Makar Maka-rovich: people plant crops, they build, they mount to the rooftops in the gray dawn to see with their own eyes one of our satellites. Everyone has his concerns, his interests. Some are writing dissertations, others are fulfilling plans ahead of schedule, still others are calling the offices of *Sovetsky Sport* to find out how our Dynamo team did in its last match in South America. But the gossips are hollow. They begin every conversation with a nauseat-ing whisper:

"Have you heard?"

"Heard what?"

"They say that vacations will be abolished after New Year's."

"What vacations?"

"Annual vacations from work."

"Why?"

"They say the Americans don't have any, so we won't either."

"It's true that there aren't paid vacations in America, but that has nothing to do with us."

"We're competing with America, aren't we?"

"We are competing in the production of milk and meat, not the production of laws. Our country's laws have always been and will continue to be socialist laws."

"You mean vacations aren't being abol-ished?"

"No, of course they aren't!"

Every day there are reports in the news-papers about the early fulfillment of produc-tion plans by territories, provinces, whole re-publics. Tass has broadcast' a report of the Central Statistical Administration on the ex-tensive overfulfillment of the plan for meat, dairy, and sausage products. These people do not listen to Tass, however; they listen to OTS.

"Have you heard about milk and butter? Prices are going up."

"Why?"

"There's not enough of them; there's a shortage."

Bukhvostov, a worker, writes to us from Mikhailovka. The day before he wrote his letter, Bukhvostov had given his wife some money and had told her:

"Buy new clothes for the children and food for the New Year's feast — goose stuffed with apples, wine, everything."

Bukhvostov's wife went shopping, but in-stead of a goose and new clothes she returned with two sacks of salt, on which she had spent all her money.

"What do we want with all that salt?" the husband exclaimed.

"For a reserve. They say that salt will cost three times as much after New Year's."

"Who says so?"

The source of information was this same OTS — "Auntie says —"

The worker Bukhvostov is furious. He de-mands that the rumor mongers be punished.

"Why should they be permitted to continue spreading all sorts of nonsense?" Bukhvostov asks.

Rumor mongers should be punished, of course, but only the deliberately malicious ones. Those who are merely gullible, like Bukhvostov's wife, need educating, not pun-ishment.

As for the question of nonsensical reports that may crop up in the future, the answer is the same as it has always been: in the future, as in the past, one should not be a simpleton, and should not lend credence to the reports of the OTS.

Skip to 300

FORCE AND TERROR

27

The Soviet Armed Forces*

General Richard Hilton

(1949)

One of the favorite topics for speculation among "kremlinologists" has been the role of the military in the struggle for power in the higher reaches of the Soviet elite. The best opinion seems to be that the military, like other technicians, accept — or at least are not pre-pared to challenge — the leadership and even

* Reprinted from "The Soviet Armed Forces," *Journal of the Royal United Service Institution,* Vol. 94 (1949), pp. 552–561, by permission of the author and the publisher.

domination of the Communist Party. The topic of Party–Army relations rests always so near the center of the balance of power that it often obscures the fact that this is one of the largest enterprises in Soviet society, encompassing millions of men in a very complex organization. Major-General Hilton, who served as British Military Attaché in Moscow, describes the organization, the personnel, and the pattern of their life.

Before embarking on a study of the Soviet armed forces themselves, I think it advisable to mention some of the difficulties which attend the collection of data for a lecture on this subject. I do so, not so much to excuse my own lack of knowledge, as to give you certain clues as to the objects of this security and the type of things that they are trying to hide.

Never having been a military attaché in any other country, I cannot of course compare, from personal experience, the Soviet practice and technique in dealing with foreign attachés with that of other nations. All that I can say with certainty is that, from a military attaché's point of view, matters could hardly be worse anywhere else. General Seraev — the officer detailed to act as sole link between foreign attachés in Moscow and the High Command, once told me candidly that, in the opinion of the Soviet authorities, all foreign attachés were *ipso facto* spies. We were certainly treated accordingly!

Not once during my sojourn in Moscow was I ever invited to attend any military parade, exercise, or demonstration (other than the bi-annual ceremonial parades in the Red Square, to which I will refer later). I was never invited inside any barracks, camp, or other military establishment except to Red Army House — a huge officers' club, to a cocktail party on Red Army Day. I was never invited to the private house or flat of any Soviet officer. I wrote many letters to General Seraev, asking to be shown something at least of mild military interest, no matter how innocuous, but he did not even answer these letters.

Nor is it only in matters strictly military that the Soviet authorities exercise this intense security. They regard the whole country and its population as being one vast war machine. There is consequently hardly a single activity of social or economic life (except perhaps the

ballet) which does not, in their view, have some bearing upon the nation's readiness for war or otherwise. Practically everything that goes on is therefore a military secret. To ask a peasant what the local potato crop had been like would most certainly be construed into an act of economic espionage. On top of all this it must be remembered that draconian laws are in force to prevent any conversation, other than officially approved conversation on restricted subjects, between Soviet citizens and foreigners. To ensure this, an elaborate technique of shadowing by plain-clothes detectives was put into force against us. Our telephones were of course tapped. Listening equipment was installed in the walls of our flats. In short, all the resources of the M.V.D. and other police forces were available to ensure that we lived ostracized within an invisible security barrier.

This intensive emphasis upon security cannot fail to give foreign observers the impression that the Soviet High Command's overruling anxiety is to conceal the true state of affairs not only militarily but also socially and economically. But are they concealing strength or weakness? That, of course, is the vitally important question. I shall not attempt to answer it this afternoon beyond indicating certain factors which may help you to form your own opinions on the matter. It would be wrong to discuss the official view, even if I knew it. My own personal opinion is no more likely to be right than yours.

In this connection may I emphasize the fact that I am speaking here today purely as a private individual — a retired officer with no official status at all. Any opinions expressed will be merely my own.

Whether you decide to think that the Soviet Union is concealing strength or weakness, one thing at least is certain — i.e., that things "are not what they seem" on the surface. The whole country is a hotbed of propaganda. Practically nothing can be accepted safely at its face value. The control of "Truth" is so complete that the authorities can almost make black seem white. It is especially important to treat with suspicion anything which is gratuitously offered to the public gaze of foreigners. This, I personally believe, applied particularly to the great military parades on the Red Square — the only warlike functions that foreign attachés (except of course those of the "satellite" countries) are ever invited to see.

Not only were we invited, but every facility was given us to have a first-class ringside view. In a country where everything else is rigidly concealed behind a profound cloak of security, this gratuitous display seems simply too good to be true. Not only are they security-minded to an intense degree, they are also past-masters in window-dressing and propaganda. It is not likely, I suggest, that we were shown much of real value on a parade of that kind; indeed, it seems far more probable that these functions are deliberately planned to give the outside world false impressions about Soviet preparedness, or to lead us to ascribe to them future trends of strategic or tactical policy which may be quite different to their real ones. I myself know of two instances at least where such a trick was attempted.

In spite of this intensive drive for security I do not want to give you too gloomy a picture of their success in keeping things from us. Even the strictest security cannot entirely prevent a foreign resident in *any* country from seeing and hearing things quite openly and legitimately, things which may enable him to make deductions and draw conclusions; and Russia is no exception: I must not forget that my words will be published in the *Journal*, and that a copy will assuredly find its way to Moscow. When General Seraev reads my last remark he will probably claim it to be a proof that all attachés are spies. He is welcome to any comfort that this may give him, but of course it is not so at all. Any old soldier who is reasonably observant can see quite a lot of the true state of affairs without in any way transgressing the correct etiquette of a diplomat. The training which one gets on many a barrack-room inspection in peacetime, and the resultant skill in spotting the dust beneath the "eyewash," stands one in very good stead on such a job as this! On the surface these Red Square parades undoubtedly look impressive, magnificent, and impeccable. But so does many a barrack-room till you peep under the beds.

The Soviet Outlook on Defence Matters

Those responsible for war-preparedness in the Soviet Union enjoy several advantages over the staffs of other nations in their approach to the problem. Firstly, they are entirely free from all "mental shackles of the past" to an extent which cannot possibly apply to fighting services with venerable traditions, such as our own. Most of us know cases where some logical reform has been delayed, or has only been applied in a watered-down form, because a completely ruthless application of logic would have offended against service tradition or upset the susceptibilities of one fighting service or another. Even our most junior service, in spite of its youth, is not free from this weakness. Not so the Soviet armed forces. With them no traditional fads or private susceptibilities of this or that arm of the services are permitted to stand in the way of logical progress, and a ruthless application of the best weapon for each job regardless of any vested interests.

Secondly, they have the enormous advantage of being able to regard the entire Soviet Union as one vast war-machine. With them this is no mere theoretical conception of how a nation *ought* to be organized for war. Every social or economic activity, even in peacetime, is subservient to the requirements of war.

Thirdly, this logical and ruthless alignment of everything on a war footing under strong centralized control has brought about an integration of the three fighting services, in strategic conception if not in outward form, far closer than has been achieved by any other nation. Though the Russians have not yet invented a word corresponding to the German *Wehrmacht*, I personally am convinced that in what really matters, namely strategic planning and perhaps also the actual conduct of combined operations, they have got much nearer than the *Wehrmacht* ever did to the ideal of one united war machine — "The Armed Forces."

If the impossible were to happen — if one could persuade a senior Soviet officer to define to you his conception of the fighting forces of his country — he would not, as most of us would, speak of three distinct services — navy, army and air force; he would, I feel sure, think of *four* distinct elements in the Soviet war machine. These four would be:

(a) *The Armed Forces* — regarded and used as one weapon.

(b) *The "Rear"* — the whole nation or "Home Front," organized as one industrial and agricultural and man-producing machine for the maintenance of the armed forces.

(c) *The M.V.D.* — the essential security police force to keep the "Home Front" up to the mark, to prevent sabotage, fifth column activities, idleness, or any other waste or diversion of war effort.

(d) *Fifth Column* — subversive activities of all kinds abroad. These may cover anything from open civil war down to the dissemination of a defeatist or "go slow" policy among the dupes of Communism. This includes "Partisans" when applicable.

It is important, I think, to realize that the Soviet leaders have got this much broader conception of what constitutes a war organization. They would no more think of planning a war without giving full consideration to these four items than an air-minded soldier of today would start planning military operations without giving full consideration to the air.

The importance attached to full development of the "Rear" can be judged by the stream of official propaganda in the papers, on the wireless, and on the cinema. In spite of several "Five Year Plans" and ruthless slave-driving by the M.V.D., this particular item in Soviet war-preparedness is still their weak point. It may not be so for long because tremendous efforts are being made and progress is visible; but they have some way to go yet. For example, the very size of the Soviet Union, immense war asset that it will be when fully developed, is a source of weakness while long-distance communications remain inadequate. The road and rail system of the Soviet Union is far below the standard of development required for the upkeep of an intense industrial effort during a long war.

I will say no more about Fifth Column activities in other countries, because it lies outside the scope of this lecture. I only wish to emphasize once more that these enter into their calculations just as much as do tanks, artillery, submarines, or any other recognized implement of war.

Likewise the M.V.D. can only be spared a few minutes of our time. This sinister force is the king-pin of the entire Soviet system. Without it the whole thing would collapse like a pack of cards. It is an army superimposed on the ordinary army, composed of carefully picked officers and men who undergo longer and more efficient military training than the ordinary run of soldiers, and who enjoy many privileges above the common herd. It is a complete fighting force of all arms — its own tanks, artillery, etc., and it is organized partially into its own mobile divisions. Above all, it enjoys the services of an intelligence system, thanks to which there is little that goes on within Soviet territory (or even abroad) without the M.V.D. knowing about it. It gets its results by terror. There is no doubt whatever regarding the effectiveness of this terror and the complete grip which it gives the M.V.D. over the entire life and activities of the nation, not excluding the Armed Forces themselves. As a sideline, the M.V.D. runs the slave-labor camps and the munition factories and mines which are worked by such labor. They also man the fire services.

The existence of this force absolves the armed forces proper of much of the onus of having to act "in aid of the civil power" against open or clandestine sedition. The effect of this is to keep relations between the Armed Forces and the civil population cordial. While the M.V.D. is hated and dreaded by the people, the Armed Forces themselves are identified very closely with the civil population. Every effort of propaganda is made to foster popular pride in "our" Red Army, Red Air Force, and Red Fleet. A strong propaganda drive is directed toward the notion of brotherhood between Red Army men (and their comrades in the other services) and the workmen and peasants who form the home front.

This relationship has obvious advantages, but there are also certain drawbacks. In a community such as the Soviet Union, with its sixteen* (nominally autonomous) states and its enormous variety of nationalities and languages, care is necessary to prevent regional patriotism from creeping into this laudable popular pride in the armed forces. It is definitely contrary to Soviet policy, for example, to foster the growth of an Ukranian Air Force, comparable to the Royal Canadian Air Force or the Royal Australian Navy. These "dominions" of the Soviet Union are allowed their own postage stamps, but not their own armed forces. It is a small point, but perhaps significant, that the expressions *Russian* Army, Navy, or Air Force, are never used by Soviet officialdom. In the Soviet Zone of Germany, when I

---

* Now fifteen.

was there, the correct term was the "Soviet Army." The expression "Red Army" was frowned upon, having recently been abolished by official decree. When I got to Moscow a year later, however, I still found the term "Red Army" in vogue even on official occasions, though the decree of abolition, as far as I know, had not been rescinded. What subtle implication (if any) lies behind this I do not know. Possibly the authorities subsequently found that sentiment for the term "Red Army" was too strong and have shut their eyes to it. At any rate, both these labels alike avoid any emphasis upon nationality.

Another disadvantage of identifying the armed forces closely with the people is that the armed forces, like the people, have to be placed under constant political surveillance. The old system of appointing a "political officer" to every unit of the army or ship of the navy, has *officially* been abolished. But, as so often happens in a propaganda-ridden country, it is one thing to abolish on paper but quite another thing in fact. The "political officers" may not be called so any more. They may not wear a distinctive uniform. But they are there just the same! After a little practice one can easily recognize them at a glance among the plain but honest combatant officers around them. I personally encountered many instances of obvious and undignified "kow-towing" by a senior combatant officer to some comparatively junior officer on his staff. I will return to this matter of "political officers" later.

Interrelationships of the Services

As I have said, in spite of wearing distinctive uniforms and being named "Red Army, "Red Air Force," and "Red Fleet," the three fighting services are united to a far greater extent than I have seen anywhere else.

The predominant partner, without a shadow of doubt, is the army — naturally, in view of their vast territories and continental situation. The Red Army exists to win any war by large-scale land operations. The other two exist to help the army in its task. That is undoubtedly still their primary function. Whether it is still their sole function or whether they are starting to study and develop a separate "air strategy" and/or a separate "naval strategy" remains to be seen.

The Red Army and Air Force. There is a Ministry of the Armed Forces, but each of the three is self-running to a limited extent. Connection between the army and air force is very close indeed. Though the latter wears a distinctive uniform it is not nearly as distinctive as that of the navy, in fact, hardly more so than of the artillery or tanks. It would not be far wrong to say that, although the air force is not integrally part of the army, to quite the same extent as the old Royal Flying Corps used to be part of our army, yet it is much more intimately connected with the land forces than is the air force of any other nation today. Until recently, it was certainly regarded exclusively as a tactical weapon of the land war, and it was so used in 1941–45. There is in the Red Army Museum in Moscow a big painting showing Soviet heavy bombers attacking Berlin by night. Indeed, I have heard propaganda claims made that the Russians were the first to attack Berlin in this way and that most of the damage was due to them! Whatever the exact truth may have been, strategic bombardment played little if any part in their use of air power. They possessed a formation called the Long Range Group, but even this was used to assist the land war by attacking the lines of communication of the German armies. It only formed a very small portion of the total air forces. The great bulk of that service was equipped with aircraft specifically designed for participation in land battles. They firmly believe that the correct use of air power was almost 100 per cent direct participation in the land battle, and who can claim, in view of their successes in land fighting, that they were wrong?

There is still undoubtedly a very strong and influential school of thought which adheres strictly to this notion of the use of air power. There may also be an opposing school of thought (headed perhaps by Marshal Stalin's son) who advocate the development of a strong strategic bomber force and the pursuit of an independent air strategy. Color has been lent to this belief by the recent appearances of heavy bombers in the "fly past" at Red Square parades. Once more I would like to suggest that what we were shown "in the shop window" in Moscow may be a very different thing from what is being prepared on a much vaster scale "under the counter," i.e., far out of sight of foreign eyes in the center of Siberia. Why should they be so obliging as to warn the world that they are taking up strategic bombing?

Before leaving the air force it may be as well to mention the activities of DOSAV — an officially sponsored society for cooperation with the Air Force. Under the auspices of this society innumerable light aeroplane clubs all over the Soviet Union are carrying out elementary flying training of the younger generation, both male and female. They have not the same ideas that we have — that flying is something only to be undertaken by carefully picked supermen who have passed through a complicated medical test. It is almost as easy for a village youth or maiden to learn to fly as it is in other countries to learn to drive a lorry. Consequently, they are able to turn out elementary pilots almost by the million.

Admittedly this training is very elementary indeed, and a great deal more would have to be done to turn any of these novices into pilots of jet fighters or heavy bombers. Not much is required, however, to turn them into quite useful tactical bombers for the land war, or to employ them in several other forms of army cooperation, some of which may seem impossibly unorthodox to our more hide-bound way of thinking. It is a factor of some importance, I think, that the whole nation is being made "air-minded," even to this limited but very practical extent. We must remember that the Soviet authorities suffer under no inhibitions against the adoption of a given tactical method of war merely on the grounds that it would cost them immense casualties.

The Red Fleet. Turning next to the navy, this has always been, and still is, the Cinderella of the Soviet fighting forces. Traditionally the Russians have never been "deep water" sailors in spite of the urge of Peter the Great and the more recent propaganda of the Kremlin. They suffer, among other disadvantages, from their geographical need to maintain, not one great fighting fleet, but several little separate ones. Thus they have to keep up:

   (a) The White Sea Fleet
   (b) The Baltic Fleet
   (c) The Black Sea Fleet
   (d) The Far Eastern Fleet
   (e) The Caspian Flotilla

I do not know to what extent there may be interchange of personnel and ideas between these, but it can hardly be as easy to arrange as between the various parts of our own Royal Navy.

I am indebted to the help and advice of two distinguished senior naval officers for what I am going to say now. Both of them have had considerable dealings with the Soviet Navy.

It does not seem likely that the Soviet Government will build an oceanic battle fleet against the Western Powers or aspire to *surface* supremacy on the oceans. It is, however, quite possible that they may aim at blockading the ocean routes by submarine and air attacks on merchant shipping on a scale more intense even than that achieved by Germany in either of her wars. They have at their disposal the services of many German scientists and technicians, and perhaps German naval officers also, experts in submarine war. Giving them the credit of having studied the Battle of the Atlantic very closely, it seems only common sense to assume that their combined strategy may aim at a seizure of certain ports on the Atlantic by the Red Army to enable submarines and aircraft to operate effectively across the western approaches to Great Britain. This strategy has nearly succeeded twice in our history. They may well think "third time lucky."

Apart from this venture into separate naval strategy, the remaining activities of the Red Fleet are likely to be limited to operations in coastal waters or narrow seas in very close cooperation with the other services. This might include getting *surface* command of the Baltic or Black Sea to facilitate an offensive move of the Red Army across one or the other of these seas.

Scientific Developments

The chief point to remember here is that the Kremlin has at its disposal the technical services of many German scientists and experts. We can be very sure that they are exploiting this advantage to the full. We must also remember that they have got the entire indusrial resources of the Soviet Union geared, as a first priority, to warlike production. Thirdly, they are entirely free from scruples against the use of any new weapon on grounds of humanity or any consideration for their own people. These three advantages are formidable, and might be expected to enable them to spring upon the World something rather unpleasant in the way of technical surprises. But fortunately they suffer from two compensating disadvantages.

The first of these is a lack of technically

educated Soviet citizens in sufficient quantities to manipulate highly complicated scientific weapons in decisive numbers. I will try to show what I mean by an example from artillery technique. As all gunners and many non-gunners know, it is not sufficient to put into the field vast numbers of powerful guns and a great mass of ammunition. You must also have quite a complicated technical organization for connecting those guns with their targets by survey or other semi-scientific methods. This demands a large staff of junior technicians of sufficient mathematical ability to work out the relevant sums. These brainy young men are needed in huge numbers to deploy artillery or any other scientific weapon in war-winning quantities. It is just this very stratum of Soviet society which is most lacking — so much so that in the recent war they were forced on account of this weakness, to deploy their artillery masses in ways that we should call "bow and arrow." It worked, but only at the expense of heavy losses among artillerymen. What is true of artillery is true of any other scientific innovation, so there is some hope that the lack of junior technicians may hinder deployment of such weapons on a grand scale.

Their second disadvantage is the all-pervading suspicion to be found everywhere in Russia. Nobody trusts anybody else. So even if some decisive new weapon is envolved, their exaggerated sense of security may prevent them from letting sufficient people into the secret so as to deploy the new weapon in decisive numbers. The German use of gas at Ypres in March 1915, and our own first use of tanks illustrate how futile it is to spring a new surprise on too small a scale for fear of letting one's own people into the secret.

Turning now to the weapons and equipment actually in the hands of the troops, it is sufficient to say that these are, on the whole, robust, practical, and up-to-date. Weapons generally are better than transport. Maintenance of the latter has improved considerably since I first saw parts of the Soviet Army on the road. There was certainly room for improvement, and there still is. The Russian as a whole is definitely not a good mechanic nor is he sympathetic to his machine.

Discipline, Morale, and Welfare

Discipline in the Red Army, as might be expected of their ideological background, is very different from our own. For all that, it is most effective. It seems to be based on two rather conflicting ideas, i.e., comradeship (of the Communist variety) when off duty, combined with a more than Prussian ferocity in all official dealings between one rank and another. You have the curious phenomenon of criticism which manifests itself in articles written to the papers by junior ranks, including N.C.O.'s and privates, condemning in very forceful terms anything which they consider to be lax or remiss on the part of their commanding officers. It is common also to see groups of young soldiers gathering round an officer or N.C.O. and arguing with him in a most friendly but off-hand manner. On the other hand, there is no other service in the world, I should think, where minor differences in rank count for so much. For example, at a conference whose presiding officer is a full colonel it would be contrary to etiquette for any lieutenant colonel to express an opinion unless he was called upon to do so, even if he happened to be the only expert on the subject under discussion. When a senior officer is giving orders to a junior officer it is quite normal for him to adopt a special "parade ground manner" — a ferocious and bullying attitude.

Officers seem far more callous of their men's comfort and welfare than is the case with us. I came across many instances of this. They are also far from punctilious in returning the salutes of their juniors. The saluted often ignores the saluter's existence altogether, or else looks at him as though he were a bit of dirt. But this curious behavior does not seem to be taken amiss. Both discipline and morale are undoubtedly very good throughout most of the Red Army. Of course, there are bad units; a few of the units in the Soviet Zone of Germany were very bad indeed. But it is fair to say, I think, that they were the exception and not the rule. Dress and general smartness in demeanor of all ranks, at any rate near Moscow, compares favorably with that of most conscript armies of the Western nations today.

Officer Class — Selection and Privileges.

As is only to be expected of a propaganda-ridden state, theoretically the officer class is in no way distinct from the rest. In reality it is very distinct. Selection, not only for junior officer ranks but also for N.C.O.'s of the permanent cadre of instructors, is based primarily upon education. Youths who have reached certain advanced standards in the universal curriculum of the state schools commence their period of military training earlier than the general mass of their contemporaries, so that by the time of the general call-up the "brighter boys" are ready to fill vacancies in the junior officer or N.C.O. training cadres.

This would be fair enough if everybody had an equal chance of attaining to this higher standard of education. Actually there is a great deal of nepotism and political bias, particularly the latter. Sons of officers, especially of the more senior officers, stand a far better chance than others. But, even more than the professional standing of the father, the political background comes very strongly into the picture. There was a time when the authorities realized that a good professional soldier need not necessarily be a fervent Communist and vice versa. Those were the days when commanders were appointed because of their ability in war without worrying too much about their zeal for the Party. That was why it was necessary in those days to have "political officers" in every unit to keep the honest fighting men on the rails. As I mentioned earlier, that system has been abolished "on paper." They may intend eventually to abolish it in reality and replace it by a system where every combatant officer is a trusty and loyal supporter of the Party.

There are signs that this is the trend, both in the selection and early education of the new generations of officers. The Lenin Academy of Political Science for the Armed Forces plays its part in this policy by indoctrinating courses of young and "middle piece" officers up to the rank of Lieut.-Colonel at least. But, on the principle that it is easier to keep a fervent young Communist fervent than to inspire enthusiasm into the middle-aged, it is reasonable to believe that growing importance is being attached to the candidate's record as an earnest *Komsomol* when selecting junior officers.

As regards officer's privileges, these differ in no special way from those enjoyed by the whole official hierarchy. The only point to emphasize here is that Communist talk about the abolition of class privilege in the Soviet Union is arrant nonsense. The entire system is based on the idea that the higher up the official tree one climbs, the better become the "perks."

On account of the leper-like isolation meted out to foreign attachés, it was harder to get an insight into the character and abilities of senior officers than it would be in a civilized country. But in the course of a year in Potsdam and another in Moscow it was possible to form a sort of composite representative picture of the average senior officer. The first impression that sticks out is that one and all of them are constantly in fear for their own futures. This impression is most marked, and I do not think that there can be any mistake about it. Many of the combatant Generals (i.e., those who were not "political officers") gave me the feeling that, if left to their natural inclinations, they might have been quite decent normal beings with whom it would have been possible to find a lot in common. But they all have to act a part, and assume the character of mannerless boors.

Most of the successful wartime commanders that I met seem to have owed their success to a ruthless force of character and toughness of "drive" rather than to the profundity of their grasp of the higher art of war.

Coming to the "middle piece" ranks, the most common characteristics are lack of personal initiative and an almost inexhaustible capacity for hard work. The former trait — lack of initiative — might almost be called the Achilles' heel of Soviet fighting efficiency as a whole. It is undoubtedly caused by the draconian penalties which attend failure, even when failure has been caused by a minor error of judgment. Nobody cares to take this risk. They all prefer, if possible, to "pass the baby" and get a ruling from higher up, even if this wastes time. I came upon many glaring instances of this.

We used to see quite a lot of the non-commissioned ranks in the Soviet Zone of Germany, e.g., by giving them lifts on the road, etc. I found the simple soldiers and junior N.C.O.'s most likeable chaps — far more so, in fact, than most of their officers. They were amazingly ignorant of the outer world, but showed no anti-foreign feelings at all. Nor, in the Soviet Zone, had they any objection to talking freely on non-military subjects provided that they were certain that they were not being observed. Most of them had the minds of peasants, and oriental peasants at that. I got the same feeling that I used to get when talking to primitive villagers in India. It was significant how many talked of a coming war with the West. They spoke of it without rancor or enthusiasm or any other strong feelings — in quite a matter-of-fact way, as of any other inevitable event, such as the snows of winter.

Summary

I have tried to give you, in the time available, my own general impressions of the Soviet armed forces — their inter-services setup, their outlook on war and politics, their principal strong and weak points, and some of the characteristics of the troops, their leaders, and their equipment. I have avoided exact figures or details, partly for security reasons and partly for lack of time.

The general impression which I should like to leave with you is that of a formidable fighting machine, but one by no means free from very serious weaknesses. However good the actual fighting forces may be, their ability to sustain a long world war will depend on the economic state of the Soviet Union and on its people's enthusiasm for the war. In both these respects the Soviet Union still has a long way to go. They know this as well as anyone and they are certainly not "marking time."

28

Forced Labor Under Stalin*

U.S. Department of State

(1952)

Purges of the elite within the Communist Party and political terror directed against the population at large were for a long time defined by many observers as distinctive and irremovable features of Soviet totalitarianism. Political controls of essentially non-political activities and restrictions on freedom of movement and expression continue to characterize Soviet society. But the formerly ubiquitous forced labor camps have apparently largely been closed down, the purging of the ranks of the Party greatly reduced, and even the treatment of defeated "enemies" at the highest levels of the Party transformed from inevitable shooting to probable demotion and "internal exile." Without taking sides in the debate as to whether the inner dynamics of the system will force a return to purging and mass coercion, we feel that any historical perspective on the Soviet system absolutely demands familiarity with the earlier practice. And since the memory of that practice lives in the mind of every Soviet citizen, an understanding of the present and future reactions of the Soviet leaders and people also assumes taking into consideration a policy which left an impression on the minds of all Soviet people deeper than that made by any other aspect of their experience under the system.

The following are Chapters I and II of a report prepared by the United States Information Service of the Department of State for distribution overseas. In view of the importance of the subject, the report is also being given limited distribution within the United States to acquaint the American public with the story of conditions within the Soviet sphere.[1]

Forced labor has been almost from the time of the October Revolution a constant characteristic of Soviet society. In seizing power the Bolsheviks were ambitious to destroy the old elite and the old institutions and to create a new society with institutions more to their liking. Use of forced labor was related to both ambitions, since it could be used to dispose of undesirable persons and perform some of the work needed to create a new society. In the first decade of rule the new Communist elite turned this weapon principally against the dispossessed elite lingering on from the former regime. In the succeeding period of construction of Stalinist socialism the rulers exploited for forced labor principally groups which the

* Reprinted from "Forced Labor in the Soviet Union," *U.S. Department of State Bulletin*, Vol. 27 (1952), pp. 428–436. This item also appeared as Department of State Publication 4716 (1952).

[1] *Forced Labor in the Soviet Union,* Department of State publication 4716. Among the sources of the report are materials which the U. S. Government turned over to the United Nations *Ad Hoc* Committee on Forced Labor; for a statement on these materials by Walter M. Kotschnig, Deputy U. S. Representative in the U. N. Economic and Social Council, see Bulletin of July 14, 1952, p. 70.

regime claimed to represent, the workers, peasants, and the new intelligentsia.

The repression, including forced labor, introduced by the Red Terror in 1918 — even if in response to opposition violence — exceeded in scale anything which had been known in Tsarist Russia. Nevertheless, the propagandists employed by Party and Government claimed that this was a temporary phenomenon which would disappear with the liquidation of opposing classes and the achievement of socialism. In fact, however, the opposite occurred. Use of forced labor against the remnants of the aristocracy and bourgeoisie was as nothing compared to the use of forced labor later against the groups supposedly allied with the Bolsheviks.

Forced labor took on mass dimensions after 1929 when ambitions of the ruling group collided with desires of the masses. The elite wanted to preserve and to extend its power. It was ambitious to increase rapidly and at all costs the power and resources within the grasp of the Soviet state while eliminating opposition to its policies within and without the ranks of the Communist Party. The peoples of the U.S.S.R. wanted the better life they had been promised, in particular release from tyrannical rule and an increase of their material wellbeing. The regime sought to increase industrial output quickly, especially in heavy industry, and to secure control of agricultural output. A policy of mass deprivation and mass expropriation followed. The resistance engendered by this policy provided great numbers of candidates for repression. Beyond any repression of dissidents, the regime used wholesale forced labor as a weapon against entire economic and ethnic groups which the rulers decided to destroy. The Soviet leaders sought to derive maximum economic benefit from these victims by organizing their labor power to serve the economic program of the state.

The Soviet Government was unwilling to employ economic incentives potent enough to attract sufficient free labor to the undeveloped areas of the Soviet Union, areas thinly populated and difficult to exploit. Consequently, the government concentrated the largest masses of forced laborers in the remote areas of Siberia, Central Asia, and the Far North. Not all persons subjected to forced labor in confinement were sent to these distant camps, however.

Many camps and colonies were located in and near the well-populated areas. Especially for "short-timers" the nearer camps could, with little waste of time and transportation facilities, usefully supplement the supply of free labor in various parts of the U.S.S.R. In addition, they served as an everyday reminder to the people of the need for conformity.

Degrees of Involuntary Labor

In a society as tightly controlled as the Soviet Union it may be asked if there is a valid distinction between forced labor and free. Much coercion is embodied in the relationship between the all-powerful Soviet state and the individual employee. A different kind of coercion finds expression in the relationship between the state and the farmer.

Compulsion or coercion of labor takes various forms. (1) Youths, often from farms, are drafted for training in labor reserve schools and bound afterwards, like graduates of higher schools, to work for 3 or 4 years on assigned jobs. (2) Workers may not leave jobs without permission, and contrariwise, certain qualified workers may be sent on obligatory assignment to other jobs in other localities. (3) Farmers are required to work a certain number of days each year in repairing roads and the like. This survival of the medieval *corvée* system has disappeared in most European countries but not in the U.S.S.R. (4) For infringement of certain rules workers may be sentenced to a type of involuntary labor with reduction of 25 per cent in wages, but they remain either at their normal place of employment, or at least outside the barbedwire enclaves. (5) Workers, peasants, and intellectuals may be exiled to remote places inside the U.S.S.R. where working opportunities are limited to a single factory or mine. Such exiles become in effect forced laborers. (6) If not exiled to a specific place, Soviet citizens may be banished from their home towns and forced to find residence and work elsewhere. Although all of these relationships involve a degree of compulsion sufficient to merit a description as forced labor, they are not of primary concern in the following text. They are discussed only as they bear upon forced labor proper.

Forced labor is a punishment meted out to those who have offended the powers that be or are considered as potential offenders. Forced laborers are persons confined for political or economic reasons in prisons, labor colonies, or concentration camps (in present-day Soviet terminology, corrective-labor camps) and compelled to work in or near the place of confinement.

Included in the great number of forced laborers are both those sentenced by courts through regular or special courts and those sentenced by administrative order. These groups are not treated separately in the present text for the simple reason that the Soviet authorities lump them together in forced labor camps. Certain distinguishing characteristics should be noted, however. Investigation of such "crimes" as those listed in Article 58 of the Soviet criminal codes is in the hands of the Ministry of State Security (MGB), an offshoot of the Ministry of Internal Affairs (MVD). The most important component of the MGB is the so-called political police, which has existed almost from the beginning of the Soviet regime and is the bearer of the "glorious tradition," to use a phrase from Soviet propaganda, of the Cheka, the OGPU, and the NKVD. The political police can decide after completing an investigation whether or not the suspect should be turned over to the courts for prosecution. If the decision is against court prosecution, the police agencies can then, without even the semblance of a trial, sentence the victim by administrative fiat to a five-year term at forced labor. If the decision is to prosecute in court, no great uncertainty arises as to the danger of the victim's being released. Judges are sufficiently well indoctrinated politically; the defendants' protections are weak; and procedures are so adjusted that a verdict of guilty can be expected. Then the victim once more enters the grasp of the political police, who administer the entire system of forced labor.

Soviet Acknowledgments of the Forced Labor System

Although a wealth of material has been accumulated describing the operations of the forced labor camps in the U.S.S.R., many facts are still not known. The gaps in outside knowledge of the Soviet labor camps relate particularly to current developments. Some of these facts will in all probability not become known, at least in the near future. The Soviet passion

for concealment and secrecy extends even to data and observations regarding routine events and processes; it would be highly surprising if secretiveness did not extend to the forced labor system, a characteristic of Soviet society which goes against the grain not only of the world's conscience but also of the Soviet leaders' own apologia.

Despite Soviet secretiveness about the nature and extent of forced labor in the U.S.S.R., much evidence regarding the system has been accumulated from Soviet documents. These documents are of several types. (1) Laws defining forced labor, establishing regimes in forced labor camps, and authorizing confinement by administrative measures without trial have been published. Although none of these is of more recent vintage than 1934, current Soviet legal publications make it clear that they are still in force. (2) When the Soviet authorities were in a mood to boast of their claimed success in reforming errant citizens through forced labor, they published material hinting at the extent to which forced labor was involved in certain construction projects, such as the canal projects. (3) Fortuitously, because disclosure was not intended by Soviet authors, the publication of a detailed Plan for 1941 disclosed the part played by forced labor in the economic life of the country on the eve of World War II. (4) Official Soviet documents given to Polish citizens upon their release early in the war from forced labor camps confirm evidence from other sources regarding the existence of literally hundreds of different camps.

Eyewitness Accounts of Soviet Forced Labor

Before World War II forced labor in the U.S.S.R. had already assumed enormous proportions. Because of Soviet censorship and tight border controls there were few witnesses who were in a position to testify to the human consequences of the system. The war changed all this. Vast dislocations of population affected Russians, Ukrainians, Azerbaijani, and other nationalities of the Soviet Union, as well as Polish citizens, former residents of the Baltic States, and, of course, Germans. Many of the Soviet citizens who had been abroad refused to return at the war's end, choosing the uncertainties of life in other countries in preference to the cruel certainties of life under a concentration-camp regime. They were justly apprehensive of Soviet measures of "re-education" following their stay abroad. This "re-education" did in fact include large doses of forced labor.

Among the displaced persons were many who had served terms in Soviet labor camps. They had a story to tell which vividly portrayed conditions in forced labor camps up to the war. Poles who had experienced similar conditions in the early years of the war brought the story more nearly up to date when their testimony was made avaliable, as in the notable book entitled *Dark Side of the Moon*.

The reconsolidation of Soviet authority has now dried up the main stream of eyewitness accounts. Nevertheless, enough Germans (ex-PW's sentenced to forced labor camps) have managed to leave the U.S.S.R. recently to show that the forced labor system continues to operate in the postwar years in the same old way.

Estimates of Size of Forced Labor Group

Neither reticent Soviet references to the forced labor system nor survivors' accounts offer a means of estimating the number of forced laborers. To fill this gap various students of Soviet affairs have attempted to estimate, on the basis of various statistics, the forced labor population. It is natural that these estimates should vary widely, but part of the discrepancies results from differences not only in the period considered but also in the definition of the group to be estimated. The definition may include — in addition to the basic group of inmates of "corrective labor" camps — forced laborers interned in colonies, exiles, persons punished by forced labor at their place of work, and prisoners-of-war.

Dallin and Nikolaevsky in their book, *Forced Labor in Soviet Russia*,[2] pass review on various estimates of the number of prisoners running up to 20 million persons and even higher. Their own guess ranges from 8 to 12 million forced laborers.

In 1948, N. S. Timasheff computed the num-

ber of forced laborers in 1937.[3] He based his estimate on the election returns of that year. Calculating that the population on January 1, 1938, was 167 million, Timasheff estimated that adults of more than 18 years constituted about 58 per cent of this total. Since only 56 per cent of the population or 94 million, registered for the 1937 election, Timasheff concluded that 3.3 million missing adults had been deprived of electoral rights. Of these a certain number, possibly one million, were either insane, feeble-minded, or ordinary criminals. The remainder were in prison camps.

An attempt was made by a research member of the Russian Research Center of Harvard University to find the number of forced laborers by making a detailed breakdown of the population as of January 1, 1939, by major occupational groups. Forced laborers become the residual category. Numbers of males and females can be found in official sources and can be adjusted to compensate for omissions and double counting. All the remaining adults not accounted for as students, pensioners, or as members of the armed forces should either be not gainfully employed (housewives, for example) or should be employed involuntarily. On the basis of this method a forced labor figure of almost 10 million for both sexes can be derived.

For 1940 Harry Schwartz estimated the number of forced laborers on the basis of the gap between payroll figures issued by the Central Accounting Administration and the "inclusive payroll for the economy as a whole." Central Accounting data cover wage and salary earners required by law to possess labor books, craftsmen working in cooperatives, and some seasonal workers. The comprehensive payroll data cover, in addition, members of the armed forces and involuntary workers. If the average annual wage of armed forces personnel or forced laborers is 2,000 rubles, the difference of 37 billion rubles would support 18.5 million persons. Five million men were assumed to be in the army. Schwartz therefore concluded that 13.5 million persons were involuntary workers.[4]

---

[2] David Dallin and B. I. Nikolaevsky (New Haven, 1947), pp. 84–87.

[3] *American Journal of Sociology*, September 1948, LIV, 150.

[4] Harry Schwartz, "A Critique of 'Appraisals of Russian Economic Statistics,'" *Review of Economics and Statistics*, February, 1948, XXX, 40–41.

Naum Jasny has presented the most recent estimate. Jasny's was based on production and investment data drawn from the State Plan for 1941. He assumed a ratio of productivity between forced labor and free labor at one-half to one. Taking into account prisoners hired out, working in a service capacity in the camps, and working in industries not mentioned in the Plan, such as gold mining, Jasny concluded that about 3.5 million were camp inmates in 1941.[5] This figure, however, does not include children, invalids, and other people who do not work.

Number of Prisoners in the U.S.S.R. and Other Countries

Because of the Soviet concealment of prison data the number of forced laborers cannot be known. Even if the number of forced laborers were only two to three million, and this is the most cautious estimate, the number is enormous in comparison either to the number confined under the Tsarist regime or to the number of prisoners confined in other countries at the present time. The *Small Soviet Encyclopedia*,[6] 2d edition, Vol. 5, Col. 361, stated that Tsarist penal labor reached its maximum in 1913 when 33,000 were confined; of these 5,000 were political prisoners. The number of people confined in regular Tsarist prisons reached a peak in 1912 with 184,000, according to Andrei Vyshinsky.[7] This figure includes common criminals as well as "politicals." In pre-revolutionary days the highest number of political exiles was 17,000, in 1907 (according to *Soviet Penal Repression*, Moscow, 1934, p. 108). All these figures are taken from orthodox Soviet publications, which do not minimize the evils of Tsarism. A comparison of these statistics with even minimum estimates for the Soviet Union reveals the great expansion of forced labor after the Bolshevik Revolution.

The Soviet figures may also be compared to the statistics of other countries, countries which, like Tsarist Russia, have published data on prison population. In the United States, for

example, portrayed in Soviet propaganda as a most barbaric dungeon, full prison statistics are published. They show that there is an average of one person out of 1,000 imprisoned, i.e., a total prison population of 150,000 in a country with a population of more than 150 million. If the U.S.S.R. had the same ratio of prisoners to population, it would have 200,000 prisoners rather than 2 to 20 million. The U.S.S.R. would have 200,000, that is, if crime were as prevalent under Soviet socialism as under capitalism. But all Soviet apologists assert that crime is disappearing under socialism. Hence a figure considerably less than 200,000 would be expected, rather than a figure from 15 to 100 times as large.

Social Effects of the Forced Labor System

Forced labor on the tremendous scale on which it exists in the U.S.S.R. brings terrible consequences in its wake.

Those most seriously affected are, of course, the victims themselves, persons confined for shorter or longer times to forced labor camps. Their lives are likely to be, in Hobbes' phrase, "nasty, mean, brutish, and short." Work is burdensome and for long hours. Skills frequently become rusty. Work conditions are hazardous to health, and hence illness comes often. Inadequacy of medical facilities delays or prevents recuperation. Human relations deteriorate in the unnatural society of the camps. Even if the victim survives his camp existence and returns to free society, he may be handicapped in rehabilitating himself either by physical or psychical defects or by the stigma attached to his name.

The forced labor system brutalizes others besides the victims. The keepers and guardians responsible for guarding the unfortunate inmates suffer a blunting of moral fibers and display tendencies to degeneration.

The system makes fear routine in the population. It shuts mouths which should speak freely and inspires the utmost caution and servility.

By its existence on a vast scale the forced labor system makes necessary the continued elevation of the political police and their continued penetration into the innermost recesses of everyday life. Since the role of the police is in turn dependent in part on the size of the forced labor establishment, a vicious rhythm

[5] "Labor and Output in Soviet Concentration Camps," *Journal of Political Economy*, October 1951, 405–419.
[6] *Malaya Sovetskaya Entsiklopediya* (Moscow, 1936).
[7] *Prisons in Capitalist Countries* (Moscow, 1937), p. 54.

is created which continues to exert deleterious effects on Soviet society.

Forced Labor Constant in Soviet Society

Forced labor has been a constant feature of Soviet society from the early days of the civil-war concentration camps to the present period of large-scale economic enterprises maintained and operated by prison labor. In the first years of the regime the Bolsheviks through proclamations promising reform of prisoners attempted to obscure the seamy reality of this institution. In recent years the Soviet authorities by their almost complete silence on forced labor have attempted to enforce secrecy about the hundreds of camps and millions of prisoners. Nevertheless, there is ample evidence not only of the economic and political significance of forced labor in the Soviet Union, but also of the inhumanities which have accompanied its application through 34 years of Communist rule.

At every stage of Soviet development the forced labor system has been adapted to changing political and economic needs. The use of forced labor as a means of political control has been constant, but the groups most seriously affected have changed in accordance with shifting emphases in political warfare. The economic significance of forced labor has varied with changes in economic programs.

Forced Labor in the Period of War Communism, 1918–1921

Forced labor camps were first opened in the fall of 1918 with the institution of the "red terror." Political repression of the former ruling groups, the *raison d'être* of forced labor in the first decade of Soviet rule, was presented as a temporary measure directed against an enemy destined to destruction. In this period forced labor was on a small scale, with perhaps less than 100,000 in camps in 1921. This number was particularly small compared with the large-scale operations in subsequent years, when the same repressive measure was directed against workers, peasants, and the revolutionary intelligentsia, the purported mainstay of the regime.

Nevertheless, it was in this early period,

1918–1921, that the forced labor system became entrenched in Soviet society. In the first months of the revolution the Bolsheviks organized a special political police agency, the Cheka, which has continued to exist under other names to the present. This police agency played a key role in the operation of forced labor camps, partly because it possessed the power to sentence victims to exile or to forced labor camps without any judicial procedure, by administrative decree only. The labor performed by the victims was in the early years of only incidental value to the state, since little attempt was made to organize it on a profitable basis. This was also true of the other widely heralded "progressive penal institutions," such as labor colonies or corrective labor houses, to which errant citizens of the working class were sent.

Forced Labor in the NEP Period, 1921–1928

Concentration or forced labor camps continued to exist all through the period of the New Economic Policy (NEP), 1921–1928, along with the system of penal institutions for nonpolitical criminals and the work projects organized for those sentenced to forced labor without incarceration. Although the NEP period represented a considerable relaxation from the stringent persecution applied during the first years of Bolshevik rule, there was little essential improvement in the status of the political prisoner. The repression carried out earlier by the Cheka found its continuation in the activities of the GPU-OGPU.

It was in this early period that the authorities formulated the legal basis of the forced labor system. One such principle involved the previously mentioned acceptance of extrajudicial methods for sentencing to forced labor, and control of forced labor camps by the political police. The criminal law codes instituted during NEP fixed forced labor as a standard penalty. These codes, typified by that of the R.S.F.S.R. (1922; revised in 1926), distinguished between forced labor with confinement and forced labor without confinement. The former involves incarceration in a labor camp, or colony, and the latter compulsory performance at a reduced rate of pay in either the person's regular job or some other assignment. These varieties of forced labor have been perpetuated to the present day.

In addition to establishing norms of the criminal law, Soviet authorities in this early period promulgated the first corrective labor code. This was issued in the R.S.F.S.R. in 1924. It was followed by codes of the other republics. These statutes established a detailed set of rules for persons condemned to all types of forced labor, and provided for a system of social stratification in Soviet penal institutions in which criminal elements were considered the elite.

The Early Plan Period, 1929–1934

With the end of NEP and the resumption of the "socialist offensive" in 1929, forced labor assumed new importance. In the earlier years forced labor was aimed at former "exploiting" classes. In the period of collectivization the farmers who held small tracts of land and a few head of livestock became the chief victims. Five million of these peasants with their families were eliminated, as Molotov acknowledged, i.e., were uprooted and transported to remote regions of the U.S.S.R. The Five Year Plans were inaugurated at this time to bring rapid industrialization to Soviet society. The greatly expanded economic activity of the state was attended by a substantial increase in the population of the forced labor camps. By 1931 the number of inmates in both prisons and corrective labor camps is estimated to have been almost 2 million for the R.S.F.S.R. and the Ukraine alone.[8]

The economic exploitation of Soviet prisoners by the OGPU and its successor, the NKVD, became more obvious as the years passed. Soviet figures relating to several projects employing prison labor were published during the 1930's. They indicate that the U.S.S.R. employed more forced laborers on *each* of several projects than the total number of prisoners forced to perform heavy labor in any year under the Tsar. According to a So-

viet source, the highest point of repression under the old regime was reached in 1913, when 33,000 convicts were engaged in penal labor.[9] In an attempt to refute Western charges about Soviet forced labor, Molotov reported to the All-Union Congress of Soviets on March 8, 1931, that there were "about 60,000" persons performing corrective labor on three highways, a railway, and the White Sea-Baltic Canal.

In actual fact, a much greater number of forced laborers was employed on these projects, which constituted only a small portion of the total forced labor activity. In 1933, upon completion of the canal alone, about 72,000 of the prisoners who had worked on the project were freed or received shortened terms by governmental decree. Similar decrees in 1937 released 55,000 prisoners who worked on the Moscow-Volga Canal and 10,000 who worked on double-tracking the Karymskoye-Khabarovsk railway.

The period of the First Five Year Plan was important for developments in the legal basis of forced labor, which since that time has remained substantially unchanged. Both the 1930 statute on corrective labor camps and the 1933 R.S.F.S.R. Corrective Labor Code (see p. 8), which regulates all other types of forced labor, are still in effect. In addition, a 1930 law of the R.S.F.S.R. introduced into the Soviet judicial system the principle of exile at forced labor, hitherto applied only administratively by the OGPU. This measure found immediate and widespread application against the kulaks in the then developing collectivization program. Exile at forced labor was widely applied to these peasants by the courts as well as by the OGPU.

During this period a definite end was written to the pretense that the political police with their powers outside the law constituted a temporary phenomenon in Soviet development. The so-called exploiting classes had been liquidated, and socialism was soon to be proclaimed. Yet the status and extra-legal authority of the political police were fully confirmed in 1934 when the U.S.S.R. established, for the first time on the All-Union level, a

---

[8] Estimate based on data in A. Ya. Vyshinsky, *Ot Tyur'em k Vospitatel'nym Uchrezhdeniyam* (from Prisons to Educational Institutions), Moscow, 1934, pp. 171, 259.

[9] *Small Soviet Encyclopedia* (Moscow, 1936), Vol. 5, Col. 361.

People's Commissariat of Internal Affairs (NKVD).

The Era of the Purges, 1935–1939

Forced labor had therefore already become a well-developed system by the time country-wide, new wholesale purges were initiated in the mid-1930's. Consequently, the administrative structure of this system was well organized and equipped to receive the additional great numbers of victims who were soon to find their way into the camps and other penal institutions.

Changes in the police structure of the Soviet Union in 1934 when the All-Union NKVD was established made it easier for the Soviet Government to sentence people to the labor camps without according them the right to court trial. This procedure was institutionalized in the form of the Special Conference of the NKVD, a police organ with the power to exile, banish, or confine in corrective labor camps for periods up to five years. Under the conditions of great internal stress prevailing in the Soviet Union following the assassination of Kirov in 1934, the police authorities exercised their extra-judicial powers freely on the Soviet citizenry.

The state found ample projects on which to employ these great masses of human material at forced labor. The NKVD's economic activity expanded tremendously in the fields of hydroelectric construction, production of industrial goods, and exploitation of the extractive industries, especially in remote localities. It was during these years, for example, that the forced labor camps of *Dalstroi* (the Far Eastern Construction Trust) became synonymous with the mining of gold in the Soviet Union.

Forced Labor on the Eve of World War II

By the time forced labor became a large-scale business in the U.S.S.R., the authorities became secretive about the magnitude and even the existence of the system. A gauge of the importance which forced labor had assumed in the economy of the Soviet Union during the late 1930's was provided by the detailed Soviet Economic Plan for 1941. This Plan, intended only for official use, fell into the hands of the Germans during World War II. The text of the Plan disclosed some dimensions of the forced labor operations in the economy and showed that a sizable part of the total production in the Soviet Union was performed by forced laborers.

War Developments in Forced Labor

With the outbreak of World War II the population of Soviet forced labor camps was augmented for the first time by large numbers of non-Soviet citizens. These consisted of inhabitants of the Baltic States and the eastern part of Poland who were considered hostile to the Soviet Government, as well as prisoners from the liquidated Polish armed forces. Many of these foreign prisoners were sent to penal labor institutions or transported to exile in the Soviet Union without the formality of judicial procedure. The inhumanity of Soviet methods of banishment to exile and forced labor is well recorded by documents on the deportations from the three Baltic States in 1941, which include long and detailed lists of individuals to be rounded up and transported, and by the depositions of former Polish prisoners.

Soviet participation in the war brought about considerable changes in the forced labor empire. Although there is little factual information on this period, because of wartime secrecy, the population of the camps seems to have decreased as a result of the need for manpower at the front. Various groups of Soviet citizens were transferred to army units. The Polish prisoners who had been incarcerated for almost two years were released by the agreement between the Polish Government-in-Exile and the Soviet Government of July 30, 1941. There does not seem, however, to have been a sharp cutback in the productive tasks assigned to the NKVD, although it is probable that the responsibilities of this agency were altered by the emphasis on functions relating to war production.

The war also brought in its wake other trends affecting the status of forced labor as an institution. Sentences to corrective labor without incarceration, always boasted of as an effective reform measure by the Bolsheviks, were to a large extent replaced by short-term sentences to deprivation of freedom. In 1942, for example, in the R.S.F.S.R. (excluding the autonomous republics) sentences to deprivation of freedom accounted for 73 per cent of all sentences by the courts, as compared with 33.5 per cent in 1934. This development seems to have been due largely to restrictive labor legislation passed at the beginning of the war.

Under the stress of war conditions, so-called "labor educational colonies" were organized in 1943 under the NKVD for minors aged 11 to 16.[10] As far as is known, this marked the first time that penal measures had been applied to children as young as 11 years of age. In the same year the old Tsarist punishment of *katorga*, or hard labor, which the Bolsheviks of earlier years had abolished with great fanfare, was instituted for terms of 15 to 20 years by an edict of the U.S.S.R. Supreme Soviet on April 19, 1943. The Soviet authorities said that this punishment was designed for certain crimes by both "German Fascists and traitors to the motherland — those giving aid to the enemy." Actually, terms of the law were vague enough so that it could be applied to political dissidents.

Developments Since the War's End

Towards the end of the war, forced labor began to assume a role of greater importance than had apparently been allotted to it during the years when the country had been in extreme danger. New contingents of people undergoing repression provided labor power for the huge amount of reconstruction which was to be undertaken. Among these the main groups seem to have been new deportees from the Baltic States and other annexed territories, collaborators with the Germans, deserters and members of the Vlasov army, and simple workers and soldiers returned from Europe who were considered to need a period of re-indoctrination. Several Soviet minority nationalities fell victim to the charge of cooperating with the enemy and were deported to other regions of the U.S.S.R. These included the Volga Germans, the Chechen-Ingush, Kalmyks, Karachai, and others. Great num-

bers of enemy prisoners of war were organized by the NKVD into productive units for the state.

Although several important functions in the construction field were withdrawn from control of the NKVD early in 1946, this agency nevertheless appears to have been one of the largest capital construction ministries in the U.S.S.R. in the postwar period. The MVD is in charge of the construction and maintenance of highways of All-Union importance and has been entrusted with a large share of responsibility for some of the greatest railway and hydrotechnical construction projects attempted in the U.S.S.R. Included in the latter are the large power plants and canals announced in the Soviet press during the latter half of 1950. The great publicity accorded the five decrees on the subject did not, of course, mention the part the MVD will play, since the Soviet Government no longer boasts of the "achievements" of its slave labor force.

The present size of the slave labor force at the disposal of the MVD is unknown. Soviet sources in recent years have seldom referred to the U.S.S.R.'s forced labor system and hardly at all to the once well-publicized institutions which administer it. Forced labor nevertheless continues to form an integral unit in Soviet planning and is without question a factor of importance to the development of the Soviet economy.

The dislocation of population caused by the war served a great purpose in enlightening the world regarding Soviet forced labor. By strict censorship over all publications and outgoing news and by strict control of travel the Soviet authorities had attempted to draw curtains on the forced labor system. As a result of the war, however, thousands of Soviet citizens had an opportunity to escape from further Bolshevik rule by refusing to return to a concentration-camp existence. In this group were many who in the prewar period had suffered as political prisoners. Their accounts of personal experiences and their knowledge of the system threw a flood of light on the operation of the regime of forced labor in the Soviet Union, as did the accounts of German prisoners of war who had spent some time in regular Soviet concentration camps and were later allowed to return to their country.

[10] I. T. Golyakov, *Ugolovnoye Pravo* (Criminal Law), Moscow, 1947. p. 80.

29

Revision of the Criminal Code*

Vladimir Gsovski

(1959)

In the "thaw" following Stalin's death, the forced labor camps were largely emptied and new arrests for reasons of purely political "prophylaxis" reduced to a very low level. To some, this meant the end of terror in Russia and, even more, an affirmation of individual rights. Western jurists remain skeptical about the meaning of such tendencies so long as they are not embodied in law and observed in practice. Professor Gsovski reviews the revisions in Soviet Russia's legal code to assess just how far the changes have gone.

The report that the Supreme Soviet of the Soviet Union passed a new Criminal Code on December 25, 1958, is not quite accurate. Actually, there has been only a partial reform of the administration of criminal justice. The ten new laws that were enacted still do not deal with all the problems usually covered by a criminal code. However, the new legislation covers not only matters pertaining to criminal law but also those of criminal procedure, civilian and military judicial organization, and military crimes.

The new laws are of varying importance. Some of the provisions, especially those related to criminal law, have the features of a true reform, others are minor amendments of present legislation. This is true of the criminal procedure, and especially of the judicial organization.

Finally, the reform is not conclusive. The administration of criminal justice is governed in the Soviet Union by a combination of Federal acts, which establish only the Basic Principles in a given field, and the laws of the

* Reprinted from "The Soviet Union's Revised Criminal Code," *The New Leader* (April 27, 1959), pp. 10–13, by permission of the author and the publisher.

individual Soviet republics, which alone are technically called codes (Criminal Code, Code of Criminal Procedure, etc.). The Federal Constitution of 1936, which is still in force, provided for the enactment of Federal codes, but no such codes have been issued, although they were promised after Stalin's death. Instead, the Federal Constitution was amended in 1957, reserving, as before 1936, the issuance of codes to the individual republics, and the issuance of the Basic Principles to Federal authorities.

The 1924 Basic Principles on criminal law did not deal with individual crimes and their penalties but merely with the general principles governing crime and punishment. Following this pattern, on December 25, 1958, the Supreme Soviet enacted only Basic Principles of criminal law, criminal procedure, and judicial organization, leaving considerable room for the legislation (the "codes") of the individual Soviet republics. In this sense the reform is not conclusive. A final opinion must be reserved for the future when the codes of the individual republics are also enacted.

Return to Traditional Concepts. Nevertheless, the reform is significant. Since 1922, when systematic Criminal Codes were enacted in the Soviet republics, Soviet theorists have claimed that they are on a new path of criminal law which departs from some of the principles of criminal justice administration in non-Soviet countries. Although every field of Soviet law is supposed to derive from Marxian philosophy, in the field of criminal law Soviet penologists borrowed ideas and terms from the Italian positivistic school. Thus Soviet criminal legislation bore distinct traces of these borrowings. It sought to treat crime not as a wrong but merely as a social danger, conceiving it in a Marxian way as a danger to the Soviet social and political order. The role of guilt in the imposition of punishment was played down.

Soviet law even provided for the direct punishment of obviously innocent persons; e.g., the exile of adult members in the household of a military traitor, or his dependents, even though they were ignorant of his treasonable plans (RSFSR Code, Sec. 58.1.c). This departure from traditional concepts, it was claimed, was not injustice but a particular form of Soviet, proletarian "class justice." For a considerable time, in fact, a special nomenclature was used. A crime was called a "socially dangerous act"; punishment, "a measure of social defense of a judicial nature"; the death penalty, an "extreme measure of social defense."

Soviet criminal law began to drift away from this terminology in 1932, but a complete return to traditional terminology and to some traditional concepts is fully expressed in the new laws of December 25, 1958. This is tacit recognition of the injustice of previous Soviet practices, and of the hypocrisy of the previous attempts to justify them. The idea of ordinary human justice has scored a victory over class injustice. This is reflected in the language of the new laws; such terms as crime, punishment, and guilt are used without any special definitions.

Instead of a vague attitude toward guilt as an element of crime, the new law emphasizes that "only persons guilty of committing a crime shall be punished" (Sec. 3). Also, the legislation formerly in force stated that "the criminal legislation of the U.S.S.R. and the Soviet republics does not have the task of retribution or of penalization" (*kara* in Russian). The new law bluntly acknowledges that punishment is one of the purposes of penalty by stating that a "penalty appears not only as a punishment for a crime committed but also . . ." and then proceeds with a recital of the reformatory purposes of penalties.

Court Monopoly in Imposing Penalties. A particular feature of Soviet criminal law from the regime's inception has been the imposition of heavy penalties not only by the courts but also by an administrative police agency free from the rules of criminal law and procedure. This agency was successively called the Cheka, Ve Cheka (1917–1921), GPU and OGPU (1921–1939), NKVD (People's Commissariat for the Interior), and after 1946 the MVD (Ministry of the Interior). It could assume jurisdiction in any criminal case and dispose of it without the interference of a court. The latest agency of this type is the KGB (Committee for State Security).

The new legislation promises a radical break with this practice. Both the Principles on Criminal Law and the Principles on Criminal Procedure state that "criminal penalties may be applied only by a court sentence" (Sec. 3

of the Principles of Criminal Law), and "No one may be declared guilty of committing a crime and be subjected to a penalty except by a court sentence" (Sec. 7, par. 2 of the Principles of Criminal Procedure). If consistently carried out, this would completely abolish the 40-year-old Soviet practice of allowing the political police to impose penalties out of court.

But these statements, important as they are, are not conclusive. Heretofore, the imposition of severe punishment out of court has been regulated only to a limited extent. It was a matter of practice on the part of certain authorities, and it was accepted as lawful by the Government. Moreover, these administrative penalties were not technically called punishments but "repressions" or "measures of social defense," or were not designated by any special term.

Past experience calls for caution. Twice before, it may be recalled, the monopoly of the courts in imposing penalties was promised. When the Ve Cheka was abolished, the Resolution of December 30, 1921, stated that the Congress of Soviets would in the future "entrust the fight against violations of the laws of the Soviet Republic to judicial bodies." Again, the Decree of the Central Executive Committee of February 6, 1922, on the abolition of the Ve Cheka, promised that "in the future all cases involving crimes which are directed against the Soviet regime or violate the laws of the RSFSR shall be subject to trial in court exclusively." Nevertheless, the new GPU, and later the OGPU, appeared with the same *de facto* powers as the abolished Ve Cheka.

Also, Section 6 of the July 10, 1934 Act on the Establishment of the NKVD expressly stated that all cases investigated by this agency had to be transferred for decision to the courts . But Section 8 of the very same Act gave the power of punishment to the NKVD. To make the provisions on the exclusive power of the court final, the powers of the Ministry of the Interior and of the KGB must be precisely and legally defined. This has not been done so far.

Moreover, penalties out of court may be continued despite the avowed monopoly of the court, but will not be called "criminal penalties." For example, as late as 1957 and 1958 laws against "parasites" were enacted in Uzbekistan, Latvia, Kazakhstan, Turkmenistan, Tadzhikistan, Azerbaijan, and Armenia. Under these laws, persons "who carry on a parasitic mode of life . . . as well as those living on unearned income" may be exiled to from two to five years of forced labor by their neighbors. The decision, passed by an open ballot, is final if approved by the local Soviet. The law does not call the incriminated behavior a "crime" or a "socially dangerous act," nor is the exile called "criminal punishment"; it is a "public censure." The fate of these laws in the near future will show whether the monopoly of the court in imposing penalties is seriously meant.

Furthermore, in order to preclude any bypassing of the announced Principles, a clear, authoritative statement must be made to the effect that punishment means any suffering or abridgment of rights to which a citizen may be subjected by the authorities. The law should also be followed by an express repeal of all laws incompatible with the monopoly of the court in the imposition of penalties.

Crime by Analogy. An essential departure of Soviet criminal law from the traditional criminal law of Imperial Russia and modern Continental Europe was the invitation to arbitrariness in the application of the Criminal Code. This was done in the first place by allowing the court to impose penalties not only for acts exactly fitting the definition of a crime given by the statute but also for acts which merely resembled the definition. This is technically called the application of penal clauses by analogy. It was prohibited in all European pre-Soviet codes, and was expressed by the Latin phrase *nullum crimen nulla poena sine lege* (an act is not a crime unless so specified by a statute and no penalty may be imposed for it unless it is specified by a statute). The Soviets' repudiation of the maxim was later followed by the Nazis, in a modified form.

The new Basic Principles expressly renounce the application of penal clauses by analogy. It is true that, as before, crime is characterized as a socially dangerous act, i.e., an act dangerous to the Soviet social and legal order. Nevertheless, such act constitutes a crime, i.e., entails penalty, only if it is "specified by a criminal statute" (Sec. 3). Dimitri S. Polyansky, who presented the draft, stated that Soviet courts should no longer "apply a

[criminal] statute by analogy, i.e., convict anyone for an act which is not directly specified by a criminal statute" (*Izvestia,* December 28, 1958).

The Soviet Codes also contained another invitation to arbitrariness: in addition to citing 20 specific counter-revolutionary crimes and crimes most dangerous to the public administration, they also contained vague group definitions of such crimes. The new law on crimes against the State, which supersedes these provisions, does not contain such group definitions and provides only for specific crimes such as treason, espionage, etc.

Finally, there is further opportunity for arbitrary application of the Criminal Codes because the definitions of individual crimes are couched in a loose, non-legal language and lack definitiveness. Definite conclusions about the new laws, therefore, must be postponed because no new definitions of individual crimes, except for political and military crimes, have been enacted. The repudiation of crime by analogy will protect citizens only if it is followed by strict definitions of individual crimes.

The definitions in the new laws on crimes against the State and military crimes are technically far superior to the old ones, but they are still very broad. For example, treason, punishable by confinement for up to 15 years or by death, includes mere "flight abroad or refusal to return from abroad."

Juvenile Delinquency. A modest liberalization has occurred in the treatment of juvenile delinquents. Prior to the reform, minors, beginning with the age of 12, were subject to the same penalties as adults for a number of specified crimes; beginning with the age of 14 they had full responsibility for all other crimes. Now the responsibility for certain specific crimes starts at 14, and for all other crimes at 16. The list of crimes for which responsibility begins at 14 now includes murder, intentional causing of bodily injury resulting in the impairment of health, rape, assault with intent to rob, larceny, malicious rowdyism, intentional destruction or damaging of Government property or the personal property of citizens which results in serious consequences, and the commission of an act with the intent to cause a train wreck.

The length of the list leaves hardly any

crimes, outside of petty offenses, for which responsibility begins at 16. A bright spot in the new law is the provision that minors may have a defense counsel during the pre-trial investigation as soon as they are told of the charges preferred against them, which as a rule is no later than ten days after arrest.

Death Penalty. In contrast to the previous provisions, the death penalty is no longer mandatory but depends upon the decision of the court. The standard language employed in stating a penalty is that the guilty person "shall be punished by confinement or death" in crimes against the State, or "death or confinement" for several military crimes.

Even after the 1958 reform, Soviet criminal law is quite lavish with threats of the death penalty. The original provisions of the Criminal Code of the RSFSR provided for 70 crimes subject to the death penalty in 47 sections. The death penalty was abolished on January 17, 1920, and restored in May of the same year. It was again abolished on May 26, 1947, but restored on January 12, 1950, for "traitors to the country, spies and subversive diversionists" without further specification of these crimes. It was later extended to murder under aggravating circumstances. The new laws on crimes against the State and military crimes provide for the death penalty in over 30 instances. This is a very modest liberalization.

Other Punishments. The number of punishments has been reduced, and some obsolete forms abolished. The 1922 Code established 10 years as a maximum period of confinement. In 1938 this was raised to 25 years for certain political crimes. Now this maximum has been reduced to 15 years, and for all other crimes the old 10-year limit has been restored.

Presumption of Innocence Still Denied. The way in which the problem of the presumption of innocence is handled reveals the authors' lukewarm attitude toward their own creation.

This problem is far from settled in Soviet jurisprudence. "A series of statements in our writings contradict each other," remarks an authoritative text on criminal procedure (Karev, ed., *Soviet Criminal Procedure,* in Russian, 1956, p. 78). The practice of the courts, especially in political trials, has shown a tendency to place the burden of the proof

of innocence upon the accused. Several recent decisions of the Supreme Court, which came out in favor of the presumption of innocence, show that it was not clear to the lower courts. Section 13 of the draft was headed "The proof of guilt is imposed upon the accuser," and stated that "the burden of proof of guilt of the defendant shall be on the prosecutor."

In discussing this formula, V. N. Sukhodrev, the deputy chairman of the juridical committee attached to the Council of Ministers, stressed the fact that the draft did not contain any clear statement of the principle that "a person should be considered innocent until his guilt is established by a final decision of the court" (*Sovietskaia Iustitsiia,* 1958, No. 7, pp. 14–16). But the report by B. S. Sharkov, who introduced the final draft to the Supreme Soviet with its pertinent section substantially changed, showed that a heated discussion of the presumption took place among the members of the drafting committee. It seems that Sukhodrev's point of view was shared by others but was, in the long run, rejected by the committee.

Sharkov did not mince words in condemning Sukhodrev's formula: "Perhaps jurists can understand the meaning of such a complicated formula, but great masses of working people could hardly understand it." He defined the presumption of innocence as an "obsolete dogma of bourgeois law," which is "in deep contradiction to the essence of Soviet Socialist law." The committee changed the draft, and the following ambiguous text was passed on December 25, 1958:

"Sec. 14, par. 2. The court, the public prosecutor, the investigator or the person conducting the police examination shall have no right to shift the burden of proof to the defendant."

It may be asked how one can "shift" a burden of proof unless it is upon one. Does the statement therefore mean that the burden of proof is not only upon the public prosecutor, but also upon the court, the investigator or a person conducting a police examination? In any event, in the light of Sharkov's report the new provisions should be taken as an indication of the unwillingness of Soviet leaders to write the presumption of innocence into their law.

Pre-trial Proceedings. The new law leaves

the most objectionable features of Soviet criminal procedure practically unchanged. In more important cases, the trial is preceeded by a lengthy pre-trial investigation, during which the accused is kept in custody. A pre-trial investigation also preceded the trial in Imperial Russia and is to be found in all other countries of Continental Europe. It is not the fact of pre-trial investigation, but its nature and methods, that singles out Soviet procedure.

In non-Soviet legal systems, the pre-trial investigation is conducted by a judge, with all guarantees of judicial proceedings and under the supervision of the court, to which any act of the judge-investigator may be appealed. A sharp distinction is drawn between such judicial pre-trial investigation, the records of which are, under certain circumstances, used as evidence in court, and mere police examination, the records of which are not used as evidence. In contrast, under the Soviets pretrial proceedings have lost their judicial character. Investigators are completely detached from the court. The investigation is conducted either by investigators directly subordinate to, and appointed by, the public prosecutors or by agencies of state security, i.e., the secret police. There is no appeal to the court, and the records of police examination have equal probative value with the records of the investigation. All this remains unchanged in the new law.

Pre-trial Custody. The new law also restates the principle of the Constitution that the public prosecutor's approval is sufficient ground for arrest without a court warrant. In fact, the prosecutor's approval may be issued subsequent to the arrest. Once arrested and under investigation, the defendant remains subject to the jurisdiction of the public prosecutor until the trial, with no resort to the court.

Under the previous laws the permissible length of pre-trial custody was most uncertain. The statutes set a normal period of two months, which could be extended to a third month. But Nikolai Krylenko, the noted prosecutor, stated in 1928 that these rules were not observed, that in fact the RSFSR Attorney General used to extend the periods. The new Principles settle the matter more definitely by allowing regional and local prosecutors to extend the period for another three months, and the Attorney General of the Soviet republic, up to nine months.

Counsel for the Defense. The participation of the defense counsel is, as before, excluded for the entire period of pre-trial proceedings. He is definitely admitted only after the investigation is terminated and the bill of charges drawn up and delivered to the defendant. However, for the first time in Soviet history, the new law affirms the counsel's right to see the defendant in custody. Exception is made for minors and incompetent persons, who may have a defense counsel as soon as charges are preferred against them.

Appeal and Reopening of Cases. Another objectionable feature of Soviet criminal procedure also remains unchanged: the unequal rights of appeal of the public prosecutor, on the one hand, and the private litigant, the defendant and his counsel, on the other. Both have the right to appeal to the next higher court only. This court verifies whether the judgment is legal and well-founded, and renders a final decision. This is as far as a private party can go — the Federal Supreme Court is closed to private parties. But the Attorney General, the public prosecutors subordinate to him, and the presidents of the courts above the lower people's court may move to reopen a closed case. This is done either by the Supreme Court or by special benches in lower courts called *presidia.* Private parties have no right to petition the court for such reopening but may, and do, petition the officers who have such right.

A case may be reopened several times, and prior to 1958 the reopening was not limited to any period of time. The new law stipulates that a judgment of acquittal may not be reopened after the expiration of one year. The same limitation also applies to a judgment of conviction which is attacked because the court applied too mild a punishment. In all other instances, reopening is not barred, as it is now, by a period of time. A case is heard on appeal, as a rule, without the defendant being summoned. If he appears, he must be heard. In deciding on the reopening of a case, the defendant may be heard only if the court expressly so orders.

Thus a case begins in an open court and is then transferred behind closed doors where it is a purely internal matter to be decided by officials charged with the administration of justice. The changes enacted on judicial organization are minor and rather technical.

They are not truly reformatory and, therefore, are not discussed here.

The general evaluation of the reform is that it represents an attempt to administer an improved Criminal Law through essentially unchanged procedures and courts.

30

The Crimes of Stalin*

Nikita S. Khrushchev

(1956)

Despite the enormous amount of evidence for the existence of terror as a pervasive feature of Soviet life, many people found it hard to accept the reality of such seemingly monstrous behavior in a society for which its rulers disseminated so profoundly different an image. It is therefore a great relief to Soviet experts simply to put forth Stalin's long-time associate and present successor to tell the story of Stalin's crimes. It is notable that this speech delivered before the 20th Congress of the Communist Party has as yet not been published in any public source in the Soviet Union — although its contents have been included in summary form in certain documents circulated by the Party.

Comrades! In the report of the Central Committee of the Party at the 20th Congress, in a number of speeches by delegates to the Congress, as also formerly during the plenary CC/CPSU [Central Committee of the Communist Party of the Soviet Union] sessions, quite a lot has been said about the cult of the individual and about its harmful consequences.

After Stalin's death the Central Committee of the Party began to implement a policy of explaining concisely and consistently that it is impermissible and foreign to the spirit of Marx-

* Reprinted from a version of the speech given at a session of the Twentieth Party Congress on February 25, 1956 released by the United States Department of State on June 4, 1956. This document was obtained from a confidential source, and is understood to have been prepared for the guidance of the leadership of a Communist Party outside the U.S.S.R.

ism-Leninism to elevate one person, to transform him into a superman possessing supernatural characteristics, akin to those of a god. Such a man supposedly knows everything, sees everything, thinks for everyone, can do anything, is infallible in his behavior.

Such a belief about a man, and specifically about Stalin, was cultivated among us for many years.

The objective of the present report is not a thorough evaluation of Stalin's life and activity. Concerning Stalin's merits, an entirely sufficient number of books, pamphlets and studies had already been written in his lifetime. The role of Stalin in the preparation and execution of the Socialist Revolution, in the Civil War, and in the fight for the construction of socialism in our country, is universally known. Everyone knows this well. At present, we are concerned with a question which has immense importance for the Party now and for the future — with how the cult of the person of Stalin has been gradually growing, the cult which became at a certain specific stage the source of a whole series of exceedingly serious and grave perversions of party principles, of Party democracy, of revolutionary legality.

Because of the fact that not all as yet realize fully the practical consequences resulting from the cult of the individual, the great harm caused by the violation of the principle of collective direction of the Party and because of the accumulation of immense and limitless power in the hands of one person, the Central Committee of the Party considers it absolutely necessary to make the material pertaining to this matter available to the 20th Congress of the Communist Party of the Soviet Union.

Opposition of Marx and Lenin to the Cult of the Individual

Allow me first of all to remind you how severely the classics of Marxism-Leninism denounced every manifestation of the cult of the individual. In a letter to the German political worker, Wilhelm Bloss, Marx stated: "From my antipathy to any cult of the individual, I never made public during the existence of the International the numerous addresses from various countries which recognized my merits and which annoyed me. I did not even reply to them, except sometimes to rebuke their authors. Engels and I first joined the secret society of Communists on the condition that everything making for superstitious worship of authority would be deleted from its statute. Lassalle subsequently did quite the opposite."

Sometime later Engels wrote: "Both Marx and I have always been against any public manifestation with regard to individuals, with the exception of cases when it had an important purpose; and we most strongly opposed such manifestations which during our lifetime concerned us personally."

The great modesty of the genius of the Revolution, Vladimir Ilyich Lenin, is known. Lenin had always stressed the role of the people as the creator of history, the directing and organizational role of the Party as a living and creative organism, and also the role of the Central Committee.

Marxism does not negate the role of the leaders of the working class in directing the revolutionary liberation movement.

While ascribing great importance to the role of the leaders and organizers of the masses, Lenin at the same time mercilessly stigmatized every manifestation of the cult of the individual, inexorably combated the foreign-to-Marxism views about a "hero" and a "crowd," and countered all efforts to oppose a "hero" to the masses and to the people.

Lenin taught that the Party's strength depends on its indissoluble unity with the masses, on the fact that behind the Party follows the people — workers, peasants and intelligentsia. "Only he will win and retain the power," said Lenin, "who believes in the people, who submerges himself in the fountain of the living creativeness of the people."

Lenin spoke with pride about the Bolshevik Communist Party as the leader and teacher of the people; he called for the presentation of all the most important questions before the opinion of knowledgeable workers, before the opinion of their Party; he said: "We believe in it, we see in it the wisdom, the honor, and the conscience of our epoch."

Lenin resolutely stood against every attempt aimed at belittling or weakening the directing role of the Party in the structure of the Soviet state. He worked out Bolshevik principles of Party direction and norms of Party life, stressing that the guiding principle of Party leadership is its collegiality. Already during the pre-Revolutionary years, Lenin called the Central Committee of the Party a collective of leaders

and the guardian and interpreter of Party principles. "During the period between congresses," pointed out Lenin, "the Central Committee guards and interprets the principles of the Party."

Underlining the role of the Central Committee of the Party and its authority, Vladimir Ilyich pointed out: "Our Central Committee constituted itself as a closely centralized and highly authoritative group."

During Lenin's life the Central Committee of the Party was a real expression of collective leadership of the Party and of the nation. Being a militant Marxist-revolutionist, always unyielding in matters of principle, Lenin never imposed by force his views upon his co-workers. He tried to convince; he patiently explained his opinions to others. Lenin always diligently observed that the norms of Party life were realized, that the Party statute was enforced, that the Party congresses and the plenary sessions of the Central Committee took place at the proper intervals.

Lenin's Suspicion of Stalin

In addition to the great accomplishments of V. I. Lenin for the victory of the working class and of the working peasants, for the victory of our Party and for the application of the ideas of scientific Communism to life, his acute mind expressed itself also in this — that he detected in Stalin in time those negative characteristics which resulted later in grave consequences. Fearing the future fate of the Party and of the Soviet nation, V. I. Lenin made a completely correct characterization of Stalin, pointing out that it was necessary to consider the question of transferring Stalin from the position of the Secretary General because of the fact that Stalin is excessively rude, that he does not have a proper attitude toward his comrades, that he is capricious and abuses his power.

In December 1922, in a letter to the Party Congress, Vladimir Ilyich wrote: "After taking over the position of Secretary General, Comrade Stalin accumulated in his hands immeasurable power and I am not certain whether he will be always able to use this power with the required care."

This letter — a political document of tremendous importance, known in the Party history as Lenin's "testament" — was distributed among the delegates to the 20th Party Congress. You have read it and will undoubtedly read it again more than once. You might reflect on Lenin's plain words, in which expression is given to Vladimir Ilyich's anxiety concerning the Party, the people, the state, and the future direction of Party policy.

Vladimir Ilyich said:

> Stalin is excessively rude, and this defect, which can be freely tolerated in our midst and in contacts among us Communists, becomes a defect which cannot be tolerated in one holding the position of the Secretary General. Because of this, I propose that the comrades consider the method by which Stalin would be removed from this position and by which another man would be selected for it, a man who, above all, would differ from Stalin in only one quality, namely, greater tolerance, greater loyalty, greater kindness and more considerate attitude toward the comrades, a less capricious temper, etc.

This document of Lenin's was made known to the delegates at the 13th Party Congress, who discussed the question of transferring Stalin from the position of Secretary General. The delegates declared themselves in favor of retaining Stalin in this post, hoping that he would heed the critical remarks of Vladimir Ilyich and would be able to overcome the defects which caused Lenin serious anxiety.

Comrades! The Party Congress should become acquainted with two new documents, which confirm Stalin's character as already outlined by Vladimir Ilyich Lenin in his "testament." These documents are a letter from Nadezhda Konstantinovna Krupskaya to Kamenev, who was at that time head of the Political Bureau, and a personal letter from Vladimir Ilyich Lenin to Stalin.

I will now read these documents:

> Lev Borisovich!
> Because of a short letter which I had written in words dictated to me by Vladimir Ilyich by permission of the doctors, Stalin allowed himself yesterday an unusually rude outburst directed at me. This is not my first day in the Party. During all these 30 years I have never heard from any comrade one word of rudeness. The business of the Party and of Ilyich are not less dear to me than to Stalin. I need at present the maximum of self-control. What one can and what one cannot discuss with Ilyich I know

better than any doctor, because I know what makes him nervous and what does not, in any case I know better than Stalin. I am turning to you and to Grigory [E. Zinoviev] as much closer comrades of V. I. and I beg you to protect me from rude interference with my private life and from vile invectives and threats. I have no doubt as to what will be the unanimous decision of the Control Commission, with which Stalin sees fit to threaten me; however, I have neither the strength nor the time to waste on this foolish quarrel. And I am a living person and my nerves are strained to the utmost.

> N. Krupskaya

Nadezhda Konstantinovna wrote this letter on December 23, 1922. After two and a half months, in March 1923, Valdimir Ilyich Lenin sent Stalin the following letter:

> To Comrade Stalin:
> Copies for: Kamenev and Zinoviev.
> Dear Comrade Stalin!
> You permitted yourself a rude summons of my wife to the telephone and a rude reprimand of her. Despite the fact that she told you that she agreed to forget what was said, nevertheless Zinoviev and Kamenev heard about it from her. I have no intention to forget so easily that which is being done against me, and I need not stress here that I consider as directed against me that which is being done against my wife. I ask you, therefore, that you weigh carefully whether you are agreeable to retracting your words and apologizing or whether you prefer the severance of relations between us.
> Sincerely: Lenin

> March 5, 1923

[Commotion in the hall.]

Comrades! I will not comment on these documents. They speak eloquently for themselves. Since Stalin could behave in this manner during Lenin's life, could thus behave toward Nadezhda Konstantinovna Krupskaya — whom the Party knows well and values highly as a loyal friend of Lenin and as an active fighter for the cause of the Party since its creation — we can easily imagine how Stalin treated other people. These negative characteristics of his developed steadily and during the last years acquired an absolutely insufferable character.

As later events have proven, Lenin's anxiety was justified: in the first period after Lenin's death, Stalin still paid attention to his advice, but later he began to disregard the serious admonitions of Vladimir Ilyich.

When we analyze the practice of Stalin in regard to the direction of the Party and of the country, when we pause to consider everything which Stalin perpetrated, we must be convinced that Lenin's fears were justified. The negative characteristics of Stalin, which, in Lenin's time, were only incipient, transformed themselves during the last years into a grave abuse of power by Stalin, which caused untold harm to our party.

Stalin Compared with Lenin

We have to consider seriously and analyze correctly this matter in order that we may preclude any possibility of a repetition in any form whatever of what took place during the life of Stalin, who absolutely did not tolerate collegiality in leadership and in work, and who practiced brutal violence, not only toward everything which opposed him, but also toward that which seemed, to his capricious and despotic character, contrary to his concepts.

Stalin acted not through persuasion, explanation, and patient cooperation with people, but by imposing his concepts and demanding absolute submission to his opinion. Whoever opposed this concept or tried to prove his viewpoint and the correctness of his position was doomed to removal from the leading collective and to subsequent moral and physical annihilation. This was especially true during the period following the 17th Party Congress, when many prominent Party leaders and rank-and-file Party workers, honest and dedicated to the cause of Communism, fell victim to Stalin's despotism.

We must affirm that the Party had fought a serious fight against the Trotskyites, rightists, and bourgeois nationalists, and that it disarmed ideologically all the enemies of Leninism. This ideological fight was carried on successfully, as a result of which the Party became strengthened and tempered. Here Stalin played a positive role.

The Party led a great political-ideological struggle against those in its own ranks who proposed anti-Leninist theses, who represented a political line hostile to the Party and to the cause of socialism. This was a stubborn and a difficult fight but a necessary one, because the political line of both the Trotskyite-Zinovievite bloc and of the Bukharinites led actually toward the restoration of capitalism and capitulation to the world bourgeoisie. Let us consider for a moment what would have happened if in 1928–1929 the political line of right deviation had prevailed among us, or orientation toward "cotton-dress industrialization," or toward the kulak, etc. We would not now have a powerful heavy industry, we would not have the kolkhozes, we would find ourselves disarmed and weak in a capitalist encirclement.

It was for this reason that the Party led an inexorable ideological fight and explained to all Party members and to the non-party masses the harm and the danger of the anti-Leninist proposals of the Trotskyite opposition and the rightist opportunists. And this great work of explaining the Party line bore fruit; both the Trotskyites and the rightist opportunists were politically isolated; the overwhelming Party majority supported the Leninist line and the Party was able to awaken and organize the working masses to apply the Leninist Party line and to build socialism.

Worth noting is the fact that, even during the progress of the furious ideological fight against the Trotskyites, the Zinovievites, the Bukharinites, and others, extreme repressive measures were not used against them. The fight was on ideological grounds. But some years later, when socialism in our country was fundamentally constructed, when the exploiting classes were generally liquidated, when the Soviet social structure had radically changed, when the social basis for political movements and groups hostile to the Party had violently contracted, when the ideological opponents of the Party were long since defeated politically — then the repression directed against them began.

It was precisely during this period (1935–1937–1938) that the practice of mass repression through the Government apparatus was born, first against the enemies of Leninism — Trotskyites, Zinovievites, Bukharinites, long since politically defeated by the Party — and subsequently also against many honest Communists, against those Party cadres who had borne the heavy load of the Civil War and the first and most difficult years of industrialization and collectivization, who actively fought against the Trotskyites and the rightists for the Leninist Party line.

Stalin originated the concept "enemy of the people." This term automatically rendered it unnecessary that the ideological errors of a man or men engaged in a controversy be proven; this term made possible the usage of the most cruel repression, violating all norms of revolutionary legality, against anyone who in any way disagreed with Stalin, against those who were only suspected of hostile intent, against those who had bad reputations. This concept "enemy of the people" actually eliminated the possibility of any kind of ideological fight or the making of one's views known on this or that issue, even those of a practical character. In the main, and in actuality, the only proof of guilt used, against all norms of current legal science, was the "confession" of the accused himself; and, as subsequent probing proved, "confessions" were acquired through physical pressures against the accused.

This led to glaring violations of revolutionary legality and to the fact that many entirely innocent persons, who in the past had defended the Party line, became victims.

We must assert that, in regard to those persons who in their time had opposed the Party line, there were often no sufficiently serious reasons for their physical annihilation. The formula "enemy of the people" was specifically introduced for the purpose of physically annihilating such individuals.

It is a fact that many persons who were later annihilated as enemies of the Party and people had worked with Lenin during his life. Some of these persons had made errors during Lenin's life, but, despite this, Lenin benefited by their work; he corrected them and he did everything possible to retain them in the ranks of the Party; he induced them to follow him.

In this connection the delegates to the Party Congress should familiarize themselves with an unpublished note by V. I. Lenin directed to the Central Committee's Political Bureau in October 1920. Outlining the duties of the Control Commission, Lenin wrote that the commission should be transformed into a real "organ of Party and proletarian conscience."

As a special duty of the Control Commission there is recommended a deep, individualized relationship with, and sometimes even a type of therapy for, the representatives of the so-called opposition — those who have experienced a psychological crisis because of failure in their Soviet or party career. An effort should be made to quiet them, to explain the matter to them in a way used among comrades, to find for them (avoiding the method of issuing orders) a task for which they are psychologically fitted. Advice and rules relating to this matter are to be formulated by the Central Committee's Organizational Bureau, etc.

Everyone knows how irreconcilable Lenin was with the ideological enemies of Marxism, with those who deviated from the correct Party line. At the same time, however, Lenin, as is evident from the given document, in his practice of directing the Party demanded the most intimate Party contact with people who had shown indecision or temporary non-conformity with the party line, but whom it was possible to return to the Party path. Lenin advised that such people should be patiently educated without the application of extreme methods.

Lenin's wisdom in dealing with people was evident in his work with cadres.

An entirely different relationship with people characterized Stalin. Lenin's traits — patient work with people, stubborn and painstaking education of them, the ability to induce people to follow him without using compulsion, but rather through the ideological influence on them of the whole collective — were entirely foreign to Stalin. He discarded the Leninist method of convincing and educating, he abandoned the method of ideological struggle for that of administrative violence, mass repressions, and terror. He acted on an increasingly larger scale and more stubbornly through punitive organs, at the same time often violating all existing norms of morality and of Soviet laws.

Arbitrary behavior by one person encouraged and permitted arbitrariness in others. Mass arrests and deportations of many thousands of people, execution without trial and without normal investigation created conditions of insecurity, fear, and even desperation.

This, of course, did not contribute toward unity of the Party ranks and of all strata of working people, but, on the contrary, brought about annihilation and the expulsion from the Party of workers who were loyal but inconvenient to Stalin.

Our Party fought for the implementation of Lenin's plans for the construction of socialism. This was an ideological fight. Had Leninist principles been observed during the course of this fight, had the Party's devotion to principles been skillfully combined with a keen and solictious concern for people, had they not been repelled and wasted but rather drawn to our side, we certainly would not have had such a brutal violation of revolutionary legality and many thousands of people would not have fallen victim to the method of terror. Extraordinary methods would then have been resorted to only against those people who had in fact committed criminal acts against the Soviet system.

Let us recall some historical facts.

In the days before the October Revolution, two members of the Central Committee of the Bolshevik party — Kamenev and Zinoviev — declared themselves against Lenin's plan for an armed uprising. In addition, on October 18 they published in the Menshevik newspaper, *Novaya Zhizn,* a statement declaring that the Bolsheviks were making preparations for an uprising and that they considered it adventuristic. Kamenev and Zinoviev thus disclosed to the enemy the decision of the Central Committee to stage the uprising and that the uprising had been organized to take place within the very near future.

This was treason against the Party and against the Revolution. In this connection, V. I. Lenin wrote: "Kamenev and Zinoviev revealed the decision of the Central Committee of their Party on the armed uprising to Rodzyanko and Kerensky . . ." He put before the Central Committee the question of Zinoviev's and Kamenev's expulsion from the Party.

However, after the Great Socialist October Revolution, as is known, Zinoviev and Kamenev were given leading positions. Lenin put them in positions in which they carried out most responsible Party tasks and participated actively in the work of the leading Party and Soviet organs. It is known that Zinoviev and Kamenev committed a number of other serious errors during Lenin's life. In his "testament" Lenin warned that "Zinoviev's and Kamenev's October episode was of course not an accident." But Lenin did not pose the question of their arrest and certainly not their shooting.

Or, let us take the example of the Trotsky-ites. At present, after a sufficiently long historical period, we can speak about the fight with the Trotskyites with complete calm and can analyze this matter with sufficient objectivity. After all, around Trotsky were people whose origin cannot by any means be traced to bourgeois society. Part of them belonged to the Party intelligentsia and a certain part were recruited from among the workers. We can name many individuals who, in their time, joined the Trotskyites; however, these same individuals took an active part in the workers' movement before the Revolution, during the Socialist October Revolution itself, and also in the consolidation of the victory of this greatest of revolutions. Many of them broke with Trotskyism and returned to Leninist positions. Was it necessary to annihilate such people? We are deeply convinced that, had Lenin lived, such an extreme method would not have been used against any of them.

Such are only a few historical facts. But can it be said that Lenin did not decide to use even the most severe means against enemies of the Revolution when this was actually necessary? No; no one can say this. Vladimir Ilyich demanded uncompromising dealings with the enemies of the Revolution and of the working class and when necessary resorted ruthlessly to such methods. You will recall only V. I. Lenin's fight with the Socialist Revolutionary organizers of the anti-Soviet uprising, with the counterrevolutionary kulaks in 1918 and with others, when Lenin without hesitation used the most extreme methods against the enemies. Lenin used such methods, however, only against actual class enemies and not against those who blunder, who err, and whom it was possible to lead through ideological influence and even retain in the leadership.

Lenin used severe methods only in the most necessary cases, when the exploiting classes were still in existence and were vigorously opposing the Revolution, when the struggle for survival was decidedly assuming the sharpest forms, even including a civil war.

Stalin, on the other hand, used extreme methods and mass repressions at a time when the Revolution was already victorious, when the Soviet state was strengthened, when the exploiting classes were already liquidated and socialist relations were rooted solidly in all phases of national economy, when our Party was politically consolidated and had strengthened itself both numerically and ideologically. It is clear that here Stalin showed in a whole series of cases his intolerance, his brutality and his abuse of power. Instead of proving his political correctness and mobilizing the masses, he often chose the path of repression and physical annihilation, not only against actual enemies, but also against individuals who had not committed any crimes against the Party and the Soviet Government. Here we see no wisdom but only a demonstration of the brutal force which had once so alarmed V. I. Lenin.

Lately, especially after the unmasking of the Beria gang, the Central Committee looked into a series of matters fabricated by this gang. This revealed a very ugly picture of brutal willfulness connected with the incorrect behavior of Stalin. As facts prove, Stalin, using his unlimited power, allowed himself many abuses, acting in the name of the Central Committee, not asking for the opinion of the Committee members nor even of the members of the Central Committee's Political Bureau; often he did not inform them about his personal decisions concerning very important Party and government matters.

Violation of Party Rules and Principles

Considering the question of the cult of an individual, we must first of all show everyone what harm this caused to the interests of our Party.

Vladimir Ilyich Lenin had always stressed the Party's role and significance in the direction of the socialist government of workers and peasants; he saw in this the chief precondition for a successful building of socialism in our country. Pointing to the great responsibility of the Bolshevik Party, as ruling party of the Soviet state, Lenin called for the most meticulous observance of all norms of Party life; he called for the realization of the principles of collegiality in the direction of the party and the state.

Collegiality of leadership flows from the very nature of our Party, a party built on the principles of democratic centralism. "This means," said Lenin, "that all Party matters are accomplished by all Party members — directly or through representatives — who, without any exceptions, are subject to the same rules; in addition, all administrative members, all directing collegia, all holders of Party positions are elective, they must account for their activities and are recallable."

It is known that Lenin himself offered an example of the most careful observance of these principles. There was no matter so important that Lenin himself decided it without asking for advice and approval of the majority of the Central Committee members or of the members of the Central Committee's Political Bureau.

In the most difficult period for our Party and our country, Lenin considered it necessary regularly to convoke congresses, Party conferences, and plenary sessions of the Central Committee at which all the most important questions were discussed and where resolutions, carefully worked out by the collective of leaders, were approved.

We can recall, for an example, the year 1918 when the country was threatened by the attack of the imperialistic interventionists. In this situation the 7th Party Congress was convened in order to discuss a vitally important matter which could not be postponed — the matter of peace. In 1919, while the civil war was raging, the 8th Party Congress convened, which adopted a new Party program, decided such important matters as the relationship with the peasant masses, the organization of the Red Army, the leading role of the Party in the work of the soviets, the correction of the social composition of the Party, and other matters. In 1920 the 9th Party Congress was convened, which laid down guiding principles pertaining to the Party's work in the sphere of economic construction. In 1921 the 10th Party Congress accepted Lenin's New Economic Policy and the historical resolution called "About Party Unity."

During Lenin's life, Party Congresses were convened regularly; always, when a radical turn in the development of the Party and the country took place, Lenin considered it absolutely necessary that the Party discuss at length all the basic matters pertaining to internal and foreign policy and to questions bearing on the development of party and government.

It is very characteristic that Lenin addressed to the Party Congress as the highest party organ his last articles, letters, and remarks. During the period between congresses, the

Central Committee of the Party, acting as the most authoritative leading collective, meticulously observed the principles of the Party and carried out its policy.

So it was during Lenin's life.

Were our Party's holy Leninist principles observed after the death of Vladimir Ilyich?

Whereas, during the first few years after Lenin's death, Party Congresses and Central Committee plenums took place more or less regularly, later, when Stalin began increasingly to abuse his power, these principles were brutally violated. This was especially evident during the last 15 years of his life. Was it a normal situation when over 13 years elapsed between the 18th and 19th Party Congresses, years during which our Party and our country had experienced so many important events? These events demanded categorically that the Party should have passed resolutions pertaining to the country's defense during the Patriotic War [World War II] and to peacetime construction after the war. Even after the end of the war a Congress was not convened for over seven years.

Central Committee plenums were hardly ever called. It should be sufficient to mention that during all the years of the Patriotic War not a single Central Committee plenum took place. It is true that there was an attempt to call a Central Committee plenum in October 1941, when Central Committee members from the whole country were called to Moscow. They waited two days for the opening of the plenum, but in vain. Stalin did not even want to meet and talk to the Central Committee members. This fact shows how demoralized Stalin was in the first months of the war and how haughtily and disdainfully he treated the Central Committee members.

In practice, Stalin ignored the norms of Party life and trampled on the Leninist principle of collective party leadership.

Repression of Innocent Party Members

Stalin's willfulness vis-a-vis the Party and its Central Committee became fully evident after the 17th Party Congress which took place in 1934.

Having at its disposal numerous data showing brutal willfulness toward Party cadres, the Central Committee had created a Party Commission under the control of the Central Committee Presidium; it was charged with investigating what made possible the mass repressions against the majority of the Central Committee members and candidates elected at the 17th Congress of the All-Union Communist Party (Bolsheviks).

The commission has become acquainted with a large quantity of materials in the NKVD archives and with other documents and has established many facts pertaining to the fabrication of cases against Communists, to false accusations, to glaring abuses of socialist legality, which resulted in the death of innocent people. It became apparent that many Party, Soviet, and economic activists, who were branded in 1937–1938 as "enemies," were actually never enemies, spies, wreckers, etc., but were always honest Communists; they were only so stigmatized and, often, no longer able to bear barbaric tortures, they charged themselves (at the order of the investigative judges — falsifiers) with all kinds of grave and unlikely crimes. The commission has presented to the Central Committee Presidium lengthy and documented materials pertaining to mass repressions against the delegates to the 17th Party Congress and against members of the Central Committee elected at that Congress. These materials have been studied by the Presidium of the Central Committee.

It was determined that of the 139 members and candidates of the Party's Central Committee who were elected at the 17th Congress, 98 persons i.e., 70 per cent, were arrested and shot (mostly in 1937–1938). [Indignation in the hall.]

What was the composition of the delegates to the 17th Congress? It is known that 80 per cent of the voting participants of the 17th Congress joined the Party during the years of conspiracy before the Revolution and during the civil war; this means before 1921. By social origin the basic mass of the delegates to the Congress were workers (60 per cent of the voting members).

For this reason, it was inconceivable that a congress so composed would have elected a Central Committee a majority of whom would prove to be enemies of the Party. The only reason why 70 per cent of Central Committee members and candidates elected at the 17th Congress were branded as enemies of the Party and of the people was because honest Communists were slandered, accusations against them were fabricated, and revolutionary legality was gravely undermined.

The same fate met not only the Central Committee members but also the majority of the delegates to the 17th Party Congress. Of 1,966 delegates with either voting or advisory rights, 1,108 persons were arrested on charges of anti-revolutionary crimes, i.e., decidedly more than a majority. This very fact shows how absurd, wild, and contrary to common sense were the charges of counterrevolutionary crimes made out, as we now see, against a majority of participants at the 17th Party Congress. [Indignation in the hall.]

We should recall that the 17th Party Congress is historically known as the Congress of Victors. Delegates to the Congress were active participants in the building of our socialist state; many of them suffered and fought for Party interests during the pre-Revolutionary years in the conspiracy and at the civil-war fronts; they fought their enemies valiantly and often nervelessly looked into the face of death. How, then, can we believe that such people could prove to be "two-faced" and had joined the camps of the enemies of socialism during the era after the political liquidation of Zinovievites, Trotskyites and rightists and after the great accomplishments of socialist construction?

This was the result of the abuse of power by Stalin, who began to use mass terror against the Party cadres.

What is the reason that mass repressions against activists increased more and more after the 17th Party Congress? It was because at that time Stalin had so elevated himself above the Party and above the nation that he ceased to consider either the Central Committee or the Party. While he still reckoned with the opinion of the collective before the 17th Congress, after the complete political liquidation of the Trotskyites, Zinovievites, and Bukharinites, when as a result of that fight and socialist victories the Party achieved unity, Stalin ceased to an ever greater degree to consider the members of the Party's Central Committee and even the members of the Political Bureau. Stalin thought that now he could decide all things alone and all he needed were statisticians; he treated all others in such a way that they could only listen to and praise him.

After the criminal murder of Sergei M. Kirov, mass repressions and brutal acts of violation of socialist legality began. On the evening of December 1, 1934, on Stalin's initiative (without the approval of the Political Bureau — which was passed two days later, casually), the Secretary of the Presidium of the Central Executive Committee, Yenukidze, signed the following directive:

> 1. Investigative agencies are directed to speed up the cases of those accused of the preparation or execution of acts of terror.
>
> 2. Judicial organs are directed not to hold up the execution of death sentences pertaining to crimes of this category in order to consider the possibility of pardon, because the Presidium of the Central Executive Committee of the USSR does not consider as possible the receiving of petitions of this sort.
>
> 3. The organs of the Commissariat of Internal Affairs are directed to execute the death sentences against criminals of the above-mentioned category immediately after the passage of sentences.

This directive became the basis for mass acts of abuse against socialist legality. During many of the fabricated court cases, the accused were charged with "the preparation" of terroristic acts; this deprived them of any possibility that their cases might be re-examined, even when they stated before the court that their "confessions" were secured by force, and when, in a convincing manner, they disproved the accusations against them.

It must be asserted that to this day the circumstances surrounding Kirov's murder hide many things which are inexplicable and mysterious and demand a most careful examination. There are reasons for the suspicion that the killer of Kirov, Nikolayev, was assisted by someone from among the people whose duty it was to protect the person of Kirov. A month and a half before the killing, Nikolayev was arrested on the grounds of suspicious behavior but he was released and not even searched. It is an unusually suspicious circumstance that when the Chekist assigned to protect Kirov was being brought for an interrogation, on December 2, 1934, he was killed in a car "accident" in which no other occupants of the car were harmed. After the murder of Kirov, top functionaries of the Leningrad NKVD were given very light sentences, but in 1937 they were shot. We can assume that they were shot in order to cover the traces of the organizers of Kirov's killing. [Movement in the hall.]

Stalin's Responsibility for Purges and Terror

Mass repressions grew tremendously from the end of 1936 after a telegram from Stalin and Zhdanov, dated from Sochi on September 25, 1936, was addressed to Kaganovich, Molotov, and other members of the Political Bureau. The content of the telegram was as follows:

> We deem it absolutely necessary and urgent that Comrade Yezhov be nominated to the post of People's Commissar for Internal Affairs. Yagoda has definitely proved himself to be incapable of unmasking the Trotskyite-Zinovievite bloc. The OGPU is four years behind in this matter. This is noted by all party workers and by the majority of the representatives of the NKVD.

Strictly speaking, we should stress that Stalin did not meet with and, therefore, could not know the opinion of Party workers.

This Stalinist formulation that the "NKVD is four years behind" in applying mass repression and that there is a necessity for "catching up" with the neglected work directly pushed the NKVD workers on the path of mass arrests and executions.

We should state that this formulation was also forced on the February-March plenary session of the Central Committee of the All-Union Communist Party (Bolsheviks) in 1937. The plenary resolution approved it on the basis of Yezhov's report, "Lessons flowing from the harmful activity, diversion, and espionage of the Japanese-German-Trotskyite agents," stating:

> The Plenum of the Central Committee of the All-Union Communist Party (Bolsheviks) considers that all facts revealed during the investigation into the matter of an anti-Soviet Trotskyite center and of its followers in the provinces show that the People's Commissariat of Internal Affairs has fallen behind at least four years in the attempt to unmask these most inexorable enemies of the people.

The mass repressions at this time were made under the slogan of a fight against the Trotsky-ites. Did the Trotskyites at this time actually constitute such a danger to our Party and to the Soviet State? We should recall that in 1927, on the eve of the 15th Party Congress, only some 4,000 votes were cast for the Trotsky-ite-Zinovievite opposition while there were 724,000 for the Party line. During the 10 years which passed between the 15th Party Congress and the February-March Central Committee Plenum, Trotskyism was completely disarmed; many former Trotskyites had changed their former views and worked in the various sectors building socialism. It is clear that in the situation of socialist victory there was no basis for mass terror in the country.

Stalin's report at the February-March Central Committee Plenum in 1937, "Deficiencies of Party Work and Methods for the Liquidation of the Trotskyites and of Other Two-Facers," contained an attempt at theoretical justification of the mass terror policy under the pretext that as we march forward toward socialism class war must allegedly sharpen. Stalin asserted that both history and Lenin taught him this.

Actually Lenin taught that the application of revolutionary violence is necessitated by the resistance of the exploiting classes, and this referred to the era when the exploiting classes existed and were powerful. As soon as the nation's political situation had improved, when in January 1920 the Red Army took Rostov and thus won a most important victory over Denikin, Lenin instructed [Cheka chief Felix] Dzerzhinsky to stop mass terror and to abolish the death penalty. Lenin justified this important political move of the Soviet State in the following manner in his report at the session of the All-Union Central Executive Committee on February 2, 1920:

> We were forced to use terror because of the terror practiced by the Entente, when strong world powers threw their hordes against us, not avoiding any type of conduct. We would not have lasted two days had we not answered these attempts of officers and White Guardists in a merciless fashion; this meant the use of terror, but this was forced upon us by the terrorist methods of the Entente.
>
> But as soon as we attained a decisive victory, even before the end of the war, immediately after taking Rostov, we gave up the use of the death penalty and thus proved that we intend to execute our own program in the manner

that we promised. We say that the application of violence flows out of the decision to smother the exploiters, the big landowners, and the capitalists; as soon as this was accomplished we gave up the use of all extraordinary methods. We have proved this in practice.

Stalin deviated from these clear and plain precepts of Lenin. Stalin put the Party and the NKVD up to the use of mass terror when the exploiting classes had been liquidated in our country and when there were no serious reasons for the use of extraordinary mass terror.

This terror was actually directed not at the remnants of the defeated exploiting classes but against the honest workers of the Party and of the Soviet State; against them were made lying, slanderous, and absurd accusations concerning "two-facedness," "espionage," "sabotage," preparation of fictitious "plots," etc.

At the February-March Central Committee Plenum in 1937 many members actually questioned the rightness of the established course regarding mass repressions under the pretext of combating "two-facedness." Comrade Postyshev ably expressed these doubts. He said:

> I have philosophized that the severe years of fighting have passed. Party members who have lost their backbones have broken down or have joined the camp of the enemy; healthy elements have fought for the Party. These were the years of industrialization and collectivization. I never thought it possible that after this severe era had passed Karpov and people like him would find themselves in the camp of the enemy. [Karpov was a worker in the Ukrainian Central Committee whom Postyshev knew well.] And now, according to the testimony, it appears that Karpov was recruited in 1934 by the Trotskyites. I personally do not believe that in 1934 an honest Party member who had trod the long road of unrelenting fight against enemies for the Party and for socialism would now be in the camp of the enemies. I do not believe it. . . . I cannot imagine how it would be possible to travel with the Party during the difficult years and then, in 1934, join the Trotskyites. It is an odd thing. . . . [Movement in the hall.]

Using Stalin's formulation, namely, that the closer we are to socialism the more enemies we will have, and using the resolution of the February-March Central Committee Plenum passed on the basis of Yezhov's report — the

provocateurs who had infiltrated the state-security organs together with conscienceless careerists began to protect with the Party name the mass terror against Party cadres, cadres of the Soviet State and the ordinary Soviet citizens. It should suffice to say that the number of arrests based on charges of counterrevolutionary crimes had grown ten times between 1936 and 1937.

Fabrication of Evidence, Police Brutality, False Confessions

It is known that brutal willfulness was practiced against leading Party workers. The Party Statute, approved at the 17th Party Congress, was based on Leninist principles expressed at the 10th Party Congress. It stated that, in order to apply an extreme method such as exclusion from the Party against a Central Committee member, against a Central Committee candidate, and against a member of the Party Control Commission, "it is necessary to call a Central Committee Plenum and to invite to the Plenum all Central Committee candidate members and all members of the Party Control Commission"; only if two-thirds of the members of such a general assembly of responsible Party leaders find it necessary, only then can a Central Committee member or candidate be expelled.

The majority of the Central Committee members and candidates elected at the 17th Congress and arrested in 1937–1938 were expelled from the Party illegally through the brutal abuse of the Party Statute, because the question of their expulsion was never studied at the Central Committee Plenum.

Now, when the cases of some of these so-called "spies" and "saboteurs" were examined, it was found that all their cases were fabricated. Confessions of guilt of many arrested and charged with enemy activity were gained with the help of cruel and inhuman tortures.

At the same time, Stalin, as we have been informed by members of the Political Bureau of that time, did not show them the statements of many accused political activists when they retracted their confessions before the military tribunal and asked for an objective examination of their cases. There were many such declarations, and Stalin doubtless knew of them.

The Central Committee considers it absolutely necessary to inform the Congress of many such fabricated "cases" against the members of the Party's Central Committee elected at the 17th Party Congress.

An example of vile provocation, of odious falsification, and of criminal violation of revolutionary legality is the case of the former candidate for the Central Committee Political Bureau, one of the most eminent workers of the Party and of the Soviet Government, Comrade Eikhe, who was a Party member since 1905. [Commotion in the hall.]

Comrade Eikhe was arrested on April 29, 1938, on the basis of slanderous materials, without the sanction of the Prosecutor of the U.S.S.R., which was finally received 15 months after the arrest.

Investigation of Eikhe's case was made in a manner which most brutally violated Soviet legality and was accompanied by willfulness and falsification.

Eikhe was forced under torture to sign ahead of time a protocol of his confession prepared by the investigative judges, in which he and several other eminent Party workers were accused of anti-Soviet activity.

On October 1, 1939, Eikhe sent his declaration to Stalin in which he categorically denied his guilt and asked for an examination of his case. In the declaration he wrote: "There is no more bitter misery than to sit in the jail of a government for which I have always fought."

A second declaration of Eikhe has been preserved which he sent to Stalin on October 27, 1939; in it he cited facts very convincingly and countered the slanderous accusations made against him, arguing that this provocatory accusation was on the one hand the work of real Trotskyites whose arrests he had sanctioned as First Secretary of the West Siberian Krai [Territory] Party Committee and who conspired in order to take revenge on him, and, on the other hand, the result of the base falsification of materials by the investigative judges.

Eikhe wrote in his declaration:

. . . On October 25 of this year I was informed that the investigation in my case has 'been concluded and I was given access to the materials of this investigation. Had I been guilty of only one hundredth of the crimes with which I am charged, I would not have dared to send you this pre-execution declaration; however, I have not been guilty of even

one of the things with which I am charged and my heart is clean of even the shadow of baseness. I have never in my life told you a word of falsehood, and now, finding my two feet in the grave, I am also not lying. My whole case is a typical example of provocation, slander, and violation of the elementary basis of revolutionary legality. . . .

. . . The confessions which were made part of my file are not only absurd but contain some slander toward the Central Committee of the All-Union Communist Party (Bolsheviks) and toward the Council of People's Commissars, because correct resolutions of the Central Committee of the All-Union Communist Party (Bolsheviks) and of the Council of People's Commissars which were not made on my initiative and without my participation are presented as hostile acts of counterrevolutionary organizations made at my suggestion. . . .

I am now alluding to the most disgraceful part of my life and to my really grave guilt against the Party and against you. This is my confession of counterrevolutionary activity. . . . The case is as follows: Not being able to suffer the tortures to which I was submitted by Ushakov and Nikolayev — and especially by the first one — who utilized the knowledge that my broken ribs have not properly mended and have caused me great pain, I have been forced to accuse myself and others.

The majority of my confession has been suggested or dictated by Ushakov, and the remainder is my reconstruction of NKVD materials from Western Siberia for which I assumed all responsibility. If some part of the story which Ushakov fabricated and which I signed did not properly hang together, I was forced to sign another variation. The same thing was done to Rukhimovich, who was at first designated as a member of the reserve net and whose name later was removed without telling me anything about it; the same was also done with the leader of the reserve net, supposedly created by Bukharin in 1935. At first I wrote my name in, and then I was instructed to insert Mezhlauk. There were other similar incidents.

. . . I am asking and begging you that you again examine my case, and this not for the purpose of sparing me but in order to unmask the vile provocation which, like a snake, wound itself around many persons in a great degree due to my meanness and criminal slander. I have never betrayed you or the Party. I know that I perish because of vile and mean work of the enemies of the Party and of the people, who fabricated the provocation against me.

It would appear that such an important declaration was worth an examination by the Central Committee. This, however, was not done, and the declaration was transmitted to Beria while the terrible maltreatment of the Political Bureau candidate, Comrade Eikhe, continued.

On February 2, 1940, Eikhe was brought before the court. Here he did not confess any guilt and said as follows:

> In all the so-called confessions of mine there is not one letter written by me with the exception of my signatures under the protocols, which were forced from me. I have made my confession under pressure from the investigative judge, who from the time of my arrest tormented me. After that I began to write all this nonsense. . . . The most important thing for me is to tell the court, the Party, and Stalin that I am not guilty. I have never been guilty of any conspiracy. I will die believing in the truth of Party policy as I have believed in it during my whole life.

On February 4 Eikhe was shot. [Indignation in the hall.] It has been definitely established now that Eikhe's case was fabricated; he has been posthumously rehabilitated.

Comrade Rudzutak, candidate-member of the Political Bureau, member of the Party since 1905, who spent 10 years in a Tsarist hard labor camp, completely retracted in court the confession which was forced from him. The protocol of the session of the Collegium of the Supreme Military Court contains the following statement by Rudzutak:

> . . . The only plea which he places before the court is that the Central Committee of the All-Union Communist Party (Bolsheviks) be informed that there is in the NKVD an as yet not liquidated center which is craftily manufacturing cases, which forces innocent persons to confess; there is no opportunity to prove one's non-participation in crimes to which the confessions of various persons testify. The investigative methods are such that they force people to lie and to slander entirely innocent persons in addition to those who already stand accused. He asks the Court that he be allowed to inform the Central Committee of the All-Union Communist Party (Bolsheviks) about

all this in writing. He assures the Court that he personally had never any evil designs in regard to the policy of our Party because he had always agreed with the Party policy pertaining to all spheres of economic and cultural activity.

This declaration of Rudzutak was ignored, despite the fact that Rudzutak was in his time the chief of the Central Control Commission, which was called into being in accordance with Lenin's concept for the purpose of fighting for Party unity. In this manner fell the chief of this highly authoritative Party organ, a victim of brutal willfulness; he was not even called before the Central Committee's Political Bureau because Stalin did not want to talk to him. Sentence was pronounced on him in 20 minutes and he was shot. [Indignation in the hall.]

After careful examination of the case in 1955, it was established that the accusation against Rudzutak was false and that it was based on slanderous materials. Rudzutak has been rehabilitated posthumously.

The way in which the former NKVD workers manufactured various fictitious "anti-Soviet centers" and "blocs" with the help of provocatory methods is seen from the confession of Comrade Rozenblum, Party member since 1906, who was arrested in 1937 by the Leningrad NKVD.

During the examination in 1955 of the Komarov case Rozenblum revealed the following fact: when Rozenblum was arrested in 1937, he was subjected to terrible torture during which he was ordered to confess false information concerning himself and other persons. He was then brought to the office of Zakovsky, who offered him freedom on condition that he make before the court a false confession fabricated in 1937 by the NKVD concerning "sabotage, espionage, and diversion in a terroristic center in Leningrad." [Movement in the hall.] With unbelievable cynicism, Zakovsky told about the vile "mechanism" for the crafty creation of fabricated "anti-Soviet plots."

"In order to illustrate it to me," stated Rozenblum, "Zakovsky gave me several possible variants of the organization of this center and of its branches. After he detailed the organization to me, Zakovsky told me that the NKVD would prepare the case of this center, remarking that the trial would be public. Before the court were to be brought four or five members of this center: Chudov, Ugarov, Smorodin, Pozern, Shaposhnikova [Chudov's wife] and others together with two or three members from the branches of this center. . . .

. . . The case of the Leningrad center has to be built solidly, and for this reason witnesses are needed. Social origin (of course, in the past) and the Party standing of the witness will play more than a small role.

"You, yourself," said Zakovsky, "will not need to invent anything. The NKVD will prepare for you a ready outline for every branch of the center; you will have to study it carefully and to remember well all questions and answers which the Court might ask. This case will be ready in four-five months, or perhaps a half year. During all this time you will be preparing yourself so that you will not compromise the investigation and yourself. Your future will depend on how the trial goes and on its results. If you begin to lie and to testify falsely, blame yourself. If you manage to endure it, you will save your head and we will feed and clothe you at the Government's cost until your death."

This is the kind of vile things which were then practiced. [Movement in the hall.]

Even more widely was the falsification of cases practiced in the provinces. The NKVD headquarters of the Sverdlov Oblast "discovered" the so-called "Ural uprising staff" — an organ of the bloc of rightists, Trotskyites, Socialist Revolutionaries, church leaders — whose chief supposedly was the Secretary of the Sverdlov Oblast Party Committee and member of the Central Committee, All-Union Communist Party (Bolsheviks), Kabakov, who had been a Party member since 1914. The investigative materials of that time show that in almost all *krais, oblasts,* and republics there supposedly existed "rightist Trotskyite, espionage-terror, and diversionary-sabotage organizations and centers" and that the heads of such organizations as a rule — for no known reason — were first secretaries of *oblast* or republic Communist Party committees or Central Committees. [Movement in the hall.]

Many thousands of honest and innocent Communists have died as a result of this monstrous falsification of such "cases," as a result of the fact that all kinds of slanderous "confessions" were accepted, and as a result of the practice of forcing accusations against oneself

and others. In the same manner were fabricated the "cases" against eminent Party and State workers — Kossior, Chubar, Postyshev, Kosarev, and others.

In those years repressions on a mass scale were applied which were based on nothing tangible and which resulted in heavy cadre losses to the Party.

The vicious practice was condoned of having the NKVD prepare lists of persons whose cases were under the jurisdiction of the Military Collegium and whose sentences were prepared in advance. Yezhov would send these lists to Stalin personally for his approval of the proposed punishment. In 1937–1938, 383 such lists containing the names of many thousands of Party, Soviet, Komsomol, Army, and economic workers were sent to Stalin. He approved these lists.

A large part of these cases are being reviewed now and a great part of them are being voided because they were baseless and falsified. Suffice it to say that from 1954 to the present time the Military Collegium of the Supreme Court has rehabilitated 7,679 persons, many of whom were rehabilitated posthumously.

Mass arrests of Party, Soviet, economic, and military workers caused tremendous harm to our country and to the cause of socialist advancement.

Mass repressions had a negative influence on the moral-political condition of the Party, created a situation of uncertainty, contributed to the spreading of unhealthy suspicion, and sowed distrust among Communists. All sorts of slanderers and careerists were active.

Resolutions of the January Plenum of the Central Committee, All-Union Communist Party (Bolsheviks), in 1938 had brought some measure of improvement to the Party organizations. However, widespread repression also existed in 1938.

Only because our Party has at its disposal such great moral-political strength was it possible for it to survive the difficult events in 1937–1938 and to educate new cadres. There is, however, no doubt that our march forward toward socialism and toward the preparation of the country's defense would have been much more successful were it not for the tremendous loss in the cadres suffered as a result of the baseless and false mass repressions in 1937–1938.

We are justly accusing Yezhov for the degenerate practices of 1937. But we have to answer these questions: Could Yezhov have arrested Kossior, for instance, without the knowledge of Stalin? Was there an exchange of opinions or a Political Bureau decision concerning this? No, there was not, as there was none regarding other cases of this type. Could Yezhov have decided such important matters as the fate of such eminent party figures? No, it would be a display of naivete to consider this the work of Yezhov alone. It is clear that these matters were decided by Stalin, and that without his orders and his sanction Yezhov could not have done this.

We have examined the cases and have rehabilitated Kossior, Rudzutak, Postyshev, Kosarev, and others. For what causes were they arrested and sentenced? The review of evidence shows that there was no reason for this. They, like many others, were arrested without the prosecutor's knowledge. In such a situation, there is no need for any sanction, for what sort of a sanction could there be when Stalin decided everything? He was the chief prosecutor in these cases. Stalin not only agreed to, but on his own initiative issued, arrest orders. We must say this so that the delegates to the Congress can clearly undertake and themselves assess this and draw the proper conclusions.

Facts prove that many abuses were made on Stalin's orders without reckoning with any norms of Party and Soviet legality. Stalin was a very distrustful man, sickly suspicious; we know this from our work with him. He could look at a man and say: "Why are your eyes so shifty today?" or "Why are you turning so much today and avoiding to look me directly in the eyes?" The sickly suspicion created in him a general distrust even toward eminent Party workers whom he had known for years. Everywhere and in everything he saw "enemies," "two-facers," and "spies."

Possessing unlimited power, he indulged in great willfulness and choked a person morally and physically. A situation was created where one could not express one's own will.

When Stalin said that one or another should be arrested, it was necessary to accept on faith that he was an "enemy of the people." Meanwhile, Beria's gang, which ran the organs of state security, outdid itself in proving the guilt of the arrested and the truth of materials which it falsified. And what proofs were offered? The confessions of the arrested, and the in-vestigative judges accepted these "confessions." And how is it possible that a person confesses to crimes which he has not committed? Only in one way — because of application of physical methods of pressuring him, tortures, bringing him to a state of unconsciousness, deprivation of his judgment, taking away of his human dignity. In this manner were "confessions" acquired.

Sanction by Stalin of Physical Torture

When the wave of mass arrests began to recede in 1939, and the leaders of territorial Party organizations began to accuse the NKVD workers of using methods of physical pressure on the arrested, Stalin dispatched a coded telegram on January 20, 1939, to the committee secretaries of *oblasts* and *krais*, to the Central Committees of republic Communist Parties, to the People's Commissars of Internal Affairs and to the heads of NKVD organizations. This telegram stated:

> The Central Committee of the All-Union Communist Party (Bolsheviks) explains that the application of methods of physical pressure in NKVD practice is permissible from 1937 on in accordance with permission of the Central Committee of the All-Union Communist Party (Bolsheviks) . . . It is known that all bourgeois intelligence services use methods of physical influence against the representatives of the socialist proletariat and that they use them in their most scandalous forms. The question arises as to why the socialist intelligence service should be more humanitarian against the mad agents of the bourgeoisie, against the deadly enemies of the working class and of the *kolkhoz* workers. The Central Committee of the All-Union Communist Party (Bolsheviks) considers that physical pressure should still be used obligatorily, as an exception applicable to known and obstinate enemies of the people, as a method both justifiable and appropriate.

Thus, Stalin had sanctioned in the name of the Central Committee of the All-Union Communist Party (Bolsheviks) the most brutal violation of socialist legality, torture, and oppression, which led as we have seen to the slandering and self-accusation of innocent people.

Not long ago — only several days before the present Congress — we called to the Central Committee Presidium session and interrogated the investigative judge Rodos, who in his time investigated and interrogated Kossior, Chubar, and Kosarev. He is a vile person, with the brain of a bird, and morally completely degenerate. And it was this man who was deciding the fate of prominent Party workers; he was making judgments also concerning the politics in these matters, because, having established their "crime," he provided therewith materials from which important political implications could be drawn.

The question arises whether a man with such an intellect could alone make the investigation in a manner to prove the guilt of people such as Kossior and others. No, he could not have done it without proper directives. At the Central Committee Presidium session he told us: "I was told that Kossior and Chubar were people's enemies and for this reason I, as an investigative judge, had to make them confess that they are enemies." [Indignation in the hall.]

He could do this only through long tortures, which he did, receiving detailed instructions from Beria. We must say that at the Central Committee Presidium session he cynically declared: "I thought that I was executing the orders of the Party." In this manner, Stalin's orders concerning the use of methods of physical pressure against the arrested were in practice executed.

These and many other facts show that all norms of correct Party solution of problems were invalidated and everything was dependent upon the willfulness of one man.

Stalin's Role in the War

The power accumulated in the hands of one person, Stalin, led to serious consequences during the Great Patriotic War.

When we look at many of our novels, films, and historical "scientific studies," the role of Stalin in the Patriotic War appears to be entirely improbable. Stalin had foreseen everything. The Soviet Army, on the basis of a strategic plan prepared by Stalin long before, used the tactics of so-called "active defense," i.e., tactics which, as we know, allowed the Germans to come up to Moscow and Stalingrad. Using such tactics, the Soviet Army, supposedly thanks only to Stalin's genius, turned to the offensive and subdued the enemy. The epic victory gained through the armed might of the land of the Soviets, through our heroic

people, is ascribed in this type of novel, film, and "scientific study" as being completely due to the strategic genius of Stalin.

We have to analyze this matter carefully because it has a tremendous significance not only from the historical, but especially from the political, educational, and practical point of view.

What are the facts of this matter?

Before the war, our press and all our political-educational work was characterized by its bragging tone: when an enemy violates the holy Soviet soil, then for every blow of the enemy we will answer with three blows, and we will battle the enemy on his soil and we will win without much harm to ourselves. But these positive statements were not based in all areas on concrete facts, which would actually guarantee the immunity of our borders.

During the war and after the war, Stalin put forward the thesis that the tragedy which our nation experienced in the first part of the war was the result of the "unexpected" attack of the Germans against the Soviet Union. But, comrades, this is completely untrue. As soon as Hitler came to power in Germany he assigned to himself the task of liquidating Communism. The fascists were saying this openly; they did not hide their plans. In order to attain this aggressive end, all sorts of pacts and blocs were created, such as the famous Berlin-Rome-Tokyo axis. Many facts from the pre-war period clearly showed that Hitler was going all out to begin a war against the Soviet State, and that he had concentrated large armed units, together with armored units, near the Soviet borders.

Documents which have now been published show that by April 3, 1941, Churchill, through his Ambassador to the U.S.S.R., Cripps, personally warned Stalin that the Germans had begun regrouping their armed units with the intent of attacking the Soviet Union. It is self-evident that Churchill did not do this at all because of his friendly feeling toward the Soviet nation. He had in this his own imperialistic goals — to bring Germany and the U.S.S.R. into a bloody war and thereby to strengthen the position of the British Empire. Just the same, Churchill affirmed in his writings that he sought to "warn Stalin and call his attention to the danger which threatened him." Churchill stressed this repeatedly in his dispatches of April 18 and on the following days. However, Stalin took no heed of these warnings. What is more, Stalin ordered that no credence be given to information of this sort, in order not to provoke the initiation of military operations.

We must assert that information of this sort concerning the threat of German armed invasion of Soviet territory was coming in also from our own military and diplomatic sources; however, because the leadership was conditioned against such information, such data was dispatched with fear and assessed with reservation.

Thus, for instance, information sent from Berlin on May 6, 1941, by the Soviet military attaché, Captain Vorontsov, stated: "Soviet citizen Bozer . . . communicated to the deputy naval attaché that, according to a statement of a certain German officer from Hitler's headquarters, Germany is preparing to invade the U.S.S.R. on May 14 through Finland, the Baltic countries, and Latvia. At the same time Moscow and Leningrad will be heavily raided and paratroopers landed in border cities. . . ."

In his report of May 22, 1941, the deputy military attaché in Berlin, Khlopov, communicated that ". . . the attack of the German Army is reportedly scheduled for June 15, but it is possible that it may begin in the first days of June. . . ."

A cable from our London Embassy dated June 18, 1941, stated: "As of now Cripps is deeply convinced of the inevitability of armed conflict between Germany and the U.S.S.R., which will begin not later than the middle of June. According to Cripps, the Germans have presently concentrated 147 divisions (including air force and service units) along the Soviet borders. . . ."

Despite these particularly grave warnings, the necessary steps were not taken to prepare the country properly for defense and to prevent it from being caught unawares.

Did we have time and the capabilities for such preparations? Yes, we had the time and capabilities. Our industry was already so developed that it was capable of supplying fully the Soviet Army with everything that it needed. This is proven by the fact that, although during the war we lost almost half of our industry and important industrial and food-production areas as the result of enemy

occupation of the Ukraine, Northern Caucasus, and other western parts of the country, the Soviet nation was still able to organize the production of military equipment in the eastern parts of the country, install there equipment taken from the western industrial areas, and to supply our armed forces with everything which was necessary to destroy the enemy.

Had our industry been mobilized properly and in time to supply the army with the necessary matériel, our wartime losses would have been decidedly smaller. Such mobilization had not been, however, started in time. And already in the first days of the war it became evident that our army was badly armed, that we did not have enough artillery, tanks, and planes to throw the enemy back.

Soviet science and technology produced excellent models of tanks and artillery pieces before the war. But mass production of all this was not organized, and, as a matter of fact, we started to modernize our military equipment only on the eve of the war. As a result, at the time of the enemy's invasion of the Soviet land we did not have sufficient quantities either of old machinery which was no longer used for armament production or of new machinery which we had planned to introduce into armament production. The situation with anti-aircraft artillery was especially bad; we did not organize the production of anti-tank ammunition. Many fortified regions had proven to be indefensible as soon as they were attacked, because the old arms had been withdrawn and new ones were not yet available there.

This pertained, alas, not only to tanks, artillery, and planes. At the outbreak of the war we did not even have sufficient numbers of rifles to arm the mobilized manpower. I recall that in those days I telephoned to Comrade Malenkov from Kiev and told him, "People have volunteered for the new army and demand arms. You must send us arms."

Malenkov answered me, "We cannot send you arms. We are sending all our rifles to Leningrad and you have to arm yourselves." [Movement in the hall.]

Such was the armament situation.

In this connection we cannot forget, for instance, the following fact: shortly before the invasion of the Soviet Union by the Hitlerite army, Kirponos, who was chief of the Kiev Special Military District (he was later killed at the front), wrote to Stalin that the German armies were at the Bug River, were preparing for an attack, and in the very near future would probably start their offensive. In this connection, Kirponos proposed that a strong defense be organized, that 300,000 people be evacuated from the border areas, and that several strong points be organized there: anti-tank ditches, trenches for the soldiers, etc.

Moscow answered this proposition with the assertion that this would be a provocation, that no preparatory defensive work should be undertaken at the borders, that the Germans were not to be given any pretext for the initiation of military action against us. Thus, our borders were insufficiently prepared to repel the enemy.

When the fascist armies had actually invaded Soviet territory and military operations began, Moscow issued the order that the German fire was not to be returned. Why? It was because Stalin, despite evident facts, thought that the war had not yet started, that this was only a provocative action on the part of several undisciplined sections of the German Army, and that our reaction might serve as a reason for the Germans to begin the war.

The following fact is also known: on the eve of the invasion of the territory of the Soviet Union by the Hitlerite army, a certain German citizen crossed our border and stated that the German armies had received orders to start the offensive against the Soviet Union on the night of June 22 at 3 o'clock. Stalin was informed about this immediately, but even this warning was ignored.

As you see, everything was ignored: warnings of certain army commanders, declarations of deserters from the enemy army, and even the open hostility of the enemy. Is this an example of the alertness of the chief of the Party and of the State at this particularly significant historical moment?

And what were the results of this carefree attitude, this disregard of clear facts? The result was that already in the first hours and days the enemy had destroyed in our border regions a large part of our Air Force, artillery, and other military equipment; he annihilated large numbers of our military cadres and disorganized our military leadership; conse-

quently we could not prevent the enemy from marching deep into the country.

Very grievous consequences, especially in reference to the beginning of the war, followed Stalin's annihilation of many military commanders and political workers during 1937–1941 because of his suspiciousness and through slanderous accusations. During these years repressions were instituted against certain parts of military cadres beginning literally at the company and battalion commander level and extending to the higher military centers; during this time the cadre of leaders who had gained military experience in Spain and in the Far East was almost completely liquidated.

The policy of large-scale repression against the military cadres led also to undermined military discipline, because for several years officers of all ranks and even soldiers in the Party and Komsomol cells were taught to "unmask" their superiors as hidden enemies. [Movement in the hall.] It is natural that this caused a negative influence on the state of military discipline in the first war period.

And, as you know, we had before the war excellent military cadres which were unquestionably loyal to the Party and to the Fatherland. Suffice it to say that those of them who managed to survive, despite severe tortures to which they were subjected in the prisons, have from the first war days shown themselves real patriots and heroically fought for the glory of the Fatherland; I have here in mind such comrades as Rokossovsky (who, as you know had been jailed), Gorbatov, Maretskov (who is a delegate at the present Congress), Podlas (he was an excellent commander who perished at the front), and many, many others. However, many such commanders perished in camps and jails and the army saw them no more.

All this brought about the situation which existed at the beginning of the war and which was the great threat to our Fatherland.

It would be incorrect to forget that, after the first severe disaster and defeat at the front, Stalin thought that this was the end. In one of his speeches in those days he said: "All that which Lenin created we have lost forever."

After this Stalin for a long time actually did not direct the military operations and ceased to do anything whatever. He returned to active leadership only when some members of the Political Bureau visited him and told him that it was necessary to take certain steps immediately in order to improve the situation at the front.

Therefore, the threatening danger which hung over our Fatherland in the first period of the war was largely due to the faulty methods of directing the nation and the Party by Stalin himself.

However, we speak not only about the moment when the war began, which led to serious disorganization of our army and brought us severe losses. Even after the war began, the nervousness and hysteria which Stalin demonstrated, interfering with actual military operation, caused our army serious damage.

Stalin was very far from an understanding of the real situation which was developing at the front. This was natural because, during the whole Patriotic War, he never visited any section of the front or any liberated city except for one short ride on the Mozhaisk highway during a stabilized situation at the front. To this incident were dedicated many literary works full of fantasies of all sorts and so many paintings. Simultaneously, Stalin was interfering with operations and issuing orders which did not take into consideration the real situation at a given section of the front and which could not help but result in huge personnel losses.

I will allow myself in this connection to bring out one characteristic fact which illustrates how Stalin directed operations at the fronts. There is present at this Congress Marshal Bagramian, who was once the chief of operations in the headquarters of the southwestern front and who can corroborate what I will tell you.

When there developed an exceptionally serious situation for our army in 1942 in the Kharkov region, we had correctly decided to drop an operation whose objective was to encircle Kharkov, because the real situation at that time would have threatened our army with fatal consequences if this operation were continued.

We communicated this to Stalin, stating that the situation demanded changes in operational plans so that the enemy would be prevented from liquidating a sizable concentration of our army.

Contrary to common sense, Stalin rejected our suggestion and issued the order to continue the operation aimed at the encirclement of Kharkov, despite the fact that at this time many army concentrations were themselves actually threatened with encirclement and liquidation.

I telephoned to Vasilevsky and begged him: "Alexander Mikhailovich, take a map" —Vasilevsky is present here — "and show Comrade Stalin the situation which has developed." We should note that Stalin planned operations on a globe. [Animation in the hall.] Yes, comrades, he used to take the globe and trace the front line on it. I said to Comrade Vasilevsky: "Show him the situation on a map; in the present situation we cannot continue the operation which was planned. The old decision must be changed for the good of the cause."

Vasilevsky replied, saying that Stalin had already studied this problem and that he, Vasilevsky, would not see Stalin further concerning this matter, because the latter didn't want to hear any arguments on the subject of this operation.

After my talk with Vasilevsky, I telephoned to Stalin at his villa. But Stalin did not answer the telephone and Malenkov was at the receiver. I told Comrade Malenkov that I was calling from the front and that I wanted to speak personally to Stalin. Stalin informed me through Malenkov that I should speak with Malenkov. I stated for the second time that I wished to inform Stalin personally about the grave situation which had arisen for us at the front. But Stalin did not consider it convenient to raise the phone and again stated that I should speak to him through Malenkov, although he was only a few steps from the telephone.

After "listening" in this manner to our plea, Stalin said: "Let everything remain as it is!"

And what was the result of this? The worst that we had expected. The Germans surrounded our army concentrations and consequently we lost hundreds of thousands of our soldiers. This is Stalin's military "genius"; this is what it cost us. [Movement in the hall.]

On one occasion after the war, during a meeting of Stalin with members of the Political Bureau, Anastas Ivanovich Mikoyan mentioned that Khrushchev must have been right when he telephoned concerning the Kharkov operation and that it was unfortunate that his suggestion had not been accepted.

You should have seen Stalin's fury! How could it be admitted that he, Stalin, had not been right! He is after all a "genius," and a genius cannot help but be right! Everyone can err, but Stalin considered that he never erred, that he was always right. He never acknowledged to anyone that he made any mistake, large or small, despite the fact that he made not a few mistakes in the matter of theory and in his practical activity. After the Party Congress we shall probably have to re-evaluate many wartime military operations and to present them in their true light.

The tactics on which Stalin insisted without knowing the essence of the conduct of battle operations cost us much blood until we succeeded in stopping the opponent and going over to the offensive.

The military know that already by the end of 1941, instead of great operational maneuvers flanking the opponent and penetrating behind his back, Stalin demanded incessant frontal attacks and the capture of one village after another. Because of this, we paid with great losses — until our generals, on whose shoulders rested the whole weight of conducting the war, succeeded in changing the situation and shifting to flexible maneuver operations, which immediately brought serious changes at the front favorable to us.

Misrepresentation of Wartime Contributions

All the more shameful was the fact that, after our great victory over the enemy which cost us so much, Stalin began to downgrade many of the commanders who contributed so much to the victory over the enemy, because Stalin excluded every possibility that services rendered at the front should be credited to anyone but himself.

Stalin was very much interested in the assessment of Comrade Zhukov as a military leader. He asked me often for my opinion of Zhukov. I told him then, "I have known Zhukov for a long time; he is a good general and a good military leader."

After the war, Stalin began to tell all kinds of nonsense about Zhukov, among others the following, "You praised Zhukov, but he does not deserve it. It is said that before each operation at the front Zhukov used to behave as follows: He used to take a handful of earth, smell it and say, 'We can begin the attack,' or

the opposite. 'The planned operation cannot be carried out.'" I stated at that time, "Comrade Stalin, I do not know who invented this, but it is not true."

It is possible that Stalin himself invented these things for the purpose of minimizing the role and military talents of Marshal Zhukov.

In this connection, Stalin very energetically popularized himself as a great leader; in various ways he tried to inculcate in the people the version that all victories gained by the Soviet nation during the Great Patriotic War were due to the courage, daring, and genius of Stalin and of no one else. Exactly like Kuzma Kryuchkov [a famous Cossack who performed heroic feats against the Germans] he put one dress on seven people at the same time. [Animation in the hall.]

In the same vein, let us take, for instance, our historical and military films and some literary creations; they make us feel sick. Their true objective is the propagation of the theme of praising Stalin as a military genius. Let us recall the film, *The Fall of Berlin*. Here only Stalin acts; he issues orders in the hall in which there are many empty chairs and only one man approaches him and reports something to him — that is Poskrebyshev, his loyal shield-bearer. [Laughter in the hall.]

And where is the military command? Where is the Political Bureau? Where is the Government? What are they doing and with what are they engaged? There is nothing about them in the film. Stalin acts for everybody; he does not reckon with anyone; he asks no one for advice. Everything is shown to the nation in this false light. Why? In order to surround Stalin with glory, contrary to the facts and contrary to historical truth.

The question arises: And where are the military, on whose shoulders rested the burden of the war? They are not in the film; with Stalin in, no room was left for them.

Not Stalin, but the Party as a whole, the Soviet Government, our heroic army, its talented leaders and brave soldiers, the whole Soviet nation — these are the ones who assured the victory in the Great Patriotic War. [Tempestuous and prolonged applause.]

The Central Committee members, ministers, our economic leaders, leaders of Soviet culture, directors of territorial-party and Soviet organizations, engineers, and technicians —

every one of them in his own place of work generously gave of his strength and knowledge toward ensuring victory over the enemy.

Exceptional heroism was shown by our hard core — surrounded by glory is our whole working class, our *kolkhoz* peasantry, the Soviet intelligentsia, who under the leadership of Party organizations overcame untold hardships and, bearing the hardships of war, devoted all their strength to the cause of the defense of the Fatherland.

Great and brave deeds during the war were accomplished by our Soviet women who bore on their backs the heavy load of production work in the factories, on the *kolkhozes,* and in various economic and cultural sectors; many women participated directly in the Great Patriotic War at the fronts; our brave youth contributed immeasurably at the front and at home to the defense of the Soviet Fatherland and to the annihilation of the enemy.

Immortal are the services of the Soviet soldiers, of our commanders and political workers of all ranks; after the loss of a considerable part of the army in the first war months they did not lose their heads and were able to reorganize during the progress of combat; they created and toughened during the progress of the war a strong and heroic army and not only stood off pressures of the strong and cunning enemy but also smashed him.

The magnificent and heroic deeds of hundreds of millions of people of the East and of the West during the fight against the threat of fascist subjugation which loomed before us will live centuries and millennia in the memory of thankful humanity. [Thunderous applause.]

The main role and the main credit for the victorious ending of the war belongs to our Communist Party, to the armed forces of the Soviet Union, and to the tens of millions of Soviet people raised by the Party. [Thunderous and prolonged applause.]

Violations of Nationality Policy

Comrades, let us reach for some other facts. The Soviet Union is justly considered as a model of a multi-national state because we have in practice assured the equality and friendship of all nations which live in our great Fatherland.

All the more monstrous are the acts whose initiator was Stalin and which are rude violations of the basic Leninist principles of the nationality policy of the Soviet state. We refer to the mass deportations from their native places of whole nations, together with all Communists and Komsomols without any exception; this deportation action was not dictated by any military considerations.

Thus, already at the end of 1943, when there occurred a permanent breakthrough at the fronts of the Great Patriotic War benefiting the Soviet Union, a decision was taken and executed concerning the deportation of all the Karachai from the lands on which they lived. In the same period, at the end of December 1943, the same lot befell the whole population of the Autonomous Kalmyk Republic. In March 1944, all the Chechen and Ingush peoples were deported and the Chechen-Ingush Autonomous Republic was liquidated. In April 1944, all Balkars were deported to faraway places from the territory of the Kabardino-Balkar Autonomous Republic and the Republic itself was renamed the Autonomous Kabardian Republic. The Ukrainians avoided meeting this fate only because there were too many of them and there was no place to which to deport them. Otherwise, he would have deported them also. [Laughter and animation in the hall.]

Not only a Marxist-Leninist but also no man of common sense can grasp how it is possible to make whole nations responsible for inimical activity, including women, children, old people, Communists and Komsomols, to use mass repression against them, and to expose them to misery and suffering for the hostile acts of individual persons or groups of persons.

The Leningrad Affair

After the conclusion of the Patriotic War, the Soviet nation stressed with pride the magnificent victories gained through great sacrifices and tremendous efforts. The country experienced a period of political enthusiasm. The Party came out of the war even more united; in the fire of the war, Party cadres were tempered and hardened. Under such conditions nobody could have even thought of the possibility of some plot in the Party.

And it was precisely at this time that the so-called "Leningrad Affair" was born. As we have now proven, this case was fabricated. Those who innocently lost their lives included

Comrades Voznesensky, Kuznetsov, Rodionov, Popkov, and others.

As is known, Voznesensky and Kuznetsov were talented and eminent leaders. Once they stood very close to Stalin. It is sufficient to mention that Stalin made Voznesensky first deputy to the Chairman of the Council of Ministers and Kuznetsov was elected Secretary of the Central Committee. The very fact that Stalin entrusted Kuznetsov with the supervision of the State security organs shows the trust which he enjoyed.

How did it happen that these persons were branded as enemies of the people and liquidated?

Facts prove that the "Leningrad Affair" is also the result of willfulness which Stalin exercised against Party cadres.

Had a normal situation existed in the Party's Central Committee and in the Central Committee Political Bureau, affairs of this nature would have been examined there in accordance with Party practice, and all pertinent facts assessed; as a result, such an affair as well as others would not have happened.

We must state that, after the war, the situation became even more complicated. Stalin became even more capricious, irritable, and brutal; in particular his suspicion grew. His persecution mania reached unbelievable dimensions. Many workers were becoming enemies before his very eyes. After the war, Stalin separated himself from the collective even more. Everything was decided by him alone without any consideration for anyone or anything.

This unbelievable suspicion was cleverly taken advantage of by the abject *provocateur* and vile enemy, Beria, who had murdered thousands of Communists and loyal Soviet people. The elevation of Voznesensky and Kuznetsov alarmed Beria. As we have now proven, it had been precisely Beria who had "suggested" to Stalin the fabrication by him and by his confidants of materials in the form of declarations and anonymous letters, and in the form of various rumors and talks.

The Party's Central Committee has examined this so-called "Leningrad Affair"; persons who innocently suffered are now rehabilitated and honor has been restored to the glorious Leningrad Party organization. Abakumov and others who had fabricated this affair were brought before a court; their trial took place in Leningrad and they received what they deserved.

The question arises: Why is it that we see the truth of this affair only now, and why did we not do something earlier, during Stalin's life, in order to prevent the loss of innocent lives? It was because Stalin personally supervised the "Leningrad Affair," and the majority of the Political Bureau members did not, at that time, know all of the circumstances in these matters and could not therefore intervene.

When Stalin received certain material from Beria and Abakumov, without examining these slanderous materials he ordered an investigation of the "affair" of Voznesensky and Kuznetsov. With this, their fate was sealed.

Stalin and Georgian "Nationalism"

Instructive in the same way is the case of the Mingrelian nationalist organization which supposedly existed in Georgia. As is known, resolutions by the Central Committee, Communist Party of the Soviet Union, were made concerning this case in November 1951 and in March 1952. These resolutions were made without prior discussion with the Political Bureau. Stalin had personally dictated them. They made serious accusations against many loyal Communists. On the basis of falsified documents, it was proven that there existed in Georgia a supposedly nationalistic organization whose objective was the liquidation of the Soviet power in that Republic with the help of imperialist powers.

In this connection, a number of responsible Party and Soviet workers were arrested in Georgia. As was later proven, this was a slander directed against the Georgian Party organization.

We know that there have been at times manifestations of local bourgeois nationalism in Georgia as in several other republics. The question arises: could it be possible that, in the period during which the resolutions referred to above were made, nationalist tendencies grew so much that there was a danger of Georgia's leaving the Soviet Union and joining Turkey? [Animation in the hall, laughter.]

This is, of course, nonsense. It is impossible to imagine how such assumptions could enter anyone's mind. Everyone knows how Georgia has developed economically and culturally under Soviet rule.

Industrial production of the Georgian Republic is 27 times greater than it was before the Revolution. Many new industries have arisen in Georgia which did not exist there before the Revolution: iron smelting, an oil industry, a machine-construction industry, etc. Illiteracy has long since been liquidated, which, in pre-Revoluntionary Georgia, included 78 per cent of the population.

Could the Georgians, comparing the situation in their Republic with the hard situation of the working masses in Turkey, be aspiring to join Turkey? In 1955, Georgia produced 18 times as much steel per person as Turkey. Georgia produces 9 times as much electrical energy per person as Turkey. According to the available 1950 census, 65 per cent of Turkey's total population are illiterate, and, of the women, 80 per cent are illiterate. Georgia has 19 institutions of higher learning which have about 39,000 students; this is 8 times more than in Turkey (for each 1,000 inhabitants). The prosperity of the working people has grown tremendously in Georgia under Soviet rule.

It is clear that, as the economy and culture develop, and as the socialist consciousness of the working masses in Georgia grows, the source from which bourgeois nationalism draws its strength evaporates.

As it developed, there was no nationalistic organization in Georgia. Thousands of innocent people fell victim to willfulness and lawlessness. All of this happened under the "genial" leadership of Stalin, "the great son of the Georgian nation," as Georgians like to refer to Stalin. [Animation in the hall.]

Stalin and Tito

The willfulness of Stalin showed itself not only in decisions concerning the internal life of the country but also in the international relations of the Soviet Union.

The July Plenum of the Central Committee studied in detail the reasons for the development of conflict with Yugoslavia. It was a shameful role which Stalin played here. The "Yugoslav Affair" contained no problems which could not have been solved through Party discussions among comrades. There was no significant basis for the development of this "Affair"; it was completely possible to have prevented the rupture of relations with that country. This does not mean, however, that the Yugoslav leaders did not make mistakes or did not have shortcomings. But these mistakes and shortcomings were magnified in a monstrous manner by Stalin, which resulted in a break of relations with a friendly country.

I recall the first days when the conflict between the Soviet Union and Yugoslavia began artificially to be blown up. Once, when I came from Kiev to Moscow, I was invited to visit Stalin, who, pointing to the copy of a letter lately sent to Tito, asked me, "Have you read this?"

Not waiting for my reply, he answered, "I will shake my little finger — and there will be no more Tito. He will fall."

We have dearly paid for this "shaking of the little finger." This statement reflected Stalin's mania for greatness, but he acted just that way: "I will shake my little finger — and there will be no Kossior"; "I will shake my little finger once more and Postyshev and Chubar will be no more"; "I will shake my little finger again — and Voznesensky, Kuznetsov, and many others will disappear."

But this did not happen to Tito. No matter how much or how little Stalin shook, not only his little finger but everything else that he could shake, Tito did not fall. Why? The reason was that, in this case of disagreement with the Yugoslav comrades, Tito had behind him a state and a people who had gone through a severe school of fighting for liberty and independence, a people which gave support to its leaders.

You see to what Stalin's mania for greatness led. He had completely lost consciousness of reality; he demonstrated his suspicion and haughtiness not only in relation to individuals in the U.S.S.R., but in relation to whole parties and nations.

We have carefully examined the case of Yugoslavia and have found a proper solution which is approved by the peoples of the Soviet Union and of Yugoslavia as well as by the working masses of all the people's democracies and by all progressive humanity. The liquidation of the abnormal relationship with Yugoslavia was done in the interest of the whole camp of socialism, in the interest of strengthening peace in the whole world.

The Doctor's Plot

Let us also recall the "Affair of the Doctor-Plotters." [Animation in the hall.] Actually there was no "Affair" outside of the declaration of the woman doctor Timashuk, who was probably influenced or ordered by someone (after all, she was an unofficial collaborator of the organs of State security) to write Stalin a letter in which she declared that doctors were applying supposedly improper methods of medical treatment.

Such a letter was sufficient for Stalin to reach an immediate conclusion that there are doctor-plotters in the Soviet Union. He issued orders to arrest a group of eminent Soviet medical specialists. He personally issued advice on the conduct of the investigation and the method of interrogation of the arrested persons. He said that the academician Vinogradov should be put in chains, another one should be beaten. Present at this Congress as a delegate is the former Minister of State Security, Comrade Ignatiev. Stalin told him curtly, "If you do not obtain confessions from the doctors we will shorten you by a head." [Tumult in the hall.]

Stalin personally called the investigative judge, gave him instructions, advised him on which investigative methods should be used; these methods were simple — beat, beat and, once again, beat.

Shortly after the doctors were arrested, we members of the Political Bureau received protocols with the doctors' confessions of guilt. After distributing these protocols, Stalin told us, "You are blind like young kittens; what will happen without me? The country will perish because you do not know how to recognize enemies."

The case was so presented that no could verify the facts on which the investigation was based. There was no possibility of trying to verify facts by contacting those who had made the confessions of guilt.

We felt, however, that the case of the arrested doctors was questionable. We knew some of these people personally because they had once treated us. When we examined this "case" after Stalin's death, we found it to be fabricated from beginning to end.

This ignominious "case" was set up by Stalin; he did not, however, have the time in which to bring it to an end (as he conceived that end), and for this reason the doctors are still alive. Now all have been rehabilitated; they are working in the same places they were working before; they treat top individuals, not excluding members of the Government; they have our full confidence; and they execute their duties honestly, as they did before.

The Role of Beria

In organizing the various dirty and shameful cases, a very base role was played by the rabid enemy of our Party, an agent of a foreign intelligence service — Beria, who had stolen into Stalin's confidence. In what way could this *provocateur* gain such a position in the Party and in the State, so as to become the First Deputy Chairman of the Council of Ministers of the Soviet Union and a member of the Central Committee Political Bureau? It has now been established that this villain had climbed up the Government ladder over an untold number of corpses.

Were there any signs that Beria was an enemy of the Party? Yes, there were. Already in 1937, at a Central Committee Plenum, former People's Commissar of Health Kaminsky said that Beria worked for the Mussavat intelligence service. But the Central Committee Plenum had barely concluded when Kaminsky was arrested and then shot. Had Stalin examined Kaminsky's statement? No, because Stalin believed in Beria, and that was enough for him. And when Stalin believed in anyone or anything, then no one could say anything which was contrary to his opinion; anyone who would dare to express opposition would have met the same fate as Kaminsky.

There were other signs, also. The declaration which Comrade Snegov made to the Party's Central Committee is interesting. (Parenthetically speaking, he was also rehabilitated not long ago, after 17 years in prison camps.) In this declaration, Snegov writes:

> In connection with the proposed rehabilitation of the former Central Committee member, Kartvelishvili-Lavrentiev, I have entrusted to the hands of the representative of the Committee of State Security a detailed deposition concerning Beria's role in the disposition of the Kartvelishvili case and concerning the criminal motives by which Beria was guided.

In my opinion, it is indispensable to recall an important fact pertaining to this case and to communicate it to the Central Committee, because I did not consider it as proper to include in the investigation documents.

On October 30, 1931, at the session of the Organizational Bureau of the Central Committee, All-Union Communist Party (Bolsheviks), Kartvelishvili, Secretary of the Transcaucasian Krai Committee, made a report. All members of the executive of the Krai Committee were present; of them I alone am alive. During this session, J. V. Stalin made a motion at the end of his speech concerning the organization of the Secretariat of the Transcaucasian Krai Committee composed of the following: First Secretary, Kartvelishvili; Second Secretary, Beria (it was then, for the first time in the Party's history, that Beria's name was mentioned as a candidate for a Party position). Kartvelishvili answered that he knew Beria well and for that reason refused categorically to work together with him. Stalin proposed then that this matter be left open and that it be solved in the process of the work itself. Two days later a decision was arrived at that Beria would receive the Party post and that Kartvelishvili would be deported from the Transcaucasus.

This fact can be confirmed by Comrades Mikoyan and Kaganovich, who were present at that session.

The long, unfriendly relations between Kartvelishvili and Beria were widely known; they date back to the time when Comrade Sergo [Ordzhonikidze] was active in the Transcaucasus; Kartvelishvili was the closest assistant of Sergo. The unfriendly relationship impelled Beria to fabricate a "case" against Kartvelishvili.

It is a characteristic thing that in this "case" Kartvelishvili was charged with a terroristic act against Beria.

The indictment in the Beria case contains a discussion of his crimes. Some things should, however, be recalled, especially since it is possible that not all delegates to the Congress have read this document. I wish to recall Beria's bestial disposition of the cases of Kedrov, Golubev, and Golubev's adopted mother, Baturina — persons who wished to inform the Central Committee concerning Beria's treacherous activity. They were shot without any trial and the sentence was passed *ex post facto*, after the execution.

Here is what the old Communist, Comrade Kedrov, wrote to the Central Committee through Comrade Andreyev (Comrade Andreyev was then a Central Committee secretary):

I am calling to you for help from a gloomy cell of the Lefortovsky prison. Let my cry of horror reach your ears; do not remain deaf; take me under your protection; please, help remove the nightmare of interrogations and show that this is all a mistake.

I suffer innocently. Please believe me. Time will testify to the truth. I am not an *agent provocateur* of the Tsarist Okhrana; I am not a spy; I am not a member of an anti-Soviet organization of which I am being accused on the basis of denunciations. I am also not guilty of any other crimes against the Party and the Government. I am an old Bolshevik, free of any stain; I have honestly fought for almost 40 years in the ranks of the party for the good and prosperity of the nation. . . .

. . . Today I, a 62-year-old man, am being threatened by the investigative judges with more severe, cruel, and degrading methods of physical pressure. They (the judges) are no longer capable of becoming aware of their error and of recognizing that their handling of my case is illegal and impermissible. They try to justify their actions by picturing me as a hardened and raving enemy and are demanding increased repressions. But let the Party know that I am innocent and that there is nothing which can turn a loyal son of the Party into an enemy, even right up to his last dying breath.

But I have no way out. I cannot divert from myself the hastily approaching new and powerful blows.

Everything, however, has its limits. My torture has reached the extreme. My health is broken, my strength and my energy are waning, the end is drawing near. To die in a Soviet prison, branded as a vile traitor to the Fatherland — what can be more monstrous for an honest man? And how monstrous all this is! Unsurpassed bitterness and pain grips my heart. No! No! This will not happen; this cannot be, I cry. Neither the Party, nor the Soviet Government, nor the People's Commissar, L. P. Beria, will permit this cruel, irreparable injustice. I am firmly certain that, given a quiet, objective examination, without any foul rantings, without any anger and without the fearful tortures, it would be easy to prove the baselessness of the charges. I believe deeply that truth and justice will triumph. I believe. I believe.

The old Bolshevik, Comrade Kedrov, was found innocent by the Military Collegium. But, despite this, he was shot at Beria's order. [Indignation in the hall.]

Beria also handled cruelly the family of Comrade Ordzhonikidze. Why? Because Ordzhonikidze had tried to prevent Beria from realizing his shameful plans. Beria had cleared from his way all persons who could possibly interfere with him. Ordzhonikidze was always an opponent of Beria, which he told to Stalin. Instead of examining this affair and taking appropriate steps, Stalin allowed the liquidation of Ordzhonikidze's brother and brought Ordzhonikidze himself to such a state that he was forced to shoot himself. [Indignation in the hall.]

Beria was unmasked by the party's Central Committee shortly after Stalin's death. As a result of the particularly detailed legal proceedings, it was established that Beria had committed monstrous crimes and Beria was shot.

The question arises why Beria, who had liquidated tens of thousands of the Party and Soviet workers, was not unmasked during Stalin's life. He was not unmasked earlier because he had utilized very skillfully Stalin's weaknesses; feeding him with suspicions, he assisted Stalin in everything and acted with his support.

The Glorification and Self-Love of Stalin

Comrades: The cult of the individual acquired such monstrous size chiefly because Stalin himself, using all conceivable methods, supported the glorification of his own person. This is supported by numerous facts. One of the most characteristic examples of Stalin's self-glorification and of his lack of even elementary modesty is the edition of his *Short Biography*, which was published in 1948.

This book is an expression of the most dissolute flattery, an example of making a man into a godhead, of transforming him into an infallible sage, "the greatest leader, sublime strategist of all times and nations." Finally, no other words could be found with which to lift Stalin up to the heavens.

We need not give here examples of the loathsome adulation filling this book. All we need to add is that they all were approved and edited by Stalin personally and some of them were added in his own handwriting to the draft text of the book.

What did Stalin consider essential to write into this book? Did he want to cool the ardor of his flatterers who were composing his *Short Biography*? No! He marked the very places where he thought that the praise of his services was insufficient. Here are some examples characterizing Stalin's activity, added in Stalin's own hand:

> In this fight against the skeptics and capitulators, the Trotskyites, Zinovievites, Bukharinites, and Kamenevites, there was definitely welded together, after Lenin's death, that leading core of the Party . . . that upheld the great banner of Lenin, rallied the Party behind Lenin's behests, and brought the Soviet people into the broad road of industrializing the country and collectivizing the rural economy. The leader of this core and the guiding force of the party and the state was Comrade Stalin.

Thus writes Stalin himself! Then he adds:

> Although he performed his task as leader of the Party and the people with consummate skill and enjoyed the unreserved support of the entire Soviet people, Stalin never allowed his work to be marred by the slightest hint of vanity, conceit, or self-adulation.

Where and when could a leader so praise himself? Is this worthy of a leader of the Marxist-Leninist type? No. Precisely against this did Marx and Engels take such a strong position. This also was always sharply condemned by Vladimir Ilyich Lenin.

In the draft text of his book appeared the following sentence: "Stalin is the Lenin of today." This sentence appeared to Stalin to be too weak, so, in his own handwriting, he changed it to read: "Stalin is the worthy continuer of Lenin's work, or, as it is said in our Party, Stalin is the Lenin of today." You see how well it is said, not by the nation, but by Stalin himself.

It is possible to give many such self-praising appraisals written into the draft text of that book in Stalin's hand. Especially generously does he endow himself with praises pertaining to his military genius, to his talent for strategy.

I will cite one more insertion made by Stalin concerning the theme of the Stalinist military genius. "The advanced Soviet science of war received further development," he writes, "at Comrade Stalin's hands. Comrade Stalin elaborated the theory of the permanently operating factors that decide the issue of wars, of active defense and the laws of counteroffensive and offensive, of the cooperation of all services and arms in modern warfare, of the role of big tank masses and air forces in modern war, and of the artillery as the most formidable of the armed services. At the various stages of the war Stalin's genius found the correct solutions that took account of all the circumstances of the situation." [Movement in the hall.]

And, further, writes Stalin: "Stalin's military mastership was displayed both in defense and offense. Comrade Stalin's genius enabled him to divine the enemy's plans and defeat them. The battles in which Comrade Stalin directed the Soviet armies are brilliant examples of operational military skill."

In this manner was Stalin praised as a strategist. Who did this? Stalin himself, not in his role as a strategist but in the role of an author-editor, one of the main creators of his self-adulatory biography.

Such, comrades, are the facts. We should rather say shameful facts.

And one additional fact from the same *Short Biography* of Stalin. As is known, *The Short Course of the History of the All-Union Communist Party (Bolsheviks)* was written by a Commission of the Party Central Committee.

This book, parenthetically, was also permeated with the cult of the individual and was written by a designated group of authors. This fact was reflected in the following formulation on the proof copy of the *Short Biography* of Stalin: "A commission of the Central Committee, All-Union Communist Party (Bolsheviks), under the direction of Comrade Stalin and with his most active personal participation, has prepared a *Short Course of the History of the All-Union Communist Party (Bolsheviks)*."

But even this phrase did not satisfy Stalin: The following sentence replaced it in the final version of the *Short Biography*: "In 1938 appeared the book, *History of the All-Union Communist Party (Bolsheviks), Short Course,* written by Comrade Stalin and approved by a commission of the Central Committee, All-

Union Communist Party (Bolsheviks)." Can one add anything more? [Animation in the hall.]

As you see, a surprising metamorphosis changed the work created by a group into a book written by Stalin. It is not necessary to state how and why this metamorphosis took place.

A pertinent question comes to our mind: if Stalin is the author of this book, why did he need to praise the person of Stalin so much and to transform the whole post-October historical period of our glorious Communist Party solely into an action of "the Stalin genius"?

Did this book properly reflect the efforts of the Party in the socialist transformation of the country, in the construction of socialist society, in the industrialization and collectivization of the country, and also other steps taken by the Party which undeviatingly traveled the path outlined by Lenin? This books speaks principally about Stalin, about his speeches, about his reports. Everything without the smallest exception is tied to his name.

And when Stalin himself asserts that he himself wrote the *Short Course of the History of the All-Union Communist Party (Bolsheviks)*, this calls at least for amazement. Can a Marxist-Leninist thus write about himself, praising his own person to the heavens?

Or let us take the matter of the Stalin Prizes. [Movement in the hall.] Not even the Tsars created prizes which they named after themselves.

Stalin recognized as the best a text of the national anthem of the Soviet Union which contains not a word about the Communist Party; it contains, however, the following unprecedented praise of Stalin: "Stalin brought us up in loyalty to the people. He inspired us to great toil and acts."

In these lines of the anthem, the whole educational, directional, and inspirational activity of the great Leninist party is ascribed to Stalin. This is, of course, a clear deviation from Marxism-Leninism, a clear debasing and belittling of the role of the Party. We should add for your information that the Presidium of the Central Committee has already passed a resolution concerning the composition of a new text of the anthem, which will reflect the role of the people and the role of the Party. [Loud, prolonged applause.]

And was it without Stalin's knowledge that

many of the largest enterprises and towns were named after him? Was it without his knowledge that Stalin monuments were erected in the whole country — these "memorials to the living"? It is a fact that Stalin himself had signed on July 2, 1951, a resolution of the U.S.S.R. Council of Ministers concerning the erection on the Volga-Don Canal of an impressive monument to Stalin; on September 4 of the same year he issued an order making 33 tons of copper available for the construction of this impressive monument. Anyone who has visited the Stalingrad area must have seen the huge statue which is being built there, and that on a site which hardly any people frequent. Huge sums were spent to build it at a time when people of this area had lived since the war in huts. Consider, yourself, was Stalin right when he wrote in his biography that ". . . he did not allow in himself . . . even a shadow of conceit, pride, or self-adoration"?

At the same time Stalin gave proofs of his lack of respect for Lenin's memory. It is not a coincidence that, despite the decision taken over 30 years ago to build a Palace of Soviets as a monument to Vladimir Ilyich, this palace was not built, its construction was always postponed and the project allowed to lapse.

We cannot forget to recall the Soviet Government resolution of August 14, 1925, concerning "the founding of Lenin prizes for educational work." This resolution was published in the press, but until this day there are no Lenin prizes. This, too, should be corrected. [Tumultuous, prolonged applause.]

During Stalin's life — thanks to known methods which I have mentioned, and quoting facts, for instance, from the *Short Biography* of Stalin — all events were explained as if Lenin played only a secondary role, even during the October Socialist Revolution. In many films and in many literary works the figure of Lenin was incorrectly presented and inadmissibly depreciated.

Stalin loved to see the film, *The Unforgettable Year of 1919*, in which he was shown on the steps of an armored train and where he was practically vanquishing the foe with his own saber. Let Klimenti Yefremovich, our dear friend, find the necessary courage and write the truth about Stalin; after all, he knows how Stalin had fought. It will be difficult for Comrade Voroshilov to undertake this, but it

would be good if he did it. Everyone will approve of it, both the people and the Party. Even his grandsons will thank him. [Prolonged applause.]

In speaking about the events of the October Revolution and about the Civil War, the impression was created that Stalin always played the main role, as if everywhere and always Stalin had suggested to Lenin what to do and how to do it. However, this is slander of Lenin. [Prolonged applause.]

I will probably not sin against the truth when I say that 99 per cent of the persons present here heard and knew very little about Stalin before the year 1924, while Lenin was known to all; he was known to the whole Party, to the whole nation, from the children up to the graybeards. [Tumultuous, prolonged applause.]

All this has to be thoroughly revised so that history, literature, and the fine arts properly reflect V. I. Lenin's role and the great deeds of our Communist party and of the Soviet people — the creative people. [Applause.]

Errors in Economic Policy

Comrades! The cult of the individual has caused the employment of faulty principles in Party work and in economic activity; it brought about rude violation of internal Party and Soviet democracy, sterile administration, deviations of all sorts, covering up the shortcomings and varnishing of reality. Our nation gave birth to many flatterers and specialists in false optimism and deceit.

We should also not forget that, due to the numerous arrests of Party, Soviet and economic leaders, many workers began to work uncertainly, showed overcautiousness, feared all which was new, feared their own shadows and began to show less initiative in their work.

Take, for instance, Party and Soviet resolutions. They were prepared in a routine manner, often without considering the concrete situation. This went so far that Party workers, even during the smallest sessions, read their speeches. All this produced the danger of formalizing the Party and Soviet work and of bureaucratizing the whole apparatus.

Stalin's reluctance to consider life's realities and the fact that he was not aware of the real state of affairs in the provinces can be illustrated by his direction of agriculture.

All those who interested themselves even a little in the national situation saw the difficult situation in agriculture, but Stalin never even noted it. Did we tell Stalin about this? Yes, we told him, but he did not support us. Why? Because Stalin never traveled anywhere, did not meet city and *kolkhoz* workers; he did not know the actual situation in the provinces.

He knew the country and agriculture only from films. And these films had dressed up and beautified the existing situation in agriculture. Many films so pictured *kolkhoz* life that the tables were bending from the weight of turkeys and geese. Evidently, Stalin thought that it was actually so.

Vladimir Ilyich Lenin looked at life differently; he was always close to the people; he used to receive peasant delegates and often spoke at factory gatherings; he used to visit villages and talk with the peasants.

Stalin separated himself from the people and never went anywhere. This lasted ten years. The last time he visited a village was in January 1928, when he visited Siberia in connection with grain deliveries. How then could he have known the situation in the provinces?

And when he was once told during a discussion that our situation on the land was a difficult one and that the situation of cattle breeding and meat production was especially bad, a commission was formed which was charged with the preparation of a resolution called "Means Toward Further Development of Animal Breeding in *Kolkhozes* and *Sovkhozes*." We worked out this project.

Of course, our propositions of that time did not contain all possibilities, but we did chart ways in which animal breeding on *kolkhozes* and *sovkhozes* would be raised. We had proposed then to raise the prices of such products in order to create material incentives for the *kolkhoz*, MTS and *sovkhoz* workers in the development of cattle breeding. But our project was not accepted and in February 1953 was laid aside entirely.

What is more, while reviewing this project Stalin proposed that the taxes paid by the *kolkhozes* and by the *kolhoz* workers should be raised by 40 billion rubles; according to him the peasants are well off and the *kolkhoz* worker would need to sell only one more chicken to pay his tax in full.

Imagine what this meant. Certainly, 40 billion rubles is a sum which the *kolkhoz* workers did not realize for all the products which they sold to the Government. In 1952, for instance, the *kolkhozes* and the *kolkhoz* workers received 26,280 million rubles for all their products delivered and sold to the Government.

Did Stalin's position, then, rest on data of any sort whatever? Of course not.

In such cases facts and figures did not interest him. If Stalin said anything, it meant it was so — after all, he was a "genius," and a genius does not need to count, he only needs to look and can immediately tell how it should be. When he expresses his opinion, everyone has to repeat it and to admire his wisdom.

But how much wisdom was contained in the proposal to raise the agricultural tax by 40 billion rubles? None, absolutely none, because the proposal was not based on an actual assessment of the situation but on the fantastic ideas of a person divorced from reality. We are currently beginning slowly to work our way out of a difficult agricultural situation. The speeches of the delegates to the Twentieth Congress please us all; we are glad that many delegates deliver speeches, that there are conditions for the fulfillment of the sixth Five-Year Plan for animal husbandry, not during the period of five years, but within two to three years. We are certain that the commitments of the new Five-Year Plan will be accomplished successfully. [Prolonged applause.]

Comrades! If we sharply criticize today the cult of the individual which was so widespread during Stalin's life and if we speak about the many negative phenomena generated by this cult which is so alien to the spirit of Marxism-Leninism, various persons may ask: How could it be? Stalin headed the Party and the country for 30 years and many victories were gained during his lifetime. Can we deny this? In my opinion, the question can be asked in this manner only by those who are blinded and hopelessly hypnotized by the cult of the individual, only by those who do not understand the essence of the revolution and of the Soviet state, only by those who do not understand, in a Leninist manner, the role of the Party and of the nation in the development of the Soviet society.

The Socialist Revolution was attained by the working class and by the poor peasantry with the partial support of middle-class peasants. It was attained by the people under the leadership of the Bolshevik Party. Lenin's great service consisted of the fact that he created a militant Party of the working class, but he was armed with Marxist understanding of the laws of social development and with the science of proletarian victory in the fight with capitalism, and he steeled this Party in the crucible of revolutionary struggle of the masses of the people. During this fight the Party consistently defended the interests of the people, became its experienced leader, and led the working masses to power, to the creation of the first socialist state.

You remember well the wise words of Lenin that the Soviet state is strong because of the awareness of the masses that history is created by the millions and tens of millions of people.

Our historical victories were attained thanks to the organizational work of the Party, to the many provincial organizations, and to the self-sacrificing work of our great nation. These victories are the result of the great drive and activity of the nation and of the Party as a whole; they are not at all the fruit of the leadership of Stalin, as the situation was pictured during the period of the cult of the individual.

If we are to consider this matter as Marxists and as Leninists, then we have to state unequivocally that the leadership practice which came into being during the last years of Stalin's life became a serious obstacle in the path of Soviet social development.

Stalin often failed for months to take up some unusually important problems, concerning the life of the Party and of the State, whose solution could not be postponed. During Stalin's leadership our peaceful relations with other nations were often threatened, because one-man decisions could cause, and often did cause, great complications.

In the last years, when we managed to free ourselves of the harmful practice of the cult of the individual and took several proper steps in the sphere of internal and external policies, everyone saw how activity grew before their very eyes, how the creative activity of the broad working masses developed, how favorably all this acted upon the development of economy and of culture. [Applause.]

The Source and Extent of Stalin's Personal Power

Some comrades may ask us: Where were the members of the Political Bureau of the Central Committee? Why did they not assert themselves against the cult of the individual in time? And why is this being done only now?

First of all, we have to consider the fact that the members of the Political Bureau viewed these matters in a different way at different times. Initially, many of them backed Stalin actively because Stalin was one of the strongest Marxists and his logic, his strength, and his will greatly influenced the cadres and Party work.

It is known that Stalin, after Lenin's death, especially during the first years, actively fought for Leninism against the enemies of Leninist theory and against those who deviated. Beginning with Leninist theory, the Party, with its Central Committee at the head, started on a great scale the work of socialist industrialization of the country, agricultural collectivization, and the cultural revolution. At that time Stalin gained great popularity, sympathy, and support. The Party had to fight those who attempted to lead the country away from the correct Leninist path; it had to fight Trotskyites, Zinovievites, and rightists, and the bourgeois nationalists. This fight was indispensable.

Later, however, Stalin, abusing his power more and more, began to fight eminent Party and Government leaders and to use terroristic methods against honest Soviet people. As we have already shown, Stalin thus handled such eminent Party and Government leaders as Kossior, Rudzutak, Eikhe, Postyshev, and many others.

Attempts to oppose groundless suspicions and charges resulted in the opponent falling victim of the repression. This characterized the fall of Comrade Postyshev.

In one of his speeches Stalin expressed his dissatisfaction with Postyshev and asked him, "What are you actually?"

Postyshev answered clearly, "I am a Bolshevik, Comrade Stalin, a Bolshevik."

This assertion was at first considered to show a lack of respect for Stalin; later it was considered a harmful act and consequently resulted in Postyshev's annihilation and branding without any reason as a "people's enemy."

In the situation which then prevailed I have talked often with Nikolai Aleksandrovich Bulganin; once when we two were traveling in a car, he said, "It has happened sometimes that a man goes to Stalin on his invitation as a friend. And, when he sits with Stalin, he does not know where he will be sent next — home or to jail."

It is clear that such conditions put every member of the Political Bureau in a very difficult situation. And, when we also consider the fact that in the last years the Central Committee plenary sessions were not convened and that the sessions of the Political Bureau occurred only occasionally, from time to time, then we will understand how difficult it was for any member of the Political Bureau to take a stand against one or another unjust or improper procedure, against serious errors and shortcomings in the practices of leadership.

As we have already shown, many decisions were taken either by one person or in a roundabout way, without collective discussion. The sad fate of Political Bureau member Comrade Voznesensky, who fell victim to Stalin's repressions, is known to all. It is a characteristic thing that the decision to remove him from the Political Bureau was never discussed but was reached in a devious fashion. In the same way came the decision concerning the removal of Kuznetsov and Rodionov from their posts.

The importance of the Central Committee's Political Bureau was reduced and its work was disorganized by the creation within the Political Bureau of various commissions — the so-called "quintets," "sextets," "septets" and "novenaries." Here is, for instance, a resolution of the Political Bureau of October 3, 1946:

> STALIN'S PROPOSAL:
>
> 1. The Political Bureau Commission for Foreign Affairs (Sextet) is to concern itself in the future, in addition to foreign affairs, also with matters of internal construction and domestic policy.
>
> 2. The Sextet is to add to its roster the Chairman of the State Commission of Economic Planning of the U.S.S.R., Comrade Voznesensky, and is to be known as a Septet.
>
> Signed: Secretary of the Central Committee, J. Stalin.

What a terminology of a card player!

[Laughter in the hall.] It is clear that the creation within the Political Bureau of this type of commission — "quintets," "sextets," "septets" and "novenaries" — was against the principle of collective leadership. The result of this was that some members of the Political Bureau were in this way kept away from participation in reaching the most important State matters.

One of the oldest members of our Party, Klimenti Yefremovich Voroshilov, found himself in an almost impossible situation. For several years he was actually deprived of the right of participation in Political Bureau sessions. Stalin forbade him to attend the Political Bureau sessions and to receive documents. When the Political Bureau was in session and Comrade Voroshilov heard about it, he telephoned each time and asked whether he would be allowed to attend. Sometimes Stalin permitted it, but always showed his dissatisfaction.

Because of his extreme suspicion, Stalin toyed also with the absurd and ridiculous suspicion that Voroshilov was an English agent. [Laughter in the hall.] It's true — an English agent. A special tapping device was installed in his home to listen to what was said there. [Indignation in the hall.]

By unilateral decision, Stalin had also separated one other man from the work of the Political Bureau — Andrei Andreyevich Andreyev. This was one of the most unbridled acts of willfulness.

Let us consider the first Central Committee Plenum after the 19th Party Congress when Stalin, in his talk at the Plenum, characterized Vyacheslav Mikhailovich Molotov and Anastas Ivanovich Mikoyan and suggested that these old workers of our Party were guilty of some baseless charges. It is not excluded that had Stalin remained at the helm for another several months, Comrades Molotov and Mikoyan would probably have not delivered any speeches at this Congress.

Stalin evidently had plans to finish off the old members of the Political Bureau. He often stated that Political Bureau members should be replaced by new ones.

His proposal, after the 19th Congress, concerning the election of 25 persons to the Central Committee Presidium, was aimed at the removal of the old Political Bureau members and the bringing in of less experienced persons so that these would extol him in all sorts of ways.

We can assume that this was also a design for the future annihilation of the old Political Bureau members and, in this way, a cover for all shameful acts of Stalin, acts which we are now considering.

Comrades! In order not to repeat errors of the past, the Central Committee has declared itself resolutely against the cult of the individual. We consider that Stalin was excessively extolled. However, in the past Stalin doubtless performed great services to the Party, to the working class, and to the international workers' movement.

This question is complicated by the fact that all which we have just discussed was done during Stalin's life under his leadership and with his concurrence; here Stalin was convinced that this was necessary for the defense of the interests of the working classes against the plotting of enemies and against the attack of the imperialist camp. He saw this from the position of the interest of the working class, of the interest of the laboring people, of the interest of the victory of socialism and communism. We cannot say that these were the deeds of a giddy despot. He considered that this should be done in the interest of the Party, of the working masses, in the name of the defense of the revolution's gains. In this lies the whole tragedy!

Comrades! Lenin had often stressed that modesty is an absolutely integral part of a real Bolshevik. Lenin himself was the living personification of the greatest modesty. We cannot say that we have been following this Leninist example in all respects. It is enough to point out that many towns, factories, and industrial enterprises, kolkhozes and sovkhozes, Soviet institutions and cultural institutions have been referred to by us with a title — if I may express it so — of private property of the names of these or those Government or Party leaders who were still active and in good health. Many of us participated in the action of assigning our names to various towns, rayons, enterprises and kolkhozes. We must correct this. [Applause.]

But this should be done calmly and slowly. The Central Committee will discuss this matter and consider it carefully in order to prevent errors and excesses. I can remember how the Ukraine learned about Kossior's arrest. The Kiev radio used to start its programs thus: "This is Radio (in the name of) Kossior." When one day the programs began without naming Kossior, everyone was quite certain that something had happened to Kossior, that he probably had been arrested.

Thus, if today we begin to remove the signs everywhere and to change names, people will think that these comrades in whose honor the given enterprises, kolkhozes, or cities are named also met some bad fate and that they have also been arrested. [Animation in the hall.]

How is the authority and the importance of this or that leader judged? On the basis of how many towns, industrial enterprises and factories, kolkhozes and sovkhozes carry his name. Is it not about time that we eliminate this "private property" and "nationalize" the factories, the industrial enterprises, the kolkhozes and the sovkhozes? [Laughter, applause, voices: "That is right."] This will benefit our cause. After all, the cult of the individual is manifested also in this way.

We should, in all seriousness, consider the question of the cult of the individual. We cannot let this matter get out of the Party, especially not to the press. It is for this reason that we are considering it here at a closed Congress session. We should know the limits; we should not give ammunition to the enemy; we should not wash our dirty linen before their eyes. I think that the delegates to the Congress will understand and assess properly all these proposals. [Tumultuous applause.]

The Tasks of the Party

Comrades! We must abolish the cult of the individual decisively, once and for all; we must draw the proper conclusions concerning both ideological-theoretical and practical work.

It is necessary for this purpose:

First, in a Bolshevik manner to condemn and to eradicate the cult of the individual as alien to Marxism-Leninism and not consonant with the principles of Party leadership and the norms of Party life, and to fight inexorably all attempts at bringing back this practice in one form or another.

To return to and actually practice in all our ideological work the most important theses of

Marxist-Leninist science about the people as the creator of history and as the creator of all material and spiritual good of humanity, about the decisive role of the Marxist Party in the revolutionary fight for the transformation of society, about the victory of communism.

In this connection we will be forced to do much work in order to examine critically from the Marxist-Leninist viewpoint and to correct the widely spread erroneous views connected with the cult of the individual in the sphere of history, philosophy, economy, and of other sciences, as well as in literature and the fine arts. It is especially necessary that in the immediate future we compile a serious textbook of the history of our Party which will be edited in accordance with scientific Marxist objectivism, a textbok of the history of Soviet society, a book pertaining to the events of the Civil War and the Great Patriotic War.

Secondly, to continue systematically and consistently the work done by the Party's Central Committee during the last years, a work characterized by minute observation in all Party organizations, from the bottom to the top, of the Leninist principles of Party leadership, characterized, above all, by the main principle of collective leadership, characterized by the observance of the norms of Party life described in the statutes of our Party, and, finally, characterized by the wide practice of criticism and self-criticism.

Thirdly, to restore completely the Leninist principles of Soviet socialist democracy, expressed in the Constitution of the Soviet Union, to fight willfulness of individuals abusing their power. The evil caused by acts violating revolutionary socialist legality which have accumulated during a long time as a result of the negative influence of the cult of the individual has to be completely corrected.

Comrades! The 20th Congress of the Communist Party of the Soviet Union has manifested with a new strength the unshakable unity of our Party, its cohesiveness around the Central Committee, its resolute will to accomplish the great task of building communism. [Tumultuous applause.] And the fact that we present in all their ramifications the basic problems of overcoming the cult of the individual which is alien to Marxism-Leninism, as well as the problem of liquidating its burdensome consequences, is an evidence of the great moral and political strength of our Party. [Prolonged applause.]

We are absolutely certain that our Party, armed with the historical resolutions of the 20th Congress, will lead the Soviet people along the Leninist path to new successes, to new victories. [Tumultuous, prolonged applause.]

Long live the victorious banner of our Party — Leninism! [Tumultuous, prolonged applause ending in ovation. All rise.]

SUGGESTIONS FOR FURTHER READING

The Role of Ideas

ACTON, H. B., *The Illusion of the Epoch: Marxism-Leninism as a Philosophical Creed*. Boston: Beacon Press, 1957.

A critical account of historical materialism and Leninist philosophy.

DANIELS, ROBERT V., *The Conscience of the Revolution: Communist Opposition in Soviet Russia*. Cambridge, Mass.: Harvard University Press, 1960.

Controversy and struggle within the Party leadership from 1917 to 1929, with special reference to the differences between the Leninists and the Leftists.

DANIELS, ROBERT V. (ed.), *A Documentary History of Communism.* New York: Random House, 1960.

> Brief excerpts from the important writings and speeches of Lenin, Stalin, Mao, Khrushchev, and other important Communist leaders. Also Party and government resolutions, theses, and other official documents.

HUNT, R. N. CAREW, *The Theory and Practice of Communism,* rev. ed. New York: The Macmillan Company, 1957.

> Critical assessment of Communist ideas from Marx to Stalin.

MEYER, ALFRED G., *Leninism.* Cambridge, Mass.: Harvard University Press, 1957.

> Leninist thought and its relation to Marxism.

MOORE, BARRINGTON, JR., *Soviet Politics — The Dilemma of Power: The Role of Ideas in Social Change.* Cambridge, Mass.: Harvard University Press, 1950.

> What happened to the pre-revolutionary ideology of the Bolsheviks after they gained power.

MOORE, STANLEY W., *The Critique of Capitalist Democracy: An Introduction to the Theory of the State in Marx, Engels and Lenin.* New York: Paine-Whitman, 1957.

> Contains much textual material.

The Communist Party

DEUTSCHER, ISAAC, *Stalin: A Political Biography.* New York: Oxford University Press, 1949.

FAINSOD, MERLE, *Smolensk Under Soviet Rule.* Cambridge, Mass.: Harvard University Press, 1958.

> Based on secret Party files for the years 1917–1938, captured in 1941 by the Germans.

FISHER, RALPH T., JR., *Pattern for Soviet Youth: A Study of the Congresses of the Komsomol, 1918–1954.* New York: Columbia University Press, 1959.

> Based on stenographic reports of the Congresses and materials from the Soviet press.

GRULIOW, LEO (ed.), *Current Soviet Policies.* New York: Frederick A. Praeger, Inc., 1953 and later years.

> Proceedings of 19th, 20th, and 21st Congresses of the Communist Party of the Soviet Union.

LEITES, NATHAN, *A Study of Bolshevism.* Glencoe, Ill.: The Free Press, 1953.

> A psychoanalytically oriented interpretation of the Bolshevik world view, with special attention to political strategy as revealed in the writings of Lenin and Stalin.

RUSSIAN INSTITUTE, COLUMBIA UNIVERSITY, *The Anti-Stalin Campaign and International Communism*, A Selection of Documents Edited by the Russian Institute, Columbia University. New York: Columbia University Press, 1956.

> Khrushchev's speech on the "cult of the individual," the reactions of Communist Parties in other countries, and the follow-up resolution of the Central Committee of the Soviet Communist Party of June 30, 1956.

SCHAPIRO, LEONARD, *The Origin of the Communist Autocracy: Political Opposition in the Soviet State, First Phase, 1917–1922.* Cambridge, Mass.: Harvard University Press, 1955.

> Political opposition to Lenin and how he handled it.

SCHAPIRO, LEONARD, *The Communist Party of the Soviet Union.* New York: Random House, 1959.

> History of the most important Soviet social institution.

SHUB, DAVID, *Lenin: A Biography.* New York: Mentor Books, 1948.

> Lenin is still the most important Soviet leader.

WOLFE, BERTRAM D., *Three Who Made a Revolution: A Biographical History.* New York: The Dial Press, 1948.

> The lives, times, and influence of Lenin, Trotsky, and Stalin.

The State

ARMSTRONG, JOHN A., *The Soviet Bureaucratic Elite: A Case Study of the Ukrainian Apparatus.* New York: Frederick A. Praeger, Inc., 1959.

> The dynamics of power at the local and regional level.

CARSON, GEORGE BARR, JR., *Electoral Practices in the U.S.S.R.* New York: Frederick A. Praeger, Inc., 1956.

> Elections to local Soviets and an analysis of their role in the Soviet system.

Current Digest of the Soviet Press. A weekly publication at Columbia University by the Joint Committee on Slavic Studies appointed by the American Council of Learned Societies and the Social Science Research Council.

> Contains translations of *Pravda* and *Izvestiya* and selected materials from other Soviet newspapers and periodicals.

FAINSOD, MERLE, *How Russia Is Ruled.* Cambridge, Mass.: Harvard University Press, 1953.

> A comprehensive account of power and authority.

HAZARD, JOHN N., *The Soviet System of Government,* rev. ed. Chicago: The University of Chicago Press, 1960.

MEISEL, JAMES H., and E. KOZERA (eds.), *Materials for the Study of the Soviet System.* Ann Arbor, Mich.: George Wahr, 1953.

> Documentary materials.

TOWSTER, JULIAN, *Political Power in the U.S.S.R., 1917–1947*. New York: Oxford University Press, 1948.
> A standard text.

The Law

BERMAN, HAROLD J., *Justice in Russia*. Cambridge, Mass.: Harvard University Press, 1950.

GSOVSKI, VLADIMIR, *Soviet Civil Law*, 2 vols. Ann Arbor, Mich.: The University of Michigan Law School, 1948.
> Volume II contains the laws and Volume I the author's analysis.

GUINS, GEORGE C., *Soviet Law and Soviet Society*. The Hague: Martinus Nijhoff, 1954.

HAZARD, JOHN N., *Law and Social Change in the U.S.S.R.* London: Stevens & Sons, 1953.

Mass Persuasion and its Effect

BABITSKY, PAUL, and JOHN RIMBERG, *The Soviet Film Industry*. New York: Frederick A. Praeger, Inc., 1955.

FISCHER, GEORGE, *Soviet Opposition to Stalin in World War II: A Case Study*. Cambridge, Mass.: Harvard University Press, 1952.
> The case of Vlassov and the Russian Army of Liberation.

INKELES, ALEX, *Public Opinion in Soviet Russia*. Cambridge, Mass.: Harvard University Press, 1959.
> How the Soviet regime has used the mass media.

Force and Terror

BECK, F., and W. GODIN, *Russian Purge and the Extraction of Confession*. New York: The Viking Press, 1951.
> An account stressing especially what went on in the minds of the victims.

BRZEZINSKI, ZBIGNIEW, *The Permanent Purge*. Cambridge, Mass.: Harvard University Press, 1956.
> A history of purges plus the thesis that they are a permanent part of totalitarianism.

DALLIN, DAVID J., *Soviet Espionage*. New Haven: Yale University Press, 1955.

DALLIN, DAVID J., and BORIS I. NICOLAEVSKY, *Forced Labor in Soviet Russia*. New Haven: Yale University Press, 1947.

DINERSTEIN, H. S., *War and the Soviet Union: Nuclear Weapons and the Revolution in Soviet Military and Political Thinking.* New York: Frederick A. Praeger, Inc., 1959.

GARTHOFF, RAYMOND L., *Soviet Military Doctrine.* Glencoe, Ill.: The Free Press, 1954.

HART, LIDDELL B. H. (ed.), *The Red Army.* New York: Harcourt, Brace and Co., 1956.

LEITES, NATHAN, and ELSA BERNAUT, *Ritual of Liquidation: The Case of the Moscow Trials.* Glencoe, Ill.: The Free Press, 1954.

WHITE, D. FEDOTOFF, *The Growth of the Red Army.* Princeton, N.J.: Princeton University Press, 1944.

WOLIN, SIMON, and ROBERT M. SLUSSER (eds.), *The Soviet Secret Police.* New York: Frederick A. Praeger, Inc., 1957.

Essays by former Soviet citizens and a historical survey.

III

Economic Life

Almost everyone approaching Soviet economic life for the first time comes forward with substantially the same set of questions: How has the Soviet economic system been organized, and is it as unique as we sometimes hear it to be? What have been the specific accomplishments or achievements of the system, what its distinctive weaknesses and failures? Whatever its attainments may be, what price has been paid by the people for this achievement? What assessment should we put on this development, especially as regards its significance for the non-Communist world?

To answer these questions fully would require a book solely devoted to economics yet as large as this volume on the entire Soviet system. We have tried to provide at least partial answers to these questions through the papers in this chapter and certain closely related articles in others. Those in this chapter give particular emphasis to the organization and functioning of Soviet economic institutions and to the economic life of the people who man industry and the collective farms. In addition, most of the other questions are at least touched upon, except for the challenge to the West posed by Soviet economic development, which is taken up by Dr. Harry Schwartz in Chapter VI.

Almost all observers of the Soviet scene are agreed that the central fact about Soviet economic development was the decision to industrialize extremely rapidly, at an exceptionally forced pace of development. A host of consequences followed from this decision: the standard of living of the population had to be drastically reduced to provide the "savings" for investment; plans had to be hastily improvised and yet rigidly followed to insure getting all possible slack out of the system; co-ordination and integration in the execution of decisions was rendered most imperfect because time was short and personnel spread very thin; and all sorts of measures to control resources, and more important to control people, had to be introduced to insure meeting planned targets.

Such a massive, indeed total, commitment of a population is certainly not unknown in modern history. It happens often in times of war. But at such times there is generally present a most essential element which was missing in the Soviet case — namely, popular consensus. The Soviet people might perhaps have accepted the plans for industrialization, but of their own volition they certainly were not committed — let alone dedicated — to achieving those plans at such great sacrifice as the regime's approach required. Although efforts at mass persuasion were useful, especially when they stressed themes like patriotism or the dangers of attack from the enemy without, they hardly sufficed to develop the consensus necessary for so great a sacrifice as the forced pace of industrialization imposed. Motivation to perform at the level the regime required was weak among managers, generally lacking among the workers, and in the peasants completely overshadowed by fierce hostility to the regime, its objectives, and its methods. Consequently the regime could attain its goals only by a series of relatively extreme measures. One element consisted of very large rewards, by Soviet standards, for a favored few who were crucial to the regime's objectives and who worked especially hard to advance its purposes. Of course this meant even less for the vast majority. The second element of the regime's response to the popular challenge was a monstrous system of controls, checks, directives, inspection, and the like, backed by general terror against the population as a whole, to enforce obedience and to drive people through fear to produce the required effort.

The price was terrible indeed. In a sense a whole generation of Soviet people was simply written off, used as the human foundation on which to erect Soviet economic progress. But out of the cauldron there emerged a complete, in many ways unique, and certainly quite effective apparatus for economic production. In addition, a large and on the whole capable and experienced modern labor force was developed both at the managerial and laboring level. Furthermore, with the end of Stalin's reign the people experienced the relief of almost complete cessation of large-scale terror and began to enjoy very noticeable improvement in their standard of living. In this more relaxed atmosphere, finally, some of the worst of the dragooning which had characterized economic life was eliminated; administration was made more rational in many respects; the whole pace of development and the internal pattern of economic activity regularized and normalized.

The capacity of the Soviet economic system for further sustained growth at a fairly high level is no longer seriously challenged. The ability of the regime to make very effective use of its productive resources — still very much smaller than those of the United States — is evident to all. In the light of their past success, which the Soviets make all the more impressive by underplaying the quite substantial base from which they started, many underdeveloped nations assume that the Soviet Union has *the* key to economic development and provides a definite model which may be easily copied. We can, of course, point to flaws in the Soviet system, give evidence of exaggeration in their statistics, expose elements of irrationality in their organization. But flaws of the same order can be found in any economic system, and this type of activity is not likely to dissuade others that in the main the key to economic development is held by the Soviet Union. To the extent that this is the case, the non-Soviet world, particularly the American–West European coalition, faces a very considerable challenge to its world leadership.

ORGANIZATION AND GROWTH

31

Interpreting Soviet Statistics*

Naum Jasny

(1958)

There is one question about Soviet economic life which falls in a category by itself, but which must be dealt with before we attempt an answer to any others on the Soviet economy: are Soviet statistics reliable? Dr. Jasny is hardly among the more complacent in accepting Soviet statistics, but he acknowledges that at least in the hands of experts they provide an adequate, although often tricky, base for the analysis of Soviet economic life. As Dr. Jasny stresses, in recent years the Soviet government has released statistical data not earlier available. In fact, shortly after his article was published, a complete revision of agricultural statistics since 1913 appeared, which makes possible interesting comparisons between official Soviet estimates and those made by Dr. Jasny and other Western experts.

I have been asked how a reasonably correct picture of the Soviet economy can be obtained

* Reprinted from "Interpreting Soviet Statistics: Penny Plain, Twopence Coloured," *Soviet Survey*, No. 26 (Oct–Dec 1958), pp. 9–14, by permission of the author and the publisher.

in spite of the inadequacy — to use a neutral word — of the relevant statistical material.

The answer is: why, it is simple. You examine carefully the statistics that are released, correct those false and inaccurate statistics that it is possible to correct, discard those which are beyond repair, putting in their place and in the gaps which have been deliberately left, your own estimates — made with the help of correct and corrected official statistics and other suitable evidence — and you then get a set of statistics permitting more or less definite conclusions.

It takes time, certainly. This is better counted in years rather than weeks or months. The present writer has been at it for more than fifteen years and cannot yet see the end.

One quality that the analyst needs, sometimes referred to as "the feel for figures," is a constructive mind which, coupled with a sense of reality, can, by a process that is both conscious and intuitive, fit together the single bricks to make a more or less comprehensive structure.

It is essential to approach this work with a reasonable lack of bias and a readiness to go your own way, whatever the demands from the outside. Those with a bloodless indifference to both sides in the present titanic conflict will most likely lack other indispensable qualifications for the task. They may well be opportunists, responding to public pressures. Only that analyst will be successful who is able not merely to reject demands from the outside, but also to conquer his own inclination to see black or pink, as the case may be.

Errors, and indeed relatively great errors, are inevitable in an analysis in which one is compelled to use such a crooked item as Soviet statistics. It is best to acknowledge such errors frankly, to get them entirely out of one's system, so that they cannot affect — and distort — further work.

These tiresome preliminaries settled, it is

possible to get a fairly correct idea of what is going on. But there is a vast difference between the knowledge of the analyst and the knowledge which has become common property. Soviet problems are usually presented in a context of heated controversy; it is at times extremely difficult to get correct findings accepted, and in this way their usefulness is diminished.

In spite of the immense amount of research into the Soviet economy being done in the United States, the sputniks came as a complete surprise except to a very few. The explanation lies largely in the bias both of those who are unwilling to give the Soviet regime due credit for its achievements, and those whose sympathies tend in the opposite direction. In either case the prevalence of wishful thinking, and the readiness of the opportunist to fall in with it, can clearly have deplorable results.

During many years of Stalin's reign and for some time thereafter almost no statistics were released in the U.S.S.R. This policy was changed in 1956, and since then a great volume of statistics has been published. They are markedly selective; for example estimates of the population, both total and subdivided into rural and urban, were published in 1956, but the age and sex composition was withheld. Among the items not covered at all or only inadequately covered by Soviet statistics are such important items as nominal wages and indices of farm production, not to speak of practically everything connected with the armed forces. A reasonably correct official price index exists only for the retail prices of consumer goods in 1947–57, with 1940 as the base year; lack of information about prices will, it is expected — and with justification — prevent even a superficial analysis of the most important economic items, such as the budget.

Sources and Degree of Distortion

The nature of Soviet statistics is in itself controversial. One extreme, and perhaps the less dangerous one, is represented by those who believe that *all* Soviet statistics are falsified. The other camp insists that Soviet statistics are not false, but that their acknowledged defects arise from methodological deficiencies. In fact, Soviet statistics cover the full range from correct to falsified, with every kind of intermediate grade in between. Concealment

of the methods of calculating the data, and of all the details of the calculations (for national income, for example, only one figure is announced for each year), frequent unannounced changes in concepts and coverage, and last but not least, the marked element of distortion introduced by the language used in commenting on the statistics, immensely enhance the difficulties.

The degree of distortion in Soviet statistics depends in the first place on the importance that an item has in Soviet propaganda and on the extent to which reality departs from the Soviet rulers' wishes or from what they want the reality to be believed to be. Other differences in reliability are related to the time factor. Correct statistics have a much greater propaganda value than false statistics; hence the release of false statistics declines in periods favorable for the regime, and soars in unfavorable periods.

The idea that all Soviet statistics are a falsification is obviously absurd. It is held mainly by strangers in the field of statistics, or by those with an anti-Soviet attitude who give free rein to their fantasy in describing what is going on (or not going on) in the U.S.S.R. This is of course much easier than making the sustained effort needed to separate the wheat from the chaff in Soviet data.

The idea that Soviet statistics do not contain falsifications — the other extreme — could have grown up only at a time when the study of the Soviet economy in the West was in its early stages. It is for reasons unconnected with research that the idea has survived until today. If this attitude toward Soviet statistics has not made the analytical work of its adherents entirely valueless, this is because they have largely disregarded the distorted official data — sometimes to an even greater extent than the present writer does.

The bulk of Soviet statistics, so far as they are released at all, are correct. Their shortcomings, if any, consist in unexpected and unannounced changes in concepts. Transport statistics, for example, seem to be entirely correct. Statistics of industrial production *in physical terms* are almost completely correct as well. Soviet statistics of acreages under cultivation and livestock herds have never been seriously doubted (possibly only because of the inability to provide proof of their unreliability).

On the other hand, most of the statistics relating to aggregate quantities, such as the indices for national income and industrial production, are incorrect. Although such data may not cover a large number of categories, they are precisely the figures to which a statesman, scholar, or journalist would in the first place turn.

Falsification reaches astronomical dimensions in statistics of real wages and real incomes. The great achievements of the U.S.S.R. in industrialization were obtained by imposing immense sacrifices on the population. Even Khrushchev admitted as much in his speech on the expansion of output of textiles and shoes in May 1958 (*Pravda*, May 10, 1958). Nevertheless, Soviet statistics are made to demonstrate immense increases in real wages and real incomes of the peasants. For example, the fantastic claim was officially made that in one year only (1948) real wages more than doubled, although such an increase is physically impossible; the actual growth is unlikely to have exceeded 15 per cent. In 1939 it was announced that real wages had more than doubled during the second five year plan; a rise of 25 per cent would have been more in line with facts. To reinforce this claim the turnover in State and co-operative trade in 1928–40 (which did not increase at constant prices by much more than 50 per cent) was advertised as having grown 4.6-fold.[1]

Falsifications and exaggerations are, in fact, strewn over the whole economy. An astonishing case was a table in an official statistical handbook, *Socialist Agriculture* (Moscow, 1939), reproduced in 1948 by M. M. Liftis, Minister of Trade, in his pamphlet *Soviet Trade*. It showed a rapid rise in per capita sales of the most important consumers' goods by the peasants in 1933–38. The table left no doubt that physical quantities were involved. Only after several years of work did the present writer realize that the quantities sold were measured in rubles of rapidly declining purchasing power.

The Soviet economy has shown great rates of growth since 1946. In the decade before the war, only the years 1934–36 were of similar nature. The period of the great purges, 1936–40, were years of near stagnation, while the period of full-scale collectivization connected with the drive to industrialize (the years 1930–32), was characterized by rapidly declining rates of growth. As might be expected, statistics covering the good periods showed in general only relatively moderate exaggerations and occasionally there were no exaggerations at all. On the other hand, the indices for the unfavorable periods are as a rule exaggerated immensely. Long-range indices for the most important items, such as national income, industrial output, and investment, embody all — even the most stupendous — exaggerations of the unfavorable periods and consequently they too are greatly exaggerated.[2]

Unexpected and usually unannounced changes in concepts are most frequent in regard to farm products. For about twenty years, until 1954, the Soviets operated with the so-called "biological" or "factual" yield of grain (for a somewhat shorter period for other crops); this departed from reality by quite substantial but never announced percentages. Recently some non-meat food was included in the estimates of meat production to make them more presentable. The milk covered by statistics was also recently expanded, without any explanation or announcement.

The idea that the errors in Soviet statistics are not deliberate implies that the Moscow central statistical office is staffed by infants. The people working there are better statisticians than most of those analyzing Soviet statistics in the West. They know better than most Western analysts the weak spots in their statistics, the great extent of falsification, the immense contradictions between them. Most Soviet statisticians would be only too happy to release honest statistics, but they operate on orders and have no choice. They may and no doubt do congratulate themselves on the great effectiveness of Soviet propaganda. The Soviet

---

[1] In 1956, the percentage increase claimed in retail trade in 1928–40 was scaled down — without any comment — to a 2.3-fold rise.

[2] Actually the statistics for the years since 1951 are much more reliable than those for 1940–50. While the rates of growth in 1946–50 were very high, the deprivations of the population were immense, and this too is a factor tending to produce greatly exaggerated statistics in the U.S.S.R.

1956 statistical handbook was published in many hundreds of thousands of copies in many languages — three editions in English alone. (Both I and my publisher would be satisfied if a few thousand copies of my *Commentary* on this handbook were to be sold.) The immensely distorted indices for the aggregates mentioned above are also repeated in virtually every speech and article, certainly in every book.

Problems and Methods of Research

The methods used in the tiresome and frustrating work of checking Soviet data vary. Here only the most important will be discussed.

The Soviet economy, as that of any other country, represents a body with an endless web of inter-connected links. Many farm products serve as the raw materials of the food industries. The output of these reaches the consumer via the retail trade. In between these two series of linked stages is the operation of the transport system. In short, there is a chain in which each stage is tied in with the preceding and the succeeding link. Other examples of such important chains of inter-connected links are: iron ore and coking coal –pig iron–steel–machinery–investment in equipment, or building materials–construction as part of investment.

In dealing with the economy of a country with good statistics, an analyst will devote attention to such chains and inter-connections only in specific cases, for example, when he is interested in the proportions of total farm output reaching the market. In general the existence of proper tie-ins is taken for granted. In work on the Soviet economy, examination of the tie-ins (most frequently the ascertainment of their insufficiency) is a major, if not the major, tool.

The degree of inexactness varies in each chain from link to link, from zero in some cases to immense proportions in others. Proper tie-ins between the individual links may consequently be absent, sometimes glaringly absent. The table on p. 34 of *Economy of the USSR in 1956*, the official statistical handbook (this is the basic table of the handbook), gives the Major Indicators of Development of the National Economy of the U.S.S.R. in 1913–56.

Some of the indicators for 1956 (1913 and 1928 = 100) in the table are as follows:

	1913–56	1928–56
Numbers of wage and salary earners	443	446
Fixed investment of the State		3527
Basic funds	1480	1089
National income	1922	1615
Gross industrial production	3021	2288
Freight transports (5 carriers)	1136	1092

Of the six series, two, those of wage and salary earners and freight transports, are reasonably correct. The other four indices are extremely high relative to those for wage and salary earners and freight transports. The contradiction in regard to the number of wage and salary earners cannot be cleared up by general considerations. It is obvious, on the other hand, that gross industrial production could not have increased in 1928–56 more than twice as much as freight transports. The transport system is engaged primarily in transporting industrial goods and the raw materials for them. Moreover, the five carriers for which the index is calculated do not include transport by horse, which declined greatly over the period. Similarly, home industry, which is as a rule conducted without or with relatively little use of transport by the five registered carriers, was still quite important in 1928, but has been greatly reduced since. Transports by the five carriers must consequently have grown substantially more than industrial production. The official indices for gross industrial production and freight transports by the five carriers imply that raw materials and finished industrial goods were making their own way from the farm to the factory, from factory to factory, and from factory to retail stores. This does not occur even in a socialist state, and since the index for freight transports is accepted as correct, the index showing a roughly 8-fold increase in industrial production in 1928–56, calculated by D. Shimkin *et al.* of the U.S. Bureau of the Census as well as by this writer, appears to accord well with the roughly 11-fold increase in freight transports by the five carriers.

The official claim of a 16-fold growth in national income in 1928–56, makes even less sense relatively to the 11-fold increase in freight transports by the five carriers, than does the 23-fold increase in industrial output. Again it may be said that, all things considered, the 4.5-fold increase in national income calculated by this writer, and the even smaller percentage rises calculated by other analysts, seem to tie in well with the officially calculated 11-fold increase in freight transports by the five carriers.

Most of the marked discrepancies between individual links in the chains and conditions point to distortions. Few of them yield reasonably exact data, as for example, determination of the grain harvest from the utilization end. Usually only a broad idea is obtained, indicating the direction in which research must be conducted.

Statistics of the national economy are normally prepared by statistical organizations. Since research on the Soviet economy in the West is mostly conducted by individuals or at best by small groups, the handling of even the available material causes great difficulties which are aggravated by the Soviet habit of concealment (wise from the Soviet point of view). A really thorough covering of the whole economy is impossible in these conditions. The choice for the Western analyst is usually between having relatively more thorough results, at prohibitive costs and with a long delay, and the use of short-cut methods (basing indices on small samples, employing semi-detective methods such as pinning down the implications, not intended for disclosure, in statements, etc.). Judiciously handled, short-cut methods yield satisfactory results, but very few analysts are able to make use of them, especially in the field of Soviet economics, and the results obtained by those who are qualified for such tasks are looked upon with more or less distrust. If this were not so, a discussion would not have been conducted in 1957–58 in the pages of *The Times* on the reliability of the funny Soviet index of industrial production (torn to shreds by Colin Clark as far back as 1939, as well as by his numerous successors thereafter).

Whatever findings on the Soviet economy are available are at best incomplete, and the disagreements between Western students in some cases substantial. The growth of national income in the five years 1951–55, for example, is estimated by this writer at 9 per cent per

year (the official figure is 11.5 per cent). Probably not many of his colleagues would agree with this estimate. The estimate of 6–7 per cent per year is generally accepted in the United States.

One of the easiest tasks is a rough calculation of real paid-out wages. Nominal wages, even when they were concealed, could have been roughly estimated from one or another tied-in item, such as retail trade. Most prices of consumer goods and services can be found, too, although a great deal more time is needed for this task than most analysts are prepared to devote. A usable index for Soviet real wages was not calculated before 1951. Calculation of peasants' incomes meets with the difficulty, which cannot be entirely surmounted, of estimating the output from their private plots and livestock; there has been a complete black-out on this since 1940. With the prices used for the index of real wages, an index of retail prices can be constructed (by changing weights), but only one attempt has been made so far, and even this needs revision.

Official estimates of the real grain crops have not been disclosed even now. The present writer's estimate for the years before World War II turned out to be accurate, while those for the post-war years were too high. Still, it was useful to have the estimate of the 1950 grain crop of 92 million tons, in face of the official estimate of 124.5 million tons, although the crop later turned out to have been equal only to about 80 million tons (implied in official data), or 85 million tons (this writer's latest estimate).[3] Calculation of the grain crops does not actually meet with serious difficulties for one who is familiar with the utilization of grain; there are only six items (food, feed, seed, technical uses, foreign trade, and waste) to consider. With the relatively small number of important farm products, and with the data on acreages and livestock herds usually available, even estimating the index for farm production available for sale and for consumption in the farm home is really not a very big task.

The calculation most frequently attempted has been that of industrial production. It has

---

[3] The Soviets do not mind underestimating an item for former years, if by so doing they can claim greater rates of growth in more recent years.

been undertaken for both gross and net output, and both by more thorough and by short-cut methods. A full coverage is impossible because of the absence of data on the output of armaments and of the great variety of machines produced and the frequent changes in models. Impressively, the results reached by most analysts for the period 1928–50 are fairly close to each other. A successful appraisal of the growth in industrial output in 1928–37 was even reached by something resembling a trick (evaluating a contradiction between two widely-diverging estimates of the share of Soviet industrial production in total world production in the same year in two different editions of the same official statistical handbook).

These are numerous factors causing considerable difficulties in estimating construction and investment. But too great errors can be avoided, because changes in investment more or less parallel changes in construction, and for construction a good check is available in the output of building materials. The main difficulties are encountered in estimating the shift of investment from 1928, when the private sector accounted for a large part of total investment, and, say, 1932, by which time this share had dwindled greatly. There are also great distortions in the official data pertaining to changes in investment during the purges (1936–40) and the subsequent years until 1946, distortions which it is not easy to eliminate completely.

All estimates of Soviet national income thus far made in the West have been produced by crude methods. The results differ greatly, depending on the selection of weights. Still, with due allowance made for this fact, the estimates do give a fair order of magnitude,[4] while the official index for, say, 1928–55, is exaggerated more than two-fold.

In conclusion, it seems to me that I may

have taken too lightly those questions on which my own mind has been made up, and that therefore the task will look too easy. I really do not see how an outsider can find his way among the various estimates, official and unofficial. Machinery output represents almost 40 per cent of total Soviet industrial production. According to official calculations, the production of machinery (including other metal-processing) grew from 1950 to 1955, a period of considerably improved Soviet statistics, by as much as 120 per cent. One organization devoted to research into the Soviet economy has given, for the output of machinery (excluding armaments) an increase of 14 per cent (1928 weights) or 23 per cent (1955 weights) in those years. Statisticians in the U.S. Bureau of the Census calculated for the output of machinery, including armaments, an increase of 72 per cent for the same period. (Let it be added that the output of armaments is unlikely to have grown during the period in question much more than the average for all machinery.) There you are: 120, 72, 14, or 23. Take your choice.

32

The Background of Soviet Economic Performance[*]

Alexander Eckstein

(1955)

To understand the Soviet economy it is necessary to see it in the context of Soviet development at large, and in particular in terms of Soviet goals. We therefore begin the substantive discussion with Prof. Eckstein's general review of the economy, its objectives, and its place in Soviet development. He calls our

---

[4] An account of estimates of the growth of national income and industrial output by the various Western analysts, and their comparison with the official estimates, is to be found in N. Jasny, *The 1956 Soviet Statistical Handbook — A Commentary* (Michigan State Press, 1957), pp. 32–33 and 57. The interested reader is referred to this source for information on the work of other analysts who helped to raise the iron curtain on the economic front.

---

[*] Reprinted with minor omissions and editorial changes from "Some Notes on Economic Development in the Soviet Union," unpublished talk given at the Fletcher School of Law and Diplomacy, Tufts University, at a conference sponsored by the World Peace Foundation, the Foreign Policy Association, and other groups on June 20, 1955, by permission of the author. Copyright © 1961 by Alexander Eckstein.

attention to the fact, often neglected, that there was once a lively debate in the Soviet Union on the alternative *paths of economic development open to a socialist country, and makes clear the implications of the decision to follow the path of forced growth under conditions of total mobilization.*

Now I would like to analyze briefly the position the Soviet Union found itself in prior to the great industrialization drive of 1928; i.e., the stage of development that the economy was in, some of the basic problems it faced, and the development dilemmas that this situation posed. Thereafter, I will try to explore some of the basic distinguishing features of the Soviet pattern of economic development, concluding with a discussion of a few of the key problems that the Soviet economy and the Soviet regime faces at the present time.

Of course, as we all know, the Russian economy of 1927–28 was highly agricultural, underdeveloped, and backward. It was an economy in which about 75–80 per cent of the population was dependent upon agriculture, as compared with 25 per cent in the United States at that time. The output of goods and services per head, or putting it in another way, per capita gross national product was one-fifth of that of the United States. This was the case in spite of relatively rapid industrialization in Russia between 1880 and World War I. But, since the Soviet Union entered upon the stage of industrial development quite late in relation to Western Europe and the United States, the industrial sector within which development proceeded so rapidly was small — i.e., the base from which the development started was quite narrow. Thus on the eve of the First World War, or as of 1927–28, the Soviet industrial sector and the Soviet industrial base were still very modest. This can be illustrated with just a very few data. Soviet coal production was 35 million tons in 1928 as compared with United States production of over 500 million. Soviet steel production was 4 million as compared with 60 million in the United States at the time. Soviet power production was 5 billion kilowatt hours as compared with 130 billion kilowatt hours in the United States. Even these few data show clearly the tremendous gap between the Soviet and United States level of industrial production in 1928.

What was the resource picture? In very brief terms, there is no question that — as shown by the studies of Chauncey Harris, Shimkin, and others — the Soviet Union is one of the most richly endowed countries in terms of mineral and industrial resources. For instance, it is estimated that about 23 per cent of world energy resources are to be found within the confines of the Soviet Union. The problem is therefore not one of the quantity of known or potential reserves. Actually, the Soviet Union was geologically quite unexplored at that time. Thus, the possibility for discovering new reserves was, and possibly still is, greater than in the United States. Therefore, the problem facing the Soviets was not one of the quantity but rather of the distribution of resources. The bulk of these resources were and are located in Asiatic Russia. The population and industrial centers of the Soviet Union were largely in European Russia, though some secondary centers were beginning to be developed in Asiatic Russia. In effect, one of the problems in Soviet economic development was that of overcoming space friction — i.e., distance. In this sense, the large territory of the Soviet Union definitely represented an economic disadvantage. Space placed a much greater burden upon the transport sector than would be the case in a smaller country such as the United Kingdom, or even the United States. This can, for instance, be illustrated by the fact that while in the Soviet Union about $\frac{1}{3}$ of coal production is consumed by railroads, the fraction in the United Kingdom is $\frac{1}{10}$ and in the United States and Canada it is $\frac{1}{5}$. Frequently, in the Soviet Union as much coal is consumed in the process of transportation as is transported from one location to another.

The Great Debates

In many respects, the Soviet development problem of 1927–28 was rather similar to that faced by many of the underdeveloped countries of today, such as India, China, and Southeast Asia. It is a problem of a basically underdeveloped agricultural economy, trying to industrialize, trying to build some mechanism, some road, some path, toward economic development. The question that needs to be posed in this context is: what is to be the objective of this economic development? and which paths should it follow? Will the patterns and objectives of economic development be focused on what may be referred to as power-oriented or welfare-oriented goals? Is the ultimate objective and the basic motivation to raise standards of welfare, standards of consumption, and standards of living of the people, or is it to achieve as rapid a rate of industrial production as is technically feasible in order to catch up with the West and, in the Soviet case, to make the country as powerful as or more powerful than any of its actual or potential enemies would be? This was a question which was not at all completely resolved on the eve of the first Five Year Plan. That is, the question of both ends and means was very much involved in the Great Industrialization Debates on the eve of the first Five Year Plan, in the middle and late twenties. These debates were most interesting and have still not been sufficiently explored by Western scholars. In a sense, they represent one of the first conscious debates on the problems of economic development that we have had in modern times. Many of the arguments and many of the basic theories that economists are groping with in the field of economic development were posed and raised in a rather sophisticated manner at that time, even though heavily overlaid by Marxist jargon and by Marxist methodology. The interesting thing about the debate is that both schools of thought — the so-called rightist and leftist groups, the Bukharin and the Preobrazhenski schools — were basically agreed on objectives. They viewed the end-goal of socialism as production for the sake of consumption; that is, the objective was to raise standards of consumption. Therefore the debate was, in a sense, one of means and rate of development.

One school, the Preobrazhenski school, adhered to the point of view held by many governments of underdeveloped areas today, that in order to develop economically it is necessary to have a very rapid rate of industrialization. This industrialization needs to be focused — at least initially and for some time to come — upon the development of producer goods industries, because without the basic, heavy industries — steel, coal, electric power, transport, etc. — it would not be possible to have rapid and rational development in the other sectors of the economy.

The other school, while not completely disagreeing, felt that it was necessary to develop agriculture as well and that agricultural development was a very important prerequisite for economic development. This divergence had also certain implications as to methods of financing economic development. The leftist group felt that, given the objective of maximizing the rate of industrial growth, it was necessary to resort to very high rates of taxation, price manipulation, and other measures, in order to check consumption and insure a high rate of savings and investment in the economy. The Bukharin faction, on the other hand, felt that much greater reliance had to be placed upon incentives — particularly in the agricultural sector — so as to stimulate agricultural development and an increase in agricultural output, thereby insuring the food supply to the cities and the maintenance of agricultural exports. This was the ideological setting.

The actual economic setting within which this industrialization debate evolved was, of course, the great scissors crisis of the 1920's. At this point it may be well to recall the fact that before the First World War, Russia was a major grain-exporting country. It exported anywhere from 7 to 10 million tons of grain a year. These exports were made possible by virtue of the prewar land tenure systems, which insured a certain share of agricultural produce being channeled from tenants, to the landlords, and therefrom to the market. After the revolution, of course, the land was distributed to the peasants, and landlordism was abolished. This made the whole problem of agricultural marketing — of getting the grain away from the peasants — a much more difficult problem. Now it was necessary to purchase the grain from the peasants in some way or to tax it away forcibly. Actually, the Soviets tried both methods. First, during the period of War Communism, they tried forcible extractions with very disastrous results. Then, during the NEP period, they tried to rely partly upon incentives, which worked to some extent but not satisfactorily enough. During the NEP period, the so-called kulaks — the wealthier peasants, who were really, from the production point of view, the progressive elements in the agricultural economy — strengthened their positions, which presented not only an economic but a political threat to the regime. This was clearly illustrated by the reluctance of the kulaks to surrender grain on terms the state trading organs were prepared to offer.

The Stalinist Road to Rapid Industrial Growth

These problems and dilemmas were drastically "solved" by Stalin, who went much, much further than Preobrazhenski or any of the leftist schools had advocated. He cut the Gordian knot by resorting to collectivization, which basically represented a mechanism for the extraction of agricultural output from the peasantry. One of the virtues and functions of collectivization from a Soviet point of view was that it constituted an effective method for attaining a high rate of involuntary saving in agriculture amidst stationary or even declining output. This was facilitated by the fact that in this way, the state gained direct access to, and control over, agriculture so that it could manipulate the terms of trade between the agricultural and urban sectors much more effectively than would have been possible in a system of private peasant land holdings. In a sense, Stalin, by resorting to this solution, threw away not only the means but also the ends of both Bukharin and Preobrazhenski. His program became very clearly a power-oriented program of economic development. This can be illustrated by a quote taken from an article which one of the leading economists of the Soviet Union wrote in the early 30's in opposition to the Preobrazhenski point of view:

> Heavy industry which produces the means of production must always outstrip the development of other branches of the economy, including light industry. This holds not only under conditions of the reconstruction period but also under conditions of the developed, classless society.

In other words, in a very real sense, industrialization, the development of producer goods industries, becomes an objective in itself, becomes an objective toward enhancing the power of the Soviet State. In this context the central objective of Soviet economic development became the maximization of the rate of growth in producer goods industries. This, in turn, revealed certain contradictions, dilemmas, so that the regime became all caught up in a vicious cycle. Thus, the Soviet planners, wishing to focus all energies on the development of heavy industry, largely neglected other sectors, particularly agriculture. In effect, by husbanding and concentrating their investment resources, they could achieve a spectacular rise in heavy industry at the cost of development in other industries. As a result, while agriculture remained in a more or less stagnant state, greater and greater demands were being made upon it, which of course produced some very serious disincentive effects even for collectivized farming. That is, the very fact of heavy farm extractions impeded the rise in agricultural output, not only because investments in agriculture were low but because even for the collective there was very little incentive to increase output. At the same time, with a growing total and urban population, the demands upon agriculture become greater and greater so the screw had to be applied tighter and tighter. This is one of the basic problems and dilemmas that the Soviet Union has faced from the very beginning of its economic development, and it still faces today.

Characteristics of Soviet Economic Development

I would now like to outline briefly some of the distinguishing characteristics of Soviet economic development. The Soviet economy is essentially a permanently, fully mobilized economy. It is akin to our war economy. This is illustrated, for instance, by the fact that while through the whole range of Soviet development about 40–45 per cent of investment went into metal and metal-products industries, in the United States this was the case only during World War II. It is an economy which is at a stage of almost permanent over-full employment. It is operated, to borrow a phrase from a colleague of mine, in a way that its commitments are greater than its resources at any one time. It is always over-extended. Its goals are maximum goals. It always attempts to proceed on all fronts at once, which, of course, is like Orwell's *Animal Farm,* in which "all animals are equal but some animals are more equal than others." Similarly, you try to proceed on all fronts at once with maximum objectives, but you have more maximum objectives in some sectors than in others. The most maximum objectives are reserved for heavy industry while the other sectors are considered from the standpoint of the Soviet planners as necessary evils. Some development in transport and in consumer goods industries is required — not necessarily because the regime is anxious to raise the standards of consumer welfare but because from a purely technical point of view, as the society becomes more urbanized and the population grows, patterns and levels of consumption shift. Moreover, standards of consumption must be maintained at levels that are conducive to raising productivity of labor in industry. Therefore, some expansion in consumer goods industries is unavoidable; in the end agriculture is really the ultimate stepchild. It isn't necessarily that the Soviet leaders say to themselves, "We do not want to develop agriculture"; rather, it is a problem of priority. Investment resources are, after all, scarce; heavy industries have greater priority than agriculture. This amounts to constant tightrope-walking. They would like to develop agriculture but they would like to develop it in a way that would not absorb an appreciable share of investment resources, and would not take too much investment away from those sectors in which they are genuinely interested. Also, they would like to develop it in a way that would insure a maximum and continuing degree of extraction.

In a more technical sense, what are some of the major characteristics of the Soviet pattern of development? First of all, it is a very rapid rate of economic development; in fact, it is the highest that we have on historical record. This may be due to the fact that the data we have and our techniques for adequately measuring rates of economic growth in the most highly developed economies date back to roughly 1850, 1870, or 1880. Britain, for instance, by the late nineteenth century had a rather highly industrialized and developed economy. It may very well be that if we had adequate records, or adequate techniques to work with inadequate records, we might discover rates of development similar to those in the Soviet Union at quite early stages of Western industrialization and economic development. As it is, Soviet rates were approximated only in Japan. Although there is some uncertainty about this, most of the available studies point to a Soviet rate of growth — as measured by gross national product or by

national income — of roughly 6–7 per cent a year, as compared to a historical rate of 3–4 per cent for the United States and a Japanese rate of 4–5 per cent. However, we would not be so confident of our findings in this respect if this were true only for national product. But it applies also to many simpler series, such as the rate of increase in industrial and non-agricultural employment, which was higher for the Soviet Union between 1928 and 1937 than for any period of the nineteenth century in the United States. The same can be said for the rate of growth in industrial production and the rate of growth of individual industries. This rapid rate of expansion is, of course, not a work of magic, but is to a large extent due to the very high rate of forced savings and investment maintained in the Soviet Union. For instance, the estimated rate of investment in the Soviet Union was around 20 per cent during much of this period, as compared to the historical rate of more or less 10 per cent in the United States.

As a result of this very rapid growth, the Soviet Union has been gradually narrowing the gap between itself and the Western economies, particularly between itself and the United States. This can be illustrated by citing a few comparative output figures for some key industries which are also of major importance from a strategic and military power point of view. Thus, in 1928 Soviet production of coal was at 6 per cent of the United States level. In 1953 it was at 63 per cent. The corresponding percentages for pig iron are 8 and 43 respectively; for steel 8 and 41; and for electric power output 5 and 29.

Future Prospects

If you project these rates forward at a stationary rate — i.e. 4 per cent growth for the United States and 7 per cent for the Soviet Union — you come to the conclusion that in 42 years the Soviet economy will be, in terms of gross national product, at the same level as the United States economy at that time. In terms of heavy industry — producers goods — it will have caught up sooner, while in per capita product it would attain the United States level later, since the aggregate national product of the Soviet Union is now at one-third of the United States level, while per capita output is about one-fourth. This projection, while interesting and, I think, in some ways significant, is in many respects spurious, because it projects stable rates of growth forward without allowing not only for unforeseen elements but even for elements which seen to emerge from recent Soviet experience. Since 1948 there has apparently been a slowing down in the rate of growth of the Soviet economy. The Soviet economy had, of course, heavily suffered from the war, but by 1948 Soviet output had roughly recovered to the prewar level. Official data on national income, on industrial production, car loadings, or rate of increase in employment, all show a slower rate of growth than for the 1928–37 period.

One may speculate that the Soviet rate of growth in the future is not likely to be quite as rapid as it was in the past. Now, what may be some of the factors that would tend to lead to such a slowing down? Before we address ourselves to this question let me summarize what were some of the key factors that could account for the rapid rate of Soviet economic development. First, the Soviet economy in 1928 began to spend its inheritance in surplus farm labor and in Western technology. At the time it had at its disposal a large reservoir of surplus labor which could be with relative ease — i.e., as compared to the present stage — extracted out of agriculture. Similarly, the Soviet economy of 1928, just because it was very backward, was able to — what Professor Gerschenkron calls — "reap the advantages of backwardness"; i.e., it was able to borrow technology from abroad, technology which corresponded to a much more advanced stage of development. Therefore, it did not have to go from a low stage through all varying, intermediate slow stages to a higher stage. It could jump, it could make a discrete technological leap from very primitive methods of production to very advanced methods of production. This discrete leap is, of course, a leap which can be made only once. It cannot be made to the same extent now because the Soviet economy is, roughly speaking, caught up — maybe not completely — with many of the Western economies. Thirdly, the Soviet economy of 1928 was able to borrow capital from the past. It was able to do this by eating into its reservoir of residential housing and transport. In the process of Soviet industrialization and urban-

ization, both housing and transport were neglected; this led to a marked overcrowding in the cities and a very rapid deterioration in housing standards, as can be illustrated by the fact that dwelling space per capita declined from approximately six square meters in 1928 to about four square meters in 1937. By 1950, housing standards deteriorated even further; war destruction was of such proportions that this process continued in spite of much larger investment allocations to housing. Now, housing has what economists call a very high capital output ratio, which means that you have to invest a great deal of capital in order to obtain an increment in output. Putting this another way, capital turnover is very slow. It takes a long time to amortize investment in housing, much longer than it takes to amortize investment in industry, so that, looking at it narrowly from the standpoint of maximizing the rate of industrial growth, housing can be viewed as a liability rather than as an asset. Thus, to the extent that Soviet planners are forced to devote a larger investment share to the high capital output ratio sectors such as housing and transport, the rate of economic growth will be slowed down. A fourth factor in the rapid rate achieved early in the Soviet economic development was the benefit derived from the tightening of the organizational and managerial framework. When an economy passes from a stagnant, passive phase to an active, dynamic phase, it is possible to capture certain economies just by going from a stage of underemployment to a stage of overemployment. The Russian economy, prior to 1928, had large pools of underemployed resources, or insufficiently employed resources. The Soviet planners drove these resources very intensively, often using three shifts in many plants. The potential margin inherent in this transition from a state of under-utilization of capital, plant, and human resources, to a state of over-utilization, is again one of the things that can be captured only once. Then it becomes a continuum; then economic development has to proceed out of its own momentum based on currently available resources.

And last but not least, there is the reservoir inherent in the ability of the regime to squeeze the agricultural sector. However, this squeezing obviously has its limits. Industrial development was extremely rapid, with industrial production multiplying three-fold between 1928 and 1937 and seven-fold between 1928 and 1953. During the same period consumer goods industries multiplied only about two-and-a-half-fold and agriculture increased only by about one-third, with per capita food availabilities remaining almost exactly at the same level in 1953 as in 1928. In such a situation a stage must be reached sooner or later where one cannot extract any more out of agriculture without really doing something seriously about increasing agricultural output. It seems to me this is what accounts for the note of urgency which you find in the pronouncements of Soviet leaders today. The Soviet economy has now reached a stage where agriculture has really become the key bottleneck sector and where without further agricultural increases progress will be inhibited. While agriculture has been collectivized, the peasant is still there and the problem of incentives for him remains to be solved. The peasantry as a human institution, the peasant way of life, is still very much there in the Soviet Union. The peasant is a creature — in terms of his psychology, in terms of his orientation and aspirations — in many ways very different from the urban worker, and this has not been too much affected by collectivization. Although the Soviet regime was able to gain much greater control over the countryside through collectivization, it has not been able to overcome the objections to onerous farm extractions, as amply illustrated by the findings of our interview project at the Russian Research Center. The Soviet peasant might be willing to accustom himself to the fact of collectives if the tax burden, the extraction burden, would not be so heavy. This is something of which I am quite sure the Soviet leaders are eminently aware. It means that either new areas of settlement have to be found, such as was done in the new lands campaign, where the problem of incentives is somewhat minimized, particularly if the new land is settled in state farms rather than in collectives, or an effort must be made to try to increase yields on existing farms. In order to increase yields, not only agricultural investment must be increased, but peasant incentives as well. This, of course, means or may imply a slowing down in the development of producers goods industry. I am not saying that this is going to take place. I am merely posing the

dilemmas that confront the Soviet leaders today.

In this sense, it may be fair to say that these dilemmas are not too dissimilar from those that they faced prior to 1928. Therefore it could be said that the Stalinist solution provided a postponement rather than a solution of the peasant problem.

Of course, the Soviet economy is much better equipped to deal with this problem today than it was in 1928. It is at a much more advanced stage and is therefore in a position to provide resources both for industrial and agricultural development; that is, if the regime is willing to pay the price in terms of lower rates of industrial expansion. Therefore the range of choice today is greater than it was in 1928. Although one cannot read the minds of the Soviet leaders nor predict what they will do, I would not rule out the possibility of a move of desperation which would be designed to create another agricultural revolution in the Soviet Union. This could take the form of a far-reaching transformation of collectives into state farms in which the tie between the peasantry and the land would be cut, and an attempt made to really and truly proletarianize the peasant and transform him into a worker in the same sense as the urban worker is. I would like to say that I am not predicting this; I do not think it is likely. I do not know whether it will take place — I am merely posing it as a possibility.

33

The Organization of Economic Planning*

Alexander Baykov

(1952)

Dr. Baykov provides a thorough survey of the organization of Soviet industry, carefully defining numerous special terms and explaining the workings of the unique institutions of Soviet

* Reprinted from "The Soviet Economic System," *Political Quarterly*, Vol. 23 (1952) pp. 49–61, by permission of the author and the publisher.

economic life. The account given here carries us to the year just before the death of Stalin. Changes made since that time are reviewed in the next contribution by Dr. Nove. It is evident from Dr. Baykov's account that the system of economic planning is itself hardly the product of planned development. At the same time there emerge certain persistent problems underlying these organizational changes — such as that of inducing adequate motivation in management and workers. This problem is discussed in depth in later contributions by Professor Berliner and Dr. Nove.

The working principles on which the present-day Soviet economic system is based are not a set of preconceived theoretical assumptions which have only been adapted to practical needs in the process of development of the Soviet economy. On the contrary, these principles are the outcome of practical measures, continual changes and adaptations made necessary over a period of 34 years, in order to put into effect the economic policy of the Soviet government. Yet in spite of the absence of theoretical foundations, in spite of continual changes in economic policy and the methods of applying it, despite alterations in the institutional framework within which the economic system has functioned in different periods of Soviet economic history, the main difficulties which have had to be solved in consequence of the repudiation of the capitalist system of economy and the building of a fully planned economy have constantly centered, during the whole of the period which has passed, in two main groups of problems: (a) how to plan the development of the country's economy efficiently, and (b) how to ensure the efficient management of this economy in the absence of the stimuli to efficiency present in the capitalist system of economy.[1]

Historically, the second of these groups of problems preceded the first. The first thing that had to be done was to solve the urgent problem of the administration of the nationalized branches of the economy: only after a basis for administration had been evolved could

---

[1] I use "capitalist system" and not "competitive economy," since competition (perfect or imperfect) is only one feature of the much larger concept of capitalist economy.

planning of the development of the national economy become possible. The task of solving the problem of the administration of the nationalized economy, in essence, then, preceded that of organizing effective planning, in spite of the fact that some planning institutions have existed since the very beginning of the Soviet regime and that the central State Planning Commission ("Gosplan") was created as early as February 1921.

Soviet Planning Institutions

Effective economic planning cannot be organized without the collaboration, in the preparation of plans, of the enterprises and establishments whose activities it is intended to plan. It also requires the creation of machinery for observing the process of fulfillment of the plans. In order to be effective, an economic plan must be based not on general economic statistical indices, but on concrete knowledge of the relevant factors, summarized in statistical indices. This concrete knowledge can be provided only by the enterprises and establishments whose activities it is intended to plan. That is why the first "control figures" of Gosplan (*not* an all-embracing plan for the national economy) appeared only in 1926 — that is, after nearly ten years of Soviet administration of the main branches of the nationalized economy; even then, the control figures of 1927-8 and 1926-7 were approved only in part, as mere directives for guiding the development of the national economy. The problem of the *preparation* of effective plans consists of organizing a two-way traffic of information: *from* the planning institution to the units whose activities it is intended to plan, and *from* these units to the planning institutions. In order to solve this problem, Soviet practice has evolved two systems of planning institutions. The first is a pyramid of *general planning institutions* which closely follow the administrative divisions of the Soviet Union, with the U.S.S.R. Gosplan as a central state planning commission for the whole Soviet Union, Gosplans in the union republics, and planning commissions in the autonomous republics, provinces, regions, districts, and towns with a population of over twenty thousand. These planning institutions are responsible for all general planning in the corresponding territory and have the right to ask all enterprises and establishments situated in their territory for any information necessary for the preparation of plans. However, none of these general planning institutions, not even the Gosplan of the U.S.S.R., have executive power either to carry out their plans or to supervise their fulfillment. The U.S.S.R. Gosplan has its representatives in the republics and regions, but they are only the eyes and ears of Gosplan and not executive officers who can interfere directly in the execution of plans. Parallel with these general planning institutions, there exists a second pyramid of *departmental planning commissions* inside the administrative hierarchy of the nationalized economy — down from the ministries of the U.S.S.R. to the ministries of Union republics and their special departments, and then to the trusts, enterprises, and institutions which manage the various units of the nationalized economy.

These two sets of planning institutions work in close collaboration, the departmental plans of the various branches of the national economy in a given territory being incorporated into the general plan of this territory by the corresponding general planning commission. The departmental planning commission is one of the executive departments in the administration of every branch of the national economy. The two-way traffic in the preparation of plans consists of sending "preliminary directives" on plans in preparation through the channels of the general planning institutions to the department planning commissions, and receiving back from them the planned targets with their comments and possibly amendments for further consideration and coordination. These are finally passed to the U.S.S.R. Gosplan. Its duty, after this two-way traffic of verification of plans is completed, is to prepare coordinated plans, which become operative plans only after ratification by the government. The operative plan is sent through the channels of the Soviet administrative hierarchy for execution by the enterprises and establishments. In this way, a clear distinction in the carrying out of plans is made between planning and administration.

Planning institutions have no executive powers and no right to give orders to the executive apparatus for the administration of the nationalized branches of the economy, but can act only by making recommendations to these executive organs of administration. They can draw the attention of the administration to defects in the fulfillment of plans, but orders for the correction of these defects can be given only by the superior administrative bodies. Credit sanctions may also be applied by the credit institutions as I shall explain below. Here I want only to stress that supervision of the fulfillment of plans is considered to be one of the essential features of planning duties. It has been learned by hard experience that however perfectly plans are prepared there always arise unforeseen circumstances not taken into account by the planners, or a dislocation of plans is caused by the uneven fulfillment of closely related parts of the plans. Only if means for supervising the fulfillment of plans can be devised in such a way that timely information on dislocation of the execution of plans becomes available, can measures for correcting their execution, or even for making modifications in the plans themselves in the process of their execution be taken. Soviet methods of supervision of plan-fulfillment are not "post-mortem," but current methods; in some branches of production and distribution there is virtually day-to-day supervision. This supervision of plan-fulfillment is considered a most essential feature, too, in the preparation of plans.

Here I must also stress that Soviet planners make a clear distinction between perspective and executive plans. All Five Year Plans are perspective plans, plans of a "directive" nature, and only those parts of them dealing with new investment have the character of executive plans for the whole period. Each annual plan, again, contains some elements both of a rigid executive plan and of a perspective plan. For example, for the most important branches of production, especially for heavy industry, the annual plan is a general executive one, with more rigid and precise quarterly executive plans. For the production of other goods — e.g., agricultural products and certain consumers' goods produced by local industries — the annual plan has the character of a perspective plan (general directives and estimates) and not that of a rigid executive plan; while for the credit system annual plans stipulate only certain limits and only quarterly plans, and in some branches of credit (e.g., the cash plan) only monthly plans, are executive ones. Owing to this flexibility in the composition of plans and the degree of their executive force, it is possible to make readjustments in the plan itself in the process of its fulfillment. For the key items in production, annual plans are detailed and precise, of a more rigid and executive nature. On the other hand, for the production and distribution of some consumers' goods susceptible to the influence of varying consumer's choice, or dependent on local sources of supply (local industries, cooperative industries, handicraft industries, the free local market for agricultural products), annual plans are very flexible. In the fulfillment of these plans, much greater freedom for local peripheral initiative is allowed — e.g., in the use of productive resources and labor, in the regulation of prices and so forth.

The Problems of Administrative Centralization

The main fundamental idea of central planning is to ensure (a) a smooth flow of production and distribution of the goods most important to the functioning of the whole national economy; (b) the fulfillment of production targets, to which priorities are given in the plan; and (c) to give a certain freedom of movement in the production and distribution of goods less important from a "national priority" point of view, relying on the initiative of the periphery in the preparation and execution of their plans as regards these goods and products.[2]

In the execution of plans as well as in the organization of the administration of the nationalized branches of the economy, the pivotal problem was to find an efficient combination of centralization of direction and decentralization of execution of plans, to find a balance between the interference of superior administrative bodies in the activities of producing and distributing units and the independence of the latter in their day-to-day activities. In the attempts made to solve these problems, many reorganizations of the institutional framework of administration in the nationalized branches of the economy took place. At the beginning, there was a Supreme Council of the National

Economy (V.S.N.Kh.) — a central body for the administration of all branches of the nationalized economy; later, this single central administrative institution was split into several institutions which each administered a major branch of the economy. By continued subdivision, nearly 30 People's Commissariats (later called Ministries) for the administration of the nationalized industries had been created by 1940.[3] This trend toward splitting central administrative institutions and an increase in their numbers did not, however, always mean a relaxation of centralization in administration. On the contrary, in certain periods of Soviet economic development it was accompanied by an increase in the degree of centralization of administration. This is another aspect of Soviet experience which could provide useful material for study by economists and industrial administrators to which, unfortunately, very little attention has yet been paid outside the Soviet Union.

After long evolution, the present-day administration of industry is now based on the principle of production-territorial organization of industry and on the principle of the unity of industrial management. From the point of view of their administration, all industries fall into three main groups: (a) All-Union industries, whose production is considered of immediate importance to the national productive plan of the whole country; they include industries producing capital goods and extracting industries, and are administered at the top level by All-Union ministries; (b) large-scale industries not of primary importance for the U.S.S.R. as a whole — i.e., mostly consumers' goods industries — which are administered by the republican ministries of Union Republics, and whose activities are only *coordinated* by the All-Union ministries (not only the administration, but also the planning of the production and distribution of these industries are in the hands of republican ministries and republican Gosplans); and finally, (c) industries of a smaller scale, practically all producing consumers' goods from local raw materials or from materials purchased in a de-

---

[2] The reader who would like to make a more detailed study of the application of these ideas of planning can find some material in Maurice Dobb, *Soviet Economic Development Since 1917,* and in Alexander Baykov, *The Development of the Soviet Economic System.*

---

[3] With ministries as specialized as electrical engineering, heavy engineering, medium engineering, general engineering, or heavy metallurgy, nonferrous metallurgy, and so on.

centralized way, which enjoy the greatest degree of decentralization of administration. They are administered by local institutions and their activities are only coordinated and stimulated by a Ministry of Local Industry. In the years immediately preceding the war, and since the war, more and more prodding has been applied to stimulate and develop local industries so as to increase the supply of locally-produced consumers' goods. (For example, these industries were granted concessions as regards the payment of turnover tax, the recruitment of labor, the regulation of the prices of their products, and so forth.)

Enterprises of All-Union or republican industries are either united in trusts on a territorial-productive basis, and through trusts subordinated to a ministry, or, in the case of very large enterprises, the intermediate layer of trusts is omitted and such enterprises are directly subordinated to a ministry.

The Role of the Manager

The principle of unity of management is embodied in a system of personal responsibility of all the directors or chiefs in the administrative hierarchy for all the business entrusted to them. Every production-unit from the lowest (brigade-shop–enterprise) to the highest (trust–ministry) has its chief or director who is responsible for the whole complex of business management of that unit. Depending on the size of the unit, the director has at his disposal a sectional administrative apparatus and functional agencies, but these functional agencies only assist the director and have no right to issue orders to lower managers or to agencies of the local administrative units. For example, the planning department of a trust can give orders neither to the director of an enterprise nor to the planning section of an enterprise, but can only pass suggestions through the chief of the trust to the director of the enterprise. Thus direct links of personal subordination and personal responsibility for the whole management of any productive unit constitute the principle of "unity of management" in Soviet industry. Each chief or director (workshop chief, director of an enterprise, head of a trust) receives his managerial tasks from a higher director and is directly subordinated only to that higher director or chief: there is but one layer of personal subordination at each stage of the admin-

istrative ladder. The selection and appointment of managerial staff are carried out in the same way. There is no "security of tenure" in any managerial post in the Soviet Union. The only safeguard against arbitrary dismissal is appeal to the superior administrative institution — or to the courts. The suitability of persons for any level of managerial activity is judged only by the efficiency of their management of the productive units entrusted to them. Soviet directors enjoy full autonomy and are held fully responsible for the actual execution of planned tasks. Their executive power in the prosecution of planned tasks is in many respects greater than that of managers of enterprises in capitalist trusts and cartels, and they enjoy more independence than the latter. They implement planned tasks by independently concluding contracts with the suppliers of their raw materials, semi-finished goods and equipment, and with wholesale purchasing organizations and the like. Their power over the employment of labor and over labor discipline is very wide. They have the right to take any reasonable production risk and carry out experimental work, and are responsible for this only to their superior director or chief. But their managerial activity is under constant supervision as regards failure or success in the fulfillment of planned tasks. Moreover, the supervision is effected not only from above, but also from below: by the workers' trade union organizations, the Party organizations and the press, as well as by the credit institutions. However, all these supervising bodies have no right to interfere directly with the management's executive decisions. They have the right to criticize and to bring any shortcomings to the attention of superior administrative bodies. Only in the case of credit institutions does there exist a right to apply immediate sanctions, namely, refusal to grant credit to an enterprise which does not fulfill its planned tasks. In this short article I cannot, of course, explain the machinery for supervising managerial activities; I can but touch on the main problems briefly and schematically.

Accounting and Financial Control

Every Soviet enterprise or establishment acts on the basis of strict *"khozraschyot,"* or economic accounting. Together with the production-plan of the enterprise, a financial plan is worked out, which includes outlays on salaries, the purchase of raw materials, fuel and the like, amortization charges, administration, and expenditures in connection with the sale of goods — that is, all those outlays necessary for achieving the fulfillment of planned tasks, which add up to the aggregate cost of production. This production-cost is a *planned* cost. It is an integral part of the production-financial plan of an enterprise. In order to carry out production plans, every enterprise has at its disposal two kinds of financial resources; its own turnover capital, and a certain amount of planned credit, both of which are administered by the State Bank. The management has an unrestricted right to dispose of its own turnover capital, but the disposal of the planned credit is conditional on its being used in accordance with the allocations earmarked for specific purposes in the financial plan of the enterprise. If the enterprise, for example, has accumulated a large stock of raw materials, or has spent more on wages than was fixed in its production-financial plan, and has asked for additional credits not earmarked for these purposes, the State Bank has the right to examine why such deviations from the planned norms have taken place, and has the right to bring these shortcomings to the attention of the superior administrative body whenever the Bank considers that they are due to a failure of the management. If, however, they are due to circumstances unforeseen by the plan or to objective circumstances outside the control of the management, the Bank can suggest amendments to the financial plan to the superior administrative body, and can grant credit from a special fund of "unplanned credit." All short-term credit operations for the whole national economy of the U.S.S.R. pass through the channels of the State Bank.

A similar control over the expenditure of credits is applied to long-term credits, and to expenditure of investment-grants and enterprises' amortization reserves. This control is performed by the specialized banks, e.g., the Industrial Bank. Any expenditure on capital construction is strictly earmarked according to approved construction-estimates, and the Industrial Bank very often opens a special office, staffed by technically qualified personnel, on the actual site of the new construction to supervise the spending of the credits allocated.

As all the financial transactions of enterprises are carried out through the channels of the State Bank, they are mutually balanced if expenditure of planned credit is going according to plan. The Bank is able to check the activity not only of an individual enterprise, but to see the whole picture of the fulfillment of the financial side of the plan.

In addition to this control over expenditure by state credit institutions, there also exists a Ministry of State Control which exercises control over the expenditure of material and monetary funds by all enterprises and organizations receiving allocations from the State Budget, as well as control over their fulfillment of government decisions on economic and similar questions. In this way, the financial organs exercise control over the process of fulfillment of production-financial plans by managements. But besides this current control, the success of the management has its final test in the profit or loss of the enterprise at the end of the year.

The Role of "Profits"

I have mentioned above only one element in the financial plan — planned costs — but every enterprise also includes in its production and financial plan a fixed planned profit and planned selling prices. Selling prices cannot be changed by the enterprise, and therefore planned profit[4] is dependent on the volume of production, cost of production, and selling prices. If the management succeeds in reducing the actual aggregate costs below planned costs, it will not only have fulfilled the requirements for the accumulation of planned profit, but over-fulfilled them; if, however, actual costs are higher than those planned, the profit will be lower than planned; *ceteris paribus* the results will be similar in the case of over-fulfillment or under-fulfillment of planned production. The negative result of the under-fulfillment of the planned production or of higher cost than that planned is quite obvious — the management will get into financial difficulties and, if it is found that this is due to defects in the management, demotion or dismissal or even prosecution for neglect of duties will follow. On the other hand, managements are actively interested in achieving

---

[4] Soviet economic literature uses the term "profit" and not "surplus" — which would be a more appropriate one for the Soviet economy.

planned profits and especially in over-fulfilling them.

Profit is used in three ways: (a) one part of it is transferred to the State Budget; (b) another considerable part remains at the disposal of the enterprise to be used for the increase of turnover capital and for capital investment; and (c) 4 per cent of the total planned profit, and 50 per cent of the profit above that planned was, in the prewar period, allocated to the "director's fund." It has been asserted that "during 1940 about 2 billion rubles went to the director's funds of the enterprises of the industrial commissariats. Of this sum, more than $1\frac{1}{2}$ billion rubles were spent during the year, of which expenditure on the building and repairing of dwellings for employees and workers amounted to 412 million rubles, on cultural and welfare service — 407 million rubles, and on bonuses to the management and workers — 125 million rubles." Thus, profits are used as a collective and individual incentive for both the management and workers of an enterprise. It is also a device for promoting efficiency in unprofitable enterprises (i.e., enterprises whose production is very important in spite of the fact that their production-costs are above the fixed selling price and which, consequently, receive subsidies; an extreme case of such an enterprise is one engaged on experimental work). Here economies achieved in adhering to planned costs, or reducing actual costs to below the planned level, entitle an enterprise's director's fund to percentages from planned or over-planned economy. Thus, even managements of unprofitable enterprises have incentives to make economies. The most characteristic feature of all Soviet annual production-financial plans is the constant drive for a reduction in production-costs. The reduction of production-costs is a prominent feature of every production-financial plan, and is taken into account in calculating the planned production-costs, selling prices, and planned profits of an enterprise. But this drive for the reduction of production-costs must not be understood as a synonym for the reduction of retail market prices of goods in the Soviet Union. The level of prices in any country is ultimately a reflection of the occupational pattern of its population. If the rate of increase in manpower employed in new construction and in services is greater than that in the production of the sum total of goods, the purchasing capacity of the population will increase more speedily than the supply of goods, and unless the increase in purchasing capacity is withdrawn by savings, and these are frozen until such time as the rate of production of goods overtakes that of increases in investment, an upward trend in prices becomes inevitable. From the launching of the first Five Year Plan in 1928 onward, throughout all the prewar years, the tempo of investment in the Soviet Union (in capital construction an "social construction" — i.e., in education, health, cultural services, and so on) was higher than that of production of consumers' goods, and especially of agricultural products, and this resulted in a constant upward trend in prices. Under such conditions of rising market prices, the device for the stimulation of managerial efficiency and the drive for the reduction of production costs described above could not be very effective. There might be a profit even where production-costs increased, because of a rise in market prices.

The Turnover Tax

The introduction of the turnover tax in 1930 made it possible to regulate market prices without directly affecting production-costs. The turnover tax (which is in some ways similar to the British purchase tax, but works more successfully in regulating prices)[5] covers the gap between the production and distribution-cost of goods and their market prices, which are determined by their supply and the effective demand for them. If demand increases more rapidly than it is possible to increase supply, and consequently the decision is taken to raise retail prices, the rate of turnover tax is increased. This, however, may have no effect either on production-costs (if the rise does not effect the prices of an enterprise's raw materials, fuel and so forth, or its wage-bill) or on the selling price at which an enterprise transfers its production to the

---

[5] For example, neither the Soviet retailer nor consumer know how much turnover tax is included in the prices of goods bought, since it is paid when the goods pass into the wholesale distribution network, the retail price giving no indication of the amount of tax included.

wholesale distribution network. In the same way, by a reduction in the rate of turnover tax, retail prices can be reduced without affecting production and distribution costs. The rate of turnover tax can also be used as an index of the scarcity of goods, and, to a certain degree, as an index for the measurement of consumers' preferences.

Role of the Consumer

I cannot describe here the very complicated and controversial problem of the influence of the consumer on the rational allocation of productive resources. The Soviet citizen, as a consumer, has the same means as a citizen in a capitalist economy of indicating his approval or disapproval of the choice of the producer who offers him these or those goods, by buying or not buying them at the price asked; but how effective this voting power of the Soviet consumer is, in comparison with that of consumers in a capitalist economy, in influencing the assortment of products marketed, is a very controversial question. Here I can only state that Soviet shops were often unable to sell some of the goods supplied to them at the prices asked, in spite of the general "famines" in consumers' goods experienced at times. These were obvious examples of bad choice by the producers. In the early years of the industrialization-drive the quality of consumers' goods was very often extremely low and the range of goods produced very limited; the Soviet press was full of complaints about defects in the quality and in the range of goods. Special penalties were introduced for the production of low-quality goods.[6] In the later years, the range of goods had considerably increased and their quality had become, in general, not inferior to goods produced in other countries, but it is difficult to assess to what degree this was due to improvements in technology, to deliberate decisions of the

---

[6] In every Soviet shop there is a "complaints book" for the use of customers, in which they can write any complaint regarding the quality of goods and defects in service, and any complaints against the management of the shop. In the immediate prewar years, the practice was introduced of exhibiting goods, the production of which was contemplated, in order to get the reaction of their potential consumers.

regulating product institutions, or to the influence of consumer demand.

Some General Comments in Conclusion

As I have mentioned above, the activity of Soviet managers is under constant observation and is stimulated not only from above but also from below — by the workers' organizations, the Communist Party, and the press.

Material incentives are absent in the Soviet economy only for entrepreneurs and shareholders. All other participants in the economic activity of a capitalist system (managers, employees and workers, and the whole population as consumers) are present, and their activity is stimulated by material incentives on what are essentially the same principles as in a capitalist economy.

Capital, in the Soviet economy, is regarded as the accumulated result of the creative activity of society as a whole, and not as a factor yielding certain returns. Of course, the cost of amortization and depreciation is taken into account in calculations of cost, but the cost of production is not geared to the cost of capital; it is based instead on the cost of obtaining materials and labor for the process of production. The drive for reducing production costs is aimed at increasing technical and economic efficiency in the use of the available productive resources, and profit or surplus is used as a technical device for the measurement of this efficiency — not as an end in itself. Increases in technical and economic efficiency are considered as a means of increasing the total productive resources at the disposal of society. Financial questions play a subordinate role to the increasing of productive capacity and production. Financial techniques have been contrived in such a way that money does not constitute the limiting factor in the planned extension of investment and production. The only limiting factors are the material and labor resources at the disposal of the society at any given time. Money and appropriate financial machinery have to be used in an economy in which wages and other payments are used as material stimuli to workers and managements, and in which freedom exists for the people to spend their incomes as they choose. But "finance" is used only as a means of measuring efficiency, and as a means of effecting mutual readjustments in the process of the society's production, distribution, and consumer activity. The main problems of the Soviet economy lie in the sphere of human relations as they affect the control and the functioning of the machinery for planning and administering the country's economic development, and not in any cardinal changes in this machinery itself. Minor modernizations and improvements in the machinery are carried out almost constantly, but in the main, it functions on firmly established principles.

34

Post-Stalin Reorganization of Industry*

Alec Nove

(1961)

A major part of the "new look" in the style of Soviet government after Stalin emerged in the field of economic administration. Khrushchev instituted an extensive reorganization of both industry and agriculture. Dr. Nove here describes and analyzes the changes in industry (as Dr. Kahan does later for agriculture.) Since there was a great deal of speculation about the possibly deep political significance of these changes, we must be grateful to Dr. Nove for placing them in perspective. He locates the specifically economic problems to which these changes were a response. In addition, he helps us to see that the break with the past is less extreme than many judged it to be. The reorganization involves many of the old basic elements, earlier described by

* Revised by Dr. Nove from "The Soviet Industrial Reorganization," *Problems of Communism*, a publication of the United States Information Agency, Vol. 6 (1957), pp. 19–25, and reprinted here with the author's permission. This, and the other essays in the present collection (Articles 36, 40, 50, 55, and 63) which were published originally in *Problems of Communism*, will appear, with some revision, in an anthology entitled *Communism After Stalin*, edited by Abraham Brumberg, and to be published in 1961 by Frederick A. Praeger.

Dr. Baykov, now arranged in new patterns.

On July 1, 1957, the Khrushchev regime launched a major reform of the Soviet economy, under which the bulk of industrial and building enterprises passed from the control of various central ministries to newly-created regional economic councils, or *sovnarkhozy*. The reform was accompanied by a drastic political shake-up in the top echelons of the CPSU, leading many commentators to interpret Khrushchev's new program as primarily an outgrowth of the political struggle for power. Khrushchev, so it has been argued, sought to smash the ministerial machines in which his enemies were entrenched while strengthening the grip of the party machine on economic life. It is clear that the power struggle played an important role in the processes of elaborating and promulgating the reform; its measures were controversial, affecting numerous vested interests, and they probably were of key significance in the conflict between Khrushchev and the so-called "anti-party group" within the leadership. On the other hand, it would be misleading to regard the reorganization as solely a power maneuver, for such a view ignores its intrinsic importance as an attempt to deal with real problems which beset the Soviet economy. The present instance would not be the first time that a major reform rooted in social or economic conditions has been carried through by an ambitious politician intent on strengthening his personal power position. Stalin, in launching his collectivization campaign in 1928–29, was no doubt plotting to isolate and defeat the Bukharin-Rykov group, but this aspect of his policy hardly merits priority in assessing its historic significance.

There were, then, economic considerations of great importance behind the recent reorganization. The background situation against which the reform must be viewed was discussed at some length in articles by Gregory Grossman and the present writer in *Problems of Communism* for March–April 1957, both of which were written prior to the announcement of Khrushchev's proposals. Briefly, as was pointed out there, the Soviet economy has long been laboring under strain. Many factors have contributed to this condition; essentially, however, the problem of the regime is one of reconciling its quest for maximum growth ("overtaking the most advanced capitalist countries at the earliest date") with other insistent demands on Soviet resources (arising out of necessary concessions to the population in the form of consumer goods, the need to increase agricultural production, the economic requirements of foreign policy, etc.) — and this in a period in which labor was no longer abundant.

These various pressures on the economy obviously called for the most efficient possible use of available resources, and the top-heavy structure of planning and control inherited from Stalin simply was not doing the job. At least as early as July 1955, at a party plenum called to discuss problems of industry, the Soviet leadership began to hint publicly that difficulties were due to failings in the economic system itself. When the strains became so great as to compel in December 1956 a downward revision of the tempo of growth envisaged in the Sixth Five-Year Plan, the issue of economic organization became manifestly urgent. It is very likely that the need for radical changes of some kind was appreciated by all leaders, though they were to come to blows over what action should be taken.

One of the more serious obstacles to efficiency arose out of the centralization of planning and operational control in Moscow, with responsibility divided among some forty economic ministries. Under heavy pressure to fulfill ambitious plans, each ministry understandably tended to look after its own enterprises, and rational cooperation between enterprises belonging to different ministries was rendered difficult. While the sins of "departmentalism" were possibly overstressed by the Soviet press in its efforts to prepare public opinion for the reform, there is little doubt that a great deal of waste was incurred as a result of the lack of coordination in the operations of ministries. Among examples cited in the press was the case of a large quarry worked by eight small quarrying enterprises, each representing a different user ministry which sought to ensure its own supplies. Another instance involved two steamer fleets operated under different ministries on the same river; one sailed empty in one direction, the other in the opposite direction.[1] There also have

been numerous cases cited of waste in transporting materials to and from factories within one ministerial system, and repeated complaints concerning delays due to the need to refer decisions to a distant Moscow.

Obviously these defects were real and there was need for corrective action. In determining what course to take, the Soviet leaders had a choice between two alternative approaches: they could delegate much wider powers at the actual production level, i.e., to the managers of enterprises, or they could create more effective operational and planning units in the localities. The first of these implied a radical departure from established methods of bureaucratic control through the governmental and party apparatuses, and would necessarily leave instead a much wider use of the price and market mechanism. Considering both Khrushchev's character and the party's traditional view of its functions, it is hardly surprising that the second alternative was chosen. However, a scheme along the latter lines could have many variants, and clearly the political struggle had a direct effect on the version finally adopted.

The essentials of the new forms of organization are doubtless familiar to most readers. The Soviet Union was divided in 1957 into 105 regions, of which 70 were in the Russian Republic (R.S.F.S.R.) and 11 in the Ukraine. In each a regional economic council, or sovnarkhoz, was established to act as the planning and operational authority for nearly all industrial and construction enterprises situated within its borders. In almost all cases, industrial ministries have been abolished both in Moscow and in the republic capitals. Within a few months, only the Ministry of Electric Power Stations was left, and this because of the necessity to control a nationally interconnected electric power system. State committees were created for the principal defense industries, and also for chemicals, and automation and machine-building; their purpose is to give general guidance in matters of design and planning, but, formally at least, they have no direct operational control. The typical Soviet enterprise, both in heavy and light industry, now takes its orders from its sovnarkhoz.[2] The

---

[1] *Pravda*, April 15, 1957.

[2] Small industrial units of purely local significance, which are under the control of municipal Soviets, are also beyond the purview of the reform and of this article.

latter is subordinated to the council of ministers of its republic (subject in turn to the usual party controls). The All-Union government, particularly *Gosplan*, and the party apparatus are supposed to ensure the necessary degree of central leadership.

These proposals were adopted after a hard struggle within the leadership; but while the existence of dissension over this and other aspects of Soviet policy became increasingly obvious, the interplay of political forces in the course of the struggle presented a confused picture. It is virtually impossible to analyze the complex motivations which governed Khrushchev or his opponents at different phases of the "debate" over economic organization, the conflicting viewpoints which determined the alignment of forces, or the extent to which differences over other policies were involved. The indications are, however, that if Khrushchev's position was ever shaky, it was in the aftermath of the Hungarian revolution in the fall of 1956. Insofar as economic policy was concerned, the decisions of a party plenum in December 1956 indicated that the prevailing opinion within the leadership favored tackling the disease of departmentalism through the subordination of almost all of the economic ministries to the State Economic Commission, with M. Pervukhin at its head. This agency had been created in May 1955 to take over responsibility for current economic affairs from *Gosplan*, whose functions were reduced at the time to long-term planning and research. Even the two ministries dealing with agricultural affairs, Khrushchev's special interest, were placed under Pervukhin, leading some observers to interpret the plan as an attempt to limit Khrushchev's interference in economic affairs.

At any rate, Khrushchev's first proposals, put forward in his "theses" of April 1957, preserved the idea adopted in December of combining planning and administrative power in one central body, though he referred to the latter by the old designation of *Gosplan*. He suggested that the old ministries be abolished (significantly, however, agriculture was now excluded from the reform) and that an undetermined number of *sovnarkhozy* be created. The latter were to be under "dual subordination" — i.e., controlled directly from Moscow as well as by the respective republic authorities. During the following month, there was an unusually open debate of the "theses" in the Soviet press, indicative of the intensive discussion and maneuvering which must have been going on behind the closed doors of the leadership councils. The result was a number of significant changes in Khrushchev's plan, as finally adopted by the Supreme Soviet in May. First, *Gosplan* was reassigned responsibility for both long-term and current planning but was stripped of all executive power, while the State Economic Commission was abolished altogether. An unknown party bureaucrat, Jusmin, was appointed to head the new Gosplan, to the surprise of all observers. The republics were given undivided control over their *sovnarkhozy* (as opposed to "dual" control, first proposed by Khrushchev; the republic governments and party organs remain subject, of course, to control from the center). It was also left to the republics to decide the number of regions into which they would be divided.

As noted, it is by no means clear how these various changes were related to the political struggle going on in the party Presidium. Thus, for example, while Khrushchev first proposed a strong *Gosplan*, he may have come to favor a limitation of its powers as a means to prevent the rise of Pervukhin as an economic "rival," if he thought the latter would be appointed its head (this might have seemed a strong likelihood in view of the December actions of the party plenum). On the other hand, Khrushchev may have decided that a weak *Gosplan* would tend to throw more responsibility for economic administration on the party apparatus; this might have seemed attractive to him quite apart from any immediate desire to down an opponent.

Political rather than economic considerations clearly influenced certain other aspects of the scheme as it was finally adopted. For instance, why were as many as 105 economic regions created? A number of voices were raised in public discussion favoring far fewer regions — one for the Urals, one for East Siberia, and so on. It was pointed out that the split-up of these and other natural economic regions under the jurisdiction of three or four *sovnarkhozy* would create awkward problems. An official of the *Gosplan* research institute, by name Omarovski, argued in print in favor of 10 to 12 *sovnarkhozy* for the R.S.F.S.R., rather than the 70 which were created. Why then, were there so many?

The only possible explanation is that the leadership wanted to avoid interfering with existing administrative boundaries, or, in political-personal terms, with the areas of influence of local party secretaries, who have always been the key personalities at the *oblast* (district) level. An *oblast* party secretary's status would inevitably be threatened if his territory were linked to a neighbor's. Suppose, for example, that the adjoining *oblasti* of Belgorod, Bryansk and Kursk were made into one economic region. Who would be the party man in charge? Either a new boss would be sent out from headquarters, or one of the three secretaries would have to be placed in authority over the others. In either case, some party officials would be aggrieved, which might result in strengthening any group of malcontents in a factional struggle. It is probably for this reason that, in the R.S.F.S.R. at any rate, the line of least resistance was followed: with very few exceptions, the boundaries of the new regions have coincided with those of existing *oblasti*.

Politics probably accounted, too, for the granting of additional powers to the republics. As was noted above, Khrushchev's original proposals gave Moscow direct access to the regions, over the heads of the republics. Such a by-passing arrangement would have tended to curtail the political-economic role of the republic governmental and party leaderships. When the proposals became known, these authorities doubtless exerted pressure to obtain full jurisdiction within the line of command, making the regions subordinate in the first instance to the republic capitals. A significant illustration of their attitude is afforded by the behavior of the then Uzbek party leader, Mukhitdinov. At first he pressed for only one region for Uzbekistan. However, when the scheme in its final form ensured that Moscow could not bypass Tashkent, he changed his mind, and in May 1957 four *sovnarkhozy* were set up in Uzbekistan.[3]

These examples suggest that Khrushchev, relying as he did on the support of provincial party secretaries, adapted the reforms to their ambitions and tried to avoid treading on their political sore spots. In this respect, as in some

others, politics seems to have played a primary role. Yet the problems which were then being tackled are real enough; they were not simply conjured up by Khrushchev in order to smash his opponents. Some action was necessary; the fact that the actual measures taken were adapted to, and influenced by, the political struggle should not be surprising. Few politicians in any country act in a wholly disinterested manner, and they seldom overlook the effects of their policies on their personal position. There is no reason why Khrushchev should be an exception.

Achievements of the Reform

Has the system worked well? Has it, at least, worked better than the ministerial system which it replaced? Experience shows that certain improvements have been achieved, principally under the following heads:

(a) The *sovnarkhozy* are able to study local productive resources and to initiate plans which, however much they may be altered at higher levels, do at least initially represent an attempt to utilize these resources in the best possible manner. This was made impossible in the past by the vertical bureaucratic structure of the ministerial system. The local plans are particularly valuable in new areas in process of development, notably in Siberia.

(b) Once an output plan for a *sovnarkhoz* is confirmed, there is a possibility of concentrating production in the most efficient local plants, and of transferring under-utilized capital assets. Unnecessary "inputs" from remote sources of supply can be eliminated if the *sovnarkhoz* is able to produce the necessary items in its own factories, thereby reducing the strain on transport.

(c) It was a weakness of the ministerial system that by-products of factories "belonging" to one ministry could not be utilized by other industries without great bureaucratic complications. The chemical industry in particular suffered from this. Much of such inflexibility has now undoubtedly been eliminated.

(d) Various minor matters which had to be referred to Moscow can now be settled on the spot, and directors of enterprises find this a considerable convenience since it reduces bureaucratic delays, and they often can exercise their local influence to useful effect.

While it would certainly be wrong to neglect

---

[3] Mukhitdinov in *Pravda*, April 6, 1957; *Partiinaia Zhizn'*, No. 7, 1957; and *Pravda Vostoka*, May 29, 1957. Subsequently a fifth one was set up.

the advantages of the *sovnarkhoz* system, the disadvantages are also considerable. The most important of them is a disease inherent in regional control; i.e., so-called localist or regionalist tendencies, in Russian, *mestnichestvo*. Any territorial authority must inevitably feel primary responsibility for enterprises under its wing. Therefore, in any choice between alternatives, it will be guided by the economic interest of its own region. This, under Soviet conditions, consists of fulfilling and, if possible, overfulfilling the plan. It is by this criterion that enterprises and *sovnarkhozy* are judged by their superior authorities. Consequently, the *sovnarkhozy*, just like the defunct ministries, must tend to insure against uncertain delivery of supplies from outside the area of their control by producing as much as possible within their own borders, and they naturally give priority to deliveries to "their" enterprises. This is not due to ill-will or lack of "socialist consciousness." In an economy based on planning and hierarchical authority, the fulfillment of plans and instructions is the essential criterion of behavior. The central and republican authorities, to be sure, issue many detailed orders to *sovnarkhozy*, and failure to obey these orders — notably in respect of planned deliveries to other regions — can lead to trouble. Nevertheless, as one object of the reform was to encourage local initiative — and in any event all contingencies cannot be covered by central orders — the *sovnarkhozy*, within the sphere of their authority, are driven towards *mestnichestvo* by the planning system itself.

To make the point clearer, we must note that, in a planned economy which is not based on the market-and-price mechanism, only the center can possibly know what the requirements of the economy are. Industries inevitably require supplies from many different regions. For example, the Minsk tractor works relies on about a hundred enterprises situated outside the Belorussian *sovnarkhoz*. This complex pattern of production and supply can be seen from the center only, and in the past the ministries underwrote important contracts and interfered to impose priorities on a national scale when things went wrong. All this cannot be done in or by any one of the supplying *sovnarkhozy*. In a market economy, the necessary signals would be transmitted through the price mechanism, but in the U.S.S.R. they can be communicated only by administrative instructions — a process which cannot be effectively decentralized and which in itself severely limits any possibilities of thoroughgoing economic decentralization.

Evidence that *mestnichestvo* would cause serious difficulties began accumulating almost immediately after the reform. Thus on September 2, 1957, the chairman of the Belorussian *Sovnarkhoz* wrote in *Pravda*:

> There are instances when officials bother only about enterprises subordinate to them, and do not think of the difficulties which their irregularities cause for enterprises in other regions. It is necessary to speak about this frankly, so that these defects do not grow worse. . . . *We have met clear instances of tendencies toward autarchy.* The Dzerzhinski factory of the Dnepropetrovsk region supplies rolled wire to the Rezhitsa nail-making works. In July the Dzerzhinski factory underfulfilled its plan by 15 per cent but sent to Rezhitsa only 300 tons of rolled wire instead of 1,020 tons. When this outrageous fact was investigated, the managers of the Dzerzhinski factory declared that they had orders from the Dnepropetrovsk *Sovnarkhoz* to give priority to enterprises in their own region and to supply them in full. (Emphasis in the original.)

In a similar case cited by the chairman, suppliers from Nikopol arbitrarily cut deliveries of pipes to Minsk by 41 per cent, while only a 7 per cent cut was made in similar deliveries to Khartov (which is in the same republic as the supplying factory). Another example came from Central Asia where *Pravda Vostoka* of March 29, 1957, reported that components from Stalingrad had stopped arriving at the Tashkent farm-machinery plant. On July 25, 1957, *Pravda* devoted an editorial to the subject of such defaults in deliveries from one region to another, and the central party organ has continued voicing similar complaints in subsequent years. One more strong editorial appeared on February 26, 1958, and as recently as June 23, 1960, the Leningrad party secretary, Spiridonov, wrote in the same paper about the difficulties encountered by the Leningrad shipbuilding industry in connection with delivery of components from outside *sovnarkhozy*.

It is true that the national interest is supposed to be defended by party secretaries in the localities. However, in practice, they frequently connive at, or even encourage, *mestnichestvo*, because ultimately they are judged by plan fulfillment in their area of responsibility. Indeed, Khrushchev himself has argued in favor of a direct connection between party officials' salaries and the fulfillment of economic plans. Party officials even encourage the use of centrally allocated investment funds for local purposes, as may be seen from an attack on several such officials published in *Partiinaya Zhizn'*.[4] On another occasion, the same party journal reported that the party office at Omsk forbade local government officials to obey an order from Moscow to send trucks to the neighboring Kustanai *oblast;* Omsk was to have 100 per cent priority, whatever anyone said.[5] Yet, local party officials, like the *sovnarkhoz* officials, have no compass to guide them — except clear orders from above — and can only strive to fulfill their own plans. Since the plans are themselves prescribed from above, the party secretary may well give his own area priority in the honest belief that what is good for Omsk is good for Russia.

Matters are not helped by the small size of most of the *sovnarkhozy*. They are not in any sense self-contained geographical-economic areas, and most decisions taken within them affect other areas in ways which the local officials usually have no means of knowing. True, *sovnarkhoz* officials who obstruct interregional deliveries were threatened with punishment by a decree announced early in 1958 by Kozlov,[6] but such punishment presupposes the existence of clear orders which have been disobeyed, rather than relating to the use made by *sovnarkhozy* of such powers of decision as they themselves possess.

Under the circumstances, an enormous weight of responsibility was necessarily thrown upon the co-ordinating agencies, i.e., primarily on *Gosplan*, which took over at the all-union level many of the planning, supply, and allocation functions of the former ministries. The problems of planners on the republic level have varied. In the smaller republics only moderate difficulties have been encountered, but in the giant Russian Republic

(R.S.F.S.R.), with its 68 *sovnarkhozy*,[7] it has been quite another matter. Numerous complaints about the republic's ineffectiveness in planning and administration have been published in the press, emphasizing not only muddle but also lack of executive authority. The latter accusation is hardly surprising, as the republic *gosplans* cannot issue binding orders and must frequently refer matters to the appropriate council of ministers.[8] These difficulties, and perhaps also some political reason, led to the dismissal of Baibakov from the chairmanship of the R.S.F.S.R. *Gosplan* in 1958. The persistent appearance of similar criticisms however, and the continuous reorganizations of the R.S.F.S.R. administrative structure indicate that the problems remain unresolved.

Old Problems in New Forms

It is essential to appreciate that this or any other reorganization cannot solve certain problems which are inherent in the Soviet system of centralized economic planning based on instructions from above. A modern industrial economy is exceedingly complex, and any investment or production decision involves a very large number of consequential decisions in many regions and many branches of industry. Thus a change of an output plan for some one commodity in a large factory affects not only the allocation of materials and components to this factory — and therefore the output and delivery plans of the industries providing them — but also the branches of the economy, anywhere in the U.S.S.R., which use the products of the factory concerned.

The cumulative complications are enormous. Of course, theoretically, an all-seeing brain at Planning Headquarters could foresee everything and make fully co-ordinated decisions, but in practice it cannot be so. The job is divided between many offices, some concerned with the common problems of an industry, some with the common problems of an area in which there are several industries, and still others with problems common to many industries and many areas (e.g., new tech-

---

[4] No. 15, 1958.

[5] No. 7, 1957.

[6] *Pravda,* January 31, 1958.

[7] There had been originally 70. The Balashov and Kamensk *oblasti* and *sovnarkhozy* were liquidated in 1957–58.

[8] See notably a vigorous article by Frolov in *Kommunist,* No. 2, 1958.

niques, labor, etc.). Naturally, different organizational forms enable certain questions to be dealt with more expeditiously, but usually at the cost of creating new difficulties in other areas. The ministerial system, superseded in 1957, neglected regional problems. The *sovnarkhoz* system registers a gain in this sector, at the cost of throwing heavier burdens on the functions of coordination. In fact, the history of the reform since 1957 is one of a steady increase in the powers of the central coordinators, and a decline in the effective importance of the *sovnarkhozy*, since the government and party strive to give effect to the central plan and to combat such regionalist tendencies as obstruct the uninterrupted functioning of at least the priority sectors of the economy. Thus, *sovnarkhozy* were forbidden to re-allocate investment funds between branches, and their powers to allocate materials and components to "their" enterprises was severely restricted.[9] Continuous gravitation of authority and control towards the central bodies, which command a bird's eye view, has been the natural result.

Newest Administrative Changes

Meanwhile, efforts have been made to mitigate the disadvantages inherent in the small size of the regions. The press referred several times to *ad hoc* committees of neighboring *sovnarkhozy*, which meet to coordinate their activities. The regions involved are: the three Baltic states, the three Transcaucasian republics, the East Siberian *sovnarkhozy*, and the eight *sovnarkhozy* in and around the Urals. It must be remembered, however, that these committees could hardly possess any powers of decision. A more important event was the setting up within the R.S.F.S.R. *Gosplan* of divisions corresponding to main geographic regions, grouping together many *sovnarkhozy*. Eminent Soviet academicians have criticized this arrangement as quite inadequate,[10] and the existence within the *Gosplan* of regional as well as functional departments caused considerable administrative confusion, which was eloquently described by

Kulyov in the party's journal *Kommunist*.[11] The substitution of big regions for the existing *sovnarkhozy*, or the grouping of them into super-regions, has consequently been widely advocated.[12] If the small size of the original regions was a by-product of Khrushchev's desire to retain the support of the *oblast* party secretaries at a time when his political future was at stake, then at present we may well expect him to advocate bigger regions, since he is surely strong enough now to opt for the more rational solution. As these lines are being written, Uzbekistan has liquidated its regions, or rather the entire republic has become a *sovnarkhoz*,[13] while the Ukraine chose to increase the number of its *sovnarkhozy* from 11 to 14.[14] This makes the all-union total 102 at the present time. More reductions are likely, affecting above all the R.S.F.S.R., with its unwieldy 68 regions.

At the all-union level, quiet, little-publicized changes which must surely have altered the balance of economic power to a marked degree, have continued. *Gosplan*, in its material allocation and its industrial branches, now has a tight grip on what the *sovnarkhozy* actually do, and its relationship to enterprises is such that I. V. Spiridonov could describe the machinery output of the Kirov (former Putilov) Works in Leningrad as "subordinated . . . to the Department of Heavy Machine-Building of *Gosplan* U.S.S.R.," and then complain that the metal production of the same factory is "an orphan" because no one at the center is responsible for it. In this context, he does not mention the *sovnarkhoz* at all, though it is the nominal master of the factory.[15] Thus it does seem as if the current planning functions of *Gosplan* had grown vast in scope and detail.

On the other hand, the political weight and area of responsibility of *Gosplan* seems, paradoxically, to have been reduced by the proliferation of other state-committees and an

---

[9] See *Promyshlenno-Ekonomicheskaia Gazeta*, September 19, 1958, and Baranov in *Planovoe Khoziaistvo*, No. 9, 1959.

[10] *Promyshlenno-Ekonomicheskaia Gazeta*, September 14, 1958 (Gerasimov and Khachaturov).

[11] No. 9, 1959.

[12] For instance, Nemchinov, in *Promyshlenno-Ekonomicheskaia Gazeta*, October 19, 1958.

[13] Decree of the Council of Ministers of the Uzbek Republic, reported in the London *Times*, July 4, 1960.

[14] By the creation of new ones for Poltava, Cherkassy, and the Crimea. Reported in *Pravda*, July 14, 1960.

[15] *Pravda*, June 23, 1960.

increase in their importance. Thus in 1960, A. N. Kosygin, who had taken over *Gosplan* from I. I. Kuzmin, was promoted to what appears to be general economic overlordship, and a little-known official, V. N. Novikov, was promoted from the R.S.F.S.R. *Gosplan* to be the head of the all-union *Gosplan*. A more senior functionary, A. F. Zasyadko, became head of a greatly expanded State Scientific and Economic Council (*Nauchno-Ekonomicheskii Sovet*) of the U.S.S.R. Council of Ministers, and it is unofficially reported that this council is now charged with long-term planning. The division between long- and short-term planning of 1955–56 is thus re-appearing once again (except that, confusingly enough, *Gosplan* was the name given in the earlier period to the body charged with *long*-term planning).

Still another body with increased, though undefined, powers is the Scientific and Technical Committee (*Nauchno-Tekhnicheskii Komitet*), and several other state committees of various grades and designations have also come into being. With the proliferation of these new committees a new problem in co-ordination arises, only this time between central bodies. It may be that Kosygin has been charged with this responsibility, or perhaps it is done within the machinery of the party's Central Committee. The details are still unknown. In the R.S.F.S.R., where presumably these various committees also exist, a dramatic change came about in June 1960 when the creation of an all-Russian super-*sovnarkhoz*, using the old designation VSNKh (or *Vesenkha*) was announced and charged with operational control over the *sovnarkhozy* of this vast republic in all matters concerned with plan fulfillment.[16] The Ukraine and Kazakhstan have followed suit.[17] It is too early to say how these new bodies will fit into the administrative and planning pattern, or whether similar changes will occur in other republics or at the all-union level. It may or may not presage a sharp cut in the number of *sovnarkhozy*. One thing, however, is certain: these newest changes add to the effective power of supervision exercised over the *sovnarkhozy* of the R.S.F.S.R. from Moscow,

and of the Ukraine from Kiev, and thus continue the trend towards restricting the area of *sovnarkhoz* autonomy.

Some Conclusions

What, then, is the conclusion we can draw from the working of the reforms of 1957?

In the present author's original article on this topic,[18] written a few months after the promulgation of the reform, the following passages appeared:

> What seems most likely, therefore, is that as difficulties become apparent, there will be a gradual return to centralization. Venturing a guess at the pattern of development, there probably will be a continuing stream of complaints reaching Moscow from enterprises and various authorities protesting the delays in production due to irregular arrival of supplies from other regions, asking for help in obtaining this or that item, and so on. The occasional interference of the center will be found insufficient. It will be necessary to set up or strengthen day-to-day organs of supervision to ensure the uninterrupted functioning of at least the priority sectors of the economy. . . . In other words, the center is likely to be compelled to limit greatly the range of choice open to the *sovnarkhozy* in order to ensure that they conform to a national plan.

This, indeed, is very largely what has occurred. Yet it would be wrong to regard the reform as purely negative in effect, or the *sovnarkhozy* as mere helpless puppets. The existence of regional authorities facilitates the initiation of local plans, and, within the national plan, all kinds of minor adjustments can still be made at the local level, various small expenditures by enterprises authorized, unused productive capacity redistributed, useful technical innovations encouraged and financed. However, we can now see how right Khrushchev was in refusing to use the word "decentralization" to describe the 1957 industrial reorganization. The *sovnarkhoz* reform was and remains a matter of reorganizing central planning.

Meanwhile, the imperfections and stresses inherent in the Soviet system of central planning are still there. Many Soviet economists are urging a major recasting of the system, to permit wider scope for free contract based on

---

[16] *Sovetskaia Rossia*, June 19, 1960.
[17] *Pravda*, July 14, 1960.

[18] *Problems of Communism*, November–December 1957.

rational prices, to reduce the area of administrative decision and increase the importance of "automatic" forces in economic life.[19] The voices of Kantorovich and Novozhilov are advocating the use of linear programming methods, which would necessitate theoretical and practical changes of the first magnitude. None of this the actual reforms so far adopted have realized. The party leadership is, by tradition and self-interest, averse to automatic economic forces and will probably resist reforms on these lines. Yet this same party leadership is actively searching for new ways of achieving efficiency in its self-imposed task of "overtaking America." Thus there will be more hesitation, more experiments, and perhaps conflict as the search for a more rational basis of economic organization continues.

AGRICULTURE

35

The Collective Farm*

Lazar Volin

(1951)

Although the organization of Soviet industry includes many unique features, the fact that its basic unit, the factory, is quite familiar makes it easier to understand the system as a whole. The collective farm, and the other basic units of Soviet agriculture, are much more distinctive forms, and this makes the whole structure more difficult to grasp. Dr. Volin identifies many of the special units of Soviet agriculture, describes their inner workings, reviews their history, and shows their

relation to each other and to the larger society. Some of these relations, as well as some internal features of the individual units, have been altered in the post-Stalin period. Those changes are reviewed and assessed in the contribution by Dr. Kahan which follows Dr. Volin's.

Three types of new Soviet farm units may be distinguished — the collective farms, or *kolkhozy;*[1] the state farms, or *sovkhozy;*[1] and the state-owned machine-tractor stations, or MTS, which themselves do not carry on farming but only serve *kolkhozy* with tractors, combines, and other farm machinery.

Collective Farms (Kolkhozy)

Organizational Structure

Collective farms were first organized shortly after the Bolshevik revolution in 1918. But, until the 1930's, despite considerable assistance from the Soviet Government, collective farming was merely a small island in the ocean of Russian peasant agriculture and its role in the Soviet agricultural economy was insignificant. In 1928, though the number of collectives had already increased considerably, they still accounted for only a little more than 1 per cent of the total area sown in crops and included less than 2 per cent of the total number of peasant households.[2]

Initially, the collective farms were organized as completely communistic associations, so-called communes, in which not only production but consumption as well was fully socialized.[2] In the late 1920's, however, the communes constituted only 5 to 6 per cent of all collective farms, the predominant form being the so-called *toz*.[3] The latter is a loose producers' association in which the peasants, while continuing private ownership of the means of production, unite for a season or longer for common cultivation of the land, sharing the product in accordance with the labor, land, and capital contributed. The *kolkhozy* during this period were small; in 1928

---

[19] For example, Nemchinov in *Kommunist*, No. 1, 1959.

* Reprinted from "Collective Farms (Kolkhozy)," *A Survey of Soviet Russian Agriculture* (1951), United States Department of Agriculture, pp. 21–48, by permission of the author.

[1] Singular of *kolkhozy* is *kolkhoz* and of *sovkhozy*, *sovkhoz*.

[2] I. A. Konyukov, *Kollektivnoe Zemledelie*, ed. 2 (Moscow, 1925), p 40.

[3] *Sotsialisticheskoe Stroitel'stvo SSSR*, 1934, p. 162.

each comprised, on the average, 13 peasant households with a total sown area of 101 acres.[4]

Since the forced mass collectivization in the early 1930's, the commune and the *toz* were supplanted by the intermediate form, the so-called artel, which, in 1932, accounted for 95.9 per cent of all collective farms. The present artel type of *kolkhoz* is a farm production unit consisting predominantly of former individual peasant farmers and organized and operated in accordance with a certain pattern prescribed and rigidly controlled by the Government. It forms an integral part of the Soviet planned economy.

In a *kolkhoz* all land that formerly was held by individual peasant farmers is collectivized, with the exception of small plots for family kitchen gardens. Boundaries are done away with, and the noncontiguous strips into which the peasant holdings were divided are consolidated into larger fields. Most of the other means of production, such as horses and, to a lesser extent, other livestock and farm implements, are also collectivized.

As it has done since the early Soviet period, the state continues to own, legally, all of the land, but each *kolkhoz* holds the land it occupies for an unlimited period, that is, in "perpetuity," as the Soviet law puts it. The title of the *kolkhoz* to the land is secured by a title deed issued on the basis of an official land survey. The land can neither be sold by the *Kolkhoz* nor leased and cannot be taken except, with proper compensation, for important public needs. Illegal leasing of land, however, has been reported from time to time in the Soviet press. Even more common has been the seizure of collective land by outsiders, mostly officials or institutions, an abuse that became so flagrant during World War II that a special Government decree (September 19, 1946) was required to control it.

In addition to land, farm capital has also been collectivized. This includes such items as draft animals and other livestock beyond certain rather narrow limits to be mentioned later, farm implements, seed, forage supplies for collective stock, stables, barns, and similar property. New members who possess such property must surrender it in good faith to the

kolkhozy. The confiscated property of some 5 million liquidated kulaks, who were driven off the land as a result of collectivization, was transferred to the *kolkhozy.*

One-fourth to one-half the value of collectivized peasant capital is counted as indivisible surplus of the *kolkhoz*, and the remainder is considered an invested share of the member, which he may recover, but in cash only, upon withdrawal from the *kolkhoz*. With the scarcities of goods in the Soviet Union, such cash payments were not to the advantage of the withdrawing members even prior to wartime inflation. Recovery in kind is permissible only when a member is transferred from one *kolkhoz* to another for reasons approved by Government authorities. The withdrawing member cannot recover his old holding but must depend upon the state to allot him land from the public domain. Allotment, however, is left to the discretion of the state, which has been trying hard to discourage individual farming.

Obviously, the kolkhoz has little in common with the old *mir*, under which there was no joint cultivation but only individual farming by peasant families. Essentially, the *kolkhoz* is an economy of socialized production and individual consumption. While the *kolkhoz* performs certain welfare and cultural functions (libraries, theaters, clubs, child nurseries, canteens, and so forth) that come under the heading of communal consumption, its present artel form is an institution primarily of production and not of consumption. The latter is basically a matter for each individual peasant household, as it was during the precollective period.

The peasant families whose holdings have been pooled in a *kolkhoz* continue to live in villages just as they did before collectivization. In addition to their dwellings, each peasant family is entitled, if land is available, to a small plot for a kitchen garden, varying regionally from 0.6 to 1.2 and, in some sections, to 2.5 acres.[5] A peasant family may also own a small number of cattle, hogs, sheep, and goats. But horses, except in the nomadic or seminomadic

---

[4] I. V. Sautin, ed., *Kolkhozy vo Vtoroi Stalinskoi Pyatiletke* (Moscow and Leningrad, 1939), p. 6.

[5] A tendency to diminish the size of the kitchen garden plots is discernible in connection with the campaign for the merger of the *kolkhozy* in 1950. See, for instance, a report of a considerable reduction in size of such plots in the Leningrad Province, by D. Brezhnev, in *Izvestiya* of August 26, 1950.

regions, are collective property. A member of a *kolkhoz* who needs a horse for his own use must ask to borrow it from the *kolkhoz;* the *kolkhoz* management may or may not grant his request.

It should be noted that the allotment of kitchen garden plots is made not to any individual member of a *kolkhoz* but to a family labor unit — the peasant household, the ablebodied members of which are supposed to participate, with some exceptions, in the work of the *kolkhoz.* Likewise, the peasant household owns jointly the dwelling, the private livestock, the few farm implements, etc. Thus, the traditional institution of joint family property among Russian peasants is retained insofar as the private farming of the peasant in the *kolkhoz* is concerned; but it does not apply to any earnings obtained from the farm operations of the *kolkhoz,* which constitute his or her personal property.[6]

Such personal farming as a member of a *kolkhoz* does on his little plot is supposed to have a strictly supplementary character, subsidiary to the basic economy of the collective farm. In practice this brings an economic dualism into the *kolkhoz* economy, resulting, as we shall see later, in competition and conflict between the collectivist and the individualist elements, which the artel organization of collective farming is supposed to reconcile.

Legally, the *kolkhoz* is intended to be a selfgoverning organization, managing its own affairs within the limits set by Government plans and regulations. Each *kolkhoz* has a charter patterned after the model charter that was approved by the Government in 1935.[7]

Although, as a rule, entrance into the *kolkhoz* has been a family affair, membership is legally an individual matter for men and women alike. The governing body of the *kolkhoz* is theoretically the general meeting or assembly of its members, which elects by majority vote the officers who constitute an executive board headed by the chairman, or manager, and who are accountable to the general assembly. The latter also elects an auditing commission, approves the budget and production program of the *kolkhoz,* and admits and expels members. In practice, however, the Government and party officials are in the habit of appointing, dismissing, and transferring officers from one *kolkhoz* to another at will, and the *kolkhoz* general assembly actually has little or no voice in the management of its *kolkhoz* affairs.

Such violations of the law have been chronic, despite frequent official censure, and they make the self-government of *kolkhozy* essentially a fiction. As a writer in the July 1947 magazine of the Soviet Ministry of Agriculture puts it:

> What kind of a democracy is there in those *kolkhozy* where chairmen are not elected by the members but are appointed by Soviet administrators, where the general assembly is either not convoked at all, or convoked very seldom, and poor preparations are made for it? In such *kolkhozy* the rank-and-file members actually are removed from the management of *kolkhoz* affairs and do not feel any responsibility for the state of affairs in the *kolkhoz.*[8]

As a result of such violations of the selfgovernment of the *kolkhoz,* the members "begin to consider the manager not as an elective official responsible to his constituents. They cease to feel that they are full-fledged proprietors of the *kolkhoz,* and this, of course, diminishes their interest in production and in *kolkhoz* affairs."[9]

Likewise, frequent interference with the *kolkhoz* manager's orders and decisions by Government officials "inevitably leads to loss of authority by him among the members of the *kolkhoz* and to the lowering of the working

---

Even the idea of a complete abandonment of personal farming by members of *kolkhozy* in the not too distant future is being broached. See I. V. Pavlov ["The Strengthening of the Organization and Economy of *Kolkhozy*"], *Sovetskoe Gosudarstvo i Pravo,* 11 (1950), pp. 50–51. The future, therefore, of this highly important element in the economic life and welfare of the collectivized peasantry appears to be uncertain in the spring of 1951.
[6] See A. N. Nikitin, A. P. Pavlov, and A. A. Ruskol, eds., *Kolkhoznoe Pravo* (Moscow, 1939), pp. 341–367. See also Vladimir Gsovski, *Soviet Civil Law: Private Rights and Their Background Under the Soviet Regime* (Ann Arbor, Mich., 1948), Vol. 1, pp. 104–105.
[7] An English translation of the charter will be found in Gsovski, *op. cit.,* Vol. 2, pp. 441–462; and in L. E. Hubbard, *The Economics of Soviet Agriculture* (London, 1939), pp. 131–147.

[8] F. Koshelev ["Democratic Basis of Management of an Agricultural Artel"], *Sotsialisticheskoe Sel'skoe Khozyaistvo 1947,* 7 (1947), p. 24. For a typical example, see ["Gross Violation of *Kolkhoz* Democracy"] *Pravda,* March 27, 1950.
[9] *Pravda Vostoka,* May 26, 1944.

discipline and order."[10] In their turn, "Some *kolkhoz* managers no longer consider a *kolkhoz* as an artel [that is, a cooperative institution]. They forget that the boss of the artel is the general assembly of the members of the *kolkhoz*. It not infrequently occurs that the general assemblies are not convoked for half a year or longer and questions which according to the charter can be decided only by the general assembly are settled by the executive board of the *kolkhoz* or the manager himself."[11]

Such an attitude of a manager usually stems from the fact that his job normally depends upon the discretion of the local "party boss" and not of the *kolkhoz* membership. Moreover, he is not likely to stay long on his job in a particular *kolkhoz*. If the manager makes mistakes and is considered incompetent, he is removed even though he may have little training or experience to gain competence. If the manager is efficient, he is often used as a "trouble shooter" to reform inefficent *kolkhozy*, a transfer that does not help the farm from which he is taken. That the rapid turnover of *kolkhoz* managers is a serious evil was repeatedly recognized in Soviet official circles, but it has never been remedied. The same condition seems to prevail in some of the newly merged *kolkhozy*, judging from an editorial in *Sotsialisticheskoe Zemledelie* of February 2, 1951, which complains that in some districts *kolkhoz* managers were selected without sufficient scrutiny and with insufficient knowledge of agriculture, or who were "previously compromised by gross violation of the *kolkhoz* charter." As a result, some managers were removed soon after the merger of *kolkhozy*. However, there are straws in the wind, such as an article dealing with selection and training of *kolkhoz* managers by a Ukrainian Provincial party official in *Pravda* of January 23, 1951, pointing to greater awareness by the Soviet bureaucracy of the need of a more tolerant attitude toward initial errors committed by inexperienced farm managers, many of whom, since World War II, have been former army officers. Special training courses for *kolkhoz* managers have also been organized.

Whereas lawless habits and greed of local officials account for some illegal interference with the *kolkhozy*, such interference is largely rooted in the very system of Soviet regimentation and control of collective farming. That the smooth functioning of collective farming requires continuous, not merely sporadic, responsibility and direction by Government and party authorities, was the thesis propounded by Joseph Stalin as far back as 1933.[12] This thesis was constantly reiterated by other important officials, such as that member of the mighty Politburo, Andreev, who at the Eighteenth Communist Party Congress in the spring of 1939 scorned the practice "of noninterference in the internal life of *kolkhozy*."[13]

Certainly, the Government has manifested a high-handed attitude towards the peasantry and the *kolkhozy* often enough to encourage emulation by the lower echelons of Soviet bureaucracy. An outstanding recent example of arbitrariness of the Politburo is the wholesale merger of *kolkhozy* to be discussed below. It is not difficult to understand, therefore, why the oft-repeated denunciations of the violations of the charter have so little effect.

But, even if the provisions of the charter are strictly adhered to, the autonomy of the *kolkhoz* is, nevertheless, circumscribed by the very fact that it must work within the plan laid down by the central government and interpreted by its local agents. This is clearly set forth in Article 6 of the charter, which states: "The 'artel' is obliged to carry on collective farming according to the plan, observing precisely the plans of agricultural production and of the obligations to the state laid down by the organs of the peasant-workers' government." The various plans which the "artel" must carry out are then again enumerated in detail. This necessity of dovetailing into the scheme of compulsory Soviet planned economy is bound to result in a large measure of control over collective farming on the part of officials charged with the execution of the plans, and . . . must restrict the self-government of the *kolkhoz*. The charter makes the *kolkhoz* legally the "boss" of its land, but a "boss" whose powers are qualified and limited by the supremacy of the national plan.[14]

---

10 *Kazakhstanskaya Pravda*, May 30, 1944.
11 *Pravda Severa*, August 29, 1944.

12 ["Work in the Rural Districts"], *Sotsialisticheskoe Zemledelie* (January 17, 1933). Reprinted in J. V. Stalin, *Problems of Leninism*, 11th ed. (Moscow, 1940), pp. 441–454.
13 *Pravda*, March 14, 1939.
14 Lazar Volin, "Agrarian Collectivism in the Soviet Union," *Journal of Political Economy*, Vol. 45 (December 1937), pp. 762–763.

In general, the Government has assumed, with respect to collective peasant agriculture, much of the responsibility for management that formerly devolved upon millions of independent peasant farmers. The Soviet Government not only has its say as to what is to be produced by collective farms and what proportion of the output is to go to the state, but is also prescribes, regulates, or plans many details of farm operation and practice with a view to increasing farm output — always the central objective of Soviet agricultural policy.

Such problems as assembling seed and forage supplies, timely and efficient sowing and harvesting, proper care of livestock, crop rotation, internal organization of the farm unit, and other details of farming, with which the Government once rarely concerned itself directly, now occupy its attention. Many of these problems, including the acreage to be sown to different crops from year to year, the number of livestock, and even the yields per acre, are dealt with by national plans, which establish goals for the various Republics and Provinces of the Union. The authorities who are responsible for execution of these plans set up local goals, including, ultimately, targets for each *kolkhoz*, on the basis of which the *kolkhozy* are supposed to prepare their annual production programs. Nonfulfilment, actual or threatened, of such goals usually involves increased intervention by state and party organs and their representatives.

Among the various kinds of plans applied to agriculture there is, first of all, the general five-year plan of economic development, which embraces all phases of Soviet economy. Three such plans were promulgated before World War II (in 1929, 1933, and 1939) and a fourth postwar five-year plan in 1946. On the basis of the five-year plan, annual plans of acreage and production for agriculture are drawn up and were published in considerable statistical detail in the 1930's. Since World War II, however, while a decree dealing with sowings and a lengthy decree pertaining to harvest and Government procurement of crops were published annually, the statistical data in such decrees have been meager. Special problems, such as the development of the livestock industry or reforestation and soil conservation or irrigation development, are dealt with by special plans.

Thus, collective farming is subjected to detailed regulations and plans laid down by Moscow and supervised by local officials who are responsible for carrying them out. State control over collective farming has been further strengthened because the Government, in the face of a severe shortage of animal draft power resulting from the wholesale slaughter of horses during the collectivization campaign, has increasingly supplied the power and machine requirements of Russian agriculture through the state-owned MTS.

Considerable rigidity and, at times, ignorance and disregard of expert opinion have characterized the control and direction of collective farming by the Communist bureaucracy. Among the numerous examples found in the Soviet press may be cited the situation in the important sugar-beet-growing district of Kharkov in the Ukraine. Here, in the spring of 1949, according to an editorial in *Pravda* of September 10, 1949, many *kolkhozy* decided to take the advice of the agronomists and postpone sugar-beet planting for 2 or 3 days because of frosts and rains. However, the secretary of the *raion* (county) party committee (the local party boss) reversed this reasonable decision and ordered planting to begin at once, overruling objections by saying, "Why do you consult with the agronomists? They don't know anything." As a result, many *kolkhozy* harvested a smaller crop of sugar beets.

Though the *Pravda* editorial does not mention it, the party official responsible in this case was doubtless influenced by the enormous stress laid by Moscow on the speedy completion of planting; and he probably feared that the delay, however well merited, might bring on him the disfavor of his superiors, the expression of which might range from a reprimand to relegation to a concentration camp. This situation illustrates not only the inflexibility, combined often with stubborness and ignorance of agricultural conditions in the lower echelons of Communist officialdom, but also the excessive centralization of authority, inspiring fear and generating rigidity in subordinates and a tendency to avoid responsibility for making decisions.

Local officials who prevent the management of a *kolkhoz* from exercising independent judgment on farm operations are bound by a hard and fast plan laid down by Provincial authorities, who, in turn, are bound by similar plans laid down by the Government of a Republic, say the Ukraine, and ultimately, of course, by

Moscow. The latter sets deadlines for the execution of its plans and directives and demands strict conformity, which often leads to falsification of achievement reports. Thus, bureaucratic regimentation stifles the initiative of those best informed and most concerned — the farmers, kolkhoz managers, and agricultural specialists — those at the grass roots.[15]

Much of the difficulty grows out of the fact that limitations imposed by nature on agricultural planning, particularly the interference of weather conditions with field work and planned crop yields, are either disregarded or at best belittled by the Kremlin. The much-publicized damage of the drought of 1946, when the U.S.S.R. was anxious to continue receiving UNRRA aid, was an exception that proves the rule.

With the dependence of the kolkhozy on plans emanating from various higher authorities, delay in making or transmitting them "often disorganized or delayed work in the kolkhozy . . . ," as a local party official put it.[16] In general, the detrimental consequences of faulty planning in Soviet agriculture are usually magnified by the large scale, sometimes nationwide, on which it is applied. . . .

Labor and Management

The membership of a kolkhoz, the kolkhozniki, constitutes its labor force. According to Article 13 of the charter, employment of outsiders (nonmembers) is permitted in cases of specialists and technicians, such as agronomists, engineers, etc. Hiring of other workers is allowed only as an exception and on a temporary basis, when the kolkhoz labor force is fully occupied and cannot complete urgent work on time. Another exception is construction labor. Actually, however, a Government decree of April 19, 1938 (Concerning the Incorrect Distribution of Income in Kolkhozy), published in the Soviet press on April 20, 1938, revealed a costly and apparently widespread employment of hired labor by kolkhozy beyond

the rather narrow scope envisaged by the charter.

In its organization of work a kolkhoz resembles a large plantation or factory. It deals separately with each worker member and not with whole families. In his day-to-day work, a member of the kolkhoz is subject to the orders and supervision of the management, just as a worker is in a Soviet factory or on a state farm. Poor or careless work, violation of the kolkhoz rules, and absenteeism are supposed to be punished by reprimands, fines, demotions, temporary dismissal from work, withholding payment for work that must be redone, and, when all other corrective measures fail, by expulsion from the kolkhoz, which also means loss of the private garden plot. Expulsion, however, must be sanctioned at a general assembly, when no less than two-thirds of the members are present, with a right of appeal to the Praesidium of the Raion Executive Committee. That expulsion from the kolkhoz, with all its dire consequences, has often been freely used may be seen from the fact that a special decree had to be passed, in April 1938, to stop this practice.[17]

The large size of many kolkhozy, with a labor force of several hundred workers and an area of several thousand acres, early posed the problem of developing a more convenient unit of actual operation and supervision of labor. Such a unit is supposed to be the brigade, or working group. It consists of 40 to 60 workers headed by a brigadier, or foreman, appointed by the management.

There are separate field-crop and livestock brigades. Large kolkhozy often employ specialists in charge of field-crop or livestock production. Field-crop brigades are supposed to be kept together for the duration of the crop-rotation period, usually for several years, to have their own equipment, and to cultivate the same plots of land. And livestock brigades are supposed to be kept together for a period of not less than three years. Judging from the Soviet press, however, these officially much-emphasized requirements are honored more often in breach than in performance, and the

[15] For a realistic description of the planning practices in the Soviet Union, see Mikh. Rozanow ["How Planning Is Done in the U.S.S.R."], *Novoe Russkoe Slovo* [Russian daily, published in New York], June 30, 1949; and Andrei Borodin ["Planning Falsifiers"], *Novoe Russkoe Slovo*, December 13, 1949.

[16] *Pravda Vostoka*, February 11, 1949.

[17] *Pravda*, April 20, 1938. See also Nikitin and others, *op. cit.*, pp. 265–268; and Lazar Volin, "Effects of the Drought and Purge on the Agriculture of the Soviet Union," *Foreign Agriculture*, 3 (May 1939), pp. 193–194.

instability of the brigades has been a frequent source of complaint. Difficulties often arising from the need to dovetail plots to be farmed by a brigade year after year with the annual acreage plan, the requirements of the crop-rotation cycle, and tractor operations of the MTS, militate against the stability of brigade plots.[18] However, the principle of stability of brigades has gained in importance as a greater role has been assigned to the performance of these units in the process of distribution of incentive payments, discussed in another section. There are also separate construction brigades, organized in connection with the extensive building activity in the newly merged collective farms in 1950–51.

In the early and middle 1930's the official emphasis was on the brigade as a unit of *kolkhoz* operation. A decree of the Central Committee of the Communist Party of February 4, 1932, stated that "A brigade must become the most important element [link] in the organization of labor in the *kolkhozy*."[19] The model charter of 1935 still further strengthened,

theoretically, the position of the brigade in the *kolkhoz* structure.

During the years immediately preceding and following World War II a smaller unit, the so-called *zveno* (literally, link), came to the fore. A *zveno* usually consists of a dozen workers under a leader. This group cultivates a plot that is supposed to be assigned to it each year. The *zveno* originated for use on, and was found especially suited to, such intensive crops as sugar beets and cotton, for the care of which a great deal of hand labor is necessary throughout the growing season.

In the late 30's, the *zveno* began to be used in grain farming also. Theoretically, it is not supposed to supplant the brigade but represents merely a section of it under the supervision of the brigadier. The smaller unit simplifies supervision and also is claimed to make for better working discipline, to arouse greater personal interest on the part of the workers, and to facilitate incentive payments based on production results. Table 1 gives an example of the distribution of crop acreage in five *zvenos* of a kolkhoz in Stalingrad Province.

It will be noted that not all of these *zvenos* have similar crops or acreages. Those that have barley, for instance, are not given oats. The idea of dividing all crops equally among the *zvenos*, with consequent fragmentation of the sown area of the *kolkhoz*, has been frowned upon.

At the Eighteenth Congress of the Com-

---

[18] A. Kholostova and M. Shestakov ["Concerning the Stability of Brigade Plots in *Kolkhozy*"], *Sotsialisticheskoe Sel'skoe Khozyaistvo 1949*, 3 (1949), pp. 18–23.
[19] ["Concerning the Current Measures for Organizational Economic Strengthening of the *Kolkhozy*"], in V. V. Kilosanidze, *Vazhneishie Resheniya po Sel'skomu Khozyaistvu*, ed. 2 (Moscow, 1935), p. 429.

TABLE 1 *Distribution of Crop Acreage in Five Zvenos of a Kolkhoz in Stalingrad Province**

CROP	ZVENO 1	ZVENO 2	ZVENO 3	ZVENO 4	ZVENO 5
	Acres	Acres	Acres	Acres	Acres
Spring wheat	202.6	215.0	148.3	264.4	182.9
Barley	86.5	98.8	98.8	. . . . . .	. . . . . .
Oats	. . . . . .	. . . . . .	. . . . . .	118.6	59.3
Millet	86.5	86.5	61.8	74.1	61.8
Sunflower seed	69.2	66.7	69.2	66.7	66.7
Melons.........................	. . . . . .	. . . . . .	9.9	9.9	. . . . . .
Potatoes	9.9	9.9	. . . . . .	. . . . . .	. . . . . .
TOTAL	454.7	476.9	388.0	533.7	370.7

* F. Safroshkin, ["Permanent *Zvenos* in *Kolkhoz* Brigades"], *Sotsialisticheskoe Zemledelie*, December 25, 1945.

munist Party of the U.S.S.R., in the spring of 1939, the *zveno* system was strongly advocated by A. A. Andreev, the spokesman of the Bolshevik leadership, or the Politburo, on agricultural matters. Andreev stated that, "The more the labor in *kolkhozy* is individualized through the *zveno* or individual *kolkhoz* workers, the more their labor is materially rewarded, the more productive it is with respect to crops and livestock. . . . Depersonalization of labor in the large brigades is the principal obstacle to the further increase of labor productivity in *kolkhozy*." The *zveno* was also endorsed by V. M. Molotov, then the Soviet Premier, and by the whole Congress in its formal resolution. Hereafter, for more than a decade, the *zveno* occupied the place of honor in the official Soviet theory and policy pronouncements and was accordingly widely used in *kolkhoz* practice.

However, a sudden turnabout with respect to the *zveno* was indicated when an unsigned article, entitled "Against Perversion in the Organization of Labor in *Kolkhozy*," appeared on February 19, 1950, in the authoritative *Pravda* (the organ of the Central Committee of the Communist Party of the U.S.S.R.). The article criticized Andreev for his advocacy of the *zveno*, attacked its use in grain farming on the ground that it is inconsistent with mechanization, reasserted the basic importance of the brigade, and only grudgingly admitted the usefulness of the *zveno* in the case of some technical and row crops and vegetables, "insofar as production of these crops is as yet insufficiently mechanized."

The article entirely overlooks the numerous claims made in Soviet publications that the crops received better care under the *zveno* system. This is highly important under Soviet conditions, even in mechanized grain farming, because of the often slipshod work of the state machine-tractor stations and the abundant growth of weeds, which require much hand labor to eradicate. Moreover, Russian grain farming, as will be shown later, was far from being completely mechanized even before World War II, and has been less so since the war.

What had influenced the Government's attitude toward the *zveno* was the apprehension that the small *zveno* unit might eventually

supplant not only the brigade but also the *kolkhoz* itself. According to the above-mentioned *Pravda* article, the substitution of the *zveno* for the brigade "would mean the breakdown of large unified collective farms into small producing cells, the dissipation of the power and means of the artel, and the changing over from advanced technology and collective forms of labor to hand labor of the individual. It would mean the shaking of the basic foundations of the large collective socialist agriculture." The shortage of machinery since World War II, with the consequent increased reliance on hand labor, doubtless tipped the scale in favor of the *zveno*. From the small *zveno* unit, it is a relatively easy step to the assignment of plots for individual cultivation and, in some cases, this was actually done. In any event, the control over the peasants from above is less difficult when the *kolkhoz* is split into a few brigades than into a large number of *zveno* units, especially when the *zveno* also takes care of the discharge of compulsory obligations for delivery of farm products to the state. Certainly, it would be necessary to secure a larger number of "politically reliable" supervisors under the *zveno* principle of organization as compared with the brigade principle. Moreover, the brigadier, who, unlike the *zveno* leader, is not a worker himself but an administrator, is likely to be a stricter supervisor. The trend toward the tightening of the state control of collective farming led, as we shall see later, to widespread mergers of *kolkhozy*, and it is reasonable to assume that it has also been at the root of the related brigade versus the *zveno* issue.

Be it as it may, the *zveno* is definitely on the wane, though the possibility cannot be excluded that another reversal of policy may revive it.

In a *kolkhoz*, unlike a small peasant farm or even a good-sized American farm, management is a specialized function and division of labor in general is carried out farther than on individually owned farms. Under such conditions the proportion of the administrative and service personnel to the labor force actually engaged in production poses a problem. Much evidence has been adduced in Soviet literature over a period of years that the *kolkhozy* have been bedeviled by an inflated and costly administrative and service apparatus.[20] [21] Its maintenance has been a heavy drain on both the income and manpower of the *kolkhozy* and has often resulted in a shortage of labor for field work. For example, an investigation in Voronezh Province showed that in one *kolkhoz* 19.4 per cent of all persons capable of work were engaged in tasks not related directly to agricultural production. The figure for another *kolkhoz* was 21; for a third, 27.5 per cent.[22]

A *kolkhoz* in Krasnodar Province, with a total of 867 persons capable of work, had 7 bookkeepers, 10 timekeepers, 12 production specialists, 15 foremen, 12 blacksmiths, 3 mechanics, 2 tinsmiths, 48 guards, 4 chauffeurs, 1 garage man (for 2 machines), 3 club workers, 1 agriculturist, and 1 horticulturist. Altogether, 136 members of this *kolkhoz* were in administrative or service jobs, and in addition it had also hired an agronomist, a physician, an animal husbandry specialist, a veterinary assistant, and an orchestra conductor.[23] Similar reports could be cited from many other regions.

A sample survey, made presumably in 1939 by the Commissariat of Agriculture of the U.S.S.R., of 132 *kolkhozy* in 26 Provinces showed that two-fifths of the *kolkhozy* had from 10 to 20 per cent of the members capable of work in administrative or service jobs, one-third of the *kolkhozy* had from 20 to 30, and one-eighth had more than 30 per cent.[23] Strong, healthy men, it was claimed, flock to the administrative and service positions in preference to field work. This was given as one important reason for the *kolkhozy's* need to hire outside help. In 1939, two-thirds of the *kolkhozy* hired outside workers, and 12 per cent of these used them for field work.[24]

In terms of the share of income going to the administrative and service personnel, the situation apparently worsened during the war. A study of collective farms in 6 regions showed that the proportion of the total earnings of the members devoted to paying such personnel increased from 7 to 10 per cent in 1940 to 12 to 18 per cent in 1945.[25] The rise was made more pronounced by the fact that the total earnings in terms of workdays increased but little or remained stationary or even declined. In the Uzbek Republic, for instance, total earnings declined 13.6 per cent, but those of the administrative and service personnel increased by 13.2 per cent. In Sverdlovsk Province, total earnings increased by 4 per cent and those of administrative and service personnel by 67 per cent.

Many of the administrative and servicing positions in the *kolkhozy* are actually part-time jobs. But when the remuneration for such work was set, it was treated generally as full time, with the result that *kolkhoz* members engaged in such activities did not lend their hands in the fields or in the barns. There was, thus, a considerable loss of manpower in production, while expenditures for administrative and service personnel were swelled at the expense of the earnings of other *kolkhoz* members.

A factor that has contributed to overexpansion of administrative and service personnel is that the small *kolkhozy* have tended to copy larger *kolkhozy* and have increased their administrative and service staffs beyond any real need. An instance was given of a *kolkhoz* in Penza Province, in which 14 out of 65 of its able-bodied members, or 22 per cent, were engaged in some managerial or servicing capacity.[26] The animal husbandry specialist of this *kolkhoz* merely supervised the 2 or 3 persons caring for 7 cows, 7 calves, and 26 sheep. There were 8 guards in the *kolkhoz*, of whom 5 were employed throughout the year. Parenthetically, the guarding of collective farm property, including crops ripe for harvest, has always been a major task, demanding considerable manpower, in the collective farm system.

[20] V. Chuvikov and F. Safroshkin ["Concerning the Reduction of Inflated Administrative and Service Set-Up in *Kolkhozy*"], *Sotsialisticheskoe Sel'skoe Khozyaistvo 1941*, 2 (1941), p. 32.
[21] V. Abramov ["Greater Role of 'Work Days' in Distribution of *Kolkhoz* Income"], *Sotsialisticheskoe Sel'skoe Khozyaistvo 1946*, 10–11 (1946), pp. 22–23.
[22] *Izvestiya*, November 15, 1940.
[23] Chuvikov and Safroskin, *op. cit.*, p. 32.
[24] *Ibid.*, pp. 32–34.

[25] V. Abramov and I. Ermolinskii ["Concerning the Administrative Structure of *Kolkhozy*"], *Sotsialisticheskoe Sel'skoe Khozyaistvo 1947*, 2 (1947), p. 22.
[26] *Ibid.*

Padding of payrolls has been another source of personnel inflation. Persons who might be connected with local administration but who had absolutely nothing to do with the *kolkhoz* were often maintained on a *kolkhoz* payroll. The extent to which all this bureaucracy had become inflated can be gathered from the fact that, after the passage of the decree of September 19, 1946, condemning this inflation, 535,-000 members of the *kolkhozy* were transferred to productive work and 213,000 persons who had no real connection with the *kolkhozy* were removed from the payrolls.[27]

Nevertheless, the problem was far from being solved, and two years later it called for yet another Government decree, which was published on September 14, 1948. This decree complained that, despite considerable progress during the two-year period, the personnel not immediately engaged in production was still excessive in many *kolkhozy* and "sometimes there are simply unnecessary positions of secretaries, timekeepers, production managers, coachmen of the *kolkhozy* executive boards, and other workers." In small collective farms the managerial personnel does not work in the fields as they could and should. In a number of *kolkhozy* the expenditures for the managerial and service personnel not only had not decreased, in accordance with the requirements of a decree of December 19, 1946, but had actually increased. New measures to reduce administrative and service personnel were prescribed by the latest decree of September 14, 1948, but past experience teaches that the road of deflation of *kolkhoz* bureaucracy is strewn with numerous stumbling blocks.

Not only has the Soviet Government been faced with the problem of deflating the over-expanded bureaucratic set-up in the *kolkhozy*, but it has also had to take steps to raise the generally low labor efficiency in many of them. It was possible to drive the majority of peasants into collectives by terror and fear of starvation, coupled with a promise of a more abundant life. It was another matter to make them work even as efficiently in these unfamiliar and often poorly managed organizations as they did when they farmed their own small holdings.

The peasant obviously did not have the same attitude toward work and property that he had on his own farm. V. M. Molotov, then chairman of the Council of People's Commissars, complained in 1933 that once the peasant ceded his horse to the *kolkhoz* he ceased to consider the horse his own and to take proper care of it.[28] Moreover, the whole problem of farm management, on which, to a large extent, the efficiency of labor depends, became a much more complicated affair with collectivization. As the former Commissar of Agriculture Yakovlev put it:

> In a farm of 4 desiatines [equivalent to about 11 acres] the peasant knew well when to plow, when to sow, when to fix things. . . . But how to organize the work in a *kolkhoz* of 2,000; 5,000; 10,000 members? Here everything must be based on a precise division of labor to avoid confusion, so that everyone should know what work he is going to do, how he will do it, and how much he will receive for it.[29]

Reports have frequently appeared in the Soviet press, especially during the early years of collectivization, of the dangerously delayed sowings, of fields overgrown with weeds, of huge harvesting losses and consequent low crop yields, and of high mortality and poor condition of such livestock as was left after the wholesale slaughter by the peasants as a prelude to their joining the collectives.

Although improvement took place during the late 1930's, still much remained to be done to bring a more efficient utilization of *kolkhoz* labor. This subject was increasingly in the spotlight of official attention during the years preceding World War II. A new urgency has been given to it since the war by manpower shortages and the swollen labor requirements of the postwar program of industrial reconstruction. In this connection one should remember that the peasant population constitutes the principal reservoir of labor that was tapped for the rapid expansion of industry under the prewar five-year plans.

Extremely high labor requirements were re-

---

27 Editorial in *Sotsialisticheskoe Zemledelie*, September 11, 1948.

28 *Ekonomicheskaya Zhizn'*, January 29, 1933.
29 Ya. A. Yakovlev, *Voprosy Organizatsii Sotsialisticheskogo Sel'skogo Khozyaistva* (Moscow, 1933), p. 262.

ported in crop production and animal husbandry by a sample survey of 428 *kolkhozy* in 10 provinces in 1937. It showed that, on the average, 46 man-days were required per cow, 21 per head of other adult cattle, 21.3 per head of young cattle, and 23.1 per calf.[30] The same survey showed that even where farming was highly mechanized before the war, as in southern Ukraine and North Caucasus, labor requirements were very high. For example, production of winter grains (predominantly winter wheat), including all preharvest and harvest operations and hauling of the crop to the delivery points, required 2.5 to 3.6 man-days per acre.

Comparison with the United States is hazardous, since corresponding data in this country are given in man-hours rather than man-days, and conversion of Russian man-days into man-hours is risky in the light of what is said below concerning the use of working time. Moreover, the great use of woman labor in Russian agriculture must be borne in mind. But despite these and other qualifications, such a comparison, for all its lack of precision, furnishes a significant clue to the relative scale of efficiency in the agriculture of the two countries. As a typical small grain we shall take wheat, a commodity in which the United States and Russia have long competed in international markets. The number of man-hours required for wheat production averages in the United States only 8.7 per acre and is as low as 4.6 in Kansas and 5.9 to 6.5 in the Dakotas.[31] The differential in favor of the United States would be even greater if the overhead expenses for such items as management were included in the figures for the two countries.

What are some of the inefficient labor practices in the *kolkhozy*? For one thing, there is often a wide gap between the time on the job and actual work. Studies made in 1939–40 in different *kolkhozy* showed that, in farm operations involving hand labor or the use of horses, an average of only 67 per cent of the working day was productively utilized.[32] This means, of course, that full utilization was not made of manpower, draft animals, and agricultural implements.

The daily working period itself in some *kolkhozy* is short, a fact that has often invoked official condemnation. Sometimes the short working period is caused by the very easy work tasks set in the *kolkhozy*. For example, in one *kolkhoz* in Kalinin Province, the daily task for plowing was 0.45 hectar (1.1 acres), although a worker was able to plow 0.11 hectare (0.27 acre) per hour and could thus complete his task in about 4 hours.[33] In the same *kolkhoz* the daily task for planting flax could be exceeded in 5 hours. Similar instances have been reported in other *kolkhozy*, though strong effort has been made since the war to correct this situation. It should be borne in mind that, unlike the farmer who owns and operates his own property, the average *kolkhoznik* is as free, on completing his task, from further responsibilities or chores in the *kolkhoz* as an average factory worker is after the whistle blows at the end of a working day. There are, of course, exceptions — the so-called Stakhanovists,[34] for example, who lavish extra care on animals or crops, particularly such intensive crops as sugar beets, cotton, or flax. But it is a safe generalization that the vast majority of the *kolkhozniki* put that extra effort into the cultivation of their own little plots and into the tending of their few personally owned animals and poultry.

There is, however, a general tendency, familiar to all foreign observers in Russia, to have two or more persons doing a job on a collective farm that is usually performed by one person in the United States. Then, such aftereffects of faulty farming as weeds, which have plagued Russian agriculture, require much effort for eradication. Russian agriculture also has less technical equipment than is found in America

---

[30] I. V. Sautin, ed., *Proizvoditel'nost i Ispol'zovanie Truda v Kolkhozakh vo Vtoroi Pyatiletke* (Moscow and Leningrad, 1939), pp. 50–51.

[31] M. R. Cooper, W. C. Holley, H. W. Hawthorne, and R. S. Washburn, *Labor Requirements for Crops and Livestock* (U.S. Bureau of Agricultural Economics, F.M. 40, 1943).

[32] F. Eliseev ["Utilization of Work Time in Spring Operations in *Kolkhozy*"], *Sotsialisticheskoe Sel'skoe Khozyaistvo 1941*, 3 (1941), pp. 31–32.

[33] *Ibid.*, p. 33.

[34] From the name of Alexis Stakhanov, a Russian miner who helped to inaugurate, in 1935, a movement for increased industrial efficiency. The term has often been applied to pace-makers employed in a sort of speed-up system to increase production.

and it is often inferior in quality. The inferiority, coupled with a lack of know-how, results in frequent breakdown of equipment, which slows farm operations. The situation is often aggravated by poor supply organization — shortages of fuel and spare parts for tractors and machinery, and inadequate repair facilities. The lower educational and, especially, living standards of the Russian collective farmer adversely affect his efficiency. The ordinarily inadequate compensation of *kolkhoz* labor does not provide sufficient incentives to work well and encourages soldiering on the job. In 1939, a compulsory minimum of labor for the farmers in *kolkhozy* was established in terms of so-called workdays, which will be discussed in a later section.

Migration from Kolkhozy

Despite the inefficient utilization of labor in the *kolkhozy*, it has been possible for the Government to divert, since collectivization, considerable manpower into industry, transportation, construction work, and similar activity. The urban, that is, the essentially industrial, population in the Soviet Union more than doubled between the censuses of January 1926 and January 1939. (The data of the census taken in January 1937 were suppressed.) Of the over-all increase in urban population of 29.6 million, 23 million migrated from the countryside.[35][36] This figure possibly included relatively few of the forced laborers from the rural areas, who swelled still further the reservoir of nonagricultural labor.

The Government took special measures to recruit labor for industry from the *kolkhozy*. A decree issued on June 30, 1931,[37] gave various privileges to the members of the *kolkhozy* who accepted employment with industrial and other state enterprises. The management of the *kolkhozy* was prohibited from interference with such employment of their members and was, in fact, encouraged to divert labor to industry and to make agreements for this purpose with various state enterprises. *Kolkhozy* making such agreements were supposed to receive priority in the distribution of agricultural machinery, in the establishment of schools, nurseries, and other educational and cultural institutions, as well as in the distribution of equipment for canteens and similar organizations.

There were thus, theoretically, two methods of approach that industry could follow in recruiting labor from the *kolkhozy*: (1) direct contact with individual members and (2) action through the *kolkhoz* management. In practice the first method was pursued to a considerable extent, and the *kolkhoz* management was neglected or side-stepped, often even to the detriment of *kolkhoz* production. Thus, the *kolkhozy* had no control over the outside employment of their members. There were many cases of so-called flying collective farmers who disappeared from the *kolkhozy* during the seasonal peaks of sowing or harvesting and reappeared in time for distribution of the *kolkhoz* income.

A new decree, therefore, was issued on March 17, 1933, which repealed the decree of June 30, 1931, and slowed recruitment of *kolkhoz* labor. Employment contracts of members had to be recorded by the executive board of the *kolkhoz* which could refuse to do so if it considered outside employment of a member contrary to the interest of the *kolkhoz*. The new regulations also empowered the *kolkhoz* management to expel those members who left the *kolkhoz* without permission.[38]

At present it is illegal for a member of a *kolkhoz* to accept employment elsewhere without permission of the *kolkhoz* management.[39] Recruiting officers are supposed to coordinate their activities with the *kolkhoz* management. If the recruiting of labor should threaten the production program of a *kolkhoz*, its management may refuse to record the employment contracts of the *kolkhoz* members and may appeal to the district (*raion*) administration. By the same token, passport regulations provide an additional stumbling block to the movement of the peasant away from the *kolkhoz* when the authorities are opposed to such a step.

The campaign for siphoning off *kolkhoz* labor

[35] Eugene M. Kulischer, *Europe on the Move: War and Population Changes* (New York, 1948), p. 107.
[36] Frank Lorimer, *The Population of the Soviet Union: History and Prospects* (Geneva, 1946), p. 149.
[37] *Ekonomicheskaya Zhizn'*, July 1, 1931.

[38] N. Aristov ["New Problems of the Organization of Migration of Labor from the *Kolkhozy*"], *Voprosy Truda*, No. 6 (1933), pp. 21–25.
[39] ["Legal Consultation on *Kolkhoz* Problems"] *Sotsialisticheskoe Zemledelie*, June 19, 1948.

into industry became intensified during the last few years preceding World War II. At the Eighteenth Communist Party Congress, Stalin stated that Soviet industry needs 1.5 million young *kolkhoz* workers annually. The labor recruiting system in the countryside, which was characterized by competition for workers on the part of different state industries and establishments, has been centralized since 1938.[40] Since the summer of 1947 this function has been assumed by special regional labor-procurement offices of the Ministry of Labor Reserves, created in the spring of 1946.

On October 2, 1940, a law was passed that permitted the Government to draft 800,000 to 1,000,000 rural and urban youth, 14 to 17 years of age, for 6 months to 2 years training in special vocational (skilled trades), railroad, and factory schools. After graduation, these draftees are obliged to work 4 years in industry, mines, and railroads, in establishments assigned by the Government. The 14- to 15-year group is assigned to vocational and railroad schools for a 2-year course, and the 16- to 17-year group to the factory schools for a 6-month course. In the *kolkhozy*, according to the 1940 regulations, 2 boys are drafted for each 100 men and women 14 to 55 years of age. Quotas for city youth are set up annually by the Government. A *kolkhoz* is supposed to provide clothing and food to last until draftees reach their schools. While attending the schools, pupils live in dormitories at Government expense. The draft first applied only to boys, but it was later extended to girls. Higher age groups are also drafted for vocational training. It was officially reported in the Soviet press on January 26, 1951, that 494,000 workers graduated from such vocational schools in 1950.

Distribution of Income and Incentives

There are, broadly speaking, three claimants to the income of the *kolkhoz*: (1) the state, (2) the *kolkhoz* as a collective enterprise interested in expansion and the growth of its capital, and (3) the members of the *kolkhoz*, constituting its labor force and managerial personnel.

The state is not only the director of but also the most important partner in collective farming and has the first claim on its production. In understanding the functioning of the collective farm system, the significance of this fact cannot be exaggerated. A *kolkhoz* must deliver to the Government at low fixed prices certain specified quantities of crops and animal products, and such deliveries have an overriding priority. Between 1933 and 1939 the basis on which crop deliveries were made was the acreage that the Government required each *kolkhoz* to plant. Since 1939–41, however, most crops have been delivered on the basis of *kolkhoz* tillable land, and livestock products on the basis of total land.

The rates of delivery per unit of land (hectare) are 15–25 per cent higher for the *kolkhozy* not served by machine-tractor stations. *Kolkhozy* that are served by the stations must make added payments in kind to them. Until 1947 the rates of delivery were uniform for each district, but, since then, lower quotas have been permitted for specified groups of collective farms that were suffering from a shortage of draft power relative to their land area and vice versa. Thus, the rates now vary.

In the aggregate, *kolkhoz* deliveries to the state and payments in kind to MTS constituted 26 per cent of their bumper grain crop in 1937 and 31 and 34 per cent, respectively, of the smaller crops in 1938 and 1939. During 1935–37, an average of 68 per cent of the meat and animal fats, 45 per cent of the milk, and 53 per cent of the wool produced collectively went to the state. No statistics are available for subsequent years, but the proportion was doubtless larger, because, as was explained above, deliveries have been based on total or tillable *kolkhoz* acreages since 1940 and not on the area to be seeded to crops or on the number of livestock. The importance that the Government attaches to the fulfillment of the so-called procuring plan for deliveries of farm products to the state is underscored by the fact that Stalin characterized this obligation of the collective farmers as a "first commandment." This term, which has penetrated into common official usage, gives a clue to the gravity with which the violation of the rule is regarded in official circles.

It will be recalled, in this connection, that to acquire farm products cheaply has always been among the main preoccupations of the

---

[40] Decree of June 21, 1938. *Sobranie Postanovlenii i Rasporyazhenii Pravitel'stva SSSR* ["Collection of Decrees and Orders of the Government of the U.S.S.R."], No. 34, August 7, 1938.

Kremlin, especially since it embarked on its ambitious industrialization program under the five-year plans. The obtaining of increased farm supplies was, as we saw earlier, at the root of agricultural collectivization.

The procuring process has involved a great deal of friction with the collective farmers, especially in the early years of collectivization, when it turned into a veritable tug of war with the peasantry. By using force without stint, and not stopping even at wholesale starvation of the countryside, the Government mastered the situation by 1933.

Although the turbulent procuring campaigns of the early years of collectivization gave way to a smoother process, difficulties still continued to be encountered, especially in years of poor crops when Government pressure for early delivery of quotas fixed irrespective of yields proved onerous to the peasants. Some *kolkhozy*, under such conditions, found themselves without seed for sowing next year's crop, and in the end the Government often had to advance grain for seed. A scheme that has been used since World War II to stimulate delivery of farm products, preferably in excess of the goals set, is to put such obligations of the *kolkhozy* in the form of public pledges to Stalin. Such pledges have an even greater driving force than an ordinary law.

It has been a stock Soviet assertion that the peasants in the U.S.S.R. do not have to pay any rental or other charges for the land and that the farm taxes are very light, constituting, for instance, in 1937, only 2.8 per cent of the total income of the *kolkhozy* from collective farming, the earnings of the members from personal farming, and other sources.[41] However, such estimates do not include the low-priced compulsory deliveries of farm products made to the state. The extent of this contribution can be gauged by considering the gap between the procuring prices paid by the state and the prices at which peasants are able to sell their products on the free market. Such information has been zealously kept out of Soviet statistical publications, however. When

some fragmentary data found their way into a pamphlet published in 1948, which dealt with the income taxes on *kolkhozy*, they revealed that free-market prices were, as a rule, 15 to more than 40 times as large as Government procurement prices.[42] This disparity had increased during the war as a result of the inflationary rise of the free-market prices. By 1951, the spread has probably become less, but it is doubtless still very large. Not only are the farmers taxed by being forced to sell their produce to the Government at very low prices, but, in common with the rest of the Soviet population, they are also subject to extremely high indirect taxation in the form of the so-called turnover tax, levied on commodities sold in Government-controlled stores, which account for the great bulk of the volume of retail trade, especially of manufactured goods.

When the *kolkhoz* has met all obligations to the state, including taxes in kind, payments to MTS, and repayment in kind of any seed loaned by the Government during the preceding year, the next step is to set aside seed supplies for the following year's sowing, forage supplies for the collectivized livestock until next harvest, and emergency reserves for these purposes. When all this is done, a *kolkhoz* is free to dispose of the remainder of its production. It may sell a part to the state at somewhat higher prices than those received for the compulsory deliveries and sometimes obtain thereby a preference in the distribution by the Government of scarce manufactured goods. A *kolkhoz* may also sell some of its products on the freemarket. But it must take the products to the market, since employment of a middleman is illegal. Moreover, free-market sale of grain and breadstuffs usually is not permitted until the grain-procuring plan for the whole Province or Republic is fulfilled.

The free market for a *kolkhoz*, therefore, is usually limited to a nearby town, though such *kolkhoz* trade has been an important factor in the over-all marketing of foodstuffs. Sometimes *kolkhozy* also sell foodstuffs to their members either for communal feeding or for individual use, at lower than prevailing free

41 I. Laptev ["*Kolkhoz* Income and the Differential Rent"], *Bol'shevik*, 16 (1944), p. 12. The existence, with certain modifications, of the differential rent as the concept is known in economic theory and its partial appropriation by the state is admitted by the author (p. 15).

42 V. S. Dankov, *O Podokhodnom Naloge s Kolkhozov* (Moscow, 1948), pp. 64–65, 70–71.

market prices. Such sales are also made to outsiders, especially Government officials, who often are able to apply pressure on the *kolkhozy*. The practice of selling below the prevailing price results in a considerable financial loss to the *kolkhozy*.[43]

From cash income, a *kolkhoz* must pay income tax, required insurance premiums, and various current expenses, including those for administration and for educational and cultural purposes. An "undivided surplus" must also be set up to cover necessary capital expenditures. Any left-over products or cash are distributed among the members of the *kolkhoz*. Thus, except for small advances in kind permitted at harvest time, the peasant is a residual claimant to the output and cash income of the *kolkhoz*. He is paid at the end of the season.

Even though the peasant in the *kolkhoz* has lost the status of an independent farm proprietor, becoming in most respects indistinguishable from a worker in the Soviet factory, still he must share in the risk inherent in farming. Thus, he has neither the advantages of a specified income that a Soviet wage worker possesses nor the degree of independence of the small peasant farmer who is his own master.

Labor contributed by a member of a *kolkhoz* is supposed to serve exclusively as a basis for distribution of income.[44][45] All earnings are required to be on a sort of task system, according to the quantity, skill, and quality of work performed by an individual and output obtained. Equal distribution and payment by the day, or on some other time basis, have been officially proscribed in the *kolkhozy*.

The arrangements by which this principle is implemented are complicated and result in a cumbersome system of remuneration. The first step is the setting up in a *kolkhoz* of daily tasks of performance for various farm operations, called norms. Standard norms developed by the Government form the basis on which the *kolkhozy* are supposed to establish their own norms. The first set of such standard norms

was developed in 1933 and was not revised for years. This explains the many official complaints of the obsoleteness of several of these norms, which were considered far too low. To insure that the norms keep pace with technological progress, the Council of Ministers of the U.S.S.R. required, in its decree of April 19, 1948, that each *kolkhoz* annually review its norms.[46]

After a norm has been established, a certain value is assigned to it. For this purpose an arbitrary unit, a so-called *trudoden*, literally translated as "workday," was adopted, which should not be confused with actual man-days of labor. All farm operations are divided into several categories on the basis of the difficulty, importance, and skill required in the performance of the work. The work requiring least skill and effort, such as that of a guard or messenger, is rated as less than one workday; whereas a skilled tractor driver, who is classified in the highest labor category, is entitled to several workdays for the performance of his daily task. Additional workdays are supposed to be accorded to those who exceed their norms, and nonfulfillment of the norm or poor quality of work theoretically involves a reduction in the number of workdays credited to the worker. The brigadier and the *kolkhoz* manager are required to inspect all completed work and officially accept or reject it. Each member has a record book into which the brigadier enters his earned (credited) workdays.

To determine how much a workday is worth in terms of cash or products, all the workdays earned by members of a *kolkhoz* are added together. This figure is divided into the amount of cash and products set aside for distribution, thus establishing the value of one workday. If, for instance, all members of a particular *kolkhoz* earned during the year a total of X workdays, then the total quantity of cash, grain, and other products subject to

---

43 L. Adrianov, in *Sotsialisticheskoe Zemledelie*, May 27, 1948.

44 Nikitkin and others, *op. cit.*, pp. 294–316.

45 L. M. Zal'tsman, ed., *Organizatsiya Sotsialisticheskikh Sel'skokhozyaistvennykh Predpriyatii* (Moscow, 1947), pp. 558–561.

46 Examples of such standard norms for a day's work proposed by this decree are: plowing of 0.7 to 0.9 hectare (1.7 to 2.2 acres) with a one-bottom plow to the depth of 20 centimeters (7.9 inches); plowing of 1.0 to 1.3 hectares (2.5 to 3.2 acres) with a two-bottom plow to the same depth; harvesting with a reaper 4.0 to 5.5 hectares (9.9 to 13.6 acres) of grain in the steppe and wooded steppe regions.

distribution is divided by X. Let us suppose, for example, that only grain and cash are distributed in a *kolkhoz* in a particular year, and that one workday is worth 4 kilograms of grain and 1 ruble in cash, and that a member of a *kolkhoz* is credited with 200 workdays during the year. His annual earnings, therefore, will be $4 \times 200 = 800$ kilograms of grain and $1 \times 200 = 200$ rubles. Those members of the *kolkhoz* who earned a larger number of workdays because they possessed certain skills that were highly valued or because they worked harder, or both, are paid more than the others in cash and in kind.

A serious complication developed, however, because many cases came to light wherein two brigades, working presumably under identical conditions on two equal plots of land, obtained various yields per acre, and sometimes higher yields were associated with the expenditure of a smaller number of workdays. As a result, the workers in a brigade that obtained higher yields earned less than those in a brigade with lower yields. This has been usually cited by Soviet spokesmen as a case of rewarding inferior work and penalizing the more efficient workers. However, the underlying assumption that two similar plots of land in a *kolkhoz* will produce identical yields if worked equally well is often unjustified. Yields of crops depend not only on human effort but also on weather and other natural and technical conditions, which frequently are highly variable even within the territory of a particular farm, especially when it is as large as the usual *kolkhoz*. It is not easy to segregate these various factors. Still, it cannot be denied that a large number of workdays may be indicative not of superior performance but of inefficiency.

Soviet leadership, in its eagerness to increase farm production, has been casting about for a better method to link output with the workday. The present system, elaborated by the decree of April 19, 1948, is to credit, in accordance with a complicated formula, a certain proportion of supplementary workdays for each brigade or *zveno* as a bonus for production in excess of the goals set by the Government plan. Similarly, workdays are deducted for failure to reach the goals, except in the event of an officially verified natural adversity.

The decree of April 19, 1948, prescribes two methods of adjusting earnings in accordance with output, either of which could be adopted by the *kolkhoz*. According to one method, for each per cent an individual brigade or *zveno* exceeds its planned production of a crop or group of crops, it is credited with one additional per cent of the total number of workdays credited to the members of the brigade or *zveno* in raising such a crop or group of crops. Likewise, when the actual outturn is below the plan, a deduction is made up to 25 per cent of the total number of workdays used in raising the crop. Thus, if the outturn of a brigade is 10 per cent above or below the plan, the total number of workdays credited to the members of the brigade for raising the crop is correspondingly increased or decreased by 10 per cent. If the brigade or *zveno* succeeds in obtaining the planned outturn, no more and no less, no increase or decrease is made in the number of workdays credited to its members. The addition or deduction of the workdays is then distributed among the members of the brigade in proportion to the number of workdays originally credited to each individual. But those *kolkhozniki* who have not earned, without a valid reason, the prescribed minimum of workdays are not supposed to be credited with any additional workdays under this system. Adolescents below 16 years of age and those who are not fully able-bodied are exempted from any deduction of workdays.

The second method is based on the comparison of the fulfillment of the planned production goals for a brigade or *zveno* with that for the *kolkhoz* as a whole. The brigade or *zveno* obtains an addition or deduction of the number of workdays to the extent that the per cent of fulfillment of the planned production goal of a brigade or *zveno* is above or below the fulfillment of the planned production goal for the *kolkhoz* as a whole. The deduction is not to exceed 25 per cent of the number of workdays credited to the members of the brigade or *zveno* raising a particular crop or group of crops. But a brigade or *zveno* that fulfills or overfulfills its planned goal, even though to a lesser extent than the *kolkhoz* as a whole meets its planned goal, is, nevertheless, not subject to any deduction of workdays. The decree also specifies that the count of workdays and production estimates must be made separately for each plot assigned to a brigade or *zveno*. In animal husbandry, the workdays are also related to outturn. A woman tending dairy cattle, for instance, must take care of from 8 to 14 cows and, for each 100 litres (227 pounds) of milk obtained during the pasturage season, she is credited with from 1.2 to 1.8 workdays and during the barn feeding period from 2.2 to 3.2 workdays; for each healthy calf born, 7 workdays; and for each calf raised from 15 to 20 days, 12 workdays.

In addition to rewarding larger output through supplementary workdays, the value of the workday itself is enhanced by special bonuses. A Government decree of December 31, 1940, first applied to the Ukraine and later extended to other regions, provided that *kolkhoz* brigades that exceed planned goals for crop yields and livestock products are to obtain a certain proportion of such surpluses in kind or the equivalent in cash. For instance, for grain, it was to be one-fourth of the amount harvested in excess of the plan; for sunflower seed, soybeans, rapeseed, and flaxseed, one-third; for milk, 15 per cent; and for sugar beets and cotton, an extra 50 per cent of the average official delivery price for each additional quintal (220.46 pounds) produced above the plan.

These bonus payments are distributed to individuals on the basis of the number of workdays earned, and they are in addition to the payments described earlier. There is, however, an important prerequisite for eligibility to these bonuses: a recipient must have put in a certain minimum number of *actual days* of labor during the agricultural season from March 1 to November 10. This requirement is in addition to the provision of the decree of May 27, 1939, and April 17, 1942, that a member of a *kolkhoz* must earn a certain minimum number of workdays during a year in order to be in good standing.

In many cases the bonus scheme was reported to have been nullified by the setting of production goals beyond the reach of even the most efficient farmers. The better *kolkhozy*, with their high standards of performance, were said to be particularly affected by this malpractice. In recent years, little has been heard of the bonus payments.

In 1937, the latest year for which detailed data are available, an average of 438 work-

days were credited to a *kolkhoz* peasant household and 194 to an able-bodied worker; 21.2 per cent of the *kolkhoz* workers were credited with 50 or fewer workdays; 15.6 with 51 to 100; 25 per cent with 101 to 200; 18.4 per cent with 201 to 300; 11.3 per cent with 301 to 400; and 8.5 per cent with more than 400 workdays.[47] Among those who earned only 50 workdays, or less, there were undoubtedly many young persons and women with family responsibilities. In the group that earned most — more than 300 workdays — there was probably a heavier representation of the more efficient *kolkhozy*, where labor is more fully and effectively employed.

By a decree of May 27, 1939, there was established a minimum number of workdays for each member of the *kolkhoz* without distinction as to sex. The country was divided into three zones, and for each a corresponding minumum of 60, 80, and 100 workdays was set up. Nonfulfillment of the minimum was penalized by expulsion from the *kolkhoz* and loss of kitchen-garden plots. The minimum was raised during the war by a decree published in *Pravda*, April 17, 1942. A novel feature of this decree was the specific allocation of the required minimum of work during different periods of the year. For instance, in a *kolkhoz* of the Moscow Province, 25 workdays "must be worked up to June 1; 25 between June 1 and August 1; 35 between August 1 and October 1, and the remaining 15 workdays after October 1." Those who did not fulfill these requirements without valid reasons are liable on conviction by court to a penalty of up to 6 months of "correctional labor" in the *kolkhoz* and a deduction of 25 per cent of their pay in favor of the *kolkhoz* treasury.

To sum up, earnings of the peasant from his work in the *kolkhoz* depend on four factors: first, on the nature of the tasks assigned to him and their rating in terms of workdays; second, on his performance of these tasks — the quantity and quality of the work done; third, on the output achieved by the brigade or *zveno*, which serves as a basis for adjusting upward or downward the number of workdays earned and for determining incentive payments in kind; and fourth, on the output and income

---

[47] Sautin, *Kolkhozy vo Vtoroi Stalinskoi Pyatiletke,* p. 38.

of the *kolkhoz* as a whole, since the higher they are the greater theoretically is the residual share distributed to members on the basis of workdays. In addition to earnings from the work in the *kolkhoz*, members derive some income from personal farming and may also obtain some earnings by working outside the *kolkhoz*, especially during the nonagricultural season.

A system of payment differing from that of the rank and file of members has been adopted for *kolkhoz* managers (chairmen). The wages of a manager comprise (1) a flat number of workdays per month, increasing with the size of the crop area of the *kolkhoz*, the numbers of communal (collectivized) livestock, and the length of the manager's service; (2) supplementary workdays as a bonus for the overfulfillment of production goals or, conversely, a reduction in the number of workdays for underfulfillment; thus, on the basis of the workdays, the manager obtains farm products and cash just as all other members do; and (3) a specified monthly cash payment, increasing with the total income of the *kolkhoz*.

In agriculture, as in industry, use has been made of pace-setters, so-called shock workers (*udarniki*), Stakhanovists, etc. Especially favorable working conditions have often been provided for such pace-setters, enabling them to earn an income far above that of the average *kolkhoz* member.

Such are the mechanics of payment for labor in the *kolkhoz*. The cumbersomeness of the system is obvious. The very complexity of computing, recording, and supervising, which has increased with the introduction of production bonuses and deductions, described above, would tax the capacity of those concerned even where educational and efficiency standards are much higher than in Soviet Russia. The workday system, however, is apparently considered the only effective means of inducing peasants to work reasonably hard and well in the *kolkhozy*, dedicated primarily to supplying the needs of the Soviet state.

Making the peasant work in the *kolkhoz* has not been an easy task. He is neither a hired man who can be as easily fired as an industrial worker (although, as we saw above, illegal expulsions have not been uncommon in the *kolkhozy*), nor does he work independently, as he once did, except in his little

kitchen-garden plot. The Soviet press has frequently complained that peasants prefer to work their little plots of land and tend a few animals, neglecting the *kolkhoz* fields and livestock. Such private farming has often proved more profitable, especially when the distance to a neighboring city makes it possible for *kolkhoz* members to sell vegetables, dairy products, and such on the private market. But the most important cause of the lukewarm attitude of many *kolkhoz* members toward collective farming, so frequently reported in Soviet publications and stressed in numerous official pronouncements, has been the low reward under the workday system.

The principal item distributed in payment for workdays in most regions has been grain, which has always constituted the most important index of the economic well-being of the Russian peasant. Skipping the starvation period of the early 1930's, or an exceptional year of bumper crops like 1937, and taking a relatively good year like 1935, we find that the per capita supply of grain distributed in the *kolkhozy* was reported at 249 kilograms (549 pounds), of which 18 kilograms (40 pounds) were obtained from the little family plots intended to serve only as kitchen gardens.[48] This quantity may be compared with the 250 to 260 kilograms[49] (550 to 570 pounds) consumed on the average during the precollective period of the middle 20's, according to special nutrition studies (which were then conducted but discontinued during the increasing statistical blackout and purge of statisticians in the 1930's). The difference is even greater when it is considered that out of the 249 kilograms the peasant had not only to feed himself but also to provide a small quantity of grain for his livestock and poultry and lay in a reserve for a possible harvest failure. Thus, the average human consumption of grain, even in a year of good harvest, was less than during the precollectivization period, when the available supply of other foods was also larger. Peasant grain consumption was doubtless much less in a poor crop year like 1936, as indicated by the

---

[48] N. Chmelevskii ["The Income of Collective Farmers in 1935"], *Plan*, 21 (1936), p. 31.
[49] A. Lositskii ["Dynamics of Grain Consumption in the U.S.S.R."], *Statisticheskoe Obozrenie 1927*, 12 (1927), p. 21. (Flour and groats converted to grain basis.)

decline of more than 30 per cent in the distribution of grain per workday compared with 1935.

While data on the payment of *kolkhoz* members since World War II are entirely inadequate, inasmuch as only occasional figures for single *kolkhozy* have been published, there is every reason to believe, judging from the size of the crops and the requirements of the Government, that the average amount of grain distributed among members was considerably reduced during the war and early postwar years and probably had not reached the prewar levels by 1950.

Another item distributed fairly widely by the *kolkhozy* is potatoes. In 1937, more than 140,000 collective farms out of a total of more than 240,000 distributed an average of 2.7 kilograms (6 pounds) per workday. As a rule, little cash is distributed in the *kolkhozy*. In 1936 and 1937, more than 30 per cent of the *kolkhozy* distributed 0.2 ruble or less per workday;[50] more than 50 per cent, 0.4 ruble or less; and 14 per cent distributed more than 1 ruble per workday.[51] Only in those *kolkhozy* that specialized in the production of valuable industrial crops needed by the Government, like cotton, or were near large cities, where they could advantageously sell their produce, were the cash receipts relatively high.

Cash receipts of *kolkhoz* members, however, were increasing before World War II. They amounted, on the average, to 108 rubles per household in 1932, 147 in 1935, and 376 in 1937. While the low prices paid by the Government for compulsory deliveries held down cash receipts, this was somewhat offset by the growing sales of surpluses on the free market. The physical volume of such kolkhoz trade from 1932, when it was initiated, to 1939 was said to have increased fivefold.[52] The importance to the collective farm economy of

trading on the free market can be gauged from the fact that such sales were claimed to have accounted for an average of 30 per cent of the cash income of all *kolkhozy* before World War II.[53]

During the Russo-German War, in those *kolkhozy* that were near enough to the cities to sell their produce on the free market, the cash receipts increased considerably. Even in 1947 when prices declined, free-market sales still accounted for 50 to 90 per cent of the cash income of six collective farms studied in Moscow and Gorky Provinces.[54]

In addition to the *kolkhozy* selling part of their produce for cash on the free market, their members were also extensively engaged in similar operations on their own account. Thus, to repeat, in districts where distance to cities made free-market sales possible, the cash receipts of *kolkhoz* members from the disbursements by the *kolkhozy* and from private sales were undoubtedly high. It should be borne in mind, however, that those were greatly inflated rubles that would buy little food and fewer manufactured goods. The peasant, of course, could and did hoard the rubles in expectation of better days. But the Soviet currency reform of December 1947, which drastically devalued the ruble (in the ratio of 1 new ruble to 10 old), largely destroyed the hoards.[55]

Other items besides grain, potatoes, and cash were distributed in various *kolkhozy* as payment for labor, but such distribution has been much less common. Data on the total earnings of members of a representative group of *kolkhozy* were published for one year only, that of 1937, which, as was pointed out above, was a year of bumper crops. These figures are based on a survey of 16,786 collective farms in 28 different regions and give the earnings per household and per capita of the *kolkhoz* population. Earnings credited for *kolkhoz* workdays and those derived from the personal farming of its members are not segregated, and payments in kind are valued in the relatively

---

[50] One ruble in 1937 was equal to 19 cents in U.S. currency at the legal rate of exchange, which, however, was considerably overvalued. Actually, the purchasing value of the ruble at that time was probably equal to not more than 4 or 5 cents in U.S. currency.

[51] Dm. Rud, *Raspredelenie Dokhodov v Kolkhozakh* (Moscow, 1938), p. 25.

[52] G. Chernyi ["*Kolkhoz* Trade and Finances of *Kolkhozy*"], *Sotsialisticheskoe Sel'skoe Khozyaistvo 1949*, 2 (1949), p. 37.

[53] *Ibid.* Presumably this refers to sales by the *kolkhozy* and not to private trading of their members.

[54] *Ibid.*, p. 38.

[55] Savings in banks were devalued at much more favorable rates, but the peasants, for the most part, did not keep their cash in savings banks.

high free-market prices. The average earnings per *kolkhoz* household were 5,843.2 rubles and per capita, 1,304.3 rubles.[56] Assuming that the actual purchasing power of the ruble equaled approximately 5 cents, U.S. currency, we obtain a per capita income of about $65 and the income of a household of $292.

Considerable variation in the income of *kolkhoz* members from region to region is shown by the 1937 figures, extending from 899.9 rubles per capita in the Armenian Republic to 1,579.0 in the Urals. Of course, there is also considerable variation within smaller districts, sometimes even among neighboring collective farms. The 10 to 30 per cent of so-called backward *kolkhozy* in each administrative district[57] have, as a rule, low per capita income. At the other pole are the so-called advanced (progressive) *kolkhozy* with an income above average.

The difference in the size of per capita income among *kolkhozy*, even of a relatively small district, may be the result of a number of causes operating singly or jointly. The efficiency, honesty, and stability of a *kolkhoz* management, the fertility of the soil, the degree of diversification of the production pattern, and the adequacy of capital equipment and labor supply are some of the important factors that influence production and income. From the standpoint of maximizing income, the importance of a *kolkhoz* location in relation to urban markets, especially considering the primitive state of Russian roads and the inadequate means of transportation, has already been emphasized. The availability of tractors and other modern farm machinery, which are concentrated in state machine-tractor stations, and, what is extremely important, the efficiency of their operations also significantly affect output and, therefore, the income of the *kolkhozy*. The production practices adopted, the extent of agronomic assistance, and, last but not least, local variations in weather conditions that affect crop yields, all play their part in varying the volume of production and the size of the income of *kolkhozy*. A favorable combination of the above-mentioned factors may place one *kolkhoz* in the millionaire class (that is, having an income of a million rubles or more), whereas an unfavorable combination may relegate another to a low-income group.

In addition to the strictly economic incentives, the Soviet Government has also striven, through so-called socialist competition propaganda, to organize a rivalry for higher production goals among individuals, separate *kolkhozy*, and even whole and sometimes distant regions. Special occasions such as the National Agricultural Exposition held in 1939 and 1940 or a national holiday such as the Anniversary of the October Revolution, for instance, are utilized for this purpose. Public pledges to Stalin by collective farmers of a whole region, promising achievement of certain goals, have been widely employed since World War II because of their value in whipping up effort on the part of Soviet citizens. Many awards of medals and honorary titles for superior performances by collective farmers have also been made. In 1947, for example, 1,931 members of *kolkhozy* and other workers in the field of agriculture were awarded the honorary title of Hero of Socialist Labor, 4,348 were awarded the Order of Lenin, 12,500 the Order of Labor Red Banner; and more than 40,000 other medals were awarded.[58]

It should be noted that, prior to January 1, 1948, the awarding of medals as a rule entailed a number of privileges, such as free transportation on streetcars, railroads, and steamers, some cash payments, reduced housing rents, and exemption from the income tax. By a decree of September 10, 1947, of the Praesidium of the Supreme Soviet of the U.S.S.R. all privileges except exemption from income tax were abolished.[59]

A special decree[60] prescribed in great detail

56 Sautin, *Kolkhozy vo Vtoroi Stalinskoi Pyatiletke*, p. 114.
57 N. A. Kulagin ["Differentiated Incomes of *Kolkhozy*"], *Izvestiya Akademii Nauk SSSR, Otdelenie Ekonomiki i Prava 1949*, 6 (1949), p. 459.

58 I. Laptev ["Socialist Competition and Labor Discipline in *Kolkhozy*"], *Pravda*, June 24, 1948. See also I. Benediktov, "Soviet Peasantry, Led by J. V. Stalin, Heads for New Victories," *U.S.S.R. Information Bulletin*, December 21, 1949, p. 768.
59 *Vedomosti Verkhovnogo Soveta SSSR*, No. 41 (November 30, 1947).
60 A decree of the Praesidium of the Supreme Soviet of the U.S.S.R., concerning the bestowal of the title of Hero of Socialist Labor and the awarding of orders and medals of the U.S.S.R. to members of *kolkhozy* and workers in the MTS and state farms, for the obtaining of high yields of wheat, rye, corn, rice, cotton, sugar beets, sunflower seeds, clover, alfalfa, and timothy grass. Issued on April 24, 1948. *Izvestiya*, April 25, 1948.

the standard conditions that had governed in 1948 and 1949 the awarding of honors in *kolkhozy* on the basis of target yields for each of 10 specified crops. It was followed by similar regulations dealing with a number of other crops. For this purpose the whole country was divided into 8 zones. For instance, if in the Krasnodar region of North Caucasus a *kolkhoz* brigade obtains 32 quintals per hectare of wheat or rye (48 and 51 bushels, respectively, per acre), on an area of no less than 60 hectares (150 acres), the brigadier is awarded the title, Hero of Socialist Labor. To warrant the Order of Lenin, the yield on the same area must be 26 quintals (39 and 41 bushels of wheat or rye, respectively, per acre). Still lower yields suffice for the awarding of other medals. For a *kolkhoz* manager or agronomist to obtain one of the honors, it is necessary to achieve these yields on a larger area, 150 hectares (371 acres) of wheat and rye. These targets vary for different zones. For example, in Kharkov Province of the Ukraine the standard yield for the awarding of the title, Hero of Socialist Labor, is 31 quintals of wheat or rye per hectare (46 and 49 bushels, respectively, per acre).

The target yields seem to be high, certainly very much above the average published figures for the various regions, even for years of excellent crops before World War II. Moreover, it appears that only the so-called barn yields are taken into consideration in awarding honors and not the preharvest figures of the Soviet official statistics, which usually are overestimated as compared with the actual barn outturn. There are obvious escape clauses throughout the text of the above-mentioned decree, which are probably placed there to facilitate the balancing of inequalities that are likely to arise where arbitrary administrative boundaries are used in regionalization. These escape clauses can probably also be used to reward staunch party members and other influential persons.

Economic incentives and propaganda are buttressed in collective agriculture, as in other branches of Soviet economy, by terror. The gruesome story of how force was used without stint during the collectivization campaign in the Russian countryside in the early 1930's, and how wholesale starvation resulted in several millions of deaths, has already been told. In the same period also came the famous law of August 7, 1932, which prescribes the death penalty as a punishment for theft of *kolkhoz* or cooperative property or, when extenuating circumstances exist, imprisonment for a period of no less than 10 years, with confiscation of all personal belongings and no possibility of amnesty. This law was applied, among others, to so-called barbers — an epithet denoting the wretched and hungry people who stole grain from the fields by cutting the ears with scissors.

Purges through expulsion from a *kolkhoz*, accompanied by the loss of the precious little kitchen-garden plot, also hang like a Damocles' sword over the peasant's head. Although there are safeguards against easy expulsion on the statute books, these regulations, as we saw above, are frequently flaunted. There is, finally, the Soviet enigma of the concentration camp or "slave labor" system.[61] This subject is, perhaps, one of the most closely guarded of Soviet secrets. But it is hardly open to doubt that the terror of the concentration camp stalks not only the cities but also the countryside, which likewise contributes a generous quota to the teeming millions of "slave workers."

36

The Peasant and Soviet Agricultural Policy*

Arcadius Kahan

(1960)

The complex history of the Soviet regime's relation to the peasants who constituted the overwhelming majority of the population is reviewed by Dr. Kahan as prologue to his examination of the changes made in Soviet agricultural policy since Stalin's death. We learn from his account that the peasant is now much better paid for his effort and that his farm has much more autonomy in running its

[61] See David J. Dallin and Boris Nikolaevsky, *Forced Labor in Soviet Russia*, 331 pp., New Haven, 1947.

* Reprinted from "The Peasant, the Party and the System," *Problems of Communism*, a publication of the United States Information Agency, Vol. 9 (1960), pp. 27–36, by permission of the author.

affairs. But it is also evident that the regime is pressing ahead relentlessly with its long-range program to deprive the peasant of his distinctive socio-economic character and transform him into merely another "worker," albeit one employed in "factories in the open."

The preoccupation of top Soviet policy-makers with problems of agriculture in recent years has been one of numerous interesting facets of the post-Stalin era. The significance of this concern in terms of further Soviet development makes it important to scrutinize closely what attitudes and policies have been adopted by the new leadership, in what sense they show continuity with past policies, and to what degree they depart from the past.

Such an examination requires an understanding of the initial basic relationship between the Soviet state and the peasantry. In spite of the fact that Russia had always been a predominantly agrarian country, few of the early Bolshevik leaders understood the "mystery" that was the Russian peasant. Among them, Lenin came closest to grasping the problem, but was very often blinded by doctrines which he believed to be true and self-evident and which he passed on to his followers. Primarily concerned with the strategy of seizing and maintaining power, Lenin viewed the peasants in terms of a potential political force that he wanted either to control or at least to neutralize. Although he recognized the peasants' deep-seated conservatism, it was apparently beyond his comprehension that they might constitute an unrelenting or permanent adversary.

In line with this attitude, he invented (or used) an explanation of peasant social behavior that was typically Russian — one, in fact, that could well have been originated by Dostoevsky. According to this theory the peasant was possessed of a split personality: on the one hand, he harbored a "diabolic" soul, characterized by attachment to private property, resistance to trends of social change, and hope for personal advancement through command over an increasing volume of resources. But there was also an "angelic" side to the peasant's soul that would accept social transformation; this side was associated with the small proprietor who could not protect himself from exploitation in the market by profit-seeking capitalists. In

Lenin's view, the latter side of the peasant's nature made it possible and indeed imperative for the industrial proletariat to seek the peasants' cooperation before and during the "bourgeois-democratic" revolution. One of Lenin's contributions to Marxist literature concerned the means of achieving such an alliance; noting the social stratification within the peasantry, he pointed out how a skillful policy making use of differences of interest at various levels could prevent the peasants as a whole from taking concerted action during the transformation of the bourgeois-democratic into the proletarian revolution.[1]

This strategy was not of course aimed at a permanent alliance with a section of the peasantry but was simply part of Lenin's blueprint for power, designed to neutralize the resistance he expected to develop, though in what form or to what degree he would not calculate. As early as 1905 he had written:

> Class antagonism between the rural proletariat and the peasant bourgeoisie is inevitable, and we reveal it in advance, explain it and prepare for the struggle. . . . At first we [will] support to the end, by all means including confiscation, the peasantry generally against the landlords, and then (or rather, not "then" but at the same time) we [will] support the proletariat against the peasantry in general. To try now to calculate the combination of forces among the peasantry on "the morrow" of the (democratic) revolution is sheer utopia.[2]

Leninism in Practice

Thus fortified with a political strategy and rules for tactical maneuvering, Lenin did not stop to analyze the socio-economic role of the peasant as a producer in the market, involving such problems as commodity prices, incomes, profits, investment opportunities, taxation, and so on. Indeed in his various writings he never exhibited a genuine interest in devising solutions for major economic problems, concentrating instead on the political expression of those problems. Thus he launched the revolu-

[1] See Lenin, "Otnosheniie Sotsial-Demokratii k Krestianskomu Dvizheniiu" (The Attitude of Social-Democracy Toward the Peasant Movement), *Sochineniia* (Works), Vol. VIII.
[2] Lenin, *Selected Works*, International Publishers, New York, Vol. III. pp. 145–56.

tion and stepped over the threshold of power without any clear notion of what ought to be the long-run objectives of his agrarian policy. The language of his speech accompanying the "Decree on Land," issued immediately after the November 7 *coup,* aptly reveals his state of mind in this respect:

> Russia is great, and local conditions vary. We believe that the peasants will be able to solve the problem [of agrarian adjustment] correctly better than we could ourselves. Whether in our spirit, or in the spirit of the program of the Socialist-Revolutionaries is not the point. The point is that the peasants should be firmly assured that there are no more landlords in the countryside, that they must themselves arrange their own lives.[3]

After embarking on the tragic (in terms of consequences) experiment of war communism, Lenin proceeded with his divide-and-rule tactics among the peasants, again in an effort to neutralize their political reaction. Specifically, he tried to foment an intra-village struggle between the poor and the rich peasants, with the medium stratum as spectators. Unmindful of the economic consequences of such conflict, he created his *"Kombiedy"* (Committees of the Poor Peasants), which acted as agents of government policy in each village in the suppression of the richer landholders. This tactic contributed to the general chaos created by "war communism," characterized on the economic side by food requisitioning, galloping inflation, and the return to a virtual barter economy. Under these conditions the peasants obstinately refused to produce any agricultural surplus, leading to a catastrophic decrease in output.

Agriculture in the 1920's

In 1921 the outbreak of peasant rebellions, along with the Kronstadt uprising, signaled the imminent political dangers of the situation confronting the regime. Unable to admit that the Kronstadt uprising represented his moral defeat by workers and sailors — the alleged pillars of his authority — Lenin hastily admitted defeat at the hands of the peasants and sounded the horn for retreat. He acknowledged this failure in plain words: "The peasants are

not content with our attitude toward them, and they will not tolerate it any longer."[4] The first battle between the Soviet state and the peasants thus ended with a victory for the peasants, and the era of the NEP (New Economic Policy) began.

The NEP's comparatively liberal policies toward the agricultural sector and internal trade demonstrated the possibilities of some sort of a symbiosis between a largely nationalised industry and a relatively free peasant agriculture, as had been visualized and advocated by the Populists in the 19th century. Simple agricultural cooperation (later used as a stepping-stone to collectivization) and an essentially free market for agricultural products proved beneficial to the task of reconstruction and recovery, the major goal of the NEP period. For the peasants themselves, the first years of NEP represented in a sense a "golden era" in their history, with incomes on the rise and investment outlays in agriculture increasing.

Yet new troubles were not long in arising. "Scissors crises" — a widening discrepancy between industrial and agricultural prices, or between peasant purchasing power and available consumer goods — in combination with faulty government price and procurement policies, led to a curtailment of the peasants' incentive to produce and thus to a decrease in the agricultural output available for the market. A major dilemma arose over conflicting demands on the short agricultural supply, for home consumption of the peasants on the one hand, urban consumption and exports on the other. Concomitantly, the regime faced the problem of deriving sources for and minimizing costs of rapid industrialization without access to foreign investment markets.

This situation led to the regime's attempts in 1928 to shift the burden of industrialization onto the peasants, by decreasing their home consumption and by procuring grain at prices below the market rate. Stalin himself best described the effect of these measures, in a speech of July 1928:

> The way matters stand with the peasantry in this respect is as follows: it not only pays the

---

[3] *Ibid.,* Vol. VI, p. 409.

[4] Lenin, speech to the 10th CPSU Congress, March 15, 1921; *Sochinenia,* IV ed., Moscow, 1952, Vol. XXXII, pp. 192–93.

state the usual taxes, direct or indirect; it also *overpays* — in the relatively high prices for manufactured goods . . . in the first place, and it is more or less *underpaid* in the prices for agricultural produce —. . . in the second place. This is an additional tax levied on the peasantry for the sake of promoting industry, which caters to the whole country, the peasantry included. It is something in the nature of a "tribute," of a supertax, which we are compelled to levy for the time being in order to preserve and accelerate our present rate of industrial development . . . to raise further the well-being of the village and then to abolish altogether this additional tax, these "scissors" between town and country.[5]

It is worth noting that Stalin's avowed intention of eventually abolishing the supertax was never acted upon in his lifetime; it remained a pious wish for the record, fulfilled only recently and only partially by the successor regime.

The Onset of Collectivization

The squeeze put on the peasants naturally met with resistance. The government forced a showdown by launching the brutal campaign against the *kulaks* and then initiating the collectivization of agriculture. Thus in the process of trying to find a short-run remedy for economic ills, the regime created a new institutional set-up for agriculture — one which from an administrative point of view solved both of its major problems, by curtailing the peasants' home consumption and procuring the required surplus at terms dictated by and favorable to the state.

Collectivization did have other important effects and purposes: the political scientist, for example, is apt to see as its main aim the tightening of control over the peasantry; the sociologist analyzes it as the preparatory stage for increased social mobility and occupational shifts from agriculture to industry, while a student of legal institutions is most interested in it as a form of land-holding. But the economist's viewpoint on collectivization comes closest to its primary purpose — the acquisition of a larger part of agricultural output at a low monopsonist price, thereby decreasing the costs borne by the state in the industrialization

process. In the implementation of the program, the chief criterion of success became the effectiveness of techniques for siphoning off the volume of output desired by the state.

The policy-makers also hoped that a change in the attitude of the peasants toward their labor, to result from the Marxian mechanics of a changing relationship between the base and the superstructure, would accompany the reorganization — in short, that the "diabolical" side of the peasant nature would disintegrate. This doctrinal supposition was combined with a strong conviction that higher efficiency in farming could be achieved more rapidly through forced collectivization than through the gradual process of eliminating marginal producers. That the institutional revamping of the farm unit would create both an optimum size, with economies of scale, and attitudes favorable to the interest of society as a whole, was a prevailing belief among many planners. Where they were mistaken is that such processes do not take place automatically, and that the impact of a particular organizational form on agricultural output itself is only incidental. In short, to collect taxes in kind efficiently and to compel or induce peasants to work harder to increase production are two entirely different tasks.

With regard to the latter, the brutal methods used to enforce the collective form of agriculture in fact produced just the opposite effect to that desired. Being motivated in part by political considerations, the regime frequently disregarded the economic rationale altogether. In the preliminary campaign to liquidate the *kulaks*, for example, it set up ostensibly economic criteria of property and income for the purpose of classifying peasant households, yet these criteria were kept vague enough to allow discrimination on political grounds when deemed expedient or necessary.[6] Unable to muster sufficient support in the rural milieu, the party simply sent thousands of its trusted urban followers to the villages to act as its agents in carrying out its policy. These agents

---

[5] I. V. Stalin, *Works*, Foreign Languages Publishing House, Moscow, 1954, Vol. XI, p. 167.

[6] For details see party and government decrees of Feb. 20 and May 21, 1929, in *Kollektivizatsia Selskovo Khoziaistva* (The Collectivization of Agriculture), USSR Academy of Sciences, Moscow, 1957, pp. 127–30, 163–64. Also Merle Fainsod, *Smolensk Under Soviet Rule*, Harvard University Press, Cambridge, Mass., 1958, pp. 238–51.

operated through the political departments of the Machine Tractor Stations; as vigilant political overseers, they were charged with the function of crushing not only actual but potential resistance — in effect, a *carte blanche* for the enormous brutalities which ensued. The peasants' reaction to these tactics was to destroy, in Samsonian fashion, the most readily destructible production assets — the livestock — during the years 1930–32. The longer-range effect of regime policies was a drastic decline in agricultural output — in fact, the precollectivization level was not reached again until about 1955.

Throughout the 1930's and 1940's the Stalin regime continued in a silent wrangle with the peasantry, mainly over their relative share in total agricultural output. The fact that the peasants resorted to passive forms of resistance, defying the spirit of the law rather than the law itself, has been erroneously interpreted in some quarters as an indication that the regime made solid inroads toward their "conversion." Yet the peasants never gave up their tacit efforts to enlarge their private garden-plots at the expense of collective farmland (leading twice — in 1939 and again in 1946 — to government decrees to reduce the size of peasant landholdings).[7] The same tenacious resistance was apparent in the "battle for the cow" — the peasants' stubborn effort to keep hold of their farm animals, in many cases a single cow, despite an enormous burden of taxation placed upon privately-owned livestock.[8]

Stalinist policy persisted in its orientation, inherited from the 1920's toward concern with distributing agricultural output rather than with devising means to increase production. As earlier, it was the size of the procurement and the efficiency of the collection apparatus which occupied most of the attention of the planners and the government bureaucracy, rather than the size of output or measures to increase it. In fact, the dictatorship kept investment in agriculture to a minimum, while at the same time imposing a standard of living on both the peasants and the urban workers below the precollectivization level.[9]

Several factors (aside from the existence of a coercive apparatus) contributed to the regime's ability to pursue its course of economic expansion without promoting any growth of agriculture. The transfer of labor from agriculture to industry, while decreasing the food requirements of the countryside, also facilitated the maintenance of urban consumption at a level to which the transplanted former peasants were accustomed. Drawing millions of women into the labor force, thus converting them from consumers into producers, in a real sense resulted in an increase of the national product without any appreciable increase in food consumption. The gradual rise in the educational level and in labor productivity also played an important role in sustaining industrial growth without a corresponding growth in agriculture. Finally, the planners were greatly "aided" by the very slow rate of population growth during the 1930's and then the grave loss of life during World War II, easing the pressures of population against the available food supply.

That such a situation could not continue indefinitely was clear, however, even to the most naive observers of the Soviet scene. The state of stagnation in agriculture toward the last years of Stalin's rule caused it to come "into conflict with the productive forces of the society," to borrow a familiar phrase from the Marxist lexicon: from being an asset in the process of economic growth, it became a definite liability. In strictly economic terms, it was unable to meet either the increasing demand for agricultural raw materials for industry or the demand for food on the part of a population which was again on the increase and could make its demands more vocal. The need for a change in agricultural policies — not to mention other spheres of Soviet life — was only too obvious. Yet Stalin was unwilling or con-

---

[7] See party-government decrees of May 27, 1939, and Sept. 19, 1946, in *Direktivy KPSS i Sovietskovo Pravitelstva po Khoziaistvennym Voprosam* (Party and State Directives on Agriculture), Gospolitizdat, Moscow, 1957–58, Vol. II, pp. 589–94, Vol. III, pp. 91–97.

[8] For a discussion of peasant resistance, see Naum Jasny, *The Socialized Agriculture of the USSR*, Stanford University Press, Stanford, Cal., 1949, pp. 363–88. Among Soviet publications which are illuminating in this respect, see the various editions of *Vazhnieishie Reshenia po Selskomu Khoziaistvu* (Most Important Decisions on Agriculture).

[9] For details see D. Gale Johnson and Arcadius Kahan, "Soviet Agriculture, Structure and Growth," *Comparisons of the United States and Soviet Economies*, Joint Economic Committee, U.S. Congress, Washington, D.C., 1959, Part I, pp. 209–10.

stitutionally unable to cope at this point in his life with problems requiring a deviation from the established pattern. It fell to his successors to meet these problems and to introduce changes which, although affecting all aspects of the national life, have had a particularly pronounced effect upon Soviet agriculture.

The Social Bases of Post-Stalin Policy

There is need for caution in defining the areas and scope of post-Stalin changes. Observers generally agree that there has been no basic shift in the priority scale of the Soviet economic planners, nor any far-reaching democratization of the political decision-making process. Where then has the change occurred? Answering this question requires a deviation from the major topic here to discuss briefly the existing relationships between the party and the rest of society in the Soviet Union.

Traditionally, the party has required from the Soviet citizen (1) acknowledgment of the supremacy of party judgment over individual judgment; (2) identification of party policies with such advantages as derive from the system; (3) dissociation of negative features of the society from party policies, and their attribution instead to imperfect execution by individuals or to outside factors; (4) acceptance of the basic doctrinal assumptions on which Soviet society and the political system are based; (5) readiness to execute party orders regardless of the effect upon individual welfare. Popular acquiescence in these requirements — doubly insured by the existence of the secret police — was taken for granted during the Stalin period, yet there is no doubt that resistance to them was on the increase. The basic change in the post-Stalin leadership's approach has been an awareness that submission on the part of the populace could not be assumed matter-of-factly and that something had to be done in order to create favorable attitudes toward the party. Two of the party's requirements seem to have come under particular question from a fairly large and influential stratum of the citizenry — namely, acceptance of the excessive and arbitrary terrorism of the political system, and obedience to party orders regardless of personal welfare. Only in the light of this changed popular attitude can one properly interpret the post-Stalin demotion of the secret police, Khru-

shchev's famous speech to the 20th CPSU Congress (shifting the blame for oppression from the party as such to Stalin personally), and the regime's various moves to appeal to the citizen's self-interest.

The changes in popular attitude were probably the inevitable result of the changes which had occurred in Soviet society. The Soviet industrialization period was marked by a build-up not only of physical capital but of human capital, possessing particular qualities. Of utmost importance in this process was the acceleration of upward mobility, encouraging traits of leadership. During this period there were two major channels of upward mobility. One — the rise through party ranks — emphasized loyalty, acceptance of discipline, and organizational ability as the tests of performance, qualities essential in a totalitarian system of administration and control. The other — the rise through professional (mainly technological) ranks — required education and special technical competence in the fields related to the urgent problems of the economy. Both channels have provided Soviet society with a steady stream of trained leadership, but one which, with the passage of time, has changed in quality and in the demands it makes.

The generation born and raised under the Soviet regime has taken for granted the existing channels of social mobility and has utilized them to the best of its abilities. While some of its forebears may have viewed the state or party in an aureate glow as their liberator from capitalist slavery, the newer generation tends much more to expect a relationship of give and take, "do ut des," with the regime, such as the relationship that exists between a seller and buyer of services. Any excessive "monopsonistic" tendencies on the part of the buyer are bound to be resented. It seems apparent that this fundamental change in attitude toward the party and state was sensed by Khrushchev and his associates — something which the old Stalinist guard was unable or unwilling to accept. The policies which in recent years have led to such trends as higher income for the farmers, increased social services for the workers, decreases in wage differentials and the like, by no means imply that Khrushchev feels greater concern for the welfare of Soviet subjects than did, say, a Molotov or a Kaganovich, but only that he is less inhibited in recognizing that the real Soviet "man in the street" is far removed from the former model of what a Soviet man ought to be.

The new course has made the Communist Party more competitively oriented with respect to other channels of upward mobility, forcing it to focus attention on ways either of attracting new leadership to itself or of controlling the alternative channels more effectively, yet without resort to former coercive methods. Toward the end of safeguarding its supremacy — without endangering the efficient operation of the economic system — the party has placed increasing emphasis on controls located closer to the local scene. The creation of the *Sovnarkhozi* (regional Councils of the National Economy), organized under a system of effective political checks, as well as the strengthening of the command position of area party secretaries, have reflected this tendency.

The trend of Khrushchev's policies has given rise to two basic questions: How far is the present party leadership willing (or able) to go in meeting the people's demands? Is there a possibility of retreat to formerly held positions? The total evidence of regime attitudes seems to suggest that it will yield only to the extent necessary to maintain the stabilty of the system and a sense of personal security among the citizenry. It will stop short of any real political concessions, and it will not change the basic priorities established for economic development. Political freedom and consumers' choice in the broadest sense are still incompatible with the Soviet system. On the other hand, though a retreat to Stalinist positions would probably be feasible under conditions of dictatorship, it is very unlikely that the regime would resort to such a course except in a dire situation of international or domestic unrest.

Against this background, let us turn to the changes of attitude on the part of the present policy-makers toward agriculture and the peasants.

Incentives and Organizational Reforms

Without question, the most important policy shift has been the regime's emphasis on the need for a substantial increase in agricultural output and its professed willingness to direct new resources toward the achievement of this goal. For the first time since collectivization was instituted, Soviet policy-makers have taken stock of their agricultural resources, openly admitted their failures, and initiated a series of measures to rescue agriculture from the dead end in which Stalin had left it.

As a preliminary step, the policy-makers showed a long overdue realization of the importance of the human element in the success or failure of any economic program or policy. Recognition of this factor — virtually ignored since the early industrialization period — led, among other early moves of the regime, to the granting of major price increases for agricultural products (since raised further, though now, under consideration for downward revision as we shall see). By raising incomes of the collective farms, the Soviet government provided the means both for a higher volume of capital investment and for a rise in individual peasant incomes, obviously designed as an incentive to raise productivity.[10]

The regime's next step was to provide a proving ground for the "new look" in agriculture which would catch the imagination of the country as a whole — the result was the campaign for the development of the so-called "new lands," glamorized as a pioneering effort on virgin soil. There were of course practical considerations involved in this project: it was hoped that the plowing up of over 30 million hectares to create a new grain region in Kazakhstan and Siberia would augment the total food and feed supply, while mitigating the fluctuations in output caused by the periodic droughts in the principal existing grain regions. These potential gains apparently outweighed considerations of the complex technical problems and risks involved in bringing vast semi-arid areas under cultivation. What the long-range outcome of this program will be is as yet difficult to tell.

Both in the "new lands" project and in agriculture generally, one of the most interesting facets of post-Stalin policy has been the regime's attitude with regard to the optimal size of farm units and to the relative advantages of state-farm as against collective-farm organization.

Soviet agricultural experts and planners have taken various positions at various times with respect to the optimal size of farms. The notion

---

[10] See *Tsentralnoe Statisticheskoe Upravlenie SSSR: Narodnoe Khoziaistvo SSSR v 1958 godu* (Central Statistical Administration of the USSR: Soviet Agriculture in 1958), Moscow, 1959, p. 367.

that economies of scale could be achieved almost indefinitely by increasing the size of
farms was very popular at the beginning of
collectivization, but was later discarded in the
face of mounting deficits and inefficiencies on
the gigantic state farms that had been created.
Nonetheless the idea again took hold after
World War II, leading to an amalgamation of
the collective farms in 1950 which reduced
their number by two-thirds and increased the
size of individual units correspondingly.

The post-Stalin period has seen a definite
trend toward the further amalgamation of the
collectives and, since 1957, toward the conversion of collective farms into state farms.
These moves have been accompanied by much
debate and a series of inquiries into the most
efficient size of farms in specific regions and
into the relative costs of output in the collective
and state-owned units. In the "new lands"
project, the planners have put heavy preferential stress on the formation of state farms of
huge acreage, on the basis that they would be
easier to administer and would show greater
labor productivity, particularly in view of the
need for the large-scale use of machinery on
the flat-lands.[11] The recent conversion of collectives into state farms in other areas is explained by the regime as a move to help out
poorer farms which were unable to effect improvements on their own, despite the increased
prices decreed for agricultural products. In
such cases it is probable that the farmers indeed preferred the guaranteed money wage of
state-farm workers (while retaining their own
livestock and a part of their garden plot) to
eking out a meager income from inferior farms.

With regard to the amalgamation of collectives, a main argument put forward in its favor
has been the possibility of a more efficient
utilization of skilled managers and agricultural
experts, who prior to 1950 were spread sparsely
over many farms. It has also been predicted
that amalgamation would result in decreased
administrative expenditures, though there is
little indication to date that such economies
have been achieved.

Income and Investment Policies

The continued emphasis on amalgamation
has been accompanied by a new focussing of
attention on the deficient quality and low
productivity of the agricultural labor force. As
noted, it has been recognized that the relative
scarcity of capital in conjunction with the relative abundance of agricultural labor (causing
the more ambitious or semi-skilled workers to
be attracted to better-paid industrial work)
have been major factors in preventing the rise
of productivity. Accordingly, in the process of
amalgamation attempts have been made to
keep the more skilled farmers and tractor
drivers on the farms through increasing their
incomes and through other incentives. At the
same time the regime has applied pressure and
devised special inducements to supply agriculture with skilled manpower from the urban
areas. Moreover, there has been a rapid increase in the quantity and quality of machinery
made available to agriculture, paralleled by
the transfer of existing machinery from the
Machine Tractor Stations to the collective farms
themselves.

The rise in the prices for agricultural commodities paid by the state to the farms has
resulted in a rapid increase in the farms' money
receipts.[12] A part of this increment has been
paid out to the collective farm members, and
attempts are now being made to recompense
them more frequently, in the form of advance
payments on a quarterly or monthly basis, with
some guarantee of a minimum income. One of
the results of this incentive policy has been an
increase in the number of days the farmers
have worked on the collective land. Incentives
— including price differentials — have also
been used to supplement administrative measures in the regime's efforts to introduce changes
in the output mix.

Out of the greater money income of the collectives, the farm administrations are ordered
to reserve a share for investment, the proportion of which has been raised in recent years
— though there are signs the government has
had to apply pressure on this score to counter

---

[11] For relevant data, see *ibid.*, pp. 518–9. The total
number of state farms in the U.S.S.R. has increased
during 1953–58 from 4,857 to 6,002, with an increase in sown area from 15.1 to 52.4 million
hectares.

[12] Major price increases were announced in September 1953 (see *Pravda*, Sept. 26, 29), February
1956 (*ibid.*, Feb. 2), and July 1958 (*ibid.*, July 1).

the peasants' desire for more labor payments. The demand for increased investment funds was attributed to the transfer of farm machinery to the collectives' charge, necessitating expenditures for repair, maintenance, and new equipment, as well as to the need for funds for a massive program of farm-building construction. The present seven-year plan envisages a further broadening of the scope of such investments.

In addition to their direct investment in physical plant and equipment, the collective farms have been charged since 1955 with the responsibility for investment in what is termed social overhead and services — the expenditures necessary for building and maintaining rural roads, providing small power plants, constructing schools and other cultural facilities, setting up bakeries, laundries, etc. The regime was probably correct in assuming that these forms of expenditure would meet with the approval of the rural population, however grudging. While the peasants are anxious for a larger share of farm income, these investment demands must seem preferable to the previous regime's indirect discriminatory taxation of agricultural producers based on vague promises of services which generally were not forthcoming.

It is difficult to measure the precise economic effect of any of the various policies outlined above — indeed, any effort to do so would be the subject of an entire paper in itself. It seems clear, however, that the collective impact of these policies has been responsible in large part for the significant increases in agricultural production and labor productivity in recent years.

Social Aims of the Agricultural Course

Turning from the economic and technical aspects of recent policy to the broader issue of the present leadership's socio-political attitudes toward the peasants, it is possible to distinguish three trends of importance: the first is the party's tighter control over the execution of its agricultural program; the second, already touched upon, is the move toward a further socialization of agriculture; the third is the attempt to raise the social status of the peasantry, conditioned upon the success of the first two objectives.

One of the major weaknesses of the party throughout its history has been its comparatively small membership in the rural areas. At the farm level, the collective chairman and possibly a few lesser administrators have been the only party members — and it is difficult to tell whether their party membership led to their farm positions or vice versa. This situation was caused by the old regime's preference for controlling agriculture through a hierarchical line of command from above. An elaborate system of party as well as government supervision was established, operating through various channels and institutions. The cumbersome functioning of this control apparatus was resented both because of its alien nature — i.e., its imposition of orders from without — and because its bureaucratic actions were often detrimental to the interests of efficiency on a particular farm.

By contrast, the present tightening of party control has had the effect of moving the center of authority closer to the farms. The new collective amalgamations, the influx of agricultural specialists and former MTS personnel (often party members) into the farm organizations, along with a drive for new party recruits in rural areas, have made it possible to organize regular party cells on most collective and state farms. The consequent opportunity to exercise control from within, and to present the party to the mass of peasants as a local rather than an alien force, has undoubtedly increased the party's influence over the behavior of the farm population. The existence of local party cells may well lead to the increased autonomy of the collectives with respect to minor internal decisions, but will also insure that major decisions are carried out in accordance with party recommendations.

An interesting indication of the party's emphasis on control at the local level — and with this condition met, its positive preference for preserving an atomized society — was provided by a recent debate during the December 1959 Plenum of the party's Central Committee. The subject of the debate was the desirability of establishing an inter-collective organization to help implement investment and construction projects involving more than one farm, particularly to represent the farms in dealings with construction agencies and other industrial branches. Although many of the speakers recommended an all-union organization of the collectives for these purposes, the final resolution — which must be presumed to have reflected the high authorities' wishes — called for organizing the farms at the county or district level. Inevitably one is reminded of the difficulties the Soviet government had in controlling the *"Kolkhoz-Tsentr"* of the late 1920's, a similar organization of the collectives which became a forum for the expression of "nonconformist" ideas against regime policies. It would seem that the party policy-makers of 1959 are mindful of this experience, and entirely unwilling to take the chance that history might repeat itself.

The March Toward Socialization

With regard to the second trend specified above, the fact that policies aimed at the further socialization of agriculture — meaning in effect a further "proletarianization" of the peasantry — were being tried out could be surmised from the following tendencies: (1) the decline of payments in kind and the increased use of money payments for the collective farmers' labor; (2) the decrease in the size of the private garden plots left to the peasantry, and in certain places their elimination; (3) the further conversion of a number of collectives into state farms. Some of the economic problems involved in these policies were discussed earlier, but their non-economic aspects are just as interesting. The trend of regime thinking is reflected in two frequently repeated slogans. The first declares that the differences between the collective and state forms of ownership are diminishing. By implication, the basis for this claim is that collective farmers are being transformed into money-wage earners and that a part of the collective's profits is being appropriated directly to tasks of a social nature, i.e., beyond the interests of a single farm.

The second slogan proclaims the disappearance of differences between town and country; the implication here is that there will be a further equalization of industrial and agricultural income, along with an increase of social services and cultural facilities (still largely restricted to urban areas) in the countryside. There is no doubt that certain policies of the regime have been directed up to now toward narrowing the differential between urban and farm income, but the gap is still very substantial. The effort represents only the dimmest hint of a start toward Khrushchev's long-professed dreams of establishing "agro-cities," his descriptions of which have raised up the vision of a modernized countryside people by educated, skilled and prosperous agricultural workers participating as equals in a smoothly-functioning utopia.

It is absolutely clear — even to the most optimistic Soviet planner — that many years will have to elapse and a very large volume of investment will have to be committed before Khrushchev's version of Fourier's "phalansteries" becomes reality. The question to be asked, then, is why Soviet politicians are talking in terms which imply that this town–country equalization is just around the corner. One explanation is that they really believe in equalization as an ultimate goal of social policy, and that they want to enlist the peasants' aid by presenting them with a dream world, the achievement of which will depend on hard work, the sacrifice of certain tangible assets for the present, and above all faith in the guidance of the party and the state. Another explanation — which may supplement rather than exclude the first — is that the regime is attempting to condition the peasants to "proletarianization" and to make its consequences more acceptable to them by visions of future rewards.

Yet at the same time — in virtual contradiction of the talk that has gone on — there have been signs of late that the start toward town-and-country equalization may be slowed down. The most crucial indication in this respect has been the paving of the way for a cut in the commodity prices paid to agricultural producers, thus reversing the trend of previous policy. Ironically, the "demand" for such a cut has been put forward by agricultural planners and executives who claim to be expressing the wishes and speaking in the name of the peasants. It is clear, of course, that the regime has instigated such talk, with an eye to immediate needs or gains and in neglect of whatever long-run plans may exist. To understand such an inconsistent and contradictory measure — as well as the tactics by which it was initiated — one must take into account the deep-rooted paternalistic attitude of the Soviet leaders toward the peasantry, their conviction that superior knowledge is a monopoly of the party and that the peasant is deficient in outlook and judgment. Changes such as the price-cut must be introduced from above, but the peasants must be cajoled along by subterfuge, by the sham impression that their opinions and "endorsement" have been taken into consideration. This paternalism, which Khrushchev apparently believes should be constantly exhibited (Stalin did not think it necessary) is in a sense the substitute for the individual freedom which is denied the peasants and indeed the whole population.

Peasant Viewpoints

In considering the peasants' attitude toward regime policies for further socialization, one is forced to cross over the boundary from facts to educated guesses. It is probably correct to assume that the idea of a return to private ownership has much less psychological appeal for the new generation on the collective farms than for its predecessor. For many of the new generation, farm work has become simply a matter of employment opportunities and income needs, rather than a preference for what used to be a "way of life." The peasants' garden plots and private cows undoubtedly still have symbolic meaning for them as the last bastion of proprietorship, but their deep attachment is also rooted in hard economic fact, since the plot is a dependable source of income in contrast to the uncertain and inadequate supply of money or income in kind from the collective farms. Not before the peasants' share in the product of their labor ceases to constitute a residual will they change their suspicious attitude toward the benefits bestowed upon them by the state. To state this in positive form, a change in their attitude will require substantial acts on the part of the regime to provide them with what they consider a fair return for their toil.

Another element in the peasants' attitude toward the state is their deep-rooted resentment over the long-professed supremacy of industrial workers in Soviet society. The innate superiority of the industrial working class over other classes of the population is a cornerstone of Bolshevik ideology — witness the basic concept of the "dictatorship of the proletariat." Until recently the distinction between the industrial worker and the peasant was often emphasized in the regime's dealings with the peasants, and in fact provided the Soviet leaders with a self-made justification for many of their policies.

A consistent policy committed to raising both the income and the social status of the agricultural population might, with time, mollify much of the existing resentment of the peasants. The rise in the status of a particular group depends much more upon government policy in the Soviet Union than in other countries, so the choice in this respect is really up to the regime — and there are signs that a change of approach is under consideration. Whereas in the past, a peasant desiring higher social status had to join the urban working force and work his way up through the ranks of industry (or, of course, rise through the party), there are now a number of indications that greater social prestige may be accorded to the upper layers of the agricultural labor force, eliminating the intermediate step of urbanization.

*   *   *   *   *

The present paper has only scratched the surface in its attempt to review the new features of Soviet agricultural policy and to compare them with former attitudes and policies. A few basic observations should perhaps be summarized. The underlying assumption here has been that post-Stalin policies make sense primarily in terms of the evolutionary social changes going on in Soviet society, changes to which the Soviet state and party, as well as the peasants themselves, are seeking to adjust. In this process the relationship between the state and the agricultural sector of the population has increasingly exhibited elements of rationality, although both sides are showing caution with respect to firm policy commitments or behavior.

If, however, the regime persists in its present course, the likelihood certainly exists that some of its policies will have a socially desirable effect upon the way of life of the peasantry. It is even possible that this course will tend to transform peasant attitudes toward the regime over a long period. To say this is not to imply by any means that the peasants could become a zealous and enthusiastic "proletariat" of the countryside. However much the regime might improve the peasants' economic lot, it will continue to deny them other rights. It would be degrading to the Russian tradition of *zemlia i volia* (land and freedom) to accept the view that the desire for material well-being could permanently displace the desire for personal freedom — though how, when, or whether the urge for greater freedom will be able to assert itself in Soviet society are questions for a distant future.

37

How to Beat the System*

from Pravda

(1958)

The peasant undoubtedly received by far the poorest share of the meager living which the Soviet regime allowed its citizens on the forced march to industrialization. In addition, the great majority of peasants felt that the collectivization of agriculture had dispossessed them of what was rightfully theirs. They learned to make ends meet by helping themselves. This tale from the distant reaches of Kazakhstan illustrates how it is done, although it does not explain why it happens so regularly.

Ust-Kamenogorsk, Kazakh Republic — The expanses of Zaisan District are vast — 2,000,000 hectares, and that's no trifling matter. It represents almost a third of East Kazakhstan Province. . . .

The lambs bleat gaily and the rams toss their horns with an air of importance. They seem to take pride in their weight and fatness

* Reprinted from "Wolves and Sheep," (feuilleton), D. Vasilyev and F. Bogatyrev, *Pravda* (Aug. 22, 1958), p. 3, translated in condensed form in *Current Digest of the Soviet Press*, Vol. 10, No. 34, pp. 28–29, published at Columbia University by the Joint Committee on Slavic Studies appointed by the American Council of Learned Societies and the Social Science Research Council. Used by permission of the publisher.

and in the good life that is theirs in these parts. . . .

But there is one thing wrong, and that is the gray wolf, the perennial enemy, crafty and wicked, of the gentle lambs and sheep. . . .

The number of these gray predators in Zaisan District has increased enormously. They have made life impossible. At first they were content with an occasional young sheep. Then they started massacring sheep by the dozen. Things have finally reached a point where hundreds of sheep are falling prey to the predators.

Energetic people have taken all kinds of steps to get rid of the gray marauders. They have set out traps and poisoned bait, they have organized hunts, they have even carried out searches for the animals by plane. Where do the wolves hide out? No one has been able to discover; it has remained a mystery. Not a trace of them is found. Invisible wolves! And yet the losses they cause are visible to everyone.

"What happened to ten of our sheep?" the state farm director asks sternly.

"The wolves ate them. The damned animals give us no peace," the shepherd replies.

The director is angry. "You're to blame! You didn't keep an eye on them."

"I am indeed to blame," the culprit readily agrees.

"That means you'll have to pay; the state mustn't suffer," the director announces firmly.

"You're absolutely right. I will pay," the shepherd acquiesces with astonishing willingness.

"And remember, you'll pay at least three times the market price for each sheep," the director warns firmly.

"Oh, you're such a big wheel and you don't even know the law! Dig around in your papers and you'll find instructions on how they're to be paid for. The law is the law. You'll get what it says you'll get!"

The director searches through his files. In one folder he comes across Advisory No. 18–299, dated June 2, 1954, from the central bookkeeping office of the U.S.S.R. Ministry of State Farms. The Ministry of State Farms has long ceased to exist, but the instructions remain in force to this day. They read:

"In claims against persons responsible for

the death of animals, claims will be assessed in the amount of one times the value of the animal . . . at procurement prices. . . ."

The director is astonished. This is strange; if a library book or even a cloakroom tag is lost, the loser is always assessed three times its value. Few people, therefore, are anxious to lose such items. But here? The procurement price is less than the market price, and — as we know from the four rules of arithmetic — one times the procurement price is always equal to one-third of three times the procurement price.

"Oh, well," the director sighs, gazing sadly at the beaming culprit, "pay according to the instructions, then. The average weight of a sheep is 50 kg., so it will come to —"

"But perhaps the sheep have grown thin during the summer. After all, a wolf couldn't carry off a big sheep! He isn't strong enough. Why not ask other state farms how they figure the weight of lost sheep?"

So the director gets on the phone. Abrakhman Belgibayev, Director of the Karatal State Sheep Farm, informs him that his farm is short more than 3,000 sheep, 600 of them breeding ewes. The loss amounts to 260,000 rubles. Sector No. 2 alone lost 36 sheep in a single month. And the average weight of the sheep is listed in the statement as 14 kg.! Never before have such Lilliputian sheep been seen in Kazakhstan!

The Buranovo State Farm "lost" 675 sheep during the drive to the Semipalatinsk Meat Combine. But the tender-hearted director, Aitmukhamed Askarov, wrote them off at prices of 80 to 120 rubles a head. . . .

Sheep also disappear at the Kenderlyk, Akzhar, and Chilik State Farms.

Quite a number of mutton lovers in wolves' clothing have appeared in the district.

They love fresh mutton, but they have refined tastes. They consume sheep only in the form of beshbarmak, plov, or shashlik. They destroy thousands of sheep without shame or conscience.

These mutton lovers operate under the protection of the obsolete ministry instructions. And they enjoy the full patronage of A. I. Izachik, director of the province agriculture administration, who observes the destruction of livestock with indifference. . . .

MANAGEMENT, LABOR, AND THE CONSUMER

38

The Situation of Plant Managers*

Joseph S. Berliner

(1959)

In an industrial society, particularly one like the Soviet Union, which is totally mobilized to attain high goals of economic development, the individual's role in production often becomes the most important fact about his life. We have therefore given substantial attention to the special situation of management and labor in Soviet industry and agriculture. Dr. Berliner draws not only on Soviet sources but on his unique experience in interviewing former Soviet managers to sketch a portrait of the rewards, the aspirations, and the problems of Soviet management. Many people feel that this yields a picture not too unlike that of management in the United States, and Professor Berliner explores the relevant comparisons and contrasts.

I. Managerial Incentives and Recruitment

The most important decision a manager has to make is made before he ever becomes a manager; namely, the decision to prepare for a managerial career. The factors influencing

* Reprinted from "Managerial Incentives and Decision-Making: A Comparison of the United States and the Soviet Union," *Comparisons of the United States and Soviet Economies,* Part I (1959), pp. 349–376, paper submitted to the Subcommittee on Economic Statistics of the Joint Economic Committee, Eighty-sixth Congress, First Session, Washington, D.C., by permission of the author.

this decision are of vital importance for our industrial society. Imagine the consequences if no one aspired to become a manager, or if young people chose management only as a last resort, or if other careers were so attractive that management got only the last pickings of each year's crop of youngsters. It might therefore be appropriate to begin with some reflections on the incentives that the United States and the U.S.S.R. offer their young people to choose a managerial career rather than some other.

The factors motivating young people to choose one or another occupation are probably not vastly different in the two countries. Family tradition is often decisive; many a youngster chooses a career simply because he wishes to be like his father (or mother). Special talents such as those of the artist, or early-conceived deep interests, like the boy who *must* be a scientist, account for the career choices of some others. But most teen-agers have no clear idea of what they would like to be. It is with respect to these youths that it is most interesting to speculate upon the incentive-pulls that the two systems offer for the choice of one career or another.

Education and Career Choice

The role of higher education in career choice is different in the two nations. Higher education is very much more of a prerequisite for the prestigeful and high income occupations in the U.S.S.R. than in the United States. To be sure, the person with a high school education or less has an increasingly difficult time entering the managerial ladder of the large American corporation. But in such fields as trade, commerce, construction, and in small business in general, the opportunities are still vast for a financially successful career. College, and education in general, is not of decisive importance. And the brute fact is that a college diploma can always be obtained somewhere in the United States, with very little effort or ability, by just about anyone who can pay the tuition and write a semi-literate paragraph. Those who don't aspire to a managerial position or who fail to make the grade can, as workingmen, nevertheless enjoy a standard of living that is the envy of the world. The point is that the young American

who is not inclined toward academic work need not feel that he is out of the competition for our society's best rewards.

This is not true in the U.S.S.R. A number of conversations with young Soviet people have convinced me that to be "worker" is something devoutly to be shunned by most young people who have reached the high school level. There are at least two reasons for this attitude, which seems to be anomolous in a "worker's state." The first is the enormously high prestige that Russian (and European) culture has always placed upon the "intelligent," the learned man, the man who works with his mind instead of his hands. The Soviet regime has striven hard to make manual labor respectable, and it undoubtedly has succeeded in endowing the worker with a social position relatively much higher than before the revolution. But the young person who has reached the educational level at which he can choose between being a worker or an "intelligent" would, other things being equal, choose the latter without question.

Other things are not equal, however. In particular, the income possibilities of a worker are far smaller than those of a college graduate, and this is the second reason for the desperate, and sometimes pathetic, drive for a higher education. Of course, a person must have reached the high school level before he can even begin to think about choosing between the career of a worker or an "intelligent." The steady annual expansion in the high school population has had the effect of presenting ever increasing numbers of young people with the choice, and few of them would freely choose to be workers. If the expansion of the school population had continued, giving more and more young people the opportunity to avoid being workers, it would have raised serious problems for the recruitment of the labor force. The radical reform of the educational system by Khrushchev was undoubtedly motivated, in part, by the wish to avoid that problem.

Thus, the undesirability of a career as a worker has intensified the desire for higher education. Add to this the fact that there is no private enterprise, no small business, in which a man could pull himself out of a worker's status and reach a position of prestige and income comparable to the self-made American businessman. I do not wish to state that the door is completely closed. By dint of hard work, ability, and certain other qualities, a Soviet citizen without the college diploma can from time to time rise to an important position in some economic hierarchy. But his chances are about as good as those of an equivalent person in a progressive American corporation. And the young person evaluating the importance of higher education understands this.

Finally, the Russian teen-ager who decides he has got to get a college diploma has very few easy ways out. He can't buy his way into college, as the American student can if he has the money. There are no private colleges that can set whatever standards they wish. To be sure, there are instances of bribery or influence, but they are certainly the exception. If the Soviet student wants a college diploma very badly, he has got to work hard to gain admission and to be graduated. The very intensity of the drive for education and the competition of many applicants for the limited number of admissions permit the high schools and colleges to maintain high standards of performance. Moreover the colleges are financially independent of student tuitions: not only are there no tuitions but most of the students earn stipends. The consequence is that the typical Soviet student works harder and has to meet higher standards of performance than the typical American student. The standards are different in the two countries, of course, because of differences in the philosophy of education. But there is no doubt that study is a much more serious business for the young Soviet student than for the American.

One final note on education and incentives. The quality of the managerial (and technical) manpower of a nation depends on the proportion of the population comprising the pool from which the managers are drawn. That is, if half the population were for some reason excluded from the pool, the quality of the managers would be lower than if the whole population comprised the pool. Both nations suffer in this respect from the fact that rural educational facilities are poorer than urban, which reduces the pool of the potential college group. Since the Soviet rural population is larger percentage-wise than that of the United States, and since their rural educational

facilities are probably relatively worse than ours, they suffer more than we from this loss. But there are other ways in which our pool is curtailed more than the Soviet. First is the fact that the private cost of education keeps a substantial portion of our talented young people in the lower income groups out of college. I admit that this fact puzzles me. With our network of free State Universities and with a fairly abundant scholarship program, I don't fully understand why any competent student who really desired it could not get a college education. It is my impression, however, that systematic studies generally show that we are losing an unfortunate number of young people to higher education for financial reasons. If this is so, we are worse off than the Soviets in this respect, for their education is absolutely free, and most students of any merit earn stipends besides. Lower-income young Soviet people may nevertheless be unable to go off to college if the family needs their earnings. A young Soviet woman told me, in reply to my question, that this was why she never went on to college. She is not a very good illustration of my point, however, for she went on to say that she really wasn't very smart anyhow.

The second group that is largely lost from America's pool of potential managerial manpower is the Negro and some other racial minorities. It may well be that the proportion of college graduates among some of the Soviet national minorities is smaller than for the Slavic nationalities; I have seen no data on this. But I would doubt that their loss from racial discrimination is as large as ours.

The third and largest group lost from our pool comprises exactly half our population — the female half. Sex discrimination certainly exists in the Soviet economy, probably more in management than in science technology. But undoubtedly the female population enlarges the pool of technical and managerial manpower much more in the U.S.S.R. than in the U.S. The difference in the role of women in the two countries must, I think, enter into the balance I am trying to strike, but it is not a subject on which I would recommend that your Committee consider writing corrective legislation. For one thing it is not perfectly clear which way sex discrimination works in the United States. Women discriminate against working about as much as jobs discriminate against women.

Let me summarize briefly this discussion of the relationship of education to career choice. Education, and particularly higher education, is more important in the U.S.S.R. than in the U.S. as the gateway to a prestigeful and highly remunerative career. Competition is keener for higher education, the cost of education to the individual is less, and the standards of admission and performance are higher in the U.S.S.R. Both nations lose part of the potential pool of managerial talent, the U.S.S.R. because of its large rural population, the U.S. because of financial burdens and racial and sex discrimination. .

Competition Among Careers

How does a managerial career compare with the attractiveness of other careers in the two nations? The young American already not dedicated to some particular field, but motivated by a roughly equal desire for prestige and money, might select some field such as law, medicine, business, or engineering. He would decidedly not go into education or science. An equivalent young Soviet person would make a somewhat different choice. He would certainly not select law, which has been assigned a most humble role in Soviet society. Nor would he select medicine, for while the prestige is high, the income is low. On the other hand, higher education or science would be an excellent choice. The very title of Professor or Scientific Worker would assure him one of the highest places of honor in the society. And an outstanding career in either of those fields would assure him of an income ranking in the upper 10 per cent or perhaps even 5 per cent (data are hard to come by) of the population. The difference in the economic and social position of the scientist and teacher in the two countries is of fundamental importance in the matter of career recruitment.

The American who decides to choose a career in the business world has a much wider range of choice than his Soviet counterpart. A great variety of fields offer roughly equivalent rewards in prestige and incomes: advertising, accounting, finance, commerce, trade, sales, light manufacturing, heavy industry. Of all these fields, it is only the last that would exert

a great pull on the young Soviet person. For forty years the government and Party have hammered home the central role of heavy industry, children are instilled with an admiration of technology, and heavy industry has been endowed with an aura of glamour that exceeds even our American fascination with technology. The ideological cards are stacked, in varying degree, against all other branches of the economy. In keeping with the ideology, the prestige and income possibilities in heavy industry are decidedly greater than in the other branches.

Not only will the student be attracted to heavy industry, but he is likely to choose engineering as his path of entry into whatever branch of heavy industry he selects. He would be attracted to engineering for the educational reasons discussed above. Engineering is, moreover, the most direct line of approach to a managerial career.

The Soviet engineering graduate will find his first job opportunities rather different from those of his American counterpart. If he is at the top of his class, the best offers will come from the research institutes, with top starting salaries and opportunities for graduate work. The poorer students will find lower paying jobs in industry. In the United States the situation is quite the reverse. The most successful students will be snapped up by recruiters from the large corporations, with the best starting salary offers. Some of the top students, will, to be sure, spurn the attractive job offers and go on to further graduate work, but I suspect that many of those who go immediately into graduate work are the men who didn't get the good job offers. To be sure, many of the top American students who join the corporations are put immediately into research and development, but as many of them will be working on new passenger car or dishwasher design as will be working on electronic development and automation technique. The Soviet researcher is more likely to be working on the latter than the former.

The young Soviet engineer who goes into industry starts at the bottom of the managerial ladder, as chief of a production shop, or in the design or maintenance departments of the enterprise. As new job opportunities develop, he faces the choice of continuing in direct production or taking one of the staff jobs in the enterprise, such as the planning department. If he stays in production proper, his career path may lead to chief engineer of an enterprise or to one of the higher economic agencies. If he moves into staff work, his career may lead to the directorship of an enterprise or of one of the higher organs. Either career leads to the pinnacle of Soviet management.

The paths that are least likely to lead to top management are finance or sales. I would guess the proportion of top management in the United States who started in such fields as finance and sales is much larger than in the U.S.S.R. There are no "Colleges of Business Administration" in the Soviet Union. The ambitious youngster who wants to work for the top of the Soviet business world studies engineering, not personnel and marketing.

Summarizing, industry in the United States has to compete with a wide variety of other branches of economic activity for its share of the best potential managerial talent. In the U.S.S.R. the values and the rewards are concentrated in relatively fewer fields, and industry is far more attractive than most others. Science and higher education, which scarcely compete with industry in the United States, are strong competitors of industry in the U.S.S.R. Among the various branches of industry, in the United States the light and consumer goods industries compete very effectively for both managerial and engineering talent. In the U.S.S.R. light and consumer goods industries are much less attractive than heavy industry. And, finally, the nature of industrial recruitment is such that technical education is much more important as part of the training of a would-be manager in the U.S.S.R. than in the United States.

My conclusion is that heavy industry, science, and higher education attract, by and large, a better and more competent crop of young people in the U.S.S.R. than in the United States. Moreover, the competition for education is keener in the U.S.S.R., so that they get a more rigorously trained (trained in different ways, to be sure) corps of managerial, engineering, scientific, and university personnel. On the other hand, such branches of the economy as sales, advertising, finance, trade and commerce, light industry, and law attract a much more competent group of people in the United States than in the U.S.S.R. Most of the outstanding people in these fields in the United States would, if they were Soviet citizens, have enjoyed successful careers in heavy industry, science, technology, or higher education. There is, after all, nothing startling in this conclusion. It is but another way of saying that each society gets what it pays for.

II. *Managerial Incentives and Decision-Making*

Material Incentives

The incentives that attract people into management are not necessarily the same incentives that motivate managers to do their jobs and do them well. What are the goals of managers? What are the considerations that impel him to make one decision rather than the other?

The moving force of our economic system is the pursuit of private gain. The worker chooses the higher paying job, the businessman accepts the more profitable contract, the investor buys the higher interest security. The usual exceptions must of course be made; the laws must be obeyed, public opinion may sometimes require that one decision be made rather than another, people make wrong decisions, a short-run loss may be accepted for a longer-term gain. But by and large — "other things being equal", as the economist likes to say — it is private gain that determines economic decision.

The Soviets have at various times experimented with other forms of incentive, for it did not at first seem quite appropriate that a socialist economy should stress private gain. But practicality won out over dogma, and private gain has for the last twenty-five years been the keystone of the managerial incentive system. To be sure, we still find references to various social incentives such as Communist enthusiasm. But we are also reminded that while enthusiasm is well and good, Communism, as Lenin used to say, must be built "not directly *on* enthusiasm but with the *aid* of enthusiasm born out of the great revolution; [Communism must be built] on private interest, on personal incentive, on business-like accounting."[1] Moreover, the incentive of private gain

---

[1] *Voprosy Ekonomiki*, 1958, No. 6, p. 74.

will be with us for a long time. According to the eminent labor economist E. Manevich, it will not disappear until the day of general overabundance arrives, until the differences between country and city are eliminated, and until the differences between mental and manual labor vanish.[2] We are safe in saying that for the next several decades at least, private gain will be the central economic incentive in both economic systems.

The form that material incentives take is of some importance. For the American businessman it is clearly profit. If you ask why did he take on this contract rather than that, why did he ship by truck rather than train, the answer would normally be, "because it's cheaper that way," or what comes to the same thing, "because he would make more money that way."

For the private businessman managing his own business, profit is clearly the guide to his actions. But most American business is not managed in this way. The men who actually run the firm are salaried managers, hired by the stockholders' representative body, the board of directors. The profit of the business does not belong to the manager but to the stockholder-owners. The fact is that the private interest of the manager need not necessarily coincide with that of the stockholder. In order to bring the manager's private interest into closer coincidence with that of the owners, most corporations have instituted some kind of bonus system, on the assumption that if the manager has a direct stake in the profit of the enterprise, his decisions are more likely to be those that will earn more profit.

In fashioning an incentive system for its managers, the Soviet government faced a problem similar to that of the American corporation. For all Soviet enterprises are run by salaried managers. If the Soviet manager's income consisted solely of his salary, it was conceivable that his private interest would not coincide at all points with the interest of the government. Accordingly a considerable variety of supplementary bonuses are available to the managerial staff. The bonuses are designed to motivate managers to make those

decisions that the government considers to be in its own interest.

The amount of income earned in the form of bonuses is substantial. In 1947, the last year for which detailed data are available to me, the managerial personnel of the iron and steel industry earned bonuses averaging 51.4 per cent of their basic income. In the food industry at the low end, the percentage was 21 per cent.[3] Since these are averages, many individual managers earned considerably more than this. Bonuses of this magnitude must be a potent incentive indeed.

But incentive for what? This is surely the crucial question. For we can readily imagine an incentive which was extremely successful in motivating action, but action of an undesirable kind. The test of an incentive is therefore not only its motivating power, but the extent to which it leads to the desired kind of decision.

Before proceeding to the relationship of incentives to decision-making, let me clarify the sense in which I use the term incentive. By incentive I mean that consideration which explains why one decision was made rather than another. If a young person decides to find employment in the electrical machinery industry rather than in the furniture industry, the difference in basic salaries in the two industries may well have been the decisive consideration. In this case, salary is the effective incentive. But once in the job, the salary does not vary according to whether one operating decision is made rather than another. When the manager decides to put one order into production ahead of another, or to substitute one material for another, it is not his salary he is thinking about. It is usually the size of the month's bonus that will depend on the decision taken. It is in this sense that the bonus is the principal incentive in the operational decisions of the Soviet enterprise.

Production Decisions

Two generations ago people debated the question of whether a socialist economy could

[2] *Voprosy Ekonomiki*, 1959, No. 1, p. 35.

[3] Documentation and further discussion of the argument in this section may be found in the author's *Factory and Manager in the USSR* (Harvard University Press, 1957).

possibly work. History removed that question from the agenda. The last generation changed the question to whether the Soviet economy could work at all efficiently. That question has also been answered. These hearings would not otherwise be taking place. My discussion takes for granted that the Soviet economy is reasonably efficient, and that the question at issue is *how* efficient.

There is little doubt that the system of managerial incentives broadly viewed, has created a corps of managers dedicated to their work and responsive to the production demands made upon them. Like their American counterparts, they are deeply involved in their work, they worry about production quotas, they demand results from their labor force. As hired managers, they are aware that if their performance is not satisfactory, there are always other persons spoiling for a chance at their jobs. I have no way of knowing whether the intensity of managerial life is greater in the U.S.S.R. than in the United States; in both countries there are variations from industry to industry. But there are two reasons why industrial life probably proceeds at a faster tempo in the U.S.S.R. than here. The first is that the absence of free trade unions makes it difficult for workers to resist pressure for intense operation. The second is that industry is under constant exhortation from government and Party for ever increasing levels of production.

But the question as indicated above is not whether management is motivated to work hard. It is rather whether the incentive system motivates them to do what the State wishes them to do; whether, in other words, they get as much mileage out of their effort as they might get.

One of the most interesting conclusions of the study of Soviet managerial incentives is that the bonus system is directly responsible for motivating management to make a variety of decisions contrary to the intent and the interests of the State. The decisions to be described go far back in the history of the Soviet economy, and have resisted countless efforts by the government to eliminate them. Most of them have survived the great organizational changes in industrial organization of the past several years. They are clearly deeply rooted in the soil of Soviet economic organization.

First, consider the matter of the reporting of information. In a planned economy it is vital that the central planners have as accurate information as possible about the productive capacity of enterprises. The bonus system, however, acts as a prevailing motivation for managers to understate their real production capacity. The reason is that the most important of the bonuses available to managers depends on the extent to which the production target of the enterprise is overfulfilled. If the manager honestly reports his full production capacity, and if for some reason something goes wrong in the course of the month, then he and his staff will lose that month's bonus. It is safer therefore to report a smaller capacity than really exists, in order that the production target will be kept low enough to allow for emergencies. The Russians call this "insurance" or "security". The consequence is that the planners can never be sure that their plans are based on accurate figures. The government is aware of the problem: "This is fully understandable," writes a Soviet economist, "because the lower the plan, the greater the opportunity to fulfill and overfulfill it. . . ."[4]

Because the higher state agencies cannot trust management's reporting of its productive capacity, various techniques have been fashioned for setting targets high enough to force the firms to operate as close as possible to capacity. One of these techniques is the arbitrary increase of targets over last year's production. As a prominent State Planning Commission economist put it, "they take as the base magnitude the level of production achieved during the preceding period and raise it by some percentage-or-other."[5] Sometimes this technique helps flush out the manager's "hidden reserves," but in other cases the arbitrary increase in targets leads to impossibly high tasks. Indeed, the spirit of planning is the use of high targets as a device for keeping managers working at as fast a tempo as possible. In the past, targets have been set so high (deliberately, one suspects) that one-third of all enterprises failed to fulfill their

---

[4] *Voprosy Ekonomiki*, 1959, No. 3, pp. 61, 67.
[5] *Voprosy Ekonomiki*, 1957, No. 4, p. 70.

annual plans. There is some evidence that in the last year or two this policy of deliberate over-planning has been modified, and we are told that in the first half of 1958 only 19 per cent of all enterprises failed to fulfill their plans.[6] This still represents one out of five enterprises, and indicates that the high level of plan targets remains a dominant fact of life for the Soviet manager. The intense pace of plant operation has its distinct advantage from the State's point of view: it elicits from management a high level of effort that might not be forthcoming if the plans were set at a more modest level. But the price paid by the State is the manager's effort to defend his enterprise by concealing his full capacity.

When the target has been set, the manager's bonus depends on the success with which he fulfills it. Most of the firm's production does indeed follow the lines laid down in the plan. But when the end of the month rolls around and, as often happens, production is far short of meeting the month's target, then managers turn to a host of time-tested techniques of meeting — or seeming to meet — the targets. In certain types of production, such as metals, the target is expressed in tons; in such cases the manager might order his shops to curtail the production of relatively light-weight products (special and quality metals) and to throw more men and materials into the production of the heavier products.[7] In textile production we read that the practice of setting targets in "running meters" (that is, in measures of length, without regard to width) causes managers to overproduce narrow-width cloth and underproduce broad-width.[8] In firms with a considerable variety of products, the production targets are expressed in value units — so many millions of rubles of production. In such cases managers tend to overproduce those products that have high fixed prices (all prices are fixed): they may deliberately use more expensive materials in order to drive up the value of production.[9] These are some of an endless variety of ways in which managers "violate the planned assortment of production"

— to use the official expression of disapproval.

How widespread are these practices? We really don't know. From time to time individual managers are publicly excoriated for such practices, and figures are published to show how widely the planned assortment of production had been departed from. But these may well be extreme cases, and it would be unwise to generalize from them. Occasionally, however, the results of special studies are published, and they give us some idea of the magnitude of the problem. The State Planning Commission recently released the results of a survey of the production practices of sixty-three enterprises. Of the total production by these enterprises in excess of the plan targets, only 43 per cent consisted of the basic products normally produced by them; 26.5 per cent consisted of "products not included in the plan when it was originally confirmed," 20 per cent consisted of "other production," and 7 per cent consisted not of finished products but of an increase in semi-fabricated parts and good-in-process.[10] While these data are not precisely in the form in which we would want them, they do provide a good indication of the managers' tendency to produce those products that are best from their own enterprises' point of view, rather than those products that the State would most wish to have produced.

Two other consequences of the bonus system (and the pressure of high targets) should be noted. One is the simple falsification of reported production. "Thus, for example," we read in a Soviet article, "if the plan is fulfilled 99 per cent, the managerial and engineering personnel receive no bonus. But if the enterprise fulfills the plan 100 per cent, they receive bonuses of from 15 per cent to 37 per cent of their salary."[11] Quite a lot of money hinges on that last percentage of production, and it is no wonder that management may succumb to the temptation to "fudge" the report a bit in order to earn the bonus. Again, the techniques of covering up for falsely reported production are myriad. To cite only one, production is "borrowed" from next month.

[6] *Planovoe Khoziaistvo,* 1958, No. 10, p. 5.
[7] *Voprosy Ekonomiki,* 1958, No. 7, p. 51.
[8] *Voprosy Ekonomiki,* 1959, No. 6, p. 19.
[9] *Voprosy Ekonomiki,* 1958, No. 6, p. 129.

[10] *Planovoe Khoziaistvo,* 1958, No. 10, pp. 5–6. The study deals only with that portion of the firm's production in excess of their planned targets.
[11] *Voprosy Ekonomiki,* 1959, No. 3, p. 67.

That is, production that is expected to occur next month is reported as having been produced this month. If things go well next month, the "borrowed" output is "repaid," if not the manager may get into trouble.

More serious than falsification, however, is the deterioration of the quality of production. The poor quality of much of Soviet consumer-goods production is well known. In other types of production the danger of detection is greater, and quality standards are less readily violated. But the explanation of management's tendency to shave on quality is the same: the high production targets are so often not attainable, and the manager wants to keep his job. Much of the quality shaving is of a kind that is not easily detected; fewer stitches in the garment, fewer screws in the piece, greener lumber in the building, more impurities in the metal. But if the pressure is keen enough, more extreme forms of quality deterioration will be adopted.

Summarizing, the bonus system is an effective device for eliciting a high level of managerial effort, but in the context of excessively high production targets, it induces management to make certain types of decisions that are contrary to the intent of the State. The production of unplanned products, the concealment of production capacity, the falsification of reports and the deterioration of quality are the unintended consequences of the system of managerial incentives.

Procurement Decisions

The high level of production targets is but half the problem facing the Soviet manager. The other half is the perpetual shortage of materials and supplies. In order to get the greatest possible production from the available stocks of materials and supplies, the State employs a variety of devices to minimize the use of materials in production and inventory. Undoubtedly these devices have served to control wasteful use of resources, and they have also helped channel the flow of resources in the direction most desired by the State. But they have been self-defeating to some extent for they have forced managers to make certain kinds of decisions which frustrate the intent of the State.

The core of the matter is that managers simply don't trust the planning system to provide them with the supplies and materials they need in the right quantity and quality, and at the right time. The recent decentralization of industrial organization may have improved matters somewhat, but the evidence we have indicates that supply problems are still the most troublesome feature of managerial life. Moreover, the reasons are similar to those we used to read about before decentralization. For all important materials the manager must still obtain an allocation order from his home office (usually the Council of the National Economy of his district), which must in turn get the allocation order from the republican or all-union planning commission. Thus, we still read of the "existing complicated system of obtaining allocation orders, under which every enterprise must submit detailed requisitions to Moscow a long time before the new planning quarter is to begin."[12] Because plans are not always finally set at the time the planning period is to begin, enterprises sometimes start with "advance allocations," that is, temporary allotments of resources designed to keep them operating until the final allocation orders are available.[13] Decentralization of the economy was supposed to have made it easier for neighboring enterprises to sell to each other without having to go through Moscow. But central purchasing agencies still exist, and agencies anywhere must find something to do. Thus the Chief Purchasing and Marketing Administration located in the republic capitals (Moscow, for example) still insist on being the middleman in purchase and sale contracts between enterprises, even when the latter are located in the same outlying city (such as Sverdlovsk).[14] Perhaps even more serious than the complex supply-planning system is the large percentage of enterprises that regularly fail to fulfill their plans, or fulfill them by producing the wrong products or substandard products. Since production of these enterprises constitutes the planned supplies of other enterprises, the supplies of the latter are delayed or simply not available. Perhaps enough has been said

---

12 *Planovoe Khoziaistvo,* 1959, No. 4, p. 58.
13 *Ibid.,* p. 65.
14 *Voprosy Ekonomiki,* 1959, No. 5, p. 75.

to explain why "managers of enterprises did not have confidence in the possibility of getting their materials on time and having them delivered to the factory by the supply depot's trucks."[15]

What does the manager do to make sure he gets his supplies? Just as he "secures" his production plan by attempting to conceal the existence of some production capacity, so he "secures" the flow of supplies in various ways. He over-orders, in the hope that if he doesn't get all he ordered, he may at least get as much as he needs. He also orders excessively large amounts of some supplies in order to be able to buy directly from the producer, instead of having to go through the maze of jobbing depots. A survey of fifteen Moscow enterprises showed a 10.4 per cent over-ordering of metals for just this reason.[16] Sometimes management's boldest efforts to obtain supplies are unsuccessful: ". . . over 300,000 construction workers undergo work stoppages daily because of the absence of materials at the workplace."[17] In other cases their padded requisitions are accepted and they receive more than they need of some materials. The consequence is the piling up of hoards of supplies of all kinds, one of the most enduring problems of Soviet industrial organization. The government has waged a long-standing war against hoarding. One of the weapons by which it attempts to hold hoarding within bounds is through the use of quotas of working capital; that is, for its annual production program the enterprise is allowed to keep on hand at any one time no more than so many tons of coal, so many board-feet of lumber, so many rubles worth of inventory. These quotas must be negotiated between enterprise and government, and the enterprise's interest demands that they be set as high as possible. The mutual attempt at outguessing the other leads to a familiar bureaucratic game: ". . . enterprises try to 'justify' and obtain as large quotas of working capital as possible. The financial agencies, aware of this, strive on the other hand to reduce the quotas of working capital."[18] This kind of planning is hardly

calculated to lead to the establishment of the optimal quotas. It is more likely that some quotas will be too large and some too small.

The most interesting of the techniques used by managers to "secure" their supply of materials is the employment of special supply expediters called *tolkachi,* or "pushers." The table of organization does not provide for this occupation, yet so great is the need that firms manage somehow to employ these people. The chief job of the expediter is to make sure that his enterprise gets the materials it needs and when it needs them. Accordingly he spends most of his time on the road, visiting his enterprise's suppliers, handing out little gifts here and there to assure that his orders are well-handled,[19] picking up supplies of one kind or another that his firm may be able to use or trade for other goods. Much of their activity is associated with the black market, that is, obtaining materials for which no allocation order has been issued. This may be done either by wangling an allocation order out of a reluctant government official by one means or another, or persuading an approachable enterprise official to sell him the things he needs without an allocation order.

Some *tolkachi* take up permanent residence in the city in which the chief suppliers are located, and only occasionally return to their home firms for consultations. To keep the record clean, they are carried on the books as "senior buyers," or "supply agents". If they are known to be particularly adept at their jobs, they may be asked by other firms to represent them. Nothing is known of their incomes, but there is no doubt that they earn many times their base pay. And they fully earn it, both because of the vital nature of their work, and because the risks they take make them vulnerable to prosecution.

How widespread is the use of these expediters? Again, we catch only occasional hints of their prevalence. The most recent outburst against them reports that the number of *tolkachi* who annually visit the typical large enterprise runs into the thousands of rubles. These, however, are only the reported expenses. More

---

[15] *Planovoe Khoziaistvo,* 1959, No. 5, p. 85.
[16] *Planovoe Khoziaistvo,* 1959, No. 5, p. 84.
[17] *Voprosy Ekonomiki,* 1957, No. 8, p. 50.
[18] *Voprosy Ekonomiki,* 1958, No 7, p. 120.

[19] The gifts are not always very little. An expediter sent out recently to get tires for his trucking firm, was given 62,000 rubles in cash for the trip. He spent 42,000 rubles for gifts. He is now in prison. *Izvestiia,* April 4, 1959, p. 2.

often than not their expenses are not reported as such but are concealed under such rubrics as "exchange of technical information," or "contract negotiations." Our latest informant, who is a Senior Investigator for the State Control Commission of the U.S.S.R., is of the opinion that despite continued official criticisms of the use of expediters, their number has actually been increasing. One of the reasons he adduces is interesting. In 1956, along with a wave of measures designed to give more freedom to plant managers, an order was issued relieving managers of the need to report in detail on all minor expenditures. Travel expenditures were among the items exempted. The measure had the unintended effect of encouraging the increased use of expediters.[20]

The economic effect of the use of expediters is difficult to assess. There is no doubt that they are of vital importance to individual enterprises, but from the national point of view much of their activity involves merely the transfer to one fortunate enterprise of resources that otherwise would have gone to another. Since the higher priority enterprises have less need for expediters, the chances are that the net effect of their activity is to cause more resources to flow in lower priority enterprises at the expense of higher priority ones. On the credit side, however, their wide knowledge of sources of supply, of who has what to sell, is of some importance, and they do arrange for the movement of supplies that otherwise would have lain idle in one plant while another had need for it. In short the expediter possesses a certain kind of knowledge that may be as important to economic organization as the knowledge of the engineer or the machinist. The planning system is able to direct the bulk of the nation's resources with reasonable effectiveness, but substantial quantities of materials and equipment elude the main stream of planning. How to get these resources back into the system is a problem that has exercised Soviet economists for a long time.[21]

In summary, the incentives that motivate managers to strive for the fulfillment of their production targets are the same incentives that motivate them to evade the regulations of the planning system. Because of the tightness of the supply system, which is deliberately engineered by the State, managers are compelled to defend their enterprises' position by over-ordering supplies, by hoarding materials and equipment, and by employing expediters whose function it is to keep the enterprise supplied with materials at all costs, legal or otherwise. The very planning system that serves to channel most of the nation's resources in directions desired by the State, serves also to misdirect a substantial volume of resources toward uses that are contrary to the wishes of the State.

Investment Decisions

If one were to ask what feature of the Soviet economic system accounts most of all for the rapid rate of growth, the answer would undoubtedly be the high rate of capital formation. The question at issue is whether it is as high as it might be, other things being equal. An examination of the system of managerial incentives will provide part, though by no means all, of the answer to this central question.

Management has a direct interest in obtaining new capital. It adds to productive capacity, and it is good for the record to show steady increases in production. Moreover, fixed capital is provided to the enterprise as a free grant by the State, with no interest charge. The problem therefore has not been one of inducing management to accept more machines; it has rather been one of dissuading management from ordering too many machines. Far back in Soviet economic history one can find expressions of the problem similar to that recently uttered by Khrushchev in connection with the dissolution of the agricultural Machine-Tractor Stations:

> The Machine-Tractor Stations accept any machine whether they need it or not. They don't grow flax, but they take flax-growing equipment. They don't grow cabbage, but they take cabbage-planting machines. Consequently many machines are not used for years and hundreds of millions of rubles worth of State resources are frozen.[22]

---

[20] *Izvestiia*, April 4, 1959, p. 2.
[21] Recently there have been numerous suggestions that enterprises and economic regions publish catalogues of the commodities they produce and the surplus materials and equipment they would like to sell. The expediters are rather like walking catalogues. *Planovoe Khoziaistvo*, 1959, No. 4, pp. 64, 96.

---

[22] *Planovoe Khoziaistvo*, 1958, No. 7, p. 121.

The reason enterprises accept any piece of equipment they can get their hands on is similar to that discussed above in connection with materials-hoarding. One can never tell when he may need just that kind of machine and not be able to obtain it. If one has a chance to get it now, order it by all means. It may come in handy some day for trading in return for something one might be able to use more readily. And above all, there is no charge for holding the equipment; there is no interest payment, and if the machine is not used there is no depreciation charge either. Hence there is everything to gain and nothing to lose by holding on to as much machinery and equipment as one can obtain.

How to induce managers to take a less cavalier view of capital has been a long-standing concern of economists. They look with some nostalgia at the effectiveness of the profit motive under capitalism in this respect. An eminent Soviet economist put it this way recently:

> In order to increase his profit as much as possible, the capitalist strives to use his equipment to the fullest extent possible, and in no case will he buy a machine that he doesn't need at the moment, since every surplus machine slows down the turnover of his capital and reduces his profit. For the same reason he strives to keep his inventories down to the very minimum and to market his finished products as quickly as possible.[23]

Recent economic literature contains a number of suggestions of ways in which Soviet managers might be induced to order only that amount of capital needed for production purposes. One of the more interesting is the proposal advanced by the author quoted above. He suggests that profit be calculated not as a ratio to total production cost (as has always been done), but as a ratio to value of invested capital. In this way the enterprise with too much idle capital will show a lower rate of profit, and profit is one of the principal indicators of over-all performance. The suggestion is interesting because it proposes that return on capital be used as a criterion of performance, a rather "bourgeois" notion. It should not, however, be thought that the proposal envisages

reliance on the "profit motive" as we know it. Profit is an important indicator of the efficiency of plant operation, but the firm does not "own" its profit, although it shares in the profit in a minor way. As a personal incentive, profit is relatively unimportant in Soviet industry, certainly by comparison with the bonus.

If the incentive system motivates managers to over-order and hoard equipment, the situation is quite the reverse with respect to technological innovation. Concern over managerial resistance to innovation is of long standing, but it has come to the fore in recent years in connection with increased emphasis on automation and modernization of plant and equipment. The reasons for the managers' tendency to drag their feet in introducing new products or production techniques are well understood by Soviet economists:

> The explanation is, first of all, that the introduction of new technology involves certain risks and requires a considerable expenditure of time; secondly, after new technology has been introduced, more difficult plan targets are set and consequently there is less opportunity for fulfilling them and receiving bonuses.[24]

When a manager has a well-running plant, when the workers have learned their jobs and have become experienced in using the existing equipment, he is reluctant to upset the cart by trying something new. A new production line means trouble. Production bugs have to be eliminated, workers have to be retrained, time is lost, and spoilage is high. The chances are that plans will be underfulfilled and the precious bonuses lost, particularly in view of the tendency for plan targets to be raised to the rated capacity of the new equipment. It is courting disaster to try new things. If the old machines are wearing out, it is safer to repair or even rebuild them rather than introduce the more complicated new models. Outlays on the rebuilding of old machines often exceed the price of a new modern machine.[25]

There is another reason why managers shy away from innovation. Even if the potential gains from new technology are great, it usually takes a number of years before they are realized. But it is Soviet policy to shift man-

---

23 *Ibid.*, p. 122.

24 *Voprosy Ekonomiki*, 1959, No. 1, pp. 44–45.
25 *Voprosy Ekonomiki*, 1957, No. 4, p. 69.

agers around from plant to plant every few years. Therefore managers have a strictly short-run point of view. Why take on all the headaches of introducing a new line when one is not likely to be around to enjoy whatever benefits may eventually accrue? Capital investment policy is by its very nature a matter of long-term planning, and therefore does not commend itself to the short-run horizon of management.

How does the State combat managerial resistance to innovation? One technique is direct pressure. Pressure exerted on and by their own superiors explains much of the innovation that does occur. Enterprise managers may drag their feet for a long time, but when the direct order comes down that the new automatic line must be installed in the next six months, it is eventually acted upon. Pressure is also exerted through the Communist Party; if the Party officials in the enterprise are under direct orders from Moscow that automation must be accelerated, they are in a position to force the manager to move faster than he otherwise might. Such pressures are important, although it must be noted in passing that both the manager's bosses and the local Party people often try to shield the enterprise from such pressures. They are as dependent for their careers upon successful plan fulfillment as are the plant managers themselves.

Direct orders from above are one way of getting management to innovate. But innovation would proceed more rapidly if managers could be made to *wish* to innovate, instead of waiting until they are forced into it. The literature of the past few years is full of suggestions on how this can be accomplished. It is suggested, for example, that attractively high prices be set on new machines, in order to stimulate the producers of those machines to put them into production more rapidly.[26] While this measure might ease the financial strain on the innovating firm, it will not remove the risk that the production plan may be sacrificed. And production is much more vital to the success of the enterprise than finance.

More to the point are the suggestions that the bonus system be employed as an incentive for innovation. Soviet economists seem to have enormous confidence in bonuses as a device

for getting management to wish to do what the State wishes them to do. But how to adapt the bonus system to this purpose is more difficult. In the course of years a variety of special bonuses have been introduced for one purpose or another, in addition to the major bonus that comes from fulfillment of the production plan. There are special bonuses available for economizing certain critical materials, for reducing the volume of goods-in-process, for conserving fuel, for increasing labor productivity, for keeping the plant clean, for reducing the volume of spoilage, for operating the plant without stoppages, for winning Socialist Competitions, and many others.[27] This dilution of the bonus system may actually weaken its power as an incentive. If the special bonuses are small, they will not be very effective. If they are large they may detract effort from what is, after all, the main objective of the State, fulfillment of the production plan. For it is interesting to note the evidence that the relative size of the bonus for this or that special purpose often determines the manager's decision to concentrate on this or that objective. There are two types of innovation: relatively small measures such as organizational improvements or inexpensive alterations, and the more dramatic large-scale changes in production techniques. The former are included in the over-all enterprise plan each year, under the name of the Plan of Organizational and Technical Measures (*Orgtekhplan*). It happens that there are certain bonuses available for the design and introduction of the large-scale innovations, but none for the fulfillment of the *Orgtekhplan*. The consequence is that research and managerial personnel concentrate on the large items, and pay little attention to the small ones, even though the latter could result in great savings with relatively little cost and effort.[28] Thus the very potency of the bonus as an incentive militates against its use for too many special purposes which may compete with each other.

To conclude this discussion, the unreliability of the supply system and the absence of a charge for the use of capital motivates manage-

---

26 *Voprosy Ekonomiki*, 1959, No. 6, p. 16.

27 *Voprosy Ekonomiki*, 1959, No. 3, p. 66. Not all these types of bonus are available to the director himself, but they are available to different groups of managerial personnel.

28 *Voprosy Ekonomiki*, 1958, No. 2, p. 136.

ment to order more fixed capital than they need and to hoard machines and equipment. This tendency deflects a certain amount of currently produced capital goods from being put directly into production in their best uses. On the other hand, the incentive system discourages management from taking the risks associated with innovation. Direct orders from above lead to a substantial volume of innovation, and in many cases management may consider certain forms of innovation to be to their interest. The provision of special bonuses for innovation, if they were large enough to compete with the production plan bonus, might help provide an incentive for innovation, and much of the current discussion in the Soviet Union seems to point to this as the next phase.

III. *Some Comparative Observations*

The preceding section has shown that Soviet managers are motivated to make a variety of decisions that are contrary to the interest of the State. Since the State's interest is paramount in the Soviet scheme of things, we may properly conclude that the incentive and decision-making system is "relatively inefficient," or "less than perfectly efficient." Let me caution the reader once more against inferring from this that Soviet managers do not do a *good* job. They do. There is no doubt that their system works well. If I have chosen to concentrate on the "pathology" of Soviet management, the purpose was not to create the impression of ineffectiveness, but to illuminate the gap that every economy shows between the actual and the ideal.

A comparison of Soviet and American management will help drive the point home. No one doubts that American management does a *good* job. But it would be fatuous to allege that it operates with perfect efficiency. An exploration of the inevitable gap between the actual and the ideal in the case of American management will help to place the corresponding gap in the U.S.S.R. in proper perspective.

A comparison of Soviet and American management is difficult for a curious reason; namely, we don't know enough about the more intimate aspects of American managerial practice. A moment's thought will make the reason clear. The American firm is a *private* enterprise in the full sense of the word. Its internal affairs are no one's business but its own. No one

has the right to pry except with special cause. To be sure, the laws of the land have, over the years, required enterprises to disclose more and more of their private affairs to public and governmental perusal. But large sectors of the enterprise's internal operations are protected from the eyes of curious outsiders.

One of the most striking differences in the conduct of American and Soviet management is precisely in this matter of privacy. The Soviet enterprise is a *public* enterprise in the fullest sense of the word. It has no right to conceal its operations from any officially recognized agent of the State. And a great range of such agents have been deliberately endowed by the State with the obligation of keeping close watch on management and disclosing any irregularities or sources of inefficiency that come to their attention. These agents include the "home office" of the firm (the regional economic council, or formerly the ministry), the State Bank, the local governmental body, the central State Control Commission, the Finance Department (tax collector), the local Communist Party boss and his staff, the Party Secretary of the enterprise itself, and indeed just about anyone in the enterprise who enjoys the extracurricular activity of attending meetings to discuss the affairs of the enterprise (the *aktiv*.) If we can imagine an American business executive suddenly placed in charge of a Soviet firm, it is this public character of the enterprise which above all would drive him to distraction. It means that any fool government official can at any time demand to examine any aspect of the firm's operations he wishes to, that at any time he can be called on the carpet by the local Party boss to explain a charge made by an irate customer, that any member of his staff (perhaps bucking for his job) can write a letter to *Pravda* exposing him for having made an irregular deal on some supplies, that any scatterbrained worker who wants to "get his picture in the papers" can rise at a public meeting that the director is obliged to attend, and compel the director to explain why he hasn't yet installed the new assembly line. The point is that the results of this authorized prying often find their way into the published Soviet economic and political literature, which gives us an insight into the more intimate operations of the Soviet firm that we can not have in the case of the American firm. But in view of this committee's expressed interest in comparisons of the United States and Soviet economies, I have attempted certain comparisons below which appear to be highly suggestive.

Managers and Owners

The original form of modern business organization was the small firm in which the owner was also the manager. The owner-manager was responsible to no one but himself for his business decisions, and his interest as manager could not conflict with his interest as owner. The development of the modern giant corporation, however, has led to that separation of management and ownership first elaborated in the work of Berle and Means.[29] Under the new conditions the private interests of the hired managers (and the controlling group) need no longer coincide at all points with the interests of the stockholder-owners. This is precisely the relationship between the hired Soviet manager and the owner-State.

Berle and Means concluded from their study that "the controlling group, even if they own a large block of stock, can serve their own pockets better by profiting at the expense of the company than by making profits for it."[30] This is precisely what Soviet managers do when they produce unplanned commodities that are advantageous to their firms but not to the State, when they over-order and hoard commodities, and when they resist innovation. Because of the differences between the two economic systems, we should expect that the precise forms that the owner–manager conflict takes would be different in the U.S.S.R. and the United States. In the United States they are to be found in such decisions as the awarding of subcontracts, the accounting of profit in such a way as to benefit the claims of the controlling group, the awarding of bonuses and other benefits to management, and in dividend payment policy. As in the Soviet enterprise, the accountant is of crucial importance in handling the books of the enterprise in such a way as make the best possible case for the manager; it is he, for example, who figures out the best way to distract the State's attention

from the large expenditures on *tolkachi*. The accounting techniques are, of course, different in the United States; they involve "the charging or the failure to deduct depreciation; charging to capital expenses which properly should be charged against income account; including non-recurrent profits as income though their real place is in surplus: and the creation of 'hidden reserves' ".[31]

A major difference between the Soviet firm and the American firm is that in the last analysis profit remains the criterion of managerial performance in the latter, whereas the Soviet manager is evaluated by a number of criteria that are sometimes mutually exclusive. Both systems have attempted to bring managerial interests into harmony with owner interests by some sort of profit-sharing system. In the Soviet case, it is clear that profit plays a very minor role, compared with bonuses, as a managerial incentive. In the United States the manager shares directly in profit to a very limited extent, and often follows other goals in his decisions. "The executive not infrequently tends to look upon the stockholders as outsiders whose complaints and demand for dividends are necessary evils. . . ." concluded one American student of management.[32] In like fashion the Soviet manager often begins to feel like the "boss" and resents the intrusion into "his" affairs of the State, which after all is the owner. I have described above some of the ways in which the Soviet manager promoted the interest of "his" enterprise by means contrary to the interests of the owner-State. In the American corporation the forms are somewhat different. ". . . profits are reinvested in the business for the sake of bigness and to protect the company, and the interests of the stockholders may be given second place to the business leader's conception of what is best for the firm itself." Executives manifest a "general unwillingness to liquidate unsuccessful enterprises" and thus put themselves out of jobs, however consistent liquidation might be with the interests of the stockholders.[33] The dramatic growth of corporate self-financing in

29 Adolph A. Berle, Jr., and Gardiner C. Means, *The Modern Corporation and Private Property* (New York: Macmillan, 1945).
30 *Ibid.*, p. 122.

31 *Ibid.*, pp. 202–203, 335.
32 Gordon, Robert A., *Business Leadership in the Large Corporation* (Washington: Brookings, 1945), p. 309.
33 *Ibid.*, p. 309.

recent years has strengthened the power of management to expand their own enterprises without having to go through the "test of the marketplace" for capital.

It was observed earlier that the desire for "security" and for what the Russians call a "quiet life" motivates a wide variety of managerial decisions such as concealing production capacity and resisting technological innovation that might rock the boat. Students of American management have also noted the change from the adventurous business tycoons of earlier days to a more professionalized managerial climate in which "greater emphasis is placed on education, training, and a scientific approach," and less on rugged, venturesome and frequently heedless individualism. The desire for security seems to have increased, and the concomitant of a growing emphasis on security is a diminishing desire for adventure for its own sake.[34] There is indeed a remarkable parallel to this development in the change in the character of Soviet managers. There would have been a great affinity between the industrial empire builders of nineteenth-century America and the Soviet directors of the first two decades of the Soviet regime. Those directors were often men of little education who came out of the romantic conflict of revolution, who dreamed great dreams of building an industrial nation and who created an ethos of bold plans and adventurous undertakings. The old Commissar of Heavy Industry. Sergei Ordzhonikidze, would have understood the spirit of the ironmonger Andrew Carnegie, and the man who built the great ZIL automotive works (now named after him) had the drives and the dreams of the auto mechanic Henry Ford. Time, and Stalin's purges, removed most of those oldtimers and their place has now been taken by Soviet-educated young men born not of revolution but of bureaucracy. Organizations seem to develop "organization men" types, whether the organization happens to be Communist or capitalist. An American reporter visiting with a group of Communist intellectuals reports that one of them had badgered him with questions about David Riesman's book *The Lonely Crowd*. "The Communist had read Riesman's book and had been fascinated by it — not, he said, because of its

application to life in the United States but because of what he maintained was its extraordinary relevance to the present conditions of life in the Soviet Union."[35] It is not, on reflection, very surprising that the job of running an industrial bureaucracy should place a common stamp on men of otherwise different backgrounds. The same would probably apply to the running of a large city or a large university.

Managers and the Laws

We have found that the Soviet manager is often compelled to evade regulations or even break laws. Part of the explanation is simply that there are so many laws. If a Chicago manufacturer fails to ship an order to a New York firm, and ships it instead to another Chicago firm, he has nothing to fear but the ire of the New York firm. But if a Kiev manufacturer fails to ship an order to a Moscow firm and ships it instead to another Kiev firm, he has injured a state enterprise and is subject to administrative action, a fine, or even criminal prosecution. If an American firm sells a substandard generator, he may lose money or his business. But if a Soviet firm sells a substandard generator, the director may go to prison. Thus, even if Soviet managers acted exactly as American managers do, we should expect to find more illegal or evasive activity in the Soviet Union than in the United States.

With the growing complexity of our society, more and more legislation is enacted to protect the public from potential abuses. With the growth of such legislation, managers find their activities more and more circumscribed by legislation. The Soviet manager apparently treats such legislation rather lightly when it conflicts with the interests of his firm (and his career and pocketbook). How does American management react when confronted by a spreading web of restrictive legislation?

It is not easy to find out very much about American managerial practice in this respect. Unlike the Soviet press, which throws its pages open to reports of the irregular activities of managers in order to warn others, the American press is likely to shy away from this kind of reporting. Moreover, the private nature of American business keeps this sort of thing from

---

[34] *Ibid.*, p. 311.

[35] *The New Yorker*, April 6, 1955, p. 52.

coming to light as easily as it might in Soviet industry. Nor is it the sort of thing that businessmen are inclined to talk about very readily. If it is true that a businessman would more readily be interviewed on his private sex life than on his private business activity, then we should require the late Dr. Kinsey to help provide the answers to the extent of unlawful or quasi-lawful business activity.

Professor E. H. Sutherland, the eminent American criminologist and sociologist, made a bold attempt to investigate the phenomenon he refers to as "white collar crime." His study is based on the decisions of a limited number of courts and administrative commissions against the seventy largest industrial-type corporations in the country. In the period 1935 to 1944 these seventy corporations were convicted 585 times for such practices as restraint of trade, misrepresentation in advertising, patent and copyright infringements, unfair labor practices, granting of rebates, and a few others.[36] The average was 8.5 convictions per corporation. These data provide some idea of the extensiveness of such practices but they clearly understate the magnitude for a variety of technical reasons. Sutherland's conclusion is that "a great deal of scattered and unorganized material indicates that white collar crimes are very prevalent."[37]

The point I wish to make is that when American management finds itself in a position approximating that of Soviet management they tend to react in ways similar to those of their Soviet counterparts. Sutherland's unique study notes many aspects of American managerial practice that are astonishingly similar to those one might find in the literature on Soviet management. "These crimes are not discrete and inadvertent violations of technical regulations. They are deliberate and have a relatively consistent unity."[38] It is in precisely this way that the Soviet manager deliberately misappropriates earmarked funds or decides to shave on the quality of production. There is evidence that the Soviet manager, aware of the fact that "everybody does it" and that the investigating agencies have restricted budgets, counts on the

law of averages (and his own superior shrewdness) to get away with it. So a member of the Federal Trade Commission wrote that "about the only thing that keeps a businessman off the wrong end of a federal indictment or administration agency's complaint is the fact that, under the hit-or-miss methods of prosecution, the law of averages hasn't made him a partner to a suit," and "Samuel Insull is reported to have remarked during his trial that he had only done what all other businessmen were doing."[39]

Similarities in managerial practice are paralleled by similarities in attitude to such violations, and toward the administrative agencies enforcing the laws and regulations. The Soviet manager does not think it is "wrong" to use influence to obtain materials unlawfully, or to fudge his reports to the government. Success is the important thing, and if you are successful you can get away with all sorts of violations. There is evidence that the manager feels contemptuous of government planners and of Party hacks who try to tell him how to run his business but who themselves had "never met a payroll." Sutherland's picture of American management's attitudes contains strains of the same kind. "The businessman who violates the laws which are designed to regulate business does not customarily lose status among his business associates. Although a few members of the industry may think less of him, others admire him. . . . Businessmen customarily regard government personnel as politicians and bureaucrats, and the persons authorized to investigate business practices as 'snoopers.'"[40]

In the first chapter of this paper, it was pointed out that a managerial career carries a great deal of prestige in the Soviet Union and attracts a large number of the better students. These youngsters have been raised in Soviet schools and have absorbed the incessant propaganda of the Communist regime. Many of them enter industry as green novices, fresh from school, filled with high ideals about building the socialist fatherland and working for the common welfare. One wonders about the process by which the naive, idealistic young Komsomol member is transformed into the

---

[36] Edwin H. Sutherland, *White Collar Crime* (New York: Dryden, 1949), p. 26.
[37] *Ibid.*, p. 10.
[38] *Ibid.*, p. 217.

[39] *Ibid.*, p. 218.
[40] *Ibid.*, p. 220.

hard-headed manager who knows all the angles for survival in the Soviet business world. Numerous incidents such as the following provide a key to the answer. A young Soviet chemist had been assigned to the quality control department of his enterprise. He was quite pleased with himself when his test showed that a sample of production, which had previously been declared acceptable by his laboratory chief, turned out to contain an excess of phosphorus. He reported the "error" and expected to get a bonus for it. Instead, his boss obtained a new sample, gave it to an outside chemist for analysis, and submitted a report showing that the batch of production was acceptable after all. The young chemist protested, was transferred to another shop, and was finally fired on trumped-up charges.[41]

What happens to such young people? Some never quite get the point and remain ordinary engineers in the plants. Others learn to adapt themselves after a few buffetings and when they decide to play the game according to the real ground-rules, begin to rise in the managerial hierarchy.

It is interesting to note that Sutherland's interviews with American businessmen turned up accounts rather similar to that narrated above. His explanation of the process by which the naive youngster is initiated into the business of selling used cars, settling insurance claims, covering up irregularities in clients' accounts — indeed, toning down the results of chemical analysis — helps explain the process of transformation of the young Komsomol member:

> In many cases he is ordered by the manager to do things which he regards as unethical or illegal, while in other cases he learns from others who have the same rank as his own how they make a success. He learns specific techniques of violating the law, together with definitions of situations in which those techniques may be used. Also he develops a general ideology. This ideology grows in part out of the specific practices and is in the nature of generalization from concrete experiences, but in part it is transmitted as a generalization by phrases such as "we are not in business for our health," "business is business," and, "no business was ever built on the beatitudes." These generalizations . . . assist the

neophyte in business to accept the illegal practices and provide rationalizations for them.[42]

Summarizing, the economic world in which the Soviet manager operates compels him to engage in a variety of illegal or evasive practices. Since the Soviet business world is enmeshed in a much greater web of laws and regulations than the American, the Soviet manager finds his interest in conflict with the laws and regulations more often than his American counterpart. But when American managers' interests conflict with the laws, they too are prepared to take the chance of violating them. Both American and Soviet managers justify their actions by an attitude of contempt for governmental controls and investigating personnel, and by a hard-headed view that "business is business" and "everybody does it." Young people in both systems who wish to achieve managerial prominence have to learn to play the game according to the rules, or disqualify themselves from the tough competition for the top.

Managers and Overfull Employment

Many of the peculiarities of Soviet management spring from the fact that the economic system works under conditions of perpetual overfull employment. By "overfull" employment I mean a condition in which there are not merely as many jobs as employables (as under full employment), but the demand for labor far exceeds the available supply. The same applies to other factors of production: materials, equipment, and commodities in general are demanded in far greater volume than the current rates of production. The ability of the Soviet government to maintain, through the planning system, a condition of permanent overfull employment is one of the greatest economic assets of the regime. We err when we interpret evidence of shortages in the Soviet economy as signs of economic weakness; they are rather indications that the economic engine is racing with the throttle wide open.

But just as an engine does not work at its maximum *efficiency* when it is working at its maximum *capacity*, so the Soviet economy pays a certain price for the advantages of overfull employment. It is the perpetual shortages of

---

[41] *Mashinostroenie*, February 17, 1939, p. 3.

[42] *Ibid.*, p. 240.

supplies that account in large measure for the losses due to over-ordering and hoarding. The hunger for goods by both firms and consumers encourages the deterioration of quality. The "sea of ink" associated with materials allocations, price fixing, priorities, and all the rigamarole of a controlled economy nurtures the spread of the *tolkach* and the use of influence for personal gain.

The normally functioning American economy does not confront our managers with this kind of problem. Hoarding makes no sense when materials are in adequate supply. Competition and consumer resistance force the quality of production up to standard. The role of influence is narrowly circumscribed when the bureaucratic machinery of government controls is removed. The biggest problem of American managers under normal conditions is marketing, not purchasing. The energy spent by the Soviet firm on obtaining materials is spent by the American firm on selling and advertising.

Thus, the major differences between the practice of American and Soviet management are to be ascribed to the differences in the economic environment. The interesting question is, how do American managers behave when placed in an environment that approximates that of the Soviet manager? The obvious test case is war. During World War II the national emergency forced us into a state of overfull employment. Along with this came the total immersion of government into economic life, with a great burgeoning of materials allocation, price-fixing, cost-plus contracting and a prevailing shortage of supplies.

It is interesting to note that the rate of growth of production during the war rose to levels rivaling the current rates of Soviet economic growth. The implication of this fact is important; it means that there is no magic in the Soviet economic system. Our economy could grow as rapidly as the Soviet economy does if our people would consent to being pushed around as totally as the Soviet people are.

But like the Soviet economy, we paid for our high rate of production in various forms of waste. One of the first consequences of the introduction of materials controls was the rise of the black market. The only full-scale study of the black market, to my knowledge, confirmed what many people felt to be the case at the time:

> During the war at least a million cases of black market violations were dealt with by the government. Illegal profits ran into billions of dollars. Business interests and government vied with one another in estimating the seriousness of the black market; business estimates, curiously, often being higher than those of the government. Such extensive conniving in the black market in illegal prices and rationed commodities took place among so many businessmen, ordinary criminals, and even the average citizen that serious questions might be raised as to the moral fiber of the American people.[43]

To understand the position of the Soviet manager, we must realize that the American black market flourished at a time when the nation was fighting for its life and public indignation acted as a restraint. But if the economic controls that led to violations could not be justified by a national emergency, they would be thought of as just irritating obstacles, as so many hurdles that the resourceful manager must overcome as part of the risks of the game. There is good evidence that the Soviet manager takes just this amoral attitude toward economic controls, and it is therefore quite understandable that the evasion of controls would be more widespread.

The high quality of American production in normal times is a byword in international markets. But the effect on the economy of shortages was similar to that in the Soviet economy. One of the techniques used by Soviet managers is to represent lower quality merchandise as of higher quality, and to sell it at the higher price. In the United States during the war, "upgrading was one of the most difficult violations to detect, particularly where no professional investigator was available who could appraise the grade or where there were no state or federal grades stamped on the commodity."[44] The reports of government investigators read like some of the indignant letters of complaint we read in the Soviet press; men's shorts made of cheesecloth, water-resistant baby's pants which permit a third of a glass of water to leak through after one laundering; "If you pick up a board by both ends

---

[43] Marshall B. Clinard, *The Black Market* (New York: Rinehart, 1952), p. vii.
[44] *Ibid.*, p. 224.

without breaking it in the middle, it's No. 1 Select," testified an American businessman.[45]

One of the features of Soviet managerial life which helps protect the manager is the feeling of "mutual support" among various officials whose fortunes depend on the success of the enterprise. The Communist Party secretary doesn't report the manipulations of a successful director because the Party benefits from the success of the enterprise; the people in the "home office" (the Ministry or the Council of the National Economy) are reluctant to fire a director who violates the laws in order to get the materials his plant needs, for while the next director may be more law-abiding, he may not succeed in fulfilling his plan. This tendency to maintain a solid front against authority is a source of great irritation to the government, which periodically inveighs against it but has not been able to eradicate it. A similar sense of common front prevailed among groups of businessmen. "Nothing better illustrates the degree of organization and consensus among businessmen than their reluctance to testify against each other. . . . Some businessmen felt that the trade would disapprove of behavior that might undermine the solid front against the government as well as interfere with supplies."[46]

One of the major differences in the position of management in the two countries is the nature of the penalty for failure. Under ordinary conditions the unsuccessful manager loses his job. But the Soviet manager faces many more situations in which the action necessary to get the job done carries with it the threat of criminal action. Indeed, whenever the government has found some managerial practice too damaging to its interests and too intractable to the normal sanctions, it has turned to the criminal courts. Immediately after the death of Stalin the punishment for economic transgressions was relaxed, but the new regime has not been able to continue operating without the courts. One of the severest economic problems following the decentralization of industry was the tendency toward "localism": that is, each economic region tended to favor the plants in its "own" region, and would discriminate against plants in other regions. When all exhortation failed, the government had to turn to the law. Today, a manager who fails to honor the orders of plants outside his own region is subject to "administrative action, fines, or even criminal punishment."[47]

Financial sanctions such as fines have rarely proved successful as restraints on Soviet managerial behavior. American managers seem to have reacted the same way to the fines imposed for black market violations. "They don't hurt anybody." "It just comes out of profits like a tax." "They make so much money on the black market they can afford to pay steep fines." But imprisonment was another matter. "Jail is the only way; nobody wants to go to jail." "A jail sentence is dishonorable; it jeopardizes the reputation."[48]

This would not be quite the same in the case of the Soviet manager. At least during Stalin's lifetime some of the best people served their time in jail, and it definitely did not destroy their reputation among their neighbors, although the neighbors might be wary of associating with them. One has the impression that large numbers of Soviet managers feel the chances are fair that some day they will do their stretch, hopefully for a minor transgression.

The wartime economy of shortages injects the government into business life not only as an agency of control but also as the largest customer of many firms. In the Soviet case we have noted the importance of the *tolkach*, the expediter, the peddler of Nazi Germany, in which government had also assumed a dominant role, also gave rise to this chap. The Germans called him the "contact man." As described by an American student of the German economy:

> To influence the powerful agencies of control, however, he [the German businessman] has good use for what might suitably be called a private relations department. Under the Nazi system of control, of business by an absolute government, the contact man, or graft, or both, take the place of the public relations executive.
>
> The contact man is primarily a political figure. His job is to pull wires. He knows the influential members of the all-pervading Nazi Party in a position to bring pressure successfully to bear upon the men in charge of controlling agencies. . . . Two types of contact man are known to

[45] *Ibid.*, p. 45.
[46] *Ibid.*, pp. 306–307.

[47] *Planovoe Khoziaistvo*, 1958, No. 7, p. 14.
[48] *Ibid.*, p. 244.

be used: one is an independent agent whom the businessman hires — or attempts to hire — whenever necessary; the other is carried on the payroll of the business in a more or less permanent capacity.[49]

The words might well have been written about the Soviet economy. In that sector of the U.S. economy in which government plays a dominant role as customer, the symbols of the mink coat or Dixon-Yates, depending upon one's political persuasion, come to mind. "Washington," wrote Senator Paul Douglas, "is indeed full of lawyers and 'representatives' whose primary commodity is 'influence.' "[50] The techniques of the American influence-pedlar differ little from those of his colleagues in the Soviet or Nazi economy. Gifts and quid-pro-quo favors are standard among Soviet *tolkachi*. Another way in which Soviet enterprises manage to exert influence is to have one of "their" men placed in other organizations that can be of use, rather like the unusually high employability in industry of retired military personnel. During the war the problem was particularly acute because of our government's desperate need for skilled managerial personnel, many of whom were on loan from corporations with which the government placed contracts. But the use of influence is not confined to government–business relations, as Senator Douglas pointed out in his critical defense of the ethics of government personnel:

> As a matter of fact, the abuses which have been exposed and properly denounced in the field of government are quite widespread practices in private business. Thus the "padding" of expense accounts is so common that they are often referred to as "swindle sheets." Purchasing agents and buyers frequently exact toll from those who seek to sell to them, and their Christmas presents and other prerequisites appreciably increase their income. Business managers and directors think nothing of awarding contracts, insurance, and underwriting privileges on the basis of friendship and relationship rather than the quality and prices of the goods and services supplied. All this is taken as a matter of course in private business, although it obviously in-

creases costs and intercepts gains which should go to stockholders and consumers.[51]

While gifts, payoffs, and bribery play their role in the Soviet scheme of things, the subtler and much more pervasive technique of influence is known as *blat*. To have good *blat* with someone means that one has an "in"; one can always count on him for a favor because of friendship or family ties or some other relationship of confidence. *Blat* may be used to obtain everything from a new apartment to a carload of coal. The prominent British observer, Edward Crankshaw, has called *blat* the most significant word in contemporary Russia.[52] The way in which the American equivalent of *blat* is cultivated is described in one final quotation from Senator Douglas:

> Today the corruption of public officials by private interests takes a more subtle form. The enticer does not generally pay money directly to the public representative. He tries instead by a series of favors to put the public official under such feeling of personal obligation that the latter gradually loses his sense of mission to the public and comes to feel that his first loyalties are to his private benefactors and patrons. What happens is a gradual shifting of a man's loyalties from the community to those who have been doing him favors. His final decisions are, therefore, made in response to private friendships and loyalties rather than to the public good.[53]

Summarizing, many of the differences between Soviet and United States managerial behavior spring from differences in the economic climate in which they operate. The stress on quality and appearance, the drive for innovation and technological development, and the interest in cost reduction reflect the force of competition and the buyer's market. Such similarities as have been observed in managerial behavior spring from features of the economic environment that are common to the two systems, such as large-scale organization and the intrusion of government into the economy. Under wartime conditions our economy takes on more of the features of normal Soviet economic life, and the consequence is that our managers adopt more of the normal practices of Soviet management.

---

[49] L. Hamburger, *How Nazi Germany Has Controlled Business* (Washington: Brookings, 1943), pp. 94–95.
[50] Paul H. Douglas, *Ethics in Government* (Cambridge: Harvard Press, 1952), p. 56.
[51] *Ibid.*, p. 25.
[52] *New York Times Magazine,* June 3, 1951, p. 35.
[53] *Op. cit.*, p. 44.

39

The Worker and His Livelihood*

Alec Nove

(1958)

Dr. Nove performs for us the same service in regard to the worker which Professor Berliner performed for the manager. With his characteristic incisiveness he poses and answers the basic questions on the life situation of the worker in Soviet industry.

The object of this article is briefly to examine the position of the Soviet wage-earner, dealing with such questions as: how are his wages determined, how far can he affect his earnings and conditions of work, how free is he to change his employment, how much does he earn, how far have there been any appreciable changes since Stalin's death in these aspects of his situation. It is not suggested that this list is exhaustive. Obviously, there are many other things which could be said which are relevant to the subject — for instance, about housing conditions, or social insurance. However, this article will concentrate more narrowly on the worker in his capacity as a recipient of wages for the work that he does.

Factors Affecting Wage Levels

Let us take an imaginary Soviet worker, Ivan Sidorov. Who determines what his wage should be? The answer to this question seems simple. The state decides what the wage scale should be in the given industry for defined grades of skill. These grades range from I for the least skilled to VII (in some industries VIII or even more) at the top. There are also geographical zones, so that, for instance, a worker in more remote areas earns more than in Central Russia. If Ivan Sidorov is deemed to be Grade IV, in the central zone, in the automobile industry, then his earnings would

* Reprinted from "The State and the Wage-Earner," *Soviet Survey*, No. 26 (Oct.-Dec. 1958), pp. 28–34, by permission of the author and the publisher.

be laid down in the appropriate wage regulation, where it is stated that persons of his grade are to earn, let us say, 500 rubles a month. This simple picture corresponds, rather curiously, to the propaganda-stories of both pro-Soviet and anti-Soviet writers. Both allege that all wages are centrally determined, though they do not derive the same conclusions from this. In a strictly formal sense both are right, but reality has been very different. There is a very powerful "built-in" tendency toward elemental increases in wages, and the state's efforts to control this tendency have been only partially effective, so that distortions in the wage structure have repeatedly appeared. To appreciate how the various pressures and controls operate, it is necessary to look more closely at how the system really works.

Let us first take another look at Ivan Sidorov, the Grade IV worker. Let us suppose that, like the majority of Soviet workers, he is paid by piece-work. He may, in certain industries, be on so-called "progressive piece-work," a system under which output in excess of the norm is paid at higher rates. A piece-worker in his grade, in our example, has a basic wage rate of 500 rubles a month. This should mean that his norm should be such that, by just fulfilling it, he would earn this sum. However, the actual work norm cannot be centrally prescribed, since no two factories are precisely alike. It has to be decided on the spot.

Now two other circumstances must be taken into account. The first is the chronic shortage of labor. The second is the strong pressure on the management to fulfill the plan. This involves attracting and retaining labor. The temptation immediately arises for the manager to set a relatively "easy" norm. But Ivan can easily exceed this lower norm; he therefore earns much more than 500 rubles, without transcending the centrally regulated "basic wage." This tendency continues, year after year, until, as we know from numerous official reports, there ceases to be any relationship between the official wage scales and the sums actually paid out. Thus in December 1956 norms were fulfilled 155 per cent on the average throughout the U.S.S.R. against 139 per cent in 1950.[1] Nor is there any necessary connection between the labor norms and the

[1] *Planovoe Khoziaistvo*, 1957, 7.

output plan of the factory. It is quite common for the output plan to envisage an average overfulfillment of work norms by 50 or even 100 per cent. Lest it be thought that a mountain is being made out of a molehill, it must be emphasized that the cumulative effect is very considerable. One has only to recall that average wages more than doubled between 1940 and 1953, although a careful compilation of every increase in *basic* wages gives us no ground for expecting an increase of more than 20–25 per cent. The difference is very largely due to the tendencies we have been describing. It was failure to allow for these tendencies which has led some economists to underestimate Soviet real wages.

It is true that the authorities repeatedly urged the upward revision of norms. The "Stakhanovite" campaigns of the thirties were indeed one of the means of ensuring such revisions. But it is now clear that the management, anxious not to lose their labor and to encourage it to work, did not carry out their orders, or did so only to a very limited extent. Faced with direct instructions to raise norms, or to determine them by work-study and stop-watch methods, they went through the motions of obeying, and then, quite unofficially, brought the real norms back to the level which would permit the payment of the customary wage by such expedients as so-called "corrective co-efficients." Thus Ivan Sidorov's scarcity value had a *de facto* influence on what he actually earned.

There is evidence, from the writer's own observations, of a deliberate use of norm-setting within the enterprise as a "corrective" to the official wage relativities. Thus in one enterprise the average worker seemed to earn about 50 per cent above his basic wage, but one occupation, that of unloading coal, was paid at a rate of 1,100 rubles a month although the basic rate was only 500. The explanation given was that the job was heavy and disagreeable and doubtless no one was willing to do it for under 1,000 rubles. So the management set a very "easy" coal-shoveling norm.

Let us now suppose Sidorov to have been a time-worker, with a fixed 500-ruble wage for a standard working month. There is now no means of raising his wages by an "easy" norm. But, with piece-workers' wages constantly creeping up, various expedients had necessarily

to be employed to raise those of time-workers. The two most common were: artificial upgrading and "phony" bonuses. The former expedient consisted simply of "promoting" Ivan Sidorov to a grade higher than his skill warranted. Indeed, in industry after industry the *lower* grades of skill (I and II) simply disappeared; there was no one in them. The "phony" bonus was paid out on a variety of pretexts, which need not be listed here.[2]

Examples of all these deviations can be found in many Soviet speeches and publications since 1953.[3] Consequently, Ivan Sidorov's wage is not settled as simply as might be expected.

The state does, of course, endeavor to stem the inflationary tide, with varying success. At certain periods, notably during the early thirties, things got out of hand. At others, money wages move forward only slowly. Of course, inflation — and the total standard of living — depends decisively on the goods available for consumption. The period of the most rapid rise in money wages — the early thirties — was also that of the most catastrophic decline in living standards in the peacetime history of the Soviet Union. This aspect of the matter must, however, be left aside here. Let us examine the state's controls over the money wages that are actually paid.

Firstly, the total size of the so-called "wages fund" is centrally determined, and this is subdivided between industries on the basis of their estimated labor force and expected average wage. The industries (and now presumably the regional economic councils) subdivide this between their various enterprises. The amounts laid down should not, in theory, be exceeded by an enterprise unless it exceeds its output plan. The local branches of the State Bank play an important "police" role in this context; thus they must refuse to honour the enterprises' checks to pay wages in excess of amounts permitted by the regulations.

Those powerful regulations would have been fully effective but for one weakness.

---

[2] *Krokodil* recently gave a few doubtless exaggerated examples, including bonuses for tact, politeness, punctuality, and coming to work sober.
[3] See, for example, *Kommunist*, 1953, No. 11, and *Pravda*, 17 July 1955.

Clearly, the failure of an enterprise to pay its workers would have most undesirable effects on production, and there could be *bona fide* reasons why an enterprise should be authorized to make extra payments. Therefore, there always had to be a proviso that these payments could be made if approved by some higher authority — for example, an economic ministry. This higher authority was primarily interested in fulfilling the output plan, and so it gave its approval almost automatically, thereby largely torpedoing the Bank's "police" role. Repeatedly one can read of enterprises, or whole industries, which underfulfill their plans while overspending their wage funds. Of course, it would be going too far to assert that the official controls were totally ineffective. They did prevent runaway inflation most of the time. It is realistic to view the process as a constant push-and-pull, of more or less strict efforts at regulation tempered by more or less successful evasion.

But evasion is not equally easy, nor is it equally tolerated by the authorities, in all sectors of the economy. And so, over the years, all kinds of anomalies developed. This was all the more difficult to check because there was no government department directly responsible for labor questions, from the abolition of the Labor Commissariat in 1933 to the creation of the Committee on Labor and Wages in 1955. Matters were allowed to drift. Each economic ministry devised its own scales — subject to the general control over the wage fund. The grading and zoning arrangements differed widely, so that fitters with similar qualifications would have different basic pay rates if the factories in which they worked came under different ministries. There was no general systematic review of the wage system between 1931 and 1956. By 1955, the situation was approximately as follows: Industrial workers, especially those on piece-work, and particularly those in priority industries (engineering, mining, etc.), had gained relatively and absolutely, compared with prewar. Those on fixed salaries, such as teachers, economists, accountants, factory foremen, and a variety of white-collar workers, had lost ground, since the government's wage controls could be much more effectively applied to them. Within the industrial working class, there was a tendency toward reduced

wage differentials, with the disappearance of workers from the lowest wage categories. Foremen found themselves earning less than their skilled subordinates.

The observant reader may have noticed a surprising similarity between these trends and those observable in Great Britain, despite the existence of a central policy in Russia and its absence here, despite the existence of trade unions here and there relatively "phony" status in the Soviet Union, and despite the fact that, for much of the period in question, a worker in the U.S.S.R. was forbidden to change his job without permission. The law of supply and demand, when the door is barred against it, often manages to climb in through the window. But, in the U.S.S.R., some windows could be effectively barred while others could not, so that the situation was full of anomalies. Any systematic effort to bring logic into the system was bound to hurt a lot of people, which is why the confused state of the wage system has been tolerated for so long. The Soviet government can easily arrest a particular person or persons, but often fights shy of outraging the feelings of fitters or instrument mechanics as a whole, because of the likely effect on production. As trade unionists everywhere well know, it is *wage relativities*, even more than the absolute level of a given category of wages, which cause most bad feelings.

In 1955, the State Committee on Labor and Wages began to tackle the mess. It is still at work. New scales have emerged for a number of industries and occupations. Norms and basic rates have been reviewed, and both have usually been raised. Some adjustments have been made where anomalies were excessive. For example, in the building industry the norms of manual laborers were lowered, as they had become too high, while those of men on machines were increased. The absurdly exaggerated "progressive" piece-work regulations in the coal industry, under which coal-getters got double pay for output exceeding 80 per cent of the norm and triple pay for anything over 100 per cent, were largely modified. The underlying object was to create a more logical wage structure without altering the general average level of wages. However, on balance it often proved simpler to raise the laggards than to cut the beneficiaries of past anomalies, and so the process of adjustment resulted in an unintended upward jump in the average. For example, wages in the building industry rose by 12 per cent as a result of the reform, imposing an additional strain on the supplies available in retail stores.

The State Committee on Labor and Wages has endeavored to base differentiation between industries on objective criteria. This has become particularly necessary with increasing decentralization of effective decisions on *actual* wage payments to republics and regional economic councils. In an interesting article in *Sotsialisticheskii Trud* (No. 2, 1958), the basis of decision in arriving at more logical inter-relationships is given as follows: Taking the worst-paid industry as 1.00, industries are graded according to certain characteristics, each being given a coefficient. The net result of the calculation then serves as a guide to the average wage in that industry. The figures shown in Table 1 are quoted from a table in the same article (the total is arrived at by multiplying together the four coefficients).

Of course, this is in part a rationalization of what already exists. True to tradition in Soviet economics, the quite important practical consideration of supply and demand is neglected, which means that real life will depart, in the near future as in the past, from the best laid schemes of Soviet mice, men, and planners.

Some Other Aspects of Working Conditions

Hours of labor were raised from seven to a standard eight a day, six days a week, in 1940, at the same time as the workers were forbidden to leave their employment of their own volition, or to be late or absent, subject to criminal penalties. Hours remained basically unaltered until 1956, when a gradual reduction to a 42-hour week was promised by 1960. Some of this reduction has already been granted. The law forbidding change of employment, and severely punishing unpunctuality, had a curious history. It was, of course, immensely unpopular. The reluctance of managers and judges to apply it could be seen from threats of punishment which were made against those who failed to act. After the war, it seems to have gradually withered away. In 1954, an unpublicized decree apparently confined the full vigor of the 1940 provisions to especially bad cases. The 1940 decrees ceased to be printed in law books. Finally, in 1957, the decrees were formally repealed. The imaginary Ivan Sidorov is now able to resign. However, as social insurance benefits depend on length of service, he will lose should he fall ill at his new job. His freedom of movement, like that of other Soviet citizens, depends on the willingness of the police to register him as a resident of the city he wishes to reside in. Thus a move to Moscow, Leningrad, or Kiev from some provincial town may be quite impossible. However, there are usually many unfilled vacancies in less desirable places. Thus the writer of these lines has seen advertisements in western towns for jobs in the Vorkuta coalfields and the forests of Tobolsk, while a local radio program announced a shortage of fitters at the Rostov farm machinery works. Notice boards often

TABLE 1

CHARACTERISTIC	INDUSTRY				
	Butter & Cheese-Making	Footwear	Fisheries	Machinery	Coal-Mining
Conditions of work	1.00	1.10	1.21	1.08	1.53
Average skill required	1.00	1.15	1.06	1.20	1.12
Geographical location	1.00	1.00	1.45	1.01	1.14
Relative economic importance	1.00	1.05	1.10	1.30	1.31
TOTAL........	1.00	1.33	2.05	1.70	2.55

tell of hands wanted. The authorities admit that they are embarrassed by a high labor turnover, so that workers really do move.

One of the objects of the new wage regulations is to increase wage differentials once again, while at the same time raising the extremely low wages of the totally unskilled cleaners, porters, watchmen, etc. (This was done in 1956, when a minimum of 300 rubles a month was decreed for urban areas.) The very considerable "spread" between unskilled and highly skilled labor in the same industry is one of the principal differences between the U.S.S.R. and most Western countries. (In England these differentials are generally 1:1.3, while the differentials which it is intended to impose in the U.S.S.R. range from 1:2 in the clothing industry to as much as 1:3.2 in mining, the average apparently being around 1:2.8.) In practice, the Soviet piece-work regulations give skilled men better chances of earning bonuses, and so the differentials are quite often even greater in practice than they are in theory, despite the tendency to undeserved upgrading of the least skilled. There appears to be some contradiction in these policies, which may perhaps be resolved by a greater increase in money wages than intended.

A word is necessary about Stakhanovism, which many think to be still a typical Soviet phenomenon. This developed into a thoroughly unhealthy form of over-publicized record-breaking, in which a few workers were given exceptional opportunities to overfulfill their norms, often at the expense of their fellows. Not only did this lead to bad feeling, but it did not effectively stimulate genuine increases in productivity, which depend on raising the general level, not on the individual record-breaker. So, gradually, the emphasis was changed, and one hears no more of Stakhanovism today. "Socialist competition" remains, and factories are urged to increase productivity and are rewarded for so doing. However, "socialist competition" also became largely fictional in character, through catching the dangerous Soviet disease of bureaucratic formalism. This was due partly to the insistence on such "competition" as a species of political obligation, and partly to the curious nature of Soviet "trade unions," which it is necessary briefly to discuss.

The Worker and His Trade Union

Ivan Sidorov may be presumed to be a member of his trade union, if only because it administers social insurance funds and would pay him only half his sickness and other benefits were he not a member. However, as an abundant Soviet literature shows, the trade union has quite failed to carry out its obligations to its membership. This is due not so much to lack of powers (of which more below) but simply to the lack of responsibility of the officials to the membership. The local officials, not to speak of the central committees of the unions, are in effect appointed, the process of "election" being no more real than most other elections in the U.S.S.R. Consequently the officials of Ivan Sidorov's branch are generally cut off from the rank and file, far more than are their equivalents in the most bureaucratized union in the West. But what functions ought a Soviet trade union be performing, apart from administering social insurance funds? So far as wage-rates are concerned, the central trade union office in Moscow does have a wages department, and must be presumed to have some consultative role in the process of deciding what the basic rates are to be, but it has no formal powers in the matter, as far as can be ascertained. In any event, at this level the "trade unions" are simply a branch of the government. They do have a more definite function in deciding what the grading system should be, since the "tariff-qualification manual" (*tarifno-kvalifikatisionny spravochnik*) bears the counter-signature of a central union secretary.

But what about the local branches? The trade union is supposed to do several things. Firstly, it must endeavor to rally the workers behind state and party economic policies, to stimulate higher productivity, to ensure fulfillment and overfulfillment of the plan, etc., etc. With this end in view it can and does influence local piece-rates and incentive bonus arrangements, which do affect actual earnings. When mass loan subscriptions were required, it was one of the duties of the trade union secretary to see that no one evaded his "voluntary" obligation. At the same time, the Union branch has a number of protective and welfare functions. Thus it is supposed to prevent breaches of the wage, hiring-and-firing, and health and safety regulations on the part of the management. Its consent is necessary for compulsory overtime working. It is associated with decisions about how to spend the various welfare funds and in the distribution of available housing space. Thus it has the twin duty of "mobilizing" the workers behind official policy and acting on their behalf.

Naturally, these two duties often contradict one another. Equally naturally, in the absence of free elections, union officials tended to hearken only to voices from above, and the representative or welfare function was neglected. Repeatedly such journals as *Trud* reported that union officials passively tolerated serious abuses at the factory. Welfare funds were misused, housing was unfairly allocated, bonus funds were largely appropriated by managerial staff, safety regulations were ignored, and so on. But these failures had a further consequence. Because of them, the members felt no sense of belonging to a trade union at all, and therefore commonly failed to respond to the union's urgings to produce more or to indulge in socialist competition. Repeated complaints appeared in the Soviet Press, and at conferences, to the effect that "socialist competitions" organized by trade unions were purely formal in character, that they (like much else in Soviet official life) were organized for the purpose of reporting to higher authority that orders had been obeyed and not to achieve anything real at all. The Soviet leaders themselves were disturbed by the ineffectiveness of the unions. For what is the good of an organization which is so artificial or phony that it fails to fulfill its functions? From the standpoint of the regime, the unions are needed not only for stimulating productivity, but also for genuinely checking abuses on the spot, since the majority of such abuses benefit managers rather than the Party or government. The trouble is, of course, that *some* "abuses" (such as, for instance, neglect of safety regulations or heavy overtime to fulfill output plans for a scarce commodity) are committed on superior orders. The balance is not easy to strike. (The word "strike" is here used for the first and only time, and not in the usual "trade union" sense, in which it is, of course, unthinkable.)

In any event, the authorities have sought to breathe some life into Soviet trade unions. A number of officials have been sacked, numerous resolutions adopted. The columns of *Trud,* the union daily paper, have, from 1956, been much more frankly denouncing abuses of many kinds. All these are still reflections of orders from above. Genuine trade union activity at the branch level, on even the most restricted scale, has yet to be shown to work. None the less, the post-Stalin period has been one in which tongues have wagged more freely, complaints have been voiced more openly, and this general trend has affected also Ivan Sidorov's right to complain about bad ventilation and unfair withholding of his bonus entitlement.

It is only fair to add that at all times, the Stalin era included, the worker had considerable rights to act on his own behalf. The rules have not greatly altered in recent years, although a decree in January 1957 simplified the procedures. Suppose that Ivan Sidorov believes that he is not receiving his full pay entitlement, or considers himself unjustly demoted or dismissed. His first recourse is to appeal to the enterprise's Conflicts Commission, on which the management and the trade union are represented. If he disagrees with the Commission's decision, he can appeal to the local trade union committee, which can (if it so decides) take up the matter or make representations to higher authority. If he remains dissatisfied, he can appeal to the courts, on the grounds that he is the victim of some illegal act. Labor cases do frequently come before the courts. For example, courts have on many occasions ordered the reinstatement of a wrongfully dismissed worker. By and large, if labor laws and regulations affecting him personally were broken, the worker was by no means helpless. He did have real protection in many instances. One recalls the situation in the British army: the colonel can sentence a soldier-tradesman to 14 days' C.B., but he cannot take away his trade qualification. In much the same way, it was often easier to arrest Ivan Sidorov than to reduce his grading from Category IV to III.

Production Councils

An interesting new development, which dates from July 1958, is the conversion of the relatively ineffective "production councils" into permanent bodies, in order, as the *Pravda* editorial puts it, to "associate the toilers with the administration of production." Experiments on these lines have been carried out in some enterprises since the December 1957 plenum of the Central Committee. The new bodies are to be elected by the workshops, offices, and department of the enterprises, and are to be closely associated with "devising and discussing current and prospective plan projects and suggestions for improving planning within the enterprise . . . to hear reports from the management about current operations and economic results . . . the organization of production, labor, wages, technical norms, the introduction of new technique, mechanization, and much else" (*Pravda*, 22 July 1958). Naturally, they are to work for the overfulfillment of the plan, the encouragement of socialist competition, and so on. Equally naturally, the local and factory Party organizations will have much to say about what the "production councils" actually do.

Only a week before the publication of the decree on production councils, *Pravda* printed a new decree which considerably strengthened the position of trade union factory committees in dealing with a variety of labor questions, including piece-work norms, bonuses, disputes, hiring and firing, etc., as well as the organization of socialist competition. These functions to a great extent overlap those to be carried out by the new production councils, and the division of responsibility remains obscure.

How far will this new organizational arrangement alter the situation of Ivan Sidorov? Will he and his fellows be able to influence their work conditions any more than hitherto? It seems to be far too soon to say anything definite on this point. It is by no means clear, either, what influence the regional economic councils will have on the whole complex of issues affecting wages and conditions of work. No doubt neither the regional councils nor the production councils will have power to alter basic wage rates, for these remain a central responsibility. But, as we have seen in practice, actual pay depends greatly on local decision. Without speculating about the future, however, it may be worth considering the purpose behind the latest measure. Three possible explanations may be mentioned. One

is that the Party really does desire to associate the workers more closely with the management of the enterprise, in the hope of encouraging harder work and facilitating the utilization of new ideas. Another is that, by this means, the leaders may hope to steal the "workers' control" thunder from the "revisionists" of Yugoslavia and Poland. Still another is this: the Party is seeking to diminish the privileges and power of the managerial strata, and, by giving powers to the "production conferences," the managers can be subjected to closer control from "below," in a manner which can be tightly regulated by the Party and which, when circumstances call for it, enables the Party to use opinions of the workers to curb undesirable managerial independence. Perhaps the truth contains all three of these elements.

The Average Wage

Finally, to return to Ivan Sidorov. What would his earnings be? Obviously, these depend on a number of factors: his grade, the zone in which he is situated, the industry in which he works, his piece-rate norm and bonus-earning opportunities, and so on. The *average* earnings are more or less known, though systematic wage statistics are still unpublished. In 1953, according to the economics textbook, the average wage was 201 per cent of 1940, which meant that it was close to 8,120 rubles per annum. In 1954, if the second edition of the textbook is to be believed, it rose to 206 per cent of 1940, i.e., about 8,360 rubles. We know from the former head of the Gosplan of the R.S.F.S.R. (Russia proper), Baibakov, that the 1958 planned average for 28 million persons in this republic was 9,170 rubles. The average relates to all kinds of state-employed persons, from managers to rural night watchmen inclusive. The R.S.F.S.R. includes some of the highest and lowest paid personnel, as well as the best-paid and least-well-paid geographical zones. It seems probable that the national average is only a little less than that for the R.S.F.S.R. As a Grade IV fitter, Ivan Sidorov is likely to earn somewhere close to the national average, perhaps 730 rubles a month, which means that his purchasing power is still modest, although he is doubtless conscious of some improvement over recent years.

40

Who Pays the Taxes?*

Leon Herman

(1959)

*The tax structure in a modern economy helps
to reveal, among other things, the way in
which the income of a society is distributed
among the population. Most governments today have adopted tax structures which are
"direct" and "progressive," that is, which are
visible to the spender and which rise progressively with increasing income level. Lenin
characterized the opposite variety, the indirect
and regressive taxes, as the most unjust form
because they fall most heavily on the poor.
Nevertheless, the indirect tax is the predominant form in the U.S.S.R. today. Mr. Herman
discusses the very important Soviet "turnover
tax," which is convenient for the government to
administer, but indirect and regressive in effect.*

In the manner of most nations around the
globe, the Soviet Union operates its economy
on a money basis. Goods and services are
regularly paid for in currency, at conventional
prices, regardless of whether they are exchanged between the government and the
population or among the economic agencies of
the state. In the course of discharging its
functions, the Soviet government also incurs
every year the standard "overhead" expenses
for defense, administration, education, and
other public services. Like its counterparts
everywhere, the regime meets its budgetary
problems with the time-honored solution of
levying taxes on the population.

At this point, however, the similarity comes
to an end. For in collecting revenue, just as
in other matters of public policy, the Soviet
government is unhampered by the constraints
of political consent. The Soviet citizen has

no voice in deciding how large his tax burden
will be, nor has he anything to say about the
methods of collection. In fact, he does not
even know how much tax money he is paying
at any given time because, unlike all modern
states, the Soviet Union chooses to collect the
bulk of its tax moneys through a system of
indirect hidden taxation. Today, nearly 50
per cent of all budget revenue, and 85 per
cent of all taxes on the population, is raised
through excise taxes on goods sold to consumers in the stores.[1] The Soviet tax system
is thus something of an iceberg: only about
15 per cent rides above the surface, while
most of the tax collecting operation takes place
out of sight, in the form of a special mark-up
over and above profits and distribution costs,
on all goods sold to the population.

In token form an income tax still survives
in the U.S.S.R. It provides currently less than
8 per cent of the total revenue in the state
budget,[2] and its fiscal role is thus quite
negligible. But by displaying prominently the
very low sums levied on income, and reporting
them officially as the only tax moneys collected
"from the population" — as opposed to the
huge excise taxes collected "from the economy"
— the Soviet regime has made the best of the
income tax in the field of political propaganda.
And so, satisfied no doubt with the ingenious
use to which the tax was put, the Soviet
leaders have long watched the downward
drift in the relative fiscal importance of direct
taxation without any visible signs of interest.

It was left to an old political practitioner
like Nikita Khrushchev to discover still another way of pressing the moribund income
tax into political service. His plan, revealed
in his seven-hour speech to the 21st Party
Congress, is quite simple. He intends to announce some time in the near future that the
Soviet Union has found a way to dispense
with this trivial item of budget revenue; and
the action will be billed as "the end of the
collection of taxes" in the U.S.S.R. Khrushchev's formal pronouncement on the subject
reads as follows:[3]

* Reprinted from "Taxes and the Soviet Citizen,"
Problems of Communism, a publication of the
United States Information Agency, Vol. 8 (1959),
pp. 21–26, by permission of the author.

[1] See annual budget report by Finance Minister A.
Zverev in *Pravda*, December 23, 1958.
[2] *Ibid.*
[3] *Pravda*, January 28, 1959.

Under present conditions the existence of taxes levied upon the population is unnecessary either from the point of view of its class significance . . . or from the point of view of securing revenue for the state budget of the U.S.S.R.; the more so, as the share of taxes raised amounts to only 7.8 per cent of budget revenue. All this will make it possible to give up in the next few years the collection of taxes from the population.

In the light of this startling treatment of the subject of "taxes," two questions are likely to arise in the mind of the reader interested in Soviet developments: (1) what is the actual tax burden of the Soviet citizen? and (2) how much does he stand to gain by the reform so solemnly adumbrated by Khrushchev?

The Size of the Turnover Tax

Ever since the basic reform of the Soviet fiscal structure in September 1930 the principal source of tax money in the U.S.S.R. has been the so-called "tax on turnover." This tax began its life as a modest special levy on all transactions involving the sale of consumer goods (there was an exception to the rule in that petroleum, a producers' good, was also made subject to the tax). The innovation proved a huge success, and it was soon extended to cover more ground, such as movie-house admissions, repairs, laundry, and other consumer services. In short, it gradually evolved into a universal excise tax and into "a means of withdrawing from circulation part of the wages and other payments made to the population."[4] This withdrawal, as will be seen later, has been carried out at a rather heavy rate.

With the aid of this new rich source of taxation, government tax receipts doubled in one year, rising from 6 to 12 billion rubles by the end of 1931. In due course, the government began to experiment with the tax rates, raising the levy on one commodity after another as much as the traffic would bear. The tax on bread, for example, went up in several successive steps from the original rate of 8 per cent of the sale price in 1931, to 76 per cent in 1934. While the price paid to the peasant for grain

remained unchanged, the government raised the price of bread to the consumer from 12 to 50 kopeks per kilogram during this three-year period.[5]

As could be expected, yields from the turnover tax rose briskly during the first decade of its life. By 1940, they were nearly ten times as large as in 1931, namely 106 billion rubles; while average wages, during the same period increased only four-fold (from 84 to 338 rubles a month). Inevitably, too, the share of this tax in total government revenue increased conspicuously, so that by 1940 it accounted for 58.8 per cent of all treasury receipts.[6] In 1959 the turnover tax is expected to yield 332.4 billion rubles, or 47 per cent of total budget revenue.[7]

Economic Functions

From the standpoint of size alone, then, the turnover tax is important enough a phenomenon to merit a position of honor in the Soviet financial system. Its economic significance, however, is even more far-reaching. What gives the turnover tax its unique influence over the economic process in the U.S.S.R. is the fact that it is employed as a device for subsidizing the state sector at the expense of the consumer sector.

More specifically, the turnover tax is deployed strategically to accomplish two basic objectives of Soviet economic policy. First, because it is levied almost entirely on consumer articles, the tax raises the price of all goods bought by the population, on the av-

---

[4] R. W. Davies, *The Development of the Soviet Budgetary System*, Cambridge University Press, Cambridge, 1958, p. 216.

[5] A. Baykov, *The Development of the Soviet Economic System*, Cambridge University Press, Cambridge, 1950, p. 371.

[6] *Finansy SSSR* (Finances of the USSR), No. 9, 1958, p. 94.

[7] The revenue resources of the Soviet Government, as planned for 1959, may be summarized as follows: (1) The turnover (excise) tax: 332.4 billion rubles, or 47 per cent of total revenue. (2) Direct taxes, chiefly the income tax: 56 billion rubles, or somewhat under 8 percent of total revenue. (3) Deductions from profits of state economic enterprises: 155 billion rubles, or about 21 per cent of total revenue. (4) The remainder, some 24 per cent of the total expected revenue, of 723.4 billion rubles, will be drawn from a group of minor revenue sources, such as the social insurance tax, the timber tax, the tax on collective farms, and others. See Zverev report, *loc. cit.*

erage, by roughly 100 per cent over and above the full economic price. By sopping up purchasing power at this greedy rate, the turnover tax acts as a powerful break on consumption and enables the government to pursue its policy of heavy investment in the capital goods and armament industries with diminished inflationary pressures in the consumer market.

Secondly, this tax, though collected from the consumer sector, does its most "creative" work in the state sector. Just how this is accomplished may be briefly described as follows: Since the Soviet government exercises a virtually exclusive monopoly of both the economic and the political authority in the country — producing, taxing, pricing, and distributing all goods with very minor exceptions — it is under no obligation to show a profit on each individual product. Neither does it have to seek an economic return in full from any large group of products. All that is required for the purpose of general economic viability is that the sum of the prices of all goods sold by the state recapture the cost of production of all goods, plus a given margin of profit. The latter is needed, of course, for the replacement of outworn equipment and for further capital expansion. Within this broad framework of economic constraint, however, there is ample room to maneuver.

Having the power to do so, the Soviet government proceeds to over-price the goods sold to the consumer by approximately the amount by which it wishes to under-price the goods it sells to itself, namely capital goods and military matériel. This herculean task of "compensation," as some Soviet economists prefer to call it,[8] is carried out by the turnover tax. Its use has made it possible over the years to depress the share of consumer goods in total industrial output from 60 per cent in the late 1920's to less than 30 per cent at present.[9]

The Tax Bite

In its own way, the Soviet government pays a special tribute to the "strategic" character of the turnover tax by taking the utmost precaution to keep all details on specific rates

out of the public view. The tax is therefore built into the sale price of each article before it is placed into retail channels. Only the total amount to be collected through this tax in the course of a year is made public. Beyond that, however, discussion of the subject is usually couched in broad, theoretical terms.

For information on actual tax rates we have to go to a few fragmentary figures released during the prewar years. According to this information, the turnover tax takes a specific "bite" out of every consumer ruble spent in the state stores. But the rates are extremely varied. Thus when the Soviet citizen buys such articles as beef, butter, or laundry soap, the final retail price he pays consists of 60 to 70 per cent tax.[10] (A tax component of 60 per cent of the selling price means, of course, in practice, that the basic economic price of the good is increased 2.5 times before it is placed into retail channels.) Other goods, such as sugar, salt, cigarettes, or vodka, are covered by a still heavier layer of tax, the latter making up as much as 70 to 88 per cent of the retail price.

Some articles sold to the consumer, like yardgoods, shoes, and apparel, appear to escape with a tax bite of "only" 40 to 55 per cent of the retail price. In fact, however, these articles are taxed twice, the first time upon emerging from the factory as intermediate products in the form of yarn, cloth, leather, etc., and the second time as finished goods.

The taxing of admission tickets to the movies provides another illustration of indirect taxation in the U.S.S.R. The Russian movie-goer pays 3.3 rubles for attending an average urban movie house, which in terms of earning power represents almost one hour's wages of the average worker. In the U.S. this cost would be the equivalent of about $1.75 for an average wage-earner. What makes the price so high is the fact that it is compounded of two charges. There is, first, the basic charge of 1.6 rubles, which represents the economic price of admission. As such, it already includes a profit for the government in its capacity as the owner of the movie house. The second, and

---

[8] See *Voprosy Ekonomiki*, No. 2, 1957, pp. 91–2.

[9] *Promyshlennost SSSR* (Statistical Handbook), Moscow, 1957, p. 13.

[10] All rates cited in this section are from the basic paper by N. Jasny, "The Soviet Price System," *American Economic Review*, December 1950, p. 853.

larger, charge consists of 1.9 rubles of turnover tax, going directly into the coffers of the treasury for the strategic expenditures in the budget.[11]

Methods of Collection

For the Soviet government, the turnover tax has two prime virtues. It is relatively painless and it is easy to collect. Because it enters into the price of all goods behind the scenes, the taxpayer is spared the agony of counting out his tax money. The government at the same time saves on the employment of tax-collectors. The retail stores throughout the country serve as the tax-gathering agencies. And so long as all citizens, urban and rural alike, must come to the stores to buy their food, clothing, and other essentials, the tax will be collected in the process, approximately as planned in the fiscal offices of the government.

For his part, the Soviet citizen enters the state stores with currency that has already been pre-taxed. In the course of making his purchases, paying the tax-laden official prices, he automatically helps to implement the government plan for recapturing a fixed proportion of the money placed in circulation. By the end of the year, when the balance sheet is drawn, it is easy to see what an impressive job of tax collecting is accomplished by the stores. In 1957, for instance, the retail trade network sold to the population a volume of goods valued at 625 billion rubles.[12] The tax component of these sales was equally imposing. Receipts from the turnover tax came to 276 billion rubles.[13] In other words, some 45 per cent of all rubles paid out by the consumer at the stores went for the payment of excise taxes, and because of the surreptitious nature of this levy, no tax receipts were issued in the process. That, too, was all to the good; the morale of the consumer was spared possible injury, while the government saved on the cost of printing receipts.

With its heavy incidence on the necessities of life, the Soviet turnover tax is of course heavily regressive. The rates are by and large determined by two basic considerations: the revenue requirements of the government and the volume of consumer goods available for distribution. Whatever the budgeted expenditures, the turnover tax must supply the bulk of the revenue. If the volume of available goods in a particular year is expected to be relatively small, the rate of the turnover tax on each commodity is raised accordingly. This is in fact what happened in the years immediately following World War II. For four consecutive years, from 1947 through 1950, the state collected through the stores about 240 billion rubles of turnover tax annually, in spite of the meager amount of goods available for sale.[14] The claims of capital investment and armament were served to the hilt; the consumer got along as best he could.

That was austerity of a high order indeed. Since 1950, however, the tax share in retail trade has been drifting downwards, dropping from 78 per cent in 1948 to 45 per cent in 1957.[15]

The Elastic Ruble

The practice of injecting varying doses of excise tax into every article the consumer buys has the effect of distorting the ruble as a yardstick of value. As a result there is no way of finding a general purchasing power equivalent of the ruble in relation to any other currency. What the ruble buys in each commodity class will depend on the amount of tax the article is planned to raise.

Measured against dollar prices the Soviet worker's expenses for food and clothing abound with incongruity. Thus when he buys a pound of meat, or fish, tea or milk, the ruble buys as much as six cents would in the United States.[16] In case of items like butter, sugar, and fruits, the purchasing power of the ruble is about three cents. In the non-food categories there is also extreme variation. When buying a shirt or nylon stockings, the Soviet citizen's ruble will command the value of only two cents. In the case of a suit, about three cents.

[11] *Economic Bulletin for Europe* (UN-ECE), Geneva, May 1957, p. 98.
[12] *SSSR v Tsifrakh* (The USSR in Figures), Central Statistical Administration, Moscow, 1958, p. 422.
[13] *Finansy SSSR* (Finances of the USSR), No. 9, 1958, p. 94.

[14] F. D. Holzman, *Soviet Taxation*, Harvard University Press, Cambridge, 1955, p. 142.
[15] F. D. Holzman, "Taxes in the USSR," *National Tax Journal*, June 1957, p. 138–47.
[16] For price calculations in this paragraph see A. Nove, "The Purchasing Power of the Soviet Ruble," *Bulletin of the Oxford University Institute of Statistics*, May 1958, 188–89.

The purchasing power of a ruble for shoes comes to four cents.

The following two examples may illustrate just how tax-packed ordinary articles of wear are in the Soviet Union. A delegation of the British weavers' trade union visiting the Moscow Oblast in September 1956 was questioned in private by a group of earnest Russian workers as to how many days they had to

TABLE 1 *Turnover Taxation in the U.S.S.R.*

YEAR	RETAIL VALUE OF TRADE	TURNOVER TAX	AVERAGE RATE OF TAX
	(In Billions of Rubles)		(Per Cent)
1940	175.1	105.9	60.5
1945	160.1	123.1	76.9
1946	247.2	190.9	77.2
1947	308.0	239.9	77.8
1948	332.0	247.3	74.5
1949	348.0	245.5	70.5
1950	359.6	236.1	65.7
1951	379.8	247.8	65.2
1952	393.6	246.9	62.7
1953	430.7	243.6	56.6
1954	481.9	224.3	46.5
1955	501.5	242.4	48.3
1956	547.0	258.6	47.2
1957	617.3	275.6	44.6
1958	668.5	301.5	45.1

Source: F. D. Holzman, "Taxes in the U.S.S.R.," *National Tax Journal*, June 1957, p. 144. Data for last two years drawn from the Annual Report of the U.S.S.R. Central Statistical Administration for the respective years.

work to earn the suits they were wearing. The Russians' findings were startling indeed. As it turned out, the British weaver had to work 7½ days, the Russian 43 days.[17] To cite another example, a shoe salesman in the U.S.S.R. earns during his workday one-tenth of the price of a pair of shoes (250 rubles).[18]

[17] *Report on Visit to the USSR* (September 16–30, 1956), Amalgamated Weavers' Association, Lewis Wright, General Secretary, Manchester, 1956, p. 8.
[18] *Steel in the Soviet Union*, American Iron and Steel Institute, New York, 1958, p. 25.

His American counterpart earns the full price of a pair in one day.

Of all consumer goods the durable variety is treated most favorably by the Soviet tax writers. But in this category, too, we find the usual range of diversity. Measured against dollar prices, musical instruments, for example, are lower-priced than cooking utensils; prices of television sets are more favorable to the consumer than the price of bicycles. Within the category as a whole, however, the ruble buys approximately as much as 11 cents would buy in the United States.

On the average, counting all the purchases he makes during the year, the Soviet consumer obtains from the ruble spent in the stores the purchasing power equivalent of 7.5 cents in the United States.[19] At this rate the average wage earner who receives 4 rubles per hour and spends 90 per cent of his money through the stores earns the equivalent of 15 dollars weekly.[20]

So far, only the consumer's ruble has been considered. The story is quite different in the state sector. There, the ruble comes close to commanding as much value as the official rate of exchange claims for it. We know, for example, from recent public Soviet statements, that it takes only 3.5 times as many rubles as dollars to buy a tank. Similarly, as shown by the official price books, the price which the government pays for a ton of steel, coal, cement, or machinery also comes close to the official rate of exchange. Within the category of investment goods, the purchasing power equivalent of the ruble lies between 20 and 30 cents.

Embarrassment for Official Theorists

The problem of explaining the turnover tax has plagued official Soviet ideologists for a long time. The tax is much too unpleasant a device to extol as a great "socialist" innovation, and too important to ignore. It should be remembered that indirect taxes of this kind have long been recognized by Marxist and liberal writers alike as "regressive" and socially iniquitous, for a tax system that taxes all individuals at the same rate without regard to their earnings imposes a relatively heavier burden on low-income recipients by exacting a

[19] A. Nove, *op. cit.*, p. 189.
[20] *Ibid.*

larger share of their income.[21] Most modern governments have therefore adopted the more equitable "progressive" tax structures — usually based on the income tax — under which tax rates rise progressively with increasing rates of income.

It is not surprising, therefore, that most of the "explanations" of the turnover tax found in official Soviet textbooks are tortured and farfetched. One can read, for example, that the turnover tax must not be compared to any other known levy because it is a unique form of "self-taxation," imposed by the workers, as the true owners of the wealth of society, upon themselves.[22] Another typical explanation will argue that the practice of singling out the consumer industries for such heavy-handed taxation is merely a matter of economy in collection, since plants in the capital goods sector are growing too rapidly.[23]

Writing on the same subject, the Soviet economist A. K. Suchkov argues that the government is justified in applying the heaviest tax rates to the food and light industries because of the shorter production cycle in these branches.[24] Hence, profit-taking can proceed at a more rapid pace. Still another explanation falls back on the old Marxian argument that only goods reaching the consumer through the market are depositories of exchange value, and

thus "commodities." By definition, then, all capital goods produced by and for the state fall outside the sphere of "commodity" production and therefore beyond the reach of the taxing authority.[25]

Within the past few years, however, Soviet economists have been encouraged to discuss the problems of price formation in the U.S.S.R. in more realistic terms. A few writers, for instance, have expressed themselves in favor of a more equal distribution of the turnover tax, and quite recently an official economic journal even admitted that some "practical workers" treat the turnover tax as a "universal excise tax."[26] But those who now attempt to treat seriously the economic function of the turnover tax tread very carefully and generally carry on their discussion in rather obscure language. Nevertheless, such meaning as does escape leaves no doubt that the turnover tax is essentially a scheme for depressing the cost of capital goods to the state. Here is a sample of the language in which the Soviet economist has recently tackled the effect of the turnover tax on prices:[27]

> The essence of the matter is as follows: Prices of producers' goods include only part (the lesser part at that) of the money accumulation in the form of profits. The other part of the accumulation, designated in practice as a tax on turnover, does not as a rule enter into that price. At the same time, prices on consumers goods contain a higher level of monetary accumulation, taking the form of profits as well as tax on turnover.

While the meaning is unmistakable, the language is painfully abstract. We need, therefore, some concrete figures to illustrate this most important point. In 1955, the state extracted from industry a total amount of "surplus product" (savings) of 321.7 billion rubles, made up of 88.7 billions in the form of "profits" and 233 billions in "turnover tax." To this amount heavy industry, which accounted for 70.5 per cent of all industrial goods produced

[21] The same policy of nominal equality, incidentally, is followed by the Soviet government in regard to rent. All occupants pay at the rate of 1.32 rubles per square meter, a charge that is admittedly below the cost of replacing any kind of housing today. The average citizen who now occupies 5.5 meters of space is thus not heavily burdened by rent, although he has to pay as much again for his utilities. Nor is he amply provided with living space. The real beneficiary is the high-paid functionary of the state. He gets ample space as well as the benefit of the low cost per unit of housing. See T. Sosnovy, "Rent in the U.S.S.R.," *The American Slavic and East European Review*, Vol. XVII, April 1959, No. 2, pp. 174–81.

[22] For a detailed treatment of the whole subject of official explanations of the turnover tax, see F. D. Holzman, *op. cit.*, Chapter 6.

[23] *Ibid.*

[24] A. K. Suchkov, *Ekonomicheskaia Priroda i Osnovnye Printsipy Organizatsii Naloga s Oborota* (The Economic Character and Basic Principles in the Organization of the Tax on Turnover), Gosfinizdat, Moscow, 1951, p. 22.

[25] See recent series of discussion articles in *Voprosy Ekonomiki*, Nos. 2–3, 1957.

[26] *Finansy SSSR* (Finances of the U.S.S.R.), No. 2, 1959, p. 37.

[27] D. D. Kondrashev, *Tsenoobrazovanie v Promyshlennosti SSSR*, (Price Formation in the Industry of the U.S.S.R.), Gosfinzdat, Moscow, 1956, p. 52.

in that year, contributed 53.4 billion rubles, or only 17 per cent of the total amount skimmed off into the treasury.[28]

This high degree of favoritism toward heavy industry has evoked the following reaction from another prominent Soviet economist:

> If prices in the capital goods sector were correlated with the value of goods, heavy industry should also have yielded about 70 per cent of the value of the "surplus product" (savings) obtained through the prices of all industrial goods produced.[29]

In other words, we have here a tax that works wonders. By its magic, every unit of currency used by the government in payment for goods becomes a "privileged" currency, exempt from paying the full economic price. By the same token, every ruble paid out by the government to the citizen is "debased" in that the price of the goods it will buy is inflated by an extra amount of profit in the form of a turnover tax.

By any test of performance, the present system of extracting tax money from the economy has worked well for the Moscow rulers. So much so, that even the reform-bent Soviet Premier seems disposed to leave the basic scheme intact. All that Mr. Khrushchev proposes to do, in effect, is to add a further refinement. Instead of relying upon indirect taxes to the extent of 85 per cent, as is the case now, he proposes to make it 100 per cent — and call it "abolition of all taxes."

In substance, nothing will be abolished, nothing sacrificed. The 50 billion rubles a year now raised through direct taxes will be collected in some other way. It is clearly not a formidable figure. To collect it, the global volume of the turnover tax would have to be increased only modestly, by some 17 per cent. As it is, the turnover tax collections have been inching upwards recently at the rate of 30 billion rubles a year. Surely from the viewpoint of the ruling New Class the prospect of governing a "taxless society" is worth the price of a modest boost in the present rates of the turn-over tax. The Soviet public will simply have to learn to view this change in the same "correct" light.

41

Economic Life in Soviet Literature*

Alexander Gerschenkron

(1950)

In the United States the sociology of industry and the school of business administration have become well established means for learning at first hand the informal details of industrial life. Study of the worker through direct contact with him has a long tradition in Europe, and even there business men are beginning to accept direct inquiries into their affairs by students of management. In the Soviet Union neither the traditions nor the channels for such studies exist. Professor Gerschenkron shows how an imaginative and informed use of literary materials can in good part fill the same function of giving us access to a more intimate and personalized picture of Soviet economic activity.

Can fiction be considered a serious source of information on *modern* economic history? In a recent article on English novels in the 1840's, William O. Aydelotte points out that information of such nature as contained in the works of the four most important social novelists of that decade (Dickens, Kingsley, Disraeli, and Mrs. Gaskell) "is highly suspect for the scholar's purpose" because "it is spotty, impressionistic, and inaccurate."[1] This is a

---

[28] Ya. Kronorod, "The Law of Value and the Problem of Price Formation in the U.S.S.R." *Voprosy Ekonomiki,* No. 2, 1957, p. 87.
[29] *Ibid.*

* Reprinted from "A Neglected Source of Economic Information on Soviet Russia," *American Slavic and East European Review,* Vol. 9 (1950), pp. 1–19, by permission of the author and the publisher.
[1] William O. Aydelotte, "The England of Marx and Mill as Reflected in Fiction," *The Journal of Economic History,* Supplement VIII, 1948 (New York, 1949), p. 43.

harsh verdict. Yet, in a somewhat milder form, it may well prove generally valid. The truth probably is that the economic historian of modern times does not need the aid of contemporaneous novels or plays. The social historian may indeed be greatly interested in inquiring as to why certain novels were written and why they were read. But this is a different matter.

No economic historian needs Balzac's *Le curé de village* in order to understand the working of the Napoleonic laws concerning inheritance. Inquiry into financial developments under the Second Empire does not require perusal of Zola's *L'Argent* or *La Curée;* and a student of the "merchant-employer" system in Silesia may safely forego reading Gerhardt Hauptmann's *Die Weber*. No additional contribution to the knowledge of peasant conditions in Russia was made either by Turgenev, or Grigorovič, or Tolstoj; and the effects of the dust bowl on the rural population of Oklahoma would not have been less clear had Steinbeck's *Grapes of Wrath* remained unwritten. Each of these authors was indeed referred to time and again in professional studies of the respective subjects, but the purpose was one of communication with the reader, that is, to strike a familiar note in the reader's mind, rather than to supply additional evidence.

Nonetheless, a fairly strong case can be made for increased preoccupation with Soviet novels, short stories, and plays on the part of Western economists who work in the field of Soviet economy. Not that the material to be found in Soviet fiction is less "spotty, impressionistic, and inaccurate" than that of Dickens' and Kingsley's. In fact, the opposite may be true. But the situation is profoundly different in other respects. Information supplied by a novelist can be disdained only if the flow from other more important sources is plentiful. This, of course, is not the case with Soviet Russia.

It has become a common practice on the part of students of Soviet economy to preface their writings on the subject with some sort of apology. This is understandable. Anyone devoting time and thought to problems of Soviet economic development must be painfully aware both of the narrow limits to the scope of his knowledge and of the distressing gaps in available information. This lack of knowledge stems essentially, although not exclusively, from the restrictive information policy of the Soviet government. Since the middle of the thirties the volume of data supplied has been steadily declining. During the war an almost complete blackout prevailed; and what has been published since its end is still very inadequate even in comparison with the low point of 1940. It is not the quantitative information alone that has deteriorated. The general descriptive Soviet literature on economic subjects has also suffered a great deal. While the volume of such literature on various portions of the current Five-Year Plan has been very considerable, its contents on the whole have been confined to a jejune repetition of official pronouncements. As a result, the innumerable books and pamphlets all seem alike. As Walter Bagehot once said, "When you have seen one Fuegian, you have seen all Fuegians — one Tasmanian, all Tasmanians."[2] The current economic literature in Soviet Russia is primitive indeed.

There is no point in exaggerating what doubtless is a very unsatisfactory situation. It is quite true that over the last decade or so a number of Western economists have impressively demonstrated that patience, imagination, and ingenuity can succeed in extracting valuable results even from such a scarce and resistant material as Soviet statistics. In order

---

[2] Walter Bagehot, *Works*, IV (Hartford, 1891), 500. The Russians are not unaware of this degradation of their economic literature. K. V. Ostrovitjanov, who was Varga's successor in the reformed Institute of Economics, said at a session of the Scientific Council of the Institute: "The fear of committing an error in posing and elaborating new problems causes economists to move away from analyses of contradictions arising in the process of development of socialist economy and reduces scholarly work to a mastication of existing resolutions, or to publication of propaganda articles and pamphlets, while serious scholarly investigation of the economic problems of socialism is avoided." He added that only a few of the recent dissertations for the degree of candidate and doctor of economics were published, because the authors did not relish having their theses printed. Cf. *Voprosy Ekonomiki*, 1948: 8, p. 74. The probable effectiveness of the speaker's admonitions for "a bolder, bolshevist approach to economic research" must be judged in the light of the recent sweeping and severe decree concerning disclosure of state secrets (*Pravda*, June 10, 1947), and Ostrovitjanov's immoderate strictures in the same speech of "errors" committed by a number of Soviet economists.

to achieve these results, the economists concerned had to pile assumption on assumption, to piece together small fragments of uncertain information into a perhaps still less certain whole, to extrapolate and to interpolate, and to unfold long inferential chains from a casually given Soviet figure or statement. Even though very often these scholars must have felt like participants in the famous game of billiards from Gilbert and Sullivan's *Mikado,* which was being played

> On a cloth untrue
> with a twisted cue,
> and elliptical billiard balls, . . .

there is no doubt that their labors have materially widened our knowledge and increased our understanding of Soviet Russia.

In many respects, however, it is precisely this increase in our grasp of the Soviet economic system that reveals and aggravates the economist's predicament. As a foundation is being laid for a scholarly study of Soviet economy with the help of tools of modern economic and statistical analysis, a growing number of new and exciting problems is brought within the purview of the economist. In the process, he becomes even more conscious of the inadequacy of his material and of a basic limitation which lies in the virtual impossibility of gaining understanding of economic processes in the Soviet Union from personal association with men who are actively engaged in these processes. The planner in the *Gosplan,* the banker in the *Gosbank* or in one of the special investment banks, the manager and the union representative of an industrial plant, the chairman of a collective farm — they all are, and, barring a radical change in Soviet policy, will remain, out of reach of the Western research worker. A scholar studying the economy of the first socialist country has not only to forego the wealth of documents which the student of capitalism once found in the British Museum; it is also unthinkable for him to have a close friend who is in charge of an industrial enterprise in the Soviet Union and moves in the very hub of the industrial life of the country. In these circumstances, no source of information, however uncertain, can be lightly rejected, and the quest for such sources deserves serious attention.

Conversations with Soviet citizens who, after the end of the war, found themselves outside Russia and her zone of influence in Europe may indeed provide valuable information. In fact, it is highly regrettable that little has been done so far to collect and to analyze information from that source, and every attempt should be made to utilize it. The matter is urgent. Memories of individuals who have suffered great tribulations in the intervening years are likely to become blurred. As times passes, and the process of their adaptation to Western ways proceeds, they must tend to lose their original viewpoints and the value of their testimonies will diminish accordingly. Finally, the accessibility of the persons concerned is dwindling through their emigration to South America, Australia, and other distant regions. At any rate, whatever information can be gleaned from this source does not transcend the years of the war. For the postwar period and for the future, one must have recourse to other sources.

The remainder of this article is devoted to a brief discussion of the possibilities of obtaining useful information from Soviet novels and plays, and to a few illustrations taken from such recent Soviet productions.

The Predominance of Economic Locales and Themes

The first question to be raised is whether or not the subject matter of Soviet literary productions is such as to arouse the economist's interest in them. The answer must be in the affirmative. Since the days of Fëdor Gladkov's *Cement,* a new type of industrial novel has developed in Soviet Russia and has been subsequently paralleled by the emergence of collective-farm novels. Very deliberately and no doubt under pressure by the government, literature has been increasingly placed in the service of the economic policies of the Soviet government. Love, friendship, the inner struggles of the individual have been pushed far into the background and sometimes eliminated altogether. Construction of factories, railroads, pipelines, and power stations; increases in mining and industrial output, application of improved methods of farming — these are the subjects to which Soviet novelists have primarily addressed themselves, if the very substantial recent crop of military novels may be disregarded. Soviet belles lettres have been dedicated to economic problems to an extent altogether unprecedented in the history of world literature, with the possible exception of the hunting songs of primitive folklore. This is a development which an economist working in the Soviet field cannot ignore.

This shift in the sphere of interest of Soviet writers, undertaken as it was under extraneous pressure, doubtless proceeded at the expense of the artistic value of their works. A pattern of monotonous uniformity has developed. Voltaire, who accepted every literary genre except the boring one, would have refused to read the average Soviet novel or play, but this is of little concern to the economist who is in search of things less exciting and more tangible than artistic values. The real problem from his point of view is whether or not this literature has been so subordinated to the propaganda interests of the government as to become worthless as a reflection of Soviet economic reality. The present writer would like to answer the question in the spirit of restrained optimism.

That Soviet literature is not only subject to a preventive censorship, but also is positively controlled and guided by the government seems reasonably certain. Otherwise it would be difficult to explain the rapidity of literary responses to changes in the Party line. A government action in the field of philosophy coupled with a campaign against Western influences immediately calls forth novels like Konovalov's *University*[3] with its brazen glorification of Russian philosophy in the face of the still valid dictum of Vladimir Solov'ëv that "what is philosophical in Russian works on philosophy is not Russian, and what is Russian in these works has no relation to philosophy."[4] The line turns against the United States and almost instantly plays like K. Simonov's *Russian Question* or Koževnikov and Prut's *The Fate of Reginald Davis*[5] are turned out. The "uprooted cosmopolitan" is put under fire, and without delay K. Simonov serves up another play, *The Foreign Shadow*,[6] where the dangers of international scientific cooperation are depicted in the darkest colors and the "cosmo-

politan" is unmasked as a spy, and, in addition, the government's policy of secrecy is glorified.

The present writer has no knowledge as to the exact nature of the actual connection: does a government agency actually present individual writers with specific assignments or is reliance on servility of the writers, in conjunction with general exhortation, considered sufficient? But strong as the ascendancy of the government is, it can hardly be absolute: a certain margin of freedom must be allowed as is shown by savage postpublication attacks in the press.[7] And this stands to reason. Complete regimentation might easily result in such an additional decline in the value of Soviet literary output as would defeat the government's purposes altogether.

Soviet discussions of "socialist realism" vs. "socialist romanticism" may be pertinent in this connection. Divested of a good deal of inane phraseology, the problem seems to be whether a Soviet writer should depict his heroes as they are or as they ought to be from the point of view of the official ideal. Presentation of society composed of Soviet *chevaliers sans peur ni reproche* should appeal to the instincts of the literary police. It may appeal to the self-preservation instincts of the authors. The result would be the "conflictless" novel as it is called in current Soviet discussions on the subject.[8] This is romanticism with a vengeance: E. T. A. Hoffman's *Die Elixiere des Teufels* without the devil. But fortunately this ideal seems to be unattainable.

Soviet economy has been one of intensive internal conflicts. As long as the ratio between investment (including military expenditures) and consumption remains so heavily weighted in favor of the former, the day-to-day economic processes in Soviet Russia are characterized by a continuous struggle between the government and the population. There is nothing sensational about these struggles. Least of all are they political in nature. But nonetheless they are very real. The government must fight the worker who is unwilling to sustain the tempo

---

[3] Grigori Konovalov, "Universitet," *Oktjabr'*, 1947: 6, 7; subsequently published in book form.
[4] Vladimir S. Solov'ev, "Nacional'nyj vopros v Rossii," *Sobranie sočinenij*, V, (St. Petersburg, n. d.), 88.
[5] K. Simonov, "The Russian Question," *Soviet Literature*, February, 1947; V. Kozevnikov and I. Prut, "Sud'ba Redzinal'da Devisa," *Zvezda*, 1947: 4.
[6] K. Simonov, "Čuzaja ten'," *Znamja*, 1949: 1.

[7] At times such attacks lead to discontinuation of the publication of a work of fiction which has been appearing serially; cf., e.g., the case of Y. German's novel "Podpolkovnik medicinskoj služby," *Zvezda*, 1949: 1.
[8] Cf., e.g., the article by N. Gribacev, "Za novyj pod'ëm sovetskoj poesij," *Znamja*, 1949: 1, p. 171.

of work in the face of inadequate increases in levels of consumption and is trying to keep the production norms as low as possible; the government must fight the manager of industrial plants who is trying in a variety of ways to evade the plan and who, conscious of inflationary pressures in the economy, is trying to hoard raw materials so as to achieve unplanned profits and the bounties and promotions which follow in the wake of such achievements; the government, in fine, must fight the collective farms, which are unwilling to surrender to the government substantial portions of their produce at prices greatly below the *kolkhoz* market prices and are employing every imaginable device to evade the obligation imposed on them.

It is not suggested that these struggles imperil the stability of the Soviet government; nor that they are inherent in the very nature of Soviet planned economy. A lower rate of investment may be relied upon to reduce the intensity of these struggles. All that is suggested here is that a literature which tries to present as "conflictless" an economy still subject to a high degree of stress and strain must inevitably and very quickly transcend the limits of verisimilitude, and that thereby literary production becomes impossible. Not necessarily so, because a strike of authors should be the answer. As Čekhov once remarked, "if you beat a hare for a sufficiently long time it may learn how to use a photographic camera." It should be not too difficult to badger a Soviet writer into submission. But the unbridgeable gulf between the "conflictless" society in the novel and on the stage and the conflict-pregnant reality would destroy all propaganda effect of literature. The Soviet discussions on romanticism and realism may perhaps be taken both as a mild form of rebellion against too great a regimentation of literature and as a sign that the regimentation is not absolute. To repeat: a certain margin of freedom must remain.

An additional point must be considered. Soviet writers, under deliberate encouragement by the government, regard themselves as apprentices to the great masters of Russian literature of the nineteenth century in matters of language and style. Their writings unmistakably reveal this influence. Ever so often in reading Soviet literature one is struck by sentences, turns of phrases, and expressions which are almost bodily lifted from *War and Peace* or *Dead Souls*. It does not seem too hazardous to suggest that style and substance are so inextricably intertwined that it is almost impossible to accept the former while neglecting the latter. It seems that despite everything, the great realistic tradition of Russian literature of the last century, the tradition of a literature that was, in many ways, the most truthful literature of all times, is still alive in Soviet Russia. It may not express itself so much in the conception and structure of the novel or the play, but it is reflected in the micro-painting of everyday life, and it is the latter that is of significance from the point of view of the problem under discussion here.

But is it possible for the non-Russian reader of Soviet works of literature to separate the wheat from the chaff, the reality from its distortion? And will the grains of truth be numerous enough to warrant the economist's search for them? A brief presentation of a number of illustrations from a few recent works of Soviet literature may be helpful in suggesting at least tentative answers to these questions.[9]

A Novel about Gold Mining

1. It may be advisable to mention first a rather singular case in which the validity of facts as supplied by the novelist was capable of being tested.

In 1948, the literary journal *Oktjabr'* published a novel on gold mining in Soviet

---

[9] Most Soviet works of fiction are first published in one of the literary journals of which at present the following should be noted: *Novyj Mir, Oktjabr', Znamja,* and *Zvezda.* The first three journals appear in Moscow, and the last one in Leningrad. For years, Mrs. Vera Aleksandrova has been publishing reviews in Russian on current Soviet fiction in various periodicals, most notably in the *Socialističeskij Vestnik,* the magazine of the Russian Social Democratic Party in exile, now appearing in New York. While Mrs. Aleksandrova's interests do not lie specifically in the economic field, she in general addresses herself to the social significance of Soviet belles lettres, and economists interested in the problems raised in this paper will find her reviews a most excellent introduction to Soviet fiction. It is, incidentally, very regrettable that these reviews are inaccessible to those who have no reading knowledge of Russian. A translation into English of at least a selection of these reviews would be desirable indeed.

Russia.[10] This novel was finished just before the outbreak of the war after its author had spent seven years in Siberia as a Party functionary in one of the gold mines. The novel describes the efforts made to increase the output of gold at a trans-Baikalian mine sometime during the thirties. The difficulties which confronted the administration of the mine and its workers are graphically presented: the inadequacy of food supplies to the miners who had been induced to move to the permafrost region by extravagant promises; the resulting low effort on the part of the workers; the hopeless primitiveness of the technological equipment; the aloofness of engineers who preferred to stay away from the mine; the deflection of sizeable portions of output into illegal channels. All this is not new to the Western economist, but this is precisely why Ganibesov's novel is of interest for the purposes of this discussion. For the Russian author's description coincides strikingly with the story of gold mining in Russia as told by a perfectly trustworthy source: John J. Littlepage,[11] the American engineer who had served for many years in a responsible capacity in the Soviet gold mine administration. There also exists a professional Soviet discussion of the subject,[12] and it is curious to see that in many respects Ganibesov's novel provides a much clearer and franker insight into the situation than did the non-fictional publication just quoted.

The Industrial Manager

2. Ever since the beginning of the First Five-Year Plan the trend in the Soviet Union has been for increased power of managers of industrial plants. "Unity of control" (*edinonačalie*) implied vesting in the manager of the enterprise the responsibility for carrying out its plan, for all matters relating to output, and to hiring and firing of workers and salaried employees of the plant. Neither the trade union through the factory committee nor the Party cell were thenceforth supposed to interfere directly in the administration of industrial enterprises. This development has raised a number of interesting problems, and economists

have every reason to search for evidence permitting them better to assess the present position of the manager within the framework of the Soviet economy. Soviet fiction does shed some light on this question. A novel by Vera Panova, *Kružilikha* (name of the plant), which was first published in 1947,[13] contains interesting material on various aspects of the question. A good deal of the novel is devoted to the relations between the manager and the chairman of the factory committee. The latter does not have much luck in his attempts to assert himself:

> Usdečkin (chairman of the factory committee) . . . came to Listopad (manager) with a number of demands concerning working conditions in the factory.
> "No, you stay out of these matters," said Listopad. "You leave all that to me."
> "Sorry, comrade manager," said Usdeckin, "but don't you know that this is a direct function of the trade union?"
> "No, I don't," said Listopad . . . "It's your business to know what your functions are." (p. 9)

The chairman of the factory committee shows some fighting spirit. He attacks the manager in the meetings of the city Party committee. But the effect is nil. The manager is unassailable, and the reason is clearly shown in the novel: he has succeeded in regularly overfulfilling the production plan. The chairman of the factory committee may protest ever so loudly against the manager's transforming the "principle of unity of control" into the "principle of autocracy." The manager knows that if the chairman should become too bothersome to him, he won't find it too difficult to get rid of this elected representative of the workers (p. 7). But would not the workers support their representative against the manager? Apparently not. And the reason is not necessarily the manager's proficiency in production. For Panova supplies an additional fact which also should be of interest to the economist. The manager had built up a secret organization of special agents who are distributed throughout the villages of the region. They watch closely the process of deliveries of

[10] V. Ganibesov, "Starateli," *Oktjabr'*, 1948: 3.
[11] John J. Littlepage, *In Search of Soviet Gold* (New York, 1938).
[12] A. P. Serebrovskij, *Na zolotom fronte* (Moscow-Leningrad, 1936).

[13] Cf. *Znamja*, 1947: 11, 12. Subsequent page references are to edition in book form (Moscow-Leningrad, 1948).

agricultural products by collective farms to the governmental procurement agencies. As soon as the quota is fulfilled and a collective farm has received the right to sell its products on a free market, representatives of "Kružilikha," who had been informed by their agents, appear on the scene, conclude the contracts and cart away grain, potatoes, and vegetables for the factory *ORS* (division of workers' supplies). By the time the other factories were officially informed of completion of deliveries to the government, Listopad had bought up the available surpluses.

The action of the novel takes place in 1945; nevertheless, this practice sheds an interesting light on the operation of the "*kolkhoz* market" in conditions of scarcity, and may have been preserved well beyond the abolition of rationing in 1947 to the extent that the latter did not necessarily mean immediate elimination of food scarcities.

It is not unlikely that the scarcities of the war period in general contributed to strengthening the position of the manager vs. the workers, thus supplementing such increases in his power as resulted from the labor legislation which tied the worker to the factory and which is referred to in the novel as "wartime legislation," even though now, four years after the end of the war, it is still on the statute book. In Panova's novel, a youth working in the factory absents himself without permission for a week. The manager can surrender him to the court. In this particular case, he decides to place no strain on the quality of mercy, and this again seems to be illuminating: the manager's power to bind and to loose must have greatly contributed to equipping him with new paternalistic traits. It is therefore not surprising to find in *Kružilikha* and elsewhere in Soviet fiction that the manager, in addressing subordinates, uses the time-consecrated feudal *ty* (thou) while the subordinates use the respectful *vy* (you).

A manager overfulfilling production plans acquires an impregnable position because of the support of his economic ministry. But Panova's novel touches on an even more important problem: the basic strength of the manager in relation to the central authorities. It describes how difficult it was to dismiss Listopad's predecessor, although, according to the novel, he had proved unable to meet the wartime plans. The manager claimed that the plans exceeded the factory's capacity. And in this, Panova informs us, he found support even from some members of the local Party committee who thought that "it would not be so bad if the plan were to be cut by about fifteen per cent. Everything would become much easier, the factory would show better performance, and come into good standing with the *Narkomat* (Ministry)" (p. 115).

The local Party functionary began a struggle against the manager, in which he was not countenanced by the city Party committee. Its chairman felt that this was a delicate matter to be decided between the *Narkom* and the manager. According to the novel, the local Party man in the plant succeeded in enlisting the help of some engineers, foremen, and skilled workers of the plant and prepared a report for submission to a special commission sent to the plant by the Ministry. His opinion prevailed, but the story carries strong implications that without this help from inside the factory the Ministry would have acquiesced in the lowering of plan goals.

Similarly, in a play by A. Sofronov, *Beketov's Career*,[14] combines which have been produced by a large Soviet factory regularly break down in the fields. The Ministry in charge of the factory sends down a representative who instantly dismisses the manager of the factory. But the Ministry's action has been provoked by a series of anonymous letters written by the factory's chief engineer who has been aspiring to the manager's position.

This is a point well worth dwelling upon. Very frequently, in professional presentations of the *modus operandi* of Soviet economy, the impression is created of a completely centralized framework within which the manager of the individual enterprise receives binding orders by the central plan as to composition and size of the plant's inputs and outputs. This may tend to disguise important developments. Even the pioneering work by Bienstock, Schwarz, and Yugow,[15] in which a good deal of information on the sphere of autonomy of industrial plant managers has been analyzed,

---

[14] A. Sofronov, "Kar'era Beketova," *Novyj Mir*, 1949: 4.

[15] Gregory Bienstock, Solomon M. Schwarz, and Aaron Yugow, *Management in Russian Industry and Agriculture* (New York, 1944).

perhaps still underestimates the actual scope of that autonomy. It would seem that in appraising the way in which the Soviet economy works and the degree of its centralization, it may be advisable to distinguish between the administrative surface and the economic core of the problem. There is no question that the Soviet administration of the economy covers by central planning overwhelmingly large parts of that economy. It is conceivable, however, that a good deal of what formally sails under the name of central planning is in fact based on decisions taken on the level of plant management.[16] It is conceivable that in reality

there are considerable limitations on the knowledge and foreknowledge of central authorities as to the actual conditions and developments in the individual plants. An economist who has been wondering about relationships in the nature of those touched upon in the preceding footnote may feel that the material contained in Panova's novel or in Sofronov's play does in some measure enhance the validity of the questions raised.

In this connection another play by A. Sofronov, which, like *Kružilikha*, was awarded the Stalin prize,[17] is also revealing. The central figure of the play is again a successful industrial manager, Potapov. His plant, which specializes in machine tool production for construction of agricultural machines, has been overfulfilling the plan. The play begins with Potapov's decision to fulfill the factory's current (Fourth) Five-Year Plan in three-and-a half years. Immediately thereafter, however, he is presented with a request from the manager of a nearby textile plant. Potapov is asked to devote some of his capacity to the output of textile machinery for the neighboring enterprise. The whole plot of the play turns around the request. Potapov first refuses and it takes full four acts of suasion and persuasion, including a decision of the district Party committee, to make him acquiesce in the wishes of the textile plant.

The details of the play need not occupy us, although some of them are illuminating (e.g., the attitude of humorous resignation which the average Russian displays toward government and Party slogans). Nor is it necessary to concern ourselves with the moral of the play, the intended propaganda effect of which is clear: the Soviet government and the Communist Party are interested not only in production of investment goods for further investment, but also for immediate use in consumption goods industries; and the play contains sharp strictures on the feeling of superiority shown on the part of representatives of heavy industry toward those of light industry, a feeling presumably intensified during the war. But while all this is certainly significant, what is of

---

[16] An example may serve to illustrate the point. Production and consumption of copper is centrally planned. Copper is included in what is called in Russia "material balances," that is, balance-sheet-like juxtapositions of output and consumption of individual commodities in terms of physical quantities. In Soviet literature very much emphasis is placed on this method of planning through "material balances." It is said to assure absence of disproportionalities. Now copper remained in short supply throughout most of the thirties. Domestic production grew at too slow a rate; imports remained substantial, and the Soviet government attempted for years to reduce the consumption of copper by introduction of substitutes in less essential lines of production. These attempts showed but a moderate degree of success, until, in 1937, the government decided to increase drastically the price of copper while keeping constant the planned cost of commodities in the production of which the metal was used. Apparently, the effect was all that could be desired. Copper was thenceforth confined to more essential uses, and substitutes began to be utilized on a significant scale. (Cf. G. Kozlov, *Khozjajstvennyj rasčët v socialstičeskom obščestve* [Ogiz, 1945], p. 65).

This obviously raises a question: why did not the central planning authority simply change the pattern of copper consumption in its "material balances." Why did the Soviet government have to have recourse to the indirect device of a price increase which surely is more uncertain and less transparent in its effects? There is a strong presumption in favor of believing that the Soviet government could not use the more direct method because it *did not know* in what segments of the copper-using industry and to what extent the restrictions should and could be applied. In other words, the central planning authority accepted decisions of the managers of the individual plants. Presumably, *after* the rise in price, the pattern of copper consumption in the "material balances" was adapted to the new situation.

[17] A. Sofronov, "Moskovskij kharakter," *Oktjabr'*, 1949: 1.

interest here is that throughout the play an important decision with respect to the production program is assumed to lie within Potapov's discretion: "If you agree, the Ministry won't have any objections!" (p. 110). And, it is interesting to add that the resolution of the Party committee does not urge the Ministry to *instruct* Potapov to accept the order of the textile factory, but merely urges the Ministry to *allow* him to do so.

This illustrates the supposition that large portions of industrial output may be in fact only very imperfectly controlled by the plan, if they are so controlled at all; that the manager, and particularly the plan-overfulfilling manager, enjoys a considerable sphere within which he can make rather independently basic decisions with respect to both the type of goods to be produced and the mode of their disposal. The latter, incidentally, becomes to a large extent a matter of personal connections. As such it introduces an element of chance and narrowness into the allocation of resources as an alternative both to the comprehensive decision of the central planner and to the objective price mechanism of the market. We shall supply presently some additional illustrations for this role of personal connections in Soviet economy. Suffice it to say here that the problem is well worth further watching. Could it be that the limitations on effective central planning in conjunction with absence of a free and broad market for industrial goods produce within the Soviet economy certain aspects of localism which in general were peculiar to the narrow economy of the medieval city?

Sofronov poses the managerial problem in Soviet Russia with a good deal of clarity, when he lets Potapov's wife tell him reproachfully: "Why do you say so often 'my factory,' 'I am the manager,' 'I am the *khozjain*' (owner, boss)? You are a *khozjajstvennik* (a responsible economic functionary), but the state, the people — that's the *khozjain*."[18] This indeed is the problem: the degree to which a *khozjajstvennik* tends to become a *khozjain*. Both

Panova's novel and Sofronov's play provide interesting fragments of information on this problem.

The increase in the power of managers of Soviet industrial plants is sometimes regarded as an irresistible evolution, which will continue unabated in the years to come. Others may feel that such strengthening in the position of the manager as has taken place in the past has been a temporary phenomenon, occasioned primarily by the fact that development of institutional machinery designed to supervise the execution of the plan has lagged behind development of an apparatus for plan-making. Naturally, fiction will provide no answer to such speculations. But the attention that at present is being devoted to the problem by Soviet fiction may be indicative of its importance and perhaps even adumbrate the approach of a period of critical decisions with regard to the relations between the managers and central authorities.

On the Kolkhoz

3. Soviet postwar literature includes a considerable crop of collective-farm novels and plays. Many of them serve to illustrate the fact that the struggle of the government vs. the peasants in evading the obligation to deliver grain to the procurement agencies has continued unabated. Both the play of Nikolaj Virta, *Our Daily Bread* and the novel by Semën Babaevskij, *Knight of the Golden Star*[19] refer to the collective farm practice of hiding grain by adding it to the "seed fund" which in the case described by Virta came to exceed the plan threefold (p. 46). In Babaevskij's novel the chairman of a collective farm becomes apprehensive of a possible inspection of the "seed fund" and distributes the surplus among the members of the *kolkhoz*. His purpose is to keep the grain for sale on the *kolkhoz* market until the spring, when prices will be high. In addition, in Virta's play, a *kolkhoz* chairman hides the grain by letting it escape into the offals during threshing with the intention of recovering it later in the winter. Such episodes must be viewed in the light of the

---

[18] For a very similar retort by which a manager of a railroad is reprimanded, cf. the recent play by A. Surov, "Zelënaja ulica," *Oktjabr'*, 1949: 5, p. 118.

[19] Nikolaj Virta, "Khleb nas nasuščnyj" *Zvezda*, 1947: 6, Semen Babaevskij, "Kavaler zolotoj zvezdy," *Oktjabr'* 1947: 4; 1948: 4, 5.

fact that grain deliveries of collective farms to the government are legally computed not on the basis of harvest, and not even on the basis of area sown (as was the custom until 1940), but on the basis of the aggregate arable land of the *kolkhoz;* computations in relation to area sown apparently either lead to a diminution of the area under cultivation in relation to total arable land, or at least prevented an increase in that ratio. In 1947, the system was rendered more flexible by varying the "delivery norms" in accordance with the existing relations between total arable land of the individual *kolkhoz* and the number of able-bodied workers available to it;[20] but the principle of government deliveries on the basis of the land available rather than on the basis of the harvest was fully maintained.

The question then arises as to the purpose pursued by *kolkhozy* in hiding their grain. It should be noted that the deliveries mentioned in the preceding paragraph constitute only a portion of the centralized deliveries to the government. A very substantial share of the aggregate[21] is delivered by the *kolkhozy* in the form of a payment in kind for work performed for them by the Machine Tractor Stations (MTS). Such payments are computed on the basis of the harvest, but for the most part the computation is made on the basis of the biological (field) yield rather than on that of the actual (barn) yield. It is only the reaping and threshing operations for which the payment is calculated in accordance with quantities actually reaped or threshed. The aim of these arrangements obviously was to render purposeless the various devices by which the *kolkozy* tried to evade their obligations. It is therefore useful to note the interest which Soviet fiction takes in those devices and to speculate as to how their continued use might be reconciled with a legal framework that *a priori* seemed to have rendered them inapplicable.

Possibly, the farm hiding grain avoids the pressure to deliver *additional* grain to the government under the so-called "decentralized deliveries." More likely is the supposition that the rigid stipulations of the legislation are im-

20 *Pravda*, March 7, 1947.
21 E.g., 50 per cent in 1937; cf. L. S. Galimon, *Dokhody Mashino-Traktornykh Stanci* (Moscow, 1948), p. 8.

possible of practical implementation and that in reality grain deliveries are determined by taking, in some manner, account of the actual production of grain. Still another possibility is that by concealment of grain the *kolkhoz* hopes to achieve a reduction of future obligations. Finally, there may be, of course, outright bribery of officials in charge of supervising the process of grain deliveries. In Virta's play the maleficent chairman of the *kolkhoz* even goes so far as to bribe the director of the MTS station into issuing a falsified certificate concerning the quantity of grain threshed and the employee of the procurement agency into issuing a fictitious receipt for grain that never has been delivered.

In the postwar collective-farm fiction the role of the hero is assigned to the home-coming veteran who immediately upon his return acquires a dominant position in the collective farm or in the local Soviet and with great energy leads the *kolkhoz* on the road of adjustment to peacetime conditions. Both in the novel and in the play the respective heroes are able to uncover the malefactors and to reform the *kolkhoz*. Neither fiction nor any other source, naturally, can provide an answer to the question of the over-all quantitative significance of evasions of government regulations by the collective farms.

Of some interest is the efficient way in which the Knight of the Golden Star, who has become chairman of the local Soviet, dismisses the guilty administration of the *kolkhoz*. He makes up his mind as to who should succeed the old chairman, and, at a late hour of night, convokes a meeting of *kolkhoz* membership and has the satisfaction of seeing that the person of his choice is spontaneously nominated by the assembly and instantly elected. This sidelight on the operation of *kolkhoz* elections is of some importance. So is the fact that at least one person in the novel protests against it and considers it a breach of the *kolkhoz* covenant.

In the collective-farm fiction considerable attention is devoted to the problem of individual plots of land of the *kolkhoz* members, and to the more intensive work devoted to these plots as compared with the work on *kolkhoz* fields. In Babaevskij's novel an interesting theory is even developed by two *kolkhoz* chairmen independently of each other to the effect that greater sowing of cereals on individual plots would tend to spread the risk so that a crop failure on *kolkhoz* fields would be compensated by a good harvest on the individual plots. While the logical persuasiveness of this theory is probably not too great, the fact that it is being expounded provides some additional insight into the attitudes of collective farmers.

The Cost of Record Performances

4. An interesting problem suggested by perusal of Soviet fiction refers to the existence of "leading" *kolkhozy*. A good deal of the novel by V. Il'enkov, *The High Way*,[22] is devoted to this question. The difference between the leading *kolkhoz*, which is managed by the father of the hero of the novel, and another one not far away is striking: "We distribute 12 kilograms of grain and in addition 4½ rubles per working day,[23] and there (i.e., in the poorer *kolkhoz*) it is years since they had enough bread to eat."[24]

The problem undoubtedly is a delicate one. The government naturally favors *kolkhozy* showing an extraordinary performance. Within a certain margin, they serve as a model for the remainder of collective farms in the region or district. The record performance, as often as not, is the result of a deliberate governmental policy. The previously quoted play by Virta shows how the local Soviet can affect the production results as among the individual *kolkhozy* by directing, in crucial moments, trucks and tractors to one *kolkhoz* in preference to others. Again, it may be noted parenthetically, the problem of personal connections comes in: in Il'enkov's novel one person expresses the opinion that unless at least the first secretary of the district Party committee, who is the actual boss of the chairman of the regional Soviet and, in fact, of the whole region, is invited to the planned bear-hunting expedition of the *kolkhoz*, it might be difficult to obtain gasoline for tractors during the summer.[25]

But the problem is a much broader one. The record performance of one *kolkhoz* may be achieved at the expense of losses by other *kolkhozy* which are greatly in excess of the increment in output realized through the record

performance. During the last war the shipyards in California from time to time would produce a Liberty boat within twenty-four hours instead of the usual 18–21 days. Impressive as such performances were, they were bought at the cost of delaying output for some fifteen boats in construction in the respective yard because all scarce equipment, such as cranes, was concentrated on the record boat. The great importance which is attributed to record performances in Soviet Russia doubtless constitutes a serious problem from the point of view of allocation of scarce resources and one may be grateful to Soviet fiction for supplying some sidelights on the question. It may be rewarding to look for analogous literary illustrations in the field of industry and mining where the problem may well be much more acute.[26]

A similar difficulty appears, in a slightly different form, in Babaevskij's novel. The hero proposes an electric power station to be built by his village, which consists of three collective farms. In the course of the execution of this proposal, he is promoted to chairmanship of the district Soviet executive committee and immediately decides to increase the capacity of the power station so as to make it serve the whole district. This action dismays the neighbors in his own village, because they had gone to great trouble in floating down the river to the village the lumber for the construction of the power station, and they are willing to share neither the fruits of their labor nor the glory of being the first electrically lit village of the region. The curious thing, however, is that when the hero is approached by a representative of a neighboring district who asks him to increase the capacity of the station further, so that it may serve more than one district, he refuses bluntly. None of the arguments on the virtues of cooperation and the dangers of selfishness with which he so eloquently allayed the misgivings of his neighbors seems to occur to him now. And the question is left uncertain except for a slight hint that the secretary of the district Party committee may take the matter

---

[22] V. Il'enkov "Bol'šaja doroga," *Oktjabr'*, 1949: 1, 2.

[23] "Working day" is a conventional measure of work performed by the members of the *kolkhoz*, and is not identical with a calendar day.

[24] Il'enkov, *op. cit.*, p. 93.

[25] *Ibid.*, p. 59.

[26] The previously quoted play by A. Surov, *The Green Street*, pivots around a sharply-criticized attempt on the part of a railroad administration to establish a record of performance merely for window-dressing purposes in lieu of sustained improvements in the speed of transportation and the volume of goods carried. Cf. *Novyj Mir*, 1949: 5.

up. The desire to monopolize achievements in Soviet economy is thus rather strikingly illustrated. The double aspect of monopolistic developments — which both promote and retard progress — may appeal to the dialectically trained minds of the Soviet leaders, but it also constitutes a grave problem calling for difficult practical decisions.

The Personal Factor

5. Perhaps it is permissible to return for a brief moment to the role of personal connections which was touched upon earlier. For Babaevskij's novel provides some additional material on the subject. When the village needs lumber for the construction of the electric power station, the first (although ineffectual) attempt to obtain it leads the Knight of the Golden Star to undertake a journey to a personal friend of the manager of the district consumers' cooperative, who is said to be in a position to arrange dealings of this sort: "There is no point in going to regional administration. They can't do anything without Moscow's consent. . . . You had better go to Pjatigorsk. I have a friend there . . . a wonderful fellow. I'll write to him, and he'll do everything."[27] When that manager is subsequently sent to Moscow to secure equipment for the station, he emphasizes in his report of the trip how helpful were the personal connections he had established, and he suggests to the "Knight" that "a certain volume of butter," if taken along, "would be extremely helpful in further attempts to purchase needed materials."

In a rather similar manner, it may be added, operates Grigori Kondrašev, an architect in K. Simonov's novel *The Smoke of the Fatherland;*[28] an additional element in this case seems to be that Kondrašev, while using personal connections for the needs of his housing projects under construction, does not forget his own person and manages to derive personal benefits from his various transactions. Interestingly enough, Simonov volunteers the information that the period of postwar distortion was particularly propitious for men of Kondrašev's type, but that Kondrašev had operated in essentially the same way before the war.

In Il'enkov's novel the chairman of the

kolkhoz, while trying to obtain copper wire, proceeds by applying to the factory in which his brother works as a foreman. It is worth noting that the request is refused because in the past the chairman of the *kolkhoz* had refused to release to the factory in question twenty *kolkhoz* members. One is struck time and again by how much of economic activities is carried out independently of the plan and of central supervision.

A Word in Conclusion

It has not been attempted in the preceding discussion to go into the novelist's or playwright's attitude to the occurrences he relates. This is a more difficult problem and perhaps a not too relevant one from the point of view of this paper. Naturally, Babaevskij and Virta both disapprove of farmers' concealing grain from the government. The perpetrators are surrendered to what presumably will be swift and merciless justice. We are told in plain words that Sofronov's manager should have complied with the demand of the textile factory and produced for them the presses they need. But it would be much more difficult to state clearly whether, for instance, Panova's sympathies are with the manager of the plant or the pathetic representative of the union whom the former bullies and badgers to his heart's content. And still more difficult would it be to express such a judgment with regard to the little facts of everyday economic life as related in fiction. Revealing as they may be to the foreign observer, the Soviet writer often takes their existence for granted and therefore does not feel under any compulsion to label them as "good" or "bad."

If some positive conclusion may be drawn from the preceding discussion, it is that it does not seem too difficult to discern in Soviet fiction descriptions of facts and relations which appear both plausible and instructive. A good deal of material an economist may find in Soviet fiction he ought to be able to place within the framework of hypotheses and questions which he has formulated on the basis of professional studies of the Soviet economic scene. While his perusal of the works of fiction will not lead to any "proofs" of his hypotheses or unambiguous answers to his questions, the cumulative effect of recurring fragments of information, all pointing in the same direction, will tend to strengthen in some measure such tentative

---

[27] Babaevskij, *op. cit.,* p. 5.
[28] Konstanin Simonov, "Dym Otečestva," *Novyj Mir,* 1947: 1, particularly pp. 32–37.

generalizations as he may have ventured upon. And contrariwise he may find Soviet fiction rather suggestive, and, very often, it may be from this side that the student of Russia's present economy may receive impulses and viewpoints which he may wish to apply in his study of the professional literature.

But the significance of Soviet fiction seems even to go beyond this. Fadeev's *Young Guard* or Popov's *Steel and Slag*[29] may be but indifferent novels, but they still give a most vivid description of the period of evacuation in the Donbas before the wave of advancing Germans, and such a description provides an invaluable background against which the economist may place such quantitative data on evacuation of factories as are, for instance, contained in Voznesenskij's book on Soviet war economy. And, similarly, Pavlenko's *Happiness*[30] allows at least a glimpse of the great migrations that must have taken place in Soviet Russia upon the conclusion of the war. It is such Soviet fiction that opens to the economist the road to acquiring some sense of the everyday atmosphere of Soviet economic life and of its human fabric without which any scholarly study must remain a lifeless shell.

— *To Here* —

42

Putting Butter in the Porridge*

from Komsomolskaya Pravda

(1958)

This little story on tipping, taken from the Soviet press, is another somewhat unorthodox source for material on consumer services and

labor conditions. It has the virtue of dealing with a bit of reality — well nigh universal — which more formal and official Soviet sources claim to have expunged. They believe tipping to be symbolic of the degradation presumed typical of the worker in bourgeois-capitalist countries.

Not enough is written about the creative processes concerned in the work of journalists. The question of joint authorship, for example, has been entirely neglected. When a reader sees an article in a newspaper or magazine and it bears a double byline, he assumes that both writers share the same views and even resemble one another, like Siamese twins. It isn't that way at all. The path of co-authorship is thorny and dangerous. This article attempts to fill this gap in journalism theory and to warn those who may lightheartedly undertake to write an article in collaboration, unaware of all the complications of doing so.

This is what happened to us. We left the editorial offices late one night. The subway had shut for the night, the last trolleybus had gone back to the depot, and we hailed a cab. The driver was in a happy mood; he joked all the way, entertaining us with amusing stories.

"All evening I've been driving a tipsy lickspittle from one address to another. A well dressed man, carrying a box of chocolates, entered the cab. 'Take me to Meshchanskaya Street!' he said. We reached Meshchanskaya. He looked at the house and said, 'This doesn't seem the right place. I think Ivan Dmitriyevich moved recently. Let's try Peschanaya Street.' Again my fare was wrong. 'Pardon me,' I said, 'but whom are you looking for?' 'I found out that today is the birthday of my boss's wife,' he replied. 'I haven't been invited, but I want to bring her a gift.' Then we went to Borovskoy Chaussee and from there to Cheremushki," the driver said, choking with laughter and slowing down the car. "Finally I let the man out at his house on Nizhnaya Maslovka."

We were so absorbed in his story that we hardly realized we had reached our destination. The driver turned off the meter and switched on the light. The meter read "10." One of us took out a ten-ruble note, thanked the driver and handed it to him. The driver's good-natured face suddenly twisted in a grimace of displeasure. He scowled at us:

"Even hack drivers used to get tips. And

[29] A. Fadeev, *Molodaja Gvardija* (Moscow, 1947); V. Popov, "Stal' i Šlak," *Znamja*, 1949: 1, 2.

[30] P. Pavlenko, "Sčast'e," *Znamja*, 1947: 7.

* Reprinted from " 'Butter in the Porridge': The Prevalence of Tipping," (feuilleton), G. Osheverov and I. Shatunovsky, *Komsomolskaya Pravda* (Jan. 14, 1958), p. 4, translated in *Current Digest of the Soviet Press*, Vol. 10, No. 2 pp. 21–43, published at Columbia University by the Joint Committee on Slavic Studies appointed by the American Council of Learned Societies and the Social Science Research Council. Used by permission of the publisher.

this is no hack, it's a modern machine! What's the price of oats nowadays?"

The second of us then reached into his pocket and handed the driver three rubles more. The driver's cheerful mood promptly returned.

"Your friend's a provincial," he said and drove off.

We remained standing on the empty street and suddenly found ourselves arguing.

"What impudence!" said the one who had been called a provincial, as he watched the red tail light of the departing taxi.

"That's not impudence at all," objected the "non-provincial." "Tipping is customary. Not only in cabs."

"Perhaps we ought to write about it."

"Let's study the problem."

We decided to do so.

Next morning we began our study. All day long we roamed the city on foot and by car, and toward evening, hungry, we entered a restaurant on Soviet Square.

The band was playing, champagne corks were popping; in a word, everything was as it should be in a restaurant. Not more than half an hour passed before a waiter named Minov noticed us. We ordered hors d'oeuvres, soup, a main course and dessert. The waiter seemed to have noted it all on his pad, but still he stood at our table, waiting.

"And how about something to drink?" He looked at us, puzzled.

"No thanks."

"This is a restaurant, not a lunchroom, you know. Well, what will you order to drink?"

He said this quite loudly, so that people seated nearby would hear.

"He's right, it's awkward," the non-provincial said in embarrassment, and added: "Bring a light wine."

Our waiter went to work busily. He kept disappearing into the kitchen and reappearing with the next dish. Strangely, however, at each reappearance Minov exuded a stronger smell of vodka. His stops in the kitchen became longer. When he brought the coffee he was swaying visibly.

Then, as the saying goes, came the time of reckoning. The waiter handed us the bill. Lord! It turned out that we owed 160 rubles. At a loss, we studied the bill and saw that the kopeks had been put down in the ruble column and the rubles in the ten-ruble column. We protested mildly.

"Of course — this isn't your bill," said the waiter. "There's been a mistake."

He left and soon returned with a fresh set of arithmetical calculations.

"Here you are: 213 rubles, no kopeks."

"This is a fraud!" protested the provincial.

"Let's pay the 213," the non-provincial urged. "Let's pay before he demands a full 500. It could be worse."

"Oh, no!" objected the provincial firmly. "Please ask your superior to come here."

The head waiter appeared at the table, then the manager. A lengthy re-count began:

"Did you order kharcho? Did you have shashlik?"

We sat there as if we were being interrogated on the witness stand. People at nearby tables shot far from sympathetic glances at us.

"You ought to know that the accepted practice in restaurants is to leave a 10 per cent tip," a dark-haired man seated across from us volunteered.

Finally the reckoning was completed. We owed 87 rubles and a few kopeks.

"Apologize to these citizens," declared the manager angrily, and went off with the head waiter.

But Minov had no intention of apologizing. He picked up the hundred-ruble note from the table and did not want to give us our change. We assumed this from the fact that he put the note in his wallet, bowed and said: "Thank you kindly!"

We rose from the table. In the cloakroom the attendant, a man past pension age, with a luxuriant Bryan mustache, brushed our jackets as energetically as though we had spent the evening shaking out featherbeds or hauling sacks of flour. Then Bryan helped us on with our coats, set out our rubbers, brushed our perfectly clean overcoats, and he gave us other touching signs of attention. No, he had not taken us for foreign ambassadors or theater stars. After having performed the full ceremonial, Bryan looked at us imploringly. The non-provincial took out two rubles, but handed Bryan only one. Bryan longingly watched the remaining ruble disappear into the non-provincial's pocket and whispered in a honeyed voice:

"My grandmother used to say you won't go

wrong if you put more butter in the porridge."

The non-provincial was embarrassed and gave Bryan the other ruble.

When you become co-authors — we feel we must note this fact in our article — you become so close that you begin to take your meals, entertainment, and relaxation together. That is how we came to decide (excuse the intimacy) to go together to the Central Baths just before New Year's.

We shall not trouble the reader with a description of details that are of no esthetic interest. Let us state merely that when we reached the cashier we acted quite differently. The provincial paid for all services in advance. The non-provincial paid only for admission.

"You'll have to pay all over again, anyway," said the non-provincial acidly.

And indeed we did have to pay the bath attendants at every step, for every small service. We had to pay one for lazily slapping our bellies [by way of massage] in the soap room, another for handing us the cluster of twigs that had already seen use on the backs of at least a dozen clients, a third for handing us a towel, for being so polite as to greet us with the traditional good wishes on completion of the bath, and for wrapping our linen in paper.

The non-provincial paid in silence, while the provincial objected in embarrassment:

"But I've paid the cashier for all this already — for the twigs and the towel and the good wishes, too."

"But you paid that to the cashier," we were told. And once again we heard the familiar parable about the grandma who told her hardly youthful grandson to add more butter to the porridge.

"That's the last of it, I hope," said the provincial as he went to the cloakroom.

Alas, a new tribulation awaited him. Two healthy young fellows, helping people on with their coats, were collecting gratuities. They stuffed the notes into their pockets and tossed the change, clattering into a dish.

"This is the last straw!" exclaimed the provincial. "We must write about all this."

We sat together at one desk in our office and pondered all that we had witnessed. We recalled visits to the theater, where we handed out a ruble for a 20-kopek program and paid triple the rental price for a hired pair of opera glasses. No one thought of giving us our change; it was kept as a tip. We had been in clubs, billiard rooms, and barber shops, and everywhere attendants asked, unabashed, for tips "for tea," and took them without a trace of embarrassment. Lovers of free and generous "tea drinking" are to be found in many stores. If you want to buy a scarce item, give a clerk something "for tea" and you will be handed a package from under the counter or receive a whispered tip-off when to come for the scarce item.

Curiously, in discussing all this the provincial boiled with wrath but the non-provincial merely smiled.

"This isn't the worst possible evil," he remarked. "What are a few tips."

"But isn't it shameful that in the forty-first year of Soviet rule the ways of the merchants should still be with us here and there?" fumed the provincial. "It was in the past that merchants on a spree went about tossing their money around, humiliating people by their tipping."

"What if those who accept tips nowadays don't feel offended by them?"

There was a pause. The provincial paced the room and exclaimed:

"Can't you see that tipping degrades both the giver, who becomes habituated to feeling superior and arrogant, and the receiver? Just think of the number of healthy young men working at jobs that yield tips. They should be working at real jobs, but instead they're copying grandma's stories about the porridge and the butter from bearded old fellows."

We argued until we were hoarse, wasted a heap of time and, having reached the point of mutual insult, parted.

Now we eat apart, go to the theater apart, ride in different taxicabs. The provincial, as a matter of principle, refuses to tip, bringing on many an ironical smile or insult. Once a taxi driver, whom he had paid precisely the amount the meter showed, said sarcastically: "If you're so poor, you can take your money back. We deliver the poor free of charge."

The non-provincial, true to himself, always has one-ruble notes handy in his pocket. And he always gets a respectful bow in restaurants and theater cloakrooms; grateful barbers have never given him a jagged haircut or snipped a tuft of hair from the top of his head to warn colleagues that the client was miserly.

We never did produce the feuilleton. We came together again only to tell the reader about the trials and tribulations of joint authorship. As for the issue itself, each has held to his own point of view, confident that the reader is on his side.

SUGGESTIONS FOR FURTHER READING

Organization and Growth

BAYKOV, ALEXANDER, *The Development of the Soviet Economic System: An Essay on the Experience of Planning in the U.S.S.R.* New York: The Macmillan Company, 1947.

> An historical approach.

CAMPBELL, R. W., *Soviet Economic Power: Its Organization, Growth, and Challenge.* Boston: Houghton Mifflin Co., 1960.

DOBB, MAURICE, *Soviet Economic Development Since 1917.* New York: International Publishers Co., 1948.

> A Marxist interpretation.

SCHWARTZ, HARRY, *Russia's Soviet Economy,* 2d ed. Englewood Cliffs, N.J.: Prentice-Hall, Inc., 1954.

> This has become the standard textbook on the Soviet economy in U.S. college courses.

SUBCOMMITTEE ON ECONOMIC STATISTICS OF THE JOINT ECONOMIC COMMITTEE, *Comparisons of the United States and Soviet Economies,* Parts 1–3. Papers submitted to the Subcommittee on Economic Statistics of the Joint Economic Committee, Eighty-sixth Congress, First Session, 1959.

> Discussions of various aspects of the economic cold war.

Agriculture

BELOV, FEDOR, *The History of a Soviet Collective Farm.* New York: Frederick A. Praeger, Inc., 1955.

> Written by the man who served as its Chairman from 1947–1949.

HUBBARD, LEONARD E., *The Economics of Soviet Agriculture.* London: Macmillan and Co., Ltd., 1939.

JASNY, NAUM, *The Socialized Agriculture of the U.S.S.R.: Plans and Performance.* Stanford University, Calif.: Stanford University Press, 1949.

LAIRD, ROY D., *Collective Farming in Russia: A Political Study of the Soviet Kolkhozy*. Lawrence, Kan.: University of Kansas Publications, Social Science Studies, 1958.

Focused largely on post-Stalin developments.

VOLIN, LAZAR, *A Survey of Soviet Russian Agriculture*. U.S. Department of Agriculture, Agriculture Monograph No. 5, 1951.

VUCINICH, ALEXANDER, *Soviet Economic Institutions: The Social Structure of Production Units*. Stanford University, Calif.: Stanford University Press, 1952.

The social context of work in the U.S.S.R., with special attention to collective and state farms.

Management, Labor, and the Consumer

BERLINER, JOSEPH S., *Factory and Manager in the U.S.S.R.* Cambridge, Mass.: Harvard University Press, 1957.

BIENSTOCK, GREGORY, SOLOMON N. SCHWARZ and AARON YUGOW, *Management in Russian Industry and Agriculture*. New York: Oxford University Press, 1944.

DEUTSCHER, ISAAC, *Soviet Trade Unions*. London: Royal Institute of International Affairs, 1950.

GRANICK, DAVID, *The Red Executive*. Garden City, N.Y.: Doubleday & Company, Inc., 1960.

HOLZMAN, FRANKLYN D., *Soviet Taxation: The Fiscal and Monetary Problems of a Planned Economy*. Cambridge, Mass.: Harvard University Press, 1955.

SCHWARZ, SOLOMON M., *Labor in the Soviet Union*. New York: Frederick A. Praeger, Inc., 1952.

The Mind and the Spirit

The Soviet system is a purposive mobilized system. It has made strenuous efforts to enlist, control, discipline, and direct the population in the interest of radical social reconstruction, rapid industrial growth and development, and the strengthening and export of a one-party political system. By comparison, the life of the mind and spirit has been neglected. Contributing to this has been the heritage of Marxist philosophy in which the life of the mind is part of the "superstructure," dependent for its form and content upon the economic base. In addition, the dynamism and power orientation of the regime has turned attention away from concern with the spirit. As with the social institutions and structures to be treated in Chapter V, the predominant Soviet tendency has been to look with favor only upon those facets of mental life which are seen as furthering the goal of developing communism. The Soviet regime seems to distinguish three main categories in the realm of the mind and the spirit. Science and practical education are in the forefront of attention, and they are heavily favored as providing support for the new system. A second category includes those ideas and their associated institutions which are seen as holding back the progress of the Revolution — such as religion, non-Marxist social science, and introspective literature. In a third class are those forms of thinking or expression which are generally, though not always, acknowledged as devoid of political content, and therefore not to be evaluated in terms of their direct contribution to the building of Communism. Into this latter group fall, for example, higher mathematics and music. In the present chapter, authoritative writers have touched upon all three of these categories, as seen from the regime's vantage point, of the life of the mind and the spirit.

From the point of view of the Soviet citizen, mind and spirit are often the locale of a struggle between the pressures imposed by the regime and his own pre-dispositions. The regime concedes little to his desire to be a unique individual, to undergo private, purely personal experiences, in a word — to be free. The precise nature of the struggle varies from individual to individual and from social group to social group. It is the older peasants, for example, who resent most strongly the anti-religious position of the regime, and of course it is the literary intelligentsia who suffer most under the strictures of "socialist realism."

Our contributors in this chapter address themselves to answering the basic questions generally raised in this realm. What has happened to religion in an atheistic state? How has Soviet educational policy changed to keep pace with modern civilization? To what does Soviet science owe its impressive achievements? The picture which emerges is neither black nor white. Alongside excellence in physical science one must range the pitiful products of Soviet social science. While admiring the excellent quality of Soviet musical creativity and performance, one must agree with Professor Simmons that the chief merit of Soviet literature is not literary.

One of the more general issues raised by the materials in this chapter is the question of how political tyranny and individual creativity are linked. Two points of view are often proposed, the stifling theory, which holds that higher culture is extinguished by political tyranny, and the inverse correlation theory, which argues that it is ultimately stimulated. Except for music and physical science, the Soviet case seems to support the first hypothesis. But many Soviet artists and writers have never lost their urge to genuine individual creativity, and many have continued producing works which are not exhibited or published. They are "for the drawer," as the current Soviet expression goes. If and when the drawers are opened and their contents displayed, we will have available an indeterminate but probably not small quantity of evidence on the question.

It should not escape our attention that in the history of changing policies toward these matters, one also finds a sensitive index to the larger trends and "periods" of Soviet history. In surveying religion, education, science, and literature, our contributors reveal certain broad parallels. A period of initial freedom and experimentation (1920's), was succeeded by a massive, almost convulsive, attempt at total regimentation and control during the height of Stalinist totalitarianism. Then came a time of relaxation, a return to more traditional forms and greater individual freedom during World War II. This was followed again by a tightening of the reins in the immediate postwar period, and then after the death of Stalin came further cautious and partial relaxation. Policies in the different fields, however, were not always correlated. For example, the 1920's and early 1930's saw the coexistence of a large measure of artistic and literary freedom on the one side, and a savage persecution of church and religion on the other. Similarly, the increase in literary freedom between 1954 and 1957 went hand in hand with a greatly strengthened campaign against "religious survivals." In the large, one can often discern a pattern similar to the "artificial dialectic" mentioned in the article by Isaiah Berlin in Chapter I. The alternating cycle of application and relaxation of control seems fully as relevant to the Bolshevik approach to religion and to literature as to economic or political life.

In spite of the artificial nature of Soviet official cultural trends — or, better, because of it — the treatment of philosophy, religion, literature, and social science in the U.S.S.R. is an important guide-post to the character of the regime. If, in the future, any or all of the basic cultural or intellectual realms are set aside as permanently independent and inviolate, this will mean that the Soviet system has truly changed its essence. More than Soviet foreign policy, the treatment of the life of the mind and the spirit serves as an indication of the trend of change in the Soviet system.

THE PLACE OF RELIGION

43

Survey of State–Church Relations*

Vladimir Gsovski

(1955)

The measure of Soviet opposition to religious ideas and the church is found in the still quoted writings of Marx, Engels, and Lenin, as well as in the record of the regime's policies. Tactical retreats and concessions, as during World War II, do not contradict the fact that the Soviet leaders continue to see in religion the strongest competition of their own "religion" — communism.

The laws and decrees relating to the Church in Czechoslovakia, Hungary, Poland, and Romania were prepared and enacted by leaders trained in the Soviet Union or inspired by the

---

* Reprinted from "Separation of Church from State in the Soviet Union," *Church and State Behind the Iron Curtain* (1955), pp. xi–xxxi, V. Gsovski, editor, Frederick A. Praeger, Inc., New York, by permission of the author and the publisher.

ideas that motivate the government of the Soviet Union. Political and legal terms used by them designate concepts which are at variance with the traditional meaning we have for these terms and they conform with Soviet ideas. This is especially true of the separation of Church and State as declared in the laws of some of these countries.[1]

Fundamental Hostility to Religion

The idea of separation of Church and State in America emerged from the struggle for religious freedom and tolerance. This principle does not imply suppression of worship but is designated to safeguard liberty in the exercise of one's faith. The State is presumed not to be hostile or beneficent to any specific Church, but is equally benevolent to every Church.

But the legislators of Soviet Russia were inspired by quite different ideas. Thus, beginning with the first Decree "On Separation of the Church from the State and the School from the Church" issued January 23, 1918 (in the third month of the Soviet regime), such a separation was not aimed toward religious freedom or tolerance, but was designed to undermine the very existence of the Church in Russia.

This was made clear in retrospect in the publication of the Central Institute for Antireligious Correspondence Courses, printed by a Soviet Government printing office in 1932.

---

[1] For Hungary see pp. 72–79, for Poland pp. 175–178.

It is necessary to emphasize that the Soviet Decree concerning the Separation of Church from State and the School from the Church, was from the beginning directed *against religion*. In the question of religion, the Soviet Government never carried a double-dealing policy of equal cooperation with religion and atheism. It would be wrong to represent the whole matter as if our government kept away from the problems of religion, washed its hands and left the matter to its natural course. . . . Therefore, this Decree cannot be considered otherwise than as *a measure deliberately directed against religion*. The advocates of "non-religious education in schools" understated the historical role of this Decree, and have misinterpreted it. In fact, according to their opinion, the Soviet Government is neither for nor against religion. No, this is not true. Soviet power fights against religion: In the first place, by means of the separation of all the Churches from the State and then by means of organization of *antireligious education* in the schools and antireligious education of the people at large. It is not that the antireligious work of our Commissariat for Education contradicts separation of Church from State, on the contrary, it follows from it. And vice versa. If, after having separated the Church from the State, our government would not have developed at the same time by all the means at its disposal antireligious propaganda, then . . . religion would have been developed and to an extent strengthened in new refined forms. . . . Therefore, it would be treason to the dictatorship of the proletariat, treason to the spirit and sense of the Decree on Separation of the State from the Church to fail to organize the fight against religion on a union-wide scale by the force and the means of the government itself. . . . In a few words, the analysis of the Decree may be summarized as follows: If the capitalistic separation of Church and State leads to the free and highest development of religion, the Soviet separation of Church and State leads to the free and final death of religion." [Italics supplied][2]

Hostility toward religion, clearly stated in this excerpt, is deeply rooted in the Communist philosophy of the Soviet leaders. For Lenin,

---

[2] *Antireligious Movement in the U.S.S.R. and Abroad* (in Russian, Government Antireligious Publishing Office, 1933), pp. 12, 15, 16

The saying of Marx: "Religion is the opium of the people," is the cornerstone of the Marxist point of view in the matter of religion. Marxism has always viewed all contemporary religion and churches, all and every kind of religious organization as agencies of bourgeois reaction, serving as a defense of exploitation and the drugging of the working class.[3]

For Engels the paramount human belief in God was merely "a fantastic reflex." Said Engels:

Now all religion is nothing else than the fantastic reflex in the minds of men of those external forces which dominate their everyday existence, a reflection in which the earthly forces assume the form of supernatural forces.[4]

Lenin went on to develop this idea:

God (as He appeared in history and life) is before all a complex of ideas produced by the stupefying oppression of man both by outer nature and class exploitations — a complex of ideas which strengthens this oppression and lulls the class struggle.[5]

The religious oppression of humanity is but the product and reflex of economic oppression within society. . . .[6]

For Lenin a good Church was worse than a corrupted one. It is religion itself and not the occasional abuses by the members of Churches that is attacked by Lenin. He says:

Any religious idea, any idea of a "good God," any coquetry even with a "good God" is an abominably nasty thing which is met especially tolerantly (often benevolently) by the "democratic bourgeoisie" and is just for that reason the most dangerous abomination, most odious infection.[7]

In Lenin's writings, antedating Communist rule in Russia, there are passages in which he

---

[3] Lenin, *Collected Works* (2nd Russian ed., Moscow, 1926), Vol. 14, p. 68; this edition is cited throughout the present work.

[4] Engels, *Anti-Duering* (English translation, 1935), p. 311.

[5] Lenin, "Two Letters to Gorky" (1913), *Collected Works*, Vol. 17, p. 85, see also *ibid.*, Vol. 14, p. 71.

[6] Lenin, "Socialism and Religion," *Collected Works*, Vol. 8, p. 422.

[7] Lenin, *Collected Works*, Vol. 17, p. 82.

insisted that the State of that time should recognize religion as a "private affair" of a citizen. However, he made plain that his aim was to deprive the Church of support given by the pre-revolutionary State. He did not expect from his party and party-dominated State any neutrality toward religion

> The [Communist] Party, while demanding of the State the declaration of religion as a "private affair" in nowise should consider the problems of the fight against the dope of the people, religious superstition, to be a private affair.[8]

Lenin vehemently condemned the attempts made by some of the Russian Marxists in 1908–09 to create a link between socialism and religion. According to Lenin:

> The party of the proletariat must be the spiritual leader in the struggle against all kinds of medievalism, including the official religion, and against all attempts to renovate it or to justify it in a new or in another way.[9]

The following passage from Lenin's article "Socialism and Religion" was recently quoted in a *Pravda* editorial of July 24, 1954, as expressing a permanent principle:

> The [Communist] Party as a union of consciously progressive fighters could not and should not take an irrelevant attitude toward unconsciousness, darkness, and obscurantism in the form of religious creeds.

A comprehensive antireligious program was adopted at a special conference on antireligious propaganda of the Communist Party of the Soviet Union and its Central Committee held on April 27–30, 1926. It called for "exposing the class essences of religious belief . . . exposing religion in its role, in Western Europe, America, and in the Orient, as the servant of capital." It asserted the "anti-scientific nature of religion," and that religion, "distorting and perverting the toiler's concept of the world, the laws of nature, and the development of human society . . . imposes upon the toilers a false concept of the world." The program stated, "where religion is victorious, Commu-

nism is weak. The Communist regime will only come into being in a society freed from religion."[10]

All religions were equally condemned by this program, but Christianity was especially disapproved. The third point of the program reads:

> The struggle with religion must be carried on by exposing religious morals as a morality imposed in a special manner upon the toilers by the ruling class. (Contemporary Christianity, for example, as a system of morals, represents by itself nothing but such a concept of duty as is in the interest of the ruling exploiters. The morals proposed to the toilers by Christianity are bourgeois — exploiters' morals, training the exploited classes for all those qualities which, from the point of view of the exploiter, his victim should have: silence, passiveness, meekness, patience.) It is necessary to condemn categorically, as the worst type of popery, every effort of approachment of Christianity to Communism. Religion must be rejected for good, without reservation and camouflage. . . . It is necessary to point out the harmfulness to the class interests of the toilers of religious emotions and sentiment.

The same hostility and determination to fight religion is also stated in *Pravda* as late as July 24, 1954:

> The victory of the socialist ideology does not mean, however, that in our society the remnants of the bourgeois concept of life and the survival of the ideology and ethics of private owners are totally liquidated. These survivals do not and will not die out by themselves, they must be fought persistently with full force. One of the most tenacious and harmful survivals of capitalism in the minds of people are the religious superstitions. These superstitions poison up to the present time the mind of a part of our people, [and] hinder their active participation in the building up of Communism.

Consequently it is the basic proposition of the Soviet rulers to combat the religious con-

---

[8] Lenin, "The Attitude of the Labor Party Towards Religion" (1909), *Collected Works*, Vol. 14, p. 74; see also Vol. 21, p. 42.
[9] *Ibid.*, p. 75.

[10] Theses adopted at the Party Conference on Antireligious Propaganda and at the Central Committee of the U.S.S.R., April 27–30, 1926, Sec. V., English translation, quoted from Hecker, *Religion and Communism* (1933), p. 279. See also Lukachevsky, *Antireligious Propaganda at the Present Stage* [of the Soviet regime] (in Russian, 1936), pp. 1, 3, 5, 9.

cept of life as an error and as a potentially inimical force. Atheism and materialism are integral parts of the Communist teaching and are its prospective standards for the popular mentality. To deprive the Churches of the possibility of exercising an influence upon the people, even outside of politics, has been the real tenor of all acts of the Soviet Russian Government. To create conditions for the replacement of religion by atheism has been its real aim.

Main Features of Religious Policy

In pursuit of this aim, the Soviet policies have varied. The years 1922–1923 and 1929–1930 are marked with the most severe suppression of Churches and persecution of high prelates and clergymen. The laws then enacted deprived the Churches of the conditions indispensable to the normal life of a religious community. Churches have been deprived of the right of property, right of teaching religion, exercising charity, of their place in public life and recognized organization over the parishes. This is all laid down in the Law of April 7, 1929 and the Instruction issued on its implementation.[11]

A sharp change took place during World War II. Suddenly, numerous concessions were made to the Russian Orthodox Church, the Church of a majority of the Russian population. The restrictive laws remained unchanged, but the government allowed a Church Council to convene in 1943 and to elect a patriarch for the first time since the death of Patriarch Tikhon in 1925. When the elected Patriarch Sergii died on May 15, 1944, another Council was convened in January-February 1945 and elected a new patriarch, Alexii. In the presence of a high government official charged with religious affairs, the same council adopted Rules on the Administration of the Russian

Orthodox Church.[12] Some provisions of these Rules imply recognition of the Church hierarchy by the Soviet Government and grant powers to the Church conflicting with the previous highly restrictive laws. The Soviet Government neither repealed nor modified the old laws nor did it extend officially any approval to the Rules. The concessions made are deprived of any authority of law, and may as easily be withdrawn as they were given. Again, they relate only to the Russian Orthodox Church and were coupled with several attacks on the Holy See.

Behind these transformations one can discern some permanent features of the status of the Church under the Soviet regime in Russia. The Church remains expressly prohibited from teaching religion, outside of special courses for training priests. Under the Law of April 1, 1929, Sec. 17, several activities are prohibited to the Churches and it is stated there that Churches "may not organize for children, young people and women, special prayer or other meetings, or, generally, meetings, groups, circles, or departments for biblical or literary study, sewing, working, or the teaching of religion. . . . Only books necessary for the purpose of the cult may be kept in the buildings and premises used for worship."

Soviet Statutes of 1918 and 1929 prohibited "the teaching of any form of religious belief in governmental, public, and private teaching, and educational establishments."[13] A Decree of 1921 prohibited also in general the "teaching of religious doctrine to persons under 18 years of age,"[14] and a Decree of 1923 prohibited any private religious instructions of children in groups comprising over three children.[15] Violation of these rules is subject to prosecution in court under Sec. 123 of the R.S.F.S.R. Criminal Code.

The Law of 1929 states that "religious in-

11 *R.S.F.S.R. Laws* (1929), text 353, hereafter cited as Law of 1929. Instruction of the R.S.F.S.R. People's Commissariat of the Interior of October 1, 1929, No. 328 (hereafter cited as Instruction 1929); *Bulletin* of the same Commissariat, 1929, No. 30, also Orleansky, *Law Concerning the Religious Associations in the R.S.F.S.R.* (in Russian, 1930), p. 27. This is the semi-official commentary to the law. For detailed analysis of the law see V. Gsovski, "The Legal Status of the Church in Soviet Russia," *Fordham Law Review*, January 1939, No. 1, pp. 8–28.

12 *The Call of the Russian Church, Report of the General Council of the Russian Orthodox Church* (London, n.d.), p. 11.
13 Decree of 1918, Sec. 9; Law of 1929, Sec. 18.
14 Decree of June 13, 1921, Section 3, note; Gidulianov, *Separation of the Church from the State in the U.S.S.R.: Complete Collection of Decrees* (in Russian, 3rd ed., 1929), p. 365.
15 Instruction of the Commissariats for the Interior and for Education, December 22, 1923, *Bulletin of the Commissariat for the Interior* (in Russian), Jan. 22, 1924, No. 3; also Gidulianov, *op. cit. supra* note 14, p. 367.

struction is permitted exclusively in special theological courses" which may be opened by a special permit by the higher Soviet authorities for the preparation of ministers of religion (Sec. 18). Several such courses were opened after 1945.

A definite task of atheistic education is clearly set in the statutes governing the Soviet schools. For example, the R.S.F.S.R. Statute on Secondary Schools of 1934[16] reads:

13. The teaching of any form of religious worship, as well as the performance of any rites or rituals of a faith, and any other form of religious influence upon the growing generation shall be prohibited and prosecuted under the criminal law.

The primary schools and secondary schools shall secure an antireligious upbringing of the students and shall build instruction and educational work upon the basis of an active fight against religion and its influence upon the student and adult population.

The more recent statutes — for example, that on teachers' colleges of 1944 — refrain from any general statements on the atheistic purpose of education. However, the same purpose is implied in the instructions for teaching the natural sciences. "The study of natural sciences must secure" [not knowledge pure and simple] "the development in the student of a dialectic-materialistic view of nature (origins of life on the earth, origin of animals and men, origin of men)."

Thus, Soviet legislation is designed not only to bar the Church from religious instruction, but also to put an end to the teaching of religious doctrine in general and achieve antireligious education.

It is significant that the early Soviet Constitution of 1918, in declaring the separation of Church and State, stated that "freedom of religious and antireligious propaganda is secured to citizens."[17] In 1929, "freedom of religious propaganda" was officially deleted[18] and it was officially announced that freedom of religious propaganda "exceeds the limits of religious freedom recognized by law."[19] The

federal Constitution of 1936, Sec. 124, which is still in force, is even more restrictive. It merely recognizes "freedom of performance of religious cults and freedom of antireligious propaganda." It was officially commented that performance of a religious cult is reduced to "prayer and performance of ceremonies and the like. Activities exceeding the satisfaction of these needs are not permitted."[20] Under the new policy, followed since 1943, the constitutional provisions were not changed and the Church activities remain restricted. Thus the 1947 and 1948 editions of the large Soviet encyclopedia state that:

The Soviet State proceeds from the proposition that the business of the Church consists only of the performance of the cult. Any kind of activities of a propagandistic, moralizing, or educative nature (on the scale extending beyond a definite religious community) should not belong to the Church as a union of believers created and existing only for the performance of the cult.[21]

The first Decree on Separation of Church and State of January 23, 1918, declared all the property of all Churches in Russia public property (Sec. 13), i.e., confiscated it without compensation. By this and later decrees and laws, the Churches were deprived of "the right to own any property" (Sec. 12), in particular church buildings, utensils, vestments, and other objects destined for liturgical or any other ceremonial use. It is especially emphasized by laws that churches "shall not enjoy the rights of a corporation (legal entity)," i.e., may not, in their own name, own anything or enter into a contract. Any assumption by a Church of the rights of a corporation or of "administrative," judicial, or other functions pertaining to public law constitutes a criminal offense (Criminal Code of the R.S.F.S.R., Sec. 126). Government ownership of any object "necessary for the cult," ie., indispensable for worship, applies not only to such objects possessed by the Church prior to the revolution, but also to any object "acquired by the believers or given to them for religious purposes" under the Soviet

---

16 R.S.F.S.R. Laws (1934), text 263.
17 R.S.F.S.R. Constitution 1918, Sec. II, ibid., 1925, sec. 4.
18 Law of May 28, 1929, R.S.F.S.R. Laws (1929), item 495.
19 Godless (in Russian), February 6, 1930.

20 Orleansky, op. cit. supra note 11, p. 11.
21 Bolshaia Sovetskaia Entsiklopediia, Soiuz Sovetskikh Sotsialisticheskikh Respublik, Moskva, 1947 (1948), columns 1783–1784.

regime. This is the express provision of Sec. 12 of the Decree of 1918 and the Law of 1929.

The only way for Soviet citizens to have a place of worship is to get it from the local soviet under a contract. Each parish, in order to obtain such a contract, even for a place which they formerly owned, has had to be organized anew as a "religious association" and register, i.e., obtain a license for their existence which can be granted or denied at the discretion of the local soviet. At least 20 parishioners should sign the contract and assume full personal liability for the upkeep of the place and the objects needed for religious ceremonies. From 1918 to 1930 each parish had to undergo two or three such registrations to survive. On any of these occasions or at any other time, the churches could be withdrawn from the use of the parish and many of them were converted into storehouses, clubs, motion picture theaters, and antireligious museums.

The Rules of the Russian Orthodox Church of 1945, Secs. 37–39, and the large Soviet Encyclopedia, 1947 edition, show that in that respect the status of the churches remains unchanged under the present policy of the Soviet government.[22]

No full account of churches withdrawn or destroyed is available. Church edifices of utmost historical and artistic value have been largely withdrawn from religious use and many have been destroyed, e.g., the Cathedral of Our Lord the Savior and many other churches in Moscow, where in 1942 only 17 churches remained in use by the parishioners from a total of over 600 before the revolution.[23] The closing of churches was particularly extensive in 1929–1930. These are the incomplete figures derived from Soviet sources: from 1921–

1923 about 722 monasteries were closed in the R.S.F.S.R. alone;[24] in 1927 some 134 churches;[25] in 1928 nearly 600;[26] but in 1929, 1,450.[27] Some newly created cities have no churches at all, e.g., Magnitogorsk, with 200,000 inhabitants; Karaganda with 120,000; and Stalinsk with 200,000.[28] Valuable articles and artistic paintings were for the most part removed in 1922–1923 (*infra*). In 1930 the Soviet press continually reported the burning of ikons and religious books in small places in such quantities as 12 wagonloads, 8 wagonloads, 4,000 ikons, and 1,000 religious books.[29] The opening of reliquaries was made on a large scale on order of the R.S.F.S.R. Commissariat for Justice of August 25, 1920, which reported 58 instances of opening of reliquaries and insisted on "complete liquidation according to a plan of relics" by placing them in museums where they were exposed to desecration. Thus the same Commissariat reported in 1921 the placing side by side with the relic of a saint a mummified rat.[30]

Beginning with the Constitution of 1918 and until 1936, present and former clergymen of all denominations (ministers, deacons, rabbis, etc.), monks and nuns were deprived of the right to vote. In 1929, 248,000 persons were disfranchised on this ground, and 161,000 in 1931, the decrease being officially explained by the "natural decrease in the number of ministers."[31] The disfranchised constituted a kind of outcaste who were officially discrimi-

---

[22] Ibid., pp. 1786 ff. For translations of sections 37–39 of Rules of 1945 see V. Gsovski, *Soviet Civil Law*, Ann Arbor, Vol. II, 1949, pp. 334–335.

[23] *Truth on Religion in Russia* (in Russian, n.p. Moskovskaia Patriarkhia, 1942), a luxuriously printed collection of articles, pictures, speeches, and reports designed to show German atrocities toward the Church in contrast to the freedom of religion under the Soviets. From the list of parishes contributing to patriotic purposes in Moscow, pp. 163–190 and passim, it follows that not more than 17 churches in Moscow remained in the use of the faithful. The pre-revolutionary number of churches in Moscow is estimated by various sources at from 400 to 675.

[24] *The People's Commissariat for Justice. Report to the 9th All-Russian Congress of Soviets* (in Russian, Moscow, 1921), p. 48.

[25] *Izvestiia*, December 29, 1936.

[26] 445 churches, 59 synagogues, and 38 mosques. *Young Guard* (in Russian, 1930), No. 22; *Izvestiia*, March 22, 1929.

[27] In the cities: 550 churches, 111 synagogues, and 96 mosques; in villages: 589 churches, 15 synagogues, and 98 mosques. *Antireligious* (in Russian, 1930), No. 3.

[28] *Izvestiia*, December 29, 1936.

[29] In Lisichansk and Denisovo, *Godless* (In Russian), March 10 and March 30, 1930. In Tver, *Izvestiia*, January 8, 1930. In Andreevka, *Godless* (in Russian), 1930, No. 5, p. 4.

[30] *Op. cit. supra* note 24, p. 44. The address of the museum given there is Moscow, Petrovka Street, No. 14.

[31] *Elections to the Soviets and the Compositions of Agencies of the Government* (in Russian, 1931), p. 35.

nated against in employment, obtaining rationed food, housing, education of their children, and taxation.[32]

The Struggle of the Church for Survival

An all-out assault on churches was made in
1922–1923. The preceding year, 1921, was
marked by famine in the central, most fertile
zones of Russia. The churches were by that
time stripped of all their assets, but there remained numerous objects made of or adorned
with precious metals, many of which were
consecrated.

The Patriarch Tikhon of the Russian Orthodox Church, elected in 1918, issued an appeal
for help for the famine-stricken in August 1921.
A Russian Church Committee was formed for
famine relief, and parishes collected food and
money. Then the government ordered them
to turn the collections over to the government
relief organizations.[33] On December 21, 1921,
the government again allowed the churches to
conduct collections and instructed the central
official relief organization *Pomgol* "to reach an
agreement with religious societies as to the
form of collection of donations and the methods
of forwarding of what is collected, having in
mind the wishes of the donors."[34] It was officially reported that such an agreement had
been reached.[35] On February 15, 1922, a message by Patriarch Tikhon was printed in
Izvestiia calling upon the parishes to donate
adornments of ikons and broken pieces of gold
and silver.[36] But on February 23 the Soviet
Government had instructed "the local soviets
to remove within one month's period . . . from

church property . . . all precious articles of
gold, silver, and precious stones, the removal
of which does not essentially infringe upon
the interest of the cult.[37] It was officially commented "that golden and silver chalices, reliquaries, metal adornments of ikons, vestments,
and the like" could not be retained.[38] The
Patriarch answered by a message to the faithful
in which he restated that he had "allowed, in
view of the emergency, the Church to donate
objects which were not consecrated and not
used in the divine services." But, he also
stated that "we cannot approve the removal
from the churches of consecrated objects even
by voluntary donations, as their use for any
purpose other than the church services is prohibited by the canons of the universal
Church."[39]

But forcible removal of all valuables from
the churches was ordered by the Soviet Government. A total of 1,414 bloody incidents
caused by resistance of the faithful was allowed
to appear in the Soviet press.[40] Numerous
trials took place before the revolutionary tribunals, which until June 1, 1922, were not
bound by any rules of statutory criminal law or
procedure and were at liberty to apply any
punishment, including the death penalty.[41] Incomplete figures show that at least 45 executions and over 500 imprisonment terms were
pronounced.[42]

---

[32] *R.S.F.S.R. Laws* (1921), item 67; Gidulianov,
op. cit. supra note 14, pp. 294–295; Decree of the
R.S.F.S.R. Commissariat for the Interior, July 30,
1929, No. 259; Resolution of R.S.F.S.R. Central
Executive Committee, Dec. 27, 1927, sec. 2; Orleansky, *op. cit. supra* note 11, pp. 56–58; Standard
Charter of Universities, *U.S.S.R. Laws* (1934), text
87(b), secs. 44, 47 (b); *ibid.* (1928), text 212, sec.
28; *ibid.* (1930), text. 462.
[33] Curtis, *The Russian Church and the Soviet State,*
Boston, 1953, p. 107.
[34] Gidulianov and Krasikov, *Church and State According to Legislation of the R.S.F.S.R.* (in Russian,
1923), XII, 5, p. 52. Emhardt, *Religion in the
Soviet Union,* Milwaukee, 1929, p. 55
[35] *Izvestiia,* January 26, 1922.
[36] *Ibid.,* February 15, 1922; Stratonov, *The Turmoil
of the Russian Church* (1921–1931) (in Russian,
Berlin, 1932), pp. 48–52.

[37] *Izvestiia,* Feburary 24, 1922; *R.S.F.S.R. Laws*
(1922), text 217, sec. 1.
[38] *Church and Revolution* (in Russian, 1923), No.
1/2, p. 5.
[39] Valentinov, *Black Book, Assault on Heaven* (in
Russian, Paris, 1925), pp. 253–254.
[40] *Pravda,* May 17, 1922, No. 108. Statement by
the priest Krasnitsky of the Living Church.
[41] *R.S.F.S.R. Laws* (1920), text 115, Secs. 1, 24,
29. "In the jurisdiction of the [revolutionary] tribunals a complete liberty of repression was advocated,
while sentencing to death was a matter of everyday practice." In these words Krylenko, the noted
prosecutor, especially in cases of the prelates of the
church, characterized the activities of the tribunals.
Krylenko, *The Judiciary of the R.S.F.S.R.* (in Russian, 1923), p. 206; see Gsovski, *op. cit. supra* note
22, Vol. I (1948), pp. 234 ff.
[42] A Soviet writer hostile to the patriarchal church
tabulated for 55 tribunals some 33 executions and
585 convictions. Brikchev, *Patriarch Tikhon and
His Church* (in Russian, Moscow, 1933), pp. 19–20,
quoted by Curtis, who considers these figures incomplete, *op. cit. supra* note 33, p. 126, but Hecker,

During one of the trials of 54 priests and laymen in Moscow in May 1922, which ended with eleven death sentences, Patriarch Tikhon was called to testify as a witness and boldly assumed the responsibility for the defense of consecrated objects. On May 2, 1922, he was indicted and placed under arrest, pending his own trial.[43] A similar trial of the prelates of the Roman Catholic Church also took place. Bishop Jan Cepliak and Mgr. Butkiewicz were sentenced to death and several other Catholic priests to long-term imprisonment.[44] This fact alone disproves the allegations of the Soviets that the prelates of the Russian Church were prosecuted because of their alleged connections with the monarchists.

A group of priests of the Russian Church, headed by the priest, Vvedensky, declared their complete acceptance of social revolution and the Soviet platform, and, as they stated in the petition to the arrested Patriarch, they "obtained permission for the opening and functioning of the chancery of the Patriarch" and for visiting him. The Patriarch conceded on May 18, 1922, that they take over the files of the Synod for the transmission to Metropolitan Agaphangel.[45] But Metropolitan Agaphangel could not come, being under house arrest in Yaroslavl. The Vvedensky group, later called the Living Church, assumed the administration of the Church affairs, setting up a Provisional Administration of Church Affairs. Metropolitan Agaphangel was arrested and exiled to Narym (Siberia). Nevertheless, he issued a message calling on the faithful to remain loyal to the arrested Patriarch and advised the bishops to administer each diocese independently until true Church authority was restored.[46]

At a gathering of the Vvedensky group of 42 persons on July 4, 1922, rules for the Living Church were adopted, the justice of the social revolution was declared, and abolition of the patriarchate and such uncanonical changes as consecration of married priests as bishops were advocated. At another convention in August, consisting of 154 delegates with only three bishops out of 143, it was reported that 60 bishops who were against the new Church administration or were noncommital were forced to retire.[47] The background for these developments is supplied by the fact that throughout these turbulent times six metropolitans, three archbishops, and 56 bishops were either arrested or exiled.[48]

The reformist movement soon became split into several groups, but a joint Sobor convened on April 29–May 9, 1923. At the Sobor, the Patriarch was neither present (he was still under arrest) nor represented; no evidence against him was produced and yet the Sobor dethroned him and reduced him to layman status on May 2, 1923. The Patriarchate was abolished and various uncanonical changes were confirmed.[49]

The trial of the Patriarch, who had been imprisoned for almost a year, was officially announced on April 23 and then postponed. Lord Curzon threatened to recall the British mission. Then on June 27, the announcement was published that the Supreme Court had set free the Patriarch on his petition of June 16. In the published text of the petition the Patriarch stated that he "was actually hostile to the Soviet power," recognized "the correctness of the court in bringing him to trial" and declared that "henceforth I am not an enemy of the Soviet Power."[50]

Upon his release the Patriarch declared the

Religion and Communism (New York, 1933), p. 209, tabulated 45 executions and 250 long-term prison sentences from Soviet sources. These figures do not include executions by the secret police — Cheka and GPU.

[43] *Izvestiia*, May 7, 1922.

[44] *Izvestiia*, March 27, 1923. See also Francis McCullagh, *The Bolshevik Persecution of Christianity*, London, 1924, pp. 99–185; Emhardt, *op. cit. supra* note 34, pp. 18–192.

[45] *Vestnik* of the Holy Synod of the Renovated Church, 1925, No. 2, p. 18; Emhardt, *op. cit. supra* note 34, pp. 59 ff.; Polskii, *Canonical Status of the Supreme Ecclesiastical Authority in the U.S.S.R. and Abroad* (in Russian, Jordanville, New York, 1948), pp. 8, 10–11; Curtis, *op. cit. supra* note 33, pp. 130 ff.; Spinka, *The Church and the Russian Revolution*, New York, 1927, pp. 201 ff.

[46] Message of June 5/18, 1922, Polskii, *op. cit.*, pp. 14–15; Curtis, *op. cit. supra* note 33, p. 134; Spinka, *op. cit. supra* note 45, p. 207; Emhardt, *op. cit. supra* note 34, p. 307.

[47] *Izvestiia*, August 10, 15, 1922; Curtis, *op. cit. supra* note 33, pp. 138–139; Spinka, *op. cit. supra* note 45, p. 213 ff.

[48] Valentinov, *op. cit. supra* note 39, pp. 257–259.

[49] *Izvestiia*, May 6, 10, and 30, 1923; Spinka, *op. cit. supra* note 45, pp. 240 ff.

[50] *Izvestiia*, June 27, 1923.

Sobor of 1923 uncanonical and his dethrone-ment illegal and assumed his office, being en-thusiastically greeted by the flock.[51] Not only parishioners but also bishops and priests who joined the Living Church repented and were admitted to the fold. Among the bishops were Sergii and Alexii, the future Patriarchs.[52]

Nevertheless, the Living Church, now re-named Renovated, continued to enjoy Soviet recognition and existed apart from the Patri-arch in spite of several attempts at reunion. On March 26, 1925, the Patriarch died. From that time on and until 1943, for eighteen years, no election of a new Patriarch was al-lowed. The late Patriarch appointed as keeper of his office, in the first place, Metropolitan Cyril, but he was placed under arrest; in the second place, Metropolitan Agaphangel, who was in exile; and in the third place, Metropoli-tan Peter, who took the office.[53] In October 1925, a Sobor of the Renovated Church con-vened, but Metropolitan Peter showed an un-compromising attitude against the Sobor and the revisionist movement in general. He was attacked in the Soviet press.[54] On December 23, 1925, Peter was arrested and in the sum-mer of 1926 exiled to Siberia where he died in 1936.[55] With him ended the unquestionable legitimate succession of authority.

Before his exile Metropolitan Peter ap-pointed as the deputy keeper of the patriarchal office Metropolitan Sergii of Nijni Novgorod and three other prelates as alternates.[56] At the same time, a group of bishops of the patri-archal Church headed by Bishop Grigorii was promised by the Soviet government legaliza-tion of Church administration. Moreover, Metropolitan Agaphangel was allowed to re-turn from exile and claimed the office under the earlier arrangement of the late patriarch. In this confusion, Metropolitan Peter (supra) being under arrest, first gave the authority to Sergii, then in January 1926, agreed to trans-fer it to Grigorii's group and then in April 1926 to Agaphangel. But Sergii, who was in and out of prison, asserted his own authority, being supported by several bishops. He suc-ceeded in persuading Agaphangel to give up his claim. In brief, out of eleven hierarchs ap-pointed to be keeper of the Patriarchal office, or his deputy, ten were in prison or exile.[57] Metropolitan Sergii, who finally assumed the office of the deputy keeper, was arrested in early 1926 during the crisis, brought to Mos-cow, then in March sent back to Nijni Nov-gorod and released. He was again arrested on December 13, 1926, and released in April 1927.[58] During all this time, he negotiated with the Soviet authorities on the conditions of the Church administration. Evidently, a com-promise was reached, since soon after his last release, Metropolitan Sergii announced the of-ficial opening of his administration and on June 29, 1927, pledged in a message not only complete loyalty but also a wholehearted sup-port of the Soviet government.[59] Since then,

---

[51] Ibid., July 3, 1923; Polskii, op. cit. supra note 45, p. 23; Mikhail Sviaschenik (pseudonym of Polskii), Status of Church in Soviet Russia (in Russian, Jeru-salem, 1931), passim; Spinka, op. cit. supra note 45, pp. 255–260.

[52] Polskii, op. cit., pp. 97–98; Timasheff, Church in Soviet Russia, New York, 1942, pp. 33 ff.; Curtis, op. cit. supra note 33, p. 168; Tserkovnye Vedo-mosti, published by the Supreme Administration of the Russian Church abroad, Sremske Karlovtsi (Yu-goslavia), No. 7/8, 1924.

[53] The events of the confusing days which followed the Patriarch's death up to the final assumption of the duties of the deputy keeper (locum tenens) of the patriarchal office by Metropolitan Sergii are to be found in Tserkovnye Vedomosti, op. cit. supra note 52, Nos. 5/6, 9/10, 11/12, pp. 6 ff.; Stratonov, op. cit. supra note 36, pp. 126–130, 150–155, 174–180; Curtis, op. cit. supra note 33, p. 27; Polskii, op. cit. supra note 45, pp. 27–41; Emhardt, op. cit. supra note 34, pp. 141–150; Spinka, op. cit. supra note 45, pp. 292 ff.

[54] Izvestiia, Nov. 15, 1925.

[55] Polskii, op. cit. supra note 45, pp. 27–28; Curtis, op. cit. supra note 33, p. 180; Emhardt, op. cit. supra note 34, p. 144; Spinka, op. cit. supra note 46, p. 310.

[56] The alternates were: Metropolitan Mikhail, ex-arch of the Ukraine, and Archbishop Josef of Rostov, later of Leningrad (Polskii, op. cit. supra note 45, p. 9). When Metropolitan Sergii was ar-rested in late 1926, the deputy locum tenens be-came Serafim of Uglich, who, according to Polskii, declined to continue in office under the conditions insisted upon by the G.P.U. (op. cit., p. 13, 15, 30). Emhardt, op. cit. supra note 34, p. 146, and Spinka, op cit. supra note 34, p. 311, mention also that Metropolitan Josef and Archbishops Cornelius and Thaddeus succeeded the arrested Sergii but were later also arrested.

[57] Curtis, op. cit. supra note 33, p. 183.

[58] Ibid., pp. 182–183.

[59] For full translation in English see Emhardt, op. cit. supra note 34, pp. 146–150.

he has repeatedly done what the government expected him to do, and only in 1943 did the government answer with some concessions. Metropolitan Sergii showed an uncompromising attitude against the Renovated Church but ordered the prayers for the Soviet Government to be said during the Church service and required pledges of loyalty to the Soviets not only from the clergy in Russia but also from those abroad.[60] Some of the bishops, clergy, and parishioners did not accept his submission to the atheist authority, and those in Russia went into exile and imprisonment. An underground Church came into being.[61]

In spite of the complete submission of Sergii to the Soviets, the attack on the Church and religion was intensified. The association of militant atheists founded in 1925 became extremely active. Numerous antireligious periodicals and numerous books and pamphlets were printed. Special atheistic courses and publishing offices were organized. In 1929, the Constitution was changed, dropping from its clauses permission for religious propaganda. The Law of 1929 sought to destroy the Church as an organized body of parishes. In 1929–1930, many churches were closed, and books and ikons were burned (*supra*). Metropolitan Sergii continued to fulfil his pledge and publicly denied any persecution of the Church in Russia before the Russian and foreign correspondents in 1930.[62]

The Policy of Limited Concessions

There was, however, a great disappointment in store for the Soviet leaders. Religion has been regarded by them as a mere "remnant of capitalism" which no longer existed in Soviet Russia. In 1936, Stalin declared that "the victory of the socialist system in all spheres of

the national economy is now a fact."[63] However, neither the social transformation of Russia according to the Communist plan nor the measures taken to deprive Churches of their influence on the people achieved the aim of putting an end to religion in Russia. In 1939, the official Communist Party periodical candidly recognized that "it is much more difficult to uproot religion from the minds of the workers than to liberate them from the exploitation of capitalism."[64] The Soviet press carried statements frankly admitting that at least one-third of the city population and more than one-half, perhaps two-thirds, of the rural population still believed in God.[65]

The Church has to be reckoned with as an independent social force which is not going to disappear in the foreseeable future despite adverse conditions created by the Soviet Government. The Soviet rulers gradually arrived at the idea of attempting to make this force serve the general Communist policies. The conduct of Metropolitan Sergii seemed to promise the possibility of such a tactic. With the beginning of World War II Metropolitan Sergii continued to show his Church's complete loyalty to the Soviet Government and identified it with the patriotic devotion to the country. Stalin was hailed "as a divinely anointed leader."[66]

A change in policy was further prompted by the news from German-occupied territories that there the closed churches were reopened and church life was revived. Both these factors induced concessions to the Russian Orthodox Church, which appeared to be willing to go along with Soviet policy. Nicholas, the Metropolitan of Kiev and Galicia, was appointed a member of the government committee to investigate German atrocities.[67] He and the Metropolitan Sergii were officially received by Stalin on September 4, 1943, and a Sobor of

[60] Curtis, *op. cit. supra* note 33, p. 187, *Izvestiia*, Aug. 19, 1927.

[61] Polskii, *op. cit.* note 45, pp. 44–57; Andreev, *Position of the Orthodox Church in the Soviet Union* (in Russian, Jordanville, 1951), *passim*; Wassilii Alexeev, *Russian Orthodox Bishops in the Soviet Union, 1941–1953*, Research Program on the U.S.S.R., in Russian, mimeographed, N. Y. C., 1954, pp. 58–62, indicates passages in the Journal of Moscow Patriarchy which suggest the existence of catacomb churches in the Soviet Union.

[62] *Izvestiia*, February 16, 1930; W. H. Chamberlin, *Russia's Iron Age*, London, 1936, pp. 323–324.

[63] Stalin, *On the Draft of the Constitution of the U.S.S.R.*, Moscow, 1951, p. 17.

[64] *Partiinoe Stroitelstvo* (in Russian, 1939), No. 11, quoted from Timasheff, *op. cit. supra* note 52, p. 98.

[65] Yaroslavsky, *On Religious Propaganda* (in Russian, 1937); *Pravda*, May 17, 1937; *The Anti-Religious* (in Russian, 1940), No. 2, p. 23.

[66] *New York Times*, November 10, 1942; *op. cit. supra* note 23, pp. 15–27, 83–86, 98–111, 168; Curtis, *op. cit. supra* note 33, p. 290 ff.

[67] *Vedomosti*, November 2, 1942, No. 40.

19 bishops (compared with 69 at the Sobor of 1917) convened on September 8 to elect Sergii the Patriarch of Russia.[68] A committee for ecclesiastic affairs of the Russian Church was created and attached to the Council of the People's Commissars (renamed, in 1946, Council of Ministers), the supreme executive body.[69] The Journal of the Moscow Patriarchy began to appear. The opening of seminaries for the training of priests was announced. Solemn church services followed each victory of the Soviet troops.

Thus, by the end of the war, when Soviet influence was spread to the satellite countries, it was a new Soviet Church policy — to refrain from direct attacks on religion and aim at making the Church an obedient instrument of government policy — which was carried into these countries. But no concession was made to the Catholic Church in Russia. The attacks on the Holy See were intensified, and attempts were made in the satellite countries to produce a separation of the lower clergy from the episcopate in the fashion of the "Living Church" in Russia (supra).

The concessions to the Russian Church in the Soviet Union were never put in the form of law nor were the restrictive provisions of old laws abrogated. Concessions today still remain a matter of policy and not of law. For its recognition as a union "existing only for the performance of the cult" the Russian Church pays the price of giving active support to all campaigns of the Soviet Government in international relations. The Church had to join the World Congress of Supporters of Peace, the Stockholm Peace Petition, and even filed with the United Nations a protest against its action in Korea, accusing the United States of aggression.[70]

Thus, the Soviet Russian Government has committed the Russian Church to a policy of unconditional fealty and blind support in exchange for precarious recognition — a policy which was soon to be attempted in the satellite countries.

---

[68] Op. cit. supra note 33, pp. 292, 293; Izvestiia, September 5, 1943; Zhurnal of the Moscow Patriarchy (in Russian), No. 1, 1943.

[69] In October, 1943. Op. cit. supra note 21, p. 1788.

[70] Zhurnal of the Moscow Patriarchy (in Russian), Special No., 1945; Nos. 2, 5, 11, 1949; Nos. 5 and 6, 1950.

44

Religious Revival in Russia?*

Robert C. Tucker

(1959)

Professor Tucker points to some evidence of a revival of religious interest among the Soviet people, and to some of the reasons for it. Resistance to the Party argument that religion is incompatible with science suggests that religious faith may find a home among some of the younger and more sophisticated elements of the population as well as among the older people and the peasantry, most of whom have never lost their faith.

The object of this article, which presents some recent observations on religious policy and religious activities in Soviet Russia, is not to reconstruct the total picture of religion in Russia but at most to etch out certain significant features of it more sharply. The observations were made during a journey which the writer was privileged to take in the latter part of 1958 as a member of the party of Governor Adlai Stevenson. In addition to Leningrad and Moscow, the itinerary included visits to Central Asia, Siberia, the Urals, and the Volga region. Impressions derived from these travels may help to bring into clearer perspective some tendencies and issues of the present moment in the field of church–state relations which show up (from the official point of view) in the Soviet press and periodicals.

The principal tendency and issue as reflected in the Soviet press can be stated quite simply: renewed tension between organized religion in the Soviet Union and the supreme political authority, the Communist Party. This renewal of tension, or more accurately the renewal of active widespread atheistic propaganda by the Party, is probably not to be described as a return to the frantic anti-religious campaign of 1954. That campaign was halted by a decree

---

* Reprinted from "Party and Church in the Soviet Union — Travel Notes," *The Russian Review*, Vol. 18 (1959), pp. 285–293, by permission of the author and the publisher.

signed by Khrushchev, "On Errors in the Conducting of Scientific-Atheistic Propaganda Among the Population." The "errors" in question were administrative acts of repression such as the closing down of churches, repressive actions against clergymen, and so forth. Whether similar "errors" are now taking place again on any appreciable scale, we do not know. But it is clear to any reader of the Soviet press that an intense organized campaign of anti-religious propapanda and agitation has been developing in the Soviet Union since the middle of 1958 and is still in progress.

A very interesting and significant, and to some extent novel, feature of the present renewed anti-religious drive is the definite note of defensiveness that is detectable in it. The Party, through its central *Agitprop* and the lesser *agitprops* down the line to the *raions*, is mobilizing an army of agitators and propagandists, to mount a sustained offensive, a campaign of verbal hostilities, against religious influences ("survivals") in the minds of Soviet citizens. But the attacker seems afraid. He seems to be actuated not by any serious hope of routing the enemy from the field but at most of repulsing his insidious advance. The goal seems to be not to defeat organized religion, but to compete with it and contain it. The official press provides numerous bits of evidence of this.

Thus, for example, we read in *Kommunist* of the need to wage a fight for the minds of a considerable segment of Soviet society that is called "the waverers" — and there arises from such language, inevitably, the image of the society as the field of a shadowy contest between two great adversaries, the Party and the Church, for spiritual influence.[1] We see official suggestions being put forward that the Komsomol create some sort of Komsomol-type religious ceremony — manifestly to combat the appeal of the religious type for young people. We learn that people are seeking and receiving moral enlightenment in problems of daily life from the pulpit; and the Party announces publication of a "Little Library of Moral Literature" to serve this need! We read querulous complaints in the Party press about various shocking new arguments of believers to the effect that there is no contradiction between Christianity and socialism since Christianity invented socialism, and that the celebrated conflict of science and religion is itself a myth.

The impression created by all this is that the churches, or some of them at any rate, have been quietly extending their influence among more and more people, that the ruling Party finds this highly disquieting, and that its present anti-religious propaganda and agitation campaign, unlike some in the past, is designed more to check the further gradual spread of religious observance and sentiment than to eliminate these phenomena. What light if any can observations made in Russia in the latter part of 1958, on a trip through numerous areas of the country, shed upon this inference?

On the affirmative side, I might mention first that informal conversation with Soviet citizens here and there brought forth a rather different general picture of the influence of the Church in Soviet society than is frequently held abroad. In the image held abroad, the Church — organized religion — occupies at best a small and precarious niche in the Soviet scheme of things, exerting less and less influence on fewer and fewer people. But this was not the picture that emerged from conversations with Soviet citizens in various places: on the contrary, one could infer from what they said that the Church has become in some ways a rather formidable power in the life of the country. Indeed, one person went so far as to affirm that there are "two powers" (*dve vlasti*) in Soviet Russia today — the state and the Church. The latter, of course, was seen as distinctly the lesser power and in a disadvantageous position in many respects, and the statement was made as a conscious exaggeration, yet as an exaggeration meant to bring out a truth. Especially the Russian Orthodox Church, it was suggested, is a force in the life of the country. A very wealthy and ramified organization and a *non-Party* organization — this was the picture conveyed of the Russian Orthodox Church in present-day Soviet Russia. And, most important, it was seen as an organization whose influence is waxing rather than waning.

While these informal Soviet views of the situation may be a needed corrective for the

---

[1] "Apart from atheists on the one hand and believers on the other, we have one other and rather large category of people — the waverers." ("*Usilit nauchno-ateisticheskuyu propagandu,*" *Kommunist,* No. 17, December, 1958, p. 93). The article (an unsigned editorial) also refers to what it calls "an activation of the *religiozniki*" as taking place at the present time.

image often entertained by foreigners of a very weak and weakening Church, other observations suggested the need for great caution in accepting the "two-power" formula. If the Russian Orthodox Church has in fact become a second "power" in the land, even in a somewhat figurative sense of the word, one would logically expect this position to be expressed in a growth of the number of functioning churches. In the numerous cities we visited, however, the only recently opened Orthodox Church seen was the Holy Trinity Cathedral in the Alexander Nevsky Monastery in Leningrad, which was reopened in 1957. Three or four hundred people were in attendance at a Sunday service, although a priest afterwards remarked that as many as 8,000 come on major religious holidays. This is one of eleven or twelve Russian Orthodox churches now open in Leningrad.

In the large cities visited in the interior of the country, the number of Orthodox churches in proportion to the Russian population was much less than in Leningrad with its dozen or so, and Moscow with its considerably larger number. In fact, observations in Gorky, Kazan, Sverdlovsk, Novosibirsk and Alma-Ata (whose population of over a half million was informally reported as being about 80 per cent Russian), suggested that the Soviet authorities have established a "norm" of two or at most three functioning Russian Orthodox churches for large interior cities with a population of a half million to a million. For example, the number reported to be open in Alma-Ata was three, in Sverdlovsk, Kazan, and in Novosibirsk, two each.

On the other hand, a small episode in Sverdlovsk — formerly Ekaterinburg and the capital city of the Urals — highlighted for a fleeting moment the spectacle of a church community pressing for a larger place and scope for activity. Inside the lovely, two-hundred-year-old Ivanovskaya Church, a lay elder, in the presence of officials of the city Soviet of Sverdlovsk, said that there were now two Russian Orthodox churches open in the city, that the church community had asked permission to reopen for services a cathedral building in an old monastery in the city, now being used for other purposes, but that the city authorities had refused this permission. "We offered to pay for it, too," he added with a glance at the silent

city officials. The statement is particularly noteworthy in contrast to that of a Russian Church dignitary met elsewhere in the country who, when asked why more Russian Orthodox churches have not been opened, said that as many are open and functioning as the believers among the people have financial means to support. Obviously, this is not the case. Clearly, there is tension between some church communities and the political authorities over the policy of restricting the number of churches permitted to function. Finally, and perhaps not so obviously, it is not the policy of the higher Church authorities to bring this issue into the open in conversation with foreign visitors, but churchmen "at the front" are not always so diplomatic in their relations with the State.

One of the points of concern to the anti-religious forces of the Party, as mentioned earlier, is the fact that some people in Russia are mentally resisting the long-standing Party argument that religious belief is incompatible with science. An interesting illustration of debate on this issue, and of one way in which debate on it takes place, was provided one Saturday evening at an open-air Party lecture forum in the Gorky Park in Moscow. Having completed her lecture on the incompatibility of science and religion, the woman lecturer was answering questions passed up to her on slips of paper from the audience. The first question ran: "How do you explain the fact that Academicians Pavlov and Filatov were believers?" The aim of the question was, of course, to say, or rather to imply, that there cannot be any real and deep incompatibility between religion and science if such eminent scientific minds as those of the physiologists Pavlov and the eye surgeon Filatov can accept religion. The Party lecturer began her answer by saying: "I get this question every time." Then she proceeded to argue that tradition is tenacious, and that some few members of an older generation of scientists remain influenced by "survivals" of older ways of thinking outside their fields of special competence.

Surely this exchange is a significant sign of the times. What it illustrates is a growth of resistance on a purely intellectual plane to the Party's essentially *nineteenth-century* conception of religion and its relation to science. In that conception religious systems of thought are seen as *competitors* of scientific truth, i.e., as poor physics. Evidently, more and more people in twentieth-century Russia are becoming too sophisticated to be influenced by such a crude misconception of what religion means. An unpleasant and unenviable dilemma may be emerging for *Agitprop:* to persist with the old line of argumentation, with less and less effect on people's minds, or to re-examine the whole issue of science versus religion in search of a more sophisticated polemical position. For various reasons the second alternative is difficult or impossible to adopt, and the Party today is simply redoubling efforts to persuade people that it is right on an issue that more and more of them, it would seem, are coming to regard as unreal.

In Tashkent the Deputy Chief Mufti of the Moslems of Central Asia and Kazakhstan, Ismail Maksum, affirmed that religious observance has increased in recent years among the Moslem peoples of this part of the Soviet Union. However, the extent of permitted organized religious activities appeared, from his own further statements, to be severely restricted. Tashkent, the capital of the largest Central Asian republic, Uzbekistan, has sixteen "large" (*sobornye*) mosques, he said, and about one hundred "small" ones. "Small" apparently means home mosques, although this was not admitted. In Uzbekistan as a whole there are two hundred of the "large" mosques and a thousand "small" ones (the population of the republic being around eight millions, the overwhelming majority of whom are Moslems). Religious education is conducted entirely in the families of the devout and through what Ismail Maksum called "groups meeting in private homes." In 1957 twenty-five or thirty Uzbeks made the pilgrimage to Mecca.

On a visit to the main Tashkent Mosque we were shown the newly opened *madrasseh* (theological seminary), which was described as a "secondary institution." It has fifty students and eight teachers, but may later be expanded and raised to the level of a higher theological institution. Its library of ten thousand volumes contained copies of the new edition of the Koran in Arabic script which was put out in Tashkent in 1957 in the pitifully small number of 3,000 copies. This edition, it was said, "sold out very quickly." A new edition of 6,000 was planned for the near future.

A visit to the Russian Baptist Church in Moscow during a Sunday morning service fortified the impression carried away by numerous foreign travelers that the Protestant movement in Russia, though relatively small in numbers, is second to none in spirit and vitality. About two thousand worshippers, mostly but not exclusively older people, and in the great majority women, were packed into the rather small church building, which serves on alternate days as the church of the Seventh-Day Adventists. Baptist churchmen with whom we spoke after the service stated that this Baptist Church has 4,400 members, that there are 530,000 Baptists in the whole Soviet Union, that there are in the country nearly 5,000 Baptist churches. The overwhelming majority of these would evidently fall in the category of "prayer-houses" comparable to the "small" mosques in Central Asia.

The only high clergyman encountered on these travels who gave a picture of a religion in decline was the new Chief Rabbi of Moscow, Rabbi Levin, although he did say that attendance at services in the Moscow main Synagogue, where he officiates, has increased in the recent past. He referred, however, to a decline of religious interest and observance among the youth of Jewish faith in the Soviet Union. This trend was treated as natural and inevitable and in no way a product of government policy. The city and province of Moscow, with a total Jewish population estimated at 400,000, have, he said, four "official" synagogues and about a hundred "home" ones, meaning regularly conducted services in private apartments for groups of not less than ten worshippers. A Jewish theological seminary was opened in 1957 at the central Moscow Synagogue to train future Rabbis. It now has twenty students in training. A Jewish prayer book was published recently, but the Rabbi could not recall the size of the edition.

It hardly needs to be emphasized in the light of all this that the "freedom of religious worship" proclaimed by Article 124 of the Soviet Constitution is honored rather in the breach than in the observance. Behind these various statistics pertaining to the different religions in the Soviet Union one feels the shadowy presence of the governmental authorities pursuing a policy of restricting the number of churches permitted to function, rationing the number of students in theological seminaries, reducing editions of vital religious texts to token numbers — in short, using the powers of the Soviet state to restrict the facilities open to organized religion. One feels in the guarded manner of the churchmen as they speak about the position of their denominations an awareness that one of the rules in this unequal game prohibits disclosure of all this "background" to the foreigner. And finally, one feels, particularly so far as the Russian Orthodox Church and Protestant movement are concerned, that there is a countervailing power which sustains the weaker party — the power of persistent, if not increasing, popular attachment to religion.

Apart from the apparently decreasing effectiveness of the established lines of anti-religious argumentation, about which I have spoken earlier, there would appear to be several possible explanations for this most interesting phenomenon. One, no doubt, is that the search for meaning which has found many forms of expression in the West in the middle of the twentieth century is going on in many Russian minds too, and there as well as in the West one of the places to which people turn to find meaning in existence is the Church. Another is the universal need for ritual and ceremony to mark the momentous occasions of human experience such as birth, marriage, and death, a need which no Komsomol weddings or Party-conducted funeral services can deeply satisfy for more than the merest few. A further explanation, somewhat subtle perhaps, but I suspect important, is that churches alone of all the organized social institutions in Soviet Russia offer in some sense a haven from "the system"; only in the most marginal sense do they belong to the ubiquitous mechanism of the Soviet political system. They alone are in it but not of it, offering some escape from politics.

One further factor remains to be mentioned. Today the motives which prompt people in Russia to go on occasion to church are operating in a changed political scene and atmosphere. The Soviet control system remains intact, but the citizen is not, at present, living in a national atmosphere permanently tinged with terror as in Stalin's later years. Party rule in all departments of the nation's life may be onerous to him, but it does not strike fear into his heart as did secret-police rule under the previous administration. Accordingly, it may

very well be that the signs of rising influence of religion reflect, in part, a feeling of greater latitude to go to church as distinguished from merely wishing to go to church. Khrushchev's attempt to operate the Soviet system if possible without the systematic use of police terror is evidently generating, as it was bound to generate, a number of more or less serious problems for the regime. Not the least of these may prove to be the problem of religious revival.

EDUCATION

45

A Historical Survey of Soviet Education*

Ruth Widmayer

(1954)

Dr. Widmayer describes the historical background and the main stages — through Stalin's reign — of Soviet policy on education, a realm in which the regime's enthusiasm balances its antipathy to religion. Within the bounds of its desire to use education for technical training and political indoctrination, the regime has experimented with various forms and approaches from one period to the next. Indeed, changes have continued since the time this article was written: full co-education was re-introduced in 1954; tuition fees were abolished in 1956; and, as subsequent articles by Nicholas DeWitt (pp. 439–443) and Robert Feldmesser (pp. 573–582) demonstrate, the pendulum has once again swung back to an increased emphasis on polytechnical training.

Education plays a vital role in the Soviet dic-

* Reprinted from "The Evolution of Soviet Educational Policy," *Harvard Educational Review*, Vol. 24 (1954), pp. 159–175, by permission of the author and the publisher.

tatorship. The Communist regime attempts to take advantage of every channel of communication to strengthen its grip over the masses. Since the schools represent the single greatest organized means of transmitting values from one generation to another, the Soviet government has a great stake in providing state-controlled education for its youth. Soviet leaders have always recognized the importance of education, but there have been vastly different views regarding the best educational methods and objectives as the Soviet system has evolved. The following pages will be chiefly concerned with the main stages through which the Soviet schools have passed in terms of educational philosophy and methodology.

Pre-revolutionary Education

When the Bolsheviks seized power in 1917 they repudiated all the major features of Tsarist education. Some aspects of the pre-revolutionary schools were doomed to complete extinction with the fall of the Romanovs, but others underwent only a temporary eclipse. It is interesting to note briefly the kind of school system which existed just prior to the revolution in order to see what type of educational system the Soviets inherited and also to observe what the elements of continuity and change have been.

In the nineteenth century, the Tsarist schools accommodated only a small number of the potential school population. After the reforms of the 1860's and 1870's, there was a substantial increase in the number of pupils attending primary schools. During the first decade and a half of the twentieth century, government expenditures on education, due largely to the activities of the *Zemstvos* (local organs of self-government), rose sharply. According to the census of 1897, the literacy rate for the country as a whole was 21.1 per cent of the total population; by 1914 this figure had almost doubled. In spite of these advances, in many parts of rural Russia and among the numerous minority peoples of the Russian Empire, educational facilities were still inadequate or lacking altogether. There were whole villages that were illiterate and some primitive tribes did not possess even a written language. Educational opportunities for women, particularly in the semi-colonial territories (the Caucasus and Central Asia) were still very restricted.

The general public school system included only the elementary grades and not the high school. The classical gymnasium, which, as its name implies, emphasized classical studies, was the traditional and most common type of secondary school in Tsarist Russia. There was also a "real school" based on the model of the German *"Real-Schule"* introduced into Russia in the 1860's. This school omitted ancient languages from the curriculum and provided instruction in more practical subjects, particularly mathematics and the physical sciences. Co-education had no place in either type of secondary school.

Authoritarian methods of teaching were prevalent. Discipline was strict and harsh: the teacher, feared and unquestioned, did not hesitate to resort to corporal punishment; emphasis was placed on memorization, drill, and rote learning; grades and examinations were an important part of school life. The teaching of Divine Law was required and many schools were controlled by ecclessiastical bodies.

While the features described above characterized the official Tsarist educational policy, there were a number of undercurrents in pre-revolutionary Russian education, which, though officially frowned upon and sometimes suppressed, were of considerable importance. A long line of eminent social critics, including Belinsky, Herzen, Pisarev, Chernyshevsky, and Dobroliubov, had protested against such things as corporal punishment and the teaching of fossilized subject matter. They proposed — among other things — that educators pay more attention to individual needs of students and that the school curriculum be revised to deal with subjects genuinely meaningful in the modern world. These men were not professional educators but their views on social problems were highly regarded by many members of the radically-inclined intelligentsia. In the late nineteenth century and early twentieth century a few real experiments in educational reforms were carried out. The most notable of these was Tolstoy's venture at Yasnaia Poliana in developing the so-called "free-school" where children were permitted unrestricted expression of their personalities. Tolstoy put emphasis on the needs and interests of children, on the importance of love and respect for the child as a unique individual. Stanislau Shatsky, who was later to become a leader in Soviet educational circles, had introduced many progressive educational principles in children's classes at a settlement house in Moscow and later in a school colony which he directed.

Marxian Theory and Early Bolshevik Policy

Bolshevik educational leaders were thoroughly familiar with these unofficial developments in pedagogy and on coming to power they elevated the views of the small minority of radical educators into a part of the official educational policy. The writings of Marx and Engels, however, supplemented by those of Lenin, provided the basic aims and objectives of the Soviet school system in terms of the values, skills, and emotional dispositions desired as a result of education. Marx and Engels wrote no systematic work on the subject of education, but a number of their writings dealt with views on the existing forms of education and recommendations for the type of education needed in a socialist-communist society.

The long-range objective of Marx and Engels was to provide through the educational system for the harmonious, all-round development of every individual, to train everyone to the limits of his capacities. This was to be accomplished by means of what Marx and Engels termed "polytechnical" education, a type of training which emphasized, in addition to mental and physical development of children, their technical proficiency. Students, whether prospective manual workers or professionals, were to be taught the general principles of all processes of production and to be given practical information regarding the use of tools. This type of education was to prevent narrow specialization of the individual and to make possible truly integral education; it was to do away with the deep chasm existing in capitalist society between physical and mental labor. The value of combining productive labor with general education Marx believed was pedagogically valuable "not only as a means for increasing social production, but as the only way of producing fully developed beings."

In education, as in other fields, Lenin accepted the basic principles laid down by Marx and Engels, applying and adapting them to the particular conditions in Russia in the twentieth century. Lenin, like Marx and Engels, was an educated, middle-class intellectual, a scholar as well as a revolutionary man of ac-

tion. Unlike some of his revolutionary contemporaries, Lenin did not conceive of Communism as a movement which would destroy all vestiges of the old "exploiting" order in the realm of culture. He believed that there had been many worthy things accomplished by past societies in spite of their oppressive character and that the Communists must utilize these treasures of the ages, carry them on and make possible their fuller flowering. Realizing that vast numbers of the Russian people lacked the most elementary education and thus were not in a position to render intelligent, thoughtful support to the things for which the Bolshevik regime stood, he urged the elimination of illiteracy as the first and foremost task of the new regime in the field of education. Lenin demanded the most rapid possible end of illiteracy not only because literacy was a basic requisite for political allegiance but also because it was a prime necessity for realizing Communist goals in the economic sphere. Millions of men and women unable to read, write, and count could not help modernize the backward Russian state. Lenin also laid great stress upon the concept of polytechnical education.

Practical Considerations and Communist Policy

The writings of Marx-Engels-Leinin provided general, over-all perspectives for education, but could not provide answers to the technical questions of educational psychology, evaluation of pupil achievement, methods of teaching, and school administration. The pre-revolutionary Russian educators discussed above shed much light upon these problems and many of their ideas were adopted by the Soviet pedagogues. In addition to the help gleaned from this source, the Communist educators drew inspiration from Western trail-blazers in the realm of education. At the very time that the Soviet educators were engaged in formulating their pedagogical plans, the progressive education movement was maturing in the United States. The principles of progressive education were avidly studied by the leaders of the new Soviet school and had a profound influence upon them. In its turn, Soviet education attracted the attention of American progressive educators, who were delighted to discover that so many of the ideas which they championed were put into practice on a nation-wide scale in the U.S.S.R. There was extensive, friendly mutual interchange of experience and ideas in the 1920's between Soviet and American progressive educators. Not only American educational advances, but those of Germany, England, and France were studied as well. Several Soviet educational journals contained special sections on educational developments abroad. Soviet teachers were strongly urged to study and apply some of the new methods in use abroad. Western educational theory contributed to the Soviet schools the idea of the "activity school," the "synthetic method" of teaching, and the general mood of dynamic experimentalism in education.

In the period of War Communism (1917–21), grandiose plans for education were proclaimed, involving the education of all children in new cooperative behavior patterns, with versatile knowledge and many-sided abilities. There were, however, also more practical and more politically partisan objectives. The school was conceived as an important "ideological arm of the Party," as a source of influence on hostile, wavering, and indifferent elements of the population. It was to popularize the ideas of socialism and the goals of the Party and to bring about the "political and social development of the population in the spirit of Communism." The schools were, in Lenin's words, "to train and educate the laboring masses in order to overcome the old customs, the old habits . . . in which the masses are so thoroughly steeped." The educational process was to make people "proletarian" in their outlook, collectivistic rather than individualistic, scientifically-minded instead of religious and superstitious, devoted to the interests of all mankind rather than only to those of their own nation. It would help them to "transform themselves."

Emotional attachment to the regime and its principles could be aroused and cemented by the schools better than by any other social institution and it was hoped to make the school the focal point of the child's existence in order to wean him away from the influence of the family, which in this period was considered a conservative force, retarding the progress of the Revolution. Pupils were encouraged to remain in the school during the day and sometimes even to return in the evenings for extra-

curricular activities of various kinds: meetings, plays, sports, social events, and gatherings of student circles. The Party teachers, Komsomol members, and often the books read by children impressed upon them that their first allegiance should be to the state and the Party and not to their immediate family. They were taught to believe what they learned in school rather than what was told them at home. A fictional character, Pavlik Morozov, who denounced his father to the secret police for hoarding grain became a popular hero among Communist youth and was held up as an example to all young people.

Communist Party and government pronouncements on education loudly proclaimed the intention of providing free and compulsory education for all children. The elimination of illiteracy was one of the major goals of the Party in the cultural field. The problem of illiteracy extended to every age group and involved more than the mere task of providing schooling for the younger generation. Numerous measures were taken to provide means of instruction for adults and youths beyond the normal school age and at the same time great efforts were made to educate the children so that the problem of illiteracy would be eliminated for the future. But there were far too few school buildings, and the number of teachers and other personnel upon which the Soviet government could draw was grossly inadequate. Unable to provide either the manpower or material necessary for new school construction, the government attempted to meet the problem, at least partially, by using a shift system in the schools which already existed. School buildings were made to accommodate two and sometimes three different shifts of pupils, operating in the evenings as well as the day-time in many places. Even the use of this device did not result in the accommodation of anything like the total number of children of school age in the Soviet Union.

The provision of genuinely universal primary and secondary education was contingent not only upon a school construction program, but upon the training of large numbers of teachers and administrators, in itself a task of formidable dimensions. It was not until the mid-1930's that enough additional schools had been built and sufficient numbers of new teachers had been trained to make possible universal attendance in even the four elementary grades for the entire Union. The problem of having to create alphabets and written languages for some of the primitive peoples of Asiatic Russia, and the difficulty of introducing schools into places where they had been totally unknown accounted in large measure for the delay in establishing universal primary education in many of the non-European sections of the country. The achievement of seven-year education for all youth took much longer; until 1949 it remained a privilege of the city youth and a small part of the rural youth. In 1949 seven-year education was made compulsory for the whole Union, but this did not automatically insure that all youth would be able to attend seven years of school. In 1950–51 the press was still speaking of "the goal of having 95 per cent of the rural child population complete seven-year education." About one-third of the children between the ages of twelve and fifteen are not in school in the rural areas at the present time.

Ten-year education has never been achieved for all youth. The goal of providing complete primary and secondary education for the entire population has never been reached, while sections of the peasantry still receive no more than four years of schooling. Although the Soviet Union has reduced illiteracy to negligible proportions, it has not come even close to providing the kind of educational opportunities for all its people which exist in the United States.

The Soviet authorities faced a perplexing dilemma with regard to school admissions policy in the years before the elementary schools were in a position to admit all youngsters. One aim of the educational system was to exert proletarian influence on the non-proletarian strata of the population and to insure the proper political orientation of youth who were not exposed to Communist ideology in their homes. On the other hand, Party leaders felt that when places in the schools were limited they should go first to the children of workers and poor peasants — the groups who had been discriminated against previously and in whose behalf the Revolution had avowedly been fought. It was the intention of the Party to give the formerly dispossessed new opportunities for culture and advancement.

The problem of admissions was answered to a large extent by the logic of events rather than by Party decree. In spite of efforts of the government to provide free clothing and food to poor pupils and official encouragement to workers and poor peasants to send their children to school, these were the groups least able financially, and least inclined culturally, to educate their children. Many of the children of the lower classes did not go to school, while considerable numbers of the children from the professional classes were able to obtain both primary and secondary education, owing to the emphasis which their families placed on education and their efforts to secure educational opportunities for their children. Children of workers and peasants constituted a majority of the pupils in the primary grades, which was natural since these groups made up the vast majority of the population, but they dropped out of school at a much greater rate, constituted the largest number of "repeaters" who had to stay in the same grade for more than one year, and most frequently failed to complete the entire school course. In the secondary school the proportion of working class youth to those from non-worker families dropped very markedly.

Some Striking Contrasts and Reforms

The first years of Communist rule represented a period of striking contrasts in the field of education. Old, time-worn, pre-revolutionary subjects and methods were maintained side by side with bizarre and unorthodox ventures in school instruction. Conservative teachers disapproved of the Revolution and wished to preserve the values of the old regime. They continued to teach the same material in the same manner as before, ignoring the government's decrees about such things as elimination of religious subjects, examinations, homework, and corporal punishments. This group was a majority in the rural areas and was numerous elsewhere. The Soviet authorities were helpless to combat the situation during the first years of its existence. No inspection system had yet been organized on a workable basis and there were not sufficient Communist forces to supervise the teachers, let alone to replace all the old teachers. Wherever possible, Communists were made directors of the schools, with the responsibility of ensuring the correct political attitudes of the teachers, but there were many rural schools with only one or two teachers which had no director; furthermore, even where Communist directors existed, the teachers were sometimes able to circumvent their scrutiny.

At the same time that the village schools remained strongholds of conservatism, many city schools were transformed into exponents of extreme modernism. In certain schools the curriculum was drastically revised. Sometimes integrated study of all subjects around one large theme (later known as the "Complex Method") was introduced. In many places the study of history was scrapped and replaced by concentration on contemporary social problems. Often students worked on problems as groups rather than individually. The old method of recitation from memory was discarded in the schools where Communist influence prevailed. One major reform in the schools was a radical altering of traditional relations between teachers and pupils. The formal, strict relationship between pupils and teachers which had characterized Tsarist schools was over-corrected in the extreme. The Communists not only wished to redress the balance between the students and instructors, but also feared that if unregenerate teachers were left to operate as respected authorities over the classrooms, they might succeed in poisoning the minds of the students against the regime. The new role of the teacher, as expressed by one of the leading Soviet educators, was to be that of "an organizer, assistant, instructor, and older comrade, but not the role of superior officer. . . ." The teacher was to maintain simple, comradely relations with the children. The extent of the change in the position of the teacher was symbolized by the custom of pupils calling the teachers by their first names. If students were rude or mischievous, the teacher did not have the right to punish them. In case the teacher treated the children harshly, the pupils were encouraged by the officials to rebel against him.

One of the principles of the new school was pupil self-government. It was through the organization of pupils in their classes and in the school as a whole that children were expected to learn the techniques of collective and cooperative behavior and to become accustomed to joint endeavors for the accomplishment of common purposes. The pupils' organizations were intended to develop active participation in useful projects. They were to be genuine expressions of pupils' needs and interests and not used as a means of discipline and order by the authorities, and they were not to be dictated to from above. Few of these aims were destined to be realized.

In addition to pupil self-government there were special student organizations with political functions. The most important of these organizations was the Union of Communist Youth (Komsomol), organized in 1918 as a junior partner of the Communist Party, whose duty was to prepare for the parent organization a "new shift" of politically tempered and trustworthy comrades. The Young Communists were leaders of the students, taking a foremost part in the organs of self-government, where they introduced and fought for measures which furthered the Party's educational innovations and general political policies. They attempted to indoctrinate their fellow students by drawing them into Marxist study circles which the Komsomols conducted in the schools.

In 1922 the Party organized the Young Pioneer movement to embrace youngsters between the ages of 10 and 16 and the following year the Little Octobrists for the 8 to 11 year group. Both these organizations were open to nearly all students and have had very large memberships. They are led by Party or Komsomol workers and strive to indoctrinate children in correct Party attitudes and to encourage them to participate actively in useful community projects.

What was done educationally in the early years of the Revolution was in the nature of make-shift, trial-and-error experiments, full of excesses and crudities. Economic hardships and ideological differences with the regime drove many teachers out of the profession and intensified the drastic shortage of trained and experienced personnel. In the years of the blockade and the famine, hunger, cold, and scarcity of goods afflicted teachers and pupils alike and prevented stable school life. Soviet authors referred to these years as a time of wholesale misery and disorder. According to the Soviet Pedagogical Encyclopedia: ". . . There was no labor in the school, no text-books, no curriculum; the teachers led a beggarly life, the schools were falling to pieces." (4, p. 1031) Nevertheless, in crude and inchoate form nearly all the basic principles of the Soviet schools during the first period of Soviet rule were laid down in these chaotic years. The structure of the school as co-educational, secular, and unified was achieved, and the nascent forms of the "complex" and "project" methods were worked out. Student self-government became rooted in school life and the role of the Komsomol as the leading organization of youth was established.

Subsequent Experimentalism in the Growing Technical Society

In the ensuing decade educational experimentalism flourished in the Soviet schools. Concrete programs were formulated to guide the teachers in the new methods, the most prominent of these being a scheme which involved the study of all school subjects in connection with three large themes — Nature, Labor, and Society. Formal knowledge in the sense of learning the traditional subject matter of the ordinary school disciplines was no longer emphasized. It was believed that reading, arithmetic, geography, grammar, etc., could be learned more meaningfully as by-products of the study of broad themes involving topics of interest to children. The Party considered the school as only one among many sources of education. It was believed that informal educational influences such as village Soviets, trade unions, theatres, libraries, and museums could provide much of pedagogical value. The school was directed to work in close cooperation with other social and economic institutions, particularly with industries and workers' organizations, in order to make pupils aware of the larger life around them and to acquaint them with productive processes.

In some respects the Soviet schools were strongholds of democracy, relatively speaking, during the 1920's. Authoritarian teachers and methods were eliminated; pupils were given the right to help decide many aspects of school policy; there was group participation in projects which the pupils themselves had a part in selecting. Racial and sexual equality was taught by verbal means and by the policy of complete equality with regard to the admission of members of racial minorities and girls in the schools. The educational leaders, who were some of the most idealistic, humanitarian, and least hide-bound of the Communists, believed in the inherent rationality and goodness of man when given the proper milieu in which to develop, and their pedagogical program reflected these optimistic views about the nature of man. However, there was never any real freedom to investigate and discuss competing social-political systems with genuine objectivity. The schools were expected to indoctrinate the growing generation in Communist ideology and the Party carefully scrutinized and censored text-books dealing with the social sciences.

By 1927–28 many of the progressive experiments in the schools had come under attack, but the introduction of the first Five Year Plan (1928) brought about a powerful resurgence of revolutionary zeal and stimulated the revolutionaries among the educators to bolder defense of their progressive methods. The exciting new environment, where industrialization and collectivization of agriculture occupied the most prominent places, lent itself admirably to the procedures of the Complex and Project methods and even some forms of the now largely discarded Dalton Plan were revived. These methods of independent study, of learning through doing, had always emphasized the study of contemporary life and they were now harnessed to the study of "socialist construction." It was quite common for schools to undertake to assist a factory in fulfilling its part in the Plan. In rural areas the collective farm frequently served as a large, many-sided "complex" theme. "Socialist competition" was all the rage in the schools: two schools, or two classes in a school, sometimes a school and a factory would pledge to fulfill certain tasks (such as achievement of 100 per cent attendance of children on religious holidays, the teaching of an agreed number of illiterates, responsibility for collectivizing a certain number of households in the region, etc.). Great pride was taken in winning these competitions.

Polytechnical education was also greatly stressed in the opening years of the first Five Year Plan. School work-shops became popular and in some cases pupils spent part of the school day actually working in a factory or enterprise.

The intensification of labor education and the introduction of socialist competition led pupils to be more concerned with the development of the Five Year Plan, or with the factory in which they worked part-time, than with the ordinary pursuits of school life. The very methods that had been intended to produce efficient, capable socialist workers had just the opposite results. Semi-literate pupils were coming out of the schools — their labor training and study of community problems had not firmly established their knowledge of the multiplication tables, of chemical formulas, or of the spelling of words. Complaints about the poor calibre of pupils coming from the Soviet schools became louder and more frequent as the need for competent workers rose under the stimulus of industrial expansion.

Trend Back to Conventionalism and Growing Nationalism

The magnitude of the problem of an ineffectual school system — which in some ways threatened the whole program of industrialization — brought action from the supreme councils of the Communist Party. In 1931 the Central Committee of the Party passed a decree relating to the schools which decisively reversed the trends in education, setting the school back on the path of conventional study. This decree emphasized the importance of a thorough mastery of the basic school subjects — mathematics, native language, geography, physics and chemistry. Subsequent decrees insisted that these basic subjects be taught in the traditional manner — that they be offered as separate subjects, using the recitation method, with individual student responsibility for mastering the material. The idea that the factory, trade-union, or village Soviet could partially replace certain school functions was thoroughly repudiated. The accent was on formal studies, involving primarily book learning. Grades and examinations were emphasized as they had not been since Tsarist times, with individual competition for high grades encouraged. The teacher was restored to a position of dignity and authority in the class-room and pupils were required to show respect and deference for the teacher. The activities of pupils' organizations were greatly curtailed and they were made completely subservient to the school authorities.

From about 1936 Soviet education has reflected in unmistakable terms the growing nationalism of the U.S.S.R., exhibited in greatly increased interest in the teaching of Russian history. History had been re-introduced into the curriculum a few years previously, but had been taught from the standpoint of classes and broad socio-economic movements, with the role of individuals, specific battles, and dates either omitted or played down. The Party approach to history changed, however, and the formerly deterministic view was largely replaced by the belief that "people make their own history," with the result that much greater importance was assigned to "the role of personality in the historical process." The existing textbooks on history were considered unsatisfactory because they were abstract and schematic in character. Three of the most prominent Bolshevik leaders, Stalin, Zhdanov, and Kirov, took responsibility for approving the outlines of new texts in the history of Russia and the U.S.S.R. By the late 1930's the Party had toned down its deprecatory approach to the Russian past and began to exploit the feats of heroes like Alexander Nevsky, Peter the Great, and Suvorov, who contributed to the glory of the Russian nation, even though they had nothing to do with revolutionary movements. Nationalism also became evident in the stress on "Soviet patriotism" which reached a high pitch during "the Great Fatherland War," as Stalin called World War II, and has not slackened since the war. Soviet leaders consider education one of the most valuable means for insuring that the Soviet citizen is properly aware of his responsibility to the state. According to a writer in the Soviet journal *Bolshevik* in 1949: "The Soviet people must be continually educated in a spirit of vitalizing Soviet patriotism. . . . There is no more important task in education than the cultivation of Soviet patriotism. . . ." (3, p. 53) The chief means of explicit indoctrination in Soviet patriotism consists of courses in the social sciences. In addition to courses in history, geography and the Constitution of the U.S.S.R. are offered in the Soviet schools. The course in the Constitution of the U.S.S.R. teaches the pupils that "the Soviet regime . . . is the highest form of democracy" and acquaints them with "the great attainments of the Soviet Union." (2, p. 26) The study of geography is utilized to deepen the pupils' love for their motherland. It "directs attention to those facts which strengthen our national pride: the vast extent of our native land, its natural wealth which is used in the interests of building socialism. . . ." (2)

As the revolutionary aspects of the Soviet

system were supplanted by the drive for stability and conformity, one by one the principles upon which Soviet education had been built originally were discarded and replaced. Following the demise of such things as the complex-method and active learning through doing came the end of polytechnical education, the most unique aspect of Marxist educational theory. The drive for mastery of the basic sciences, for accurate spelling, correct grammar, and ability to add and multiply correctly and rapidly was impeded by the time spent on labor. Another factor which contributed to the abandonment of labor education was the fact that much of the work performed by children in school work-shops had become anachronistic. The machinery, tools, and techniques which were used in the work-shops were usually simple and fairly primitive, best suited to handicraft labor and not to complicated large-scale industrial production. The learning of such crude labor processes was of little help to the pupil when he went to work in a modern factory equipped with the latest mechanical devices and machinery.

Polytechnism was re-interpreted to mean simply the study of the scientific subjects upon which industry is based, such as mathematics, physics, and chemistry. The curriculum of the Soviet schools continues to be heavily weighted in the direction of the natural and physical sciences. Many of the secondary schools offer, in addition to such customary subjects as algebra, geometry, biology, physics, and chemistry, astronomy, trigonometry, anatomy, and geology. Russian language and literature, history, geography, foreign language,[1] and physical education (military training for boys) constitute the rest of the program. Soviet secondary schools operate from September 1st to July 1st, six days a week, from 8:30 A.M. to 2:30 P.M. — a rigorous schedule for adolescents! The curriculum of the elementary school consists of language study or reading (including history, geography, and natural science) and arithmetic in the first two years, with natural science offered as a separate subject in the third year and geography in the last year. Physical education, art, and music are part of the program and often a foreign language is also included. Children in non-Russian schools study in their native tongues but must study the Russian language as a required subject.

The Tuition Fee Issue

In 1940 still another of the basic aspects of Soviet education was dealt a severe blow. The long-cherished aim of providing free education for all Soviet youth was abandoned with the introduction of tuition fees in the last three grades of the secondary school and in higher educational institutions. The fees were modest (200 rubles a year in cities; 150 in rural areas — less than a month's salary for even the lowest paid workers), and there were categories of students who continued to be admitted free,[2] but along with other accompanying measures they had the effect of limiting the educational opportunities of the great mass of Soviet youth to seven years of general education. The scholastically gifted child is still given a chance to continue his education regardless of the ability of his parents to pay tuition fees, but the average pupil whose parents can afford to pay the fees is now able to secure a complete secondary education, whereas his classmate coming from a poor family may not be able to finish the final three grades. This is especially likely to be the case where there are a number of children of secondary school age in a low-income family or where the family is anxious to have the child become a wage-earner as soon as possible.

Whether a student completes the secondary school or not is a determining factor in the whole future life of the boy or girl, for those who complete the secondary school are in a position to enter the higher educational institutions which provide training for the more lucrative and respected professions, while failure to finish secondary school means that the young person has no choice but to enter an unskilled or semi-skilled occupation, the only types open to graduates of incomplete secondary schools. There are a few exceptions, however, as a certain percentage of the graduates of technical schools are permitted to enter higher educational institutions.

There is a possibility that as a result of the

---

[1] Of the foreign languages, English, French, and German are the most common offerings, with schools often providing only the foreign language in which their teachers are qualified. Latin was re-introduced into the secondary schools in 1952.

[2] War orphans, children of sick or disabled parents, or of men in the armed forces, and those with outstanding scholastic records.

fee system the upper income groups will be able to perpetuate their privileged positions in Soviet society. However, the careful consideration given to genuine merit indicates that the youth must prove his worth and cannot actually get too far simply on the prestige and financial position of his family. For example, a mediocre student who completes secondary education by the payment of fees, will probably be unable to pass the stiff competitive examinations required for admission to the higher institutions of learning and thus may be forced to enter a middle-grade Technicum, leading to a middle-grade job. There is no doubt, however, that children of prominent Party officials obtain educational privileges, as teachers and school administrators are eager to retain the good-will of influential parents. Furthermore, one of the determinants of "merit" in the judging of pupils is a complete knowledge and acceptance of Party doctrine, so-called "Marxism-Leninism."

The reason given by the government for the introduction of tuition fees was the need for additional revenue to increase and improve school facilities, and the fact that the average Soviet citizen was now in a position to be able to afford to pay part of the expense of educating his children. Probably a more compelling motive was the desire to bring as many new workers as possible into industry by discouraging the intellectually dull pupils from continuing general education and obliging them to enter trade schools which prepare for productive jobs in a relatively short period of time.

The Co-education Issue

A further break with previously held educational principles of the Communists took place in 1943 when co-education was abandoned in the secondary schools in the large cities and industrial settlements. It was emphasized by the Party and educational authorities that this move did not indicate any change in the Communist attitude toward sexual equality, but was an effort to provide more adequate and meaningful schooling for youth, since it was held that boys and girls mature at different ages and can be taught more effectively in segregated classes. It was also hoped that having boys and girls separated from each other during adolescence, when they are beginning to become preoccupied with the opposite sex, would

have a salutary effect on the problem of discipline, which had long plagued the Soviet schools. Also of prime significance were considerations relating to the military needs of the country. Separate schools facilitated increased military training for the boys. While physical education requirements differed in the segregated schools (girls were given rudiments of nursing, cooking, sewing, and child care in place of military training), the rest of the curricula remained the same for both boys and girls, and both were equally eligible for admission to any higher education institution upon graduation from the tenth grade. Almost half the students in higher educational institutions in the U.S.S.R. are women.

The partial abandonment of co-education in the secondary school does not necessarily signify any basic modification in the Communist belief in the equality of women, for so long as the Soviet economy is expanding there will be need for the services of women as doctors, teachers, chemists, and factory workers, as well as home-makers. For several years there has been wide-spread discussion in the Soviet press airing the pros and cons of co-education and the opponents of segregated middle schools have been encouraged to express their views. It may be that the experiment in segregated education will be given up, especially in light of the fact that it has only been carried out in some areas anyway.

Increasing Centralization

Centralization in the field of education increased measurably during the 1930's and 1940's. Today there are hardly any variations in methods, text-books, curricula, examinations, and grading standards from one part of the union to the other. In some subjects, such as the local language, history and geography of the region, material pertaining to local conditions is permitted, but in these cases the study of the Russian language and of the over-all history and geography of the entire U.S.S.R. are also required. By and large, the Soviet pupil, whether in Samarkand, Moscow, or Archangel learns the same mathematics, history, and literature, is trained in the same pattern of Soviet patriotism, and is encouraged in much the same manner to become a sober, steadfast, and dutiful citizen.

Communist Party domination over the schools was greatly expanded during the past two decades. The practice of employing Party or Komsomol members as school directors and teachers of history and social science continued while the numbers of Party inspectors was increased. By the time of the return to traditional education, the teachers as a whole were trusted by the Party. Many of the teachers were young people trained in Soviet schools and thus thoroughly imbued with Communist ideology. Furthermore, the older teachers who had been trained under the old regime for the most part welcomed the changes in educational policy which the Party fostered in the 1930's.

Prior to 1931 the Party had not prescribed in detail the methods and curriculum of the schools. It devoted its attention only to such broad general matters as the establishment of universal compulsory primary education, the admission of children of poor peasants and workers, and the organization of Communist youth groups in schools. In sharp contrast with the earlier general directives were the long and detailed decrees of the 1930's and subsequently, regarding such intimate aspects of school life as the length of the lesson, the manner of conducting examinations, the precise form of grading to be used in all schools, and the type of instruction to be provided in the classroom. The textbook was an object of special concern to the Party in its efforts to make the school a fully effective weapon in the struggle for the mind of youth. It was recognized that uniform textbooks presenting the views of the Party, distributed to all the schools of the U.S.S.R., could be a mighty weapon for providing homogeneous knowledge and thus the basis for unity of thinking of all youth.

The growth of totalitarianism in the Soviet system was accompanied by a growth in Party strength, making possible the penetration of effectual control into formerly neglected spheres. The school was one of the first of those institutions which had previously been permitted some measure of internal freedom to be brought under complete political domination. This was because formal education had become the surest means of creating the kind of attitudes, beliefs, and abilities desired by the Party. Embracing millions of children and youth from all elements of the population, the school has a huge captive audience upon which to impose the ideology of the regime. Party concern about the schools was due not

only to the expectation that the school would produce a future generation of loyal and devoted citizens, but because it was recognized by the Communist leaders that the school is the most powerful link of the state with the entire population of the country. A Bolshevik leader expressed this idea very aptly in an article in a Soviet journal: "The school is essentially the greatest mass organization in the country. The school is literally connected with everyday life. It is connected with the millions of workers and Kolkhoz families through their most intimate tie — the children, and the workers and Kolkhozniks often judge the Soviet authorities, judge how the Soviet authorities deal with bureaucracy, etc., from the way the school functions." (1, p. 20)

Conclusions

In the first decade of Communist rule, Marxist, pre-revolutionary Russian-radical, and Western progressive influences were predominant in the Soviet schools. From Marx, Engels, and Lenin were taken the socialistic purposes of the educational system: the emphasis on labor and polytechnical training; the antireligious, materialistic bias; the Marxist-Leninist dogma. The Russian radical heritage contributed such things as the stress on natural sciences, elimination of corporal punishments, and humane treatment of children. From Western educational theory came the concept of the teacher as a guide and not a disciplinarian; the teaching of subject matter related to the lives of the pupils; and emphasis on the importance of active methods of instruction based on direct experience.

After 1931–32 Western ideas were bitterly repudiated and many of the Marxist educational theories were rendered only lip-service, while a significant number of the practices of the traditional Russian school were brought back, including the grading and examination system, inculcation of fervent patriotism, passive teaching methods, fees, and segregation of boys and girls. The latter two features are not strictly comparable to Tsarist practices, since they do not apply to every level of the school system, but only to the secondary schools and even there are limited in application; however, even their partial reintroduction is significant.

The present Soviet schools have, in some

ways, more in common with the schools that existed before the October Revolution than with the school envisioned by Marx and the Russian educational reformers, or with the schools in existence in many sections of the Western world. Great advances have been made over the Tsarist educational system in terms of the numbers of students embraced by the Soviet schools, but this prodigious achievement has not been accomplished for the purpose of liberating the masses or of making possible the fullest development of all the varied potentialities of the child and youth, but in order to produce an ample supply of competent workers for industry and agriculture, and to ensure the devotion and allegiance of the rising generation to the Soviet state and the Communist Party.

REFERENCES

1. Epshtein, M. S. "Ob Organizatsii Uchebnogo Goda i O Soderzhanii Uchebnykh Zaniatii v Novom Uchebnom Gody," *Kommunisticheskoe Prosveshchenie*, No. 5, 1935, p. 20.
2. Medinsky, E. *Narodnoe Obrazovanie v SSSR*, Moscow, 1947, p. 26.
3. Mishakova, O. "The Building of Socialism and the Communist Education of the Working People," *Bolshevik*, No. 4, Feb. 28, 1949, p. 53.
4. "Organizatsionye Voprosy Narodnogo Prosveshcheniia," *Pedagogicheskaia Entsiklopediia*, Moscow, 1927, p. 1031.

46

Recent Trends in Soviet Education*

Nicholas DeWitt

(1960)

In this era of science and technology, education has become a weapon of national policy. Mr. DeWitt assesses the Soviet educational system in this light, with particular reference

* Reprinted from "Soviet Science Education and the School Reform," *School and Society*, Vol. 88 (1960), pp. 297–300, by permission of the author and the publisher.

to the recent reforms (see also Article 63 by R. A. Feldmesser), and in comparison with American education.

In the last few years, since so many people in American educational circles have gained an opportunity to travel to Russia, the new phrase, "Soviet commitment to education," has become popular. But much of the fancy talk about the Communist commitment to education comes dangerously close to missing the really important point: what we must ask ourselves is the basic question — *commitment to what kind of education?* The answer is disarmingly simple: first, last, and always, the Soviet commitment to education is a commitment to scientific education, to technological education, to an education which will enable Soviet citizens to perform specialized functional tasks to the best of their ability in their expanding industrial society.

The Russians orient their educational efforts so as to maximize the returns from it for the advancement of their political, military, and economic objectives. The Communists do not believe in education for education's sake. They do not believe in education for the individual's sake. The Russians want no part of liberal or general humanistic education. They want no generalists — only specialists. Their main objective is to offer *functional education* so as to train, to mold, to develop the skills, the professions, and the specialists required by their long-run development programs — specialists who are capable of performing the tasks of running the industrial and bureaucratic machinery of the Communist state. And in order to accomplish this, the Russians *were, are,* and *will be* training an army of scientists and technologists.

Although professing the aims of general and well-rounded education, the Soviet educational system in reality is uniquely geared to the training of specialized manpower. By means of mass persuasion, of coercion if necessary, and of bold incentives, the Soviet state makes every effort to channel the best and largest share of available talent into professional occupations and into engineering and scientific professions in particular. This is clearly evident when we compare the professional manpower situation and current training trends in the Soviet Union and the U.S. The total stock of professional higher education graduates in the U.S.S.R. at the end of 1959 was 3,300,000.[1] Projected additions of higher education graduates in the next five years amount to 335,000 annually. The total number of Soviet higher education graduates is less than one-half the number of college graduates in the U.S. The Soviet Union's annual number of graduates will be probably 10 per cent less than ours. The comparison of graduates by field in the U.S. and U.S.S.R. is shown in Table 1.

The score card looks unfavorable, no matter how many reservations one makes about the validity of such numerical comparisons. It is all the more disheartening because, during the last ten years, there has not been a single study in the U.S. or in Western Europe which could

[1] This figure and those in the comparisons below refer to professional higher education graduates employed in the civilian economy of the U.S.S.R. The Soviet census of population in 1959 revealed (*Pravda*, Feb. 4, 1960) that, as of January 1959, the U.S.S.R. had 3,778,000 higher education graduates, of whom 3,027,000 were employed in the civilian economy. The remaining 750,000 professionals were in the armed forces (estimated at about 350,000), retired graduates, and women graduates who were not gainfully employed (estimated at about 400,000 for both categories).

challenge the proposition that, in qualitative terms, Soviet science and engineering education is not inferior to that in the West. Soviet faults are many and complaints about shortcomings are monotonous; but the basic proposition of qualitative comparability (and, at times, superiority of Soviet science and technical education) remains in force.

Although many American educators may dispute the theory, Soviet leaders believe that engineers and scientists can perform managerial, administrative, economic, and business coordination jobs *better* than any generalist or any non-technically trained specialist. This is the simple consideration behind the fact that Soviet engineers manage Soviet industry, Soviet engineers supervise planning and distribution, and a significant part of the Soviet government is even run by engineers and scientists. Perhaps one should not question the wisdom of the presence of American liberal arts graduates and generalists as golden nuggets in the American business world. The fact remains, however, that there are no such nuggets in the Soviet setting, and, what is more, the Soviet regime wants none of them.

Soviet success in training large numbers of

TABLE 1   *U.S.S.R. and U.S. Professional Graduates*

Field	Stock of Soviet Professional Graduates at the End of 1959	Projected Annual Additions of Graduates in the Next Five Years	U.S.S.R. — U.S. Comparisons
General education, cultural, and socio-economic fields	1,686,000	146,000	Soviet stock only ⅓ as large as ours. Annual additions half as large.
Agricultural fields	248,000	35,000	Soviet stock about ⅓ higher than ours. Annual additions ⅓ higher.
Health and medical fields	383,000	28,000	Soviet stock about ¼ larger than ours. Annual additions four times as large.
Engineering fields	974,000	125,000	Soviet stock ⅓ larger than ours. Annual additions three times larger.

specialists on the professional level depends, to a large degree, upon the secondary school training. Today Soviet education is in a state of flux. During the 1950's, two central problems emerged. The first relates to the educational policy of the Soviet regime, and the second to current demographic trends in the Soviet Union. It was not until recently that the goal of universal secondary education has even begun to be approached. As late as 1952, less than 10 per cent of 17-year-olds were able to complete the entire ten-year program of Soviet primary and secondary schooling. Either because of personal circumstances or the stringent academic requirements, some 90 per cent of youngsters fell by the wayside. But by 1956, there were close to 1,500,000 secondary school graduates. In relation to the corresponding age cohort, the rate of completion of the ten-year school increased from less than 10 to 35 per cent. Admission quotas in higher education, however, did not expand appreciably in the intervening period, and, consequently, the *majority* of ten-year-school graduates found themselves outside the walls of institutions of higher learning. Meanwhile, although there have been some revisions in the primary and secondary school curriculum (the introduction of manual training and workshop activities are to be particularly noted), the program of skilled training and vocational preparation has *not* made much headway. As a result, in the course of the last few years, the problem has reared up with full force as to what should be the next step to prepare secondary school graduates for practical occupations.

The second problem is that World War II not only made for tremendous physical devastation within the Soviet Union, but also played havoc with the Soviet population. In 1959, the Soviet population was 208,000,000, while 20 years earlier, just before the outbreak of the war, it was already 192,000,000. Had it not been for the war, the Soviet population would be 30–40,000,000 more than it actually is today. Also, the birthrate declined drastically during the war, and it is only natural to expect that the heavy losses in population were reflected in the school enrollment. While, in the fall of 1948, in the elementary grades (1–4) of Soviet schools there were some 24,000,000 youngsters, by 1953 their number had been cut in half, to only 12,000,000. This

staggering decline occurred in the course of five years. Recovery since 1953 has been very slow, and in 1958 there were still only 18,000,000 pupils in the elementary grades. The obvious implication is that the prime age groups for new additions to the labor force, as well as for those who are to serve in the armed forces or to continue their training in Soviet institutions of higher learning, are now considerably reduced. This deficit will continue to be felt throughout the 1960's, particularly during the early years of the decade.

These two social forces were the most influential in triggering off "Khrushchev's Educational Reform." No doubt, political factors also had a role, but the economic considerations predominated. For a year or so, Western observers were quite puzzled by what the future of Soviet education would hold. Now we have enough evidence to state conclusively that the reform will not diminish but, in effect, will *intensify* the scientific and technical orientation of Soviet schooling. As far as general education and as far as the social sciences and the humanities are concerned, the ax will fall. The new educational reform envisages a reorganization of the Soviet complete secondary school from ten to eleven years. The first eight years will be compulsory. After completion of the eight-year school, most youths at age 15 or 16 will be integrated into productive activity in the labor force directly, and their schooling will be continued on a *part-time* basis only. The three upper grades, 9–11, will be called "general polytechnical school with production training," and these grades will be more selective than were grades 8–10 in 1956. The scientific and technical content will be intensified in these three upper grades, as well as through the general school structure itself, as revealed by a brief comparison of the present ten-year and the new eleven-year curriculum (Table 2).

The bulk of the additional 2,041 hours of instruction will be allocated to vocational subjects (1,454) and workshop and industrial practice. The sciences will gain 395 instruction hours and the addition to the humanities will be only 192 classroom hours. But what this redistribution overlooks is that the "polytechnical subjects" will be science- and technology-oriented. Over one-third of polytechnical instruction will be technology-applied science,

TABLE 2 — *Changes in Soviet Curriculum*

CURRICULUM	10-YEAR 1957 CURRICULUM		11-YEAR PROPOSED 1963 CURRICULUM		NET GAIN IN INSTR. HOURS
	Instr. Hours	%	Instr. Hours	%	
General (language, literature, humanities, and social sciences)	4,692	44	4,884	38	192
Scientific (sciences and mathematics)	3,332	31	3,727	29	395
Applied activities and vocational skill subjects	2,763	25	4,217	33	1,454
TOTAL	10,787	100%	12,828	100%	2,041

and two-thirds will be industrial arts and skill subjects. In other words, although the content will be of an applied nature, it will be closely tied in with regular science and mathematics instruction.

In addition to the curricular changes, one must emphasize the very favorable situation in the supply of teachers. Of the total 1,800,000 teachers on all levels of the Soviet school system, about half are teachers in secondary schools. Among these 900,000 secondary school teachers, 340,000 are science or mathematics teachers. The current trend in teacher training is that of the 110,000 teachers trained annually, about 25,000 are science or mathematics teachers.

Another factor which should give us pause is the question of money. All education, and particularly science and technological education, requires money — and much of it. The Soviet state controls all types of education, and most educational expenditures are borne by the state, which spends annually 7 per cent of the Soviet gross national product. In proportionate terms, this is *twice* as much as we spend on education; in absolute terms, we are about even. This actually means that a country which is less than half as rich as we are spends as much on education as we do. We, who can afford most, are saving most on an effort which matters critically for the long-run welfare of the nation. Most education in the Soviet Union is tuition-free. A successful student

through a system of stipends and scholarships gets paid for going to school. And it is largely by lessening the economic burden of education upon the individual and his family that the Soviet state is able to apply such stringent selection and to channel by means of incentive the national talent into fields of specialization it deems most desired.

Soviet science and education *do* serve the state's military, political, and power objectives. But in pursuing these objectives, they often fulfill their self-purposiveness and thus get full benefit and full credit. We often fail to grasp this in trying to understand the Soviet effort. Today the Soviet Union is in a new phase in its economic evolution: more hands doing physical labor have to be replaced as rapidly as possible by machines and higher quality of skills. The army of Soviet scientists, engineers, and technologists which the Soviet Union has trained in recent years and will continue to train is to be deployed to achieve this task. In order to succeed in this, what the Soviet Union apparently needs most of all today is higher quality in the laboring and technical skills. And Soviet education, as in the past, is being called upon to perform a specific, functional task in developing these skills. This is the essence of Khrushchev's educational reform which has been largely overlooked by many in the West. The age-old issue of education — what kind and what for — is again being resolved *not* in favor of the individual, but in favor of the Soviet state. There is a lesson in this, too. I hope we never will have to resort to such devices, but, in order to avoid them, we will have to begin to do much more for the betterment of our own education before it is too late. For education can be no better than society is willing to make it.

47

Soviet Books for Children*

Helen Rapp

(1958)

Children's literature shows a warm human side in a society where daily life has often been quite gray and grim. It also reveals another aspect of the official approach to life, and suggests the kind of people the Soviet rulers want children to become.

In 1948 the Soviet Ministry of Education published a scholarly work by A. P. Babushkina, entitled *The History of Russian Children's Literature*. This book is interesting because it emphasizes the educational element of books for children in Russia from the times of the seventeenth-century *Entertaining ABCs* of Karion Istomin, through the ideas of the nineteenth century to the precepts laid down by Maxim Gorki after the Revolution. Babushkina gives the following definition of children's literature: "It is a literature which performs through the medium of artistic images the task of educating children. . . . A clear idea, a bright, gay or dramatic plot, clear composition, a hero as an ideal to be emulated . . . the serious use of the word . . . those are the necessary elements of the artistic organism of the works for children."

Such principles, surely, are at the basis of serious books for children anywhere, and it is not surprising therefore that much of today's Soviet writing for children, if translated into

English, would easily gain parental approval and be read by English children with pleasure. Some might even give great delight and gain much popularity. Children in Russia and England are, after all, mainly just children and the things they like to read are much the same. Neverthless there are striking and quite fundamental differences between English and Soviet books for children, not the least being that in Russia children's books are published by the State, on a systematic and planned basis, whereas in the West they sprout in publishers' lists in a free, ungoverned, and incalculable way. This very marked element of planning in the production of Soviet children's literature makes it possible, far more than it would be in the West, to generalize from a few examples chosen almost at random — and were it not so, the subject would be quite unmanageable, for the most striking thing about Soviet children's literature is its sudden and prolific growth.

Before the Revolution there was no regular publication of children's books — they cropped up from time to time, and, as in England, many books initially intended for adults were used as children's reading matter (Aksakov's *Childhood of Bagrov's Grandson* or Tolstoy's *Childhood*). Some of Russia's great writers tried to fill the gap, but at the end of the nineteenth century Chekhov still found reason to complain: "There are no books for children. There are books about cats and dogs (a deliberate hint at his own story about a stray dog Kashtanka) — that's not children's literature: it's dogs' literature."

Shortly before and after the Revolution Maxim Gorki and Kornei Chukovsky made a first attempt to tackle the subject systematically. Chukovsky wrote several interesting articles on children's language, stressing their creative approach to words, and produced some wholly delightful verses for children in the spirit and rhythm of language which he was advocating. Gorki, who still dominates the Russian literary scene, formulated guiding principles which, to some extent, foreshadowed the books that were to follow. Children, he proclaimed, should be brought up to be life's masters, not its slaves. Real life was the best teacher. Children, in Gorki's words, "have a love for the unusual and colorful. The unusual and colorful in the Soviet Union are all those new things which the revolutionary energy of the working class is achieving." He called, for

* Reprinted from "Noddy and the Commissar: Soviet Children's Literature," *Soviet Survey*, No. 23 (January–March 1958), pp. 18–23, by permission of the author and the publisher.

instance, for a book about how man became a giant, about how science increased human sight (telescope, television), hearing (telephone, wireless), legs (transport), hands (remote control), etc. These achievements of man were to be presented entertainingly, without moralising and above all in beautiful and simple language.

One can trace these precepts of Gorki's in the books Soviet children read today. The first thing that strikes the Western parent is what they do *not* read. They have no comics, no Wild West tales, no detective stories, no romances glorifying violence. I do not wish to pronounce any judgments, but I have the impression that — whatever else they may do — Soviet children in their day-dreams do not rush around waving six-shooters or fighting battles against gangsters. Altogether — except for the traditional Russian fairytales which are a thing apart — the fantastic, for better or worse, is absent. The unusual and colorful are provided by the more eventful moments of Russian history (the Crimean war, the revolutionary period, or the last war) or in the romantic setting of some of the far-flung and little known regions of the Soviet Union (Siberia, the Altai mountains) or in adventure stories where childish credulity is not strained beyond, say, the possibility of an outsize submarine linked with the shore by an underwater tunnel. There is a whole class of books, published as "A Library of Adventure," which presents adventure in the form of exciting historical, ethnographical or scientific instruction, but which, stripped of their narrative, would not disgrace a text-book. The approach to children's literature in the Soviet Union is serious, even earnest, and as the books are published not by individual and uncoordinated firms but by the state, there is a certain amount of uniformity and a great deal of system in the aims of the books issued.

As in the West, they are roughly divided into three groups suitable for three different age levels, but in Russia each book clearly states the age group for which it is intended.

For the Older Children

The greatest variety is found among the books for teenagers where you have adventure tales, straightforward stories of children's everyday life at home and at school, historical

novels, and purely scientific books such as a story of experiments with plants in a botanical garden outside Leningrad, to produce bigger, better, and juicier berries. This age-group also comes in for the greatest amount of teaching, by which I mean the whole range from general moral and character-forming instruction to the repetitive drumbeats of Communist and patriotic propaganda. Children's literature, where it does not seek merely to amuse or thrill, is necessarily educational. Propaganda apart — and Soviet children get their propaganda in magazines more than in books — it is interesting to get a glimpse of what is good or bad in the eyes of Soviet pedagogues.

The virtues extolled are on the Spartan side: self-discipline, honesty towards oneself and others, simplicity, the importance of being natural, comradeship, and, overshadowing all others, the dominant virtue of perseverance, hard work, and collective rather than individual effort. If there is one theme which Soviet children's books stress a little more than any other, it is that of the need to face and master difficulties, of doing things the hard way. Prilezhaeva's book *The Youth of Masha Strogova* — a book for teenage girls — urges naturalness, simplicity and perseverance. Oseyeva's very popular *Vasyok Trubachov and His Friends* — for slightly younger children — speaks for comradeship, discipline, the importance of school education and — perseverance. Its underlying pedagogic purpose comes through openly enough in the postcript to the young readers which says: "You have read the last page. Together with Trubachov and his friends you have lived through everything that came their way. You love your country as much as they did and if danger comes, you will be ready to defend her from her enemies, to preserve your school, your happy childhood. . . . In your school life, like Trubachov and his friends, you have many great and many little things to do, you educate yourself and steel your will in order to join the ranks of better children. . . ."

It is perhaps not entirely my fault if all this tends to seem just a little on the drab side, although I should add that all the books I have mentioned present their stories entertainingly and probably have no difficulty in holding the attention of their young readers. But rather more color is brought into the young Russian's reading matter by the historical novels. It may be worth noting in passing that those I have read make no attempt to distort or misrepresent the past to suit any present Soviet purpose. The political approach to books for young children is quite different from that to books for the older ones. Changes in the party line are not reflected in them to anything like the same extent. In line with a tradition of writing of which Tolstoy was the outstanding example in Russia, it is the people rather than the isolated statesman or leader who are the protagonists in Soviet historical novels for children. Their aim is to make history lessons more palatable and with a sensitive and intuitive touch characteristic of some Russian writing they achieve this by viewing history through the eyes of a small child. There is one about the Crimean war by Grigor'yev which describes the defence of Sebastopol as seen by a sailor's small son who takes an active part in everything that goes on. He meets personally the great admiral Nakhimov and witnesses the admiral's death. And *The Lone White Sail*, a famous historical novel by Valentin Kataev, is also a profound study of a child's psychology. It deals with children caught up by the revolution, caught in it and bewildered and making sense of it all in their own childish way. "Daddy," says one little boy, "what is Tsar?" "How do you mean: what is Tsar?" — "Well, *what* is it?" — "A Tsar is a Tsar." — "No, but what *is* it?" — "I don't know what you mean. He is the anointed, if you like." — "Anointed with what . . .?" Little snatches of conversation which children overhear from the grownups, together with their elders' nervousness, fear, or indignation which the child senses, are understood in a peculiar child perspective. Out of chaos the child creates a world which has no bearing on reality but which, to him, is very vivid.

This way of presenting the world from inside a child's mind is a peculiar achievement of Russian literature from the time of Aksakov's *Family Chronicle* and Tolstoy's *Childhood*. It is a tradition that is being kept alive, but is now presented about children *for* children, whereas in the last century its appeal was to the adult.

The same understanding for what is un-sophisticated, natural, and alive comes out in the books about plants and animals. Some of them, in the wealth and beauty of their language, and in their refreshingly unsentimental approach, remind one of Williamson's *Tarka the Otter*. Armilov's book *In The Hunter's Tracks* gives short accounts of the various birds and animals he hunted with his grandfather. There is no false sentimentality about killing: the description of a bear's death is stark in its realism, stark as the Siberian forests where man must kill to survive. But one is at the same time left aware of the educational aim of instructing the child and of enriching his vocabulary.

Soviet books for children thus preach the virtues of friendship, courage, education, and perseverance, entertain with plausible adventures and provide information about nature and human scientific achievement. With regard to the latter, a brief summary of recent publications would show the range. There are books like B. Lyapunov's *Struggle For Speed* (1956) which is an easily worded handbook on the achievements of technology. It discusses above all the latest discoveries in aviation, automation, electronics, and all those branches of science that go into the making of them and poses at the end the following question: Is all this super science-fiction? Does this mean that the machine will replace man? No. Man the controller remains. Nothing can replace the human brain. And Lyapunov quotes the words of Gorki: "We live in an age when the distance between the most unbelievable fantasies and reality is being reduced with incredible speed." This book looks ahead to future achievements, to the time when man will take more from the earth and the sun than they at the moment yield. The purpose of the book, clearly, is not only to instruct young readers, but also to kindle their imagination and to draw them into the ranks of scientists and technologists. The same can be said of A. E. Fersman's *Attractive Geochemistry* (1954), a long, well written, comprehensible work on the study of the atom which ends with the words: "We must study nature in order to conquer it. We must master the atoms so that we can do with them whatever we want, we must, for instance, find super-hard alloys, which will be harder than diamonds . . . we want to subjugate the atom, to bend it to our will, to the will of triumphant man who turns all the threatening and harmful forces of nature into useful ones. The whole of nature we want to put at the feet of hard-working humanity. . . . With these words we end this book. . . . But, dear friends, is there an end to science or to study?" Or again there is M. Vasil'yev's *Journey Into Cosmos* (1955), which in this Sputnik age I personally found fascinating. It deals with the possible victory of man over cosmic space. "From a nebulous dream this problem has become a concrete task of science and technology. It is no longer science-fiction writers who work out the details of cosmic routes, but scientists and engineers. Metallurgists are already testing those metals, whose job it will be to visit other planets . . . the first pilots of the first cosmic ships have already finished their secondary education. . . ." The author considers Professor V. V. Dobronravov's prediction that men will visit the moon by the year 2000 to be a somewhat pessimistic one. Vasil'yev — in his own words — writes about how "man came to the fulfilment of such a dream, about the history of the discovery first of one planet — man's own earth, and about the future discovery of the Universe, outlining the difficulties which man has overcome and those which still stand in his way to the stars." Discussing aeronautics as opposed to aviation, Vasil'yev must necessarily touch upon different branches of science, engineering, technology, etc., all of which he does lucidly and entertainingly and makes his book more thrilling than any science fiction. And once more the purpose and the message are explicit and clear. His young reader is made to feel proud of the achievements of man, proud to belong to the human race which, having pitted itself against dark and mysterious forces of nature, is beginning to emerge victorious. Science, he is told, is a constructive and a hopeful thing, it is there for the benefit of humanity. Its destructive powers are not discussed, they are not even mentioned. The reader is urged to participate in or to admire its achievements. (Although the achievements of Soviet scientists are stressed again and again, tribute is paid to what has been and is being done abroad.)

Sometimes Soviet science books may appear to a Western reader excessively dry in their earnest informativeness: as in a story about gooseberries and how to grow them and how to improve them by grafting and how to classify the various types of gooseberries and how to test suitable soils and so on.

By and large, the virtues of collective effort, courage, optimistic faith in the achievements of the human mind are normally the total extent of "indoctrination" in Soviet books for children, with one startling exception that came my way. A book was published in 1951 under the title *The Story of the Miraculous Dandelion*. It is written in collaboration with an agricultural scientist and tells of the discovery of a rubber plant in the Soviet Union. But with the tale of the discovery, investigation, and cultivation of this miraculous weed there is also woven into the book a history — if history it can be called — of rubber in the capitalist world which is the crudest anti-Western propaganda I have come across. Germany, the arch-enemy, and America, the potential enemy, are uncommonly interested in getting hold of this weed, and some foreign scientist even tries to steal the seeds at an agricultural exhibition. The book is such a jumble of botanical information, defence of Lysenko theories, and anti-capitalist propaganda as to stand out sharply from the general run of children's books. It is a bad book also from the point of view of mere presentation, for no child can absorb so much different and diverse information even if the information were correct.

For the Youngest Readers

I have saved up for the end the pleasure of looking at the books Soviet Russia produces for her youngest readers. The books for older children are marked by a certain uniformity and a certain amount of implicit political teaching — it is a good child's ultimate aim to be accepted into the *komsomol*. Their style and language are usually simple and on occasions pedestrian.

The nursery of Soviet literature presents a different picture. One is tempted to think that where politics do not have to enter, the writer is glad to be able to let himself go, in imagination, in language, in illustration.

There is a veritable fairground of fun, of color, rhythm, and humor. There is more imaginative grasp of a child's young eagerness and far less whimsicality than our children are sometimes exposed to and none of that facile foreshortening, that false child's perspective which is really designed with an eye on the delighted adult. Where the older children read mainly prose, the small children have much of their reading in verse. This is naturally of uneven quality but sometimes reaches flashes of genius, as in some of the poems of Marshak, of Barto, and in those of Chukovsky, that master of Russian jingle and rhyme. The poems, intended to teach children their native language, have marked rhythm and very clear rhymes, and there is great play on words, puns being a great favorite with children. Marshak has a delightful little poem about a garden, a garden which wakes up in the morning, washes, goes for a walk, has lunch, sleeps, plays with toys . . . and is of course a Kinder-Garten. These verses for children are about the seasons of the year, about different regions of the Soviet Union, about the various fruits that grow in different climates, about animals, and about toys. The animals, incidentally, rarely behave like human beings, as for instance in Grahame's *The Wind In The Willows.* If they are made to talk, it is usually to show up their own characteristics, much as in fables. And there seem to be no animated toys, in the manner of, say, Enid Blyton. Russian toys do not make off on their own to take a trip to the seaside or in other ways try to parallel human life. They remain starting points for the childish imagination: the boy beats his drum and *sees himself* on a parade-ground, he strides his rocking-horse on *imaginary* excursions. Ultimately, it is what the child does with the toys that goes into Russian children's books, not what the toys do on their own. No confusion is created about the world surrounding the child, his toy cupboard is not full of pathetic fallacies.

These books for the small children also stand out by being printed more legibly and on better paper than the average Soviet product and there is color and originality in the illustrations. This applies also to the traditional fairy tales which are republished periodically with colorful pictures in the old Russian style and of which admirable children's films have been made. But there is something in the very presentation and approach of a fairy tale which prevents all these witches, hunchback horses, and underwater princesses from getting mixed up in the child's mind with his everyday world, a careful though not derogatory setting apart of this world of magic in which the retention of the traditional stylized illustrations plays no small part. The draftsmanship of Soviet book illustrations is often of a very high order. In children's books it is supported by strong and imaginative colors, a free and powerful use of, say, dark greens and reds or purple, a readiness to exploit the darker, deeper, even gloomier end of the palette which seems very alive, seizes the child's visual imagination in no uncertain manner and appeared to me very welcome after the faint and sweetish pastel shades feebly decorating some Western publications for children.

The Detgiz — or Publishing House for Children — provides its reading public also with a wide range of monthly periodicals. In many of these political propaganda is far more marked than in the books — I have some issues where nearly the first half of each paper is devoted to poems and songs in praise of Stalin, the Soviet Union, various youth movements, and the international peace campaign. But apart from this the periodicals, like the books, cater for different age groups and for a great diversity of interests. There are geographical and technical magazines and others which encourage music, singing, dancing, and hobbies like woodwork. Much attention is devoted to using these magazines to stimulate interest in schoolwork, in the experimental side of science, in overcoming a child's aversion to mathematics by showing its practical applications. These papers, which are printed in large numbers, suffer from a somewhat uninspiring appearance — faded small print on yellowish paper — with the exception again of the magazine for the small children called *Murzhilka.*

I would like to end by quoting from a poem for children by Chukovsky, translated by Mr. Richard Coe, of Leeds University. Chukovsky, who was already a well-known critic at the time of the Revolution, is not altogether typical of today's Soviet literature for children, but is still very popular.

'The Knight of the Bath' is a poem about a boy who did not want to wash:

The eiderdown fled
From my bed
And the sheet
From my feet,
And the pillow-slip
Sped
Hop-a-skip
From my head;
And the light
Took fright
And nipped
Into a drawer:
And my books and my toys
In a trice
With a pattering noise
Like mice
Hurried
And scurried
And slid
All over the floor
And hid!

I wanted a drink,
And what do you think?
The coffee pot
Shot
Straight into the sink!
What's the matter?
Skitter-scatter
Every plate
And every platter
Whirling,
Twirling,
Swirls around
In the air
And on the ground!
A watering can
And a steak
Play catch-as-catch can
With a cake;
And the cake
With a trowel,
And the trowel
With a towel,
And the towel
With a bowl
(A big bright bowl)
And a rake!

With a crash like a big brass drum
Which shook every nail in the floor,
The Bath Tub strode through the door
Bad-tempered and scowling and glum!

"O, dirty-face, you slimy
Gutter-snipey little hog!
Chimney sweeps are not so grimy
Sweeping chimneys in a fog!
Look!

There's mud on your nose,
And there's ink on your toes,
And your hands are so filthy,
That even your shoes,
Your shoes and your trousers,
Your trousers, your trousers,
Your very own trousers,
Ashamed and forlorn,
Have hidden themselves,
And refuse to be worn! . . .

"I am the Tub
The Great Lord of the Water!
My name is King Scrub
And the Soap is my daughter.
One tap of my foot
And down will come howling:—
'Into the wash with him,
Into the Wash!'—
A mountain of soap,
And a mile of towelling,
Floods of suds,
And the Great Scrubbing Brush.
And the sponges and flannels
Like hounds from their kennels,
Will snap at your heels
And nip at each limb,
And you'll see how it feels,
You dirty young snorter,
To be washed in each quarter,
With water, with water
With icy cold water
And pumice
And vim!"

48

Recreation and Social Life
at Moscow University*

Rex V. Brown (editor)

(1956)

*All students spend long hours with their books
and lectures, and Soviet students perhaps*

* Reprinted with minor editorial changes from
"Social Life," Part IV, pp. 34–39 of "Moscow

study as hard as any. How do they spend their free hours? What kind of social atmosphere exists among them? In these English students' comments, we get an admittedly impressionistic but quite revealing picture of the less organized and less serious side of student life at Moscow University.

Our information on the social life of Moscow students is less complete than on other sections, though we trust it may still be of value.

Patterns of Recreation

In general, students who are accommodated on the Lenin Hills, spend most of their days entirely within the precincts of the University, which has most of the conveniences of a small city. They will occasionally go into Moscow for a football match, a film, the theatre, or some purchase which they cannot make in the University shops, but normally they find enough to occupy them inside. Regularly Komsomol groups will organize a visit to the ballet, art exhibitions, etc., for which free tickets will often be procured.

The local Park of Rest and Culture does not attract many students, but the pleasant countryside and ornate gardens adjoining the University are often the setting for strolls after a tiring day in the class-room.

"Students seem to spend their leisure time more passively than at Cambridge, and this is probably directly related to the long hours spent in the class-room, and to the fact that almost any activity must be under the auspices of some official organization. In general, the Moscow students we were in contact with seemed rather poor at organizing their own amusements, and tended to rely very largely on the official apparatus of entertainment. They did not, for example, even appear to make conversation very easily among themselves — at least when we were present. They

did organize spontaneously what seemed to us to be rather childish games — such as the physical tilting games we used to play in the playground at school — and were very fond of community singing. The whole social atmosphere reminded me very much more strongly of a vast grammar school than a University."

"There is no doubt that Soviet student groups are more closely integrated than is the case at Cambridge. The Soviet student is not a member of a number of separate groups — college, faculty, societies, sports groups, etc. — but tends rather to work together closely with other members of his year in his faculty, both in academic work and in his social life. The student organizations — Trade Union, Komsomol and societies — are generally organized on a faculty basis, much more centrally than in British Universities, and the proliferation of clubs and societies, often overlapping, to which we are accustomed, has no place."

"As far as informal social relations are concerned, Soviet students appear to participate much more fully in each others' lives than we should do. An individual's problems and plans — whom he should marry, his uncultural habit of whistling in the street, his nostalgia for his home Ukraine — would be common conversational currency among his particular in-group."

"Here, too, a wedding is a much more communal affair, something for a whole course to get excited about and arrange together. If a member of a course falls ill, there is much more general concern than there is with us. If a student falls behind with his work, the rest of the students do all they can to help him. This latter is officially encouraged, but it is my strong impression that this feeling would exist even without the official backing."

"Cultural activities are organized by the interested students themselves and we were told that individuals are free to initiate the organization of new activities. Where activities are so popular as to require some subdivision, this is arranged on the basis of faculties and year of study. Cultural activities are financed by the students' Trade Union, with the exception that any staff required (e.g., teachers of musical instruments, sports trainers) are paid by the University. Such activities include: all

University, September 1956," (an unpublished account of a four-week visit to Moscow State University by five Cambridge students, from September 1, 1956 to October 8, 1956), by permission of the editor. Copyright © 1961 by Rex V. Brown. The material in quotation marks has been selected by Mr. Brown from his group's diaries.

kinds of musical circles, choirs and a dance band, dancing (ballet, folk, and ballroom), photographic, linguistic and scientific societies, and the publishing of a university newspaper, etc.

"The University has excellent athletics and sports facilities and there are more than 30 different sports clubs. These include acrobatics, yachting, mountaineering, boxing, table-tennis, archery, cycling, riding, etc."

The focus of much of the University's social life is the University club, which occupies several floors in the new University building. The club is, of course, modern and the amenities are very impressive.

"The auditorium is magnificent, with a capacity of about 800 — it was packed to overflowing the evening we were there. Club activities are arranged by a committee on which both the Trade Union and the Komsomol are represented and details of these activities are advertised on hoardings at four or five points in the University. On an average two activities are advertised for each evening, and the following are a selection: documentary films on Milan and Indonesia; a Mussorgsky concert — for certain concerts, e.g. Oistrakh concerts, an entrance fee is charged; film shows, sometimes foreign films, e.g. Italian (some students said they went three times a week); scientific lectures, e.g. on interplanetary travel; a concert and dance until 11 P.M. every Saturday."

"Amateur dramatics, however, appear to have no part in the club program, except for the Saturday concert, consisting of individual turns, and the *kapustniki* or satirical plays. These are sometimes organized by the students, criticizing and ridiculing well-known University figures, and range from farce to serious criticism. It is possible, although very rare, for the *kapustniki* to be directed against someone outside the University."

A popular form of mass entertainment is a concert-cum-social called a *Vecher*, which usually takes place once a week, and may also be organized for special occasions.

One such *Vecher* was organized for the students to meet their current foreign guests, of whom we were only a few. This was advertised as "A meeting with English, Danish, and Italian students". With the exception of

the speeches and discussions it was a fairly typical *Vecher*.

"First of all there was a concert, which was quite well done. An English girl who has lived all her life in Russia sings some English songs very sweetly. Gymnasts pirouette to tinkly tunes on a piano. This is rather funny. A man in a cheap suit over a Ukrainian shirt sings a terribly sad and complicated aria about, or by, or with, or to, or from Dubrovsky. It goes on for hours and hours, and to indicate his sadness he clasps his hands and stares soulfully, first at the footlights and then at the gallery. People laugh, I am afraid, and also sing the last note for him because he is off-key."

"Then the three Western student 'delegations' are introduced and their respective leaders are called upon to deliver short speeches. These speeches are greeted by vigorous ovations — quite independent, it seems, of the actual content of the speeches — not at all like the mild applause which greeted the concert items, which by comparison were very competent." "Rex got a particularly good ovation — and a cheer at his first words — because he was the only one to dispense with an interpreter and address the students in Russian."

For the second half of the evening we all moved into the adjoining foyer — an ornate marble hall — where we danced to a professional five-piece orchestra. Almost immediately we five were beset by eager questioners.

"First of all three girls trap me to practise their English on me. Then I keep on being taken aside to meet students of philosophy and journalism. Soon I have my back to a pillar, and am surrounded by a dense press of Arts students, all asking questions. I move aside to drop a cigarette in an ash-tray, and find myself in a new crowd, natural scientists this time. From then on until one in the morning, I can scarcely move for people, who stand around firing questions at me."

Apart from this special *Vecher*, we also attended the regular Saturday evening ones, including one in the old University buildings. "The clubroom in the old building has a large auditorium with ponderous pillars, heavy archways, and brilliant blue velvet curtains. Everyone streams into the adjoining room for dancing and it is very crowded. There is a marked contrast between the majority of the girls, dressed very shabbily and without taste, and a few with self-conscious bright eyes, make-up, and stylish dresses. At one side of the room there is an enormous white bust of Lenin, and on the opposite wall a vast painting in pastel shades of a steel-faced young Soviet man and woman thrusting their clasped hands into the future, against the background of the new University, over which is the slogan: 'Soviet citizens have a right to education.' "

"In addition to the *Vecher*, there is dancing on alternate floors of the several University buildings every Saturday and Sunday. The students dance rather grimly, and without elegance, the regular ball-room steps. At the same time as these dances, private parties are often organized in students' rooms. It was difficult for us to judge what regular parties were like because almost certainly the character of the parties we attended was affected by our attendance. We tended to be treated as guests of honor and in many cases, I suspect, the parties were given specially for us and may even have had official backing."

"After dinner Rex and I go to Q's party. It fluctuates between two student rooms and the large local vestibule where there is a general dance going on. Almost everyone is a journalist. Some of the men at the dance have long hair and pipes; one is trying to grow a beard. It's difficult to hear over the noise of the conversation, but the records on the gramophone seem to be near-jazz. Paul Robeson is singing 'When the Evening Sun Goes Down.' Later we danced in the two little rooms to the Voice of America and any other station we could find broadcasting dance music. We drank toasts. Our glasses were whole tumblers of port-wine which were supposed to be downed in one gulp. A great array of sweets had been prepared for us. (There was some confusion on that evening because it appears that another group of journalists had also organized a party for us which we had not realised to be distinct.)"

A student wedding may be the occasion of organized festivities. "Two of us attended the nuptials of two of our acquaintances in the Journalism Faculty. A group of their friends organized a large banquet attended by most of the students of their year in the Faculty, and to which all contributed their share. The marriage had been formally registered several days previously. Vodka, caviar, and various delicacies prepared by the girls were in generous evidence. (I frequently came across the phenomenon of students depriving themselves over long periods in order to make possible the occasional exuberant luxury.) There were speeches, toasts, and a general joyous tumult. When we arrived, we were ourselves cheered and toasted before we added our congratulations to the newlyweds. The evening closed with dancing in the corridors. I have never seen a more happy human throng."

Another form of entertainment is the *pokhod*, a sort of mass hike and camp-fire. We went on one organized by the History Faculty Sports Club — only we were told that this one was not really a *pokhod*, because we didn't walk very far.

"We travelled first of all by train to Malye Vyasemy — a small village about forty kilometres out of Moscow on the Mozhaisk highway — and then set off into the forest. After walking a few miles we met other members of the club who had camped out overnight to prepare the site. Although only September, it was very cold and snowed from time to time. A net was set up and volleyball played; a football was kicked about and a relay race was organized while others sat around a fire and cooked millet-porridge."

"People sang their faculty songs, which were either sentimental, about seeing old friends again, or funny (not very, actually), or in praise of things like discipline . . . No one really seemed to be enjoying himself . . . Things settled down to a frozen monotony until we came home."

Boy and Girl Relationships

"Boy and girl relationships seem to follow a similar pattern to the West, but manifestations of a liaison were much more difficult to detect. Kissing, cuddling, and holding hands in public I never saw. I playfully teased a man with my disappointment at finding no evidence of the passionate Slav soul. "Our passion is as great as any," he said, "but it is for four eyes alone to see." Light-hearted flirtatiousness and the flippant tendentiousness, not uncommon in British student small-talk, is frowned upon.

"This is consistent with the model of behavior urged in Komsomol groups and in the national press. (A Soviet student delegation, which I acted as interpreter for in England, when taken to see a spicy French film, registered a combination of moral indignation and school-girl giggles. One male student shut his eyes in protest during a display of female legs on Cinerama.) However, the *de facto* sexual relations among the students appear to be rather free, though our documentation on this is, not surprisingly, scanty. Men and women may occupy adjacent sets on the same landing (though not adjacent rooms within a double set) and, although there is a University rule that students must be in their own rooms after midnight, it seems that this is not rigidly enforced. The official attitude appears to be rather matter-of-fact. The authorities apply no sanctions against girls whom they believe to be "immoral" but discourage their contact with foreigners and students whose studies are lagging.

"Quite a large number of students get married while still at the University, though such marriages often appeared to be unstable. Children are looked after in a university creche and the parents visit them often no more frequently than once a week."

Vacations

"During vacations, students are expected to continue to do practical work connected with their subject. For members of the science faculties, this often means going on expeditions — very often to those underdeveloped parts of the Soviet Union which are being opened up. Those who are eminent in the sporting sphere will be exempted from some of this practical work.

"In theory, students of the humanities are expected to take some sort of work which may have bearing on their subject, such as work in a publishing house. In practice, this is not always so. For example, Alek had spent one vacation on a geological expedition, because it afforded a chance of sightseeing in areas he would not otherwise visit.

"Many students work on collective farms, where the system is that members are paid in proportion to the work days they accomplish. If, in a given day, they do not fulfill their 'norm,' they are paid for only half a day; if it is overfulfilled, one and a half days are paid. If other members of a family come to help, their work done contributes to the member's work-unit output. Similarly, when students help, their production is divided among the members of the collective. Students are provided with bed and board, and the collective organization sees to it that they are satisfied with what they are given so that they will return.

"At harvest time, students are often released from their lectures in order that they may help on the collective farms. This was the case when we visited Leningrad University, so we were told."

Holidays (as opposed to vacation employment) are often taken by large groups of students within a single faculty. (We saw photographs of one such holiday incorporated in a faculty wall-newspaper.) Again, holiday tickets (*putyovki*) are sold or allocated free to deserving students, permitting the holder to spend, say, two weeks at a rest center or seaside resort. Holidays organized on individual initiative are apparently unusual, though we have little information on this subject as a whole.

Hitch-hiking is not uncommon as an adjunct to holidays. "We learned that some students had gone in for hitch-hiking when in the Caucasus. Lorries appear to be the best bet and money is often paid for the lift, about 20 rubles for 100 kilometres. V. volunteered to hitch with me along the road out of Moscow, but he was not at all happy about this, as normally hitch-hiking is only done where normal transport fails. In actual fact, we did not find time for this venture."

Home Conditions

We did not often manage to visit the homes of our student friends. There was a natural reluctance even on the part of the most cooperative to give us their addresses and a few even asked us to delete the addresses from our notebooks after having given them to us.

In Leningrad one student was extremely embarrassed by a direct request from us to visit her home.

"We visit the home of a student. It is in an old block of flats which are nearing collapse. The block is long overdue for demolition but instead it is covered in scaffolding and the facade is being repaired. We step over puddles in the back yard and go up some stone stairs in complete darkness. The kitchen is shared by three or four families, which they say is better than the average. It is a small room, things are broken, and the clothes all have holes. An old babushka neighbor is cooking at the stove, sometimes making sudden remarks and muttering away to herself. Another gloomy and wrinkled old babushka potters in and out of the door from her room to the kitchen. . . . Five families live in five small rooms in this apartment.

"We go into the room where F. lives with her aunt and cousin. They have only one room although apparently F. sleeps elsewhere. The room is about six feet wide and nearly filled by a grand piano, past which one can just squeeze through into a little space where there is a cupboard and chair and where F.'s aunt changed her dress while we sat at the other side of the piano. Here there is just room to sit, with one cupboard, a small round table, two chairs, and a divan. The cousin is 18, very kind and gentle; she says she loves English people. They serve tea, rusks, and sweets. The aunt is a handsome woman of 43, at first ready to be embarrassed about the room. Soon we are in the midst of a very friendly conversation and play the piano to each other."

"I visited Ph. in his family's flat in one of the better quarters of Moscow. The block was built in the 1930's and faces onto a park. Ph.'s father is a scientific worker and one of the privileged of the regime. They have occupied this flat since the 1930's although they were evacuated during the war when Moscow was threatened. Formerly they only occupied two of the flat's three rooms, but when the occupant of the third room died they applied for, and obtained, the room for Ph. Since he has a mania for tape recordings, life is very much less irritating for his parents now that

he has his own room — of which he is immensely proud and which he will continue to occupy in the event of marriage, unless he has too large a family! Because I had on a previous occasion offered him coffee, he had now prepared coffee in lieu of the usual glass of tea — with biscuits.

"The rent of the flat in August 1956 was 187 rubles, but it is usually between 200 and 250 rubles, depending upon the amount of electricity consumed. It has three quite large rooms, furnished mostly with very plain wooden furniture. Even in this professional family there were no carpets on the floors, the kitchen equipment was shabby, the toilet seat was missing and when I peered through the bathroom door the bath appeared to be full of oddments of ironmongery. Ph.'s parents apparently occupy one room with a resident servant; his brother, aged 13, has a room to himself. An uncle occasionally stays with them, using the spare bed in Ph.'s room. The wallpaper in Ph.s room has a Victorian air, and a Chinese rug looks rather ludicrous pinned against it above the bed, the latter with the usual spotless white covers."

Alek told us that he had a flat of his own, consisting of two small rooms but no bathroom. Like many other Moscow families, he uses the public baths. This flat was his family's when his parents were alive (they died during the war). During a conversation on a quite different subject he said that he lived with a friend of the family for a time after the war, so it is not quite clear whether or not he was able to maintain tenancy of this flat all along.

We were unable to ascertain the number of married students living within the University, although we did meet a few. Other than these few, all the married students with whom we were in contact — except one — lived with one or other of the in-laws, probably occupying one room of the communal house. One graduate scientist whom we met, and whose parents were dead, regretted that his wife's mother did not live in Moscow and they had thus to live by themselves. His wife is also a scientist, and although she did not work for some time after their daughter was born she now prefers to continue her research and so they have a resident maid.

PHILOSOPHY, SCIENCE AND THE ARTS

49

The Poverty of Soviet Philosophy*

J. M. Bochenski

(1951)

Totalitarian systems are notoriously intolerant of free thought. The Soviet Union is no exception to this. It recognizes that philosophy can be the means for stimulating and expressing aspirations for freedom of inquiry, and has therefore made it a total monopoly of the Party. Professor Bochenski clarifies the paradox of the importance of Soviet "philosophy" in a land where genuine philosophy is barely alive.

The first thing one must understand in order to grasp the nature of Bolshevism is its philosophical character.[1] There are, of course, other factors which contributed to the formation and which influence the activity of the Party; but the Party considers itself as acting in the name and for the sake of a philosophical creed. That is why philosophy is considered an overwhelmingly important matter in the contemporary Soviet Union. As this point is often overlooked by Westerners (who are still very much influenced by the positivistic tradi-

* Reprinted from "On Soviet Philosophy," *Review of Politics*, Vol. 13 (1951), pp. 344–353, by permission of the author and the publisher.
[1] The present paper is based on the author's book, *Der Sowjetrussische Dialektische Materialismus*, Bern, A. Francke, 1950. Only a few new things have happened, as far as may be known, in Soviet philosophy since it was published. One of them is the celebrated condemnation of the linguistic theory of N. Marr (1864–1934) by Stalin himself (*Pravda*, May 30, 1950).

tion), it is useful and necessary to substantiate it.

Importance

According to the Bolshevik theory, as expressed in the "classics" and constantly repeated by everyone dealing with the subject in the Soviet or in sovietized countries, dialectical and historical materialism — that is, philosophy — is the "basis" and the most important tool of the Party in its fight against the bourgeois world. Without it the Party could not do anything. This theory may be explained by the Marxist principle of "dialectical" interdependence of theory with practice — for philosophy is considered among Soviets as the "general theory" of the Party. Another factor which strongly influenced contemporary Soviet thought in such a direction is doubtless the attitude of Lenin, who was not only a political leader, but also a passionate thinker.

That this theory is taken seriously may be seen from the effort of the Party to disseminate philosophical books. Consider some figures on this effort: no less than 327,000,000 copies of the work of Marx, Engels, Lenin, and Stalin — a part of which is philosophical — are said to have been sold over a period of twenty-two years; and the *Short History of the Party*, containing the strictly philosophical chapter by Stalin, had a sale, according to Zelenov, of 35,762,000 copies. But even non-Marxist philosophers have been published on an enormous scale: the edition of Aristotle's *Metaphysics* amounted to 783,000 copies, Hegel's works to 200,500, and Spinoza's to 55,200, Diderot's to 139,100, and so on. Even abroad, for example in France, the Party publishes a great many philosophical books. Philosophy — Soviet brand — is also thoroughgoingly taught in the schools of the Soviet Union and of the countries under its control. The present author recently received, for example, a letter from a humble schoolmaster in a small Polish village. The letter was full of Soviet philosophy which that schoolmaster evidently had to learn. As far as leaders are concerned, a considerable part of their training is devoted to philosophy: in an evening course for leaders in 1945, out of 340 hours of courses and exercises no less than 126 — that is, more than a third — were devoted to academic philosophy and its history.

But the most convincing evidence of the importance attached to philosophy by the Party are the numerous interventions of its highest authorities in strictly philosophical matters. Here are some of the best-known facts of this kind: on January 25, 1931, a leading philosopher, A. M. Deborin, was condemned by the Central Committee of the Party. On November 11, 1938, the same committee issued a solemn declaration concerning the teaching of philosophy. Six years later, on May 1, 1944, certain errors of philosophers were condemned. Then on June 25, 1947, A. A. Zhdanov, speaking on behalf of the committee and of Stalin himself, condemned another leading philosopher, G. F. Alexandrov, and issued rules about the development of philosophy in the Soviet Union. The small Armenian Republic imitated the Union in condemning, in November 1947, two of its local philosophers, V. Tchakhoyan and A. Adamyan. The Russian minister of higher education condemned, by a decree of March 23, 1948, formalism in logic. Likewise many condemnations issued against students of other domains were based on philosophical reasons: for example, the verdicts concerning ethnographers (1932), "idealistic" novelists and poets (1934), the so-called "paedologists" (1936), the "intellectual" in general (1946), and the Mendelian biologists (1948). These are only a few among many instances in which the highest authorities of the Party showed a very keen interest in philosophical questions.

Origins

If we ask what this all-important philosophy is, the members of the Party answer that it is Marxism-Leninism-Stalinism. This is a pretty good description of its origins, but needs some explanation to be understood correctly. Let us note, first of all, that the identification of Soviet philosophy with Marxism is a mistake: there are several kinds of Marxism, some of them very much opposed to Soviet philosophy. Marx is, of course, one great source of the doctrine; but Engels is far more often quoted than Marx by Soviet philosophers — and it may be remarked that the (Leninist) identification of Marx with his friend and collaborator does Marx an injustice. However, Lenin took

to Engels, adding some new elements to the stock of "Marxism." These are partly of Russian revolutionary origin, partly the work of Lenin himself. We may cite, among the most striking features of Lenin's philosophy, the following: a rather personal explanation of dialectics (with the stress laid on the "struggle"), the stress laid on human will (as against economic determinism), and a shift of emphasis concerning religion, a central problem with Lenin, although a rather secondary one with the Western Marxists. As far as more technical details are concerned, Lenin undertook a defense of realism against some more recent trends in physics and philosophy, and while doing so elaborated a theory of "matter" which, if followed to its consequences, would have led him to the rejection of materialism.

In any case, the real founder of contemporary Soviet philosophy is neither Marx, nor even Engels, but Lenin. Stalin can hardly be called a philosopher at all; all he wrote about philosophy is a short resumé of Leninist teaching. This is skillfully done, but its very brevity made Leninism as superficial and vulgar as possible. The doctrines of Lenin as presented by Stalin form actually the foundation and, it is only fair to say, nearly the whole content of contemporary Soviet philosophy.

Development

Philosophy *has* a history among the Soviets. This history may be divided into three periods, roughly corresponding to similar periods in the social and political history of the country. Its beginning may be placed in 1921, in which year all non-Leninist philosophers were eliminated and no more non-Leninist books on philosophy were allowed to be published. This first period is one of discussions between the two wings of Soviet philosophers of that time: one stressed the materialistic element in dialectical materialism, the other, dialectics, or at least was accused of doing so. After a period of heated discussions the quarrel was ended by the decree of the Central Committee of 1931, already mentioned.

A second period followed which, compared with the first, may be called the "dead period." Since philosophers were linked in 1931 with political "deviationists," it became highly dangerous to philosophize. All we have in this period are vulgarizations of the "classics" and some irrelevant comments on them. Only one work published in this period has real importance: the second half of the fourth chapter of the *Short History of the Party* by Stalin. This became, from that time on, the canon of Soviet philosophy.

A third, if very short, period was opened with the celebrated speech of Zhdanov in 1947. The late political leader condemned in this speech not only the unfortunate Alexandrov, but also the whole community of Soviet philosophers, and asked them to be courageous and productive, to develop speculative thought. That is what they tried to do — and for a few years some rather interesting discussions were carried on among them. We may note, for example, the discussion on realism in microphysics between M. A. Markov and A. A. Maximov, or the polemic of B. M. Kedrov against over-chauvinistic tendencies — also some rather curious discussions on psychology and logic. In 1947 a big review of philosophy, the *Voprosy Filosofii* ("Problems of Philosophy") was founded, and the authors writing in it distinguished themselves by violent polemics against recent Western philosophers, such as Ayer, Carnap, Maritain, Russell, Sartre, and others.

It appears that this period is already ended. At any rate the most brilliant Soviet thinkers, who courageously said something of interest during those few years, were nearly all defeated and condemned. One gets the impression from the last issues of the *Voprosy* that a new dead period has begun after a short interlude of relative freedom.

Two remarks concerning these various discussions should be made, as several misunderstandings are widespread. First, all Soviet philosophers are Leninists; a different trend is unimaginable in the Soviet Union. Discussions bear only on the interpretation of the mind of Lenin and Stalin. Second, a philosopher who is condemned for his philosophical errors is not "liquidated," that is, killed, or sent to a concentration camp, if he submits, as most of them do. There are, of course, cases of "liquidation," but normally the condemnation results only in the guilty man's loss of his leading position; often he even remains on the team which he formerly led, but in a lesser position.

External Organization

It is not easy to get adequate information about the external organization of Soviet philosophy. There are, however, some data which may give an idea of it. The Academy of Sciences has a department for history and philosophy, which publishes a Bulletin containing some philosophical papers. It also includes a Philosophical Institute which is the main school for graduate studies in philosophy in the Soviet Union. Eighty-two students were enrolled in this institute in 1948; ten dissertations were presented during 1947. Other philosophical institutes (of less importance, of course) are to be found, according to V. S. Iovtchouk, only in the Ukraine and in Azerbaidjan. Three universities (among the thirty existing in the Soviet) have philosophical faculties: Moscow, Leningrad, and Kaunas. Some other academic schools, however, provide philosophical learning; for example the Academy of Social Sciences accepted in 1947 no less than thirty-two strictly philosophical dissertations, and some similar works were accepted by the Moscow State Institute of Education, the Moscow Town Institute of Education and the Institute of Political Economy.

The teaching in the Moscow Philosophical Institute includes three branches: dialectical and historical materialism, logic, and psychology. The organization is different from ours: the study and teaching are directed by professors who are called "managers of a *cafedra*," which seems to correspond to something like an institute in our departments of natural sciences.

As far as publications are concerned, one is struck by the fact that they are rather few. The unique philosophical review, *Pod Znamenem Marxisma* ("Under the Banner of Marxism"), which was founded in 1922, ceased to appear in 1944. It was followed by two volumes of the *Filosofskie Zapiski* ("Philosophical Notes") in 1946 and 1948. Then the *Voprosy Filosofii* was founded (1947). This is a very voluminous review, more voluminous than any outside the Soviet. It was supposed to appear three times a year; but as a matter of fact the issues were always late until recently. The *Voprosy Filosofii* carries, along with systematic and historical papers, discussions among Soviet philosophers and polemics against foreigners — also some detailed reviews of Soviet books. But very few such books are reviewed: for example there were only ten reviews in the *Voprosy* of 1948.

Quite elaborate plans are being made by the Institute for the future: about forty volumes should be produced during the next few years. But the publication of a philosophical book is not an easy thing in the Soviet Union. Generally it is first published in a limited number of copies which are not for sale and which are supplied only to the leading specialists in order that the book may be thoroughly discussed. Only if the result of such discussion is favorable to the author is a larger edition printed. But even the favorable verdict of many philosophers is no warrant against condemnation. The *History of Western Philosophy* by Alexandrov is an instance: it was approved by about fifteen leading Moscow philosophers after many discussions in the Institute; yet it has been condemned.

As to the number of philosophers now existing in the Soviet Union, the following figure may give some idea: at the great meeting of 1947 some 150 philosophers seem to have been present. In 1949, 140 teachers of logic took part in another meeting.

On the whole one gets the impression that, in spite of the importance philosophy has among the Soviets, it is quantitatively rather weak — in any case comparatively far weaker than in any Western country. To make but one comparison, the annual Congress of Italian Philosophers is a far bigger affair than the most important Soviet Congress of similar type, in spite of the fact that the Soviets have four times as many inhabitants.

Spirit

We come now to a description of the methods and of the attitudes of Soviet philosophy. They are thoroughly theological — without religion, of course. In fact, the methods and the general spirit of Soviet philosophy bear a striking resemblance to Catholic theol-

ogy. Thus Soviet philosophy has a set of "sacred" books called "classics" which are used in exactly the same way as the Bible is among Christian theologians. They cannot be contradicted, are employed as decisive arguments in discussions, and the main effort of Soviet philosophers is directed toward a minute exegesis of their texts. Such are all the works of Marx, Engels, Lenin, and Stalin — and of those writers alone. Some other writings occupy a lesser position — for example the speeches of the late Zhdanov. There is also a constant and very severe control by the Party (of which we quoted some instances above) concerning the interpretation of the "classics" and, in general, of all philosophical works. The Party, represented by its Central Committee, makes important decisions as to the right doctrine to be held, and sometimes proclaims such decisions in solemn decrees. Whoever does not follow the right path is declared a heretic ("deviationist": the name is different, but its meaning corresponds closely to that of the Christian word). When the Party condemns a doctrine held by some philosopher, the duty of the victim is to submit humbly.

It may be remarked that all this is highly paradoxical, as Bolshevists do not acknowledge the authors of their "classics" as anything other than men; one hardly understands what may be the logical ground for attributing infallibility to them or to the Party. But, if the word is not used, all attributes of infallibility are claimed by the leaders, above all by Stalin, and woe to him who does not submit to this infallibility.

At any rate, such is the spirit of Soviet philosophy. Moreover, as Bertrand Russell noticed as early as 1921, it is rather an Islamic than a Christian spirit. Bolshevist philosophers are not only extremely dogmatic — they are sure they possess the truth — but also very aggressive. Discussions, even among the Bolshevists, are very uncharitable; and when a Soviet philosopher turns his pen against a non-Leninist, he becomes always — I do not know a single exception — violent and vulgar. In recent years this phenomenon is perhaps more apparent than it was some time ago; it is rendered more disagreeable still to a Western reader by the wild chauvinism — I am sorry I cannot find another word to describe it — of all authors concerned.

Let us add one more characteristic of this literature: it uses a peculiar terminology in which Western words — such as "materialism," "idealism," etc. — are used in an arbitrary way, quite different from that of the Western philosophers. On the whole, no one who has any contact with the original works of Soviet philosophers can avoid being impressed by the fact that their philosophy is, from the point of view of method, something completely different from what we call "philosophy" in the West. In fact, according to our view, it is not philosophy at all, but a kind of emotional explanation and Talmudic exegesis, under the severe control of the Party, of texts held sacred.

Content

The content of Soviet philosophy is well known; anyone wishing to know everything essential in it need only read *Dialectical and Historical Materialism* by Stalin. Even such a conscientious and well-informed scholar as Father G. A. Wetter, who made a thorough study of Soviet philosophy, did not find in it anything of any importance which was not already in the Stalin pamphlet — or was not condemned. Therefore, we shall not try to summarize again the Stalinist summation but rather endeavor to make some remarks on its general characteristics.

What strikes one who reads Stalin and his commentators without prejudice is, above all, the amount of good common sense which is contained in these writings. We find there, for example, a sound realistic attitude, a high appraisal of reason which does not degenerate into merely empty speculation, a thorough acknowledgment of the existence of truth, an honest fight both against positivism and idealism, a right idea of the role of philosophy with stress on its supremacy and independence, and so on.

It is perhaps less known that Soviet philosophy defends some important doctrines in common with Thomism. The Soviet philosophers have an amazingly clear idea (due to the Hegelian root of their teaching) about categorical pluralism. As developed, for example, in S. L. Rubenstein's work, this be-

comes a sound psychology, equally opposed to the well-known Western unilateralities of behaviorism and introspectionism, of Cartesian dualism and of gross monism. Some Marxist elements, such as the stress on social environment and on genetic method, are also to be positively evaluated. Even where Soviet philosophy defends indefensible doctrines, these nearly always have some aspect which is certainly good common sense.

Unfortunately, the great amount of common sense contained in Soviet philosophizing is vitiated by two factors. On one side, it is thoroughly corrupted by a kind of decadent Hegelianism, which causes many parts of the Soviet writings (for example most of what they write about dialectics) to be simple nonsense; it is doubtful that they understand it themselves. On the other hand, the level of explanation is incredibly low: on the whole, one can say without exaggeration that when Soviet philosophers are not repeating certain nonsense of Engels, they speak a very primitive and vulgar language. The late F. Orestano once said that Soviet philosophy is pre-Socratic. And as a matter of fact this is an excellent characterization of it: the level on which problems are discussed, for example, realism, or the mind–body problem, or logic, is astonishingly low.

Moreover, even if this were not so — there is no reason why Soviet philosophers should always keep babbling — there are more serious sins in the very fundamental doctrines. These are due mostly to a mechanical union of two completely opposed philosophies: of Hegelianism, with its categorical pluralism, its moralizing attitude, its stress on man — with the gross nineteenth-century materialism which denies all idealism. This situation is rendered all the more complex and paradoxical by the introduction of historical materialism. This teaches an extreme social pragmatism, whereas dialectical materialism stands for an intellectualistic and absolutistic doctrine. One of the most curious consequences of these contradictions is to be found in ethics. A philosophy pretending to be quite "scientific" is, at the same time, a prophetic and moralizing doctrine which preaches salvation, duty, heroism, and so on.

To be brief, Soviet philosophy must appear

to a Western philosopher, regardless of his own creed, as a set of contradictory statements, expressed partly on a pre-Socratic level, and formulated partly in a way which has no meaning at all.

Soviet and Western Philosophy

Thus a collaboration of Western philosophers with the Soviet specialists in Marxism-Leninism-Stalinism can hardly be conceived. Not only is there little to be learned from them — even the objections they propose are always very primitive — but also they confess outspokenly that what they wish is not a search for truth but propaganda for their creed. And a fanatical creed it is. If it were imposed on the world — and that is the avowed aim of all Soviet philosophers — then our philosophical life would have to die. Those who consider Western philosophy a valuable part of our spiritual heritage must avoid giving to Soviet philosophers any occasion for spreading their deadly doctrines.

Soviet philosophy, however, has considerable relevance as a phenomenon. It belongs, as such, directly to sociology; but it is a phenomenon which has many aspects highly interesting to the philosopher. One such aspect is the important fact that, in spite of the iron rule of the Party, *our* philosophical ideals have never completely died, up to now at least, in the Soviet countries. Again and again we find there some thinkers who apparently try to *think*, and object to the enslaving and debasing of philosophical thought. It may be important to stress that many such thinkers are completely Soviet-educated, that they know Western philosophy only through distorted comments of the Party writers. And yet, some resistance rises from time to time. This seems to show that the human spirit has, fundamentally, a common structure, which was adequately expressed in the Greek foundations of our thought.

Another interesting problem is the influence of Soviet philosophy. Everybody knows that many intelligent people follow it even in non-Soviet countries — with enthusiasm. How is this possible? Certainly the social creed based on that philosophy has some relevance here; but the present writer believes that it does not constitute the main force of the Bolshevik

ideology today. It may be noticed that Bolshevism is a social doctrine only in its applications. Soviet philosophers never tire of asserting that historical materialism (which contains the basis of Bolshevik social teaching) depends wholly on dialectical materialism, which is metaphysics and cosmology, not a social or moral doctrine. It seems pretty clear that many young intellectualists are seduced not by the social corollaries of Bolshevism, but by its very metaphysics.

Why is this so? The answer is perhaps that one aspect of this metaphysics is essentially Hegelian, that is, romantic. It promises to the young man an infinite heroic struggle for the transformation of the world — a world in which man is alone, without any helping power. This idea of an eternal Promethean struggle with nature might be considered as one of the main forces which allow to Soviet philosophy its successes with many intellectuals. Of course, the ideal is clad in an impossible form; but it is still a creed, and a romantic creed. That creed is proposed in a dogmatic way as an absolute truth. And truth — certitude — is one thing for which modern un-Christian men crave today. For only a creed can give meaning to life.

And yet it is a strange creed. It appeals to the noblest aspects of the human soul — especially of the soul of the young — in order to impose its materialistic, somber view, in which there is no place for any heroism, any enthusiasm, any soul at all. Soviet philosophy is, in fact, a combination of these two elements: of romantic dialectics with the old nineteenth-century materialism. This is not only a paradox and a contradiction, but, as we are here on moral ground, something far worse. G. Miche is probably not wrong when he says that it is properly evil.

How, in the face of all this, some Christians can feel attracted by Soviet philosophy is another problem. The problem is, however, not so difficult to resolve, as it seems the reason for the attraction is simply the lack of information on their part. And that is one more reason why Soviet philosophy — and its significance — should be grasped. Without interest for a philosopher so far as it is a doctrine, Soviet philosophy remains as a social factor one of the most important things of our day.

50

A Survey of Russian Science*

Eugene Rabinowitch

(1958)

The Soviet Government has given strong support to science, staking the future of communism upon, as this author notes, "the power of science to transform the economy." The road to success has not always been easy. Dr. Rabinowitch enlists concrete episodes and case history material to prove that even though less constrained than other areas of mental and spiritual life, science, too, has had its ups and downs in the U.S.S.R. He concludes with a distinction between fundamental and applied science, which serves to balance the current tendency to overestimate Soviet scientific achievement.

The recent outstanding successes of Soviet technology and science can be baffling only to those who forget that Russia has had a long and honorable tradition of scientific achievement dating back to the early eighteenth century. The most famous of early Russian scientists was Mikhail Lomonosov (1711–1765), who was instrumental in making the Russian Academy of Sciences, founded by Peter the Great in 1724, a great and justly renowned scientific institution. He was the precursor of many other men whose contributions in the succeeding two centuries placed Russia prominently on the scientific map of Europe.

Lobachevsky and Chebyshev in mathematics, Mendeleyev in chemistry, Lebedev in physics, Ivanovsky — discoverer of the first virus — in plant physiology, Dokuchaev and Pryanishnikov who originated soil science, Zhukovsky who pioneered in aerodynamic research, Pavlov and Mechnikov whose contributions in biology and medicine were rewarded with the Nobel Prize — all these names surely

* Reprinted from "Soviet Science — A Survey," *Problems of Communism*, a publication of the United States Information Agency, Vol. 8 (1958), pp. 1–9, by permission of the author.

testify to the fact that Russia could match the most advanced countries in Western Europe in its achievements in many fields of scientific endeavor.

To be sure, after the mid-nineteenth century the backwardness of Russia's ruling classes hindered and delayed progress in academic and applied science. The best scientific minds had to work in small, poorly equipped laboratories with little official encouragement. Nor did the growing conflicts between the reactionary government and the liberal intelligentsia fail to touch the scientists. Many prominent ones, among them Mechnikov, Sophia Kovalevskaia, and Bakh, went abroad. Even the conservative-minded Mendeleyev had his share of troubles with the government over academic freedom and the autonomy of the universities.

Nevertheless, when the revolution came, the ground was already well prepared for further scientific advance. A tradition of high-grade, forward-looking research was firmly established at the leading universities — of St. Petersburg, Moscow, Kharkov, Kiev and Kazan — as well as at various technological institutes and specialized military academies. The overthrow of the Tsarist regime encouraged widespread hopes among scholars and intellectuals generally for the advent of a new climate of freedom favorable to academic and scientific progress.

The Early Years

These hopes were soon disappointed. After seizing power from the shortlived democratic provisional government, the Bolsheviks established a dictatorship and proceeded to change everything by force. Laboratories stood empty, without gas, heat, or electric power. Students went off to fight in the civil war campaigns. Professors, seeing their cherished dreams of freedom and representative government trampled upon, adopted an attitude of non-cooperation toward the Communist regime. Many scholars fled to the regions still occupied by the Whites, later escaping abroad.

Bolshevik policy, however, soon began to discriminate between the natural sciences on the one hand and the social sciences and humanities on the other. At an early stage the regime proclaimed its intention to foster the advance of science and to stake the future of Communist society upon the power of science to transform the economy. It implemented this intention by offering material inducements and public recognition to scientists, and cooperation by the latter was rendered easier by the fact that it did not entail the same moral capitulation that was required of historians, economists, and philosophers. The result was to place scientific talent back in charge of teaching and research.

For the first fifteen years of the Communist regime, science continued to develop under relatively favorable conditions, an oasis of intellectual freedom in the desert of compulsory conformism. The ruling party largely refrained from restricting the choice of subjects of scientific study and the objective interpretation of results. This freedom, coupled with economic encouragement and social recognition, led to a rapid expansion of scientific education. The pent-up desire for knowledge released by the social revolution flooded the classrooms and research laboratories with eager but poorly prepared young men and women aspiring, as the saying went, to bite into the granite of science.

There were, however, numerous difficulties. Apart from the deficiencies in preliminary educational preparation, there was a shortage of trained scientists to serve as teachers. Many had to teach simultaneously at several institutions, often rushing from town to town to do so. The scientific books produced during this period were preponderantly elementary textbooks, and the professional publications reflected the influx of newly-trained scientists, often giving evidence of immaturity and provincialism. Scientific research was frequently hampered also by lack of the simplest laboratory instruments. This resulted, in part, from official pressure on the academic laboratories and research institutes to prove their "usefulness," the demands being carried to the point of requiring them, at one time, not only to produce their own scientific instruments but to turn out machinery for industry.

Little by little, these difficulties were gradually overcome between 1920 and 1930. The quality of high school education was restored, permitting the selection of well-qualified students for scientific study. The science faculties were augmented by an influx of competent graduates. Dependence upon imported scientific instruments was reduced by the crea-

tion of a domestic instrument manufacturing industry, which was to develop so successfully that one of the things which most strikes visiting observers today is the lavish equipment of Soviet laboratories.

But while the situation of Soviet science improved rapidly in respect of these material and human factors, another menace loomed in the growing pressure for ideological conformism. Suspicions had already been voiced in the early years of the regime regarding certain scientific theories that were viewed as heretical from the standpoint of dialectical materialism, but such attacks had been sporadic and ineffectual. Thus, the theory of relativity had come under fire, but physicists continued to teach and use it.[1] The situation was less happy in biology, because of its greater vulnerability to the inroads of extra-scientific Marxist dogma. In fact, even before the revolution, certain trends had begun in Russian biology that helped prepare the way for its eventual emasculation under Stalin.

Ideological Inroads

Among those originally responsible for injecting an ideological note into biology was Timiriazev, one of the most influential figures in modern Russian scientific development. An outstanding plant physiologist, Timiriazev was well ahead of his age in the application of physio-chemical principles to biology. But he was also an early devotee of Marxism and one of the few senior scientists who enthusiastically embraced the Bolshevik revolution. When he died soon afterward, he was enshrined as one of the revolution's patron saints, and even now Soviet scientists dare not admit that any of his theories was mistaken. For example, Timiriazev claimed that the absorption maximum in the spectrum of chlorophyll coincided with the energy maximum in the solar spectrum, and he held this alleged coincidence to be striking evidence of Darwinian adaptation of organisms to

---

1 For a discussion of Soviet views regarding the incompatibility between Einstein's theory of relativity and dialectical materialism, see Gustav Wetter, S. J., "Dialectical Materialism and Natural Science," in *Soviet Survey* (London), January–March 1958; also Paul S. Epstein, "The Diamat and Modern Science," *Bulletin of Atomic Physicists* (Chicago), August 1952 (referred to hereafter as *Bulletin*).

external conditions. Already in 1883 Engelmann had pointed out the error of Timiriazev's theory, but all Soviet treatises on the subject still hail it as a great "discovery" and proof of Timiriazev's genius.

In one region of biological theory, Soviet ideologists found themselves in agreement with the leading scientific school. Pavlov's theory of conditioned reflexes was considered to fit perfectly into the dialectical theory of the development of higher nervous activity in organisms in response to external challenges. The old master was therefore given generous support — and even the unique privilege of criticizing the official philosophy in his lectures.

In spite of the stagnation that affected many of the biological disciplines, the first fifteen years of the Communist regime were generally a period of rapid growth and expansion for Russian science. By 1930 scientists were well on their way to becoming a privileged class in Soviet society not only in respect of economic status, but also of freedom to choose their field of work, to publish their research findings in Russian and foreign journals, and to maintain contacts with foreign scientists, including the privilege to travel and work abroad. All through the 1920's and early 1930's, Soviet scientists were permitted to spend months and even years working in the leading laboratories of Germany and England. Foreign scholars were invited to scientific conferences in the Soviet Union and lavishly entertained; some prominent ones went to the U.S.S.R. to work — for example, the American geneticists, H. J. Muller and R. Goldschmidt, who contributed a great deal to the development of a flourishing Russian school of genetics.

One of the Soviet scientists who worked abroad in this period was Peter Kapitsa, a promising young physicist. Taken to England by his professor to get over a crisis in his personal life, he was permitted to stay more than ten years at Cambridge, where he rapidly acquired an outstanding reputation in low-temperature research. Several times he made temporary trips back to the Soviet Union to attend scientific meetings; in 1935, during one of these visits, it was announced that he had decided to stay in Moscow. He was never again seen abroad, and the Soviet government later purchased his laboratory equipment in Cambridge so that he might continue his work in Moscow. Another outstanding young theoretical physicist of this period, George Gamov, managed to remain abroad permanently, first in Denmark and later in America, where he is now well known among scholars as an astrophysicist, and to the public as a popular science writer.

The Destruction of a Science

Gamov's departure in 1933 was one of the signs that the honeymoon between Russian science and the Soviet regime was over. With the consolidation of Stalin's personal dictatorship, terror — which until then had been confined, more or less, to the political arena — invaded other areas as well. As in domestic and foreign policy, so in science and art the personal whims, views, and phobias of the omnipotent dictator became decisive. In art, only things pleasurable to Stalin's eye, or melodious to his ear, were tolerated; in science, it was Stalin who decided whether Marr's theories of the origin of languages, or Mendel's laws of genetics, or Pauling's theories of resonance in chemistry were in agreement with dialectical materialism.[2]

The best-known case history of Stalin's personal intervention in science was, of course, the destruction of genetics, with the role of executioner played by the self-made selectionist, Trofim Lysenko. The official motivation for Lysenko's campaign against scientific genetics was as absurd as it was invalid. Briefly, genetics teaches that species can be changed only by selection of the few desirable mutations among many random ones; the number of mutations can be increased artificially, but it is (at least as yet) impossible to direct them. Therefore, patient selection of progeny through many generations, ultimately producing genetically pure strains, and crossing them to obtain the desirable combination of heritable characters, is needed to produce improved and hereditary stable breeds of plants and animals.

Now, these theories do not seem to fit in with the cardinal assumption of dialectical

---

[2] On Marr's linguistic theories, see J. Kucera, "The Linguistic Controversy," *Problems of Communism*, No. 2, March–April 1954; on Pauling's theories vs. dialectical materialism, see John Turkevich, "Soviet Physics and Chemistry," in *Soviet Science: a Symposium* (Horn-Shafer Co., Baltimore, 1952).

materialism — namely, that "being determines consciousness," that all phenomena in life can be explained purely in environmental terms. Nor does genetics fit in with the aims of a government which claims to be able to change human nature by altering the economic and political structure of society. Finally, the theories of genetics seemed to imply that the improvement of agricultural plants and animals, so sorely needed by the Soviet state, would not be as rapid as its leaders desired. All of which made it easy for Lysenko to attack genetics as "fatalistic," contrary to the tenets of dialectical materialism, and highly impractical to boot. According to Lysenko, heritable changes can be created to order and on short notice, by changed feeding of plants or animals, by grafts, by selections of individual seeds, or by seed treatment prior to germination. Genetics scoffed at his claims — so genetics had to be suppressed.[3]

Lysenko's campaign reached its climax in August 1948, during a "scholarly" meeting of Soviet biologists, at which he dramatically announced that his theories had been "examined and approved" by the Central Committee of the Communist Party — in other words, by Stalin himself.[4] An orgy of persecution against "academic" geneticists was soon unleashed. Institutes of genetics were closed, textbooks destroyed; professors disappeared from their laboratories. Lysenko was made President of the Lenin Agricultural Academy, founded by Lenin on the insistence of the leading Russian geneticist, N. A. Vavilov. (Vavilov himself had been attacked by Lysenko as early as 1940. At the beginning of the German-Soviet war, he was accused of planning to flee abroad and was deported to Magadan in northeast Siberia, where he soon died.) Within a short time, the young but flourishing school of Russian genetics was totally destroyed.

At the present time, several years after Stalin's death, the status of genetics in the U.S.S.R. is still obscure. True, Lysenko was demoted from the presidency of the Agricultural Academy, and his theories have been subjected, now and again, to critical comment by bona fide scientists. Yet Khrushchev has on several occasions gone out of his way to praise Lysenko's abilities, and as recently as December 1957, *Izvestia* carried Lysenko's article (entitled "Theoretical Successes of Agronomic Biology") which boldly repeated all his former claims and prevarications. Whatever Lysenko's personal position at the present time, the fact remains that very few of the Russian geneticists survived the reign of terror, and the surviving ones have given scant indication of having resumed their work.

The Scientist's Dilemma

The saddest aspect of the persecution of genetics was that distinguished scientists were used as tools of Stalin's purge. The president of the Soviet Academy of Sciences at that time was S. I. Vavilov, younger brother of the geneticist and himself an outstanding physicist with considerable achievements in physical and physiological optics. A believer in true science, a liberal European in his philosophy, an admirer of his older brother, he had to sign orders for the destruction of his brother's life work and the purge of his pupils. He had to praise publicly the quackery of Lysenko and the scientific genius of Lysenko's patron in the Kremlin.[5]

Western scientists are apt to ask of Vavilov, and others like him: if they could not rebel, could they not at least resign? Was it only fear of the dictator which caused them to deny their principles, and to forget their personal attachments? Or were the glitter and economic rewards of the presidency of the Soviet Academy sufficient to buy a man's conscience? Or did the prospect of leadership in the broad expansion of scientific work for the benefit of one's country lead to a rationalization which made capitulation in any single area appear justified? Was solace provided by the hope that, by remaining in an exposed position and offering oneself as willing executioner of the dictator's orders, one could protect other victims, and thus soften the blows? Would it not

---

[3] See Theodosius Dobzhansky, "The Suppression of a Science," *Bulletin*, May 1949; also *Death of a Science in Russia*, by Conway Zirkle (University of Pennsylvania Press, 1949.)

[4] The highlights of the proceedings of the session of the Agricultural Academy can be found in Zirkle, *op. cit.*, and *The Country of the Blind*, by George S. Counts and Nucia Lodge (Houghton Mifflin Co., Boston, 1949), Chapter 9.

[5] See Eric Ashby, *A Scientist in Russia*, Penguin Books, New York, 1947.

have meant opening the door to greater evil to withdraw and let the presidency of the Academy be taken over by an adventurer like Lysenko — perhaps Lysenko himself?

It is difficult for those who did not experience the debilitating pressure and the moral dilemmas of life under terror to comprehend the rationalizations (and self-deceptions) which permit men to carry on under these conditions. We cannot but wonder how intellectual and scientific life could continue at all and bear fruit, in daily expectation of arrest, deportation and death, in constant dissimulation of one's true feelings and convictions.

The historic fact is that Soviet science *did* function and bear fruit even during the darkest days of Stalin's terror. True, genetics was wiped out. The blight soon spread into other branches of biology and for a while invaded some sectors of physics and chemistry.[6] From his vantage point as president of the Agricultural Academy, member of the Academy of Sciences, director of a great research institute, boss of all Agricultural Research Stations and protégé of the almighty dictator, Lysenko threatened to become the master of biology (if not of all science) in the U.S.S.R. Distinguished physiologists and embryologists — Orbeli, Shmalgauzen and others — were censured and made to recant in public. Strict "Pavlovism" was proclaimed obligatory in the physiology of the nervous system, and in psychology.[7] The quackery of Madame Lepeshinskaia, who claimed to have proved the existence of extracellular "living matter," was rewarded with a Stalin prize.[8]

Physicists Under Fire

In physics, the most persistent attack was directed against the statistical interpretation of quantum mechanics — the indeterminancy principle of Heisenberg, the complementarity concept of Bohr. The tendency of many modern theoretical physicists to discard the concept of "reality" of physical phenomena, and replace it by a system of mathematical relations between "observables," was a challenge to dialectic materialism, which is based on belief in

[6] See Turkevich, *op. cit.*
[7] See I. D. London, "Soviet Psychology and Psychiatry," *Bulletin,* August 1952.
[8] See I. D. London, "Toward a Realistic Appraisal of Soviet Science," *Bulletin,* May 1957.

the inherent capacty of the human mind to perceive the realities of the psysical world (and on the narrow nineteenth-century postulate that these realities must consist entirely of different "modes of motion" of matter). Many physicists in the West, including Einstein, de Broglie, and Schroedinger, refused to accept statistical "laws" predicting, within definite limits, the results of practically possible experiments, as an adequate substitute for causal laws connecting real phenomena of nature — on an atomic scale as well as an everyday scale. No wonder that the search for a reinterpretation of quantum mechanics on a strictly causal basis was — and still is — officially encouraged in the Soviet Union.

However, no sustained effort was made to destroy those sharing the prevailing Western ideas in quantum mechanics as thoroughly as the geneticists were destroyed in 1948. True, rejection of the "idealistic Copenhagen school of theoretical physics" (Bohr, Heisenberg, Born, and the majority of Western theoretical physicists) became obligatory, and may still be so. Some venerable Soviet physicists — such as Joffe and Frenkel — were taken to task for being lukewarm in their conversion to dialectic materialism, applying it only in the introductory chapters of their books in the hope that censors would not read farther. They had to publish recantations and promise better behavior in the future, but the threat to them, though ominous for a while, has subsided in recent years.

The purges, however, did not entirely spare Russian physicists. German-Jewish physicists, who went to Russia after Hitler's ascension to power, were summarily expelled after the Soviet-Nazi rapprochement in 1939; some of them (like Houtermans) were arrested and kept imprisoned for many years. The most brilliant theoretical physicist of the new Soviet generation of scientists, Landau, also went to prison. Khrushchev himself has reportedly stated that the dean of Soviet experimental physicists, Joffe, was on the list of people to be shot in one of the purges, but that his name was crossed out by Stalin because "he may still prove useful to us." According to apparently reliable reports, Kapitsa was punished — allegedly for refusing to take part in work on the atomic bomb — by spending several years under house arrest in the country.

One reason why physics and chemistry have, on the whole, been treated much more gently than biology may have been the vital interest of the Soviet leaders — including Stalin himself — in the contribution these disciplines could make to the military and industrial might of the Soviet Union. They were the hens expected to lay golden eggs, and therefore not to be killed. And useful they did prove. Spurred by material encouragement, by pressure from the political leadership, and by patriotic spirit (which has always been a strong impetus to Russian science, especially during the German invasion of 1942–45), Soviet physicists rapidly mastered the new techniques of nuclear physics. They produced the first Soviet atom bomb in 1949, only four years after Hiroshima. They arrived, almost simultaneously with American scientists, at a practical solution of the problem of thermonuclear explosions. They now hold the lead in the construction of great particle accelerators. Finally, continuing the tradition of Russian pioneering in aerodynamics and ballistics, they stayed well ahead of American development in rocketry and produced, in 1957, the first man-made satellites and the first "intercontinental" missiles.

With this last success, Soviet science has emerged as a great international force, its prestige enormously enhanced. Speculations are rife as to what influence this new force will exert on Soviet society and on the future world policy of the Soviet Union.

Stunted Branches on a Growing Tree

The idea that the Soviet Union may be a hell politically, but a paradise for scientists (at least in some areas) is difficult to accept. True, scientists in the West took this view in the 1920's, but as more and more sciences — and scientists — came under Moscow's fire, as Lysenko trampled over genetics, and quantum mechanics was bombarded by the heavy guns of dialectical materialism, even these Western observers began to think that Soviet science faced a hopeless future, that ideological perversion would eventually cripple it, and that freedom of science can never be secure in a country which has no respect for freedom of thought in general. The material and societal inducements offered by the totalitarian dictatorship of the East appeared to be inadequate substitutes for independence of thought and

personal freedom offered by the libertarian societies of the West — even if the latter were much less actively interested in science, and much stingier in its support.

However, the discounting of Soviet science in the 1940's was as exaggerated as had been its exaltation in the 1920's. A climate of spiritual freedom is certainly important for the development of science, but so are adequate education and proper support. While the Soviet Union was deficient in the first, it provided plenty of the other two. Discussing the state of Russian science in 1952, during the period of Lysenko's ascendency, this author wrote:

> One is left with the impression of a flourishing community stricken by an epidemic. Here and there, houses are closed and quarantined. Nobody knows for certain how to protect himself from the scourge. A certain ritual of pacifying the angry gods is followed. It includes praising their wisdom at the beginning and end of each printed or spoken communication, and loudly denouncing all those stricken by the plague as sinners who have brought it upon themselves. . . . However, as men do in real epidemics — as they did during the war under the bombs — those who are still hale go to work as usual.

And in conclusion:

> It is wrong to think of contemporary Soviet science as being largely paralyzed by the ideological dictatorship of ignorant politicians. Some branches may be dead or stunted, but it is still a vigorous, growing tree. Limbs that have been cut off sprout new shoots; those prevented from growing in their natural direction, grow around the obstacle.[9]

There is not much to change in this appraisal now, except that the situation has improved considerably since Stalin's death. The areas of ideological oppression have narrowed, and its intensity decreased. Not that Soviet science is now quite free; far from it. Occasional pressure is still exerted to restrict activity to immediately practical ends; no group of scientists is quite immune from censure for doing things which are deemed of no use to the state. Lysenko continues in the picture as research director and editor of "agrobiological" journals. When Nikita Khrushchev recently

---

[9] In *Bulletin,* August 1952.

proclaimed that the Russian dairy industry would overcome the American lead within a few years, his optimism was based on Lysenko's promise that Russian cows can be induced to double their production of milk — one should add, by means as "scientific" as those which he once promised would transform agricultural plants. Physicists using the principles of relativity, uncertainty, or complementarity are still exposed to ideological heckling. Obeisance to dialectic materialism as the mainspring of all true science remains obligatory. But science, which has weathered the days of Zhdanov and Stalin, will not be stunted by today's much milder forms of control.

A point to be underscored is that science in Russia, even under worst conditions, has been freer than all other areas of intellectual endeavor. Compared to historians and sociologists, economists and writers, who have lived in constant jeopardy, trying to guess what tomorrow's party line would be, recanting today what they said yesterday, scientists have been much more their own masters. This has made scientific careers particularly attractive to those among the younger generation who most value their independence. Thus it is erroneous either to compare or to contrast the pressures and restrictions which have impaired the attractiveness of science in the West with the much greater pressures and tighter restrictions in the Soviet system. In America, only a little pressure can cause the most valuable young intellects to seek expression in other fields. In the Soviet Union, much heavier restrictions have not prevented science from seeming a haven of intellectual freedom.

It is difficult to decide whether general restrictions on independent thinking and the training of Soviet youth for conformity discourage to any extent truly creative scientific thought (as contrasted to good scientific workmanship). Scientists with revolutionary new ideas are rare under all conditions; it is difficult to apply statistics to such essentially unique phenomena. Does systematic indoctrination in philosophic dogmatism and political docility — the basic feature of instruction in all Soviet schools and colleges — make the appearance of a Darwin, an Einstein, or a Lobachevsky less likely? Despite the vast quantitative growth and steadily improving average level of sci-

entific achievement in the Soviet Union, so far, at least, no great new ideas have come from there. Since 1904, when Pavlov won a Nobel award, this prize has gone only once to a Russian scientist: the chemistry prize awarded to N. N. Semenov for his work on chemical chain reactions — a highly creditable but not revolutionary achievement.

In the same period, over twenty Nobel prizes in science have gone to scholars in the United States. The majority of them were for achievements similar to that of Semenov, but in a few cases revolutionary new concepts were involved. An outstanding example was last year's award of the physics prize to two young Chinese-American physicists, Yang and Lee, for the overthrow of the parity principle.

Is a similar revolutionary idea less likely to occur to a Soviet scientist because he has been discouraged early in his career from questioning the prevailing concepts? Or will pressure for conformity merely provoke the keenest minds to doubt? Some of the greatest scientific geniuses — Copernicus, Galileo, Kepler — conceived their heterodox ideas despite prevailing pressures to conform. Some competent Soviet scientists seem to have accepted the tenets of dialectic materialism as a matter of conviction, not merely of compunction or convenience; yet it seems a fair guess that there are plenty of Russian scientists — old and young ones alike — who see in the official philosophy only cant, to be used occasionally for self-protection.

Incentives and Motivations

Whether or not the general discouragement of free inquiry in Soviet academic and public life also inhibits the inquiring mind in science, there is no doubt that other forces at work in the Soviet Union are powerfully assisting scientific progress.

In the first place, Soviet secondary education introduces youth to the ideas and techniques of mathematics and science. The curriculum itself — except for the emphasis on ideological studies and the disappearance of classical languages — is not very different from that offered by high schools in prerevolutionary Russia (or for that matter in many other countries now). What is, of course, radically different from prerevolutionary days is the enormous spread of secondary education and the opportunity given to gifted children to qualify for further training in scientific careers.

Two other factors favoring the development of science are more uniquely typical of Soviet society. The first is the prestige with which science is endowed, and which finds expression both in the financial rewards of a successful scientific career and in the high standing of scientists in public opinion. The second is the lavish support the government gives to institutions of higher learning and to research institutes. The facts relevant to these considerations have been widely discussed since the launching of the first satellite: they include the larger numbers of scientific and engineering graduates in the U.S.S.R. compared to the U.S.; the relatively high salaries and other benefits in science; the conviction of Soviet scientists that "money is there for the asking" — so different from the often precarious financial status of the most important research projects in the United States.

There is another factor which deserves more attention than it has received from the West; that is the Soviet glorification of science as a way to achieve happiness and prosperity for the peoples of the U.S.S.R. and of the whole world. This faith in science as a creative force in society is, perhaps, even more important in attracting the best minds to science than the expectation of financial rewards and social recognition. Soviet youth grows up in a world of poverty and privation. It is not hard to instill in them the desire to transform society, through science, into something much happier and more prosperous. Small wonder, then, that in publicizing the aims of scientific development, the regime puts less emphasis on the enhancement of Soviet military might than on such attractive and appealing aspects as the exploration of space and interplanetary travel, which are calculated to arouse the enthusiasm of youth.

While world attention remains glued on Soviet successes in producing thermonuclear weapons, ballistic missiles, and space satellites, there is a tendency to forget that this is only one aspect of the broad development of Soviet science. The regime aims at making the U.S.S.R., through science and technology, not only the most powerful but also the most productive country in the world, and to induce other nations to accept its technical and scientific help and leadership. It is to this wider aim that the enormous organization of scientific research in Russia is directed.

The direction of this effort is centered in the Soviet Academy of Sciences. In contrast to similar institutions in the U.S. and Western Europe, the Soviet Academy is not merely the leading learned society in the country; it is also the operating agency for much of the research done in the U.S.S.R. According to a recent study by A. Vucinich of Stanford University, the Academy now has 118 institutes in the various natural sciences. Besides sixteen local branches of the central academy, there are twelve affiliated academies in the constituent republics of the U.S.S.R.[10]

In viewing the work of this vast institute, Western scholars are inclined to note primarily its subordination to party control and to the political aims of the regime. If they are sociologists (like Professor Vucinich), they are impressed by the low scholarly level of the historical, sociological, and economic sections of the Academy, and the subservience in all these fields to the current party line. Attention is called to the hollowness of the autonomy of the Academy, the powerlessness of its supposedly supreme General Assembly, and the influence of its party-dominated Presidium and permanent secretariat.

All this is undoubtedly true. However, in most of its important *scientific* functions, the Academy is a highly competent and largely independent body. It is composed of a fair selection of the best minds in Soviet science, including a considerable number of older men with prerevolutionary education. Those who owe their membership to considerations other than scientific prominence (such as Lysenko) are small in number. While Nesmeyanov, the present head of the Academy Presidium, and Topchiev, the chief scientific secretary, are both Communist Party members, they are also prominent scientists, not party hacks or bureaucrats (both are organic chemists).

The academy has been described as the "general staff" of a scientific army, throwing its

---

[10] A. Vucinich, *The Soviet Academy of Sciences,* Stanford University Press, Stanford, Calif., 1956.

columns to this or that decisive segment of the "scientific front," in response to the directives of the Communist leadership; in fact, this is the picture that the Presidium itself likes to paint in official reports. Science is visualized as a centrally planned activity; its most spectacular achievements are interpreted as results of planned concentration on a few "targets."

This is only partly true. Efforts in *applied science* can be planned; if considered of national importance, they can be speeded up by a crash program. The United States' "Manhattan Project," which produced the atom bomb in 1945, is an example. It is quite likely that the Soviet space satellites were the result of a similar crash program.

The advance of fundamental science is much more difficult to plan. It has been reported that when the requirement of planning was first imposed on the research institutes, the directors presented, as the "plan of research for the next year," the actual results of the previous year's research in order to assure 100 per cent fulfilment.[11] As in other fields, probably a good deal of this type of deceptive manipulation of the plan goes on, but this is not to say that central planning is totally ineffectual. To cite an example, in 1946 a conference was called by the Academy to review the state of photosynthesis research; it was found to be backward, and a decision was taken to promote it. By 1957, a second conference on photosynthesis saw the presentation of about 150 research papers as against 10 at the earlier gathering. In a similar way, research in electronic computers and automation has been spurred by resolutions of the Academy.

However, pressures of this type are much more likely to spur progress in fields where Soviet science is recognized as backward compared to the West than in forays into new, unexplored regions. They can bring up the rear, but not lead the van. Resolutions proclaiming the necessity of achieving breakthroughs into unexplored areas of physics or biology are bound to remain mere words until a creative scientific mind shows the way, usually in an unexpected direction.

All attempts at central planning notwithstanding, the decisive determinant of new achievements in science remains the personal interest and dedication of individual scientists — and this cannot be planned. The recent development of areas of science which require expensive instrumentation and the cooperation of large groups of reseachers has not invalidated the fact that science is what individual scientists make it. Particle accelerators were developed in America, not because a central agency had planned it, but because of Ernest Lawrence; Soviet science owes its success in the same area largely to Wechsler. In short, the development of fundamental science in Soviet Russia proceeds in about the same way as in the West, through the interplay of individual talents.

As to the alleged "unevenness" of scientific progress in the Soviet Union, attributed to planned concentration on a few sectors — this again, if true at all, affects *applied* science only. If one takes wide classifications (such as "nuclear physics," "molecular physics," "atomic physics," "organic chemistry," "enzymology," etc.) and counts the numbers of papers in these classes published in the U.S.S.R. and in the United States, one finds a more or less constant ratio, indicating that Soviet science — insofar as broadness of coverage is concerned — has generally caught up with Western science. One does find wide differences in special areas, but differences are easy to find in the scientific record of every country. What is significant is that this kind of statistics, extended over several recent years, reveals continuous increase in the relative contribution of Soviet research to most if not all areas of science — an increase that will probably become more and more conspicuous in the years to come. However, scientific leadership does not consist in numbers — be it numbers of scientists or of scientific papers; it is based, above all, on great individual achievements (Holland and Denmark, for example, have played a role in science out of all proportion to the numbers, not only of their population, but also of their scientists and scientific publications). Whether such achievements will come in increasing numbers from the U.S.S.R., because of the growth of its total scientific manpower and resources, or whether they will remain disproportionately small because of the general prevalence of conformism and discouragement of unorthodox thinking, only time can tell.

---

[11] See Ashby, *op. cit.*

51

Political Controls and Soviet Literature*

Ernest J. Simmons

(1952)

Here is the history of how Soviet literature has been transformed from an alive and exciting art in the 1920's into the dreary fabrication known as "socialist realism." Here too we find a depiction of the institutions and behind-the-scene processes by which the imaginative writer is made to subordinate his art to politics. The brief period of relaxation of control in 1956, most welcome inside as well as outside the Soviet Union, has now given way again to Party regimentation, though not as severe as was usual under Stalin.

During the early 1920's the Soviet literary scene presented a striking contrast to that of today. Freedom — one might almost say a certain degree of anarchy — inspired by the tremendous release of energy brought about by the Revolution, prevailed among writers. The passionate desire of radical writers to make a clean sweep of the old was countered by a cautious policy, encouraged by the party, that the best of the classics of the past must be preserved and understood and a new socialist literature built on this foundation. Liberal convictions of the rights of authors to express themselves freely without fear of persecution, a heritage of nineteenth-century Russian Marxism, persisted and were shared by prominent Communists in the government. Anatoly Lunarcharsky, the first Commissar of Education, declared publicly that a revolutionary government ought to preserve the right of individual creation. Though at first publishing was nationalized, beginning with 1921 and extending through the period of the New Economic Policy, private publishers were allowed to operate, subject to rather nominal

* Reprinted from "Controls in Soviet Literature," *Political Quarterly*, Vol. 23 (1952), pp. 15–31, by permission of the author and the publisher.

censorship controls of the newly established central government publishing firm — *Gosizdat.* By 1922 there were 220 private publishers in Moscow alone, and they had published 803 titles up to this point with a record of rejection through censorship of only 5.3 per cent.

In this revolutionary atmosphere of release and comparative freedom, numerous independent writers' organizations sprang up, each with its manifesto declaring a variety of artistic aims and ideological loyalties. Groups such as the Proletcult, the Serapion Brothers, and the Formalists boldly asserted their intentions of pursuing literature and criticism without benefit of any government controls. Leading Communists both encouraged and denounced them in print, and the brilliant party literary critic and editor of *Red Virgin Soil*, Alexander Voronsky, published in this leading review in the early 1920's the works of members of various groups — party writers, fellow-travelers, and even bourgeois authors. As an editor he made it clear that he was less interested in ideological matters than in good literature, for he felt that every work of art had an esthetic as well as a class or sociological aspect. Art, he believed, should not be devoted to agitation and propaganda, or to the service of a proletarian state or to the conscious promotion of any set of ideas or values.

Of course, the genuine democratic spirit of early Russian Marxism and the feeling of release afforded by successful revolution do not account entirely for this atmosphere of freedom. The party in these early years was too absorbed in the fierce struggle to maintain the government and its own existence to be effectively concerned with the problems of literary controls. Yet a warning of the direction that future party action might take occurred as early as 1920. For in that year, through the medium of the Central Committee of the Party, Lenin forced upon a Congress of the Proletcult a resolution which, in effect, ended that powerful organization's insistence that proletarian literature should be allowed to develop free of any control by the government or the party. The Central Committee, however, felt it necessary to soften this degree of interference by publishing a letter in *Pravda*, which, among other things, assured workers in the field of artistic creation that "full autonomy" would be guaranteed them.

In fact, instead of dictator, the party played the role rather of referee in the major literary struggle of the time — that between the various left-wing proletarian groups which demanded hegemony, party sanction, and government support for the development of proletarian literature, and the right-wing and fellow-traveler groups which insisted upon complete freedom to create as they wished. The battle raged with much acrimony in the press. Well-known party officials publicly expressed their opinions on both sides of the issue. It is interesting to observe that Bukharin favored the position of the right wing, maintaining that the party should scrupulously avoid issuing directives on literature since such problems were not susceptible to methods used in politics

At a meeting of the Press Section of the Central Committee in May 1924, representatives of all factions in this controversy were invited to present their views. Nothing appears to have been lacking in democratic procedure in the discussion or in the formulation of or in the voting on the resolution that was passed. This meeting was followed by others of a special commission of the Central Committee (February 1925) to work out a policy statement to settle the quarrel. The conclusions of the commission were embodied in the famous resolution of the Politburo (July 1, 1925) on literature. In substance it repudiated the extreme position of the proletarian literary groups without failing to promise them future support, but it definitely encouraged the efforts of non-party, right-wing, and fellow-traveler authors.

The ambivalence of the party in the matter of literary controls and the very liberalism of the 1925 resolution were no doubt connected with both the social and economic conditions of the country at this time and with the struggle for power within the party. That is, the political struggle was reflected in the literary struggle — the right, believing that literature should be immune to the direct influence of the party, emphasized the emotional, esthetic, and individual element in the creative process; the left demanded firm party control and stressed the primary educational, propaganda, and utilitarian functions of literature.

The Growth of Party Domination

It was inevitable, however, that in a totalitarian form of government the single party in power should ultimately secure full control over literature as over every other ideology. And it would be easy to offer a Marxian rationalization of this development: in a socialist state the ideological superstructure must necessarily reflect the socialist economic base. Since there is little formal treatment of literature in the works of Marx and Engels, and certain "deviations" were soon discovered in the more extensive efforts of Plekhanov in this direction, Soviet critics eventually elaborated a Marxian literary theory of their own with Lenin and later Stalin as the "authorities," which justified in terms of historical materialism the several shifts and changes in the national literature on its way to absolute party control.

However, neither socialism nor a real totalitarian status had been achieved as yet. But with the triumph of Stalin over Trotsky and his other enemies and the inauguration of the First Five-Year Plan in 1928, the party felt able to move further in the direction of literary controls. In the summer of 1928 the Central Committee called an All-Union Conference on questions of agitation and propaganda. Among the resolutions passed was one on literature, the theater, and cinema which ordered that they be mobilized to reach the whole population in order to fight for a new cultural outlook in keeping with the operations of the Plan. Out of this conference, in December 1928, came a formal resolution of the Central Committee which was a primary statement of the Communist Party in literary matters for the entire period of the First Five-Year Plan. It is in the form of a directive to publishing houses, indicating the kinds of books they are to select for publication and the nature of the subjects to suggest to writers. The resolution is a frank departure from the tolerant policy of 1925 and must be regarded as the first positive effort of the party to "take over" literature and use it as an instrument to support a national program.

During this campaign the party quietly dropped another of its policies — its decision not to favor any of the rival literary groups. It gave its support to the most powerful organization, the Russian Association of Proletarian Writers (R.A.P.P.), as the one best suited to organize literature as a propaganda instrument to promote the success of the Plan.

With party support and under the able leadership of Leopold Averbakh, R.A.P.P. was soon able to assert its control over many of the literary journals and publishing firms and thus could discipline recalcitrant authors who failed to heed the "social demand" of the Plan by denying them an outlet for their works and even by exposing them as "enemies of the people." In many respects R.A.P.P. was able to achieve an extraordinary thematic conformity in plays, novels, and poetry, which uniformly acclaimed the achievements of the Five-Year Plan.

Despite R.A.P.P. regimentation, writers within the organization and other literary groups fought back publicly, though not with much success, against these dictatorial methods. And even the leadership of R.A.P.P., once it had obtained extensive controls, ambitiously developed its own theory of literature, which had little in common with the party's stark determination to use belles lettres to propagandize the virtues of the Plan. Though Averbakh felt it important to help writers to be conscious of the social demand, he is on record as declaring that it was impossible to dictate themes to an author. Not dictated themes, he said, but a proper view of the world was the important thing for a writer. If his view of the world is a Marxian one and is based on dialectical materialism, he will fulfill his mission to the proletariat. He even borrowed from Voronsky's theorizing, by now officially discredited, the idea that art is cognition of life, but, contrary to Voronsky, a form of cognition of reality as an instrument of the class struggle and as a means of changing social reality. Further, the leadership of R.A.P.P. advocated a literature devoted to the realistic and psychological portrayal of the "living man," and to a "tearing away of the masks" of Soviet life, revealing its evils as well as its virtues.

Such presumption on the part of a favored organization could not be tolerated, and after several unheeded warnings, the Central Committee issued a resolution on April 23, 1932, dissolving R.A.P.P. The resolution also suggested the formation of a single Union of Soviet Writers, which was actually organized in 1934 after all other literary groupings had obligingly dissolved themselves. This move was hailed as a charter of liberty in the Soviet literary world and even abroad, for it brought to an end the regimentation of R.A.P.P. Actually the evidence appears to indicate that the party had at last reached a point where it felt that it could safely take over control of all literary endeavor in the Soviet Union and bend it to its own purposes.

The relative success of the First Five-Year Plan had helped mightily to assure the power of the party and Stalin's sole leadership of it. Contrary to the contention of R.A.P.P., it was now maintained that there was no real need for a proletarian literature, for with the great progress towards socialism all literature in the Soviet Union must be socialist in essence.

There is good reason to believe that Stalin played a personal role in the dissolution of R.A.P.P. and fathered the idea of one big union of writers for the whole of the U.S.S.R. Dividing the opposition in order to conquer it is a familiar party tactic, but so also is the device of combining organizational fractions into one large organization in order to control diverse activities more effectively. In a field so resistant to control as culture, this latter device is possible only when the party has great power, and by 1932 the party had reached that stage. Far from conferring more freedom upon writers, as was widely imagined at the time, the organization of a single union made for more sweeping controls.

In what turned out to be a final exercise of the freedom of individuals and organizations to oppose in print the official decisions of the party in literary matters, the leadership of R.A.P.P. bravely published a firm criticism of the 1932 resolution in their own journal *On Literary Guard*. In effect, it was a criticism of Stalin. They denounced the party line on the publicist function of art and also those people who, knowing nothing about literary criticism, try to impose their ideas on it. In fact, this spirit of opposition to party interference died hard among literary men. Numerous meetings of authors throughout the country and much manipulation and party pressure over a two-year period were necessary in order to establish the proper attitude of compliance in which to launch, in 1934, the organization of a single union of writers.

From this time on to the Nazi invasion in 1941 Soviet literature developed in an atmosphere of conformity to party dictates. The conservatism of a revolution growing old, which had already begun to affect literature, was intensified by the enveloping domination of the party. In general, the party still preferred to remain behind the scenes, exercising its controlling influence largely through the medium of the party fraction in the Union of Soviet Writers. Only occasionally did it show its claws in public as in the case of the vitriolic denunciation of formalism in the arts in *Pravda* in 1936.

Instead of the varied and often highly individualistic schools of criticism which, before 1932, had made a brilliant and impressive contribution to Soviet literary theory, there now existed the single authority of Lenin and the official artistic credo of socialist realism. Fatuous attempts were made during this period to elevate Lenin to the position of a universal authority on literature on the basis of a few random remarks scattered through his works, several brief essays on Tolstoy, which are more social than literary criticism, and his 1905 article, "Party Organization and Party Literature." This latter piece became an unfailing touchstone for all literary critics, largely by way of justifying party direction of literature, Communist and non-Communist, though there is reason to doubt that this was Lenin's precise intention in the article. Some measure of the success of this apotheosis of Lenin as a literary critic may be gained from a typical declaration of a later writer that "there is no important problem of the historical development of Russian literature that was not dealt with in his writings" (*Soviet Literature*, No. 1, 1951, p. 151).

After 1932 critics were asserting in concert that only an author with the Marxist-Leninist-Stalinist world view could correctly portray life in the Soviet Union and abroad, and hence only literature written from this point of view could be considered as real art. The Marxian interpretation of socialist realism ended in the closed and vicious circle of declaring that only the reality of socialism is real and that therefore everything hostile to socialism is unreal. Such a position was the logical outcome of party dictation, and its relation to the truth of art in literature is well summed up in a typical statement of one of the critics, M. Serebryansky, in 1938: "Artistic truth is the ability to tell everything necessary but to tell it correctly,

that is, from a definite, Bolshevik point of view" (*Literaturnye Ocherki*, p. 231).

Shortly after the war began and the propaganda emphasis had shifted from its focus of the directing genius of the Communist Party to that of the unity and patriotism of the multinational peoples of the Soviet Union in defending the motherland, one could detect a relaxation of party controls on all the media of art and intellectual life. In the spirit of this unexpected freedom writers poured forth sentiments and feelings in their works which often had little connection with the former prescribed pattern of Communist emotions. Even direct and implied criticism of party dictation may be found in this deeply patriotic war literature. And at the end of the war a public report of the tenth plenum of the Executive Committee of the Union of Soviet Writers recorded frank expressions of hope by prominent authors that interfence in the arts would be discontinued.

These hopes were blasted by the resolution of the Central Committee of the party on literature shortly after the war (August 14, 1946) and by the related speech of the late Andrei Zhdanov, member of the Politburo, in which he clearly indicated not only what literature was considered anti-Soviet, but also defined the kinds of books that ought to be written by postwar authors of belles lettres. As is now well known, this resolution touched off a vast frontal attack by the party on all aspects of Soviet artistic and intellectual life. In this period of "the gradual transition from socialism to communism," the shift in the ideological line must be understood as a reflection of the new postwar national and international policy of the party. Specifically in the "purification" drive that followed there were no doubt several objectives, but certainly one of them was the determination that all intellectual and artistic effort must be utterly subservient to party control and should have as one of its aims the glorification of the Soviet Union and its accomplishments over the capitalist West and America.

In fact, the most obvious feature of the interference in belles lettres in this new period, as contrasted with the earlier ones, is the direct, openly declared, and total domination of the party in the whole literary direction of things. In its blatant public identification with literature, the party now demands from all writers adherence to the guiding principle of *partiinost* — of party spirit — which assumes an all-pervading organic connection between literature and politics.

Such inclusive and rigid controls in literature require an omniscient authority as an infallible point of reference for authors and critics. Naturally Stalin, who has pretty much usurped Lenin's position in this respect, has been readily and apparently uncomplainingly pressed into service. (It should be recalled that Lenin achieved this unearned reward only after his death.) However, Stalin's comments on belles lettres, even more sparse than Lenin's, have been diligently collected and used again and again by critics, appropriately and inappropriately, to illuminate the new "line" in literature. Nevertheless, it should be added that Stalin's personal decisions behind the scenes, not recorded though occasionally hinted at, have probably played a significant part in the direction of literature, music, and the theater since 1930. Speaking of the fact, not altogether certain, that Stalin was responsible for the description of the writer as "an engineer of the human soul," a Soviet critic writes: "Indeed, how deep is the love and respect for man and the writer's labor contained in this famous definition by Stalin! Only he, the educator of the millions, the mentor of mentors, for whom there is nothing more precious on earth than man, could have defined the significance of the writer in the new society in terms so full of love and wisdom. All of Stalin's precepts on art and the artists' tasks constitute a creative development of Lenin's views on art, and primarily of Lenin's cardinal, fundamental principle of socialist esthetics — the principle of the Bolshevik Party spirit of Literature" (V. Yermilov, *Soviet Literature*, No. 4, 1950, p. 126).

Techniques of Control

By now a formidable control apparatus has been developed to enable the party to carry out its declared intention of using literature for its own purposes. Since the whole manufacturing process of the printed word (paper, presses, publishing houses, distribution) is ultimately under government control, the party has an economic stranglehold on the output and content of literature. The propaganda line that determines the broad direction of literary content is usually initiated in the Politburo and announced in resolutions of the Central Committee which have almost the force of law. The Propaganda and Agitation Department of the Central Committee has as one of its main duties to compel active observance of the ideological line in literature and to expose through various means what it considers important deviations from it. From time to time it may also promulgate a new aspect or interpretation of the line or emphasize the need for special concentration on some theme by writers. This is ordinarily done through inspired articles in *Pravda, Literary Gazette,* or some other important party organ.

Lower down in the hierarchy of controls, though capable of bringing more immediate pressure to bear on authors, is the Union of Soviet Writers, which is divided into committees corresponding to the various branches of literature. Though Communists do not predominate in the membership of the Union, they do occupy most of the key posts and control it. Authors are encouraged to read their works in progress to the relevant committee of the Union, and there the critical emphasis is on whether the writer has embodied in his work the true spirit of the party line. A further check takes place in the editorial offices of the so-called "thick" magazines, for the best literature, even novels as serials, appears first in these publications. Their editorial boards in turn are made up largely of Communists, and one of their principal functions is to pass on the ideological correctness of manuscripts submitted to them. The same is true of the editorial boards of the huge government book publishing firms. Finally, all literary works must receive the approval of the official government censorship office (*Glavlit*).

Should a literary work pass safely through this formidable array and appear in printed form with some undiscovered ideological impurity, which occasionally happens, it is almost certain to be pounced upon by reviewers (literary magazines as well as books are reviewed). And if there is any hesitation to review the work, which is sometimes the case, or if reviewers have failed to criticize offending ideological faults, an officially inspired statement appears in the press to set matters aright. This invariably elicits recantation all around — from the author, officials of the Union of Soviet

Writers, the editorial head of the responsible magazine or publishing house, the incautious reviewer, and often from the editor of the publication in which the erring review appeared.

It may be observed from this brief treatment of the subject that the history of literary controls in the Soviet Union over the last thirty-four years is closely connected with the history of the party. For the party's interference in literature progressed from its early, hesitant, and ambivalent attitude, when the party was relatively weak and divided and permitted much freedom in literary expression, to its present position of absolute control which derives from the monolithic power of the party today. Further, there has been a close correlation between the party attitude toward literature as an ideology and over-all shifts in party domestic and international policy: the 1925 resolution of the Central Committee on literature reflected the gradualist, compromise position during the N.E.P., as well as division within the party; the 1928 resolution to the publishing houses tied literature to the service of the "second revolution" — the First Five-Year Plan — and at the same time signified the growing unity and power of the party under Stalin's leadership; the 1932 resolution removed the emphasis upon proletarian literature and placed it on socialist literature, reflecting the conviction that the corner to socialism had been turned, and concurrently the dissolution of all literary groups and the establishment of the single Union of Soviet Writers marked the still greater confidence of the party in its power to control literature; the 1946 resolution on literature is an ideological reflection of the new period of the gradual transition from socialism to communism, in which the party in various ways has publicly asserted its absolute control over all ideological matters in a national and international policy of far-reaching consequences. Early literary freedom under the party has given way to complete subjection to the party. If the whole of Christian art was devoted to the greater glory of God, today the whole of Soviet art is devoted to the greater glory of the Communist Party.

The Writer and His Art

What effect has such a system of dictated party ideology and rigorous controls on the Soviet literary artist? In conjuring up the familiar image of numerous artistic lives polluted or wrecked by the regimentation of a totalitarian regime, it is well to remember that in modern times the bulk of so-called imaginative literature is the product of skilled craftsmen rather than of indubitable literary artists. Mass production in publishing and a vast market of readers have made a commercial business of literature. Those who write literature, in the Soviet Union as elsewhere, with the sole purpose of making a livelihood out of it are primarily interested in producing what the publishers want. What Soviet publishers want is dictated not only by reader interest, but also by compliance with the latest party line in literature. In this sense it is safe to say that most writers conform to the publishers' demands in theme and the ideological treatment of it without any severe wrenching of conscience.

The case of the real literary artist subjected to the withering touch of such controls may be quite another matter. It has always been supposed that complete freedom was a vital condition for the proper functioning of the creative spirit. Perhaps there is some point, however, in Lenin's generalization that man cannot live in a society and be entirely free from it. Clearly the literary artist, whether his métier be realism or fantasy, cannot escape the compelling influence of the imperatives of his social environment or the idols of his own creative personality. He is never a wholly free spirit. But whatever open or hidden controls may exist for the Western artist — economic, social, legal, or personal — the fact remains that he has freedom of choice to select his subject and treat it as he desires. In a sense he enjoys a larger freedom, for the very essence of a work of art is centered in the variety of all possible relationships in exercising artistic judgment in freedom of choice. In this process the author lives his own version of freedom.

The Soviet artist today does not enjoy this complete freedom of choice. Limits are placed on the area of human experience he can reflect in art, and his creative mind is restricted to the pattern of ideas, beliefs, and loyalties prescribed by the party. Punishment for failure to comply usually takes the form of public denunciation. If recantation does not follow, accompanied by reformed practice, the artist may be driven from literature and he may ultimately suffer a worse fate. By now the annals of Soviet literature contain scores of names of writers, some of great distinction, who have unaccountably disappeared from the field or whose unfortunate fate is known with reasonable certainty. Some of these may well have vanished for reasons other than literary "deviations," but in most cases the evidence indicates literary non-conformism.

The psychological effect of such enforced conformity on the individual artist and his creative process can only be guessed at. As we have seen, in some instances it has resulted in rebellion, with deplorable consequences for the artist. Among those who endeavor to effect a compromise in order to continue to write and to live, the normally free-ranging mind and imagination of the true artist must stumble in constant pain and a sense of self-violation in a compulsive, suffocating atmosphere of creation.

One cannot dismiss this subject without dwelling for a moment on the speculation that profound belief in the party and all it stands for may enable the sincere communist writer to accept control as an article of faith in no sense inhibiting his artistic functioning. The obvious analogy is the mediaeval Christian artist for whom the controls of the Church were an inseparable part of his religious convictions. How passionate a faith Communism can be for its true devotees requires no substantiation. Like the Church in the Middle Ages, the Communist Party in the Soviet Union provides a hallowed pattern of life that takes its faithful hopefully from the cradle to the grave. Where faith begins, reasons ends; the artist believes and hence does not question the ends achieved by instruments of control, for they have become a fighting conviction. Such Communists understand party discipline not as a frame that binds from without, dictating solely their political behavior, but as an internal, ideological force directing them in all their living reality. In some strange but believable manner the party and literature, like freedom and authority, become identical in the minds of writers with such faith. "Both the party and artistic literature in our country," declared the prominent Soviet writer Alexander Fadeyev at Paris, "have one and the same purpose. Neither the party nor governmental power in the Soviet land interferes in the individual creation of the artist; they have never dictated and have never attempted to dictate themes and characters, to say nothing of artistic forms" (*Literaturnaya Gazeta*, March 2, 1949). Numerous similar declarations of faith on the part of Soviet Communist authors have a ring of fanatical sincerity. For example, another prominent author, Konstantin Simonov, wrote in *Pravda* (November 26, 1946): "Publicly, from the tribune of art, for all the world to hear, we say, and will keep on saying that we are fighting for Communism, that we consider Communism to be the only path for humanity to follow in the future, that our Communist ideals have been, are, and shall be immutable, and that no one is going to change them."

Out of such faith, no doubt, can come inspired, genuine art in which ideological limitations and controls cease to be impediments to the creative process because they do not exist as such for the artist. The act of artistic creation becomes an act of faith in the system that controls it.

Literature and Soviet Social Reality

It is against this background of the development of controls and their effect on the writer that one must appraise the value of Soviet literature as evidence of the reality of life which it describes. If good literature promotes revolution, it does not logically follow that a revolution promotes good literature. The vast volume of fiction, poetry, and drama produced in the Soviet Union over the last thirty-four years may be set down as literary reportage tendentiously conceived in the spirit of official demands. But a very appreciable part of it, judged by the usual canons of critical taste, possesses artistic qualities of high worth. Nearly all of it, however, is of evidential value to the serious student of the Soviet Union.

On the negative side, it must be admitted that literary conformity to changing ideology has been enforced in varying degrees. But of this one never need be in doubt. As has been indicated, the periodization of Soviet social, political, and economic development has been clearly reflected in literature, so much so that one may see it in operation in the textual changes made in novels that are reprinted after a lapse of years, in order to bring them up to date ideologically. Herein lies a type of evidence that has its own peculiar value. Yet no one could scientifically estimate from the evidence of literature the extent of real popular opposition to the regime. Many subjects are obviously forbidden to the writer. However, hostile elements are frequently treated under the familiar designation of "bourgeois survivals." A careful investigation of these manifestations would yield significant evidence of the kind and extent of the opposition in the country and at least some of the methods employed to overcome it. Finally, an official version of Soviet life, especially since 1946, dominates this literature, and one must take care to distinguish it from Soviet reality.

On the positive side there is much to be said for the value of Soviet literature over the years as a body of evidence revealing the variegated life of the people, provided the student takes the proper precautions in the interpretation of this evidence.

Until the formation of a single writers' union in 1934, when the party was able to exercise more effective control, literature reflected with varying degrees of faithfulness the central problem of Soviet life over those early years — the mortal struggle between the old and the new in the rapid building of a socialist society. This problem took numerous forms in the poetry, plays, and novels treating successively the periods of revolution and civil war, the N.E.P., and the First Five-Year Plan, but the reality of its abiding tragedy was rarely sacrificed to Communist doctrine. Party motivation is nearly always there, but what is commonly forgotten in this annoying omnipresence of the party in belles lettres is that it is quite true to the experience of Soviet life.

Over these early years the amount of freedom that prevailed permitted criticism of the actions of both government and party. There were many novels, plays, poems, and short stories in which the sympathetic treatment of opposition plainly revealed the reality of it in Soviet life. And out of the wealth of literature emerged the changing behavior pattern of Soviet men and women as we see them portrayed in the fierce struggle of civil war and in the titanic efforts of industrial reconstruction and the merciless business of agricultural collectivization. Five-Year Plan novelists and dramatists, who often gathered their material on the spot, bore their readers and audiences with the technical details of huge building operations. Everywhere in this literature the individual is sacrificed to the drama of collective effort in an atmosphere of ceaseless struggle and incredible human privations. And Communist bureaucracy, peculation, and widespread Philistinism were fearlessly satirized, especially in the literature of the N.E.P. period.

The party began to thrust upon writers an official version of Soviet life in the early 1930's. Although it has changed in points of emphasis and new facets have been added since then, the fundamental content of the picture has remained pretty constant. In this official version the Soviet Union has become something of a socialist utopia. Stakhanovite workers perform prodigies of labor in the factories, overfulfilling their norms amid general jubilation, and peasants on the collective farms overcome every conceivable hostile element of nature to win through to a bumper harvest in the end. Both workers and peasants are richly honored by the state for their achievements, and all join in attributing their success to the inspiring influence of Stalin. All types portrayed seem to live lives of beauty, labor heroism, and the honest joy of accomplishment. The essential human conflict is usually between sterling Communist virtues embodied in the masses and stray "bourgeois survivals" still persistently lodged in the nature of an occasional villain. Of course, there is never any doubt of the final triumph of socialist principles.

Literature did not absorb this official version of Soviet reality all at once; life, in no sense idealized, appeared in plays and novels written up to the time of the war. The early concentration in literature upon the collective was replaced to a considerable extent by an emphasis upon the individual and his adjustments to the new socialist reality. Numerous types are portrayed — the factory manager, *Kolkhoz* manager, engineer, country schoolteacher, scientist, oil worker, railroad worker, the brigade leader in different kinds of labor. In socialist realism, Soviet literary critics insist, the typical does not coincide with the commonplace but reflects rather a tendency to development that is implicit in real life. However much the types may be idealized, their activities in their respective milieus provide a fund of social, political, and economic data the veracity of which may be checked by elements of consistency and by other known relevant facts. A revealing study could be made, for example, of the factory manager as portrayed in Soviet plays and novels. It would yield information difficult or impossible to obtain from other sources: the factory manager's pattern of daily life, his social status, relations with his ministry, his workers, the district party committee, the party nucleus in the factory, the factory trade union committee, the planning system, and with many other aspects that make up the functioning and economy of a Soviet factory. About such facts, the Soviet writer is usually well informed, for in selecting a locale of this kind he would ordinarily feel obliged to learn the facts from actual experience in a factory.

Literature during the war pursued a rather free and unorthodox course and thematically is concentrated almost exclusively on the struggle with the invaders. In descriptive power it marks a return, however fugitive and unequal, to the spirit of the unvarnished realism of the great Russian classics of the nineteenth century. Pictures of stoic suffering in the rear, the amazing feats of the partisans, and the heroism at the front reveal the perennial qualities of the Russian people in time of war, now curiously emancipated from Communist direction and inspiration, although these factors appear repeatedly. This war literature is filled with abundant details of the life and character of the Red Army officer and soldier, and nearly every novel and play contains a native "enemy of the people," which serves to remind us how misled we were by reports of the early elimination of all fifth-column elements in the Soviet Union before the war.

One must make a distinction between literature written during the war and that devoted to this theme, of which there is much, after the war. The latter bears the impress of the hindsights suggested by the 1946 resolution of the Central Committee on literature — in this case a marked anti-Western fervor and a glorification of Communist leadership in the fighting. As pointed out earlier, the new policy resulted in the public identification of the party with literature and its exercise of complete control over it. The policy was quickly reflected in the thematic direction of literature: writers were to concern themselves with exalted praise of the Soviet part in the war (frequently amounting to claims that they had won the war in spite of their allies), and to themes of postwar re-

construction and the rehabilitation of returning Red Army men. Later another category was added — the hostile designs of the West, and especially of America, against the Soviet Union.

One may well wonder whether postwar literature, under the burden of such uncompromising controls, can have any relevance at all to the reality of life in the Soviet Union. A recent interpretation of socialist realism in keeping with the new policy in literature conveys the notion of utter irrelevance. A sample passage reads: "In describing whatever contradictions he notices in life, in depicting the struggle between the new socialist principles and the vestiges of the past in the minds of people, the Soviet writer knows that to show all this correctly he must have a clear understanding of the fact that under conditions of Soviet reality the new is bound to win. . . . The writer who, in depicting the vestiges of the past in the minds of people, merely records events, without 'interfering' in their course, without taking sides as a champion of the new . . . such a writer is not a socialist realist, his position is that of an adherent of trends hostile to realism . . ." (Anatoly Tarasenkov, *Soviet Literature*, No. 5, 1949, p. 145). And then this critic goes on to condemn certain characters in recent Soviet fiction as "non-typical" and a "gross violation of the truth of life," because the cowardice of one, an army officer, leads to the destruction of a whole division, and because a soldier in another displays weakness. These attributes, declares the critic, are "slanders against reality."

In short, it would appear that in this new world of Soviet reality vice can never triumph over virtue, evil over good. The cards are stacked against the bad man; he is not even real, at least if he succeeds. It is apparently acceptable to write about "officially" bad people, but only as foils for the good. They must never win out; they are either reformed in the end or jailed or killed off. Socialist realism in postwar literature must contribute to the forward progress of Soviet life in all its aspects or it is not realism. Thus present-day socialist realism seems to have been transformed into the unreality of the conventional fairy tale.

By and large postwar literature supports this conception of socialist realism in its unvarying black-and-white character portrayals. However, real problems of Soviet life are dealt with, and often against carefully described backgrounds of village or town, of factory or huge construction efforts — all of which provide important social data for the investigator. And a whole new field has been recently opened up in the growing number of novels centered in the far outlying districts of the Soviet Union. These novels present fascinating material on the life and peoples of these distant regions under the impact of Soviet socialism. However, the psychological presentation of character is hopelessly stereotyped, plainly and tiresomely manufactured out of the whole cloth of official ideology. The positive hero is now nearly always a Communist, cast in the father-image of Stalin.

In its postwar development Soviet literature has become the perfect propaganda instrument, for it is presenting for popular consumption a series of consistent, idealized Communist heroes who, the party no doubt hopes, will stand in their personal lives, heroic actions, and unswerving loyalty to the regime as instructive models for the average Soviet citizen. It is in this negative sense of reality — the idealization of life which the party foists upon the public both as a mirror of Communist aspirations and as an opiate to minister to its discontent — that Soviet literature today can best serve the purpose of the social historian.

52

Social Science in the Service of Politics*

Philip E. Mosely

(1950)

The fate of Soviet social science runs a close parallel to that of philosophy and literature.

* Reprinted from "Soviet Research in the Social Field," *Proceedings of the American Philosophical Society*, Vol. 94, No. 2 (1950), pp. 105–110, by permission of the author and the American Philosophical Society.

Professor Mosely's brief but eloquent statement, and the examples he cites, suggest the conclusion that lack of freedom for the conduct of inquiry in social science may in the long run be one of the most self-defeating features of Soviet Communism.

For reasons which are familiar, work in the social sciences is doubly accessible and vulnerable to criticism by laymen, in comparison with that of the natural and biological sciences. In so far as social scientists are engaged in analyzing and interpreting, or sometimes merely in commenting upon, events and processes in the society around them, they cannot escape entirely from the assumptions and presuppositions common to their own times and peoples. Similarly, the points of departure or arrival of their trains of thought may be of considerable consequence to their fellow-citizens.[1]

True, if social scientists state their processes of thought and their conclusions in esoteric phrase, as psychologists and economists so often do when conversing with one another, the eaves-dropping layman is likely to tiptoe away somewhat mystified. In so far as the social scientist deals with the data lying about him in our society and speaks in plain words about matters requiring action, he must expect reactions, mild or fierce, from his fellow-citizens. The real question is the way in which lay holders of power express their reactions to the activities of social scientists. Here the question of the dispersion or concentration of power is of capital importance.

Social Science and the Soviet State. In Soviet society the position of social scientists differs greatly from that of their American counterparts. Soviet scholars also work in a society in which they and their product are judged by laymen. But judgment is rendered by busy administrators who have no time to be practitioners of the sciences. The lay judges are not individuals, struggling to be heard against a cacophony of divergent opinions. They are the supreme leaders of a monolithic Party. This Party claims to possess a monop-

[1] Cf. Carl L. Becker, "Everyman His Own Historian," in his book of the same title, 233–255, New York, Crofts, 1935.

oly of wisdom, embodied at any given time in the selected texts of Marx, Engels, Lenin, and Stalin.

Intellectual monopoly is in turn exercised through an administrative monopoly of power, which can be used to regulate the welfare and life of each individual. Thus the role of the lay "consumer" of social science research, which is dispersed widely through American society is, in Soviet society, concentrated in a few men, possessed of absolute power. Yet these men are laymen concerned basically with the uses of power within the Soviet Union and with the world-wide Messianic role of the Soviet state.

Since the emergence of the Soviet regime its leadership has been deeply concerned with the content of the social sciences, as well as of literature, music, and the arts. After an initial period of toleration, or, perhaps, of neglect, the heavily charged atmosphere of the First Five-Year Plan (1927–1932) brought with it a tightened control and direction of the sciences and the arts. A new period of relative toleration (1933–1936) was followed by the wild self-immolation of the period of the purges.[2]

The war with Germany, with its appeal to humane revulsion from Nazi barbarities and pseudo-scientific stupidities and its final rehabilitation of Russia's national past, brought with it a widening of the range of "permitted" thought, provided, naturally, that it contributed its part to the upsurge of the patriotic will to self-defense and victory. Many observers, in Russia and abroad, believed that victory in the war, in alliance with Great Britain and America, would strengthen and preserve the enlarged sphere of intellectual elbow-room and would allow Soviet scholarship quietly to re-enter the general community of learning. As one Soviet writer said to me in 1943 with deep conviction, "The regime *must* trust the people now, for the people have saved the regime."

Postwar Return to Intellectual Autarchy. Even before the end of the war the shift back to an intensified "Bolshevist vigilance" was under way. The system of party schools, in

which local party leaders and propagandists are trained to transmit the will of the party to Soviet society, was notably strengthened in November 1944. Instead of, as previously, ascribing the victory to "the Russian people," this merit was now reserved to the party, alone acclaimed henceforth as "the organizer of victory." The idea of a community of thought with Russia's democratic allies in the victory, which was referred to with some cordiality as late as 1945, was now repressed forcibly.

In view of the political direction of the social sciences, as well as of art and literature, it is in the pronouncements of political leaders that the key to the postwar trend must be sought. Two such landmarks are Marshal Stalin's election speech of February 9, 1946, and the late Andrei Zhdanov's address to the Moscow Union of Writers, on September 17, 1946.[3] Marshal Stalin's speech laid special stress on the theme that the war had proven the absolute superiority of the Soviet system over all others. By implication it emphasized the revival of Soviet autarchy, in cultural as well as in political life.

Zhdanov's speech to the writers of Moscow was mainly directed against elements of irony, lyricism, and similarly individualist and apolitical manifestations of Soviet literature. In it only one paragraph foreshadowed an all-out attack on "bourgeois" influence in Soviet intellectual life. This paragraph is worth citing, however, since it gave the keynote to the turmoil of the years which have followed:

> It is no accident that in the literary journals of Leningrad people have been carried away with enthusiasm for the contemporary, low-caliber bourgeois literature of the West. Some of our literary people have begun to regard themselves not as teachers but as pupils of bourgeois and petty-bourgeois literati, have fallen into a tone of kow-towing and self-prostration before petty-bourgeois foreign literature. Is such kow-towing fitting for us, Soviet patriots, for us who have built the Soviet order which is a hundred times loftier and better than any bourgeois order? Is kow-towing before the narrow-

[2] Cf. P. E. Mosely, "Freedom of Artistic Expression and Scientific Inquiry in Russia," *Annals Amer. Acad. Pol. and Soc. Sci.,* 200: 254–274, 1938.

[3] A. A. Zhdanov, "Doklad o Zhurnalakh *Zvezda* i *Leningrad,*" *Literaturnaia Gazeta,* 39 (2302): 2–3, 1946.

minded petty-bourgeois literature of the West fitting for our progressive Soviet literature, the most revolutionary literature in the world?

Attack on Soviet Economists. On this call to self-sufficiency and self-isolation the changes have been rung ever since September 1946. After the scourge had swept through literature and music, it descended upon the economists. The chief target was Eugene Varga, long a leading figure of Soviet economics, editor for many years of *World Economy and World Politics* and Director of the Institute of World Economics in Moscow. At a series of official conferences, held in Moscow on May 7, 14, and 21, 1947, Varga's study of *Changes in the Economy of Capitalism Resulting from the Second World War* was subjected to severe criticism. The author was accused of neglecting political factors of power in favor of "objective" economic factors, of asserting that the bourgeois state is capable of regulating the economy for a general, classless or non-class purpose, and of stating that colonies could be liberated from metropolitan control without a revolutionary struggle. Above all, Varga was accused of ignoring the "general crisis" of capitalism, the precursor of its eagerly anticipated downfall.[4]

It is significant that the Varga controversy was not carried to the point of eliminating Varga himself from the field of economic study. Personal factors may have played a role, although thirty years of work as a prominent party member do not necessarily provide immunity. Varga's Institute was merged with the Institute of Economics, headed by Ostrovitianov, his relentless critic.

---

[4] Stenographic transcript of the discussion of Varga's book, on May 7, 14, and 21, 1947, approved for publication on December 8, 1947, published as a supplement to the November 1947 issue of *Mirovoe Khoziaistvo i Mirovaia Politika;* available in English translation as *Soviet Views on the Post-War World Economy,* Washington, 1948, Public Affairs Press in cooperation with the Russian Translation Program of the American Council of Learned Societies. See also Frederick C. Barghoorn, "The Varga Discussion and Its Significance," *Amer. Slavic and East European Rev.,* 7 (3): 214–236, 1948; and Ruth Amende Rosa, "The Soviet Theory of 'People's Democracy,'" *World Politics,* 1 (4): 489–510, 1949.

Ostrovitianov and the work of his Institute have also been subjected to severe criticisms. *Culture and Life,* which rivals the *Literary Gazette* in pointing out the shortcomings of Soviet scholars, made a slashing attack on the Ostrovitianov Institute in its issue of August 31, 1949:

> . . . Of late the Institute has produced few works summing up economic processes going on in the Soviet and the foreign economy. Economists do not devote the necessary attention to working out such very important questions of Soviet economics as expanded socialist reproduction, the organization and payment of labor, the disposition of productive forces, cost accounting, lowering of prime costs, accumulations in excess of plan, acceleration of turnover of working capital, price formation in the Soviet economy, questions of mass production, and the formation and utilization of state reserves.
>
> In the Institute, questions of the economy and politics of the people's democracies are poorly examined, changes are not analyzed which took place after the second world war in industry and agriculture in the capitalist countries, and processes connected with the advent of the economic crisis in capitalist countries are not studied.
>
> The Institute of Economics does not fulfill its plan of research work from year to year. For example, out of nineteen works laid down by the 1948 plan only two works were accepted by the directors of the Institute. . . . The Institute of Economics and its director, Comrade Ostrovitianov, are under obligation to reorganize their work in Bolshevist fashion. . . .[5]

Attack on Soviet Philosophers. The wave of repudiation of "Western" thought spread in 1947 to the field of philosophy. Georgii Aleksandrov had emerged before and during the war (he is now forty-one) as the leading academic philosopher and as chairman of the Party's key Committee on Propaganda. His one-volume *History of Western European Philosophy,* published in 1946, was widely

---

[5] "Overcoming Shortcomings in the Work of the Institute of Economics," *Kul'tura i Zhizn',* 3, August 31, 1949; cited from the summary published in the *Current Digest of the Soviet Press,* 1 (35): 12–14, 1949, with slight adjustment in the translation.

acclaimed and received the accolade of a Stalin prize. However, at a conference held on June 24, 1947, at the Institute of Philosophy of the Academy of Sciences, Zhdanov turned the barbs of his criticism against Aleksandrov's book. Among his criticisms were those of underestimating the originality of Marxism in relation to earlier German philosophies, a condescending attitude towards Russian philosophers of the nineteenth century, a failure to imbue his work with "party spirit."[6]

> Concerning almost all older philosophers Comrade Aleksandrov finds occasion to say a kind word. The greater a bourgeois philosopher, the more incense is offered up to him. All this results in Comrade Aleksandrov, possibly without himself suspecting it, falling into captivity to the bourgeois historians of philosophy, whose starting-point is to see in each philosopher an ally in the profession and only then to see him as an adversary. If such conceptions were allowed to develop among us, they would inevitably result in objectivism, in kow-towing before the bourgeois philosophers, in an exaggeration of their merits, in depriving our philosophy of its militant offensive spirit. That would mean departing from the basic principle of materialism — its sense of direction, its party-spirit.[7]

Aleksandrov was removed from his post as Chairman of the Party's Committee on Propaganda, but was appointed Director of the Institute of Philosophy.

Zhdanov's role in defining the postwar trends in Soviet social science was further clarified in his speech of September 1947, delivered at a conference held in Poland, at which the Communist Information Bureau, or Cominform, was organized. In his analysis of "aggressive" American policy and "peaceful" Soviet policy Zhdanov accuses the United States of seeking to rob country after country of its independence, of a "design to enslave Europe," of maintaining the largest army in the world, of "hatching a new imperialist war." According to Zhdanov,

> The war-mongers realize that long ideological preparation is necessary before they can get their soldiers to fight the Soviet Union. . . .
>
> One of the lines taken by the ideological campaign that goes hand in hand with the plans for the enslavement of Europe is an attack on the principle of national sovereignty. . . .[8]

Attack on Soviet Jurisprudence. The Soviet conception of "sovereignty" has been spelled out by Dr. I. D. Levin in a recent issue of *Soviet State and Law*. According to Levin, the exercise of national sovereignty "presupposes the formation of a sovereign national state or of a sovereign multinational state based on the voluntary union of equal nations." Soviet foreign policy ". . . is a model of a consistent policy of respect for the sovereignty of all peoples and states, large or small. . . ." On the other hand, "imperialist cosmopolitanism is the worst enemy of the self-determination and freedom of peoples. . . ."[9]

The attack on "bourgeois cosmopolitanism" in the field of jurisprudence has been pressed forward steadily. The task of Soviet jurists is not an easy one. As Dr. V. Chkhvikvadze wrote in the *Literary Gazette* of September 7, 1949:

> . . . it must be recorded that until now the decree of the Central Committee of the Communist Party concerning preparation of textbooks on such important subjects as the theory of state and law, the history of the Soviet state and law, and the history of political science and bourgeois public law has not been carried out. The U.S.S.R. Ministry of Higher Education has ordered the textbooks *The Criminal Trial* and *Soviet Public Law* excluded from the list of recommended literature because they abound in serious mistakes. However, many of the text-

[6] A. A. Zhdanov, *Vystuplenie na Diskussii po Knige G. F. Aleksandrova "Istoriia Zapadnoevropeiskoi Filosofii,"* Moscow, 1947, *passim*. Cf. varying treatments of this episode by Percy E. Corbett, "The Alexandrov Story," *World Politics*, 1 (2): 161–174, 1949; and J. and M. Miller, "Zhdanov's Speech to the Philosophers: An Essay in Interpretation," *Soviet Studies*, 1 (1): 40–51, 1949.

[7] A. A. Zhdanov, *op. cit.*, 19.

[8] A. A. Zhdanov, *The International Situation*; Speech delivered at the Informatory Conference of representatives of a number of Communist Parties, held in Poland in the latter part of September 1947, 27, 29, 31, Moscow, 1947.

[9] I. D. Levin, "On the Essence and Significance of the Principle of Sovereignty," *Sovetskoe Gosudarstvo i Pravo*, 6: 33–46, 1949; cited from condensed text published in *Current Digest of the Soviet Press*, 1 (39): 3–7, *passim*, 1949.

books which the students of juridical higher educational institutions will have to use likewise contain many serious shortcomings. . . .

The task of Soviet jurists [he concludes] is to show the profound ideological decay experienced by bourgeois juridical science, to show that there is no branch of bourgeois juridical science which might not fall under the baneful influence of imperialist reaction.[10]

The "Classless Society" and "Cosmopolitanism." What is the source of this intensified demand for intellectual autarchy? Of course, a period of "cold war" may have its intellectual casualties anywhere. Since the Soviet government is engaged in a desperate struggle to enlarge the area of its domination, a period of extreme tension in intellectual life, of extreme demands for "party spirit," is also to be expected.

The source of the tension goes far deeper, however. According to the Soviet philosophy, the dialectic of history has already destroyed "classes as such" as the moving forces in Soviet society. It might be thought that the establishment of an officially classless society — which may be proclaimed any month now — would lead to a relaxation of tensions and of controls within that society. This view, which is a derivative from the notion of the "withering away of the state," is, of course, heretical in the Soviet Union today, and has been heretical there since the purge of Soviet political science in 1937.

The present-day Stalinist analysis holds, on the contrary, that the closer Soviet society approaches to the stage of communism, the more the agencies of compulsion and coercion must be strengthened, that the greater the "success" of Soviet power the greater is the danger of attack by a coalition of hostile states. Having allegedly eliminated all class conflicts within its own society, danger can henceforth come only from without. In the political field the dangers are attributed to the United States, its chief rival in the polarization of power. In the intellectual field the main danger is the influence which foreign "bourgeois" and "cosmopolitan" science, art, and letters might exert upon Soviet intellectuals.

Domestically, there is a complete denial of any internal Soviet conflicts of interest which might provide the soil for the slightest deviation from pursuit of the tasks set by the state and Party. Any failure to achieve the goals set is now attributed to foreign machinations or to influences or suggestions emanating from the "bourgeois" world. In the intellectual field deviations from the goals set by the Party-state are attributed to the influence of "bourgeois pseudo-science." Vulnerability to foreign suggestions is called "cosmopolitanism." As the breast-beating historians proclaimed earlier this year:

> Servility and obsequiousness toward bourgeois science — in any manner and any form — are particularly ruinous for historians of modern and recent times; servility toward bourgeois science frequently takes the form of objectivism, of rejecting the party and class point of view on historical events and on their interpretations in bourgeois historiography. . . .[11]

Attack on Soviet Orientalists. "Misery loves company." The historians, having been castigated for their sins, turned upon the Orientalists. The leading historical journal accused the historians of the East of avoiding the study of recent and contemporary history.

> *Soviet Orientology* . . . impresses the reader with the almost complete lack of any really timely subject matter in its articles and reviews. For instance, the fifth volume of *Soviet Orientology* (1948) contains ten articles in the "History" section. Two of these are devoted to ancient history, three to the period from the third through the sixth centuries, two to the fourteenth century, two to the eighteenth, and only one to the 1850's. *Soviet Orientology* just did not reach the twentieth century. . . .
>
> We lack comprehensive works expounding as a whole the history of China, Iran, India, Korea, Mongolia and other countries of the East. . . .
>
> American Oriental studies and American bourgeois historians diligently assist the present-day imperialist claimants to world domination, attempting by every means to justify the "right" of the United States of America to a leading role with respect to Eastern countries. It is the direct duty of Soviet historians of the East to expose

---

[10] Dr. V. Chkhvikvadze, "On Major Shortcomings in Juridical Science," *Literaturnaia Gazeta*, 72: 2, 1949; cited from condensed text published in *Current Digest of the Soviet Press*, 1 (39): 16–18, *passim*, 1949.

[11] "Tasks of Soviet Historians in the Field of Modern and Recent History," *Voprosy Istorii*, 3: 3–13, 1949; cited from condensed text published in *Current Digest of the Soviet Press*, 1 (35): 7, 1949.

the true predatory role of American imperialism in the East, to expose by countless historical examples the hypocrisy and perfidy of American aggressive policy, particularly in China, the Philippines, Korea, and the Near East.[12]

Attacks on Soviet Historiography. This extreme emphasis upon the role of history writing as a tool of immediate policy has not always been so pronounced in Soviet social science. In contrast to the present demands upon historians it is refreshing to turn to a review of Soviet historiography, entitled *Twenty-five Years of Historical Science in the U.S.S.R.*, published during the war by the Institute of History of the Academy of Sciences.[13] This collective study, edited by several of the best historians of present-day Russia, passed in review the achievements of Soviet historiography in each field, appraising the principal sources and publications and noting the deficiencies in an impartial way. It noted the superiority of Soviet studies of early Russian history, as well as the almost complete absence of study of the other Slavic countries and of the Soviet period. It was a work of historians written for historians, not for politicians.

Like historians of the East, Soviet historians in general have been found guilty of neglecting modern and recent history. *Culture and Life* has taken them severely to task for this retreat to the past.

> As yet the members of the Institute [of History] staff have not written scientific works on the history of the Soviet state, the history of the working class in the U.S.S.R. and the history of the revolutionary movement. . . . The work of exposing Anglo-American imperialism and the reactionary essence of social-reformism is poorly conducted. . . .
>
> The magazine's [*Voprosy Istorii*] unsatisfactory treatment of problems of the history of the Soviet state is explained to a great extent by the fact that the editorial board oriented itself on a small group of historians headed by Academician I. Mints, who considers the history of the Soviet state his indefeasible monopoly. Yet it is

known that Academician Mints and a number of his supporters, who permitted errors of a cosmopolitan nature, have not written important works in the field of history. . . . *Voprosy Istorii* is not conducting an intensive attack against Anglo-American and other bourgeois falsifiers of history. . . .[14]

Conflict Between Monolithic Power and Freedom of Inquiry. The quandary of the historian is no greater, perhaps less, than that of other social scientists in the Soviet Union. The political leadership, which has an absolute power over the livelihood and life of the individual, to a degree hardly imaginable for people who have not lived under a totalitarian system, demands studies of current and actual problems. The scholar flees to the past or to esoteric problems not too closely connected with current policy. The conflict between the demand of policy-makers and the need of the scholar to think out his own answers is always present in latent or active form. At present the conflict is unusually acute, although actual exclusion from scientific work or physical extermination appears to occur infrequently, in comparison with the purges of the 1930's.

Loyalty to the state and to the Party is no protection for the need of the scholar to have room to think. A work of scholarship may receive the highest rewards, academic and material, only to be cast into the limbo within a few years or even a few months. The party line changes, but the written words of the scholar remain. It is no excuse for the Soviet scholar to allege that a given work was in accord with the party line at the time it was published. If the line has subsequently changed the scholar may be punished just as if he had written it under the new dispensation. As one Soviet scholar expressed his predicament, in a private conversation, scientific work is a lottery in which the scholar can never win but can always lose.

Because political power is concentrated in a few hands, power to direct scientific work is also closely held. There is sufficient information available for preparing a sociology of

[12] "Urgent Tasks of Soviet Historians of the Orient," *Voprosy Istorii*, 4: 3–8, 1949; cited with slight adaptation in translation from *Current Digest of the Soviet Press*, 1 (36): 3–6, *passim*, 1949.

[13] V. P. Volgin, E. V. Tarle, and A. M. Pankratova (eds.), *Dvatsiat' Piat Let Istoricheskoi Nauki v SSSR*, Moscow-Leningrad, 1942.

[14] A. Mitin and A. Likholat, "For a High Ideological and Scientific Level: Concerning the Magazine *Voprosy Istorii*," *Kul'tura i Zhizn'*, April 21, 1949; cited with slight adjustment of translation from condensed text published in *Current Digest of the Soviet Press*, 1 (26): 22–23, *passim*, 1949.

Soviet scholarship. The key figure seems to be the party entrepreneur who is able to interpret the party line to the scholars working under his direction, to secure political "protection" (in Russian, *protektsiia*) for the work of his institute, to satisfy some still higher figure in the party leadership of the value of the work of his institute for the Party, and thus to secure political and financial support.

When such a mediator falls from grace, the anatomy of his power is laid bare. When *Culture and Life* turned upon Academician Mints, other historians spoke up against him. At a meeting [in March 1949] of the Learned Council of the Institute of History, Professor Sidorov accused Mints of "servility toward German historiography as far back as 1928." "Somewhat later Academician Mints came out with anti-Party views on problems of the history of our Party." "Academician Mints was able to monopolize the treatment of the history of Soviet society."[15]

In its philosophical claims Marxism aspires to represent a highly rational concept of human society and human progress. It claims to represent the intellectual methodology by means of which man can ultimately escape from the operation of blind forces and take control of his own social destiny. As applied in the Soviet state, scholarship is deprived of access to important materials, and it is forced to acknowledge and "prove" a detailed set of conclusions which are laid down for it by political authority. It is forced to abandon any idea of self-propelling intellectual evolution and exploration and to follow the continual shiftings of the Party line. Under these conditions it is remarkable how many scientific achievements have emerged from the work of Soviet scholars, how much patient labor has gone into answering the questions which the scholar must ask of his data, not of political authority. The Soviet regime needs the work of its social scientists, in order to manage an increasingly complex society, but it rejects, as a matter of philosophical principle and of daily political practice, the spirit of free inquiry under which alone social science can flourish and serve society.

---

[15] "Meeting of the Learned Council of the History Institute of the U.S.S.R. Academy of Sciences, March 24–28, 1949," *Voprosi Istorii*, 3: 152–155, 1949; cited from *Current Digest of the Soviet Press*, 1 (35): 9–12, *passim*, 1949.

53

Musical Expression in the U.S.S.R.*

Cecil Parrott

(1959)

We conclude this section of our chapter on the world of ideas and emotional life with a discussion of Soviet music. Mr. Parrott points to the strong and weak sides of Soviet musical activity, in which the former predominates, and he views the future with optimism.

Whatever may be said in the West about Soviet literature, drama, or art, Soviet music seems to have justified itself. If anyone were to dispute this, he could be referred to the superb artistry of instrumentalists like Oistrakh, Gillels, Rostropovich, and Rikhter, the popularity outside Russia of the works of Shostakovich and Prokofiev, the almost legendary performances of classical ballet and native opera at the Bolshoi and Marinsky theatres, and, perhaps most important of all, the astonishing triumphs of Soviet youth at the various world *concours*. The facts speak for themselves and Soviet propaganda has no need to embellish them.

A Privileged Position

Music today has a privileged place within Russia. The regime regards it as an important adjunct to the pomp and pageantry of state and invokes its aid at all major diplomatic ceremonial. Is there any other country where every distinguished foreign visitor from Chou En-lai to Tito and from the Queen of the Belgians to the President of Finland is regaled not only with special performances at the opera and ballet but with concerts in the royal or presidential palace, where the finest artists in the land perform? As a result of their appearances at the Bolshoi and in the Kremlin the musicians see more of the present rulers of Russia than any other class of the population.

---

* Reprinted from "The Soviet Concert Hall," *Soviet Survey*, No. 27 (Jan.–March 1959), pp. 25–31, by permission of the author and the publisher.

There are several reasons why music should be accorded this favoured position. For one thing it offers the negative advantage of presenting fewer dangers to the current ideology than the spoken or written word, and the positive advantage of being able to project its appeal across all frontiers. In the 19th century, with the help of Pushkin and the Russian national school of composers, music spread abroad the glory of the national epos. Today it can be used to foster abroad a concept which is already axiomatic inside the Soviet Union, namely that no regime has done more to preserve and advance culture than the present one and that modern Soviet art is the legitimate heir to traditional Russian art and in no way inferior to it.

None the less, even in this sheltered and privileged corner of Soviet life, the path of the artist has not been an easy one, and it is only thanks to his natural genius, his devotion to his art, and his peculiar skill in finding a compromise between his own individualistic strivings and the ideological demands of the society in which he lives, that he has managed to preserve continuity with the great tradition of which he is the inheritor. A certain amount of "give and take" has been necessary on both sides. The composer has had to submit to a measure of self-discipline. He has been required to abstain from excessive "modernistic" experiments and to concentrate on themes of national and ideological importance, so that he is, albeit reluctantly, transformed into a potential Composer Laureate. In return the Party has tempered the wind to the shorn lamb by not insisting too rigidly on a literal application of Marxist principles to the sphere of music. A happy result of this understanding is that Soviet music has neither gone to seed nor bloomed in isolation. Even before the War, and much more since, Soviet musicians travelled widely and their experience has been enriched and their status at home enhanced by their rewarding contacts with the Western world.

Soviet music had its growing pains in the twenties and suffered severe setbacks under the Zhdanov decrees of 1948, but it has survived as a native force and has suffered less from Marxist distortion than any other art-form. There is no parallel to *Dr. Zhivago* in Russian musical history. Although *Lady Macbeth of Mtsensk* is no longer performed,

Shostakovich is reported to be preparing a revised version of it. And in spite of all the strictures passed on Prokofiev's *War and Peace*, the opera did at last appear. Even if some of the so-called "formalistic" works of these two outstanding composers remain still under a cloud, and are not performed, the composers themselves have been exonerated from blame and honorably rehabilitated. Today there is no Russian composer, past or present, whose works are not played and admired in the Soviet Union, except Stravinsky, and even some of his early works are given a hearing from time to time.

Problems Facing Soviet Composers

When the death of both Zhdanov and Stalin released fresh ideas about music, as about everything else, what problems confronted the Soviet composers and how are they solving them today? Their crying need is inspiration. The Party is always at hand to offer this, but the composer does not always feel the divine spark. Art evolves and the artist must advance. It is difficult for him not to stand still if he is cut off from the main stream of development in the world around him. According to Soviet thinking musical art attained its apogee with Tchaikovsky and "The Mighty Handful," just as pictorial art did with the "Itinerant" school in the Tretyakov Gallery. Everything composed or painted since bears the seeds of decay. The Russians honor the great composers of their national school on this side of idolatry and no one will quarrel with them for that. Unfortunately, canonization of the composers has gone hand in hand with canonization of the tastes and prejudices of the age in which they lived, and this has a narrowing effect on Soviet musical life. It is not enough to say that young composers are discouraged from seeking inspiration in the work of twentieth-century masters like Strauss, Bartok, and Stravinsky (not to speak of Schönberg, Berg, and Webern); they are not even offered the chance of hearing Wagner's Ring or Bruckner's symphonies. Instead they are given overdoses of Tchaikovsky, Rachmaninov, and Western romantics like Chopin, Schumann, Grieg, and Liszt. In fact they are fed on the musical fare of their fathers and grandfathers before them and it is a very one-sided diet. Steering between the reefs of "formalism" (trying to write like Stravinsky) and "epigonism" (attempting to reproduce the sweeping melancholy lyricism of Tchaikovsky and Rachmaninov), young composers find it hard to establish an idiom which will be at once original, personal, and acceptable. "Bold creative searching" is praiseworthy, but if the searching proves too bold, the composer finds himself on the rocks and denounced for formalism. Most of them try to follow the preachings of their masters and take refuge in folk-motives, but everyone knows how a composer's individuality and creative genius are cramped if he allows himself to be submerged by an excess of national melodies. The use of folk-motives requires exceptional skill and sense of proportion. As a great Soviet musician said some years ago when criticizing the indiscriminate way in which some Stalin prizes had been awarded to composers for works which had no merit whatsoever: "The mere evidence of folk-lore in the thematic material does not necessarily mean that the composition is genuinely national and shows mature craftsmanship."

In these circumstances many of the younger composers seek their inspiration in the works of beloved Russian "moderns" like Prokofiev and Shostakovich; but even this results in a good deal of in-breeding, since it is naturally the more orthodox rather than the more experimental works of these masters which they tend to take as models. Nor does it necessarily earn a composer a good mark to write like Shostakovich, as has been the experience of the youthful composer from Tomsk, Denisov, whose symphony was pleasantly spiked with the little angular and vivacious figures which Shostakovich loves to use. A critic soon detected that if the hands were the hands of Esau the voice was the voice of Dmitri!

There is no such thing as "art for art's sake." Soviet composers are not encouraged to write "pure music," i.e. music without a label, of the kind Bach wrote in his concertos or Bartok in his quartets. Shostakovich may have written Preludes and Fugues on the model of Bach's "Forty-Eight," but this would not be considered constructive in a young composer. Just as a Soviet painting must tell a story, so even a symphony or a quartet should have some sort of ideological theme. A Soviet critic once praised Shostakovich's Eleventh Symphony because he said it was "saturated with working-

class revolutionary songs" and was an "assertion of the approaching victory of communism." The Tenth Symphony, however, which at its first performance seemed to have no identifiable program, was pronounced to be "somber." Although each work is a masterpiece in its way, there is no doubt which of the two enjoys the greater official favor. It is the symphony with the label "1905."

It is axiomatic in the Soviet Union today that music must appeal to the masses and strengthen their faith in Communism. With this in view the authorities are always pressing the composers to write operas, since a spectacle is always likely to draw bigger audiences than a concert work. Unfortunately the spectacular appeal of the modern opera suffers from the further official requirement that operas and ballets should not depict Tsars and enchantresses but events of contemporary life. Alas, too often the finished product, after heavy and prolonged birth-pangs, plays before empty houses, and after the first opening nights the director sends an enthusiastic report to the Ministry of Culture and puts the score on the shelf. But when the day of reckoning comes he does not escape a rebuke for having failed to keep in step with the demands of modern Soviet society. A difficult problem indeed, since Russian audiences are very conservative in their tastes and never seem to tire of seeing bearded boyars and tiaraed princesses on the stage. And how much easier it is to weave folk-motives into the story of Novgorod the Great than the building of the Kuibyshev dam! It is understandable that Shostakovich, who has so far resisted pressure to write another opera, is now engaged in composing an operetta!

None the less composers are free to write as they like and there is no censorship. It has sometimes happened that the Conservatoire has refused to accept students' work because of its formalism. In 1954 a minor stir was caused by three Moscow students, Ledenev, Chugaev, and Volkonsky. Ledenev, who held a diploma from the Moscow Conservatoire, submitted a pianoforte sonata as his graduating work. The director of the faculty felt impelled to forbid the public performance of the work because of its "serious defects in style and ideology." The octagenarian composer Glier publicly criticized all three of them. The interest in these cases lies in the fact that the young men had prepared their works under the benign aegis of some of the most distinguished composer-teachers of the day. We are now in 1959 and the talented Volkonsky is still composing controversial music. Writing of his Second String Quartet (recently discussed at the December Plenum of the Union of Soviet Composers), Kabalevsky found that the second movement "exceeded the limit beyond which chaos begins and where the complexity of the artistic scheme degenerates into a sheer piling up of sounds." A few years ago Karen Khachaturian, the young nephew of the eminent Armenian composer, wrote a symphony which the critics condemned as riddled with formalism. Shaporin (one of the composer-teachers referred to) defended Khachaturian in the Union of Soviet Composers, saying that he admired his talents and found much that was interesting and valuable in the first two movements of his symphony. The young composer received some publicity for this, but adverse publicity is not so advantageous in the Soviet Union as it sometimes is in the West.

The composer is free, but if he wants to make a living he must get his work performed. Shostakovich and Prokofiev could afford to take risks and make experiments which might not find favor because they had many successes to their credit and their reputation carried a great deal of weight. But the young composers must write a work which will either achieve popularity on its own merits or gain official recognition as something which the authorities think worth subsidizing. The first step toward official recognition is to submit the manuscript to the appropriate section of the Union of Soviet Composers, where it will be discussed and criticized and where the composer may be advised to rewrite some portions of it. This process sounds horrifying to Western observers, who could with difficulty imagine Sir William Walton submitting the score of one of his new works to the Arts Council and cheerfully taking it home to rewrite it because someone had said it was out of touch with the demands of the time. But in Russia it is different. Even before the Revolution, Russian composers were in the habit of submitting their manuscripts to the judgment of their fellow composers and critics before they

finalized them, and docilely accepting correction from them. The members of the *Moguchaya Kuchka* discussed their scores with their leader Balakirev ("We obeyed him absolutely," wrote Rimsky-Korsakov), and with the critic Stassov, while Rimsky-Korsakov took it upon himself to correct and improve upon Mussorgsky and Borodin. The idea of discussion in a collective is by no means so abhorrent to the Russian artist as one might think, but there is little doubt that it slows up and complicates the process of composition. Prokofiev had to revise his opera *War and Peace* four times, and Khachaturian took several years to steer his music to the ballet *Spartak* through the discussions in the Union. Generally an honorable compromise is reached and a finished work emerges. It would be a mistake to assume that discussions of this kind cannot be fruitful and rewarding or that the artists do not accept the criticisms as just. When Shostakovich's Tenth Symphony was being discussed in the Union the composer admitted quite frankly and sincerely that he had failed to write a proper *allegro* movement. He had never been able to manage it, he said, and had made the same mistake in his other symphonies.

Some Recent Developments

Soviet composers can now take part in discussions with composers from other countries. Soviet musicians tour all parts of the world and get the chance of hearing much music which they would not find in their concert repertoire at home. The public in its turn has heard orchestras, conductors, and artists from Britain, America, and other countries, who have profited by the occasion to give the Soviet people their first hearings of many modern works. Strauss, Hindemith, Stravinsky, Walton, Britten, and Bartok — to name only a few — have all been heard (though by no means the whole range of their works). The names of composers like Vaughan-Williams and Honegger are now mentioned in the same breath as Beethoven and Tchaikovsky, even if their music is still performed only on a very selective basis. (Here copyright problems come in also.) It can at least be said that the Communist composers, such as there are, receive no privileged treatment in this respect. Although Alan Bush attended the Congress of

Soviet Composers in 1957 and left it in no doubt of his political views, there has been no sign on the part of the Russians of any undue eagerness to perform his works.

Indeed, if concert and opera repertoires are still very conservative and limited by our standards, the range has become in recent years a much wider one. For one thing, the choice of works is no longer confined to the romantic school. A particularly welcome development has been the "rediscovery" of Bach. This year the Riga choir sang the St. Matthew Passion and the Leningrad Academic Choir the B Minor Mass. Performances of the *Magnificat* and the Matthew Passion (again) are planned for next year. Some few years ago a chamber orchestra was founded by the viola player, Rudolf Barshai, which was dedicated to the study and performance of the works of Bach and his contemporaries and gives excellent concerts at Moscow. In the present season he is extending his repertoire to include Hindemith and Honegger. Professor Gedike, who died two years ago, will be greatly missed for his organ recitals of Bach, but he has many successful pupils and his organ at the Conservatoire (as well as several others in the country) is being enlarged and modernized.

Western music of the kind which had never been favored under Stalin is gradually making its way into Russia. Last season the *Sinfonia Domestica* of Strauss and Hindemith's *Metamorphoses* were performed for the first time. Bartok and Janacek are becoming quite popular (mostly due to the visits of Hungarian and Czechoslovak and other foreign artists). All this may not sound very advanced, but it must be understood that there is no wide-spread demand for very modern music. Soviet taste has advanced some twenty years since Stalin died, but it would be a mistake to think that that rate of progress will be maintained. Russia's taste in music has always been conservative and when Communist critics attack Schoenberg it would be an error to think that they are necessarily putting forward an unpopular reactionary view. The Soviet public would like to see more examples of modern painting from the West and learn more about the state of art there, if only to know exactly what is wrong with it. So much is clear from the letters which the editor of the Soviet

journal *Art* receives. But they would probably be ready to take on trust that the "Tone Row" is not for them. If the Party taboo were relaxed, it is doubtful whether there would be much active interest in very modern music, even among the most musical. Some of the more discriminating musicians feel none the less that the musical public should be given a chance of knowing what dodecaphonic music is, before final judgment is passed on it. From this point of view an article by an East German critic, translated by the Soviet conductor Anosov, which was recently published in *Soviet Music* and which did make some attempt to analyze the dodecaphonic system, was an advance on the stock way of dealing with this problem, which is to take out of their context remarks by various musicians of the past (such as Ysaye!) condemning modernism without providing any preliminary analysis of what the term really implies.

If modern Western music is slowly securing a wider hearing in the Soviet Union today, what is the position with modern Soviet music? Some five years ago one often heard complaints that the state was not doing enough for the propagation of contemporary works. The works of new composers were seldom performed and it was even difficult to hear the works of established Soviet composers. A student of music found it hard to hear performances of works which were being talked about in the Conservatoire or written about in *Soviet Music*. (The selection of recorded music was very limited and records often unobtainable.) This was due to the general disorientation which prevailed in Soviet musical life after Zhdanov's ill-fated interventions. The importance of propagating Soviet music was appreciated, but most of the music which was being currently written was, when weighed up in the scales of Zhdanov, found to be wanting, and it was not considered healthy to propagate it. Zhdanov discouraged the composition of symphonies, chamber music, and song-cycles in their traditional forms. He tried to induce composers to go in for "mass songs," oratorios (of a secular ideological kind), and operas (on contemporary themes). The authorities were then more preoccupied with the ideological aberrations of the Soviet intelligentsia than they were with Soviet prestige abroad. After the death of Stalin, when artists began to travel abroad in far greater numbers and music became a valuable diplomatic asset, it was realized that Soviet music could not begin to command respect abroad again unless it won laurels in the traditional forms and that an overdose of ideology would spoil the taste of the commodity for the foreign consumer. Moreover composers showed a certain reluctance to have their art forms dictated to them. As the Polish musical critic, Stefan Jarocinski, wrote in an article reproduced in *Soviet Music* in 1955, composers were being told: "If your mass-songs do not succeed and people will not sing them, then write cantatas and program music." The Polish critic argued that though they had the right to demand from the artist that he should help the people in their struggle to build socialism, they exceeded their authority if they suggested to him not only his thematic material (i.e., folk-motives) but also the means of expressing it and the language in which he should clothe his ideas. There is no doubt that discussions on this important question influenced the party to modify its attitude and composers were encouraged to return to the traditional forms of composition. In a series of some dozen concerts which the Union of Soviet Composers organized in 1955 in connection with their Plenary Meeting, symphonic music took pride of place, and it was agreeable to find how much good music was being written by the younger composers such as Galynin, a pupil of Shostakovich, whose pianoforte concerto was performed; Shchedrin, a pupil of Shaporin, who himself executed his own pianoforte concerto; Boris Chaikovsky (Serenade), and others. Since then a great deal has been done to propagate contemporary symphonic works. In the present season in Moscow, for instance, it is planned to perform no fewer than one hundred symphonic works of Soviet composers, including works of the younger school. One uses advisedly the word "planned" because in the Soviet musical world not all promises are fulfilled!

But this brings the Soviet authorities face to face with a problem which is identical in all countries. As elsewhere, young and little known artists and composers perform before empty halls. Beethoven and Chopin, if performed by celebrities, will always fill them. The only Soviet composers who draw are Shostakovich and Prokofiev (who are inciden-

tally the only two who are popular in the West, which only goes to show that, underneath, the musical pulse beats the same on either side of the Iron Curtain). But of the rich fund of music which these two composers have bestowed on a not too ungrateful people too little is performed even today. The Second, Third, and Fourth Symphonies of Shostakovich are never played and the Eighth and Ninth very rarely. His ballet and opera music are likewise left on the shelf. Soviet audiences are allowed to hear only a very limited selection of Prokofiev's works — of that great Sergei Sergeyevich, who is today almost canonized in Soviet musical circles. Yet Western gramophone companies have recorded a much wider range of his works than can be heard in his native land. It is of course the benign and romantic Prokofiev of *Romeo and Juliet, Peter and the Wolf,* and the Seventh Symphony, rather than the spicy and mordant one of the Scythian Suite, the Fool, the Love of Three Oranges and some of the pianoforte concertos, who is presented to the people. It is likewise the Seventh Symphony of Shostakovich and his Cantata *The Sun Shines on Our Country* which is most often coupled with the composer's name in articles and speeches. But what if the artists were consulted and said that they agreed with this choice? Shostakovich does not seem to have accepted the verdict on the Eighth and Ninth Symphonies and in any case the public likes to make its own choice and posterity does not necessarily endorse an author's own judgments on his work.

No one who has lived in the Soviet Union could come away without feeling that he had been among a people who are exceptionally gifted musically and where the regime does a great deal for the musicians, handling them now with greater tact and understanding, even if its Jehova-like paternalism would not be to every artist's taste. But one cannot conceal some disappointment at finding how little is done for the musical education of the masses, of which so much is written, and in particular for the forming of their tastes. In this classic country of planning there is a conspicuous absence of it in the musical sector, where musical programs often appear to be put together in a haphazard and indeed somewhat amateur fashion. Perhaps one should regard this as one of the healthier features of Soviet musical life and express relief at finding so little direction. But, as in many other spheres of Soviet life, direction lives side by side with the lack of it, and to the outsider it sometimes appears as though the missionary zeal was misplaced. There is no doubt that countless opportunities are lost by the failure of the authorities to provide for properly planned repertoires in the concert seasons, designed to show music in its historic perspective or composers in their varying stages of development. Last year it was complained that Brahms' First Symphony was performed three times in the course of one season in Moscow and his Third and Fourth not at all. It was also mentioned that no attempt was made to present a cycle of all Beethoven's pianoforte sonatas or string quartets. Concert notes are totally inadequate for the general public, and worst of all, the main national newspapers advertise few of the concerts in advance and seldom comment on them afterwards, with the result that most of the population have no idea of who performed what, when, or how. Here the admirable *Soviet Music* steps into the breach, but it reports the concerts some two months after they took place, has in any case a very limited circulation among specialists, and can exercise little influence on the masses. The new fortnightly *Musical Life* should be quicker off the mark with musical information and be more accessible to the public, but it has not so far thought of providing a special column for concert reviews. It is also doubtful whether it will touch a much wider circle than *Soviet Music*, even though it is written in a more popular style.

If, in this particular respect, arrangements today fall far behind what was the practice in

Tsarist times, we must not forget that the Soviet regime has done a great deal to develop musical life in the non-Russian parts of the Union, which lay pretty fallow before the revolution. Today the nationalities play a vital part in the musical life of modern Russia. Many of the best musicians come from the Republics: Khachaturian, Arutiunian, Taktakishvili, Kara Karaev, to name only a few. In the list of composers who were Stalin laureates in 1953 over half were non-Russian. It was the Riga Opera who came to Moscow to remind the Russians what a musical treasure they had in *The Invisible City of Kitezh*, Rimsky-Korsakov's great opera, hitherto put on the shelf because of its mystical Christian ideals. The Latvians gave Moscow an electrifying rendering of it and moved the audience deeply by their fine choral singing, an art to which the Russians are always peculiarly responsive. Now the Bolshoi are going to stage it themselves. It was a Riga choir which gave the first performance for a quarter of a century of the Matthew Passion. The Russians will follow their example next Easter. The inauguration of "decades," i.e., ten-day festivals in Moscow, held by opera and theatre companies from the Republics, has done much to encourage interest in music in the provinces.

Thanks to the more liberal attitude adopted to music in the last few years, and to the fruitful results of cross-fertilization with the Republics and the countries of Central and Eastern Europe, and last but not least, thanks to the exchange of ideas and impressions with the West, Russian musical life is undergoing great changes and one can view its future with optimism.

SUGGESTIONS FOR FURTHER READING

The Place of Religion

ANDERSON, PAUL B., *People, Church, and State in Modern Russia*. New York: The Macmillan Company, 1944.

BACH, MARCUS, *God and the Soviets.* New York: Thomas Y. Crowell Company, 1958.

> Observations reported by a professor of religion.

CURTISS, JOHN S., *The Russian Church and the Soviet State.* Boston: Little, Brown and Co., 1953.

TIMASHEFF, NICHOLAS S., *Religion in Soviet Russia.* London: Sheed and Ward, 1943.

Education

BEREDAY, GEORGE Z. F., and JAAN PENNAR (eds.), *The Politics of Soviet Education.* New York: Frederick A. Praeger, Inc., 1960.

> Essays on "polytechnical" education, foreign language teaching, Party control, etc.

BEREDAY, GEORGE Z. F., *et al.* (eds.), *The Changing Soviet School: The Comparative Education Society Field Study in the U.S.S.R.* Boston: Houghton Mifflin Co., 1960.

> Consists mostly of data and impressions gathered in 1958 by an American cultural exchange mission.

COUNTS, GEORGE S., *The Challenge of Soviet Education.* New York: McGraw-Hill Book Company, Inc., 1957.

> A lot of attention is given to political and moral education.

DEWITT, NICHOLAS, *Soviet Professional Manpower: Its Education, Training, and Supply.* Washington, D.C.: Government Printing Office, 1955.

Education in the U.S.S.R. Washington, D.C.: Government Printing Office, 1957.

> A general survey.

Philosophy, Science and the Arts

ASHBY, ERIC, *Scientist in Russia.* New York: Penguin Books, Inc., 1947.

> The organization of science and personal experiences of an Australian scientist.

BAUER, RAYMOND A., *The New Man in Soviet Psychology.* Cambridge, Mass.: Harvard University Press, 1952.

> What happened to psychology as an academic discipline.

CHRISTMAN, RUTH C. (ed.), *Soviet Science.* Washington, D.C.: American Association for the Advancement of Science, 1952.

> Results of a symposium held on December 27, 1951 at Philadelphia.

COUNTS, GEORGE S., and NUCIA LODGE, *The Country of the Blind: The Soviet System of Mind Control.* Boston: Houghton Mifflin Co., 1949.

> How the regime has sought to use literature, science, drama, and even music as instruments for political indoctrination.

OLKHOVSKY, ANDREY, *Music Under the Soviets: The Agony of an Art.* New York: Frederick A. Praeger, Inc., 1955.

SIMMONS, ERNEST J., *Russian Fiction and Soviet Ideology.* New York: Columbia University Press, 1958.

Lives and works of three leading novelists, Leonov, Fedin, and Sholokhov.

STRUVE, GLEB, *Soviet Russian Literature, 1917–1950.* Norman, Okla.: University of Oklahoma Press, 1951.

A standard text.

VUCINICH, ALEXANDER, *The Soviet Academy of Sciences.* Stanford University, Calif.: Stanford University Press, 1956.

Science and scientists and how they fit with the Soviet system.

WETTER, GUSTAV A., *Dialectical Materialism: A Historical and Systematic Survey of Philosophy in the Soviet Union.* London: Routledge & Kegan Paul, Ltd., 1958.

ZIRKLE, CONWAY (ed.), *Death of a Science in Russia: The Fate of Genetics as Described in Pravda and Elsewhere.* Philadelphia: University of Pennsylvania Press, 1949.

A detailed account of the Lysenko controversy.

V

Everyday Living

The institutions and patterns of Soviet everyday life make up one of the limiting conditions under which the regime's leaders pursue their own purposes. It has been characteristic for the regime to underestimate the compelling and tenacious nature, the "drag," from its point of view, of traditional ways. In this respect, Soviet leaders have been handicapped by Marxist sociology, which treats the economic base as the prime mover in social change, and sees the conditions and institutions of everyday life as epiphenomena. For many years the Soviet leaders, fanatic about hurrying along the process of change, concentrated their attention on economic problems and treated everyday life as of secondary importance. Like law, the state, and religion, it was expected that undesired patterns of living would disappear or change and that, in general, everyday life would fall into place on its own, so to say, as part of the superstructure. Inequality in the treatment of the sexes, pronounced differences among social classes, nationalistic separatism, material hardship, and criminal behavior were stated to be "typical" of capitalist systems, and were expected to disappear under Soviet socialism. Nevertheless, they persisted. The leaders placed the blame not on a "system" but on the people and their past, labeling these features of Soviet life "survivals of capitalism in the consciousness of the people."

Could something be done about such "survivals"? Or did one concentrate attention upon economic problems and wait for economic reforms and achievements to have their anticipated effects? Here Marxist opinion split. Lenin and Stalin *chose* opted strongly for active intervention into the patterns of everyday life, and in the U.S.S.R. the principle of concurrent change of daily life patterns came to be known as the "cultural revolution." It goes without saying that it was a revolution from above. As time passed, two developments could be observed.

493

First, practical experience caused the regime to lower its expectations; some of the most hallowed traditions of the Marxist utopia were repealed by Stalin's fiat. The renovation of the family is a prominent example. Second, the Party and Soviet state took an ever more active role in seeking to shape directly the activities and institutions of everyday living.

And yet the tradition of Marxist economic determinism somehow also continued. Furthermore, the world situation seemed to the Soviet leadership to require that the best possible face be put on the Soviet domestic scene. As a result the regime has been caught in a curious dilemma, on the one side taking forceful measures to bring about the patterns it desires, and on the other side asserting that, since socialism has been achieved in Russia, the desired patterns are already in existence. From this comes the typical Communist style of discussing Soviet daily life, sometimes called the "imperative-indicative." For example, Soviet propaganda asserts that "in the land of socialism there are no antagonisms between classes and nationality groups." Soviet citizens and experienced observers understand that this assertion is not literally true — that is, it does not reflect Soviet social reality. The meaning of the statement, rather, lies in its being an expression of (1) the concern of the Soviet leadership about the presence of such antagonisms in the U.S.S.R. and (2) their desire to eradicate them. In effect, propositions of Soviet origin about social life in the U.S.S.R. must always be suspected of being composed for purposes of propaganda and "education." The Soviet leaders have long subscribed in practice to their version of what Western propaganda analysts refer to as the bandwagon principle.

Such is the official approach. It in turn has several consequences. For one, there is no genuine social science profession or research tradition of the sort known in the West. Second, and this probably has been a more or less conscious aim of the Soviet leaders, there has been substantial ignorance both in the West and inside the U.S.S.R. about the true state of affairs. Among the rank and file of the population, for instance, there is still a great deal of ignorance about the behavior and state of mind of their fellow citizens.

Of course, the Soviet people are neither blind nor deaf, and one fact has long been apparent to them — that there is a considerable discrepancy between Soviet propaganda and Soviet reality. This in turn has produced a striking feature of the Soviet scene — a second culture, unofficial, informal, somewhat "underground," including opinions, moral values, and patterns of behavior which diverge from official expectations. Ironically, these views owe their origin in good part to the very fact of official intervention in every realm of daily life. For example, the regime's massive effort to shape the mind of the youth has apparently generated alongside the official values and activities of the Young Communist League (*Komsomol*) an unofficial and more or less rebellious "youth culture," indeed several of them.

About the range and distribution of such patterns we can learn little from Soviet sources. Such information about them as is released is virtually always for didactic purposes, such as the article from the Soviet press about the young "stylists" included in this chapter. In spite of a few fairly respectable studies published in the years since Stalin's death, it is not likely that we will see a quick improvement in the situation, for this is above all the ground on which the struggle between totalitarianism and individual freedom takes place. In Soviet parlance, the matter at issue is known as the relation of "public" to "private" life. The regime avows that the two are inseparable, or "non-antagonistic," but the people know better. The preservation of "private life" — a euphemism, we would say, for individual freedom — has become one of the main personal goals of many Soviet people.

The patterns of everyday life tend to be less visible than economic, political, and artistic activity. For that reason, the contrast between official sources and Soviet reality in this sector of society is very great. The contributors to this chapter have been obliged to use a number of special sources and devices, to say nothing of a generous measure of inference, to enable them to penetrate the propaganda screen and probe social reality. Among these are interviewing and opinion polling of Soviet political refugees, analysis of the sociological significance of changes in the law or in national policy, and interpretation of the relationship between literature and life.

SOCIAL WELFARE

54

Soviet Living Standards*

Legislative Reference Service of the Library of Congress

(1957)

The welfare of the individual, claimed to be one of the ultimate goals of Communism, has in practice taken a back seat during most of Soviet history. By now the story is a familiar one; the greater part of Soviet economic resources has gone into reinvestment. This survey rightfully stresses, however, that the problem of comparing living standards is quite complex,

*Reprinted from "Levels of Living," *Soviet Economic Growth: A Comparison with the United States* (1957), pp. 107–123, a study prepared for the Subcommittee on Foreign Economic Policy of the Joint Economic Committee, Eighty-fifth Congress, First Session, by the Legislative Reference Service of the Library of Congress, Washington, D.C. Tables and footnotes are omitted.

and that comparisons other than between the U.S.S.R. and the U.S.A. deserve attention.

Levels of living and allocations to consumption in most Western societies are considered to reflect the effectiveness of the economic system in providing for the material needs of individuals of the society. To Soviet planners, however, security and enrichment of state power are paramount, with allocations to individual consumption viewed not as an ultimate goal of the economy but rather as an expense necessary to preclude disaffection and to induce required growth in productivity of labor. This basic difference between the United States and the Soviet Union must be kept in mind along with the usual cautions about international and intertemporal comparisons of levels of living.

Measurement and evaluation of levels of living are complex and difficult tasks and the answers vary widely according to the yardstick chosen. This is true whether the yardstick is that of some previous time in the history of a nation or that of some other nation, or whether it is food or all goods and services actually consumed or produced, or simply measurement of purchasing power of the average worker (real wages). The variations are especially large if, as is true here, there have been very significant changes in the consumption pattern within one or both of the nations (particularly the Soviet Union in this case), or if the consumption pattern of the nations compared is significantly different. Even though quantities of goods and services can be put into a common price system, the social valuations put upon them cannot be made comparable. This assessment, therefore, must be remembered as being viewed in United States values.

In approaching the problem, this study has used several yardsticks, resulting in these findings: (1) Soviet living levels are far below those in the United States; they have been widely reported to be significantly or noticeably below those in Europe; and they appear to be considerably higher than those in neighboring countries of Asia. (2) Soviet levels of living in 1955 were not necessarily above those of 1928 at the start of the Soviet planning era, even though they have risen sharply during the past five and ten years, recovering from wartime losses. By contrast, although levels of living in the United States have not risen as rapidly during the last five years as those in the Soviet Union, they are half again the levels of 1928. (3) There is no apparent reason why living levels should not continue to rise in both countries. The rise in Soviet living levels seems unlikely to continue at the high rates achieved during the period 1950–55, but the rate is likely to be higher than in the United States for some time to come, because the Soviet base is so much lower. No conceivable rise, however, could result in Soviet living standards approaching those of the United States within the next decade or two. The Soviet authorities boast that they can win a straight per capita production race with the United States, as Khrushchev claimed in late May 1957. Secretly, they probably believe that a collapse of the United States economy in the doctrinaire Marxist sense would provide their only hope. But our economy has no intention of collapsing.

Comparison of Soviet Levels of Living with Those in the United States and Other Countries in 1955

International comparisons of living levels must be approached with a healthy skepticism. However, questionable though the quantification of results may be, the mere attempts often reveal significant points that otherwise might be overlooked in less detailed analysis. One approach to international comparisons is by means of purchasing power comparisons of respective currencies for significant commodities or categories.

In 1955 an estimated 670 billion rubles were expended in the U.S.S.R. on goods and services for private consumption, in contrast to about 270 billion dollars so spent in the United States. As a result of a series of recent studies of Soviet and United States prices by the Rand Corporation, the ruble expenditures can now be converted into United States dollars. Naturally, the dollar purchasing power of each ruble varies according to how it is spent. For example, in the purchase of foods, a Soviet ruble would purchase from about a penny's worth of lard to about 25 cents worth of carrots; in manufactured consumer goods, from 1½ cents in the purchase of a rayon dress to about 33 cents in a thermometer; and in services, a ruble was worth from 3 cents in dry cleaning to about 50 cents in a haircut. For that reason, it makes a great difference how much weight is given to each of the commodity-price-relatives in computing an average ruble–dollar price index. The procedure followed in the RAND studies was to weight the individual price ratios by the proportion each represented in Soviet consumption to obtain an average ruble–dollar ratio based on Soviet consumption habits. For the purposes at hand, it can be assumed that a "true" ruble–dollar index lies somewhere between the two averages computed, but the RAND Corporation itself would probably be more cautious in stating such a conclusion considering the coverage uncertainties and gaps in some of the underlying data, as well as the for some purposes insoluble conceptual and methodological problems involved.

Based on Soviet consumption habits, a ruble in 1955 was worth not more than about $0.10½, contrasted with a purchasing power of not more than $0.07 based on a United States consumption pattern. Total Soviet personal-consumption expenditures in 1955, therefore, amounted to from about 46 billion to 70 billion United States dollars, depending on the price index chosen — or only about one-fourth to one-sixth the household consumption expenditures in the United States. When converted to a per capita basis, the personal consumption in the U.S.S.R. turns out to be only about one-fifth to one-seventh as great as personal consumption in the United States.

About the same results on comparative levels of living were obtained through a crude comparison of real wages of nonagricultural employees in the U.S.S.R. and the United States. That is, division of the U.S.S.R.–United States ratio of average money earnings in 1955 by the ruble–dollar price ratios indicates that the Soviet wage or salary earner could buy on the average only from about one-quarter or one-fifth to one-seventh as much as the average United States wage or salary earner. The similarity of results is not surprising because of the basic similarity of the underlying data. However, it conceals some important coverage differences which tend to be offsetting. First, the real-wages approach covers basically only nonagricultural employees, plus the relatively few hired farm employees in each country; that is, it excludes the very large number of collective farmers in the U.S.S.R. and the independent farmers in the United States. Second, government services are included in the personal-consumption, but not the real-wages, approach. Finally, the ratios of wage earners to dependents are different in each country.

Although the ratios of real wages and salaries given above cannot be used as precise measures of relative levels of living in the two countries, they indicate, as do the estimates based on gross national product data given in Chapter VI of this study, that the average consumption level in the U.S.S.R. is far below that in the United States. The orders of magnitude are supported by the reports of nearly all Western visitors to the Soviet Union, and are supported (though not quantified as to extent) even by statements in the Soviet press. Further, it is supported by inspection of relative production and consumption figures on individual items of consumer goods in the U.S.S.R. and United States in 1955.

Relative to the United States, Soviet per capita consumption of consumer goods is greatest for soft goods and food products, except animal products. They lag the furthest behind (and are improving the fastest) in expenditures for such durable consumer goods as passenger automobiles, washing machines, and television sets. The amount and quality of housing available is miserable but, unlike consumer durables, is difficult to improve.

Suppose, for example, that an average-size house in the United States, of about 1,000 square feet or 93 square meters, housed about 20 persons; or suppose about 40 persons were crowded into one of the middle-class or older homes. That degree of crowding would approximate the housing situation in the U.S.S.R., where most families have only a single room in which all members sleep.

If quality could be taken into account, the differential is further increased, because the quality of Soviet housing is notoriously low. Judged from reports and pictures made by Western observers, as well as statistical data, most United States housing is incomparably better built and maintained. Further, nearly three-fourths of all dwelling units in this country (rural plus urban) have inside bathrooms; about the same percentage have hot and cold running water; 80 per cent have mechanical refrigerators; and an additional 11 per cent have iceboxes. By contrast, except for a small proportion of the new urban housing, most Soviet housing — both new and old — has been widely reported by Westerners as rivaling the houses in our slum areas. Although many of the newer urban units have individual inside bathrooms, such "luxuries" are practically unknown in rural areas, and bathrooms shared among a number of families are the rule even in urban areas. Kitchen facilities in the U.S.S.R. also are usually shared by a number of families, and such items as refrigerators are luxuries still beyond the reach of the bulk of Soviet citizens.

The frame of reference of this study is one of Soviet and United States comparisons. However, in view of Soviet activities in Asia, it would be more relevant to compare Soviet living standards with those of countries other than the United States. United States living standards are much higher than those in any other country, so that the U.S.S.R.–United States comparison is interesting but not as relevant to policy problems as certain other comparisons. A provisional conclusion, based on reported observations of many competent Westerners, is that Soviet levels of living are significantly lower than those of industrialized nations such as England and France, but observably higher than those of the neighboring countries of Asia. This conclusion, probably accepted in most of the uncommitted nations of Asia, is of more than academic interest, since a great deal of the reported attractiveness of Soviet Communism to some Asians is based on their belief that the Soviet way of industrialization is more adaptable to their circumstances than is the free-competitive-enterprise method. These people ignore the heavy human costs and center their attention on the alleged results of Communism in raising living standards in the U.S.S.R. They are not aware that per capita consumption on the average has improved very little in the 1928–55 period in the Soviet Union. Any increase in opportunities for Soviet citizens to compare higher levels of living in Europe with their own lower levels can cause trouble for the Soviet authorities, too, if this is added to previous comparisons restricted to the Soviet economy.

Trends in Levels of Living Within the U.S.S.R. and the United States

Analyses of trends of levels of living within the U.S.S.R. and the United States are of interest, as were the comparisons of present Soviet–United States levels made above, principally because such trends are the standards normally used by the so-called uncommitted nations in evaluating progress within the Soviet Union, and also because comparisons with his own experience over time probably dominate the judgments of material satisfaction or dissatisfaction of the Soviet citizen toward his government. Reliable information for the first purpose has not usually been available to the uncommitted nations, so that evaluations have often been made on the basis of unsupported Soviet claims or a limited number of Communist-directed visual observations. It is relevant to note, regarding the second purpose, that although Soviet citizens are allegedly very interested in comparing their living levels with those in other countries, they have had little opportunity to do so in most years; but they have always been able to compare their own living levels at any time with that which they remember from some earlier year, or with that related to them by others. Such recollections, incidentally, may not always coincide with reality.

Measurements of price movements within a single country, especially when there have been significant changes in consumption habits during the period, are subject to difficulties at least as great as those described above for international comparisons of price levels. There is also an additional complication in this instance, inasmuch as the average money earnings exclude those of collective farmers and independent peasants in the Soviet Union, and of self-employed farmers in the United States, and the BLS consumer price index covers only families of urban wage earners and clerical workers. For all practical purposes, therefore, the results may be interpreted as referring only to urban workers.

Changes in urban real earnings are not equivalent to changes in urban consumption levels. First, the number of wage earners per family appears to have increased during the period in both the U.S.S.R. and the United States, so that increases in consumption levels would be greater than indicated. Also, there have been changes in hours of work and leisure time available. In the Soviet Union, on the other hand, new direct taxes and near-compulsory bond purchases must be subtracted from the apparent improvements. There was also during this period a tremendous flow of people to urban areas; and since living levels in rural areas were lower, even a maintenance of urban levels would indicate an increase in over-all living levels, unless rural levels declined correspondingly. And finally, the questions of availability of consumer goods at the prices indicated during the years compared, as well as the stocks of goods in the hands of consumers — especially housing — may be fully as important in indicating changes in living levels as the indexes of real wages.

Despite the qualifications referred to, however, the indexes of average real wages reflect the general order of magnitude of changes since 1928 and 1950. For the period, 1928 to 1955, as a whole, Soviet money wages increased very sharply, but price inflation may have been even greater, so that by 1955 the estimated range of real wages in the Soviet Union had only just re-attained a zone which straddled the 1928 level, meaning they could as easily be below the 1928 level as above it. By contrast, during approximately the same period, real wages of the United States urban workers increased by nearly 80 per cent. The possible bare re-attainment of Soviet real wages after 27 years of Soviet planning and economic controls — especially when contrasted to the United States record — illustrates the lopsided character of Soviet economic development. During this period, the U.S.S.R. increased its total industrial production about eightfold, and, partly because of newly acquired territory, increased its agricultural output by perhaps 35 to 50 per cent. The increases, however, were largely in goods not available for personal consumption, so that increases in output of consumer goods barely kept pace with the increases in population. The peasant population fared even more poorly than the average for the U.S.S.R. By contrast, the increases in United States industrial production (of "only" 136 per cent) during the period 1929 to 1955, and in agricultural output of about 50 per cent, were reflected in roughly proportionate increases in levels of living. (Further, in 1929 production in the United States was at a peak.)

Of interest, too, is the trend in real wages during the past five years. Real wages increased, according to Soviet statistics, by about 39 per cent in the Soviet Union, compared to an increase of about 14 per cent in the United States from 1950 to 1955. The Soviet claim is almost certainly too high in light of other evidence, even though it would be an admission of abysmally low levels in 1950. Juxtaposition of the longer-term trends in both countries from 1928(29) to 1955 and the United States trend from 1950 to 1955, together with an examination of other aspects of the U.S.S.R. economy, suggest that the real wage trends in the U.S.S.R. during the past five years were not normal in any sense of the word. In 1950, at a time when over-all reconstruction of war-damaged areas had been largely completed and prewar industrial production levels exceeded, Soviet real wages were significantly lower than in any late prewar years, and were possibly only somewhere in the range of from 60 to 85 per cent as high as in 1928. Obviously, then, the rapid rise to approximately 1928 levels by 1955 represented something of a dramatic effort to regain lost ground rather than a necessarily continuing and stable phenomenon of Soviet growth. It reflects both the increased domestic output of manufactured consumer goods by the early and middle fifties, and also the woefully low postwar level of Soviet real wages in 1950.

Changes in Per Capita Consumption

Data on per capita consumption of products important to Soviet living standards have been compiled . . . for the years 1928, 1950, and 1955. For reasons alluded to at the start of this section changes in real wages would differ from changes in per capita consumption, so a comparison of the two is only a partial check, even with the best of data; and since the data for 1928 are understated in the case of shoes, and undoubtedly understated in the case of a few other commodities, the comparison also has statistical limitations. For example, urbanization in the Soviet Union has increased the need for many products over those of an agricultural era. . . . The comparison at least suggests that the previous measures of trends in real wages are probably fairly correct in general order of magnitude. Per capita consumption of grain, meat, and dairy products all declined during the period, the decline being approximately offset by increases in consumption of such products as fish, potatoes, sugar, soap, fabrics, and perhaps shoes. The decline in grain could be expected if consumption of meat, dairy, and other food products had increased correspondingly. But these more desired products did not increase sufficiently over-all to assure the unimportance of the grain decline. Urban housing in being also declined by about 20 per cent, per capita, during the period. There are new consumer durable goods being turned out today which were not made in 1928, but the limited amounts available must be spread over so many people as not yet to enter very seriously into the calculations. Services of education and health protection improved, although they are not measured with these commodity data. Even so, the data suggest over-all, as did the trends in real wages, that Soviet living standards have improved little if at all during the past 27 years.

The Future

Reliable forecasts of future trends are particularly hazardous in the case of Soviet living standards, because of their direct dependence upon planning decisions of the central government. There is little question but that the Soviet economy could double or triple its output of manufactured consumers' goods (that is, those not dependent upon agricultural materials) in a relatively short time, say, a single decade, if it were willing to forego increases in output of the producer and defense goods to which it has always given priority. This is not an astonishingly large increase simply because such a small percentage of industrial resources are presently devoted to consumer needs. The increase referred to is not an over-all measure of consumer levels of living which are much harder to improve rapidly. Even after a 2- or 3-fold increase, Soviet output of such manufactured goods would still lag far behind the United States. All the indications point to continued emphasis on investment goods, if one places any credence in the statements of Soviet leaders. But even slight shifts in emphasis would produce significant percentage results in the consumer-goods sector. Large increases in personal consumption of foodstuffs must be predicated, also, on greatly increased availability of agricultural products, either through imports or increased domestic production, which will not be easy, despite the boasts of Khrushchev in late May 1957.

However, further intensification and rationalization of Soviet economic activity in the course of further rapid growth of the industrial sector will inevitably require allocation of additional increments for consumption. The tendency to substitute incentives for coercion to achieve the desired placement of labor throughout the economy, while it persists, is an important factor working to reinforce this requirement. Preferential allocations of scarce consumer goods to those retail outlets serving priority sectors of the economy serve to tie consumption to priority production activities in much the same way that company-provided fringe benefits augment nominal wages in attracting labor to a particular plant in the United States. That the Soviet planning authorities and leaders consider this aspect of consumption significant is clear from their attempts to induce what is called material interestedness of the worker in production, and is reflected in the relative importance of the Directorates of Workers' Supply for the various economic ministries in retail trade distribution (almost a fifth of state and cooperative retail sales were through these outlets in 1955). An important reason for the current emphasis on housing construction, especially in new industrial complexes remote from existing urban centers, is the need to attract adequate labor by the provision of housing facilities. Thus, increments to consumption are increasingly apportioned in a manner consistent with the desired distribution of the labor force — and

are considered, therefore, by Soviet leaders as a necessary "cost" of increased labor productivity arising from "better" distribution of the labor force.

On balance, it seems likely that Soviet levels of living will continue to rise in the foreseeable future. The rise has already slowed down during the past two or three years, so that future increases are unlikely to be nearly as high as the average increases attained while principally recovering from low postwar levels. On the other hand, they are unlikely to be anywhere near as low as the average increase, if any, for the entire period 1928–55. (The trends of both these periods should be ruled out, unless similar circumstances could occur in the future: forced industrialization and the "agricultural revolution," war devastation and extremely low consumption levels even by Soviet standards, and rapid recovery once the more "basic" production goals had been met.)

In summary, given the present disparity in levels of living between the United States and the U.S.S.R., the prospect of Soviet living levels approaching those of this country in the foreseeable future seems very remote. Soviet authorities know that they lag far behind the United States in providing consumer goods with little prospect of catching up in a straight production race. They take comfort in the doctrinaire assumption that the United States will collapse into economic depression, affording the U.S.S.R. an opportunity to surpass us. This hope should certainly be in vain.

55

Is the Soviet Union a Welfare State?*

Alec Nove

(1960)

Hunger and cold have not been strangers to the masses of the Soviet people, and nagging shortages of almost everything needed by the consumer, trifles as well as the staples of daily

*Reprinted from "Social Welfare in the USSR," *Problems of Communism,* a publication of the United States Information Agency, Vol. 9 (1960), pp. 1–10, by permission of the author.

life, have been characteristic. It is important, however, to realize that the Soviet man in the street has seen noticeable improvement in his living conditions in the past decade. Moreover, as Alec Nove points out in his provocative article, the Soviet system has welfare features which often go further than, or find no parallel with, those in the West.

As some critics see it, the Soviet state is exclusively an organ of oppression. The motivations of its leaders, they believe, are to be found solely in the pursuit of world revolution, of national aggrandizement, of personal power — or of all these at once. The attitude of the Soviet leaders toward their own people is often represented as if it were mainly inspired by the objective of keeping the mass of Soviet citizens on the lowest possible living standard consistent with the necessity of providing minimum work incentives.

Hence such critics are inclined to view all Soviet measures which seem to increase public welfare as "concessions" wrung from a reluctant regime by irresistible force of circumstance or popular pressure. It is but a short step from this view to the conclusion that such measures are, in themselves, proof of the regime's weakness or instability. If more was done to improve welfare in the first years after Stalin's death, these critics might argue, it was only because the struggle for power among Stalin's successors was undecided, and because the police apparatus had lost much of its capacity to intimidate. Inversely, now that Khrushchev has become unquestioned boss, they should logically expect a return to the old ways.

The purpose of the present article is to inquire into the validity of such interpretations of the "welfare" aspect of Soviet rule. But it is necessary first of all to define the area of discussion. To take a negative approach, the author does not propose to discuss such matters as wage rates and consumer goods production. It is acknowledged fact that real wages in the Soviet Union have been rising slowly but steadily, that peasant incomes and retail trade turnover have gone up, and that the present Soviet leadership has declared its intention to continue this process through the period of the Seven-Year Plan (1958–65). It is also true that the upward trend in these areas is highly relevant to welfare in the general sense and should be duly noted. In the present paper, however, attention will be concentrated rather on activities of a more direct "public welfare" nature, i.e., on the various social services (health, education, etc.), on housing, and such other state measures as affect the everyday life of Soviet citizens.

A Look at the Record

Before inquiring into the question of motivation, it is also necessary to set forth a few facts showing what actually *has* been done, or is being done, by the Soviet Union in the area of welfare. Such a survey of the record may best begin with a look at budget allocations for social and cultural expenditures during the 1950–59 period, presented in Table 1. Keeping the general trend toward increased outlays in mind, the individual categories of welfare listed are reviewed below with particular attention as to whether or not there has been any recent change of policy.

Health. There is no evidence that Soviet policy in this field has undergone any basic change in recent years. Vigorous efforts to expand medical and health services were already a feature of Stalin's reign, and the progress that was achieved is clearly indicated by the fact that the Soviet Union, as the following figures attest, has since 1951 boasted a larger number of doctors per thousand inhabitants than most Western countries:

U.S.S.R. (1951)	13.9
U.S.S.R. (1957)	16.9
United States (1954)	12.7
United Kingdom (1951)	8.8
West Germany (1955)	13.5

(Source: *Dostizheniia Sovetskoi Vlasti za 40 Let* [The Achievements of the Soviet Government in 40 Years], Moscow, 1957, p. 348).

Thus, while the 1957 and 1959 budget figures show relatively sharp increases in health expenditures, it is clear that these are not a new departure in Soviet policy, but rather a continuation of past trends.

It is true that the equipment of many Soviet hospitals is antiquated, that drugs are often scarce, and that the general level of health facilities is not up to the best Western standards. Nevertheless, a great deal has certainly been done to spread hygiene, combat epidemics, and reduce infant mortality. The services of state doctors and hospitals are free, although most medicines have to be bought by the patient.

TABLE 1 U.S.S.R. Social-Cultural Budget: 1950–59 (In Billions of Rubles)

WELFARE ITEM	1950	1953	1957	1959
Total Health	21.4	24.2	38.3	44.0
(of which)				
Hospitals & clinics, urban	10.3	12.3	18.6	....
Hospitals & clinics, rural	2.6	3.1	4.6	....
Total Education	56.9	61.1	80.7	94.3
(of which)				
General schooling (a)	30.4	32.2	37.6	....
Higher and technical	18.3	19.3	24.2	....
Science and research (b)	5.4	6.2	13.6	23.1 (c)
Total Social Security	22.0	22.8	52.8	88.2
Total Social Insurance	12.7	16.2	23.5	....
Total Maternity Assistance	1.2	4.5	5.2	5.5
TOTAL, SOCIAL-CULTURAL	116.7	128.8	200.5	232.0

Source: Raskhody na Sotsialno-Kulturnye Meropriiatia po Gosudarstvennomu Byudzhetu SSSR (Expenditures for Social-Cultural Measures in the State Budget of the USSR), Moscow, 1958; also Finance Minister Zverev's speech, reported in Pravda, December 23, 1958.

Notes: (a) Includes kindergarten and adult education. (b) As most all-Union expenditures for science and research are kept secret, no complete breakdown of this item is given in the budget, but nuclear research is doubtless a major element. The item as a whole has practically no relevance for "welfare" in any sense. (c) Part of the big increase in 1959 is accounted for by a change in definition hinted at in Zverev's budget speech.

Education. Here again, recent Soviet policy has not basically altered Stalin's approach insofar as the latter aimed at a large-scale expansion of the educational system, but there have been important changes in emphasis and direction. Thus, the decision of the 20th CPSU Congress (February 1956) to extend full-time secondary education to all has since been modified in favor of part-time education after the age of 15, and Khrushchev's reform of higher education also seems likely to result in a reduction of the number of *full-time* university students. It is not, of course, within the scope of the present article to discuss the detailed causes and consequences of Khrushchev's reforms of Soviet education. Regardless of the effect they may have on academic standards, however, it can be stated that these reforms are unlikely to result in any modification of the upward trend in Soviet educational expenditures (except for a possible large saving in student stipends).

One notable reason for this assumption is the evident rise in the school building program, partly as a result of an overdue effort to remedy the overcrowding which at present necessitates

a two-shift, and sometimes even three-shift, system of attendance, and partly to set up the new-type boarding schools in which Khrushchev plans to train the "new Soviet man." It is only fair to add that, in contrast to the continuing shortage of physical facilities, the situation of Soviet schools with regard to the ratio of teachers to pupils compares very favorably with that in many other countries including the United States, as evidenced by the following figures:

	Pupils (in thousands)	Teachers (in thousands)	Pupils per Teacher
U.S.S.R. (1956–57)	30,127	1,811	16.6
United States (1955)	30,531	1,135	26.9
United Kingdom (1956)	7,981	309	25.8

(Sources: For the U.S.S.R. Dostizheniia. . . . p. 274; for the U.S. and U.K., United Nations Statistical Yearbook, 1958.)

Mention should also be made of the Khrushchev leadership's action in 1956 to abolish all fees in schools and universities, which reversed one of Stalin's counter-reforms.

It will be recalled that free education had been a feature of the Soviet regime from the beginning and was explicitly guaranteed by the 1936 Stalin constitution. Despite the constitutional guarantee, however, educational charges were imposed in the top three grades of secondary schools and in universities by a simple decree of the Council of Ministers in 1940. Although the action did not have such a serious effect on university students because of the fact that the large majority were receiving stipends from which the fees simply were deducted, its impact on children of poor families enrolled in secondary schools, where stipends were not payable, was much more severe. Without doubt the restoration of free education was a highly popular act.

Social Insurance, Social Security, and Pensions. Sick-pay benefits in the Soviet Union have long been on a relatively generous scale, and there have been no significant changes in rates of payment in recent years, although overall expenditures for this purpose have increased as a result of the upward trend in total numbers of employed and in the average wage. As part of the campaign launched in the 1930's to reduce the high rate of labor turnover, full rates of sick pay were made conditional upon a minimum period of work in the same enterprise or office, except in cases where workers had transferred under official orders. These rules remain in force, although with some modifications in favor of the worker.

Provided he is a trade-union member, a worker who falls ill is paid the following proportions of his actual earnings (non-members receive one-half these rates, subject to the minima referred to below):

Years of service	% of Earnings
Less than 3	50
3–5	60
5–8	70
8–12	80
More than 12	90

Present regulations provide for minimum monthly payments of 300 rubles in towns and 270 rubles in rural areas, and a maximum payment of 100 rubles per day. Those who are injured at work or suffer from diseases caused by their work are entitled to sickness benefits at the rate of 100 per cent of their earnings regardless of length of service. Where a worker leaves his job of his own volition, he is not entitled to sickness pay for ordinary illness until a period of six months has elapsed, but this limitation does not apply (since February 1957) to cases of accident or disease caused by a person's work.[1] Of course, the social insurance rates described here apply only to disability for a limited period of time, permanent disablement being dealt with under pension regulations.

The maternity benefit rate itself also has not been changed in recent years, but in 1956 the period of paid maternity leave was lengthened to 112 days.[2] This was, in effect, a return to the regulation which had been in force up until 1938, when the period of maternity leave was reduced from 112 to 70 days.

The biggest improvements in this general area recently have been in the field of old-age and permanent disability pensions. Their effect, according to Finance Minister Zverev, was to raise the average rate of all pensions by 81 per cent,[3] but certain groups of workers who had fared relatively worse under the pre-1956 pension regulations secured much bigger gains than this, for the following reasons: The previous regulations nominally entitled a worker qualifying for an old-age pension by length of service to receive payments at the rate of two-thirds of his final wage. This looked extremely generous until one noticed the proviso, often omitted from propaganda statements, that the two-thirds was to be calculated on the basis of a *maximum* "reckonable" wage of 300 rubles per month, meaning an effective maximum pension of 200 rubles per month. This figure, when originally fixed some 25 years earlier, was quite legitimate, but wages and prices subsequently multiplied without any upward revision of the allowable maximum. The result was considerable hardship for ordinary workers, while on the other hand exceptional treatment was granted to certain categories including not only the professional and official classes but also workers in some priority occupations. For example, coal miners, steel workers, and those engaged in electricity

---

[1] These details are taken from S. A. Mitin (ed.), *Spravochnik po Trudu i Zarabotnoi Plate v Stroiteltsve* (Reference Book on Labor and Earnings in Construction), Moscow, 1957, pp. 438–41.
[2] G. A. Prudenski (ed.), *Voprosy Truda v SSSR* (Problems of Labor in the USSR), Moscow, 1958, p. 66.
[3] In *Finansy SSSR* (Finances of the USSR), No.

generation were allotted a much higher reckonable maximum. Similar discriminatory rules applied also to pension benefits for surviving dependents and victims of industrial accidents and the like.

The reform of 1956, while reducing certain very high pensions, established an all-round minimum old-age pension of 300 rubles per month for those qualified by length of service, an advance of great importance. In addition, it put into effect a new scale of payments benefiting lower-paid workers, so that those earning up to 350 rubles per month now receive pensions amounting to 100 per cent of earnings, with progressively smaller percentages for those with higher earnings, and with a maximum over-all ceiling of 1200 rubles per month. An average worker earning, say, 750 rubles per month qualifies for a pension of 487 rubles under the new rules, as against probably only 200 under the old.[4] One offsetting feature of the reform is that working pensioners are no longer permitted to receive full pensions on top of their wages.[5] (This provision, together with the better pension rates, has very probably encouraged many old people to retire.) On balance, however, the net gain to Soviet pensioners can readily be measured by the increase in pension expenditures shown in the following table (in billions of rubles):

	1950	1956	1957 (prelim.)	1958 (plan)
Total pensions	30.1	36.5	59.9	66.0
(of which)				
Non-working pensioners	8.7	12.6	27.6	34.2
Working pensioners	4.7	5.1	5.3	5.8
Ex-military & families	15.6	17.5	23.5	23.4

(Source: A. Zverev, in *Planovoe Khoziaistvo*, No. 12, 1957, p. 24.)

The improvement in old-age pension benefits was accompanied by substantial increases in pensions for those suffering permanent disability of varying degrees and for dependents, the increases reportedly amounting to 50–65 per cent.[6] Further sizable increases in min-

imum pension rates have also been promised under the Seven-Year Plan, along with a raising of minimum wages. No doubt exists regarding the general popularity of these measures.

There has also been a good deal of talk about extending social insurance and pension rights to collective farmers, who have thus far never enjoyed them. Some farms are reported to have adopted a system of paying fixed amounts of money and produce to their sick and aged members, which represents a step forward from the normal collective farm practice of extending relief to such members out of a small fund set aside for this purpose. Cases where fixed payments have been instituted are still the exception since the vast majority of collective farms do not yet have sufficient revenues for this purpose, but it is a fact that the number of such exceptions is steadily growing, and the extensive publicity given to them in the Soviet press indicates that the new system is officially regarded as a desirable development. It must be noted that, at present, all such payments are made out of the resources of each farm, and that the state has no responsibility, financial or otherwise. However, as the regime's policy toward the peasants is, in principle, to reward regular collective work with regular pay, and to bring the status of the peasant gradually closer to that of the industrial worker, it seems to follow that the state eventually will have to accept some responsibility for at least ensuring that the collective farms are financially capable of providing social-insurance benefits. This is all the more necessary because the collective farms have now absorbed the workers of the disbanded Machine Tractor Stations, who were promised the continuation of the benefits they formerly enjoyed as state employed workers. It is too soon, however, to say how the problem will be tackled.

Other Welfare Benefits

Holidays. Turning to other kinds of social welfare benefits for state-employed persons, there appears to have been no appreciable change in the rules governing paid holidays, which already were on a fairly generous scale under Stalin. These regulations compare favorably with those of West European countries, especially for workers in what are deemed to be arduous or unhealthy occupations. For example, miners, steel workers, and bus drivers

---

10, 1957, p. 17.

[4] Prudenski, *op. cit.*, p. 357.

[5] The normal payment to working pensioners is now only 150 rubles per month.

[6] See *Vedomosti Verkhovnogo Soveta* (Supreme Soviet Gazette), July 28, 1956.

are allowed up to four weeks of paid vacation per year. Over-all statistics showing the distribution of the total working force according to numbers of paid (working-day) holidays per year are as follows:

Days of vacation	% of Total Workers
12	43%
15	12
18	11
21	3
24	19
Over 24	12
	100%

(Source: *Vestnik Statistiki*, No. 10, 1958, Statistical Supplement.)

A less desirable feature of the Soviet holiday system is the practice of spreading vacations over the whole year, so that many are on vacation when the weather is unfavorable. There is also a grave shortage of holiday accommodations: despite the existence of much-publicized trade-union rest homes charging low prices, these can accommodate only a small fraction of the workers.

Working Time. There has been significant improvement in respect of hours of labor, although here again the reform effected by the present leadership so far represents, in large part, a return to the more liberal regulations which prevailed prior to Stalin's oppressive labor legislation of 1938–40. A 1940 decree lengthened the standard workday from seven to eight hours, increasing total hours for the six-day work week to 48. This remained unchanged until 1956 when the Khrushchev leadership, implementing its promise at the 20th Party Congress to reduce working hours, took an initial step to cut down Saturday work to six hours, leaving most of the afternoon free and thus creating the beginnings of a Soviet "weekend."

During 1957–58 further reductions of working hours were made effective in certain industries, notably mining and metallurgy.[7] These were followed by still greater promises at the 21st Party Congress in January 1959, when the leadership explicitly pledged a standard 40-hour week (and a 35-hour week in unhealthy occupations) by no later than 1962, with further reductions to follow later in the

decade. There was even talk of achieving "the shortest working week in the world" by 1967. The promises have been so definite and attended by such great publicity that it will be hard indeed for the leadership to go back on its word, except in the event of dire emergency. Reduced hours are in fact already being put into effect in several key industries. A statement jointly issued by the CPSU Central Committee, the Council of Ministers, and the central trade union organization, and published in the Soviet press on September 20, 1959, announced a detailed time schedule for the gradual extension of the seven-hour day to "all workers and employees in the national economy." (With six-hour Saturdays, this will reduce the standard working week to 41 hours.) The process began October 1, 1959, and is to be completed in the fourth quarter of 1960.

Some Western critics, pointing to the fact that planned productivity increases are greater than would be necessary to compensate for the reduction of working hours, conclude from this that the reform is in some way not genuine since there will have to be greater intensity of effort in the shortened work period.[8] Such a view hardly seems justifiable. It is obvious, in the first place, that a shorter working week requires greater work intensity and higher productivity not only in Russia but in the United States or any other country. If output per hour remained the same while hours were reduced by 15 per cent, then — other things being equal — total output would go down by 15 per cent and everyone would be correspondingly poorer, a situation which no one could possibly want. Nor is it true that the Soviet Union intends to increase productivity solely, or even mainly, by imposing heavier physical burdens on labor. This is quite evident from the great attention being paid to the mechanization of labor-intensive processes, especially in auxiliary occupations (loading, moving of materials, etc.).

The charge that weekly wages are being cut as part of the reduction in working hours is equally untenable. The fact that a major reform of the Soviet wage system has coincided

---

[7] See *Pravda*, January 27, 1958, and November 4, 1958.

[8] This was argued, for instance, by Dr. E. Kux, writing in the *Neue Zürcher Zeitung* (December 16, 1958), in tones suggesting that the reform was practically a fraud.

with the reduction of the working week makes it difficult to determine the precise effect of either change, but average wages appear in any event to be displaying their usual tendency to rise slowly. Thus, the cut in the working week is as genuine as these things can be in an imperfect world. Those who assert the contrary are guilty of using against the Soviet Union the very same — quite unfounded — arguments by which Soviet propagandists seek to explain away the reduction of the working week in the United States.

Other Employment Reforms. Brief mention should also be made of recent steps extending the special privileges of juvenile workers. Since May 1956 workers between the ages of 16 and 18 have enjoyed a working day shortened to six hours, with extra piecework pay to make up any loss in earnings. In addition they are allowed a full month's vacation each year and special facilities for study.[9] These privileges have, indeed, caused many managers to try to avoid employing juveniles — a tendency which has aroused official criticism and contributed to the difficulties experienced by high school graduates in seeking employment.[10] The compulsory drafting of young people into labor reserve schools, introduced in October 1940, had already been terminated by a decree of March 18, 1955, and has been replaced by voluntary recruitment.

For another thing, the worker's right to change his occupation, while not explicitly recognized, has been made more real by the present regime's abolition, in 1957, of criminal penalties for leaving one's job without permission. These penalties, as well as others for worker absenteeism and unpunctuality, had been instituted by decree in 1940. Although the decree gradually became a dead letter under Stalin's successors and was no longer mentioned in Soviet legal textbooks from 1954 on, it apparently survived on the statute books until 1957.

In still another reversal of Stalinist policy, the 1936 decree which required the rural population to give six days' unpaid labor per year for working on roads was repealed by the present leadership in November 1958. Instead,

responsibility for building and repairing local roads has been placed on the "collective farms, state farms, industrial, transport, building and other enterprises and organizations." Of course, the job still has to be done, but presumably the individual is now entitled to be paid for doing it.

Wage Questions. Although wages as such are outside the province of this discussion, it may be useful to refer briefly to changes in this field insofar as they are indicative of political attitudes. The practice of the Stalin period was to maximize wage differentials, which indeed reached record dimensions; on the contrary, the trend in recent years has been in the opposite direction. In 1956, a minimum wage law was adopted, fixing a floor of 300–350 rubles per month in urban areas and 270 rubles in the country. The measure particularly benefited the appallingly underpaid groups of auxiliary personnel (janitors, cleaners, messengers, etc.) and the lowest grades of shop assistants, railroad workers, and others. This process of raising the level of the lowest-paid workers is to continue. The decree on the Seven-Year Plan provides for increasing the minimum wage to 400–450 rubles monthly during 1959–62, and to 500–600 rubles during 1963–65, as well as for a consequential (but smaller) upward revision of the pay of middle-grade workers. Since the average increase in all money wages is to be only 26 per cent, it is evident that the spread between top and bottom will be sharply reduced.

This policy is reflected in other aspects of wage reform now in progress. Apart from introducing smaller differentials in basic rates, the reforms are tending to eliminate the more exaggerated forms of progressive piecework bonuses, which will cut down disparities in actual earnings. The gap between skilled and unskilled workers' pay on collective farms is also being significantly reduced.[11] There have apparently been cuts in very high salaries, such as those of government ministers and university professors. (Though no statement to this effect seems to have appeared in print, the cuts are apparently a matter of general knowledge in the Soviet Union and have been confirmed to

---

[9] A. I. Denisov (ed.), *Trudovoe Pravo* (Labor Law), Moscow, 1959, p. 441.
[10] A decree to combat this was issued by the party Central Committee and the government on September 12, 1957.

[11] Some farms are adopting a pay ratio for unskilled as against skilled labor of 1:3 instead of the previously "recommended" 1:5. See *Voprosy Ekonomiki*, No. 2, 1959, p. 114.

the writer several times.) The relative position of the lowest-paid has also been improved as a result of a decree of March 23, 1957, reducing direct taxation on incomes below 450 rubles per month. All this certainly does not indicate that the Soviets are embracing hitherto-condemned "petty-bourgeois egalitarianism," but it does show that the *excessive* inequalities of the Stalin era are being corrected.

Housing. Something must also be said about housing, since the fact that rents in the Soviet Union are far too low to bear any relation to housing costs justifies treating it as a social service rather than as a species of commercial transaction. At 1.32 rubles per square meter per month (somewhat higher for new apartments in some cities), rents are generally insufficient even to cover bare maintenance, which may explain why this is so often neglected.[12] At the same time, the miseries caused by the shortage of housing and consequent overcrowding are too well known to require comment here. Khrushchev has declared that his aim is eventually to provide a separate apartment for every Soviet family instead of the single room which is the usual situation today. It is evident from the housing provisions of the Seven-Year Plan, however, that the separate apartments will be very small by Western standards: the plan calls for the construction of 15 million apartment units with a total floor space (including corridors, bathroom, and kitchen) of 650–60 million square meters — or, at most, 44 square meters (430 square feet) per apartment. A British working-class family would be shocked at having to live in so little space. Still, no one can doubt that Soviet citizens will be much happier if and when each family can have its own front door and no longer have to share the kitchen with several neighbors.

There is no question about the sharp acceleration of housing construction under the post-Stalin leadership. This is fully evident from the following figures showing housing space (excluding private rural housing) completed in four different years from 1950 to 1958, and the Seven-Year Plan goals:

Year	Total	State	Urban Private
	(in million sq. meters of total space)		
1950	24.2	17.8	6.4
1953	30.8	23.2	7.6
1957	52.0	38.5	13.5 (a)
1958	70.1	45.6	24.5 (a)
1959 (plan) ..	80.0	—	—
1960 (plan) ..	101.0	—	—
1959–65 plan, total	650–60.0	—	—
do., annual average	93.0	—	—

(Source: *Vestnik Statistiki*, No. 5, 1959, p. 94). (a) These figures include private house-building by state-employed persons engaged in agriculture and forestry.

Despite the sharply-increased effort since Stalin's death, it is clear that there is still a very long way to go before tolerable housing conditions will be achieved, since a large part of new construction is necessary merely to keep pace with urban population growth. It has been pointed out that the Soviet *per capita* rate of house-building, even allowing generously for peasant construction, remains below that of the (West) German Federal Republic.[13] Nonetheless, the facts reveal considerable progress in the U.S.S.R. The ambitious plans for rebuilding villages in connection with Khrushchev's contemplated revival of the *agrogorod* necessarily call for a still greater expansion of housing construction in rural areas, although the financial burden involved is to be shouldered by the collective farms.

Services. Finally, brief mention must be made of improvements in badly needed consumer services — restaurants, cafes, shops, repair facilities, and the like. This is a very backward sector of Soviet life. To cite just one example, an article in *Pravda* (March 14, 1959) estimated the total capacity of shoe-repair establishments in the Russian republic (R.S.F.S.R.) at 15 million pairs annually, although 100 million pairs of new shoes are sold each year and may be presumed to require repair at least once annually. A recent decree embodied plans for increasing the turnover of service and repair shops of all kinds to 10.3 billion rubles in 1961, as against 6.2 million

---

[12] In Moscow, for example, the average revenue from tenants for rent and "other items" is 1.75 rubles per square meter, while running costs, inclusive of capital repairs, average 4.31 rubles per square meter. See *Novyi Mir*, No. 10, 1959, p. 211.

---

[13] S. Wolk, in *Bulletin* (of the Munich Institute for the Study of the USSR), No. 5, 1959.

rubles in 1958.[14] There have also been measures to increase the number of shops and restaurants.

Motivations of Recent Policy

This, then, is the actual Soviet record in social welfare. It suggests, first of all, that even under Stalin's rule much attention was paid to the expansion and improvement of health services and education, and fairly generous rules adopted in regard to such things as sickness benefits and paid vacations. In the late 1930's, however, some steps backward were taken, particularly affecting hours of labor, maternity leave, and the worker's right to change his occupation, and it was only after Stalin's death that moves got underway to restore the conditions which had prevailed until the mid-1930's. In the last few years, the record shows, much more has been or is being done to improve old-age pensions and disability pay, to reduce working hours, to build more housing, and to provide more consumer services, even though the Soviet citizen certainly still has — and probably will continue to have — much to complain about.

Only the willfully blind will refuse to take all this seriously. But more than *what* has been done, the vital question is *why* has it been done, and what significance, if any, do these developments have from the standpoint of assessing the nature of the Soviet system? No single, definitive answer is possible of course, but here, for what they may be worth, are a few thoughts on the subject.

While it is arguable that the Soviet rulers do as little as possible for the citizen in order to devote the largest possible share of national resources to heavy industry and weapons, such a formulation begs the question. One could reverse it and say that they devote as much as possible to improving the citizen's lot, subject to the necessary investment in heavy industry and weapons — which would sound better from the Soviet point of view, but mean equally little. Is the glass half-full or half-empty? In any case, neither formulation explains why more is being done for the Soviet citizen today than in the past.

One relevant factor may simply be that the U.S.S.R. is now powerful enough economically to permit the diversion of an increasing amount

of resources to the satisfaction of the needs of its citizens, without curtailing ambitious plans for the expansion of heavy industry. To carry out the first Five-Year Plan (1928–32), Stalin found it necessary to reduce living standards drastically, but it would be foolish to take this to be what lawyers term "evidence of system." It is obviously no part of Communist ideology to make people poorer; on the contrary, communism lays great stress on abundance. The "abundance" of communism may well be — in the author's opinion it definitely is — a meaningless, even nonsensical concept, but it surely was the intention of all Soviet leaders, including even Stalin, to raise living standards at some future date, once the painful sacrifices of "primitive accumulation" were no longer necessary. The Soviet citizen was, and still is, denied adequate housing, but it would be a mistake to conclude that the leadership believes in bad housing in the same sense that it believes in the undesirability of private peasant enterprise. Soviet leaders have been willing to sacrifice a generation, to neglect urgent needs for years, but it would be patently foolish to represent them as favoring poverty and hardship as such. They surely would concede, and even advocate, improvements in popular welfare if doing so would not interfere with the pursuit of their basic aims.

Before leaving the subject of ideology, two other points are worth making. One is the enormous attention which Communists always pay to education: however they may twist its content to suit their purposes, they have invariably lavished resources on its development, whether under Stalin or under his successors. It is true that this effort is due, in part, to the urgent need of developing technical skills, but this is far from the whole explanation. Indeed, the promise made at the 20th Congress to extend full-time secondary education to all went far beyond practical necessities, and its implementation even tended to aggravate social tensions, which was one reason for Khrushchev's subsequent counter reforms.

The second point is the great importance, from the standpoint of Communist ideology, of appearing to be doing something to improve the lot of the working masses. Even when nothing or little is actually being done, the party leaders must of necessity claim to be acting in that direction. Too great a contrast between words and deeds, however, can lead

---

[14] *Pravda*, March 13, 1959.

to general cynicism, as in fact it did under Stalin. Khrushchev is now engaged in an evident effort to revive the fervor of the party and to replace passive bureaucratism with initiative. It is reasonable to suppose, therefore, that with this aim in view he wants to show that the party is genuinely doing something to carry out its promises to the people.

One example of this ideological influence is the regime's insistence, for political reasons, on cheap bread and low rents even when these are economically irrational and administratively inconvenient. Thus, Khrushchev recently reasserted the *political impossibility* of raising bread prices despite the fact that, at these prices, it pays to feed bread rather than regular cattle feed to private livestock. In short, cheap bread is essential to the party's outward picture of itself.[15]

The Role of Incentives

Other factors, too, have a bearing on the regime's attitude in regard to welfare. For a number of reasons too complex to be analyzed here, the functioning of the Soviet economy is coming to depend more on incentives and less on compulsion. Prisoners can be kept working even when forced to live in overcrowded barracks on a minimum diet, but unless there is some emergency to spur them, free men work better when they can expect to live better by greater effort. To achieve the leadership's ambitious plans, better work, more efficient organization, more initiative at the grass roots are all objective necessities. To some extent, of course, this was also true under Stalin and was acted upon, as evidenced by the lavish rewards given to Stakhanovites. But few analysts question that there has been a shift toward much *greater* reliance on incentives in recent years, paralleled by scaling down of the number and powers of the police. To give but one of many examples of how this works in practice, the author, during a tour of the Soviet Union, was shown a new apartment block in Kiev,

which he was told was being erected by the building industry for its own workers because, now that they could change employment without incurring criminal penalties, they would not remain in the industry "unless we replaced the barracks and hostels with decent housing."

Of course, people's attitudes and expectations are relevant to the efficacy of incentives as well as to political stability. The more the Soviet Union boasts of its great technical progress, of its Sputniks and moon rockets, of its equality with or superiority over the United States in weapons, the more impatient its citizens become with their backward living conditions, and the less reasonable it seems to them that nothing drastic is done to improve them. Confronted by such a popular state of mind, an intelligent leadership is likely to see the wisdom of taking some action to satisfy it.

The increasing range of contacts between Soviet citizens and foreigners plays a dual role in this process. Many more Soviet citizens are now learning at first or second hand how the other side lives, and this affects their own expectations. Then, too, with the increasing flow of foreign visitors to Russia, it must certainly appear politically advantageous to the leadership to impress them with higher standards of living. This is much more than a matter of impressing unsophisticated tourists from the West, who can if necessary be fobbed off with Potemkin villages. Much more important are the thousands of students and others from underdeveloped countries, as well as from the Soviet Union's own allies, who actually spend some time living among the Russians and cannot help learning the truth. Khrushchev is well aware that relative living standards will play an important role in the world impact of the two opposed systems.

Some Points of Logic

For all its simplicity, one should not overlook still another point: Khrushchev wants to be popular. He may genuinely care to reduce poverty, or he may be acting on the basis of cold political calculation — it does not matter which. He may even aspire to go down in history as the man who brought prosperity to the Soviet people — on the foundations laid by his grim predecessor. There are some Western observers who seem to shy away from even considering such motives possible, as if to do so would label them as pro-Soviet. This

---

[15] This picture has been obscured in the West by denunciations of an allegedly huge Soviet turnover tax on bread. Although it is true that the tax was for years the major constituent of the price of bread, the reason for this was that the tax was calculated on the basis of a ridiculously low procurement price for grain. The real economic incidence of the tax was not on consumers, but on the producers — the peasants.

is clearly an illogical attitude. What is primarily objectionable about the Soviet system is its totalitarian character, its lack of intellectual and political freedom; and this character is not directly affected by the shortening of working hours or the provision of a separate apartment for every family.

It is indeed true that certain features of the Soviet economy are inconsistent with the proper satisfaction of consumer demand. It may also be true that the ultimate logic of a better-educated and materially more satisfied citizenry is incompatible with the totalitarian one-party state. Let us hope that it will prove so. But that is no reason for closing one's eyes to the realities: much is being done on the Soviet "welfare" front, and there is no sign that Khrushchev's consolidation of his political power will cause any change in this respect, especially since the policies being followed must, in his judgment, appear rational, right, and necessary.

56

Doctors and Patients*

Mark G. Field

(1953)

To most American families medical expenses are a prominent part of the household budget. In the U.S.S.R. medical care is free, although Soviet citizens are required to pay for medicines. Within this setting, Dr. Field explores some of the pro's and con's of the practice of medicine in Soviet totalitarian society. One of the most interesting points is his revelation of the protective and supporting function which the rank and file of the citizens often have asked the Soviet doctor to perform.

Sociology views the work of the physician as part of the general division of labor in society and attempts to relate his functions to

*Reprinted from "Some Problems of Soviet Medical Practice: A Sociological Approach," *The New England Journal of Medicine,* Vol. 248 (1953), pp. 919–926, by permission of the author and the publisher.

other aspects of the social order.[†][1,2] Of particular interest in this respect is the problem of the issuance by the physician of sickness certificates as valid excuses to obtain relief from certain obligations or to by-pass certain regulations.

It is a general premise, in a "rational" system of medicine, that true illnesses or injuries are not the result of the motivation of the patient, and that he must not be held morally or legally accountable for what he does or fails to do on account of illness or injury. To be a "patient," therefore, not only entails certain obligations, such as obeying the doctor's orders and "making an effort to get well," but also relieves the person of certain duties and endows him with certain privileges that he would not get under "normal" circumstances. But, as Boisseau[3] remarks:

> If it is true that the first man who saw his neighbor suffer must have sought ways to help him, it is also certain that seeing the care lavished upon the sick, the deference that was granted them, the advantages that their patient status conferred upon them, the idea of simulation must not have been late in arising.

Certification of illness (or self-certification)

† Research sponsored by the Harvard University Russian Research Center and supported in part by the United States Air Force under Contract Number AF 33 (038) — 12909, monitored by the Air University, Human Resources Research Institute. This paper, especially written for presentation to the medical profession, is a revised version of an article that appeared under the title "Structured Strain in the Role of the Soviet Physician" in the March 1953 issue of the *American Journal of Sociology.* The latter article, however, accents the sociologic angle and does not include matters of fact and interpretation of particular interest to physicians. The author gratefully acknowledges the assistance and guidance of Albert C. England, Jr., M.D., for reading the first draft, offering valuable suggestions, and seeing the manuscript through to its final form. This paper is presented as a contribution to the rapprochement of the medical and the social sciences, in the hope that it will yield results of practical value to the physician and of theoretical import to the sociologist.
1 T. Parsons, "Illness and the Role of the Physician: A Sociological Perspective," *Am. J. Orthopsychiat.,* 21: 452–460, 1951.
2 R. H. Shryock, *The Development of Modern Medicine,* Philadelphia, University of Pennsylvania Press, 1936.
3 E. Boisseau, *Des Maladies simulées et des moyens de les reconnaître,* Paris, Baillière, 1870.

cannot be left, in the majority of cases, to the person who claims the patient role. It is the physician, then, as the only person technically qualified to do so, who must "legitimize" sickness in the eyes of society. This also means that abuses of the medical system will be oriented toward deceiving the physician into believing one's sickness or injury to be independent of one's conscious motivation whereas it actually is not. This introduces a complicating element in the sense that the classic assumption that the person who comes to the physician must necessarily be sick (independently of motivation) is no longer tenable; the opposite assumption may, in certain cases, be just as valid. This has, in turn, important implications and consequences for both the physician and the "genuine" patient. Some of these implications are taken up in detail below.

It is the contention presented here that claims for medical exemptions on non-medical grounds do not constitute a random phenomenon, solely dependent on the personalities of the patients seen by the physician, but are rather the end product of a complex of social, cultural, and economic forces. (A man stranded alone on an island does not malinger.) It is further hypothesized that a relatively high rate of such claims is an index of social malintegration and malaise, which the physician, through a judicious use of the medical dispensation in non-medical cases, may, to some extent, reduce. An inquiry into some aspects of Soviet medical practice affords an opportunity to test the validity of this hypothesis.

The Soviet Medical World

Generally speaking, access to the Soviet medical world has been denied Western observers, and consequently little is known about its organization or even its technics.[4] During World War II, when sympathy toward the Soviet Union ran high, organizations such as the American-Soviet Medical Society and its journal, the *American Review of Soviet Medicine*, hoped that medicine, a field traditionally removed from political considerations, might pave the way to peaceful international cooperation in the postwar years. Unfortunately, this hope has not been realized, and at this writing Soviet and Western physicians are more iso-

lated from each other than they have ever been. The *Review of Soviet Medicine* stopped publication in 1948, not because Soviet materials were not forthcoming but because of the general political situation.[5]

In the absence of direct, quantitative, and objective data on the Soviet world one must fall back on other sources of information. One such source, available only since the end of World War II, consists of the many former Soviet citizens who failed to return home from Western Europe after the end of hostilities. Although the reasons for defection are many and too complicated to be examined here,[6] the former Soviet citizens remain, in many cases, the only source of eye-witness information on Soviet Russia. An a priori and unqualified refusal to listen to these persons is clearly untenable under the present conditions of scarcity of knowledge. Whereas the Displaced Persons do not constitute a random or representative sample of the Soviet population, they can — with the proper precautions, reserve, and due qualifications — give the West valuable (and otherwise unobtainable) insight into some of the workings of the Soviet world. This insight is, of course, indirect, qualitative, and subjective. Its accuracy, reliability, and validity are the result of three elements: the internal consistency of the Displaced Persons sample; general knowledge of societies in general and of Soviet society in particular, confirmed and documented by reports of Western observers; and the official Soviet sources themselves, many of which are available in the West. It is only in this perspective that an approach to the study of Soviet society may be more than mere speculation and wishful thinking.

Methods

A general investigation into the nature and functioning of the Soviet social system was undertaken by a team of social scientists affiliated with the Harvard Russian Research Center. Approximately 2500 former Soviet citizens were either interviewed or asked to fill in detailed questionnaires on certain aspects of Soviet life. In the course of this study, 21

---

[4] H. E. Sigerist, *Medicine and Health in the Soviet Union,* New York, Citadel Press, 1947.

[5] *Idem.* Editorial. *Am. Rev. Soviet Med.,* 5: 162, 1948.

[6] G. Fischer, *Soviet Opposition to Stalin: A Case Study of World War II,* Cambridge, Mass., Harvard University Press, 1952.

former Soviet physicians were intensively inter-viewed; in addition 1600 Displaced Persons filled in questionnaires on their reactions to the Soviet type of medicine; finally, research was carried on in the official Soviet sources, primar-ily in *Meditsinski Rabotnik* (The Medical Worker), the semi-weekly organ of the Ministry of Health for the U.S.S.R. This paper presents certain findings concerning the role of the physician in Soviet society.

Claims for Medical Exemptions

Generally speaking, Soviet physicians dis-tinguished three types of claims for medical excuses on non-medical grounds. They were as follows: malingering; direct requests for the medical certificate, with or without an attempt to motivate the physician by arousing his sympathy; or requests for the medical cer-tificate by genuine patients without request for medical attention (residual type).

Malingering

Malingering is not, of course, a phenom-enon peculiar to Soviet medicine. Physicians have met it from the earliest days of medicine and are still faced with it in institutional, military, insurance and compensation claims, and in certain aspects of legal medicine.[7-11] There has been until now, however, little evidence that malingering was a problem that concerned the "workers' state." If the evidence given by the physicians interviewed is any indication (an attempt will be made later to confirm it), malingering is an issue that also confronts the Soviet physician in his daily practice, at least at the dispensary level where medical certificates are delivered. For example, a Ukrainian doctor[12] who finished her medical

---

[7] E. Littre, *Œuvres complètes d'Hippocrate*, Vol. 2, Paris, Baillière, 1840, p. 64.
[8] F. B. Lund, "Galen on Malingering, Centaurs, Diabetes, and Other Subjects More or Less Re-lated," *Proc. of the Charaka Club*, 10: 52–55, 1940.
[9] W. Derblich, *Die simulierten Krankheiten der Wehrpflichtigen*, Vienna, Urban & Schwarzenberg, 1878.
[10] W. P. King, *Perjury for Pay*, Kansas City, The Burton Company, 1906.
[11] J. Collie, *Malingering and Feigned Sickness*, 2d ed., New York, Longmans, Green, 1917.
[12] *Protocols of the Harvard Refugee Interview Project, B – Schedule on Professions*, Report No. 1379, 1950, 1951, pp. 28–29.

training in 1937 had this to say on the problem:

> It was hell . . . I still have nightmares about it. Many of the malingerers appeared when the law on tardiness came into effect. A good 50% of the cases at the Railroad Clinic where I worked were fakers . . . there were people who overslept and came late to work. People had to stand in line after shifts and work and cook . . . life was very hard . . . sleep was a dead-man's sleep and it was hard to get up in the morning. As soon as he sees he is late he will go to the doctor. You will think of some disease to excuse him.

A Georgian physician, who was chief of Clinic,[13] reported on the same subject as fol-lows:

> Georgia is not very large and always has been agricultural. When industrialization started the peasants went into the factories, as it was better than entering collective farms. But the small peasant household remained with its little garden plot. And in the spring you must cul-tivate this plot. And as soon as spring starts and we all knew it, all the patients try to fake illness. And even if a man had a grippe and you gave him five days off, a doctor who would check at his home would not find him there be-cause he went to the village . . . the socialized system of medicine is not bad, but it is the entire system which is bad, which does not give the people enough food nor interest in their work.

Guarded references to the malingering prob-lems may be gathered in the medical journals. For example, in an article entitled "An Ideological Sketch of the Soviet Physician," S. Tikhodeev[14] addresses himself to what the Soviet doctor should be like:

> [In a dispensary the doctor who] uses formal-istic methods can find in every individual he examines symptoms of pathological processess; he can label these as "hypertonic" or "vegeto-neurotic." Such "humanism" has no connec-tion with reality, it has no scientific basis. The Soviet doctor must sift from the total mass of virtually healthy individuals these few who are really sick and need immediate medical atten-tion . . . working in a factory dispensary the physician could deprive production of a great many workers if he were to approach the prob-lem only from the viewpoint of the delivery of

---

[13] *Ibid.*, No. 607, pp. 24, 25.
[14] *Meditsinski Rabotnik*, June 19, 1947, p. 3.

sick certificates. (How shall we solve the "problem": not give the certificate and consider the patients as malingerers or aggravators, or on the contrary give them an unlimited number out of "humane" considerations?)

In another case, the son of a patient wrote to the editor of *The Medical Worker* that his mother, who had severe pains in the region of the liver, had been hospitalized in the clinic of a Professor Voronov. While she was there she received no treatment, and her complaints only threw the Professor into a state of unexplainable exasperation: "She is malingering," yelled Voronov, addressing the writer. He further relates that after his mother was released she then went into another clinic, where her trouble was diagnosed, an operation was performed, and she quickly recovered.[15]

Further confirmation of the existence of Soviet malingering was gathered in the questionnaires. More than 600 former Soviet citizens were asked whether they thought many people faked illness in the Soviet Union to escape obligations. Of the 569 who answered the question, 256 answered in the affirmative, and 313 in the negative. They were then asked whether — and, if so, why — they had ever faked illness in the Soviet Union. Although only 20 per cent answered that they had simulated illness (perhaps the phrasing was unfortunate in that it asked admission of an irregular act), the reasons given for engaging in such behavior were varied. They could be divided into two general groups: to avoid certain undesirable things, such as unpleasant work, military service, and punishment for minor infractions of the law; and to obtain certain desirable things, such as a better, different job, rest, and leisure time. Other reasons given were as follows: "I did not want to be evacuated with the Reds" (when the Germans invaded the Soviet Union); "to obtain time to attend to the children" (by a woman collective farmer); "to avoid going to a demonstration"; "to avoid being arrested"; "to arrange urgent family affairs"; "to obtain a 1,000-kilometer transfer to be with my relatives"; "to stand in line to buy a coat and shoes"; "I did it only in a concentration camp because I was there without adequate clothing and shoes."

---

15 Letter to the Editor, "Only Heartless," *Meditsinski Rabotnik*, January 13, 1952, p. 4.

The respondents were also asked whether they had heard or knew of any methods of simulating illness and if so to indicate one or two ways of going about it. There were more than 200 responses, which ranged from the artificial production of fever, to methods for increasing the heart beat, complaints difficult to check, self-inflicted wounds and the retarding of healing (particularly in extreme situations such as Army service or concentration-camp life) and, finally, simulation of nervous diseases, which was least in frequency. One person indicated "soaking a thread in kerosene and its passing through the skin with a needle." Another wrote that one should pierce the cheeks and blow water through them and "this will cause swelling." Still another stated that many simulated sciatica pains: "After recovering from this illness the patient knew the symptoms well and easily and repeatedly received (medical) excuses." Another reported that "they irritated the skin by rubbing it with garlic or produced burns with cigarettes. At best we introduced a hair under the skin, but many cases ended in prison." A woman indicated that one of her friends was allergic to pyramidon:

> When she badly wanted a rest she swallowed two pills half an hour before going to the doctor. This caused a big, red rash on her face, her back, and her breast. Usually she got two days' exemption from work.

Although, again, the sample is not claimed to be typical, there is thus ground to believe in the existence of a malingering "folklore" or culture in Soviet society.

Malingerers, in any large numbers, have several implications for medical practice. First of all, the physician begins to suspect that every claimant for medical attention may be trying to deceive him. One is reminded, for example, of the humorous (though fictional) account in *The Good Soldier Schweik*, in which every sick soldier was considered, on principle, a malingerer, and particularly of the one who was "dying of consumption, pretending he had tuberculosis." Indeed, physicians who have written on this subject point to the great danger and injustice of mistaking a sick person for a malingerer.

This element of suspicion destroys the mutual trust between doctor and patient that is of paramount importance for therapy.[16-18] Secondly, the malingerers force the really sick persons to convince the physician they are not shamming. As one interviewed physician declared: ". . . every patient who was sick and knew about fakers tried to aggravate his case in order to receive the medical treatment to which he was entitled."[19] Finally they overload medical facilities and reduce the medical care available to the sick population.

Direct Requests for the Medical Certificate

Although malingering remains the most universally used method of attempting to obtain a medical certificate, there are additional ways in which medical dispensations may be obtained. One of these consists in a direct appeal to the sympathy of the physician.

It may be true, though not often enough appreciated, that the role of the physician does not limit itself to the treatment of the sick organism. The physician addresses himself to a total human being, and influences, by his behavior (his art) as well as his technical skill, the recovery of his patient. There was, for example, among the Babylonians, the Jews, the Greeks, and the Romans no great distinction between medical and priestly functions.[20] To this day the Catholic Church maintains shrines for which miraculous cures are claimed. There is, for instance, at the shrine at Lourdes (France), a medical bureau where claims for cures are verified by physicians.[21] Finally, an exclusive preoccupation with the biologic aspect of illness was partly responsible, in the nineteenth century, for the rise of such movements as Christian Science, which completely denied the biologic approach, and for health cults such as homeopathy, Thomsonianism, osteopathy, hydropathy, and Grahamism.[22]

16 T. Parsons, *The Social System*, Glencoe, Ill., The Free Press, 1951, pp. 428–479.
17 L. J. Henderson, "Physician and Patient as a Social System," *New Eng. J. Med.*, 212: 819–823, 1935.
18 N. Siletskaia, "Important Element of Therapy," *Meditsinski Rabotnik*, January 17, 1952.
19 *Protocols*, B, No. 607, p. 23.
20 H. E. Sigerist, *Medicine and Human Welfare*, New Haven, Yale University Press, 1941, pp. 1–52.
21 F. Leuret and H. Bon, *Les Guérisons miraculeuses modernes*, Paris: Presses Universitaires de France, 1950.
22 R. H. Shryock, *op. cit.*, pp. 114, 115, 250, 264.

The need for a sensitive physician is particularly acute in highly secularized societies such as the Soviet Union (and the United States), where he tends perforce to assume some of the priestly functions and is expected to lend a sympathetic ear to those who need his assistance. In many cases refusal to give help would be the practical equivalent of imposing suffering, a proposition that is foreign to all the canons of medicine, Soviet or Western. As one physician related in an interview: "How do you think we felt when women came to us, crying, begging, 'Comrade doctor, give me just one day off. I want to go to my mother's in the village and get some food for my starving children.' "[23] And a gynecologist reported that an old woman asked for a certificate of a bad heart so that her son, who had been sent on a work project to Siberia and had not been home in ten years, could get permission to come and see her:

> At that moment she burst into tears. This is another conflict situation between your professional conscience and human feelings. You witnessed the terrible situation of those people, and you said to yourself "I must help this person. I cannot obey the regulations."[24]

Requests for help have some of the following implications. First of all the physician is requested, point blank, to affix his name to a statement that is known to be untrue and may make him a partner in crime either *de facto* or *de jure* or both. In view of the severity of Soviet laws this may have dangerous consequences for the physician. At the same time, such requests introduce an element of moral evaluation, which then tends to spread to all patient–doctor relations, in which the main question that the doctor seeks to answer is no longer "*What* is *wrong* with this person?" but rather "Does he or does he not deserve a medical excuse?" or "Is he or is he not trying to fool me with a pathetic but exaggerated and untrue story?" This tends to destroy the traditional *neutrality* of the patient–doctor relation (exclusive concern with problems of health independently of moral and other judgments) and is, in the long run, prejudicial to effective medical practice. (This absence of moral judgment and standards seems to be the pre-

23 *Protocols*, B, No. 1800, p. 4.
24 *Ibid.*, No. 1758, pp. 41, 42.

requisite of successful medical practice.[24a] A Soviet physician,[25] writing on this subject in *The Medical Worker* noted that "when speaking with a patient we must eliminate every value judgment. . . ." This may also tend to irritate and frustrate the physician, because he must make moral decisions, a function for which he does not have the training or preparation that a priest, for example, has. Finally, his inability, in many cases, to grant help may only highlight his own powerlessness.

Requests for the Medical Certificate Without Medical Treatment

There is finally a third and residual category of claimants for the Medical Certificate, consisting of persons who come to the dispensary physician and ask for a certificate while they seek medical treatment elsewhere or, in other words, consult a physician privately. It should be noted that private practice, although heavily taxed, is not forbidden by law. Schedules of taxes for private medical practice were published as late as 1946.[26] In this respect the German occupation of Soviet territory almost provided a controlled experiment. It appears that as soon as Soviet authorities disappeared, almost every physician opened up private practice.[27] It thus seems that unless socialized medicine can exactly duplicate, in this sphere, the private patient–doctor relation there will always be a tendency, on the part of the patient, for the "little extra" that is of such great importance in situations of crisis. (The certificates are required, of course, not only to escape certain provisions of the law but also to draw disability pensions and sickness insurance.)

This went so far that in certain cases a physician, calling at the home of a patient, would ask him whether he wanted an examination and treatment or only the certificate, in which case he would ask the patient for the diagnosis established by the privately consulted physician. Since he had many calls to make he would not mind the saving of time and effort. Or as one doctor[28] put it:

If you need a certificate you go to the dispensary doctor, but if you have a couple of rubles you go to a private doctor. The young lady physician who delivers the certificate is not a doctor in the eyes of the patient. She is a State employee who delivers the necessary papers.

Under these circumstances, the original function of the physician (treatment of patients) has completely disappeared and has been replaced by the secondary function (issuance of medical certificate). This means that the physician has entirely lost the mission for which he has been trained for so many years and has become nothing more than a cog in the organization of labor discipline, a proposition that cannot fail to be disturbing to at least some members of the profession.

The Soviet doctor, faced with a host of problems and decisions that bear little relation to traditional medical practice, finds it difficult to steer a course between compassion and indifference and may acquire a sense of hopelessness as evidenced in the outcry of the Ukrainian doctor quoted above:[29]

. . . Sometimes we got together after work and asked ourselves: "What good are we doing to the people?" We just sat there and decided which one we would give a dispensation and which one we would not . . . Of course we helped some . . . but morally it was great suffering.

Causes of Soviet Malingering

The word "malingering" is used here to denote both the simulation of illness or injury and the requests for medical care on non-medical grounds described above. Generally speaking, physicians have paid scant attention to the social circumstances surrounding the presence of malingering, although they have been quick to detect that it was, in some respect, a cultural phenomenon, "a deplorable tradition" transmitted from person to person in certain classes or types. For example, a French doctor, writing on self-mutilations, mentions a list of thirteen methods of malingering taken from a prisoner.[30] There is little doubt that military hospitals and prisons are

[24a] Henderson, *op. cit.*
[25] Siletskaia, *op. cit.*
[26] G. L. Mariakhin, *Nalogi i Sbori s Naselenia i Kolkhozov,* Moscow, Gosfinizdat, 1946.
[27] *Protocols,* B, No. 1379, pp. 37, 52.
[28] *Ibid.,* No. 1800, p. 37.

[29] *Ibid.,* No. 1379.
[30] Huguet, *Recherches sur les maladies simulées et mutilations volontaires,* Paris, Henri Charles-Lavanzelle, 1900, p. 270.

fertile grounds for malingering knowledge, which in wartime attains the rank of a science. Physicians have, at times, suspected that there were special courses given on the subject.[31] As a matter of fact, in World War II, Germans dropped propaganda leaflets on British troops, entitled "Better a few weeks ill than all your life dead," which contained a complete set of instructions in simulation.[32] In this country the *Infantry Journal* made a reference to courses in psychoneurosis guaranteed to obtain either a rejection or a discharge from the Army,[33] and druggists were arrested for selling "goof balls," also known as "4-F pills," to cause rejection from Selective Service on "nervous grounds."[34] Physicians who have dealt with the subject have been prone to attribute it to dishonesty, lack of courage, sloth, and desire for gain. They have also noticed that malingering was most prevalent in military and industrial life, where monotony, danger, alienation, and low remuneration were prevalent.

To return to the Soviet situation, Soviet physicians interviewed suggested the hypothesis that two complementary elements accounted for the high rate of malingering. The first was the result of the decision taken in the early 1930's by the Soviet leaders to industrialize their country under forced draft without borrowing capital from abroad and without an adequately trained and disciplined labor force. This in turn led to a drastic decrease in the standard of living of the masses of the Russian population. The inability of the regime to provide adequate motivation for faithful and accurate work and the ever increased tempo of industrialization necessitated the imposition of ever stricter discipline and regulations in all spheres of Soviet life and particularly in production. For example, a series of decrees first introduced in the early 1930's tightened regulations on absenteeism and tardiness, unless for a justifiable reason, and these became legal offenses punishable by a court sentence of compulsory labor without confinement at the usual place of employment

for a maximum period of six months with a maximum wage deduction of 25 per cent. In view of the generally low standard of living of the greater part of the Soviet masses, the application of such regulations often results in undeserved and sometimes unbearable hardships for the "guilty" parties, who find themselves accused of "crimes" that they never intended to commit or committed through no fault of their own (for example, through a breakdown of the transportation system). At the same time a low standard of living, coupled with certain fixed expenses, means that a wage cut will affect the food budget. (According to figures recently obtained and valid for 1948, a man supporting a wife and two children would see his food budget cut by 38 per cent as a result of a 25 per cent wage cut; recent evidence, however, points to a definite increase in the standard of living.[35]) It is natural that the physician should be looked upon as the logical person to see in case of trouble. It may be assumed that as long as the social and economic situation remains the same, there will be a consistently high demand for medical certificates and that this demand per se is relatively independent of the fact that medical services are "socialized."

Resulting State Pressure Upon the Physician

It stands to reason that a large-scale exploitation of the medical system would lead to a short-circuiting of social controls, and the "business" of the society would not get done. There are, then, certain "mechanisms" that to some extent cope with this problem. First of all, it may be assumed that the physician may well believe that if his attitude were too permissive the system would collapse. Sir John Collie[36] spelled out this principle more than thirty years ago when he wrote: "Surely it is the duty of the medical man to help the State count amongst her citizens the maximum number of units capable to work." Secondly, the doctor, as a professional, does not like the idea of being deceived by clever malingerers or sob-story spinners. Thirdly, he may believe that, pressures upon everyone, including himself, being fairly heavy, there is no justification for "undeserving" persons to exploit the

[31] "Progress in War Medicine: Method of Simulating Used in Germany by Men Who Wish to Evade Military Service," *Science Digest*, 9: 69, 1941.
[32] Editorial, *Lancet*, 1: 318, 1945.
[33] E. D. Cooke, "Gangplank Fever," *Infantry J.*, 58: 35–39, 1946.
[34] "Drugs for Dodgers," *Newsweek*, 24: 105, 1944.

[35] M. Gordey, *Visa to Moscow*, New York, Knopf, 1952.
[36] J. Collie, *op. cit.*, p. 30.

medical system. Fourthly, the physician realizes that malingerers deprive the genuinely sick person of medical attention. Fifthly, there is the fear of *agents provocateurs* who request a sick-certificate and then report the physician to the authorities. As one doctor[37] said: "The physician is afraid, like everybody else. . . . every patient could be an agent, the crying woman may be one, who knows?"

There is, in addition, a set of pressures applied directly upon the doctor. He is sensitive to these pressures because he is, in the majority of cases, a direct employee of the state, working for a salary and subject to the orders of the Ministry of Health and of its local organs. At the same time the physicians, like any other social and occupational group, are not allowed to organize themselves into independent professional associations that would enable them to take a stand against the encroachments of the state. Physicians may join the Union of Medical Workers (*Medsantrud*), which embraces everyone working in the field of health, including doctors, *feldshers* (doctors' assistants), nurses, attendants, and cooks, and within this union, the physicians' sections. But these sections cannot in any respect be likened to local chapters of a national medical association.

The discretion of the physician is restricted by two conditions. In the first place, patients who claim that they are sick must show a temperature above a certain minimum. This minimum fluctuates with the necessities of production and the urgency of the situation. Although temperature is not always a valid criterion for the diagnosis of illness and can easily be artificially produced, this condition definitely restricts the power of the physician. It is, of course, also possible for the physician to indicate in his record a temperature higher than the one observed, but even this small area of discretion is often narrowed down by the practice of having, in most cases, the nurse take and record the temperature herself. Under those circumstances the physician is reluctant to engage in forgery, since this would involve a third party and the possibility of a denunciation.

The second control mechanism (less generally used) consists in the issuance of definite and limited norms of sickness certificates to be granted in any one period. These norms,

which can also be revised according to the situation, usually consist of a percentage of the number of persons on the physician's panel. The doctor who consistently exceeds his norms will be called upon to explain his actions, and may be threatened with sanctions unless he observes the quotas. A Soviet-trained physician, who was also chief of clinic and thus directly responsible for the work of his colleagues under him, said that he asked doctors who had gone over the norms: "How come, doctor, last week you delivered 15 certificates, and this week 17?" And the doctor had to explain and prove — in other words to justify — his actions.[38] Another doctor reported that after exceeding his norm, he had been threatened with being accused of sabotage and hostility to the Soviet regime.[39] In the Soviet Union such an accusation is not to be taken lightly, since loyalty to the regime is the primary basis of personal security. There are, in addition, special commissions that check on the work of physicians, particularly in the spending of funds for social insurance and in areas of lagging productions.[40-42]

These control mechanisms make the performance of medical work difficult, and sometimes even dangerous. At the same time it might be easy to infer that under these circumstances the physician can well afford to disregard the interests of his patients by obeying all the orders he receives and thus playing it safe. This assumption is not, however, borne out by the evidence. There again, other mechanisms force the physician to be concerned with the welfare of the persons he sees.

Pressures of the Patients and the State Against the Physician

In spite of the manifold elements that interfere with the work of the Soviet physician, his primary function and *raison d'être* remain the maintenance of an adequate level of health among the population, on the assumption that illness and injury reduce production. In the scheme of Soviet production the doctor has his

---

[37] *Protocols,* B, No. 1800, p. 5; No. 426, p. 30.

[38] *Ibid.,* No. 607, p. 23.
[39] *Ibid.,* No. 353, p. 11.
[40] G. Golozhinski, "Insurance Physician of Trade Union," *Trud,* June 28, 1951.
[41] E. Kirtenko, "Medical Care for Workers and Employees," *Trud,* February 5, 1949.
[42] V. Abakumora, "Beginning of Great Enterprise," *Meditsinski Rabotnik,* January 13, 1952.

place as a preventive maintenance and repair engineer dealing with the human cogs of the industrial machine. The proposition is simple: "Sick or injured workers do not produce." It thus behooves the physician to lessen, as far as possible, the impact of illness upon society. The first mechanism may be said to be inherent in the nature of medical work itself and in the desire of the physician to perform his work by helping individuals. As one Soviet-trained doctor[43] declared:

> . . . In principle the doctor must not behave as a technician working for financial rewards, but exclusively from the medical viewpoint . . . the very low pay that he received made it so that there was no financial motivation attached to the job of physician . . . most of them were idealists.

Or as another Soviet physician[44] put it: "Our work was our inner emigration." It is also relatively easy for the average physician to identify himself with the majority of his patients since his standard of living does not differ significantly from that of the Soviet masses.

There are, in addition, a set of formal pressures originating with the Ministry of Health, which is vitally interested in the good performance of its physicians and in the downward trend of time lost through illness; it thus urges the physician to prevent and detect illness that might become serious. Another source of pressure is the Soviet population itself in the following manner. The regime, in its propaganda, claims that, among other blessings, everything is done for the welfare of the population. Socialized medicine is presented as still another brilliant achievement of the Soviet system that could not be duplicated in capitalistic countries:

> The Soviet Union is the first country where the principle of free and socialized medical-sanitary assistance for everyone is realized. This is one of the many manifestations of the Stalinist concern for the individual. . . . all the efforts of medical science are used in our country to protect the health of the workers. . . . In the capitalistic countries medical assistance is

available only to the rich. . . . this is what happens when the working man does not count . . . where all is done for profits.[45]

It is also clear that these statements do not always correspond to reality and that medical care often falls short of expectations. In addition to the difficulties cited above, Soviet medicine is plagued with shortages of medical equipment, drugs, and facilities, the poor quality of instruments, the bureaucratic procurement system, and the lack of cooperation shown by local authorities and enterprises.[46–49] Soviet citizens are told that the deficiencies are faults of execution and not of design and are the result of bureaucratic apathy; they are then encouraged to report all such shortcomings. These reports usually take the form of critical letters to editors of newspapers, and are known as "Bolshevik self-criticism."[50,51] These letters, an example of which has been given above, permit the release of aggression upon suitable targets and thus deflect it from the regime. The physician is in no way immune from such criticisms, which are, in the words of one of the physicians interviewed, a constant source of anxiety. As *Trud* (Labor) stated in an editorial: "Each fact of inattentive attitude to the patient, each case of insolence and irresponsibility, must become the subject of a social investigation and action."[52]

It may be assumed, then, that, regardless of the motives that may have urged (or even forced) the physician to behave in a certain manner toward patients (and Soviet conditions as described above are prone to produce end-

---

[43] *Protocols*, B, No. 1725, p. 1.

[44] *Protocols of the Harvard Refugee Interview Project*, A — *Life Histories*, No. 139, p. 9.

[45] "Persistently Improve Medical Care of Toilers," *Trud*, July 5, 1951.

[46] Letter of doctor, *Literaturnaia Gazeta*, September 17, 1949.

[47] "They Don't Care About Clinic," *Trud*, October 19, 1949.

[48] "Disorder and Waste," *Meditsinski Rabotnik*, October 12, 1950.

[49] "Once More About Bad Quality of Hypodermic Needles," *Meditsinski Rabotnik*, February 15, 1951.

[50] A. Inkeles, *Public Opinion in Soviet Russia*, Cambridge, Harvard University Press, 1950, pp. 194–222.

[51] A. Inkeles and K. Geiger, "Critical Letters to the Editors of the Soviet Press," *Am. Sociol. Rev.*, 17: 694–703, 1952; 18: 12–22, 1953.

[52] *Trud*, July 5, 1951.

less irritations and frustrations), he will not relish seeing himself attacked or accused of negligence by laymen, particularly since these accusations may have dire consequences in the form of drastic punishment. Again, the letter[53] mentioned above states:

> Of course, one cannot demand that in every case the doctor make a faultless diagnosis. Mistakes are possible but that is not here or there. What is completely intolerable is that a physician who cannot determine the nature of an illness should insult his patient. This is precisely the way doctor Cherkessova and Professor Voronov behaved toward their patients. They call this being heartless. Is that all?

In the same issue of *The Medical Worker* it is reported that readers wrote about the inattentiveness of a certain doctor in a district clinic:

> A check-up by the Volynsky Regional Health Department confirmed the reported situation and Doctor Portnoy was removed. Also, Comrade Leontiev head of the Manevichsky District Health Department received an administrative reprimand for the lack of supervision of clinic work.

The Ministry of Health and its lower echelons also maintain specially designated bureaus, which deal with the investigation and appropriate action to be taken in these cases. Another article in *The Medical Worker*,[54] for example, reports on the work of these bureaus and notices "some improvement in the examination of complaints and statements of workers." In some cases the State arranges "show trials" to demonstrate its concern with the "health of the toilers"; in these trials the doctor may be prejudged guilty regardless of the medical merits of the case. In this respect the lack of a strong professional organization prevents other physicians from helping their colleagues, particularly when these colleagues are considered as "enemies of the people." To testify in their favor would mean siding against "the people". In this respect, it is significant that in the fantastic accusations of "medical murder" leveled at nine prominent Soviet doctors in mid-January 1953 no physician or body of

physicians demanded an impartial investigation of the charges. Rather, one physician, Lydia F. Timachuk, was awarded the Order of Lenin for the assistance she gave the government in "unmasking the doctor-murderers."[55] (When subsequently the doctors were released on the grounds that the accusations had been fabricated, their jailers were in turn sent to prison; Dr. Timachuk also lost her order.)

The Soviet physician finds himself in an anomalous situation. Trained and urged to behave "like a doctor," he is often prevented from doing so, and must often pay for this failure. There appears to be enough evidence in official Soviet sources to prove that this situation is not unique with the doctors who were interviewed, but is part of medical practice under Soviet conditions.

Discussion

The difficulties experienced by the Soviet physician are the result of factors present both in the Soviet situation and in a system of socialized medicine. Undoubtedly, a low standard of living, coercive measures, and totalitarian controls, as well as the low priority accorded the life and health of the worker (except as a producing instrument), exacerbate rather than mitigate certain inherent defects of socialized medicine such as excessive bureaucratization and unwarranted layman interference in professional matters. (At the same time, it must be recognized that, whereas it is true that medicine has become one of the links in the Soviet system of controls, to claim that state-supported medicine in other societies would bring a Soviet regime is tantamount to saying that the Army Medical Corps makes casualties unavoidable.) It may be supposed, in addition, that if the fundamental ideologic and political commitments of the Soviet leaders moved toward a more humanitarian form, this change would be reflected in better medical care for the population and easier working conditions for the physician. Indeed, the Displaced Persons as a whole, and most of the interviewed physicians, considered the design (if not the execution) of socialized medicine as one of the most positive elements in the

---

[53] See footnote 15.
[54] *Meditsinski Rabotnik,* January 27, 1952.

[55] *Trud,* January 21, 1953.

Soviet scheme (ranking second only to popular education) and one they would like to retain and improve upon if a change of regime were feasible. There is, furthermore, reason to believe that under certain specific types of social organization, some form of "socialized medicine" is the only solution to the problem of medical care. (It would, for example, be difficult to conceive of private medical practice in the armed forces.)

It may finally be argued that strain in the role of the Soviet doctor reflects, to some extent, a degree of social malintegration and malaise but that the physician cushions or softens the impact of the regime upon the individual. Thus, from the point of view of the society as a functioning system, the work of the physician may be seen as one of the many "adjustive mechanisms" that keep the social organism going by limiting discontent and hence disaffection. Although this role is undoubtedly hard on the doctor, he appears to realize the positive functions he performs and apparently derives some satisfaction from it. As one physician, employed in a concentration camp, declared to Elinor Lipper, who was at that time an inmate: "Camps are made to tighten the screws on the prisoners, and we physicians are here to loosen them a bit."[56] With some modification, this applies to the work of the Soviet doctor in general.

Summary

Besides his medical functions, the physician delivers socially recognized excuses from normal obligations and sanctions.

In Soviet society, for a variety of reasons noted, attempts are made to manipulate these excuses for non-medical purposes. The Soviet State consequently applies pressure on the physician to reduce this manipulation and to ensure the highest industrial and agricultural productivity by its citizens.

Although malingering is a sign of social disorganization, the physician, by mitigating the impact of the regime on his patient, is a source of stability and integration.

The excesses of malingering in Russia appear primarily to be due to coercive work measures and a considerable disregard for the individual's

[56] E. Lipper, *Onze ans dans les bagnes soviétiques*, Paris, Nagel, 1950, p. 218.

welfare. They are not directly related to the organization of Soviet medicine.

57

Leisure-Time Activities*

David Allchurch

(1958)

As Soviet industrial progress advanced, an increasing part of the population began to have significant leisure time and faced the question of what to do with it. This is not to say that leisure is a "problem" as it is for some in the West. For most Soviet people free time, and the facilities to enjoy it, are as yet too new and too precious to be anything but most welcome. If, as Mr. Allchurch points out, there is a certain heavy-handed seriousness and a tendency toward over-organization about the regime's approach to guiding the use of leisure time, one still cannot gainsay the fact that such time and facilities are available to many of the people for the first time.

There is an exact equivalent in Russian for our word "leisure," but it is nowadays seldom used except for humorous or archaic effect. With its suggestions of idleness and frivolity, or at best of doing what you please instead of what you must, it does well enough to describe the lives of old-time gentry and modern parasites, or the off-work hours of bourgeois individualists. For the honest Soviet toiler, "rest" has superseded "leisure." We urge our friends to enjoy themselves, have a good time, or take it easy, according to circumstances. The Russian exhorts his friends to "rest," whether in fact they are bound for the easy chair, the theater, or the ski-run. If he is sententious by profession or inclination he may repeat the schoolroom incantation: "Rest and gather strength for new labors and new successes." The Soviet citizen has a constitu-

*Reprinted from "Diversions and Distractions," *Soviet Survey*, No. 26 (October-December 1958), pp. 49–55, by permission of the publisher.

tional right to work and to rest; and in the bulky literature on the subject rest is treated as above all a preparation for more work. There must, we read, be a regular alternation of work and rest on peril of disturbance to the conditioned reflex stereotypes, with a consequent reduction of working capacity and resistance to illness. Rest should be active, and its content should be a change of work, physical culture, social activity, or the satisfaction of cultural needs. This mixture of ideas from Pavlov with others more reminiscent of William Morris gives an unexceptionable prescription for the right use of leisure. Doubt sets in when we reflect that in the Soviet Union the state, with its somewhat arbitrary opinions on the legitimate needs of its subjects, and its rigid views on desirable forms of social and cultural activity, has a virtual monopoly in the provision of amenities for leisure.

How Much Free Time?

Soviet town-dwellers today enjoy more free time than they did even two or three years ago, and enjoy it more. The industrial working week is 42–46 hours, against 48 until early 1956. Since the Stalinist laws on labor discipline were modified, the worker no longer needs to rise hours too early for fear that a transport failure will earn him savage punishment. Compulsory after-work meetings are less frequent, and attendance less strictly enforced. Most industrial workers have at least a fortnight's annual leave, those who work in particularly arduous occupations get a month, and the normal allowance may be doubled in underdeveloped areas with severe climate. The pension scheme of 1956 makes it possible for workers to retire at 60 (55 in the case of miners, workers in hot shops, and women) without serious hardship.

Changes in rural life have followed a different pattern. The peasant is usually required to work harder in the communal sector of the economy than he did a few years ago. The penalties for failure to put in the obligatory minimum of labor days remain unchanged. Some collective farm managements ignore and most of them scamp their obligation to provide for their superannuated members. On the other hand, peasant incomes have risen greatly as a result of Khrushchev's agrarian reforms, so that many peasants may feel that although they work harder they now have leisure instead of just time on their hands.

In this country, students, schoolchildren, and women without children under school age often enjoy more than the average share of leisure. In the Soviet Union all three groups are sadly underprivileged. Students do their reading and their written work, and if they are ambitious make their political observances, after a full day of compulsory lectures. It is now generally recognized that younger schoolchildren have in the past borne an excessively heavy burden of homework, but there is little prospect of relief for those who must enter the increasingly sharp competition for places in higher educational institutions. Able-bodied women usually have full-time jobs in addition to their domestic duties.

The inconveniences of everyday life fritter away far too much of the Soviet citizen's time, especially in the towns. Even Moscow is full, like Dickens' London, of people trudging surprisingly long distances, because public transport is inadequate. At home, you may have to wait your turn at a communal stove. The provision shops are too few and always crowded. Delivery services are almost unknown. Customers queue twice, first to pay and then to claim their purchases. Service in shops and restaurants is slow and sullen.

Current housing programs will make life easier for millions within a decade or two, but so far the pressure on accommodation in the bigger cities has decreased only slightly since 1953. There have been improvements in marketing methods and shopping facilities — a wider range of ready-packed goods and some self-service stores — but only on a small scale. The expanding, though still inadequate, network of *stolovye* (public canteens), where service is quick and food cheap and reasonably good, is a great boon. Better still, the list of goods in short supply shrinks from year to year, and the labor of shopping with it.

The town-dweller's life then, though wearisome and uncomfortable enough by our standards, is far less exhausting and exasperating than it was. The social atmosphere is much less oppressive. Opportunities for simple enjoyment have increased: food is plentiful in most places and travel much freer. For many people, more spare time means above all a better chance to improve their living conditions, and the state goes some little way to help them, even providing loans and allocations of material for those who want to join in a communal building project or to build a family house or *dacha* of their own. Still, most people have more leisure than ever before, and they hanker after more varied and satisfying forms of relaxation and amusement.

The Restaurant

The Soviet citizen cultivates, with an enthusiasm which we have most of us lost, the simplest pleasures: eating, drinking, and rest, in the most literal sense of the word. Partly no doubt because hunger and weariness have been more familiar to him than to most of us in the recent past.

On Saturday nights, special occasions, paydays (1st and 15th of each month), he makes if he can for the restaurant, which does duty as nightspot, pub, and social club as well as eating-house. It is not an entirely satisfactory arrangement for anybody. Not for the couples jostling each other around the tiny dancefloor to the same old handful of Soviet ballads and faded Western pop-tunes in palm-court arrangements. Not for the drinkers, fixed to their bib-and-tuckered chairs over half-consumed token orders of food and a litter of cardboard cigarette ends, with each round more agonizingly slow and uncertain to arrive than the last. Certainly not for the bona fide diners who have to share with or follow a drinking party. Least of all for the angry and suspicious queue in the vestibule or outside the tactically locked front door.

Of course, you can dance elsewhere. Workers' clubs, houses of culture, the local officers' house, and many other institutions organize dances. If you don't want to dance in an organized fashion, you will find at the very least an open-air concrete floor, and in big towns a hall no barer nor less inviting than an English small-town palais, in the local Park of Culture and Rest. You can eat and drink elsewhere too: in cafes, tea rooms, beer halls, *stolovye*. Most of these establishments keep short hours, and their equipment is strictly utilitarian. Worse, they often have gravely deficient menus: vodka, always available in first-class restaurants, is not always sold in lesser eating houses, though you may get more expensive — and deleterious — cognac instead, or even "viski" from the highlands of Armenia.

The determined drinker can fall back on a variety of informal and illegal arrangements. There are illicit "pop-ins" usually selling homemade hooch. If you are hard up, there are obliging persons with a stock laid in against such emergencies, ready to exchange a bottle for a "pledge," which may be, as in a recent case reported by *Krokodil*, the clothes off your back.

But there is no substitute for the restaurant. To sit with his feet on a carpet, amongst pillars like glazed brawn or under a dropsical *empire* ceiling, with a hubbub of music and talk about him and black-garbed waiters however sluggishly at his beck and call — this is the ordinary Russian's ideal of luxury, ease, and glamour. The sophisticated may sneer at the "merchant taste" of the furnishings and decorations: the dizzy chandeliers, the female statues in difficulties with their marble shifts, the messy canvases (bears in a wood, the three fat, mounted Kievan warriors, a wishy-washy view of some old Russian town from across its river). To the common man these things are an assurance that he has come up in the world and is entitled to his share of its luxuries. There is more to it than this of course. Many of the lesser restaurants are unpretentious, and even the greatest are less imposing than many a House of Culture. What they all have to offer is a sense of ease and independence, of relative freedom from regulation, of asserting if only with partial success your consumer sovereignty, of spending freely and receiving service.

People make many complaints about the restaurants, some of which are echoed in the press. But the only really bitter complaint is that there are too few of them. Moscow has over a thousand eating-houses, but only about thirty of these are restaurants. In the provinces, the park in the summer and the railway station in the winter is often the only resort for an evening of sociable eating and drinking.

For many Soviet citizens the restaurant is almost the only opportunity for conspicuous consumption. There are many more occasions for conspicuous leisure, and the Soviet citizen eagerly dons its uniform, the pyjama suit, not only at holiday resorts, or at the *dacha* settlement, but on train journeys or even in his own backyard. Pyjamas are comfortable too, of course, and save wear on everyday clothes, but in chilly weather they may even be worn above an ordinary suit. Many a pyjama suit is economically removed and replaced by non-symbolic attire — often singlet and shorts — at bedtime.

Vacation Period

Rest, in medically supervised therapeutic conditions, is the officially favored form of annual holiday. If you can obtain a pass you go to a *kurort* and stay in a sanatorium if you need medical treatment, or a house of rest if your health is good. In the Caucasus or the Crimea if you are lucky, but more likely in some salubrious pinewood or on some refreshing hill just out of town. Most resorts offer excursions, concerts, physical training classes. But most of the time you will rest, which means lying, sitting, or walking around in your pyjamas. If you are at all susceptible to medical suggestion, you will find yourself on a diet and drinking strong waters. It is all rather like what Count Witte and Tsar Nicholas did at Bad Nauheim, and for good or ill, not a bit like what Mr. Malik saw at Blackpool. Such holidays are popular enough, though of course more so with the elderly and middle-aged than with young adults. About five million people find a place in these establishments, and for every successful applicant there are probably a dozen who would be glad of the chance.

There are some facilities for organized tourism, and of course camps for the young. But most Soviet workers spend their annual holiday at home, or, if they can afford it, traveling for a change of scene. Shortage of accommodations in hotels and indeed on trains curtails opportunities for private travel. Nonetheless, in the last few years the trains in summer have been crowded with people "going away" for a week or two, often to stay with already overcrowded relatives, adding to the difficulties of railway travel by carrying with them bulky goods in short supply at their places of destination. And still, for most people, an annual holiday means no more than staying away from work, sunning themselves on the nearest riverbank, perhaps painting the town a little more lavishly than usual.

Unique Institutions for "Culture and Rest"

The most important monument to the state's theory of leisure is the social and cultural club:

called a Palace of Culture, a House of Culture, or merely a Club according to size and scope. There were nearly 130,000 of them in 1956, of which nine-tenths were small rural clubs. Two-thirds of the total belong to the Ministry of Culture; others, including most of the largest urban clubs, to Trades Unions, and roughly one *kolkhoz* in three has a little club of its own. These institutions provide facilities for political instruction, group cultural activities, hobbies, and, to a lesser extent, amusement without motive of self-improvement. In large towns the accommodations and equipment are impressive by any standards: a large library, comfortable reading rooms, at least one concert hall, rehearsal rooms for amateur dramatics and musical activities, a special children's section, often a cinema and a dance hall. If the numerous lectures on political and artistic subjects are hackneyed and ill-attended, instruction in hobbies (especially radio and photography) and amateur cultural activities are on a high level, and quite popular. Small mining towns sometimes produce a folk-dance team which it would be hard to match outside the Soviet Union. There are thousands of amateur choirs of a quality which was common enough in industrial England and Wales thirty years ago but is very rare today.

It is uncertain how many people use these facilities, but official figures for participation in group activities give some indication. At the beginning of 1956, roughly 4.8 million people were enrolled for various group activities, of which choral singing and amateur dramatics, each with more than a million participants, were the most popular.

Life in the Soviet Union would be duller without the clubs, but even in the towns figures suggest that comparatively few adults visit them except to see a film or a concert or to attend a dance. In the country, the clubs are often open only intermittently, and have a small range of attractions.

Like similar institutions elsewhere, the clubs attract more youngsters than adults, more women than men, the socially militant rather than the merely sociable. They are run by professional *kulturniki,* committed to raising the ideological and cultural tone of their flock, and they give little opportunity for popular initiative or informal enjoyment. Sometimes the masses, with their longing for gaiety and novelty, triumph over their sober-minded organizers, as the film *Carnival Night* showed us. Sometimes the *kulturniki* pander to popular taste. But for the most part the clubs offer the same synthetic sham-popular entertainment of which the Soviet man-in-the-street has long ago wearied.

The Park of Culture and Rest gives visiting foreigners an excellent synoptic view of Soviet leisure activity. "Parks" were originally just enclosures, and associations with "park-land" should be forgotten. A really cultured Soviet park has little room for rough grass and copse. A ruble takes you through an elaborate classical gateway on to graveled or cemented walks, flanked alternately with flower-beds and rows of hoardings bearing political messages. Here and there you may rest on a balustrade and enjoy a cultured view: flowers, fountains, statues — athletes modest in vest and drawers, the long-trousered proletarian male and the petticoated peasant maid threatening heaven with hammer and sickle, Lenin with his high exhortatory gesture (forward to the future) and Stalin, hand smugly extended (look what I have given you). There are rooms where you can read the newspaper or play chess, a dance hall or at least an open-air dance floor and open-air stage in summer, skating in winter, sometimes a cinema. On summer holidays troupes of dancers, usually amateurs in bright national costumes, will attract a few bored stares, and "mass-workers" will try to involve a half-hearted public in open-air party games.

Less cultured amusements are not entirely forgotten. Big parks have at least one restaurant, and even the smallest provincial park usually has a beer-hut. In summer the parks are favorite resorts for drunks and hooligans.

Very occasionally, the parks provide fairground "*attraktsiony.*" The "wall of death" recently enjoyed a run in Gorky Park, Moscow, and though few and far between, there are even Coney Island installations for administering retrospectively pleasurable shocks to the stomach and nervous system.

Sport

The Soviet state yields to no English headmaster in its enthusiasm for sport, builder of strong bodies and disciplined characters. Last year, some 19 million people were enrolled in sports clubs, and 15 million of them regularly practised. Light athletics (with 3.5 million participants), volleyball (2.5 million), skiing (2.5 million), and football (1 million) enjoyed greatest popularity. (Comparison of spectator statistics, if available, would probably show that these figures are affected by relative availability of facilities.) Members of sports clubs are expected to undertake rigorous training under state instructors, and to submit to a series of graded tests. The aim is to produce good all-rounders, and an expert in one sport is sometimes held back by his lack of interest in others.

The Soviet Union's international record in sport can surprise no one who has marveled at the proficiency of unknown athletes in little provincial clubs. But officialdom is dissatisfied with the condition of Soviet sport. There are three main complaints. First, that, because of organizational complications, facilities are inadequately used, so that, as *Komsomolskaya Pravda* put it, "pitched battles are fought on vacant lots and in backyards while stadia remain empty." Second, that the "consumer approach" is hindering the growth of mass participation in sport. Third, that commercialism and the "star cult" are perverting the true ends of Soviet sport which may be summed up in the name of the national body in charge of sports standards: "Ready for Defence and Labor."

The Theater

Statistics for the development of the entertainment industries show interesting contrasts with the pattern in the West. It is rather as though two phases of Western development — the movie age and the television age — had been telescoped, with a general shortage of facilities further distorting the pattern.

There were many more theaters in 1941 (908) than in 1956 (503), and most of the missing 400 were closed by 1951. The reduction is accounted for partly by the building of bigger and better theaters, partly by the conversion of obsolete or unsuccessful provincial theaters into cinemas. At the same time, while theater audiences increased only by one-seventh between 1950 and 1955, cinema audiences more than doubled during the same period. They showed a further 50 per cent increase between 1955 and 1957, while theater audiences hardly increased at all.

There are now 6 or 7 million television sets in the Soviet Union. It is not difficult to imagine how much more comfortable a cramped Soviet apartment becomes in semi-darkness, with the family hypnotically immobilized. The theater has suffered severely from the impact of television, the cinema hardly at all. Theater-going is more expensive and time-consuming than a jaunt to the corner cinema. Perhaps more important, the cinema offers nowadays a steady flow of new films, while theater repertoires are notoriously stale and in any case form the staple of television broadcasts. Jealous jokes about television can be heard on the Soviet as on the Western stage:

"There's nothing on the telly nowadays."
"Never mind, there'll be a second channel soon."
"Then there'll be twice nothing."

But jokes of this sort are even less fair in the Soviet Union than elsewhere. From year to year the theater offers the same circumscribed repertoire: hackneyed classics and modern plays which are little more than crudely dramatized slogans. Theatrical people and cultural overlords alike grumble about the poverty of the repertoire. Even a technically excellent company like MKhAT complained of falling attendances: a month after its 1956–57 season opened, MKhAT's average audience was only three-quarters of capacity, and the three perennial Gorky plays in the repertoire were only half-filling the theatre. The Maly — home of Ostrovsky and of the best acting in Moscow — was in even worse plight.

Stale plays and bad new ones lower acting standards. Ilyinsky, perhaps the finest satirical actor in Europe, has complained about the lack of good fresh plays to stretch and tone up his talent. The more successful Soviet plays are often artistically parasitical. Sofroniv's *Money*, for instance, enjoyed a certain popularity because one of the Soviet theater's grand old ladies, Pashennaya, gave a virtuoso reading of comic female rascality which owed nothing to Sofronov and everything to her experience in Ostrovsky. Young actors without a rigorous classical schooling can neither ape their elders convincingly nor lend a semblance of personality to the abstract creatures talking like newspapers who people the run-of-the-mill Soviet play. Frequenters of the opera and the ballet are of course less avid of novelty than the theater-goer. The simpler sort revel in luxurious spectacle, the connoisseur is there to study fine points of performance. The true balletomane cares little more for the "story" than does the *aficionado* for the name of the bull. Nonetheless, there is a growing feeling among artists and public alike that many shows have gone on too long, that most of the new ones are not good enough, and that performances are becoming stale and perfunctory as a result.

The art director of the Bolshoi spoke recently of a "certain stagnation," and Western audiences who have succumbed to the magnificence of its spectacles and the incomparable technique of its stars can scarcely imagine the dreariness of a routine second-team performance at Moscow's greatest theater.

In 1956–57 the repertoire was enlivened by a few revivals (including two or three old Meyerhold productions) and a curious assortment of Western importations. Some of these have since been swept from the stage by official protests, others have survived. There were eager audiences for plays as diverse as Lillian Hellman's *Autumn Garden*, *Dial M for Murder*, Priestley's *Dangerous Corner*, Erdman's *Mandate* (a witty romp from the NEP era), and Mayakovsky's *Bedbug* (in the hilariously funny and ideologically suspect first production at the Satira Theatre). Under official pressure managements have since become more orthodox and cautious. The list of new productions for 1957–58 included no appetizing novelties, and there was a depressing plethora of safe new plays about the war.

The Cinema

The cinema has fared much better: 144 full-length films were produced, and 70 foreign films shown, in 1957. A few years ago Soviet films could not compete for popularity with the few allowed in from abroad. In the lean years many cinema-goers looked back to wartime importations (especially weepies like *Waterloo Bridge*) as the high point in their cinema-going experience. Even in 1956 *La Strada,* and less understandably *Lady Hamilton*, caused more excitement in Moscow and Leningrad than any Soviet film. Any Western European film — they included a deliciously naughty old-fashioned farce from Austria, Italian films built around shots of girls removing their stockings in tenements — was a certain success. But from 1956 on, Soviet studios have produced a series of love stories, musicals, and melodramas, made up to Western (often Hollywood) recipes which have won genuine popularity. Some of them have also achieved the difficult double feat of satisfying Soviet officialdom and impressing Western audiences. It is not at all sure, however, whether the cultural overlords will long tolerate the new type of Soviet films, with its healthy vulgarity, its skillful exploitation of romantic clichés, and its lack of ideological urgency. At a conference of cinema workers in 1958, self-congratulation on quantitative increase was mingled with complaints of qualitative decline, and there is an increasingly strident demand for strong propaganda films on themes of labor heroism.

For the present a visit to the cinema is among the most pleasurable of leisure activities. The cinema-goer's one serious complaint is that he cannot go as often as he would like. Cinemas are too few and too small. Peasants may have to travel many miles to a mobile projection unit, which often shows films without sound. Even in big towns it is necessary to queue for advance tickets, and to sit in poky unventilated, and often unheated rooms. There are not enough copies of new films to go round, and distribution is erratic, so that small towns and country places may receive the same old film over and over again. A few years ago the press regularly complained that some *kolkhozniki* saw nothing but episodes in the career of Tarzan year in and year out; and that saga of rampant individualism in a crowded natural setting may still be intriguing tight little collectives out on the featureless plain. But the state has impressive plans for more and better cinemas and a further great increase in film output. In ten years or so, the quantitative needs of the Soviet cinema-goer may be fully met.

The Problem of Leisure, Soviet Style

The problem of leisure is perhaps more acute in the Soviet Union than in more leisured but less closely organized industrial societies. The state claims an unlimited right to regulate the use of leisure, and exercises it not to gratify man as he is, without damage to society, but to refashion him at all costs. Soviet man has proved highly resistant to refashioning, because the state works to a sociologically unrealistic blueprint. There is no reason to believe that Soviet man, in adjusting himself to more prosperous and leisured circumstances, will draw nearer to the state's ideal; nor yet that the state will become more accommodating to man as he is.

The state wants its citizens to "rest in preparation for new work," to make themselves "ready for defence and labor," to "raise their political and cultural level" until they fully identify themselves with its purposes and its prejudices. The individual wants to relax, to enjoy his free time freely, to please himself as a change from pleasing the boss. He may be disposed to seek his gratifications in sport, in the arts, or even in politics. But all these fields of activity are circumscribed and subject to a distressing degree of official interference: politics so much so that no well-balanced person takes an active interest in it except for bread and butter reasons, the arts sufficiently to make their pursuit frustrating to people of critical intelligence and refined taste, even sport to such an extent that adults are more and more inclined to watch rather than to play.

In practice, of course, there has always been a compromise between the desires of the people and the "interests of society." The state fulminates against drunkenness — and keeps up a supply of alcohol which would be excessive in a reasonably sober society. The state deplores the consumer approach in sport — and builds the colisea which encourage it. The state disapproves of sloppy and vulgar entertainment — but tolerates and even rewards a few (scrupulously un-American) exponents of vulgar sentimentalism.

A compromise, or should we call it a tug-of-war? During the period of social relaxation and ideological confusion in 1956 and early 1957, the public had the cultural overlords off-balance, and the long haul back is still incomplete. For a brief spell, magazines were readable, and eagerly bought; frivolous foreign films and plays drew full houses; jazz and pop-songs broke into the forty-year-long tinkle of balalaikas. "Johnny," "Besame Mucho," and home-made imitations like "Perhaps" and "My Boyfriend Is So Handsome," yearningly mooed by respectable Soviet artistes and recorded by state studios, vied in popularity with the black marketer's X-ray plate transcripts of foreign broadcasts. It is clear from the series of official pronouncements on the arts and entertainment in 1957–58 that the state has realized how tame and tedious the Soviet public finds its normal cultural diet; and equally clear that the state has little idea what to do about it.

In the West we are uneasily conscious of the widening gap between highbrow and popular culture; we may have doubts about the health of both, but there is no denying that both on the whole satisfy their consumers. In the Soviet Union there is a single, synthetic official culture, which makes a few concessions to vulgar tastes and far fewer to those of the elite. It has no rotten spots; it is just dead. Ehrenburg has asked authority to recognize the existence of different levels of taste, and authority was unwise to reject his plea. As it is, both the uneducated and the elite are terribly vulnerable to foreign cultural influence. Soviet literature, written primarily for the censor, cannot stand the limited competition even of the translations published in *Inostrannaya Literatura;* significantly, the provincial nonentities hoisted to literary power by Khrushchev have begun to blame an excessively liberal translation policy for symptoms of decadence in the work of young Soviet writers. The purveyors of popular entertainment are no less weary than their audiences of synthetic folksiness and hearty balladry; for want of fresh native material they relay Americana whenever their invigilators nod. Even more serious from the official point of view than the danger of foreign cultural penetration is the evidence that official culture is inadequate to its task of indoctrination by pleasurable means.

The state's answer to the problem of leisure is "more of the same": more palaces of culture, theaters, cinemas, stadia, a 50 per cent increase in the output of publishing houses within five years, and of course more lectures, study circles, carefully controlled opportunities for mass participation in public affairs. Improved amenities will obviously help to combat the worst abuses of leisure — drunkenness, hooliganism, petty crime — which flourish most vigorously in the more primitive industrial areas. More cinemas and clubs in the Komi ASSR will mean fewer drunken knife-fights. But the quantitative approach can have only a partial success. It is increasingly clear that Soviet man is restlessly dissatisfied with approved forms of leisure activity even where amenities are adequate.

High living standards are in themselves the best — though by no means a complete — answer to the problem of leisure in industrial societies. But even if it had the means, the Soviet state would for political and ideological reasons be reluctant to put any considerable part of its population into militantly self-contained dwellings, seal them in envelopes of cash-conscious egoism, provide them with gardens to hedge off from the neighbors, clubs to keep exclusive, cars to get away in. For many years to come, gradually increasing prosperity will probably aggravate the problem of leisure. Perhaps, as time goes by, the Soviet state will see the need to find more effective methods of satisfying and influencing a vast urban population with time on its hands and money in its pocket, uncomfortable at home, bored with permitted pleasures, increasingly eager for luxury, amusement, and excitement.

58

Have a Glass of Vodka*

A Soviet Doctor Writing in Izvestiya

(1958)

The Soviet man, like his cousin in countries all over the world, finds it hard to be a model citizen, especially in his time off. Indeed, the pressures of daily life and the often unrealistic standard of behavior expected of him make it more difficult for him than is the case in other nations. In this short story by a Soviet doctor we have a sample of the critical and didactic literature with which the Soviet regime has sought, since the earliest period of its power, to bring about moderation in the use of alcohol.

Last fall a tall man in worn, dirty clothing came up to me.

"Can you spare me a ruble, citizeness? I've run short."

*Reprinted from "A Doctor's Notes: A Glass of Vodka," Lydia Bogdanovich, *Izvestiya* (March 2, 1958), p. 4, translated in the *Current Digest of the Soviet Press,* Vol. 10, No. 9, pp. 29–30, published at Columbia University by the Joint Committee on Slavic Studies appointed by the American Council of Learned Societies and the Social Science Research Council. Used by permission of the publisher.

His gray hair and dark, puffy face were literally covered with dust. There was something very familiar about his eyes, which were extraordinarily like a mermaid's with their greenish glow, and about his wide, soft mouth. I gave him a ruble and about 70 kopeks in change. Taking the money, he hastily tossed off.

"Thanks."

Going off to one side, the man opened his fist and counted the change. Then with hurrying, heavy step he cut across Semyonovskaya Square and disappeared into a shop with the sign "Beer, Soda Water."

"So that's what he wanted the money for!" I thought angrily. Then something in me clicked. I recalled my youth and an exhibition of paintings in Krasnodar. One of the pictures at the exhibition was entitled "Comrades." It showed a green pine grove with a sunny clearing through which a clear brook ran; two village youths were standing beside an oak tree with snares for catching siskin. There was always a crowd in front of this picture. It had been painted by a young artist named Ryzhov, who lived in a nearby apartment. The artist had two young sons and a lovely wife. I had gone to the exhibit with them and my parents. Ryzhov met us there. No doubt he had already had several drinks since morning; he swayed a little as he stood. There was a look of reproach on his wife's face. With the particular bitterness that had become habitual with her, she said:

"Have you done it again, Alyosha?"

Ryzhov smiled a broad, happy smile in reply.

At that time the young artist was acclaimed. He acquired many friends and fans, and their expressions of respect for some reason took the form of frequent rounds of drinks. Soon Ryzhov began to fight with his family. He would drink and become hung over. He became pathologically jealous of his wife, who by that time had become emaciated and had a lung disease. She died soon after. Then I lost sight of Ryzhov.

And now — the man who had asked me for money reminded me for some reason of Ryzhov. I went over to the beer hall. He was coming toward me with the burdened step of a man loaded with alcoholic beverages. I touched him on the hand:

"Are you from Krasnodar? Are you Ryzhov?"

"Yes, I am the artist Ryzhov. There is no other and never will be!"

This man's immense pride, coupled with his dirty, swollen hands and dirty clothing, made a strange impression on me. I reminded him that we had been neighbors in Krasnodar. We sat on a bench in a flower garden near the Motherland Motion Picture Theater. Ryzhov told me briefly that he had long been "on a pension," even though he was "in perfect health." He boastingly but hesitatingly shared his secret "creative plans" with me. He told me that one of his sons had died and that the other was "in a children's home somewhere."

I suggested to the artist that he "build up his nervous system" at the hospital where I work. He was deeply touched. A film of tears covered his watery, greenish eyes. He thanked me volubly, then wrote his address for me in a shaky hand and excused himself. But after I had turned the corner he caught up with me.

"I'll come to see you. I'll come for sure. Then you'll see what kind of a person Ryzhov is capable of becoming. But today — just for today — let me have three rubles, won't you?"

Ryzhov never came. Maybe he lost the address. I made inquiries about him, but it was too late. The artist had been run over by an automobile driven by a reckless drunken driver. The militia report on the incident said "the victim was also drunk."

And so liquor led a talented man to his death. Unfortunately, this incident is not unique. Drunkenness is a legacy and a terrible survival from the past. It brings people a great deal of unhappiness, breaks up families, puts healthy people in psychiatric hospitals, pushes cowards into crime, damages the health, and causes the Soviet state immense losses.

It is a known fact, for example, that 50 per cent of all accidents happen to people who are heavily under the influence, and that 70 per cent of all crimes are linked to drinking. Drunks make up the majority of the persons who violate labor discipline at enterprises and on collective farms.

Alcohol has a pernicious effect on higher nervous activity. Such disease as hypertension, diseases of the heart, liver and kidneys, and various malignant tumors are frequently caused by alcohol.

And how many of the various mental and nervous disorders are caused by drunkenness! Mentally and physically deficient children suffering from idiocy and mental defects are most often born of drinking parents.

People frequently ask:

"If liquor causes such immense harm, then why isn't the use of alcoholic beverages forbidden in our country by law?"

Many years of experience have shown that even very strict administrative measures in the struggle against that evil have not succeeded. Suffice it to recall the prohibition of the sale of vodka and liquor in various countries, such as the "dry law" in the U.S.A. They only led to the development of bootleg trade. Unchecked speculators flooded the country with both alcoholic beverages and poisonous narcotics.

This means that it is impossible to forbid the sale of alcoholic beverages. We do not mean that a person should never take a drink; it is drunkenness that we are objecting to. Like all pathological social phenomena, alcoholism must be combated daily, in a well-thought-out, purposeful manner. And naturally a reasonable limitation on the consumption of alcohol must play an important role in that fight. Working people unanimously welcomed the intensification of the struggle against the production of illicit liquor. The prohibition against selling vodka in market stalls has been a great help.

True, the carrying out of this sensible ordinance of the Moscow City Soviet is being poorly supervised. The street drink shops have been done away with, but go into one of the large Moscow delicatessens, let's say the one on Smolensk Square, on paydays and days off. Liquors and vodka are sold there "without waiting." There is a legion of "regulars" standing beside the counter and the wrapping table. They pass a glass around among those who want a drink. Right before the eyes of the administration and the customers, Moscow Bitter Vodka is poured out in "rounds." And no one pays any attention to it. Vodka is even sold to adolescents in the stores and market booths. There are still many market booths that supply glasses on request with the sale of a half liter, and a round of drinks is poured on the spot.

The spread of alcoholism is greatly aided by the harmful habits and pseudo-folk customs that drinkers frequently pass off as time-honored folk traditions.

A young fellow from a working family went to work at a factory after finishing secondary school. On his first payday he came home late and very drunk. Having taken off his coat, the fellow gave his mother a few rubles.

"Why so little, Tolya? Or did you work poorly?" asked his mother disappointedly.

"No, no. I earned enough, all right. But you know I had to stand treat for the foreman, the brigade leader, and the boys. We went to a beer hall and had a bit to drink."

His mother shook her head in distress.

"And I wanted to buy you a silk shirt — a blue one. But you went off to the beer hall."

"Leave off nagging the boy, Mother. You've got to understand that it's his first pay check," the father interceded sympathetically. "That's the way it's been done for years. It's the custom."

To a lot of people, visiting, getting together with friends and passing the time of day means, above all, drinking. Invite friends to dinner or for tea and pastry without vodka and they are offended. Drinking is done on the sly at student evening affairs. The young men consider it "bad form" not to drink, and so they make wry faces, but they drink; they mix vodka with beer and they serve drinks to the girls. And Young Communist League organizations take a complacent view of this situation. But among Young Communists it used to be considered shameful and unethical to drink vodka.

I had occasion to spend New Year's Eve with a certain family. The room we were in was large and attractive; a crystal chandelier hung from the white ceiling. The guests sat around an oval table and drank. Our host's son, a boy of four, rode around and around the table on a three-wheeler. He was very pale and skinny.

I turned to my hostess, a plump woman in the pink of health, and said:

"Was your son ill recently?"

"No, it's just that he eats so terribly."

The youngster rode up to his father and asked for some wine.

"Give him some. Give Valerya some Cahors wine. Let him celebrate the New Year," came a chorus of drunken voices.

The father poured a bit into a glass, and the son drank it off with the practiced hand of an adult.

"Misha, why are you teaching him bad habits?" the wife said angrily.

But the guests butted in:

"That's nothing! Let him learn. You have to make a real man of him!"

For some people, alcohol has become their companion in happiness and sorrow, and a measure of the recompense for one's labor. The purchase of an overcoat or moving to a new apartment necessarily "calls for a little drink." Moving one's things and reaching an agreement on redecorating the apartment are all measured out "in half-liters."

It seems to me that our public, the *aktiv* of Soviets, trade unions, and the Young Communist League must all wage a decisive and merciless battle against these old customs which cannot be reconciled with the norms of Communist morality and which are doing enormous harm to the people's health and to socialist society.

Much can be done by our art: by the theater, the motion pictures, and vaudeville. Unfortunately, these media very rarely raise the theme of the fight against alcoholism. Aside from K. Finn's very weak play *Anna's Mistake,* not a single play has been produced in recent years dealing with this important social theme.

In 1955, the Leningrad Film Studio put out two popular scientific films attacking alcohol. But since that time the movie-makers have not returned to this important problem. What is more, it is a rare film today that does not present some sort of drinking scene — either individual or collective drunkenness — with relish. On the screen, the drinking by both the positive and the negative characters is made "attractive." The films and plays that show the growth of our country's well-being laud alcoholic joys above all else. The pictures of happy families on television and in the newspapers necessarily show a bottle on the table.

Mass hygiene propaganda is being poorly conducted. In 1954, publishing houses and hygiene education centers published only 38 pamphlet articles; in 1955, only 24; in 1956, seven; and in 1957, five. Depressing figures! Do not such facts attest to a lack of concern? In 1957, the All-Union Society for the Dissemination of Political and Scientific Knowledge published only one lecture in Moscow against alcohol. Last year no lectures at all against alcoholism were given in the Society's central lecture halls in Moscow.

There are many ways to fight alcoholism. It is necessary above all to put an end to in-difference. It is time to declare drunks disturbers of the peace and violators of the working people's interests. Various measures can be taken. After drunks have been sent to the drunk sobering-off cells, they should not be let off scot-free, but it should be mandatory that their conduct be reported to their place of work.

I believe the time has come to create a mass public society "For Healthy Everyday Life" that would combat harmful habits, customs and prejudices; that would propagandize the principles of people's hygiene and help the Party and the Soviets to bring up the younger generation hale and healthy.

I am not urging asceticism. Our country consumes less alcohol than many capitalist countries. But Soviet society cannot be indifferent to alcoholism. We must conduct hygiene education work among the masses on a broader basis — particularly among young people. The interests of the Soviet people's health, happiness, and welfare demand it.

THE FAMILY

59

Family and Inheritance in Soviet Law

Vladimir Gsovski

(1947)

The fate of the family in Russia has excited as much interest as that of any other institution. In classical Marxist theory the family is seen as essentially an institution for the purpose of holding and transmitting property, and thus as quite thoroughly corrupted. What happened to it, and to what seems an equally indispensable institution, inheritance, is revealed in this suggestive analysis by Dr.

*Reprinted from "Family and Inheritance in Soviet Law," The Russian Review, Vol. 7 (1947), pp. 71–87, by permission of the author and the publisher.

Gsovski. Although the article was written in 1947, there appear to have been no significant changes in the relevant Soviet laws since that time.

Marriage, divorce, and inheritance were among the first institutions to be affected by Soviet revolutionary decrees.† In December 1917, during the second month of the Soviet regime, two decrees appeared. One introduced divorce upon consent of both spouses or even upon the request of one. In both instances, no statement of grounds was required. As Brandenburgsky, professor of law, commented later: "A dissoluble marriage, and not a life-long union, was the first principle of the new legislation." The second decree substituted civil marriage for religious marriage, which had been the dominant form of marriage under Russian pre-Soviet law.

The meager provisions of these decrees were replaced in 1918 by a *Code of Laws Relating to Acts of Civil Status* — marriage, family, and guardianship. The Code followed in the main the decrees but showed a radical departure from the traditional family concept. "Birth itself," declared the Code, "shall be the basis of the family. No differentiation whatsoever shall be made between relationships by birth, whether in or out of wedlock." This provision was given a retroactive effect. Brandenburgsky commented upon this principle, which was sustained until 1944, that "Soviet legislation has completely detached the family relationship from the marital relationship. Family relationship or consanguinity is not based with us upon marriage but upon birth." The Code emphasized that children have no rights to the property of the parents and vice versa. While stating the parental duty to take care of the minor children and their education, the Code failed to provide for the parental authority or for the responsibility of parents for their children. The duty of parents to give maintenance to their children as well as the duty of children to support parents was conditioned by the fact of childrens' or parents' destitution and inability to work. This duty of support was recognized only insofar as the children "were not pro-

---

† The present article is derived from a chapter in the author's *Soviet Civil Law*, 2 vols., Ann Arbor, Mich., University of Michigan Law School, 1948.

vided for from public or state funds," and the parents did not receive old age pensions or other forms of social security.

However, the most radical departure from the traditional concept of marriage and divorce was carried out much later in the *Code on Domestic Relations* enacted in 1926. In this respect the Soviet law took a course contrary to the doctrine of Marxist philosophy according to which family relations are conditioned by "the mode of production of commodities." Little credence may be given to the contention of a Soviet law textbook of 1938 that "the Socialist Revolution which has created new social relations in the production and distribution of commodities and in the sphere of culture and everyday life, is also creating new Socialist family relations." Thus, it was the Code enacted in 1926, at the time of a general relaxation in the pursuit of Socialist reconstruction, that showed the most radical departure from the family law known to the capitalist countries. Declaration of the victory of a Socialist economic order made in the 1936 Constitution was followed by gradual withdrawal of the innovations in family law.

The fate of inheritance under the Soviet regime was somewhat different. As early as the fourth month of the Soviet regime the abolition of inheritance was bluntly declared. It was admitted, within certain limits, with the advent of the New Economic Policy in 1922, when several concessions to capitalism were made in law. Since then, the inheritance of property has become firmly entrenched, and its original restrictions have been progressively reduced.

Under the First Five Year Plan (1929–1933) the rigid enforcement of a socialist economic order was resumed, private enterprise was completely eliminated, and the Constitution of 1936 officially announced that socialism was achieved in the Soviet Union, all the basic instruments of production having been assigned to government property. However, the inheritance of property was written into the Constitution, succession rights were gradually extended, and a greater freedom in bequeathing individual property was recognized.

Thus, both the family and inheritance were challenged by the early Soviet laws, but both have shown a stubborn vitality and proved to be indispensable institutions even in a Socialist regime, which the Soviet State officially claims to be. In the following pages an analysis is offered of the successive stages in the transformation of Soviet legislation affecting family and inheritance.

Marriage and Divorce

The Code on Domestic Relations enacted for the R.S.F.S.R., the largest and leading state of the Soviet Union, on October 22, 1926, was in the main followed by all other Soviet republics. This Code was not only at variance with the former Russian law, but also made Soviet civil marriage totally different from civil marriage in any other country. The Code of 1918 prescribed that "only a civil (Soviet) marriage registered in the Civil Status Record, should produce the rights and duties of spouses"; it denied any legal status to religious marriage. (The effect of religious marriage antecedent to the law or the establishment of the Soviet regime in a given locality was maintained.)

The Code of 1926 used a different language. A more than terminological significance was attached to the word "registration." The provisions of the Code suggested that such registration was not, strictly speaking, equivalent to the celebration of a marriage. It supplied only the best proof that a marriage existed, until the contrary was established in court. "The registration of marriage," read the Code, "shall furnish conclusive evidence of the existence of the state of matrimony."

In accordance with the concept of registration as mere evidence of marriage, the Code instructed the courts what "evidence of marital cohabitation, in case the marriage was not registered," should be sufficient for the court. These were "the fact of cohabitation, combined with a common household, evidence of marital relations before third parties or in personal correspondence and other documents, mutual financial support, the raising of children in common if supported by circumstantial evidence, and the like." Moreover, "persons who live in a state of *de facto* matrimonial relations, not registered in a manner prescribed by law, shall be entitled to legalize their status at any time, stating the period of actual cohabitation." Thus, on the one hand, any informal cohabitation had the effect of marriage with respect to marital property rights and succession rights of the spouses and children, if duly proved. On the other hand, a religious marriage had no legal effect in itself, but if it was followed by factual marital relations, it assumed the status of a *de facto* marriage with all the legal consequences thereof.

The rights of children to maintenance and succession did not depend on their being born in registered wedlock. The parent–child relationship remained totally independent of marriage, registered or not. Fatherhood, if established in court, entailed the liability of supplying maintenance and support and gave the right of succession to children born in or out of wedlock. But the qualifying clause making the duty of mutual support of parents and children dependent upon the absence of public or government support, was omitted. The State evidently did not visualize a social security system as a substitute for support by next of kin.

Soviet divorce under the Code of 1926 had no less striking features than Soviet marriage. Either spouse had complete freedom to register the discontinuance of marital life without stating the reasons therefor. The divorce was recorded by the Civil Registry Office, not only upon a declaration by both spouses, but also upon a unilateral declaration by either spouse of his or her desire to discontinue conjugal life. Neither a statement of reasons for such action nor any judicial proceedings were required. The other party was summoned, but in case of failure to appear the entry of the divorce in the Civil Registry Record was made, and the party had no right to oppose the divorce. In other words, just as Soviet marriage was merely a registration of existing marriage, the Soviet divorce was not a divorce, but a registration of the fact that marital life was discontinued.

Several other provisions of Soviet statutes contributed to a new background for sexual life in the Soviet Union. In 1920 abortion was permitted. The Soviet Criminal Code did not provide for punishment of bigamy, incest, adultery, and homosexuality. Polygamy was punishable only in regions where Mohammedanism prevailed among the population. Other provisions of Soviet law sought to undermine the importance of family ties and make children independent of parents and irresponsible. Prior to 1935, children were not held criminally responsible before the age of 16. Juvenile delinquents were handled not by courts but by special boards which were supposed to apply only measures of an educational nature. Minors under 14 were not liable for any damage caused outside of criminal offenses (torts). On the other hand, parents were not liable for damage caused by their children who reached the age of 14.

There may still be doubt in respect to the social objectives sought then by the Soviet legislators. Was such legislation visualized as a preparatory step toward a society without the family, where the State takes care of the children and the union of man and woman is left to the unlimited freedom of personal inclination, or did the legislators believe in the monogamous family as a union for life, considering only any legal safeguards for such family superfluous? Many statements bluntly supporting the first hypothesis were made by prominent Soviet leaders in the early years of the Soviet regime. For instance, Madam Kollontay, at one time diplomatic representative of the Soviet Union in Norway, writer on the family under Communism, and a prominent member of the Old Bolshevik guard, wrote in 1919 that "the family has ceased to be a necessity both for its members and for the State." Likewise, Bukharin, who, though later executed as a traitor, was for a long time a recognized theoretician of the Soviet regime, characterized the family as "a formidable stronghold of all the turpitudes of the old regime." An anticipation of the disappearance of the family in the Socialist state is evident in the following explanation of the *Soviet Code on Domestic Relations* given in 1927 by Professor Brandenburgsky, the author of standard texts on the subject:

> Until Socialism is achieved the individual family is inescapable. . . . We undoubtedly are approaching public upbringing of the children, free labor schools, the widest social security at the expense of the State. If at present we maintain the duty of mutual support within the family, we do it because the State cannot yet, for the time being, replace the family in this respect. . . . The family creating a series of rights and duties between the spouses, the parents and children, will certainly disappear in the course of time and will be replaced by governmental organization of public education and social security.

Moreover, certain provisions of the Code led the Supreme Court of the R.S.F.S.R. to a tacit recognition of the legality of bigamy and

a loose sexual life. Thus, the court affirmed a decision of a lower court by which two women were declared *de facto* wives of a decedent and awarded both a share in the estate.

A reverse trend began about 1935. In that year the parents were made responsible for disorderly conduct and hooliganisms of their children and held liable to fine, up to 200 rubles, by police authorities. Parents and guardians were also made liable jointly with minors, who reached the age of 14, whenever these caused damages. It was also enacted in 1935 that "minors who have reached twelve years of age and are indicted for larceny, violence causing bodily injury, murder, or attempted murder shall be tried by the criminal court, which may impose upon them any measure of punishment." In 1940 this rule was extended to minors who have reached twelve years of age and who committed acts endangering railroad traffic, such as loosening of rails, placing objects on the rails, and the like.

In the middle thirties, a series of laws were enacted making divorce slightly more difficult and expensive. Abortion was made a punishable offense in 1936, and homosexuality in 1934.

In palpable discord with the concept of marriage advocated before, with the statutory provisions and rulings by the courts, new principles were announced in the Soviet press. On May 28, 1936, *Pravda* commented on the prohibition of abortion and the increase of fees for divorces:

> So-called free love and loose sexual life are altogether bourgeois and have nothing in common either with Socialist principles and ethics or with the rules of behavior of a Soviet citizen. Marriage is the most serious affair in life. . . . Fatherhood and motherhood become virtues in the Soviet land.

Quoting these statements, Boshko, a Soviet professor of law, wrote in the official periodical of the Attorney General:

> Marriage, basically, and in the spirit of Soviet law, is in principle essentially a lifelong union. . . . Moreover, marriage receives its full life-blood and value for the Soviet State only if there is birth of children, proper upbringing, and if the spouses experience the highest happiness of motherhood and fatherhood.

The author sought to reconcile these ideas with the then existing laws. Boshko argued that: "Freedom of divorce is not in conflict with marriage as a lifelong union, but on the contrary it presupposes such freedom as its foundation [which may admit of some exceptions]." However, this reconciliation was only verbal. The tenor of the discussion sounded like the inauguration of a program of support of the family along traditional lines, and the recent Soviet legislation on marriage and divorce was the implementation of such a program. It has gone even further than in many countries where only civil marriage is recognized. It bars common-law marriage and bastardy proceedings, and relieves a father of the duty of supporting his illegitimate child. It also creates illegitimacy.

Since July 8, 1944, only a marriage registered with the Civil Registry Office has had the legal effect of a marriage and created the rights and duties of husband and wife and fatherhood uniformly in the whole of the Soviet Union. Persons who were living in *de facto* marital relations prior to July 8, 1944, were allowed, however, to legalize their marital status by registering the marriage and indicating the time which had elapsed since the beginning of their conjugal life.

The mother of a child born before July 8, 1944, outside of a registered marriage may claim alimony for the child from the person who is the natural father of the child only if he has been entered as such by the Civil Registry Office, and such children have succession rights to the property of the person so entered. But all children born after July 8, 1944, outside of a registered marriage have no succession rights to the father's property and may not claim the father's name. Nor are such fathers liable for maintenance and support of children born outside a registered marriage. However, mothers of children born after July 8, 1944, outside a registered marriage receive aid from the government in a small fixed amount. Thus, children born outside a registered marriage after July 8, 1944, are comparable to illegitimate children in other countries, even if such terminology is not used. It remains to be seen whether the change in legal status will be followed in daily life by a social stigma on illegitimacy. This at least has been the story of illegitimacy in the past.

It is also significant that a recent law seeks to create an atmosphere of solemnity for the registration of Soviet marriage. Local authorities have been ordered to supply the Civil Registry Offices with well-furnished quarters appropriate for the celebration, with separate waiting room, and to keep them in good order. The date for registration must be arranged in advance; it takes place in the presence of the prospective bride and groom, and, if they wish, of their parents and friends. A certificate is then handed over to the newlyweds in the presence of a representative of the local administration. The managers of the government establishments and the collective farms are advised to furnish the newlyweds transportation to the Registry Office and to help them buy furniture, bedding, etc., for cash at fixed government prices.

No less radical is the change with regard to divorce. Since July 8, 1944, divorce has been granted only by the courts and only for reasons which the courts deem justifiable. Such reasons are not specified by statute and are left to the discretion of the courts. Divorce proceedings pass through two stages, each in a different court. The petition for divorce must be filed with the lower court, the people's court, by either spouse or both of them jointly. The petitioner must specify the reasons for which divorce is sought and must present witnesses and other evidence of the facts alleged. The people's court orders notice of the filing of the divorce suit to be published in the local newspaper at the expense of the plaintiff. The people's court does not decide the case but merely prepares it and attempts to reconcile the spouses; it summons the spouses to appear in person, hears them and the witnesses in order to ascertain the reasons for divorce, and takes steps toward their reconciliation. Should this court fail to reconcile the spouses, the petitioner may then file a complaint for divorce with the next higher court, which hears the case in public and grants the divorce if it finds the petition is based on good reasons. At the request of either party, the court may order the case to be heard *in camera*. The divorce decree may be appealed in accordance with the general rules. The Government fee for filing the petition for divorce is one hundred rubles and from five hundred to two thousand rubles for registration of the divorce according to the determination of the court. Thus, it is now more difficult to obtain a divorce in Soviet Russia than in many capitalist countries.

The unlimited discretion of Soviet courts of first instance in granting or refusing the divorce signifies a departure from the original Soviet philosophy. The latitude of the departure appears striking upon comparison of this power with the following statements of Lenin:

> Reactionaries are against the freedom of divorce. They are calling for a cautious treatment of such a freedom and are shouting that it means dissolution of the family. But democracy considers that the reactionaries are hypocritical and are, in fact, defending the omnipotence of the police and the bureaucracy, the privilege of one sex, and the worst kind of oppression of women, that, in fact, freedom of divorce does not mean dissolution of family relations, but, on the contrary, their strengthening on democratic grounds, the only possible and stable grounds in a civilized society. . . . It is impossible to be a democrat and a socialist without immediately demanding complete freedom of divorce, because the absence of such freedom is the utmost oppression of the subdued sex, woman — although it does not take brains to gather that the recognition of freedom to leave one's husband is not an invitation for all wives to leave their husbands.

As late as 1938 the Soviet jurists insisted that the Soviets "do not have and could not have what is known in the capitalist countries as divorce proceedings." Yet, the Soviet divorce proceedings, after 1945, are stricter and offer the parties less privacy and certainty as to the final outcome than those of many capitalist countries.

Thus the Soviets have rediscovered the value of family life and strong family ties for the maintenance of sound public morals and the increase of population of a country which went through the calamity of a devastating war. Soviet marriage has at present the features of a normal marriage. But, on the other hand, recent Soviet legislation, though inconsistent with the earlier Soviet laws, shows a consistency of policy of interference of the State with the family life of the citizen. In the early stage, Soviet laws sought to disrupt and weaken the family ties. At present the interference goes the other way. Under the old provisions of the Code of 1926, a religious marriage not followed by a civil registration but coupled with actual marital life may have

passed for a *de facto* matrimony and given the spouses and the children rights of succession and maintenance. Since 1945, such possibility is altogether excluded. Again, divorce, regardless of the ground, is not a matter of right, but is left to the unlimited discretion of the Soviet court, which is an obedient instrument of government policy. Any quarrel between the conjugal partners, if brought before the court, may result in divorce only if the court considers it in conformity with "the general policies of the Soviet government," to which the court must resort under Section 4 of the Code of Civil Procedure in absence of statutory provisions bearing upon the case. No party, on the other hand, is guaranteed by law that the guilt of the other party will be deemed a sufficient ground for divorce. Moreover, the Soviet Attorney General may enter any civil suit, at any stage of proceedings, and may petition the Supreme Court to reopen *ex officio* a case settled by a final judgment. The spirit of recent Soviet legislation on marriage is best exemplified perhaps by the law enacted in April 1947 which flatly prohibited marriage between Soviet citizens and aliens.

Inheritance

From the time of the Communist Manifesto of 1848, abolition of inheritance of property has been considered a cornerstone of the Socialist program. In fulfillment of this program, the first Soviet decree dealing with inheritance, proclaimed on April 27, 1918, bore the title "Concerning the Abolition of Inheritance" and stated outright: "Testate and intestate succession are abolished. Property of an owner (movable as well as immovable) becomes after his death the domain of the Russian Socialist Soviet Federal Republic."

However, a consistent application of the repeal of succession seemed to be beyond the power of the Soviet government. The same decree permitted an estate not exceeding 10,000 rubles to "pass to immediate management and disposal" of the decedent's close relatives who had lived with him (Art. IX). Furthermore, "until a decree on universal social insurance is issued" close relatives of a decedent who left an estate exceeding 10,000 rubles were allowed to receive from the estate a sum necessary for self support (Art. IX).

Further exemption was made on May 21, 1919, regarding the estates left by the peasants.

It must be borne in mind that, under the Imperial law, the general inheritance law (Vol. X, Part I, of the Imperial Code of Laws) was not applicable to the succession among the peasants regarding the land which they received at the time of the Emancipation Act in 1861 (the so-called "alloted" land or *nadel*), and property pertaining to farming on such lands. These lands constituted roughly 80 per cent of the total area of arable land held by the peasants on the eve of the Revolution. The tenure of such land and property incidental to farming (buildings, livestock, implements, and the like) were considered to be undivided property of all the members of a household (*dvor*), blood relatives, and strangers living and working under the same roof. A peasant, even if he were the head of the household, could not dispose of such property by testament, and it descended according to the local customs. Although these customs varied considerably from place to place, the principle of the undivided joint ownership of the entire household was very much in evidence everywhere and was recognized by the governing Senate, the supreme court of Imperial Russia.

Now, in spite of the abolition of the inheritance in 1918, the Commissar of Justice issued on May 21, 1919, an "interpretation" to the effect that properties belonging to a peasant household are not subject to the 10,000-ruble limit of an estate and were to remain in the possession and use of the spouse and the relatives of the deceased who had lived in his household, regardless of the value of the estate. Soviet legal writers later considered this provision to be a tacit recognition of the peasant customary law of succession.

In any event, the Soviet government had, at the time, no adequate apparatus to check upon all the estates in Russia. With regard to the peasants, the retreat from the abolition of inheritance was officially recognized by the above interpretation, while in the cities, according to Soviet writers, nobody had reported the estates of decedents to the authorities, these usually being divided among the individuals who happened to be present at the time of death. No estate actually taken by the State was recorded during the time that the law abolishing succession was in force. It remained a purely declaratory statement. There was,

however, not much left to be inherited. The confiscatory Soviet decrees practically destroyed private ownership of all objects except those serving bare consumption needs. Private ownership of land was abolished, the bulk of private housing, major industrial and commercial enterprises, the means of transportation, banks, stocks, and bonds, as well as private bank accounts, were confiscated.

With the advent of the New Economic Policy in 1922, protection of property rights and inheritance was promised, and the Soviet Civil Code which went into force on January 1, 1923 introduced inheritance, although with some restrictions (Section 416 *et seq.*). However, the Soviet leaders did not at that time consider inheritance to be a sound institution. Goikhbarg, the principal compiler of the Civil Code, bluntly characterized the recognition of inheritance as a concession to the capitalist law "in principle and in practice," a concession permitted within strict limits for temporary economic reasons, *viz.*, "to stimulate the accumulation of private wealth as permitted by law." This view was professed by Soviet jurists for a considerable period of time.

Thus as late as 1938, after the completion of the First Five Year Plan, the official textbook edited by Ginsburg and Pashukanis stated plainly that there is no place and no need for inheritance of property under a Communist regime. There is no place for it, because there must be no unearned income in the Communist system; because the able-bodied will work and thus have their living secured, while the disabled will be taken care of by the State through social insurance.

The actual development of Soviet legislation, however, shows a different tendency.

The Civil Code, as promulgated in 1922, sought to limit inheritance: (a) by setting at a fixed amount of 10,000 rubles the maximum permissible net value of an estate (Section 416); and (b) by restricting the circle of persons to whom the estate might descend by intestate succession or by will (Section 418).

Thus, estates exceeding 10,000 gold rubles net value were declared to be the property of the State. However, rights arising from contracts between private persons and the government descended without any limitation in value to the heirs, and the value of these rights was not computed as part of an estate. The same was true of certain insurance premiums, according to the amendment of June 1, 1925 (Section 375a of the Civil Code).

If the net value of an estate exceeded 10,000 gold rubles, the estate was held in joint ownership by the State and the takers, and a special procedure was prescribed for the dissolution of the joint ownership and the distribution of the estate.

Again, the limitation of inheritance by the fixed value of 10,000 rubles met with practical difficulties. Moreover, the Soviet government decided "to aid the possibility of the continued existence of commercial and industrial enterprises after the decease of their owners and to establish more attractive conditions for the creation and influx into the country of material and resources." Consequently, this maximum permissible value of the estate was abolished on February 15, 1926. Since then, a heavy progressive tax, up to 90 per cent, has alone served as a check upon value passing by inheritance. However, even this restriction disappeared in 1943, when the inheritance tax was abolished.

Thus, there is today no limitation on the value of an inheritance in Soviet Russia. A governmental fee is collected for the issuance of inheritance certificates; the scale is progressive, and the highest rate is 10 per cent. There remains, however, an indirect practical limitation based upon the monopoly of the U.S.S.R. State Bank in dealing with precious metals and foreign exchange: if such "foreign exchange values" belong to the estate, they must be deposited with the State Bank, and the inheritors receive only their equivalent in Soviet currency according to the official rate.

Another limitation on inheritance under the Civil Code consisted in restricting the circle of persons who may inherit. Although testaments were permitted, the testator had to select the beneficiaries from among the persons to whom the law assigned the estate in absence of a testament. Consequently, in fact, the testator could only change the shares of his heirs as defined by law or deprive one or all of them of succession. In such a case, the share of the disinherited person reverted to the State. Thus, whether under a will or in absence of a will, only the following persons could inherit until March 15, 1945: direct descendants (children, grandchildren, and great-grandchildren), the surviving spouse, and disabled and destitute relatives or strangers who were dependents of the deceased for at least one year before his death. Descendants inherited regardless of whether they were born in or out of wedlock. Neither parents nor collateral relatives such as brothers, sisters, nephews, etc., had any succession rights. After 1928, it was allowed to bequeath to the State, the Communist Party, and other organizations. Since 1928, children of the deceased under the age of 18 were guaranteed a share in the estate regardless of the will of the deceased.

The narrow limits of succession were gradually extended by Soviet legislation: first, in 1930 and 1935, some exceptions with regard to specific types of property were introduced; later, in 1945, the circle of eligible heirs was radically changed. The scheme of limitations on free disposition by will was abandoned first in regard to certain types of property. This was accomplished by declaring such property not part of the estate. In this category were included in 1930 insurance premiums, several kinds of government loans, stocks and bonds, and, in 1935, other deposits with government banks, including money deposits. The owner may dispose of such assets freely, not by a will but by a written assignment addressed to the bank and indicating the person to whom deposits shall be paid after the death of the depositor.

Thus, in addition to property that forms the estate of a deceased person and comes under the limitations prescribed for inheritance, there is property not included in the estate. This descends at the discretion of the owner and has not been subject to the inheritance tax. Property of this nature, money deposits and securities, are considered in any capitalist country to be *prima facie* capital. The Soviet regime started some thirty years ago with the abolition and confiscation of such property. At present, in theory, there exists the possibility of unlimited accumulation of private wealth in money and securities in Soviet Russia, if deposited in certain government banks. However, one circumstance is supposed to limit this possibility. This is the lack of legitimate and profitable avenues of activity that would facilitate such accumulation of capital, because private industrial and commercial enterprises are practically eliminated.

The rigid scheme of testate and intestate succession has been radically changed by the

Edicts of March 14, 1945, and of June 12, 1945.

With regard to intestate succession, the Edict introduced a system of inheritance by classes somewhat similar to that of the Code Napoleon, the German Civil Code of 1900, and other European codes. Three classes of heirs by operation of law were established so that the heirs of the second class inherit only in the absence of any heirs of the first class, or on their refusal to take the estate, and the heirs of the third class inherit in the absence of heirs of the second class.

As before, the first class embraces children and their descendants, the spouse, and actual dependents, whether or not related to the deceased, but adds to this group disabled (unable to earn) parents of the decedent. In the absence of these persons, the heirs are the able-bodied parents of the deceased. In their absence, the estate devolves upon the heirs of the third class — the brothers and sisters (Section I of the Edict; Section 418 of the Civil Code as amended June 12, 1945).

The testator, in making his will, is at liberty "to bequeath all his property or a part of it to one or several persons from among those belonging to either of the three above-mentioned classes." Consequently, in contrast to the situation under the old provisions, he may leave bequests to either of his parents or to any of his brothers or sisters. He may not, however, "deprive his minor children, or other heirs who are unable to earn, of the portion which would belong to them under intestate succession." In addition, the testator may, subject to certain limitations, leave bequests to "governmental agencies and public institutions." The Communist Party is not specifically mentioned, but there is no doubt that it comes within the meaning of a "public organization."

If there are no persons belonging to either of the three classes of heirs outlined above, "the property may be bequeathed to any person."

In line with the general tendency toward broader recognition of succession rights, the original provisions of the Civil Code creating an especially favorable condition for the acquisition· of estates by the government (escheat) were also changed. The Code required the heir absent from the place of estate to appear within six months and expressly declare the acceptance of the estate. In case of

failure to do so or the renunciation of the estate, the share of the heir reverted to the State. But several court decisions and executive orders sought to soften the rigidity of this rule. The renunciation was construed very strictly and authorities handling the estate were ordered to advise the absent heirs. Finally, on March 15, 1945, it was enacted that the share of an heir who renounced inheritance or failed to accept it in due time goes to the other heirs.

There is also another aspect of the reform affecting children born out of wedlock (registered marriage). Under the original provisions, children born out of wedlock had succession rights equal to those of children born in wedlock (marriage registered with civil authorities). Under the Edicts of the Presidium of July 8, 1944, and March 15, 1945, children born out of wedlock have no right of succession after their fathers. Such a child may not claim the name of its father. Nor can its mother use the father for maintenance and support of the child. Thus, though the name illegitimate child is not used, the children born out of wedlock obtain a legal status totally different from that of children born in wedlock and all conditions are now in evidence to produce the stigma of illegitimacy.

The inheritance law as outlined in the Civil Code and its amendments has only a limited application to farming families. Like the peasant household under the Imperial law, the farming households in the collective farms remain units with a community property of its own kind. The membership in a collective farm is individual. Every member of a household belonging to a collective farm receives his own share in collectively obtained income in proportion to his personal contribution of labor. This share forms his own personal ownership, constitutes his estate, and descends according to general rules of the Soviet inheritance law. But the house and garden plot (not more than 2.47 acres) appurtenant to the dwelling are assigned by the collective farm to a household, a family, not to an individual. Likewise the house itself is the property of the family. Each family is allowed to conduct its own "midget" farming on this plot and sell the produce on the open market. All the properties appertaining to such farming constitute the community property of the family. The share of a deceased member remains in the joint ownership of the household and does not descend by inheritance. These rules established by the Land Code of 1922 for independent farming households under the N.E.P. are still applicable to households in the collective farms, according to Soviet jurists. The Soviet law itself is silent. The old-fashioned peasant family household, though unwelcome, is an indispensable element of the collectivized system. Thus it is allowed to exist without explicit provisions of law defining the relations of the members of the household.

It may also be mentioned that Soviet law introduced community property of husband and wife in urban families in contrast to complete separation of property under Imperial law. Thus, in case of death the surviving spouse is entitled to his or her share in the common marital property, in addition to sharing as an heir in the estate.

Recent Soviet legislation concerning inheritance is in obvious contradiction with the theory of disappearance of inheritance with the advent of Socialism, professed by Soviet jurists after the restoration of inheritance in 1922. The Soviet Constitution of 1936 officially terms Socialism the social order achieved in Soviet Russia, yet inheritance under this social order bears all the essential features of inheritance in a capitalist country. As a result, Soviet legal theory has recently shown an astounding shift. Legal writings on the eve of World War II were mostly silent on the future disappearance of inheritance (e.g., Textbook on Civil Law of 1938). More recent works (Textbook of 1944) definitely shelve such disappearance to the most remote idyllic future beyond any human prediction, when, according to the expectations of Marx, "together with the many-sided development of individuals, the productive forces shall also grow and all the sources of collective wealth flow in a full current." But at the present stage of "victorious Socialism," Soviet jurists argue that inheritance "promotes protection of personal property of the toilers, increases the productivity of labor, strengthening the Soviet family and fortifying the relationship of the citizens of the U.S.S.R. with the Socialist society." They rightly emphasize that "descent of property cannot be an irrelevant matter for a citizen of the U.S.S.R.," and that "succession appears to be

one of the stimuli for the development of personal ownership — for increasing the productivity of labor, and for fortifying the Socialist family." The earlier legal theories which characterized inheritance as a capitalist institution and declared inheritance under Soviet law to be a "private form of, or substitute for, social security" are at the present time declared "subversive" and their authors branded wrong-doers and wreckers. Paradoxically, in 1926 the removal of limitation of inheritance was officially motivated by the intention of securing "continued existence" of private enterprise (*supra*) but in 1938 and 1944 the abolition of this very private enterprise in Soviet Russia is given as the reason for inheritance of property as a sound institution of Soviet Socialist law.

Even the "abolition of inheritance" by the decree of 1918 is attempted to be explained away. Thus, a Soviet professor, Serebrovsky, who in 1927 wrote that the exceptions made to the law abolishing inheritance for small estates in 1918, "had nothing in common with the succession," has come to believe in 1945 that it is wrong, and that the "abolition of inheritance" declared at that time was not abolition but merely a transformation of inheritance. Other legal writers also share this opinion. At the present time, private enterprise is practically barred in the Soviet Union; there is no "capitalist private ownership" but "socialist ownership of the means of production" and "personal ownership" of articles of consumption and small housing. Therefore, the Soviet jurists argue that inheritance of property can no longer result in the resurrection of private enterprise and of capitalism. This, of course, is a matter of future development. It may be pointed out, however, that economic leveling is no longer attempted but is directly condemned in Soviet Russia. High wages for the executive and the technical personnel in government, industry, and commerce, extra remunerations and bonuses given to the above as well as to the inventors, scientists, writers, and artists, useful to the regime, permit very considerable accumulations of money and properties as compared to the meager earnings of ordinary laborers. Such capital can be invested in government stocks and bonds and may bring winnings in government lotteries. Only the future will show what will happen with this capital, if inherited and engrossed in the course of two or three generations. One thing is clear: the possibility of an unearned income for the coming generations is established under the Socialist regime of present-day Russia. Thus, in this field, as in many others, the Soviet leaders have had to sacrifice many of their original Socialist principles in order to keep things going and maintain the Communist Party in power.

60

Sex: From Free Love to Puritanism*

Vera S. Dunham

(1951)

Marx and Engels had little to say about sex, but what they did say leaned in favor of sexual freedom. Partly for this reason, and partly because of the breakdown in sexual mores often attendant upon war and revolution, the outside world often thought of the U.S.S.R. as the land of "free love." In fact, the official attitude has gone from one extreme to the other. Dr. Dunham maps these changes for us with excerpts from Soviet literature.

In Soviet eyes the Kinsey report is a revelation of the dirt and depravity into which American civilization has fallen. We Americans have sunk so low that we are interested only in sexual pathology. Our family has decayed, our morals have disintegrated. We are hardly human anymore. All this, say Soviet ideologists, was, of course, in the bourgeois cards. Therefore, "the bourgeois family decays and rots in the same measure as bourgeois society decays and rots!"

By contrast, true morality is possible only in the Marxist-Leninist-Stalinist part of the world. For only there has woman been liberated, only there is the moral code divested of its medieval

*Reprinted from "Sex in the Soviet Union," *The Russian Review*, Vol. 10 (1951), pp. 199–209, by permission of the author and the publisher.

shackles, only there is sex purified, and marriage become a voluntary union of free persons.

To be sure, the Soviet position on sex must seem, to the average American, as topsy-turvy as the proposition that South attacked North Korea. In the mind of the average American the notion that free love is a Communist invention is deeply entrenched.

The Years of Sexual Freedom

It is impossible to deny that one of the most important changes which came with the Russia Revolution of 1917 was the destruction of the traditional family. This was most certainly not planned by Lenin, architect number one, but it happened just the same. The family was literally torn apart by the impact of the external conditions such as Civil War, starvation, and mass migration in search of food.

But the family was torn apart internally also. Traditional values collapsed and revolutionary ones emerged out of the chaos. There was a quite sudden and jarring emancipation of woman, to whose emancipation, incidentally, the whole liberal world in the West had been looking forward. There emerged also the new idea that the child should belong to the State. There were indeed millions of disease-ridden, abandoned children — direct and cruel result of war and revolution — whom the State had to take care of.

Out of this atmosphere of seething uncertainty, changing values, and social disorganization there emerged an anarchistic attitude toward sex. "Free love" it was called and it became the reigning conception in the 1920's.

The new government declared that "marriage is a private act of the citizen which does not concern the state . . . a voluntary relationship undertaken by two citizens." Contraceptive information was disseminated, abortions were allowed, the stigma was taken from illegitimate children, divorce by mutual consent became a matter of course. Marriages, if they were contracted at all, were "registered" in a matter of minutes. All this was widely spread practice in the Marxist-Leninist part of the world during the 1920's.

The record of it is to be found in the literature of the period. For instance, in a comedy by Kataev, entitled *Squaring the Circle*, two married student couples, under the impact of the housing shortage, switch wives in no time at all. A crude treatment of the same theme is to be found in Malyshkin's novel, *Moon from the Left,* which dealt with sexual promiscuity within Communist Youth Organizations and which, incidentally, is banned today. In another novel of that period, also on the black list today, Pilnyak's *Mahogany,* a woman addicted to free love who expects a child from an unknown father, says:

> In the center of my attention was neither love nor my partner, but I myself and my emotions. I chose men, different men, in order to learn everything. I did not want to become pregnant, sex is joy; I did not think of the child. But I will manage it, and the State will help me. As to morals, I don't know what it means, I have been taught to forget it. Or perhaps I have my own morals. I am responsible only for myself . . .

Accompanying this sex-is-joy attitude was a great emphasis on the unadorned physiology of sex, a brazen depoetization of love. Take these harsh lines from Mayakovsky, a poet-laureat of the revolution, for example:

> We are fed up with heavenly candies,
> Give us rye-bread to feed on!
> We are fed up with cardboard passions,
> Give us a live wife to live with!

But the sex-is-joy attitude and the call for rye-bread did not outlast the 1920's.

The average Russian, the nondescript majority of those who endured the revolution (as distinct from those who brought it about), early became very critical of the fundamentally destructive nature of free love. In the late twenties a flood of jokes sprang up on the instability of marriages, on licentiousness, on seductions, on abortions, on alimony, on ludicrous judicial efforts to establish fatherhood. A husband, for example, comes home after a hard day's work anticipating domestic bliss. Instead, he finds at the door his suitcase packed with a note attached to it: "My dear, you are divorced."

The one and only great Soviet satirist, Michael Zoshchenko, tragically silenced in the purges of 1946, devoted much effort to uncovering the uglier sides of Soviet free love. He pictures for us a bridegroom who cannot locate the bride at his own wedding, because he had seen her before the ceremony only once, in a streetcar at that. The groom has a good time with assorted female wedding guests and gets a divorce the next morning without in the meantime having spotted his life's companion. Zoshchenko has also a shrewd lover who ahead of time extorts from his partner a written statement that she will have no claims on him should "something happen." In another Zoshchenko sketch, an alert business-like wife marries her own dapper husband off to another woman in order to collect matchmaker's fees. In still another, a judge busies himself in court with anthropological comparison of an infant nose and the proboscis of a denying-it-all reluctant father.

Sex and Love in the Service of the Revolution

Whether as a concession to public opinion, or whether simply capitulating in front of unshakable family preservation instincts, or whether because of a new policy of increasing population, the Soviet government, in due time, intervened and brought an end to the "free love" era.

Abortions became illegal in 1936. Divorce laws were revised, so that by 1944 simple mortals found it extremely difficult to obtain divorces. Motherhood medals, carrying with them lucrative state subsidies for large families, were instituted.

The reign of free love — or Red love — was succeeded by the regime of Stalinist Virtue. (The latter emerged as anything but red or flamboyant, but on the contrary enormously rigid and oppressive.)

No doubt the average American will be as suspicious of Stalinist Virtue as he was disdainful of earlier Communist Free Love. And he will be right. For if the notion of free love violates the American's sense of fair play, Stalinist Virtue will appear to him as an unbelievable attempt to regiment the individual through regulation of sexual impulses. A Soviet journal, *Novyi Mir,* explains what is meant by Stalinist Virtue, which has come into its own since the end of World War II: "A Soviet person cannot 'simply' love someone without criticism, without political and moral watchfulness." That is to say, political watchfulness must preside at the bed of two lovers. Or, more broadly: "Our Soviet citizen can no longer love only because of a natural drive. He wants his beloved to be worthy of his feeling, to possess the best Soviet qualities." That is to say, doctrinal orthodoxy must play a formative role in the love relationship.

Let us take for example, a love poem, "Tanya," recently published in *Oktiabr'*, a leading Soviet literary journal. In this poem, a young collective farmer visits his beloved, a crack team leader on a neighboring collective farm. In the room of his beloved there are not only geranium plants, but a map of the world hung on the wall. From another wall the portrait of Lysenko, the "great" Soviet biologist, the pupil of the yet greater Michurin, "leans over her table." The young man begins by insisting that he came only for technical advice. He is puzzled by his sweetheart's phenomenal successes in harvesting and he wants to know her secret. With a twinkle in her eye she tells him:

> Michurin leads my brigade
> In the field.
> It's very simple.
> In our work
> We are one
> With science.
> Every husk
> We can account for,
> Of every blade
> We take stock.

But the young man is not too bright, for he wants to know what else goes into the secret of her miraculous productivity. Somewhat annoyed, the lady retorts:

> You didn't get it?
> *This is* the whole secret.

Unaccountably jumping several associations, the young man suddenly asks:

> You don't love me, Tanya, do you?
> You don't love me, no?

Dumbfounded by his own audacity, the meek young man departs without waiting for an answer. But as he passes under the window, his true love calls him back.

> Listen, lad!
> As farewell
> I want to tell you something.
> If you win in competition,
> Send your go-betweens,
> But if not,

> If you lag behind,
> Don't come near me!

This is not a parody. Nor is it the joke of some lightheaded Soviet editor. On the contrary, it is considered in the Soviet Union an admirable flight of poetic imagination. Of all things, this is a love poem, or as much of a love poem as a Soviet reader can find these days.

The puerility of this poem, garbed in the cheap and phoney diction of village folksiness, is obvious to the American reader even in translation. But to hold an across-cultural-barriers trial of Soviet esthetics would be futile. It's the ethics of the poem, the didactic message which it contains that is of interest to us. Here we have the perpetual glorification of competitive Stakhanovism, of the overfulfilment of labor norms (with the help of Michurin's ghost and Lysenko's portrait at that). But most fantastic of all, love is conceived as reward, as a mere device for stimulating competition in the collection of grain.

But at least, we now have some conception — if only a very partial conception — of the objective of Stalinist Virtue, namely, the attempted subordination of the sex drive to the requirements of the Five Year Plan. Stalinist Virtue has, however, broader implications.

There was published in Soviet Russia not long ago a popular pamphlet entitled *Love, Marriage, and the Family in Socialist Society*. In this pamphlet the author imprudently admitted that the stability of happiness in marriage could be destroyed because "the depth, intensity, and durability of human feelings differ from individual to individual." This being the case, the author had further to admit that divorce occasionally was necessary even in *socialist* society. "The right of divorce is exercised only in exceptional cases when a common life becomes unendurable for biological, psychological, or other reasons."

This author was at once attacked in the Soviet press. He was "guilty" of placing the Soviet family at the mercy of "biological factors," whereas he should have known, as any good Soviet citizen knew, that the reasons for which divorces are sometimes permitted in *socialist* society are quite different. What are they? They are not biological, but *civic*. Divorce is possible only when one spouse realizes that his or her partner is an *unworthy* citizen. This "Soviet truth" is well illustrated by a recent novel, loudly acclaimed, Mal'zev's *With the Whole Heart,* in which a wife curses her love for her husband and refuses to have anything to do with him when she discovers that, during the war, he fled from the front. In the Soviet motherland, a potent Soviet literary critic remarks approvingly,

> it is impossible to speak of the life and fate of a family as of something specifically personal, independent, and separate. The Soviet family is a particle of the socialist nation. Therefore its life is inseparable from the life of the country.

And so the virtuous wife spurns the husband who failed to defend the socialist society.

The Soviet family is thus, on the surface, more stable by far than its American counterpart, for the Soviet couple is divorced only in case one of the partners is guilty of treason. This extraordinary stability is a stability based not on biological factors (much less the moonlit nonsense of decadent and shameless Hollywood) but rather upon "respect for work":

> Respect for work [is] one of the tenets of Communist morality. Love does not, consequently, evolve independently of work, but is fused with work. Work is the cementing basis, the source of close comradely ties between lovers.

What emerges as solely formative in intimate human relationships is WORK. And we must bear in mind that WORK is always defined as that which *directly* and *immediately* serves the needs of the Soviet State.

We may summarize all this by saying that the Stalinist Virtue which replaced the original Communist free love, means, first, the de-erotization of love and, secondly, the subordination of the sexual drive to the political and economic exigencies of the Soviet state. But there still remains a third aspect of Stalinist Virtue, and this aspect is the most sinister of all: its use as a device for invading the one sphere of personal privacy yet remaining to the Soviet citizen.

Public Life and Private Life

In 1946, before the postwar controls had as yet been brought effectively into force, Ilya Sadofyev wrote a love poem entitled "Tart Wine." Because it became involved in a Soviet purge, we have undug and translated it in its entirety.

> Whether my sorrow is blessed
> Or ridiculous — I do not care —
> As long as they do not mix honey
> Into this tart wine.
>
> Any spiteful slander I can endure
> More resigned than a simpleton
> As long as you don't pour
> Bland drops of consolation
> In my glass.
>
> When in sleepless restlessness,
> I understood we had to part,
> All I could do was drink and drink
> This wine not sharing a drop.
>
> And so — whether enviable or stupid
> Is my sorrow — I do not care —
> I can't forget the way we drank together
> Of love the sweetest wine.
>
> We drank in festive drunkenness
> Sharing with no one a single drop.
> A joy then spilled over our hearts.
> Of all earthly gifts the best.
>
> Unexpected and mute, fate,
> Like a thief, like the last hour,
> Entered . . . and at once imperiously
> Divided us through space . . .
>
> And proud of its might twisted
> My thoughts in a whirlwind.
> From that time on, sorrow
> Fills my veins, the strongest wine.
>
> And pain is unquenchable,
> And even days it is night.
> It is easy if past me flows
> Of love the transparent wine?
>
> No, no. I don't want peace
> Unless the insult is burnt out,
> Unless we shall drink our wine
> With no one sharing a drop.
>
> Take away my hearing and sight,
> Take away my tongue and my rights,
> But leave me my anxiety,
> The seething of my sleepless thoughts
> And memory, my memory.

The poet emphasizes the notion that love is a

private, not a collective experience. Three times he repeats the phrase: "with no one sharing a drop."

In the fall of 1946, the Politburo began an all-embracing purge on the "cultural front" and the poem just cited was among the first objects of its vociferous attack. What was wrong with the poem? Here is the explanation of Andrei Zhdanov, chief purger in the field of culture:

> In Leningrad journals, there began to appear works . . . which relapsed to a position of idealess-ness and defeatism. I have in mind such works as those of Sadofyev. . . . In some of his poems, Sadofyev . . . began to cultivate moods of sadness, longing and loneliness . . . Needless to say, such moods . . . can exercise only a negative influence on our youth with the rotten spirit of idealess-ness, of apoliticism, of despondency. And what would have happened had we educated our youth in this spirit of despondency and disbelief in our goals? We would not have won the Great Patriotic War.

No less than treason is laid at the feet of a poet who dares to bemoan the loss of his beloved and dares to indulge in the tart wine of a purely private tragedy.

The essence of the matter, that is to say of Stalinist Virtue, is that the wall which separates the private life of individuals from the public life of the collectivity must be destroyed. "Private life and family life are an intrinsic and inseparable part of public life." Sex, as a private matter, is looked upon with great suspicion by the rulers in the Kremlin. They believe that the intimate world of the individual, with its loves, hates, and fears, must be carefully investigated and controlled by the collectivity, that is to say by the Party. Such scrutiny is obviously far more embracing than a mere check on the political reliability of a citizen. Such scrutiny includes an investigation of how a man treats his girl or his wife or his children. Preoccupation on the part of an individual with his own emotions is considered futile, obsolete, anti-social, and above all time-consuming. Time translated into work hours is the supreme collective good. The dogmatically established interference of the State with private lives is perhaps one of the most difficult things to understand about the Soviet Union. If the private is absolutely subservient to the public interest, it follows that "biological factors" in human life must be denied. It also follows that love — or rather love for love's sake — is treasonable. Such reasoning is quite logical within the Stalinist framework of thinking. Art for art's sake is no less treasonable than love for love's sake, as for that matter the raising of carrots for the sake of raising carrots would be. For all such self-enclosed and self-sufficient activities, drives, and inclinations detract from the sole purpose of human existence: that of service to the State.

Some Literary Premonitions

A remarkable novel was written, but never published, in the Soviet Union back in 1922. It was entitled quite simply *We*. Its author, Evgenii Zamyatin, was one of the truly important Russian prose writers of the twentieth century. The publication of *We* in the Soviet Union was prohibited and the book exists today only in English and French translations now out of print. Its author died in exile.

The action of this curious novel takes place in the twenty-sixth century. Consequently, it has been mistaken by some interpreters for a utopia, which it is not. There were good reasons, even in the early period of Soviet rule, to banish the book as a dangerous satire on Soviet actuality. For *We* is a grim denunciation of socialist collectivization and regimentation. What is depicted here is a "scientifically" controlled society in which any manifestation of individuality has been destroyed, and citizens have become mechanized puppets. The underlying philosophy of the "Benefactor," the totalitarian ruler, is that freedom and crime are interrelated. Where there is no freedom, there is no crime. All this has been anticipated, of course, by Dostoyevsky in his *Grand Inquisitor*. But Zamyatin tackles this problem, if less profoundly, with great courage and with vivid sensitivity to concrete details. The plot is largely concerned with the unsuccessful rebellion of two lovers against standardized slavery, in the name of freedom and decency. In Zamyatin's dreary vision of the Communistic future, sex and love are as mechanized and as strictly regimented as any other manifestation of life. To control sex and love is easy for the rulers because numbers (people have no longer names, but numbers) do not any longer possess individual consciousness. Individual consciousness and imagination have been classified as diseases and people are about to be cured of them once and for all by means of brain operations. To provide for sexual needs, pink tickets are issued to the citizens and these are used, under the supervision of guardians, at certain rationed "sexual" hours.

Very few people today know of Zamyatin's book. But it did not get lost. It inspired one of the most frightening imaginative documents of our own epoch. George Orwell was deeply impressed by Zamyatin's book and tried unsuccessfully to provide for its republication. In idea, plot, and in many details Orwell's *1984* has been deeply influenced by Zamyatin's *We*. Orwell's satire of totalitarianism has, however, that air of grim finality, that dead-end atmosphere of ultimate conclusions at which Zamyatin did not arrive. Unlike Zamyatin, Orwell shows the process of how all that is human in man is destroyed not from *without*, by means of Zamyatin's external surgical operations, but from *within*. Orwell's rebels, however, like Zamyatin's, find their strength precisely in their forbidden love for each other. And Orwell's rebels labor under the delusion that when they are caught, even if they are forced to "confess," they will not betray each other. They presume that the torture experts of the secret police have no means of getting *inside* a human being. But the message of Orwell's book is that "they" can. The rebels are destroyed from the *inside* so thoroughly that they are even permitted to go on living after torture. They are morally destroyed precisely by being forced to betray *each other,* to betray their *love.*

In Orwell's grim vision of our totalitarian future, individuals are spied upon day and night by telescreens. And according to that all-pervasive loud-speaker system, in Orwell's tragically witty *newspeak* (the emasculated and moronic language of our cheerless future), *ownlife* is a crime while *sexcrime* is punishable by death. *Goodsex* is thoroughly de-eroticized intercourse between husband and wife with the sole purpose of begetting children for the State. All else is *sexcrime.*

The aim of the Party was not merely to prevent men and women from forming loyalties which it might not be able to control. Its real undeclared purpose was to remove all pleasure from the sexual act. Not love so much as eroticism was the enemy, inside marriage as well as outside. . . . The Party was trying to kill the sex instinct, or, if it could not be killed, then to distort it and dirty it.

Of course, Orwell is what may be called an expressionist. He exaggerates shreds of reality for the sake of his warning message. But this great English guardian of human dignity found the basis for his nightmare not only in his apprehensions but also in what he managed to decipher of contemporary Soviet reality.

Isn't the ludicrous poem "Tanya" with its conception of love as reward for overfulfilment of the working norm sufficient evidence of *goodsex* in Soviet morality?

Isn't Zhdanov's wrath against a lyrical poet further evidence that Soviet rulers have already decreed the existence of *sexcrime?*

Isn't the verbose official justification of the rigidity of Stalinist Virtue sufficient evidence that love, which implies the loyalty of two people to each other, is considered to be treason?

But why?

Orwell provides also an answer to this question. In the words of his monstrously inhuman secret police agent:

We have cut the links between child and parent, and between man and man, and between man and woman. No one dares trust a wife or a child or a friend any longer. But in the future there will be no wives and no friends. Children will be taken from their mothers at birth, as one takes eggs from a hen. The sex instinct will be eradicated. Procreation will be annual formality like the renewal of a ration card. We shall abolish orgasm. Our neurologists are at work upon it now. There will be no loyalty, except loyalty toward the Party.

The need of absolute loyalty to the Party is what requires therefore the moral and emotional castration of the human individual.

Is Soviet life *already* as tragic as Orwell's parody on it — or — *not yet?* This is an important question. Is *goodsex*, synonymous with Stalinist Virtue and prohibitive of any kind of *sexcrime* the direction into which the Politburo is pushing its subjects with all its might, or is it already so thoroughly established as a fact that no more pushing need be done? The mere

existence of such loud and persistent propaganda indicates the former: that "private
worlds," with all their latent and hidden possibilities of *sexcrime* and other heresies, still
exist.

That Soviet reality *cannot* be (not yet) a
docile thing shaped according to the Stalinist
blueprint is precisely the point. That men and
women over there sleep together, or fall in
love, or get married for reasons other than
successful mastery of Michurin's agricultural
theories is guaranteed to us not only by common sense but also by high Soviet birthrate
statistics.

Soviet novels reveal, needless to say inadvertently, that Soviet life is very, very hard,
that the standard of living is low, very low,
that the struggle for sheer physical survival is
grim. Perhaps the worn-out woman who at
thirty looks all of fifty, forced to work as much
as a man and on top of it to take care of her
family, perhaps this overburdened slave finds
solace only in communion with her husband.
And the husband, living in fear of committing
a deviation, for which he will be punished,
finds comfort only in the warmth of his wife's
body. We speak, of course, not of the privileged bureaucratic and professional classes,
but of the grey masses who are caught in the
stagnant drudgery of the "socialist" economic
system. That kind of solace and communion is
perhaps not yet subject to control. And perhaps never before did the average Soviet individual need such solace and such communion
so badly.

61

Winning Over the Youth*

Kent Geiger

(1956)

*The next selection takes up another aspect of
what the Soviet people would like to regard
as their private life. In the Soviet Union, as*

*Reprinted from "Changing Political Attitudes in
Totalitarian Society: A Case Study of the Role of
the Family," World Politics, Vol. 8 (1956), pp.
189–205, by permission of the publisher.

*elsewhere, parent–child relations have been
the cause of many misunderstandings. Not infrequently, indirect pressures created by the
regime and by Soviet conditions have forced
parents to relinquish or suppress cherished
values.*

There is general agreement among Western
scholars that the modern totalitarian state is
distinguished in part by its possession of a
unitary and systematically elaborated ideology.
While it will be found that expert opinions vary
considerably in regard to the importance of
the role played by ideology in the origin and
continuation of totalitarianism,[1] there is little
question but that the ruling power of the totalitarian society is not indifferent to the relationship between national ideology and popular
attitudes. Indeed, history shows that the rulers
of twentieth-century totalitarian states have
devoted considerable effort to the development
among their citizenries of attitudes of acceptance toward the social philosophies and goals
associated with their regimes.

However, a realistic sense of the limits to
which popular psychology can in the short run
be reshaped has seemed to direct the totalitarian leadership sooner or later into feeling
that the older generation will not respond to
the desired extent, and that major emphasis
should be placed upon the recruitment of
youth. Thus, we find in the writings of the
totalitarian ideologues that considerable importance is attached to the increasingly great
devotion and loyalty expected of the younger
generations.[2] We also find that state-sponsored,

[1] Carl J. Friedrich, ed., *Totalitarianism: Proceedings of a Conference Held at the American Academy of Arts and Sciences,* Cambridge, Mass, 1954.
See especially the papers and discussion included
in Part III — "Totalitarianism and Ideology," pp.
87–137.
[2] "Only by radically remolding the teaching, organization, and training of the youth shall we be
able to ensure that the result of the efforts of the
younger generation will be the creation of a society
that will be unlike the old society, i.e., a Communist society." V. I. Lenin, "The Tasks of the Youth
Leagues, Speech Delivered at the Third All-Russian Congress of the Russian Young Communist
League," October 2, 1920, in *Lenin: Selected
Works,* II, Moscow, 1947, p. 661.
"A few words about the members of the Young
Communist League, young men and women, in
the collective farms. The youth is our future, our

closely controlled youth movements have been characteristic of totalitarianism.[3] /

---

hope, comrades. The youth must take our place, the place of the old people. It must carry our banner to final victory. Among the peasants there are not a few old people, borne down by the burden of the past, burdened with the habits and the recollections of the old life. Naturally, they are not always able to keep pace with the Party, to keep pace with the Soviet Government. But that cannot be said of our youth. They are free from the burden of the past, and it is easiest for them to assimilate Lenin's behests." Joseph Stalin, "Speech Delivered at the First All-Union Congress of Collective-Farm Shock Workers," February 19, 1933, in J. Stalin, *Problems of Leninism*, Moscow, 1947, p. 451.

"The youth of today is ever the people of tomorrow. For this reason we have set before ourselves the task of inoculating our youth with the spirit of this community of the people at a very early age, at an age when human beings are still unperverted and therefore unspoiled. . . . This Reich stands, and it is building itself up for the future upon its youth. And this new Reich will give its youth to no one, but will itself take youth and give to youth its own education and its own upbringing." Speech given by Adolf Hitler on May 1, 1937, published in the *Frankfurter Zeitung*, May 3, 1937, and cited in Norman H. Baynes, ed., *The Speeches of Adolf Hitler, April 1922–August 1939*, London, 1942, p. 549.

"Some other system of government, a system not ours, the demoliberal system, the system of those whom we despise, may think it proper to renounce the education of the younger generations. We not! In this respect we are intractable. Ours must be the teaching! These children must be educated in our religious faith; but we have the duty of integrating this education, we need to give these youngsters the sense of virility, of power, of conquest; and above all we need to inspire them with our faith, and to inflame them with our hopes." Benito Mussolini, "Report to the Chamber of Deputies on the Agreement with the Lateran," 1929, cited in Herman Finer, *Mussolini's Italy*, London, 1935, p. 428.

[3] Accounts in English of various aspects of totalitarian youth movements may be found in the following: Merle Fainsod, "The Komsomols — A Study of Youth Under Dictatorship," *American Political Science Review*, XLV (March 1951), pp. 18–40; Herbert S. Lewin, "Hitler Youth and the Boy Scouts of America: A Comparison of Aims," *Human Relations*, I (1947), pp. 206–27; Robert A. Brady, *The Spirit and Structure of German Fascism*, New York, 1937, especially Chapter v, "Training the Youth to Become Soldiers of Labor," pp. 161–98; Finer, *op. cit.*, especially Chapter xv, "The Fascist Party: Youth Organizations," pp. 426–54.

But here the aim of the totalitarian state collides with an obstacle. In the crucial early years, children are trained and their personalities shaped predominantly within the family, and the family is not a public, but a private, association of individuals. Within the family, interpersonal relations and behavior tend in the main to be governed by the force of tradition, that is, by relatively inflexible norms which frequently are not in accord with those viewed favorably by the totalitarian regime. Therefore, the rapid and radical changes in the orientation of youth fostered by the totalitarian dictatorship are virtually certain to clash with certain of the traditionally sanctioned attitudes of parents.[4] This situation is not infrequently considered prototypical of parent–youth relations in modern totalitarian societies and has become known in popular parlance as the "struggle" between family and state for the minds of the young.

In this struggle (as popularly conceived) it cannot be denied that the totalitarian state disposes of powerful resources for shaping the minds of the young in the desired direction. These include a carefully controlled school system, the suffusion of the output of the mass media with propaganda themes, and, of course, the closely supervised youth organizations. On the other hand, the resources of the family are frequently seen as equally strong; they include the presumed complete control of parents over children in the earliest years, and influence achieved through mutual ties of loyalty and affection at later ages.

It is the purpose of this article to explore the dimensions of this contest of forces, with special attention to the way in which the situation is viewed and managed by parents in a totalitarian society. The data to be presented enable us to make some estimate of the degree of success attained by one contemporary totalitarian state, the U.S.S.R., in modifying and controlling for its own purposes this aspect of the process of socialization of young persons within the family.

---

[4] Compare Kingsley Davis, "The Sociology of Parent-Youth Conflict," *American Sociological Review*, V (August 1940), pp. 523–35. Davis notes that rapid social change, when taken in conjunction with the slower rates of socialization of older persons, results in a general tendency for attitudes of parents to lag behind those of their children in modern industrial society.

Source and Nature of the Data

Ideally, of course, investigation of such a problem would be conducted on the spot, but the Soviet Union, unfortunately, has been exceptionally vigorous in denying Western investigators access to its population. However, owing to circumstances associated with the Second World War, it has become possible in the last few years to make extensive use of political refugees as first-hand sources of information about the Soviet Union. The data to be analyzed below were obtained from former Soviet citizens who were interviewed in Germany and in the New York City area in 1950 and 1951 by members of the Harvard Project on the Soviet Social System.[5] There is no doubt that former Soviet citizens who are now refugees in the West constitute a group which in certain respects must be considered unique, and which is far from a random sample of the Soviet population still resident in the U.S.S.R. In particular, by their very presence in the West and by virtue of their prolonged exposure to Western influence, we may assume that they are considerably more hostile toward the Soviet regime and its institutions and ideas than the rank and file of the Soviet people. But such a fact does not preclude their effective use as sources of information about the Soviet system if sufficient account is taken of the bias, and if care is exercised in the way the results are interpreted.

To investigate the impact of the Soviet system on the transmission of political attitudes within the Soviet parent–child relationship, data were obtained with two different instruments and from two different refugee subsamples. The first group of materials consists of extended life-history interviews with 141 Soviet young persons who were born in the period 1915–1929. Project interviewers were instructed to cover at some time during the

[5] This Project has been conducted by the Russian Research Center of Harvard University under the sponsorship of the Officer Education Research Laboratory of Air Research and Development Command, Maxwell Air Force Base, Montgomery, Alabama, under contract No. AF 33(038)–12909. Reproduction of this article in whole or in part is permitted for any purpose of the United States Government. Grateful acknowledgment is here made to the Russian Research Center for the assistance which has facilitated completion of this study.

course of the two or three days of the interview the role of the respondent's parents in the development of his attitudes toward the Soviet regime and its works. For the bulk of respondents, this proved to be a topic of considerable meaning and interest, and they freely discussed their relationships with their parents vis-à-vis the Soviet regime.

The first part of the analysis which follows will be devoted to the responses secured in interviews from these young people. They were members of families from all social levels, of both rural and urban residence, and include a few representatives of the Soviet minority nationalities, although 93 per cent of the total were members of the dominant Slavic majority — Great Russian, Ukrainian, and White Russian. Although occasional quotations from persons outside the 1915–1929 age range will be given for illustrative purposes, the percentage figures and tables from the interview materials represent exclusively the responses of the younger persons in the interview sample.

The second body of data was obtained with the use of a check-list questionnaire from persons who were themselves parents in the U.S.S.R. and whose first child was born in the 1915–1930 period. Thus, in terms of age, these respondents correspond roughly to the parental generation of the young persons in the life-history sample. Their responses, which will be discussed after the results of the interviews are presented, serve in part as a check on the validity of the latter.

Varieties of Parental Behavior

As a starting point for the analysis of the family–state relationship, let us consider the descriptions of parental attitudes toward the Soviet regime given by the sample of young refugee respondents. Most frequently, as might be expected from this group, the respondents reported that their parents were likely to show hostility, skepticism, or a lack of appropriate enthusiasm in regard to the Soviet regime. For example:

My father always spoke openly. Prior to the war he said that the purges, the closing of the churches, the collective farms, and the 1940 labor laws were all slavery. (23-year-old male, father a shop foreman)[6]

[6] All ages are as of 1950; father's occupation is the last one reported prior to World War II.

In fact, 94 of the 141 cases available, or 67 per cent, said that their parents had had predominantly anti-Soviet attitudes. At the other extreme, only 9, or 6 per cent, reported that their parents had been in the main pro-regime. The remaining 27 per cent gave no information about the attitudes of their parents, gave inconsistent or contradictory information, or did not live in families as they grew up.

Of the 103 young persons who gave adequate responses to the question, then, 91 per cent came from families in which the parents had been at heart anti-Soviet in feeling while living in the U.S.S.R. This was a situation which posed a sharp problem for the parents: How, if indeed at all, should they teach their children to understand the real nature of the Soviet regime? How far should they go in transmitting openly their own attitudes and values to their children? As a Soviet mother put it:

> . . . in raising our son we immediately faced the question: Should we raise him in the spirit of the Soviet Union or not? At that time we were changing our views toward the Soviet Union; we were both strongly against the Soviet power. (64-year-old female, doctor)

In the meantime, other forces were at work — forces which served to restrict the parents' freedom of choice. Since school, youth organizations, informal peer groups, cinema, radio, and reading materials of all description strive to make the young person a loyal adherent to the works and symbols of the Soviet order, it is not surprising that children were regularly led in the direction of enthusiastic acceptance of Bolshevik ideology. In fact, within the anti-Soviet family there frequently appeared a young political activist who did not hesitate to display his sentiments:

> The child comes to the conviction that the Communist propaganda tells the truth, and if he hears from his parents the opposite opinion, he feels insulted and tries to explain these things to his parents, who are not politically conscious. In short, he becomes a convinced Communist, a Pioneer, fired by the Pioneer literature, activism, and so on. (57-year-old male, accountant)

Actually, for very young children, the matter of "parental influence" was pretty much a closed issue, since divulgence of suspect interpretations and sentiments to the partly developed consciousness and incomplete sense of responsibility of the child could have serious repercussions. One of the most widely cited norms of family conduct under Soviet conditions was the requirement that non-conforming attitudes were not to be expressed in front of small children:

> Everyone was afraid of his children. A small child can betray his parents unwittingly, and therefore my parents were always careful in what they said before me and my brother. (20-year-old female, father a secondary-school teacher)

In the close and continuous interaction within the family, this constituted a problem which could not be lightly dismissed. Gross differences in regard to emotionally significant value orientations between persons in intimate relationships are hard to tolerate. In fact, such differences set forces in motion which in the end serve either to make homogeneous the values of the individuals concerned, or disrupt the relationship because of a distressing increase in interpersonal tension.

The distribution of power in the parent–child relationship is generally thought of as markedly asymmetrical; indeed, a good part of the process of socialization can be seen as the exercise of power and influence by the parent in the interest of transmitting his own attitudes to his children. Under Soviet totalitarianism, however, it is clear that parents could not easily control the views of their young children. Moreover, the problem areas in the parent–child relationship applied not only to matters which a Westerner would consider "political," and in which, it might be argued, children have little interest or involvement, but to matters which had traditionally been of central importance to the parent–child relationship. Two stand out as of particular relevance — the mode in which parental authority was exercised, and the transmission of traditionally hallowed attitudes toward religion and the church. Consider, for example, the following comments:

> . . . they told you you have no right to punish a child. And if a child was punished, he would go and complain to the authorities. (51-year-old male, unskilled worker)

> . . . in the schools they were developing a child of the worst sort. There were denunciations,

lack of respect for elders, and denial of God. (51-year-old male, bookkeeper)

The psychological immaturity of children thus constituted a definitely weak link in the family's struggle against the state, and provided in effect a point of entry into the family for elements of the totalitarian ideology. Such a situation must be reckoned as a basic source of tension in the prewar Soviet family. In the Project materials, it was a prominent target for parental complaints. However, as the child grew older, the situation changed. From the age of 12 to 15 or 16, when an enlarged sense of awareness and personal responsibility had developed, it was possible, if the parent so desired, to open more fully the channels of communication between himself and his child. From the parental point of view, only then could the child be "trusted" with information which clearly showed a gap between family values and the official sponsored ideology:

(Was your child a member of the Komsomol?) No. Komsomols are young people in their teens — that is to say, children who are already able to reason. Consequently, at that age they may be influenced by their parents. (47-year-old male, office clerk)

To explore the way in which Soviet parents managed their relationships with older children, the reactions of "anti-Soviet" parents were sorted into categories. These fell into three groups. The most numerous, occurring in 67 out of the 94 cases of anti-Soviet parents, or 71 per cent, was that group in which the parents reportedly took the youngsters into their confidence and freely communicated to them their doubts about and antipathies to the regime.[7] The following are typical of the responses in this category:

The strongest influences in my life were those of my mother, my father, and my grandmother. All of them were always opposed to the Soviet government, and I, of course, was raised in such

---

[7] It was frequently noted that this was done only after the children were old enough to be trusted, or that the children were carefully warned to keep silent about such matters when outside the family.

opposition. (28-year-old male, father an engineer)

Since my early childhood our family had been anti-Soviet, and very often I heard my parents say that now the situation was no good, and that before it had been better. (29-year-old male, father a store clerk)

The second group consisted of those families in which the parents were reported to be relatively uncommunicative about their attitudes toward the regime. There were 18 of these — 19 per cent of the total. An example is:

. . . my father never told me, "Here is what it says in the paper, but the fact is this." He never talked about political matters. My father was in no way in accord with the Soviet regime, but he was always silent about it. (26-year-old female, father a director of postal-telegraph office)

A reservation about this category must be entered in terms of the inherent difficulty of "hiding" a deeply felt sentiment from one's family intimates. Some of the respondents did in fact indicate that although nothing was said, they "knew" what the parental view was. For example:

The parents avoid direct talk on political questions. They only try to strengthen the child in his general moral position. (Were there any discussions between you and your parents?) What kind of discussions could there be? I was just a kid, but they tried to deflect my attention from Communism by making me read classical literature or other instructive and interesting books rather than the Pioneer literature. (Did you know their political views?) They did not tell me that, but I felt that it did not support the view which was developing in me. (How did you know that?) My feeling was quite definite. I tried to propagandize them and show them they didn't understand. (Did they oppose your ideas?) They did not oppose me directly. They only said, "Wait until you get older and then you will understand more." (And did this influence you?) It did not influence me directly, but it put some doubt in me. These words and remarks became more frequent and they accumulated. (When did they start accumulating?) Between the age of 10 and 15 years. . . . (24-year-old male, father a stage director in theater)

Finally, the least numerous group, 9, or 10 per cent of the total, was composed of the individuals whose parents adapted to this problem by supporting the official doctrines of the regime:

> How were we educated? We were educated in the spirit of Communism, the Soviet Union only, we did not know anything else. . . . My parents were afraid to tell about life under the Tsarist regime. . . . My father was very enclosed within himself in the family. He never told about the past. He always said, "You must do what you are told to do." (23-year-old male, father a trust director)

How may one explain the differences revealed by these patterns? For the open and frankly anti-Soviet response, in the majority of cases little rationale was offered. This can be accounted for in part by the anti-Soviet milieu in which the respondents had been living for some time, that is, the Western world, in the context of which the interviews took place. The reporting of an anti-Soviet atmosphere in the family was a response more likely to be approved by DP groups and also by Western interviewers, and apparently most respondents felt that an overtly expressed anti-regime attitude did not have to be justified in terms of other values or aspects of the family's situation. However, there does seem to have been a prior motivational element in the picture which, although not mentioned by the respondents, helps to account for the predominance of the openly anti-Soviet pattern. This is the trait of impulsiveness, the spontaneous emission of feelings with little regard for their consequences. For instance:

> My mother often cursed the Communists, and said, you should excuse the expression, "It is the Communists who —— over everything." And my brother was a Komsomol and a Party member. My mother would often say, "We have gone through so much, and for what? We have nothing and we never will. During Tsarist times we lived better." Sometimes we got fed up with her raving and told her to keep quiet. (Did she say such things even when your brother was around?) Yes. She would say, "Our comrades! What have they done for us? We have gotten nothing good from them." She

would say this every day and she would always cry. My mother felt that she had lived better before. Then she often had arguments with my brother over religion, too. (27-year-old male, mother a waitress separated from husband)

Further evidence of such lack of future-oriented calculation is to be found in the fact that in 29 of the 67 cases in the openly anti-Soviet group, the frank expression of parental views did not win over the child, but led instead to conflict, or enhanced the seriousness of an already existing conflict. According to these respondents, parental opposition to the ideas they learned at school brought them into a position where they rebelled against their parents and rejected their values. For example:

> Whenever I stayed with my family, I quarreled with my parents, especially my father. He tried to tell me that the Party line was nothing but a lie, that I should open my eyes and see what's behind it all. But I had faith. I was very young and thus very enthusiastic and I thought my parents were old, clinging to old-fashioned ideas, that they couldn't see the truth, that they couldn't understand our new socialist reforms. (33-year-old female, father a physics teacher)

Here is another sample of parent–child tension over political opinions:

> When I started to go to school, the agitation and propaganda began in my life. They used to say we lived better than anybody anywhere. School had a very great influence on me. I did not believe anything my mother said about their having a servant and a cow and everything. Mother often used to tell me about this. She would tell me about her mother and her father, and how satisfied they were with their life. But when I joined the Pioneers I was torn away from my family. I doubted that my mother told me the truth, because they [at school] used to tell me about the exploiters before the Revolution, and that people were not able to live. (30-year-old male, mother a cook, widowed in 1930)

There is no doubt but that with increasing age the intellectual maturation of the child made him both more fully interested in political ideas, and also potentially able to admit and handle the conflict between his parents' views and the outlook broached in extra-familial contexts. On the other hand, another accompaniment of aging is emotional maturation, and in modern industrial societies one of the central problems connected with emotional maturation concerns the "emancipation" of the child from close emotional ties with his parents. Such emotional emancipation is a process which ordinarily accompanies adolescence, and thus occurs concurrently with the young person's greater consciousness of his parents' political views. If the latter are dissonant with those which he has learned to idealize in school and youth group organizations, then they will become the focus for conflict with his parents. Consequently, it is quite plausible and probable that in Soviet society emotional problems of the parent–youth relationship become "politicized" to an exceptional degree or, to put it the other way around, that a great proportion of parent–youth conflicts over differing political viewpoints can be explained as a displacement associated with the struggle to overcome dependency feelings which are no longer culturally approved.

Nonetheless, the central point to be noted in the parent–child relationship in those families in which parents frankly expressed their anti-regime sentiments is the high frequency with which political differences were a sore point, and the widespread tendency of children to reject their parents' views.

Let us turn now to those parents who did not express their views so openly. Although they themselves were in fact opposed to the regime, they adopted either a "neutral" or a "pro-Soviet" position in regard to the ideological development of their children. The predominant explanation given for such parental behavior was expressed in terms of how best to contribute to the present and future welfare of the child:

My mother never tried to convince me of the rightness of her ideas. She was extremely cultured and knew I had to live my own life, that I had to live in Soviet society, and she did not wish to make it difficult for me. (32-year-old male, mother a typist, widowed in 1928)

In a number of interviews, respondents who were themselves parents in the U.S.S.R.[8] responded in effect in the same way:

[8] Responses from this group are not included in the textual or tabular numerical totals.

(What kind of character did you try to impart to your child?) I will tell you exactly what my attitude was. Inasmuch as we were living in the Soviet Union, we knew that our children would have to continue to live in the Soviet Union even after we were gone, and so we tried to introduce them to Communist ideas. What can I say about the education of our children? It was of a different sort than I would have preferred, but I didn't object. (59-year-old female, scientific research worker)

In a few cases, a different explanation was offered — namely, that the frank transmission of their own feelings to their children would have jeopardized the physical or economic welfare of the parents themselves:

In the majority of instances, the influence of parents on their children was insignificant in the Soviet Union. Many questions of ethics are absorbed by the children in school from their classmates and the school's environment, and the parents are forced to accept it. Otherwise there can be very serious consequences. For instance, one can be reported for "political discussions." (54-year-old male, university professor)

(What was your attitude toward religion?) We did not have any icons in our house. All depended on my father. In the position he was in we could not have done it. My father's sister was a very religious woman and she always laughed at us because we were godless. (What was his internal attitude toward religion?) Since my father occupied a good position, he could not display any religious feelings. Maybe they [the parents of the respondent] talked somewhat differently between themselves. I couldn't know it, but it was not in our presence. We, the young people, were educated in an anti-religious spirit. (23-year-old male, father a trust director)

Finally, there is some indication that still another explanatory condition deserves mention. The modal type of family in the U.S.S.R. is a small, structurally isolated[9] group in which emotional intimacy is highly valued. In such circumstances it becomes especially important to maintain expected levels of mutual accept-

[9] Isolated, that is, in the sense that members of the larger kin group are in the typical case not particularly close in either a residential or emotional sense to the members of the immediate individual

ance and stability in interpersonal relations. For this reason, it may be supposed that Soviet parents were not infrequently moved to avoid serious conflict with their children simply in order to maintain peace and harmony within the family. Moreover, the burden of adaptation or adjustment could be seen as rightfully belonging more to them than to their children, since by virtue of their age and experience they were better able to "understand" the reasons for the attitudinal patterns of their children than were their children able to appreciate the parental point of view. Moreover, in the adolescent period during which the child is engaging in the struggle to become emotionally independent from his parents, he may be notably unwilling to compromise those principles he calls his own. For these reasons, it is perhaps not too surprising that some Soviet parents were likely to engage in a measure of adaptation to the views of the younger generation, and were willing to pay the price of suppressing their dissatisfaction with the Soviet system.[10] The most popular private rationalization for this seems to have been something on the order of: "Someday they'll find out the true state of affairs for themselves."

The result obtained from analysis of reported parental attitudes in the families of these 94 young respondents appears to be an important datum for appraisal of the role of the family in Soviet totalitarian society, for it indicates that in a majority of cases anti-Soviet parents were unwilling or unable by their own efforts to raise anti-Soviet children. Twenty-seven, or 29 per cent of the 94, seem to have made little attempt to do so, and either did not contradict what their children learned in school, or in

fact reiterated and reinforced what they had learned there. As a justification of this attitude, the predominant view in this group was that the children should be raised for their own good, or for the good of the family as a whole, in the spirit of the social system in which they had to live. And of the 67 parents who were reported as attempting to influence their children in an anti-Soviet direction, 29 of the 67 cases, or 43 per cent — a not inconsiderable proportion — were relatively unsuccessful. If these 29 are added to the two groups of families in which the parents, in effect, cooperated with the regime, 27 in all, the resulting 56 families constitute 60 per cent of the total number of 94 respondents with anti-Soviet parents. Now, if the 9 respondents who came from predominantly pro-Soviet families are also added to this number, the proportion of families represented by young respondents in the interview sample which were relatively powerless to oppose effectively the pressures of the Soviet system is even greater — 65 out of 103, or 63 per cent. Considering the circumstances under which the interviews were conducted, and the disaffected, political-refugee status of the respondents, this is indeed a remarkable finding, and testifies in sinister fashion to the ability of the Soviet regime to destroy ideological opposition even within the private family group.

It is not necessary that the above result stand alone, for rough corroboration was obtained from a different group of refugees and with the use of a different instrument. Sixty-six respondents who had themselves been parents in the U.S.S.R. were administered paper-and-pencil questionnaires concerned primarily with their experiences in family life. The first child of these respondents was born in the 1915–1930 period; thus they comprise a group which corresponds in age quite closely to that of the parents of the young respondents whose experiences were examined above. These former Soviet parents were confronted with the following check-list question:

---

family. In this respect the Soviet family, at least in its urban Slavic variety, does not differ from the predominant family type in the United States. See Talcott Parsons, "The Kinship System of the Contemporary United States," *American Anthropologist*, xlv (January 1943), pp. 22–38.

[10] The advantage to the individual parent of peace within the family is clearly expressed in the following exchange:

(How did you explain to your children those events in the U.S.S.R. whose negative side was clear to you?) On this question, the children had much instruction in school, and in order not to become upset, I kept silent. (56-year-old female, bookkeeper)

How did you explain to your child(ren) those events in the U.S.S.R. whose negative side was clear to you, such as purges, repressions, the Terror, etc.?

a —— I explained to them as best I could in such a fashion that they would see no contradictions between what I told them and what they heard in school.

b —— I told them the complete truth although it contradicted the things they were taught in school.

c —— I tried as best I could to avoid such topics and remained silent.

d —— Something else. (Please explain)

Results were as follows: the most frequently chosen responses were "c," indicated by 36 per cent of the group, and "b," also chosen by 36 per cent. Five per cent chose alternative "a," and nine persons, or 14 per cent, answered in their own terms ("d") or checked more than one response. Five, or 9 per cent, did not answer.

In Table 1, these results are compared with the parental attitudes toward the regime reported by the respondents who were themselves children in Soviet families.

This table merits several comments. In the first place, it indicates that not only when the situation is reported from the point of view of the child, but also from the point of view of the parents themselves, a sizeable proportion of Soviet parents were not able or not willing to express their views to their children with complete frankness. Indeed, the table suggests that parents are quite a bit less willing than

are children to signify the presence of overt opposition to the Soviet regime within the home.

The table also indicates that parental attitudes as characterized by young people tend to be concentrated at the extremes of the three major response patterns, while parental attitudes as characterized by parents themselves are bunched more on the middle, or non-committal, alternative. This difference may be in part a function of the way in which the information was gathered. In the interview situation, because of the use of probes by the interviewer, the respondent may have felt more pressure to characterize the attitudes of his parents as either actively "for" or "against" than was felt by the questionnaire respondents. However, another interpretation is possible: the table may reflect the fact that the same process is being viewed, and interpreted, from two different points of view within the family — points of view which are in themselves different. Parental silence on vital topics may be seen *by the parent* as a compromise solution to the conflict between his own negative attitude and the more positive interpretation of the Soviet scene which he feels is expected of him by his children. But such behavior may be seen *by a young person* as

TABLE 1   *Mode of Interpreting Soviet Regime to Children of Anti-regime Parents* as Reported by Children in Interviews and by Parents on a Check-List Questionnaire***

POSITION OF RESPONDENT IN FAMILY	MODE OF INTERPRETING REGIME			TOTAL
	Overtly Anti-regime	Non-committal	Favorable to Regime	
Child	71%	19%	10%	100% (N = 94)
Parent	47%	47%	6%	100% (N = 51)

* Parents best described as holding genuinely pro-Soviet attitudes while in the Soviet Union ($N = 9$ in the interview sample, and $N = 1$ in the questionnaire group) are excluded.
** There is a distinct social class difference in the parental mode of interpreting the regime to children, a pattern which is discussed further below. There are also somewhat different proportions of social class representation in the two sample groups being compared. This does not, however, change the tendency for children to report parental behavior differently from the way it is reported by parents themselves. Essentially the same pattern of differences between the parental version of events and the child's version continue to appear when each social class group is analyzed separately.

behavior corresponding to the old Russian pro-verb, "Silence gives consent," or, more likely, as failure to respond in the prescribed way and thus as opposition to the regime.

The first major conclusion suggested by both sources of data is that the regime was quite successful in opposing the anti-Soviet views of parents and thus in molding the attitudes of young people. Clearly, the first step in the process consisted in gaining the loyalty of children at an early age. The predominant reaction to this on the part of parents was a feeling of fear and helplessness. Little could be done to prevent their indoctrination. As their children grew older, however, and de-veloped a sense of responsibility for the wel-fare of their parents, it was possible to intro-duce them to non-conformist ideas. But as might be expected, and as these data indicate, by this time it was in many cases too late, and if the parents persisted in contradicting what the children had learned in school, conflict was likely to develop. Parent–youth conflict, actual and potential, then served as a social pressure within the family which often led to greater parental conformity with the attitudes and values of the new Soviet culture. It there-fore actually served the purposes of the regime by helping to weaken the family as a source of opposition to Bolshevik ideology.[11]

It is perhaps of greater import, however — particularly in view of the anti-Soviet bias of the respondents in this case — to emphasize that such a substantial number of parents made no attempt to pit their strength against the tide of events while they were in the U.S.S.R.,

and failed to oppose the new Soviet *Weltan-schauung* even within the privacy of their homes. They thus collaborated with the regime in spite of themselves in the task of developing their children into loyal young Soviet citizens. It is in fact quite probable that political con-formity in this sense has been for some time the modal response among the population still resident in the Soviet Union.

Social Class Differences

Still and all, the fact remains that in some cases Soviet parents failed to surrender to the course of events, and within the home actively resisted the new ideas propagated by the Soviet regime. This raises the question: which were the families more likely to become "Sovietized," and which were those internally more resistant to the new ideas? To some degree, of course, the answer to this question depends upon the pattern of specific experiences undergone by the members of the family under consideration. For instance, the arrest and sentencing for political reasons of a member of a family made it difficult for the rest of the family to maintain any semblance of a neutral or pro-Soviet orientation.[12] However, consideration of cer-tain more general aspects of Soviet social con-ditions and social structure leads one to expect significant differences in this regard among the various Soviet socio-economic groups.

Comparisons for the three major socio-economic groups of Soviet society are made in Table 2. In both samples dealt with, the young life-history respondents and the ques-tionnaire respondents of the parental genera-tion, the variation by socio-economic group was in the same direction, and the two samples were therefore combined. Also, the question-naire respondents who checked more than one category or answered in their own words were assigned to a single, most appropriate category. The difference quite conclusively favors the Soviet peasant family as furnishing the most active anti-regime family environment. On the other hand, the least actively anti-regime family is the white-collar level family of in-telligentsia and employees.

[11] Compare with the role of children in the first-generation immigrant family in the United States. For example: "In the face of this whole develop-ment [i.e., the pressures and attractions of Ameri-can life] the immigrants were helpless. They had neither the will nor the ability to turn their off-spring into other directions. The nominal authority of the fathers was often halfheartedly used; they were cruelly torn by the conflicting wishes that their sons be like themselves and yet lead better lives than they. Sensing that the school and street would tear the next generation away, the parents knew not how to counteract those forces without injuring their own flesh and blood." From Oscar Handlin, *The Uprooted*, Boston, 1951, pp. 252–53. See also W. Lloyd Warner and Leo Srole, *The Social Systems of American Ethnic Groups*, New Haven, Conn., 1945, especially Chapter VI, "The Family," pp. 103–55.

[12] Changes in family relationships subsequent to regime-induced deprivations are discussed at length in Kent Geiger, "Deprivation and Solidarity in the Soviet Urban Family," *American Sociological Re-view*, XX (January 1955), pp. 57–68.

TABLE 2 *Overt Attitude Expressed in Family by Anti-Soviet Parents* Toward Soviet Regime, by Socio-economic Level*

SOCIO-ECONOMIC LEVEL	OVERT ATTITUDE TOWARD SOVIET REGIME		TOTAL
	Not Overtly Anti-regime	Overtly Anti-regime	
Non-manual	47%	53%	100% (N = 81)
Worker	35%	65%	100% (N = 34)
Peasant	23%	77%	100% (N = 39)

* This table includes respondents from both the life-history interview and the questionnaire on family life and only those cases in which the parents were reported as "anti-Soviet." Respondents from the interview sample group were born in the 1915–1929 period, while respondents from the questionnaire sample had children of which the first was born within the same time period. The distributions over these periods of precise years of birth of the children as among the three socio-economic groups in the samples are approximately equivalent.

How may these differences be explained? In the first place, area of residence is an important factor. The school system, the youth-group organizations, and the mass communications media through which the regime's agitation and propaganda are mediated are much more effectively developed in urban areas than in the Soviet countryside.[13] Therefore, the young people in the cities, and probably to some degree the entire urban population, tend to be much more influenced by current ideology than do their country peers. It is of course not only in totalitarian societies that social change occurs more rapidly in the city than in the country. Insofar as such pressures are effective, we would expect to find a stronger trend toward conformity among urban parents than among rural parents.

Closely connected is the strength of the traditional peasant orientation toward religion, and the relative weakness of religious attitudes among the urban population.[14] Essential contradictions between Bolshevism and traditional religious views quite effectively precluded the adoption of other than an anti-Soviet frame of reference within a strongly religious household.

The latter consideration also applies in some measure to social group differentiation among the urban population. Owing to the rapid rate of urbanization characterizing recent Soviet history[15] and the fact that newly urbanized peasants generally become workers, a positive attitude toward religion and other attitudinal and behavioral patterns of the peasantry tend to be found more frequently in the urban working class than among the urban non-manual population.

---

[13] Consult Fainsod, *op. cit.*, especially p. 36, for information on the weaknesses of youth organizations in rural areas. The differential exposure of various population groups to the mass media is discussed in Peter H. Rossi and Raymond A. Bauer, "Some Patterns of Soviet Communications Behavior," *Public Opinion Quarterly*, XVI (Winter 1952–1953), pp. 653–70. Rossi and Bauer characterize the Soviet collective farmer as a person who is "almost isolated from the communications network" (p. 658).

[14] In 1937 E. Yaroslavsky, head of the League of Militant Atheists, estimated that about two-thirds of the urban adult population over 16 called themselves atheists, whereas in the country from one-half to two-thirds were believers. Cited in N. S. Timasheff, *Religion in Soviet Russia, 1917–1942*, New York, 1942, p. 65. Harvard Project data on refugee attitudes toward religion also indicate that religious belief increases in strength as one descends in the social class hierarchy.

[15] Lorimer concludes that the net migration from rural areas to cities must have been at least 23 million persons in the inter-census period, 1926 to 1939. Frank Lorimer, *The Population of the Soviet Union: History and Prospects*, Geneva, 1946, pp. 145–50.

It is also widely recognized that Soviet society since the mid-1930's has become highly stratified,[16] and that the material lot of the Soviet peasant and worker has been a hard one. Hence one might expect parents in these categories to manifest genuine hostility toward the Soviet regime purely on the basis of neglected "class interests."[17]

One additional factor deserves mention. It concerns the close connection in Soviet society between access to and retention of responsible, well-paid jobs and attitudes of political orthodoxy. Soviet parents who were highly placed in the Soviet system usually felt they could ill afford to take any chances in jeopardizing their position.[18] Thus part of the price paid by the Soviet upper class for their material advantages was a greater degree of ideological conformity, genuine or simulated, whereas the lower classes seemed to have the compensatory advantage of being allowed more liberty to blow off steam. In their case, politically deviant beliefs and attitudes could be shrugged off by Soviet authorities as a case of the "backwardness of the masses."

The implications of this class difference in family patterns extend in several directions. In the first place, Table 2 makes it apparent that it is in some measure misleading to make general and unqualified statements about the role of "the family" in changing political attitudes. The role of the family evidently varies considerably from class level to class level. Second, since overtly expressed opposition to the regime on the part of parents varies inversely with class level, we would expect parent–youth solidarity in terms of political conflict also to vary inversely with social class level. The best data available indicate that at least for the urban population such is actually the case. Solidarity in Soviet "intel-

ligentsia" families apparently is greater than in families of lower ranking non-manual categories (bookkeeper, schoolteacher, clerk, etc.) and in these latter greater than in worker level families.[19] Finally, it is quite likely that considerable variegation as well as a high incidence of underlying ambivalence characterize the political attitudes of young people in the peasant and working class groups. Particularly in the case of the peasant youth, ambivalent feelings about the Soviet regime seem to have given rise to the typical reaction of political apathy, a trend which is related in mutually supporting fashion to the weakness of rural Komsomol and Party organizations.

Conclusion

The broad problem with which this paper has been concerned has been the struggle between totalitarian state and family for the control of the mind of youth. The prewar Soviet Union has served as a test case, and the data have been furnished by Soviet political refugees. If the experiences reported by such persons differ from those of the rank and file of the Soviet population, it may be assumed that they incline in the direction of more parental hostility toward the Soviet Government. Thus any conclusion reached which seems to be favorable to the aims of the Soviet regime would probably be even more strongly substantiated if it were possible to investigate the problem within the contemporary U.S.S.R. itself.

A basic conclusion is warranted. The family has on the whole not been a significant force in resisting the ideological indoctrination of Soviet young persons. While there is some evidence that politically tinged parent–youth conflict was a prominent feature in the prewar Soviet family, of equal or greater importance is the fact that Soviet parents so frequently minimized such conflict by their adaptive-conforming responses to the regime's ideology. Although a number of considerations must enter into a full explanation, two deserve special prominence since they underline essential differences between the totalitarian and the democratic way of organizing society. The first is the systematic use of coercion and ter-

---

[16] Alex Inkeles, "Social Stratification and Mobility in the Soviet Union: 1940–1950," *American Sociological Review,* xv (August 1950), pp. 465–79.

[17] There is, however, some evidence to the contrary. It is likely that a considerable portion of the frustration engendered by difficult material living conditions is expressed and dissipated within the context of the family itself. See Geiger, *op. cit.*

[18] Note, for example, the case of the trust director's son (p. 197 above) who felt that a man "in his father's position" had to use more than the usual amount of care.

[19] Geiger, *op. cit.*, pp. 65–66.

rorism as a means of inducing conformity. In substantial measure, Soviet parents went along with the Soviet regime because they feared to act otherwise. Secondly, the family, like an army, travels on its stomach — and the Soviet regime holds the key to the larder. Under Soviet conditions, in which all opportunities are government opportunities, attitudes of political conformity have come to be seen as a basic prerequisite for the obtaining of the good things of life — education, good jobs and, ultimately, decent food, clothing, and shelter.

It is also of some interest to note that the connection between a semblance of political loyalty and personal welfare is most relevant for parents in the upper class family, and that it plays a less prominent role in the worker and peasant family. This reflects a general feature of social structure in contemporary urban industrial society. Adaptation and close conformity to the needs of the existing order are part of the cost involved in the attainment and preservation of high status and its privileges.

A final commentary on the findings reported above takes us back to the general question of evaluating the role of the family in resisting the creation of those homogeneous political attitudes associated with totalitarianism. To what extent can the present results be generalized to other totalitarian societies? It is probable that the Soviet regime in the years preceding World War II enjoyed less mass support than any other totalitarian system of modern times. If the family was of so little importance in blocking the influence of externally induced sources of attitudinal change in this extreme case, one might conclude that it can be reckoned as even less significant a conservative force in other totalitarian societies. But popular support is only one factor. The realities of the Soviet scene differ in a number of additional respects from those obtaining in other systems of the totalitarian type. In the extent to which basic social changes[20] have been carried through, in the isolation of the population from outside influences, and in the very longevity and manifest stability of the system itself, the Soviet experience has as yet not been matched by other regimes. The implications of such contrasts as these suggest

that the Soviet pattern cannot easily be generalized to other totalitarian systems. For they emphasize the fact, which has been a consistent interpretive motif in this case study, that parental action within the family is partly determined by factors over and above traditionally grounded personal predispositions.

SOCIAL STRATIFICATION

62

Myth and Reality of Social Classes*

Alex Inkeles

(1950)

Differences in economic position and prestige are regarded by many sociologists as functionally necessary to the operation of a society, especially the modern urban-industrial variety. Yet the Marxist heritage includes a generous strain toward equalitarianism. The following article tells us what actually happened when these two opposing forces met during the reign of Stalin.

In introducing the new Soviet Constitution in 1936 Stalin stated that the Soviet population was divided into two major classes, the working class and the peasantry, and a third group, the intelligentsia, which as a genuflection in the direction of Marxian orthodoxy he called a *stratum*.† The members of all three groups

---

[20] Forms of property ownership, relations between church and state, etc.

---

*Reprinted from "Social Stratification and Mobility in the Soviet Union: 1940–1950," *American Sociological Review*, Vol. 15 (1950), pp. 465–479, by permission of the American Sociological Association.
† Expanded version of paper read at the annual meeting of the American Sociological Society held in New York, December 28–30, 1949. The author is indebted to the Russian Research Center of Harvard University for making available research assistance in the persons of Arnold Horelick and Hans Rogger.

were defined as being "equal in rights" within Soviet society, and Stalin further asserted that under Soviet conditions the amount of social distance and the political and economic contradictions between the groups was diminishing and indeed was being obliterated.[1] Even as he made these declarations, however, the actual relations between and within the major social groups were moving in a very different direction under the impact of social forces which Stalin had himself largely set in motion in 1931.

For in that year, faced by severe problems in relation to the productivity of labor and an extraordinarily high rate of labor turnover under the First Five Year Plan,[2] Stalin launched an attack against "equality-mongering" and wage equalization and began a movement for personal incentive based on differential rewards. No working class in history had managed without its own intelligentsia, he asserted, and there were "no grounds for believing that the working class of the U.S.S.R. can manage without its own industrial and technical intelligentsia." There were in every shop and factory, furthermore, certain "leading groups" of skilled workers who are "the chief link in production." In consideration of these facts he called for an end to the "baiting of specialists" and its replacement by a new policy "of showing them greater attention and solicitude, displaying more boldness in enlisting their cooperation . . . [and] creating suitable conditions for them to work in, without stinting money for this purpose." In regard to the skilled workers, he ordered that they be treated to promotion to higher positions and to payment of higher levels of wages, to "a system of payment which gives each worker his due according to his qualifications." The unskilled workers were to be given a similar "stimulus and the prospect of advancement"

by this pattern of wage payment. And, Stalin affirmed, "the more boldly we do this the better."[3]

Rapidly implemented in the succeeding years, Stalin's campaign produced a series of new institutions for differential economic reward and strengthened those which existed only in rudimentary form: on the collective farms, the labor-day and the piecework system of payment; in industry, more precise gradings between the various skill categories, increasingly great spreads between the wages of the least skilled and the most skilled workers, and the extreme extension of the progressive piece-rate system; and in the case of managers and technicians, pay scales separate and distinct from those for workers, special "personal salaries," and bonuses taken out of the enterprises' profits.

The Soviet Class System

As a result of these and related economic and political measures the Soviet Union possessed by 1940 an elaborately and precisely stratified status system within which at least ten major social-class groups could be distinguished for purposes of sociological analysis. Unfortunately, limits of space permit neither full description of each of the groups nor a detailed statement of the method by which they were delineated, and we must restrict ourselves here merely to enumerating them.[4]

The intelligentsia was actually divided into at least four sub-units:

[1] Joseph V. Stalin, *Voprosy Leninizma,* 11th ed., Moscow: Ogiz, 1940, pp. 510–512, 516.

[2] In 1930, for example the average number of workers engaged was 174 per cent and the average number who left jobs was 152 per cent of the total average in employment during the year. See Alexander Baykov, *The Development of the Soviet Economic System,* New York: Macmillan Company, 1947, p. 125. Also see Maurice Dobb, *Soviet Economic Development Since 1917,* New York: International Publishers, 1948, pp. 239–243.

[3] See his speeches of February 4 and June 23, 1931, addressed to Soviet economic managers in J. Stalin, *Selected Writings,* New York: International Publishers, 1942, pp. 194–202 and 203–221.

[4] The class structure of the Soviet Union has not yet been given adequate extended treatment in the sociological literature. Some brief general treatments of varying quality are available. See David Dallin, *The Real Soviet Russia,* New Haven: Yale University Press, 1947, pp. 108–226; Rudolph Schlesinger, *The Spirit of Post-War Russia,* London: Dennis Dobson, Ltd., 1947, pp. 21–47; Nicholas S. Timasheff, *The Great Retreat,* New York: E. P. Dutton, 1946, pp. 203–331; Julian Towster, *Political Power in the U.S.S.R. 1917–1947,* New York: Oxford University Press, 1948, pp. 313–343; A. Yugow, *Russia's Economic Front for War and Peace,* New York: Harper Brothers, 1942, pp. 220–243, 256–259.

1. The ruling elite, a small group consisting of high Party, government, economic, and military officials, prominent scientists, and selected artists and writers.

2. The superior intelligentsia, composed of the intermediary ranks of the categories mentioned above, plus certain important technical specialists.

3. The general intelligentsia, incorporating most of the professional groups, the middle ranks of the bureaucracy, managers of small enterprises, junior military officers, technicians, etc.

4. The white collar group, largely synonymous with the Soviet term for employees, which ranges from petty-bureaucrats through accountants and bookkeepers down to the level of ordinary clerks and office workers.

The working class was also markedly differentiated, incorporating:

1. The working class "aristocracy," that is, the most highly skilled and productive workers, in particular large numbers of the so-called Stakhanovites.

2. The rank-and-file workers, those in one of the lesser skill grades earning slightly above or below the average wage for all workers.

3. The disadvantaged workers, estimated to include as many as one-fourth of the labor force, whose low level of skill and lack of productivity or initiative kept them close to the minimum wage level.

The peasantry, although relatively homogeneous, also was divided into distinguishable subgroups:

1. The well-to-do peasants, consisting of those particularly advantaged by virtue of the location, fertility, or crop raised by their collective farms — i.e., those living on the so-called "millionaire" farms — and those whose trade, skill, or productivity pushes them into the higher income brackets even on the less prosperous farms.

2. The average peasant, shading off into the least productive or poor peasant groups.

There was, in addition, a residual group of those in forced labor camps who are really outside the formal class structure, although available reports indicate that these camps have an internal class structure of their own which derives its main lines from the class structure of the society as a whole.

The sequence in which the subgroups are listed above may be taken as reflecting their rank order within each of the three major categories, but this does not apply to the list as a whole. The rank order within the structure as a whole appears to be as follows: ruling elite (1); superior intelligentsia (2); general intelligentsia (3); working class aristocracy (4); white collar (5.5); well-to-do peasants (5.5); average workers (7); average peasants (8.5); disadvantaged workers (8.5); forced labor (10). It must be recognized, however, that the complexity of the structure and the degree of variation within each of the subgroups was such as to make any such rank ordering a very rough approximation. In addition, this type of rank ordering does not reflect the actual degree of social distance between strata.

Membership in any one of these major social-class groups[5] was predominantly determined on the basis of a complex of conditions, of which occupation, income, and the possession of power and authority were the main elements. Thus, the system was essentially based on differences in the functions performed by individuals in the productive process, the administrative apparatus, and the power structure rather than on either hereditary and semi-hereditary factors, which were primary in defining social position in Tsarist Russia, or on ideological considerations, which predominantly determined the stratification patterns during the earlier years of the Soviet regime.

Yet while these divisions were essentially economic and functional, the evaluation of the different occupations was markedly affected by cultural factors, such as the traditional tendency to rate brain work above physical labor. The strength of such tendencies, inadvertently strengthened by the regime it-

---

5 The term "social-class group" as used here represents a composite, based on the criteria used by Max Weber to distinguish "economic class" and "social status group." See From Max Weber: Essays in Sociology, H. H. Gerth and C. W. Mills, eds., New York: Oxford University Press, 1946, pp. 180–195; The Theory of Social and Economic Organization, A. M. Henderson and Talcott Parsons, eds., New York: Oxford University Press, 1947, pp. 424–429.

self,[6] is strikingly reflected in the following criticism directed at Soviet parents:

> Many of us are to blame for spoiling our children, asking them when they are still in rompers, "What do you want to be when you grow up?" and falling into raptures at their answers — an academician, a ballerina, or something else of that sort. And now these same children are called upon to be steel smelters, rolling mill operators, forge hands — dirty, hot, and hard jobs.[7]

Furthermore, despite the fact that the range of income and special privilege available to each of the major groups was fairly distinct, there was a significant degree of overlapping. Thus, an appreciable number of workers and peasants had incomes on the average higher than those of large segments of the white collar group and in some cases equaling the incomes of many individuals in the general and even in the superior intelligentsia.[8] Highly

---

[6] Both because of its desire to capitalize on the promise of social mobility for all strata of the population, and because of the extreme need for technically competent personnel created by the expansion of the economy, Soviet propaganda in the thirties glorified the status of the professionally trained. The consequences of such emphasis were apparently far from fully foreseen by the leaders. Note the comment of the late President Kalinin: "Formerly we educated people to become intellectuals and not persons doing physical labor. I personally consider this incorrect, since in our state the majority of the population is, after all, occupied in physical labor." Quoted in *Oktyabr*, No. 10, 1944, p. 119.

[7] A. Loginov, "Young Complements of the Working Class," *Oktyabr*, No. 10, 1944, pp. 120–121, quoted in Philip R. Lever, the "State Labor Reserves System of the Soviet Union," unpublished M.A. thesis, Columbia University, 1948.

[8] See Abram Bergson, *The Structure of Soviet Wages*, Cambridge: Harvard University Press, 1946, *passim*, and William Schumer, "Incomes of Selected Professions in the U.S.S.R.," unpublished M.A. thesis, Columbia University, 1948. Unfortunately, both of these works deal only with the period up to the mid-thirties, after which the dispersion of incomes within and between particular occupations generally increased. For comments on later developments see: Gregory Bienstock, S. M. Schwarz, and A. Yugow, *Management in Russian Industry and Agriculture*, Oxford University Press, 1944, pp. 91–95, 163–169; Baykov, *op. cit.*, pp. 339–350; Dobb, *op. cit.*, pp. 424–429; Naum

skilled workers, particularly the Stakhanovites, were also granted greater privileges in the access to scarce goods and services — especially under rationing — and were awarded more formal prestige and status by the regime than most ordinary employees. Finally, the major groupings based on income and power had begun to develop fairly definitive styles of life, to elaborate differential patterns of association, and to manifest varying degrees of group-consciousness.

As a result of these conditions the component social-class groups were enmeshed in a complicated system of interrelationships producing a pattern of social stratification which was certainly not as simple as Stalin's description of it. Neither did it conform to some of the descriptions of it in Western literature on the U.S.S.R., in which the error was frequently made of placing all Party members — regardless of income, power, or prestige — at the head of the social hierarchy, or of assuming that the divisions between the *occupational* groups were so sharp and distinct that all employees ranked above all workers, and all workers above all peasants.

Social Mobility

Although a relatively precise system of social stratification had been elaborated by 1940, this system was the product of a recent and enormous shifting of population into the newly developed positions opened up as a result of the expansion of the national economy under the industrialization and collectivization programs from 1928 on. It is to be noted that while the total number of workers and employees more than doubled in roughly the first decade of the Plans,[9] the size of the intelligentsia increased at the striking rate of 3.8 times between 1926 and 1937. In the same period the number of responsible managers of large- and small-scale enterprises increased by 4.6 times, and other categories showed even more marked expansion — the number of engineers and architects being 7.9 times, and the number of scientific workers (including professors) being 5.9 times greater in 1937 than in 1926. In

---

Jasny, *The Socialized Agriculture of the U.S.S.R.*, Stanford University Press, 1949, pp. 688–705.

[9] *Sotsialisticheskoe Stroitel'stvo Soyuza SSR, 1933–1938*, Moscow: Gosplanizdat, 1939, p. 20.

the case of agriculture alone some 580,000 positions, almost all newly created, were filled by collective farm chairmen and their deputies.[10]

Comparable opportunities for advancement became available at other levels as the changes in the socio-economic and political structure created a demand for enormous numbers of lower managerial personnel, semi-professionals, and skilled workers. During 1938, for example, the program for giving initial and refresher training for those in industry and allied fields encompassed 6,580,500 people outside of the universities and secondary schools. The great bulk (5,418,000) were enrolled in "courses" designed to impart rudimentary industrial skills, but almost 300,000 were training to be foremen and Stakhanovites. Similarly in the field of agriculture, 1,211,387 persons completed brief training courses during 1937 and 1938 to qualify for positions as combine operators, mechanics, veterinary assistants, field brigade leaders, etc.[11]

A description of mobility in this period must, finally, give attention to the marked changes in the position of women in the Soviet Union. The proportion which women constituted of the total labor force increased from 28 per cent in 1928 to 38 per cent in 1938,[12] which meant that the absolute number of women workers and employees was more than doubled. Throughout this period women comprised a large part, in some cases over half, of the students at industrial training schools, and as a result they came to represent a significant proportion of the skilled workers in Soviet

industry.[13] Their advance in fields requiring higher training was even more impressive. Between 1928 and 1938 the proportion of women in the universities increased from 28 per cent to 43 per cent, and from 37 per cent to 51 per cent in the specialized secondary schools.[14] The effect of this upward movement was reflected in the fact that they constituted about 40 per cent of all specialists in the Soviet Union before the war.[15] The shifts in the rural regions were no less striking, as large numbers of women assumed positions of responsibility and skill on the collective farms.[16]

Thus it may be said that on the eve of the war decade the Soviet Union possessed virtually a completely open class system, characterized by a high degree of mobility. This mobility was created predominantly by the tremendous expansion of the national economy, but was given additional impetus by the high rate of natural attrition accompanying the revolutionary process, by the declassing — and in part physical elimination — of major portions of the former upper and middle classes, and by a political system which periodically removed large numbers of people from responsible positions by means of the *chistka* or purge.

---

[10] K. Seleznev, "On the New Soviet Intelligentsia," *Partiinoe Stroitel'stvo*, No. 13, 1939, p. 40. *XVIII S'ezd Vsesoyusznoi Kommunisticheskoi Partii*, Stenographic Report, Moscow: Ogiz, 1939, pp. 309–310.

[11] *Kul'turnoe Stroitel'stvo SSSR*, Moscow: Gosplanizdat, 1940, pp. 136, 138.

[12] *Planovoe Khozyaistvo*, No. 10, 1939, p. 114. This increase was not bought cheaply. Women worked very largely because of the need to supplement family income. Despite considerable strides in the provision of creches, kindergartens, and communal services, the available resources were far from enabling women to work without extreme hardships arising from their continuing responsibilities as wives and mothers.

[13] In 1941, for example, women constituted 32 per cent of the electricians in electrical substations, 29 per cent of the machine molders, and 27 per cent of the compressor operators. It is important to note that they were represented as well in occupations most unsuited for women, being 17 per cent of the stevedores and 6 per cent of the steamboiler stokers. N. Voznesensky, *The Economy of the U.S.S.R. During World War II*, Washington: Public Affairs Press, 1948, p. 66.

[14] *Kul'turnoe Stroitel'stvo*, p. 113.

[15] By 1949 women constituted 44 per cent of all specialists in the Soviet Union. The prewar percentage was, of course, somewhat lower. *Izvestiya*, March 8, 1949.

[16] In addition to providing concrete opportunities for training and advancement, the collective farm introduced a more general and far-reaching change in the position of women. For under the labor-day system of payment each woman was paid directly for her work, rather than having the rewards for her labor go into the general family funds through the person of her husband or father. Sir John Maynard regarded this change as having produced one of the fundamental social sources of support for the regime, by putting the village women "on the side of the Soviets." *Russia in Flux*, New York: The Macmillan Co., 1948, pp. 399–400.

Class Structure During the War Decade

The war decade must be recognized as having provided an extreme test of the stability and solidity of the system of stratification existing in 1940. For on the two former occasions when the Soviet Union had experienced extensive social upheaval and strain there had been a marked tendency for the society to move away from stratification towards social equalization and the elimination of economic class differences.[17] This tendency was most evident in the period of War Communism from 1918 to 1921, and was perhaps best reflected in the fact that in the latter year the wages of the most skilled workers were only 102 per cent of those of the least skilled workers, that is, they were in effect equal.[18] A similar tendency, although less marked, was manifested during the early turbulent years of the First Plan. In industry this took most concrete form in the tendencies toward wage equalization, which Stalin later fought. And in agriculture it was apparent in the tremendous leveling effect of the forced collectivization, which swept away the entire stratum of rich peasants or *kulaks* along with many of the middle peasants, and reduced the remainder to the common, and initially relatively impoverished, status of collective farm members.

In sharp contrast, during the war years the system of stratification was in no major respect subjected by the Communist leaders to measures designed to press equalization and to erase the lines of stratification. On the contrary, almost all of the wartime measures respected the major prewar lines of demarcation. This applied in the realm of monetary rewards; in the structure and operation of the

rationing system, particularly through the use of "closed stores" open only to specified segments of the population; in the application of differential patterns for evacuating populations from threatened areas, and so on.

Not only did the system of stratification demonstrate its durability during the war years, but there was an intensification of the process of lending greater precision to the lines of division and of more fully formalizing and institutionalizing the differences between the major social-class groups. This was most strikingly indicated, indeed it was symbolized, by the regulations established to govern the award of the most important military decorations created during the war. For the first time in Soviet history it was provided by law that certain awards such as the Order of Victory, formally defined as the highest Soviet military decoration, were to be granted only to commanding personnel of highest rank, and so on through the hierarchy of military command down to such medals as the Orders of Glory, which were awarded only to junior officers and enlisted personnel.[19] This was in marked contrast to the conditions for granting the military awards in existence before the war, such as the Order of the Red Banner, granted without distinction to the rank and file, officers, and high commanding personnel alike.[20]

Thus, the Soviet regime has adopted the principle that recognition and reward are to be determined not only by the *extent* of a man's contribution beyond the call of duty, but also by the *status* he held when he made this contribution. A comparable development occurred with the creation in 1939 of special "Stalin Prizes" for outstanding contributions in the arts, sciences, and industry. The prizes are awarded annually to as many as a thousand persons, and range from 50,000 to 300,000 rubles in cash.[21] Ordinary citizens, of course,

---

[17] This applied, of course, only in regard to those segments of the population considered eligible for membership in the new society, especially workers and poor peasants. The policy in regard to the former so-called "possessing classes" was not merely to equalize but to eliminate them. The old technical and administrative intelligentsia were associated with the possessing classes in this respect; but since they could not be destroyed without irreparable loss to the society, the initial goal in their case was the more limited one of declassing them and bringing them to the same or even a lower status level than workers or peasants.

[18] Baykov, *op. cit.,* p. 43.

[19] For a description of the major decorations created during the war (up to 1944) and the conditions for their award, see *Sbornik Zakonov SSSR: Ukazov Prezidiuma Verkhovnogo Soveta SSSR 1938–1944,* Moscow: 1945, pp. 260–286.

[20] *Malaya Sovetskaya Entsiklopediya,* Moscow: Ogiz, 1938, Vol. 7, p. 767.

[21] For the decree which initially established the Prizes, then limited to 100,000 rubles, see *Pravda,* December 21, 1939.

have very slight chances of qualifying for awards in the arts and sciences, but even in the case of prizes granted for inventions and fundamental improvements in production methods there is almost no representation of the rank-and-file worker or even of the lower ranks of industrial management such as foremen.[22]

Perhaps even more striking has been the recent practice of providing large cash grants and substantial annuities for the widows and heirs of prominent Soviet officials, scientists, and artists. To choose some examples more or less at random: the wife of Peoples' Artist of the U.S.S.R., A. V. Aleksandrov, was given 50,000 rubles and a personal pension of 750 rubles per month, and his son Yuri a pension of 750 rubles per month until completion of his higher education; the widow of Lt. General of Engineering Troops D. M. Karbyshev was granted a pension of 1,000 rubles a month, and his daughter and son each 700 rubles per month until the completion of their education.[23] No instances are known to this writer of comparable grants made to persons of lesser social rank who made outstanding contributions at the level of *their* occupational skill.

A second major development which tended further to formalize the distinctions between the major social groupings was the adoption of a series of laws which placed several millions of Soviet citizens in civilian uniforms. At the present time all officials and responsible personnel, and in some cases rank-and-file employees and workers, in the railway and river transport systems, in the coal and iron ore industries, in the Ministry of Foreign Affairs and the Procuracy, as well as students in State Labor Reserves Schools, must wear either uniforms — which vary in quality, color, and style according to the status of the wearer — or distinctive insignia of rank in the form of collar tabs and sleeve markings similar to the insignia worn by military personnel.[24] The main reason stated for this innovation was its importance for improving discipline and increasing the authority of those in positions of responsibility, which is itself significant.[25] But this was not simply a wartime emergency measure since in the majority of cases the decision to adopt this system came near the end or after the formal cessation of hostilities, and there has been no indication that a shift in policy is forthcoming.

The fact that large numbers of Soviet citizens now wear insignia of rank formally designating their position in the hierarchy of income, power, and prestige, must be recognized as giving the most direct, formal, and official sanction to a precise system of social stratification. Thus, in effect, the Bolshevik leaders have restored to the Soviet Union the system of *chiny*, or formal civil service ranks, which was a central aspect of the Tsarist system of social differentiation and had traditionally been treated by the Bolsheviks as one of the paramount symbols of class exploitation and stratification.[26] In addition, the insignia of rank will probably serve as a focus around which informal patterns for demanding and giving social deference will develop, and this in turn may be expected to go far in institutionalizing the existing system of stratification.

A third major development was the removal of several economic restrictions which formerly tended to exert an equalizing influence. Among the more striking measures was the abolition of the inheritance tax, in force since 1926,

---

[22] Of 121 awards made in 1948 for inventions and fundamental improvements in production methods, only 4 went to persons with the rank of foreman and below — to a shepherd, a chief drill master, two foremen, and in one case "the workers of the plant." In each instance, the prize was given *jointly* to these persons and to a man of higher rank — engineer, director of the plant, senior scientist, etc. Based on the notice of awards published in *Pravda*, July 3, 1948.
[23] *Pravda*, August 17, 1946.

[24] For examples see *Vedomosti Verkhovnogo Soveta*, 1943, Nos. 22, 32, 39; *Pravda*, September 5, 12, 24, 1947
[25] See, for example, the quotation from the 1945 text on *Soviet Administrative Law* cited by V. Gsovski, *Soviet Civil Law*, 2 vols., Ann Arbor: University of Michigan Law School, Vol. I, p. 144. Also see the *Information Bulletin*, Embassy of the U.S.S.R., Washington, D.C., Nov. 7, 1943, pp. 33–37.
[26] The first major shift in Soviet policy in this respect came with the restoration of regular military ranks in the Soviet armed forces in 1935. See Gsovski, *op. cit.*, pp. 142–143. Special significance, however, attaches to the extension of this practice to status groups in civil life, and particularly to restoration of the term *chin*.

which had provided for taxes graded progressively according to the size of an estate up to 90 per cent of its total value. Under the new law only a governmental registration fee is collected and this fee may not exceed more than 10 per cent of the estate's valuation.[27]

This new inheritance law must be seen in the context of the Soviet personal income tax structure. Under the scale established in 1943, progressive rates are applied only up to the level of 1,000 rubles of income per month, with a single flat rate of 13 per cent for all earnings beyond that point. Thus, a man earning 6,000 rubles per year would pay 5.2 per cent of that sum as income tax, whereas a man earning 60,000 rubles, or ten times the approximate average annual wage in industry, would pay only 12 per cent of his earnings.[28] Incomes of 60,000 rubles per year are by now common in certain segments of the population, and are frequently greatly exceeded. It is significant, for example, that the income tax law of 1940 included provisions for a special tax on income in excess of 300,000 rubles made by writers, actors, and other artists.[29] Finally, it must be noted that the large special awards such as the Stalin Prizes are tax free, as is the total income of those who hold such awards as Hero of the Soviet Union and Hero of Socialist Labor,[30] categories which include many of the country's high income earners.

Since only certain groups — such as the ruling elite, the superior intelligentsia, the highly skilled workers, and some *kolkhoz* members[31] — are capable of accumulating large sums of money, these laws act further to reinforce the stratification system. They do so by protecting large income differentials during the life of the earners,[32] and by providing families with the means to maintain their socio-economic position for protracted periods after the death of the head of the household.

As a fourth point here, brief notice must be given to shifts in the relations to the power structure of the various social-class groups. The 18th Communist Party Congress in 1939 placed members of the intelligentsia on an equal footing with workers and peasants seeking to enter the Party, and in fact since that time the Party has given first priority to the enrollment of intellectuals.[33] This shift in the

[27] *Vedomosti Verkhovnogo Soveta SSSR*, 1943, No. 3. See V. Gsovski, "Family and Inheritance in Soviet Law," *The Russian Review*, 1947, Vol. 7, No. 1.

[28] A. K. Suchkova (ed.) *Dokhody Gosudarstvennogo Byudzheta SSSR*, Moscow: Gosfinizdat, 1945, pp. 133–136; K. N. Plotnikov, *Byudzhet Sotsialisticheskogo Gosudarstva*, Leningrad: Gosfinizdat, 1948, pp. 278–282. The new tax law of 1943, in comparison with the previous law, actually provided slight tax relief for those in the lower brackets and a slight increase in the rates for the upper brackets. The striking fact about the law was that it continued in force a tax system involving only the most modest progression in rates for higher income brackets. This pattern was set in the early thirties at a time when there were relatively few incomes over 600 rubles per month, and the general income spread was relatively slight.

[29] V. P. D'yachenko (ed.), *Finansy i Kredit SSSR*, Moscow: Gosfinizdat, 1940, p. 321.

[30] Plotnikov, *op. cit.*, p. 281.

[31] Special income tax provisions (and inheritance laws) govern peasants on the collective farms. Major segments of the peasantry accumulated very large sums of cash holdings during the recent war through the sale of extremely scarce food products. It was largely to prevent this money from flooding the consumers goods market that the monetary reform of 1947 was carried out. See B. Alexandrov, "The Soviet Currency Reform" *The Russian Review*, Jan., 1949, Vol. 8, No. 1, pp. 56–61.

[32] Probably of even greater significance than the modest direct income tax in protecting existing income differentials is the Soviet system of indirect taxation. The turnover tax — not seen by the consumer since it is included in the price — is leveled primarily on consumption goods, about 85 per cent of the collections in 1940 being derived from food and textile products. The importance of this tax is clear when it is recognized that it regularly accounts for about 60 per cent of the total budget receipts of the government and that this budget, unlike those in most countries, includes almost all of the nation's allocations for new industrial capital investment in the coming year. Its impact on personal income is highlighted by the fact that it represents from 50 to 80 per cent of the selling price of most mass consumption items. It appears to be, in its social effect, a regressive tax. Yugow, *op. cit.*, pp. 125–138. For an opposing view see Dobb, *op. cit.*, pp. 360–374.

[33] See B. Moore, Jr., "The Communist Party of the Soviet Union: 1928–1944," *American Sociological Review*, IX (June, 1944), 267–278; Merle Fainsod, "Postwar Role of the Communist Party." *The Annals of the American Academy of Political and Social Science*, 263 (May, 1944), 20–32.

value system and in the practice of the Communist leaders was also reflected more subtly in the manner in which they evaluated the contribution to the war effort of each of the major social groups. The intelligentsia were at all times given full credit for at least an equal share in the victory, and indeed were at times assigned a foremost role.

Changes Affecting the Chance for Mobility

Just as the system of social stratification emerged essentially intact from this period so did the fact of high social mobility. Indeed, severe wartime personnel losses vacated many positions and thus created new opportunities for advancement. In addition, the restoration of the devasted economy and the further program of expansion undertaken in the Fourth Five-Year Plan have encouraged relatively rapid mobility. It is perhaps sufficient to indicate that by 1946 the number of students in higher educational institutions had reached the prewar levels, after having fallen to about a third of the former enrollment during the early part of the war, and a large expansion beyond that point has been undertaken.

Yet, it must also be stated that during the war decade forces were set in motion which may in time act seriously to restrict social mobility and to transform the present pattern of stratification into a much more closed class system. There are at least five such developments which deserve mention here.

1. *Restrictions on access to educational opportunities.* On October 2, 1940, the Soviet government simultaneously introduced a labor draft of up to one million youths per year between the ages of fourteen and seventeen for training as industrial workers,[34] and tuition fees at higher schools and for the last three years of secondary education.[35] Both laws

continue in effect and appear to be intended for extended operation.

In terms of human freedom, the state labor-reserves draft serves to restrict the right of millions of Soviet youths to choose their occupation and place of work,[36] and the fee system was certainly a departure from standard Soviet practice and ideology — the original decree being in violation of the explicit provisions of the Constitution, since amended to eliminate the discrepancy.[37] But specification of the implications of these measures for social mobility must be approached with caution, and certainly the evidence does not support sweeping assertions, such as have been made, that these measures introduce hereditary social status into the Soviet system.

The labor draft, for example, places prime emphasis on those not attending school, and is in part designed to get rural youths off the farms into industry.[38] Although most of these youths undoubtedly come from families low in the social-class hierarchy, there is no reason to believe that they would have been upward mobile even if not drafted as industrial laborers. Indeed, the training they receive may increase their opportunities for mobility. Graduates of the six-month factory training schools, for example, are given a skill rating in the third or fourth category, and those from the two-year craft and railway schools are placed in the relatively high fourth to sixth skill cate-

---

[34] *Vedomosti Verkhovnogo Soveta SSSR,* 1940, No. 37. The initial decree provided for the drafting of boys only, but a later decree of June 19, 1947, provided as well for the drafting of girls in the 15–18 age group, and extended the age of eligible males up to and including 19 years.
[35] The following fees were established: for the eighth through the tenth grades of regular secondary and specialized (*tekhnikum*) secondary schools — 200 rubles per year in Moscow, Leningrad, and capital cities of union republics, 150 rubles elsewhere; for higher educational institu-

tions — 400 rubles per year in Moscow, Leningrad, etc., 300 rubles elsewhere. Students at higher schools for the study of art, music, and the theater must pay 500 rubles. Students studying through correspondence courses pay half fees, as do those studying at comparable night schools. *Sobranie Postanovlenii i Rasporyazhenii Pravitel'stva SSSR,* 1940, No. 27, Sect. 637; 1940, No. 29, Sect. 698.
[36] For a description of the structure and functioning of the system see Philip R. Lever, *op. cit., passim.*
[37] Article 121 of the 1936 (Stalin) Constitution had provided for "free education, including higher education." (*Konstitutsiya Soyuza Sovetskikh Sotsialisticheskikh Respublik,* Moscow, 1938, p. 87). It was amended by the Supreme Soviet on Feb. 25, 1947, to read: "free education, up to and including the seventh grade. . . ." *Constitution of the Union of Soviet Socialist Republics,* Moscow, 1947 (in English).
[38] For relevant citations and discussion see Lever, *op. cit.,* pp. 39–45.

gories.[39] Thus, the graduates of these schools are placed at a distinct advantage over unskilled workers entering Soviet industry without training. They are, in addition, trained free of charge, provided with room, board, and clothing, and may receive some small cash payment for the value of the goods produced during their training.[40]

As for the tuition fees, it must be recognized that admittance to higher educational institutions remains on the basis of uniform, nationwide competitive examinations. The law specifies that those with the highest grades among the examinees shall be selected for admission, and that those not accepted in the field in which they took their examination may be admitted to fill vacancies in higher schools in related fields. Students with grades of distinction in their secondary school work are admitted without examination. Persons who served in the recent war are admitted directly, i.e., on a non-competitive basis, so long as they receive a passing grade on the examinations.[41]

Students in higher and specialized secondary schools who earn "good" grades, and this apparently includes almost 80 per cent of the total,[42] are granted stipends by the government. The stipends are graded according to the type of institution attended and the student's year of study, with a bonus of 25 per cent for those with excellent grades in all subjects. Thus, students receiving the smallest sums, e.g. those in the first year of a secondary school for teacher training, can pay the cost of the full year's tuition with two of their monthly stipend payments; a senior in a major university, such as one for training transport engineers, can cover the full cost of a year's tuition with one monthly payment of his stipend if he makes excellent grades.[43] In addition, students from many of the national minority groups in several of the union-republics are exempt from tuition payments,[44] as are those students with good or excellent grades who can prove that they are "needy."[45] The stipends, furthermore, are not subject to income tax.[46] Finally, legal provision is made for low cost rooms and meals.[47] As a result, the stipends should enable many students to cover a very large part of the costs of their

[39] *Bolshevik*, Nos. 7–8, April, 1943, p. 21, cited by Lever, *op. cit.*, p. 59.

[40] Order No. 1, Chief Administration of Labor Reserves under the Council of Peoples Commissars, Article 17, provided that one-third of the funds received for goods and services produced by the schools should be paid to the students. *Izvestiya*, October 5, 1940.

[41] Decree of the Central Committee of the All-Union Communist Party (Bolshevik) and the Council of Peoples' Commissars of the U.S.S.R., of July 11, 1940, No. 1228; Instruction of the Ministry of Higher Education of the U.S.S.R. of February 25, 1947. *Vysshaya Shkola*, Moscow, 1948, pp. 81–86.

[42] Since September 1, 1948, stipends are granted only to students who have either excellent or good grades, with the exception of those in certain important schools, such as those for mining and metallurgy, in which all passing students receive stipends. In 1946 S. Kaftanov, Minister of Higher Education, reported that more than 78 per cent of the students had passed all their courses with grades of "good" or better. Previously, with the exception of the war years, 1940–43, stipends had been granted on a more liberal basis, being given to all with "passing grades." This change has meant some reduction in the number receiving

stipends, since in 1939 90.6 per cent of all students in higher schools received them. *Byulleten' Ministerstva Vysshego Obrazovaniya SSSR*, No. 10, October, 1948, p. 7; *Vestnik Vysshei Shkoli*, No. 11–12, 1946, p. 2; *Vysshaya Shkola*, p. 496; *Kul'turnoe Stroitel'stvo*, p. 115.

[43] Students in most secondary schools receive from 80 rubles per month in the first year to 140 in the fourth. In particularly important transport and industrial *tekhnikums* the rates are from 125 to 200 rubles per month. In most higher schools the basic rates range from 140 rubles for the first year to 210 in the fifth, whereas the rates at the most important industrial and transport higher training institutes range from 210 to 315 rubles per month. *Vysshaya Shkola*, pp. 496–497.

[44] For the relevant decisions of the Council of Peoples' Commissars see *Vysshaya Shkola*, pp. 554–555.

[45] Decision of the Committee on Higher Schools under the Council of Peoples' Commissars, October 12, 1940, No. 857, *Vysshaya Shkola*, p. 548.

[46] Plotnikov, *op. cit.*, p. 281. This applies on amounts up to and including 210 rubles per month.

[47] Dormitory fees (including bedding) are 7 rubles per month for students at secondary schools, and 15 rubles per month for those at higher educational institutions. In 1938 the proportion of all students living in dormitories at higher schools and *tekhnikums* for training specialists (industrial, transport, and agricultural) ranged from 56 to 80 per cent. See *Vysshaya Shkola*, p. 537; *Kul'turnoe Stroitel'-stvo*, p. 127.

education independent of their parents' finan-cial resources.

These reservations being made, however, it still seems justified to conclude that the fee system and the labor draft act to a significant degree to restrict the mobility of some and to facilitate maintenance of status of others. The labor draft, for example, is conducted on a very large scale involving a significant proportion of the eligible youths. Nine hundred thousand boys and girls were to graduate annually from the labor-reserves schools during the years of the postwar Fourth Five Year Plan, and they were expected to account for two-thirds of the anticipated increase in the labor force during the Plan years. The youths called up are regarded as "mobilized," and are subject to penalties of up to a year of forced labor for desertion from the school or gross violation of labor discipline while in training. And upon graduation they must work for a period of four years at an enterprise designated by the state.[48]

Undoubtedly some segment of this group which might otherwise have gone on to further schooling will find its chance for upward mobility seriously reduced, if not effectively cut off, because of the accident of the draft. This remains true despite the fact that a special system of schools for working youths was developed after 1943 to permit those whose education was interrupted by the war, and of course those drafted into the State Labor Reserves, to complete their secondary education. Instruction in these schools is apparently free. There are forty-four weeks in the school year, with sixteen hours of class instruction and four hours of consultation in each week. Similar schools are established for working peasant youths. Students at the end of the seventh year (incomplete secondary) and those at the end of the tenth year (complete secondary) classes may obtain fifteen and twenty days of leave with pay, respectively, in which to prepare for the nationwide matriculation examinations. If they perform successfully, their certificate has equal weight with the diploma from regular secondary schools. These students are at an obvious disadvantage, however, since their instruction is very limited in time, and since they must continue to carry

virtually a full-time job in production while attending school.[49] And the youths so affected are most likely to be from families of lower social-class standing because of the operation of the fee system, the labor draft, and other factors not touched on in this paper.

Similarly, there is no doubt that the fee system will place some segment of the eligible youth at a disadvantage in obtaining a higher education in competition with other youths of only equal or even inferior aptitude whose parents can spare the loss of their earning power, support them, and provide them with the money to pay the fees. It is significant that of the students who dropped out of higher school in the Russian Republic (R.S.F.S.R.) between the school year 1940–41, during which the fees were introduced, and 1942–43, some 20 per cent left due to "the sifting out in connection with the introduction of fees for tuition and the changes in the method of allotting stipends."[50] Although the system for allocating stipends was liberalized once again after 1943,[51] and although the magnitude of the percentage of withdrawals given above was undoubtedly affected by wartime financial strains,[52] there is no mistaking the initial impact of the introduction of the fee system.

But beyond this direct effect, the tuition fees act more subtly to permit a class influence

---

[48] See Lever, op. cit., passim.

[49] Narodnoe Obrazovanie (compiled by A. M. Danev), Moscow; Uchpedgiz, 1948, pp. 247–265.
[50] Narodnoe Obrazovanie v RSFSR v 1943 gody (Otchet Narodnogo Komissariata Prosveshcheniya RSFSR), Moscow, 1944. p. 42.
[51] In October 1940, it was provided that only students making excellent progress should receive stipends. In 1943 the prewar system of granting the stipends to all students who made passing grades was restored. See fn. 42 above. Pravda, October 3, 1940; Vysshaya Shkola, p. 496.
[52] In the first war year in the Russian Republic 130,000 students, almost half of the enrollment in higher schools and teachers' institutes in the R.S.F.S.R., withdrew for various reasons. In the school year 1943–44, as judged by a small sample of the schools, 26 per cent of the enrollment, then much reduced, left the schools. Of these only 2.5 per cent were dismissed for non-payment of fees or left for reasons of their "material conditions," and 11.3 per cent because of family obligations other than illness in the family. Narodnoe Obrazovanie v RSFSR v 1943 Gody, p. 42. Narodnoe Obrazovanie v RSFSR v 1944 Gody, p. 72.

on that type of social mobility which is based on the acquisition of higher education. Although the tuition fees are the same for regular (academic) and technical or specialized secondary schools, no stipends are granted to students in the academic secondary schools.[53] Under Soviet law graduates of academic secondary schools are permitted to enter higher schools directly if they qualify. But only 5 per cent of the graduates of the technical and specialized secondary schools are permitted to do so, the remainder being obliged to spend three years "in production" as technicians, teachers, etc., according to their speciality.[54] Thus of those entering higher schools in 1938, 58.8 per cent came from regular secondary schools, 12.9 per cent from technical and specialized secondary schools, and 22.9 per cent from the *rabfak* (workers' faculty), i.e., special schools for preparing working and peasant youths and adults whose education had been interrupted for admission to higher educational establishments.[55] The *rabfak* appears to have gone out of existence during the war, and has apparently been replaced by special secondary schools for working urban and peasant youths described above. Students from the less well-to-do homes are obviously more likely to gravitate toward the technical and specialized secondary schools to become eligible for the stipends.[56] In 1938, for example, the social composition of the students in technical and specialized secondary schools was as follows: workers and their children 27.1 per cent; employees, specialists and their children, 16.1 per cent; collective farmers and their children, 49.8 per cent; and others, 7 per cent. A comparable distribution for the regular secondary schools is unfortunately not available, but these figures will be seen to differ sharply from the social composition of the student body in higher educational estab-

lishments as given below.[57] It would appear, therefore, that there is a much higher probability that students from less well-to-do homes will find their attendance at a higher school long postponed, if not put off indefinitely, while their age mates from richer homes are pursuing their higher education.[58]

2. Changes in the inheritance taxes. The new inheritance and income tax laws, mentioned above, when combined with the fact that some members of Soviet society now earn cash incomes of up to 100,000 rubles — quite apart from the valuable services they may obtain free, such as assignment to a desirable apartment or the use of an automobile — make it possible for some families to have large sums of cash savings.[59] Such savings receive interest at the rate of 3 per cent, or 5 per cent if deposited for fixed terms, and this interest is not treated as income for tax purposes.[60] In addition, families may accumulate significant quantities of physical property in the form of houses,[61] and household and personal goods, easily convertible to liquid assets because of the Soviet goods scarcity. Although this fact

---

[53] *Vysshaya Shkola*, pp. 496–497.

[54] Those who have served three years on active military duty may substitute such service for the requirement. *Vysshaya Shkola*, p. 83.

[55] *Kul'turnoe Stroitel'stvo*, p. 127.

[56] There is, of course, a "cultural" factor operating here as well. Students of parents in the intelligentsia are more likely to be oriented in childhood toward the academic secondary schools, and are more likely to be better qualified to pursue such courses.

[57] *Kul'turnoe Stroitel'stvo*, p. 114.

[58] It appears that of those graduating from the regular or academic secondary schools about 75 of 100 graduates succeed in entering higher schools, but of the graduates of the specialized secondary schools only 13 of 100 are able to go on. Estimates based on data given in *Kul'turnoe Stroitel'stvo*, pp. 109, 111–112, 127.

[59] In 1935, the last year on which adequate data have been published by the Soviet government, 64 per cent of all depositors had savings accounts of below 25 rubles, and these represented less than 6 per cent of the value of all deposits; in contrast, less than 3 per cent of all depositors had accounts of more than 1,000 rubles, but these represented almost 43 per cent of the value of all deposits. This pattern apparently still prevailed in 1940, with a very large percentage of the total deposits in accounts of over 3,000 rubles. *Sotsialisticheskoe Stroitel'stvo SSSR*, Moscow, Tsunkhy, 1936, pp. 668–669, Plotnikov, *op. cit.*, p. 201.

[60] The currency reform of 1947 served, however, as a progressive tax on these savings accounts, since savings of up to 3,000 rubles were refunded on a 1–1 basis, those from 3,000–10,000 on the basis of 2 new rubles for 3 old, and sums above 10,000 on the basis of 1 new for 2 old rubles. See B. Alexandrov, *op. cit.*

[61] Use of such houses for income purposes through rental is of course sharply circumscribed by the legal proscriptions against "speculation."

does not necessarily restrict the upward mobility of other individuals, it does to some degree prevent or forestall the downward mobility of some individuals whose earning power would reduce them to a much lower standard of living if they were dependent on it alone.

3. *The tendency to make access to certain desirable statuses dependent at least in part on birth.* For example, it appears that in admitting boys to the recently created military cadet (*Suvorov* and *Nakhimov*) schools for training the Soviet equivalent of "an officer and a gentleman," preference was given to the children of high officers.[62] At a lower point in the social scale the regulations governing admittance to the State Labor Reserves Schools for training railroad workers provide that preference shall be given to children whose parents are railway workers. Thus, a provision which makes access to an occupational status partially dependent on kinship has now been made a part of Soviet law.[63] Such provisions by no means freeze anyone in the social-class position into which he is born. But by restricting access to desirable training opportunities on the basis of kinship they give preferential advantage to some in maintaining the class position of their family, and by thus reducing the number of training opportunities open to all they indirectly restrict the mobility of others who might seek to acquire that training.

4. *The tendency to draw individuals for important managerial posts predominantly from the ranks of those trained in the regular programs of secondary and higher technical education.*[64] During the first decade of Soviet rule,

---

[62] See Gsovski, *Soviet Civil Law*, Vol. I, p. 147, citing *Krasnaya Zvezda*, August 22 and December 1, 1943.

[63] Article 4, Order No. 1, October 4, 1940, Chief Administration of Labor Reserves under the Council of Peoples' Commissars. (*Izvestiya*, Oct. 5, 1940). Up to 1943, of course, provisions of this type were used to keep children of the disfranchised former "ruling" classes from obtaining a higher education.

[64] For a description of the development of Soviet policy on this question see Solomon M. Schwarz's analysis in *Management in Soviet Industry and Agriculture*, pp. 104–124. Mr. Schwarz's conclusions go beyond what is warranted by the available data, and should therefore be used with caution.

and particularly during the first years of the Five Year Plan, large numbers of adults who were regarded as politically reliable were rapidly trained and then advanced to high managerial positions. In the last decade the personnel newly entering into the ranks of management in Soviet industry have tended to come almost exclusively from among the graduates of Soviet higher schools. The Party ruled in 1941, for example, that the position of foreman, lowest rung in the administrative hierarchy, should be filled predominantly by persons possessing specialized technical training — skilled workers being utilized only when engineers and technicians are not available.[65]

Insofar as political and social conditions permit it to do this, the regime is of course acting logically and rationally. But the fact does remain that movement from the status of worker to high managerial positions within the *same* generation, the Soviet equivalent of the American dream of rags to riches, is now becoming less usual whereas it was commonplace, if not the standard practice, in an earlier period. In this sense and to that degree social mobility has decreased in the Soviet Union in the last decade.

5. *The strengthening of the family.* The Soviet regime has sought to rehabilitate and strengthen the family through a series of measures inaugurated in 1936 and considerably extended during the wartime decade.[66] If we accept the proposition that strong emphasis

---

[65] See the address of Malenkov to 18th Party Conference and the Resolutions of the Conference, *Izvestiya*, February 16 and 19, 1942; also see *Planovoe Khozyaistvo*, No. 7, 1940, p. 19. This ruling should not be misunderstood, however, as being designed to inhibit the mobility of skilled workers. Its intent — as against its effect — was to secure persons of a higher technical skill at the working level, to get the technically trained out of offices and down to the production level, and to give recently graduated engineers first-hand practical experience. It should also be noted that in 1940 of the "directors of shops" in industry, a position far above that of foreman, only 22 per cent were specialists with higher education. But 32 per cent of the *assistant* shop directors had higher education, indicating the nature of the trend.

[66] See Alex Inkeles, "Family and Church in the Post-war USSR," *The Annals of the American Academy of Political and Social Science*, 263 (May, 1949), 33–44.

on kinship ties in any social system acts to inhibit social mobility, then the measures adopted warrant at least the presumption that, as the family is strengthened in the Soviet Union, kin relations will play an increasingly important role in determining Soviet youths' opportunities for mobility. It should be noted that stories about persons in responsible positions exerting influence to favor their kin have appeared with considerable frequency in recent years, both in the Soviet press and in the reports of first-hand observers.

Ideology, Social Classes, and the Soviet System

It would appear that the Communist regime has not been highly successful in preventing the stratification of society into social-class groups, and is certainly a long way from having eliminated them. In contrasting these facts with the relevant doctrines of Soviet ideology, however, it must be recognized that Lenin was very explicit in stating that inequality of reward would persist — *and be protected by the state* — for a protracted period after the revolution transferred ownership of the means of production to the workers.[67] But Lenin certainly did not envision anything like the present *pattern* of stratification, nor did he imagine that the differentiation would be nearly as intensive as that currently manifested in the Soviet Union. He assumed, for example, that all persons in administrative positions would receive the same salary as an average worker.[68]

It seems relevant to state, therefore, that Lenin seriously underestimated the degree to which strong tendencies toward social differentiation inhere in the organization of modern industry and mechanized agriculture. Indeed Lenin assumed that the development of this complex organization of production, with its attendant rationalization and routinization of function provided the necessary basis for social equalization.[69] Actually, Soviet experience indicates that the very fact of modern large-scale production — involving extreme division of labor, precise differentiation of function, emphasis on technical competence, and elaborate hierarchies of authority and responsibility

— provides a natural basis for the development of distinct social groups.[70]

Such differences in the relations of individuals to the productive process tend to yield inequalities in economic reward because of the differential position of certain persons in the labor market. This was particularly marked in the Soviet case, where the initial economic backwardness of the country combined with the exceptionally rapid tempo of industrialization to produce an extreme scarcity of skilled labor and technically trained personnel. The occupational structure, furthermore, is so important a focus in contemporary large-scale social systems that occupational status can serve very largely to determine the *general* social status of individuals. It requires only the appearance of distinctive patterns of speech, manners, and dress, differential patterns of association, and social group consciousness, to lay the foundation of a system of stratification based on social-class groupings. Once established, such stratification, as Max Weber indicated, "goes hand in hand with a monopolization of ideal and material goods or opportunities in a manner we have come to know as typical."[71] Thus, in the Soviet case, as stratification has become instutionalized there has been a noticeable tendency for social mobility to decline and for the system to become less an open class structure.

These facts must in part be attributed to the decreasing opportunities made available by the economic system as it passed beyond its initial period of enormous growth and approached a more modest and stable rate of development. Soviet university officials, for example, report that the number of applicants for each vacancy in the higher schools grows greater every year. Full weight must also be given, however, to the fact that there is now a large group of people who have achieved high status by means legitimate within the existing social system, and who wish to pass some of their benefits and privileges on to their children. This creates strong pressures for the establishment of conditions which make it easier for children from this group to main-

---

[67] Vladimir I. Lenin, *State and Revolution,* New York: International Publishers, 1935, pp. 75–78.
[68] *Ibid.,* p. 92.
[69] *Ibid.,* p. 83.

[70] For a fuller discussion of this point see Barrington Moore, Jr., *Soviet Politics — The Dilemma of Power: The Role of Ideas in Social Change,* Cambridge: Harvard University Press (in press).
[71] Gerth and Mills (eds.), *op. cit.,* p. 190.

tain or improve their position and simultaneously constitute obstacles to effective competition from the children born into families lower in the scale of stratification. It is certainly not accidental that since 1938 the Soviet Union has not published statistics on the social composition of the student body in higher educational institutions, since at that time — even before the introduction of school fees and the labor draft — it was already true that children of the intelligentsia and employees constituted 47 per cent of the student body although the group made up only some 17 per cent of the total population.[72]

None of this is meant to imply that there are any absolute reasons why stratification could not have been kept at a minimum and mobility at a maximum in the Soviet Union. However much the "objective" conditions which existed may have structured the situation in favor of the course adopted, it was nevertheless a choice among alternatives. For even granting that the speed of industrialization severely limited the supply of consumers goods and the simple necessities of life,[73] this merely posed in more acute form, but did not answer, the question: "Who will get what share?" The decision made under Stalin's guidance was in the direction of maximizing the rewards of the relative few whom Stalin defined as crucial to the productive process, and who were in tremendous demand because of the shortage of skilled hands. But there was always the alternative of spreading the available resources in a relatively uniform, albeit thin, manner.

Yet the Soviet leaders today remain formally committed to the goal of attaining a classless society. What then is the prognosis for the future development of the present structure of stratification? An unequivocal answer appears warranted. The present system of stratification seems to be not merely stable, but is of such an order that it would probably require a new social and political revolution to restore the kind of dynamism necessary to create even an approximation of a classless society as defined in classical Marxism terms.

To state that the system is highly stable is by no means to indicate that the particular individuals in the intelligentsia and other favored groups have absolute security in their positions. For the ruling political elite at the head of the Party recognizes the ever-present possibility that group-consciousness might develop in these favored strata with the implied threat of a challenge to the authority of the present leaders. This possibility is met in part by the incorporation and absorption of groups like the intelligentsia, foremen, and Stakhanovites into the Party,[74] where their members can be indoctrinated, subordinated to the Party's discipline and purposes, and carefully watched. It is also met by maintaining what appears to be an almost calculated degree of relatively constant instability — by means of rapid and sudden turnover in personnel, by intensive criticism, purging, and at times police action, and by consistent bidding up of the lower strata. But although these measures introduce an additional element of dynamism, and aid the top leaders in controlling some of the potential consequences of their policy, they do not represent in any sense an attack on the system of stratification *as a system*.

The reasons for this inhere in the very structure of contemporary Soviet society. For the social classes which are currently most highly rewarded in income, status, and power are precisely those social groups on which the present regime relies most heavily as its basis of social support. A new program aimed at social equalization could, therefore, be accomplished only at the expense, and hence with the alienation, of those groups on whose support the regime rests. Any such effort would consequently subject the whole system to real jeopardy. The interest of the ruling elite in social stability as a foundation for its programs of internal and foreign expansion is such that it seems most unlikely that it would undertake

---

[72] *Kul'turnoe Stroitel'stvo* SSSR, p. 114.
[73] The decision to industrialize at so rapid a tempo was itself not inevitable. Industrialization based on a significantly lower rate of investment, particularly if combined with greater emphasis on consumers goods industries, would have had a profound effect on Soviet internal conditions. In particular, it would have made it possible to have much less intensive economic stratification, since the striking aspect of the Soviet system in this respect is not the absolute level of luxury at which the richer groups live but rather the relatively low level at which the population as a whole finds itself.

---

[74] See fn. 33 *supra*.

a program designed to effect one phase of its ideological goals at the expense of the stability of the system as a whole. It may in fact be said that despite recurrent affirmations of the aim of achieving a classless society, this goal can no longer be realistically regarded as one towards which the present leadership is actively and effectively oriented. Indeed, there is no absolute reason to assume that the present rate of social mobility, which probably equals that in the United States and possibly surpasses it, will be maintained. But if it is not, major consequences for the structure and functioning of Soviet society as now "traditionally" constituted may be expected.

63

Toward the Classless Society?*

Robert A. Feldmesser

(1960)

Since the death of Stalin, the Soviet system has remained a totalitarian dictatorship. This does not mean that no significant changes have occurred. Nor does it mean that pre-Stalinist ideas have lost all influence. Moreover, while the main goals and political structure of the U.S.S.R. have evolved little, if at all, some of the changes described by Professor Feldmesser have moved firmly in a direction opposite to the least attractive features of Stalin's time.

A great deal has been written on the emergence of gross inequalities of wealth, privilege, and official honor in Soviet society. The process, fully described and documented, may be said to have begun with a famous speech by Stalin in 1931, in which he denounced "equality-mongering" in the wage structure and

*Reprinted from "Equality and Inequality Under Khrushchev," *Problems of Communism*, a publication of the United States Information Agency, Vol. 9 (1960), pp. 31–39, by permission of the author. Professor Feldmesser very kindly made some minor corrections in the article as originally published.

called for a new attitude of "solicitude" toward the intelligentsia; it manifested itself in highly differentiated incomes, in a change in the composition of the Communist Party, in the establishment of tuition fees and other more subtle obstacles to higher education, in elegant uniforms and elaborate titles, and in a host of other ways. By the end of World War II, and particularly during the last years of Stalin's life, the trend was clear: the Soviet Union was well advanced along a seemingly irreversible course toward a rigid system of social stratification, in which the upper classes would remain upper, the lower classes lower, and the twain would rarely meet.

Yet the irreversible has now been reversed. With that breathtaking facility which so often startles us, the Soviet leadership has launched a series of measures calculated to reduce the degree and rigidity of differentiation in Soviet society to a very considerable extent. Many observers have not yet fully apprehended this turn of events, if only because all its component parts had not been assembled in one place: to do so is one objective of the present study. But partly, too, the lack of comprehension is due to a reluctance to credit Soviet leaders with the desire or ability to achieve so "virtuous" an aim as social equality — or rather, it is due to a failure to appreciate the *meaning* of equality in the Soviet system. A second objective here is to define that meaning.

The "Revival of Democracy"

[He] began to trample crudely on the methods of collectivity in leadership . . . to order people around and push aside the personnel of Soviet and economic organizations . . . [He] decided questions great and small by himself, completely ignoring the opinions of others.

[He] flattered himself with the belief that all [improvements] were due only to his own merits. The more successfully things went, the more conceited he became, the more airs he gave himself.

. . . you get the impression that everything other people do is bad, and only the things [he] does are good.

These scathing remarks could well have been taken from Khrushchev's secret speech to the 20th Congress of the CPSU exposing the incredible extremes to which Stalin's method of one-man rule had gone. A common reaction to this speech abroad was to see in it a confirmation of the trend toward inequality. The intelligentsia, or the "state bourgeoisie,"[1] despite their privileges *vis-à-vis* other elements of the population, had long resented the Stalinist tyranny. Now, as a result of their increasing power in an industrialized and militarized state, they had reached the point where they could force Khrushchev to confess that they had been unjustly treated, to promise them the freedom of decision-making, and to guarantee the security of their status.

Subsequent comments in the Soviet press have belied this interpretation. The quotations do not come from the secret speech; they are attacks on, respectively, a *raion* party secretary, the chairman of a city soviet executive committee, and a factory director.[2] For, as it now appears, the secret speech was directed not only at the one big Stalin, but also at all the other little Stalins who had grown up in his image. It has been followed up not with praise for Soviet administrators, but with denunciations of *"administrirovanie"* — the highhanded, arrogant ways of officials who have exercised "petty tutelage" over their subordinates; who have glossed over shortcomings, suppressed criticism, and persecuted their critics; who have been "inattentive to the workers and their needs"; who have, in short, violated the letter of Soviet law and the spirit of "Communist morality."

Denunciations of this sort are not, of course, a new phenomenon; but what is interesting today is not only the frequency and vehemence of such attacks but the implicit admission that the inspiration for bad administrative habits came from very high up. Accordingly, Khrushchev's own behavior, so sharply at variance with Stalin's, has been held up as an example for others to follow: Soviet officials have been urged to get closer to the people, to pay more attention to them, and not to rely exclusively on existing channels of authority. Sessions of local soviets are being held more frequently; there have been occasional reports of ministers

and department heads being subjected to questioning by deputies; in some instances, agendas of meetings have been posted and public hearings held on the items under discussion. The number of deputies in local soviets has been increased by 1,800,000, and unpaid activists have been taking on tasks formerly performed by the executive staff — as if housewives were indeed to run the state.[3] Along the same lines, there has been a large-scale effort to reinvigorate the system of worker and peasant correspondents, to protect them from reprisals by the targets of their criticism, and to have them do more of the newspapers' work in place of the professional journalistic staff.[4] A party journal has told *raion* newspapers that they were not limited to criticizing "only rank-and-file workers and 'second-rank' officials of *raion* organizations."[5]

The appeal for "popular participation" to reform the deeply ingrained bureaucratic habits of Soviet officialdom has even been extended to the party-controlled trade unions, which have been urged to shake off their submissiveness to factory executives and to offer vigorous opposition when necessary.[6] Instances of rambunctious local trade-union committees have been held up for emulation, and workers enjoined to criticize "without being afraid that it will upset some director or other," and without having their remarks "prepared" or "cleared" by higher authorities.[7]

Another indication of the new spirit antedating the 20th Congress, has been the abolishment of the uniforms, insignia of rank, and titles which had been authorized for many civilian occupations during and after the war.[8]

---

[1] The term is Hugh Seton-Watson's, in an article presenting this interpretation: "The Soviet Ruling Class," *Problems of Communism*, No. 3 (May–June), 1956.

[2] Respectively in *Pravda*, Nov. 23, 1957, and *Izvestia*, Jan. 16, 1958, and June 13, 1959. These are samples from a plethora of similar articles.

[3] See especially the editorial in *Sovetskoe Gosudarstvo i Pravo*, No. 3 (May), 1956, pp. 3–14; *Izvestia*, May 22 and 23, Oct. 12, and Nov. 24, 1957; Aug. 1, 1958; and May 24, 1959.

[4] *Pravda*, June 8, 1959, and many earlier sources. This matter as well as the treatment of readers' letters were the subjects of Central Committee resolutions: *Pravda*, Aug. 26, 1958, and *Izvestia*, Oct. 11, 1958.

[5] *Partiinaia Zhizn*, No. 14 (July), 1959, p. 55.

[6] Report to the 20th Congress, *Pravda*, Feb. 15, 1956.

[7] *Pravda*, July 11, 1959; see also *Izvestia*, June 25, 1957.

[8] Decree of July 12, 1954, in *Shornik Zakonov SSSR i Ukazov Prezidiuma Verkhovnovo Soveta SSSR*, Moscow, 1959, pp. 411–13.

There has been an appeal for more informal relations and less social distance between those of high rank and those of low, and for an end to such practices in the armed forces as separate dining rooms for the several ranks.[9]

In general, the party seems to have been going out of its way to assert its respect for "ordinary" workers and peasants, a development reminiscent, as are many aspects of this campaign, of the attitude prevailing during the first decade after the October Revolution. Reversing a trend of more than 20 years' duration, the party has made a deliberate attempt to recruit more workers and peasants into its ranks: so much so, that Khrushchev was able to report at the 21st Congress that two-thirds of current admissions were in those categories, a figure which he accurately called a "considerable increase."[10] In addition, the Soviet press has published numerous editorials, articles, and letters passionately proclaiming the honor and worth of manual labor in a socialist society, filled with glowing words about citizens who are not afraid of soiling their hands, who are "creating material values for the people," rather than "sitting in offices and filing papers." This is not a new line, either, though it had lain dormant for some time. In recent speeches and articles, the third member has often been missing from the traditional trinity of "workers, collective farm peasants, and intelligentsia."

The rights and privileges mentioned thus far may seem to be only honorific. To be sure, they do not signify any real diffusion of the locus of power in Soviet society. Nevertheless, their importance should not be underrated: they do, after all, attempt to raise the ordinary worker's self-respect, and to imbue him with the consciousness — denied to him under Stalin — of his own contribution to the country's industrial progress. Having for years been exposed to harassment, incessant exhortations, and an attitude on the part of the authorities bordering on contempt, he is not likely to scorn even this — however mild — token of recognition and respect.

Adjustments in the Income Structure

In any event, more tangible rewards have also resulted from the new policy. Although we need not take too literally all of the promises made by Khrushchev — and by Malenkov before him — to increase the output of consumers' goods, there is every indication that the lowest-paid Soviet workers and peasants have been placed in a better competitive position to buy whatever is available.

On the one hand, minimum wages were raised in 1956, and two more increases scheduled in the current plan will bring the wage floor up to 500–600 rubles a month by 1965 — hardly a level of luxury, but approximately twice what it is now; raises have also been promised to "medium-paid workers and employees."[11] Old-age and disability pensions have been increased, too. Income taxes have been revised in favor of the lowest income brackets.[12]

On the other hand, there has been a good deal of talk, and some action, aimed at reducing the incomes of managerial and scientific personnel. In particular, the awarding of lavish bonuses to administrative, party, and other officials has been repeatedly attacked, and it is almost certain that the worst abuses are being corrected, "voluntarily" if not otherwise. A decree of the Council of Ministers has warned against excessive expense accounts on *komandirovki* (business trips) — another common source of added income for economic staffs.[13] Sputniks notwithstanding, the scientists have come in for their share of criticism, too, for holding multiple jobs and for receiving high incomes "merely" because they have higher degrees.[14]

The range of differentiation is being contracted not only between manual and nonmanual workers, but within the manual group as well. Wages in a number of industries have been sporadically revised over the past five years, the guiding principle being "a rise in the proportion of basic wage rates in workers' earnings." Although the primary motives seemed to be economic and bookkeeping con-

[9] *Krasnaia Zvezda*, Aug. 21, 1957.
[10] *Pravda*, Jan. 28, 1959. See also T. H. Rigby, "Social Orientation of Recruitment and Distribution of Membership in the Communist Party of the Soviet Union," *American Slavic and East European Review*, No. 3 (October), 1957.

[11] *Pravda*, Sept. 9, 1956, and Nov. 14, 1958.
[12] *Sbornik Zakonov* . . . , pp. 505–506.
[13] *Izvestia*, April 4 and June 6, 1959.
[14] *Kosomolskaia Pravda*, March 20 and April 6, 1956; *Pravda*, July 2, 1959.

cerns — to restrain inflationary forces and restore simplicity to the wage structure — it was
implied that many of the premiums and increments which had permitted the rise of an
inner aristocracy among the workers would
be curtailed or eliminated. It has now been
authoritatively stated that greater equality of
wages is a deliberate intention. A. Volkov,
who succeeded Kaganovich as head of the
Committee on Labor and Wages, has declared
that, "with the aim of decreasing the gap between maximum and minimum wage rates,"
such measures as these are to be undertaken:
a reduction in the number of skill categories
and in the ratio between the highest and lowest
rates to "no more than" two to one; a "sharp"
decrease in the use of progressive piece-work
rates; and a replacement of individual bonuses
by collective bonuses, spreading the benefits of
a single worker's accomplishment to his whole
work team.[15]

Rural Remedies

Even more striking have been the changes
in the agricultural sector. Adjustments in crop-
purchase prices and agricultural taxes and other
steps taken since 1953 have raised the income
of collective farmers in general while diminishing the range of earnings among and within
the collectives.[16] On several occasions, Khrushchev has referred to the "excessively high incomes" of some collective farms (as he has to
the "unjustifiably high incomes" of some
workers). One remedy, analogous to the industrial wage reform, has been the establishment of a uniform pricing system for agricultural purchases, without bonuses for exceeding the purchase plan, with the result, according to Khrushchev, that "many collective farms
will undoubtedly get more, while the leading
collective farms will receive . . . somewhat less
than now. And this," he added, "will be entirely fair."[17] Especially interesting is his implicit denial of the principle laid down by Stalin
in 1931: that wide income differentials were

needed as incentives to raise production.
Khrushchev, on the contrary, has asserted
that the farms with low income due to poor
production are discouraged from increasing
their output:

> . . . collective farms that did not achieve the
> planned harvest . . . were penalized, as it were.
> . . . This, of course, did not spur them on. . . .
> The goal here must be a more correct determi-
> nation of pay . . . in order to provide incentive
> not only to the leading but to all collective
> farms.[18]

In connection with the shift, now apparently
under way, from payment by workdays to
guaranteed cash payments, the whole problem
of income differentiation in agriculture was
recently discussed in three articles in the Soviet Union's leading economic journal. Among
situations they cited as "unjustifiable" are: income differentials among collective farms due
to varying locations, soil fertility, or crops;
those between peasants and farm executives,
due to the closer linking of peasant earnings
to the volume of output; and those among
the peasants themselves, due to too many
pay-rate categories with too steep increases,
and to inequitable discrepancies in output
norms. The remedies are fairly obvious, and
cases are cited in which they are already being
applied.[19]

Reform in Education

The school system initiated in the 1930's
was one of the major props of social differentiation. Its salient features, for present purposes,
were these: seven years of education were
nominally compulsory, although it has been
revealed that as late as 1958 only 80 per cent
of the young people were completing the
course.[20] After the seven-year school, a youngster might: (1) go to work in a job requiring
little or no skill; (2) be drafted into a labor-
reserves school, providing training of up to
two years for occupations of moderate skill;

---

[15] *Pravda,* Nov. 25, 1958. At the 21st Congress,
Khrushchev remarked that it was also time to
eliminate the differential paid for work in remote
places: *Pravda,* Feb. 1, 1959. Premiums evidently
will be preserved for hot or underground jobs and
hard physical labor.
[16] Lazar Volin, "Reform in Agriculture," *Problems
of Communism,* No. 1 (Jan.–Feb.), 1959.
[17] *Pravda,* June 21, 1958.

[18] *Ibid.*
[19] *Voprosy Ekonomiki,* No. 2 (Feb.), 1959, pp.
80–88, 113–22, 143–49. In addition, see *Izvestia,*
Nov. 30, 1958, in which a collective farm chairman reports that his own earnings now vary according to the volume of output, but are not to
exceed 1500 rubles a month.
[20] *Literaturnaia Gazeta,* July 3, 1958. Khrushchev
has used this figure on several occasions.

(3) enter a *tekhnikum*, a three- or four-year school for highly-skilled manual and some non-manual occupations; or (4) proceed to the upper grades of a ten-year school for essentially "academic" training, preparatory in almost all cases to matriculation at a higher educational institution (*vuz*). Tuition fees were charged in the *vuzes*, ten-year schools and *tekhnikums*. Scholarships were available at *tekhnikums*, while room, board, and uniforms were free in the labor-reserves schools, but no such aids were offered to pupils of the ten-year school. For both material and "cultural" reasons, therefore, the tendency was for children from lower-status families to attend the vocational schools and enter the same sort of occupations already held by their parents, while children of the "elite" were more likely to take the academic sequence preparing them for professional and administrative positions. The greater informal influence which highly-placed parents could exercise on those responsible for *vuz* admission strengthened this tendency. The schools thus contributed to the cleavage between manual and nonmanual groups.

The decision, adopted at the 19th Congress and re-affirmed at the 20th, to implement universal ten-year education wreaked havoc with this arrangement. Since ten-year schooling was to be compulsory, tuition fees made little sense, and they were accordingly abolished.[21] On the other hand *vuz* enrollments were not expanded; most of the ten-year graduates were expected to go directly to work, or into *tekhnikums* or other vocational schools.[22] This meant, in turn, a revision of the ten-year-school curriculum: physical education, music, art, mechanical drawing and other "practical studies," were increased at the expense of academic courses, and the latter were simplified in content, with fewer examinations and less homework. The effect of these changes — again in part intended — was to make school more accessible and more comfortable for the children of workers and peasants, improving their chances for scholastic success; and to blur the distinction between education for the manual worker and education for his occupational and social superior.

[21] *Izvestia*, June 10, 1956.
[22] Nicholas DeWitt, "Upheaval in Education," *Problems of Communism*, No. 1 (Jan.–Feb.), 1959.

New Problems and a New Program. But the reform proved unsatisfactory in important respects. In particular, graduates of the ten-year schools clung to the idea that they were entitled to a higher education. Many of them resented going either to work or to a vocational school, preferring to wait until they could gain admission to a *vuz* — and this in the face of an imminent labor shortage caused by the birth deficiencies of the war years. One attempt at solving this problem was the campaign, referred to above, stressing anew the dignity of manual labor; but it proved futile. Khrushchev then struck boldly: rejecting the ten-year principle, he declared that eight years of education were all that was necessary, and that such training should be "close to life" — i.e., primarily vocational. He proclaimed a "sacred slogan": "All students must prepare for useful work" and take a full-time job upon completion of the eighth grade.

> This . . . will be democratic since more equal conditions will be created for all citizens: neither the position nor the pleas of parents will exempt anyone, whoever he may be, from productive labor. . . .[23]

This program met two related goals: a labor force would be trained, in a minimum amount of time, for the kind of work that would be the lot of most;[24] and the notion of an automatic transition from secondary school to higher education would be dispelled. The purpose and atmosphere of the new type of school are suggested by the fact that pupils will combine their studies with productive work and with such chores as cleaning classrooms, tending shrubbery, and preparing and serving lunches. After the educational overhaul is completed, in three to five years, all students who wish to receive full secondary schooling (now to be of eleven years' duration)[25] will do so by correspondence or in evening or off-season

[23] Memorandum to the Central Committee, *Pravda*, Sept. 21, 1958.
[24] Khrushchev estimated an annual increment of 2 to 3.5 million youths in the labor force two years earlier than under the old program (*ibid.*); this gain is exclusive of the part-time work to be performed by pupils in most grades.
[25] It should be pointed out that the eight-year school is not a condensation of the ten-year curriculum but an expansion of the seven-year school — again indicative of the relaxation of academic rigor.

schools, without taking time away from their jobs. Although there was much discussion of schools for the "gifted," which would not require students to work while studying, it is significant that no provision was made for them (except in the areas of music and dance) in the reform as it was finally enacted. The labor-reserves system as such now seems to be a dead letter, though it might be more accurate to say that in effect it has been extended to embrace all schools and all young people.

Regulation of Vuz *Admissions.* At the same time, changes have been effected to improve the chances of workers' and peasants' children competing for entrance to higher educational institutions. Khrushchev and others had repeatedly deplored the handicaps faced by children of lower-status families, scoring in particular the fact that the "competition of parents" with influence was as important in determining *vuz* admissions as was the competition in entrance examinations.[26] In Moscow's higher schools, said Khrushchev, children of workers and collective farmers made up only 30 to 40 per cent of the enrollment. The abolition of tuition fees in the *vuzes*, along with those in the secondary schools, was one move calculated to alter this situation. It is particularly revealing that this step was taken at a time when pressure for admission to higher education from the growing ranks of ten-year graduates was reaching its peak — that is, when selectivity in admissions was becoming most necessary. If there were truth in the hypothesis of growing class stratification under pressure from a powerful "state bourgeoisie," just the opposite might have been expected — i.e., a rise in the tuition fees as a convenient way of shutting out low-income applicants.

Very different rules of competition were instead set up. A rising proportion (currently, 80 per cent) of *vuz* admissions was reserved for applicants with at least two years of work experience or military service;[27] presumably, this will become a universal requirement when the secondary-school reform is complete. Meanwhile, honor graduates of the ten-year

schools and the *tekhnikums* are now obliged to compete in entrance examinations along with everybody else — and, for the sake of "objectivity," the written part of the examinations is turned in under a pseudonym.[28] In most fields, the first two or three years of higher education are to be combined with full-time work, in order both to weed out the less serious students and to impress the future *vuz* graduates with the "glorious traditions of our working class and collective-farm peasantry" — i.e., to blunt the forces making for social separateness.[29] The method of awarding scholarships has been revised to take more account of the material needs of the student, and somewhat less of his grades; special courses are being organized to help *vuz* applicants who have not completed secondary education, or who have been out of school for a while; and all applicants must present recommendations from places of work and also from party, Komsomol, or trade-union organizations, whose representatives in addition sit on admissions boards[30] — all of which recall the days when the official aim was to "proletarianize" the higher schools. Given the recent Soviet willingness to publish more figures (so long as they "look good"), it may be predicted that we shall soon have, for the first time since 1938, comprehensive data on the social origins of students in higher education.[31]

---

26 See especially Khrushchev's speech to the 13th Congress of the Komsomol, *Pravda*, April 19, 1958, and his memorandum to the Central Committee, *ibid.* Sept. 21, 1958.

27 *Ibid.*, June 4, 1958.

28 *Ibid.*, June 4 and Nov. 12, 1958; *Izvestia*, April 4, 1959. Since honor graduates formerly were admitted without entrance examinations, high-status parents (according to Khrushchev) often put pressure on secondary-school teachers to give their children good grades (*Pravda*, Sept. 21, 1958).

29 See Khrushchev's memorandum, *Pravda*, Sept. 21, 1958, and the Central Committee resolution on school reform, *ibid.*, Nov. 14, 1958; also Minister of Higher Education Yelyutin's discussions of the problem, *ibid.*, Sept. 17, 1958, and *Izvestia*, Dec. 24, 1958.

30 See *Komsomolskaia Pravda*, Aug. 16, 1956; *Vestnik Vysshei Shkoly*, No. 9 (Sept.), 1957, pp. 3–5; *Pravda*, June 4, 1958; and *Izvestia*, Dec. 24, 1958, and April 4, 1959.

31 Another prediction which might be ventured is the resurrection of intelligence and aptitude tests, abolished in the 1930's on the grounds that they emphasized inherited rather than acquired traits and discriminated against children of workers and peasants. In effect, the criteria of "ability" became instead school examinations, grades, and *vuz* entrance examinations, which actually discriminate

The subject of educational reform cannot be passed over without taking notice of the boarding schools. When Khrushchev first broached the topic at the 20th Congress, observers assumed (as in the case of the secret speech) that his proposal demonstrated the influence of the elite and that the new schools — despite his protestation to the contrary — would be exclusive institutions for the privileged.

The reality of the boarding school has been a far cry from these suppositions. Priority in admission has gone — as, after all, Khrushchev said it should — to children from large or low-income families, and to others from disadvantaged environments. Fees are charged, but they have been waived for those who could not afford them — again in accord with Khrushchev's original suggestion. Moreover, the curriculum has been strictly polytechnical, providing training for such occupations as lathe operators, electricians, farm machine operators, stenographers, typists, etc. — hardly pursuits becoming to an aristocratic caste.[32]

Is the Classless Society Coming?

The scope and force of the trend away from extreme differentiation are unmistakable. There are many clues other than those which have already been cited: criticism of the practice of assigning chauffeured cars to officials; a pervasive, if still partial, change in the method of awarding medals and orders; a demand that the Soviet fashion journal concern itself less with evening gowns and furs and more with "everyday" clothes. To dismiss all this evidence as mere window-dressing, as ritual obeisance to an ideology, explains nothing: for why is it happening *now?* Why should Khrushchev feel compelled to renew

---

more heavily against low-status students in terms of the motivational or "cultural" influences in their lives. Intelligence-test scores are now considered less immutable than was once thought to be the case, and Khrushchev may "discover" that IQ tests are a more "objective" (i.e., less class-biased) measure of ability than achievement tests.
[32] On the schools, see *Pravda*, Feb. 15 and July 1, 1956; *Uchitelskaia Gazeta*, June 27, 1956; *Trud*, July 27, 1956; *Pravda*, Oct. 9, 1958. It might be noted that many, if not most, of the boarding schools have been converted from former seven- or ten-year schools, probably due to insufficient construction funds.

rituals that Stalin had long neglected, rituals that offend the sensibilities of the "elite"? What, then, does account for the change? Is one facet of the "transition to communism" to be the end of class distinctions?

Stalin, it seems clear, had felt that a high degree of differentiation was necessary to achieve his overriding goal — a very rapid process of industrialization subject to his absolute control. This meant, in the first place, that a group of loyal and competent administrators and other brain-workers had to be created, and quickly. It also meant that large segments of the population would have to be deprived, at least "temporarily," of material returns from their labor, in order that greater proportions of production could be applied to the expansion of industrial capacity. The consequently depressed condition of the workers and peasants Stalin sought to turn to good purpose, by offering them great rewards for joining the administrative and technical corps — hence the wealth, privilege, and prestige which came to define the upper end of the occupational hierarchy. The need for upward mobility to escape a life of privation would induce people to strive for educational training and vocational achievement, and would encourage obedience to Stalin's dictates, while the chance for upward mobility would serve as a substitute for the more prosaic benefits of a slow and moderate rise in the general standard of living.

The gap thus generated between the higher statuses and the lower ably served Stalin's purposes in some respects. Those in high position came to live a different kind of life, free from the material anxieties of those over whom they stood. They became, in short, "insulated" from the less fortunate: blind or indifferent to the needs and wishes of the masses. For they learned that success was to be had by winning the favor not of those below them but of those above them, which was exactly what Stalin wanted them to learn. Now that the policy has come under fire, the attitude which it engendered has been amply described in the Soviet press, for example in this criticism of the "self-willed" official as a type:

Tell such an official that he has disturbed his subordinate's state of mind, and he will probably be amazed: "His state of mind? Brother, we're having trouble meeting our plan here, and I have no time to look into all sorts of cases of melancholia."[33]

The Problems of Stalinist Policy

Nevertheless, extreme social differentiation had its less desirable aspects, too. For one thing, it "over-motivated" the population: anything less than a higher education, and the higher occupation it brought, was regarded as a disgrace for an upper-status child and as a sad fate for a lower-status child — hence, the intense pressure exerted on the educational institutions, the reluctance of youths to commit themselves to factory jobs. For another and more important thing, it interfered with the operation of the impersonal selection system necessary to an efficient economy and to the reward-function of upward mobility. Those in higher and better-paid positions were able to use their influence and their money to assure similar places for their children, at the expense of potentially more capable or more loyal children from less-favored families. Perhaps even worse, some children from well-to-do families neither studied nor worked, but lived off their parents' income — an idle existence which not only meant a loss to the labor force but also, if the Soviet press is to be believed, led in many cases to alcoholism, crime, or even to the acceptance of "bourgeois ideology."[34]

This excessive measure of status security perverted adults as well as children. Once a man was granted local power, he was able to suppress or punish, if not ignore, criticism from his inferiors, and he cooperated with his colleagues to evade the regime's cross-checks on him. This had been intermittently acknowledged in the Soviet Union under the label of *semeistvennost* ("family-ness"), but the full dimensions of the problem are only now being revealed. Among many instances, one may be cited concerning the chairman of a city soviet executive committee who "forbade his assistants and the heads of the city executive committee departments to appeal to party organs without his consent."[35] Thus, higher authorities were

precluded from receiving the information they needed to keep tabs on their own subordinates. Or, if the party did manage to find out about and remove some incompetent or dishonest official, he often reappeared in another responsible position — partly, at least, as the result of friendships formed and mutual obligations exacted. Indeed, an integral part of the pattern has been the concern of officials to find places in the *apparat* for friends and relatives who could reciprocally provide a haven if necessary.

All of this was simply the obverse side of the arbitrary power delegated to local officials, for the sake of allowing them to carry out their instructions from above without interference from below. But it was ironically self-defeating: by being freed of criticism from below, administrators were able to free themselves of supervision from above. This threatened to contravene the cardinal dogma of the Soviet system, which has come to be known as Stalinism though it could as well be called Leninism or Khrushchevism: that ultimate power belongs exclusively to the party — or more accurately, to the head of the party. Whenever any group jeopardizes that principle, it must be struck down, and that is what Khrushchev is doing. Stalin, in other words, forgot his Stalinism; and Khrushchev is not repudiating Stalinism, he is, if anything, reinstating it.

Khrushchev's Two-Sided Task

No doubt, the Soviet press, in characteristic fashion, has exaggerated the threat. Stalin was not a complete fool, and when all is said and done, he does seem to have kept things pretty well under control. If the group whose growth he fostered was an "elite," then surely no elite has ever proved so utterly helpless in preventing actions which, like those at present, so adversely affect it. The danger was a distant cloud — but a good Bolshevik tries not to wait until the storm has swept away his fortifications. Khrushchev's task, then, is to rid the "state bourgeoisie" of its cockiness, to disabuse it of the notion that it is safe whatever it does, to infuse into it fresh blood, personnel more responsive to orders. Just because of the kinds of positions these people occupy, the task will not be easy, and the plan may be "underfulfilled." But given the Soviet political structure, the odds are on Khrushchev's side.

---

[33] *Izvestia,* Jan. 18, 1958.

[34] Mark G. Field, "Drink and Delinquency in the U.S.S.R.," *Problems of Communism,* No. 3 (May–June), 1955; Allen Kassof, "Youth vs. the Regime: Conflict in Values," *ibid.,* No. 3 (May–June), 1957.

[35] *Izvestia,* Jan. 16, 1958.

The nature of the targets at which Khrushchev has taken aim makes his crusade sound like an echo of earlier revolutionary periods; but in actuality, the development does not connote a return to the situation that prevailed in the early 1920's, for Khrushchev has learned something from Soviet history. The extremes of high and low incomes are to be moderated — but "equality-mongering" is still wrong. Mass participation and criticism from below are to be permitted — but not "violations of state discipline" or "slander of the party and its leaders." Executives should be more humble, more attentive to their subordinates — but the principle of "one-man management" is to be preserved. "The struggle against the cult of the individual does not at all mean a belittling of the significance of leadership and leaders. . . . The party does not advocate the denial of authorities."[36] Moreover, Khrushchev has expressly defended the nonmanual pursuits — "those who work in offices are not at all bureaucrats, they are the creative people who originate that which is new . . ." — and he has strongly implied that, even under communism, there will still be the bosses and the bossed: communist society will be "highly organized."[37] Complete equality is not just around the corner, nor even being contemplated.

"Classlessness" Defined

Nevertheless, Khrushchev *is* seeking a classless society, in the proper sense of the term. If an "upper class," for example, means anything, it means a group of people who share fairly distinctive values and advantages which they are able to hold on to for some length of time, even against the resistance of others. Yet in the totalitarian scheme of things, it is essential to the preservation of party supremacy that no group become so entrenched in positions of strength as to become insulated against further demands from the party. An "upper class," or any other "class," is no more admissible than an autonomous trade union or ethnic group. Hence the party must insist — in the long run — that every man be individually and continuously on trial, that status and rewards remain contingent and ephemeral. The greatest threat to the party is the development of a

sense of identification or solidarity within a group — or class — and this is precisely what was happening to the Soviet elite. Khrushchev's war against the bourgeoisie is, in fact, only an extension of the battle with the bureaucrats which has long been a part of Soviet policy, even if it was sometimes muted. In short, "classlessness" is essentially a corollary of Stalinism.

Khrushchev, however, believes himself to be in a better position to attain it than Stalin ever was. The creation of a substantial industrial base has relieved him of the urgency which Stalin so acutely felt. Automation, as he has frequently pointed out, really has diminished the differences between mental workers and manual. The spread of education has freed him from dependence on a relatively small group as the only source of administrative and intellectual personnel; workers and peasants can now be brought into the *vuzes* with less risk of lowering the quality of education (as happened in the 1920's). Finally, he evidently presumes that a long period of enforced political homogeneity has led to the withering away of deviant values among Soviet citizens. Criticism from below would thus be less dangerous, since it is more likely to accord with what the party wants. The only agency left which has enabled Soviet man to maintain and transmit both "hostile" values and favored positions, with even a small degree of success, is the family — whence the significance of the boarding schools (and other attempts to loosen family bonds). For the boarding schools are destined to be not elite institutions, but universal ones: the instrument by which the regime hopes finally to achieve control over the last remaining semi-autonomous activity, the rearing of children.[38] This, too, is an objective which will be familiar to students of Soviet history, but unlike the situation earlier, Soviet leaders may well feel that they now have, or can produce, the material facilities with which to realize it.

Yet it is unlikely that the regime has solved,

---

[36] *Partiinaia Zhizn,* No. 7 (April), 1956, p. 5.
[37] *Pravda,* July 2, 1959; also Khrushchev's report to the 21st Congress, *Pravda,* Jan. 28, 1959.

---

[38] "The sooner we provide nurseries, kindergartens, and boarding schools for all children, the sooner and the more successfully will the task of the Communist upbringing of the growing generation be accomplished": Khrushchev's theses on the Seven-Year Plan, *Pravda,* Nov. 14, 1958. See also the decree on the boarding schools in *Pravda,* May 26, 1959.

once and for all, the problem of inequality. Power corrupts — even delegated power. Workers and peasants, no less than intelligentsia, will sooner or later try to put their privileges to uses which, so far as the party is concerned, are "selfish." They may, for example, try to develop a monopoly of their own on higher education, or act "prematurely" to increase the production of consumers' goods or raise wages, in a kind of latter-day "workers' opposition." Or, once terror is removed, they may turn out not to have lost all their hostile values, after all. When that happens, they will once more be put back in the inferior position they knew up to Stalin's death. No end is in sight to this ancient practice of playing one off against the other, this alternate granting of status privilege within a basically classless framework, as the Soviet system struggles with its perennial and fundamental problem: the need to control the controllers.

NATIONALITIES

64

The Regime's Nationality Policy*

Hugh Seton-Watson

(1956)

The Soviet attitude toward the nationality question has been in some ways similar to the attitude toward religion, the family, and social stratification. National differences and national loyalties were expected to give way with the Revolution and the establishment of socialism, to be replaced by unity and solidarity under the red flag. That such has not been

*Reprinted from "Soviet Nationality Policy," *The Russian Review*, Vol. 15 (1956), pp. 3–13, by permission of the author and the publisher.

the case is clearly seen in this history of the regime's policies.

At the outset it should be stated that I do not believe that Russia and her problems are unique. They have, of course, their special features, but in many ways they are comparable with other peoples and other lands. I do not believe that Russian nature is something that human reason cannot penetrate. Some Russians will, it is true, contemptuously reject this view. "We are different," they will say. "You will never understand us." Here argument ends. Esoteric revelations and irrational rhetoric are unanswerable. All that one can say with absolute confidence is that there is nothing unique at all in the dogma, "My nation is unique." This attitude is as old as the human race. In our own life-time it was used by Adolf Hitler. In a different setting it was used by Dr. Malan in South Africa. In yet another setting it was used by the Bolsheviks. It is a dangerous dogma, used by dubious people. It makes all human intercourse impossible.

I believe, then, that we must look for enlightenment on the problems of any country which we study, whether it is Russia, or Britain, or Abyssinia, not only to the historical documents of the respective country, but also to comparable problems and situations in the experience of other countries. For the problem of Soviet nationality policy I suggest that it is worth looking at the experience of Austria-Hungary and of the small Balkan states and on the other hand at the British and other European colonial empires. If one can separate those features of Soviet national policy which are characteristic of all multi-national states or colonial empires from those which are peculiar to the Soviet regime, one will have made some real progress.

A History in Brief

Lenin's doctrine on the national question is no doubt so well known that I need spend little time on it. He upheld in principle the right of every nation to self-determination, including the right of secession. At the same time he upheld the international solidarity of the proletariat, and the consequent duty of every working class to prefer the working class of a neighboring nation to the bourgeoisie of its own nation. The contradiction between these two principles could not be, and has not been, resolved either in theory or in practice.

Whether, during the stormy years after the October Revolution, any given nationality remained within Soviet Russia or had an independent state of its own was decided not by theoretical examination of the conflicting principles, but by the geographical position of the respective nationality and by military force. Thus the Poles, Finns, Lithuanians, Letts, and Estonians established independent states because they were first occupied by the invading German army and then defended by the victorious Western Powers, whose naval might was dominant in the Baltic Sea. The Georgians, Azerbaidjanis, and Armenians had a few years of independence, but they were conquered because Soviet Russia and Turkey had a common interest in their suppression, because they quarreled with each other, and because they antagonized the Western Powers. The other main nationalities of the Russian Empire, Ukrainians, Volga Tatars, and Central Asians, were inaccessible to Western help and were conquered in turn by White and Red armies.

Once the Bolshevik regime was established, its official policy, as we know, was based on the principle of "a culture national in form and socialist in content." In theory, there were two dangers, to be combated with equal energy and vigilance. One was Great Russian Great Power chauvinism, the other, local bourgeois nationalism. In actual fact, however, Bolshevik treatment of the nationalities after 1921 was as opportunist as it had been during the Civil War. The most important single fact about the history of Bolshevik nationality policy is that its phases coincide with, and were determined by, the phases of Stalin's general policy.

The years of N.E.P. were a period in which, though the Bolsheviks held dictatorial power, they exercised it with relative mildness. This was true not only in the peasant economy but also in religious and cultural life and in nationality policy. During these years some of the nationalities enjoyed a real measure of self-government. In the Ukraine, the official policy of Ukrainization enjoyed true popular support. In Transcaucasia, though the vindictive intrigues of Stalin caused injustice and discontent, at least it was true that power was held by local men. But in the other parts of the Soviet Union conditions were different. After the disgrace of Sultan-Galiev, the Volga Tatars lost most of their autonomy. In Central Asia, official Soviet sources show beyond doubt that power was concentrated in the hands of the local Russian minority, and the Asian peoples were kept in subjection. Occasional interventions by Moscow did not substantially change this state of affairs.

Stalin's second revolution of 1929, with its drive for collectivization of agriculture and rapid industrialization, brought a fundamental change of nationality policy, as of all other departments of policy. Ruthless centralization in the economic field was not compatible with self-government for the nationalities. Economic misery and political oppression created bitter hatred, and in the national areas this inevitably took the form of national hatred. Already, in 1930, Ukrainization was abandoned. The famine of 1932–33 in the Ukraine was followed by the appointment of Postyshev as Second Secretary of the Ukrainian party and Stalin's governor-general in the Ukraine. The massacre of livestock in the Kazakh steppes was followed by the starvation or flight of nearly half the Kazakh nation and the Russification of Kazakhstan.

In the national areas as in Russian lands, the years 1935 and 1936 were a period of relaxation of pressures. But the *Yezhovshchina*, beginning at the end of 1936 and extending till early 1939, hit the nationalities with special severity. In the Ukraine, Postyshev himself was swept away, together with all members of the Ukrainian Politburo and the Ukrainian Sovnarkom, besides hundreds of thousands of lower party and state officials and Ukrainian intellectuals. In North Caucasus and the Transcaucasian republics, Avtorhanov tells us that 3 to 4 per cent of the population were arrested. In Central Asia, the Uzbek Prime Minister Hodzhaev and First Secretary Ikramov were only the most eminent of tens of thousands of victims. The purge also ravaged the autonomous republics of Tataria, Bashkiria, and Buryat Mongolia.

The war brought not only an understandable exaltation of patriotism in official propaganda, but a rigid identification of patriotism with subservience to the Stalinist totalitarian regime and ruthless punishment as traitors not only of the regime's enemies, but of whole nations regarded as potentially disloyal. To this period belong the genocide of the Volga Germans, Crimean Tatars, Chechens, Karachays, and Kalmyks.

The postwar period is marked by the emergence of the Soviet Union as one of the two giant powers of the world, with an imperialist policy affecting every part of the globe. This new phase of Soviet imperialism has required still further blows to the national individuality and national traditions of all the peoples of the Soviet Union. The most striking examples of this phase are the suppression of the national epics of the Moslem peoples and the falsification of the history of North Caucasians, Kirgiz, Ukrainians, Rumanians of Bessarabia, and other nations. The campaign against "cosmopolitanism" has the same significance. For example, Tadjiks must not show pride in the common culture which they share with Persians; rather they must stress the links between Tadjik and Russian culture.

The Russification Question

This brief survey of the past leads to the important question: Is the nationality policy of the Soviet Union today one of Russification?

This raises two separate questions. The first is, "Does Russification exist?" The second, "Is Russification the driving force of Soviet nationality policy? Is it the motive of this policy, or only its result, or its instrument?"

The answer to the first question must be "Yes."

There are great differences between different parts of the Soviet Union. In Georgia and Armenia there has hitherto been absolutely no Russification. These republics are ruled exclusively by their own nationals. In the Ukraine and Azerbaidjan the problem is more complicated. On the whole it would seem to me that the Ukraine is ruled by Ukrainians, though the formerly Polish provinces form an exception and though, in general, the Russian resident element in the Ukraine certainly possesses influence out of proportion to its numbers. In Azerbaidjan the city of Baku has a large Russian population, which no doubt is well represented in the state and party apparatus. But the study of such sources as have

been available — admittedly imperfect — suggests that even in Baku most important posts are held by Azerbaidjanis, and that in the rest of the republic this is definitely so.

A special case are certain border provinces. Here there have been massive deportations of local people and massive colonization of Russians. This is true in Western Ukraine, the Baltic states, and probably Western White Russia. It is also true in Bessarabia. In the Far East the same is true of Sakhalin and the Kurile Islands. The motives of these actions are clearly strategic.

But the most important examples of Russification are to be found in the economically developing regions of Asiatic Russia, inhabited by Moslem, Buddhist, or Shamanist nations. Here Russification takes several distinct forms.

Colonization of Russians and Ukrainians affects in the first place the new industrial centers. The capitals of the Central Asian republics are largely Russian cities — Tashkent rather less so than the others. So are Izhevsk, capital of the Udmurt A.S.S.R.; Ufa, capital of Bashkiria; Ulan Ude, capital of Buryat Mongolia. But in certain areas colonization extends even to the countryside. After the mass starvation in Kazakhstan during collectivization Russian and Ukrainian peasants were brought in. Khrushchev's new drive to develop the agriculture of Kazakhstan will take the process further.

To insist that Russian should be taught as a compulsory second language in national schools does not seem to me to be unreasonable. Every great state must have a first language and in the Soviet Union it is obvious that this must be Russian. Much more dubious is the tendency to make Russian the only language in secondary and higher education in areas of mixed population. The universities of Central Asia, of which Soviet propaganda to Asia makes so much use, have for the most part Russian as the language of instruction and a very large proportion of their students are not Asians but resident Russians. Another element of Russification is the imposition of the Cyrillic alphabet for Asian languages and the systematic introduction into those languages of Russian words which go far beyond technical vocabulary in the strict sense.

In recent years we have seen the systematic falsification of the history of the nationalities. In Ukrainian history all links with Moscow are stressed, while links with Poland and with southern or western Europe are minimized. Shamil[1] is represented as a reactionary agent of Anglo-Turkish imperialism. The conquest of Kirgizia by the Tsar's armies is interpreted as a progressive action as it furthered the social development of the Kirgiz nation and brought it into contact with progressive Russian culture. This argument is simply the Marxist-Leninist-Stalinist equivalent of the arguments used by the nineteenth century theorists of European and American imperialism. The same tendency can be seen in the suppression of the Moslem national epics — *Dede Korkut* in Azerbaidjan; *Korkut ata* in Turkmenia; *Alpamysh* in Uzbekistan and *Manas* in Kirgizia.

Of the subordination of the republican governments to the Union government there is of course no doubt. It is clear even in the text of the Constitution and it is clearer still if one takes into account the hierarchy of the Communist Party. But here too the problem of Russification arises. In Central Asia the Second Secretaries of the Central Committees of the republican parties and in most cases the Second Secretaries of *oblast* committees are Russian. In Kazakhstan, of course, at present both the First and Second Secretaries are Russians, but this is perhaps due to temporary exceptional circumstances. It is interesting to note that postwar purges in the Central Asian parties appear to have affected Russian Second Secretaries more than Asian First Secretaries. This would seem to show that it is the Second Secretaries who wield the real power. In the case of the Ukraine the problem is not that the Ukrainian party is run by Russians — this does not seem to be the case — but that the Ukraine is extraordinarily under-represented in the leadership of the All-Union party.[2]

Now comes the second question — "Is Russification the driving force, the motive, of

Soviet nationality policy?" It is tempting to argue that Bolshevik policy is a continuation of the Russification policy of Alexander III and Nicholas II. There are some striking similarities. I have already mentioned the imperialistic interpretation of the suppression of Shamil and the Kirgiz. I am myself inclined to the view that the dominant social type which is emerging in the Soviet Union is a kind of bureaucratic state bourgeoisie, whose ideas and general mentality are a curious combination of those of the nineteenth-century European capitalist bourgeoisie and the nineteenth-century Russian bureaucracy. One might thus argue that there is likely to be a continuity of outlook between Plehve and Khrushchev.

Nevertheless I believe this idea to be wrong. I do not think that the Soviet government is interested in Russian nationalism. The conflict is not between the Russians and the smaller nationalities, but between these nationalities and a centralized totalitarian regime. The regime suppresses the nationalities as it suppresses all groups not created by itself. For the suppression of the nationalities it uses Russians as its instruments. It does this because the Russians are the most numerous, and culturally and economically the most advanced, of the peoples of the Soviet Union and because Russians, as Russians, are less likely to be disloyal to the regime. It may well be that individual Russians used by the regime in national areas act in a contemptuous and chauvinistic manner towards members of other nationalities. The sum total of such arrogant actions may produce a very large volume of indignation. But Russification is not the government's aim.

The government's aim is total power. It intends to exploit every human being, and every economic resource in the country. If there is oil in the territory of Bashkiria or Azerbaidjan, that oil must be made available for the purposes of those who control the totalitarian machine, centered in Moscow. If it is to their advantage that Uzbeks and Tadjiks should grow more cotton and less grain, they will be made to do so. When the British ruled Egypt, they developed cotton at the expense of grain and have been severely criticized for doing so. But there are three important differences between British treatment of Egypt and Bolshevik treatment of

---

[1] Shamil (1797–1871) led the Caucasian tribes in a long war to maintain independence from Russia; defeated and captured in 1859.

[2] The All-Union Central Committee has among its full members thirty-six First Secretaries of *obkoms* or *kraikoms* of A.S.S.R.s within the R.S.F.S.R. and another twelve as candidates. Only two First Secretaries of Ukrainian *obkoms* are candidates; none are full members. *Oblasts* of such industrial importance as Kharkov, Stalino, Kiev, and Dnepropetrovsk are not represented.

Turkestan. Firstly, the greater part of the profits of Egyptian cotton-growing went to Egyptians, while all the profits of Uzbek cotton *kolkhozy* go to Moscow. Secondly, no British government would ever have considered, or did consider, withholding grain supplies from Egypt to starve its people into submission, whereas this threat was used by the Soviet government. Thirdly, Egyptians could and did bitterly attack not only British cotton policy but British rule itself. For Uzbeks or Tadjiks such criticism would be fatal.

In order to achieve total power over its subjects, the Soviet regime systematically atomizes society. All associations of citizens for whatever purpose must be directed by the Party and infiltrated by the M.V.D. This applies as much to groups of musicians or sportsmen or butterfly-lovers as to political groups. The regime has a special distrust, which, granted its premises, is perfectly just, for any association derived from some principle that is independent of, and older than, the regime. The two most important associations of this kind are religious communities and nations. By its very nature the regime is unable to tolerate the existence of either. It is determined to destroy the nationalities, not in the interest of the Russian nation, but because the totality of its power demands it. It will not be content until no Uzbek feels that he is linked to another Uzbek, because he is an Uzbek, by a link stronger than that which binds him to his hierarchical superior in the totalitarian power system.

Soviet policy is a war of extermination against the principle of nationality. It can also fairly be described as imperialism. But it is not inspired by the desire to Russify the nationalities.

It would, however, be quite wrong to deduce from this that Soviet policy does not appear to the nationalities that suffer from it as a policy of deliberate Russification. Thousands of examples can be found to show that oppression whose instruments are people of another nation is felt by objects to be something different from oppression at the hands of their own compatriots. In the 1930's in Czechoslovakia the German workers of the western border regions suffered heavily from unemployment. This was a result of the world economic depression of that time, but these Germans regarded it as an act of oppression by

the Czech government. In Transylvania under the Rumanian King Carol the corruption and brutality of the bureaucracy caused equal suffering to its Rumanian and Hungarian inhabitants. But whereas to the Rumanians this seemed a matter of political or class oppression, the Hungarians felt that they were being victimized as a nation.

In the Soviet Union the famines in the Ukraine and Kazakhstan seemed to their victims to be measures of extermination directed against their nations, though this was not in fact the conscious aim of Stalin.

The attitude of the Moscow government to Islam seems to be especially important. Bolshevik persecution of Orthodoxy was persecution by Russians of Russians. Persecution of Islam is persecution by Russians of Asians. The evidence shows without doubt (1) that ever since 1917 the number of Communists among the Moslem nations of the Soviet Union has been very small, and (2) that these Asian Communists have always been most reluctant to attack Islam, even though they personally may have ceased to be believers. The campaigns against Islam have always come from Moscow and their active exponents in the Moslem areas have been the resident Russian elements. Those Asian Communists who have supported the campaign have appeared to the population as mere puppets of the Russians. The attack on Islam in fact has been imposed from outside, by members of another nation with other religious traditions. Such a situation inevitably creates nationalist reaction.

Orientation of the Intelligentsia

There is a special problem to be considered — the formation of a new intelligentsia among the nationalities. It is beyond dispute that the Soviet regime has given the nationalities greater opportunities of education and of careers for their talents than could have been dreamed of under the Tsars. Ukrainians, Transcaucasians, Tatars, and Central Asians now have hundreds of thousands of university students, teachers, engineers, scientists, and bureaucrats of all sorts. These men owe their careers to the Soviet regime. It is often assumed that they are grateful for this and that they form most loyal and reliable support for the Stalinist regime among their compatriots.

In my view this opinion is quite wrong. In the Kingdom of Hungary before 1914, Slovaks or Serbs or Rumanians who learned the Hungarian language and went to a Hungarian university could acquire the best education and make good careers. But those who did this did not become exponents among their own peoples of the Hungarian regime to which they owed their careers. On the contrary, they used their new knowledge and skill to make themselves leaders of the struggle of their peoples for independence from Hungary. The intelligentsia of the Asian nations was created by the opportunities of modern secular education created by the European powers. Moslems, Confucians, and Buddhists of course had had schools of their own type, with their traditional form of culture, which may have been equal or superior to ours for centuries. But for survival in the modern world, modern secular education is needed. This was imported by the Europeans. The new Asian intelligentsia which arose from study in the schools and universities of the West, or in schools of the Western type created in their countries, owed their careers entirely to the Westerners. But this did not make them exponents among their own peoples of Western colonial rule. On the contrary, like the intelligentsia of the subject peoples of Hungary, they became leaders of their peoples' struggles for independence. Pandit Nehru was educated at Harrow, one of the best schools in England (which had among its pupils Sir Winston Churchill), and at Cambridge University. Ho-Chi-Minh studied in France, loves French literature and civilization and has had many French friends. The pioneers of the small Communist parties of the Arab lands include many former students of the American University of Beirut.

I do not believe that the same result is not also produced among the intelligentsia of the nationalities of the Soviet Union and especially among the Asian element. It is of course true that there are no independence movements in Central Asia like the Indian National Congress or the Egyptian WAFD or the Tunisian neo-Destour. But, as we all know, this proves only that totalitarianism is different from democracy, that the M.V.D.'s function in Soviet society is different from that of the police in Britain or France. It does not prove that the Central Asian intelligentsia are not thinking in terms of nationalist movements. The campaigns of the Soviet Communist Party against "bourgeois nationalism," with all their fantastic excesses, provide indirect evidence.

Pattern of the Future

In conclusion, a few words about the future. The record of Russian imperialism before 1917 was, it seems to me, neither worse nor better than that of other European imperialism. Bolshevik imperialism is a horrible tyranny, but the Russians are its victims as well as the other nations of the Soviet Union. There are positive elements in the historical relationship between the Russian people and their neighbors, at least in the east and south. Strong arguments can be found in favor of preserving a single great state, reorganized on a genuinely federal principle. But there is no iron law of history that states must be big.

The Nazis loved to declaim about the merits of a *"Grossraum,"* within which the Germans should rule over dozens of smaller client peoples. To adopt their doctrines on behalf of the Russian people would be perilous. Let us put aside all rhetorical phrases and metaphysical dogmas. The economies of the Ukraine and Russia are complementary. They must trade with each other on a massive scale. But this does not prove that there cannot be an independent Ukrainian State. National independence does not need to bring with it tariff barriers and economic boycotts. An independent Georgia would be a very small state. But Switzerland is a small state and has survived, although it lies between France, Germany, and Italy, which have often fought wars with each other. Central and South America contain many small states which have survived for a hundred years or more. When Stalinism has ceased to exist — which we may or may not live to see — we must assume that a system of international order and security will be established, within which it will be possible for both small states and large federations to exist.

One thing, however, is absolutely clear. Neither the United States, which has granted independence to the twenty million people of the Philippines, nor Britain, which has granted independence to the four hundred and fifty million people of India, Pakistan, Burma, and Ceylon, can undertake to support a free Russia of the future in preventing Ukrainians or Uzbeks or Georgians or Letts from seeking their own independence. The future of the nationalities of the Soviet Union must depend on their own wishes, freely expressed in a clear manner. Meanwhile we must regard the question as open and we must do everything to promote real friendship between the Russian people and the other peoples oppressed by the common totalitarian enemy. And I am using the word, not as a piece of rhetoric, but in its exact sense. By "friendship" I mean not imperialism hiding under a mask, but friendship.

65

Assimilation and the Muslims: A Case Study*

Richard Pipes

(1955)

Our knowledge of what has been happening at the grass root level to the various national groupings of the U.S.S.R. has been conspicuously deficient. Prof. Pipes' study of the Muslims of Soviet Central Asia is a rare and happy exception. His thorough canvass of the different sides of their social and cultural life indicates that social change in the form of assimilation to the dominant great Russian industrial pattern has gone quite far indeed.

The crucial question in the entire future of Soviet Central Asia is the degree to which the native population of that region is succumbing to the process of Russification, actively fostered by the Soviet regime.[1] If the Central Asian

natives are gradually losing their ethnic peculiarities and assimilating, either by being absorbed into the Great Russian population or by dissolving in a new "Soviet" nationality, then Soviet Central Asia may be expected in time fully to merge with the Russian core of the U.S.S.R. If, on the other hand, they are resisting alien pressures and retaining their ethnic and cultural complexion, then Central Asia will continue to be set apart from the remainder of Soviet territories, and to merit distinct political treatment. In either event, the fate of Central Asia as a Russian frontier and a potential buffer zone between Russia and China may be said to hinge primarily on the cultural tendencies of its Muslim population.

In view of the great shortage of reliable, objective printed materials dealing with the inhabitants of contemporary Soviet Central Asia, an inquiry of this nature must of necessity have recourse to some unorthodox sources of information, among them the testimony of refugees from this area. It must also be confined to the broadest aspects of the question. Neither limitation is quite satisfactory from the point of view of scholarship, but since scholarship is a means for the discovery of truth and not an end in itself, it must be capable of adapting itself to the circumstances.

The primary sources of information for this essay consisted of the standard literature on Central Asia, pre-Revolutionary and Soviet, and of materials collected in the course of interviews conducted with 31 Muslim refugees from the Soviet Union, most of them from Central Asia.[2] These interviews concentrated on the personal experiences of the informants, and avoided, insofar as possible, references to politics, in order to reduce to a minimum the likelihood of deliberate concealment or lying. All the informants were male, and consisted, in their majority, of persons 30 to 50 years of age,

*Reprinted from "Muslims of Soviet Central Asia: Trends and Prospects," *The Middle East Journal*, Vol. 9 (1955), pp. 147–162 and 295–308, by permission of the author and the publisher.
[1] By Soviet Central Asia are meant here both the steppe regions and Turkestan, i.e., the territory covered today by the republics of Kazakhstan, Kirghizia, Uzbekistan, Tajikistan, and Turkmenistan. Prior to the Revolution they embraced the General Gubernie of the Steppe and of Turkestan, the Gubernie of Uralsk and Turgai, and the dependent principalities of Khiva and Bukhara. By the term "Russians" is meant not only the Great Russians, but also the Ukrainians and Belorussians, because statistical and other information for Central Asia rarely distinguishes among these Slavic subgroups.

[2] These interviews were conducted in the summer of 1953 under the auspices and with the generous assistance of the Institute of Intercultural Studies and the Ford Foundation. I wish to express my particular gratitude to Professor Philip E. Mosely of Columbia University, who first suggested this task and was instrumental in enabling me to carry it out. I also would like to thank the Center for International Studies of the Massachusetts Institute of Technology for its kind help in completing this inquiry.

with a high school or *tekhnikum* education, who had left the Soviet Union as laborers or prisoners of war in the course of the Nazi-Soviet conflict. They represented, in other words, largely the middle-aged Soviet "intelligentsia" (in the Communist sense of the word). The conclusions derived from the interviews were placed against the historical background of Central Asia for the purpose of separating the accidental from the essential, on the assumption that generalizations obtained from interviews were both more reliable and more significant in terms of the future when in agreement with pre-Soviet developments in Central Asia. The fact that in the main there is such agreement seems to the author an added reason for confidence in the correctness of the conclusions thus derived.

The main criteria used in investigating the cultural tendencies of the Central Asian Muslim were five: religion, customs, language, ethnic identity, and the character and trends of the native intelligentsia. An attempt was made in each case to determine the extent and nature of the changes which had occurred under Soviet rule; to ascertain whether these changes agreed with or ran contrary to the spontaneous developments taking place prior to the 1917 Revolution; and finally, to evaluate their meaning in terms of the probable future.

Religion

The term "religion" comprises at least three distinct phenomena: a belief in the existence of one or more supreme beings; a set of rituals which gives this belief external expression; and a way of life based upon the principles explicitly and implicitly enunciated by the belief's founders. In analyzing the religious life of a community, these aspects must be clearly differentiated.

Russian Central Asia consists of two main parts, distinguished from each other by historic tradition, culture, and topography: the northern half, the steppe region (today's Kazakhstan), and the southern half, Turkestan (comprising the remaining four Central Asian republics). The population of the former was traditionally nomadic, Turkish, and in religious matters fairly indifferent. Turkestan, on the other hand, being predominantly urban and agricultural, and inhabited by Iranians and considerably Arabicized and Iranicized Turks, was until the Soviet period one of the great centers of Islamic learning and practice. This difference between the religious background of the two regions must be kept in mind when studying contemporary Central Asian Muslims.

The most striking feature of the religious attitude of the Muslim refugees is their strong and articulate hostility toward all forms of established religion, including Islam. Time and again, the informants expressed the conviction that all religion is a form of superstition incapable of standing the test of "science," of serving society as a means of attaining social progress. The typical opinion ran as follows: "Yes, I believe in a Supreme Being, but it doesn't matter whether He is called Allah, God, Christ, or anything else. Nor does He care whether I pray or not. Religion is a superstition which keeps people backward. Look at the Arabs and Persians, where religion has gotten them: they are poor and ignorant. To achieve progress, we must not allow religion to interfere, though religion should not be persecuted because it does help some people in facing life." The general assumptions behind such reasoning are fairly obvious: the belief in a conflict between faith and reason, religion and science; a pragmatic, utilitarian scale of values; scepticism of certain aspects of religion, leading to a wholesale rejection of all religion.

In the long run, this attitude may well determine the whole future of Islam in Central Asia. The intelligentsia displays the same cult of reason, and of its concomitant, secular society, in an extreme, uncomprising way, as do the educated groups of other Asian societies. Here as there, progress, the ultimate good, is conceived as incompatible with religion. Against such hostility to established religion the revival of Islam in its pre-1917 form, even under conditions of complete freedom, does not seem likely.

This conclusion is strengthened by the picture given of the religious practices of Central Asian Muslims. Islam in the Soviet Union has to operate under extremely difficult conditions, due in part to the specific repressive measures undertaken by the regime against religion, and in part to the general conditions of Soviet life. In the first category are the physical destruction of the Islamic leadership undertaken between 1927 and 1932 through the arrest and deportation of virtually all persons enjoying some religious status in the Muslim com-

munity, from the top hierarchy to the lowest
village mullah; the closing of nearly all the
village mosques and most of the city mosques;
the threat of dismissal hanging constantly over
every Soviet citizen in any position of responsibility if known to engage in religious practices; and the nearly complete suppression of all
religious literature through the change of the
native alphabets (from Arabic to Latin in
the late 1920's, and again from Latin to Cyrillic
ten years later), the impounding of religious
texts, including the Qur'an, and the total cessation of all publication of a religious nature.
These antireligious policies would of themselves make an active religious life most
difficult.

The interviews, however, indicate that
equally important in hampering the religious
life of Central Asian Islam are forces not
directly connected with the Communist antireligious policies, such as the general impoverishment of the population, which compels
the inhabitants to devote all their time and
energies to attain bare survival, and leaves little
freedom for time-consuming actions required
by religion; the shortage of animals used in
certain Muslim festivals; and the requirements
of a highly dynamic society, geared primarily
for production and not for the satisfaction of
the needs of its citizens. If, despite such
formidable difficulties, Islamic practices have
not altogether vanished from Central Asia, the
reason must be sought both in the great hold
which this religion exercises on its followers
(Bartold had once observed that history knows
many cases of mass conversion *to* Islam, but
not a single instance of a society being converted *from* Islam), and the secondary role of
leaders and institutions in that religion; the
latter factor permits Muslims, like the Jews,
to survive better under extreme oppression
than other religions for which the clergy, the
hierarchy, the supreme spiritual authority are
essential.

One of the most important — perhaps the
single most important — element in the Muslim
ritual are the five daily prayers. This practice
seems to have declined among Soviet Muslims
to such an extent as to have all but vanished.
The principal cause for its disappearance is the
inability of Soviet Muslims to take time off
from work in order to recite the prayers; such
stoppage of work is considered "economic

sabotage" and involves serious retribution. The
fact that since the 1930's Friday — the day of
rest and public prayer — is considered a
regular working day in Central Asia prevents
the adult population from engaging in communal worship as well. The only times of the
day when a Muslim may perform his prayers
undisturbed occur at sunrise and at sunset —
the first and the last of the daily prayers; that
is, when he is at home, with his family. This
is the reason why, to the extent that the daily
prayer is observed at all, it survives largely
among that part of the population which is
not gainfully employed: above all, the women
and the elders.

The younger generation is further handicapped by its ignorance of the prayers. Only
a few of the refugees interviewed knew how
to perform the regular daily prayers; none of
those belonged to the younger generation. It
may also be added that not one of these
refugees had cared to learn the prayers since
his arrival in the West.

Another important duty of Muslims is to
observe daytime fasting during the entire 28
days of the month of Ramazan. Prior to 1917
the fast was faithfully observed by the
Turkestan natives; those of the steppe region
were less strict, prevented as they were by the
exigencies of nomadic and seminomadic life.
During Ramazan, Muslim communities in
Central Asia customarily reversed their routine,
resting daytimes, eating and entertaining at
night. Shortly after the end of the fast there
occurs a major holiday, *kurban bayram* (feast
of sacrifice), attended by the slaughter of sheep
and by festivities.

The difficulties of observing the Ramazan
fast in the Soviet Union are obvious at first
sight. To eliminate or even reduce daytime
work for a period of a month is possible only
for a people economically independent; it is
inconceivable in a society in which virtually
every breadwinner is an employee of the state,
and the state drives relentlessly to increase
production. Furthermore, a worker who fasts
all day is, even when compelled to do a full
day's work, a poor worker. As a result, the
Ramazan fast is severely repressed by the
authorities and can survive only in a greatly
modified form.

Several of the refugees recalled instances of
Communist Party officials subjecting Muslims

suspected of fasting to "tests." Thus, for example, many Muslim employees of state institutions were called in for conferences with their superiors sometime during the month of Ramazan and there offered a drink or a cigarette; refusal to accept the offer was tantamount to an admission of fasting and could lead to expulsion from work. Similar "tests" were recalled by schoolteachers — during Ramazan teams of officials from neighboring towns often visited schools and checked on both the teachers and the students.

Nevertheless, the observance of the fast, although severely restricted, appears to have partly survived. Some Muslims, unable to fast for 28 consecutive days, compromise by abstaining for three days only: the 1st, 15th, and last days of Ramazan. Others, compelled to eat in order to have strength for work and to avoid the suspicion of authorities, eat and drink as little as possible. It is quite likely — although there is no direct evidence — that the fast may be observed more regularly among those who are not gainfully employed.

The *kurban bayram*, despite its originally religious significance, appears to have suffered the fate of most religious festivities in societies which are secularized or on their way to becoming so: the religious element has largely been forgotten, and the holiday has acquired a predominantly secular, national character. This, in part, may be one of the reasons for its survival. Almost all the informants agreed that the *kurban bayram* was widely observed at least until the outbreak of the war, even by members of the Communist Party. The main difficulty in observing this holiday is the shortage of sheep, which are essential for the ceremony. Not only are almost all the sheep in the hands of the *kolkhozy* (collective farms) and *sovkhozy* (state farms) — four-fifths, according to the Soviet Encyclopedia — which do not release them for religious purposes, but the over-all number of sheep and goats in Turkestan has declined from 3 per native in 1913 to approximately 1.5 per native in 1938. Compromises and subterfuges are resorted to to overcome this difficulty. In some collective farms the sheep are stolen or slaughtered under one pretext or another, often with the tacit acquiescence of the collective's chairman. In the cities, the well-to-do purchase sheep on the free market, while the less affluent either enter into partner-

ships with other families to purchase and divide one ram, or else, if they are even too poor for that, sacrifice a chicken instead. The *kurban bayram* seems to be observed less publicly than in pre-Revolutionary years, and usually only in the circle of the immediate family, "with the windows shut and the doors locked," as several refugees put it.

The third fundamental Muslim duty is that of regular alms giving, known as *zakat*, traditionally set at 2.5 per cent of earnings. In Central Asia the *zakat* had lost even before the Russian conquest in the nineteenth century the character of a purely philanthropic measure, having been transformed into a *de facto* tax, collected for the benefit of the local secular authorities. The tsarist administration did its best to suppress this practice in territories under its control, replacing it with its own system of taxes. Today, nothing seems to remain of the *zakat* in Soviet Central Asia. The practice had no deep roots to begin with; the population is too impoverished to keep it up; and there is no one to collect it. Almost none of the refugees even knew the meaning of the term *zakat*, and upon being informed, denied ever seeing it practiced.

Finally, there is the obligation of performing the pilgrimage to Mecca, the *hajj*. Of all the duties incumbent upon a Muslim this is the one most difficult to fulfill under Soviet conditions, inasmuch as the regime forbids travel of private citizens abroad for any purpose whatsoever. Occasionally, as in 1953, the Soviet government itself dispatches to Mecca official delegations headed by government-appointed muftis and shaykhs, but it is quite obvious that such delegations consist only of carefully screened individuals, liberally interspersed with employees of the security police, and that their primary purpose is not religion but foreign propaganda. For the private individual, the road to Mecca is barred. It appears, however, that pilgrimages to the graves of local saints continue to be popular, and in some sense may serve as a substitute for the forbidden *hajj*.

Thus, of the four practices which constitute the central elements of the Islamic ritual, the five Pillars of the Faith (the fifth being the profession of faith), one (prayer) is almost entirely neglected by the younger and middle-age groups, one (fasting) is observed rarely and even then imperfectly, and two (*zakat* and *hajj*) have completely disappeared. Religious *ritual* thus may be said to have declined considerably and no longer to play an important role in the life of the Central Asian Muslims of the Soviet Union.

Let us now turn to other Islamic customs and practices. Circumcision appears from the interviews to be almost universally observed by Central Asian Muslims. One of the reasons for its prevalence is its tolerance by the regime, caused by the fact that this practice requires neither abstention from work nor the transfer of personal allegiance from the state to the religion, and in fact may be justified by hygienic reasons. It is performed by mendicant "specialists," who visit villages and towns, or by anyone else skilled in the use of appropriate instruments, such as local barbers. Communist Party members and other persons in positions of responsibility who may be incriminated in the eyes of the regime by observing this practice, send their children to relatives away from home, where they can be circumcised without the knowledge of the local authorities. Circumcision seems to have lost its festive character, and is carried out so as to attract the minimum attention. Its prevalence among all layers of Muslim society, including Communist Party members, has been attested to by every one of the refugees interviewed.

The religious ceremonies attending births, weddings, and burials require the presence of religiously trained figures such as the mullahs, and it is the great shortage of such persons which more than any factor deprives them of their religious character. The vast majority of mullahs and other Muslim leaders disappeared during the terror of 1928–32. Careful questioning of refugees revealed that in some villages and towns mullahs did remain all throughout the 1930's. These "hidden mullahs" earned their livelihood as ordinary workers (e.g., *kolkhoz* laborers, night watchmen, etc.) and often as janitors in mosques and other religious buildings, but when the occasion arose could also conduct religious ceremonies if the latter were organized by trusted friends and within a closed family circle. Almost every one of the refugees interviewed remembered either knowing of such a clandestine mullah or of having heard of one. But they are few and live under the perpetual threat of exposure and arrest; hence, they cannot make a great

impression on the religious life of their communities. Where there is need for persons with religious training, the natives are far more likely to use the services of an elderly layman from their own midst than risk engaging a person who is difficult to locate and may involve them in trouble with the authorities.

As a consequence of the disappearance of the religious leaders, births, weddings, and burials appear to have largely lost their religious complexion and become transformed into occasions for mere family gatherings. The entire institution of betrothal — which will be described at greater length below — conforms closely to secular local traditions, but is no longer accompanied by religious ceremonies. Occasionally, refugees indicate, after a formal lay wedding ceremony, the parents of the bride and bridegroom may engage the services of a mullah or another trained person to read in secret the *nikah,* the wedding formula, but this is an exception rather than the rule.

As for the *shari‘ah* — representing for the Muslims the religious "way of life" — it has been eliminated not only by the Soviet liquidation of native religious courts and the introduction of a single system of justice throughout the Soviet Union, but also by the spontaneous development of Muslim society itself. Even prior to the 1917 Revolution there had emerged among the Central Asian intelligentsia a powerful secular reform movement known as *jadidism* (*dzhadidism,* in Russian transliteration), the followers of which adopted as one of their principal aims the separation of religion and state. The jadidists fought the clerical groups, gathered around the Ulema Dzhemieti (Association of Ulema), with as much fervor as they fought Russian colonial officials and settlers. Indeed, on this basis of a united effort against the religious influence on everyday life, there occurred in the early period of the Soviet regime an alliance between the Communists and left-wing jadidists which lasted until the purges of the 1930's. The desire to transform Central Asia into a modern, secular, Western country — a desire which is as deep-seated in the post-World War II refugee as it was in the pre-1917 jadidist — has as one of its prerequisites the elimination of religion from a position of influence in the everyday life of the Muslim community, and its confinement to the "proper" sphere, that is, ritual. Islam as a way of life has thus been destroyed by the combined pressures of Soviet antireligious policy and the hostility of the native intelligentsia. The trend in the direction of secularization is so distinct as to make a return to the *shariʿah* as unlikely as a return of Western Europe to the medieval theocratic ideal.[3]

Without doubt the religious life of the Islamic community in Central Asia is stronger among the lower strata of society, among the mountain peoples, and among the elders and women than it is among the groups represented in the interviews. But it is equally certain that the most active elements of society — the adult males, and especially the rural and urban "intelligentsia" — reject religion. A certain measure of religious revival in the event of the return of civic freedom in Central Asia is not unlikely. It may lead to a reopening of the mosques, the reinstitution of Friday prayers, the emergence of mullahs and the introduction of some religious education for the young. But a return to the religious life of the pre-1927–32 period seems entirely out of the question. Islam still survives as a powerful social bond because it serves to differentiate the native from the Russian; but instead of constituting the substance of ethnic identification, as it did before the Revolution, today it forms merely one of its many attributes.

Customs

Although most national customs of the Central Asian Turks are in one way or another connected with Islam, they are by origin and function sufficiently distinct from it to be treated independently, the more so that they are affected differently by Soviet policies: whereas Communism is openly hostile to religion, it either tolerates customs or attempts to take them over for its own purposes.

National customs have fared much better under Soviet rule than religious practices, in part as a result of this tolerant attitude of the regime and in part because they can be better

reconciled with the spirit of Westernization. While Islam has suffered a serious decline, national customs have either remained intact or undergone a transformation which has modified somewhat their outward manifestations without diminishing their hold on the population. In regard to customs, the following seems to be the general rule: the natives abandon or modify those customs which are utterly incompatible with the improvement of living standards, but they cling tenaciously to the traditions which either do not interfere with material progress or can be modified to serve it. Where abandonment or adjustment is necessary, the natives often prefer to adopt the customs of their more advanced Muslim neighbors than those of the Russians or other Europeans.

This pattern emerges clearly in the institution of marriage, which can be analyzed in its three main aspects: the method whereby the marriage is arranged; the formalities connected with the engagement; and the wedding ceremony.

Traditionally, in Muslim communities of Central Asia marriages were arranged not by the couples concerned, but by their parents. Engagements were frequently made when the prospective bride and bridegroom were still in their childhood, and occasionally even before they were born. This custom was in keeping with the elevated position of the father in the Muslim family, and with the seclusion of women in the urban and rural communities of Turkestan; among the nomadic Turks, the high bride price (*kalym*) was a further factor inhibiting marriage outside parental authority.

Inasmuch as this practice runs contrary to the breaking up of family control and the emancipation of women implicit in Westernization, it is being abandoned. Everywhere, and particularly in the urban centers, the youth is becoming less and less dependent on the family, and, with the active encouragement of the regime, frees itself from its control. Coeducational schools, participation in sports, the growing practice of social dating, employment of men and women in offices and stores — all these factors tend to break down the wall between the sexes. The Muslim youth today is not only increasingly able to plan its future without regard to the wishes of parents, but also has many opportunities to mingle freely

---

[3] In this connection it is interesting to note that recently a Constitutional Commission of Pakistan declared that a republic based on the principles of the Qur'an, as desired by the Pakistani ulema, could not be a democratic one, because of the fundamental incompatibility between Islam and democracy. See *New York Times*, April 24, 1954.

with members of the opposite sex. All this
helps undermine the traditional habits in marriage selection. Among the urban Muslim
intelligentsia it appears now to be the rule for
the young couples to decide upon marriage first
and to ask parents for permission afterwards,
as is done in Western societies. In the villages,
where the hold of tradition is stronger and the
family more closely knit, the parents still do
play an important, and perhaps even decisive,
role in the arrangement of marriages; but here,
too, the tendency seems to run against tradition.

An influential factor in the marriage arrangement among Central Asian Muslims was the
kalym, or bride price. The *kalym* was paid to
the parents of the bride by the parents of the
bridegroom prior to the wedding. In the steppe
regions, it consisted usually of livestock, averaging in pre-Revolutionary days from 50 to 100
horses and an equal or larger number of sheep
— a sizeable fortune by local standards. In
Turkestan, the *kalym* consisted of gifts of
money, jewels, or other valuables. The payment of the *kalym* is one of the few traditions
of a nonreligious nature outlawed by the Soviet
regime, ostensibly as "degrading" to women,
but its illegality explains only in part its actual
decline, which is probably due more to the
impoverishment of the native population over
the past 25 years. What Kazakh disposes of
50 horses or sheep? Poverty seems to have
reduced the tradition of the *kalym* to a purely
symbolic significance. It apparently continues
to survive in one form or another throughout
Central Asia, but it no longer performs any
important economic function.

One of the more startling results of information gathered from refugees is the impression
of strict sexual morality prevailing among Soviet Muslims. Despite the freer mingling of
sexes, there is little opportunity for sexual
promiscuity because of the close watch exercised over the girls by their families and the
great value attached by the natives to virginity.
Most of the refugees agreed that an unmarried
Muslim girl who has lost her virginity — no
matter under what circumstances — is considered to be on the same level as a common
prostitute. Her chances of marriage are almost
nonexistent, because it is generally accepted
that a marriage contract is void if the bride is
found on the wedding night not to be a virgin.

On the whole, sexual licentiousness seems rare:
it is prevented by tradition and by the control
exercised by the family, to whom a deflowered
daughter not only brings public disgrace but
also represents a lasting financial liability.[4]

So far as the Communist authorities are
concerned, the actual wedding act should consist merely of a registration in the local office
of the ZAGS (*Zapis' aktov grazhdanskogo
sostoianiia* — Registry of Civil Acts); any festivities connected with it should preferably be
organized by the local Young Communist
League, Trade Union, or other organization to
which the young couple belongs. In fact, however, the natives prefer to celebrate weddings
in a more traditional manner. Among the inhabitants of the steppe and desert, for instance,
it is still customary on the wedding day for
the bride (properly veiled) to wait at her
parents' home for the friends of the bridegroom
to take her to her new home — but whereas
before the Revolution she was transported on
a camel or a horse, she is now brought to the
wedding place in a rented automobile. It is
still customary, while the wedding party is
in progress, for the young pair to retire to a
separate room, and there have sexual relations,
in order to be able to prove to the relatives of
both parties the virginity of the bride. The
entire wedding ceremony in Central Asia assumes ever more the character of a purely
secular festivity, but insofar as possible it is
carried out within the framework of traditional
nonreligious forms and rituals.

The food habits of the natives seem to have
undergone little change. Through contact with
Russians they have been exposed to such novel
foods as potatoes, bread, and boiled eggs, but
their preference is for traditional native dishes:
pilau, kumys, etc. They are often compelled
to eat Russian food, including pork, in government and other restaurants and in the army,

[4] Newspapers and periodicals from Central Asia
indicate that, despite Soviet efforts aimed at changing native attitudes toward women, tradition persists. It seems apparently to be quite common
practice for natives to withdraw daughters from
school when the girls attain the age of adolescence;
the local press reports occasionally instances of
high-school graduating classes being completely
devoid of girls, all of them having dropped out a
few years earlier. See *Central Asian Review*, Vol.
I, No. 3 (1953), pp. 47–53; Vol. II, No. 1 (1954),
pp. 71–72.

but they avoid it if at all possible. The natives seem to prefer to partake of their main meal in the evening, rather than at midday, as the Russians are in the habit of doing.

In clothing the natives of Central Asia appear to tend in the direction of a synthesis of traditional and Western garb. The basic articles of wear, their cut, and ornamentation are native; but some items of clothing are adopted from the Russians. Adult males have almost everywhere taken to wearing leather shoes, which are superior in comfort and durability to their native counterparts; Muslim girls like to wear, together with their national costumes, Western-style blouses. Soviet sources report a general tendency on the part of natives to wear mixed clothing, part Western, part native — the former apparently for comfort, the latter for national identification. In the cities, especially among the youth, Western clothing predominates; in the village, the opposite is the case. In clothes, as in other customs, the principle enunciated earlier holds true: the natives discard what is patently inconvenient and adopt from the Russians what is more practical, i.e., Western. They do not discard traditions for reasons other than utility.

The same principle applies to housing and furniture. The natives adopt freely and widely articles of utility, such as kerosene lamps, samovars, and iron stoves. But they resist efforts of the authorities to introduce chairs, tables, and bedsteads, which to them seem quite unnecessary. "Not only those collective farm families sleep on the floor which as yet have no bedsteads," writes a recent Soviet observer of conditions in the Kirghiz republic. "Sometimes a purchased bedstead, instead of being used for its purpose, stands all made up as a decoration, while the family continues sleeping on the floor."[5] Even the most Westernized Muslim intelligentsia in the cities demonstrate a desire to preserve a link with tradition by decorating a single room of an otherwise Western-style apartment in the native manner.

House construction among the old settled groups of the population seems to follow traditional lines, with minor innovations, such as the use of whitewash for the walls and floors. Among the recently settled nomads, whom the Soviet regime wishes to have acquire permanent buildings, a curious compromise has been attained: the natives spend one part of their time in the permanent structures and another part in the traditional *yurt* (nomadic tent) erected alongside the houses. On the whole, one gains the impression that among the Turkic groups which had been settled during and since the period of collectivization, the *yurt* continues to prevail, while in the mountains it is still the exclusive shelter of native inhabitants.

The general picture which emerges from a survey of native customs indicates that they are adhered to far more loyally than are religious traditions. The causes for this are threefold. In the first place, a considerable part of the native population of Central Asia was only superficially affected by Islam, while remaining loyal to local traditions. In the second place, national traditions are on the whole not contrary to the spirit of Westernization, and can in most cases be well adapted to the demands of a secular, utilitarian society. And, finally, the Soviet regime treats local customs far more gingerly than religion, trying to destroy them more through example and infiltration than through outright suppression. The native population clings to its customs, surrendering them only when they are utterly incompatible with material progress of society, and when it does modify traditions, it tries to synthesize the innovations with tradition. The native may be persuaded that it is a good thing to possess an iron bedstead, but often he cannot be convinced that sleeping on a bed is preferable to sleeping on the floor. Similarly, he may agree that eating by fork and spoon is hygienically preferable to eating by hand, but he refuses to agree that pork and potatoes are superior to lamb and rice. This attitude gives native customs a considerable resiliency to external pressures.

Language

With the exception of the Tajiks, virtually all the Muslims of Central Asia speak local dialects of one and the same Turki language group. Varying cultural influences to which the in-

---

[5] S. M. Abramzon, *Ocherki kul'tury kirgizskogo naroda* (Frunze, 1946), p. 75. Abramzon's book supplies interesting data on the culture of the Kirghiz in the post-World War II era, much of which supports the conclusions derived from interviews with refugees.

dividual subgroups have been subjected in the course of history have led to a certain differentiation in the vocabulary and grammar of the principal dialects. Uzbek especially, having been exposed to strong Iranian and Arabic influences, has changed much, even to the extent of losing the vowel harmony common to the sound system of the Turki languages. By and large, however, it is possible to speak of the Central Asian Muslims as possessing linguistic unity: the dialectical differences, significant as they are to the philologist, neither prevent effective communication among the Turkic inhabitants nor preclude the eventual emergence of a single Turki literary language for Central Asia. The latter, however, had not yet been formed when the Communists conquered Central Asia in the 1920's and suppressed its further development.

The importance of language for national consciousness is self-evident: language represents the most ready means of national identification, available alike to the literate and illiterate. While not absolutely indispensable for nationality (witness the Jews), it is so intimately connected with it as to make it one of nationality's very best criteria.

Soviet linguistic policy in Central Asia has two principal aspects, both of which follow closely the general lines of Soviet nationality policy. In the first place it strives at all costs to prevent the formation of a single Turki literary language in Central Asia on the assumption that such a language would serve as a powerful weapon for the forging of a united Central Asian national movement. In the second place, it endeavors to promote the acceptance of Russian as the primary language of communication among persons of different groups. The first goal is fostered by exploiting all, even the minutest, dialectical differences among the various Turkic subgroups, and by granting the status of full-fledged national-literary languages to local variants of one and the same Turki language. The second is fostered through the official change of Turki alphabets from Arabic to Latin, and then from Latin to the Russian Cyrillic; through the gradual introduction of Russian words in their original form and spelling into the native vocabularies; through compulsory Russian language instruction in all schools above the elementary level; and, finally,

through the requirement of a good knowledge of Russian for all citizens, regardless of nationality, desirous of making any kind of a career. It is apparently the hope of the authorities that, given sufficient time, such policies will make Russian the language of all the socially dynamic elements of the Muslim population and relegate Turkic to the status of a peasant dialect devoid of political importance.[6]

This policy of linguistic Russification is far more subtle than that practiced by the tsarist regime in some of its borderlands during the darkest days of modern Russian autocracy (1881–1903), and, if successful, could deal a very considerable blow to Muslim prospects in Central Asia. Thirty-five years is admittedly too short a time to judge the effects of a set of measures apparently designed to operate for several generations; but certain evidence permits us to draw some conclusions about its efficacy and prospects of success.

Soviet linguistic policies seem to have had very little effect on the speech habits of the bulk of the Muslim *rural* population. Living in their own fairly closed communities, which offer little continuous contact with Russians, the Muslim peasants continue to use exclusively their local dialects. They seem to be as ignorant of Russian as their ancestors had been. None of the peasants interviewed knew more

---

[6] An alternate interpretation of Soviet linguistic policies in Central Asia is suggested by a British authority, G. E. Wheeler: "[The Soviet authorities] evidently hope to achieve by russification an effect similar to that produced by the 'Arabization' of the indigenous languages of the peoples who came under Arab Islamic domination. The adoption of the Arabic script and of numerous Arabic words and phrases was a powerful factor in the perpetuation of Islam, and thus of Arab culture, even after the tide of Arab conquest had receded. But it was the *result* of conversion to Islam, not the cause, and while the Arabs may have insisted on the use of Arabic for official purposes, just as Tsarist Russia and Britain insisted on the use of Russian and English, there is no evidence that they ever instituted a policy of Arabization of existing languages. The Soviet government is attempting to achieve the same end by arbitrary means: it is insisting on the russification of Central Asian languages by the introduction of the Cyrillic script and Russian loanwords; and it even envisages the modification of grammar and phonetics." G. E. Wheeler, "Cultural Developments in Soviet Central Asia," *Royal Central Asian Journal*, vol. 41 (July–Oct. 1954), p. 181.

than a few words of Russian; after ten years in Germany several could speak better German than they could Russian after several decades of residence in the Soviet Union. For most of the rural Muslims in the U.S.S.R., the first important contact with Russians and the Russian language comes with entrance into military service. After being drafted they are distributed among Russian soldiers and are expected to learn the language as best they can. For many of them, the military service is the first and most efficient school of Russian.

The situation is somewhat different in the cities and small towns, where Muslims live side by side with Russians, and where a large proportion of Muslim youths attend high schools and institutions of higher learning. It is difficult to obtain a clear picture of the linguistic training in Central Asia, because it varies from area to area and from time to time. If there is a general principle, it seems to consist in a direct correlation between level of education and Russian language instruction. In the elementary schools, the instruction is predominantly in the prevailing local language, either Turki or Russian, and in areas where both groups are numerous, in both. In the secondary schools Russian is either the principal language of instruction (in schools attended largely by Russian students) or else it is taught as an important second (but "foreign") language; passing a Russian language examination seems to be a graduation prerequisite for all high-school students, regardless of nationality. Every graduate of a Soviet high school is thus expected to possess a knowledge of Russian. Whether or not this knowledge actually exists probably depends more on what the student does after graduation than upon the intensity or quality of his training. For the average Muslim girl who marries a Muslim and then raises a family, her high-school Russian language instruction is wasted, for at home she speaks her native tongue and soon forgets all she has learned; the same is probably true of the Muslim youth who returns to the village after his studies. For the more enterprising wage earner, however, the Russian training is of greater and more lasting importance: it represents the key to all further academic or professional advancement, as well as to membership in the vast party and state

apparatus, which comprise and circumscribe a "career" in Soviet society.[7]

At one time the Communists made serious attempts in the direction of founding university-level training in the native languages, but these endeavors were not very successful, in part because of the shortage of qualified native teaching personnel and in part as a result of the general trend in the direction of Russification. Today most of the university-level instruction, except that which by its very content requires the use of local languages (Central Asian archeology, anthropology, philology, folklore, etc.), appears to be conducted in Russian.

A young Muslim, in order to succeed in life, must learn Russian and learn it well. Among the Muslim intelligentsia, therefore, a knowledge of Russian is widespread. But — and this is essential for the present inquiry — by acquiring a knowledge of Russian the local Muslims do not, as is apparently anticipated by the regime, lose command of their own language; instead, they become bilingual. Russian is the language of business, and the means through which it is possible to establish some contact with the culture of the outside world; it is not the language of daily life, in use at home, in the family, and among friends. The refugee informants were unanimous in asserting that neither they nor their friends, even those active in the Party, ever spoke Russian elsewhere than at work. They were equally firm in maintaining that they knew no Muslims who had lost command of their native speech. This assertion is reinforced by the observation that the Muslim refugees in Germany do not communicate with each other in Russian, even on occasions when, because of diverse ethnic origins, communication in Turki presents considerable difficulties.

It is as yet too early to estimate the effects

---

[7] According to the *Central Asian Review*, admission to the State University of Turkmenia and the Turkmen Academy of Sciences is "dependent upon students passing an examination in Russian and Russian literature." On the other hand, "Russian students at the Academy of Sciences are only required to have a knowledge of the Turkmen language if they intend to make a special study of Turkmen language and literature." There is no reason to suppose that the pattern is different in the other republics of Central Asia. *Central Asian Review*, Vol. I, No. 3 (1953), pp. 65–66.

of Soviet linguistic policy aimed at Russification through methods which are both negative (division of Muslim groups) and positive (the imposition of Russian through compulsion, linguistic infiltration, and career inducements). On the eve of World War II the Muslim rural masses seemed to have been quite unaffected by Soviet linguistic measures, and so were the poorer and less educated elements in the cities. These groups continued, as before, to communicate exclusively in their native dialects, being ignorant of Russian. Soviet policies did cause the numerous and growing Muslim intelligentsia to acquire a working knowledge of Russian; but instead of becoming Russified these groups became bilingual, using Russian for the purposes of work, and Turki or Persian, as the case may be, for all other purposes. Of linguistic assimilation there does not seem the slightest evidence; on the contrary, all signs point to a remarkable ability of the local languages to survive in the face of strong external pressures.

Ethnic Identity of Central Asian Muslims

Until the beginning of the twentieth century, Central Asia preserved its ethnic homogeneity remarkably well. The tsarist government discouraged the migration of Slavs into the steppe region for fear of native rebellions, while Turkestan, which in the centuries prior to Russian conquest had been one of the world's most isolated areas, virtually closed to non-Muslims, absorbed only a small trickle of Russian officials and merchants. Khiva and Bukhara continued even after the establishment of the Russian protectorate to admit only a small number of Russians. At the turn of the century Muslims formed over 90 per cent of

the total population of all Central Asia; in Turkestan itself they accounted for 97 per cent of all the inhabitants.[8] (See Table 1.)

Perhaps the most significant single change which has occurred in Central Asia during the last half century has been the destruction of its ethnic homogeneity, brought about by Russian and Ukrainian immigration.

The first great migratory wave of Russians entered between 1906 and 1911, during the ministry of P. Stolypin, as a result of the deliberate effort of the tsarist regime to reduce the land hunger of the Russian villages by settling some of their excess population in the sparsely inhabited steppe regions of Central Asia. This colonizing enterprise brought to Central Asia about one million peasants, most of whom made their home in the eastern parts of the steppe region and in the Semirechensk province of Turkestan. The newcomers were provided by the government with generous land allotments (transferred from the Crown, which claimed as its property all the nomadic grazing lands) and inventory, and settled in compact villages, apart from the Kazakh-Kirghiz natives, most of whom continued their traditional nomadic or seminomadic habits. The colonization program had only a limited success, for after the outbreak of World War I the large-scale Russian influx into the steppe regions ceased; the Russians living in the Kazakh Republic in 1939 still consisted in their majority of the original Stolypin colonists or their direct descendants. The proportion of

---

[8] These statistics, and those which follow, are based mainly on three sources: *Aziatskaia Rossiia*, Vol. I (St. Petersburg, 1914); *Ts. St. Upr. SSSR. Narodnost' i rodnoi iazyk naseleniia SSSR* (Moscow, 1928); and *Strany mira* (Moscow, 1946).

TABLE 1 *Russian and Native Population of Central Asia,* in Round Figures*

	1897	1911	1926	1939
Muslims	9,300,000	10,400,000	10,700,000	c. 11,700,000
Russians	700,000	2,000,000	2,700,000	4,500,000
Others	300,000	600,000	300,000	400,000
TOTAL	10,300,000	13,000,000	13,700,000	16,600,000

* Including estimates for Khiva and Bukhara.

Russians in the total population of the steppe region would not have grown appreciably, therefore, were it not for the fact that the upheavals which had occurred in that area during World War I and the Russian Revolution (the 1916 Kazakh-Kirghiz revolt, and the famine of 1920–21) led to a considerable decrease in the native population. While the Kazakh-Kirghiz population remained virtually constant between 1911 and 1926, the local Russian population increased during the same period through natural growth by one-fourth. As a result of these demographic changes, Muslims constituted by 1926 only two-thirds of the population of the Kazakh Republic. (See Table 2.)

Turkestan succeeded in maintaining its ethnic homogeneity somewhat longer than the steppe region. The Russian influx into Turkestan prior to the Revolution was predominantly urban, consisting of officials, merchants, military personnel, and other groups connected with this area's administration and economic development. Thus, in 1926 the Russians still constituted merely 7.4 per cent of the population of Turkestan.

The next important change in the demography of Central Asia occurred around 1930 as a consequence of Russian immigration and the further decrease of the native population. The Russians who migrated into Central Asia during this period were both victims of collectivization seeking to find refuge and to make a living on the Asiatic frontier, and settlers who followed in the wake of the newly constructed Turkestan–Siberian (Turksib) railroad. These migrants — whose number may be tentatively estimated between 1926 and 1939 at 1,300,000 — settled not in the steppe but in Turkestan.

While the 1939 census did not provide ethnographic breakdowns for the individual republics (with one exception noted below[9]), it is possible, by comparing the growth of the population within the individual republics with the total growth of the major Central Asian ethnic groups (both reported by Soviet sources), to arrive at a reasonably close estimate of the distribution of the Russian newcomers:

In the Uzbek Republic 720,000
In the Kirghiz Republic 285,000
In the Tajik Republic 155,000
In the Turkmen Republic 135,000

More than one-half of the migrants, in other words, settled in the Uzbek Republic, where in all probability most of them moved into the towns (Tashkent especially) and the expanding industrial centers of the Ferghana valley. In the Tajik and Turkmen Republics most of the Russian newcomers probably also settled in the cities, while in Kirghizia, where there were numerous Russian agricultural settlements of pre-Revolutionary vintage, they moved into the countryside as well (the total urban population of the Kirghiz Republic grew, between 1926 and 1939, only by 150,000, whereas the total Russian population there increased in the same period by an estimated 285,000 immigrants).

———————

[9] The Turkmen SSR is the exception. Official Soviet statistics for 1939, when the total population of this republic was 1,251,900, break down its ethnic structure as follows: Turkmen 59.2 per cent; Russians 18.7 per cent; Uzbeks 8.5 per cent; Kazakhs 4.9 per cent; other nationalities 8.7 per cent. Z. G. Freikin, *Turkmenskaia SSR* (Moscow, 1954), p. 84.

TABLE 2   *Distribution of the Russian Population in Central Asia,* in Round Figures*

	1897	1911	1926	1939
Steppe	500,000	1,600,000	2,100,000	c. 2,600,000
Turkestan	200,000	400,000	600,000	c. 1,900,000
Per Cent of Russians in Total Population of Central Asia...	6.8	15.3	19.7	c. 27.1

* Including estimates for Khiva and Bukhara.

Another factor which increased the ratio of Russians to Muslims in Central Asia was the decline in the Muslim population of the steppe due to the terrors of the period of collectivization. According to Soviet census statistics, the Kazakh population of the Soviet Union decreased between 1926 and 1939 from 3,960,000 to 3,099,000 — a decline of about a million and a half if one takes into consideration the normal rate of growth.

Thus, by 1939 the Muslims probably formed less than one-half of the inhabitants in the steppe region and about four-fifths of those in Turkestan. The ratio of Muslims to Russians in all of Central Asia dropped from 15 to 1 in 1897 to less than 4 to 1 in 1939. Obviously, such a rapid demographic change was bound to have profound effects on the ability of the natives to preserve their ethnic identity, the more so since the influx of Russians appears to have continued undiminished after 1939, becoming particularly rapid during the period of war-time evacuation (1942–44) and the new program of Russian and Ukrainian settlement in the Kazakh steppes since 1952.

On the face of it, Russian migration threatens the natives with eventual destruction. Central Asia appears to be faced with ethnic Russification, which may bring about the complete assimilation of the natives. However, in order to determine the effect of the Russian influx upon the natives it is necessary to go beyond mere statistics and to analyze the nature and scope of relations between these two groups. What matters is not so much how many Russians come to live in Central Asia, but whether, through intermarriage, social contact, cultural and other means, they actually exercise a denationalizing influence upon the Muslims. The answer to this question is not as discouraging for Muslim prospects as might appear from the mere survey of demographic statistics.

The Russians who migrate into Central Asia do not displace the natives, but settle side by side with them. The Russo-Ukrainian influx into Central Asia resembles not so much a demographic inundation, which gradually spreads over and submerges the whole native population, as a stream which penetrates the area following the path of least resistance and covers the regions which are least populated. It thus splits the population into two unequal parts, both of which retain their national character.

As has been pointed out above, the Russians inhabiting the steppe region in 1939 were largely the descendants of the pre-1914 colonists, living in the separate Russo-Ukrainian villages (now collectivized) or in the predominantly Russian-inhabited cities. When the Kazakhs were collectivized in the 1930's, and in many instances forcefully settled as well, they were formed into separate *kolkhozy* (collective farms), apart from the old and established Russo-Ukrainian villages. The establishment of ethnically mixed collectives was impractical, partly because the Russians were already settled in their own communities and partly because the basis of the native economy, sheep and livestock grazing, was different from that of the predominantly agricultural Russian villages.[10] The overwhelming majority of the Russian and Kazakh peasants in Kazakhstan, therefore, continues to live in separate settlements. Interviews with refugees from this region indicate that until the outbreak of World War II, at any rate, there were practically no ethnically mixed *kolkhozy*, although closely situated villages were frequently combined for administrative purposes into a single *sel'sovet* (village soviet), even when consisting of differing ethnic groups. Occasionally stray Russians may be found working on Kazakh collectives: doctors, nurses, bookkeepers, and so forth — as often as not persons who found it expedient for one reason or another to leave their native regions. Kazakh shepherds and laborers are also employed by some Russian collectives. But these are cases affecting individuals which do not change the general picture of ethnic separation in the rural areas.

The situation is somewhat different in the *sovkhozy* (state farms), which are operated like large enterprises with hired labor (there were

---

[10] Attempts to mix collectives apparently had little success: "Instead of organizing the greatest possible mutual assistance of Russian and Kazakh collective farms," writes an official Kazakh Republic publication, "[the authorities] permitted instances of formation of international collective farms, ignoring the fact that the mass of the collective farmers was not as yet prepared for them." *10 let Kazakhstana — 1920–1930* (Alma-Ata, 1930), p. 216.

191 *sovkhozy* in the Kazakh Republic in 1938). The *sovkhozy* carry out diversified agricultural functions, and hire many Muslims to tend the sheep and livestock — a task they can carry out better than the Russian workers. They also employ some Muslim white-collar workers.

A similar picture of ethnic separation exists in Turkestan. In pre-Revolutionary times the Russians moving into the cities of Turkestan followed the custom of Europeans in other colonial areas of the world, and rather than make their home in the Oriental quarters, insanitary and overcrowded by Western standards, or build new cities from scratch, they constructed separate European sections adjoining the native towns. In this way, nearly all the cities in Turkestan were split into two halves: native, or Old, and European, or New. Significant exceptions to this rule were only Vernyi (Alma-Ata), whose geographic location did not permit the planning of a separate Russian sector, and Kokand, in the Ferghana valley, which the Russians left entirely to the natives, erecting the European town some 8 miles away, in Skobelev (Fergana). After the advent of the Communists this basic pattern remained, with one important change: leaving the Old and the New sections of the towns intact, the Soviet authorities constructed in most towns new quarters to house the officials, employees, and other privileged elements of Soviet society, who are predominantly, but not exclusively, European. Thus, most Central Asian towns today are divided into three parts: one predominantly native, another predominantly European, and a third one mixed, with Europeans dominant. The new quarters house alike native and Russian employees of the state; the natives living there, however, belong exclusively to the so-called "intelligentsia," which is Westernized and bilingual and constitutes a relatively small segment of the total native urban population. The majority of Russians and of natives continue, as before the Revolution, to live in their respective quarters, though the lines separating these quarters seem less sharp than they were before. A general mixing of the urban population has certainly not occurred.

As a result of this situation, the large influx of Russians into the cities does not have the effect of submerging the native population.

Rather it leads to a great expansion of the European and Soviet sectors, a development which has no direct effect upon the native parts of the towns. The settlement of newcomers in the native quarters is quite unlikely, if only because of the overcrowding which prevails in almost all of them, as in most Oriental towns.

The next question which arises is whether, despite the residential separation, the Russians and Muslims actually assimilate through intermarriage and social contact. Here we must rely for answers entirely on interview material.

Intermarriage is by far the most effective means of breaking down ethnic barriers. Prior to the Revolution, Russians and Muslims did not intermarry. If the interviews are correct, this continues to be the case today. A number of factors prevent intermarriage: the enormous cultural gap between Russians and Muslims, which ranges from such everyday matters as language, food, and type of residence to more subtle differences of national character and sexual customs; the considerable control which Muslim parents continue to exercise over their female children; and the great difficulty which a mixed family would have in finding a place in the Muslim or Russian community. The informants unanimously agreed that in Central Asia marriage between a Muslim girl and a Russian would be utterly unthinkable, since it would be prevented by the parents and the male relatives of the girl. Several of the refugee informants stated the opinion that a girl who would evade parental disapproval and marry a Russian would be assassinated by her male relatives; one recalled a specific instance of an Uzbek opera star who was killed by her brother for having married a Russian. Intermarriage is considered an insult to the family and to the nation. As one informant put it: "There are never enough girls for all the available Muslim suitors anyway; if a Muslim girl married a Russian that would mean that we weren't good enough for her."[11] None of the informants — who, it must be remembered, came from the ranks of the most Westernized

----

[11] Indeed, the ratio of males to females in Central Asia was always high: in 1926 the proportion was 10 to 9 in favor of the males. Among the Russians, on the other hand, the ratio is reversed.

Central Asian Muslims — knew personally any native girl who had married a Russian.

It appears much easier for a Muslim male to marry a Russian woman, and in some cases this happens because of the shortage of Muslim girls and the not inconsiderable number of Russian widows and prostitutes living in Central Asia. But such occurrences, too, seem rather rare. The informants who knew of such cases could recall only instances of Muslims living with Russian women without benefit of formal marriage; such Muslims are largely people whose homes have been broken up and who live with their wives or mistresses outside both Muslim and Russian communities.

The fact that the mere act of marrying an outsider leads to instant exclusion from the two dominant communities and forces the family to live in a social no-man's land is a strong deterrent to intermarriage. Consequently, the overwhelming majority of Russians and Muslims in Central Asia marry persons of their own ethnic group. Intermarriage appears very rare; insofar as it exists at all, it seems confined to the marginal groups of society, to persons who lack families and hence have little contact with their respective ethnic groups, or those who have left Central Asia and taken up residence in other parts of the Soviet Union.

Social contact, too, seems to be limited, even among the groups which by virtue of their occupation are constantly in touch with representatives of other nationalities. Muslim refugees who had been employed in Soviet agencies and offices together with Russians were unanimous in asserting that contact with the Russians ceased after working hours. Much the same seems to be the case among soldiers on active service in peace time.

Russo-Muslim relations vary considerably, depending upon the social status and level of education of the groups concerned. On the whole, the interviews indicate that national friction is in an inverse ratio to social status and education: the higher the status, the less friction. Racial hostility appears strongest among the poorest rural inhabitants, among the plain soldiers, and the unskilled laborers; it seems least prevalent among the intelligentsia, the state and party officials, the well-to-do peasants and workers, and the army officers. By and large the refugees — despite their strong anti-Russian bias — agreed that the relations between Russians and Muslims are good, and they attached little significance to various incidents of national friction which, being prompted, they had been able to recall. There seems to be a deep-seated feeling that whatever the differences dividing them, both these groups suffer from the same regime, that they are "in the same boat."

In the universities, *vuzy, tekhnikums,* and other places where work is combined with residence, Muslims and Russians frequently tend to separate from each other on their own initiative. A number of refugees reported that Muslim and Russian students, when given the choice, preferred to live in separate dormitories.

The greatest single Russifying force in the Soviet Union is the army. In the 1920's, in the initial stage of the Soviet nationality policy, the Communists had created separate military divisions for the major nationality groups in the U.S.S.R. These units were gradually broken up in the early 1930's, first by withdrawing regiments and battalions from their national commands and dispersing them among other regular Soviet divisions, and then by disbanding their commanding staffs as well. From then until World War II there were no separate national units. At one time in the course of World War II, when Soviet military fortunes were at their nadir, attempts were made to create separate all-Muslim units in Turkestan, possibly to serve as Home Guards. However, as soon as the Soviet army began to gain the initiative at the front, the formation of these units was suspended, and its personnel was eventually dispersed in the regular Red army. Since the 1930's the army has scattered Muslim draftees throughout regular Soviet units in such a manner that no more than a few Muslims are assigned to any one infantry company; Muslim officers, too, are distributed as thinly as possible.

Naturally, such a system does not permit Muslim recruits to maintain their ethnic separateness. For many a Muslim, entry into military service represents the first contact with an alien nationality. The Muslim recruit is expected at once to understand Russian commands, even though he is often completely ignorant of Russian. This linguistic difficulty, coupled with the general ineptitude of most Central Asian Muslims for army life (due to the exemption granted them in tsarist days), makes military service for many a shocking and bewildering experience. Sooner or later, however, most Muslims, except the dullest or most recalcitrant, learn enough Russian to get along and communicate with their Russian superiors and comrades. Several of the refugees stated that they had first learned Russian in the army; for some others, the army was actually the first experience with life outside their own Muslim communities. On many recruits the effect of such an experience, though violent, is not long-lasting; having completed his military service, the recruit returns to his village and soon forgets most of what he has learned. For others, however, it constitutes a radical break which affects their entire life. The Red army represents the only Soviet institution — save for the forced labor camps — where Muslim and Russian societies are forcibly compressed together, and where the cultural and ethnic walls usually separating them are to some extent broken down.

Evidence obtained from refugees who had lived in Soviet concentration camps and Nazi prisoner-of-war camps indicates that in conditions of great distress the ethnic barriers break down most rapidly, for in neither was there much separation between Muslims and Russians.[12] After an initial period of very harsh treatment by the Germans as "Asiatics," the Central Asians were separated out by the Germans under the influence of Turkestani émigré organizations and were formed into numerous small military units, commanded by Germans; these units served as military police and anti-partisan units and in some cases as front-line combat units.

An important factor in the demography of Central Asia is the settlement of the nomadic and seminomadic populations of the steppe and desert regions. The abandonment of nomadic habits had begun long before the Revolution; one of the main themes in the entire history of the Turkic tribes since their appearance in Central Asia and the Middle East a thousand years ago is the gradual transition from pure nomadism to a settled existence. This process was in part caused by the encroachment of agricultural peoples of neighboring territories upon the extensive nomadic lands, with the resultant shrinkage of grazing areas, and in part by the economic advantages to be derived from a combination of cattle and sheep herding with agriculture. Both these factors caused a rapid decline in nomadism in Central Asia in the latter half of the nineteenth century, under Russian rule. In 1926 (i.e., on the eve of collectivization) in Kazakhstan — the main area of nomadism — 26 per cent of all the Kazakh families were fully settled, 66 per cent practiced nomadism in the summers (transhumance), and only the remaining 6 per cent to 8 per cent were nomadic the year around. Of the major group, i.e., those practicing summer nomadism, more than two-thirds moved within a 25-kilometer radius of their winter quarters.[13] Soviet collectivization thus completed a process of settlement that was already well on its way, and given another few decades might have been accomplished quite naturally. A by-product of settlement is the decline of the tribe as a unit of social organization, and with it the disappearance of the tribal divisions and feuds which in the past have constituted one of the most serious deterrents to the development of a national consciousness among the Central Asian natives. The natives of the steppe and desert chafe greatly under the severe limitations imposed upon their movement by the Soviet regime, and, given freedom, would probably like to return at least in part to some form of nomadism; nevertheless, the tribal structure is probably destroyed beyond repair. This fact greatly strengthens the development of modern nationalism.

Thus, despite the considerable Russian influx into Central Asia, the Muslims living there appear to maintain their ethnic distinctiveness. This is thanks both to the character of Russian settlement, which leads to the establishment of

---

[12] More recent evidence, however, indicates that this has not been the case in Soviet forced labor camps since World War II. Repatriated inmates of Vorkuta, one of the largest Soviet forced labor camps, indicate that national differences are very prominent in the camp, and the prisoners tend to group strictly along national or religious lines. See, for instance, J. Scholmer, *Vorkuta* (New York, 1955). It is not certain whether this contradiction is due to some unknown factors operating in post-World War II camps, or whether there is no clearcut pattern permitting generalization on this subject.

[13] *10 let Kazakhstana*, pp. 82–83.

Russian centers *side by side* rather than *among* the natives, and to the wide cultural gap, which hinders intermarriage and more intimate social contact. Indeed, it may be said that Russian migration and Soviet policies have rather contributed to the development of national consciousness, first by exposing all natives to contact with representatives of an alien culture and thus forcing them to question their own status, and secondly by helping to destroy — through settlement — the tribal divisions which had always been a most formidable obstacle to native unity vis-à-vis the foreigner.

The Intelligentsia

An important factor in the transformation of an ethnic group into a full-fledged nation with a developed sense of national consciousness is an articulate class with sufficient education and experience to provide the population with intellectual leadership. In societies which have only recently begun to undergo such a transformation, this function is usually assumed by what the Russians call "intelligentsia" — a class composed of individuals of diverse social background whom a common middle or higher education, qualifying it for professional or white-collar work, turns into a new social estate.

The Russian Muslims already possessed such a class prior to 1917, consisting largely of professional people, especially lawyers, teachers, journalists, and engineers from the Kazan and Baku areas. This intelligentsia played a leading role in the Muslim national movements during the Revolution and the period immediately following it; many of its members cooperated with the Soviet regime in the 1920's, during the era of Communist "softness" toward Muslim nationalism; others, especially those who had been connected with the White Guard movement during the Civil War, went into hiding or disassociated themselves from all further political activity.

Most of the older Muslim intelligentsia of the Soviet Union — pro-Communist and anti-Communist alike — was physically destroyed in the course of the purges, arrests, deportations, and executions of the 1930's. On the eve of World War II Soviet Muslims found themselves without national leadership, since the only other classes capable of providing it — the landowners, merchants, and the clergy

— had also been liquidated in the course of the simultaneous drives for collectivization and against the Islamic religion in the late 1920's and early 1930's.

It is a perennial dilemma of the Soviet system that its dynamic totalitarianism requires an unusually large body of trained officials, and yet it cannot permit these officials the freedom of thought and action which they demand in consequence of their training. The principal solution which Communism has so far been able to devise for this problem consists of periodic purges, causing the destruction of the established bureaucracy and its replacement with ever new personnel — a procedure very costly in terms of manpower, but roughly serving the purpose for which it is devised. However, the system of purges, mass as well as local, requires constant repetition, for purge as it may, the Soviet regime cannot alter the fact that the intelligentsia, whose growth it is actively promoting, chafes under the yoke of totalitarianism and constitutes one of the major sources of tension within the established order.

It is this feature of its system which compelled the Soviet regime to replace the old intelligentsia of Central Asian Muslims destroyed by it with a new one. The new intelligentsia is largely Soviet-educated, and comprises people most of whom are today under 40 years of age. This new intelligentsia is, by comparison with the old, pre-Revolutionary one, very numerous. According to Soviet statistics for 1939, in the 5 republics of Central Asia there were 66,000 active students in technical and other specialized schools above the high-school level, and 35,000 active students in universities and other institutions of higher learning. Central Asia also had 758,000 persons with a completed high-school education and 57,000 with a completed higher education. Even allowing that a sizable proportion of these persons consists of Russians and other Europeans, the number of Muslims among them must be very considerable. Measured by Western European standards, the training of these "intellectuals," even graduates of universities, is quite poor. What matters, however, is not their level of knowledge, but their position vis-à-vis the rest of the population and the attitudes and aspirations resulting from their training.

Evidence indicates that the graduates of

schools consider themselves superior to manual labor, and expect to be rewarded for their schooling with administrative or other office work. The Muslim intellectual seems to feel that education entitles one not so much to greater rewards as to a reduction of the working load. It is a professional intelligentsia which aspires to national leadership and is strongly interested in political action.

The Central Asian Muslim intelligentsia possesses many of the characteristics which distinguish the Soviet intelligentsia as a whole, but in addition it also displays certain traits engendered by special conditions prevailing in Central Asia.

The Muslim intelligentsia occupies in Central Asia a peculiar position: by origin, language, culture, and family ties, it is connected to the Muslim population; by training, work, and much of its world-outlook, it is identified with the Soviet regime. It thus belongs fully to neither of the two groups, constituting something of a third element which functions as a connecting link between the Russian-dominated regime and the native population. Such a class had existed, of course, in Central Asia prior to the Revolution, and it arises in most colonial systems, but it has never before been so numerous and ubiquitous as it is in Soviet Central Asia. What are its ideas, attitudes, and prospects? Upon the answer to this question depends to a large extent whether the potentialities of a Muslim revival in Central Asia can ever be realized.

Evidence secured from interviews indicates that Muslim intellectuals in Central Asia consider themselves full-fledged Europeans. Startling as this may be to a Westerner, it must be remembered that to many an Asian "Europe" means not so much a geographic concept as a way of life, characterized by technology and secularism, which had been brought to Asia by Europeans. None of the Central Asian refugees interviewed considered himself to be an Asian, and several took offence at the very suggestion that this may be the case. Most of the refugees have a vivid contempt for the non-Soviet East. For instance, several of the refugees who had served in the Soviet army in Iran during World War II spoke with utter contempt of the natives of that country as "Asiatics." Even Turkey, where several of the DP's found refuge after the war, appeared to them backward and "Oriental." Many Muslim DP's left Turkey for Germany or the United States after having been received there with open arms, because, as they put it, they found life there strange and difficult.

Despite its superficial Westernization and Sovietization, this new intelligentsia has not severed the ties binding it to the remainder of Muslim society in Central Asia. It is connected with the population culturally: the intellectuals communicate with each other in the local Turki dialects, not in Russian; they retain the customs, traditions, and other cultural traits previously discussed; they marry Muslims. They also retain a sense of loyalty to their people, a loyalty which is sufficiently strong to be seemingly unaffected by the close ties between the intellectuals and the regime. It is noteworthy that the majority of the refugees, though outspokenly anti-Communist in their sentiments, agreed that there is little friction between Muslim Communists and the rest of the Muslim population. The population does not transfer its dislike of the regime to its individual Muslim representatives, nor does it seem to regard Muslim Communists as apostates. On the contrary, Muslim Party members are regarded rather as friends and protectors, capable of shielding the inhabitants from the full brunt of Soviet policies. Many refugees recalled instances of receiving special consideration from Muslim Communists. The population is inclined to regard Muslims connected with the Communist machine as unwitting instruments of an evil system and to judge them entirely on their individual merits. Conversely, interrogation of Muslim refugees who had at one time belonged to the Communist Party indicates that in their minds they have not changed their national status by virtue of their Party allegiance. The notion of an all-embracing "Soviet" patriotism, fostered by the regime in its borderlands, apparently has had little if any success among the intellectuals.

This combination of Westernism and ethnic loyalty leads to the development of a sense of national consciousness on the part of the intelligentsia. However, because of Soviet cultural measures in the borderlands, this feeling appears to be as yet rather formless, inchoate, and devoid of a well formulated ideology.

For one thing, the Muslim intelligentsia is woefully ignorant of the history of Turkestan.

This is hardly surprising, since the first histories of that area were published only after World War II (if one excepts the very scholarly and inaccessible monographs of Bartold and a few other scholars). The Soviet government deliberately minimizes the history of the Central Asian Turks and exaggerates the role of the Russian conqueror in order to undermine local nationalism and facilitate Russification. But the effect of these measures appears to be quite the opposite of what the Communists intend. Objectively speaking, the history of Turkestan is largely the story of the gradual conquest and destruction of a great Iranian civilization by barbarian Turkic nomads, resulting in perpetual internecine wars, isolation from the rest of the world, and cultural petrification of that area. In other words, the history of the Central Asian Turks is by no means a glorious one, either politically or culturally. By suppressing the study of native history, the regime actually helps stimulate the imagination of the native population. Ignorant of the facts, the natives glorify their past and create a mental picture of greatness which is quite unwarranted by the historical record. Several of the more educated refugees presented a completely distorted conception of Central Asian history; it was so idealized as to be a model for the stimulation of nationalist emotions.

The refugees also know very little about Central Asian history of recent times. The jadidist movement, the All-Russian Muslim movement, the events of the Revolution and civil war, the Kokand and Alash-Orda governments, are meaningless names to most of them. Most of the younger refugees knew of these events from the Soviet trials of the 1930's; none of them knew what these parties really stood for. *Basmachestvo*[14] was somewhat better known, because of its resurgence during the period of collectivization. Almost all of the refugees from Central Asia had had some personal experiences with the Basmachis, and could discuss the activities of these rebels in their region, though also tending to exaggerate their feats.

_____
[14] *Basmachestvo* was a native resistance movement directed against the Soviet regime; it was particularly active in the period 1918–1922. See Richard Pipes, *The Formation of the Soviet Union* (Cambridge, Mass., 1954), pp. 178–80, 255–60.

Conclusions

Speaking broadly, Soviet Central Asia may be said to have undergone in the course of the past fifty years two parallel developments: the native population has been transformed from a loose agglomeration of diverse tribes and ill-defined ethnic groups into several distinct nationalities, and the Russians residing in Central Asia have grown from an insignificant minority to an important segment of the total population. Both these developments are intimately connected; both may be expected to continue in the foreseeable future.

The first of these two processes has been by and large encouraged by the Soviet authorities because of their fear of pan-Islamism and pan-Turanianism. Faced with the choice of a movement aspiring to integrate all the Central Asian natives into a single nationality bound by the ties of a common religion or racial descent, and the formation of several separate nationalities, they selected the latter alternative as less dangerous to their political hold on the area. This course, however, had its price, for it compelled the Communists to encourage the growth of national consciousness among the major native ethnic groups.

But it would be a mistake to seek in Soviet strategy the *cause* of this process of nationality formation. The cause lies far deeper. The growth of nationalism in Central Asia, as in other parts of the world recently affected by European ideas, institutions, and technology, must above all be ascribed to the fact that the encounter of Westernism and tradition rarely results in a clear-cut victory for either force, but rather leads to a synthesis of both. *Nationalism represents such a synthesis of imported Western and traditional native values.* It owes its success to the fact that it permits the adoption of all the essential features of European civilization without the surrender of the local ethos. It is strongest and most vital in societies which, like the mid-twentieth-century Muslims of Central Asia, are in the very throes of this process of cultural fusion.

The Russian influx, uninterrupted since the beginning of the present century, does not hinder this development except where it is accompanied by large-scale physical destruction of the natives (as was the case with the Kazakhs). On the contrary, it rather strengthens it. In the Central Asian context, the Russian population with its Russian culture must be regarded primarily as an agent of Westernization, and hence as a force accelerating the transition of the natives to full-fledged nationhood. The Russians not only tend to promote the spread of such ideas as secularism, utility, and anti-traditionalism, but also by their very presence and cultural cohesion, to induce the native to define his own national status. The Russian influx thus has not led to the emergence of a new, third nationality, "Soviet" in its culture, but to the split of the population of Central Asia into two parts: this split has tended to crystallize the national consciousness of both groups.

Without indulging in the dangerous and fruitless game of prediction (which always presupposes some degree of historical predetermination), it is still possible, on the basis of the evidence adduced above, to arrive at some general political conclusions from the cultural tendencies discernible in Soviet Central Asia.

In the first place, Soviet Central Asia may be expected to grow in importance as an internal problem for the regimes, present and future, ruling Russia and its possessions. The Muslim natives, formed into full-fledged nationalities with settled populations, well-defined cultures, and indigenous intelligentsias, will be far more troublesome to their rulers than the disunited, half-nomadic, Islam-dominated Muslim tribes and ethnic groups of the past have been. In the second place, the entire area of Central Asia, including Chinese Turkestan with which Russian Central Asia has always been closely connected, may well tend to move with time in the direction of independent statehood. It is not inconceivable that this vast territory may some day be encompassed in a new Turkic, Muslim state, oriented toward the Middle East, and serving as a buffer among Russia, China, and India. In the past this has been prevented by Russian conquest and Russia's policy of supporting Chinese authority in Sinkiang out of fear of British and Japanese activity in this sensitive region. With Britain and Japan out of Central Asia, Russo-Chinese cooperation may be less intensive than before, and any possible disagreements among the great powers bordering on this area will only benefit the national aspirations of the local

Muslims. Whether or not this will occur cannot, of course, be foreseen. But so long as the Central Asian Muslims continue to preserve their cultural peculiarities and, under Communist pressures, to evolve the characteristics of modern nationalities, as they have done in Soviet territories, so long will the cultural and ethnic bases for such a development be present.

TYPES OF SOVIET MEN

66

Studies of Russian National Character*

Clyde Kluckhohn

(1955)

What has happened to the personality of the Soviet man? To many people this is the most interesting question about the Soviet scene. Professional as well as amateur analysts have made efforts to deal with this important problem. Professor Kluckhohn provides a thorough summary of the methods and findings of Western psychologists who have studied the psychological structure of great Russians.

By "national character" I mean those modalities of behavior and of view of the world and experience in it which are found or claimed to be characteristic of a specified national or ethnic population at a particular period in time.[1] In this instance I shall not be talking

---

*Reprinted from "Recent Studies of the National Character of Great Russians," *Human Development Bulletin,* University of Chicago (Feb. 5, 1955), pp. 39–60, by permission of the publisher and Florence Rockwood Kluckhohn.
[1] I am under particular debt to my colleagues in the Project on the Soviet Social System (Russian Research Center, Harvard University) and especially to Drs. Eugenia Hanfmann, Helen Beier, Alex Inkeles, and Raymond Bauer. Participation in

about "all Russians" or all the citizens of the U.S.S.R. but rather only about recent inhabitants of Great Russia, speakers of the Russian language proper. It is on Great Russians that we have the richest materials. I shall avoid methodological and theoretical discussion as much as possible, though the discussants will doubtless raise some of these points. I must inevitably sketch some central facts concerning data utilized and basic viewpoints and methods. Otherwise, for purposes of this paper, I shall assume that, while there are certainly methodological and theoretical issues of great urgency, the over-all approach is a tenable one and that problems of sampling and other aspects of method have been sufficiently met to warrant our taking some findings seriously. It is my impression that the blaze of controversy over conceptual and procedural questions has too much deflected our gaze from the empirical substance that has gradually emerged in the shadows not highlighted by the fires of dispute. This afternoon, therefore, I want primarily to summarize for you what seem to me the most interesting generalizations thus far made by behavioral scientists who have studied Great Russians.

The first statement I know by a social scientist on Russian "national character" is Sapir's in the early twenties.[2] Though based upon reading and experience rather than upon systematic research, it still seems to me so penetrating and so fundamental as regards the traditional Russian character as to be worth quoting at length:

> ... the tendency of the Russian to see and think of human beings not as representatives of types, not as creatures that appear eternally clothed in the garments of civilization, but as stark human beings existing primarily in and for themselves, only secondarily for the sake of civilization. . . . The one thing that the Russian can take seri-

ously is elemental humanity, and elemental humanity, in his view of the world, obtrudes itself at every step. . . . For his environment, including in that term all the machinery of civilization, the Russian has generally not a little contempt. The subordination of the depths of personality to an institution is not readily swallowed by him as a necessary price for the blessings of civilization. We can follow out this sweeping humanity, this almost impertinent prodding of the real self that lies swathed in civilization, in numberless forms. In personal relations we may note the curious readiness of the Russian to ignore all the institutional barriers which separate man from man; on its weaker side, this involves at times a personal irresponsibility that harbors no insincerity. The renunciation of Tolstoi was no isolated phenomenon, it was a symbol of the deep-seated Russian indifference to institutionalism, to the accreted values of civilization. In a spiritual sense, it is easy for the Russian to overthrow any embodiment of the spirit of institutionalism; his real loyalties are elsewhere. The Russian preoccupation with elemental humanity is naturally most in evidence in the realm of art, where self-expression has freest rein. In the pages of Tolstoi, Dostoyevski, Turgenev, Gorki, and Chekhov personality runs riot in its morbid moments of play with crime, in its depressions and apathies, in its generous enthusiasms and idealism. So many of the figures in Russian literature look out upon life with a puzzled and incredulous gaze. "This thing that you call civilization — is that all there is to life?" we hear them ask a hundred times. In music, too, the Russian spirit delights to unmask itself, to revel in the cries and gestures of man as man. . . . It is hard to think of the main current of Russian art as anywhere infected by the dry rot of formalism; we expect some human flash or cry to escape from behind the bars.

There have been many subsequent speculative essays on "Russian personality" and its changes during the Communist period. Some of them have contained fragmentary observations not without interest.[3] A few studies have had some philosophic and historical

---

informal discussions with them over a period of years as well as reading their published and unpublished papers are largely responsible for whatever knowledge I have of this subject. They, however, must not be held responsible for views I express in this paper, except insofar as these are documented in their own writings, published or forthcoming.

[2] "Culture, Genuine and Spurious," *American Journal of Sociology*, 29 (1924), 401–429. Cited with the permission of The University of Chicago Press.

[3] E.g., A. S. Steinberg, "Um das Individuum im alten und neuen Russland," in Th. Brugsch and F. W. Lewy (eds.), *Die Biologie der Person*, Vol. 4, Berlin and Vienna, 1929, pp. 699–735.

depth.[4] But here attention will be concentrated upon the results obtained by two American research teams operating during the last seven or eight years.

Columbia University and American Museum of Natural History Studies[5]

This multidisciplinary group organized originally by Ruth Benedict but directed during most of its course by Margaret Mead utilized literary, historical, and other published materials; personal documents, folklore; films and photographs; and some interviews (mainly with individuals who had been away from the U.S.S.R. for some years). The essential assumption was that one is dealing "with a system which can be delineated by a small number of very highly specified samples." Mead spells out the detailed implications of this assumption in a fashion that deserves careful attention:

> The anthropological use of informants is closer to the historian's use of *documents* than it is to the sociologist's use of respondents or the social psychologist's use of experimental *subjects*. Each informant is evaluated individually against a wide knowledge (on the part of the interviewer) of the culture of the informant, the social structure of which the informant is a part, and the particular subject about which the informant is being interviewed. Here the anthropological interviewer's skill parallels that which an historian, trained in a particular period, brings to the interpretation of the reliability and significance of a new document from the period in which he is a specialist. So, for example, it is possible to judge whether Informant Kom-3 is basing a statement about the Komsomol mainly on reports on — or experience of — a particular congress; to check statements from an informant in Rostov against a knowledge of movements and countermovements of the Russian and German armies through Rostov in World War II; to judge whether the vo-

cabulary used by an elderly informant is congruent with the particular educational claims which he puts forward. Furthermore, each interview or series of interviews with a single informant is studied as a whole; different statements are viewed contextually, in the sequence within which they occurred, and in connection with the affect displayed by the informant (using here the methods of interview evaluation developed within clinical psychology, psychiatry and psychiatric social work). Statements of opinion are placed within this depth context and are treated not as matters of fact, but as parts of a total response; so in this method there is no use for percentage statements, such as, "Twenty per cent of the informants said they never read the front page of *Pravda*," or "Fifteen per cent claimed that the ritual creation of Stakhanovites was necessary," which would not be any more meaningful than the statement, "Of the surviving documents on the early history of New England, fifteen per cent said that Providence was good." Interviews are cross-compared for pattern and within the pattern apparently contrary factual statements are fitted together, such as: "I never read the papers because it was all just what the regime wanted you to think," and "I read the papers very carefully to give me a clue to what was going to happen next, to be prepared." Both are statements about the informant's belief in the amount of control exercised over the press. The contrasting statements about reading and not reading can in turn be related to the position, age, and personality of the two informants and to statements by other informants. From such study, significant relationships between status — or type of involvement within the system — and dependence upon clues from the press, may or may not emerge. If systematic interviewing of carefully selected groups within the Soviet Union were possible, the contrast between those who do and those who do not report reading the press could be investigated and perhaps systematic relationships to age or sex or echelon or type of activity could be found. But we still would not know how this was related to whether people actually did or did not read the press; quite separate methods would be necessary to determine this. But, as with the use of available historical documents on a period which is past, the reports of informants — whose availability has been determined, not by some ideal sampling process, but by a series of historical accidents often arbitrarily rather than systematically related to each

---

[4] E.g., Fritz Lieb, *Russland Unterwegs*, Bern, Switzerland, 1945; D. Tomasic, *The Impact of Russian Culture on Soviet Communism*, Glencoe, Illinois, 1953.

[5] Actually, there were three distinct but overlapping projects, variously entitled and supported by different organizations (the Office of Naval Research, RAND Corporation, and the Center for International Studies at M.I.T.)

other — cannot be used to make statistical statements. Nor is the number of informants or the number of interviews with single informants of very much importance — subtracting any given informant or any given interview from the total would produce a change, not by diminishing the reliability or validity of the whole group, but by impoverishing in a specific way the fullness of the pattern which can be derived from the whole. For example, because these statements could be examined *both* in the light of Dr. Dinerstein's experience (during another piece of research) in examining procedures of the Soviet provincial press *and* in connection with a growing body of materials on how hearsay was believed insofar as it reflected wholeness of response, the statements of Informant #16 (BC) — a highly sophisticated student of communication — became an essential clue to an understanding of the way *feuilletons* were used to atomize accounts about corruption into small particular events occurring in widely scattered places and, thus, to reduce the impact of such news. But taken alone, this informant's discussion would have had an entirely different value, and could not have been coded into a series of statements of comparable value. Unless these methodological considerations are kept in mind, there is danger that the approach will be misinterpreted.

A brief discussion is also necessary as to the validity of the pattern delineation which is given here. This has been validated against our available knowledge of Great Russian traditional behavior and contemporary Soviet behavior, as well as against systematic psychological theory. Further validation could take the following forms: collection of more interview material and its subjection to the same kind of analysis; observation — under some sort of controlled conditions — of a group of Soviet defectors, and the analysis of their behavior into categories which would make possible a comparison of the patterns derived. These statements are statements about Soviet behavior, not about human behavior which is culturally unspecified. The question arises whether the construction of experimental situations approximating conditions obtained in the Soviet Union, and the exposure of American experimental subjects to such conditions, would throw light upon the validity of the conclusions about Soviet behavior. There is at present no body of theory on this question, but the following tentative suggestions may be made.

When an American psychologist conceptualizes conditions in the Soviet Union as delineated by systematic anthropological work, these anthropological findings are retranslated into American terms in this process of conceptualization. For example, an experiment might be set up to show the effect on individuals of being lied to in two or three quite predictable ways — one type of lying (e.g., the statement of the exact opposite) for one type of material, another type of lying (e.g., an alteration of fact and falsehood, or a systematic alteration in scale, or a falsification of sequence or of time perspective) for another type of material, etc. The responses of American subjects might then be studied. Whether or not their responses conformed to those which had been found to be characteristic of the Soviet informants would not be definitive for the following reasons: we do not know to what degree the totality of behavior of individuals who are members of one culture is reset when they are presented with a stimulus situation that is a *patterned* representation of another culture, and we do not know to what extent the construction of the situation which is meant to represent the Soviet situation at a more abstract level has or has not been transformed into an American situation. Another possibility is one in which the experimental psychologist would be able to operate at a tertiary level so that his American experimental situation would stand in the same relationship to American cultural behavior, in respect to the crucial variables, as a *different* experimental situation would stand to Russian cultural behavior. The use of such a validating method requires a handling of cultural pattern which it is possible to prefigure, but for which we have at present no model — the closest model being probably in the field of structural linguistics. (1952, pp. 9–15)

Numerous publications have appeared.[6]

6 See G. Gorer and J. Rickman, *The People of Great Russia*, London, 1949; E. Erikson, *Childhood and Society*, New York, 1950, Chapter 10; M. Mead, *Soviet Attitudes Toward Authority*, New York, 1951; M. Mead (ed.), *Studies in Soviet Communication*, 2 vols., Center for International Studies, M.I.T., 1952; M. Mead and R. Métraux, *The Study of Culture at a Distance*, Chicago, 1953 (contains methodological information and some substantive material on Russians that is not elsewhere available); M. Mead, "The Swaddling Hypothesis: Its Reception," *American Anthropologist*, 56 (1954), 395–410; N. Leites, *A Study of Bol-*

In my selective summary of conclusions and hypotheses I shall for the most part give preference to those that seem to have at least some support from more than one publication of this project and/or from other sources. In certain instances, however, this will not be the case, and you must therefore not take it that any particular idea is necessarily propounded by more than a single scholar. But let us start with some proposition that would win wide acceptance.

1. There is a sizable gap between the modal personality type advocated by the Soviet leadership (and attained to varying degree by many of the elite) and that most characteristic of Great Russians in general.

Although Soviet intellectuals strenuously deprecate American culture and personality studies, nothing could be more certain than that Soviet leaders in fact believe that personalities can be shaped more or less according to specifications by employing carefully chosen techniques of socialization, education, environmental control, and indoctrination. Many of the utterances and acts of the leadership also strongly suggest that the Soviet elite hold a view of the traditional Russian national character similar in many respects to that of Western social scientists.

2. The people are warmly human, tremendously dependent upon secure social affiliations, labile, non-rational, strong but undisciplined, needing to submit to authority.

3. The counteractive Bolshevik ideal demands stern, ascetic, vigilant, incorruptible, obedient personalities who will not be deflected from the aims of the Party and the State by family or personal ties and affections. Instrumental rationality must prevail. At any given point in history there is only one "truth" that describes a particular situation. But since those who are not for the Party line of the moment without reservations must be presumed to be altogether disloyal and since every individual (alike from the people and the elite) must be assumed to harbor some forbidden attitudes,

any person is capable of complete betrayal. In spite of the theory of the remorseless working out of the "laws of historical materialism," the leadership operates in practice upon the premise of intensely personal causation. When something goes wrong, some individual must be at fault. Genuine guilt is less important than preservation of the principle that the pattern of personal responsibility be preserved by punishment rationalized with standard clichés. This is in accord with the general tendency of the elite to build "as complete a semblance as possible of the world as they wish to see it."

4. The regime's program of educating the masses toward independent and conscious action which is highly goal-directed, self-stimulated, and self-sustained is contradicted by the varied pressures constantly applied, producing apathy or cynical indifference among the people and the so-called "inner emigration" among frustrated or disgruntled elite. Conflicts of conscience beset many of the recruits to leadership.

5. The attitude of the people remains, on the whole, that strong external authority is both hateful and essential.

Let us now turn to some points that are interesting but perhaps less solidly established. In Erikson's luminous chapter he makes much of "vasomotor excess" in a people both "isolated and effusive." "It is as if each individual were strangely imprisoned in himself as in a restraining box of strangled emotions." Erikson sees the Bolshevik movement as "delayed Eastern Protestantism" which tolerates no sectarianism, trying to liberate "swaddled souls" from "apathy, lethargy, and serfdom." The people must escape from the mother image, "the manic identification of earth and woman," from "the imagery of an ancient agricultural revolution," from their weakness in enduring what enslaves them. The Bolsheviks explain and excuse their imparting further suffering by the fact that suffering is part of the human condition. "To leave the ruins of men and systems behind seems a job which does not call for any expenditure of emotion." Discipline rather than atonement is central. Parents, sacrifice, ego restriction are unimportant compared to exclusion from a creditable part in the historical process. Leaders can wait patiently but eventually they must act, must

shevism, Glencoe, Illinois, 1953; N. Leites and E. Bernaut, *Ritual of Liquidation,* Glencoe, Illinois, 1954. The bibliographies in the foregoing references list many other articles emanating from this project.

"grasp life," must at all costs avoid "sinking back into dependence" or "regressing to the traditional morality and the ancient folkways of the people."

In two fragmentary but highly suggestive working papers in Mead and Métraux (1953), Leopold Haimson makes notes on thinking in the traditional culture (reversibility; lack of specificity, consistency, and completeness; readiness to equate whole and a part or the outside and inside of an object) and sketches the Russian style of playing chess. This latter, he hints, may constitute a small paradigm of the elite's ideal of "conscious activity" which should be a central characteristic of the "new Soviet man." The Soviet chess masters, according to Haimson, study carefully the opponents' favorite style of play and predilections. They try to seize and maintain the psychological and material initiative, gaining advantages on position and tempo and committing their adversaries to static and passive defense. When the other player has an initial advantage, they "direct the game into tense and complex positions, introducing new and relatively untested variations." They strive to hold to positions that are familiar to and psychologically suitable to themselves and unfamiliar and psychologically inappropriate for their opponents. Soviet players are adept at developing relatively short-range combinations. Now some of this has an oddly familiar ring when one thinks of the Soviet style of political maneuver. It is perfectly true, as Haimson freely admits, that chess as a game played internationally is influenced by new modes of play developed in various countries. Nevertheless, he makes a good case for there being some distinctive elements in the Soviet style. Anthropologists and others can think of many parallels. For example, Australian cricket playing has its own special flavor, though the "test matches" bring together teams from many countries in the British Commonwealth.

One can hardly speak of the work of the Mead group without paying one's respects to the most controversial of its members, namely Geoffrey Gorer. That he is guilty of loose statements, unwarranted assumptions, dubious analogies, factual errors, seems to be unarguable. I agree with most of Goldman's crit-

icisms.[7] And it cannot be emphasized too strongly that the reader hardly ever knows where he stands on evidential grounds. Gorer speaks of "three or four hundred interviews" but never makes it clear how many of these were with Russians, how many with men and women of specified ages, whether given generalizations represent a consensus of informants or a particular category of individuals, etc. On the other hand, I believe that one must take Gorer's work seriously in the face of all these methodological deficiencies. He seems in many significant respects to have been right in spite of inadequate evidence, perhaps in some cases to have been right for the wrong reasons. Dicks,[8] in whose clinical judgment on this matter I have the most trust, writes:

> For the earliest level, only Geoffrey Gorer has so far evolved a coherent hypothesis. His critics have done the very thing he warned them against; mistaken the paradigm for the theory. Nothing in my observation has contradicted his views.

Even on the "swaddling hypothesis" Erikson, another sensitive clinician, speaks of "smoldering vasomotor madness." True, Erikson was influenced by Gorer (and perhaps vice versa). In any case, I agree with Mead[9] that much of the furor over swaddling was misplaced (though Gorer is at fault for placing his qualifications mainly in brief footnotes). I do not agree that data on the frequency of swaddling by time period and social class is irrelevant. To my knowledge, the first information, other than impressionistic or inferential, on this point consists in the following figures gathered by the Harvard Project. On the general theoretical issue Mead's most recent (1954) formulation is:

> Stated concretely, the Russian institution of a strong leader, whether called Czar or Stalin,

[7] "Psychiatric Interpretations of Russian History," *American Slavic and East European Review,* 9 (1950), 151–161.
[8] "Observations on Contemporary Russian Behavior," *Human Relations,* 5 (1952), 111–175.
[9] *Op. cit.* (1954). Much of Gorer's argument in his main text still seems reducible (though he does not use these words) to an oversimple formula for "Russian character": "If I accept constrainment, I get milk (i.e., food and general support)."

is not to be attributed to swaddling. But the forms of the acceptance of such a leader are grounded in the way children are reared to be members of Russian culture. . . .

From an analysis of the way Russians swaddle infants, it is possible to build a model of Russian character formation which enables us to relate what we know about human behavior and what we know about Russian culture in such a way that Russian behavior becomes more understandable. (Original in italics).

It is impossible in brief space to do justice to the fascinating books by Leites and by Leites and Bernaut. They are, to be sure, the products only in part of the projects under review and they are based almost exclusively upon published writings rather than a full repertory of national character instruments. Nevertheless they give us the most extensive and intensive explorations we have to this point of the "mentality" of the Soviet elite — its historical origins in the broad sense and in the nature of family life among Russian nineteenth-century intelligentsia. The compulsive need for certainty, cruelty as a reaction formation against the sentimentality of nineteenth-century Russian intellectuals, the implicit and explicit conceptions of the enemy within and the enemy without — all these and many other characteristic traits of Bolshevik leaders emerge within the framework of a developmental and psychoanalytic model.

Russian Research Center: Project on the Soviet Social System

With the second recent study, I am more intimately familiar. The materials are still largely unpublished. This circumstance requires a warning. My colleagues must not be held responsible for what I say here today. I have ventured to select from their unpublished documents, to modify in some instances, to combine. My own connection with this project was largely administrative and advisory. At best, I have the fairly comprehensive overview of the educated dilettante.

One of the various pilot studies of this project has been rather fully reported.[10] Dr. Dicks lived eighteen years in Russia and speaks Russian as he does English. He had previously

---

[10] Dicks, *op. cit.*

had intensive and highly successful experience doing work of this sort with German prisoners of war when he served as a psychiatrist attached to British intelligence. In the Russian case he had only 29 subjects, but all of them had left the Soviet orbit in the years after 1947, and the interviews lasted between 15 and 18 hours. Only five of the subjects were 45 or over. Dicks' central theses appear in the following quotations:

> One of the dominant and persistent conflicts in Russian society (both pre-Soviet and especially recent Soviet) is that between the ancient Russian *oral* character structure typical in many ways for the culture, and an *anal-compulsive* ("puritan") pattern characterizing the *elite*. Further, this same conflict operates to a marked extent within members of the *elite* itself, under the pull of its own recent emergence from the traditional pattern, and of its identification with the norm-models demanded by an originally "Western" type of industrial and administrative social development . . . . it would not be amiss to apply to the analysis of Soviet *elite* behavior the categories and concepts subsumed under the term of "the authoritarian character" (Fromm, 1941).
>
> . . . . the outstanding trait of the Russian personality is its contradictoriness — its ambivalence. . . . Russian behavior oscillates in large swings in relation to self, to primary love objects, authority figures, and outgroups. I think of the quality of these swings in terms of the oral character: at one end the "omnivorousness," the lusty greed, the tendency to rush at things and to "swallow them whole," the need for quick and full gratification, the spells of manic omnipotence feeling and optimistic belief in unlimited achievement, the overflowing vitality, spontaneity, and anarchic demand for abolition of all bounds and limitations. At the other end, the melancholy, dreary apathy, frugality, closeness and suspicion, the anxious and sullen submissiveness, moral masochism and grudging idealization of a strong and arbitrary authority which is thought of as the only safeguard against the excesses of the Russian nature. In this mood we find the capacity for subtle introspection and ruminative self-doubt and self-torment. Outward servility and secret mulish obstinacy co-exist, as if one could bend the knee to Caesar in outward conformity and yet inwardly remain wholly on the side of God,

before whom all men are equally small and fallible. The Russian can feel that he is no good, yet also superior to all the rest of mankind. Whether in his bacchanalian mood or in his depression, he always needs direct, spontaneous, heart-to-heart contact and communication, and respects that need in others. He is intolerant of hauteur, formalism, and bureaucratic protocol and hierarchy, preferring the direct, informal, face-to-face handling of problems, and spontaneous improvisation in tackling difficulties. Elaborate hierarchy troubles him, as does any kind of rigidly and uniformly controlled activity.

. . . . this behavior is in great contrast to that expected of and by the elite. . . . Charisma attaches . . . to those who can demonstrate their mastery over oral gratification needs. . . . The surrender of passivity and oral spontaneity in favor of leader-like abstinence requires defense mechanisms. . . .

. . . . *manic denial* — shown by the stress on unlimited achievement, on restless organizing ability and on tempo; by the great importance they attach to technology, machines, and other "assurances of mastery" over nature and internal threats. Manic denial could also be responsible for the contemptuous avoidance of and, one might almost say, taboo on depressive moods, pessimism, doubt, sentimentality — all the "minor key" sides of Russian personality. There must be no guilt and no bad objects which cannot be "controlled."

. . . . *persecutory anxiety* — On the one hand there is the pressure to project the tormenting bad object into foreign aggressors — capitalists and imperialists. On the other hand there is an identification with the aggressors manifested in the persecution of "Id" qualities within "the people" as projections of the Self; the scenting of revolt, ill-will, or opposition in everyone's motivations; the anxious and organized analysis of these motivations amounting to a paranoid interpretation of minimal misdemeanors as deliberate; the intoleration of sloth, "bourgeois" individualism, or easy-goingness, and the progressive petrification of an ideological orthodoxy in the world of beliefs, including the same kind of condemnation of subjective art which the Nazis once labeled *"Kulturbolschewismus."*

The materials used by the Project on the Soviet Social System are much more sizable:

Extended life-history interviews and Sentence Completion Tests from 330 subjects.

Intensive clinical interviews, projective questions, Rorschach Tests, two TAT Tests, Episode Tests with 55 subjects.

All of these are interpreted in the light of the information coming from a much larger population which gave us more than ten thousand written questionnaires, twelve hundred short answer items, and about fifty manuscripts written by escapees on their personal observations and experiences within the U.S.S.R. Finally, a group of interviews and psychological tests was done on a group of Americans matched for age, sex, and occupation with 100 of the Soviet émigrés. In general, the findings from this much larger body of data square well with Dicks' interpretations. The major discrepancies would appear to be:

(1) We did not discover the Russian people to be psychologically driven to be submissive. They do desire supportive and nurturant superiors. (We also found little evidence to support Erikson's "masochistic identification with authority.")

(2) We did not find the outstanding aggressiveness reported by Dicks, even though our sample was weighted toward the young Soviet male middle elite.

(3) Our Russian data, when compared with our American, do not give clear-cut evidence for the "oral" emphasis in the traditional character structure of Great Russians.

In addition, the findings of the main project add many details of interest and put some flesh on the bones skillfully X-rayed by Dicks. I shall draw primarily on a synthesis recently completed in manuscript by our two senior clinicians, Drs. Eugenia Hanfmann and Helen Beier,[11] although many others, including one of our discussants today, Dr. Getzels, had a significant part in the analysis of these data.[12]

The "modal national pattern" to be delineated is found in its extreme "primary" form among workers and peasants, is attenuated among those upwardly mobile, and almost disappears at the top of the social hierarchy. "Modal" subjects showed a great need for

---

[11] Also on an unpublished paper by Alex Inkeles ("Modal Personality Characteristics of Former Soviet Citizens") and on papers by Raymond Bauer.

[12] See Eugenia Hanfmann and J. G. Getzels, *Interpersonal Attitudes of Former Soviet Citizens as Studied by a Semi-Projective Method*, Vol. 68, No. 18 (1955), whole number 389.

intensive face-to-face relationships with others, skill in creating such relationships, and deep satisfactions from them. They "welcomed others into their lives" but were not tensely anxious about the opinions of others nor compulsive about clinging to relationships once established. They see others in immense concreteness yet make their judgments less on the basis of the behavior of others than upon their conception of the basic qualities and attitudes of their friends and acquaintances. They value people in terms of what they are rather than in terms of what they have done. They are unthreatened by mutual dependence, whether in the family or in the peer group.

These Russians are expressive and emotionally alive. They exhibit fewer defense mechanisms than do Americans of comparable age and occupational position. The issue between isolation and conformity is less pronounced than among Americans. Russians, as might be expected, do show greater fear of external authority. In general, they express fear, depression, and despair more frequently and openly than Americans. "They viewed the ambiguous situations presented in the tests in terms of danger and threat on the one hand, of privation and loss on the other." They accept the need for impulse control but are nevertheless rather prone to excessive indulgence. They are, however, seldom punitive toward themselves or others for giving way to impulses. They are less perseverant than Americans and more acceptant of the passive sides of their nature.

While a little "Puritanical" about verbal discussion of sex, the Russians exhibited little conflict in this area and showed less confusion about their sex identification than did the Americans. Aggressive content emphasized the material realm: robbing, stealing, depriving. Among the Americans "aggression" appeared more often diffuse or displaced onto trivial external annoyances. The Russians more often focused it on inimical and depriving people and situations. Defenses of the Russians were not only less prominent but also less stabilized; they were supplemented by the utilization of the sympathy and support of others for the expression and management of disturbing emotions.

Some other Russian–American points are worth summary. American stress upon autonomy, social approval, and personal achievement appears little in the Russian protocols. Russians demand and expect moral responses (loyalty, respect, sincerity) from their group. Americans care more about just being liked. Neither the Russian nor the American groups reveal marked needs for dominance or aggression — two trends often emphasized in previous national character studies. Americans are more optimistic, former Soviet citizens more pessimistic. In spite of the passion of the Russians for close social interaction, they exhibit considerable mistrust of others. They ask, "Is he wearing a mask?" "Where does he really stand with respect to me?" But the dilemma is much more "outside" in the relationship rather than within the self. Americans, on the other hand, exhibit more acute self-awareness, self-examination, doubt of their own inner motivations.

Americans are appreciably more worried about their failures in achievement, lapses in approved etiquette, inability to meet social obligations. Russians are shamed most deeply by dishonesty, betrayal, and disloyalty. Americans are less aware of other individuals as unique entities as opposed to performers of familiar roles. The Russians value identification with and participation in the larger collectivity more than Americans. At the same time they are less timid about expressing their individuality within the group. Yet they are extremely sensitive to public humiliation, to impersonal treatment by superiors, to what appears to them as violation of the dignity of the unique personality. In approaching new interpersonal situations Russians characteristically take a very large view initially, then make a very detailed and specific analysis which usually takes an individualized and unstereotyped form. Russians and Americans both love material things, especially gadgets. The desire for "mastery" is stronger in Americans than in non-elite Russians, but Russians of all kinds often manifest great bursts of activity. Non-elite Russians are less likely to project their own hostile impulses on to others. They see mothers as nurturant and supporting, fathers as arbitrary and demanding more markedly than do Americans. Americans exhibit more inner conflict as to the dilemma of "rebelling or submitting."

The elite group are notably less expressive emotionally, less socially committed, much more strongly characterized by defense structures, less unequivocal in their sex identifications. They are more capable of unconditional obedience, ruthlessness, disciplined and orderly behavior. They are more persistent in goal trends. They are more prepared to shoulder responsibility for socially unacceptable actions. Hanfmann and Beier suggest that the marked discontinuity between the top layer and the rest of the population indicates a strong selective factor "beyond those coincident to advanced education and training."

Among the elite, Raymond Bauer[13] has distinguished three personality types (idealist, conformist, and careerist) corresponding to three dominant motivation clusters. The "idealist" has, as a youth, interiorized the more utopian values of theoretical Communism. However, he tends to make increasingly his own interpretations of how these ideals should be implemented and hence becomes disillusioned with the regime or rationalizes his conflicts over loyalty. The more intelligent and genuine of this type become concerned with the violation of their psychological selves through compromises with the regime. Those who finally turn consciously against the status quo usually withdraw into the "inner emigration." This type appears to be becoming more and more rare among adults in the Soviet Union.

The person motivated primarily by a need for psychological security (the "conformist") finds this by submerging his identity in Communism and by giving complete obedience to the strong system and its leaders. Both "idealists" and "conformists" have an external aspect of devotion and dedication. The "conformist," however, is more rigidly correct in his behavior and never swims against the current of the times. He is seldom able to let his doubts become conscious unless the leaders with whom he has personally identified himself fall or he loses faith in the strength of the system. He then becomes directionless or apolitical or suffers mental collapse.

The type more and more prominent among the younger elite is the cynical "careerist." He pursues his own immediate self-interest — material gains, personal recognition, leisure, recreation — within the established system of rewards and controls, but is really apolitical in his approach. He makes the appropriate political noises when necessary and conforms where this is necessary to his objectives. These ambitious men appear to be more correct in their behavior than the members of the Presidium, but this conformity is instrumental. Actually, he is neither loyal nor disloyal to the system. He is intensely loyal to himself, using his intelligence and energy to advance and to protect such position as he has gained.

Swaddling

In view of the controversies among "experts" as to swaddling practices in Great Russia within the last two generations, it seems worth while to make a preliminary report upon perhaps the only systematic body of data available in the West. Of 172[14] Great Russian respondents interviewed on their life histories only three (all young) professed unfamiliarity with the practice, while another four or five refused in effect to discuss the subject. A majority of the subjects manifested some tension or uncomfortableness with this part of the interview. They laughed or smiled nervously or expressed irritation by verbal or other behavior. Often this took the form of an explicit rejection of the Gorer hypothesis of which a considerable number had heard, though usually in vulgarized or distorted form. The theory as such received no support from any of our interviewees, though some appeared to agree with the empirical generalizations on which it is based. Usually the theory was termed inadequate,

[13] See "The Psychology of the Soviet Middle Elite," in C. Kluckhohn, H. Murray, and D. Schneider (eds.), *Personality in Nature, Society, and Culture*, New York, 1953, pp. 633–650; "The Development of Attitudes Towards the Soviet Regime: Selected Case Histories" (mimeographed, Russian Research Center, 1952); and (with Helen Beier) "Oleg, A Member of the Soviet 'Golden Youth'" (to appear in the *Journal of Abnormal and Social Psychology*).

[14] This and all following figures must be taken as approximate because of problems of interpretation and coding. For example, is one to consider a family as Great Russian where the mother was Great Russian but the father was Ukrainian? (In this case, I coded as Great Russian because the infancy of the individual in question was spent in Great Russia with a Great Russian mother and her extended family.)

"stupid," or "ridiculous." Some said plainly that questions of this sort "hurt one's feeling of self-respect", or that, "This question implies that Russians are wild animals."

On many points our subjects were in rough agreement. In the pre-Soviet period swaddling was "compulsory" or "obligatory" in almost all sectors of the society. During the past generation it has gradually become less frequent. It is much more common in rural areas, and in urban areas in recent times it is seldom practiced except among families of workers and "the uneducated." Swaddling is "old-fashioned," "primitive," and "not cultured," though a few of our informants (including two individuals under thirty) defended the custom.[15] The medical profession has opposed swaddling for some time. The attitude of the Government was generally agreed to be unfavorable, though the dates of an official pronouncement were variously given as between 1924 and 1936 and there were accounts of instruction in swaddling in Government nurseries as late as immediately before World War II.

There was good consensus on cultural rationalizations for swaddling. About half of the interviewees stated that swaddling was "to keep the child from harming himself." The most frequent specific instance was to prevent the infant from scratching his face or his eyes. Prevention of thumb or finger sucking was mentioned only a few times. Some informants spoke of protection when the child had to be left alone in a room. Others said their families had believed that swaddling was an insurance against colds. Straight limbs and avoidance of spinal curvature were frequently stated as being prominent in folk belief. The same may be said for swaddling as an aid to the child's sleeping long, "quietly," "peacefully." Such grounds were often connected with a more practical justification. Busy parents were less disturbed if the child was swaddled. They had more peace and could do their work better. At least one subject said that this factor entered into the practice in Government nurseries. If there was only one nurse for ten or more children, there were practical reasons why the children had to be swaddled.

Some of the reasons invoked by those who rejected swaddling were interesting:

"Why should I torture my children? I was educated."

"We should all be free to grow up normally."

"Doctors say it isn't healthy."

"It is really a terrible thing to torture babies with swaddling."

"I did not swaddle my child so that he would not be tortured and would develop."

"But I probably was not swaddled because my father loved me very much."

The wide variation in reports of swaddling customs may plausibly be interpreted as reflecting wide variation in actual practice. The modal figure for the duration of swaddling was three to five months, but a number of informants extended the period to a year and one to a year and a half. Some said that after three or four months "the bones are stronger," and hence the child needs to be swaddled less if at all. Others insisted indeed that full swaddling occurred only when the child was taken out of doors in cold weather. Some stated that hands and/or feet were left free "after the child could sit up" or "after eight months." Apparently "tight" and "loose" swaddling were rather consistently contrasted, and different families and regions followed varying patterns. Our informants, however, disagreed among themselves as to whether the two Russian terms ordinarily applied to swaddling could be differentiated according to the "tight" and "loose" categories. There was likewise disagreement as to the extent to which standard practice required the pinioning of the arms. Some insisted that this was usual throughout the swaddling period, others that this was true only at night or during the earlier months. A few reported that their mothers freed the arms of those children who did not show a tendency to scratch their faces or suck their thumbs. The richness of detail on the materials used, the actual techniques of binding and cleanliness, and other ethnographic data would demand a small monograph for adequate presentation.

Ninety-six Great Russians said that they themselves had been swaddled. Only two of these were born before 1895; 35 were swaddled during the Soviet period. Of these latter all

---

[15] "The child could kill itself." "The baby is straighter and stronger if swaddled." ". . . just like sticks. It's good that way. He is firm and supported and can't hurt himself."

except 10 came from rural backgrounds. Five were reared in large cities and five in small cities. Of informants who had themselves been swaddled, 12 reported that their children had also been swaddled. However, of the individuals so reporting all except four were born before 1900 and only one was born in the Soviet epoch. In one instance the swaddling of the second generation was attributed to the grandmother rather than the parents. Eight individuals in the group who had been swaddled specifically stated that their children had not been. Twenty-six Great Russians said that they themselves had not been swaddled. Of these only 7 had definitely rural backgrounds. Twenty-two individuals explicitly professed ignorance as to whether they had been swaddled or not. In a number of these instances there are grounds for suspecting that in fact they had been. The context of the interview often indicates that the subject was reluctant to admit the fact to an American. In another case the respondent gave the information that his own child had been swaddled: "If you don't, their legs will be crooked or their arms will be crooked." The remainder of the 172 Great Russians either evaded this question or made equivocal statements.

Discussion

The interpretations made thus far by both the New York City and the Cambridge teams[16] are all points of departure, not points of arrival. And yet on some issues it is possible to make with considerable confidence statements about the relatively enduring and salient personality characteristics of the contemporary Great Russian population. Different observers and analysts, using different methods and data, are in excellent agreement among themselves — and indeed with the Russians. The findings obtained by the use of a variety of psychological instruments are also in some respects remarkably congruent. For example, the Russians

---

[16] In addition to the references already cited, forthcoming publications will include a case in detail presented by Dr. Hanfmann in a volume of clinical cases edited by Burton and Harris; and *Authoritarian and Egalitarian Attitudes of Former Soviet Citizens as Studied by the Projective Questions Technique,* by Helen Beier and John Orton (about to be submitted for publication).

when compared with Americans and other groups stand out for their passion for affiliation, for belongingness, and for their warmth and expressiveness in human relations. All students likewise agree on a strong need for dependence, for, to quote Dicks, "a positive drive for loving protection and security . . . care and affection. . . ." There is, however, disagreement as to the extent to which dependence and submission blend. Similarly, the consensus as to the contrast between the modal personality of people and elite does not extend to an acceptance of Dicks' typology of "oral" versus "anal-compulsive." Compare the historical "explanation" advanced by Tomasic (*op. cit.*): the elite are nomad Eurasian warriors; the peace-loving peasants and workers are the old Slavs. The reality of some contrasts between people and elite is irrefutable, but no theory, either psychological or historical, thus far set forth is entirely convincing. It is clear, however, that social changes and aspects of the general social situation under the Soviets (as well as historical tradition and child-rearing practices) have had their perceptible consequences in modal personality.

A national character drama is now being played out in the U.S.S.R. The plot centers on the following themes:

warm, expressive expansiveness versus formality, control, and orderliness

personal loyalty, sincerity and responsiveness versus distrust and conspiratorial mentality

strong identification with the face-to-face groups of which the individual is a member versus a single tolerated loyalty (upward to people not known personally)

being versus doing, or dependent passivity versus ceaseless instrumental "conscious activity."

This spectacle cannot fail to engage us as scientists as well as from the point of view of the potential consequences of various outcomes for the future lives of ourselves and our children. This is an experiment on the grand scale. Can a small minority, under the spell of a fierce and intolerant ideology, remold a people in a direction quite contrary to the most fundamental propensities of their traditional national char-

acter? If so, how soon and after how much destructive activity at home and abroad? While
we must not evade the fact that there are some
traits in the contemporary character structure
of the Russian *people* which tend to make for
support of the present dictatorship, personally
I think Riesman is along the right track when
he writes:

> . . . . many of the defenses I have discussed
> are little better than forms of paralysis which,
> by their presence, evidence the resistance men
> put up against seemingly implacable destinies.
> I would prefer to see men fighting back through
> paralysis than succumbing through active in-
> corporation of the enemy. But this is hardly an
> optimum way to live one's life, and we cannot
> be — even apart from the danger to ourselves
> — unmoved by the plight of those now living
> and dying under Communist regimes. All we
> can do while we seek ways to bring those re-
> gimes down without war is to find our way to a
> more robust view of man's potentialities, not
> only for evil, about which we have heard and
> learned so much, not only for heroism, about
> which we have also learned, but also for sheer
> unheroic cussed resistance to totalitarian efforts
> to make a new man of him.[17]

Dicks is really saying somewhat the same
thing when he writes:

> . . . the Soviet system works chiefly because
> of the obstinate persistence of unofficial, un-
> Communist, but uncommonly Russian patterns
> of "backsliding" into fraternal, affectionate, and
> easy-going human relations; because of the
> capacity of the Russians to tolerate and cope
> with bad objects in virtue of the undoubted
> deep optimism created by the good though fitful
> nurturance they experience as infants, and be-
> cause any developing society gives some scope
> for constructiveness and the kind of achieve-
> ment which raises morale.

These valid points must not, however, be interpreted in too optimistic a fashion. The situation is not static, and there is evidence that
larger and larger segments of the young people
are moving closer and closer to the type of personality advocated and planned for by the
regime.

---

[17] "Some Observations on the Limits of Totalitarian
Power," *Antioch Review* (1952), 155–168.

67

Three Generations of the Soviet Intelligentsia*

Leopold Haimson

(1959)

*There are many sides to man's nature. Equal
in importance to psychological character as
treated in the preceding article are the more
conscious and complex attitudes and general
orientations toward life. Professor Haimson
describes these and notes considerable variation
from generation to generation among the Soviet
intelligentsia. His contribution gives us a rare
glimpse of the weakened as well as the abiding
spirit of man under totalitarianism.*

After forty years of Communist rule the Soviet intelligentsia is still far from homogeneous.
Each generation has been subject to quite different influences as gradually the vision of an
unrealized revolutionary Utopia has been transformed — partly into a set of ritualistic utterances and practices, partly into stabilized institutions. There have been changes, too, in
the intelligentsia's relationship to authority, as
the still relatively free and even anti-authori-
tarian intellectual climate of the early and middle 1920's was replaced little by little by the
rigidly orthodox intellectual atmosphere and
ubiquitous controls of the Stalin era. There
also have been changes in the social composition and in the sense of social identity of the
intelligentsia, which reflected in turn the great
social overturns and dislocations of the late
1920's and early 1930's and the subsequent
stabilization of Soviet society. And, last but
not least, there have been changes of emphasis
in the intelligentsia's intellectual pursuits and
concerns, following the "Second Socialist Offensive," with the emergence, full grown, of

---

°Reprinted from "Three Generations of the Soviet
Intelligentsia," *Foreign Affairs*, Vol. 37 (1959),
pp. 235–246, by permission of the author and publisher. (Copyright, 1958, by the Council of Foreign Affairs.)

a society oriented toward science and technology. Each of these processes and patterns of change has left its mark in differing degree on the different generations of the present Soviet intelligentsia.

A visitor to Russia today quickly draws the impression that there are gaping chasms — which almost no continuities or points of contact seem to bridge — between major age groups in the intelligentsia. Three major groups stand out: the generation that had already reached intellectual maturity before the Bolshevik seizure of power, or at least before the imposition in the 1930's of totalitarian controls over Soviet intellectual life; the middle generation, including those between, say, the ages of 35 and 50, who spent almost all their adult life stifling under what has come to be called "the cult of personality"; and finally the group of young men and women who, while largely educated under Stalin, have begun to make their presence felt on the Soviet intellectual scene only under the more clement and chaotic conditions of the post-Stalin "thaw."

The survivors of the pre-revolutionary generation of the intelligentsia are now few in number. Yet one is struck by their extraordinary prominence and influence on the intellectual and particularly the academic scene. One finds these aging symbols of the past — complete down to their redingotes, pinces-nez and small Vandyke beards — still occupying the major chairs in Russian universities. One finds them still editing the major works published by the Academy of Sciences and still scurrying, with a busy and proprietary air, about the halls and offices of its various institutes; occasionally one even finds them, in their studios or salons, eagerly presiding over gatherings of young adepts of literature and the arts.

How do these men seem to be faring after four decades of war, revolution, penury, and terror? They seem much older, of course, more frayed and more fragile, but at the core remarkably unchanged. Through these years of continuous pressure and stress most of them have managed somehow to hold onto the basic interests, values, and personal style of life that they originally carved out for themselves, and even their energy, their zest for existence, seems unimpaired. While talking with these aging figures one sometimes feels as if one were resuming a conversation, interrupted for thirty

or forty years, exactly at the point where one had left it: the names of the same authors, the titles of the same books are cited; the same intellectual and aesthetic standards, the same basic likes and dislikes are expressed.

All this is not to imply that these men have maintained an active or even a passive hostility toward the Soviet regime. Quite the contrary, most of them seem to have made their peace with it, if only by burying themselves in the confines of their professional work. Indeed, at critical moments when the world threatened to engulf them, many made the pragmatic, crass compromise of writing books or delivering lectures in which they believed not one word. And even now, basking in the measure of recognition that the post-Stalin era has brought them, they generally display wily circumspection. Yet it is worthy of emphasis how slight an impress the events of the past forty years seem to have made on them. Though the regime did largely succeed in controlling the nature of their writings and public utterances, there apparently were many (particularly among the litterateurs) who continued even at the height of the Stalin era to seek their own truths; and while their thoughts could not usually be published, they often received wide circulation in manuscript form. (To this day, some of the poems most popular in certain intellectual circles have never appeared in print.)

I vividly recall the passing comment of a prominent literary historian of this older generation as we were browsing in a book store. Pointing to the more recent volumes in a series that he himself had edited, he explained to me, with complete aplomb, and in impeccable if somewhat dated French slang: "These particular volumes still smell, I'm afraid — they appeared a little too early." I remember another conversation, about Russian historiography, with a formidable-looking old scholar, the author of monumental works on the early history of Russia. At the end of this talk, during which he had cited only standard pre-Soviet works on the subject, he observed, in the most casual manner: "It is a pity that Miliukov never finished his book on Russian historical thought; nothing to make up for it has been published in recent years." The fact that Miliukov, a prominent leader of the liberal Kadet party and the first foreign minister of the Provisional Government in 1917, has been denounced for many years as an arch reactionary had not apparently entered his mind. And finally I recall a talk with an aged and sickly writer, a Jew who had suffered much at the hands of the regime during the last years of Stalin's life. Despite all his disappointments, this ailing old man, brushing aside my own expressions of skepticism, valiantly strove to infuse me with his rosy, nineteenth-century faith in the inherent goodness of the Russian people and in the vast promise of modern scientific progress.

The sources of the inner resilience, security, and assurance that the members of this generation commonly display appear to have been drawn largely from the traditions and style of life of the past, with manifestations as varied as their own pre-revolutionary or pre-Stalinist experiences. Those who spent some of their student years in Western Europe have kept the thoughts and values — even the speech and mannerisms — of the universal European culture. Others have sunk their roots deep in the history and culture of the Russian past, and have found there a secure basis for their own identity. Others still have somehow kept intact — despite the post-revolutionary experience — the touching cult of the People, the innocent Golden Populist credo of the old leftist intelligentsia. It might perhaps be said that for many of these men life came to a standstill thirty or forty years ago, but that the experiences of those earlier times still uphold and nourish them.

II

The contrast between these old men of the Russian intelligentsia and those who immediately followed in their footsteps is of dramatic and tragic proportions. If the survivors of the old generation impress one with their continued pre-eminence, the members of the second generation, who spent all of their adult lives under Stalin's rule, are striking for their lack of real vigor and influence on the contemporary scene. What has happened to this middle generation which usually exercises so prominent a role in a country's intellectual life?

To a degree, the impression that it is largely absent from the stage is literally true; for this, we must recall, is the generation that was most nakedly exposed to, and most heavily decimated by, the great purges of the 1930's, the carnage of the war years and the obscurantist reaction of the postwar period. Yet physical bloodletting provides only part of the explanation.

These survivors are not all of a type. Some have the somewhat abrupt and "businesslike" manner, the rigidity in personal intercourse, the broad, squarish physical features characteristic of the "new" intelligentsia largely recruited from the ranks during the great social overturns of the 1920's and early 1930's. Others seem to reflect in speech and mannerisms their upbringing by the old intelligentsia. Many are found in positions of bureaucratic or official responsibility; they are administrators in universities and institutes, Party hacks of the press, literature, and the arts. But some have also survived among the scholars and artists who were compelled to carry on their work somehow under the vigilant eyes of the official keepers of orthodoxy.

The differences between the eldest generation of the intelligentsia and their own immediate descendants, particularly in the fields of literature and the arts, are largely of an emotional rather than an intellectual character. In contrast to the impression of vigor and zest conveyed by most of the old men, many of their "children" appear to be facing the future with a feeling of futility and hopelessness. Indicative of their general mood is the answer I received from a quite successful middle-aged dramatist — a pupil of Vakhtangov, and thus one of the few prominent survivors of the golden age of the Soviet experimental theater — when I asked what one might expect of the still younger (the third) generation of the intelligentsia. "Nothing," was his reply, "nothing at all. The young people don't really want anything. They just want to construct little boxes. Art is dead; it will be hard, very hard to resurrect it."

This aura of futility and defeat continues to be evoked despite the fissures in official orthodoxy that have appeared since Stalin's death — the hesitant, limited, almost intangible sense of movement that then began to permeate certain spheres of Soviet intellectual life. Why this deep-seated pessimism? It might be argued (particularly in the light of the official reaction following the Hungarian uprising) that the pessimism has been justified, but this would not be particularly germane, for what needs to be explained is an attitude which is largely confined to the members of this one generation. Perhaps the most relevant fact is that these middle-aged intellectuals have had to spend almost all their lives in a world out of control, a world which subjected many of them to early disillusionment and which compelled them, in order to survive, to make abject submissions or compromises. And, unlike their elders, they have had to make their arid journey without the support of a personal set of values, without even a brief or remote memory of an unsullied past, in short, without the basis for an independent identity that could stand up against their engulfing contemporary environment. Some of them will occasionally refer wistfully in conversation to the intelligentsia's traditional heroes and their works. But they are memories at second hand. These men appear to have come out of the long Stalin night utterly spent, and they look to the future with apprehension, in part, perhaps, because they face it with no inner reserves of energy, faith, or self-respect.

It should be noted that intellectuals in this age group who were subjected to administrative exile or imprisonment during the Stalin era — and who, therefore, had little occasion or tendency to compromise — present a striking contrast to those who remained "free." Surviving deportees who have returned since the governmental amnesty appear remarkably unbroken. They seem assured, fearless, not unhopeful, and it is they who provide whatever intellectual leadership this generation is still able to offer.

The smell of defeat does not hang only about those descendants of the old intelligentsia who remained in the main current of Soviet intellectual life throughout the Stalin era. To a lesser degree, signs of uncertainty and disorientation may be discerned among the "new" intelligentsia recruited from lower social strata and hastily trained in the late 1920's and early 1930's. When one first sees them sitting behind their big desks or presiding at the head of their long green-felt conference tables, these heavy-set cultural bureaucrats look quite formidable, and they display considerable authority as they deliver themselves of the latest platitudes of the Party line. And yet an observer quickly draws the impression, as he watches their dealings with their younger subordinates, that these men are largely going through empty motions, that they have lost much of their confidence in

the importance of their positions and the significance of their acts.

What has happened since Stalin's death to upset the confidence and self-esteem of men who have successfully weathered so many crises? No doubt they were somewhat puzzled and embarrassed by the ensuing modest reassertion of traditional cultural values and by the attendant confusion in government policy. To a Western visitor, the manifestations of their plight may be quite comical. I recall a session at one of the Institutes of the Academy of Sciences at which one such "official type" solemnly reproached himself for having failed to pay adequate attention in the past to, of all people, the Russian Idealist philosophers of the nineteenth century.

But the harshest blow that these bureaucrats have had to suffer has been the destruction of their sense of the importance of their role in the creation of a new Russian culture. With all their servile conformance to the twists and turns of government policy, with all the personal ruthlessness that most of them displayed in "ideological" and bureaucratic in-fighting, many in this segment of the middle generation were sustained throughout the Stalin era by an ideal which gave them energy and purpose. They viewed themselves during those long years not just as policemen or sycophants, but as agents in the birth and shaping of a new and different culture, in the creation of a new and different intelligentsia that would be as energetic, disciplined, and down-to-earth as the old one had seemed to them anarchic and divorced from practical realities.

To understand the naïveté and crudeness of this vision, to account for its survival through the Stalin era, one needs to recall that its keepers entered Russian intellectual life as outsiders, with no backlog of intellectual traditions or experience to guide them. The official ideology and cosmogony provided literally their only intellectual frame of reference; the role defined for them by the Party provided their only conception of proper activity in the development of Russian culture. Being themselves so much creations as well as agents of the Party in a world utterly divorced from their earlier experience, few of them had occasion to question the Party's objectives or their own mission. But now, after 30 years, this sense of historic destiny has finally been undone, partly as the result of the recent changes in the Party's policies, but mainly, I think, because the culture these men had dreamed of finally came to life and in the chaos of the post-Stalin era began to assert its presence.

What appears to have been most unsettling for these men in the post-Stalin "thaw" has not been so much the Party's vague, hesitant gestures at ideological liberalization — gestures often retracted almost as soon as they were made — but rather its increasing tendency to acknowledge that the achievement of success, even in certain cultural spheres, depended more on practical skill and experience than on the rituals of theory and dogma. It is, after all, precisely in this realm of professional ability that the "new" intelligentsia of the middle generation cannot help but sense its inferiority to the young men and women now beginning to assert their presence.

Indeed, the men of the Stalin era have been partly defeated by the very measure of their success. They are finding the youth, in the main, as rational, purposeful, down-to-earth, devoid of the "fatal" inclination to vast and "frivolous" theoretical flights — in short, as seemingly "useful" and politically safe — as they could have dared to dream. At the same time, these younger men and women are as steeped in certain scientific values and skills, as acclimated to certain intellectual experiences and pursuits, as their forerunners were not. And it is by virtue of these intellectual accomplishments — and limitations — that in many areas of intellectual life they have begun to express the sense of their superiority over the "new" intelligentsia of the Stalin era and to show that they consider its tutelage superfluous.

The sense of conflict and psychological distance that many in the Stalinist intelligentsia have begun to feel in their contacts with the young also reflects the measure of their historic failure. The young who have come to the fore appear to be politically safe. Yet while they may have adopted the general ideological framework and values of their makers, they perceive these as the limits rather than as the center of their world. Observing the intelligentsia of the Stalin era, they must have an attitude of indifference or even repugnance and disdain. Themselves dreamless, or animated by quite different and far more personal dreams, they cannot believe in, or indeed

often perceive, the large and impersonal visions that animated their forerunners — their striving and straining for the realization of vast collective endeavors. They can see in them only despotic, "uncultured," obsolescent men, ignorant of the intellectual skills and scientific values in the name of which they purport to speak.

"We still have far too many people who talk about things they don't know anything about," a young Soviet scholar told me within the hearing of an official of his institute who had just delivered a long and windy speech. In the face of such verdicts, the bureaucrats of the Stalin era, and, generally, most of the "new" intelligentsia of the middle generation (whatever the power and authority they still hold), have finally begun to feel their age.

III

The young men and women between 25 and 35 who are now making their way in Soviet intellectual life are truly the children of the Stalin era. All their lives, they have known no other social order, no other ideology, no other vision of man and society, than those which the regime imposed upon them. And yet the gloomy forecasts of an all-pervasive state giving birth to a new race of de-personalized subjects have somehow not come to pass.

This is not to say that the failure of the regime has been unqualified or that the nature of the failure is immediately apparent. Indeed, a Western visitor is likely to draw from his first contacts an impression of almost universal ideological uniformity among the younger generation. There is an appalling kind of sameness about the assumptions they voice, and particularly about the terminology they employ in discussing broad political, social, or philosophical questions. Thirty years ago, a significant percentage of the generation then young would have rejected, or at least ignored, official ideological categories; but today those of the same age almost uniformly consider themselves "socialist" in politics and "materialist" in philosophy, believe in the "Marxist" interpretation of history and venerate the "Leninist heritage" — about as unquestioningly as American schoolboys accept a stereotyped image of the American "Revolution."

Only as a visitor's acquaintances become more intimate and the conversation turns from generalities and abstractions does he discover that, although members of this generation abide by official ideology and use approved terminology, these are not reliable guides to their individual tastes, attitudes, and thoughts. A young logician may call himself a "materialist," and if you prod him will comfortably defend the basic tenets of materialist philosophy; but this surface orthodoxy has not deterred him from absorbing the positivist outlook of most Western logicians in his thinking about specific problems encountered in his work. A young artist may consider himself a realist even while searching in Western and Russian aesthetic traditions for richer and more complex aesthetic forms. Young intellectuals, generally, may proclaim themselves to be "Leninists" and yet hunger for a political and social climate that would be more open to free and individual self-expression. (An extreme illustration of this was the argument advanced by a friend to the effect that, after all, Lenin himself had included representatives of other parties in the cabinet formed immediately after the October Revolution.)

All this is not to imply that the official ideology has now become easier to discard. On the contrary, as already observed, it is now almost automatically accepted by the young, partly because it provides the only general conceptual framework and language that they know, but chiefly, I think, due to the fundamental change in meaning that it has come to hold for them. Three decades ago, this ideology was supported by a distinct vision of Utopia; now that it has been at least partially realized in relatively stable institutions it has become largely indistinguishable from the diffuse ethos in which the members of this generation have been inextricably absorbed since childhood. While this transformation undoubtedly made them more prone to accept the ideology, it has also made them likely to give it a personal interpretation. Since it no longer rests on an abstract vision of the future but is merged with concrete and differentiated current perceptions, it no longer can be the same sort of guardian of their thoughts and feelings. The nature of this immediate experience has become the chief influence in shaping their attitudes and values, especially in their professional pursuits.

The past three decades have transformed the character of professional roles so radically that the very meaning of the word "intelligentsia" has altered. As late as thirty years ago, the term still meant the selected few who were presumably engaged in exploring new ideas, new forms, new values, and in criticizing existing ones. Now it applies simply to all those who are engaged in occupations that require a degree of intellectual and technical skill. The change can be traced not merely in the increased proportion of young men and women now engaged in scientific or technical pursuits, but also very clearly in the general climate of this generation's intellectual life. Indeed, this "technocratic" orientation has become almost as characteristic of young historians or philosophers as it seems to be of young scientists and technicans, in that all show an interest in implementing "general truths" rather than in discovering them.

What are typical intellectual attitudes and values of the young? There is a genuine desire for professional competence, an urge to assimilate facts and to master the techniques required to organize and manipulate them skillfully. These traits are combined with a certain narrowness of outlook, a lack of urgent desire to explore new intellectual horizons or question basic theoretical assumptions. There is a relatively unquestioning acceptance of what are conceived to be the basic institutions and values of the existing political and social order, combined with a deeply felt urge to acquire autonomy in one's professional role and in a sector of private life. As one goes down the list of characteristics, the composite portrait that emerges differs little from the picture often drawn today of intellectual life in contemporary Western societies, and especially in the United States, under the impact of modern technology and mass communications. The analogy should not, of course, be pushed too far: even if certain universal tendencies of the modern age have been at work in Russia, they take distinctive shape and flavor in the Russian context.

Some of the differences are only of degree. For example, the concern of most members of the younger generation to become professionally competent is even more serious and sustained than in the West, while at the same time their intellectual horizon tends to be even narrower, their interest in any broad ultimate questions even flabbier. I might cite as example an extremely able and well-trained young Soviet logician who is very well read in the whole history of Western epistemology, from Aristotle, Leibnitz, and Kant to Russell and Whitehead, but who is not in the least interested in the fundamental problems that preoccupied these great philosophers.

This narrowness of intellectual interest might be accounted for by the political controls and the observance of official orthodoxy within which this generation must operate. But I think other factors are more significant.

First, one is struck by a certain self-consciousness shown by this generation about the presumed attributes of their professional roles — about their skills, their manners, even their dress. One is reminded of the attitudes of the nascent Russian intelligentsia in the eighteenth and early nineteenth centuries following the first flush of westernization. There is a similar concern with techniques, manners, and forms rather than with basic objectives, a desire to be, and especially to appear, "cultured," a consciousness of station and some uncertainty as to precisely what are the prerequisites for it, a deeply felt sense of patriotism combined with a vivid sense of emulation of, and competition with, the West.

The intense and narrow professionalism of this generation also represents, I believe, a genuine form of self-emancipation. Their insistence on the all-importance of facts and techniques provides the safest as well as the most direct escape from the political hacks of the Stalin era. (And, by the same logic, the insistence of the latter on the "ultimate" implications of various intellectual and professional concerns, and therefore on the continued importance of ideological conformity, has constituted their chief defense.) Just as in the most innocuous manifestations of their attitudes — the desire for a private apartment, the urge to join in informal leisure activities of their own choosing (even if only the collection of postage stamps) — they reveal a deep desire for some individual autonomy, some personal privacy.

The same urge is expressed, more forcefully and directly, in the one area of intellectual life in which, occasionally, ultimate problems of value are squarely faced and explicitly discussed, namely in literature and the arts. Literature has always been the inner fortress of the Russian intelligentsia, and in the contemporary

works of young writers, and particularly of young poets, its traditional visage is even now to be discerned. To be sure, the intelligentsia's traditional concern with ultimate questions and ulitimate values is no longer expressed in the affirmation of broad, generous, and ambitious world views, pregnant with immediate political and social implications. After forty years of Soviet experience, it has now taken the form of a search for more modest, more personal, perhaps more human values. The rediscovery of truthfulness rather than the discovery of truth; the defense of a code of personal dignity and personal honesty; the apprehension of beauty in nature and in love; the determination to endure but not to compromise — these themes are frequently expressed in the poems (many of them unpublished) of the younger generation of writers and occasionally sift through the net of official censorship into published works of prose.

What does all this portend for the future? With all the urgency of their desire for some personal autonomy, most of these young people, it must be recalled, continue to feel loyal to the foundations of their social order — to socialism and its values, as they variously choose to define them. But we must also remind ourselves that the pattern of values and thoughts that a person consciously entertains at a particular moment does not necessarily reflect precisely the complex and unstable balance between those elements that attract him to, and those that repel him from, the social order under which he lives. A sense of loyalty often represents the only real alternative to the almost intolerable bitterness and loneliness that come from a feeling of total alienation.

As to the future attitudes of this generation of the Russian intelligentsia, much will depend in the last analysis on the future policies of the regime. In my view, most of its members still appear willing to support an authoritarian political order, in which — as has been the case through most of Russia's history — respect for higher authority is combined with the recognition of some priority for the needs of the State. But most of these young men and women do not appear to expect, nor will they willingly tolerate, the all-pervasive controls, the invasions of all areas of human privacy, that have been characteristic of the past. Such a diagnosis should not lead us to feel excessively despairing or especially superior. Authoritarianism, after all, assumes a variety of forms; and through most of human history individuals have had to seek, and often have managed to find, despite its restrictions, a measure of inner freedom and dignity.

68

Young Men Gone Astray*

from Komsomolskaya Pravda

(1956)

Clinical and social psychological studies of the sort familiar to the West are not published in the U.S.S.R. However, concrete sketches, often carried to the level of caricature, do suggest that at least some Soviet youth share the exuberance and irresponsibility known to young people in other urban industrial societies. The stilyaga, or stylist, accused of excessively individualistic behavior, is a characteristic deviant social type in Soviet cities today.

This one? He is dressed in a wide-shouldered jacket and extremely narrow short trousers from beneath which flash brightly colored socks. He spends a large part of his time on his appearance. He wears his hair long and sprinkles his speech with such words as "colossal!" "charming!" "simply," etc. If he is Boris, he calls himself Bob, and if he is Ivan, he calls himself John.

He lives off his parents and "burns" his money in restaurants. Sometimes he is registered as a student, but he "despises" "cramming" and "crammers" and therefore does not study. He "adores" everything foreign and is ready to give his right arm for a fashionable

*Reprinted from "Which of Them is the Stilyaga," Ye. Rusakova, *Komsomolskaya Pravda* (August 11, 1956), p. 2, translated in *Current Digest of the Soviet Press*, Vol. 8, No. 33, pp. 8–9, published at Columbia University by the Joint Committee on Slavic Studies appointed by the American Council of Learned Societies and the Social Science Research Council. Used by permission of the publisher.

record. He thinks nothing of deceiving a girl and he boasts about it. He likes to dance, dumbfounding the public with his magnificent steps. He is disillusioned with life.

Or this one, perhaps? When he speaks he favors his speech richly with insulting words of abuse. If those around him take offense, he replaces his "expressions" with the phrase ———, "get it?"

He works and earns a good salary but does not even think about helping his parents, although they are not too well off. What is more, after squandering his regular salary, he "borrows" money from old people, "forgetting" to give it back, or else he is "kept and fed" by his parents for a long time.

Sometimes he is "tipsy" when he comes to work, but he doesn't overdo it.

"I wouldn't give a darn. Get it? But your wages are less when you're drunk. Get it?"

He is not averse to talking about girls. Not that he boasts about his conquests. He just evaluates his girl friends in a businesslike way, as people evaluate a "piece" of merchandise. He is full of enthusiasm when the conversation turns to suits. He rails angrily against narrow trousers, constantly exclaiming:

"What am I, some sort of stilyaga, to wear trousers? Get it?"

Indeed, he wears wide trousers and a white shirt. His hair is cut short. The only "distinguishing feature" is two perfectly good front teeth that have gold crowns for adornment.

Or perhaps this one can be called a stilyaga? He is proud, a man of few words. He always has the air of being offended. No matter what happens to him, "people" and the "situation" are to blame. He never is.

"The Russian language teacher is a 'fool.'" he stated and stopped studying Russian. For this reason he remained an ignoramus. He began working, but the work turned out to be "uninteresting" and his fellow workers "crude" people who lacked "understanding" and "sensitivity." He sent in his resignation. Nobody tried to stop him. Insulted, he returned to the bosom of his family and, after resting a year or so, joined, let us say, the district club as an accordian player.

But the director of the club was a "dunderhead," a "blockhead," and the film operator a "stupid robot."

"It's better not to work at all than to work

without inspiration, among dull, indifferent people," our friend said and again returned to the bosom of his family.

And so he is again sponging off his parents. He plays volleyball with enthusiasm. He allows himself to be loved by an ordinary girl but has no intention of marrying her. He despises the latest fashions, and a spot of grease invariably decorates the front of his pink soccer sweater.

Perhaps this one, the fourth, can be called a stilyaga? He is dressed impeccably, according to the latest fashion, with taste, just right. He is handsome, and his manners are refined. If he studies, he studies well but without interest. If he works, it is without enthusiasm and only to have a "good reputation."

He is polite and charming when he deals with people who can be of use to him. He may fail to greet a person who has no "influence." At meetings, he always supports the strongest, often repeating their very words.

"You want help? Sorry, I have no time." This is how he answers a friend.

"We're going to have a child? I love you very much. If you want to be a mother, that's up to you, but I will not be a father." This is how he answers his girl friend.

Which of these four, then, is the stilyaga?

In every language there are words which keep one meaning for a long time, and then, as time passes, they are "enriched" with a second or a third meaning. Take the word to "saw," for example. You can saw a tree, but you can also "saw," i.e., nag, a person for something. In sound and action both are very similar, hence the two meanings are combined in one word.

Sometimes the opposite happens, however: a word suddenly becomes "impoverished" and for no reason at all assumes only one — an offensive — meaning. This has happened to the word "style." This is a Greek word and means a combination of distinguishing features. But there are various features — good and bad ones. Here in our country the word "style" has come to mean only bad things and the word "stilyaga" to denote a person of bad style. . . .

Aimlessness, indifference to everything that does not affect the petty, narrow world of egotistical interests, the desire to get as much as possible from society, from friends and relatives, giving them as little as possible or nothing at all in return — these are bourgeois, narrow-minded features.

It is against these bourgeois features that the Young Communist League is fighting. But what sometimes happens is that the blow is directed not against these bourgeois ways but against dress, against the details of one's appearance and behavior.

As always in cases where secondary things begin to obscure what is essential, a multitude of errors is committed.

Here is one such incident. It takes the form of letters.

"In our region there lives a certain young man who works as a lawyer in the Chkalovskoye legal advice service, Gennady Avgustovich Antonov, who was born in 1931. He has been a Y.C.L. member since 1945. He graduated from the Kazan Law Institute and was active in the district Y.C.L. committee. He was elected to the bureau of the district Y.C.L. committee in 1954 and was re-elected in 1955. But in 1955 a district Y.C.L. committee plenary session did not make him a member of the district committee bureau after noting his inadequate work over a period of one year. He is a good skier, a district champion. But the fact is that he is very peculiar. This he was told at a meeting of the apparatus and bureau of the district Y.C.L. committee. At the meeting a speech was made by Comrade Shakurov, former secretary of the district Y. C. L. committee. This is what he said: 'Today I wish to rebuke Gena Antonov in a comradely way for his somewhat abnormal behavior among the young people in the club. He differs from everyone else in all respects: he combs his hair differently, his clothes are different and he has a turned-up collar.' "

This is part of a letter from Comrade Krasnov, Secretary of the Chkalovskoye District Y.C.L. Committee of the Chuvash Autonomous Republic.

Here is an excerpt of a letter from Gena Antonov himself:

"A satirical newspaper called Crocodile Covers the District is published in our district. One of its issues carried a caricature with the caption: 'Who is he?' It was not hard to answer this question: The caricature had me in mind. The reason for publishing it was that the editors saw an imitation of stilyagas in the way I dress. I feel that it was wrong to publish the caricature, since there is nothing of the stilyaga in the way I dress. I tried to prove this to Comrade Krasnov, secretary of the district Y.C.L. committee, the day after the paper appeared. In answer to my arguments Krasnov said: We live in Batyrevo and so let's dress in the Batyrevo way.

"Confident that the editors of the satirical newspaper had acted wrongly, I spoke at a regular district Y.C.L. committee plenary session and, in addition to other mistakes in this newspaper, I pointed to this instance too. A dispute flared up on this question, and two proposals were put to a vote:

"1. To consider removing the caricature from the display window. Six of the 28 persons present voted for this motion.

"2. Not to remove the caricature from the display window but to make a copy of it and send it with my photo to *Komsomolskaya Pravda* for clarification of the question of whether or not I dressed like a stilyaga. The remaining members of the district committee voted for this motion."

And so we have Gena Antonov's photo before us on the desk. His cap is pulled so far down over his eyes that even his ear is twisted a little. He is wearing a raincoat with a turned-up collar, slacks, and loafers.

Is this form of dress pleasing to the eye? No. The turned-up collar and the cap pulled down over the eyes give a man an unpleasant appearance. These things obviously show Gena's bad taste. This should have been proved to him. But just because a man, a comrade and Y.C.L. member, has bad taste in clothes is no reason at all for making him a laughing stock.

Does this mean that we should completely avoid powerful devices like caricatures in a satirical newspaper? Of course not! But they can be used only in instances where it is really necessary, and then only after a careful checkup on all the circumstances and facts involved.

Good taste must be cultivated. But in order to cultivate it in others, one must first cultivate it in himself. Then it is easy to prove what is pleasing and what is ugly without resorting to strong devices.

Apropos of the formula: "In Batyrevo one must dress in the Batyrevo way." Special clothing is issued in the army and in sports societies. There it is necessary, practical and therefore pleasing to the eye. But why must the in-

habitants of Batyrevo all be dressed alike? On the contrary: the greater the variety in young peoples' clothes, the better.

Then there is the story of the moustache. It was told us in a letter from B. Pedyash, a Y.C.L. group organizer and a student at the Odessa Polytechnical Institute.

When the Y.C.L. membership cards were being renewed, Comrade Navolokina, Second Secretary of the Water Transport Borough Y.C.L. Committee, suddenly asked B. Pedyash:

"Tell me, Comrade Y.C.L. member, why do you wear a moustache?"

"Because I like to," he replied, thinking it was a joke.

But Comrade Navolokina was quite serious and stated that Comrade Pedyash looked strange with a moustache and that it seemed to her that he didn't belong in the Y.C.L. On these grounds she refused to give B. Pedyash his Y.C.L. card.

"Let the borough committee bureau decide whether you are worthy of the high calling of a Y.C.L. member in connection with the fact that you have a moustache."

All this was so incredible that the comrades in our editorial office telephoned Odessa. Navolokina confirmed everything.

"Pedyash is a good fellow. But his moustache! If everyone wore a moustache or if there were some sort of rule about it, things would be different. What sort of a Y.C.L. member is it who has a moustache? First a moustache, then a tie with parrots painted on it, and the result — a stilyaga."

"And what if a girl wears earrings?"

"We're against it. It's not suitable for a Y.C.L. member."

Both these stories are lamentable. Insulted Y.C.L. honor, bitterness, hurt, the torment of unmerited shame, undermined authority and, finally, animosity — these are the result.

These stories also reveal something else — that some Y.C.L. leaders have grown accustomed to stereotyped ideas and do not have the ability to settle even the simplest question without a special "regulation" on it.

The struggle against suits, rings, and moustaches, which supplants the struggle against real bourgeois elements, has another side to it: The Y.C.L. members cease to respect such leaders.

And real bourgeois elements, perhaps dressed entirely in the "Batyrevo way," under the clamor raised by this "struggle," idle away their time, insult girls, hold life back, and themselves shout: "Down with narrow trousers!" Of course no Y.C.L. member — the "fighter against fashion" — desires such an "ally" but actually that is what sometimes happens.

You can have a moustache and a fashionable suit and still be a good Y.C.L. member. An elegant ring on the beautiful hand of a girl can make her hand still more beautiful. Y.C.L. honor does not suffer from this. Look at a portrait of Avdotya Panayeva, the friend and companion-in-arms of Nekrasov: How the pendants set off the Russian beauty of her face! And you cannot reproach Panayeva for bourgeois ways.

The desire to dress well is natural: It is bourgeois only when it becomes almost the main concern of one's life.

The point is not the suit, the earrings, or other details of one's appearance, but who wears them and how they are worn. If all this is done with taste, if it suits a person and makes him look better, then why not wear them? After all, we very often quote A. P. Chekhov's words: "Everything in a person should be beautiful."

On the other hand, if you do not like narrow trousers, if earrings, moustaches, and rings do not suit you, don't wear them. After all, there is nothing compulsory about fashion.

Y.C.L. members in the first years after the revolution also regarded fine clothing as something belonging to bourgeois elements. But their marked asceticism was justified by the times: it expressed both the stern heroism of those days and hatred for everything "bourgeois."

The situation has changed, and this concept is part of the past. Sometimes, however, it springs to life again, but now, without any reason, it begins to impede life: it extinguishes joy, brings hurt, and deflects one from what is important.

SUGGESTIONS FOR FURTHER READING

Social Welfare

ALT, HERSCHEL and EDITH, *Russia's Children*. New York: Bookman Associates, 1959.

> The report of what two social workers were able to find out in a summer visit.

FIELD, MARK G., *Doctor and Patient in Soviet Russia*. Cambridge, Mass.: Harvard University Press, 1957.

PARKINS, MAURICE F., *City Planning in Soviet Russia*. Chicago: The University of Chicago Press, 1953.

PUBLIC HEALTH SERVICE, *Report of the United States Public Health Mission to the Union of Soviet Socialist Republics*. Public Health Service, Department of Health, Education and Welfare, 1959.

> Impressions of medicine and public health from the Mission's tour in several Soviet republics in 1957.

SOSNOVY, TIMOTHY J., *The Housing Problem in the Soviet Union*. New York: Research Program on the U.S.S.R., 1954.

WORTIS, JOSEPH, *Soviet Psychiatry*. Baltimore, Md.: The Williams and Wilkins Company, 1950.

The Family

LUKE, LOUISE E., "Marxian Woman: Soviet Variants," in Ernest J. Simmons (ed.), *Through the Glass of Soviet Literature: Views of Russian Society.* New York: Columbia University Press, 1953.

     Women in Marxist ideology and Soviet literature.

SCHLESINGER, RUDOLPH (ed.), *The Family in the U.S.S.R.* London: Routledge & Kegan Paul, Ltd., 1949.

     Translations of family law and important Soviet writings, with an essay by the editor.

Social Stratification

DALLIN, DAVID J., *The Changing World of Soviet Russia.* New Haven: Yale University Press, 1956.

     Part I, "Social Revolution in Russia," contains a comprehensive analysis of the Soviet class structure.

DJILAS, MILOVAN, *The New Class: An Analysis of the Communist System.* New York: Frederick A. Praeger, Inc., 1957.

     A critical indictment of the Soviet order by a Yugoslav Communist theoretician, stressing the role of Communist functionaries, the "new class."

Nationalities

ARMSTRONG, JOHN A., *Ukrainian Nationalism, 1939–1945.* New York: Columbia University Press, 1955.

BARGHOORN, FREDERICK C., *Soviet Russian Nationalism.* New York: Oxford University Press, 1956.

KOLARZ, WALTER, *Russia and Her Colonies.* New York: Frederick A. Praeger, Inc., 1952.

     The non-Russian, minority national groups and Soviet policies toward them.

KOLARZ, WALTER, *The People of the Soviet Far East.* New York: Frederick A. Praeger, Inc., 1954.

     A continuation of *Russia and Her Colonies.*

SCHLESINGER, RUDOLF, (ed.), *Changing Attitudes in Soviet Russia: The Nationalities Problem and Soviet Administration.* London: Routledge and Kegan Paul, 1955.

     Readings from Soviet sources, with an introductory essay by the editor.

SCHWARZ, SOLOMON H., *The Jews in the Soviet Union.* Syracuse, N.Y.: Syracuse University Press, 1951.

Types of Soviet Men

BAUER, RAYMOND A., *Nine Soviet Portraits*. New York: John Wiley & Sons, 1955.

Soviet social types and life experiences, based on refugee accounts.

X GORER, GEOFFREY, and JOHN RICKMAN, *The People of Great Russia: A Psychological Study*. London: Cresset Press, 1949.

The statement of the swaddling hypothesis.

MEAD, MARGARET, *Soviet Attitudes Toward Authority*. New York: McGraw-Hill Book Company, Inc., 1951.

The psycho-cultural approach to understanding the individual and society.

X MEHNERT, KLAUS, *Youth in Soviet Russia,* tr. by Michael Davidson. New York: Harcourt, Brace and Co., 1933.

The life and atmosphere of youth at an important period in Soviet history.

VI

A Forward Look

To see into the future has always been one of man's fondest dreams. Today the rapidly diminishing size of the world and the rapidly increasing power of man to destroy it have made it more than a fanciful exercise to seek some pattern in the future course of events in Soviet Russia. There is no single key to this pattern. Perhaps more than anything else, detailed knowledge of what has gone before is helpful. This we can acquire through the study of Soviet history and the projection of established trends. Yet the same item of information, especially when it becomes necessary to take many into account simultaneously, can be differently weighted by various people.

Take, for example, the well-known fact that the Soviet people are becoming more "educated." How should one interpret its significance? Does it mean that they will also become more dissatisfied with the inanities of Marxism? More willing and able somehow to press for more cultural freedom? Or does it perhaps mean that they will become more regimented, more chauvinistic, will more closely approximate the "new Soviet man" of the official propaganda?

Moreover, acquaintance with Soviet history shows that the unique personalities of Lenin and Stalin did much to make the Soviet Union what it is today. Obviously the U.S.S.R. of tomorrow depends heavily upon the man who now occupies the posts of First Secretary of the Soviet Communist Party and Chairman of the Council of Ministers of the Supreme Soviet. The limits to our knowledge about Khrushchev, the man, hence set another limit on our ability to look ahead.

On the other hand, Khrushchev is today much more caught up in the established patterns of an on-going system than were his predecessors, and his personal ability to shape Soviet destiny is thereby diminished. In the light of this circumstance, it is not unreasonable to expect that the main secular trends in Soviet economic and political life will continue.

Khrushchev's personal power is also diminished by the relatively recent entrance of the Soviet Union into the game of maintaining the world's balance of power through alliances with other nations. The power and anticipated behavior of Communist China will also influence the future course of events in the U.S.S.R.

Then there is, finally, the question of our own influence. Not only in our foreign policy, but in future domestic developments within the free societies, in economic and social policy, is to be found one of the factors which will have relevance to the Soviet future.

69

The Future of Communist and World Society*

Nikita S. Khrushchev

(1959)

What will happen next in Russia? As much as upon any other single factor, the future of Soviet Russia depends upon the intentions of the Soviet leadership. In the past, in the words of Marx, the Communists have disdained to conceal their aims. For these reasons we start our final chapter with a portion of the address given by Khrushchev at the Extraordinary 21st Congress of the Communist Party of the Soviet Union in 1959. In it we find a good sample of the regime's image of Soviet society — its purpose, achievements, and future. Khrushchev also discusses a number of problems which pre-

* Reprinted from "New Stages in Communist Construction and Some Problems of Marxist-Leninist Theory," Part IV of speech to Extraordinary Twenty-first Congress of the Communist Party of the Soviet Union, *Pravda* (Jan. 28, 1959), pp. 2–10, translated in *Current Digest of the Soviet Press*, Vol. 11, No. 5, pp. 13–19, published at Columbia University by the Joint Committee on Slavic Studies appointed by the American Council of Learned Societies and the Social Science Research Council. Used by permission of the publisher.

occupy the Soviet leadership both on the domestic scene and in international affairs.

The Transition to Communism

Comrades! Now that our country has entered a new historical period of its development, special importance attaches to problems of Marxist-Leninist theory connected with the transition from socialism to communism.

First of all, the question of *the two phases of communist society* — of the laws governing the evolution of socialism into communism — should be mentioned.

The founders of scientific communism — Marx, Engels and Lenin — indicated that, following the overthrow of capitalist and landlord domination, society would pass through two stages. The first would be socialism, and the second, higher stage would be a classless communist society.

The development of Soviet society has confirmed the Marxist-Leninist prediction of two phases of communism. Having built a socialist society, the Soviet people have entered a new period of historical development in which socialism grows into communism.

Marxist-Leninist theory and the practical experience of building socialist society provide grounds for some important conclusions concerning the nature of society's advance to communism.

First, the transition from the socialist stage of development to the higher phase is a logical historical process that one cannot arbitrarily violate or bypass. The Marxist-Leninist parties consider the building of communist society to be their ultimate goal. But society cannot leap from capitalism to communism, skipping the socialist stage of development. "From capitalism," said V. I. Lenin, "mankind can pass directly only to socialism, i.e., to public ownership of the means of production and the distribution of goods according to the work performed by each individual. Our party looks farther ahead: Inevitably, socialism must gradually turn into communism, upon the banner of which is inscribed the motto, 'From each according to his ability, to each according to his needs.'" ("Works" [in Russian], Vol. XXIV, p. 62)

Of course, some comrades may say that the principles of communism should be introduced sooner. But to pass prematurely to distribution according to needs when the economic conditions for this have not yet been created, when an abundance of material goods has not yet been achieved and when people have not been prepared to live and work in a communist way would harm the cause of building communism. It must be borne in mind that with the present level of development of production there is still not enough to satisfy fully the requirements of all the people. Such "equalitarian communism" would only eat up accumulated funds and make impossible the further successful development of the economy and expanded reproduction.

We must advance step by step, creating the material and spiritual requisites for a planned transition to communism.

Second, nothwithstanding all the differences between communism and the socialist stage, there is no wall separating these two stages of social development. Communism grows out of socialism and is its direct continuation. It would be wrong, erroneous, to assume that communism will somehow appear suddenly. Communist forms of labor and industrial organization as well as such forms of satisfying the requirements of our people as public catering, boarding schools, kindergartens, and day nurseries are already developing more and more widely. Our society has many tangible and visible communist features which will be developing and improving.

There is no calendar date marking the entry into communism. There will be no given moment at which we shall shut one door and announce: "The building of socialism is completed," then open another door and say: "We have now reached communism." The transition from socialism to communism is a continuous process. We are already opening the door to communist society, we are now engaged in building communism. Our country has now entered a period of extensive communist construction, one in which all the material and spiritual requirements for communism are being created. Communist construction will be completed when we shall have provided a complete abundance of everything needed to satisfy the requirements of all the people, when all the people learn to work according to their ability, so as to multiply and accumulate communal wealth.

Third, gradual transition to communism should not be understood as a slowed movement. On the contrary, it is a period of rapid development of modern industry and large-scale mechanized agriculture, rapid progress in all of the economy and culture with the active and conscious participation of the millions upon millions of builders of communist society. This law-governed evolution of socialism into communism can be accelerated on the basis of the high level of material production attained in the period of socialism. One cannot hurry and hastily introduce what is not yet ready for introduction. This would lead to distortions and to discrediting our work. But one cannot rest content with what has been achieved; this would lead to stagnation.

Is the time far off when it will be possible fully to satisfy the essential requirements of all Soviet persons? Evidently not so far off, considering our immense potentialities for increasing social production and raising the cultural standards of society. But this will be accomplished not all at once, but step by step; not by a single act, but progressively, as the material production conditions are prepared.

Full satisfaction, within necessary and reasonable limits, of all the Soviet people's requirements of food, housing, and clothing can probably be attained in the near future. Not very much time is needed before, say, free lunches and dinners are provided for school children and all children can be accommodated in kindergartens, nurseries, and boarding schools with full maintenance at the expense of society. As for the adult population, it must be borne in mind that man's requirements of means of existence are not limitless. A person cannot, for instance, consume more bread and other foods than his organism needs. There are also definite limits to the amounts of clothing and housing that can be used. Of course, when we speak of satisfying people's requirements, we have in mind not whims or claims to luxuries, but the wholesome consumption of a cultured person.

It will take a longer time for people to acquire the inner need to work in accordance with their abilities. As long as this is lacking, society cannot dispense with definite regulation of working time in order that every able-bodied person contribute a definite amount of labor to the production of the goods and services that the community needs.

Our country's basic practical task at this time is *to establish the material and technical base of communist society, to secure a great new expansion of socialist productive forces.*

Why is this now our principal task in economic development of the country? At the present level of socialist production we are still unable to create the full abundance of material goods and cultural benefits necessary to satisfy the growing requirements of our people, necessary for their full development. But communism is impossible without this. Consequently, it is necessary first of all to develop the productive forces further and to increase the production of goods. Communism can be achieved only if we surpass the level of production in the developed capitalist countries and raise labor productivity to a new level far above that of capitalism.

Creation of the material and technical base of communism presumes, first of all, a highly developed, modern industry, complete electrification of the country, scientific and technical progress in all branches of industry and agriculture, complex mechanization and automation of all production processes, maximum utilization of new power sources and of our wealth of natural resources, new synthetics and other materials, a higher cultural and technical level of all the working people, further improvement in the organization of production, and higher labor productivity.

It would be an oversimplification to assume that if we overtake the United States economically, that will signify completion of communist construction. No, that is not the final limit of our advance, only a decisive stage in the competition with capitalism.

While competing with America, we do not regard America as our yardstick of economic development. Although the U.S.A. has a highly developed economy, the defective capitalist mode of production and distribution prevails there. Along with a profusion of every kind of goods, there are millions of unemployed, and millions poorly provided for, who cannot satisfy their most elementary needs. The communists do not want to imitate this order, but, on the contrary, to put an end to such injustice on earth. And if America's production level is taken as a yardstick for the growth of our economy, it is only in order to compare this economy with the most developed capitalist economy. When we win the economic competition with the U.S.A., we shall only have completed the first stage of communist construction. The level of economic development reached at this stage will not be the end of our road, but only a way station at which we shall be able to overtake the most highly developed capitalist country, leave it behind, and push ahead. [*Stormy applause.*]

As our productive forces grow, socialist production relations, which are based on principles of comradely cooperation, friendship, and mutual assistance of all the toilers of society, will be perfected. In our country social labor has already become the expression of new, socialist relationships among people and an index of the lofty moral qualities of man.

As socialist production develops further on a new material and technical base and as education is steadily more closely linked with work, the essential distinctions between mental and manual labor will gradually disappear. The rounded development of our people will turn into a prime need of man. The contemplated reduction of working hours and further improvement of working conditions will facilitate this. When all branches of industry are automated, when man becomes a commander of machines, he will have to spend less time and energy to produce the means of existence. Labor, which is now at times still arduous and tiring, will become a source of joy and pleasure for the healthy, rounded man.

In laying prime emphasis in the coming period on the creation of the material and technical base of communism we proceed completely from Marxism-Leninism and the experience of the Soviet Union and all the socialist countries.

The development of society presents another major problem of scientific communism, the problem of *distribution of society's material and cultural product among all of society's members.* Marxism-Leninism teaches that in social development distribution is not a determining but a derivative factor and that its forms and principles depend on the mode and volume of production.

In socialist society distribution is based in the main on the principle: "From each according to his abilities, to each according to his labor." This means that the greatest part of the material and cultural product is distributed among society's members in accordance with their labor contribution to social production.

It must be borne in mind, of course, that even under socialism a considerable and ever increasing portion of the material and cultural product is distributed among the members of society independently of the quantity and quality of their work — that is, gratis. Society carries immense costs of free education, free health services, pensions, grants to large families, free club services, free libraries, etc.

The following facts illustrate the part played by government expenditures and expenditures out of the communal funds of the collective farms in increasing the well-being and improving the material status of the working people. There are approximately 100,000,000 workers, employees, and collective farmers engaged in social production in our country. Approximately 20,000,000 pensioners are supported by the state, collective farms, and public organizations; 5,000,000 children are accommodated in kindergartens, nurseries, and children's homes; 3,300,000 in higher and specialized secondary educational institutions, public schools, and labor reserves schools receive state stipends and dormitory housing; boarding-school pupils are fully provided for by the state. The Young Pioneer camps, summer playgrounds and tourist camps accommodate 5,600,000 vacationing children annually. More than 3,000,000 workers, employees, and collective farmers vacation or obtain treatment at sanatoriums or rest homes every year at the expense of the social insurance fund or the collective farms. In addition, approximately

7,000,000 mothers of large families or unmarried mothers receive government grants.

State expenditures for these purposes will increase in the future. As we advance toward communism society's care of each individual from the cradle to old age will increase more and more.

At the present stage the chief yardstick of the share each citizen receives from society in the distribution of the social product is the quantity and quality of his labor. Lenin said: "Until a higher phase of communism arrives, socialists demand the most *stringent* control by society *and by the state* over the amount of labor and the amount of consumption. . . ." ("Works" [in Russian], Vol. XXV, p. 441)

The history of the development of our country included a period of "war communism," when we were temporarily obliged to depart from the principle of distribution according to work and adopt equalitarian "distribution according to the number of mouths." This was not due to abundance, but to an acute shortage of food and consumer goods. By the most stringent discipline in food distribution, the state was able to avert mass famine and to supply the fighters of the Red Army and the urban population with regular, if meager, rations, at times only an eighth of a pound of bread a day.

This method of distribution, however, could not be a normal economic system. Its defects became evident as soon as the country set about reconstruction and development of the economy. V. I. Lenin most directly stated then that, without a material stake for all personnel in the results of their work, the country's productive capacity could not be raised, a socialist economy could not be built and the millions of people could not be led toward communism.

With the change to peaceful construction, monetary pay for workers and employees was introduced. Its underlying principle was distribution according to work. With the triumph of the system of collective farming this principle of distribution was established in the collective-farm countryside as well.

In articles and lectures, some social scientists voice the view that distribution according to work signifies application of bourgeois law to socialist society. They ask whether the time has not come to shift from this principle to equalitarian distribution of the social product among all personnel. One cannot agree with this view.

True, Marx and Lenin spoke of survivals of "bourgeois law" that are inevitable under socialism, but what they had in mind was juridical forms which were left over from the old society and will disappear under communism.

Socialist distribution on the principle of equal pay for equal work means that one and the same legal yardstick is applied to different people. That single, equal yardstick is labor. Socialism excludes class inequality; there remains only the inequality of the share received in the distribution of goods. Inasmuch as different people have different skills, talents, and working ability and different sized families, it is natural that with equal pay for equal work they have in fact unequal incomes. But this system is inevitable in the first phase of communist society.

We should not confuse legal forms with the substance of the social relationships which they express. Bourgeois law recognizes individual private ownership of the means of production, whereas socialism makes them public property and in this respect completely breaks with bourgeois law. Under socialism all people stand in equal relationship to the means of production and are paid according to their work. In socialist society the rule applying to all able-bodied members of society is: He who does not work, neither shall he eat.

Under capitalism distribution is in fact based not on work, but primarily on capital, and is regulated by the laws of value, profit, and rent. For that reason greater income is received not by those who work more, but by those who have more capital.

As we see, there is a fundamental difference between capitalism and socialism in the distribution of the values produced.

The socialist principle of distribution according to work is based on the recognition that equalitarian distribution is impossible in the socialist period. Distribution according to work is the only reasonable and just principle under the given conditions. One cannot fail to see that leveling would lead to unjust distribution: the bad worker and the good one would receive an equal share, which would be to the advantage of the slackers only. The

material incentive for people to work better, to raise productivity and produce more, would be undermined. Leveling would signify not transition to communism, but discrediting of communism.

Distribution according to work provides a material stake for people in the results of production, stimulates labor productivity, the acquisition of higher skills, and technical progress. It also performs an important educational function by accustoming people to socialist discipline and making labor universal and obligatory. In socialist society labor enthusiasm rises higher and higher and the moral incentives to work acquire even greater importance. Thanks to the material incentive, as a result of higher consciousness and through habit, work becomes a vital inner need for the millions of working people of socialist society.

The need for regulating the distribution of goods among the members of society disappears only under communism, when the productive forces will have expanded so much that an abundance of all the necessary consumer goods will be attained and when all people, voluntarily and irrespective of the share of material goods that they receive, will work to the full of their ability, knowing that this is necessary for society.

Communist society will of course have a planned and organized allocation of labor among the various branches of production and social regulation of working time in accordance with the specific requirements of various production processes. Production by machine has a definite rhythm that is impossible without a corresponding scheduling of people's work.

Some persons have a vulgarized conception of communist society as a loose, unorganized, anarchic mass of people. No, it will be a highly organized and closely coordinated community of men of labor. Operation of machinery requires that each person perform his job and meet his social obligations at definite times and in definite ways. The highly mechanized and automated industry of the future will not require long hours of work; there will be a great deal of free time for study, art, literature, sports, etc.

The Organization of Agriculture

The question of *the ways of developing and bringing closer together the collective-farm and public forms of socialist ownership* acquires great theoretical and practical importance in resolving the tasks of communist construction.

It is quite clear that in the future the collective-farm–cooperative and state forms of ownership will merge completely into a single form of communist ownership. Why, then, it may be asked, are we not pressing for their merger now, why do we consider that at the present stage it is necessary to develop collective-farm–cooperative ownership in every way, along with state ownership?

Forms of ownership are not changed arbitrarily, but develop on the basis of economic laws and depend on the nature and level of development of the productive forces. The collective-farm system fully accords with the present level and developmental requirements of today's productive forces in agriculture. It permits the most effective use of modern farm machinery, which is impossible with fragmented, small-scale peasant holdings. Now that powerful modern machinery is going directly to the collective farms, their communal output is increasing more rapidly.

Some branches of agriculture lagged in the recent past not because the collective-farm form hampered development of the productive forces, but because inadequate use was made of the potentialities and advantages offered by the collective-farm system. The successes achieved in agriculture in the past five years are most convincing evidence that the collective-farm–cooperative form of production relations, far from having exhausted its potentialities, serves and for a long time can continue to serve the development of agriculture's productive forces.

With the further development of the productive forces there will be a rise in the degree of socialization of collective-farm production, and collective-farm–cooperative ownership will come to approximate public ownership more closely; gradually the line dividing the two will be obliterated. This is indicated by the following characteristic processes:

First, there is a steady increase in the indivisible funds of the collective farms, constituting the economic basis for further development of collective-farm production and for gradual approximation of collective-farm–cooperative and public property.

Second, communal collective-farm production is coming more and more fully to embrace all the branches of agriculture, one after another. As the communal economy grows, the collective farmers' needs not only of bread, but of meat, milk, butter, vegetables, potatoes, and fruit will be met more and more not from their unproductive private plots and private livestock but from the economically advantageous communal production of the collective farms.

Third, intercollective-farm production ties and various forms of cooperation among collective farms are developing more and more widely and inevitably will grow. Joint construction of power stations, irrigation canals, enterprises for processing farm products and for manufacturing building materials, and road building will require more and more systematic unified efforts by numbers of collective farms.

Fourth, agricultural electrification, mechanization, and automation will lead to the pooling — in a certain sense, the merging — of collective-farm means of production with state and public means of production; farm labor will gradually turn into a variety of industrial labor.

The historically inevitable merger of the collective-farm–cooperative and public forms of property will occur in the future not by shutting down collective-farm–cooperative ownership but by raising its level of socialization with the aid and support of the socialist state.

The merger of collective-farm–cooperative property with state property into unified public property is not a simple economic-organizational measure, but is the solution of the profound problem of overcoming the essential difference between town and country.

In the coming seven years we intend to take a decisive step in further advancing agricultural output and on this basis radically improving the cultural level and living conditions of the rural population. The Party is aiming to convert the collective-farm villages into urban-type communities with all the latest communal, cultural, and service facilities.

The Administration of Public Affairs

Along with the problems of economic development, there likewise urgently arise *problems of the political organization of society, the state structure and government in the period of extensive building of communism.*

Marxism-Leninism teaches that under communism the state will wither away and that the functions of public administration will lose their political character and will turn into management of society's affairs directly by the people. But one cannot oversimplify and conceive of the process of the withering away of the agencies of state as something like the turning of leaves in autumn, when the branches are left bare as the leaves fall.

If we approach it dialectically, the question of withering away of the state is a question of evolution of the socialist state toward communist public self-government. Under communism, too, there will remain certain public functions similar to those now performed by the state, but their nature and the methods by which they will be accomplished will differ from those obtaining in the present stage.

The chief trend in the development of the socialist state is the utmost unfolding of democracy, the enlisting of the broadest strata of the population in the management of all affairs of the country, enlistment of all citizens in participation in the management of economic and cultural construction.

The Social-Democratic theoreticians and revisionists try every variation to discredit and vilify socialist democracy. In their view, "democratization" should mean renunciation of the leading role of the working class and its party under socialism, a return to the forms of bourgeois democracy. Without this, in their view, there is neither democracy nor socialism. To them democracy is the opportunity to engage in glittering parliamentary oratory, to play at political deals among the parties, to set up a flowery screen of "free elections" behind which capital is omnipotent and the people are actually disenfranchised. To us, democracy is genuine rule by the people, the fullest development of the initiative and activity of the masses of working people, self-government of the people. [*Applause.*]

It is already clear that many functions performed by government agencies will gradually pass to public organizations. Take, for instance, certain aspects of cultural services. It is not at all essential that they remain in the hands of government organizations. Public organizations can deal with them successfully.

Life suggests also that it is necessary to change the organization of health services and resort facilities. Evidently the conditions are ready for turning over more and more public

health matters in the cities to the trade unions and in the countryside, at the present stage, directly to the local Soviets.

Up to now the physical culture movement in our country has been directed by a government agency, the Committee on Physical Culture and Sports. Now a more expedient structure for the physical culture movement has been formed; public organizations participating in this movement will play the decisive role in it. A Federation of Public Sports Societies, not a governmental but a public organization, is being set up.

Problems of enforcing public order and the rules of the socialist community should likewise come increasingly under the jurisdiction of public organizations. There are now no cases in the Soviet Union of people being tried for political crimes. This is undoubtedly a great achievement. It testifies to an unprecedented unity of political convictions of our entire people, to their solidarity with the Communist Party and Soviet government. [*Prolonged applause.*]

But there are still many instances of violation of public order, and a resolute struggle must be waged against them. Can the Soviet public cope with the violators of socialist law and order? Of course it can. Our public organizations have no less adequate capacities, means, and forces for this than the militia, the courts, and the Prosecutor's Office!

Matters are approaching a situation in which public organizations, alongside and parallel with such state agencies as the militia and the courts, will perform the functions of safeguarding public order and security. This process is now under way. The size of the militia has been sharply reduced; the state security agencies in particular have been considerably reduced.

Socialist society forms such voluntary organizations for safeguarding public order as the people's militia, comrades' courts, and the like. They all employ new methods and find new ways of performing public functions. The voluntary detachments of people's militia should undertake to keep public order in their respective communities and to see that the rights and interests of all citizens are respected and protected.

The time has come when more attention should be paid to the comrades' courts, which should seek chiefly to prevent assorted kinds of law violations. They should hear not only cases concerning behavior on the job but also cases of everyday deportment and morality, cases of improper conduct by members of the group who disregard the standards of social behavior.

When the comrades' public courts function actively and the public itself delegates persons to ensure public order, it will be much easier to combat transgressors. It will be possible to spot a transgressor before he commits a misdemeanor or crime, when he first shows a departure from the standards of public behavior that might lead him into antisocial acts. People could exert timely influence on such a person to curb his evil propensities. Measures are required that will prevent and subsequently completely preclude individuals' commission of acts harmful to society. The chief thing is preventive, educational work.

Of course, definite functions will remain with the courts, the militia, and the Prosecutor's Office. These agencies will continue to function in order to exert influence on persons who maliciously refuse to submit to socialist society's standards of behavior and are not amenable to persuasion.

The transfer of some functions of state agencies to public organizations should be carried out without undue haste. In some circumstances it should be done more resolutely; in others only the first, exploratory steps should be taken in order to accustom people to safeguard public order themselves.

Obviously, the transfer to public organizations of some functions now performed by state agencies does not at all mean weakening the role of the socialist state in the building of communism. The fact that public organizations will perform a number of the present functions of the state will broaden and strengthen the political base of socialist society and will ensure further development of socialist democracy.

It is not only we Communists and Soviet people who see that the Soviet system rests on firm foundations. This must be admitted even by the persons who come to us from abroad to see whether the Soviet system is not breaking down and who go back with sour mien when the picture they find is not the one they had wished to see. They put off to a future date their hopes that the Soviet state

will be weakened, but the future prospects for our country are brighter than ever. [*Stormy applause.*]

In the future, the Soviet Union will be able to concentrate more attention on developing the economy, the material base of our system. "Under the bourgeois system," Lenin said, "the bosses and not state agencies ran the economy, but in our society economics is the affair of all. This is the politics that interests us most." ("Works" [in Russian], Vol. XXXII, pp. 406–407)

The World Situation

The tasks of the socialist state in safeguarding peace, in the sphere of defense against the threat of armed attack by the imperialist powers, are especially important and great. As long as the Western powers' aggressive military blocs exist, we are obliged to strengthen and improve our glorious Armed Forces, which stand guard over the great achievements and peaceful labor of the Soviet people. [*Stormy, prolonged applause.*] The state security agencies, which direct their spearhead primarily against agents sent into the country by imperialist states, must be strengthened, as must other agencies which have the mission of blocking the provocational actions and intrigues of our enemies from the imperialist camp. Our enemies are spending enormous sums on subversive work against the socialist countries. How, then, can we abolish agencies which have the duty of safeguarding the security of the socialist state! That would be foolish and criminal.

The Yugoslav revisionists criticize us for the fact that our Party devotes great attention to strengthening the Soviet state, alleging that this does not accord with the Marxist-Leninist doctrine on the withering away of the state.

As I have already stated, we do not now have prisoners who have been jailed for political reasons. It would be a good thing if the Yugoslav leaders, who like to talk about the withering away of coercive agencies, were to release all the Communists now languishing in Yugoslav prisons for disagreeing with the new program of the League of Communists of Yugoslavia, for holding dissenting views on the building of socialism and the role of the Party. [*Stir in the hall. Stormy, prolonged applause.*]

Leninism teaches that the state will wither away with the complete triumph of communism. To weaken the socialist state in present conditions would be to help our enemies. The imperialists cannot crush us now, but the revisionists are inviting us, in effect, to disarm, abolish the state agencies that ensure defense of the country and thus leave ourselves to the mercy of our enemies. The functions of defending the socialist Fatherland, now performed by the state, can wither away only when the danger of an imperialist attack on our country or on countries allied with ours is completely removed.

Now that the building of socialism is no longer confined to one country and a world socialist system has been formed, *new theoretical problems of the struggle for the victory of socialism and communism* have arisen.

Not so long ago the Communist movement was facing and discussing the question of whether socialism could be built in one country separately, the question of its complete and final victory.

When the Soviet land had only just set about building socialism and when for many the country's path ahead was hidden in the mist of the future, V. I. Lenin opened up clear and broad vistas before the country. He said that we have ". . . everything necessary for building a complete socialist society." ("Works" [in Russian], Vol. XXXIII, p. 428) Unswervingly guided by Lenin's instructions, the Soviet people, inspired by the Communist Party, worked perseveringly, amid the constant menace of armed attack by capitalist states, to build a socialist society, advanced along uncharted paths, and achieved the complete triumph of socialism in our country. [*Prolonged applause.*]

But this victory was not final. By the final victory of socialism Marxists mean its triumph on an international scale. Having built socialism, our country for a long time remained the world's only socialist state, in a hostile capitalist encirclement. It could not consider itself fully guaranteed against armed intervention and the danger of a forcible restoration of capitalism by international reaction. The capitalist states then surrounding the land of socialism were much stronger economically and militarily.

Now the world situation has changed fundamentally. The capitalist encirclement no longer exists for our country. There are two world social systems: capitalism, living out its day, and socialism, filled with growing, vital forces and enjoying the support of the working people of all lands. [*Applause.*]

The Soviet country, like any other socialist country, is not guaranteed against the possibility of aggression by the imperialist states. But the correlation of real forces in the world now is such that we shall be able to repel any attack by any enemy. [*Stormy applause.*]

There are no forces in the world now that could re-establish capitalism in our country or crush the socialist camp. The danger of capitalist restoration in the Soviet Union is ruled out. This means that *the triumph of socialism is not only complete but final.* [*Stormy, prolonged applause.*]

Thus it can be considered that the questions of building socialism in one country and its complete and final victory have been decided by the world-historic course of social development.

The victory of socialism in the U.S.S.R. and the formation of the world socialist system immeasurably strengthen the forces of the international workers' movement and open up new vistas for it. The brilliant scientific prediction made by Vladimir Ilyich Lenin in his last pronouncement is now coming true. "In the final analysis," he said, "the outcome of the struggle will be determined by the fact that Russia, India, China, etc., represent the overwhelming majority of the population. And it is precisely this majority that in recent years has been drawn into the struggle for emancipation with extraordinary rapidity, so that in this sense there cannot be the slightest shadow of doubt about the final outcome of the world struggle. In this sense the final victory of socialism is fully and absolutely assured." ("Works" [in Russian], Vol. XXXIII, p. 458) [*Stormy applause.*]

How will the further development of the socialist countries toward communism proceed? Can one imagine one of the socialist countries attaining communism and introducing the communist principles of production and distribution, while other countries are left trailing somewhere behind in the early stages of building socialist society?

This prospect is highly improbable if one

takes into account the laws governing the economic development of the socialist system. From the theoretical standpoint it would be more correct to assume that by successfully employing the potentialities inherent in socialism, the socialist countries will enter the higher phase of communist society more or less simultaneously. We base ourselves on the fact that new laws of development, laws unknown to human society in the past, operate in the socialist economic system. For instance, a law operating under imperialism is that of uneven economic and political development of different countries. The course of development under that system is such that some countries push ahead at the expense of others and oppress and exploit these others. The ones that have pushed ahead take care to safeguard their privileged position so as to keep the backward countries in dependence and subjugation.

The law of planned, proportional development operates in the socialist economic system, with the result that formerly economically backward countries rapidly make up for lost time and raise their economic and cultural levels by drawing on the experience of other socialist countries and on cooperation and mutual assistance. Thus the common line of the economic and cultural development of all the socialist countries is evened out.

There is no doubt that, with the further growth and strengthening of the world socialist system, all the socialist countries will develop with increasing success. The conditions necessary for the transition from the first phase of communism to its second phase will be established at an increasingly faster pace in these countries.

One should recall the brilliant way that life has confirmed Lenin's proposition that, with the support of the advanced socialist states, some formerly backward countries could go over to the socialist system and advance through definite stages of development to communism, bypassing the capitalist stage. Everyone now sees the tremendous progress achieved along the path of socialist development by the peoples of Kazakhstan and Central Asia, who at the time of the socialist revolution in our country either had been at a pre-capitalist stage or were only just entering the capitalist stage. These peoples did not have to go through the entire tormenting stage of capitalist

development; they were able to bypass it and change over to socialism with the support and help of the more developed socialist nations, in particular the Russian socialist nation. Separate mention should be made of the Mongolian People's Republic, which, bypassing the capitalist stage, long ago set out on the socialist path and has made great progress in economic and cultural construction.

In surveying the prospect of mankind's advance to communism, we must bear in mind the tremendous diversity of historical conditions in the different countries. Hence inevitably there arises a diversity of methods, ways and forms of applying the common laws of mankind's advance to communism. But, for all this, it must be emphasized that the principal, determining aspect in the development of all countries along the path to communism is the laws common to all of them, not the particular ways in which these laws are manifested. Marxism-Leninism requires the ability to apply the theory of scientific communism to the specific conditions of each individual country at the various stages of its development.

The Yugoslav leaders talk a great deal now about the alleged fact that the Communist Parties are speaking out against them because they, the Yugoslav leaders, take as their starting point in building socialism the features peculiar to their own country and do not follow the example and experience of other socialist countries. That, of course, is a distortion of the truth. The Marxist-Leninist parties recognize that each country has its own specific features of development. But this does not mean that one can reach socialism by some other road that lies to the side of the common path indicated by Marxism-Leninism. The particular features of the situation and period in which one country or another is developing — these must be taken into consideration. For example, some measures applied in socialist construction in the Soviet Union in the past cannot be mechanically applied in other countries. All the socialist countries are building socialism, but they do not do it by stereotype.

The Communist Party of China is employing many original forms of socialist construction. But we have no disagreements with this party, nor can there be any disagreements.

The Yugoslav revisionists are now concentrating their fire on the Chinese People's Republic, disseminating all sorts of inventions about alleged differences between the Communist Parties of the Soviet Union and China. As the Russian saying puts it, "the hungry man dreams of bread." The revisionists are searching for discord among our Communist Parties, but their illusory hopes are doomed to failure. [*Stormy, prolonged applause.*] We are in full and complete agreement with the fraternal Communist Party of China, although in many respects its methods of building socialism do not resemble our own. We know that China has its specific features of historical development, size of population, level of production and national culture. Therefore it would be a mistake to ignore these specific features and to copy what is good for one country but unsuitable for another.

Why have we no differences with the Communist Party of China? Because we share the same class approach and class conception. The Chinese Communist Party stands firmly on Marxist-Leninist class positions. It is waging a struggle against the imperialists and exploiters, a struggle to refashion life along socialist lines; it abides by the principle of international proletarian solidarity and is guided by Marxist-Leninist theory.

The chief thing is to maintain and strengthen class solidarity in the struggle against capitalism, for the liberation of the working class, for the building of socialism. And on this score there is no divergence, there are no conflicting conceptions, among Communists, nor can there be. This is the main point that divides us from revisionists. [*Stormy applause.*]

Questions of the methods and practice of socialist construction are the domestic affair of each individual country. We have no controversy with the Yugoslav leaders on the establishing of workers' councils or other matters of their domestic affairs. When the declaration of the conference of representatives of the Communist and Workers' Parties of the socialist countries was being signed, there were no arguments and no controversies on such matters.

One can say to the Yugoslav revisionists: Don't look for cracks where they don't exist. Presumably, you want to encourage yourselves and mislead the Yugoslav people by asserting that there are differences not only between us and you, but also between the Soviet Union

and the Chinese People's Republic. It won't work. You will never see such differences, any more than you can see your own ears. [*Stir in the hall. Applause.*] The Communist Party of the Soviet Union and the Communist Party of China are doing everything to strengthen the friendship of the two great socialist countries. [*Stormy, prolonged applause.*]

For the international workers' movement, for the triumph of communism, the ideas of Marxism-Leninism have the same life-giving power as sunshine and warmth have for plants, for life on earth. As life itself is boundless in its progress, in its diverse manifestations, so Marxism-Leninism is limitless in its development and enrichment by new experience and new propositions. . . .

70

Russia and Western Civilization*

Arnold J. Toynbee

(1952)

Arnold Toynbee, the famous British historian, seeks to fit the meaning of Russia into the broad pattern of world history. He has some provocative things to say about the elements of continuity and discontinuity with the Russian past in Soviet policy, and about the significance of Communism as a creed. However, his assertion that Russia has captured the spiritual initiative from the West must be qualified by the ever growing awareness throughout the world of a substantial gap between the claims and realities of Soviet Communism.

In the encounter between the world and the West that has been going on by now for four or five hundred years, the world, not the West, is the party that, up to now, has had the signif-

* Reprinted with minor editorial omissions from "Russia and the West," *The World and the West* (1952), pp. 1–17, Oxford University Press, by permission of the author and publisher. This article also appeared in *Harper's Magazine*, Vol. 206 (March 1953), pp. 54–58.

icant experience. It has not been the West that has been hit by the world; it is the world that has been hit — and hit hard — by the West.

A Westerner who wants to grapple with this subject must try, for a few minutes, to slip out of his native Western skin and look at the encounter between the world and the West through the eyes of the great non-Western majority of mankind. Different though the non-Western peoples of the world may be from one another in race, language, civilization, and religion, if any Western inquirer asks them their opinion of the West, he will hear them all giving him the same answer: Russians, Moslems, Hindus, Chinese, Japanese, and all the rest. The West, they will tell him, has been the arch-aggressor of modern times, and each will have their own experience of Western aggression to bring up against him. The Russians will remind him that their country has been invaded by Western armies overland in 1941, 1915, 1812, 1709, and 1610; the peoples of Africa and Asia will remind him that Western missionaries, traders, and soldiers from across the sea have been pushing into their countries from the coasts since the fifteenth century. The Asians will also remind him that, within the same period, the Westerners have occupied the lion's share of the world's last vacant lands in the Americas, Australia, New Zealand, and South and East Africa. The Africans will remind him that they were enslaved and deported across the Atlantic in order to serve the European colonizers of the Americas as living tools to minister to their Western masters' greed for wealth. The descendants of the aboriginal population of North America will remind him that their ancestors were swept aside to make room for the west European intruders and for their African slaves.

This indictment will surprise, shock, grieve, and perhaps even outrage most Westerners today. Dutch Westerners are conscious of having evacuated Indonesia, and British Westerners of having evacuated India, Pakistan, Burma, and Ceylon, since 1945. British Westerners have no aggressive war on their consciences since the South African War of 1899–1902, and American Westerners none since the Spanish-American War of 1898. We forget all too easily that the Germans, who attacked their neighbors, including Russia, in the First World War and again in the Second World War, are Westerners too, and that the Russians, Asians, and Africans do not draw fine distinctions between different hordes of "Franks" — which is the world's common name for Westerners in the mass. "When the world passes judgment it can be sure of having the last word," according to a well-known Latin proverb. And certainly the world's judgment on the West does seem to be justified over a period of about four and a half centuries ending in 1945. In the world's experience of the West during all that time, the West has been the aggressor on the whole; and, if the tables are being turned on the West by Russia and China today, this is a new chapter of the story which did not begin until after the end of the Second World War. The West's alarm and anger at recent acts of Russian and Chinese aggression at the West's expense are evidence that, for us Westerners, it is today still a strange experience to be suffering at the hands of the world what the world has been suffering at Western hands for a number of centuries past.

II

What, then, has been the world's experience of the West? Let us look at Russia's experience, for Russia is part of the world's great non-Western majority. Though the Russians have been Christians and are, many of them, Christians still, they have never been Western Christians. Russia was converted not from Rome, as England was, but from Constantinople; and, in spite of their common Christian origins, Eastern and Western Christendom have always been foreign to one another, and have often been mutually antipathic and hostile, as Russia and the West unhappily still are today, when each of them is in what one might call a "post-Christian" phase of its history.

This on the whole unhappy story of Russia's relations with the West did, though, have a happier first chapter; for, in spite of the difference between the Russian and the Western way of life, Russia and the West got on fairly well with one another in the early Middle Ages. The peoples traded, and the royal families intermarried. An English King Harold's daughter, for instance, married a Russian prince. The estrangement began in the thirteenth century, after the subjugation of Russia by the Tatars. The Tatars' domination over Russia was temporary, because the Tatars were nomads from the Steppes who could not ever make themselves at home in Russia's fields and forests. Russia's lasting losses as a result of this temporary Tatar conquest were, not to her Tatar conquerors, but to her Western neighbors; for these took advantage of Russia's prostration in order to lop off, and annex to Western Christendom, the western fringes of the Russian world in White Russia and in the Western half of the Ukraine. It was not till 1945 that Russia recaptured the last piece of these huge Russian territories that were taken from her by Western powers in the thirteenth and fourteenth centuries.

These Western conquests at Russia's expense in the late Middle Ages had an effect on Russia's life at home, as well as on her relations with her Western assailants. The pressure on Russia from the West did not merely estrange Russia from the West; it was one of the hard facts of Russian life that moved the Russians to submit to the yoke of a new native Russian power at Moscow which, at the price of autocracy, imposed on Russia the political unity that she now had to have if she was to survive. It was no accident that this new-fangled autocratic centralizing government of Russia should have arisen at Moscow; for Moscow stood in the fairway of the easiest line for the invasion of what was left of Russia by a Western aggressor. The Poles in 1610, the French in 1812, the Germans in 1941, all marched this way. Since an early date in the fourteenth century, autocracy and centralization have been the dominant notes of all successive Russian regimes. This Muscovite Russian political tradition has perhaps always been as disagreeable for the Russians themselves as it has certainly been distasteful and alarming to their neighbors; but unfortunately the Russians have learned to put up with it, partly perhaps out of sheer habit, but also, no doubt, because they have felt it to be a lesser evil than the alternative fate of being conquered by aggressive neighbors.

This submissive Russian attitude toward an autocratic regime that has become traditional in Russia is, of course, one of the main difficulties, as we Westerners see it, in the relations between Russia and the West today. The great majority of people in the West feel that tyranny is an intolerable social evil. At a fearful cost we have put down tyranny when it has raised its head among our Western selves in the forms of Fascism and National Socialism. We feel the same detestation and distrust of it in its Russian form, whether this calls itself Tsarism or calls itself Communism. We do not want to see this Russian brand of tyranny spread; and we are particularly concerned about this danger to Western ideals of liberty now that we Franks find ourselves thrown upon the defensive for the first time in our history since the second Turkish siege of Vienna in 1682–83. Our present anxiety about what seems to us to be a postwar threat to the West from Russia is a well-justified anxiety in our belief. At the same time, we must take care not to allow the reversal in the relation between Russia and the West since 1945 to mislead us into forgetting the past in our natural preoccupation with the present. When we look at the encounter between Russia and the West in the historian's instead of the journalist's perspective, we shall see that, over a period of several centuries ending in 1945, the Russians have had the same reason for looking askance at the West that we Westerners feel that we have for looking askance at Russia today.

During the past few centuries, this threat to Russia from the West, which has been a constant threat from the thirteenth century till 1945, has been made more serious for Russia by the outbreak, in the West, of a technological revolution which has become chronic and which does not yet show any signs of abating.

When the West adopted firearms, Russia followed suit, and in the sixteenth century she used these new weapons from the West to conquer the Tatars in the Volga valley and more primitive peoples in the Urals and in Siberia. But in 1610 the superiority of the Western armaments of the day enabled the Poles to occupy Moscow and to hold it for two years, while at about the same time the Swedes were also able to deprive Russia of her outlet on the Baltic Sea at the head of the Gulf of Finland. The Russian retort to these seventeenth-century Western acts of aggression was to adopt the technology of the West wholesale, together with as much of the Western way of life as was inseparable from Western technology.

It was characteristic of the autocratic centralizing Muscovite regime that this technological and accompanying social revolution in

Russia at the turn of the seventeenth and eighteenth centuries should have been imposed upon Russia from above downward, by the fiat of one man of genius, Peter the Great. Peter is a key figure for an understanding of the world's relations with the West not only in Russia but everywhere; for Peter is the archetype of the autocratic Westernizing reformer who, during the past two and a half centuries, has saved the world from falling entirely under Western domination by forcing the world to train itself to resist Western aggression with Western weapons. Sultans Selim III and Mohammed II and President Mustafa Kemal Ataturk in Turkey, Mehemet Ali Pasha in Egypt, and "the Elder Statesmen," who made the Westernizing revolution in Japan in the eighteen-sixties, were, all of them, following in Peter the Great's footsteps consciously or unconsciously.

Peter launched Russia on a technological race with the West which Russia is still running. Russia has never yet been able to afford to rest, because the West has continually been making fresh spurts. For example, Peter and his eighteenth-century successors brought Russia close enough abreast of the Western world of the day to make Russia just able to defeat her Swedish Western invaders in 1709 and her French Western invaders in 1812; but, in the nineteenth-century Western industrial revolution, the West once more left Russia behind, so that in the First World War Russia was defeated by her German Western invaders as she had been defeated, two hundred years earlier, by the Poles and the Swedes. The present Communist autocratic government was able to supplant the Tsardom in Russia in consequence of Russia's defeat by an industiral Western technology in 1914–17; and the Communist regime then set out, from 1928 to 1941, to do for Russia, all over again, what the Tsar Peter had done for her about 230 years earlier.

For the second time in the modern chapter of her history Russia was now put, by an autocratic ruler, through a forced march to catch up with a Western technology that had once more shot ahead of hers; and Stalin's tyrannical course of technological Westernization was eventually justified, like Peter's, through an ordeal by battle. The Communist technological revolution in Russia defeated the German invaders in the Second World War, as Peter's technological revolution had defeated the Swedish invaders in 1709 and the French invaders in 1812. And then, a few months after the completion of the liberation of Russian soil from German-Western occupation in 1945, Russia's American-Western allies dropped in Japan an atom bomb that announced the outbreak of a third Western technological revolution. So today, for the third time, Russia is having to make a forced march in an effort to catch up with a Western technology that, for the third time, has left her behind by shooting ahead. The result of this third event in the perpetual competition between Russia and the West still lies hidden in the future; but it is already clear that this renewal of the technological race is another of the very serious difficulties now besetting the relations between these two ex-Christian societies.

III

Technology is, of course, only a long Greek name for a bag of tools; and we have to ask ourselves: What are the tools that count in this competition in the use of tools as means to power? A power-loom or a locomotive is obviously a tool for this purpose, as well as a gun, an airplane, or a bomb. But all tools are not of the material kind; there are spiritual tools as well, and these are the most potent that Man has made. A creed, for instance, can be a tool; and, in the new round in the competition between Russia and the West that began in 1917, the Russians this time threw into their scale of balances a creed that weighed as heavily against their Western competitors' material tools as, in the Roman story of the ransoming of Rome from the Gauls, the sword thrown in by Brennus weighed against the Roman gold.

Communism, then, is a weapon; and, like bombs, airplanes, and guns, this is a weapon of Western origin. If it had not been invented by a couple of nineteenth-century Westerners, Karl Marx and Friedrich Engels, who were brought up in the Rhineland and spent the best part of their working lives in London and in Manchester respectively, Communism could never have become Russia's official ideology. There was nothing in the Russian tradition that could have led the Russians to invent Communism for themselves; and it is certain that they would never have dreamed of it if it had not been lying, ready-made, there in the West, for a revolutionary Russian regime to apply in Russia in 1917.

In borrowing from the West a Western ideology, besides a Western industrial revolution, to serve as an anti-Western weapon, the Bolsheviki in 1917 were making a great new departure in Russian history; for this was the first time that Russia had ever borrowed a creed from the West. But it was a creed particularly well suited to serve Russia as a Western weapon for waging an anti-Western spiritual warfare. In the West, where Communism had arisen, this new creed was a heresy. It was a Western criticism of the West's failure to live up to her own Christian principles in the economic and social life of this professedly Christian society; and a creed of Western origin which was at the same time an indictment of Western practice was, of course, just the spiritual weapon that an adversary of the West would like to pick up and turn against its makers.

With this Western spiritual weapon in her hands, Russia could carry her war with the West into the enemy's country on the spiritual plane. Since Communism had originated as a product of uneasy Western consciences it could appeal to other uneasy Western consciences when it was radiated back into the Western world by a Russian propaganda. And so now, for the first time in the modern Western world's history since the close of the seventeenth century, when the flow of Western converts to Islam almost ceased, the West has again found itself threatened with spiritual disintegration from inside, as well as with an assault from outside. In thus threatening to undermine Western civilization's foundations on the West's own home ground, Communism has already proved itself a more effective anti-Western weapon in Russian hands than any material weapon could ever be.

Communism has also served Russia as a weapon for bringing into the Russian camp the Chinese quarter of the human race, as well as other sections of that majority of mankind that is neither Russian nor Western. We know that the outcome of the struggle to win the allegiance of these neutrals may be decisive for the outcome of the Russo-Western conflict as a whole, because this non-Western and non-Russian majority of mankind may prove to hold the casting vote in a competition between

Russia and the West for world power. Now Communism can make a two-fold appeal to a depressed Asian, African, and Latin American peasantry when it is the voice of Russia that is commending Communism to them.

The Russian spokesman can say to the Asian peasantry first: "If you follow the Russian example, Communism will give you the strength to stand up against the West, as a Communist Russia can already stand up against the West today." The second appeal of Communism to the Asian peasantry is Communism's claim that it can, and that private enterprise neither can nor would if it could, get rid of the extreme inequality between a rich minority and a poverty-stricken majority in Asian countries. Discontented Asians, however, are not the only public for whom Communism has an appeal. Communism also has an appeal for all men, since it can claim to offer mankind the unity which is our only alternative to self-destruction in an atomic age.

It looks as if, in the encounter between Russia and the West, the spiritual initiative, though not the technological lead, has now passed, at any rate for the moment, from the Western to the Russian side. We Westerners cannot afford to resign ourselves to this, because this Western heresy — Communism — which the Russians have taken up, seems to the great majority of people in the West to be a perverse, misguided, and disastrous doctrine and way of life. A theologian might put it that our great modern Western heresiarch Karl Marx has made what is a heretic's characteristic intellectual mistake and moral aberration. In putting his finger on one point in orthodox practice in which there has been a crying need for reform, he has lost sight of all other considerations and therefore has produced a remedy that is worse than the disease.

The Russians' recent success in capturing the initiative from us Westerners by taking up this Western heresy called Communism and radiating it out into the world in a cloud of anti-Western poison gas does not, of course, mean that Communism is destined to prevail. Marx's vision seems, in non-Marxian eyes, far too narrow and too badly warped to be likely to prove permanently satisfying to human hearts and minds. All the same, Communism's success, so far as it has gone, looks like a portent of things to come. What it tells us is that the present encounter between the world and the West is now moving off the technological plane onto the spiritual plane.

Some light on this next chapter of this story, which for us still lies in the future, may be found in the history of the world's earlier encounter wtih Greece and Rome.

71

The Durability of Soviet Totalitarianism*

Bertram D. Wolfe

(1957)

Perhaps Professor Toynbee has put his finger on the meaning of Russia in the long stretch of history, but the world of the twentieth century views with more immediate alarm the rise of a mighty industrial state, armed with the weapons of modern warfare, and headed by men (and all too frequently, only one man) whose power is not adequately restrained by world opinion nor by the opinions of their fellow Soviet Russians. Bertram D. Wolfe, long a leading student of Soviet affairs, expresses what many of the most experienced observers in the West consider to be the hard face of reality. It revolves around understanding the meaning of modern totalitarianism as a political phenomenon.

I

At every turn the historian encounters the unpredictable: contingency, historical accident, biological accident intruding itself into history, as when the death of a history-making person brings a change of direction; changes of mood,

---

*Reprinted, with the author's permission, from "The Durability of Despotism in the Soviet System," a paper presented at a symposium on "Changes in Soviet Society Since Stalin's Death," sponsored by St. Antony's College, Oxford University, in association with the Congress for Cultural Freedom, and held at Oxford in June 1957. Copyright 1957 by Bertram D. Wolfe. The paper was first published in The Russian Review, Vol. 16 (1958), pp. 83–93 and 163–175.

emergence of new situations; sudden leaps that seem to turn an accretion of little events into a big one; the complicated interaction of multiple determinants on the production of every event; the unintended consequences of intended actions.

Still, history is not so open that any event is conjecturally just as likely as any other. As in the flux of things we note continuing structures, as in biology we note heredity as well as variation and mutation, so in history there is an interrelation between continuity and change.

Though all lands go through a history, and all orders and institutions are subject to continuous modification and ultimate transformation, there are some social orders or systems that are more markedly dynamic, more open, more mutable, even self-transforming, while others exhibit marked staying powers, their main outlines continuing to be discernibly the same through the most varied vicissitudes.

Though it may be difficult to determine except in retrospect just when a system may be said to change in ways so fundamental as to signify a transformation of the system, still it is possible and necessary to distinguish between self-conserving and self-transforming systems, between relatively open and relatively closed societies and between changes so clearly of a secondary order that they may be designated *within-system changes*, and those so clearly fundamental that they involve *changes in the system* or basic societal structure. That this distinction may be hard to make in practice, that there may may be gradations and borderline cases and sudden surprises, does not relieve us of this obligation. Merely to reiterate endlessly that all things change, without attempting to make such distinctions, is to stand helpless before history-in-the-making, helpless to evaluate and helpless to react.

If we look at the Roman Empire, let us say from the time of Julius Caesar to the time of Julian the Apostate, or perhaps from Augustus to Romulus Augustulus, through its many vicissitudes and changes, we can nevertheless perceive that for three or four centuries the Roman Empire continued in a meaningful and determinable sense to be the Roman Empire. In similar fashion we can easily select a good half millennium of continuity in the Byzantine Empire. Or if we take one of the most dynamic regions, Western Europe, in one of its more dynamic periods, we can note that monarchical absolutism had a continuity of several centuries. This is the more interesting because monarchical absolutism, though its was one of the more stable and monopolistically exclusive power systems of the modern Western World, was a *multi-centered system* in which the monarch was checked and limited by his need of support from groups, corporations, and interests that were organized separately and independently of the power center; the castled, armed, and propertied nobility; the Church with its spiritual authority; the burghers of the wealthy, fortified towns.

It is the presence of these independent centers of corporate organization that makes Western monarchical absolutism an exception among the centralized, long-lasting power systems. It was these limiting forces, organized independently of the central power, that managed to exact the charters and constitutions, the right to determine size and length of service of armed levies, size and purpose of monetary contributions, thus ultimately transforming the absolute monarchy into the limited, constitutional monarchy of modern times. And it is from our experience in the milieu of this exceptional evolution that we derive many of our unconscious preconceptions as to the inevitability, sweep, and comparative ease of change. To correct our one-sided view it is necessary to compare the characteristics of multi-centered Western absolutism with other more "complete" and "perfected" forms of single-centered power and despotism.[1]

In the *samoderzhavie* of Muscovy we find a more truly single-centered power structure, stronger, more completely centralized, more monopolistic, more despotic, more unyielding in its rigid institutional framework than was the absolutism of Western Europe. The Tsar early

---

[1] This comparison is a central part of Karl A. Wittfogel's *Oriental Despotism: A Comparative Study of Total Power*, Yale, 1957. His attention is centered on the countries in which "the state became stronger than society" because of the need to undertake vast state irrigation and flood control works by corvée organization of the entire population, with the consequent assumption of enormous managerial functions. But his study is full of insights into modern, industry-based totalitarianism highly suggestive for the purposes of our inquiry and the theme of the present paper.

managed to subvert the independent *boyars* and substituted for them a state-service nobility. The crown possessed enormous crown lands and state serfs. Bondage, both to the state and to the state-service nobility, was a state-ordained and state-instituted bondage, adjusted to the purposes of the recruiting sergeant and the tax-gatherer. When in the nineteenth century the Emancipation came, it came as a state-decreed "revolution from above" (Alexander's own words for it), and carried with it state supervision and the decreeing of collective responsibility to the state of the village *mir*.

To this universal state-service and state-bondage, we must add the features of Caesaro-papism, signifying a tsar- and state-dominated church in place of an independent one. In addition there was the administrative-military nature of the Russian towns, which checked the rise of an independent burgher class with independent corporate organization. Industrialization, too, came with state initiative and an enormous preponderance of state ownership and management. From Peter I to Nicholas II there were two centuries of state-ordained and fostered industrialization, with continuing powerful state-owned and state-managed basic industry, mining, metallurgy, munitions, railroad construction and ownership, and some state commercial monopolies, all crowned with a huge and predominant state banking and credit system.

The rudiments of a more multi-centered life were just beginning to develop in this powerful, single-center organized society when World War I caused the managerial state to add to its concerns the total mobilization of men, money, materials, transport, industry, for history's first total war. The "model" country in this new form of State enterprise was wartime Germany. The system of total management by the state for total war has been variously, but not very intelligibly, termed "state capitalism" and "state socialism." In any case, Lenin was quick to welcome this development as the "final transition form." In it, as in the heritage from the Tsarist managerial autocratic state itself, he found much to build on in making his own transition to the new totalitarianism.

From Ivan the Terrible on, for a period of four centuries, "the state had been stronger than society" and had been ruled from a single power center as a military, bureaucratic, managerial state. Amidst the most varied vicissitudes, including a time of troubles, wars, conquests, invasions, peasant insurrections, palace revolutions, and revolutions from above, the powerful framework endured. Weakenings, even power vacuums, were followed by swift "*restoration*" of its basic outlines. When the strains of total war, of a magnitude beyond its inflexible powers to organize, finally caused its collapse, there came a brief interlude of the loosening of the bonds. Then Lenin, even as he revolutionized, likewise "restored" much of the four-century-old heritage. Indeed, it was this "*socialist restoration of autocracy*" which Plekhanov had warned against as early as the 1880's as a danger inherent in, or at least potential to Russia, whenever the longed-for revolution should come. He warned the impatient Populists that unless all the bonds were first loosened and a free "Western" or "bourgeois-democratic" order were allowed to develop and mature, the seizure of power by would-be socialists could only lead to a "restoration" of Oriental, autocratic depotism on a pseudo-socialist foundation with a pseudo-socialist "ruling caste." Things would be even worse, he warned Lenin in 1907, if this new "Inca ruling caste of Sons of the Sun" should make the fatal mistake of nationalizing the land, thus tightening more than ever the bonds that bound the peasant to the autocratic state.

The term *Oriental despotism,* applied to Russia in the course of this controversy among Russian socialists, reminds us that there are yet more durable social formations with yet greater built-in staying powers than those we have so far noted. These reckon their continuity not in centuries alone but even in millennia.

As a Chinese historian once observed to me: "Your Renaissance was a fascinating period. We had seven of them." If we substitute Restoration for Renaissance, both in the sense of restoration of vigor and restoration of basic structure, he was right.

For though China knew changes, suffered upheavals, invasions, conquests, falls of dynasties, rebellions, interregna, and times of troubles, a Chinese villager or a Chinese official of the nineteenth century, if transported to the China of two thousand or more years ago, would have found himself at home in a familiar institutional and ideological environment.

With the exception of Western monarchical absolutism, what all these enduring social structures had in common was a single power center, a managerial state, a lack of independent social orders and forms of property, an absence of checks on the flow of power to the center and the top, a powerful, self-perpetuating institutional framework.

It is the view of this paper that modern totalitarianism is one of these comparatively closed and conservative societies with a powerful and self-perpetuating institutional framework, calculated to assimilate the changes which it intends and those which are forced upon it, in such fashion that — barring explosion from within or battering down from without — the changes tend to be either inhibited or shaped and assimilated as within-system changes in a persistent system with built-in staying powers.

At first glance the word conservative may seem out of place in speaking of a society that is organized revolution. And indeed there is a striking difference between Communist totalitarianism and all previous systems of absolute, despotic, undivided (and in that sense, total) power. For whereas despotism, autocracy, and absolutism were bent on preserving the *status quo,* Communist totalitarianism is dedicated to "the future." This powerful institutional structure which tolerates no rival centers of organization has a vested interest in keeping things in flux. It maintains the omnipotence of its state and ideology by carrying on, within and by means of its power system, a permanent revolution. Like Alexander's, it is a revolution from above. Indeed, much more truly that Alexander's and much more sweepingly and exclusively is it a revolution from above. Its aim is nothing less than to keep society atomized and to create, as rapidly and as completely as the recalcitrant human material and the refractory surrounding world will permit, a new man, a new society, and a new world.

Like the earlier systems referred to, and much more than they, it possesses a state that is stronger than society. Like them it represents a system of total, in the sense of undivided, power. Like them it lacks any organized and institutionalized checks on the flow of power to the top. Like them it possesses a state-centered, state dominated, state-managed, and for the first time, a completely state-owned economy.

If the other societies are distinguished by the high specific gravity of state ownership, state control, and state managerial function within the total activity of the society in question, under Communist totalitarianism, state ownership and state managerialism aspire to be total in a new sense. In the other cases, we have been contemplating total power in the sense of undivided power: power without significant rival centers of independent organization. But now we must add to the concept of *undivided power*, the concept of *all-embracing power*.

No longer does the state limit itself to being "stronger than society." It now strives to be *coextensive* with society. Whereas the earlier power systems recognize certain limitations in their capacity to run everything, leaving room, for example, for pocket-handkerchief-sized farms and the self-feeding of the corvée population, for private arts and crafts unconnected with the managerial concerns of the state, for certain types of private trade, and even finding room for village communal democracy under the watchful eye of the state overseer (what Wittfogel has aptly called "beggars democracy") — the new totalitarianism strives completely to fragment and atomize society, to co-ordinate the system of dispersed villages completely into its centralized power system, to eliminate even the small private parcel of the *kolkhoznik*, already reduced from a "pocket handkerchief" to a mere swatch.

For the first time a total-power system in the earlier sense of undivided and unchallenged power aspires to be totalist or *totalitarian* in the further sense of all-embracing power as well, and to convert the state-stronger-than-society into the state-coextensive-with-society.

We cannot deduce much from a comparison with other modern totalitarianisms. For historical and physical reasons Italian Fascism was more totalist in aspiration than in realization. And, though Nazism and Stalinist Communism suggestively moved towards each other, Nazism did not last long enough to complete its evolution. But it did live long enough to dispose of certain illusions concerning the supposed incompatibility of totalitarianism with certain aspects of modern life.

Thus it is widely held that the monopoly of total power and the attempt to embrace the totality of social life and activity are incompatible with modern industry and advanced technology. But Germany adopted totalitarianism when it was the foremost country of Europe in industry and technology. This should also dispose of the idea that totalitarianism is the appropriate form for industrializing.

Indeed, it is precisely modern technology, with its all-embracing means of communication, its high speed transmission of commands and reports and armed force to and from any point in a country, its mass communication and mass conditioning techniques and the like, which for the first time makes it possible for total (undivided) power to aspire to be totalist (all-embracing) power. That is what Herzen foreboded when he wrote: "Some day Jinghis Khan will return with the telegraph." If total power tends to arise wherever the state is stronger than society, totalitarian power can rule over a great area and in great depth only where the state is both stronger than society and in possession of all the resources of modern technology.

Closely akin to the illusion of the incompatibility of totalitarianism with modern technology is the view that totalitarianism is "in the long run" (a run not generally conceived of as very long despite the slow geologic time implied in the popular metaphor of "erosion") incompatible with universal literacy, with advanced technological training, and with widespread "higher" or secondary school education. Once more it is Germany that serves to remind us that one of the most highly literate and technologically trained peoples in the history of man adopted Nazism when that people was both universally literate and possessed a high proportion of scientists, scholars, and persons with secondary school training.

Whereas in pre-literate societies it took long periods of conflict followed by ages of the development of tradition to indoctrinate a people into customary acceptance of centralized total power and customary acceptance of their lot as obedient servitors of a managerial-priestly bureaucracy, Nazi ideology spread like wildfire among a people who already knew how to read. For modern totalitarianism requires that everybody be able to read so that all can be made to read the same thing at the same moment. Not the mere ability to read, but the possibility of choosing between alternative types of reading, is a potential — and only a potential — liberating influence.

When Stalin died in 1953, Bolshevism was fifty years old. Its distinctive views on the significance of organization, of centralization, and of the guardianship or dictatorship of a vanguard or elite, date from Lenin's programmatic writings of 1902 (*Where to Begin; What Is to Be Done?*). His separate machine and his authoritarian control of it dates from the split of 1903.

During these fifty years Bolshevism had had only two authoritative leaders, each of whom in turn set the stamp of his personality upon it. Lenin, as we have suggested, inherited much from Tsarist autocracy, yet, his totalitarianism is different in principle from the old Muscovite despotism. He regarded himself as a devout, orthodox Marxist, building upon and enlarging some aspects of Marx's conceptions while ignoring, altering, or misrepresenting others. His Marxism was so different from Marx's that a not unfriendly commentator, Charles Rappoport, called it *Marxisme à la Tartare*. Stalin's Leninism, in turn, differed enough from Lenin's that we might term it *Marxisme à la mode Caucasienne*. Yet there is discernibly more continuity between Stalin and Lenin than between Lenin and Marx. The changes Stalin introduced involved the continuation and enlargement of certain elements in Lenin's methods and conceptions, along with the alteration of others. He inherited and used, now in Leninist, now in his own "Stalinist" fashion, a powerful institutional framework involving a party machine, a state machine, a doctrine of infallibility, an ideology, and the determination to extend the totalization of power to transform the Russian into the "New Communist Man," and win the world for Communism.

With Stalin's death, once more there are new leaders or a new leader. It is impossible to believe that this new personal imprint will not make alterations in Stalinism as Stalin did in Leninism. But it seems to me useful, after four years of unsystematic talk about changes, that we should remind ourselves at the outset, that the "new men" are not so new, that they have inherited a going concern with a powerful institutional framework, a dynamics and a momentum already powerful and powerfully established, and that actually we are examining changes in — or rather I think we should say *within* — a single-centered, closed, highly centralized society run by a power that is both total in the sense of undivided and totalist in its aspirations. Such societies, as I have indicated, have tended to exhibit built-in staying powers and a perdurability despite changes like the death of a despot, an oligarchial interregnum, or a struggle for succession.

As for these "new men," they are, of course, Stalin's men. They would not now have any claim to power over a great nation were it not that they managed to be the surviving close lieutenants at the moment of Stalin's death.

It is my impression that they are smallish men. There is a principle of selection in personal despotisms which surrounds the despot with courtiers, sycophants, executants, yes-men, and rules out original and challenging minds. This almost guarantees a crisis of succession where there is no system of legitimacy, until a new dictator emerges. Moreover, the heirs are no longer young (Khrushchev is 64), so that a fresh crisis of succession may well supervene before the present muted and restricted crisis is over.

I would not consider these "smallish men" too small, however, for when you have a sixth of the earth, 200,000,000 population, a total state economy, and a great empire to practice on, you learn other trades besides that of courtier or faction lieutenant. Even so, not one of them at present exhibits the originality and the high charge of energy and intellect that characterized Lenin. Nor the grosser but no less original demonic force of Stalin.

Whenever a despot dies, there is a universal expectation of change. The new men have had to take account of it, and have taken advantage of it to introduce changes which the old tyrant made seem desirable even to his lieutenants: to rationalize elements of a system which has no organized, independent force to change it from below, and to make limited concessions while they are consolidating their power. But the institutional framework they have inherited is one they intend to maintain. It is a solid and durable political system dominating a society that has been totally fragmented or atomized, and the state, or rather the party which is its core, is the controlling core of all extant organizations.[2]

Some of the parts of this power machine are now more than a half-century old, others date from 1917, others from the consolidation of the Stalinist regime in industry, agriculture, politics, and culture in the thirties. But even these last

---

[2] This does not apply to the Empire but only to the Soviet Union. In general in this article I have omitted any consideration of the Empire.

have been established for more than two decades.

In short, what the epigoni have inherited is no small heritage: an atomized society; a centralized, monolithic, monopolistic party; a single-party state; a regime of absolute force supplemented by persuasion or by continuous psychological warfare upon its people; a managerial bureaucracy accustomed to take orders and execute them (with a little elbowroom for regularized evasion); a centrally managed, totally state-owned and state-regulated economy including farms, factories, banks, transport and communications, and all trade, domestic and foreign; an established dogmatic priority for the branches of industry which underlie the power of the state; a bare subsistence economy for the bulk of the producers; a completely statized and "collectivized" agriculture which, though it has never solved the problem of productivity, continues to reach out after greater gigantism and statification and threatens to reduce even the small parcel to a mere "garden adornment"; a powerful, if one-sided, forced-tempo industry, centralized even beyond the point of rationality from the standpoint of totalitarianism itself; the techniques and momentums of a succession of Five-Year Plans of which the present is the Sixth; a completely managed and controlled culture (except for the most secret recesses of the spirit which even modern technology cannot reach); a monopoly of all the means of expression and communication; a state-owned system of "criticism"; an infallible doctrine stemming from infallible authorities, interpreted and applied by an infallible party led by an infallible leader or clique of infallible leaders, in any case by an infallible "summit"; a method of advance by zigzags toward basically unchanging goals; a system of promotion, demotion, correction of error, modification of strategy and tactics, and elimination of differences, by fiat from the summit, implemented by purges of varying scope and intensity; a commitment to continuing revolution from above until the Soviet subject has been remade according to the blueprint of the men in the Kremlin, and until Communism has won the world.

It is in this heritage that these men were formed. In this they believe. It is the weight and power and internal dynamics of this heritage that in part inhibits, in part shapes such changes as these men undertake, and enters as a powerful shaping force into the changes which they make involuntarily.

II

It would require a separate study to attempt an inquiry into what is fundamental to totalitarianism so that a change in it would represent a "change in the system," and what is of a more superficial order so that a change in it may readily be recognized as a "within-system" change. Here we shall have to limit ourselves to a glance at a few post-Stalin political developments for purposes of exemplification. The first change that obtrudes itself is "Collective Leadership."

The Party statutes do not provide for an authoritative leader, a dictator or a *vozhd*. Just as this the most centralized great power still professes to be federal, a mere union of autonomous republics, so the party statutes have always proclaimed party democracy and collective leadership.

It was not hard to predict that Stalin's orphaned heirs would proclaim a "collective leadership" at the moment of his death, even as they began the maneuvers for the emergence of a still narrower ruling group (triumvirate, duumvirate) and a muted struggle for the succession. Stalin, too, found it necessary to proclaim a "collective leadership" and pose as its faithful wheel horse for more than half a decade, and he took a full decade before he killed the first of his "rivals."

Stalin's heirs had the same reasons as he for proclaiming the "collective leadership" of the Presidium and some additional ones. The harrowing and demoralizing experiences of the thirties, the signs of the beginnings of a new mass purge just a few months before Stalin died, the state of terror in which even his closest collaborators lived, and the justified fear of each of the others, all combined to make necessary the proclamation of a "collective leadership."

To be sure, there is nothing inherently incompatible with total (undivided) nor with totalitarian (all-embracing) power, in the rule of an oligarchy, or in a shorter or longer interregnum between despots or dictators. What is harder to understand is the seriousness with which experts discussed and are still discussing "collective leadership" as if it were a permanently institutionalized feature, or even the beginning of the dispersal of power. What is noteworthy in the case of this "collective" is the swiftness with which the first triumvirate — Malenkov, Molotov, Beria — were demoted and disgraced. It took Stalin ten years to shed the blood of potential rivals; Beria disappeared in a few months. In less than two years, the skeptical were obliged to recognize that Khrushchev was "more equal than the others," was demonstrating in a score of fields that "power is knowledge" and making all the important programmatic declarations with his hand on the lever of the party machine.[3]

The important point to remember is that triumvirates, duumvirates, directories, are notoriously transitional in the succession to a despot where there is no legitimacy to provide a successor, and where there are no *socially organized* checks, below and outside the central power, to restrain the flow of power to the top.

The whole dynamics of dictatorship calls for a personal dictator; authoritarianism for an authority; infallible doctrine for an infallible applier and interpreter; totally militarized life for a supreme commander; centralized, undivided, all-embracing, and "messianic" power for a "charismatic" symbol and tenant of authority.

As long as "collective leadership" does not swiftly and determinedly broaden itself instead of narrowing; as long as it does not openly recognize itself as "pre-legitimate" in the sense of aiming to replace itself by a broader, non-dictatorial organization of power; as long as power does not flood down into the basic units of the party (where it did not inhere even in Lenin's day), and then overflow the party dikes and spill out into self-organizing corporate bodies independent of the state and party, thus restoring some initiative to society as against party and state; as long as there do not develop rival organized or corporate bodies, freely functioning factions and ultimately parties; as long, in other words, as there develop no organized checks upon the reflux of power to the top, not merely a slowing but actually a reversing of the whole trend of totalitarianism —

[3] This was presented at Oxford *before* Khrushchev ousted Malenkov, Molotov, Kaganovich, Zhukov, and Bulganin. Yet as this is published there are still experts who talk solemnly of "collective leadership" because Khrushchev, like Stalin and Lenin, finds it desirable to have his underlings ratify and approve his pronouncements.

there is reason to regard any "directory" or "collective leadership" as a mere interregnum between dictators.

Both purge and terror were instituted by Lenin and "perfected" and "over-perfected" by Stalin. Leaving on one side the purely personal element (paranoia and relish for vengeance), both purge in the party and terror in society as a whole serve many of the "rational" purposes of the totalitarian regime: the establishment of the infallibility of the party, its summit, and its doctrine; the maintenance of the party in a "state of grace" (zeal, doctrinal purity, fanatical devotion, discipline, subordination, total mobilization); the atomization of society as a whole; the breaking up of all non-state conformations and centers of solidarity; the turnover in the elite, demotion of deadwood and promotion of new forces; the supplying of scapegoats for every error and dramatization of every needed change of line; the maintenance of the priority of heavy industry, of forced savings for capital investment, of unquestioned command and relative efficiency in production, of "collectivization" in agriculture, of control in culture, and a number of similar objectives of the totalist state.

All of these institutions have been so well established that to a large extent they are now taken for granted and have become to that extent "second nature." Stalin himself promised in 1939 that there would never again be a mass purge. Except in the Army and among Jewish writers, the purge became physically more moderate, until, with increasing signs of paranoia, Stalin gave every sign of opening another era of mass purge a few months before his death. The first thing the heirs did around the corpse was to call off this purge, both because it had no "rational" purpose and because it had threatened to involve most of them.

But it would be a mistake to believe that the "moderate" purge has been dispensed with or is dispensable. In the preparation of the Twentieth Congress the Heirs showed how well they had mastered the "Leninist norms" which had prepared every congress since the Tenth by a prior purge of the organization. All the regional Secretaries and leading committees were "renewed," 37 per cent of those who attended the Nineteenth Congress disappeared from public view, 44 per cent of the Central Committee failed to be elected as delegates or to be reelected to the new Committee. All we can say is that the purge today resembles those of Stalin's "benign" periods or of Lenin's day. Yet the liquidation of Beria and at least twenty-five of his friends shows that the techniques of the bloodpurge have not been forgotten, only held in reserve in case of need. That the party ranks breathe easier and are glad of the self-denying ordinance of the leaders in their struggle for position we do not doubt. But there is no evidence that the party ranks ordered this change or could do so, or would venture to try.

The terror in society as a whole has also diminished. No longer are there such bloody tasks as forced collectivization to carry through. Habitual obedience, the amnesties and concessions of an interregnum, the shortage of manpower for industry, agriculture, and the army due to continued expansion and the deficit of wartime births that should now have been reaching the labor age — these and many other things account for the fact that artists and writers, workmen and peasants and managers do not at this moment feel that public reproof (which they are quick to hearken to) must necessarily be followed by arrest and concentration camp. With manpower shortages the concentration camp is the most wasteful and least productive way of using up a man. The camps are gentler now, yet the camps are there. Their size is shrinking, but no one dares to propose their abolition or take notice of them.

The police has been downgraded and, in a regime so in need of naked force, the army has been upgraded, i.e., given more internal political functions. The public prosecutors have been given more control of trials and pre-trial inquisitions — like making the fox the guardian of the chicken coop. There are some other minor law reforms. Above all there has been much fuss about a promise of a codification and regularization of the laws.

This new code was begun in Stalin's last months. It was promised "within sixty days" by Lavrentii Beria when his star seemed in the ascendent. It has not yet been issued, four years after Stalin's and almost four years after Beria's death. Sight unseen, we can predict that the new code will not touch the foundations of the totalist state, i.e., not alter the subservience of courts and laws and prosecutors and judges and police to the will and purposes of the oligarchy or the single leader. It is necessary to remember that any total power, and *a fortiori*, any totalist power, may obey its own

laws whenever it suits it to do so without giving those laws power over it or making them into limits upon its powers. A power center that is both legislator and administrator and judge and enforcer and even self-pronounced infallible "critic" of its own acts, may declare any activity a crime which it pleases. In the Soviet Union even loyalty to the underlying principles on which the state itself was founded has been declared a degrading crime and punished with incredible cruelty. How easily this totalist state may set aside its laws and negate its most solemn and "binding" promises is evidenced anew — after the repeated proclamation of "socialist legality" — by the sudden repudiation by the "workers' state" of the state debt to the workers themselves, without so much as the possibility of a murmur. The owners of the repudiated bonds and investors of their now wiped out compulsory savings were even obliged to hold meetings and pass resolutions in which they expressed their delight at being expropriated.

The longer such a regime endures the more it has need of regularization of the duties and expectations of its subjects, even as it keeps undiminished its powers of sudden reversal and unpredictable and unlimited intervention. The only guarantee against a totally powerful state is the existence of non-state organizations capable of effective control of or effective, organized pressure on the governmental power. Otherwise, to attempt to check, or limit, or even question, is to invite the fury of exemplary punishment for the purposes of preserving atomization.

"Betwixt subject and subject," Locke wrote of Despotism, "they will grant, there must be measures, laws and judgments for their mutual peace and security. But as for the ruler, he ought to be absolute, and is above all such circumstances; because he has the power to do more hurt and wrong, it is right when he does it. To ask how you may be guarded from harm or injury on that side . . . is the voice of faction and rebellion . . . The very question can scarcely be borne. They are ready to tell you it deserves death only to ask after safety. . . ."[4]

It is well for us to remember that the most despotic rulers have on occasion handed down elaborate law codes. The famous and in many

---

[4] *Second Treatise on Government,* Chapter VII, 593.

ways justly admired Roman Code was compiled and proclaimed only after the emperor himself had become a god, no longer subject to question or limitation, only to worship. Though laws must multiply and be regularized so that the subjects may know what is expected of them, and even what they can count on in their relations with each other where the central power is unaffected, the lack of independent courts, of independent power groups or corporate bodies, of an independent press and public opinion deprives these laws of any binding force upon the rulers. In Communist totalitarianism, the place of imperial divinity is taken by the infallibility of doctrine, the dogmatic untouchability of the dictatorship, the infallibility of the masters of the infallible doctrine, and by such spiritual demiurges as "revolutionary consciousness," "historical necessity," and "the interests of the revolution and of the people." Those who *know* where History is going, surely have the right and duty to see to it that she goes there.

"The scientific concept, dictatorship," Lenin reminds us with beautiful simplicity, "means neither more nor less than unlimited power, resting directly on force, not limited by anything, not restricted by any laws or any absolute rules. Nothing else but that."[5]

And to Commissar of Justice Kursky, when he was elaborating the first law code, Lenin wrote:

[My] draft is rough . . . but the basic thought, I hope, is clear: openly to set forth the proposition straightforward in principle and politically (and not merely in the narrow-juridical sense), which motivates the *essence* and *justification* of terror, its necessity, its limits.

The court should not eliminate the terror: to promise that would be either self-deception or (simple) deception, but should give it a foundation and a legalization in principle, clearly, without falsification and without embellishment. It is necessary to formulate it as widely as possible, for only a revolutionary consciousness of justice and a revolutionary conscience will put conditions upon its application in practice, on a more or less wide scale. (Emphasis in the original)[6]

In these regards the new men do not have to

"return to Leninist norms," for they have never been abandoned for a moment.

If we can hope for, perhaps count on, the diminution of the apocalyptic element in the ideology of a going and long-lasting society, we must remind ourselves that Leninism was peculiar in that its central "ideas" were always ideas about organization.

Bolshevism was born in an organization feud: what the statutes should say about the definition of a party member, and who should control the majority on a paper (*Iskra*), which should act both as guardian of the doctrine, and core of organization of the party. "Give me an organization," Lenin wrote at the outset of his career as a Leninist, "and I will turn Russia upside down." The organization he wanted, he explained, must be one in which "bureaucratism" prevailed against "democratism," "centralism" against "autonomy," which "strives to go from the top downward, and defends the enlargement of the rights and plenary powers of the central body against the parts." When at the 1903 Congress, an exalter of the Central Committee urged that it should become the "omnipresent and one," the all-pervasive, all-informing, and all-uniting "spirit," Lenin cried out from his seat: *"Ne dukh, a kulak!"* ("Not spirit, but fist!") The idea of the rule of the elite, the idea of a vanguard party, the idea of the repulsiveness of all other classes, and the untrustworthiness of the working class, the idea that the working class also required a dictator or overseer to compel it to its mission — these "ideas" about organization form the very core of Leninism as a special ideology. Far from "eroding" or growing "weak" and merely "decorative," it is just precisely these structural ideas that have grown and expanded, become implemented and systematized.

It is these concepts of organizational structure and the dictatorship of an infallible elite which set their limits on the possibility of *organized* public opinion. Resentments, pressures, discontent, longing for a less oppressive regime and an easier lot, exist under despotisms, autocracies, total-power states, and totalist states, even as in other social orders. Indeed, whenever hope or expectation stirs they are apt to become endemic and intense. The problem of "statecraft" in a despotism is that of preventing the discontent and longing from assuming *independent* and *organized* form. Since the totalist state penetrates all social organiza-

[5] *Collected Works,* 4th Edition, Vol. 31, p. 326.
[6] *Collected Works,* Vol. 33, pp. 321–2.

tions as their leading core and uses them as transmission belts (framing up and destroying whatever organization it cannot coordinate into its structure), it is particularly adapted to keeping discontent thus fragmented and unorganized. The earlier despotisms spied on their people not merely to weed out trouble-makers, but often to find out what changes it should introduce to lessen such discontents, where the changes did not affect its fundamental powers and aims. Here, too, the totalist state is better adapted by virtue of its universal police and espionage penetration than was the primitive "espionage" of an incognito Haroun al-Raschid or Peter the Great.

By 1936, Lenin's central idea of an elite, single-centered dictatorship had gotten into the "most democratic Constitution in the world" as Article 126 which proclaimed the party to be "the vanguard of the working people and the leading core of all organizations both social and state." And in the summer of 1956, when Khrushchev and Co. were summing up the Stalin discussion, they declared in *Pravda*:

"As for our country, the Communist Party has been and will be the *only master* of the *minds*, the *thoughts*, the *only spokesman, leader and organizer* of the people." (Emphasis added).

It is foolhardy to believe that they did not mean it, self-deluding to convince ourselves that the forces pressing for concessions within the country are likely to find the road open to separate and effective corporate organization, which is the condition precedent to the development of a limited, multi-centered state and society.

Even before Stalin died, we got evidence that the spirit of man is wayward and not as easily subjected as his body — the mass desertions at the war's end; the escape of millions who "voted with their feet" against totalitarianism; the two out of three "Chinese Volunteers" in the Korean prison camps who, for the first time after any war, preferred exile under precarious and shameful "displaced person" conditions to return to their native scenes and homes.

Since Stalin's death there have been East Berlin and Pilsen, Poznan and Vorkuta, Warsaw and Budapest, to prove that men will sometimes stand up unarmed to tanks and cannon and machine guns. They have proved too that the armies of the conquered lands have never been the pliant instruments of the Kremlin that faint-hearted men thought they were.

We have seen that forty years of *Gleichschaltung*, corruption, and terror have not rooted out of the artist the ineradicable notion that sincerity to his creative vision is more to be desired than *partiinost* and *ideinost*. We have seen that the youth, though the faint-hearted thought they would be turned off the conveyer-belt as "little monsters," are still born young, and therefore plastic, receptive, doubting, capable of illusion and disillusion, capable of "youthful idealism" and youthful questioning of the elders and of the established, and of youthful rebellion. Now the expulsions among the university youth are for the first time providing a pariah elite as a possible leadership to future undergrounds that may form under even this most terribly efficient atomizer of society.

Both Zamiatin in *We* and Orwell in *1984* with appropriate symbolism made the love of a man and a woman the crime of treason against the totalist state, because love represents a solidarity outside the purview and control of the state, an antidote to total atomization. Even Ivan Petrovich Pavlov, he of the "Conditioned Reflexes" by which those who believe man to be infinitely manipulable chart their course, found among the primary reflexes in the inborn nature of men and animals: "the reflex of freedom."[7]

I would not have it thought, in presenting these remarks on the power and durability of the institutional framework of despotism in general and the totalist state in particular, that I do not take account of the "freedom reflex" and of the fact that the nature of man, too, is tough and durable, so that when the screws are relaxed ever so little, it tends to spring back towards a more human shape.

Nor do I underestimate the power of illusion. Because of the ideology which they inherited, and because of the very nature of man and their contest to win man's allegiance on a world scale, the men in the Kremlin are compelled to engage in semantic subterfuge. While this is actually one of their devices for dominion over and atomization of those over whom they

---

7 "The Reflex of Freedom" is the title of Chapter 28 in Ivan Petrovich Pavlov's *Lectures on Conditioned Reflexes*, New York, 1928, pp. 282–6.

rule, it bears within it the possibility of vast and fateful misunderstandings. If in general it is dangerous to relax the screws ever so slightly or to measure out homeopathic doses of freedom, there is an additional specific danger that big announcements and big promises may seem to mean more than they intend. Illusion, to paraphrase Marx, once it takes possession of great masses of men, becomes itself a material force.

Nor, finally, have I ever for a moment ceased to cast about for grounds of hope: that weaker heirs might make less efficient use of the terrible engines of total power; that a struggle, or succession of struggles for the succession, might compel a contender to go outside the inner circles and summon social forces in the lower ranks of the party or outside of it into some sort of independent existence; that the army, disgraced as no other in all history by the charge that it gave birth to traitors by the thousands in its general staff, might develop the independence from the party sufficient to make it a rival power center or an organized pressure body; that intellectuals, that technicians, that students, might somehow break through the barriers that hinder the conversion of discontent into an organized, independent force.

If then, this analysis puts the emphasis on the nature of the institutional framework and its built-in staying powers, it is by way of bending the stick in the direction I thought it had to be bent in order to straighten it out. For, or so it has seemed to me, the Western World has found it hard to gaze straight and steadily at the head of Medusa, even if only in the reflecting shield of theoretical analysis. Brought up in a world of flux and openness, we find it hard to believe in the durability of despotic systems. Our hopes and longings are apt to betray us again and again into readiness to be deceived or to deceive ourselves. And the "journalistic" nature of our culture has made us too ready to inflate the new, because that alone is "news," while we neglect to put it into its tiresomely "repetitious" historical and institutional setting.

From the NEP to Socialism in One Country; from the Popular Front and Collective Security to the Grand Alliance and One World; from "Peaceful Coexistence" to the "Geneva Spirit" — the occupational hazard of the Western intellectual has been not to read too little but to read too much into planned changes, involuntary changes, and even into mere tactical maneuvers and verbal asseverations.

Each has been hailed in turn as the softening of the war of the totalist state on its own people and the war upon the world; as the long awaited "inevitable change" or "fundamental transformation," "the sobering that comes from the responsibilities of power"; "the response to the pressure of the recognition of reality"; "the transition from terrorist to normal modes of societal regimentation"; the growing modification of totalist power by "a rationalist technocracy"; the sobering effect of privilege upon "a new privileged class"; the "rise of a limited and traditionalist despotism"; a "feeling of responsibility to Russia as against World Revolution"; the "quiet digestion period of a sated beast of prey" no longer on the prowl; the "diffusion of authority which could lead to a constitutional despotism"; the "mellowing process that sooner or later overtakes all militant movements"; the second thoughts on the struggle for the world which have come at long last "from the recognition of the universal and mutual destructiveness of nuclear war"; the "preordained downward curve in the parabola of revolution"; the "inevitable work of erosion upon the totalitarian edifice." (Each of these expressions is quoted from some highly respected authority on Soviet affairs in the Anglo-Saxon world.)

Because of the nature of our mental climate and our longings, because, too, of the injection of "revolutionary methods" into diplomacy in a polarized and antagonistic world, we are not nearly so likely to overlook change and to test perhaps without sufficient scepticism the meaning of each verbal declaration. No, "the main danger," as the Communists would say, has not lain in insensitivity to hope, but in too-ready self-deception.

When Hitler's attack on Russia threw Stalin into our camp during World War II, I wrote an article, entitled "Stalin at the Peace Table," which contended that there would be no peace table or general settlement as after other wars, and that the peace would be settled piecemeal by the strategic acts of the war, so that, if the war were not planned accordingly, there would be no decent peace. The illusions of the Grand Alliance were such that this view could not get a hearing.

This is not surprising in the case of a

"Cassandra" who is merely a free-lance writer on totalitarianism and Soviet affairs. But Winston Churchill, participating in the directing councils of the Grand Alliance, tried in vain to get an agreement on a strategy for the joint occupation and liberation of the Balkans and Eastern Europe, and even he could not prevail against the overpowering Grand Alliance illusions of both Anglo-Saxon lands. As a result, where the Soviet Army was in sole occupation, there are conquered countries. Where there was joint occupation, there is a divided Germany and a divided Korea. Where the Soviet Army was not admitted, there is a Japan free to criticize its occupier and determine its own destiny. Thus an awareness of the nature of Soviet totalitarianism and its aims would have made a difference in the freedom of hundreds of millions of human beings.

The case is, to be sure, exceptional in that the War created an exceptionally fluid world. But what we are trying to understand and estimate is at no time a mere exercise in sociological abstraction or historical generalization. For literally every judgment in the estimation of the nature of totalitarianism and the scope of the changes in it is fraught with fateful significance for the fate of millions of men.

72

The Economic Challenge to the American Way of Life*

Harry Schwartz

(1959)

The Soviet leaders like to see the essence of the world situation today as a struggle between socialism and capitalism. We prefer to see it more as a struggle between democracy and totalitarianism, for we see our economy as a mixed and flexible one, and feel that the Soviet brand is one of the less happy varieties of socialism. In any case, however the issue be posed, the Soviet way of life and conduct of world affairs constitute a challenge to us, and one realistic way of taking its measure is in terms of economic productivity. Dr. Harry Schwartz, of The New York Times, tells us what we can expect of the Soviets in the future by way of economic policy and production.

The Subcommittee on Economic Statistics of the Joint Economic Committee of Congress has performed a major public service by its initiative in focusing public attention on Soviet-American economic comparisons. The two volumes of materials on this issue already released are the richest systematic treasure trove of information on this subject which have become recently available in the public domain.[1]

I am appreciative both of the honor and of the responsibility involved in being invited to comment on these materials. In offering the comments below, however, I am giving only my own opinions and do not speak for *The New York Times*, my employer.

A General Statement

The picture presented by the bulk of materials prepared for the subcommittee may be summarized somewhat as follows: Soviet production is still well below that of the United States, but is increasing far more rapidly and — what should not be forgotten — far more steadily than is that of the United States. Moreover the increasing Soviet output consists to a much larger degree of goods which serve to further the national power of the Soviet Union than does the product and services mix of the U.S. economy. As a result the standard of living of the American people is far higher than that of the Soviet people, but the efficiency of Soviet utilization of resources for power purposes is far greater than our own. Any long continuation of these trends must pose the most serious questions about the future of our society and our way of life.

George F. Kennan, former U.S. Ambassador to the Soviet Union, has recently stated the

*Reprinted from "Reflections on the Economic Race," *Comparisons of the United States and Soviet Economies*, Part III (1959), pp. 609–616, paper submitted to the Subcommittee on Economic Statistics of the Joint Economic Committee, Eighty-sixth Congress, First Session, Washington, D.C., by permission of the author.

[1] *Comparisons of the United States and Soviet Economies* [see footnote above], Parts I and II. These volumes will be referred to below simply as Part I or Part II as appropriate.

issue in words which seem to me to deserve the most serious consideration:

> If you ask me — as a historian, let us say — whether a country in the state this country is in today: with no highly developed sense of national purpose, with the overwhelming accent of life on personal comfort and amusement, with a dearth of public services and a surfeit of privately sold gadgetry, with a chaotic transportation system, with its great urban areas being gradually disintegrated by the head-long switch to motor transportation, with an educational system where quality has been extensively sacrificed to quantity, fanned with insufficient social discipline even to keep its major industries functioning without grievous interruptions — if you ask me whether such a country has over the long run good chances of competing with a purposeful, serious, and disciplined society such as that of the Soviet Union, I must say that the answer is "No."[2]

Behind Mr. Kennan's anxiety, which I share, is, I believe, this unpleasant fact. The Soviet Union, with a gross national product less than half of ours, is today effectively our military equal and our superior in the most exciting contemporary adventure of the human race: the exploration of space. If Soviet world power and prestige have risen so high on such a relatively small economic base compared to ours, one can only look forward with foreboding to the situation which will develop as Soviet production increases and the economic gap between us and the Soviet Union diminishes, as diminish it will. Moreover in this world where abysmal poverty is still the lot of most of the world's people, the example of superior Soviet speed in raising production is exercising and, if continued, will exercise the greatest attraction upon the masses and leaders of South America, Asia, and Africa where most of the world's people and most of the world's poverty are concentrated.

We know that the rulers of the Soviet Union are dedicated to maximally rapid increase of the production base for their power position. Against the record of their disturbing achievements since 1945 we must expect they will continue to progress relatively rapidly in the years ahead. If we are to remain an effective bulwark for democracy, we must improve our own performance in terms of speed and amount of economic advance. We must also improve the allocation of our resources so as to get a mix of products and services more nearly corresponding to our national needs in this competition for survival.

Recent and Future Soviet Industrial Growth

The key to the policy problems facing us lies in the speed of the future growth of Soviet heavy industry. On the basis of the evidence already presented to this committee, I think we may assume that other fields of the Soviet economy — agriculture, standard of living, transportation, etc. — will continue to improve at rates which will probably be adequate to keep the Soviet people quiescent, even if still far from fully satisfied, and the Soviet economy operating. Premier Khrushchev's recent speeches in Siberia made clear his knowledge of the desire of the Soviet people for lower prices, more and better goods, and the like. But the concessions already given — for example, the increased durable consumer goods production goals for 1961 — and those he could make if pressed seem adequate to prevent serious political trouble. But the emphasis on heavy industry continues and will continue.

It seems useful at this point to introduce into the record the latest data on recent growth of Soviet key heavy industrial raw materials production, and the plans for their increased output next year (see Table 1).

This is not an unimpressive performance, especially when we bear in mind that our recent evidence regarding the principles governing Soviet industrial planning suggests that the 1960 goals shown above have been estimated realistically and will probably be attained or very closely approached. As I have pointed out elsewhere in detail,[3] the published 1960 goals for Soviet industry are — with the exception of oil and gas — below the original goals of the sixth Five-Year Plan for that year. Those original goals, the data suggest, may be reached in 1961 or 1962 at the latest. But even though the sixth Five-Year Plan had to be abandoned, the production increase that now appears likely for the 1956–60 period can in no way encourage complacency on our part.

One value of the data above, I believe, is

---

[2] Quotation is taken from the text of Mr. Kennan's speech last October 22.

[3] *The New York Times,* November 2, 1959.

TABLE 1 *Soviet Production of Key Commodities: 1955, 1959, and 1960 Plan*

COMMODITY	UNIT	1955	1959	1960 GOAL	1960 GOAL AS PER CENT OF 1955
Pig iron	Million metric tons	33.3	43.0	47.0	142
Steel.	Million metric tons	45.3	60.3	65.0	143
Coal	Million metric tons	391.3	507.0	516.0	132
Oil	Million metric tons	70.8	129.2	144.0	203
Natural gas	Billion cubic meters	10.4	35.0	53.0	510
Electricity	Billion kilowatt-hours	170.2	262.8	291.0	171
Cement.	Million metric tons	22.5	38.5	45.5	202

Sources: 1955 — Narodnoye Khozyaistvo SSSR v 1958 Godu, pp. 158–165. 1959 — Steel, oil, and electricity figures from A. I. Mikoyan's speech in Izvestia, October 24, 1959; remaining figures estimated on basis of 9-month production figures in Pravda, October 15, 1959. 1960 goal — Aleksei N. Kosygin's speech in Pravda, October 28, 1959.

that they provide information useful for making minimum estimates of likely Soviet production of these key commodities in 1965 and 1970. We can do this by adding to the 1960 goals the apparent absolute increases in outputs of these commodities since 1955. The result is an estimate of Soviet 1965 production on the assumption merely that the indicated absolute increase achieved during 1956–60 will be repeated in the next half decade. This is a minimal estimate of possible 1965 Soviet production because this technique implies immediately a significant slowdown in the rate of growth of the production of these commodities. In addition, it will be a far easier task for the larger Soviet economy of the early 1960's to achieve a given absolute amount of production increase than it was for the smaller Soviet economy of the late 1950's. Adding the same absolute figures for apparent 1956–60 production increase to the minimal 1965 estimates gives us similarly an even more minimal estimate of Soviet production of these commodities in 1970. Table 2 shows the

TABLE 2 *Minimum Estimates of Soviet Output of Key Commodities in 1965 and 1970, Soviet Goals for 1965, and U.S. Output in 1958*

COMMODITY	UNIT	MINIMUM ESTIMATES		SOVIET 1965 GOALS	U.S. 1958 OUTPUT
		1965	1970		
Pig iron . . .	Million metric tons	60.7	74.4	65–70	52.4
Steel	Million metric tons	84.7	104.4	86–91	77.2
Coal	Million metric tons	600.0*	700.0*	596–609	382.8
Oil.	Million metric tons	217.2	290.4	230–240	330.8
Natural gas	Billion cubic meters	95.6	138.2	150	311.9
Electricity . .	Billion kilowatt-hours	411.8	532.6	500–520	724.0
Cement . . .	Million metric tons	68.5	91.5	75–81	53.1

* Arbitrary estimates which are below the minima calculated by the technique otherwise applied in these tables because of announced Soviet intention sharply to reduce growth of coal output.

Sources: Soviet 1965 goals from Izvestia, November 14, 1958. U.S. 1958 output from Survey of Current Business, March and April 1959.

results of these calculations, and compare them with the official Soviet goals for 1965 and also American production of these commodities in 1958.

My own belief is that, barring war or unlikely major political disturbance in the Soviet Union, the minimum estimates are very likely to be reached or even exceeded, particularly in 1970, by the dates indicated. Let us look at some of the implications of this belief, bearing in mind that the minimum estimates for 1965 are very conservative and imply a substantial failure of the current Soviet Seven-Year Plan to reach even its minimum targets for 1965:

1. In 1965 Soviet heavy industry will be producing substantially more than did the corresponding industry of the United States in 1958. It should be noted that the minimum 1965 estimates for pig iron, steel, coal and cement are all well above actual production in this country last year. Moreover, bearing in mind the fact that Soviet output of automobiles and other consumer durable goods in 1965 will certainly be still far below the corresponding output of these goods here last year, Soviet production of heavy machinery, armaments, and other goods important primarily from the point of view of national power is likely to be far greater in 1965 than was corresponding American production last year. The implications of this for the magnitude of the Soviet challenge in such fields as international trade and foreign economic aid would seem to be both obvious and disturbing.

2. Even on the basis of these minimum estimates, the Soviet output of these commodities is growing so rapidly that within the next very few years it will be perfectly feasible for Soviet production of pig iron, steel, and cement to exceed ours if we have only a moderate recession or suffer anything resembling this year's prolonged steel strike. Last year already the recession-caused reduction in our steel output permitted Soviet steel production to exceed 70 per cent of our own for the first time in Soviet history.

3. Looking ahead to 1970, we may note that the estimates of minimum likely Soviet output for that year are, in the case of pig iron and steel, approximately of the magnitude of this country's record production. Bearing in mind too the fact that far less of Soviet electricity output is used for direct consumer needs than is true here, the conclusion seems in-escapable that by 1970 the Soviet Union's heavy industry will be capable of producing at least as much as, and probably more than, our heavy industry ever has in our history. And here, too, of course, the differences in product mix between our heavy industry — with its emphasis on consumer durables — and Soviet heavy industry is very pertinent.

The conclusion seems inescapable that we are in the eve of a tremendous increase in Soviet capabilities of all kinds and of a vast expansion in Soviet competitive power against us. It also seems likely that the next decade will see Soviet capabilities outstrip our own in many different fields unless the United States substantially lifts its output not only above the levels of recession-ridden 1958 but also above past record levels, or changes its patterns of resource use, or both.

Present and Future Communist Bloc Strength

But it is important to remember that growing Communist capabilities are not restricted by the Soviet Union's potentialities. For many purposes of policy formation it is essential to bear in mind the growing economic strength of the total Communist bloc. Premier Khrushchev has already boasted that in 1965 he expects the Communist nations to be producing over half of the world's industrial output.[4] While we need not accept this prediction as certain of fulfillment, it is worth taking a brief look, in Table 3, at the growing output of the Communist bloc as compared with that of the non-Communist world and also at a minimal estimate of what the Communist bloc output may be in 1965.

The minimal nature of the 1965 estimates given above must be stressed. The estimates were arrived at rather mechanically by assuming merely that at the very least the Communist bloc economies will be able to increase the absolute amount of output of these commodities as much during the 7-year period 1959–65 as they actually did during the 8-year preceding period 1951–58. Actually, bearing in mind the still vast potentialities of economic growth in Communist China, it would not be at all surprising if in 1965 Communist bloc production equalled or exceeded the following somewhat higher figures: pig iron, 120 million metric tons; steel, 150 million metric

---

[4] *Izvestia,* November 14, 1958.

TABLE 3 *Output of the Communist Bloc in 1950 and 1958, Free World Output in 1958, and Minimum Estimate of Communist Bloc Output in 1965*

COMMODITY	UNIT	COMMUNIST BLOC OUTPUT			FREE WORLD 1958 OUTPUT
		1950 Actual	1958 Actual	1965 Estimate	
Pig iron	Million metric tons	24.7	64.8	104.9	134.8
Steel............	Million metric tons	36.1	80.1	124.1	189.5
Electricity	Billion kilowatt-hours	140.0	362.5	585.0	1,400.0*
Cement..........	Million metric tons	21.0	61.6	104.6	150.0*

* Very rough estimate.

Sources: Communist bloc 1950 and 1958 figures from *Voprosy Ekonomiki*, No. 9, 1959, p. 76. Free world figures based on U.N. data.

tons; electricity, 650 billion kilowatt-hours; and cement, 120 million metric tons. And, of course, in comparing the free world and Communist block output totals we must bear in mind how very differently the Communists use their steel and electricity as compared to the way we use them.

But even the rather minimal 1965 estimates given in the table above show that we must be prepared to witness a very great expansion of total Communist bloc production and economic power in the years immediately ahead. The free world as a whole has no more right to complacency than does the United States alone. Moreover, it should be borne in mind that the Communist bloc as a whole has only about half as many people as does the free world. Hence when population is considered even the minimal 1965 estimates of the table above give Communist bloc per capita 1965 production estimates substantially exceeding the actual per capita free world figures for 1958 in the case of pig iron, steel, and cement. This is a useful reminder that the free world consists not only of highly industrialized countries such as our own and the nations of Western Europe, but also of many underdeveloped countries in Asia, Africa, and South America which at present contribute very little indeed to the industrial strength of the non-Communist world.

Some Policy Implications

The policy implications of the above analysis obviously depend upon one's assumptions as to the likely future relations between the Soviet Union and the United States. So far as I can see, the most likely assumption here is that a state of uneasy absence of armed conflict will prevail between these two great states in the foreseeable future. And instead of shooting at each other, the two States — and the kinds of societies they represent — will be competing for the minds of men everywhere in terms of performance. This is what Premier Khrushchev obviously has in mind when he talks of peaceful coexistence and peaceful competition. And he has said often enough that he expects to show the superiority of his way of life by superior performance, most particularly by way of superior performance in raising production.

There would seem already to be in this country a substantial amount of informed and responsible opinion which recognizes that we must meet this challenge and this competition within the framework of our democratic institutions. I take it that this recognition is, at least in part, behind such suggestions as President Eisenhower's proposal last January for a committee to set up long-range national goals as well as last year's recommendation by the Rockefeller Brothers Fund study group on the national economy that this Nation seek to expand its output more rapidly and more regularly than in the past, perhaps by 5 per cent per annum. Others, such as Prof. J. K. Galbraith, of Harvard University, in his influential book, *The Affluent Society*, have stressed also the need for reallocation of our national resources so that social needs for education, housing, medical care, and the like are relatively better met in the future than they have been even in the past prosperous post-World War II decade and a half. It seems to me that these and related trends in our public opinion provide important component parts of any adequate attempt to frame a national policy capable of meeting the massive and growing challenge of the Soviet Union and its allies. Certainly, the record of recession-ridden 1958 and of 1959, when roughly 85 per cent of our steel capacity was shut down by a strike which lasted almost 4 months, does not inspire confidence that business-as-usual attitudes have any hope of meeting the challenge.

President Eisenhower has repeatedly called in recent months for national self-discipline. By that I take it the President means that the different elements in our economy and our society must take the Nation's needs into account, as well as their own self-interest, in determining their actions. Certainly the perspectives we meet in facing the challenge of the Soviet Union, where discipline is coercively applied to the entire population, strengthens the importance of the American people heeding the President's appeal.

Against this background it is disturbing to read the statement of Howard C. Petersen.[5] The over-all impact of his statement, I am afraid, will be to give aid and comfort to those who would prefer not to compete, to continue business as usual in the Micawberish hope that something will turn up which will change and improve the unhappy perspectives before us. Mr. Petersen properly disparages the "vaguely felt fears that we cannot afford to do what is necessary" for defense and foreign aid. Yet it is precisely those who hold such fears who are likely to be most receptive to Mr. Petersen's not so vague hints that any real attempt to compete economically with the Soviet Union must inevitably mean the fastening of socialist bondage upon our economy. At least that is my reading of his assertion that any serious effort to raise our growth rate would require "a degree of governmental intervention in economic life that would change the very character of our free economy." The implied notion that the distinguished persons involved in the Rockefeller Brothers Fund report

on the national economy may be in some way heralds of American socialism is curious, to say the least.

I would suggest that there are at least two basic errors in Mr. Petersen's thinking:

First, I believe Mr. Petersen seriously underestimates the flexibility and viability of our private enterprise economy, and its potentialities for adapting itself to the changing needs of our society. A quarter of a century ago, in the 1930's, there were those who similarly raised the specter of socialist slavery against laws providing for social security, unemployment insurance, wage and hour regulation, and the like. With the wisdom of hindsight we have come to understand that these changes strengthened rather than weakened our free economy. I would argue rather that there are still very large and untapped reservoirs of flexibility and adaptation which can be drawn upon for fruitful partnership between all key elements in our economic life and government so as successfully to resist a challenge which threatens the very existence of private enterprise and of freedom. After all, defeat in the economic war could be as disastrous as defeat in a shooting war used to be before nuclear weapons made shooting wars involving their use intolerable.

We have, I would point out, social and political mechanisms which would permit leaders of all key elements in our society to hammer out needed national policy without the Draconian government coercion Mr. Petersen fears. Why cannot the top leaders of Government, business, labor, agriculture, and other key groups meet at the American Assembly or some similar forum to face the serious problems posed before us by the Soviet challenge and come to an agreed set of solutions? The attempt, at least, would seem worth while. Obviously if each group in our society puts maximization of its own interest before all other goals, such common policy would be difficult indeed to secure. But in the face of the common danger can we not hope for the voluntary self-discipline of all groups to play a greater role in the future than it has played in the past? We are often told these days, by Walter Lippmann, George Kennan, and others, that as a nation we lack a sense of national purpose. Could not such meetings define the purpose of our Nation and measures to implement those purposes?

[5] Part II, pp. 517–527.

To create the climate of public opinion which would make possible fruitful cooperation of the type suggested above obviously requires leadership. That is the challenge before all responsible public figures today. We have recently seen effective leadership exercised in mobilizing public resentment and anger against those who practiced fraud via the television screens in our homes. Is it unreasonable to hope that we may have leadership to mobilize public opinion for solution of the far more serious problem of the future survival of the free society and free economy we treasure?

Mr. Petersen's second error, I believe, lies in his estimate of the order of magnitude of the resources required to raise our rate of growth. On the basis of what he himself recognizes is the flimsiest possible kind of evidence he raises the specter that it would take something like $75 billion a year in extra expenditures to raise our growth rate from 3 to 5 per cent annually.

My own suspicion is that Mr. Petersen radically underestimates the potentials for rapid expansion of production in our economy, supposing the markets can be provided to give incentives for maximum production and productivity. Surely Mr. Petersen is aware of the significant fraction of our resources which is inefficiently, wastefully, or partially employed because of lack of markets. Moreover we are living at the beginning of the automation revolution, in an era when technological progress is moving exponentially to give us better ways of making old goods as well as new goods we never had before. We have had some glimpses of the fantastic potentials for production increase in our economy in the performance of our war industry during World War II and in the astonishing rise of our agricultural productivity since 1940.

As will be clear from the above, my belief is that Mr. Petersen takes too static, even unimaginative, a view of our potentialities within the framework of our democratic and private enterprise institutions. Those institutions have successfully met all previous tests in our history, and I see no reason to suppose they cannot meet the present test if we use to the full our resources of imaginativeness, inventiveness, and intelligence. That this will require changes in some of our past practices and habits, is clear, of course, but then all life is a process of change and adaptation to new circumstances. What I do not believe is that the changes we

need carry the dangers Mr. Petersen raises so gloomily. And I am particularly baffled by his attitude when I see that in the same statement he supports higher taxes for defense and foreign aid, higher taxes which cannot help — to use his own words — "curtailing the freedom of families to choose between consumption and saving and between work and leisure. . . ." The real danger, I fear, is that we will do too little and too late to meet the Soviet economic challenge, rather than that we will engage in any mindless, reckless rush to change our basic institutions.

Some months ago a speaker at the National War College began his lecture by reminding his audience that the barbarian tribes which conquered Rome had a far smaller gross national product than did the rich, effete civilization they overcame. We need not labor the analogy, and of course our Soviet competitors are not barbarians, though there have been barbaric periods in not too distant Soviet history. I shall end by noting that the remark is a useful reminder that what is important for survival is not only the size of total production, but also the composition of that production and what it is used for.

73

Beyond the Containment Policy*

Marshall D. Shulman

(1958)

American policy toward the U.S.S.R. has for more than a decade been based on a premise and a proposition. The first was that Soviet expansionism could be contained by a firm stand. The second held that containment would lead to a certain mellowing, in accordance with which the U.S.S.R. would come to see its own welfare more closely associated with the international status quo. We conclude our selection of writings with a contribution by

────────

*Reprinted from "Changing Appreciation of the Soviet Problem," *World Politics*, Vol. 10 (1958), pp. 499–511, by permission of the author and the publisher.

Dr. Marshall D. Shulman, who poses a sharp issue succinctly by arguing that the "containment policy" has not worked, and that something more is needed if America is to remain a live force in shaping the future.

Whether we articulate them or not, the assumptions that we make concerning the future development of the Soviet system are fundamental to our thinking about American foreign policy.† The objectives toward which we can reasonably direct our efforts, the philosophy of our situation, are in a very large measure a function of the image we have in our minds of the changes we discern or anticipate in the character of the society and the government of the Russian people.

In recent years, we have come to learn a great deal about aspects of the Soviet Union, certainly much more than is reflected in public discussion. But of the actual distribution of power within the Soviet system, or of the laws governing the development of a modern totalitarian state, we still know very little. Necessarily, our thoughts regarding the changes which time can be expected to produce in this confrontation lead us into the realm of speculative projection from rather tenuous data.

The data at our disposal are, however, constantly increasing, and the assumptions on which we are operating require constant examination. It is evident that the present period is witnessing changes of a profound character in the Communist world, although it is certainly too soon to say with assurance what these changes signify, let alone to describe what they are. Even such fragments of information as are suggested by recent developments in the Soviet situation open up perspectives of the problem more profoundly challenging for American policy, both foreign and domestic, than have yet been faced in current discussion of these matters.

I

Whatever one might think of the Soviet regime, the Soviet achievements in World War II made it necessary to think about it in a somewhat longer-term perspective than many had been accustomed to before the war. As Stalin justifiably boasted in his electoral speech of 1946, the Soviet Union could no longer be regarded as a transient phenomenon.

For the most part, the prevailing conception which was brought to this longer perspective was of the Soviet Union as a variant of the Western pattern of political and economic development. Those who were sympathetically inclined continued to see the Soviet Union as an advance in Western social development, and analogized from Western revolutionary experience in deriving their expectations of its future course. Projecting a normative life cycle for revolutions, they anticipated that time could be expected to bring about a diminution of its harsher aspects, and that the social advance would remain in a domesticated form. To those who were more critically disposed, it was also possible to conceive of the Soviet order as an aberration from the normal, i.e., the Western, pattern of development, the degree of aberration representing the extent of the contradiction between reality and the Soviet path of development. In this view, it was anticipated that events would oblige the rulers of the Soviet Union to realize the error, if not the unfeasibility, of their ways, and in time to return to a more "normal" pattern of development and of relationship with other nations. If the Soviet leaders persisted in their error, it was felt, they would in time be replaced by another and more realistic regime.

In his remarkable article, "The Sources of Soviet Conduct," published eleven years ago, under the pseudonym "X,"[1] Mr. George Kennan proposed that the frustration of Russia's expansionist tendencies would be likely to lead either to the breakup or to the "gradual mellowing" of Soviet power. The argument was based upon the assumption that the Soviet Union was faced with powerful internal strains: economic weakness and imbalance, the exhaustion and disaffection of the population, the problem of succession, the difficulty of bring the younger generation into the system of power, and other factors which added up to the strong possibil-

† Acknowledgment is gratefully made to the Russian Research Center, Harvard University, under whose shelter this article was prepared.

[1] *Foreign Affairs*, XXV, No. 4 (July 1947), pp. 566–82. [See pp. 90–99 of the present volume.]

ity that the Soviet power bore within itself the seeds of its own decay in a less-than-ultimate sense. These strains would, if Soviet external pressures were met and blocked by counterforce, produce fundamental changes in the character of the regime, presumably moderating the features responsible for the situation of conflict with the rest of the world. Leaving aside the question of the validity of the general proposition, whose essential condition was only partly realized in the following period, the question involved here is what expectation was suggested by the concept of the "mellowing" of Soviet power. What Mr. Kennan himself had in mind was more fully set forth in another essay, "America and the Russian Future," which he published in 1951.[2] There are many aspects of this landmark essay deserving of attention, but our interest at the moment is in the nature of the image it projected of the possible forms of development of the Soviet system.

Recognizing that the primary responsibility for enduring change in the Soviet system would have to come from within, and that there were rather narrow limits to what could be achieved from abroad, Mr. Kennan set forth a course of action for the United States that he believed most likely to influence Soviet development in the desired direction. His emphasis was upon perfecting our own society, so that we might set an example of "spiritual distinction." He took for granted the mounting of military strength and cohesiveness in the Western world, the necessity for which had been generally accepted by this time, and said that the purpose of this policy should be "to convince the masters of the Kremlin that their grand design is a futile and unachievable one, persistence in which promises no solution of their own predicaments and dilemmas."[3]

Mr. Kennan believed it possible, but unlikely, that desired changes could come about by evolution, "by erosion from despotism rather than by the violent upthrust of liberty." Chiefly, this was because he felt that the modern police state, unlike the despotisms of the past, does not have behind it "a driving political will," does not concern itself with the well-

being of the people over whom it rules, does not recognize an obligation to the future, relies chiefly upon terror and coercion to maintain its power. He saw not only a dichotomy but a smoldering hostility between the small ruling group and the Russian people, and expressed faith that any such system, "based on the evil and weakness in man's nature," could never achieve genuine stability.

It was no use, Mr. Kennan warned, expecting Russia to become capitalist and liberal-democratic, with institutions like our own. We had to anticipate a continuation of the collective tradition, although in agriculture, which he saw as the Achilles' heel of the Soviet system, one could anticipate voluntary co-operatives instead of forcible collectives. Three minimum changes were required, however, for Russia to become the kind of a country we could live with in peace: abolition of the iron curtain, elimination of imperialist expansion and oppression, and elimination of totalitarian controls over the Russian population. These apart, the Russian people should be allowed to work out their internal problems in their own manner.

Subsequent thinking on the possibilities for change in the Soviet system has been substantially influenced by two developments: first, the death of Stalin and the transfer of power to his successors have been handled by the regime, not without incident, but so far at least without the upheaval that many had anticipated; and second, Soviet economic and technological progress has continued at an extraordinary rate, and has so far at least managed to surmount agricultural, transportation, and other vulnerabilities as problems rather than as crises.

Perhaps the highest degree of optimism in the period following the death of Stalin was to be found in the writings of Mr. Isaac Deutscher, who argued that economic progress and the spread of literacy in the Soviet Union made possible — indeed, had already begun to produce — a transmutation of the Soviet system to a form of social democracy.[4] Although few other writers went as far, many began to explore the implications of the impact of industrialization upon Soviet society, and speculated on the ultimate effects of the emergence

[2] *Ibid.*, XXIX, No. 3 (April 1951), pp. 351–70.
[3] *Ibid.*, p. 370.

[4] *Russia — What Next?* Oxford, 1953.

of a middle class, of a class of bureaucrats and technicians, with varying expectations.[5]

Even before the appearance of the Soviet earth satellite brought this point home forcibly and perhaps traumatically to the American public, it had become evident to students of Soviet affairs that the remarkable Soviet economic and technological progress made obligatory a revision of any expectations of a collapse of the regime resulting from the unsoundness of its economic base.

In 1956, for example, Mr. Henry Roberts, in his excellent summation of the Soviet problem, based upon a two-year study by a group of prominent Americans, indicated the impact of these developments on our thinking. "There is no question," he wrote, "but that the Soviet regime has made some remarkable achievements, and has been able to exploit the potentialities of twentieth-century technology and organization to a degree greater than we might have thought its cumbersome and doctrinaire outlook would permit."[6]

And when, in 1957, Mr. Kennan returned to the subject in his Reith lectures over the BBC, now published in the United States as *Russia, the Atom, and the West,* he began his series by acknowledging freely that Soviet economic progress had surpassed anything he had thought possible at the time of the "X" article ten years before.

However, he is concerned lest we exaggerate the significance of this fact. In a part of his analysis which has received less public attention than other sections of the series,[7] Mr. Kennan endeavors to strike a new balance of the strengths and vulnerabilities of the Soviet system, and its prospects for change. He points to the imbalance of the Soviet economy, particularly in agriculture, and cites the familiar assurance that the Soviet rate of growth is likely to slow down as it runs out of the advantages of backwardness and begins to experience the problems common to other advanced industrial societies. In any case, material progress is not everything. The Russians, he finds, are inclined to be "Babbitts" about their economic growth just as we were some years ago, and they will become more mature about it in time. Despite Mr. Khrushchev's challenge, we are not in a contest between the two economies; rather we should welcome each advance of the Soviet economy. As to its effects upon the Soviet power position, Mr. Kennan is inclined to deprecate this concern, since "the danger is already so great that variations in degree do not have much meaning."

Mr. Kennan's equanimity about Soviet economic progress is strengthened by his estimate of the deepening crisis of Soviet political life. He holds that the Communist Party is in an unstable situation because of the existence outside of the Party of groups and interests that do not find, under the present system, representation in the political process. Another source of instability lies in the pressure of Soviet intellectuals, artists, and students for "complete intellectual and cultural freedom," which the Communist leaders cannot grant without undermining their own rule.

Mr. Kennan suggests, although he does not explicitly say so, that his expectations of an evolutionary pattern of development in the Soviet system are somewhat greater than they were at the time of his earlier writings, and he expresses the wish that "Russia's progress toward more mature political institutions might proceed with as little violence and trouble as possible."[8] In the meantime, as he has urged before, the chief means of countering the Soviet threat will be found in remedying our own failings: the racial problem, urban development, education, and so forth.

The impression this suggests is that, in his anxiety to counteract errors of emphasis in the public mind, Mr. Kennan has unbalanced his argument in the other direction. He is out to dispel the overmilitarized and frenetic cold warrior in us, and to induce instead a state of dignified composure and moral perfectibility. The posture he evokes is appealing, but the question is whether it represents an appropriate

[5] E. H. Carr, "The Structure of Soviet Society," *The Listener,* LIV, No. 1379 (August 4, 1955), pp. 167–68, and a letter by Hugh Seton-Watson to the editor of *The Listener* on the above article, *ibid.,* No. 1380 (August 11, 1955), pp. 222–23; Barrington Moore, Jr., *Terror and Progress — USSR,* Cambridge, Mass., 1954; Carl J. Friedrich, ed., *Totalitarianism,* Cambridge, Mass., 1954.
[6] *Russia and America: Dangers and Prospects,* New York, 1956, p. 20.
[7] *Russia, the Atom, and the West,* New York, 1958, pp. 2–31.

[8] *Ibid.,* p. 14.

or an adequate response to the problem in its present form.

II

What we know about the events of the past few years in the Soviet Union, fragmentary and inconclusive as the evidence may be, is suggestive of a much more complex and disturbing image of the pattern of development of the Soviet system than we have yet acknowledged. Although not necessarily contradictory of all that Mr. Kennan and others have been anticipating, the changes which seem to be in process lack some of the benignity and promise connoted by the term "mellowing" and, instead of bringing us closer to a "normalization" of our relations, seem more likely to effect our defeat.

Whereas ten years ago our policy proceeded on the confident assumption that "time is on our side," it is now the case that, unless we respond more adequately than we are doing to the situation created by Soviet internal and external developments, the reverse assumption appears the more probable.

Indeed, many things have happened in the Soviet Union in recent years which may in time turn out to have been part of a "progress toward more mature political institutions." But if the changes that have taken place turn out to be more than the cyclical alternations which have characterized Soviet policy from the beginning, the "maturity" they adumbrate represents a greater rather than a lesser challenge, different in character perhaps from the one we are accustomed to, but more profoundly threatening over the course of time.

Ferment has been reported among Soviet students, artists, and intellectuals, and the intermittent widening and narrowing of the latitudes of discussion and of creative activities which have been permitted by the regime suggest an experimental approach to the question of the limits to be accepted. While a lessening of the degree of Party control over the arts would constitute in that measure progress toward a less totalitarian society, it is not necessarily a question of absolute control or absolute freedom, as is suggested in Mr. Kennan's image of the pressure from these quarters for "complete intellectual and cultural freedom." Insofar as one can judge from the outside, the pressure of the intellectuals appears to be directed chiefly at a reduction in the

interference by the Party in cultural matters, and does not imply a widespread political dissidence toward the regime, or an espousal of an alternative form of government.

The administrative decentralization, apart from its other significance, may permit a degree of local initiative, although ample means for central control remain through Party and planning channels. The elimination of the Machine Tractor Stations not only may portend a change in the collective farm system, but even more importantly reflects a greater pragmatism in dealing with the organization of agriculture than would have been thought possible a few years ago. In responding to trouble in the satellites, the regime seems to be involved in a critical experiment as to the degree of variation in local patterns it can accept within its sphere, providing the adherence of the area to the Communist bloc is not in question. The somewhat greater emphasis on the production of consumer goods, the reported reduction in reliance upon military and administrative tribunals in the legal system, the less overt use of police surveillance, and the possibility of greater travel abroad and of more widespread cultural contacts with the non-Communist world — all these elements may portend a refinement and a modification in the nature of Soviet totalitarianism, although it would be disproportionate to regard these measures as "democratization" in any Western sense of the word.

While it is possible, as some writers maintain, to picture these measures as reluctant concessions by the leadership to threatening pressures from within, it is at least as plausible to suggest that the easing of controls in certain areas of administrative and cultural life is possible because the fundamental allegiance of the population can be taken for granted, and that the interests of efficiency are better served by reliance upon voluntary service to the interests of the state. Such samplings as exist of present or former Soviet citizens indicate substantial dissidence only among the peasantry,[9] whereas the predominant view of the population as a whole appears to be one of acceptance of the regime because it "works," because it

---

[9] R. A. Bauer, Alex Inkeles, and Clyde Kluckhohn, *How the Soviet System Works,* Cambridge, Mass., 1956.

provides opportunity for individual advancement, some improvement from year to year in living conditions, and has had external successes. If a smoldering hostility exists between the Russian people as a whole and the Soviet regime, it is not reflected in the evidence available abroad.

Further, the Communist Party has shown skill in identifying and absorbing potential interest groups outside itself, and thus in preventing the growth of independent power elements in the society. As the Roberts study pointed out to those who count upon the army or the managerial elite to threaten the position of the party, "while the Communist regime has been bureaucratized, the bureaucracy (including the military) has been Communized."[10] In a recent study of the position of the Party, Professor Merle Fainsod comes to the conclusion that, at least to the present, the Party has shown a capacity for adaptation and growth, and that this has assisted it to maintain its primacy in Soviet society. "Better-educated than their Stalinist predecessors, more technically-oriented in their training and experience, the present-day party functionaries have had to learn to balance zealotry with the pragmatic skills required to manage a complex industrial society."[11]

Although he feels that the authority of the present ruling group in the Party rests upon a precarious equilibrium which will be tested by the next succession crisis, Professor Fainsod finds no evidence in recent Soviet experience to suggest that the interests of the men who run the factories cannot be accommodated within a framework of totalitarian party control without yielding them political power. "There is no iron law," he says, "which dictates incompatibility between one-party rule and a highly-developed industrial society."[12]

In considering the consequences of Soviet economic growth, while it might be unseemly, as Mr. Kennan instructs us, to groan each time the scoreboard shows a Soviet advance, it would be foolhardy to ignore the dangers for us in the relative statistics. At the very least, we cannot afford to ignore the dilemma that

while Soviet economic progress may over the long run present the hypothetical advantage of having certain desired effects upon Soviet society, it results in the meantime in a threat which is not hypothetical of a significant improvement in the Soviet power position relative to our own.

It may very well be true that, to the extent the Soviet regime commits itself to the production of consumer goods, this may over the long period circumscribe the freedom of action of the Soviet leadership in disposing of the nation's resources. So far, however, it must be said that the Soviet leaders have been able to make enough of a concession in the direction of consumer goods to have a beneficial political effect, domestic and foreign, without significantly reducing their capabilities in heavy industry and defense.

It may also be true that there are factors in the Soviet situation which may lead to a slowing of the rate of industrial growth, and indeed this may already be the case, but the comfort this affords is small, considering that the rate of growth of gross national product still remains and seems likely to remain something on the order of double our own. It is a milestone of enormous portent that the steel production of the Sino-Soviet bloc for the first time surpassed that of the United States in the first quarter of this year, according to the Director of the Central Intelligence Agency.[13]

That this is not just a matter of being out-pointed at some game devised by Mr. Khrushchev is soberly documented in the account presented by Mr. Allen Dulles of the ways in which the advances in the Soviet economic and technological capabilities are leading to a strengthening of the relative power position of the Soviet Union in the world.

What is involved is not simply the production of a larger quantity of weapons, which Mr. Kennan perhaps rightly feels would not alter the situation a great deal, but a number of other uses of Soviet economic power which would indeed alter the situation qualitatively and for us disastrously. Apart from the possibility of a technical breakthrough in weapons development — which becomes ever more pos-

---

[10] Roberts, op. cit., p. 27.
[11] "The Party in the Post-Stalin Era," in *Problems of Communism*, VII, No. 1 (January–February 1958), p. 13.
[12] *Ibid.*

[13] Allen W. Dulles, speech to the U.S. Chamber of Commerce, *New York Times*, April 29, 1958, p. 8.

sible, given the increased Soviet capabilities in this direction — the more direct and immediate danger is the use by the Soviet Union of economic means to affect the political orientation of other countries. It is already the case that both advanced industrial areas and economically underdeveloped areas have shown susceptibility to the appeal of Soviet trade, credits, and other instruments of economic penetration. It does not require an exercise of the imagination to anticipate the possibility of a number of areas of strategic importance becoming, not necessarily Communized, but oriented toward Soviet policies and away from our own, as a result of the increased capabilities of the Soviet Union in the economic realm. The influence of the Soviet system as a model of rapid industrialization is reported as a tangible political factor by all who visit Asia and Africa. Technical breakthroughs by Soviet science and technology in matters that bear upon the living conditions of these populations would further contribute to the expansion of Soviet influence and power.

There is another point which should be mentioned in this connection. In his lecture on "The Soviet Mind and World Realities,"[14] Mr. Kennan finds one of the sources of conflict in the persistent misunderstanding by the Soviet leadership of the motives of the West. Distorted by the Marxist-Leninist ideology, their perceptions of "the things that make our life tick as it does" mislead the Soviet leaders and tend to perpetuate the situation of conflict. Presumably this error can be eradicated only by confronting the Soviet leadership over long periods of time with situations which will require them at last to make an adjustment in their mode of thought.

But what seems more to the point is not so much their understanding of our *motives* — a subjective factor which the Communists have been inclined to dismiss — as the extent to which their analysis of the dynamics of our political and economic system appears to them to have validity. And here it must be said that the events of recent years seem more likely to strengthen than to weaken the faith of the Soviet leadership in the validity of their conception of the dynamics of our society. Writing

at this moment, under the impact of dramatic Soviet technological and economic achievements, contrasted with the current recession in the American economy, there may be a tendency to overemphasize this consideration, but even before sputnik and the recession, the contraction of American power and influence cannot have appeared to the Soviet leaders to have contradicted their expectations. Soviet ideology has shown resilience in many respects, particularly in the realm of the tactics of transition to communism, and Soviet ideologists did experience some difficulty in explaining the high rate of industrial output in the United States, but the central element of the ideology, which rests upon a Marxist interpretation of the dynamics of our economic system, has for the most part survived the four decades of Soviet experience intact. What is most difficult for us to face is this: that events do not appear to have contradicted the conviction of the Soviet leaders that their directed economy has competitive advantages over the free market economy of the West in an age of advanced industrialism. Nor, barring fortuitous developments in our behalf or a substantial change in our policies, do they appear likely to do so in the future.

What this brief reference to current trends in the Soviet system suggests is the possibility of a pattern of development toward a form for which we have neither the conceptual framework nor a nomenclature. Bearing in mind always that imponderable and fortuitous factors may influence the course of development of the Soviet system in ways that we cannot anticipate, we are obliged to face the hard implications of the direction pointed by present trends. There is at least the possibility that the Soviet system shows signs of development toward a more highly differentiated and stabilized state, perhaps less totalitarian in the degree of intervention of the Party in all aspects of the society, but still collectivized, authoritarian, and heavily centralized under the direction of a single party, which encompasses within itself the pluralist interests of a complex industrial order. There does not appear to be reason to believe that this development will be accompanied by a process which can be described as the "normalization" of its external relations, in the sense that it involves a diminution of the Soviet commitment to the ultimate emergence

---

[14] Kennan, *Russia, The Atom, and the West, op. cit.,* pp. 21–24.

of a Communist world system. On the contrary, it seems more probable that the Soviet system, evolving in its own terms, strengthening its military and economic capabilities, may represent an increasingly effective challenge for world influence with the passage of time.

Luck, of course, may be with us, and this picture may turn out to have been too dark. It is always possible, in a situation containing so many imponderable factors, that difficulties impossible to anticipate may rise up to alter the balance radically, but we cannot base our planning on a less sober estimate of the Soviet challenge than these indications present.

If this is the assumption on which we can reasonably base our thinking about the future, what follows from it? One thing certainly is that, separate from the plane of moral judgment, it is necessary for us to take the full measure of the Soviet system as an alternative form of the organization of society in the age of industrialism. That is to say that the pursuit of virtue in our democratic life, although by no means irrelevant, is not a substitute for the effective utilization by our society of its human and material resources. Questions of the ultimate values of our society are, of course, involved; the word "effective" immediately raises the question: "Toward what ends?" But the implication of this challenge is that the validation of our convictions regarding the values of a democratic society will depend on whether we are able to relate them to the conditions of a highly advanced industrialism.

Beyond the problem of maintaining some kind of military equilibrium with the Soviet bloc over a long period of time under conditions of a rapidly changing military technology, and of countering Soviet political and economic maneuvers, there is the more difficult and more fundamental question of whether over the years we shall be able to find ways of expressing a national sense of purpose in the utilization of our resources more effective than the centralized planning and direction of the Soviet system. It is likely that the measure of effectiveness in this confrontation will be taken in terms of national power in the broadest sense, military and non-military, tangible and moral, including the satisfaction of the needs of the respective populations.

The ultimate question, in short, is not merely the wisdom of our policies, but the adequacy of our institutions for the conduct of our affairs both at home and abroad.

III

In the mood of collective introspection which the Soviet earth satellite induced in the American people, many aspects of American life have been looked at as though they had never been seen before, from professors' salaries to automobile tail-fins. But even before the general public was aroused by this dramatic Soviet technical achievement, here and there isolated sectors of the discussion over foreign policy problems opened heretical chasms for examination.

In a study entitled *Foreign Policy and the Democratic Process*, the British writer, Max Beloff, takes note of the "sustained and serious debate" going on in the United States, and observes that it is "bound to continue to probe until it calls into question the most fundamental of all American beliefs: that of the absolute validity of the American philosophy of government and of the institutions in which it has become embodied."[15] The question to which Mr. Beloff addresses himself is the adequacy of democratic processes for the conduct of foreign policy in the face of the Communist challenge, and in the light of the advantages possessed by a totalitarian society for concentration of effort, secrecy, and speed of action.

Another writer — also British, as it happens — Mr. G. L. Arnold, has invited our attention to the question "whether democratic politics can in time produce agreement on the degree of public planning necessary to preserve the social health of the non-Communist world." In a sketchy and neglected book entitled *The Pattern of World Conflict*, Mr. Arnold defines the cold war as "competitive attempts to alter the balance of power without overt resort to force,"[16] and urges upon us a planned international investment policy, providing for the interrelated needs of the advanced industrial and the economically underdeveloped areas of the non-Communist world.

Mr. Arnold is a member of what he describes as "the new hard-bitten generation of post-totalitarian liberals [which] is distinguished by

---

15 Baltimore, Md., 1955, p. 12.
16 New York, 1955, pp. 228–35.

a reluctant acceptance of the need for more centralized power."[17] In his analysis, totalitarianism is merely a perverted expression of the impulsion toward centralized state control provided by the industrial revolution. The answer to it is to be found in democratic planning — national and, for the non-Communist world, international. Mr. Arnold doubts the capacity of private investment and the free play of market forces to offer much competition to communism's efforts to integrate itself with the nationalist movements in the underdeveloped areas of the world.

Doubtless the debate has only begun, and if the American economy and the Soviet leaders combine to administer further traumatic shocks to the American public, the national self-inquiry is likely to go forward with that zeal which characterizes all pursuits of American public opinion. The outcome of this period of inquiry involves as many imponderables as the question of the future of the Soviet system; indeed, some of them are the same.

Certain elements of the problem appear evident, although just to enumerate them plunges one immediately into a painful awareness of the conflicts they involve. Certainly some more effective form of expression of a sense of national purpose in the use of our resources will need to be found, as the anomalies and irrationalities resulting from leaving matters to the interplay of private interests are contemplated by the American public.

Just as certainly, it is not in the nature of our

society to follow doctrinaire solutions, and what is most likely to occur is a period of pragmatic development and expansion of the many instrumentalities already available to us. This may lead us to direct our attention to the quality and effectiveness of the administrative agencies we have developed, a revision of procedures for the selection and responsibility of administrative personnel, review procedures, and measures to ensure a greater degree of political responsibility of these agencies. Perhaps at this conjuncture, the politics of administration becomes a critical sector in considering the adequacy of our institutions to meet the problems of an increasingly complex industrial society under competition from a centralized and controlled society.

This is of course the central dilemma: whether we can accept the need for a higher degree of centralization in certain areas of our national life to provide for a more rational and effective use of our resources, and at the same time vigilantly distinguish and preserve the pluralist values of our society in the cultural and spiritual realms. The full measure of political genius of the American people will be needed for the task.

We have enormous advantages in this competition. Our resources and our technology are a source of strength; even more so, the limitless potentialities of our free society. But the quality of our leadership may be the decisive factor, for this is less a matter of devising new and different institutions than of suffusing the ones we have with a sense of national purpose.

---

[17] *Ibid.*, p. 15.

SUGGESTIONS FOR FURTHER READING

COMMITTEE ON FOREIGN RELATIONS, UNITED STATES SENATE, *United States Foreign Policy: U.S.S.R. and Eastern Europe.* Prepared at the request of the Committee on Foreign Relations, United States Senate, Eighty-sixth Congress, Second Session, by a Columbia-Harvard Research Group, February 14, 1960.

DEUTSCHER, ISAAC, *The Great Contest: Russia and the West.* New York: Oxford University Press, 1960.

> Post-Stalin developments, the new mood in the U.S.S.R., and implications for the future.

DEUTSCHER, ISAAC, *Russia in Transition,* rev. ed. New York: Grove Press, Inc., 1960.

> Essays on recent events in Soviet history and their meaning for the U.S.S.R.'s future path of development.

KENNAN, GEORGE F., *Russia, the Atom, and the West.* New York: Harper & Brothers, 1958.

> Strengths, weaknesses, and sources of change in the Soviet system.

MOORE, BARRINGTON, JR., *Terror and Progress, U.S.S.R.: Some Sources of Change and Stability in the Soviet Dictatorship.* Cambridge, Mass.: Harvard University Press, 1954.

> Analysis of the present with an eye to foreseeing future developments.

ROBERTS, HENRY L., *Russia and America: Dangers and Prospects.* New York: Harper & Brothers, 1956.

> The implications of Soviet totalitarianism and the requirements imposed by it and the world situation upon American policy.

ROBINSON, GEROID T., "Stalin's Vision of Utopia: The Future Communist Society," *Proceedings of the American Philosophical Society,* Vol. 99 (1955), pp. 11–21.

> Man and society in the future according to Stalin.

Biographical Notes

DAVID ALLCHURCH   Pseudonym for a British observer of the Soviet scene who prefers to remain anonymous.

RAYMOND A. BAUER   Professor of Business Administration, Harvard Graduate School of Business Administration, and author of *The New Man in Soviet Psychology, Nine Soviet Portraits, How the Soviet System Works* (with Inkeles and Kluckhohn) and *The Soviet Citizen* (with Inkeles). Mr. Bauer's main interests at the moment are in problems of communications, political behavior, and the functioning of organizations.

ALEXANDER BAYKOV   Professor of Russian Economic Studies and Head of the Department of Economics and Institutions of the U.S.S.R., Faculty of Commerce and Social Science, University of Birmingham, Mr. Baykov has studied Soviet economics since 1923, first in Prague (1923–39), then in Great Britain. His best-known work is *The Development of the Soviet Economic System*.

DANIEL BELL   Formerly staff writer and managing editor for *The New Leader* and labor editor of *Fortune* magazine, Mr. Bell is now Professor of Sociology at Columbia University. Among his writings are *The History of Marxian Socialism in the U.S.* and *The End of Ideology.*

ISAIAH BERLIN   Sir Isaiah has been First Secretary of the British Embassies in Washington and Moscow in addition to holding academic positions in England and America. At present he is Professor of Social and Political Theory at Oxford University. His books include *Karl Marx* and *The Age of Enlightenment.*

JOSEPH S. BERLINER   Presently Associate Professor of Economics, Syracuse University, Mr. Berliner has also been a Research Fellow of the Russian Research Center, Harvard University, and worked as an economist for the Corporation for Economic and Industry Research, Inc. His major publications are *Factory and Manager in the USSR, and Soviet Economic Aid.*

HAROLD J. BERMAN   Professor of Law,

Harvard Law School and member of the Executive Committee of the Russian Research Center, Harvard University. Author of *Justice in Russia: An Interpretation of Soviet Law*, *The Russians in Focus*, *Soviet Law in Action: The Recollected Cases of a Soviet Lawyer* (with Boris A. Konstantinovsky), *Soviet Military Law and Administration* (with Miroslav Kerner), and other books, as well as numerous articles on Soviet law.

CYRIL E. BLACK   Professor of History, Princeton University, and Editor of *World Politics*. He has written (with E. C. Helmreich) *Twentieth Century Europe: A History*, and edited *Rewriting Russian History: Soviet Interpretations of Russia's Past*, and *The Transformation of Russian Society: Aspects of Social Change Since 1861*. In March 1958 he visited the U.S.S.R. as a member of the U.S. delegation to observe the elections to the Supreme Soviet.

J. M. BOCHENSKI   Joseph M. Bochenski, Ph.D., D.D., is Professor of the History of Contemporary Philosophy and Director of the Institute of East-European Studies at the University of Fribourg, Switzerland. He is the author of *Soviet Dialectical Materialism* and has served as editor of the *Handbook on World Communism* and the series *Sovietica*.

REX V. BROWN   In 1956, Rex Brown, then studying social sciences at Cambridge, privately arranged a month's stay at Moscow University to report on Soviet student life. Four other Russian speaking students went with him — Michael Frayn (journalist), Angela Hobbs (university research), James Woodburn (anthropologist), and Margaret Armstrong (psychologist). The selection is based on their diaries. Mr. Brown has pursued his interest in Russian affairs through research and other activities, including the production of a television film on England for Soviet audiences. He is now in marketing research.

E. H. CARR   E. H. Carr is a Fellow of Trinity College, Cambridge. At present he is engaged on a monumental *History of Soviet Russia*, of which the following installments have been published: *The Bolshevik Revolution 1917–1923*, 3 vols.; *The Interregnum, 1923–1924; Socialism in One Country, 1924–1926*, 2 vols.

ROBERT V. DANIELS   Assistant Professor of History, University of Vermont. Mr. Daniels has been on the staff of the Russian Research Center, Harvard University, and has also taught at Bennington College and Indiana University. He is particularly interested in studying the development of Communist ideology, and has written or edited *A Documentary History of Communism*, *The Conscience of the Revolution: Communist Opposition in Soviet Russia*, and *The Nature of Communism*.

ISAAC DEUTSCHER   Mr. Deutscher is the author of *Stalin: A Political Biography* and other books and articles on Soviet Russia. He has worked as journalist, staff writer and editor for periodicals in Poland and England.

NICHOLAS DeWITT   Research Associate, Office of Scientific Personnel, National Academy of Sciences — National Research Council, Washington, D.C.; and Associate, Russian Research Center, Harvard University. Mr. DeWitt does research in the area of Soviet education, professional manpower, and science, and has written *Soviet Professional Manpower* and *Education and Professional Employment in the USSR*.

VERA S. DUNHAM   Assistant Professor, Department of Slavic and Eastern Languages, Wayne State University. Dr. Dunham, who looks at the social implications as well as at the artistic side of Soviet belles-lettres is now working on "humanism" in Soviet fiction and poetry as it expresses itself in the debate between the generations of the Soviet intelligentsia.

ALEXANDER ECKSTEIN   At present Professor of International Economics at the University of Rochester, Mr. Eckstein has in the past been associated with the Food and Agricultural Organization of the United Nations, the Department of State, and the Russian Research Center, Harvard University. He is a co-author of *Prospects for Communist China: Moscow-Peking Axis*.

MERLE FAINSOD   Among Mr. Fainsod's books are *How Russia is Ruled* and *Smolensk Under Soviet Rule*. He is Professor of Government and Director of the Russian Research Center, Harvard University.

ROBERT A. FELDMESSER Assistant Professor of Sociology, Brandeis University, and engaged in the study of social stratification and mobility in the U.S.S.R., Mr. Feldmesser has also been a Research Fellow at the Russian Research Center and Instructor in Social Relations at Harvard University.

MARK G. FIELD Now Associate Professor of Sociology at the University of Illinois, Mr. Field was formerly Research Associate at the Russian Research Center and Lecturer in Social Relations, Harvard University. Dr. Field is the author of *Doctor and Patient in Soviet Russia,* a joint author of *New Perspectives on Mental Patient Care,* and has written numerous articles on the Soviet Union. He is presently engaged in a study of Soviet socialized medicine.

KENT GEIGER Associate Professor of Sociology, Tufts University, formerly Research Fellow at the Russian Research Center, Harvard University, he is preparing a monograph on Soviet family life.

ALEXANDER GERSCHENKRON Among Mr. Gerschenkron's works are *Economic Relations with the U.S.S.R.* and *A Dollar Index of Soviet Machinery Output.* He is Professor of Economics at Harvard University and also a frequent commentator on modern Soviet literature.

VLADIMIR GSOVSKI Born in Russia, Mr. Gsovski is now Chief of the European Law Division, Law Library, Library of Congress, and is Professorial Lecturer, Georgetown University School of Foreign Service. Among his publications are *Soviet Civil Law* and *Russian Administration of Alaska.*

WALDEMAR GURIAN At the time of his death in 1954, Professor Gurian was Professor of Political Science at Notre Dame University. His works include *Bolshevism* and *The Rise and Decline of Marxism.*

LEOPOLD H. HAIMSON Associate Professor of Russian History and Director of The Project on the History of Menshevism, University of Chicago. Mr. Haimson's major research interests center on the history of Russian culture, with particular emphasis on the intellectual and social history of modern Russia. His publications include *The Russian Marxists and the Origins of Bolshevism.*

CHAUNCY D. HARRIS Professor of Geography at the University of Chicago, Mr. Harris's main interest in Soviet affairs centers on economic and urban geography. He is editor of the English translation of *Economic Geography of the USSR* by Balzak, Vasyutin, and Feigin.

JOHN N. HAZARD Professor of Public Law, Columbia University, and author of *Settling Disputes in Soviet Society,* and *Law and Social Change in the U.S.S.R.* Mr. Hazard was a Fellow of the Institute of Current World Affairs in the Moscow Juridical Institute from 1934–1937.

LEON HERMAN Mr. Herman follows economic developments in the Soviet Union for the Library of Congress, where he serves as a senior staff member of the Legislative Reference Service. His recent writings have appeared in *Nation's Business, The New Leader,* and *Problems of Communism.* In July 1960 he visited six large Soviet industrial centers for the purpose of making first-hand economic observations as a member of a six-man exchange team sponsored by the Committee for Economic Development.

RICHARD HILTON A British regular army officer from 1913 to 1948, Mr. Hilton served in both World Wars, in British India, and as British Military Attaché in Moscow from 1947–48. Since his retirement he has been a journalist, lecturer, and author. Among his books is *Military Attaché in Moscow.*

ALEX INKELES Professor of Sociology and Director of Studies in Social Relations at the Russian Research Center, Harvard University; author of *Public Opinion in Soviet Russia* and other works on Soviet affairs.

NAUM JASNY Mr. Jasny does free-lance research on the Soviet economy and has published numerous books and articles on that subject.

ARCADIUS KAHAN   Assistant Professor of Economics, University of Chicago, Mr. Kahan's area of specialization is economic history. He has done research in Soviet agriculture and labor and is co-author of a forthcoming study on Soviet agriculture. He is presently at work on a book entitled *The State and Entrepreneur in Russian Economic Development.*

JOHN F. KANTNER   Mr. Kantner has taught at the College of William and Mary, served as Associate Research Professor with the University of California staff at the University of Indonesia and worked as a statistician with the Foreign Manpower Research Office, U.S. Bureau of the Census. He is currently with the Population Council.

GEORGE F. KENNAN   Professor, School of Historical Studies, Institute for Advanced Study, Princeton, N.J., Mr. Kennan was formerly U.S. Ambassador to the Soviet Union. His major publications on Russia are: *Soviet–American Relations, 1917–1920:* Vol. I, *Russia Leaves the War,* and Vol. II, *The Decision to Intervene;* and *Soviet Foreign Policy, 1917–1941.*

N. S. KHRUSHCHEV   First Secretary of the Communist Party of the Soviet Union and Chairman of the Council of Ministers of the U.S.S.R.

CLYDE KLUCKHOHN   Professor of Anthropology at Harvard University until his death in 1960, first director of the Russian Research Center, former president of the American Anthropological Association, Mr. Kluckhohn numbered Soviet affairs among his many interests. He was co-author of *How the Soviet System Works.*

FRANK LORIMER   In addition to his books on the Soviet and Eastern European populations, Mr. Lorimer, who is Professor of Sociology at American University, has also written *Dynamics of Population* (with Frederick Osborn) and *Culture and Human Fertility.*

DONALD G. MacRAE   First University Lecturer in Sociology at Oxford and Reader in Sociology in the University of London. Mr. MacRae is also Managing Editor of the *British Journal of Sociology,* and has been Visiting Professor, University College of Ghana and the University of California, Berkeley.

BARRINGTON MOORE, Jr.   Dr. Barrington Moore, Jr. of Harvard's Russian Research Center is the author of *Soviet Politics: The Dilemma of Power, Terror and Progress USSR: Some Sources of Change and Stability in Soviet Society,* and a series of theoretical and historical essays on the problems of authority, *Political Power and Social Theory.* For some years he has been working on a comparative historical study of the rural origins of dictatorship and democracy.

PHILIP E. MOSELY   Since his first period of research, 1930–32, in the Soviet Union, Philip E. Mosely has devoted a major part of his scholarly efforts to the study of Soviet developments. After serving as director of the Russian Institute of Columbia University from 1951 to 1955, he is now Director of Studies at the Council on Foreign Relations, Inc.

ALEC NOVE   An economist at the London School of Economics, Mr. Nove writes with expertise on many sides of contemporary Soviet affairs.

CECIL PARROTT   A member of the British Foreign Service who has spent many years studying musical developments in the Soviet Union.

RICHARD PIPES   Associate Professor of History and member of the Executive Committee of the Russian Research Center, Harvard University. Mr. Pipes' main interest is modern Russian history, especially political thought and institutions and the nationality problem. He has written *The Formation of the Soviet Union,* translated and edited *Karamzin's Memoir on Ancient and Modern Russia,* and edited *The Russian Intelligentsia.*

EUGENE RABINOWITCH   Born in St. Petersburg (Leningrad), educated there up to the third university year, Mr. Rabinowitch is at present Research Professor of Botany and Biophysics, University of Illinois. He has been writing on Russian problems for some 35 years, and has served as editor and editorial writer of *The Bulletin of the Atomic Scientists* since 1945.

HELEN RAPP   Miss Rapp was born in Yugoslavia of Russian parents, educated at Oxford (B.A., M.A.) and London (Ph.D.), and is on the teaching staff of the Slavonic Department of the University of Oxford and of the School of Slavonic and East European Studies of the University of London.

THOMAS H. RIGBY   Associate Professor of Russian, Australian National University, Canberra. Mr. Rigby has held positions as Senior Research Officer, London School of Economics and Political Science, member of the Research Department of the United Kingdom Foreign Office, and, in 1957–1958, Second Secretary in the British Embassy in Moscow. He has published a number of articles on Soviet politics and administration, and is currently preparing a book on the selection and composition of leading cadres in the U.S.S.R.

HARRY SCHWARTZ   Harry Schwartz is a specialist on Soviet Affairs for *The New York Times* and a member of its Editorial Board. He is the author of *Russia's Soviet Economy* and numerous other publications dealing with the Soviet economy. He was formerly Professor of Economics in the Maxwell School of Syracuse University, and has served with the Department of State, Office of Strategic Services, War Production Board, and Department of Agriculture of the United States Government.

HUGH SETON-WATSON   Among the books written by Mr. Seton-Watson, Professor of Russian History in the School of Slavonic and East European Studies, University of London, are *Eastern Europe Between the Wars,* and *The Pattern of Communist Revolution.*

MARSHALL D. SHULMAN   Associate Director of the Russian Research Center, Harvard Uni-

versity, formerly Special Assistant to the Secretary of State, Mr. Shulman has written and lectured extensively on Soviet foreign policy.

ERNEST J. SIMMONS   Has taught at Harvard and Cornell, was Chairman of the Department of Slavic Languages at Columbia, was the Editor of *The American Slavic and East European Review* from 1947 to 1950, and was General Editor of The Columbia Slavic Studies. Among his works the best known are *Pushkin, Dostoevski: the Making of a Novelist, Tolstoy,* and *Russian Fiction and Soviet Ideology.* He is presently devoting his time to research and writing, and is preparing a book on Chekhov.

NICHOLAS S. TIMASHEFF   Born in St. Petersburg, Russia, in 1886, Mr. Timasheff has been Professor of Jurisprudence and Criminal Law, School of Economics, Polytechnical Institute, St. Petersburg, 1916–21; Professor of Law, University of Prague, Czechoslovakia, 1923–28; Professor of Russian Institutions, Sorbonne, Paris, 1928–36; Visiting Professor of Sociology, Harvard University, 1936–40; and Professor of Sociology, Fordham University and Marymount College, since 1943. He is the author of many books and articles on Soviet affairs.

ARNOLD J. TOYNBEE   Professor Emeritus of International History, University of London, and former Director of Studies, Royal Institute of International Affairs, London, Mr. Toynbee was also a member of the U.K. delegation at the Paris Peace Conferences of 1919 and 1946. Among his many works are the ten-volume *A Study of History,* and the Royal Institute's *Survey of International Affairs,* of which he is joint author with his wife.

ROBERT C. TUCKER   Professor of Government, Indiana University. Attaché, U.S. Embassy, Moscow, 1944–53. Author of *The Alienated World of Karl Marx* and various short studies, primarily in the field of Russian thought and politics.

LAZAR VOLIN   Lazar Volin has been a specialist on Russia for the U.S. Department of Agriculture for more than 30 years, and most recently has been a Research Associate, Russian Research Center, Harvard University. He has written extensively on Russia.

RUTH WIDMAYER   Associate Professor of Political Science, Portland State College. Fullbright Professor in India, 1958–60, at Jadavpur U., Calcutta, and Osmonia U., Hyderabad. Dr. Widmayer has written on Soviet education and other aspects of Soviet affairs and has made two trips to the U.S.S.R. in recent years.

BERTRAM D. WOLFE   An independent scholar and writer, Mr. Wolfe is well known in the

field of Soviet studies for his account of Lenin, Trotsky, and Stalin, *Three Who Made a Revolution.*

FREDERICK S. WYLE   Frederick S. Wyle is an attorney practicing in San Francisco. He is a student of Soviet affairs and is active in a number of groups in the foreign policy area. In 1950 and 1951 he participated in the Refugee Interview Project in Germany and Austria of Harvard's Russian Research Center and was associated with the Russian Research Center at various times from 1951 to 1954.

Glossary

advocate Member of a collegium of lawyers engaged in law practice

Agitprop Department of Agitation and Propaganda of the Communist Party

agrogorod Agricultural city

aktiv Leading group, most active members of a given organization

apparat The Party or governmental structure

apparatchik Influential member of the Party or government

artel Cooperative work association

A.S.S.R. Autonomous Soviet Socialist Republic

blat "Pull"; especially the obtaining of products, etc. through "connections"

cadre Staff or personnel of an organization

Cheka Extraordinary Commission for Struggle Against Counterrevolution (1917–1921); predecessor of O.G.P.U., N.K.V.D., and M.V.D.

chernozyom Black-earth region

chiny Tsarist system of formal civil service ranks

chistka Purge

collegium A board or collective body exercising administrative responsibilities

Comintern Communist International; an international organization composed of all the Communist Parties; dissolved in 1943

C.P.S.U. Communist Party of the Soviet Union

dacha Villa; house in the country

Dalstroi Far Eastern Construction Trust

desyatina A measure of area, 2.7 acres

diamat Dialectical materialism

Dosav Society for the Promotion of Aviation

Duma Tsarist parliamentary body

dvor Household

edinonachalie One-man control; single rule or authority

Ezhovshchina Terror and purges of 1936–1938; so called after Ezhov, head of the N.K.V.D.

feldsher Medical worker who is intermediate in training between a physician and a nurse

feuilleton Critical or satirical newspaper article

F.Z.U. Trade school attached to a factory

Generalny Prokuror Attorney General of the Soviet Union

Glavlit Chief Administration for Publishing and Literary Affairs

Gosarbitrazh Arbitration board; special system of courts which hears cases involving state business enterprises

Gosbank State Bank

Gosplan State Planning Commission

hectare Measure of area, 2.471 acres

ideinost Ideological content, especially of Communist ideas

ikon Holy image in form of painting, bas relief, mosaic, etc.

Iskra The Spark, pre-Revolutionary newspaper of the Russian Social Democratic Party

istmat Historical materialism

jurisconsult Lawyer acting as legal adviser in an enterprise

kafedra University chair

kapustniki Satirical plays

katorga Hard labor

khoziain Boss, owner

khoziaistvennik A responsible economic official

khozraschyot Cost accounting; economic accounting

khuliganstvo Rowdyism

kolkhoz Collective farm

kolkhoznik Collective farmer

komandirovka Business trip

kombedy Committees of the poor peasantry

Komsomol Communist League of Youth

Komsomolskaya Pravda Central newspaper of the Komsomol

kopeck Penny; small coin
krai Territory

kraikom Territorial committee of the Party or the Komsomol

Krokodil Soviet humor magazine

kulak A wealthy peasant in the pre-collectivization era

Medsantrud Union of Medical Workers

Mensheviki Right wing of the Russian Social-Democratic Workers Party

mestnichestvo Regionalism, localism

M.G.B. Ministry of State Security

mir Pre-Revolutionary village community with communal land tenure

M.Kh.A.T. Moscow Art Theater

M.T.S. Machine-Tractor Station

muzhik Peasant (derogatory)

M.V.D. Ministry of Internal Affairs

narkom People's commissar; now called minister

narkomat People's commissariat; now called ministry

Nepman Private trader or businessman (during the N.E.P. period)

N.E.P. New Economic Policy

N.K.V.D. People's Commissariat of Internal Affairs

obkom Regional committee of the Party or the Komsomol

oblast Region

Octobrists Communist organization for youngest children

Ogiz Central Government Publishing House

orgtekhplan Organizational and technical plan

O.R.S. Workers' Supply Section

Otzovists "Recallists," pre-Revolutionary Bolshevik faction demanding the immediate recall or withdrawal of the Party delegation to the Duma

partiinost Communist Party spirit; state of being imbued with and motivated by Party aims and principles

Pioneers Communist organization for young children

Pionerskaya Pravda Central newspaper of the Pioneers

Politburo Political Bureau, highest organ of the Central Committee of the Communist Party, known since 1952 as the Presidium

pokhod Hike; campaign

proteksiya Political protection, patronage

Pravda Official newspaper of the Soviet Communist Party

putyovka Holiday ticket or pass

rabfak Workers' institute or school

raion District

raikom District committee of the Party or the Komsomol

R.A.P.P. Russian Association of Proletarian Writers

R.S.F.S.R. Russian Soviet Federated Socialist Republic

samoderzhavie Autocracy

samokritika Self-criticism

seksot Secret police informer

selsovet Village soviet

semeistvennost Nepotism

sobor Council; synod

sledovatel Examining judge

S.D. Social Democrat

S.R. Social Revolutionary

soviet Government body; council

sovkhoz State farm

sovnarkhoz Regional economic council

Stakhanovite Worker rewarded for setting the highest norms on a given job

steppe Grassland or prairie

stolovaya Public canteen; dining hall

sukhovei Desiccating wind

taiga Coniferous forest occupying most of northern U.S.S.R.

Tass Soviet news distributing agency

tekhnikum Vocational high school or special technical school on secondary level

tolkach Expediter

toz Association for joint land cultivation

trudoden Workday

Ts.I.K. Central Executive Committee of the U.S.S.R.

tundra Treeless plain in Arctic region

Ultimatists Pre-Revolutionary Bolshevik faction which insisted that an ultimatum be dispatched to the Duma delegation with the proviso that its members be recalled if the instructions contained in the ultimatum were rejected

ukase Decree; order

vecher Organized evening of entertainment

verkhushka The top leadership

V.K.P.(b) All-Union Communist Party (Bolshevik)

Vlasov Army Army of prisoners of war and deserters that fought on Axis side in World War II

Vperyodists Dissident group expelled from the Party by Lenin in 1909; so called for the name of their journal, *Vperyod*

V.S.N.Kh. Supreme Council of the National Economy

vuz Higher educational institution

Y.C.L. Young Communist League; Komsomol

zakon Law

zemstvo Agency of rural self-government in pre-Revolutionary Russia

zvenevoi Leader of *zveno* (link)

zveno Link, a small work unit of the kolkhoz

Index